Also by **HOWARD M. SACHAR**

THE COURSE OF MODERN JEWISH HISTORY

ALIYAH: THE PEOPLES OF ISRAEL

FROM THE ENDS OF THE EARTH: THE PEOPLES OF ISRAEL

THE EMERGENCE OF THE MIDDLE EAST, 1914–1924

EUROPE LEAVES THE MIDDLE EAST, 1936–1954

THE MAN ON THE CAMEL

EGYPT AND ISRAEL

DIASPORA: AN INQUIRY INTO THE CONTEMPORARY JEWISH WORLD

A HISTORY OF ISRAEL: FROM THE AFTERMATH OF THE YOM KIPPUR WAR

A HISTORY OF THE JEWS IN AMERICA

FAREWELL ESPAÑA: THE WORLD OF THE SEPHARDIM REMEMBERED

ISRAEL AND EUROPE: AN APPRAISAL IN HISTORY

DREAMLAND: EUROPEANS AND JEWS IN THE AFTERMATH OF THE GREAT WAR

A HISTORY OF THE JEWS IN THE MODERN WORLD

A HISTORY
OF ISRAEL

HOWARD M. SACHAR

A HISTORY

OF ISRAEL

FROM THE RISE OF
ZIONISM TO OUR TIME

Third Edition, Revised and Updated

ALFRED A. KNOPF · NEW YORK · 2010

THIS IS A BORZOI BOOK
PUBLISHED BY ALFRED A. KNOPF, INC.

Published in the United States by Alfred A. Knopf, a division of
Random House, Inc., New York, and in Canada by Random
House of Canada Limited, Toronto.

Library of Congress Cataloging-in-Publication Data
Sachar, Howard Morley, [date]
  A history of Israel : from the rise of Zionism to our
time / by Howard M. Sachar. — 3rd ed., rev. and updated.
      p.   cm.
  "This is a Borzoi book"—T.p. verso.
  Includes bibliographical references and index.
  ISBN 978-0-375-71132-9
1. Israel—History.   2. Zionism—History.   3. Palestine—
History—1917–1948.   I. Title.
DS126.5.S155 2007
956.94—dc22   2006101970

Manufactured in the United States of America
Published October 21, 1976
Second Edition, February 9, 1996
Third Edition, May 15, 2007
Second Printing, April 2010

For Daniel

CONTENTS

MAPS

STYLISTIC NOTE

In transliterated Hebrew words appearing in the text and bibliography, the consonant *ch* is pronounced from the back of the palate, rather than as in the English word *chain*. Similarly, the consonant *z* in transliterated words as a rule is pronounced *tz*, as in *Eretz Israel*, *kibbutz*, and *kvutzah* (three common transliterations where the *tz* is left intact). While Arabic words listed in the bibliography follow the classical form—although without diacritical markings—transliterations more familiar to Westerners also are used in the text.

PREFACE

This is a long volume for a small country. After four far-ramifying Middle Eastern crises in one generation, however, it may be assumed that the seismic impact of Israel upon the contemporary world is too palpable to require elaboration. One may even argue that the Jews, with or without statehood, have exerted an uncommonly protean influence upon organized society from ancient to modern times. Ironically, the theorists of Zionism had anticipated that revived nationhood in the Land of Israel finally would lift this unique and burdensome afflatus from the backs of the Jewish people; for, aside from the religionists among them, the Zionists were animated less by a sense of mission than by a search for normalcy. In the ensuing chapters, we shall have opportunity to evaluate the ambivalent results of that quest.

Although this work is intended in large part for university students and general readers, I venture to hope that specialists in modern history may find useful certain extended treatments that relate to the Middle East as a whole. (To that end, I have not hesitated—particularly in Chapters V, IX, X, XI, XII, and XIII—to borrow material appearing in my own specialized works in this field, *The Emergence of the Middle East* and *Europe Leaves the Middle East*.) The bibliography, too, has been organized with concern for those who may wish to probe more thoroughly into selected topics of their own research. It should be noted here that the selections are less formidable than they may initially appear. While the list plainly is more than introductory, it is far from exhaustive. An endless source of fascination for social scientists, the Jewish nation has evoked and produced an immense literature, one as out of proportion to its size as the role of Israel altogether in the twentieth century.

The book owes much to the help of several good friends and respected colleagues. The Faculty Research Committee of George Washington University under the chairmanship of Dean Henry Solomon generously underwrote the expenses attendant upon the completion of this manuscript. Professor Joseph Nedava, chairman of the political science department of the University of Haifa, graciously read and offered corrections for many of the prestate chapters. Mr. S. Z. Abramov, Knesset Member and distinguished historian, provided invaluable marginal commentary on the chapters dealing with Israel's political and ideological evolution. Mr. David Kochav, presently economic adviser to the Israeli ministry of defense, supplied many incisive observations for the chapters on Israel's economic life; while Mr. Moshe Raviv, director of the United States department of the Israeli foreign ministry, made numerous crucial suggestions for the chapters describing Israel's international relations. In the same spirit,

Professor Jacob Neusner of Brown University contributed his insights into the question of links between Israel and the Diaspora.

During my period of teaching and research in Israel, Rabbi Herbert Friedman, formerly executive vice-president of the United Jewish Appeal, gave unstintingly of his time to clarify the role of Western philanthropy in Israel's growth and development. Mr. Zelig Chinitz of the Jewish Agency opened out useful data on the immigration and settlement of Soviet Jews. General Mordechai Gur, then chief of Israel's northern military command, kindly made available to me opportunities to study Israeli defense problems along the Golan frontier; even as Colonel Arieh Shalev, then deputy director of military intelligence for the Egyptian front, extended similar courtesies for the Sinai-Suez area. Mr. Yehoshua Almog, foreign ministry representative for the administered territories, and Mr. Anan Safadi, Arab affairs correspondent of the Jerusalem *Post,* shared with me their detailed knowledge of Arab-Israeli relations on the occupied West Bank. I am equally indebted to Mr. Netanel Lorch, formerly director of the African department of the Israeli foreign ministry, who provided me with many hours of background information on Israel's aid program among the underdeveloped nations.

My warmest thanks go out as well to an old and cherished friend, Dr. Lawrence Marwick, director of the Hebraica section of the Library of Congress, for his indispensable help in acquiring source materials in Hebrew and Arabic. For other bibliographical courtesies I herewith express my appreciation to Mr. Aaron D. Rosenbaum, senior research associate of that estimable weekly, the *Near East Report;* to Mrs. Michelle Bitters, director of interlibrary loans of the George Washington University Library; and not least of all to my brother-in-law, Mr. Eri Steimatzky of Tel Aviv. Once again Mrs. Elnora Carter gave to the ordeal of manuscript-typing an expertise that transcended the stenographic and approached the editorial. Lastly, my wife, Eliana, shared with me her own rich knowledge of Israeli history and life, serving as always as my most devoted critic and collaborator.   *Kensington, Maryland, 1975*

Thirty years have passed since the first edition of this volume appeared, almost eleven years since the second edition. Some of the individuals whose help I have acknowledged earlier are no longer with us. My original expression of warm appreciation to them will of course remain.

The passage of three decades, however, brings with it a far larger accumulation of indebtedness. It is true that many of my benefactors are listed in others of my publishing efforts, specifically those that relate to the Middle East or to various aspects of Israel's growth and development. Even so, over the years many scores, if not several hundred, of additional specialists and friends—in Israel, the United States, and other countries—have contributed significantly to the revisions and enlargements of my two later editions. They are far too numerous, and it is far too late, to thank each one of them on the written page. If any of them should peruse this book, I hope and trust that they will remember our meetings or correspondence, and sense the full measure of my silent gratitude.
                                      Kensington, Maryland, 2006

A·HISTORY
OF ISRAEL

THE RISE
OF JEWISH NATIONALISM

ACCULTURATION AND HISTORICAL MEMORY

On February 9, 1807, an honor guard of French grenadiers beat a military tattoo on their drums at the entrance to the Hôtel de Ville in Paris. Thereupon a procession of seventy-one men filed in to take their seats in the hotel's ornate banquet hall. Solemnly, the chairman, a bearded rabbi in dark clerical attire, gaveled the meeting to order. The delegates were all Jews. They had gathered to participate in a Sanhedrin, a modern version of the council that had issued and enforced the laws during the Jewish Commonwealth of antiquity. The ancient body plainly had languished following the destruction of Jewish statehood at the hands of the Romans. Now, however, much to the astonishment of Frenchmen and Jews alike, the Sanhedrin was being revived at the explicit orders of Napoleon Bonaparte. It was the emperor's intention that the Jews of France, to whom the General Assembly had granted equality of rights only fifteen years before, should accept the responsibilities of citizenship in as "official" and ceremonial a manner as the Jewish tradition itself provided.

Although the nation's 40,000 Jews had been emancipated in 1791, this was hardly attributable to their popularity in a Christian state. The determining factor, rather, was the unsparing rationalism that already had overthrown the *ancien régime,* and that seemed capable of final validation only if applied without distinction to all the inhabitants of the land. In any case, both the revolutionary government and Napoleon, its successor, appreciated that France no longer could sustain itself as a Great Power while tolerating the relics of corporativism, including the ghettoized autonomy of the Jews. Nor was it possible to ignore the tangible dividends to be accrued from the unlocked mobility of Jewish wealth and enterprise. If Napoleon appreciated these fraternal advantages, however, and indeed bestowed them on Jews in the territories he conquered elsewhere in western and central Europe, he expected certain commitments in return. He demanded specific assurances that rabbinical jurisdiction in Jewish civil and judicial affairs was a thing of the past, that the Jews had turned their backs forever on their separate nationhood, on their corporative status, and not least of all on their traditional hope for redemption in Palestine.

The French emperor received his assurances. Grateful for the honor paid their religious sensibilities, the members of the revived Sanhedrin affirmed their determination to "gallicize" all elements within their own community. Formally, too, they declared that rabbinical laws henceforth would be applied exclusively to matters of religious tradition and practice; that France alone had claim on their political allegiance; that French Jews "no longer formed a nation"; and that they had renounced forever their dream of collective exodus to the ancestral Land of Israel. As it transpired, these commitments were destined to exert a far-reaching influence on Jewish life, and well beyond the borders of France itself. Although the Jews of western Europe—those emancipated by the Revolution, by Napoleon's armies, or, grudgingly, by local regimes—numbered scarcely half a million in 1807, and at most three-quarters of a million fifty years later, they represented the "aristocrats" of Jewish life. By mid-century, they had consolidated the rights tentatively awarded them during the revolutionary-Napoleonic era, and were free to build homes, to travel, to engage in business, and to practice their professions as they chose. In their hearts they were certain, too, that their own efforts, more even than Gentile toleration, had achieved this equality of status. Faithful to the Sanhedrin's historic affirmation, they had shown themselves loyal comrades-in-arms, public-spirited citizens, sensitive interpreters of their various national idioms.

To protect what they had achieved in civic freedom, moreover, Western Jews, in the United States and Europe alike, tended to accept the emerging nineteenth-century consensus that loyalty to a national state was incompatible with pluralism in cultures. In increasing numbers, they dropped the traditional allusions to Zion in their ritual observances and spoke of the messianic age less in terms of return to the Land of Israel than of a miraculous "end of days," or of an era of "universal brotherhood." Ultimately the Sanhedrin's nationalist commitment provided a rationale for Germans, Frenchmen, and Americans of the "Israelitish" or "Mosaic" faith—for Jews in a hurry to assume the protective coloration of their Gentile neighbors. The affirmation's most substantial impact, therefore, lay not so much in its repudiation of Jewish corporative autonomy or of nostalgia for Zion, as in the increasing sanction it provided for Western Jews to reject their historic civilization in its wider ethnic and cultural implications.

On the other hand, the lineaments of Western Jewish emancipation and acculturation differed strikingly from the pattern of the *Ostjuden,* the 3 million Jews of eastern Europe who represented nearly 75 percent of world Jewry in 1850. The largest numbers of Jewish "Easterners" were to be found in Russia, where they comprised some 4 percent of the Romanov Empire's population and by far its most despised and oppressed minority. To the tsarist government, no less than to the backward, largely illiterate native peasantry, the Jews were regarded in terms of their medieval stereotype: as Christ killers, well poisoners, or at best as usurious traders and parasitic middlemen. The government's approach to these unwelcome infidels, whom it had inherited in the eighteenth-century partitions of

Poland, was simply to cordon them off from integral Russia in a "Pale of Settlement" that consisted essentially of the newly annexed western provinces. Even within this extensive territorial ghetto, the Jews were driven from sensitive border communities, restricted in their opportunities for a livelihood, and denied a share in local government. Under the harshly autocratic Nicholas I, who ruled to mid-century, their communal self-government was abolished and their children subjected to thinly disguised conversionary pressures in the army and the "Crown" school system. Ironically, all these tsarist efforts proved counterproductive to Jewish "amalgamation." Driven more tightly into themselves, insulated by force and choice from the surrounding Gentile population, the Jews of Russia continued unshakably ethnocentric and grimly intent upon maintaining the full skein of their religious and communal traditions, their unique diet and dress, their Hebrew worship and Yiddish vernacular.

Among the most cherished features of the Russian Jewish cultural heritage, surely, was the memory of the ancestral homeland, the lost and lamented Zion that was enshrined in the ceremony and folklore of virtually every believing Jew. The truth was that throughout all the centuries of Jewish dispersion until modern times, Zion, hardly less than the Deity, functioned as a binding integument of the Jewish religious and social experience. Rabbinic and midrashic literature, the prayer book, medieval literary treatises, all displayed a uniform preoccupation with the Holy Land. Poets, philosophers, mystics, liturgists in Spain, North Africa, and Europe traditionally vied with one another in expressing the yearning of the People of Israel for the ravished cradle of its nationhood. In the West, to be sure, the memory of Zion unquestionably was fading by the nineteenth century, was even being exorcised by reformers and secularists. But for Russian Jews, distraught and quarantined under the tsars, clinging fast to their accumulated sacred literature, the Holy Land was no mere featureless idyll, to be embellished in lullabies and fireside tales. The recollection of its loss was a visceral wound. On the ninth day of the Hebrew month of Av, commemorating the destruction of Solomon's Temple, east European Jews fasted and mourned as though they had been witnesses and victims of that ancient catastrophe. Three times a day they prayed for the restoration of Jerusalem. Their appeals for timely rains and harvests were phrased in terms evocative not of ice-bound Russia but of the subtropical Holy Land. Jewish festivities and holidays—Passover, Chanukkah, Sukkot, Shavuot—all evoked and refined memories of the departed national hearth. In the manner, then, of other ethnic-religious Eastern communities—of the Greeks and Armenians, for example—Russian Jews continued to nourish the vision of a future apocalypse, the redemption of sacred soil.

On the other hand, the Jews of the Pale resisted all attempts to "force the end." In the seventeenth and eighteenth centuries the excesses and perversions of a series of false messiahs had burned them badly. Messianism was transformed, rather, into attendance upon a halcyonic era that alone would signal final redemption in the Land of Israel. *"You'll* never bring the Messiah any nearer," an aged rabbi once cautioned the youthful Chaim Weizmann. "One has to do much, learn much, know much and suffer much before one is worthy of that." Even so, it was no generalized Western Jewish conception of universal amity that brooded in the folk memory of east European Jewry, but rather the mesmeric vision of the Jewish people transplanted to a Zion physically restored.

FORERUNNERS OF ZIONISM

If, then, in the earliest phases of its gestation, Jewish nationalism drew extensively from the messianic dream, it was less than surprising that one of the first to translate prophecy into a more contemporary framework should have been an Orthodox rabbi. Admittedly, there was little in the career of Rabbi Judah Alkalai to portend this insight. Born at the end of the eighteenth century, Alkalai was an obscure preacher in a little Sephardic community, Semlin, near Belgrade. In 1839, however, he astounded his congregants by publishing a Ladino-Hebrew textbook, *Darchei Noam* (Pleasant Paths), in the introduction of which he alluded to the need for establishing Jewish colonies in the Holy Land as a necessary prelude to the Redemption. In his later writings, of which the best-known was *Sh'ma Yisrael* (Hear, O Israel), Alkalai observed that self-effort toward this climactic physical and spiritual achievement was justified by the very "proof texts" of tradition. Had the Cabalah not intimated that the struggle of devoted Jewish common people everywhere would prefigure the coming of the Messiah? In 1840, moreover, the efforts of influential Western Jewish leaders achieved the release of several unfortunate Jews imprisoned in Damascus on blood libel charges. Alkalai detected in this "miracle" of vigorous secular action a precedent for future stages of redemption—in Palestine. In his booklet, *Minchat Yehuda* (The Offering of Judah), issued in 1843, Alkalai declared:

It is written in the Bible: "Return, O Lord, unto the tens of thousands of the families of Israel." . . . [But] upon what should the Divine Presence rest? On sticks and stones? Therefore, as the initial stage in the redemption of our souls, we must cause at least 22,000 to return to the Holy Land. This is the necessary precondition for a descent of the Divine Presence among us; afterward, He will grant us and all Israel additional signs of His favor.

During his remaining thirty-five years, Alkalai continued to publish his ideas extensively, and in the end he himself settled in Palestine as an example to others. Before his death in 1878, the energetic rabbi managed to organize a small group of followers. One of his disciples, interestingly enough, was Simon Loeb Herzl, the grandfather of Theodor. In truth, the link between Alkalai and Theodor Herzl was more than one of generational accident. Like Herzl later, the Rabbi of Semlin favored Jewish national unity through an all-embracing organization, and particularly through the intercession of affluent Western Jews.

Alkalai's views were paralleled to a remarkable degree by a contemporary and colleague, the Orthodox rabbi Zvi Hirsch Kalischer. Serving a large congregation in the Polish-speaking city of Thorn, East Prussia, Kalischer enjoyed a rather substantial following. As a consequence, he was given an immediate and respectful hearing when, like Alkalai, he too discerned in the progressive triumph of Western Jewish emancipation an augury of messianic redemption in Palestine. In 1843, Kalischer published his views in a two-volume work entitled *Emunah Yesharah* (An Honest Faith), and in 1862 completed his presentation in a final volume, *Drishat Zion* (The Search for Zion). Three principal theses were developed in these writings, supported by an impressive array of biblical texts and talmudical responsa. They were: that the salvation of the Jews, as foretold by the Prophets, could take place through natural means, that is, by self-help, and did not require the advent of the Messiah; that the colonization of Palestine should be launched without delay; and that the revival of sacrifices in the Holy Land was permissible. "Pay no heed," he wrote,

> to the traditional view that the Messiah will suddenly loose a blast on the Great Shofar and cause all the inhabitants of the earth to tremble. On the contrary, the Redemption will begin with the generating of support among philanthropists and with the gaining of the consent of the nations to the gathering of the scattered of Israel into the Holy Land.

Only when many pious and learned Jews volunteered to live in Jerusalem, Kalischer explained, would the Creator hearken to their prayers and speed the Day of Redemption.

Prayers would not suffice, however. Moving so far beyond traditional Orthodoxy that some colleagues branded his views heretical, Kalischer urged: the formation of a society of rich Jews to undertake the colonization of Zion; settlement by Jews of all backgrounds on the soil of the Holy Land; the training of young Jews in self-defense; and the establishment of an agricultural school in the Land of Israel where Jews might learn farming and other practical subjects. Far from undermining the study of the Torah (the first five books of the Bible), "the policy we propose will add dignity to the Torah. . . ." Kalischer's notion of "practical messianism" in fact was appealing enough to win over a small but influential group of contemporaries who joined him in founding a "Society for the Colonization of the Land of Israel." At Kalischer's initiative, too, the Alliance Israélite Universelle, a renowned French Jewish philanthropy, provided the initial subsidy for a Jewish agricultural school in the Holy Land. Established near Jaffa in 1870, the institution was called Mikveh Israel (Hope of Israel). It is worth noting, however, that Alkalai's and Kalischer's major activities took place during the heyday of mid-nineteenth-century liberalism, an era that inspired almost universal optimism on the future of Jewish emancipation in Europe. Indeed, at no time had the two rabbis ever based their appeal for settlement in Palestine on physical need. It was this lack of urgency, therefore, as well as an underlying Orthodox hostility toward "forcing the end," that accounted for a generally cool reaction to the proto-Zionist vision. At best, the ideas of the two rabbis could be regarded as a modern, but lineally descended, expression of the historic messianism that continued to infuse Jewish life in eastern Europe.

By mid-century, too, a messianic age of sorts appeared to have opened in Russia itself. In 1855, Alexander II ascended the tsarist throne and set about launching a vigorous program of domestic reforms, including a notably more humane approach to the Jews. Rejecting his father's notion of enforced conversion, the new ruler summarily did away with Jewish military "cantonment," the six-year preconscription horror of Russian Jewish life. Thereafter, a succession of imperial ukases allowed greater numbers of Jews to move into the Russian interior, to participate in a new scheme of zemstvo local government, to attend universities, and to practice their professions. The response of east European Jewry to the new and millennial epoch was not simply one of hope and gratitude; it was one of self-examination. For by mid-century a rather considerable Jewish middle class had developed in Galicia, along the border areas of the Pale of Settlement, and in the port city of Odessa. It was this new element that first reacted to the winds of humanism sweeping across Russia from the West.

With fresh opportunities suddenly opening for Jewish enterprise, the Jewish bourgeoisie now asked if the time had not come for all Jews in the tsarist empire to "modernize," to "productivize" themselves, by moving into more useful and dignified livelihoods and by wresting themselves free from the constricting lock-step of parochial Jewish education. This secularist awakening is known in Jewish history as the Haskalah, the mid-nineteenth-century period of east European Jewish "enlightenment." The earliest of the humanists, seeking an alternative to the squalid Jewish village and the insularity and cultural backwardness it represented, placed a new emphasis on nature and beauty, on love and physical action. Thus, the Haskalah poet Micah Joseph Lebensohn could write yearningly:

> Once in a leafy tree, there was my home.
> Torn from a swaying branch, friendless I roam,
> Plucked from the joyous green that gave me birth,
> What is my life to me, and of what worth?

For the Russian Jewish essayist Moshe Lilienblum and for the great Haskalah poet Judah Leib Gordon, there were "normalcy," insight, and enrichment to be gained from discourse with the surrounding Gentile population. "Be a Jew at home and a man in the street," argued Gordon, in the Haskalah's most radical credo—that is, observe one's Jewish traditions in the privacy of household and synagogue, but live a hearty, "normal" Russian life in the outer world.

By placing its faith in cultural emancipation and secular activity on Russian soil, Haskalah literature at first seemingly deemphasized the traditional messianic yearning for Zion. Yet Jewish humanism was responsible as well for a number of features that later were absorbed into the very mainstream of Zionist ideology. In its demand for vocational "productivization," for example, Haskalah literature extolled the merits of physical labor in the fields and factories, a conception that later was to become the very bedrock of Labor Zionism. It idealized, too, a new secular Jew who appraised the world about him realistically, emancipated from the cloisters of religious obscurantism. Most important, the Haskalah revitalized the Hebrew language. Until mid-century, Hebrew had been consigned to the synagogue and the religious school; Yiddish remained the daily vernacular of east European Jewry. Now, however, the writers of the Jewish enlightenment consciously revived Hebrew as their vehicle of expression. One of their motives conceivably was social, to differentiate themselves from the Yiddish-speaking proletariat. But the principal reason unquestionably was ethnocentric, to assure that the Jews who wakened from their insularity would not become simply educated Jewish Russians, in the manner of the German salon-Jews of preceding decades, but enlightened Russian Jews, aware of the treasured values of their heritage. And for whatever purpose, the secular, literary use of this classical tongue inevitably evoked a rich skein of historical associations. Thus, in Hebrew, it was natural to describe the conditions of Jewish life, even its straitened parochialism, in terminology rich with biblical allusions; to contrast the circumstances of the Russian Jewish village with the legendary (and idealized) glories of ancient Zion.

Zion, then, as envisaged by the Haskalah writers, became a kind of mythic idyll—in the words of Lebensohn, "the land where the muses dwell, where each flower is a Psalm, each cedar a song divine, each stone a book and each rock a tablet." In the ornately tapestried historical romances of Kalman Schulman and Abraham Mapu, biblical Palestine was projected as the terrain of ancient glory, inhabited by robust farmers and soldiers, by epic heroes and men of action. During the 1870s the Hebrew-language journals enlarged upon this biblical ideal in a kind of pre-adumbrated Zionism. At the same time, however, their pages reflected a growing concern lest "enlightenment" divert the new generation of secularly educated Jews from a basic identification with their people's fate and fortunes. It was a cautionary theme that received its most eloquent treatment at the hands of Perez Smolenskin. A White Russian Jew, the founder-editor of the Hebrew literary monthly *HaShachar* (The Dawn), Smolenskin was the author of six novels and of innumerable essays that, more than any other body of work, laid the foundations of literary realism in the Hebrew language. Not less significantly, he was the first of the major Hebrew writers to warn against the extravagances and dangers of Haskalah.

Like the Russian Slavophiles, disenchanted with the false blandishments of the West, Smolenskin feared that Haskalah extremism was inducing thousands of Jewish humanists to reject their ancestral loyalties. In 1872 his most widely read essay, "Am Olam" (Eternal People), appeared in the pages of *HaShachar*. It was a trenchant defense of Jewish peoplehood:

> The willfully blind bid us to be like all other nations, and I repeat after them: let us be like all the other nations, pursuing and attaining knowledge, leaving

off from wickedness and folly. . . . Yes, let us be like all the other nations, unashamed of the rock whence we have been hewn, like the rest in holding dear our language and the glory of our people.

The western European conception of Judaism as a religious confession was bankrupt, Smolenskin asserted. So, too, was Gordon's concept of the duality of the Jew—"in the home" and "in the street." The time had come to gird for the moral, even political, resurrection of the Jewish people as a national entity. In later essays, Smolenskin made plain that all methods were legitimate in sustaining the national ideal, not excluding the physical colonization of the Land of Israel (p. 14). Yet in this earlier phase of his writings, too, and well before the tsarist pogroms of the 1880s, Smolenskin's unerring instinct for his colleagues' latent ethnic pride fulfilled a decisive role. He launched the first intellectually effective counterattack against the current Haskalah illusion that secular modernism, rather than national revival, was somehow the answer to the Jewish problem in Europe.

EUROPEAN NATIONALISM AND RUSSIAN UPHEAVAL

If the regenerative impulse latent in both messianism and humanism kindled a Zionist spark among Russian Jewry, so also did the emergence of other nineteenth-century nationalist and irredentist movements. "Let us take to heart the examples of the Italians, Poles and Hungarians," wrote Rabbi Kalischer in one of his articles. "All the other peoples have striven only for the sake of their own national honor; how much more should we exert ourselves, for our duty is to labor . . . for the glory of God who chose Zion!" The Jung Deutschland movement powerfully impressed Micah Joseph Lebensohn, who lived for three years in Berlin; even as Hungarian and Slovakian nationalism deeply affected Smolenskin and Leo Pinsker (p. 14) in the course of their respective sojourns in Vienna. Eliezer Perlman (Ben-Yehuda), a witness to the Pan-Slavism sweeping the Balkans during the Russo-Turkish War of 1877, asked: "Why should we be any less worthy than any other people? What about our nation, our language, our land?"

Perhaps the most original response to the nationalist awakening was that of Moses Hess, the son of an Orthodox Jewish family of Bonn. Reared in the early post-Napoleonic era, exposed to the influences of German scholarship and literature, Hess as a young man gradually lost interest in religion —of any variety—and ceased to be a practicing Jew. His punishment was ejection from his father's business. Thereafter he wandered across Germany, fitfully trying his hand at teaching and writing. Enrolling for a while at the University of Bonn, a "tall, scrawny man, with benevolent eyes and a cock-like curve to his neck," as he was described later by his fellow student Karl Marx, Hess preached mildly of love, humanity, justice, and sympathy for the poor. In fact, he was preaching a kind of utopian socialism; and in Paris he went so far as to marry a prostitute out of socialist compassion. Reflecting, too, the Hegelian interest in history then current in Germany,

Hess in 1837 published his first book, *The Holy History of Mankind by a Young Spinozist.* It sank without a trace. The young man subsequently occupied himself with political journalism.

Hess's Jewish interests were revived by the apparently ineradicable anti-Semitism of "cosmopolitan" western Europe. In 1857 the writings of Rabbi Kalischer were drawn to his notice, and Hess was impelled to begin a systematic study of Jewish history. Almost simultaneously, too, he became deeply engrossed in the works of the Italian nationalist Mazzini, and was moved by the apparent fulfillment of the latter's dream of a united Italy. It was the combination of these social and intellectual influences that resulted in Hess's second volume, *Rome and Jerusalem,* published in 1862. "Here I stand again in the midst of my people," he admitted at the outset, "after being estranged from it for twenty years." Hess thereupon confessed that his encounters with European nationalism, his studies in ethnicity, had persuaded him that his original cosmopolitan vision of a single homogeneity of nations was outdated. Each people, he wrote, nurtured its own individual traits, its own unique ambitions and "mission"; the events "now transpiring in Italy" confirmed that view, for "on the ruins of Christian Rome a regenerated Italian people is rising." Hess insisted, then, that what the Italians and others had achieved must also be achieved by the Jews, who represented the "last great national problem" in Europe. If the Italians had a mission, so, no less, did the Jews in Palestine. "Only a national renaissance can endow the religious genius of the Jews . . . with new strength, and raise its soul once again to the level of prophetic inspiration."

Rome and Jerusalem was unique in its prefigurations of later and better-known Zionist doctrines. It anticipated the writings of Ber Borochov and of other Labor Zionists, for example, by asserting that return to the Land of Israel was indispensable if the Jews were to shed their function as a historical anomaly, a social parasite in the lands of other peoples. Only on ancestral soil would Jewish labor find it possible to organize on "correct Socialist" principles. Two decades before Pinsker, Hess issued the warning that a national homeland offered the Jews their last, best chance of self-transformation into a "normal" people, emancipated from the vulnerable phantom status that historically had provoked anti-Semitism. Predating Herzl, Hess envisaged the self-interested collaboration of other governments in reviving a Jewish protégé nation in the Middle East, and the active help of the "Jewish princes"—Rothschild, Montefiore, and other millionaires—who would fund and organize Jewish colonization in Palestine. With these and other insights, Hess's book was a dazzling tour de force of ideological prophecy. Even so, *Rome and Jerusalem* ignited no fires in the Jewish world—not in 1862. Only two hundred copies of the work were sold in the five years after its appearance. It found no English translator for fifty years and was published as a book in Hebrew only in 1899. Hess's role as an authentic visionary of Zionism awaited the centenary of his volume in 1962, when his remains at last were flown from Germany to Israel, and reinterred on the shores of Lake Galilee in a state ceremony.

It is of significance that Hess's writings carried a pungent warning that more than Jewish religious or national ideals awaited fulfillment in Palestine; sheer physical existence was also at stake. For Hess's ethnic theories alluded not only to differences between nations and peoples, but to the fundamental antipathy between them, and particularly to the animus of the German toward the Jew. "We shall always remain strangers among the nations," he insisted. The validity of this jeremiad was almost instantly confirmed. At first, however, it was less the pseudoscience of German racism than a cruel outburst of Russian nationalism that transformed Zionism from an intellectual theory into an urgent survivalist movement. In the 1860s and 1870s, Slavophilism, a curiously hybrid fusion of Byzantine Orthodoxy and Great Russian nationalism, gained momentum in the tsarist empire. Subsequently Alexander III's accession to the throne in 1881, upon the murder of his father at the hands of revolutionaries, ushered in the grimmest period of chauvinist oppression in modern Russian history. Committed to national homogeneity as the foundation of imperial power, the new tsar regarded the ethnic minorities in his dominions as a standing challenge to his autocracy. Almost immediately, therefore, the non-Russian races—Poles, Estonians, Latvians, Finns, Armenians, Turkmenians, among others—found themselves subjected to a far-reaching campaign of discrimination in public employment and in educational and cultural self-expression.

By no coincidence, the Jews once again were the victims of an especial refinement of persecution, for they remained the most suspect and vulnerable of the empire's minorities. Numbering approximately 5 million at the time of the 1897 census, they remained confined by and large to their Pale of Settlement, an area encompassing 20 percent of European Russia. Half of them lived in towns and cities, the rest in villages and hamlets. To the tsarist regime, moreover, this vast, closely knit Jewish enclave was the object not merely of enforced "Russification," but of organized counterrevolutionary diversion. The bureaucracy was shrewdly determined now to stigmatize "revolutionarism" as nothing less than a Jewish plot. Thus, in 1881, a chain reaction of officially inspired pogroms erupted throughout the dense Jewish hinterland of southern Russia and the Ukraine, taking dozens of lives and wreaking extensive physical damage. The following year a government committee under the chairmanship of the minister of the interior, Count Nicolai Ignatiev, issued a report stating bluntly that the late Alexander II's policy of toleration had failed, that harsh measures were now in order against Russian Jewry. Thereupon Alexander III issued a new series of anti-Jewish decrees on May 3, 1882, in the form of "temporary regulations." Far from being temporary, however, the regulations continued in effect, with mounting stringency in their enforcement, until the March Revolution of 1917.

By the provisions of these "May Laws," all further rural areas were closed to Jewish settlement. Within the Pale, Jews by the hundreds of thousands were driven from the countryside into the city slums. A much tighter *numerus clausus* was imposed in Russian high schools and universities, and Jews were systematically uprooted from the professions. As a consequence both of oppression and of developing industrialization, the economic base of Russian Jewish life was soon all but fatally undermined. By the end of the century, nearly 40 percent of the empire's Jews were at least partially dependent on charity or remittances from kinsmen living abroad, and their sheer physical survival was placed in gravest jeopardy. In this fashion, then, the government's intentions were being fulfilled admirably. "One-third will die out," Konstantin Pobedonostsev, the tsar's closest adviser, blandly observed in 1894, "one-third will leave the country, and one-third will be completely dissolved in the surrounding population." Elsewhere too in eastern Europe, in Austrian Galicia and Rumania, the industrial crisis was almost as serious. Vocationally expendable as a consequence of technological change, inundated by floods of Russian Jewish refugees, burdened (in the case of Rumania) with heavy legal disabilities, the indigenous Jewish communities gradually were reduced to the narrowest margin of subsistence.

PALESTINE AS REFUGE AND RENAISSANCE

The May Laws, and the pogroms of 1881–82 and their aftermath, shattered Russian Jewry's final lingering illusions of equality and achievement under tsarist rule. Even their faith in the redeeming value of enlightenment was blasted, for Russian academicians and university students, no less than government officials and illiterate muzhiks, joined enthusiastically in the new anti-Jewish campaign. "I intended to devote my strength and energy to serving the interests of my country," Chaim Chissin, a Jewish medical student, lamented in his diary, "and honestly to fulfill the obligations of a good citizen. . . . And now suddenly we are shown the door. It is too much for a sensitive Jew." Lev Levanda, one of the paladins of the Haskalah, opened his heart in the Russian Jewish journal *Rassviet* (Daybreak): "When I think of what was done to us, how we were taught to love Russia and the Russian word, how we were lured into introducing the Russian language and everything Russian in our home . . . and how we are now rejected and hounded . . . my heart is filled with corroding despair from which there is no escape." But of course there had to be some escape. One response was the growth of Jewish socialism, a movement ultimately destined to embrace hundreds of thousands of Jewish workers and their families. Even among the Jewish proletariat, however, there was a strong undertow of awareness that the most effective immediate solution was emigration from Russia altogether. The United States was regarded as the most likely sanctuary.

Nevertheless, for other Jews a continuation of minority status among Gentiles anywhere was no longer an answer. Moshe Lilienblum, the distinguished Jewish humanist, had spent two days cowering in a basement as Russian mobs churned through his neighborhood. "All the old ideals left me in a flash," he wrote afterward. "There is no home for us in this, or any, Gentile land." Henceforth he regarded departure for Palestine as the one remaining solution of the Jewish question, and he pressed this view in innumerable articles. In 1882 he wrote:

This is the land in which our fathers have found rest since time immemorial—and as they lived, so shall we live. Let us go now to the only land in which we will find relief for our souls that have been harassed by murderers for these thousands of years. Our beginnings will be small, but in the end we will flourish.

Smolenskin, too, the last and greatest figure of Haskalah, now abandoned his earlier conception of the Jews as a uniquely "spiritual" nation and called for mass emigration to Palestine. "Now is the time to circulate this idea," he wrote in 1881, "and to raise funds to help settle those who will go to the Land of Israel. And now for the sake of resettlement in Zion, let us neither be still nor quiet until the light dawns and causes our healing to begin."

Lilienblum's and Smolenskin's focus on Palestine as asylum may have emerged naturally from the messianic tradition, from the Hebraic strain in Haskalah, even from the example of other European nationalist movements. Yet, whatever their disillusionment with the "exile," neither Smolenskin nor Lilienblum, any more than Alkalai or Kalischer before them, offered compelling evidence that the tide of Gentile prejudice might not eventually crest, perhaps even be dissipated by political change within Russia itself. Hundreds of thousands of Jewish liberals and Socialists continued to nurture that dream, after all, and in western Europe and America they were witnessing its apparent realization. If, then, ancient folk memories of Palestine failed to arouse the enthusiasm of these secular leftists, what other compelling incentive was there for them to return to the wilderness of Zion? One such inducement existed, as it happened. It took the form of a rigorous "scientific" analysis of the Jewish condition.

Leo Pinsker was the son of an "enlightened" family of Odessa, a city that functioned as the nerve center of mid-nineteenth-century Haskalah. Educated in the Russian school system, he had studied medicine at the University of Moscow. Afterward, during the Crimean War, he had volunteered as an army doctor and had won high esteem for his performance battling a cholera epidemic. During the benign reform era of Alexander II, Pinsker shared in the prevailing optimism of the 1860s. Indeed, as a loyal Jew and a frequent contributor to *Rassviet,* he publicized his faith in both Russian toleration and Jewish enlightenment. His vision of the Jewish future at this stage was, like Smolenskin's, one of cultural self-expression within a pluralistic Russia. In 1871, however, an anti-Jewish outbreak erupted briefly in Odessa. Deeply unsettled by the episode, Pinsker withdrew from all Jewish public activities for the next seven years and brooded upon the evident failure of his cherished ideal of enlightenment. His disillusionment was reinforced by the political events of 1881 and their aftermath. It was then, at the age of sixty, that Pinsker departed Russia to visit leaders in central and western Europe and to offer them his plan for Jewish survival. "I put all my soul into the argument," he wrote Lev Levanda afterward. "I made use of all the facts, trying to play upon all the strings of the human heart." Apparently Pinsker was less than successful. Nevertheless, he remained for several months in Berlin, where he organized his views in writing, and published them (in German) in September 1882.

His lengthy essay bore the straightforward title *Selbstemanzipation* (Auto-emancipation).

In this work Pinsker outlined his central thesis: normal dealings between peoples were founded on mutual respect, not love; and it was unlikely the Jews ever could be accorded such respect, for they lacked its prerequisite of national equality. "The Jewish people has no fatherland of its own," Pinsker observed, "no center of gravity, no government of its own, no official representation." Rather, the Jews were perceived as a kind of "phantom people," bearing many of the characteristics of nationhood without the final indispensable ingredient of a land of their own. "There is something unnatural about a people without a territory, just as there is about a man without a shadow." Worse yet, as a phantom people, the Jews inspired fear among the non-Jewish majority; and whatever people feared, they hated. If, then, "the prejudice of mankind against us rests upon anthropological and social principles, innate and ineradicable," it was futile to seek the disappearance of these "natural laws" through enlightenment, assimilation, dispersion, or Jewish ultrapatriotism. The solution to the Jewish condition, Pinsker insisted, lay not in reliance upon the will-o'-the-wisp of emancipation, but in a concerted attempt by the Jews to utilize their waning moment of opportunity to restore a national home of their own. Only on such a basis could the Jews achieve the recognizable physiognomy of other nations. "Let 'now or never' be our watchword!" he exclaimed. "Woe to our descendants . . . if we let this moment pass by!" It was illustrative of Pinsker's "scientific objectivity," however, that he attached no especial sentimental importance to Palestine. "The piece of land might form a small territory in North America, or a sovereign Pashalik in Asiatic Turkey. . . ." What counted most was recognized nationhood on a land, any land.

Until Pinsker, the vulnerability of the Jews as a homeless people had never been demonstrated quite so systematically. For the first time Jew-hatred was analyzed as a deeply complex social phenomenon, bearing little relationship to education or progress in conventional terms. Almost immediately, therefore, *Selbstemanzipation* evoked a responsive chord among its readers. Gordon and Lilienblum praised it effusively, as did other Haskalah spokesmen. Very quickly, Pinsker became one of the most admired men in Russian Jewry. Indeed, for a while he was the very heart of the gestating Zionist movement. Like Herzl later, Pinsker would have preferred that the headquarters of the movement be established in the West. He had little faith in Russian Jewry, impoverished and straitjacketed as it was by tsarist restrictions; as he saw it, only Western Jews, especially German Jews, commanded the political influence and financial means to secure a national territorial base. And yet, over the next year and a half, in 1882–83, it was specifically among the Western Jewish "aristocrats" that Pinsker failed to elicit a meaningful response. As a result, he was obliged increasingly to turn his attention to his Zionist following in eastern Europe. "It is our most wholesome, most reliable element," he admitted. In 1884, encouraged by Dr. Max Mandelstamm of Kiev and Professor

Hermann Schapira of Heidelberg, Pinsker finally set about organizing his amorphous collection of followers into a national movement.

THE CHOVEVEI ZION

By the late 1870s, several years before the outbreak of Alexander III's pogroms, Zionist study circles and clubs had begun to function in hundreds of the Pale's cities and towns. Some called themselves "parties" or "assemblies." A number adopted such titles as Ezra or Maccabi. But all were generally known as Chovevei Zion—Lovers of Zion. Their common ingredient was acceptance of the credo "that there is no salvation for the People of Israel unless they establish a government of their own in the Land of Israel." In the classic pattern of other European nationalist movements, a few of these early groups simply offered courses in the Hebrew language and history. Others established choirs or gymnastic and self-defense organizations. The meetings were conducted secretly, for Zionism, like other varieties of minority nationalism, was quite illegal in the tsarist empire. More inhibiting yet, there was no central direction to the Chovevei Zion cause.

It was under these circumstances that Pinsker, by prestige and general recognition the natural leader of the burgeoning Zionist movement, took the initiative in 1884 of summoning a national conference of the various Chovevei Zion societies. To circumvent the Russian authorities, the meeting was convened in Kattowitz, a German Silesian city. Thirty-four delegates attended the initial gathering, and reached a consensus on the financing of Jewish settlement in Palestine as their first priority. Only in the Land of Israel, it was agreed, could the People of Israel be transformed into a viable society and nation. The organization's central office was established in Odessa. As president there of the Chovevei Zion, Pinsker was charged with directing a growing stream of Jewish emigrants to Palestine. There was a certain irony in this task, for Pinsker himself opposed the piecemeal approach to settlement. He would have favored strengthening the Zionist ranks in Europe, afterward summoning an international Jewish Congress to place the Jewish question before the governments of the world. Failing to win conference support of his views, however, Pinsker was obliged to devote his energies thereafter to a colonization effort in Palestine that he regarded at best as of minimal value.

As it turned out, Pinsker, like Herzl after him, underrated the importance of this gradualist effort. It was uniquely as a "Society for the Support of Jewish Agriculturists and Artisans in Palestine and Syria," rather than as a nationalist organization, that the Chovevei Zion in 1890 won a certain unofficial toleration from the St. Petersburg government (Chapter ii). Afterward, too, Pinsker's propaganda efforts throughout Europe on behalf of migration to the Holy Land were remarkably successful. Indeed, before his death in 1891, he managed to provide the Chovevei Zion with a coherent ideology and an organizational framework, to strengthen the foundations of Palestine colonization, and to achieve a quasi-legalization for the movement in Russia.

In the 1890s the Chovevei Zion grew rapidly in many parts of Europe and overseas. It took strong root in Rumania, where the Jewish position was hardly less marginal than in Russia. In the Habsburg Empire the movement was led primarily by east European Jews living in Vienna. One of these was Smolenskin, and another, later, was Dr. Nathan Birnbaum, who first coined the term "Zionism." In Berlin, too, Chovevei Zion groups were founded by Russian Jewish students, prominent among them Leo Motzkin, Chaim Weizmann, and Shmaryahu Levin. Similar groups later were organized among German Jewish students, including the future leaders of German Zionism—Victor Jacobson, Willi Bambus, and Arthur Hantke. In England a Chovevei Zion organization was founded under the leadership of eminent Sephardic Jews, Colonel Albert Goldsmid and Eli d'Avigdor (its branches were called "tents"). Even in the United States, a philo-Zionist group was sponsored in the early 1880s by Russian Jewish immigrants and several distinguished rabbis, Gustav Gottheil, Benjamin Szold, and Marcus Jastrow. Thus it was, by the time Herzl appeared on the scene, that he encountered in Europe and America the nucleus of a thoroughly respectable Zionist movement. Its various societies provided him with the largest number of his followers, including 90 percent of the delegates attending the First Zionist Congress in 1897.

To be sure, Zionism still remained an avant-garde within the Jewish world in the late nineteenth century. Yet it was by no means an insignificant force. As has been seen, its origins traced back in part to Jewish liturgy and tradition, where the messianic image of Zion remained as tactile as the geography of the Diaspora itself. In fact, Zionism strengthened its bonds with the Orthodox religionists by adopting as its own symbols a number of traditional Jewish holidays, those memorializing heroic moments in Jewish history or celebrating Palestinian harvests or sowing seasons. Accordingly, while flight from persecution offered the key to Jewish survival after 1881, the Jewish religious leadership could regard emigration to a Jewish ancestral land more benevolently than departure to the *terra incognita* of emancipated secular countries in the West. It was from European nationalism, meanwhile, that the Zionists derived example and inspiration, even as they adopted from the Haskalah two particularly vital features of their movement: the Hebrew language, with its biblical evocations; and the conviction that the Jewish problem must be solved logically and dynamically, rather than by a fatalistic immersion in traditional Orthodoxy. But for this tough-minded pragmatism, it is questionable whether members of the Russian Jewish intelligentsia would have been as capable of accepting Pinsker's unsparing analysis of the Jewish condition. Their willingness to do so enabled Zionism to exploit the general east European Jewish mood of migration, and to infuse it with an ideological élan that survived even the cruelest realities of pioneering settlement in the Land of Israel itself.

THE BEGINNING

OF THE RETURN

THE LINK WITH THE LAND

Halfway between Safed and Naharia in northern Israel, the angulated, terraced slope of Mount Ha'ari, 3,300 feet above sea level, commands a simultaneous view of the Mediterranean to the west and of Lake Galilee to the southeast. Branching off westward, a road leads directly into the sheltered little village of Peki'in, a somewhat nondescript enclave of limestone houses, inhabited by mixed communities of Druze, Arabs, and a few Jews. A synagogue guards the flank of the entryway. It is an ancient structure. We are informed that the two carved stones in its walls once belonged to the original Temple of Jerusalem, destroyed by the Romans more than 1,900 years before. The Zainati family that worships here traces its origins equally far. Indeed, its members note with pride that they are the only Jews in Israel whose forebears have lived uninterruptedly in the Holy Land since the days of the last Jewish Commonwealth. Small of bone, dark-skinned, bilingual in Hebrew and Arabic, the Peki'in Jews cultivate the land, breed silkworms, and devotedly guard their shrines and historic memories. Perhaps with quiet bemusement, too, they endure the glances of visitors who are fascinated by the sight of "authentic" Hebrews.

But authentic they are, these little Arabized Jews, the embodiment of a physical Jewish connection with Palestine that never quite expired. The Romans may have laid the entire nation waste between A.D. 70 and 135, slaughtering as many as 600,000 Jews, and carrying off half that number in bondage. Yet even in the wake of this monumental dispersion, a few thousand Jews somehow remained on in the country. Heavily taxed, denied the right to visit their ancient capital, the survivors made their homes in Galilee, where they farmed their land and plied their trades. In the late Roman era this decimated Jewish community actually managed something of a revival. For three centuries, its towns, villages, and farms extended as far as the coastal plain, and were reasonably affluent. Its culture showed signs of a certain uneven vitality. During this period, for example, the Palestinian Talmud was compiled. Moreover, the Jewish population sustained its growth well beyond the Arab conquest in the seventh century, and even under the Seljuk Turks, ultimately reaching 300,000 inhabitants by the year 1000.

This promising interlude ended abruptly, however, and quite terribly, with the arrival of the Crusaders. Thereafter, the butchery of Jews was so extensive under Christian rule that in 1169, when Benjamin of Tudela, a Spanish Jewish traveler, visited the Holy Land, he found only a thousand Jewish families still alive. Yet even then the foothold was tenaciously maintained. Eighteen years later Salah-ed-Din (Saladin), sultan of Egypt, won a crushing victory over the Latin Kingdoms and began the process that ultimately evicted the last of the Crusaders a century later. Subsequently, under a tolerant Moslem regime, pilgrimages of Jews from overseas augmented the tiny Palestinian remnant. The immigrants arrived from North Africa, from Europe, and most particularly from Spain, the largest Jewish community in the Diaspora. Well before the pressures of the Inquisition, in fact, some 5,000 Sephardic Jews (from Sepharad, the Hebrew word for Spain) had already established their preeminence among other Jews in the Holy Land, swallowing up the Musta'aribin (Arabized Jews) and imposing their own Ladino dialect as the lingua franca of Palestine Jewry.

Yet it was most notably the Spanish Inquisition, and finally the Spanish expulsion decree in 1492, that propelled tens of thousands of Sephardim into all corners of the Mediterranean world, and not less than 8,000 of them into Palestine. By fortunate chance, their arrival corresponded with the Ottoman conquest of the Levant (1517), and in its first century the rule of the Turks proved unexpectedly benign. Thus, in ensuing years, other Jews made their way to Palestine from the Mediterranean littoral. Most of them were Cabalists, followers of the *Zohar*, a volume of Jewish mysticism that prophesied the final redemption of God's Spirit in the outer world. Not surprisingly, the Cabalists had discerned in the Spanish upheaval a timely injunction to return to ancestral soil in expectation of the "End of Days." Large numbers of them settled in the abandoned Crusader city of Safed, precisely because Safed was located only a half-hour's donkey ride from the tomb of Rabbi Shimon Bar-Yochai, the *Zohar's* putative author. They were joined in the seventeenth and eighteenth centuries by fitful migrations of Ashkenazim, Jews from central or northern Europe (literally, from Ashkenaz, the Hebrew word for Germany). Moreover, the largest numbers among the Europeans called themselves Chasidim, "Followers of the (True) Way." Like many of the Sephardic Jews, the Chasidim also were devotees of Cabalistic literature and similarly regarded themselves as mystics, although of a more emotional and rapturous variety. Sephardic and Ashkenazic newcomers alike, then, increased Safed's Jewish population to 16,000 by the opening of the eighteenth century. Many of the pilgrims remained dependent on charity from abroad, but most of them became self-supporting as tinkers, shoemakers, spice merchants, even occasionally as farmers.

Elsewhere in Palestine, Jewish habitation was less impressive. A brief Sephardic attempt to establish a community in ancient Tiberias, on a tract provided by the Ottoman sultan, failed to attract settlers. Later efforts were abandoned in the face of local Arab opposition, although a limited nucleus of dark-skinned, Arabic-speaking Jews is still to be found (among more recent Jewish immigrants) in this modest, lakeside town. Similar efforts were mounted in Hebron, revered as the birthplace of King David and as the reputed gravesite of the Hebrew patriarchs. But at its high point, in 1890, Jewish settlement in Hebron comprised barely 1,500 souls, most of them clustered around three or four talmudical academies. The most tenacious redemptionist effort, rather, was devoted to Jerusalem, home of the ancient Temple and thereby queen over Safed, Hebron, and Tiberias in the hierarchy of Palestine's four "holy" cities. At the outset, to be sure, the likelihood of revival there seemed almost foredoomed. During the three and a half centuries of Roman dominion after the first century A.D., not a single Jew had been permitted to set foot in the ravaged capital. Under Arab rule, handfuls of Jews returned to Jerusalem, and a small number of them continued to live there even under the Crusaders. After the first century of Ottoman rule, however, the Turks proceeded to make life increasingly difficult for Christians and Jews alike. In 1700 one last group of 1,500 Ashkenazim, under Rabbi Judah the Chasid, ventured a heroic attempt to take up domicile within the city's Turkish wall. Some 500 of these pilgrims died even before arriving in the Holy City; of the rest, only a tiny enclave of thirty families survived a bare two and a half decades. "Tax-farmers lie in wait like wolves and lions to devour us," wrote one of the settlers. Simon van Geldern, a Dutch Jew who visited in 1776, found perhaps 2,000 Arabic-speaking Sephardic and Moroccan Jews dwelling in Jerusalem, but only the meagerest residue of European Jews. "In fifty years' time no Ashkenazim will be living in this land anymore," he wrote.

Van Geldern hardly exaggerated. Under an increasingly brutal Ottoman administration, even the once flourishing Jewish population of Safed declined to 3,000 souls by 1800. From then on, Arab bandits roamed unchecked through the Galilee and periodically despoiled the little mountain city. Finally, in 1837, Safed was convulsed by a massive earthquake, the most fearful natural disaster in the history of modern Palestine. Having buried their dead, the more enterprising survivors moved away to Jerusalem and Hebron. The 2,000 or so who remained in Safed were largely aging pietists, mirror images of their kinsmen in Jerusalem. No more than 6,000 Jews altogether lingered on in the four holy cities. Taxed and tyrannized as they were to within an inch of their lives, they regarded their ordeal essentially as a testament of repentance.

PALESTINE AND EUROPEAN CONSCIOUSNESS

If there were auguries of hope, nevertheless, for this remnant Jewry in the nineteenth century, it was because Palestine itself was emerging from its legendary mists and entering the realm of public interest. Napoleon's invasion of Egypt in 1798, the emergence of the Russian threat to the Ottoman Empire at the turn of the century, Mehemet Ali's conquest of Syria in the 1830s, the Crimean War in the 1850s, Britain's occupation of Cyprus in 1878 and of Egypt in 1882—all opened up the East as a critical new arena of world politics. With other nations of the Middle East, Palestine once again was restored to the map, and it became the object of general European attention, of improved communications, and of growing tourism and archaeological exploration.

These developments coincided with, and indeed contributed to, the rise of British Protestant evangelicalism. At once fundamentalist and visionary, this uniquely mid-Victorian brand of pietism included a renewed and vested interest in the Holy Land. Theological concern was directed as well toward the Jews, who were regarded now less as deicides than as sacred exiles from sacred soil, a living witness to God's truth in an unredeemed world. Typical of the upsurge of millennialism was the proto-Zionist career of Edward Ashley, seventh earl of Shaftesbury. An influential political figure in the mid-nineteenth century, Shaftesbury nurtured a compelling spiritual vision of the People of Israel restored by Britain's grace to the Holy Land, in this fashion setting in motion the whole chain of divine events leading to the Second Coming. So widely diffused was the mood of nineteenth-century evangelicalism that Shaftesbury and his fellow millennialists were not regarded as mere eccentrics. Even as impassioned a proto-Zionist as Laurence Oliphant was taken seriously by English men of affairs. The son of an intensely devout family, married to a woman equally pietistic, Oliphant had joined the diplomatic corps, had served in posts ranging from Canada to Japan, and had traveled widely on his own. Ardently he shared his wife's dream that "God's Holy People" soon would be restored to the cradle of its birth, thus hastening the Millennium and the Advent. Like Shaftesbury, he hurled himself into endless propaganda work and public meetings on behalf of a Jewish national restoration.

So respectable by mid-century was the concept of Zion redeemed that it won the approbation of several of Britain's most distinguished romantic poets and novelists. Thus, the arch-romanticist of his time, Benjamin Disraeli, flaunted the cause of Jewish restoration in *Alroy*, one of his earliest novels: "You ask me what I wish: my answer is, a national existence. . . . You ask me what I wish: my answer is, the Land of Promise." Other Victorian writers imputed to the Jews (as to the Scots, Greeks, Bulgars, and other historic races) the pageant-struck nationalism that was universally recognized as the wave of Europe's future. In "Oh! Weep for Those," one of the more widely quoted of his *Hebrew Melodies*, Lord Byron wrote poignantly:

The white dove hath her nest, the fox his cave.
Mankind their country—Israel but the grave.

For Sir Walter Scott, the tantalizing dream of a restored Zion was expressed through the person of Rebecca, the exotic Jewess of *Ivanhoe*. It was through the Jewish hero, too, of her novel *Daniel Deronda* that George Eliot projected an identical Christian-romantic vision "[that] the outraged Jew shall have a defence in the court of nations. . . . And the world will gain as Israel gains." Ironically, these romantic and millennialist fantasies embodied no practical yearnings by the Jews themselves, who distrusted them as blatantly conversionary.

While suspect in Jewish eyes, however, proto-Zionism fulfilled an increasingly useful purpose for European leaders obsessed with the developing Eastern Question. Thus, marching on Palestine in April 1799 during his Oriental campaign against Britain, Napoleon issued the Jews of Asia and Africa a florid invitation to gather under his flag and reestablish their ancient capital of Jerusalem. "Israelites, arise!" the proclamation declared.

> Ye exiled, arise! Hasten! Now is the moment which may not return for thousands of years, to claim the restoration of civic rights among the population of the universe which have shamefully been withheld from you for thousands of years, to claim your political existence as a nation among nations, and the unlimited natural right to worship Jehovah according to your faith, publicly and most probably forever. . . .

The wretched Jewish settlement of Jerusalem, let alone the other Jews of Asia and North Africa, did not so much as hear of this pronunciamento. The next month, in any case, the French army was routed by the British outside Acre, and Napoleon hurriedly led his shattered columns back to Egypt.

Forty years later, however, Europe's foreign ministers assembled in London to deal with the crisis precipitated by Mehemet Ali's invasion of Syria and Palestine. Cornered by Shaftesbury and other millennialists, British Foreign Secretary Palmerston swallowed whole the notion that the Jews themselves were champing at the bit to return to Zion and that their presence in the Holy Land would serve Ottoman (and British) interests. Thereupon, Palmerston wrote his ambassador in Constantinople:

> There exists at the present time, among the Jews dispersed over Europe, a strong notion that the time is approaching when their nation is to return to Palestine. . . . It would be of manifest importance to the Sultan to encourage the Jews to return . . . because the wealth which they would bring with them would increase the resources of the Sultan's dominions; and the Jewish people, if returning under the sanction and protection and at the invitation of the Sultan, would be a check upon any future evil designs of Mehemet Ali or his successor.

Later yet, during the Crimean War and the Lebanese crisis of 1860, Christian proto-Zionists in France suggested that their government's foreign-policy goals might well be advanced by a Jewish buffer state in Palestine. The Congress of Berlin of 1878 provoked even further interest in the idea. It will be seen later (Chapter v) with what extraordinary fidelity this seemingly arcane notion would be revived during World War I.

THE "OLD SETTLEMENT"

Loosely divided between the provinces of Beirut and Syria, the Palestine of the early 1800s was hardly less than an administrative shambles. Centuries of Turkish indifference and misgovernment had encouraged recurrent warfare between local pashas and had permitted Bedouin robber bands to terrorize the country's 400,000 inhabitants (by 1840). Trade was minimal. The entire region was agriculture-based, but stunted in its growth by the depredations of tax farmers, by army recruitment, forced labor, drought, and locusts. Concentrated by and large in the four holy cities, the Jews numbered between 5,000 and 6,000 at the opening of the nineteenth century. Had Palestine remained a neglected backwater of the Ottoman realm, it is unlikely that this meager settlement would have transcended its status as a fossilized curiosity. But the emergence of the Eastern Question witnessed a growing Ottoman dependence upon western Europe, and the price of that support—against Russia—was not merely Constantinople's assurances of reform, but a reassertion in 1840 of European Capitulations throughout the Turkish Empire. The capitulatory arrangement in its essence simply guaranteed resident European nationals a kind of legal and financial immunity under the protection of their respective consuls. Moreover, by an Anglo-Turkish understanding achieved in 1864 through the good offices of the British consul in Jerusalem, this protection was extended equally to Jewish residents of the Holy Land. The Capitulations thereafter provided the stimulus for a growing European Jewish immigration. Indeed, by 1856, the Jewish population of the Holy Land exceeded 17,000.

Most of the newcomers were devoutly religious, and as a result more than a third of them chose to settle in Jerusalem. Otherwise, the city offered few enough material or social inducements. While its predominantly Moslem inhabitants were not unwilling to tolerate the acculturated, Arabic-speaking Sephardim and other Mediterranean Jews, they regarded the immigrant Ashkenazim with open hostility. Notwithstanding their new capitulatory status, the lot of the newcomers for many years remained ghettoization, dhimmi (legal inferiority), and exposure to ridicule, stonings, even occasional lynchings. For that matter, even the veteran Sephardim disdained the hand of friendship, concerned lest their own nativized status be jeopardized by the presence of these European coreligionists. Nevertheless, under consular protection, the Ashkenazic settlement in Jerusalem continued to grow. Religious and communal rights were slowly, if grudgingly, extended to them.

Even had the newly arrived pietists enjoyed adequate financial means, however, their life in Jerusalem would barely have been tolerable. The ancient capital, now shrunken behind its medieval wall to a provincial Ottoman town of 17,000, vegetated in unspeakable squalor. Hygienic facilities were all but nonexistent. Year in and year out, Jerusalem was racked by summer epidemics of typhoid and typhus. Yet those who chose to live there found no alternative to this walled congestion. The city gates were locked at twilight, and the unfortunates who delayed were compelled to spend the night in the open, likely victims of Bedouin robbers. Nor did any of Jerusalem's inhabitants suffer a more painful constriction than the Jews. The Ashkenazim sought a measure of physical protection by erecting their dwellings around courtyards, most of these impacted into a tiny quarter known as the Churva, the "ruin" of Rabbi Judah the Chasid's eighteenth-century settlement. As a rule, the little enclaves were owned and supported by the European Jewish communities of origin. Thus, the immigrants from Warsaw were subsidized by the "Klal" Warsaw; those from Vilna by the "Klal" Vilna; those from Hungary by the "Klal" Ungarn, and so on.

It was evident in any case that few of the Jews, in Jerusalem or elsewhere in Palestine, were really self-supporting. The name attached to them in Zionist history was HaYishuv HaYashan—the "Old Settlement." As pietists who were animated exclusively by the sacred mission of living, worshipping, and dying on holy soil, they depended heavily upon the charitable generosity of Jews abroad. By the 1860s the systematic collection and distribution of these remittances—known as Chalukkah (division)—amounted to over a third of the aggregate income of Palestine Jewry and fully half the income of Jews in Jerusalem. An observer, Ludwig August Frankel, noted that as late as 1856, out of a Jewish population in Jerusalem of approximately 6,000, not more than 47 persons were engaged full-time in trade, nor were more than 150 of them craftsmen.

Notwithstanding these limitations of circumstance and purpose, the conditions of life in Palestine gradually were improving in the latter half of the century. Public safety at least was somewhat better assured, and it was even possible to travel in the countryside unarmed. In 1869, the first road was cut in the mountains between Jaffa and Jerusalem. The economy profited from the mounting expenditures of Christian religious orders and Jewish philanthropies alike, and from more advanced methods of farming. Assured, then, of increased European consular protection, sharing in augmented communications between Europe and the Levant and within the Holy Land itself, the Jewish population, between 5,000 and 6,000 in 1800, nearly 17,000 at mid-century, surpassed 25,000 in 1881. Some 9,000 Jewish settlers were to be found in Tiberias, Safed, and Hebron, with a modest scattering in the port of Jaffa and other localities. The rest, equally divided between Ashkenazic and Sephardic-Oriental Jews, were concentrated in Jerusalem, where they formed over half the city's population. With few exceptions, they remained an inanimate community, parochial and inbred, almost entirely mendicant, living in a paralyzed dream world of ancient myths and brooding memories.

THE "OLD SETTLEMENT" STIRS

Yet all was not night within the Yishuv HaYashan. From the 1830s onward, intermittent attempts were launched to "productivize" Jewish settlement in the Holy Land. The first of these efforts were associated with the most revered Jew of the nineteenth century, Sir Moses Montefiore, whose life and career were largely intertwined with the golden era of Jewish emancipation. A wealthy bullion broker and financier of London, knighted by Queen Victoria for his innumerable philanthropies and good works, Montefiore devoted the largest portion of his energy and funds to the welfare of his coreligionists in every land. During the course of his 101 years, he interceded on behalf of his fellow Jews with two Russian tsars, two Turkish sultans, a king of Prussia, a shah of Persia, a viceroy of Egypt, a sultan of Morocco, as well as a host of princes, prelates, diplomats, and statesmen.

No cause of his life was more important to Montefiore than the establishment of a viable Jewish community in Palestine. Devoutly Orthodox, inspired by a quasi-messianic vision of the Chosen People restored to Holy Soil, Montefiore made seven voyages to Palestine between 1827 and 1875 in fulfillment of this sacred calling. He recognized from the outset, too, that the fundamental problem of Jewish indigence in Palestine would have to be solved by creative manual labor and self-help. To that end, Montefiore negotiated in 1838 with Mehemet Ali, viceroy of Egypt and (in those days) ruler of Syria and Palestine, for the purchase of land on which Jews might live and earn their bread without interference. Endlessly thwarted, however, by the avariciousness of Turkish and Egyptian officials, Montefiore failed to secure a charter for widespread Jewish settlement. He was rather more successful in establishing loan funds and dispensaries for impoverished Jews, in buying up modest tracts for Jewish habitation outside the polluted congestion of walled Jerusalem, and land sites elsewhere in Palestine for future Jewish agricultural enterprises. On each of his successive visits, Montefiore added to his largess: founding a girls' school in Jerusalem to offer instruction in domestic subjects, erecting a windmill for Jewish flour needs, building almshouses with money provided by himself and other affluent Jews. The revered philanthropist admitted later that he had underestimated the challenge of transforming ghetto dwellers and passive religionists into "creative" farmers and workers. Yet he was not altogether without influence in his practical ambitions for the Holy Land. At his initiative, in 1855, a group of Jerusalem Jews bought the land on which the settlement of Motza ultimately would be established forty years later. It was similarly at Montefiore's intercession that Adolphe Crémieux, a distinguished French Jewish statesman, turned his attention to the circumstances of Oriental Jews. In 1870 the Alliance Israélite Universelle, founded originally by Crémieux, established Mikveh Israel, the first Jewish agricultural school in Palestine.

Events in the Holy Land itself also began to make tentative inroads into Chalukkah passivity. During the Crimean War, Palestine was blockaded and deprived of European charitable funds. The country's Jews very nearly perished, as a result. It was then that many even among the Orthodox recognized that their children would have to practice a trade or face starvation. Accordingly, in 1856, several dozen Jewish youngsters were enrolled in the Lämel School. This institution had recently been established in Jerusalem with funds bequeathed by Simon Lämel, an Austrian Jewish industrialist, and offered a mixed general and religious curriculum. The Ashkenazic rabbinate of Jerusalem, however, fearing the possibly heretical consequences of secular education, immediately threatened a ban of excommunication on families whose children were registered. The warning had its impact on the Ashkenazim; for a while, Sephardic youths were the school's only pupils. Despite this setback, there were others to be found, themselves men of unimpeachable Orthodoxy, who were persuaded that the institution of Chalukkah was baneful by any criterion of reverence or survival. In 1869 the leader of this group, Joel Moshe Salomon, and six of his friends bought a tract of land outside the city wall. Later entitled Nachlat Shiv'ah (Plot of the Seven), the purchase represented Jerusalem Jewry's first voluntary, self-financed undertaking beyond the ancient Jewish quarter. In 1875 another group of Jerusalemites procured a second tract on the other side of the wall, to be known as Mea Sh'arim (Hundred Gates). These ventures signified more than a desire to escape the congestion of the Old City; they were motivated, as well, by a determination to engage in productive life and labor free from the immediate scrutiny of the Jerusalem rabbinate. The ambition evidently was shared by many, although it was not until after World War I that the Jewish population of the "New City" outnumbered that of the Old City.

In 1875, too, with the help of friends and colleagues, Salomon embarked on a quest for cultivable land. The search took nearly three years, and was carried out in the face of dire imprecations from the Ashkenazic rabbis, whose mistrust of "profane" labor was not uninfluenced by fear of losing charitable income from abroad. Finally, in 1878, an available tract was located and purchased in the Sharon Valley, six miles from Jaffa. It was a wild and desolate stretch, lacking roads or assurance of Ottoman police protection. Even so, the soil appeared fertile, and water was available from the nearby Yarkon River. Mud huts were quickly erected for the twenty-six initial families. Salomon and his companions dubbed the settlement Petach Tikvah (Portal of Hope).

Unfortunately, the river was a source not only of water but of the anopheles mosquito. During the project's first year many of the farmers were struck down by malaria. Some died. Others were deserted by their families. Until the first grain harvest, too, the survivors were continually racked by hunger as well as disease. And when at last the crops were reaped, they found no market among the Jews of Jerusalem, whose religious leaders were unforgiving of Salomon's "heresy." Worse yet, during the second year the Yarkon overflowed its banks and flooded the settlement, inundating the mud houses. Broken by then in body and spirit, the Jewish farmers abandoned their effort and returned to Jerusalem. Petach Tikvah lapsed into wilderness. Nothing appeared capable any longer of reviving the flagging morale of these initial Orthodox pioneers.

THE FIRST ALIYAH

Then, between 1882 and 1903, fully 25,000 Jews entered Palestine, the largest single influx since the Spanish Expulsion decree. This upsurge of immigration is usually described as the First Aliyah—the first immigration wave—but in fact it consisted of two main waves, of 1882–84 and 1890–91. Many of the immigrants were consciously Zionist and had come under the influence or auspices of the Chovevei Zion (p. 16) and the Bilu (below). But many more, probably the majority, were simply refugees from tsarist oppression, or religionists intent upon spending their years in study and prayer. All but 5 percent of the newcomers settled in the towns—Jerusalem, Jaffa, Hebron, and Haifa. A few opened stores or workshops. Others subsisted on Chalukkah. It soon became evident that the Chovevei Zion movement in Europe, while attracting numerous followers, remained quite ineffective as an agency of immigration. To be sure, many of its individual societies were led by able and resolute personalities, among them the writers Lev Levanda and Joseph Finn in Vilna, the historian Saul Rabinowitz in Warsaw, Rabbi Samuel Mohilever in Bialystok, Dr. Max Mandelstamm in Kiev. Yet for a number of years the Chovevei Zion leadership naïvely pinned its hopes on the support of the Alliance Israélite Universelle and of other Western Jewish organizations. None of these powerful philanthropies evinced the slightest interest in Zionism.

It was rather a group of youthful idealists that decided finally to take the initiative in establishing a creative foothold in Palestine. In January 1882, thirty young men and women gathered in the Kharkov lodgings of a university student, Israel Belkind, to discuss the "plight of the nation." Most of them had been reared in middle-class families. All either were attending university or, in some instances, had received professional degrees. They were all imbued, too, with a mixture of ardent Jewish nationalism and fiery Russian populism. In their minds, as in those of most of the Russian students of their generation, social reform and national fulfillment were interlinked. Thus, after extended discussion, the group decided that the revival of Jewish life in the Holy Land on a "productive" basis must begin immediately, without awaiting full-scale support from the wider Jewish community. Then and there they formed an emigration society, later to be known as "Bilu"—a Hebrew biblical acrostic of "House of Jacob, let us go." In ensuing meetings, nineteen of the youths made the commitment to abandon their studies or professions in favor of immediate departure to the Land of Israel; the others would recruit new members to establish a model agricultural colony in Palestine. "We have no capital," noted Chaim Chissin, a founding member, in his diary, "but we are certain that once we are [in Palestine] we shall be established. On every side we find an enthusiastic display of sympathy for the idea of the colonization of the Land of Israel and we have already received promises of aid from societies and influential persons."

The source of that promised help was less the impoverished Chovevei Zion network than the devout English millennialist Laurence Oliphant (p. 21). Visiting Rumania in 1879 during a series of anti-Semitic outbreaks, Oliphant witnessed at first hand the tragedy of the Jewish refugees. Afterward he attended a Chovevei Zion conference in Jassy, where he instantly sensed the potential of the emergent Zionist movement. The indefatigable Englishman thereupon departed for Constantinople in the hope of persuading the Ottoman government to grant the Jews a charter for colonizing the Holy Land. He was given short shrift by the Turks. Undaunted, Oliphant traveled on to Palestine to examine the state of the country. In 1880 he published a book, *The Land of Gilead*. The volume elaborated upon its author's by then well-familiar theme that Jewish resettlement under British protection would offer Britain a valuable enclave of influence in the Middle East. Developing at considerable length his initial blueprint for the revival of Palestine, Oliphant emphasized that the scheme was entirely feasible once money was available. And money, he later assured his Jewish friends, he would secure from the British government or from Anglo-Jewish philanthropists.

Accounts of this promise reached the young Biluites, and for weeks, then months, they awaited its fulfillment in tense expectation. Unfortunately for them, Oliphant was quickly apprised that the British government, having occupied Ottoman Cyprus only four years earlier, was distinctly uninterested now in provoking further Turkish suspicion. As for the wealthy Jews, Oliphant soon enough discovered the home truth that those Jews who possessed money and influence were almost unanimously opposed to the Zionist ideal. By July 1882, news of the Englishman's lack of progress reached Kharkov. The Biluites accordingly decided not to wait. Instead, anticipating that Oliphant's failure was only temporary, they shifted their headquarters from Kharkov to Odessa, and at the end of the month seventeen members of the group sailed for Constantinople. There, after several weeks, they received the melancholy intelligence that Oliphant had exhausted his resources and apparently could do nothing further for them. Whereupon all but three of the Biluites grimly prepared to continue to Palestine on their own. Before departure, however, they drew up a rather florid pronunciamento of goals. In typically populist language, the document attacked capitalist land ownership as the evil of civilization and warned against settlement in Palestine on the "rotten basis" of the old order. The Biluites further stipulated that every bachelor member of their organization must serve the Jewish people and its land for three years in a model communal farm; afterward, each of them would fulfill the role of instructor in a network of other, newer settlements. "And Israel on its land," concluded the declaration, "the Land of the Prophets, will combine a new society with social justice, for that is the function of Israel in the Land of Israel."

At the end of July the advance guard of thirteen young men and one young woman sailed for Palestine, reaching Jaffa five days later. Their initial contact with the squalid port town was hardly encouraging. Registering in a malodorous dormitory-hostel, they encountered their first "authentic" Palestine Jews—caftaned pietists, visibly undernourished, urgently awaiting ships to return to Europe. Undeterred, nevertheless, and intent upon securing at least a minimum of agricultural experience before launching upon a farm of their own, the young pioneers eventually received their first opportunity at Mikveh Israel, the training school established twelve years earlier by the Alliance. There they were set to work at a pittance under the direction of hard-bitten French agronomists, none of whom evinced the remotest sympathy for the newcomers' Zionist "fantasies." Rather, the Biluites were driven mercilessly in their field work, eleven and twelve hours a day, until they neared collapse. "The overseers kept pressing us," lamented Chissin, "giving us not a moment's rest. They had been instructed . . . to drive this 'spirit of folly' out of us and compel us to leave." Nor was the morale of the young idealists improved when reinforcements and financial support from Odessa did not arrive. Indeed, the Ottoman authorities were systematically restricting immigration now and forbidding land sales to European Jews. Later these measures were circumvented by bribery and other techniques; but in the summer of 1882 the Biluites had little reason to be optimistic. Sickness was undermining their will to go on. Where were the funds that at least would enable them to develop a model colony of their own—their very *raison d'être* for having traveled to Palestine?

Almost at the last moment, help of a sort materialized in the form of two Jerusalem Jews, Zalman Levontin and Joseph Feinberg. During the previous year, these men had collected money for land purchase from investors in both Jerusalem and Europe. Through the usual intermediary of a Sephardic Jew, an Ottoman subject, they had managed to acquire a tract of 400 dunams (roughly 100 acres) eight miles inland from Jaffa. Erecting their first tiny shacks there, the participating Jerusalem families enthusiastically dubbed their new settlement Rishon l'Zion—"First to Zion." At this point, touched by the dedication of the Biluites, Levontin and Feinberg persuaded the others to allow the youngsters to join the venture. Immediately, then, eleven of the Biluites took up shelter in a makeshift dormitory hut that was set aside for their use. Pooling their last remaining piasters in a common fund, the would-be farmers set about clearing the soil and planting maize and vegetables. Unfortunately, the harvest season already had passed. After two months, both food and money were exhausted, and the settlers—the Biluites among them—faced the very real threat of starvation. Completely dispirited, five of the original pioneer group decided to return to Mikveh Israel, six to Russia.

By then, actually, a number of other Jewish farm communities had been established. Petach Tikvah, abandoned several years earlier, was being resettled by newcomers from Europe. Several hundred newly arrived Chovevei Zion members from Rumania purchased a tract on the western ridge of Mount Carmel, which they named Zamarin. Others of the group moved on to the Galilee, founding the village of Rosh Pina. Early in 1883 another Galilee farm settlement, Y'sod HaMa'aleh, was organized by a group of Polish Chovevei Zion. None of these early villages was established on the Bilu principle of cooperative self-help; the settlers were middle-class individualists, each working his own plot. Yet their commitment to the land was not less intense than that of the young visionaries of Rishon l'Zion. Neither was the pain of their ordeal. Hardly any of the farmers had acquired experience on the soil in Europe. Eaten alive now by flies, periodically robbed of their livestock by Bedouins, the settlers and their families quickly began to wilt under disease, heat, and sheer exhaustion. Some drifted off to the cities. Others eventually returned to Europe. One way or another, like the Biluites of Rishon l'Zion and G'dera (p. 31), they had reached the limit of their strength and were prepared to abandon an evidently hopeless cause.

"THE WELL-KNOWN BENEFACTOR"

Their rescue came from an unanticipated source. Although the Rothschilds traditionally had been the first port of call for every Jewish philanthropy, the celebrated banking dynasty was opposed to Jewish nationalism and repeatedly had turned down earlier Chovevei Zion appeals for funds. It happened, nevertheless, that Baron Edmond de Rothschild, a scion of the French branch, occasionally had supported efforts to transform the Jews into a "productive," "normal" people, capable of laboring once again on the soil. In the autumn of 1882 he granted an audience to Joseph Feinberg, one of the two founders of Rishon l'Zion, who had returned to Europe in a desperate fund-raising effort to save his languishing colony. The eminent banker was moved to tears by Feinberg's account of the pioneers' self-sacrifice. Immediately he offered 30,000 francs for the purpose of drilling a well at Rishon l'Zion, and intimated that additional help would be forthcoming. Soon after, Rothschild dispatched an expert French agronomist to Palestine to instruct the Bilu farmers and hired the director of the Mikveh Israel school as overseer of Rishon l'Zion. The baron arranged, as well, for twelve additional families to study at Mikveh Israel, and promised to set them up later with a plot of their own (it became the colony of Ekron). Afterward he took the struggling colonies of Zamarin (eventually renamed Zichron Ya'akov, in memory of his father) and Rosh Pina under his protection. In return for his help, Rothschild stipulated only that his contributions not be made public. His wish was honored for many years. Somewhat cryptically, the settlers referred to their patron, whose identity was not unknown to them, as HaNadiv HaYadua—"the well-known benefactor."

With the passage of time, the Zionist colonies became Rothschild's major philanthropic interest. Between 1884 and 1900 he spent $6 million on the purchase of land and houses for the colonists, on training, machinery, livestock, and waterworks, on the construction of dispensaries, synagogues, and old-age homes. Hardly one of the fledgling settlements was denied his largess. Even Petach Tikvah turned to Rothschild for support, and by 1888 twenty-eight families there relied on him for their daily income. Other villages—Mishmar HaYarden, Chadera, Ein Zeitim, Metulla, Hartuv—were established initially upon the tacit understanding that HaNadiv HaYadua would be available if the settlers failed to manage on their own.

Yet Rothschild's support by no means took the form of a blank check for the colonists to operate their farms according to their own judgment. That was not the baron's way. The experts he sent from France and from Mikveh Israel became his overseers, charged with the day-to-day administration of the settlements. Before long, a radical change took place in the farmers' status. No longer did they collect subsidies according to the work they performed, but rather according to the size of their families, or even by virtue of their willingness to ingratiate themselves with the overseers. Eventually they were stripped of all authority to determine the crops they might plant and sell. It was the decision of the overseers, for example, that Rishon l'Zion and a number of other colonies should specialize in viticulture. Thus, at the baron's expense, vast wine cellars were constructed at Rishon. When the wines proved noncompetitive on the European market, Rothschild himself bought them up at 20 percent above the going price.

This kind of paternalism not only eroded the farmers' initiative, it undermined their morale as well. They resented their dependence upon the caprice of the overseers, who soon took to interfering in the most personal minutiae of their existence. Although well aware by then that they might starve without Rothschild's funds, the colonists openly voiced bitterness at their transformation into "serfs." They complained, too, that repeated changes of crop culture, from grapes to almonds, from olives to wheat—all at the discretion of Rothschild's overseers—were a waste of effort, that the years were passing and leaving them insecure and uncertain of the future. The Chovevei Zion committees in Odessa and Constantinople reinforced these misgivings, accusing the Rishon l'Zion settlers of "betraying" their original goal of a model cooperative settlement. The criticism reached the mark. The nine Biluites continuing on at Rishon and Mikveh Israel were fully as despairing under Rothschild's supervision as they had been in their earlier, hungrier days.

Once again, in the fall of 1884, an alternative solution developed unexpectedly. Yechiel Pines, a Russian Jew who had emigrated to Palestine in 1878, had brought with him a modest sum collected from the various Chovevei Zion groups. With this and other—borrowed—funds, Pines had established a craftsmen's society for the Biluites in Jerusalem in 1882. Now, with the remainder of the money, he purchased 2,800 dunams of land near Yavneh, a few miles inland from the coast, and similarly turned it over to the Biluites. In December of 1884, therefore, the youths, cruelly chastened but still not without hope, their number reduced to eight, made the trip to the farm. They called the tract G'dera (Sheepfold). Once more they were obliged to live in a single wooden shack. Again they lacked oxen and milch cows, and their funds were scarcely adequate for more than a few months of staples and the barest minimum of vine cuttings. With the land apparently best suited for viticulture, the Biluites would have to wait at least three and a half years for a paying harvest. Meanwhile they would survive on what they could grow, on winter wheat and barley and summer dura.

It was not enough. Deprived of access to Rothschild's experts, the Bilu youths misplanted their subsistence crops and in the end were reduced to meals of radishes and potatoes. By the opening of 1886 their situation was quite desperate. Too weak to protect their land, they watched helplessly as the Arabs grazed their herds on G'dera's fields. Chissin wrote in his diary:

And when our Arab neighbors saw us dressed in tatters, without adequate housing, and a prey to want . . . they violated our boundaries and dispossessed us of whole tracts of our land—and we were helpless. . . . The arrogance of the Arabs reached the point where they even began to beat us, and we were compelled to stifle our wrath in bitterness. . . . Full of shame and broken in spirit, we sat, each lost in his own painful thoughts.

For most of the farmers the ordeal no longer was bearable. "What a hopeless existence!" Chissin admitted. "I am leaving the country and shall return only when I am able to build my life here with my own hands."

It seemed a less than reasonable possibility. G'dera itself survived, but only through Rothschild's largess. The handful of settlers who remained abandoned the notion of a cooperative community. Like the colonists at Rishon l'Zion, Petach Tikvah, and other villages, they began to accept handouts from Paris and to hire cheap Arab labor. The original Biluites, in any case, refused to endure this moral surrender. By the end of the decade all of them had abandoned G'dera, some for the cities, some for Europe. Their experiment in "social justice" manifestly had failed.

THE BRIDGEHEAD WIDENS

In eastern Europe, as in Palestine, the Zionist enthusiasm that had been kindled at the onset of the 1880s had subsided by mid-decade. Partly as a consequence of the malaise that afflicted the settlement effort, and partly as a result of Turkish obstructionism, emigration to Palestine dwindled to a trickle. For the next several years the Chovevei Zion organization itself remained in the doldrums. Denied legal status in Russia, it was unable to collect funds in the Pale. The opportunity to widen the base of support opened only in 1890, when the tsarist regime permitted the Chovevei Zion to conduct their activities under the rubric of a Society for the Support of Jewish Agriculturists and Artisans in Palestine and Syria (p. 16). The distinction was important to the Russian authorities. Minority nationalism was one matter, but encouragement of Jewish departure to another land was not unattractive to the government. Thus, from 1890 on, with a permanent office in Odessa, the Society consolidated its efforts, raised between \$20,000 and \$30,000 annually, and encouraged and directed emigration. In 1890–91, as a result, no fewer than 3,000 Russian and Rumanian Jews departed for Palestine.

That same year, too, the Odessa Committee—as the Chovevei Zion organization was known henceforth in the Zionist world—opened a bureau in Jaffa under the direction of Ze'ev Tiomkin, a Russian Jewish engineer. Exuberant and warm-hearted, Tiomkin hurled himself confidently into the effort to secure land and jobs for new immigrants. His initial success was quite remarkable. Unfazed by Ottoman government restrictions, he managed through intermediaries to purchase several large tracts on behalf of the Chovevei Zion, which he then resold to settlers or land companies. It was in this fashion that two important farm colonies, Rehovot and Chadera, came into Jewish hands outside Rothschild administration, and a number of other, smaller communities were later established. G'dera also began to revive with financial help from Tiomkin's office, and by the late 1890s a group of new settlers at last began producing impressive vegetable and cereal crops. Elsewhere immigrants were finding jobs in the towns, working in handicrafts and commerce. Jaffa became a teeming center, filled with Chovevei Zion members, with pietists, colonization agents, merchants, and workers, all arriving by the hundreds each month. Avraham Yaari, an editor of early immigrant writings, quotes the exuberant recollections of a Rumanian pioneer of that time:

> It is hard to describe the romance—the hope, light, and joy—that filled their hearts . . . as they set sail for the land of their fathers to be pioneers of Jewish agriculture. Each man painted in the brightest of colors a picture of his farm-to-be in the Land of Israel. . . . Each man would have his own wheat field, vegetable garden and chicken run. . . . In the land flowing with milk and honey, of course, all this would be supplemented by olives, almonds, figs, dates, and other delicacies.

Nevertheless, the experience of the Rumanian immigrants who settled the agricultural colony of Beer Tuvia was less than idyllic. Ravaged by malaria, they soon abandoned their village. So did other would-be farmers in other colonies. As it turned out, the brief upsurge of the 1890s had rested on shaky foundations. Tiomkin, whose enthusiasm for acquiring tracts exceeded his financial judgment, inadvertently had driven up land values. Many of the newcomers lacked sufficient funds to acquire plots; and those who managed to buy usually failed to recoup their initial costs. Eventually an investigating commission was dispatched by the Odessa Committee. It promptly closed down Tiomkin's operation, and Tiomkin himself returned to Europe. But the damage was already done. Disenchantment was not with the Odessa Committee alone. The sheer hardships of farming in Palestine, a series of lethal malaria and typhoid epidemics, and the endless legal obstacles interposed by the Ottoman authorities, who tightened their restrictions on land transfers—all proved too heavy a burden for many hundreds of settlers. By the latter 1890s ships reaching Jaffa were loading more passengers for Europe than they were disembarking.

Apprised, meanwhile, of the continuing unrest in his own network of subsidized colonies, Rothschild visited Palestine on his yacht in December 1898. He was not unimpressed by the progress he saw about him. The Jews he met—bronzed, sinewy, many of them galloping on their horses to escort him to their colonies—appeared at least physically to fulfill his dream of a new race of vigorous Jewish farmers. Nevertheless, the baron also recognized the symptoms of eroded initiative, of a Jewish plantocracy increasingly dependent upon hired Arab labor. Accordingly, he informed the colonists that he had decided now to phase out his subsidies. He would not yet abandon them completely. He would continue to provide them with schools and communal buildings. But he expected that the farmers henceforth would meet their day-to-day responsibilities on their own. Upon returning to Paris, therefore, the baron terminated his subsidy of Rishon l'Zion's wine crops. More significantly, he appeared to disengage himself from personal control of the settlements by turning over their management to a separate and ostensibly independent body, the Palestine Colonization Association—the PICA.

Yet, with some exceptions, the transition to agricultural self-reliance continued nominal, at best, for many years. Few of the settlers were left entirely to their own resources. In delegating the PICA as an "independent" managing agency, for example, Rothschild provided it with 14 million francs of his own money. An elaborate credit system was established for the farmers. PICA "representatives" (no longer called overseers) continued to provide expert advice, to manage accounts, even—despite the baron's misgivings—to hire increasingly larger droves of Arab workers. In fact if not in name, then, the "well-known benefactor" remained in charge. He made this plain in 1901, rejecting alternative suggestions for the PICA farms. "I created the Palestine Yishuv [Jewish settlement]," he insisted. "I and no one else. Therefore neither the colonists nor any organization has the right to interfere in my plans and to offer opinions on the subject."

Such were the circumstances of the Yishuv by the end of the nineteenth century. Nearly 50,000 Jews were living in Palestine. The great majority of them, however, were ensconced in the four holy cities, and half their numbers were fully or partially dependent on Chalukkah charity. The rural population of the First Aliyah comprised at most 5,000 souls living in twenty villages (nearly that many had been abandoned), and fifteen of these were subsidized by the PICA. Whatever their progress, their economics remained heavily dependent on a bottomless pool of cut-rate Arab labor. In 1898, the fields of Zichron Ya'akov were tended by more than one thousand Arabs working for two hundred Jews. In Rishon l'Zion, thirty-eight Jewish settler families depended on the labor of over three hundred Arab migrant families encamped in nearby huts. Schooling in the Jewish villages was essentially French, underwritten either by the PICA or by the Alliance Israélite Universelle. It was this blend of Gallic education and surrounding Arab village mores that appeared to doom any hope of an indigenous Jewish culture. Indeed, the likelihood of any meaningful growth in the Jewish population overall seemed equally remote, as Turkish officials raised innumerable obstacles to further settlement.

The crisis was perceived at the very outset by Asher Ginzberg, a leading member of the Chovevei Zion in Russia, who wrote under the *nom de plume* of Achad HaAm (One of the People). As early as 1889, in an article entitled "Lo Zeh HaDerech" (This Is Not the Way), Achad HaAm had warned his fellow Zionists not to fasten on scapegoats for disappointments in Palestine, to avoid blaming Rothschild or even the institution of Chalukkah. He insisted rather that the basis of Jewish national revival in Europe itself was not capable of supporting a major pioneering venture in the Holy Land. When Achad HaAm visited Palestine two years later, his worst fears were confirmed by the mood of despair he encountered throughout the Yishuv. From then on, remorselessly, he lashed out at the "bankruptcy" of "piecemeal" settlement. It was a shock to him, for example, that on a second trip, in 1893, he was unable to land at the port of Jaffa without paying baksheesh to Turkish officials, and was forbidden so much as to visit Jerusalem (although he managed a trip to the city two years later). One recourse alone was open, Achad HaAm insisted. This was to mobilize the help of Western Jews in organizing an international society for building the Yishuv. Only such a body was capable of negotiating a charter of Jewish settlement with the Ottoman regime, and afterward of buying and preparing land for "systematic and orderly habitation."

Here, surely, was an irony of Jewish history. Achad HaAm was destined to become the most influential of "cultural"—as distinguished from "political"—Zionists, and later the severest critic of those who placed their emphasis upon an autonomous Palestine Jewish homeland (Chapter III). Yet, in describing the vulnerability and impending atrophy of the Yishuv, his was the first authentic Jewish voice, speaking from the depths of the Hebraic tradition and in the Hebrew language itself, to anticipate the climactic Zionist vision of Theodor Herzl.

HERZL

AND THE RISE

OF POLITICAL ZIONISM

THE COMPLETE EUROPEAN

On June 2, 1895, Baron Moritz de Hirsch received a visitor in the drawing room of his Paris mansion. A Belgian Jew, master builder of the Trans-Balkan railroad network, de Hirsch was one of the financial giants of his era, and an outstanding figure in the sphere of Jewish philanthropy. Earlier in the decade he had poured millions of francs into a scheme for transporting Russian Jewry en masse to the Argentine. The experiment had failed. Fewer than 3,000 Jews had allowed themselves to be re-settled in de Hirsch's colonies, and at the beginning of the twentieth century there were in all perhaps 7,000 Jewish farmers in Argentina. Never-theless, the Belgian tycoon had persisted in expending vast sums on refugees in Europe and Latin America. His acumen and generosity had continued to evoke the highest respect of Jews and Gentiles alike. Then, on May 24, 1895, a request for an interview had arrived in his morning mail. The writer was Theodor Herzl, an author and journalist of interna-tional reputation; and the letter, reflecting this dignity, was in marked contrast to the fawning solicitations that ordinarily reached the baron's desk. "What you have undertaken until now was as magnificent in con-ception as it has proved futile in actuality," Herzl had written. "Until now you have been only a philanthropist. . . . I want to show you the way to become something more." Annoyed and intrigued in equal measure, de Hirsch had consented to the meeting.

The man who was ushered now into the baron's presence was ex-ceptionally striking in appearance, with dark burning eyes, chiseled fea-tures, and a rich "Assyrian" beard. His demeanor was consciously aristo-cratic. The self-assurance, too, with which the visitor presented his case to de Hirsch was magisterial to the point of arrogance. "You breed beggars," Herzl calmly informed his host. "As long as Jews are passive recipients of charitable funds, they will remain weaklings and cowards." What the Jews required, he insisted, was political education for self-support, and ultimately for self-government, in a land of their own. But when Herzl began elaborating upon this theme, de Hirsch, provoked and incensed, in-terrupted with vigorous objections. The discussion soon collapsed in a mutual shouting match. The next day, in yet another less-than-ingratiating letter, Herzl repeated his objections to de Hirsch's program of subsidies:

"Do you know that you have adopted a frightfully reactionary policy— worse than that of the most absolute autocrat? Fortunately your powers are not great enough to carry it out." De Hirsch did not bother to respond. What manner of man was this Herzl, he was later to ask Zadoc Kahn, the Grand Rabbi of Paris, to utter thoughts so shockingly at variance with the affirmation of Europeanism, the Sanhedrin's dominating tradition in Western Jewish life?

In truth, Herzl was the very paradigm of Europeanism. Born in Budapest in 1860, the son of an affluent banking family, he was taught devoutly to cherish the opportunities of Habsburg citizenship. His parents maintained a nominal Jewish allegiance, attending the Liberal (Reform) temple each week and observing the major Jewish festivals. Theodor Herzl himself underwent Bar Mitzvah, and even attended a Jewish communal school. Yet his own ambitions, as those of his family, were to excel in the realm of German culture. He attended the University of Vienna, enrolling in the faculty of law. Receiving his doctorate of jurisprudence in 1884, he accepted a quasi-official position in the ministry of justice. Virtually his every free moment, however, was spent in the writing of plays and literary essays, and before a year had passed he had abandoned the law entirely.

Herzl's chosen medium was the feuilleton, a popular European literary form that offered commentary on the social and cultural events of the time. He became an instant success. His pieces, crafted with an instinctive elegance of theme and style, won enthusiastic audiences. In 1887 he was installed briefly as feuilleton editor of the *Wiener Allgemeine Zeitung*, later held other senior editorial positions, and four years afterward accepted the envied post of Paris correspondent for the *Neue Freie Presse*, Austria's leading newspaper. By then, at the age of thirty-one, Herzl seemingly had reached the apogee of his financial and professional ambitions. Only emotional satisfaction was lacking. His wife, the beautiful and wealthy Julie Naschauer, was high-strung and unstable. Following the birth of their first two children, she lived in a state of near-chronic hysteria, possibly exacerbated by the intrusiveness of Herzl's adoring mother. Separations of the couple were frequent; after the birth of their third child, they lived together only intermittently.

Herzl was increasingly preoccupied, too, by the Jewish question. During his university days, he had accepted the fashionable liberal view that religious and racial prejudices ultimately would vanish in an enlightened age. That faith remained unshaken even into the years of his early manhood. Indeed, he himself shared a certain assimilated distaste for the "wrong kind" of Jews. Yet the mounting intensity of nationalist anti-Semitism began to leave its mark, particularly as displayed in the writings of Eugen Dühring in Germany and Edouard Drumont in Paris. So, too, did the political exploitation of Jew-hatred by Karl Lüger, Vienna's Christian Socialist candidate for mayor. In 1891, moreover, the suicide of a friend, Heinrich Kana, possibly for reasons of Jewish *Weltschmerz*, shook Herzl to his depths. The optimism of his youth never returned. From 1892 on, his columns from Paris devoted increasing attention to anti-Semitism in the

French capital. Privately, he began to grope for an answer to this debilitating social illness. One solution that occurred to him was "a voluntary and honorable [mass Jewish] conversion" to Christianity. In his notes, he envisaged the act taking place "in the broad light of day, at noon on a Sunday, a solemn and festive procession accompanied by the pealing of bells . . . proudly and with a gesture of dignity. . . ."

If Herzl soon dropped this approach, he rejected equally the notion of a proto-Zionist solution, a theme he first encountered upon reading a novel, *La Femme de Claude*, by Dumas the younger. Yet it was no less illusory, as Herzl saw it, to anticipate a change of attitude among the peoples of Europe themselves. In November 1894 he dashed off a play, *Das Neue Ghetto*, that represented his first major literary effort directed exclusively to the Jewish question. The central character in this *Tendenzstück* was a high-minded Jewish lawyer, Dr. Jacob Samuel, who was engaged by a Christian aristocrat as attorney for a mining company. When the mine flooded and the company went bankrupt, its owner angrily denounced Samuel as a *"Judenpack"*—"Jewish rabble"—and in the ensuing duel mortally wounded him. With his last breath, Samuel cried out: "Jews, my brothers, you won't be allowed to live again until you—get out of the Ghetto."

But if Herzl's despairing obsession with the Jewish question predated the Dreyfus Affair, it was markedly intensified by the arrest and degradation of that unfortunate French Jewish army captain. Herzl wrote later that the anti-Semitism of the mob, as it taunted Dreyfus with shouts of "À la mort les juifs," was his own critical moment of recognition. For the first time in his adult life he began attending Jewish religious services, even plotting a Jewish novel that envisaged the revival of the Promised Land by a suffering race. Sometime, surely, in the winter and spring of 1895, the Zionist idea took form in Herzl's mind. It was on May 24, 1895, then, that he dispatched his letter to Moritz de Hirsch, and nine days later he held his acrimonious interview with the railroad baron.

DER JUDENSTAAT

Far from discouraging Herzl, the abrasive meeting with de Hirsch impelled the journalist into an urgent formulation of his new Zionist idea. Within days thereafter he began transcribing his thoughts on the Jewish question in a notebook:

> For some time now I have been engaged in a work of indescribable greatness. . . . It has assumed the aspect of some powerful dream. But days and weeks have passed since it has filled me utterly, it has overflown into my unconscious self, it accompanies me wherever I go, it broods above all prosaic conversation . . . it disturbs and intoxicates me. What it will lead to is impossible to surmise as yet. But my experience tells me that it is something marvelous, even as a dream, and that I should write it down—Title: "The Promised Land."

So began Herzl's astonishing diary. He would continue to record entries into it methodically for the ensuing nine years of his Zionist career, until shortly before his death. Eventually reaching half a million words, the diary became Herzl's outstanding literary achievement. The opening pages described an electrifying vision that left its author breathless, that possessed him "walking, standing, lying down, in the street, at the table, at nighttime. I must above all master myself," he wrote. "I believe that for me life has ceased and world history begun. . . . The Jewish State is a world necessity." An early "chapter" of the diary was especially titled "An Address to the Rothschilds." Herzl intended to read it to the banking family assembled in council, and if necessary to rework it later into a book.

In July 1895, meanwhile, Herzl persuaded the owners of the *Neue Freie Presse* to accept him as feuilleton editor, thus enabling him to return home, where he might conduct his Zionist negotiations. The following month he consulted Dr. Moritz Güdemann, Chief Rabbi of Vienna, and read him the "Address to the Rothschilds." The rabbi evidently was moved, and suggested that the document be published. Herzl discussed the suggestion with a friend, Dr. Max Nordau. Eleven years older than Herzl, the thickset, grizzle-bearded Nordau had been trained as a physician, but subsequently had achieved a distinguished literary reputation as the author of numerous volumes exposing the foibles and hypocrisies of contemporary European society. For most of his adult life, too, Nordau had considered himself a cosmopolitan—until he, like Herzl, had witnessed the degradation of Captain Dreyfus. When now Herzl read the "Address," Nordau was enthralled. Embracing his friend, he cried: "If you are mad, we are mad together! Count on me, I am with you!" From then on, Nordau remained Herzl's most intimate collaborator.

It was Nordau who proposed at this point that Herzl visit Israel Zangwill, a close friend of the physician-writer, an eminent Anglo-Jewish novelist, and a man of considerable reputation among British Jewry; the contact might prove to be important. Herzl agreed, and crossed the Channel to meet Zangwill in London in November 1895. Zangwill heard out his visitor respectfully, even presented him to the Maccabeans, a society of Anglo-Jewish businessmen. "An unknown Hungarian," Zangwill wrote later, "dropped from the skies, gave to the world the first exposition of his scheme in an eloquent mixture of German, French, and English." The reception of Herzl's ideas was courteous, if generally noncommittal. Encouraged by the visit, nevertheless, Herzl returned to Vienna, where he set about pruning, taming, and organizing the notes for his "Address to the Rothschilds" into a formal sixty-five-page essay. What emerged from this effort was *Der Judenstaat*.

The title has been translated loosely as *The Jewish State*. In fact, it is *The Jew-State*, a word Herzl flung into the teeth of the anti-Semites and of those acculturated Western Jews who preferred such euphemisms as "Hebrew" or "Israelite." The subtitle, "An Attempt at a Modern Solution to the Jewish Question," was hardly less forthright. As Herzl declared in his preface:

> The idea which I have developed in this pamphlet is an ancient one. It is
> the restoration of the Jewish State. . . . I shall do no more than suggest
> what cogs and wheels comprise the machinery I propose, trusting that better
> mechanics than myself will be found to carry the work out. . . . The world
> needs the Jewish State; therefore it will arise.

The first chapter opened with the bald assertion that Jew-hatred was an
ineluctable fact of life; it would not be wished away. Indeed, the Jewish
question was neither social nor religious. "It is a national question, and in
order to solve it we must, before everything else, transform it into a political world question, to be answered in the council of the civilized peoples."
Herzl then developed his central thesis. "We are a *people—one* people,"
he insisted. "We have sincerely tried everywhere to merge with the national communities in which we live, seeking only to preserve the faith of
our fathers. It is not permitted us." Only one solution remained. It was an
exodus, a gathering together of the Jews from their worldwide dispersion
into a land of their own. "Political principle will provide the basis, technology the means, and the driving force will be the Jewish tragedy." It
was Herzl's contention, moreover, that Europe itself would cooperate in
the Jewish departure. "There will be an inner migration of Christian citizens into the positions abandoned by the Jews. The outflow will be gradual,
without any disturbance, and its very inception means the end of anti-
Semitism." The greater part of the essay consisted of a detailed discussion
of the Jewish exodus and transplantation. What was needed, Herzl argued,
was a dramatic break with the principle of "gradual Jewish infiltration" as
it was then being carried out in Argentina and Palestine. International
recognition of the right of collective Jewish settlement would have to come
first. Either Argentina or Palestine might be useful sites, although Palestine,
"our unforgettable historic homeland," logically would be the first choice.
Two organs would be created, the "Society of the Jews" and the "Jewish
Company." The first would serve as legal representative of the idea, the
latter as a joint stock company with a share capital of 50 million pounds to
be provided by "the big financial Jews." If this failed, popular subscrip-
tion would be resorted to. Emigration to the Jewish land admittedly
would require decades. Once established in a state of their own, however,
the Jews would develop their commonwealth on the latest scientific, technical, and social principles. For example, private initiative would be encouraged, but obliged to serve the public interest. Women would enjoy
full equality. Herzl was somewhat vaguer on cultural matters. He hardly
made reference to the national language except to record his doubt that it
would be Hebrew or Yiddish. Possibly, he speculated, a linguistic federation would emerge, as in Switzerland. These details in any case were less
important than the sheer compulsion to emigrate and build a Jewish
nation. And to that end mass propaganda was needed.

> The idea must radiate out until it reaches the last wretched nests of our
> people. They will awaken out of their dull brooding. Then a new meaning
> will come into the lives of all of us. . . . I believe that a race of marvellous
> Jews will grow out of the earth. The Maccabees will rise again! . . . We

shall at last live as free men on our own soil and die peacefully in our own homeland.

Der Judenstaat was published in Vienna on February 14, 1896. English and French translations soon followed.

As one assesses the phenomenon of a Europeanized, nontraditional Jew producing a work of this startling nature, it is worth recalling that Herzl was a citizen of a multinational, multilingual empire. Both as a Jew and as a Habsburg citizen, he was in no sense the outsider that Lilienblum or Pinsker had been in tsarist Russia. Habsburg society was pluralistic by definition, and well accustomed to the spectacle of ethnic and national minorities contending for power within the larger framework of the empire. Indeed, not a few of the lawyers who pleaded the cause of their kindred Czechs, Croats, or Slovenes were themselves entirely Germanized in language and culture. There was nothing especially strange, therefore, in a German-speaking, agnostic Jew like Herzl propounding Jewish separateness, without being steeped himself in the Jews' own language and historical traditions. Yet, if there were precedents for this sort of advocacy within the Habsburg tradition, there were none whatever within the Jewish experience. Earlier formulations of Jewish nationalism, even Pinsker's "scientific" tract, had issued directly from a more than superficial understanding of Jewish traditions and folklore. Herzl, conversely, writing in ignorance of Smolenskin and Pinsker, was uninhibited by the emphasis these and other Hebraically oriented east European Jews laid on cultural awakening as the first priority in revived Jewish nationhood. On the contrary, he made no distinction between the "Jewish" Jew of Russia and the assimilated Jew of western Europe. His famous sentence, "We are a *people—one* people," expressed a universal sweep of vision that emerged more naturally from Western humanism than from a devout, but insular, Russian Jewish traditionalism.

Herzl's Zionism was unique in other respects, as well. It was Zionism articulated for the first time by a man of the world, a distinguished political observer and broadly traveled journalist. The *Judenstaat,* therefore, in its transfixing eloquence and orderly exposition, introduced Zionism to European readers, to editors, university men, statesmen, and other molders of public opinion, in the kind of language they were accustomed to reading. More important yet, Herzl stood alone in his attempt to resolve the Jewish question not merely through the dramatic and far-reaching notion of a Jewish state but through the active collaboration of leading European powers. From the very outset, he projected Zionism into international statecraft.

FROM THEORIST TO ACTIVIST: THE ZIONIST CONGRESS

Notwithstanding these credentials of authorship and presentation, the initial reception of *Der Judenstaat* was less than auspicious. The central European press, shocked by the "aberration" of one of its most distinguished contributors, ridiculed Herzl as the "Jewish Jules Verne." Typical was the reaction of the *Münchener Allgemeine Zeitung*, which described the essay as "the fantastic dream of a feuilletonist whose mind has been unhinged by Jewish enthusiasm." Stefan Zweig recalled:

> I was still in the Gymnasium when this short pamphlet . . . appeared; but I can still remember the general astonishment and annoyance of the middle class Jewish elements of Vienna. What has happened, they said angrily, to this otherwise intelligent, witty, and cultivated writer? What foolishness is this that he has thought up and writes about? Why should we go to Palestine? Our language is German and not Hebrew, and beautiful Austria is our homeland. Are we not well off under the good Emperor Franz Josef? Do we not make an adequate living, and is our position not secure? . . . Why does he, who speaks as a Jew and who wishes to help Judaism, place arguments in the hands of our worst enemies and attempt to separate us, when every day brings us more closely and intimately into the German world?

Even Chief Rabbi Güdemann, whose loyalty Herzl had felt was assured, now changed his mind and published an article decrying the "*Kuckucksei*" of Jewish nationalism.

Scorn and exasperation were by no means the only reactions, however, even in the West. The *Judenstaat* was received warmly by Kadima, the Zionist student society of Vienna, which now deluged Herzl with praise and lecture invitations. David Wolffsohn, a leading Zionist of Cologne, was entirely overwhelmed by the *Judenstaat*. Indeed, he immediately traveled to Vienna to meet Herzl. It was through Wolffsohn in turn that Herzl was introduced to the leaders of the German Chovevei Zion—to Hantke, Löwe, Bambus, and others. Through them, too, he first learned of the writings of Pinsker and Hess, and of the tremendous Zionist renaissance in eastern Europe.

One of those who rushed to meet Herzl in the spring of 1896 was a Protestant clergyman, the Reverend William Hechler, chaplain of the British embassy in Vienna. Hechler was yet another of that remarkable millennialist breed, obsessed by the notion of a worldwide Jewish return to Zion. He had written a book on the subject, *The Restoration of the Jews to Palestine According to the Prophets*. The appearance of the *Judenstaat* convinced the Englishman that Herzl was indeed the prophet sent by God "to fulfill prophecy." Through Hechler, afterward, Herzl secured an interview with the Grand Duke of Baden, uncle of the German kaiser. One of Germany's more liberal princes, the grand duke reacted well to Herzl's vision of a Jewish state; he promised to discuss the matter with his nephew. Yet another Gentile contact was a debt-ridden émigré Polish aristocrat, Count Philip Michael de Nevlinski, who maintained important friendships among the demimonde of European royalty. Intrigued in equal measure by the Zionist idea and the likelihood of Jewish subsidies, Nevlinski volunteered to serve Herzl as an official emissary, particularly to the Ottoman court. Herzl accepted the count's help willingly and opened his private purse to him. On June 15, 1896, the two men departed for Constantinople in quest of an audience with Sultan Abdul Hamid II.

With Nevlinski's connections and his own liberal distribution of bak-sheesh, Herzl eventually was received by the Turkish grand vizier and foreign minister. The two officials listened with interest to their visitor's striking proposal. As it had been outlined earlier in the *Judenstaat*, the scheme was for "influential Jewish financiers" to relieve the chronic economic distress of the Ottoman government in return for a charter of Jewish settlement in Palestine. Upon being relayed to the Seraglio, however, the proposal failed to impress Abdul Hamid. "When my empire is divided," he sent back word, "perhaps they will get Palestine for nothing. But only our corpse can be divided. I will never consent to vivisection." Herzl was not unduly dismayed. For him, the dream was only postponed.

He traveled on, then, to London, a city he envisaged as the headquarters of his "Society of Jews." Addressing the Maccabeans again, he described the Society—cautiously, this time—as an instrument for "the acquisition of a territory secured by international law . . . for those Jews who cannot assimilate." This time Herzl was politely rebuffed; the acculturated Anglo-Jewish gentlemen regarded his scheme as farfetched. He returned to Paris. There, on July 18, 1896, he finally secured an interview with Baron Edmond de Rothschild. It was a strained meeting. Rothschild launched into an angry monologue against the very notion of Jewish statehood. When Herzl managed to get in a word, offering to hand over political leadership of the "movement" to Rothschild himself, the baron curtly dismissed the notion as one that would simply bring 150,000 "schnorrers" (beggars) to Palestine. "You were the keystone of the entire combination," Herzl observed sadly. "If you refuse [support] . . . . I shall have to do it in a different way. I shall launch a great agitation which will make the masses still more difficult to keep in order."

It was no idle warning. By then, Herzl had reached a far wider audience than he had ever dared hope. Although the tsarist censorship forbade publication of the *Judenstaat* in Russia, central European Jews began smuggling copies of the book into the Pale, where Herzl's name and legend grew. As Chaim Weizmann recalled in his autobiography:

> It was an utterance which came like a bolt from the blue. . . . Fundamentally, *The Jewish State* contained not a single new idea for us. . . . Not the ideas, but the personality which stood behind them appealed to us. Here was daring, clarity, and energy. The very fact that the Westerner came to us unencumbered by our own preconceptions had its appeal. We were right in our instinctive appreciation that what had emerged from the *Judenstaat* was less a concept than a historic personality.

Telegrams and letters of thanks poured in to Herzl from Chovevei Zion societies in Bulgaria, Galicia, Russia, and Palestine, calling upon the "new Moses" to accept leadership of the movement. Moreover, returning to Vienna from his first visit to Constantinople, Herzl was met at the Sofia railway station by hundreds of Jewish admirers, who carried him off the train to the synagogue; there people greeted him as a new Messiah and insisted upon kissing his hand. During his otherwise unsuccessful visit to London, too, he was cheered by a tumultuous mass meeting convened in his honor by Russian Jewish immigrants in the East End. "About me a faint mist is rising," he admitted in his diary, not without pleasure. Finally, on July 21, 1896, three days after his abortive meeting with Rothschild, he wrote Jacob de Haas, who had served as his "aide-de-camp" in London: "There is only one reply to this situation: let us organize our masses immediately."

The notion of calling "a general Zionist day," which ultimately evolved into a Zionist congress, was first suggested to Herzl in January 1897 by Willi Bambus and Theodore Zlocisti, members of the German Kadima society. Several months of consultations with western European Zionists followed. The Austro-Hungarian Zionist Convention, meeting in Vienna in early March, added its endorsement for a later international congress. But when, finally, official invitations were issued for the gathering, scheduled for late August in Munich, the Western Jewish response was one of outrage. Editorials in German Jewish newspapers denounced the proposed Zionist assembly as treason to the Fatherland and a danger to Judaism. The B'nai Brith Lodge of Munich was beside itself, and eventually forced the Munich Jewish community to deny cooperation to Herzl. A letter issued by the Executive Committee of the Association of German Rabbis accurately reflected German Jewry's reaction to Zionism:

> The Association of Rabbis in Germany regards it as proper to make the following explanations: 1. The efforts of so-called Zionists to found a Jewish national state in Palestine contradict the messianic promises of Judaism as contained in Holy Writ and in later religious sources. 2. Judaism obligates its adherents to serve with all devotion the Fatherland to which they belong, and to further its national interests with all their heart and with all their strength. . . . Religion and patriotism both lay upon us the duty of asking all who are concerned with the welfare of Judaism to stay away from the above-mentioned Zionist endeavors and most particularly from the Congress which is still being planned, despite all the warnings against it.

The site of the Congress was finally shifted to Basle, Switzerland. It was the only compromise Herzl was prepared to make. The austere Viennese feuilletonist had now become a dynamic man of action. He threw himself heart and soul into the preparations, launching into extensive correspondence with Zionist leaders throughout Europe, ensuring the distribution of the agenda in every major European Jewish community, urging the election only of "the most eminent" representatives. He traveled to Basle on August 5, in advance of the event, to supervise the final details. Soon the delegates began to arrive—from fifteen countries, including the United States, Algeria, Palestine, as well as western and eastern Europe. There were 204 representatives in all.

They began their sessions on August 29 in the Stadt Casino, a concert and dance hall on the Steinenberg. A modern Zionist flag was hanging at the building's entrance. Dignity was the keynote; Herzl had requested delegates to wear frock coats and white ties. The galleries were packed with visitors, Jews and Christians alike. The leading newspapers of Europe had sent correspondents, testimony to the thoroughness of Herzl's public relations. And when Herzl himself rose to address the Congress, the delegates jumped to their feet in a thrilled ovation that lasted a quarter of an hour. Ben-Ami, one of the Russian delegates, was so moved by this "marvelous and exalted figure, kingly in bearing and stature, with deep eyes in which could be read quiet majesty and unuttered sorrow," that he wanted to cry out, "Yechi HaMelech!"—Hail to the King! It was an appellation that Herzl would not have disdained. The only son of adoring parents, a prodigy, a *succès d'estime* of Europe-wide reputation, acutely conscious of his sheer physical beauty, which he enhanced by the regality of his manner, he found the position of leadership the only one worthy of his talents. If at last he was cast into dealings with the Yiddishist world of east European Jewry, it was a role he could only have accepted as "the King of the Jews." ("My father will be the first Senator of the Jewish State," he wrote in his diary.)

When the applause finally died down, Herzl began his speech. Its opening words were as unequivocal as those of the *Judenstaat:* "We are here to lay the foundation stone of the house which is to shelter the Jewish nation." He noted that modern communications at last had made possible the gathering of the dispersed elements of the Jewish people. "Anti-Semitism has given us our strength again. We have returned home. . . . Zionism is the return of the Jews to Judaism even before their return to the Jewish land." The Congress accordingly would occupy itself with "the spiritual means of reviving and nursing the Jewish national consciousness." Having paid his respects to the east European cultural tradition, however, Herzl then went on to emphasize that it was the physical circumstances of the Jews that most urgently cried out for attention. The older methods of piecemeal colonization in Palestine, deprived of international legal recognition, no longer were adequate. A new, permanent, and "official" body was required henceforth in order to cope with the Jewish question more directly and forcefully.

The address was solemn and impressive, but temperate and restrained, as well. Herzl allowed the fire and oratory, rather, to come from Nordau, who met the challenge superbly. Touching only briefly on the misery of east European Jewry, the physician-writer analyzed the failure of emancipation, the social and political dilemma of Western assimilated Jews in modern times, whom he described as a race of new Marranos (the secretly professing Jews of Catholic Spain). "It is a great sin," Nordau declared, in ringing tones, "to let a race whose abilities even its worst enemies do not deny, degenerate in intellectual and physical misery. . . . The misery of the Jew cries out for help. The finding of that help will be the great task of this Congress."

Thereafter Herzl, who had learned much of parliamentary techniques during his years covering the French Chamber of Deputies, presided skillfully over the discussions. Adhering to the prepared agenda, he entertained reports on the condition of Jews from spokesmen of the various countries —except Russia, whose delegates had agreed to remain meaningfully silent. Nordau then submitted a program that had been formulated in advance by the "Commission of the Preliminary Conference." In order to avoid arousing Turkish suspicions, the lawyers in the commission circumspectly described "the aim of Zionism [to be] a Jewish homeland openly recognized, legally secured" (*"öffentlich-rechtlich"*). For the achievement of this goal, the Congress approved: the encouragement of settlement in Palestine by Jewish agricultural workers, laborers, and artisans; the unification of all Jewry into local and general (Zionist) groups; the strengthening of Jewish self-awareness and national consciousness; diplomatic activity to secure the help of various governments.

Thereupon the Congress established as its instrument a permanent Zionist Organization—the "Jewish Society" of Herzl's essay. The executive organ of the Zionist Organization would be a General Council, to be known as the "Greater Actions Committee," and composed of representatives of the various national Zionist federations; and a Central Executive (a "Smaller Actions Committee") whose members all lived in Vienna. Membership in the Organization was to be conferred on everyone who subscribed to the Basle Program and who paid the annual fee of a "shekel," an ancient Hebrew coin, deemed the equivalent of a single Austrian schilling. Herzl was unanimously elected president of the Zionist Organization. The three days of discussion finally concluded with the singing of a Hebrew anthem, "HaTikvah" (The Hope), written by Naphtali Herz Imber, and with a vote of thanks to Herzl. The assembly then rose as one man and embraced one another, weeping. To tumultuous applause, Herzl was carried through the hall on the shoulders of the younger delegates. In his diary, he later wrote: "If I were to sum up the Basle Congress in a single phrase—which I would not dare to make public—I would say: in Basle I created the Jewish State."

Probably Herzl's single most valuable experience at the gathering was his first intimate contact with east European Jewry. Its strength was much greater than he had expected. Far from being the culturally deprived semi-mendicants he had imagined, many of the Russian Jewish delegates were brilliant, polylingual lawyers, doctors, and scholars. He was impressed by their moral stature, as well. "They possess that inner unity which has disappeared from among the Westerners," he admitted in his diary. More than he had anticipated, too, the Congress gave powerful impetus to Zionist propaganda throughout the world. Hundreds of societies were formed to augment the old Chovevei Zion groups in affiliation with the Zionist Organization. Zionism (and anti-Zionism) now became the leading Jewish question of the day, infusing new vitality into Jewish communities everywhere.

In the Zionist Organization, Herzl had created his "Society of Jews." Now he was determined to organize the "Jewish Company," a bank to be entitled the Jewish Colonial Trust. At first, he intended to establish the bank in London, with a share capital of £2 million. As events developed, however, few wealthy Jews were interested in making generous contributions, and it soon became clear that the dreary, but vital, task of fund-raising would be the acid test of Zionist progress in the years ahead.

The prospect did not intimidate Herzl. Membership in the Organization was climbing steadily. In August 1898, a Second Zionist Congress was convened, also in Basle, and this time the number of delegates rose to 349. The Russian delegation, for example (including Caucasian mountain Jews wearing boots and bandoliers), was twice its former size. Among the new representatives were those who would emerge subsequently as the future giants of the movement: Chaim Weizmann, Nachum Sokolow, Professor Richard Gottheil of Columbia University, and the young American Reform rabbi Stephen Wise. From England came Chief Rabbi Moses Gaster, Norman Bentwich, and Leopold Greenberg. It was an outstanding gathering. Herzl was euphoric.

At the Second Congress, too, detailed reports were given not merely on the circumstances of Diaspora Jewry, but of Palestine Jewry as well. Leo Motzkin, whom the Zionist Organization earlier had sent to Palestine, now warned that under current legal restrictions a mass migration to the Holy Land was impossible. On the other hand, in Herzl's view, infiltration was equally out of the question; it was the very opposite of his entire purpose. A third choice accordingly was endorsed by the Congress. This was simultaneously to improve the coalition of the Yishuv—Palestine Jewry—by colonization and industrialization, and to endorse once again all possible diplomatic efforts to acquire a charter of Jewish settlement in the Holy Land.

THE KAISER AND THE SULTAN

Herzl hardly needed to be reminded of the importance of a charter. It had transfixed his thinking even during the vital organizational period of the Zionist Congresses. As instruments of imperial policy, charters had been in widespread use for nearly three centuries, and entire nations in fact had been settled in this fashion, including the American colonies. During the 1890s, moreover, as German engineers constructed the Berlin-to-Baghdad Railroad and German banks underwrote sizable investments in Turkey, the Ottoman Empire gradually moved into the German economic and diplomatic orbit. A keen student of international diplomacy, Herzl appreciated, then, that if the Ottoman government were to be favorably disposed to a charter of Zionist settlement in Palestine, it was Kaiser Wilhelm II who must exert the necessary leverage. Nor had Herzl neglected to formulate an inducement for that leverage. As he explained to the Grand Duke of Baden, the leaders of the Zionist movement were German-speaking Jews, the language of their Congresses was German, and Zionism accordingly would introduce a German cultural element into the Orient. "We need a protectorate," he observed meaningfully, "and the German would suit us best." In September 1898, Herzl was received by the German ambassador in Vienna, Count Philip zu Eulenburg, a friend and confidant of the kaiser. The ambassador was impressed with the Zionist plan, and scheduled an interview for Herzl the next day with Prince Bernhard von Bülow, the German foreign minister (soon to be chancellor), who was visiting in the Austrian capital. The meeting was unsuccessful, as it happened; Bülow was cool to the idea.

Then, in October, Eulenburg suddenly informed Herzl that the kaiser had agreed to an audience during the impending royal visit to Constantinople. At first, the Jewish journalist was stunned. He still did not have the bank, the financial instrument he had regarded as crucial to both negotiations and colonization. Nor, in the ensuing weeks, did he succeed in raising additional funds in London. Even so, Eulenburg urged Herzl not to make this financial uncertainty a reason for delay; the kaiser was already sold, he insisted. "Wunderbar! Wunderbar!" Herzl exclaimed in his diary. "The intervention of Germany, the protectorate, is a *fait acquis*." On October 13 he departed by train for Constantinople, taking with him David Wolffsohn (p. 42) and two other German associates. After a wait of several days in the Ottoman capital (the Turks had not been informed of the meeting), the audience took place on October 18, at the Yildiz Kiosk, where the kaiser and Bülow were housed.

The Zionist leader by then was self-assured. Having made a careful background study of the kaiser, he was convinced that Wilhelm could be reached through vanity. "I dressed with care," he wrote later. "The shade of my gloves worked out especially well: a delicate grey." Herzl's bearing, his regal poise and eloquence, unquestionably impressed the German ruler. Wilhelm did imply, to be sure, during the hour-long meeting, that his interest in Zionism was at least obliquely anti-Semitic. "There are among your people certain elements whom it would be a good thing to move to Palestine," he said. Unruffled, Herzl explained that prejudice always affected the "best" rather than the "worst" Jews. Whereupon Bülow, standing nearby, spoke of Jewish membership in the "revolutionary" party. Again Herzl replied that Zionism would dissipate that membership. Then, unfolding his plan for a charter of Jewish settlement in Palestine, Herzl emphasized the advantages a German protectorate might offer both Turkey and Germany. The kaiser reacted warmly to this approach and intimated that he would discuss it with the sultan. "Write out your address and give it to von Bülow," he stated at the end of the interview. "I will then work it out with him. Only tell me in brief what you want me to ask of the Sultan." "A chartered company—under German protection," Herzl replied. "Good, a chartered company," repeated the kaiser, who then shook Herzl's hand and left.

Herzl and his colleagues worked feverishly the rest of the day to prepare the address, then delivered it to Bülow. Soon afterward the little Zionist group departed by ship for Jaffa, in expectation of a second meeting with Wilhelm on the next stage of the royal tour. As the shore of Palestine at last came into view, Herzl and Wolffsohn embraced, tears in their eyes, and whispered softly: "Our country, our mother Zion!" Herzl was eager to take in what he could of the Yishuv before his next audience with the kaiser. Visiting Mikveh Israel and Rishon l'Zion, he was greeted enthusiastically by the settlers. Although distressed by the poverty he saw around him, Herzl tactfully praised Baron Rothschild's "magnificent generosity." At Ness Ziona and Rehovot, his spirits were at least partially revived by the spectacle of bronzed Jewish cowboys galloping out to meet him. A day later, as the imperial cortege passed Mikveh Israel, the kaiser recognized Herzl amid the awe-struck throng, bent down from his horse, and shook hands.

On November 12, he was called to his second interview with the German ruler, in a tent outside Jerusalem. Herzl used the occasion to read an address he and his colleagues had drawn up while en route to Palestine. This time, to avoid provoking Turkish hostility, the document referred not to a charter but merely to a "land company" for Jewish settlement under German protection. In contrast to the first meeting, however, the kaiser was now distinctly reserved. He limited himself to compliments on the Jewish villages he had seen. It would take much money to irrigate the land, he remarked, but he supposed the Jews had plenty. After a few more amenities, the interview was terminated. Several days later, en route back to Europe, Herzl read the German press communiqué on the events of November 12. It was studiously noncommittal, referring only to the kaiser's "benevolent interest" in agriculture in Palestine and the welfare of the Turkish empire.

Objectively, Herzl understood Wilhelm's hesitation in raising the delicate subject of a Zionist protectorate with Abdul Hamid. He assumed that Bülow must have pointed out its dangers. Indeed, this assumption was correct: the foreign minister was the obstacle. In his memoirs, years later, Bülow even denied that an audience with the Zionists had so much as taken place:

> Wilhelm II was at first fired with enthusiasm for the Zionist idea, because he hoped by this means to free his country from many elements [i.e., radical Jews]. However, when the Turkish Ambassador in Berlin, who accompanied us on our . . . tour, had made it clear that the Sultan would have nothing to do with Zionism and an independent Jewish kingdom, he dropped the Zionist cause and refused to receive its advocates in Zion.

Bülow had informed friends at the time that the rich Jews were uninterested in Zionism anyway, and he wanted nothing to do with the "scurvy Polish Jews." For months afterward, nevertheless, Herzl urgently sought to pick up the thread of the broken relationship, and visited Eulenburg and the Grand Duke of Baden. Both remained sympathetic, but without further influence.

It was a bleak period for Herzl. He feared that he was returning from his Eastern trip exposed as a visionary, perhaps a faker. Yet if he resumed his Zionist activities without his former mystic fits of elation, he was not less committed to the diplomatic route. This time, however, he decided to focus his major attention on the sultan. On March 30, 1899, at heavy personal expense, he sent Nevlinski back to Constantinople to seek a royal audience. Three days later, Nevlinski died. Herzl was shaken, but determined to go on. He reminded the Third Zionist Congress, meeting in August of that year, that the immediate aim of Zionist policy had not

changed. It continued to be the acquisition of a charter of settlement in
Palestine. He then asked Nordau, Professor Gottheil of New York, and
Max Bodenheimer, a German lawyer who had accompanied him on his
recent Ottoman trip, to prepare drafts of a charter. As models, he suggested the Chartered Company of Rhodes and the New Guinea Company.
In his attempt to establish contact with the sultan, meanwhile, Herzl
distributed large quantities of his personal funds among Turkish officials
in Europe.

Notwithstanding these efforts, impatience with his diplomacy was growing within the Zionist movement, particularly among the east Europeans.
As the years passed, the Jewish situation in Russia and Rumania was becoming intolerable, with tens of thousands of refugees flooding into central
and western Europe in search of asylum. Not surprisingly, the Fourth Zionist Congress, meeting in London in August 1900, was confused and dispirited in its proceedings. Herzl's employers, meanwhile, the publishers of
the *Neue Freie Presse,* warned him against ignoring his journalistic duties.
His fortune was rapidly being depleted by his Zionist expenditures. "The
wind blows through the stubble," Herzl wrote in his diary on January 30,
1901. "I feel my autumn approaching. I see before me the danger of leaving no achievement to the world and no inheritance to my children."

In the summer of 1900, Herzl began cultivating yet another potential intermediary with the sultan. This was a seventy-year-old Hungarian Jew,
Arminius Vambéry. At successive phases of his career an explorer, scientist,
and political agent for England and Turkey, Vambéry now held the title of
Professor of Oriental Languages at the University of Budapest. He had
gone through five religions in his lifetime, and despite his Jewish origin
had evinced meager interest in his people. To Herzl, nevertheless, Vambéry's possible usefulness lay in his special relationship with the Ottoman
royal family, which he had established years before as a language teacher
to Abdul Hamid's favorite sister, Princess Fatima. Eventually, through the
dependable technique of generous private subsidies, Herzl won Vambéry
to his cause. For a while, to be sure, the funds appeared as misspent as all
Herzl's earlier baksheesh. But on May 7, 1901, a telegram suddenly reached
Herzl from Vambéry in Constantinople to come at once: the sultan would
receive him. Three days later, accompanied by Wolffsohn and Oskar
Marmorek, Herzl was in the Turkish capital. His expectations were cautious by then. "Here I am," he wrote in his diary, "after five years, sitting
in the same suite of the Hotel Royal where I stayed with Nevlinski at the
beginning of the business. I look out the window, a changed man, and
see the unchanging Golden Horn. Beauty no longer moves me." Days
passed; additional baksheesh was disbursed to Ottoman officials. At last,
on May 17, Herzl was received by Abdul Hamid at a royal banquet. He
wrote later:

> I still see him before me, this Sultan of a dying robber empire. Small, shabby,
> with a badly dyed beard. . . . The hook nose of a Punchinello, long
> yellow teeth with a large gap in the right upper jaw, the fez pulled down
> over his head—which is probably bald—the protruding ears. . . . I see the

enfeebled hands in the loose gloves, and the big, ill-fitting shirt cuffs. The bleating voice, the diffidence in every word, the timidity in every glance. And that apparition rules!

The sultan went to great lengths to be amiable, presenting Herzl with a medal, repeatedly emphasizing his friendship for the Jews.

Herzl, in turn, responded by quoting the old fable of Androcles and the lion. "His Majesty is the lion, perhaps I am Androcles, and perhaps there is a thorn which I could withdraw." He went on. "I consider the Ottoman Public Debt the thorn. If this could be removed, then the life-strength of Turkey . . . could unfold anew." The Zionist leader then intimated that his Jewish associates might supply funds in return for "the proclamation of a measure particularly favorable to the Jews." Whereupon the delighted sultan offered to make a friendly statement on the Jews to his court jeweler, who was a Jew. Herzl smiled, indicating that he himself was prepared to formulate the text of a declaration. After two hours the conversation ended with mutual protestations of respect. The next day Herzl discussed with the grand vizier and the minister of finance his plans for refunding the Ottoman Public Debt. He indicated that a syndicate of Jews might buy up the Debt bonds over a period of three years. The sultan, for his part, would grant Jews a charter for a land settlement company in Palestine. Leaving the officials to chew over this proposal, Herzl then returned to Vienna, convinced that years of effort were approaching fruition at last.

Indeed, once news of the interview with Abdul Hamid was publicized, it significantly enhanced the reputation of the Zionist movement and its leader. Herzl was sure now that he had finally achieved the leverage necessary to raise a down payment of £1.5 million for the charter. But again he was doomed to disappointment. None of the Rothschilds expressed interest. Neither did the Montefiores in London. Worse yet, some of his closest associates, including Nordau, remained unimpressed by the sultan's professed goodwill. Funds were nowhere available. Herzl was in despair. "I have run myself ragged," he wrote Dr. Max Mandelstamm on August 18, "and I haven't obtained a hearing from the wretched crew which controls the money. . . . It is something utterly unheard of, and fifty years from now people will spit on the graves of these men. . . ." When the Fifth Zionist Congress assembled in Basle on December 26, 1901, Herzl could speak only of the "highest hopes" he entertained following his spring interview with the Turkish ruler.

He wrote Abdul Hamid, too, intimating that he was holding useful discussions with colleagues in Paris and London and soon would be able to make a tangible offer. The sultan took Herzl at his word. On February 5, 1902, he summoned the Zionist leader back to Constantinople to "furnish information" on current progress. Upon meeting with Ottoman officials in their capital nine days later, Herzl could only fight for time. In a desperate maneuver, he suggested that before any funding of the Public Debt was possible, the sultan should take the initiative in offering the Jews the general concession of a land colonizing company. The grand vizier did not take the bait. The most he was prepared to offer instead was a statement of protection for refugee Jews who could be dispersed throughout the empire, "everywhere but in Palestine," which the sultan would not give up. Herzl declined. The Jews already enjoyed protection in Western countries, he explained; what was required now was a "national" assurance. The Turks reserved their answer.

Entraining for Vienna, Herzl mulled over an approach that had been suggested by Izzat Bey, Abdul Hamid's first secretary. It was to establish a base of influence by purchasing mining concessions in Turkey. "Take our finances in hand," Izzat Bey had said, "and you will become the master." Afterward, presumably, the issue of colonization would be taken up again. Herzl found the idea appealing. With some effort, he finally secured the Zionist Actions Committee's reluctant approval to deposit letters of credit totaling 3 million francs in Ottoman banks; the sum would be guaranteed by the Jewish Colonial Trust. Yet by then it was too late even for indirect measures. When Herzl returned to Constantinople in July 1902, for still another meeting with Ottoman officials, he made a shocking discovery: the Turks evidently had been using the Zionist offer as a bargaining pawn with a visiting commission of French financiers, represented by Foreign Minister Maurice Rouvier, in the hope of securing a major loan from Paris.

THE BRITISH CONNECTION

In 1902 Herzl's melancholy was compounded not simply by the apparent failure of his years of diplomatic effort, but by the growing mood of restlessness within the Zionist Organization itself (p. 58). He took little solace in the quiet but impressive growth of Zionist membership throughout the world; the increasing numbers of delegates who attended the Congresses; the Hebrew cultural revival gestating throughout eastern Europe; even the establishment at last of a modestly funded Jewish Colonial Trust and a Jewish National Fund for land-buying purposes in Palestine. All this represented precisely the kind of gradualism he had intended to transcend by a single, dramatic coup of statecraft.

If the Zionist ideal was gaining in articulation, moreover, so was anti-Zionism. Some of the outstanding intellectual representatives of German Jewry, men of the stature of Hermann Cohen and Ludwig Geiger, discerned in Zionism a movement "fully as dangerous to the German spirit as are social democracy and ultramontanism." In Austria, Zionism won few intellectual supporters, and in France virtually none. In England, Lucien Wolf, secretary of the Joint Foreign Committee of the Anglo-Jewish Association and the Board of Deputies of British Jews, regarded Herzl's ideas as blatant treason, and a provocation to anti-Semitism. The reaction in the United States was hardly more sympathetic. A convention of American Reform rabbis, meeting in Pittsburgh a decade before the appearance of the *Judenstaat,* had declared in their "official" platform: "We consider ourselves no longer a nation but a religious community, and therefore expect neither a return to Palestine . . . nor the restoration of any of the laws concerning the Jewish state." After the First Zionist Congress, the Reform rabbis branded Herzl's action as "Zionmania" and purged Zionist sympathizers from the Union of American Hebrew Congregations.

It is only in the context of these failures and the mounting animus of the anti-Zionists that Herzl's evident shift in tactics can be understood. In 1902 he remained fully committed to Palestine—indeed, much more so than at the time he wrote his *Judenstaat;* for contact with the Russian Zionists had enlightened him on the centrality of Zion in Jewish tradition. But it was equally plain that he had underestimated the difficulties of securing a charter of settlement for the Holy Land. As early as 1898, moreover, witnessing the critical circumstances of Jewish life in Galicia, Herzl gave momentary thought to "finding a closer territorial objective for the movement, while retaining Zion as the ultimate aim." In his diary on July 1, 1898, he wrote: "We can perhaps ask England for Cyprus; we may even consider South Africa or America until the day of Turkey's dissolution." Yet in the next few years, during his German-Turkish negotiations, he neglected these various alternatives.

It happened, then, in early 1902, that the British Parliament appointed a Royal Commission to study the "threat of cheap labor" posed by the influx of Russian Jews into London's East End. At this point Leopold Greenberg, a London journalist and well-known British Zionist, sensed an opportunity to provide Herzl with an important forum. He arranged for the Commission to offer Herzl an invitation to testify as a "Jewish expert." Herzl thereafter appeared before the parliamentary body on July 7 to describe the wretched conditions of east European Jewry and to express hope that Britain would continue to offer asylum for fugitives. He added, however: "If you find that they are not wanted here, then some place must be found to which they can migrate without raising the problems that confront them here. These problems will not arise if a home be found for them which will be legally recognized as Jewish." In this fashion, Herzl delicately adverted to his Zionist solution.

In fact, before testifying, he had met with Lord Nathaniel Rothschild, himself a member of the Royal Commission, and a man whose support Herzl urgently needed for the "chartered company." Herzl then raised the idea of the Sinai Peninsula or of Cyprus as possible alternatives for collective Jewish settlement. Rothschild did not object. On his own, now, Rothschild took Herzl's written speech to Joseph Chamberlain, the British colonial secretary. An ardent and vigorous spokesman for the "Greater Englanders," Chamberlain was known to favor the use of client peoples as dependable instruments of British imperialism. Conceivably the Jews might play such a role. He listened with interest, then, as Herzl, in his stumbling English, indicated that Palestine was still the ultimate goal of Zionism, but that negotiations were dragging. "Now I have time to negotiate," the Zionist leader explained, "but my people have not. They are starving in the Pale." Chamberlain, in turn, professing his "friendship" for the Jews, suggested that if Herzl could show him "a spot among the British possessions which was not yet inhabited by white settlers, then we could talk."

Encouraged, Herzl proceeded to outline for Chamberlain his scheme for the colonization either of Cyprus or of al-Arish, in the northern Sinai Peninsula. The Englishman ruled out Cyprus immediately but considered the notion of Egypt feasible. "No," smiled Herzl, "we will not go to Egypt. We have been there." Instead, he pressed specifically for al-Arish, a tract of desert land that was not part of "integral" Egypt and that hopefully might lend itself to wide-scale cultivation. Presumably, al-Arish also would exert an emotional appeal to the Zionists as the site of Mount Sinai. The proposal intrigued Chamberlain, who accordingly set up a meeting between Herzl and the foreign secretary, Lord Lansdowne, for the next day. Lansdowne was equally cordial and suggested that Lord Cromer, the British agent-general of Egypt, negotiate the matter directly with a Zionist mission. Herzl was delighted. After preparing memoranda and holding further discussions with officials in London, he selected Leopold Greenberg as negotiator with Lord Cromer; he also appointed a technical commission headed by a Zionist engineer, Leopold Kessler, and including a land expert, another engineer, an architect, several agronomists, and a physician. Greenberg then left for Cairo in advance.

Almost at once, however, the Zionist negotiator began encountering difficulties with Cromer and with the Egyptian prime minister, Boutros Ghali. Both men were less than enthusiastic about the plan. Herzl himself departed for Cairo in March of 1903. He found Cromer "the most disagreeable Englishman" he had ever met, and Boutros Ghali even less amiable. Somewhat fearfully, he presented them with the interim report of Kessler's technical commission. It had found al-Arish suitable for Europeans, for the cultivation of tobacco and cotton, provided irrigation were available; and irrigation from the Nile, while expensive, was not unfeasible. Two months later, nevertheless, Cromer informed the Zionists that the Egyptian government was rejecting the plan on grounds of "inadequate irrigation." The argument in fact was a bluff. It was discovered later that Cromer and the Egyptian authorities had simply disliked the notion of a Jewish enclave in their territory. Herzl now fell into black despair. "It's simply done for," he wrote in his diary on May 11.

It is at least conceivable that Herzl was at this point willing to abandon Palestine altogether as his intended state. Unquestionably, the torment of Russian and Rumanian Jewry affected him deeply. He was obsessed similarly by the need to present his followers with a tangible diplomatic coup in the early future; otherwise, he feared, the Zionist movement would collapse for lack of encouragement. For that matter, Herzl did not know how many more years of leadership he could offer. He was suffering from cardiac arrhythmia, and his personal estate had been gravely depleted by massive expenditures in travel, baksheesh, and subsidies. One gains insight into his thinking through the novel, *Altneuland* (Old-New Land), that he dashed off in this period of ebbing morale. The initial impulse for the book had been supplied by his visit to Palestine in 1898. He sketched an outline in July 1899 and returned to it finally in March 1902.

Altneuland's weakness was that of all Herzl's plays and of many polemical novels. Its figures were one-dimensional, essentially spokesmen for ideologies and programs. The hero, Friedrich Löwenberg, was transparently Herzl himself, a world-weary attorney of Vienna. Disappointed in love, shaken by the corrosive anti-Semitism of Habsburg Austria, he accepted an invitation to join a wealthy German aristocrat, Kingscourt, on a private yacht tour around the world. In the course of their journey the two men stopped off in Palestine. They were repelled by the backwardness of the country, and not least all by its moribund Jewish settlement. Despite occasional encouraging glimpses of Zionist villages, of Jewish farms and cowboys, Löwenberg concluded that "nobody can be deader than the Jewish people." The travelers sailed off.

And then, twenty years later, in 1923, Löwenberg and Kingscourt paid a return visit to the Holy Land. They were dumfounded by the changes that had taken place. Their port of entry, Haifa, had become a glittering international city, the "safest and most comfortable harbor in the Mediterranean." Wherever they traveled in Palestine—renamed Altneuland by its Jewish inhabitants—they encountered other, equally flourishing cities and a thriving, irrigated agriculture. Supplied with electricity by the flow of the Jordan River, the country was a model of technological advancement. A race of Jewish fugitives had been transformed by orderly Zionist direction into a nation of successful farmers, industrialists, and businessmen. A new social and economic order had been created, too, based on a cooperative economy. Women enjoyed equal rights. Ample employment opportunities, medical facilities, health and old-age insurance benefits were available for all. Education was free. Arabs and Jews lived in friendship side by side. "The Jews have enriched us," observed one Arab notable, Reshid Bey. "Why should we have anything against them? They live with us like brothers, why should we not love them?" Altneuland similarly had enriched Jewish life throughout the world. With the departure of Jews for Palestine, Jewish economic competition had declined in Europe, and anti-Semitism with it. Emancipation at last had become a reality. Was this all a dream, a mere vision? Löwenberg asked himself. The novel closed with the epilogue: "But if you will it, it is no fable."

While less than a commercial success, the book achieved a respectable audience within the Zionist movement itself. It was also among these readers, however, that the novel's lacunae were noted most acutely. Herzl's description of Altneuland's emergent culture, for example, a refinement of Jewish linguistic and intellectual accomplishments in Europe, was curiously pedestrian. Hebrew, to be sure, occupied a place in the new society; but so did French, German, Italian, Spanish, even Yiddish. Critics of the book insisted that Herzl neither foresaw nor evidently favored a Hebrew school system, a Hebrew theater, a Hebrew press; nor did he anticipate a life thoroughly rooted in the Hebraic idiom. Altneuland, in sum, was viewed as a political and technological answer to Jewish oppression, little more. In actual fact, Herzl was not less eager than the "practical," ideological Zionists for an authentic Jewish culture in Palestine; but he expected that this phenomenon would develop spontaneously on the basis of a normal, independent existence, which Zionism had first to create. Even so, the bitter exchange over the novel between the "practicals," a majority of them east European Jews, and the "politicals," the advocates of a diplomatic solution, merely accentuated a rift that had been widening for several years, and that soon threatened to fracture the Zionist movement itself.

ACHAD HAAM, EASTERNERS, AND THE DEMOCRATIC FRACTION

The principal intellectual opponent of Herzl's leadership was a didactic, somewhat irascible Russian-Jewish writer, Asher Ginzberg, better known since his early criticisms of the Chovevei Zion by his pen name of Achad HaAm (Chapter II). Born in the Ukraine of a Chasidic family, Achad HaAm endured the classic Jewish youth of a sensitive mind imprisoned by the obscurantism of the Pale. He was married off at the age of seventeen to a girl he had never set eyes on until the day of the wedding, then was locked into a modest family business for which he exhibited neither enthusiasm nor aptitude. His escape from material circumstances was almost entirely cerebral. Like other, often forgotten, geniuses of the Haskalah era, he became an omnivorous reader in virtually all European languages. His horizons were additionally broadened when he took up residence first in Odessa, a major Jewish intellectual center, and then, early in the twentieth century, in London, where he served as an auditor of the English branch of the Wissotzky Tea Company.

Almost from the beginning of early manhood, this spare, narrow-shouldered little man, goateed and pince-nezed, devoted his phenomenal erudition and stylistic perfectionism to one cause—"The Solution of the Jewish Problem" (the title of one of his essays). Despite Achad HaAm's later emphasis upon "spiritual" or "cultural" Zionism, his earliest writings suggest that initially it was anti-Semitism that aroused his Jewish nationalism no less than Herzl's. Moreover, in the aftermath of a brutal series of pogroms, he, too, like Herzl, briefly entertained the notion of voluntary racial assimilation. It was only upon reaching Odessa that Achad HaAm eventually became an active member of the Chovevei Zion, and it was from that Black Sea port that he launched his criticism of Zionism's early infiltrationist methods. In "Lo Zeh HaDerech," we have noted (p. 34), he urged his fellow Chovevei Zion to reconsider their emphasis upon actual physical settlement in Palestine. Yet his purpose was not merely to postpone colonization until juridical and diplomatic guarantees were secured from the Turks, but to ensure that the national spirit of the Jewish people was fully ignited. "Not twenty agricultural colonies, not even a hundred," he wrote, ". . . can automatically effect our spiritual salvation. . . . Let us then return to the proper approach, of working and strengthening the ideal of [spiritual unification] until the day comes when it can be transformed into reality."

The essay aroused wide resentment among the members of Chovevei Zion, and Achad HaAm's subsequent reports on the precariousness of Jewish life in the Holy Land evoked even more criticism. How was it possible, asked his readers, to launch a Jewish cultural revival except on the basis of a healthy social and economic infrastructure in the Yishuv? Somewhat taken aback by this reaction, Achad HaAm later modified his views, conceding that agricultural settlement in Palestine was indeed a worthy idea. He proceeded nevertheless to elaborate upon his conception of the Land of Israel as essentially a "national spiritual center" for the revival of Judaism throughout the world—the proper goal of the Zionist movement. His obsession with spiritual and cultural awakening, expressed in an austere lucidity of style unknown until then in the modern Hebrew language, began to exert its impact, even among the most relentless "practical" Zionists. His pen name soon became the most important in the Zionist world. Weizmann recalled of him: "He had the profoundest effect on the Russian-Jewish students in Europe . . . the appearance of one of Achad HaAm's articles was always an event of prime importance. He was read and discussed endlessly. . . . He was . . . what Gandhi had been to many Indians, what Mazzini was to Young Italy a century ago."

It was to cultivate the spiritual-cultural ideal, moreover, that Achad HaAm in 1899 founded a select, elitist group, the B'nai Moshe, within the Chovevei Zion. The society's accomplishments were important, if unspectacular. It founded a national land-purchasing fund, which in later years was handed over to the "official" Jewish National Fund; published a series of newsletters in Jaffa giving accurate information on developments within the Yishuv; established the first Hebrew-language school, also in Jaffa—and later a collection of Hebrew libraries throughout Palestine; organized a nucleus of secular, Hebrew-language day schools in Russia proper, as well as the influential Achiasaf (Hebrew-language) Publishing Company. The B'nai Moshe subsequently was dissolved in the aftermath of the early Zionist Congresses. It was inevitable by then that Herzl's dynamic activist Zionism, with its intoxicating vision of political sovereignty, should arouse greater enthusiasm among European Jewry than Achad HaAm's rather austere vision of a Judaic renaissance.

Nevertheless, it was the little Russian Jewish essayist who came to serve as the conscience of tens of thousands among the east European Jews who flocked to the Zionist movement. Nor did Achad HaAm err on the side of understatement. Detecting and mercilessly exposing the lack of Hebraic content in Herzl's *Judenstaat,* he chose to attend the First Zionist Congress as a visitor rather than as a delegate—"like a mourner at a wedding feast," he wrote afterward. In later articles he insisted that political Zionism, far from developing naturally out of Jewish tradition, was hardly more than an artificial concoction of Europeanized Western Jews. From the late 1890s on, then, Achad HaAm's campaign against "mere" political Zionism and Herzl's diplomatist leadership transformed him into the most feared and respected critic in the Zionist world. His scathing attack on *Altneuland,* when it appeared late in 1902, his contempt for Herzl's vision of a Europeanized polyglot society in the Land of Israel, dramatized the emerging ideological fissure within the movement.

Years later, Weizmann described the misgivings shared by Russian Jewish delegates even at the earliest Zionist Congresses. For one thing, the "Easterners" did not like the note of "elegance and pseudo-worldliness" that characterized the central European leadership; it seemed to belie the folk-democracy of the Pale of Settlement. Moreover, "Herzl's pursuit of great men, of princes and rulers, who were to 'give' us Palestine, was the pursuit of a mirage. . . . We, on the other hand, had little faith in the benevolence of the mighty. . . ." (Weizmann himself would change his views on this subject within a few years.) Of decisive concern to all the Easterners, however—many of whom were ardent followers of the "cher maître," Achad HaAm—was the palpable lack of Judaic "spirit" in the activities of Herzl and his closest collaborators. To express their misgivings, Weizmann, Leo Motzkin, and a group of younger Russian Jewish delegates to the Zionist Congresses summoned a Zionist Youth Conference in December 1901. Its intention was to formulate a "realistic" cultural desideratum for the movement. Thirty-seven members participated in the gathering and reached agreement that the "culturists" henceforth should be welded together in an organized "Fraction" (in effect, a party) within the Zionist Congress.

The Fraction was not altogether without influence. At the Fifth Zionist Congress, it presented a resolution—one that Herzl decided to accept—affirming that "the education of the Jewish people in a national spirit is an essential part of the Zionist Program," and advocating the election of a cultural commission whose members would include Weizmann and Achad HaAm. In subsequent years, too, the Fraction's program of a Zionist school system was brought to life throughout eastern Europe. On the other hand, one of Weizmann's most cherished ambitions, the establishment of a Jewish university, turned out to be premature. The group served essentially as the rallying point for those devoted to the goals of "spiritual, cultural" Zionism. This was no minor function. It was the heritage of Judaic culture, after all, that ensured the centrality of Palestine in the minds and hearts of Russian Jewry. Moreover, while Achad HaAm, no less than Herzl, deplored "infiltrationism" as a technique for reviving the Jewish nation, the former's disciples—Weizmann, Motzkin, and the largest numbers of east European Jews—still preferred gradual and methodical colonization in the revered Holy Land to a paralysis of suspended animation, waiting breathlessly for Herzl's diplomatic achievement of a charter. Well prior to the Sixth Zionist Congress in August 1903, it became evident that the al-Arish project had reached a dead end. This fresh setback further confirmed the Fraction's view that renewed emphasis simply would have to be placed on the grudging, tedious, but vitally important consolidation of the Yishuv—Jewry's indispensable bridgehead in Zion.

A FINAL DIPLOMATIC EFFORT AND THE "UGANDA" CRISIS

Returning from his visit to Cromer in Egypt, meanwhile, Herzl stopped off in London in April 1903 to report to Chamberlain. The Zionist leader remained optimistic that something tangible would yet emerge from the al-Arish project. Nor had Chamberlain given up hope of exploiting the Jews as talented agents of British imperial policy. It was to that end that the colonial secretary unexpectedly dropped another proposal in Herzl's lap. "On my travels," he said, "I saw a country for you: Uganda. [The reference to "Uganda" was erroneous; the territory was known as British East Africa and lay within the area that ultimately became Kenya.] On the coast it is hot, but in the interior the climate is excellent for Europeans. You can plant cotton and sugar. I thought to myself: that's just the country for Dr. Herzl. But *he* must have Palestine and will move only into its vicinity [that is, al-Arish]." "Yes, I must," Herzl responded. "The base must be in or near Palestine."

But as it soon developed, Herzl's commitment to the Holy Land or its proximity was shaken by the onrush of events in Russia. The following month a savage pogrom in Kishinev, Bessarabia, took the lives of 45 Jews, wounded 86 more, and destroyed over 1,500 Jewish homes and shops. Herzl was shattered by news of this atrocity, and by the evident impending doom of Russian Jewry altogether. Soon afterward, therefore, when Chamberlain again proposed East Africa to Leopold Greenberg, Herzl wrote back to London: "We will see what they offer us. Even if, under pressure of immediate need, we accept such a proposition we still do not give up Sinai." He notified Chamberlain that a Zionist commission of investigation shortly would be sent to British East Africa. At the same time he requested Greenberg to prepare a charter of Jewish autonomy there. Greenberg thereupon commissioned the law firm of Lloyd George, Roberts, and Company to prepare a charter document.

When Herzl broached Chamberlain's offer to Nordau on July 2, 1903, his old friend was not enthusiastic, and Herzl was obliged to reassure him that East Africa was not intended as a substitute for Palestine, but rather as a training ground for it. Indeed, it might serve as a bargaining weapon with the sultan. "We must give an answer to Kishinev," Herzl emphasized, "and this is the only one. . . ." He added: "If we acknowledge Chamberlain's offer with thanks . . . we strengthen our position in his sympathies, we involve him in the necessity of doing *something* for us in the event that our commission . . . brings in a negative recommendation; and we have, in our relationship with this gigantic nation, acquired recognition as a state-building power. . . ." The rationale was not unimpressive, and

Nordau was persuaded. The British Foreign Office, meanwhile, which held formal authority for the East Africa Protectorate, informed Greenberg that the question would require closer examination once the Zionists themselves completed their investigation. "Afterward, if a mutually appropriate area were found, [Foreign Secretary] Lord Lansdowne will be glad to consider favourably proposals for the creation of a Jewish colony. . . ." It was an encouraging beginning.

Even as these exchanges took place, Herzl was making preparations for an urgent trip to St. Petersburg. He had learned that Vyacheslav von Plehve, the tsarist minister of the interior, had ordered new and crippling measures against organized Zionism in Russia. Already the tsarist police were banning Zionist meetings, forbidding the sale of Jewish Colonial Trust shares and solicitations for the Jewish National Fund, and arresting and jailing individual Zionist leaders. It was clear that the entire practical foundation of Russian Zionism now was threatened. Herzl accordingly reached the tsarist capital on August 7, 1903, where he secured an immediate meeting with von Plehve. The interior minister ("the arch anti-Semite, a restrained panther," in Herzl's description) chatted amiably with his visitor in French. He showed himself remarkably well informed on the Zionist movement and emphasized his government's interest in the departure of the "unassimilable" portion of the Jewish people. But of late, von Plehve added, the "Achad HaAmist" group was placing more stress upon Jewish nationalism than upon emigration, and this was inimical to Russia's need for a "homogeneous population."

Herzl then explained that it was in Russia's interest to allow collections for the Jewish Colonial Trust and the Jewish National Fund. These institutions not only would foster emigration but would provide an outlet against socialism. This argument impressed von Plehve, who promised to discuss it with the prime minister and with the tsar himself. In fact, Herzl's diplomacy proved astute. Within a week, sanctions against Zionist fund-raising were lifted; the legal status of Zionism as an emigrationist movement was revalidated. Stopping off in Vilna en route home, Herzl was tendered an immense reception by thousands of grateful Zionists. He was shaken, nevertheless, by evidence he saw everywhere of Russian police brutality toward the Jews. Unless this vast minority population found refuge, he knew, its sheer physical survival no longer could be assured.

The mood of urgency was shared by all factions within Zionism. In the aftermath of the Kishinev pogrom, Weizmann recalled, "normal activity seemed meaningless. . . . Our dreams of Palestine, our plans for a Hebrew University, receded into the background. Our eyes saw nothing but the blood of slaughtered men, women, and children, our ears were deaf to everything but their cries." Entering the Basle assembly hall for the Sixth Zionist Congress, on August 22, 1903, the delegates suddenly recognized the extent to which the rescue effort obsessed the movement's leadership. It had been a tradition in earlier Congresses for a map of Palestine to be hung on the wall behind the dais. This now had been replaced by a map of East Africa. Herzl confirmed the new approach when he informed the delegates of London's offer "to consider favourably" proposals for the establishment of a Jewish colony in East Africa. "Zion this certainly is not," Herzl emphasized, "and can never become. . . . It is, and must remain, an emergency measure which is intended . . . to prevent the loss of these detached fragments of our people." Nordau then followed Herzl to the platform to assure the audience that "Uganda" could be envisaged at most as a *"Nachtasyl"*—an asylum for a night—and as a thrilling new connection with the British government.

Initially, these hopeful auguries seemed to register on the Congress. A leading Russian Zionist, Shmaryahu Levin, watched the effect produced by the announcement on the delegates. "It was one of almost agonized attention," he recounted in his autobiography. "On the faces were written astonishment and admiration—but not a sign of protest. . . ." As the rousing applause died down, however, and the implications of the offer sank home, a muffled disquiet became evident in the hall. It was given its first expression on the rostrum by Yechiel Tchlenow, a fervent admirer of Herzl and a leader of the east European delegates. "There fills us all an inexpressible joy," he declared, "that a great European Power, for the first time since the destruction of the Temple, has recognized with this offer the national demands of the Jewish people. But therewith is linked the great sorrow that we must refuse this offer, because our needs can only be satisfied by Palestine." Other speakers were far less moderate. The debate became impassioned. Warnings and accusations—"Suicide!" "Criminal!" "Treachery!"—began flying from all sides. Thus, when a vote was taken on the seemingly innocuous resolution to dispatch an investigative commission to East Africa, it passed by the unimpressive tally of 295 to 177, with 100 members abstaining.

Even this "victory" became a Pyrrhic one for Herzl. The Congress was soon polarized. Some delegates sat on the floor and wept. Others, mainly east Europeans who had opposed the measure, stormed out of the hall to gather as a rump caucus in another room. There they voted against consideration even of the most temporary alternatives to Palestine. When Herzl insisted on addressing the defectors, they received him coldly. In the manner of an admonishing father, the Zionist leader reviewed the whole story of his diplomatic travels. He was fully as committed to the goal of Palestine as they, he insisted, but warned that the opportunity of developing a relationship with Britain should not be forfeited. The next day the two groups reached an understanding of sorts. There was agreement that a mission would be sent to East Africa, although strictly for investigation and without powers to commit the organization. To balance the decision, however, a Palestine commission also was appointed to study the circumstances of the Yishuv.

It is an oversimplification to assume that the cleavage was simply between "political" Westerners, on the one hand, and "practical-cultural" east Europeans, on the other, for whom Palestine alone enjoyed a mystic significance. Nordau, for example, privately opposed the notion of sending a commission to East Africa. Other Westerners voted against the proposal, including Martin Buber, Berthold Feiwel, Heinrich Löwe, Richard Gottheil, and Jacob de Haas. Conversely, many east Europeans voted in favor of the measure, including the Labor Zionist leader Nachman Syrkin, Weizmann's own father and brother, and fully eighty-one others. Among those abstaining, too, were the respected Russian Zionist leaders Leo Motzkin, Nachum Sokolow, even Yechiel Tchlenow. Yet the largest groundswell of opposition unquestionably came from the Pale. Ramifications of the East Africa issue, oversimplified and ultimately distorted, soon were to be felt in every corner of the Zionist world. In a white heat of indignation, Achad HaAm published an article, "HaBochim" (Those Who Weep), in which he proclaimed the final bankruptcy of "political Zionism."

The most implacable opponent of "Ugandism" turned out to be the Russian Zionist leader Menachem Ussishkin, a dynamic, stocky bull of a man, who concentrated on land-purchasing missions in Palestine. Indeed, Ussishkin had been in Palestine during the recent Congress. Returning hurriedly now to Europe, he immediately announced his intention of "declaring war" on Herzl. To that end he summoned an emergency conference of leading "practical" Zionists in Kharkov, at the end of October 1903. Repudiating the "Uganda project" overwhelmingly, the conference thereupon sent a delegation to Vienna, where it insisted that Herzl abandon his method of "authoritarian decision" and submit all further policy resolutions to the Greater Actions Committee (on which the Easterners were heavily represented). Herzl similarly was warned to drop the "Uganda" scheme forthwith, on pain of losing east European funds for the Zionist Organization. It was a tough ultimatum, and Herzl was obliged to muster all his forbearance to assure his visitors that he had not abandoned Palestine as his central objective. His restraint, however, was to no avail. The "practicals" were not appeased, nor did the storm abate. Meanwhile, outraged by the challenge to their leader, Herzl's supporters launched impassioned protests of their own in the Zionist house organ, Die Welt, against the "rebels of Kharkov." By then, too, violent disputes on the "Uganda" issue had erupted not only among European Zionists but among the pioneer colonists of the Yishuv who were experiencing at first hand the bitterness of life in Palestine. Ironically, the farmers of Zichron Ya'akov went so far as to detach the signpost from "Ussishkin Street" in repudiation of its namesake's position on East Africa. From Jerusalem, Eliezer Ben-Yehuda, the preeminent creator of the modern Hebrew language (Chapter IV), wrote articles in defense of the East Africa proposal. Throughout the Zionist world, family bonds and lifelong friendships were shattered on the issue.

In any case, while the crisis precipitated a major upheaval of the "practical-cultural" Zionists, who for years had been champing at Herzl's "diplomatism," the availability of East Africa itself rapidly was becoming academic. English colonists there strenuously opposed the very notion of a mass influx of Russian Jews. As a result, Foreign Secretary Lansdowne's communications to Herzl and Greenberg became increasingly evasive, and at last Chamberlain suggested that the area probably was too small for extensive Jewish habitation. For his part, Herzl was almost relieved by then that the project seemed to be fading. The contact with England was all that mattered. "You will see," he told Max Bodenheimer, "the time is coming when England will do everything in her power to have Palestine ceded to us for the Jewish state." By April 1904, with the prospect of alternative settlement no longer meaningful, the Zionist Greater Actions Committee met in a spirit of reconciliation. Herzl offered his solemn assurance that Palestine alone thenceforth would be the cynosure of his efforts. Tchlenow responded with gratification that Herzl was "making every attempt to further the work in Palestine programmatically, energetically, and wisely."

HERZL: A LAST ASSESSMENT

The bitter internecine struggle had taken its toll. A friend was startled by the change in Herzl. "The imposing figure was now stooped," he wrote later, "the face was sallow, the eyes, those mirrors of a fine soul, were darkened, the mouth was drawn in pain and marked by passion." In the late spring of 1904, Herzl suffered a mild heart attack, and on June 3 he left for Edlach in the Semmering resort area to recuperate. But on July 1 his breathing became stertorous, he coughed blood, then lapsed into a coma. His mother and children were summoned. Chaplain Hechler, a devoted ally since Herzl's earliest Zionist career, rushed to his friend's bedside. On the afternoon of July 3, 1904, Herzl died at the age of forty-four.

In his will, the Zionist leader had requested that his body be interred in Vienna, next to his father's grave, "to remain there until the Jewish people carry my remains to Palestine." During the last trip back to the Austrian capital, news of his passing spread rapidly throughout the Zionist world. Ended, immediately, were all factional recriminations. The sheer vacuum of his departure was numbing. Even Achad HaAm admitted now that Herzl had given the Jews a personal image of great and messiahlike grandeur. Joseph Klausner, an eminent Zionist literary historian, observed that "something regal" had departed the Jewish people. The similes most frequently invoked in Herzl's obituaries were of a "king," a "prophet," a "great eagle." "Herzl made great mistakes," Weizmann wrote his fiancée, "but he had the outlook of an eagle and was a great force." He then instructed her to wear black. The funeral took place in Vienna on July 7. Six thousand people walked behind the cortege. Stefan Zweig recalled that the huge procession was dignified, when suddenly

> a tumult ensued at the cemetery; too many had suddenly stormed to his coffin, crying, sobbing, screaming in a wild explosion of despair. It was almost a riot, a fury. All order was overturned through a sort of elemental ecstatic mourning such as I have never seen before or since at a funeral. And it was this gigantic outpouring of grief from the depths of millions of souls that caused me to realize for the first time how much passion and hope this

lone and lonesome man had borne into the world through the power of a
single idea.

Herzl's personal shortcomings were not trivial. His manner transcended
the regal and approached the dictatorial. Unconsciously, perhaps, he emulated the approach of Baron de Rothschild, and did not know that it had
failed. For all his courage and imagination, too, Herzl never resolutely
faced the issue of dual loyalty. Instead, he tabled it, hoping that an imminent diplomatic victory would preclude the need for an ideological choice
between Jewish cultural solidarity in the Diaspora and emigration, pure
and simple, to a Jewish state. Yet Herzl's redeeming greatness was his
ability to elevate a domestic misery, one that traditionally had been coped
with through stopgap measures, into a challenging international issue. He
removed the Jewish problem from the waiting rooms of philanthropy
and introduced it into the chancelleries of European diplomacy. In Marvin
Lowenthal's apt phrase, Herzl put Zionism on the map; and, in creating
the Zionist Organization, he gave the Jewish people an address. The very
term "Zionism" soon fell naturally from the lips of world leaders and became an item on the agenda of prime ministers and princes. Even the
young Russian Chovevei Zion learned from Herzl the techniques of international diplomacy—without which Zionism would have been doomed to
remain at best an object of emotion and philanthropic relief.

It was significant, also, that Herzl bequeathed to future Zionist leaders
—Weizmann and Sokolow, among others—far more than precept and example. In his own career, he actually developed the contacts they later
would exploit. Arthur James Balfour, for example, was prime minister in
1903, when Herzl secured the British offer of territory in East Africa. Three
years later, when Balfour first met Weizmann, the British statesman recalled Herzl's vision of a Jewish homeland. At Herzl's request, Lloyd
George had drawn up the initial draft charter for a Jewish regime in East
Africa and had actively espoused the Zionist cause during the parliamentary debate on the offer in 1904. Sir Edward Grey and Lord Milner,
both of them vital to Weizmann in 1917, had been politically attracted to
Zionism by Herzl and his agents in the course of the al-Arish and East
Africa negotiations. Much that Herzl had anticipated, from high diplomacy
to the patient and tedious cultivation of individuals and solicitation of
funds, he himself put into action. "Everything directed from one center
with purposeful and far-sighted vision," he had written Baron de Hirsch
after the abortive meeting of 1895. "Finally, I would have had to tell you
what flag I would unfurl and how. And then you would have asked in
mockery, 'A flag, what is that? A stick with a cloth rag?' No, a flag, monsieur, is more than that. With a flag you can lead men where you will—
even into the Promised Land."

On August 16, 1949, Herzl's remains were flown to Israel. The next day
they were interred on a ridge facing Jerusalem and bearing the name
Mount Herzl.

THE GROWTH
OF THE YISHUV

ZIONISM AFTER HERZL

It seemed unlikely that the void opened in the Zionist Organization after Herzl's death could be filled by individual leadership alone. Nor was the moment opportune for a renewed and indefinite prolongation of high-echelon statecraft. The confrontation between the "politicals" and the "practicals" remained unresolved, after all, with neither diplomacy nor physical settlement in Palestine offering evidence of dramatic success. As a result, the Seventh Zionist Congress, meeting in Basle from July 27 to August 2, 1905, was obliged to give urgent attention to its future stance. In overwhelming numbers, the delegates rejected any colonizing activities outside Palestine, and voted unequivocally in favor of emigration and settlement there, with active encouragement of Jewish agriculture and industry. It was a less than oblique rebuke to the Herzlian fixation with purely governmental negotiations. So was the choice of a new president. Nordau was the one man of stature who had been most closely identified with Herzl. Accordingly, he was offered the presidency, but chose to disqualify himself on the grounds that his wife was a non-Jew. He sensed, too, however, that as a "political," he would not have been assured the full-hearted support of the Russian Jewish majority. Eventually the choice fell on David Wolffsohn, who represented a compromise between the two factions. A genial, stocky man of forty-nine, Wolffsohn almost ideally linked the ethnic and the ideological components within the Zionist organization. Born in Lithuania, the son of a rabbi, he had settled in Cologne at the age of twenty and had achieved success in the lumber business. He had been a prominent member of the German Chovevei Zion when the *Judenstaat* appeared, and from then on rendered Herzl invaluable service as the latter's "emissary" to the Russian Jews.

It was a role Wolffsohn intended to continue upon assuming his new duties. To be sure, the glamour and excitement inspired by Herzl never returned. The high diplomacy of earlier years faded; negotiations with the Turks all but ceased. Although markedly inclined to the "politicals," Wolffsohn felt himself constrained to shift steadily toward practical work, and it was here, indeed, that he fulfilled the responsibilities of his office with much competence. Even before Herzl's death, he had organized the Anglo-Palestine Company for work in Palestine and had encouraged the establishment of the Jewish National Fund for land purchase. Now, during his own incumbency, Wolffsohn made it increasingly clear that he was charting a course of routinized consolidation in Palestine, an approach the Easterners repeatedly had advocated.

These compromises notwithstanding, at the Tenth Congress in 1911 Wolffsohn was displaced from his leadership in favor of a presidium heavily weighted with east Europeans. Actually, the shift was less a repudiation of the man's policies than evidence of the functional, day-to-day spadework Zionism had become. It was also at the Tenth Congress, for example, that the Organization voted to approve the extensive land-purchasing activities of the Palestine office in Jaffa, under Dr. Arthur Ruppin (p. 77). At Weizmann's insistence, too, the Congress resolved that Hebrew from then on should be recognized as the official language of the Zionist movement, and its teaching intensified in the Diaspora. The body similarly endorsed the participation of distinct Jewish blocs in parliamentary and local elections, and notably in the Habsburg Empire, thus underscoring the existence of specifically Jewish national interests in multinational states.

If Zionism did not gain dramatically from this commitment to the seemingly pedestrian, neither did it lose thereby. The structure of the Organization took on shape and order. Congresses were meeting biennially, the number of their delegates growing continually. Local federations were becoming stronger now. In Russia, Zionists participated as a bloc in the initial Duma elections of 1905, returning five of the fourteen Jews who were elected (the number fell sharply in 1906, during the Stolypin reaction). In Germany, membership in the Zionist Federation grew from 1,300 in 1901 to 8,000 in 1914; and while the figure hardly compared with that of the burgeoning Russian Zionist movement, participants included at least several of Germany's most distinguished Jewish figures, among them Otto Warburg, Kurt Blumenfeld, and, later, Albert Einstein. One of the most influential of the early members, Martin Buber, born in Vienna of Galician parents, captivated hundreds of German and Austrian Jewish students with his neomystical vision of Zionism reuniting a holy people on holy soil.

By 1914, then, 127,000 Jews throughout the world were paying the "shekel" of Zionist membership. Zionist associations were functioning even in South Africa and North and South America. Hebrew schools were being organized. Zionist literature was being translated into many languages. The little blue-and-white Jewish National Fund box could be found in growing thousands of Jewish homes and hundreds of synagogues. Thus it was that *Gegenwartsarbeit*—"work in the present," practical Zionism—embracing both colonization in Palestine and cultural activity in the Diaspora, became a meaningful Jewish force.

THE GROWTH OF ZIONIST PARTIES

It was a testimony to Zionism's emergent strength, too, that a variegation of approaches and philosophies within the movement began taking political form. From 1902 on, individual doctrinal organizations, among them the Mizrachi and the Poalei Zion, existed side by side with national federations and transcended national boundaries. We recall, for example, that Zionism drew much of its emotional commitment from religious messianism. Yet, in addition, a specifically religious Zionism, a conscious blending of Orthodoxy and Jewish nationalism, also played an important minority role within the Congresses. Its inspiration was provided by Rabbi Samuel Mohilever, an erudite Lithuanian talmudist who was impelled into practical Zionist labors by the tsarist reaction of the 1880s, and who became one of the early stalwarts of Chovevei Zion. Mohilever's decision to continue in the movement, cheek by jowl with avowed secularists like Herzl, reflected his intention of working pragmatically to induce his fellow Zionists into religious observance. Thus, in his message to the First Zionist Congress, Mohilever affirmed that the revival of the Land of Israel was one of the most important commandments of the Torah, but emphasized that "Torah-true" Judaism was not less obligatory upon Zionist settlers if the Holy Land were once again to be the arena for Jewry's "spiritual" mission.

As early as 1893, Mohilever had founded a society for promulgating his views. It was called the Merkaz Ruchani (spiritual center), or simply "Mizrachi." It was not until the organizational efforts of Rabbi Isaac Jacob Reines, however, one of the authentic giants of Zionist history, that the Mizrachi became a conscious political movement within Zionism. An unusually eclectic personality, Reines had made it a point to introduce secular as well as religious studies into his yeshivah in Swintzan, Russia. He too became an early partisan of the Chovevei Zion, then subsequently of Herzl's political Zionism, and eventually in 1902 he restructured the Mizrachi organization as a faction within the Zionist movement. Yet Reines's accommodation with Jewish nationalism was the outer limit of his flexibility. Both as a delegate to successive Zionist Congresses and as an author of numerous books on religious philosophy, he preached a form of dual redemption: of the Land of Israel and of the Jewish spirit. Neither could be accomplished, he argued, except within the precepts of strict Orthodoxy. The Mizrachi party seldom returned more than a dozen representatives to the various Zionist Congresses before the war (its membership grew dramatically afterward). Nevertheless, its ideological rigidity was the despair even of the "cultural" Zionists, followers of Achad HaAm. The latter, in turn, underestimated the degree to which the Mizrachi made Zionism palatable to traditional elements within Jewish life, those who otherwise would have been alienated not merely by Zionist secularism but by an emergent and powerful new strain of Zionist socialism.

The roots of this "Labor Zionist" movement could be traced directly to the circumstances of Jewish life in eastern Europe. While Marxism was a formidable influence altogether during the early years of Russian industrialization, it elicited a particularly devoted response from Russian Jewry. No nationality in the tsarist empire suffered quite so bitterly from the combined impact of economic change and Romanov oppression. The Russian census of 1897, for example, indicated that more than half the country's Jewish population had become proletarianized, working in textile, metal, building, and other, lighter, industries. Impacted by the May Laws into the cities of the Pale, this Jewish working class was economically marginal at best, and was being reduced daily to a state of virtual pauperization. A Jewish demographer, Jacob Lestschinsky, has left a graphic account: "poverty and privation, need and hunger . . . sweating-system . . . sick and tubercular lungs—these are the conditions under which the Jewish worker had to fight for social reform, and for the future ideal of socialism."

As literate and sentient as they were oppressed and impoverished, Jewish working-class families hurled themselves into the Socialist movement with a passion born of desperation. Indeed, nearly half the delegates to the Second Russian Social Democratic Party Congress of 1903 were Jews. It was true that the party conducted its activities in the Russian language, and that there was nothing specifically Jewish in its tone. But the imbalance apparently was rectified by the emergence of a separatist Jewish Social Democratic party—the Bund—which offered itself as a vehicle both for the class struggle and for the assertion of Jewish communal rights. During the Russian revolutionary epoch, between 1904 and 1906, 30,000 Jews were dues-paying members of the Bund, and tens of thousands of others were active or passive sympathizers. Obsessed as they were with the campaign to achieve political and economic liberation on Russian soil, they tended to regard Zionism as a kind of "bourgeois utopianism." For them, Zionism implied dependence upon the goodwill of the reactionary Turkish sultan and of other rightist governments, and upon the endless largess of Jewish capitalists. Worse yet, Zionism seemed to ignore the political and economic aspirations of Jews within Russia proper. An outraged Bundist leader could shout at a Zionist gathering: "Pack your belongings! Turn your backs on our life, on our struggle, on our joys and sorrows. . . . Well, leave [us] in peace. Don't show your generosity by throwing alms . . . [to us] . . . from the window of your rail carriage." Weizmann, in turn, could describe the Bundists as "poorly assimilated as regards Judaism, degenerate, rotten, lacking in any moral fibre."

The competition between Zionism and socialism was waged with particular ferocity for the minds of Russian Jewish students at Western universities, the intellectual elite of European Jewry. In a letter to Herzl on May 6, 1903, Weizmann lamented the growing inroads of "radicalism" among Russian Jewish youth. "Our hardest struggle everywhere," he admitted, "is conducted against the Jewish Social Democrats." It was a tragic confrontation; for both groups, the Zionists and the Socialists, were often equally committed in their Jewish loyalties, equally driven by the need to build a Jewish society grounded in freedom and justice.

LABOR ZIONISM

Although efforts to reconcile Zionism and socialism were launched a number of years even before the first Zionist Congress, it was Nachman
Syrkin in 1898 who first mounted a serious intellectual attempt to bridge
the gap. The son of a middle-class Russian Jewish family, Syrkin was a
university student in Berlin when he embarked on the effort to achieve a
synthesis of the two ideologies. He outlined his scheme initially before
a Zionist group in Zurich in 1898, then later published it as an essay,
Die Judenfrage und der Sozialistische Judenstaat. "Socialism will solve
the Jewish problem only in the remote future," he declared. Anti-Semitism
was a fact of life that would not immediately be cured by normal Socialist
evolution, "and in any case the class struggle can help the Jewish middle
class but little if at all." A Jewish state was therefore the one decisive
answer to Jewish oppression. "The *form* of the Jewish state," Syrkin
argued,

> is the only debatable issue involved in Zionism. Zionism must be responsive
> to the opinion of the Jewish masses, for, without them, the movement will be
> stillborn. . . . Zionism must of necessity fuse with socialism. . . . Con-
> temporary political Zionism is striving for a Jewish state based on the right
> of private property. . . . For a Jewish state to come into being, it must,
> from the very outset, avoid all the ills of modern life. . . . Its guidelines must
> be justice, national planning, and social solidarity.

Yet Syrkin's manifesto and his later writings aroused little response
among either Socialists or Zionists. The former had only contempt for his
espousal of utopian Socialism over orthodox Marxism. One Bundist
mocked him in verse:

> Half-Marxist and half-Herzlian,
> Half-savage and half a lout,
> Half-donkey—but he soon will be
> A whole one without a doubt.

Syrkin thoroughly alienated the non-Socialists, on the other hand, by playing the role of *enfant terrible* at the Zionist Congresses. Persistently heckling the "rabbis" of Zionism, needling the "bourgeois" seekers after royal
goodwill, he ensured that socialism remained a dirty word among the
middle-class majority in the Organization. But his most fatal decision was
actively to support the "Uganda" plan. The moment Herzl submitted the
East Africa proposal to the Sixth Zionist Congress, Syrkin greeted it joyously and immediately launched into a denunciation of "romantic attach-
ments" to arid Palestine under the patronage of reactionary sultans, tsars,
and kaisers. A partner later with Israel Zangwill in the Ugandist "Jewish
Territorial Organization," Syrkin never recovered his brief, if limited,
influence even among the Zionist Left.

This lapse notwithstanding, Syrkin's career reflected a growing instinct
toward accommodation between Zionists and Socialists. Even as he was
conducting his propaganda in Berlin, isolated Labor Zionist groups were

surfacing intermittently in Russia under the name Poalei Zion (Workers of Zion). At first, these cells appeared spontaneously in different communities, and their only questionable divergence from other Zionists at the turn of the century was their essentially working-class membership. Some experimented with more original formulations of Zionism along national lines. Others, in Austria, preferred to structure the movement territorially, while a few in southern and central Russia were fixated by classical Marxism. Among this latter group, however, the city of Poltava, a kind of exile center for revolutionary agitators, nurtured an unusually active Labor Zionist branch. It was here that Ber Borochov, a twenty-five-year-old university student, already expelled from the Social Democratic party for Zionist "deviationism," formulated his unique theory of Marxist Zionism.

Tortuously working through a synthesis of the two ideologies, Borochov in 1905 appeared before the Poalei Zion leadership in Poltava and for three hours read through his (Yiddish-language) essay "The National Question and the Class Struggle." The party executive committee instantly seized upon the document as their long-awaited philosophical rationale. Borochov's approach was structured in terms of dialectical materialism, and brimmed over with conventional Marxist formulae on labor, capital, prices, and wages. It was within this determinist context, Borochov pointed out, that the Jews as a landless nation were incapable of adapting effectively to a foreign system of economy. Perhaps the Jewish bourgeoisie had managed the adjustment, but the Jewish proletariat hardly could duplicate the feat. The latter was concentrated for the most part in secondary industries that were distant from natural resources, from basic communications, from the tools of heavy production; and it was unable as a result to organize properly against its exploiters. As Borochov described it, then, the shortcomings suffered by the Jewish proletariat would be eliminated only by departure of the Jews to a land of their own. Only on its own territory could the Jewish working-class movement develop finally under normal conditions. Only from such a base could Jews mount their class struggle and achieve their social revolution.

As a Marxist, Borochov did not justify the choice of Palestine along romantic, nationalistic lines. Rather, he argued that Palestine was a site dictated exclusively by "stychic" (automatic, ineluctable) factors. In other nations, he explained, the absorptive capacity for immigration was limited. What was needed was a land in which Jews could freely enter all branches of the economy, where Jewish workers could participate in basic industries and agriculture. The land must be semiagricultural and thinly populated. Such a country, in fact, was Palestine, for Palestine alone was lacking in a national tradition of its own, in attraction for European immigrants, or in significant cultural and political development. Only in Palestine, therefore, "parallel with the growth of [Jewish] economic independence will come the growth of [Jewish] political independence."

From the contemporary vantage point, Borochov's formulation may seem riddled with inconsistencies. But for the intensely class-conscious Jewish proletariat of early twentieth-century Russia, it appeared as if he had devised a theory of Zionism that evolved deductively, almost mathematically, from Marxist premises. And precisely for this reason Borochov made Zionism intellectually respectable at last among tens of thousands of Socialist Jewish youth. Yitzchak Avner (later Ben-Zvi, the second president of Israel), who collaborated with Borochov in the early Poltava days of Poalei Zion, recalled that Borochov was "the teacher" of a whole generation of Zionists. One must add, too, that Borochov's own latent *Judenschmerz* probably reflected the unconscious Jewish romanticism of even his devoutest Marxist supporters. Fleeing to the United States after the collapse of the 1905 uprising, Borochov did not return to Russia for twelve years, until the March Revolution of 1917. Then, hurrying back— to attend a Poalei Zion convention—he was felled suddenly by pneumonia and died in Kiev in December 1917 at the age of thirty-six. It was during his American interregnum, however, that Borochov began to write of a full partnership of "all Jewish groups" in Zionism, of Palestine as a home for the "entire Jewish people." In his essays there reappeared such forgotten terms as "the Jewish masses," rather than simply the "proletariat," and even the ancient phrase "Eretz Israel"—the Land of Israel. Avner's fiancée, Rachel Yanait, like other thousands of her Socialist generation who admired Borochov, felt as if she "were reliving the Jewish past, stepping at the same time into the Jewish future." Inadvertently, but typically, she too revealed a thoroughly non-Marxist obsession with Palestine when "suddenly, in the spirit of one trying . . . 'to hasten the coming of the Messiah,' I asked [Avner]: 'And *when* is the inevitable stychic process going to start?' "

THE SECOND ALIYAH

Until the revolutionary epoch and its failure, even the Poalei Zion had been unwilling to "hasten the coming of the Messiah." Ben-Zvi's (Avner's) response to his fiancée was typical: "In his deliberate manner," she recalled, "[he] explained that according to Socialist theory, it was essential first to reform the Turkish feudal regime and then to strengthen the organization of Jewish labor—also it was still a long way. . . ." This seemed a fair appraisal of the circumstances in Palestine. At the turn of the century, we recall, both the "old" Yishuv and the "new" Yishuv still depended mainly on outside help—Chalukkah charity for the old, Rothschild or Zionist philanthropy for the new. Although more than 50,000 Jews were living in the Holy Land by then, only 5,000 were to be found in the twenty rural colonies. The First Aliyah had been less than successful in producing the "new" Jewish farmer. Arriving in Palestine in 1907, Arthur Ruppin witnessed a dismal sight. As he wrote later:

> There are few things sadder to imagine than the state of mind of the old colonists. . . . The older generation had grown weary and sullen with the labor and toil of a quarter of a century, without the faintest hope for the future or the slightest enjoyment of the present; the younger generation,

brought up in French schools, wished but one thing, namely to leave agriculture, which could not provide their parents with a secure living, and to find a "better" occupation in the outside world.

The "inevitable stychic process" began in earnest with the failure of the Octobrist Revolution of 1905. The upheaval was suppressed in a nationwide chain reaction of pogroms. For the Jews, in fact, the attendant political and economic oppression was the grimmest yet in their modern experience. Their survival as a people now literally hung in the balance. Accordingly, a massive new Jewish emigration overseas resumed, and gained momentum each year until the outbreak of World War I. Yet those who departed for Palestine—only a small minority of the total exodus—were affected not simply by the course of events in Russia, nor even by Labor Zionist ideology. Ben-Zvi's generation was powerfully moved as well by an appeal issued in 1907 from the Yishuv itself; and specifically by one Yosef Vitkin, a schoolteacher in a remote Galilee farm colony. Departure for Palestine, Vitkin insisted, should neither be determined by mere doctrine nor be inhibited by earlier failures in the Holy Land. What was required now was simple courage, a mighty joint effort of "chalutziut"—of pioneering. Vitkin wrote:

> The major causes of our blundering are our search for a shortcut, and our belief that the attainment of our goal is close at hand. Out of this belief we have built castles in the air . . . and have turned aside with contempt from the longer and harder road, which is perhaps the surest, and, in the end, the shortest. . . . Awake, O youth of Israel! Come to the aid of your people. Your people lies in agony. Rush to its side. Band together; discipline yourselves for life or death; forget all the precious bonds of your childhood; leave them behind forever without a shadow of regret, and answer to the call of your people. . . .

It was an eloquent plea, and it reached the mark in the postrevolutionary ferment of eastern Europe. Indeed, it was virtually memorized by Poalei Zion orators and endorsed even by such non-Socialist writers as Yosef Chaim Brenner (p. 74) and A. D. Gordon (p. 75). Ben-Zvi, traveling from one Poalei Zion meeting to another, suddenly asked himself the question posed by thousands of other young Russian Zionists: "Why am I here and not there? Why are we all here and not there?" The vision of becoming chalutzim—pioneers—suddenly exerted a new and compelling attraction. Not all those who made the commitment for emigration were idealists. Some intended to evade tsarist military conscription; others envisaged Palestine simply as an alternative refuge from Russian oppression. But for a majority of the 30,000 Jews who departed for Palestine in the Second Aliyah years between 1905 and 1914, Labor Zionism, ignited by Vitkin's pioneering challenge, was the catalyst.

The circumstances awaiting the newcomers were bleak. Rachel Yanait wrote later that in each of the farm colonies she visited the identical complaints were heard: of exhaustion, lack of jobs, and resentment at the sheer harshness of life. In the largest Jewish village, Petach Tikvah, the attitude of the established capitalist planters was distinctly unfriendly, even hostile. Israel Shochat, a young immigrant, recalled that the main task of the Petach Tikvah farmers

was to ensure that the Arabs worked properly. . . . In the market in the center of town, all the produce came from Arab villages in the area, and was sold by Arabs. Before dawn, hundreds of Arab laborers daily streamed into Petach Tikvah, to look for work, and mostly they found it. Then there was the matter of language; the villagers all spoke Yiddish. To speak Hebrew was regarded as absurd, as a Zionist affectation. And the most serious thing was that Jews were considered virtually unemployable.

The farmers' dislike of the newcomers was influenced not only by the immigrants' lack of experience but by their Socialist theories. The orange growers' journal (later entitled *Bustenai*) warned that the new "Jewish workers aren't just interested in work and food. . . . They want power, economic and social dictatorship over the agricultural domain and those who own it." Faced with this antagonism, the immigrants wandered from settlement to settlement, in rags, on the edge of collapse from malnutrition. David Ben-Gurion, a nineteen-year-old former student, succumbed to malaria and nearly perished. A doctor urged him to return quickly to Europe. "My well-meaning friends all pointed out that this was hardly a disgrace," Ben-Gurion wrote afterward. "Half the immigrants who came to Palestine in those early days took one look and caught the same ship home again." Indeed, more. Possibly 80 percent of the Second Aliyah returned to Europe or continued on to America within weeks or months of their arrival.

If perhaps 2,000 of the chalutzim hung on, it was the little necklace of Jewish farm colonies that often made the difference. Limited as these villages were as a source of employment, they provided more jobs at least than the Biluites had found during their ordeal in the 1880s. Companionship, too, was a factor. In somewhat larger numbers than during the First Aliyah, the new immigrants were able to meet at night, in Jaffa or Petach Tikvah, crowding into small rooms where they articulated their dreams and theories. "They would assemble for a few hours," recalled Shmuel Dayan, father of the general, "engage in discussion and debate, and go their several ways again, reinvigorated and with renewed determination to strive for a solution to the main problem of our existence—the 'Conquest of Labor.'" Almost from the moment they reached Palestine, in fact, the immigrants organized Poalei Zion groups, declaring themselves "the party of the Palestinian working class in creation, the only revolutionary party of the Jewish worker in the Ottoman Empire." In a platform worked out at a gathering in Ramle in 1906, Ben-Zvi, Ben-Gurion, and other Labor Zionists emphasized the centrality of the class struggle, and later added to their ideology a full-blown, if somewhat meaningless (for arid, impoverished Palestine), demand for "public ownership of the means of production." It was evident that these were not the usual kind of colonists, not even within the older Zionist tradition of the nineteenth century. Their notion of pioneering was a kind of secularized messianism.

THE CONQUEST OF LABOR

They had come, too, not merely to establish a Socialist commonwealth but to rebuild their nationhood, their very manhood, by the sweat of their brows. The emphasis of the Second Aliyah was upon physical labor on the soil of Palestine. The youthful visionaries who fled the misery of the Pale evinced a genuine sense of guilt for having been alienated from the land. It was a Russian, no less than a Jewish, reaction. Slav writers, from the populist Narodniki to the universally venerated Tolstoy, had been accustomed to extol the peasant as the repository of all virtue; and notwithstanding the Slav muzhik's affinity for pogroms, the Jewish intelligentsia subscribed to this romanticized image. Their obsession with the soil also expressed unconscious resentment at the creeping industrial revolution in eastern Europe, a social transformation that dislodged the Jews economically and confronted them with the new and more vicious anti-Semitism of the urban lower-middle class. Agriculture alone, then, would make the Jews independent. As members also of the Poalei Zion, the newcomers appreciated that Socialist thinkers from Marx to Lenin had cited the absence of a Jewish peasant class as evidence that the Jews were not a nation, but rather a peculiar social or functional entity. It was this assertion that had now to be disproved.

It was significant, at the turn of the century, that virtually all the influential Zionist writers shared a common antipathy to the rootless, marginal existence of the Diaspora. As early as 1894, Chaim Nachman Bialik, the greatest of the Hebrew poets, captured the anguish of a people deprived of its soil:

Not my hands formed you, O ears of corn,
Not my hands fostered your growth;
Not I have spent my strength here,
Not I will enjoy your harvest.

The newly awakened reverence for physical labor was shared by Bialik's contemporary, the Hebrew essayist and novelist Micah Joseph Berditchewski. A Nietzschean, Berditchewski loosed a series of withering blasts against a Judaism that had sapped his people's capacity to act. In his biblical criticism, he glorified Joshua at the expense of Moses. His preference was for the earliest Hebrew tribes, those barely removed from heathenism, who at least had exhibited a primordial instinct for action, violence, even sexual libertinism.

This disdain for a purely cerebral Judaism was amplified by Yosef Chaim Brenner, the first of the literary figures whose writing career spanned both the Pale and the Yishuv. Born in the Ukraine in 1881, Brenner early identified himself with the Socialist movement, was imprisoned for his revolutionary activities, then escaped to London, where he briefly edited a Hebrew paper. In 1909, at the age of twenty-eight, he made his way to Palestine. There he became a part-time teacher in a Jewish high school, and an essayist of considerable influence in the Yishuv. His following was the more remarkable for his caustic indictment not only of the doomed Pale, but of many of the Second Aliyah pioneers. The latter, in his articles, were exposed as naïve and windy idealists, given to Marxist rationalizations of their newborn attachment to the soil. For Brenner, on the other hand, labor was exclusively an act of self-preservation. "I, a Zionist," he wrote,

> can have no truck with this prattle about a renaissance, a spiritual renaissance. . . . We are not Italy. My Zionism commands: "The hour has struck for . . . the Jewish people to end their sojourn among non-Jews and their dependence upon non-Jews". . . . The Jewish spirit? Wind and chaff. The great heritage? Sound and fury. . . . It is time for an honest self-appraisal: we bear no value, we command no respect. Only when we will have learned the secret of labor and committed to memory the hymn of those settled on their own soil shall we have deserved the title Man. . . . We have sinned through not working: there is no statement except through labor.

Without manual skills himself, Brenner nevertheless accompanied the Zionist work gangs across the land as a Hebrew teacher, sharing their tent life, their illnesses and hunger, often lecturing and presiding over group discussions. He was killed in the Arab riots of 1921 (Chapter vi).

It was the added dimension of individual commitment that transformed Brenner's contemporary, Aaron David Gordon, into the foremost prophet of the "religion of labor." Unlike Brenner or Berditchewski, certainly unlike Syrkin or Borochov, Gordon was the practitioner of his own message. Russian-born, educated in Orthodox Jewish schools, he had followed the classical Haskalah path, teaching himself Western languages and history. In adulthood he took, and held for twenty-three years, a comfortable position as financial manager of the rural estate of Baron Horace de Gunzburg. It was during his leisure hours that Gordon immersed himself in the writings of Nietzsche and Tolstoy and began to develop his own unique philosophy of Zionism as an act of personal redemption. When the Gunzburg estate was sold in 1903, leaving Gordon without employment at the age of forty-eight, he made a soul-searching decision that was not unlike Tolstoy's flight to Yasnaya Polyana. He departed for Palestine. There he was offered an office job at Petach Tikvah, but shunned it in favor of manual labor in the orange groves. Afterward he worked in various farm settlements. A contemporary recalled of him: "There were many in the Second Aliyah who exceeded [Gordon] in labor and worked with great devotion. But in their labor one felt their efforts to excel and to prove that the Jews, and not only the Arabs, knew how to work. The work of Gordon was of another sort entirely. It was a kind of worship, a pure prayer."

For Gordon, as for Berditchewski, nationhood was the wave of the Jewish future. Yet, as Gordon saw it, the vital element in nationhood was creativity, and labor was the bedrock of creativity. Without labor, the Jews would remain an island in an Arab sea. "The land will not be ours and we shall not be the people of the land. Here, then, we shall also be aliens." Gordon's concern transcended the political, however. Work alone was the force that unlocked the individual—and ultimately the national—

energies of a struggling race. In "Some Observations," perhaps his best-known essay, Gordon developed this theme:

> A living people always possesses a great majority to whom labor is its second nature. Not so among us. We despise labor. . . . There is only one path that can lead to our renaissance—the path of manual labor, of mobilizing all our national energies, of absolute and sacrificial devotion to our ideal and our tasks. . . . Our people can be rejuvenated only if each one of us re-creates himself through labor and a life close to nature.

Gordon's exhortation far transcended the written word. Indeed, his literary efforts ordinarily were restricted to candlelight in the small hours of the morning. His days were the proving ground of his ideology, and these were spent with the young pioneers in the field. Until the last weeks of his life, he dwelt among the immigrant workers, sharing a room and tilling the soil with them, participating in their communal life. An aged and beloved figure, with his great Tolstoyan beard, he was an unquench-able source of encouragement to younger men who faltered. His wife, who came to share his life in Palestine, died of malaria before the war. His only surviving son died in postwar Russia. Afflicted with cancer, he rejected pity. To those who visited his bedside, he insisted merely on preaching his faith in the redemptive significance of labor.

It was surely Gordon's magnetism alone that transcended the class dogmas of the Poalei Zion. He himself scorned Marxism as an appeal to "the herd instinct in man," one that "diverts him from seeking his power within himself. . . ." During his years in Palestine, he fought bitterly the establishment of schools based on party ideology and class consciousness. To combat this sectarianism, his followers organized themselves in 1905 as HaPoel HaZair—the Young Worker. An ideological society more than a political movement, it disdained to match the Poalei Zion in organized activities or propaganda. Yet even the most doctrinaire Socialist immigrants found an unspoken communion of purpose with Gordon. Respect for work and the worker, after all, had similarly been inherent in the First Aliyah of the 1880s and 1890s. It was simply that in those earlier decades physical exertion had been equated with the pastoral ideal of a return to the Land of Israel and had been fused with a biblical glorification of life "under one's own vine and fig tree." Only in the years before World War I did the concept of work as social redemption become imperative. Like Gordon, the post-1905 immigrants insisted on earning their bread as hired workers, and shunned occasional easier livelihoods that came their way. They dressed as Russian peasants, lived on the simplest food, despised luxury, scorned the "materialism" of the veteran capitalist farmers. Their common goal, Gordonian no less than Borochovian, was well expressed in a pioneer folk song of the time: "Anu banu Artza, liv'not u'l'hibanot ba"—We've come to the Land of Israel to build, and to be rebuilt, here.

THE COLLECTIVE SETTLEMENT

The onset of the Second Aliyah coincided with a growing momentum of Jewish agricultural settlement in Palestine. It was helped in considerable measure by Baron Rothschild's PICA. New colonies included Sejera, Mescha, Menachemia, and Yavne'el founded in 1901–02, and Beit Gan in 1904. Later Mizpah (1908) and Kinneret (1909) were added. The settlers initially were farmers or sons of farmers from villages that previously had been under the baron's administration. By and large, they were capable agriculturists. With land and loans supplied by PICA, the new colonies eventually showed modest profits. Substituting mixed farming for viticulture, meanwhile, the older plantation villages in the coastal zone became economically viable for the first time. In Petach Tikvah and elsewhere on the Plain of Sharon, citrus fruits became an increasingly lucrative crop. The fact was, however, that the PICA administrators were less interested in fostering employment for newcomers than in "productivizing" established villages, often by taking fullest advantage of cheap Arab labor. Had this trend continued, the survival of the tenuous Zionist enclave would have been unlikely.

Well within Herzl's lifetime, the Zionist Organization recognized that more active encouragement would have to be given to the settlement effort in Palestine. That help first materialized in 1903, with the establishment in Jaffa of a subsidiary of the Jewish Colonial Trust. Known initially as the Anglo-Palestine Company, later as the Anglo-Palestine Bank, it granted loans at low interest to merchants and manufacturers, to farmers and building societies. In the aftermath of the Young Turk Revolution of 1908, moreover, the promise of a liberalized Ottoman administration encouraged the Zionist Organization to open its first Palestine Office in Jaffa. From these headquarters, it was anticipated that Jewish National Fund properties would be administered and additional land purchases negotiated. The office's first director was a thirty-two-year-old German Jew, Dr. Arthur Ruppin. A graduate of the Universities of Berlin and Halle, Ruppin had earned a wide reputation for his sociological writings on contemporary Jewish life and as director of the Bureau of Jewish Statistics in Berlin. Before taking on the new Zionist assignment, Ruppin spent five months in Palestine investigating settlement possibilities there. His conclusion, incorporated in a memorandum to the Zionist Smaller Actions Committee, observed that the Yishuv was not yet ripe for an autonomous existence within the Turkish Empire. A Herzlian vision of that magnitude could be realized only when Jews formed a much larger proportion of the inhabitants and owned substantial amounts of land in Palestine. The immediate task, therefore, was to create employment opportunities for thousands of new immigrants. And to that end, Ruppin now proposed buying up to 2 million dunams of land in Judea and Galilee (as JNF funds became available), to sell them on easy terms to Jewish immigrants, and to train farm workers on "auxiliary" farms before settling them on the soil.

These recommendations were accepted. In theory, all activities of the

Palestine Office fell within the scope of the Zionist Organization. In practice, Ruppin showed much initiative and flexibility in interpreting his mandate. Thus, upon embarking on his assignment, he launched immediately into urban housing and agricultural development. With a JNF loan of £ 10,000, he organized an estate company, Achuzat Bayit, to establish a modern Jewish quarter on the town limits of Jaffa, and a Palestine Land Development Company to purchase and populate tracts in the countryside. With the help of a veteran Jewish land buyer, Joshua Chankin, who had developed a special knack for doing business with Arabs and Turks, the PLDC acquired extensive holdings in Judea and Galilee, prepared them for cultivation, and divided them into modest plots suitable for farmers. In this fashion the company added to the Yishuv nine new villages in six years, and land acquisitions totaling 50,000 dunams in various parts of the country. Immigrants were given shelter and agricultural training at farms in Kinneret, Ben Shemen, and Chulda. Ruppin's program occasionally was audacious in the liberties it took with JNF and other funds. But in justifying his expenditures to the Zionist Congress in 1913, the young sociologist emphasized to the business-minded delegates that "our farms must, for the time being, serve other and larger purposes than the production of a profit. . . . Instead of dividends [the farms] will provide us with something more necessary: men."

This was the vision, too, that Ruppin applied in fostering one of the Yishuv's most noteworthy social innovations, the kvutzah—the collective settlement. In fact, there had been prefigurations of collectivism well before Ruppin's arrival. It is recalled that the Biluites went through a passing collectivist phase before their efforts were stamped out by the Rothschild administration. Afterward, too, even non-Socialist immigrants managed to survive only by pooling their funds and sharing common staples. Other Jewish pioneers hired themselves out on a group basis to work in the citrus groves and vineyards. These contracting "cooperatives" also appeared in the towns. When Tel Aviv was founded in 1909, for example (p. 88), one group assumed the task of leveling the sand dunes, another graded roads, another cut stones, yet another built the houses. Cooperative laundries, kitchens, and bakeries sprang up in many places. In the end, however, it was oppressive labor conditions on the PICA farms that drove the youthful immigrants of the Second Aliyah into an urgent quest for other alternatives. "They could not become individualist farmers, planters, exploiters of others," wrote one of their members, Manya Wilbuschevitch (afterward Manya Shochat); "their Socialist principles forbade that. And they could not continue their competition with Arab labor. . . . For my part, I had never believed in the Conquest of Labor through adaptation to the Arab standard of living."

In the winter of 1907–08, Manya Shochat and several of her comrades persuaded the director of the PICA training farm at Sejera, which chronically ran a deficit, to let them operate the tract on their own responsibility. Thereupon, with livestock, seed, and equipment advanced (against earnings) by the PICA, the fourteen young men and four young women launched the venture on a purely collectivist basis. They arranged their own division of labor, organized a communal kitchen, and shared a common period of rest and reflection and a common determination to rely exclusively upon the sweat of their own brows, and under no circumstances to hire Arab labor. It was a backbreaking life, but the little group was charged with the mood of excitement and pioneering. Eventually their numbers reached fifty, including several Yemenite Jewish immigrants. After a year and a half, the Sejera farm harvested an adequate crop and repaid the PICA loan with a fifth of its produce. "We demonstrated once and for all," wrote Manya Shochat, "that a collectivist economy was a possibility." Having made their point, the original eighteen youths returned the tract to the PICA. They envisaged their role as that of an advance guard for the permanent settlers who would follow.

The problem henceforth was to secure additional land. Here Ruppin's support was crucial. In 1909, on behalf of the JNF, he had acquired a 1,200-dunam stretch of uncultivated land, Um Juni, on the shores of Lake Galilee. Shortly afterward, he funded a group of immigrants who proceeded to work the tract along conventional lines. They failed. A year later, however, thirty-six members of HaPoel HaZair—disciples of A. D. Gordon—asked permission to farm Um Juni on a collectivist basis. It was a measure of the sheer functionalism of collective settlement that even non-Marxists were drawn to this approach. Once more Ruppin approved, this time providing the farmers with a rather larger stretch of land adjacent to Um Juni, complete with two mud-brick "dormitories," some basic farm equipment, and a half-dozen mules. The experiment was a grim ordeal; the Jordan Valley was an inferno, and malaria took a heavy toll of the little group. Nevertheless, discipline and organization saw the farmers through. An elected leadership committee decided each day who went into the fields, who manned the night watch. The women shared the housework, cooking, laundering, and feeding of the animals. Fullest equality was maintained between the sexes. It was straightforward collectivism, and it worked. The farm brought in a decent harvest in 1911, and its members purchased additional livestock. By then, they had given the little kvutzah the name of Degania—Cornflower. Its fame spread rapidly. Shmuel Dayan, who joined Degania the following year, was thrilled with his first taste of an independent existence. He wrote later:

> To work in freedom! The words seemed to convey a deep breath, in contrast to the servitude of the [capitalist farms]. There is a feeling of creativity in the work performed by the worker himself, even in the services, in administration, and in the very thought of work. . . . We are free employers and overseers. . . . We are responsible to ourselves.

Inspired by the success of Degania, other groups moved onto JNF land to found collective farms of their own. Numbering between ten and thirty, these little bands established kvutzot (the plural of kvutzah) at Merchavia and Gan Shmuel. On this basis, too, the moribund old Chovevei Zion settlement of Beer Tuvia was revived. By 1914, there were fourteen such farms, half of them barely more than outposts, but all dedicated to collectivism as the proper ideological approach to the Conquest of Labor. It was perhaps the most functional approach, as well. The kvutzot returned a somewhat higher per capita income than the existing capitalist small farms. The return may have been pitiably meager by any Western standard, but if the kvutzah members were poor, none was poorer than his fellows. All regarded themselves as equal owners of the farm and responsible for it. They shared an awareness of moral superiority, too, as pioneers of a venture dedicated to equality and social justice. Perhaps they were not wrong. The collective was to become Zionism's most innovative and influential experiment in human relations.

THE GUILD OF WATCHMEN

In September 1907 ten young men gathered in the attic of Yitzchak Ben-Zvi's rooming house in Jaffa. Addressing the group, Israel Shochat reminded it that the Conquest of Labor also necessarily embraced the Jewish right to self-defense. For several months, in fact, Shochat had been traveling through the Yishuv, entreating his fellow agricultural workers to assume responsibility for guarding the lands they were plowing. It was unthinkable, he insisted, to maintain the baneful practice of hiring Arab or Circassian guards to protect Jewish property and lives. This was no way to revive a Jewish nation. On the contrary, the guards themselves were hardly more than bandits masquerading as watchmen, holding the Jewish settlers in contempt, blackmailing them, extorting from them. The future of a Jewish nation was at stake, Shochat warned. If the Jews were capable now of farming their land, should they not be capable of defending it? Back in Russia, for that matter, in Shochat's native Homel, the Poalei Zion had been effective in organizing self-defense units against tsarist pogroms. The precedent in reinforced self-esteem had been crucial. In Palestine later, a number of informal meetings had taken place before the decisive gathering in Ben-Zvi's attic. Now, finally, in September 1907, a program was drafted for a secret society of Jewish watchmen, to be called Bar-Giora, after the celebrated Jewish warrior of antiquity. The founding members pledged themselves to accept employment as guards wherever the opportunities arose. They resolved as well to speak only Hebrew, and to live together whenever possible on a collectivist basis—for the Labor Zionist goal remained basic to their outlook. It was significant, for example, that the Bar-Giora members were among the first to pioneer the embryonic kvutzah at Sejera.

It was at Sejera, too, that the would-be Jewish guards requested jobs as watchmen from the manager of the neighboring PICA farm school. When the man proved skeptical, the young activists proceeded to steal a mule from under the nose of the hired Circassian and to return it the following morning. The director was convinced. From then on, the PICA farm remained under Jewish protection. The little Bar-Giora group subsequently offered itself out to other, neighboring villages. The gesture was not without its risks. By late 1908, in the aftermath of the Young Turk Revolution, Ottoman authority had loosened in Palestine and Arab bandits roamed the countryside at will. Nevertheless, the Jewish village of Mescha (later Kfar Tabor) ventured to dismiss its Moroccan watchmen and hire two of the Bar-Giora group. The Jewish youths thereupon proceeded to offer Mescha the best protection it had yet known, accompanying workers to the fields on horseback, rifles slung, an effective deterrent to interlopers.

With two villages won over by 1909, Shochat and his friends recognized that a small, clandestine society no longer was adequate. Additional watchmen were needed to offer protection elsewhere throughout the Yishuv. To achieve that goal, Bar-Giora was reincarnated under a new title, HaShomer—the Watchman. Its new charter laconically defined the guild's purpose as the formation of a society of Jewish guards. Nothing was said about quality. Even so, requirements for admission were so inflexible that after two years the original group of eight increased to only twenty-six. The training program was exceptionally rigorous. Candidates were drilled in night maneuvers, scouting, direction finding, and conversational Arabic. Those few who were accepted into the society were known as exceptional horsemen and crack shots. Mounted, armed, brawny, and confident of bearing, they evoked respect among the Arabs, who described them as "Moscoby"—Russians, brave men and good hunters. Often, in fact, the exploits of the Jewish watchmen provided themes for Arab folklore, tales that subsequently were embroidered and exaggerated upon each repetition.

Soon all Lower Galilee came into HaShomer's fold—Yavne'el, Beit Gan, Menachemia, Sarona, Mizpah, Kinneret. By 1911 the guild had acquired a foothold in Samaria. From there its fame spread to Judea, then to the coastal plain, where the large capitalist plantation villages invited HaShomer to take charge of the watch. Few settlers ever regretted their choice of protection. Despite repeated Bedouin attacks, the Shomrim (guards) kept security tight. Other villages subsequently were added to their clientele: Rishon l'Zion, Ben Shemen, Beer Ya'akov. By 1914, the watchman's guild operated four squads in Judea alone, one hundred men throughout Jewish Palestine, all on instant call whenever danger threatened.

By then, the Yishuv was demanding more guards than the Shomer could supply, and the guild's three-man executive agreed that Jewish self-defense would have to be deprofessionalized; in time of danger all farmers and workers should be capable of bearing arms. Although the training program could not be enlarged significantly before the outbreak of the World War, the pattern of self-defense nevertheless was accepted by growing numbers of farm colonies. There was wide recognition, too, that the achievement of the watchman's guild was more than simply functional. It was at once an embodiment of Socialist doctrine, of self-defense, of communal living, and of nationalist solidarity. By the eve of the war, HaShomer's legend of valor had dramatically raised the morale of the Yishuv. No longer did the Arabs flout the Jews as "children of death." The Zionist pioneers had before them at last a tangible inspiration for future cohesion and self-sacrifice.

THE CONQUEST OF HEBREW

During the prewar years, a crucial linguistic framework was similarly being established for the Zionist redemptive effort. It was altogether as impressive an achievement as the Conquest of Labor, for Hebrew educational facilities were virtually nonexistent in Palestine until the twentieth century. Indeed, until the late 1870s, the handful of Jewish schools operating in Palestine were almost entirely religious, and conducted in the Yiddish language on antiquated Orthodox lines. The Lämel School (Chapter ii), founded in Jerusalem in 1856, taught its courses in German and Yiddish. In the network of elementary and vocational schools sponsored by the Alliance Israélite Universelle, French remained the principal language of instruction for the—essentially—Sephardic youngsters. It developed, then, that the emergence of modern Hebrew, a language capable of secular, vernacular use, awaited the heroic achievements of a sparrow-chested little Russian Jewish philologist, Eliezer Perlman—better known by his adopted surname of Ben-Yehuda.

Born of Orthodox parents, the recipient of a parochial religious education, Ben-Yehuda joined other thousands of his generation in turning from pietism to Haskalah secularism, and then to Zionism. Although he was an enthusiastic student of Hebrew literature, his vision of language as the decisive component of modern nationhood awaited his years as a student at the Sorbonne, when he became acutely conscious of the role of literature in the growth of French nationalism. "I have decided," he wrote his fiancée in 1880, "that in order to have our own land and political life it is also necessary that we have a language to hold us together. That language is Hebrew, but not the Hebrew of the rabbis and scholars. We must have a Hebrew language in which we can conduct the business of life." The following year, Ben-Yehuda, aged twenty-three, married his fiancée, aged twenty-seven, and they departed for Palestine. From the moment they boarded ship, they vowed thenceforth to speak no other language but Hebrew. We are told that the pledge was never broken.

The couple's next years in Palestine were as agonizing in their poverty as any endured by the early farmers of Zionist settlement. In Jerusalem, Ben-Yehuda earned a wretched pittance teaching Hebrew for an Alliance school. His every free moment was devoted to editing a succession of Hebrew-language newspapers, the circulation of which in the early 1880s rarely exceeded two hundred. There were occasions when he and his growing family were evicted from their room for lack of rent money. At times they nearly starved. Nor did Ben-Yehuda ease his circumstances by his incessant attacks on the Orthodox: for their opposition to the use of Hebrew and to secular labor, and for their "social crime" of fostering a

Chalukkah community. The outraged pietists retaliated, stoning his office, denouncing him to the Ottoman authorities for "treason" (once he was briefly jailed), placing him under a rabbinical ban of excommunication. When Ben-Yehuda's wife died of tuberculosis in 1891, leaving behind five children, the Orthodox refused her burial in the Ashkenazic cemetery.

Nevertheless, Ben-Yehuda's proselytizing efforts began to have their impact. Virtually all the agricultural colonies subscribed to his newspapers and purchased his textbooks. He became a power in the Yishuv, and eventually in the Zionist world at large. By the turn of the century he was well launched on the project that would absorb the remainder of his life, the creation of a modern Hebrew dictionary. Pursuing his research with books and other materials sent him by disciples in Europe, he relentlessly tracked down the Semitic roots of words that ultimately he incorporated into a contemporary vernacular. In 1904, modestly endowed at last by grants from the Zionist Organization, from Baron Edmond de Rothschild, and other Jewish sources, Ben-Yehuda published the first volume of the dictionary. It was virtually a thesaurus—indeed, an encyclopedia—of the Hebrew language, a monumental work of scholarship. He would complete three more volumes before his death, and afterward the undertaking would be expanded by his successors into a seventeen-volume series, the definitive basis for a revived spoken and written medium.

In putting Hebrew to vernacular use, moreover, Ben-Yehuda counted heavily on the Yishuv's teachers. At the turn of the century the largest number of these was employed by the Hilfsverein der Deutschen Juden. By 1914, the Hilfsverein operated a network of fifty schools throughout the Yishuv, from kindergartens through secondary institutions, providing instruction for 7,000 youngsters. Although German was used predominantly as a second language, it was due mainly to Ben-Yehuda's efforts that the Hilfsverein laid renewed emphasis upon Hebrew studies. The Alliance schools, too, were conducting the major portion of their instruction in the Hebrew language, as were the schools in the Zionist agricultural colonies. Additionally, sixty Zionist schools in the towns and outlying farm colonies, comprising 2,600 pupils, were using Hebrew as their sole medium of instruction. This program was decisively augmented by the iron willpower of the Zionist settlers themselves, and notably the immigrants of the Second Aliyah. Plainly it was an excruciating ordeal for Yiddish- and Russian-speaking Jews to employ Hebrew as their daily idiom at home and in the field, when every instinct cried out for relaxation. But they submitted to this discipline as tenaciously as they faced the other hardships of life in Palestine. Most of the Zionist farmers and workers by then had accepted fully Ben-Yehuda's contention: a nation was its language, no less than its sweat and blood. The teachers in the various schools shared the little philologist's sense of commitment. In 1903 they organized themselves into a Hebrew Teachers' Association, which instituted its own qualifying examinations for instructors.

Ironically, it was Germany's *Drang nach Osten,* an imperialist expansion into the Middle East during the last years before the World War, that threatened the impressive progress of this Hebraization. As conscious or unconscious agents of German influence in Palestine, the directors of the Hilfsverein schools began offering a number of courses taught exclusively in the German language. Examinations were conducted increasingly in German. Yet the issue of Hebraism versus Germanism did not become urgent until plans were laid to establish a Haifa Technical Institute. Funds for such a "Technion" (or Technikum, in German) had been made available by the estate of Wolf Wissotzky, the Russian Jewish tea magnate. The JNF supplied the land in Haifa, with the Hilfsverein and individual philanthropists contributing additional sums. As the administering agency, the Hilfsverein was determined that the Technion should be the very capstone of the Yishuv's educational structure—and also, not incidentally, a spectacular example of *Deutsche Kultur*. In recognition of this goal, the German foreign undersecretary, Dr. Arthur von Zimmermann, personally sought and obtained Constantinople's approval to erect the school's first building, which was completed in 1913. Meanwhile, the German Jewish members of the Technion's board of governors proposed that all technical subjects be taught exclusively in the German language. More than national pride animated this recommendation. German was widely recognized as the lingua franca of science. Hebrew, by contrast, was woefully deficient in technical vocabulary.

The decision nevertheless produced a wave of indignation among the Zionist settlers. Ben-Yehuda was all but apoplectic. "Blood will flow on the streets," he warned the Hilfsverein's director. At Ben-Yehuda's instigation, too, protest meetings were organized by Jewish students and teachers throughout the Yishuv. In October 1913, the Hebrew Teachers' Association proclaimed a strike in all Hilfsverein schools, and students demonstrated outside the German consulate in Jerusalem. Like the East Africa issue a decade earlier, the Technion crisis seemingly threatened the entire Hebraic nature of the Zionist renaissance. Aware of what was at stake, then, the Zionist Organization immediately set about establishing more than a dozen new Hebrew-language schools for Palestine and launched a worldwide campaign for additional funds. At last, four months later, in February 1914, the language controversy ended when the board of governors reconsidered the matter and agreed that all Technion courses thenceforth would be taught exclusively in Hebrew.

From then on, the commitment to a Hebrew vernacular for the Yishuv was never in doubt. In the aftermath of the Technion battle, the Hebrew Teachers' Association, subsidized by the Zionist Organization, founded a board of education to administer the curriculum and establish teaching guidelines for all Jewish—non-Orthodox—schools in Palestine, including the Hilfsverein network. By 1916, the fulfillment of Ben-Yehuda's dream was in sight. A census that year indicated that 40 percent of the Yishuv's population (outside of the old Orthodox community) spoke Hebrew as their first language. The little philologist's accomplishment was in every way as formidable as Herzl's, and as widely recognized. When Ben-Yehuda died in Jerusalem in December 1922, 30,000 people escorted his body to its grave, and Palestine Jewry observed three days of official mourning.

THE YISHUV STRIVES FOR POLITICAL IDENTITY

One of the Zionist settlers' fondest hopes was to prove themselves worthy of Ottoman toleration, and thereby to overcome the government's endless legal obstacles to immigration and land purchase. With the best of intentions, however, the Yishuv failed to accommodate itself to the political realities of the country. To begin with, Palestine was disjointed under Turkish rule into separate administrative units. Individual governors in Beirut and Jerusalem wielded all but unlimited powers and issued decrees that often conflicted. In both provinces, to be sure, administrative councils included leaders of the various religious communities, together with a handful of elected local citizens. Yet the capacity of these bodies was purely advisory. After the 1908 Revolution, the inhabitants of Palestine were entitled to send representatives to the Ottoman Parliament, and the country did in fact return five such deputies. Again, their actual powers were negligible. By the same token, municipal councils were based on a restricted property franchise and wielded no visible influence.

Whatever the limited theoretical opportunities for representation in government, these applied to the Jews hardly at all. Few Jews were Ottoman citizens; from the outset, they had learned that they were better off as foreign nationals remaining under the capitulatory protection of the European consuls. Elections to the Ottoman Parliament took place virtually without Jewish participation, as a result. The Sephardic Chief Rabbi, the Chacham Bashi, sat in the administrative council of Jerusalem, a smiling ornament. In 1912 a provincial council was established for the sanjak (district) of Jerusalem; the Jews failed to return a single one of the thirteen elected members. With voting rights restricted to property owners, municipal councils had few Jewish members. In Jerusalem, for example, where Jews constituted a majority of the city's population, only three of their number were included among the ten representatives on the municipal council in 1910. In 1912 there were four Jews; in 1914, one.

Yet, among themselves, at least, the inhabitants of the Yishuv appreciated the need for some form of collaboration that would protect their uncertain tenure in the Holy Land. The main stumbling block was the heterogeneous nature of the Jewish population, divided as it was into Ashkenazim, Sephardic-Orientals, pietists, secularists, and various political factions among the Zionist immigrants. Even so, an initial effort to organize a representative body was launched in the agricultural villages, where communal life was fractionally more active than in the cities. Through the efforts of Achad HaAm, who visited Palestine in 1900, several hundred Jewish farm workers elected a delegation with the intention of petitioning Baron Rothschild to loosen PICA's grip on Jewish rural life.

The appeal failed. Three years later a "Congress of Palestinian Jewry" was "elected"—by a meager 2,157 Jews from all parts of the country. This group, too, soon dissolved, as a consequence of the East Africa episode.

On the other hand, among the newcomers of the Second Aliyah were to be found large numbers of individuals with experience in the organized (Jewish) communal life of eastern Europe. In 1907 several hundred of these immigrants founded a Palestinian Council, with the intention of coordinating the work of the Zionist agencies in the Yishuv. The Council met on a haphazard basis during the ensuing two years, then splintered into factionalism; the Sephardic majority in Jerusalem and Safed was uninterested in joint ventures with the Russian Labor Zionists. The organization expired in 1908. This series of failures notwithstanding, Jewish interest in communal affairs persisted. It was evidenced in the large number of political parties, clubs, and unions that continued to surface in the Yishuv well after the Young Turk Revolution. Thus, in 1913, journeying by horseback through the Yishuv's towns and villages, Israel Belkind renewed the effort to establish a Jewish representative body. Once more the response was favorable. In the spring of 1914 the plan was discussed and endorsed by the Executive Council of the Federation of Judean Colonies (below). The outbreak of the war doomed the scheme.

Nevertheless, a certain rudimentary self-government developed on the local and regional level. Villages frequently consulted each other on matters of joint interest, such as the building of synagogues or the drilling of wells. At the opening of the century, the inhabitants of the PICA colonies assembled in town meetings to issue occasional local regulations that would fill the vacuum of effective Turkish government. And in the last years before the war, two regional federations of colonies actually were organized. One of these, the Federation of Judean Colonies, concentrated on establishing marketing societies, acquiring modern farm implements, organizing a livestock insurance company, hiring a veterinarian, and circulating agricultural information. In 1913 the farm communities of lower Galilee joined in a federation of their own to cope with the danger of marauding Arab bandits. Unlike its Judean counterpart, this body survived the outbreak of war, appealed to the government for police protection, helped the needy with loans, and evacuated Jews from areas threatened by heavy fighting.

Despite the absence of formal structure, therefore, the lineaments of a distinct, self-aware, and increasingly assertive Jewish community were plainly visible on the eve of the World War. It was also a community that was growing more rapidly than at any time since the rise of the Zionist movement. During the first six months of 1914, no fewer than 6,000 Jews immigrated into Palestine, while the flow of emigration back to Europe slowed appreciably. By then, too, some 85,000 Jews were living in the Holy Land, a higher Jewish ratio to total population than in any other country, and enjoying a far wider occupational diversity. New shipping services and railroad lines offered hope of accelerated economic growth for Palestine. So did the first Jewish workshops and small industries, including

JEWISH SETTLEMENT (YISHUV) IN PALESTINE, 1881–1914

Approximate populations

1881: 470,000 Arabs   24,000 Jews
1914: 500,000 Arabs   85,000 Jews

● Major Jewish settlements established between 1881 and 1914
○ Other Jewish settlements
□ Major Arab towns

0   MILES   15

LAKE CHULA
Y'sod HaMa'alah ●
Mishmar HaYarden ●
Safed ●
Rosh Pina

GALILEE

LAKE GALILEE

Tiberias ●
Sejera ●

Kfar Tabor ●   Degania ●

Merchavia ●   Menachemia

● Atlit

● Zichron Ya'akov

M E D I T E R R A N E A N   S E A

Chadera ●

S A M A R I A

□ Nablus

Jordan River

● Kfar Saba

Jaffa ●
● Mikveh Israel

Rishon l'Zion ●
Ness Ziona ●

● G'dera
● Hartuv   ● Jerusalem
● Beer Tuvia

J U D E A

□ Gaza   ● Hebron

DEAD SEA

□ Beersheba

○ G'vulot

a cement and brick factory, a sugar beet refinery, and engineering work-shops. Jaffa, with its port facilities and access to Europe, was now an important Jewish cultural and administrative center for Zionist enterprises. There the first Hebrew schools were established and the first workers' federations opened their offices.

It was also from Jaffa, with its 6,000 Jews, that a new suburb emerged that was destined ultimately to become the metropolitan center of Jewish life in Palestine. The port city was squalid, and largely Arab. For some years Ruppin had been intrigued by the notion of building an all-Jewish satellite community. With the endorsement, then, of the Eighth Zionist Congress, the director of the Palestine Office agreed to lend JNF funds to a private development company, the Achuzat Bayit. The latter in turn sold individual plots, in both Europe and the Yishuv, to future Jewish settlers. In 1909 construction began on the sand dunes outside the Jaffa town limits, and by 1914 a modest garden quarter had grown up, encompassing 139 houses and 1,419 Jewish inhabitants. The community was named Tel Aviv (Hill of Spring), from a site mentioned in the Bible, and used by Nachum Sokolow as the title for his Hebrew translation of Herzl's *Altneuland.* Jewish agriculture matched this urban growth. The villages founded by the original nineteenth-century Chovevei Zion immigrants had recovered, especially the plantation settlements along the coastal lowland. Citrus and grapes of profitable quality and quantity were being cultivated. By 1914, the Jewish rural population had climbed to 12,000.

How far, then, had the return to Zion materialized? Far enough so that by 1914, only three years before the Balfour Declaration, the notion of a Jewish homeland was worth taking seriously in European governmental circles. The awakening was made possible not merely by the growth of the Zionist Organization, nor by the agencies of that body, the Jewish National Fund and the Anglo-Palestine Bank. It was accomplished, too, by the presence of a rather considerable Jewish enclave in Palestine, 14 percent of whose settlers were living in farm villages, many of them speaking Hebrew, their hands on their own plows, even on their own guns. Had the "practical" approach of building the Yishuv not been followed, had the Zionist movement worldwide been allowed breathlessly to await a miracle of future statecraft, there is little doubt that the redemptive effort in Palestine would have died of inanition. It was between 1905 and 1914, therefore, that the foundations of the Jewish National Home were laid and its ideological configuration charted. "Above all," reflected Weizmann, "we got the feel of things, so that we did not approach our task after the Balfour Declaration like complete beginners."

CHAPTER V THE BALFOUR DECLARATION

For all its impressive progress, the Yishuv itself remained the most vulnerable component in the Zionist movement after the outbreak of the World War. Since the nineteenth century, we recall, Palestine's Ashkenazic Jews had learned to rely upon the European consuls to ensure their elementary physical security. Now, with the rescission of the Capitulations and Turkey's entrance into the war, that assurance was gone. Even after hostilities began, few European Jews were inclined at first to seek the dubious advantages of Ottoman citizenship, with all this entailed in arbitrary taxation and capricious justice. It was simple government brutality that changed their minds. On December 17, 1914, Beha-a-Din, the aged and irascible Turkish governor of Jaffa, ordered the immediate expulsion of the 6,000 Russian Jews living in his port city. The same day, then, the police rounded up their first 700 victims, loaded them on an Italian steamer, and shipped them off to Alexandria. Aghast at this development, Jews throughout the Yishuv hurriedly began packing for departure. Within one month, 7,000 of them had fled the country. The rest—the majority—unable to pull up stakes at short notice, remained paralyzed in uncertainty of their future course. Guidance at this juncture, therefore, was provided by the Jewish religious and communal leaders themselves, who urged their coreligionists to apply immediately for Ottoman citizenship as the only alternative to disaster. Within several weeks, 12,000 Jews followed the suggestion. The number doubled in the ensuing year. Gradually the threat of large-scale expulsion declined.

Other dangers remained. Before the war it had been the tradition for Christians and Jews to buy exemption from military conscription by paying special taxes. That alternative was out of the question now. The best non-Moslems could hope for, as members of an educated elite, was privileged "labor" service on the home front close to their families. Yet by the winter of 1915 even this opportunity was foreclosed. Indeed, labor service became all but penal. Young men and old were drafted, set to work paving roads or quarrying stone, consigned to verminous barracks and starvation rations. Those who fell ill were imprisoned for malingering. Others died. Punitive as the treatment was, it failed at first to discourage the Labor Zionist leaders. Many welcomed the opportunity of proving their loyalty to the Ottoman regime. Ben-Gurion and Ben-Zvi, for example, were among those who petitioned the Turkish authorities for a Jewish militia to share in the defense of the country. And in fact Djemal Pasha, commander of the Ottoman Fourth Army and military governor of Palestine, favored the idea. He was dissuaded from accepting it only at the last moment by Beha-a-Din, who was irredeemably hostile to the non-Turkish minorities. Undaunted, nevertheless, other young Jews volunteered for regular armed service. In the early months of the war, some were accepted. Moshe Shertok and Dov Hoz—both, in later years, prominent figures in the life of the Yishuv—were among those sent to officers' training schools and eventually assigned to Turkish battlefronts.

The initial ambiguity of Turkish policy toward the Zionists was soon resolved by Djemal Pasha. In February 1915, Djemal returned from a disastrous military expedition against the Suez Canal. In a black mood, determined to reduce the country's non-Turkish population to a state of terrorized submission, he appointed Beha-a-Din as his "secretary for Jewish affairs." At the latter's orders, the Anglo-Palestine Bank was closed, together with Zionist newspapers, schools, and political offices. All Zionist public activities were banned. More ominously yet, Jewish land titles were called into question, and Arabs were encouraged to pillage Jewish villages. When Ben-Gurion and Ben-Zvi ventured to protest these measures, they and other Zionist leaders were summarily exiled. The circumstances of the Jewish "labor battalions" became increasingly grim. Many hundreds of young men were marched off in chains to prisons in Damascus, others exiled to Brusa and Constantinople, yet others sentenced to a living death in the granite pits of Tarsus.

It was not Djemal's hostility alone that threatened the survival of Palestine Jewry. The "normal" hardships of war were painful enough. The British naval blockade choked off food imports and philanthropic remittances from abroad. The citrus crop withered and died on the trees. Crushing war taxes were levied on Jewish and Arab farms. Livestock and foodstuffs were confiscated, reducing many thousands of Jewish and Arab families to maize grits as their basic staple. During the first two years of the war, some 35,000 inhabitants of Syria, Lebanon, and Palestine died of starvation or hunger-induced disease; perhaps 8,000 of these were Jews. If even more widespread hunger was avoided in the Yishuv, Jewish self-discipline was one factor. An emergency committee of Jewish organizations distributed food among the poor and unemployed, even assumed the quasi-legal responsibility of "taxing" Jews in Jaffa and Tel Aviv for improvised public works projects and soup kitchens.

The intercession of strategically located Western Jews also proved timely. One of these was Arthur Ruppin. As a German citizen who was known to enjoy the esteem of Foreign Minister Arthur von Zimmermann, a pro-Zionist, he was allowed to distribute funds received from German Jewish sources. Even more important was the solicitude of the United States ambassador in Constantinople, Henry Morgenthau. A Jew himself, Morgenthau inclined at first toward studied restraint in his dealings with

Ottoman officials. Yet as the representative of a powerful neutral government, he was bound to be taken seriously in his concern for Jewish and other minorities. It was principally in deference to Morgenthau that Djemal eased the worst of his repressive measures in the spring of 1915 and called a halt to the wave of expulsions and arrests. Morgenthau secured permission, too, for American naval vessels to bring occasional relief shipments and money to the Holy Land. Until diplomatic relations between Washington and Constantinople were ruptured in April 1917, it was this uncertain trickle of supplies and funds from abroad that enabled the Yishuv barely to hold out.

Nevertheless, Ottoman brutality was not forgiven by those who had been driven into exile. By March 1915 some 10,000 Palestine Jews had found asylum in Egypt. Half of them were lodged in refugee camps at Gabbari and Mafruza, where they were sustained by Jewish communal funds. In their hurried exit from Palestine they had left homes, farms, and families behind. Vegetating now in enforced and bitter idleness, they gave close attention to circulated accounts and rumors of Allied operations in the Middle East. It was among these restive young émigrés, moreover, that the first efforts were launched to recruit a Jewish legion for battle service against the Turks in Palestine. Initiated by Vladimir Jabotinsky, a Russian Jewish journalist (p. 102), the appeal aroused a mixed response. On the one hand, Britain was an ally of the hated tsar. On the other, if the Palestinians refused to take up arms, they feared the alternative of deportation to Russia and conscription into the tsarist army (although the British in fact turned down this Russian request).

Notable among these Palestinians was Joseph Trumpeldor, one of the most attractive and charismatic personalities in Zionist history. A handsome six-footer, Trumpeldor originally had been trained as a dentist. As a volunteer officer in the Russian army, he had lost an arm and had been decorated for heroism in the Russo-Japanese War. In more recent years he had been serving as a farmer-pioneer on a kvutzah in Galilee. After the war began, Trumpeldor was one of those deported by the Turks. Immediately, then, he made his way to Alexandria to volunteer for the British army. There he met Jabotinsky in the Mafruza camp, and the two promptly collaborated in the effort to recruit a Jewish legion. While the British authorities in Egypt were not unreceptive to the notion, they preferred to limit it to a Jewish transport unit for service in an alternative Allied war theater. Despite Jabotinsky's initial misgivings, Trumpeldor favored the scheme. As long as the enemy was the Turk, the latter insisted, "any front leads to Zion." Thus, in March and April of 1915, some five hundred Jews were accepted for enlistment in a special transportation unit, the Zion Mule Corps, and allowed to wear their own shoulder flashes bearing the Shield of David. Their assignment was the impending Dardanelles campaign. A British officer, Lieutenant Colonel John Patterson, was placed in charge of the force, but its animating spirit was Trumpeldor, now commissioned a captain in the British army.

Upon disembarkation at the beaches of Gallipoli, the Zion Mule Corps performed creditably enough, the men leading their supply mules to the front trenches through heavy fire. Eight of the troops were killed, fifty-five others wounded, among them Trumpeldor. Another 150 young Jews from Egypt promptly volunteered as replacements. With the subsequent evacuation of Gallipoli in the winter of 1915, the Mule Corps was among the last of the units to be withdrawn. Its reputation by then had spread throughout the Zionist world. Yet for the Jews remaining in Palestine itself, news of this military enterprise was a source of concern; the Turks might be tempted to retaliate against the Yishuv. Indeed, to forestall that threat, bands of Jewish loyalists marched through the streets of Jerusalem and Jaffa, shouting their contempt of the "traitors." The muleteers' performance failed in any case to influence the British command, which dissolved the unit once the Gallipoli campaign ended. Nevertheless, unrecognized at the time by British and Jews alike, the episode of the Zion Mule Corps represented the first tentative step in a developing Anglo-Zionist collaboration.

THE MIDDLE EAST AND BRITISH WAR POLICY

It was the outbreak of the World War that suddenly invested Palestine with a new importance in Allied military calculations. From then on, England based its Near Eastern policy on a central and immutable criterion, the security of the Suez Canal. This vital passageway for British commerce, the artery of transport for the military manpower reserves of the overseas empire, was threatened twice in the course of hostilities by Ottoman invasion expeditions of January 1915 and August 1916. Although repelled each time, the Turkish offensives fixated British attention on the vulnerability of Suez to assault from neighboring Palestine. To cope with the threat, military headquarters in Cairo devoted increasing attention to a new political strategy. It was to mobilize the Ottoman Empire's restive subject peoples in a joint military effort against the Turks. In fact, the idea initially had been mooted by a distinguished Arab personality, the Emir Abdullah, eldest son of Hussein, the Hashemite sherif of Mecca and Medina. Even before the war Abdullah had visited General Kitchener in Cairo to request British help in protecting his father's dynasty against its suspicious Ottoman overlords. Negotiations were resumed by the British later in the year, and then were continued upon the outbreak of war, in direct correspondence between Hussein himself and Sir Henry McMahon, Britain's high commissioner in Egypt.

Following an exchange of several letters, a bargain was worked out between McMahon and the sherif in the autumn of 1915. The crucial letter, from the high commissioner to Hussein on October 24, stated that Britain was prepared "to recognize and support the independence of the Arabs in all the regions within the limits demanded by the Sherif [namely, the entire Arab rectangle, including Syria, Arabia, and Mesopotamia]," with the exception of those "portions of Syria lying to the west of the districts of

Damascus, Homs, Hama, and Aleppo. . . ." In return for British support, so the understanding went, the Hashemite Arabs would join the Allied war effort against Turkey. Moreover, after the war, the newly established Arab government would "seek the advice and guidance of Great Britain only. . . ." On this basis the Arab revolt finally began in June of 1916, under the leadership of Hussein's second son, the Emir Feisal, and later with the help of such British liaison officers as T. E. Lawrence. During the subsequent year and a half, the uprising of between 10,000 and 20,000 Arab irregulars played a not inconsiderable role in the British military effort against Turkish forces in Arabia and eastern Palestine.

Yet if the British made a commitment to the Hashemites, they scrupulously protected not only their own postwar interests but also those of France. The Ottoman Empire, after all, was more than a source of danger to the Suez Canal; with its untutored Moslem populace, it also provided a far likelier terrain than Europe for Western imperial aggrandizement. In recognition, then, of this territorial opportunity, Britain dutifully apprised the French and Russian governments of its impending compact with Sherif Hussein. And at the same time, even as McMahon was preempting for Britain the key "advisory" role over a future Arab government within the Fertile Crescent, he also made clear to Hussein in the letter of October 24, 1915, that western Syria was being reserved by implication for a special French relationship.

Indeed, during the winter of 1915–16 this implication was confirmed in a series of negotiations among the British, French, and Russian governments themselves. It was in January 1916 that Sir Mark Sykes, the British representative, and Charles François Georges-Picot, the French emissary, reached a meeting of minds on the allocation of postwar spheres of influence in the Arab world. Britain would be invested with supervision over Arab territories encompassing the largest part of Mesopotamia, most of Transjordan, and southern Palestine. The agreement seemingly was not inconsistent with the understanding reached earlier between McMahon and Hussein. Neither did it violate the provisions currently worked out on behalf of France. These authorized the French to exercise varying degrees of ascendancy over southern Turkey, Syria, northern Palestine, and the Mosul area of upper Mesopotamia.

What was the fate of Palestine under this arrangement? If, over the years, France had carved out for itself preemptive economic and cultural rights in Syria—interests now given territorial formulation in the Sykes-Picot agreement—it was the not illogical view of Paris that those rights applied to the Holy Land as well. The largest sector of Palestine (except for the Jerusalem sanjak) was an integral part of the Ottoman-Syrian administration, after all. Nevertheless, as early as January 1915, the tsarist government began expressing its own grave concern about rumored French ambitions for Palestine. St. Petersburg surely was not unaware that the Franciscan Order had been a principal European religious influence in the Holy Land, operating a wide network of churches, convents, monasteries, and hospices. Yet Russian Orthodox interests hardly were less extensive or jealously guarded than those of the Roman Catholics, and notably in the Jerusalem-Bethlehem area. Nor was Britain's preoccupation with the Holy Land, finally, less extensive than that of France or of Russia; although here the concern admittedly was dictated less by religious than by military considerations. From London's viewpoint, terrain of this strategic proximity to the Canal simply could not be allowed to fall into the grasp of another power. To be sure, Foreign Secretary Sir Edward Grey was too astute a statesman to offend his allies by demanding unilateral control for Britain. He came up rather with a compromise formula that in the end proved acceptable to Paris and St. Petersburg. It was for a joint Allied condominium over the largest part of the Holy Land.

In their January 1916 agreement, therefore (later endorsed by Russian Foreign Minister Sergei Sazonov), Sykes and Georges-Picot reached an understanding for the promulgation of a Franco-Russian-British condominium in a "Brown Zone" that would include, essentially, central Palestine. Under these terms, neither France nor England fully abandoned its respective interests in the Holy Land. Skirting the central zone, for example, Britain would control Acre and Haifa Bay; a British railroad would connect Haifa and Baghdad, with a right of easement through French Syria. Additionally, Britain's sphere of influence embraced southern Palestine and the country's Transjordanian hinterland, thus assuring that the "Brown Zone" would be surrounded on three sides by territory under British domination. To the French sphere of influence would be allocated northwestern Palestine, including all of upper Galilee, with its fertile wheat fields, water sources, and venerated religious shrines. Later, by the terms of the Treaty of St. Jean de Maurienne of September 1917, Italy too was permitted to share in the condominium area of Palestine (see map, opposite).

Meanwhile, from the summer of 1916 onward, Sinai and Palestine were to function increasingly as Britain's chosen battlefield against the Turks. Early British expeditions in the Middle East, in the Dardanelles and Mesopotamia, had turned out to be sanguinary failures. By contrast, the Sinai Peninsula offered a possibly more direct and manageable invasion route toward the Ottoman Levant. Once this consensus was reached by the imperial general command, in June of 1916, British military headquarters in Cairo set about organizing and equipping a 150,000-man "Egyptian Expeditionary Force" in anticipation of a straight-line plunge into Palestine. On December 22, 1916, the massive army ventured out against the Ottoman post of al-Arish and captured it. Early in January 1917, Rafa was overrun. Finally, in March, the expeditionary force moved against Gaza, the gateway to Palestine. And here it was stopped twice in the next three weeks by a formidable Turkish defense. The British commander was replaced forthwith. His successor, General Sir Edmund Allenby, an energetic, hard-bitten cavalry officer, immediately set about reorganizing his divisions and making plans for a climactic breakthrough toward the north of Palestine's Negev Desert.

Even as Allenby's troops were preparing for their thrust into the Holy

Land, however, British Foreign Office and military officials shared growing misgivings about the prize their diplomacy seemingly had forfeited. The compromise of quasi-internationalization may have been inevitable at a time when the British were hurled back onto the defensive in the Middle East, licking their wounds after Gallipoli and Kut. It was also the period when the French were carrying the heaviest burden of the struggle on the Western front. Nevertheless, as the months passed, the prospect of a French military enclave in Palestine, even linked to an Allied condominium, became increasingly unpalatable to London; and

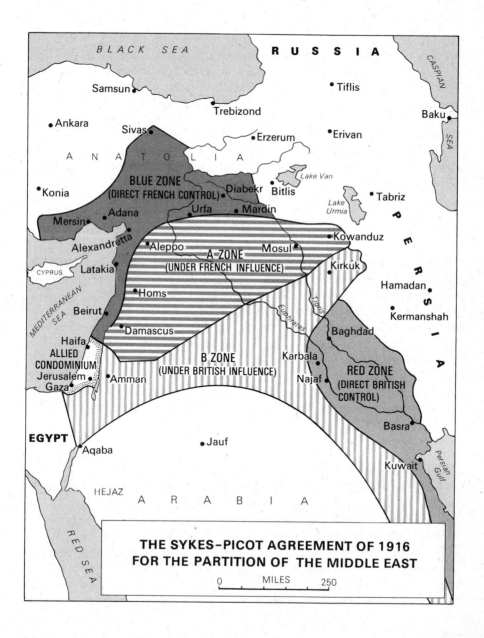

THE SYKES–PICOT AGREEMENT OF 1916
FOR THE PARTITION OF THE MIDDLE EAST

0   MILES   250

all the more so, in the spring of 1917, when Allenby was marshaling tens of thousands of imperial troops for the offensive into the Holy Land. It was as a consequence of these misgivings that the War Cabinet had summarily vetoed repeated French demands to participate in the operation.

On April 19 a special Committee on Territorial Terms of Peace, under the chairmanship of Lord Curzon, unanimously emphasized the importance of British postwar control in Palestine. Two days later, Lloyd George informed Lord Bertie, his ambassador in Paris, that "the French will have to accept our Protectorate over Palestine." The prime minister noted subsequently that an international regime in the Holy Land "would be quite intolerable to ourselves. . . . Palestine is really the strategic buffer of Egypt." Even so, for the Lloyd George government, the fact of Britain's military predominance was less than an appropriate basis for dealings between wartime allies or for staking any kind of postwar claim to the Holy Land. At the least, it would have violated the principle of non-acquisition of territories by war enunciated by President Woodrow Wilson and by the newly established Provisional Government in Russia. A more "idealistic" rationale would still have been preferred at a time when Sir Mark Sykes's signature was not yet dry on the 1916 agreement with Georges-Picot. Initially, Whitehall failed to grasp that such a rationale already existed. It had been provided by a rather unlikely source, the Jews.

THE ORIGINS OF THE ANGLO-ZIONIST ALLIANCE

The Zionist Organization hardly was in its strongest bargaining position at the outbreak of the war. The fact was that in no part of the world, not excluding eastern Europe, had Zionism yet won overwhelming support even within the Jewish community. In Russia, the Bund vigorously contested for the loyalty of the Jewish working classes, while Orthodox Jews by and large remained suspicious of Zionism. In the Western nations, the acculturated Jewish "establishment" opposed Zionism with vigor and spleen. The war itself, finally, ruptured the precarious unity of the Zionist movement. In the hope of preserving at least a functional contact between its members throughout Europe, the Zionist Organization in 1914 established a special "Bureau for Zionist Affairs" in neutral Copenhagen. The device was notably ineffective. The principal Zionist leaders remained in their native countries. As a result, the movement suffered a diffusion of centralized authority.

Not less critically, the Zionists shared the general patriotic enthusiasm of their fellow countrymen. In Austria the Zionist Federation announced that it expected all its young members to volunteer for military service. In Germany the official Zionist weekly "recognize[d] that our [Jewish] interest is exclusively on the side of Germany." Throughout Europe, in fact, efforts were mounted not simply to identify all Jews with the various national causes, but to identify the Zionist movement itself with the war aims of the respective governments. This was particularly true in Germany, where

Arthur Hantke and Richard Lichtheim courted officials in Berlin, urging them to take the initiative in establishing a Jewish homeland in Palestine —which then surely would form a "bastion" of German influence in the Levant. In the event, the Wilhelmstrasse rejected these overtures; it was not prepared to alienate its Turkish ally.

Other foreign ministries shared a widespread indifference, even hostility, to Zionism. The government of France, as an example, was aware that Herzl, Nordau, Wolffsohn, and other early Zionist leaders were central European Jews by training and culture, and it therefore suspected Jewish nationalism as "the advance guard of German influence." In St. Petersburg, the tsarist regime hardly was likely to evince sympathy for Jewish nationalism at a time when it was driving half a million Jews like cattle into the Russian interior. England, finally, appeared an even less promising source of help for the Zionist cause. Although its quarter of a million Jews consisted largely of Russian immigrants, most of these were too poor or harassed to exert a significant influence in public or communal affairs; while Britain's acculturated Jewish families generally rejected the idea of Jewish nationalism altogether. Meanwhile, the British government remained as indifferent as any other Great Power to the Zionist renaissance.

Yet, in the eyes of at least some British politicians and statesmen, Zionism was no longer either unknown or suspect. Articles on Zionism had appeared in British periodicals for several years even before Herzl's negotiations with Chamberlain. In August 1902, the Fourth Zionist Congress was held in London, and its sessions were given considerable publicity. Afterward, the al-Arish and East Africa schemes were raised and debated in a parliament that included Lloyd George and Balfour. Lord Milner was high commissioner in South Africa during Herzl's negotiations with Chamberlain, and was well familiar with the Zionist idea from then on; eventually he became a great friend of the movement. Henry Wickham Steed, later editor of the *Times*, had met Herzl twice, in 1896 and 1902, and had been impressed by the Zionist leader and his views.

If the earlier Anglo-Zionist connection revived and developed with unanticipated warmth after 1914, one of the explanations was the quality of new Zionist activists who by chance were living in England at the outbreak of war. Their acknowledged spokesman was Dr. Chaim Weizmann, then forty years old, a chemistry instructor at the University of Manchester. Russian-born, university-trained in Germany and Switzerland, Weizmann proved to be as lucid and convincing a propagandist in England as in his youthful leadership of the "Fraction" during the early Zionist Congresses (Chapter iii). He soon won a loyal following for Zionism among a number of distinguished personalities in the Anglo-Jewish community. The most influential of these after Weizmann himself was Herbert Samuel, president of the Local Government Board, and afterward home secretary in the Asquith government. In fact, Samuel had taken a mild interest in Zionism even before the war. Once hostilities broke out, and well before meeting Weizmann, Samuel already was contemplating the likely diplomatic advantages of a British protectorate over a Palestine Jewish homeland. On this basis of unalloyed national self-interest, he mooted the idea to Asquith and Sir Edward Grey, both of whom initially expressed reservations.

Samuel persisted, however. Upon meeting Weizmann (through the auspices of Charles P. Scott, editor of the *Manchester Guardian*), Samuel and the brilliant Anglo-Jewish lawyer Harry Sacher made it their business to introduce him to several eminent public figures. One of these was Steed of the *Times*, whose interest in Zionism was now rekindled. Through Scott and Steed, in turn, Weizmann made the acquaintance of the nation's political leaders, including Lloyd George, Winston Churchill, and Lord Robert Cecil. His relationship with these men was further strengthened by a vital service he performed for the British Admiralty. In March of 1916, Weizmann was summoned to London to help solve the shortage of acetone, an ingredient in the naval explosive cordite. After two years of laboratory research, he accomplished the task by devising a special fermentation process.

During this period, too, the friendships Weizmann had made earlier were cemented at the highest level. Indeed, the Zionist leader's extraordinary gift for friendship was a not inconsiderable factor in the unfolding diplomatic triumph of the next half-decade. His sheer physical presence was arresting, for one thing. The brow of his massive bald head was finely etched with veins, his eyes were piercing, his mustache and goatee elegant, his clothing always superbly tailored. A slight Russian accent lent a touch of exoticism to his perfect command of English. More important, he possessed a rare, inner charisma. Years later Sir Ronald Storrs described Weizmann as

> a brilliant talker with an unrivaled gift for lucid exposition. . . . As a speaker almost frighteningly convincing, even in English . . . in Hebrew, and even more in Russian, overwhelming, with all that dynamic persuasiveness which Slavs usually devote to love and Jews to business, nourished, trained, and concentrated upon the accomplishment of Zion.

Sir Charles Webster, who first met Weizmann at the War Office in 1917, considered him the greatest statesman of his time. "With unerring skill," wrote Webster,

> he adapted his arguments to the special circumstances of each statesman. To the British and Americans he could use biblical language and awake a deep emotional undertone; to other nationalities he more often talked in terms of interest. Mr. Lloyd George was told that Palestine was a little mountainous country not unlike Wales; with Lord Balfour the philosophical background of Zionism could be surveyed; for Lord Cecil the problem was placed in the setting of a new world organization; while to Lord Milner the extension of imperial power could be vividly portrayed.

As Webster intimated, Weizmann's efforts were buttressed by other advantages. One was the mystical veneration with which many devout Anglo-Saxon (or Welsh or Scottish) Protestants regarded the Old Testament traditions, the Children of Israel, and particularly the Holy Land itself. Lloyd George wrote later that in his first meeting with Weizmann, in December 1914, historic sites in Palestine were mentioned that were "more familiar to me than those of the Western front." Balfour, too, had evinced a lifelong interest in the Holy Land and its traditions, as had Jan Christiaan Smuts, the South African member of the War Cabinet. These men felt deeply Christianity's historic obligation to the Jews. That debt was compounded not merely by Weizmann's personal services to the Allied war effort, but also by his uncompromising devotion to Britain, his repeated insistence that the fate of Zionism was inexorably linked to that of the Allies. Thus, a letter written by Weizmann in 1916, terminating relations with the "neutralist" Zionist Bureau in Copenhagen, was kept by Scotland Yard (unknown to Weizmann) and further influenced the authorities in his favor.

Against this background of Anglo-Zionist cordiality, Weizmann's allusions to a "British protectorate over a Jewish homeland" struck an increasingly responsive chord among government officials. The moment of decisive reappraisal in Middle Eastern policy came in the last weeks of 1916, when Lloyd George and Balfour became prime minister and foreign secretary, respectively. As the new government recognized, the Sykes-Picot Agreement no longer was a sufficiently watertight guarantee for British interests in Palestine. Perhaps, then, the Jews as a client people might be as useful an opening wedge for British domination as were the Arabs? Since the beginning of the war, in fact, Lloyd George had proposed annexing the Holy Land. In his eyes, British rule over a Jewish Palestine would have represented a logical and climactic tour de force of imperial diplomacy. He had had no part anyway in making the Sykes-Picot Agreement, which he regarded as a "fatuous document" based on erroneous calculations. The Zionists might open new possibilities of revision. A partnership with the Zionists similarly was advocated now by Lord Milner, Lloyd George's closest friend in the War Cabinet; by Lord Robert Cecil, undersecretary of foreign affairs; by Philip Kerr, the prime minister's adviser on foreign policy; and most importantly, by the War Cabinet's three young undersecretaries for Middle Eastern Affairs: Sir Mark Sykes, Leopold Amery, and William Ormsby-Gore.

A CRUCIAL INTERMEDIARY

Sykes was the most influential of this group, the official who served as "marriage broker" in the progressively intimate relationship between the government and the Zionist leadership. The role was an unusual one for the cabinet undersecretary, for he had never really cared much for Jews, particularly the "diluted" Jews who were beginning to make their way in British society. It was only during his travels in Palestine that Sykes had come to admire the Zionist colonies and to sense their potential rejuvenating influence among the Jewish people. Plainly more than concern for the future of the Jews animated his emerging Zionism, however. Although initially hesitant to upset the 1916 agreement with France, during ensuing months Sykes came to share his colleagues' interest in a revised approach to a Middle Eastern settlement. Thus, the chain of liberated national groups —Armenians, Arabs, Greeks—whom Sykes envisaged as Britain's logical Middle Eastern clients against the Turks, necessarily would include the Zionist Jews. The idea did not spring full-blown from his own mind. It was suggested to him in October 1916 by Dr. Moses Gaster, Sephardic Chief Rabbi of London, by the Zionist agronomist Aaron Aaronsohn (p. 103), and by James Malcolm, a Persian-born Armenian who had been raised in England. Malcolm attached himself to the Zionist cause early, partly out of conviction and partly in the hope "that Jewish *haute finance* will help the Armenians. . . ." Through Malcolm and Gaster, Sykes met Weizmann on February 7, 1917. By then, it had become Sykes's mission in life to wed Zionist and British interests. "From the purely British point of view," he told Amery, "a prosperous Jewish population in Palestine, owing its inception and its opportunity of development to British policy, might be an invaluable asset as a defense of the Suez Canal against attack from the north and as a station on the future air routes to the East."

Speed now became decisive, for by the opening days of 1917 the British military offensive in Palestine already had been launched. In the meeting of February 7, therefore, Sykes hinted to the Zionist leaders that the government might be prepared to favor a Jewish national entity in the Holy Land. He could not yet reveal the existence of the agreement he had signed with Georges-Picot and the restrictions this treaty placed on the War Cabinet's liberty of action, although he hinted that Britain was not yet a free agent in the Middle East. He observed simply that the Zionists themselves would have to take the initiative in persuading the Allied governments to endorse the notion of a Jewish national home in Palestine. Once this thesis was accepted, the corollary of a British protectorate would be easier to negotiate. Weizmann and the others agreed and set about immediately presenting their case in Paris and Rome.

Sykes, in the background, carefully stage-managed the negotiations. Nachum Sokolow, Weizmann's most intimate collaborator in these Allied discussions, wrote later:

> As I was crossing the Quai d'Orsay [in Paris] on my return from the Foreign Ministry I came across Sykes. He had not had the patience to wait. We walked on together, and I gave him an outline of the proceedings. This did not satisfy him; he studied every detail; I had to give him full notes and he drew up a minute report. "That's a good day's work," he said with shining eyes. The second [meeting] was a day in April, 1917, in Rome. Sykes had been there before me and could not await my arrival. . . . I put up at the hotel; Sykes had ordered rooms for me. I went to the British Embassy; letters and instructions from Sykes were waiting for me there. I went to the Italian Government Offices; Sykes had been there, too; then to the Vatican, where Sykes again prepared my way.

These efforts were not unsuccessful. Although the French Foreign Ministry left no doubt of its opposition to any change in the Sykes-Picot Agreement, it expressed a friendly interest in the Jewish homeland. Apparently it had little choice, for rumors of an impending pro-Zionist statement by Berlin (which turned out to be false) convinced Paris that in Jewish nationalism it was "up against a big thing." On June 4, the Quai d'Orsay dispatched a letter to Sokolow assuring him that "the French Government . . . can but feel sympathy to your cause, the triumph of which is bound up with that of the Allies." In Rome, Pope Benedict XV evinced a similar cordiality. In the pontiff's case, friendship was as tactical as it was atypical: a British-sponsored Jewish enclave in Palestine at least would forestall a Russian Orthodox presence.

In truth, none of the Allies was obtuse in discerning Britain's purpose in fostering Zionism. As early as April 6, 1917, Sykes frankly informed Georges-Picot that Britain's military efforts in Palestine would have to be taken into account at the peace conference. "[Picot] is convinced," President Poincaré of France wrote in his diary on April 17, "that in London our agreements are now considered null and void." Neither were the Zionists ignorant of their function as an extension of British policy. On the contrary, they welcomed the role; for the support and friendship of this mighty imperial power was now all but official. Specifically for that reason, Weizmann and the others, impatient for a public declaration from the War Cabinet, were mystified that support continually fell just short of open commitment. They knew nothing of the prior understanding with France, of course. "It was *not* from [Sykes] that we learned of the existence of the agreement," Weizmann recalled, "and months passed before we understood what it was that blocked our progress." C. P. Scott of the *Manchester Guardian* was the first to uncover the details of the Sykes-Picot understanding. Inadvertently, he let the information slip to Weizmann, who was appalled. When Weizmann in turn confronted Lord Robert Cecil with the information, the undersecretary neither confirmed nor denied it. Cecil intimated, on the other hand, that conceivably more yet could be done in persuading the government officially to declare the identity of British and Zionist goals. It would be helpful, the undersecretary observed, if Jews not simply in England but in other lands should express themselves openly in favor of a British protectorate in the Holy Land. The hint was plain, too, that the government's benevolent interest in Zionism merited the fullest Jewish loyalty, worldwide, to the Entente cause.

THE QUID PRO QUO OF JEWISH FRIENDSHIP

The hoary myth of the power and wealth of international Jewry could be traced to the Baroque era, when Jewish court bankers functioned as reliable supporters of central European dynasties. It was taken with equal seriousness in the nineteenth century, the heyday of the Rothschilds, when, as we recall, Palmerston importuned the Ottoman government to allow large-scale Jewish settlement in Palestine "because the wealth they would bring with them would increase the resources of the Sultan's dominions. . . ." Nor was it regarded with less solemnity in the twentieth century. In February 1917, Sykes wrote Georges-Picot: "If the great force of Judaism feels that its aspirations are . . . in a fair way to realization, then there is hope for an ordered and developed Arabia and Middle East." Nearly all the major belligerent governments shared this awe for the—essentially legendary—power of world Jewry. It was significant that both Germany and France included Jewish "advisers" among their wartime missions to the United States, individuals capable, it was hoped, of mobilizing American Jewish support for their respective causes. Until the United States entered the war, moreover, it appeared for a while as if that support inclined toward Germany. The American Jewish "establishment" was largely of German origin. The eminent financier Jacob Schiff and others like him made no secret of their pro-German sentiments. Neither did the Russian Jewish immigrant community, with its bitter memories of tsarist persecution.

Lloyd George, too, expressed the prevailing conviction concerning Jewish "influence" in other lands. If the notion was entirely spurious, this was less important than what the prime minister believed. And Lloyd George's beliefs in 1917 were conditioned by the worst crisis of the war: Russia virtually *hors de combat;* France exhausted, its troops mutinying; Italy demoralized after Caporetto; German submarines taking a fearful toll of Allied shipping; not a single American division yet in the trenches. The need to exploit America's resources, to keep Russia in the war, was overpowering. "In the solution of these two problems," Lloyd George wrote, "public opinion in Russia and America played a great part, and we [believed] . . . . that in both countries the friendliness or hostility of the Jewish race might make a considerable difference." Actually, the potential hostility or friendship of American Jewry was a negligible factor once the United States entered the war. The Russian Zionist attitude toward the Entente, on the other hand, seemed hopelessly poisoned by hatred of the tsarist regime. This became evident in June 1917, when Ussishkin and other Russian Zionist leaders sent word to Louis Brandeis (p. 108) and Weizmann that they were unprepared to identify the cause of Zionism with one or another of the combatant powers. Their animus toward the Russian Entente partnership was barely disguised.

Vladimir Jabotinsky discovered this opposition the hard way. A Russian Jewish writer, orator, poet, and linguist of remarkable virtuosity, thirty-four years old when the war began, he served as correspondent on the Western front for the liberal Russian newspaper *Russkiye Vyedomosti.* The moment the Ottoman Empire joined the Central Powers, Jabotinsky sensed the unique opportunity that would accrue to Zionism if the Turks could be driven from Palestine. To emphasize the Zionist commitment to the Allied cause, therefore, Jabotinsky hurled himself into the endeavor to organize a Jewish legion for "the liberation of the Holy Land." The first fruit of that effort, it is remembered, the Zion Mule Corps, was sent to Gallipoli instead and afterward disbanded. Early in 1915, Jabotinsky paid a return visit to Russia. There he found himself ostracized by the Zionists, who regarded any military effort on behalf of the Entente as simply another attempt at succoring the despised Romanov government. In his hometown of Odessa, Jabotinsky was branded as a traitor from the synagogue pulpit. His mother was accosted in the street by Ussishkin, who remarked that "your son should be hanged."

From then on, Jabotinsky concentrated his recruiting efforts in London. There also he nearly met disaster. Addressing crowds of Russian Jewish immigrants in the ghetto of the East End, he was furiously hooted and shouted off the platform. It was evident that in England, as in Russia, the Jews wanted no part of a legion or of any other unit dedicated to fighting the enemies of the tsar. Most of the leaders of British Zionism, too, except for Weizmann, were equally cold to Jabotinsky's scheme, although for different reasons. They recognized that the Jewish settlement in Palestine was an Ottoman hostage. If it became known that Jews abroad were mobilizing specifically to liberate the Holy Land, the Yishuv conceivably might suffer the fate of the Armenians, whom the Turks recently had all but annihilated as potential traitors.

This analogy was by no means farfetched. In 1916 the same tragic result was almost provoked by a small group of Palestine Jews engaged in transmitting military data to the British. A certain Aaron Aaronsohn was the driving force behind the clandestine operation. The son of a Zionist farmer, Aaronsohn was an agronomist of recognized genius. In 1906 he won international acclaim for discovering a weather-resistant primeval wheat. Four years later, encouraged by the United States Department of Agriculture and funded by a wealthy American Jew, Aaronsohn set up an experimental station in Atlit, a coastal village at the tip of the Carmel range. There, in succeeding years, he carried out extensive research on dry-farming techniques. Even as he explored methods of reviving Palestine's soil, however, Aaronsohn and his associate, Avshalom Feinberg, were driven to the conclusion that neither the Land of Israel nor the Jewish settlement there had a future under the slothful, brutish Ottoman regime. The outbreak of the war, the expulsions and sequestrations carried out against Jews and Arabs alike, the horror visited upon the Armenians, whose pathetic refugees straggled in dying bands through the countryside, appeared to confirm this premonition. The Jews' best hope, Feinberg and Aaronsohn were convinced, was simply to wrest Palestine away for themselves. This view was shared by a small group of associates, including Aaronsohn's father, brothers, and sisters, and, besides Feinberg, several other young Palestinians who worked in the research station.

Aaronsohn and his companions had anticipated a British invasion once the war began. When the landings occurred instead at Gallipoli, the Atlit research team decided on its own to establish communications with the British and to offer the Allies systematic information on Ottoman troop movements in Palestine. Aaronsohn and his co-workers were in a unique position to supply this intelligence. They were veteran settlers, known and respected for their agronomical work, and generally permitted freedom of movement throughout Palestine in organizing antilocust campaigns. As a result, Feinberg and Aaronsohn's brother Alexander managed to pass successfully through the Turkish lines and reach Egypt. At first British officials in Cairo showed little enthusiasm for dealing with the Jewish spies. In the autumn of 1916, however, Aaron Aaronsohn received ominous information that the Turks were concentrating large numbers of troops for a second invasion attempt against the Suez Canal. Somehow the British had to be warned. It was vital, too, that they appreciate another danger: unless Palestine were swiftly liberated, its inhabitants might not survive the famine that was penetrating into every corner of the land. Aaronsohn's problem was to find a way of getting to England and speaking directly there with the appropriate British officials.

An invasion of another kind—of locusts—gave him his chance. In a meeting with Djemal Pasha, he persuaded the Fourth Army commander to let him depart for Germany in order to carry out "research on a variety of sesame rich in oil." But once in Germany, Aaronsohn traveled on to neutral Copenhagen, and through the Zionist Bureau there worked out a plan to reach England without appearing to defect. He set sail for the United States in October 1916. En route, by prearrangement, a British destroyer intercepted the ship, "arrested" Aaronsohn as an Ottoman citizen, and carried him back to England. Within hours of his arrival in London, he was pouring out his information to Sir Basil Thomson, chief of Scotland Yard. The agronomist offered compelling evidence of Turkish vulnerability to an invasion through Palestine. Thomson was impressed, and in late November sent Aaronsohn on to Egypt for discussions with the military commanders there. The latter were as intrigued as Thomson had been, and this time promised active collaboration with the Jewish spy ring. Aaronsohn remained in Cairo as liaison between the British and the Atlit group. It is worth noting, too, that during the first weeks of Aaronsohn's earlier sojourn in London, others who met him—among them Sykes, Amery, and Ormsby-Gore—were profoundly stirred by his Zionist idealism and his dream of a British protectorate over a Jewish homeland in Palestine. Indeed, from then on, virtually all Ormsby-Gore's memoranda dealing with Palestine bore the stamp of Aaronsohn's ideas.

The NILI organization, meanwhile, as the Jewish spy network was called (from the initials of its Hebrew password, "Nezach Yisrael Lo Y'shaker"—The Eternal One of Israel Will Not Lie), worked for the next eight months under the very noses of the Turks. Aaronsohn's sister Sarah, and an associate, Joseph Lishanski, directed the effort, collecting extensive information on Ottoman military bases and army movements and transmitting it to a British frigate that anchored off the Atlit coast every two weeks at nightfall. The intelligence was of critical importance to the British. When Allenby assumed command of the Egyptian Expeditionary Force in the spring of 1917, he asked the NILI spies for particulars on Turkish defenses around Beersheba, the site of his intended offensive. Sarah Aaronsohn and her associates at once set about fulfilling the assignment. Their dispatches included vital data on the weather, on the location of water sources and malarial swamps, on the precise condition of every known route to Beersheba from the Negev. "It was very largely the daring work of the young spies . . . ," wrote Captain Raymond Savage, Allenby's deputy military secretary, "which enabled the brilliant Field-Marshal to accomplish his undertaking so effectively."

The espionage came to an end in September 1917, when one of the NILI carrier pigeons fell into the hands of the Turks. Two weeks later, a member of the group, Na'aman Belkind, was caught trying to reach Egypt. Eventually the police traced the spy network back to Atlit. Most of the ring was seized, including nearly all of Aaronsohn's family. Their fate was predictable. Sarah Aaronsohn turned herself in to spare her aged father additional beatings. She, in turn, was tortured to divulge her information. On the third day of her ordeal she seized a revolver from a drawer and shot herself; paralyzed, she lingered for several days before dying. Other members of the organization were similarly tortured. One of them, Reuven Schwartz, committed suicide. Belkind and Lishanski were hanged in Damascus. Although the merest handful of Palestine Jews were aware of the NILI plot, it was only the imminent British capture of Jerusalem that saved the Yishuv from mass arrests and possibly mass hangings and deportations. Under these conditions, most of Palestine's Zionist settlers took an ambiguous, even hostile, attitude toward the espionage. They had always disliked Aaronsohn anyway for his known antipathy to socialism. Many of the Poalei Zion, too, we recall, had gone to considerable lengths to affirm their loyalty to the Ottoman regime. The Yishuv accordingly refused to give aid or comfort to the NILI survivors. There were few enough of these, in any case. Aaron Aaronsohn himself, living in Cairo, managed to survive the war. With a certain classic inexorability, however, the NILI story ended in May 1919, when Aaronsohn's plane crashed into the English Channel en route from London to the Paris Peace Conference.

A DECLARATION IS ISSUED

The fate of the NILI spies unquestionably was one of the dangers the British Zionist leadership had in mind when it hesitated at first to endorse Jabotinsky's plans for a Jewish legion. The vulnerability of the Yishuv might also have inhibited Weizmann and his colleagues in their attempt to extract a pro-Zionist declaration from the British government. But their discovery of the Sykes-Picot Agreement convinced them that any risk was worth taking now to avoid the dismemberment of Palestine, and its Jewish settlement, into isolated zones of conflicting sovereignties. With Allenby's Palestine offensive imminent, too, both Weizmann and the War Cabinet sensed the urgent need for a government declaration that would imply future unilateral British control over the Holy Land.

The remote possibility also existed that the Turks still might extricate themselves from the war, and thus avoid losing Palestine or the rest of their empire. Indeed, Washington was convinced that such a possibility might usefully be explored with Henry Morgenthau's "reliable" Ottoman sources. In May 1917, therefore, the State Department requested the former ambassador (who had left his post in April, following the severance of United States–Turkish relations) to embark upon negotiations with certain "intermediaries" in Switzerland. Morgenthau accepted the task with enthusiasm. At first London concurred in the mission, but shortly afterward Whitehall began to have second thoughts as it contemplated Morgenthau's German background and connections. The eve of Allenby's offensive in any case was hardly the moment to give the Turks an opportunity to defect. The Zionists shared these misgivings. Thus, at the behest of the Foreign Office, Weizmann agreed to intercept Morgenthau and his traveling companion, Felix Frankfurter, in Gibraltar. The extraordinary meeting took place on July 4. During the course of a lengthy interview, the Zionist leader explained to Morgenthau and Frankfurter the unlikelihood of Turkish agreement to a separate peace that would end Ottoman rule over Armenia, Syria, or Palestine; and the Allies were committed to the freedom of these lands. As Weizmann recalled: "It was no job to persuade Mr. Morgenthau to drop the project. He simply persuaded himself."

By then it was quite evident both to Weizmann and to Balfour and his staff that the risks of delay were mounting, and that an official declaration of governmental support for a Jewish homeland no longer could be postponed. Sykes and Ormsby-Gore were convinced (wrongly, as it turned out) that Berlin was about to steal a march on the Allies by issuing a pro-Zionist declaration of its own. In May, too, the "Conjoint Committee," a body representing the nativized Anglo-Jewish "establishment," had issued a sharply anti-Zionist statement to the *Times*—thereby revealing an embarrassing ambivalence of Jewish attitude toward the Holy Land, and a seeming uncertainty of British footing on the Palestine question. Balfour, therefore, did not have to be convinced that Zionism now required an official imprimatur. As it happened, the foreign secretary's interest in Jewish nationalism was neither recent nor altogether opportunistic. As early as 1906, at his Manchester constituency, he had been the first of England's public figures to meet Weizmann. "It was from that talk with Weizmann that I saw that the Jewish form of patriotism was unique," he stated later. "Their love of country refused to be satisfied by the Uganda scheme. It was Weizmann's absolute refusal even to look at it that impressed me." The friendship between the two men was renewed in 1917, and Balfour's sympathy for Zionism evidently had not waned. Like Smuts and Lloyd George himself, the foreign secretary had been nurtured on the Old Testament, and his extensive study of Jewish history had filled him with inner remorse about Christendom's treatment of the Jews. "They have been exiled, scattered and oppressed," he told Harold Nicolson in 1917. "If we can find them an asylum, a safe home, in their native land, then the full flowering of their genius will burst forth and propagate." Imperial self-interest obviously was paramount in the government's calculations. Yet, in Balfour's case, a genuine vein of Zionist mysticism unquestionably strengthened commitment to the Jewish national home. In response, then, to an urgent appeal by Weizmann on June 17, 1917, the British statesman urged the Zionists themselves to formulate an appropriate declaration. He would submit it to the War Cabinet with his endorsement.

Weizmann's closest associates, Sacher and Sokolow, immediately launched into the preparation of a suitable text. With the War Cabinet anxious to legitimize its tenure in Palestine, the moment was ripe for a maximalist document. For his part, Sacher favored governmental recognition of Palestine as "a Jewish State and the National Home of the Jewish People." Sokolow, more cautious, would have limited the government's approbation to Palestine as the "National Home of the Jewish People." The compromise draft eventually reflected Sokolow's approach. Numerous consultations with Ormsby-Gore further modified the text. Yet even the final version, submitted on July 18, did not lack forthrightness. "His Majesty's Government," it stated, "accepts the principle that Palestine should be reconstituted as the National Home of the Jewish People. His Majesty's Government will use its best endeavours to secure achievement of this object and will discuss the necessary methods and means with the Zionist Organization." When the letter was formally discussed in a cabinet conference of September 3, it elicited the ministers' warm approval.

Ironically, the only forceful opposition came from the one Jew in the Lloyd George government, Edwin Montagu, secretary of state for India —and a cousin of Herbert Samuel. Although reared in affluence (his father was Lord Swaythling), Montagu had fought an uphill battle to escape his Orthodox Jewish origins and to win acceptance in the privileged circles of government. In this case, a "national home" for the Jews seemed to raise for him embarrassing questions of dual loyalty. "I view with horror the aspiration for a national entity," he had written Sir Eric Drummond on August 8, 1916. "Did I accept it, as a patriotic Englishman, I should resign my position on the Cabinet and declare myself neutral. . . ." Now, on September 3, 1917, Montagu insisted that a pro-Zionist statement would at once alarm the Moslems of India and embarrass the Jews of England. The vehemence of his opposition to Zionism as "a mischievous political creed" persuaded the cabinet to leave the matter unresolved for the time being.

Neither the Zionists nor their supporters in the government accepted the setback as more than temporary. Lloyd George confidently put the matter of the declaration on the agenda for the next cabinet session. Yet when the meeting took place on October 4, Montagu opposed the draft with even more intensity than before. "I understand the man almost wept," Weizmann wrote later. Montagu's opposition and that of his supporters, Lord Curzon and Gertrude Bell, had the effect not of changing the minds of Balfour, Smuts, Lloyd George, or other Zionist sympathizers, but of persuading them that a milder text was needed simply to dispose of the question. Even as Weizmann and his colleagues maintained their pressure on the government, therefore, Amery and Milner labored over a compromise formula—one that became the essential draft of the Balfour Declaration. The earlier phrase, "that Palestine should be reconstituted as the National Home" of the Jews, was dropped in favor of a somewhat more equivocal statement (p. 109). The Zionists were deeply chagrined by the alteration. Nevertheless, they were fearful of tampering with it.

Lloyd George was prepared at last to force the issue through. Before taking the final step, however, the prime minister was determined to win a firm commitment of diplomatic support for Zionist aspirations. It was by then open knowledge in Western circles that the very notion of a Jewish national home was wedded to the corollary of a British protectorate. Lloyd George accordingly required assurance that a declaration implying such a protectorate would not encounter serious opposition at the peace conference later. Ultimately, it was the prestige and influence of the American government that resolved the matter. Washington had not declared war on the Ottoman Empire, to be sure. Even so, the United States unquestionably would exert a major impact on all phases of the peace settlement, including the future of the Holy Land.

President Wilson could not have been ignorant of American Jewish sentiment by then; for in the United States, too, Jewish opinion was veering increasingly toward Zionism. Moreover, as it adopted this orientation, American Jewry was influenced by its new role as host to the Zionist movement's de facto headquarters "in exile." When the war first began in August 1914, a member of the Zionist Executive, Shmaryahu Levin, was en route from the United States to Europe. His ship turned back immediately and Levin remained in New York to establish a "Provisional Executive Committee for General Zionist Affairs." It was this committee's vigilant liaison that ultimately helped save the Yishuv. Its intercession with the State Department fortified Morgenthau's humanitarian efforts on behalf of Palestine Jewry. Additionally, the committee's president, Louis D. Brandeis, was a man of national prominence in American life; in 1916 he became the first Jewish appointee to the United States Supreme Court. It was at Weizmann's suggestion, then, and with Balfour's full concurrence, that Brandeis was asked to use his influence with the president on behalf of London's impending pro-Zionist statement. At first the jurist's efforts were unsuccessful. When the original draft declaration was brought to Wilson's attention on September 11, the president opposed it as too extensive a commitment. But the British persisted, and on October 6 London cabled Washington the more pallid Amery-Milner version. Wilson then dropped his objections. "I find in my pocket the memorandum you gave me about the Zionist movement," Wilson wrote Colonel House, his closest adviser, on October 13. "I am afraid I did not say to you that I concurred in the formula suggested [by London]. . . . I do, and would be obliged if you would let them know it." The moment House's cable arrived in London, on October 16, the pro-Zionist faction had what it needed.

The War Cabinet voted for the declaration on October 31, over Montagu's and Curzon's last forlorn objections. Significantly, the principal rationale by then was no longer the need to avert French participation in a Palestine condominium—Allenby's army was on the verge of conquering the Holy Land, and the issue unquestionably would be decided by the substantial presence of the Egyptian Expeditionary Force. Rather, it was the obsessive desire to win the friendship of world Jewry that influenced the War Cabinet's decision. Lloyd George was counting on this support. "The Zionist leaders," he wrote later, "gave us a definite promise that, if the Allies committed themselves to . . . a National Home for the Jews in Palestine, they would do their best to rally to the Allied cause . . . Jewish sentiment and support throughout the world. They kept their word in letter and spirit. . . ." Other factors similarly determined the cabinet's vote. One was the genuine personal affinity of Balfour (and Smuts and Lloyd George) for the Holy Land and the Jewish people. "Near the end of his days," wrote Lady Dugdale, Balfour's niece, "he said to me that on the whole he felt that what he had been able to do for the Jews had been the thing he looked back upon as the most worth doing." Others in the cabinet may have been animated by even more complex motives—for example, Protestant millennialism, an uneasy conscience about Jewish suffering, conceivably the need to endorse a humane and productive act in the midst of the holocaust of war.

The declaration itself seemed curiously bland, however, and devoid of religious or mystical overtones of any kind. It took the form of a letter on November 2 to Lord Rothschild, president of the British Zionist Federation, and stated:

> Dear Lord Rothschild, I have much pleasure in conveying to you, on behalf of His Majesty's Government, the following declaration of sympathy with Jewish Zionist aspirations which has been submitted to, and approved by, the Cabinet: "His Majesty's Government view with favour the establishment in Palestine of a national home for the Jewish people, and will use their best endeavours to facilitate the achievement of this object, it being clearly understood that nothing shall be done which may prejudice the civil and religious rights of existing non-Jewish communities in Palestine, or the rights and political status enjoyed by Jews in any other country." I should be grateful if you would bring this declaration to the knowledge of the Zionist Federation.

The original Zionist draft of the declaration had called for the reconstitution of Palestine "*as* [italics added] the National Home of the Jewish people." The phrase "national home," employed in both versions, actually was unknown in international usage. The Zionists had coined the expression at the 1897 Congress, to avoid the term "Jewish state," which the Turks might have found provocative, and Sokolow's draft in 1917 had followed this circumspect approach. Now, however, the Balfour version dispensed with the need for outlining the boundaries of a Jewish settlement *in* Palestine. The "national home" might be no more than a small enclave within the country. Only five years later, as shall be seen, the broad uplands of Transjordan were cut away, and fifteen years after that yet a further amputation would be proposed by a Royal Commission—all without violating the letter of the declaration. Moreover, the need to protect "the civil and religious rights of existing non-Jewish communities in Palestine" could, and ultimately would, be interpreted as justification for limiting, even foreclosing, Jewish immigration in order to placate Arab nationalism.

The eventual fate of the declaration was not necessarily consonant with the original intention of its authors, however. "My personal hope," Balfour told a friend in 1918, "is that the Jews will make good in Palestine and eventually found a Jewish State." That same year Lord Robert Cecil declared: "Our wish is that Arabian countries shall be for the Arabs, Armenia for the Armenians, and Judea for the Jews." In 1920, Churchill, who had served as minister of munitions when the Balfour Declaration was issued, spoke of "a Jewish State by the banks of the Jordan . . . which might comprise three or four million Jews." And in 1919, Smuts, also a former member of the War Cabinet, envisaged the rise of "a great Jewish State." Lloyd George was quite explicit in his description of the cabinet's proposal:

> It was contemplated that when the time arrived for according representative institutions in Palestine, if the Jews had meanwhile responded to the opportunity afforded them by the idea of a National Home and had become a definite majority of the inhabitants, then Palestine would thus become a Jewish Commonwealth. The notion that Jewish immigration would have to be artificially restricted in order to ensure that the Jews should be a permanent minority never entered into the heads of anyone engaged in framing the policy. That would have been regarded as unjust and as a fraud on the people to whom we were appealing.

It is worth assessing the effectiveness of the appeal to "world Jewry." The Jews of England were thrilled and grateful, as their public meetings throughout the country and their innumerable resolutions of thanks made evident. Heartened by this response, in turn, and intent upon duplicating it in other countries, the government established a special Jewish section within the department of information, staffing it primarily with Zionists. The department's task was to prepare literature for distribution in Jewish communities throughout the world. Copies of the British statement were circulated by the millions, including leaflets dropped from the air over German and Austrian towns. When news of the declaration reached Russia three weeks later, it evoked wild rejoicing. Huge, cheering crowds gathered outside the British consulates in the larger cities. Petitions and cables of gratitude flooded in on Balfour from Jewish communities as far removed as Shanghai, Alexandria, and Capetown.

If the War Cabinet's major objective was to swing "neutral" Jewish opinion toward Britain, it succeeded beyond all expectations. It was a hopeful omen, for example, that Salonica Jewry, formerly regarded as the "brain and nerve center" of the Young Turk movement, applauded the British gesture warmly. Indeed, so fearful were Britain's enemies of the propaganda value to be reaped by the declaration that belated efforts were launched to match it. In Constantinople, Talaat Pasha, the powerful minister of the interior, announced his intention of canceling restrictions on Jewish immigration to Palestine. In January 1918, at the suggestion of Emmanuel Carasso, a Jewish deputy in the Ottoman parliament, Talaat approved the establishment of a chartered company to foster Jewish settlement in Palestine on an autonomous basis. In Berlin, two days later, Undersecretary of State von dem Busschi-Haddenhousen formally endorsed the Turkish proposal. To sustain the momentum, meanwhile, Talaat invited leading German and Austrian Jews to Constantinople to discuss Jewish land colonization and autonomy in Palestine. In August, the Turks sent Chief Rabbi Chaim Nahum on a tour of the Netherlands and Sweden to recruit Jewish support for Turkey.

Yet it is doubtful if these matching offers significantly influenced the commitment of Jews living within the various belligerent nations. One of London's expectations was that the Balfour Declaration, through its impact on Jews abroad, would meaningfully enhance the Allied cause. Thus, embarking on a redoubled effort to mobilize Jewish support against the Central Powers, Weizmann and Brandeis cabled friends in Russia, entreating them to intercede with the new Bolshevik government on behalf of the common Entente war effort. Ultimately, this was wasted effort. The War Cabinet's notion that Russian Jewry could exert meaningful pressure on the emergent Soviet regime was totally naïve; the fifteen or twenty Jewish Bolsheviks possessed of any real influence were entirely hostile to Jewish nationalism. The Jews of Germany and the Dual Monarchy, meanwhile, remained steadfastly loyal to their countries. The Zionists among them (Bodenheimer, Warburg, Hantke, Franz Oppenheimer) sought only to persuade their governments to match Britain's offer—and in this they were unsuccessful. The Jews of France, more limited in number than their British counterparts, responded to news of Balfour's declaration with a certain mild enthusiasm. Henri Bergson, Edmond Fleg, and other eminent French Jewish figures expressed their satisfaction. But the official Consistoire Central des Juifs Français maintained an ambiguous posture on the subject of Jewish nationalism.

There was nothing equivocal about the reaction of American Jewry, to be sure. Its members hardly were less exhilarated by news of the declaration than were the Jews of Britain and Russia. Among them, too, public expressions and demonstrations of gratitude were evoked in the same full measure, with large parades in New York, Philadelphia, Chicago, and other major cities. But the United States was already at war. The hated Russian tsar had fallen. Nothing remained to inhibit the enthusiastic participation of American Jews in their war effort, and nothing further was required to stimulate it. The sum of Jewish reaction was well described by Sir Ronald Storrs in 1937: "The American loan [to Britain] went much as had been expected; no sympathies for Britain accrued from the Soviet (which shortly denounced Zionism as a capitalist contrivance); and the loyalty of German Jewry remained unshaken—with the subsequent reward that the world is now contemplating."

THE JEWISH LEGION
AND THE LIBERATION OF THE YISHUV

Perhaps the one tangible military result of the declaration was Jabotinsky's belated success in organizing a Jewish legion. With the overthrow of the tsar in March 1917, Jewish opposition to the plan began to weaken. Moreover, in late spring, the imminence of a British offensive in Palestine largely dispelled fears of Turkish reprisals. In the interval, Jabotinsky had persuaded Lord Derby, the war secretary, that Zionist and British interests would equally be served by a Jewish military unit entrenched in Palestine. In August, therefore, Lloyd George and Balfour officially confirmed the decision to establish a special Jewish infantry regiment, which would be assigned for combat exclusively on the Palestine front.

At this juncture the task of organizing the regiment's first unit, the Thirty-eighth Battalion of Royal Fusiliers, was given to Colonel John Patterson, former commander of the Zion Mule Corps. Patterson was an Irish Protestant. The millennial purpose he discerned in his special relationship with the Jews was not unlike Balfour's. "Indeed," he wrote later, "by many it is held that the British people are none other than some of the lost tribes; moreover, we have taken so much of Jewish national life for our own, [due] to our strong Biblical leanings, that the Jews can never feel while with us that they are among entire strangers." Predictably, the colonel's first recruits were some 120 veterans of the original Mule Corps. This time, too, with the active proselytizing efforts of Jabotinsky, who had volunteered as a private but later was promoted to lieutenant and Patterson's aide-de-camp, the unit's members were supplemented from the immigrant Jewry of London's East End. The volunteers—stunted, ill-nourished, ghetto-bred—were less than impressive fighting material at first. Yet basic training had its effect. When at last, in February 1918, the Thirty-eighth Royal Fusiliers marched with gleaming bayonets through the City of London and Whitechapel, even those who initially had opposed the Legion were consumed with joy and pride. The Lord Mayor took the unit's salute in front of the Mansion House.

The recruitment effort was not limited to England. Patterson and Jabotinsky ensured that circulars were distributed among Jewish communities in North and South America. The Balfour Declaration had been issued by then, the tsar had abdicated, the Labor Zionist parties no longer actively opposed the Legion, and in the United States and Canada volunteers soon began registering at British consular and recruitment offices. Among the first of 6,500 to enlist were Ben-Gurion and Ben-Zvi, whom Djemal Pasha had exiled from Palestine in 1915 and who had traveled halfway around the world to New York. They were sent on now with the others to basic training camp in Nova Scotia, and by August 1918 were on their way across the Atlantic as members of the Thirty-ninth and Fortieth battalions of the Royal Fusiliers. After further preparation in England, the troops were loaded on transports and escorted across the Mediterranean by Japanese destroyers. The initial vanguard of the Thirty-eighth

Royal Fusiliers disembarked at Alexandria as early as March 1918 and received training outside Cairo.

Their arrival was hardly premature. During 1917 the circumstances of the Yishuv in Palestine had become critical. In late March of that year, with the British offensive anticipated at any time, Djemal Pasha ordered the evacuation of all remaining Jewish inhabitants of Jaffa and Tel Aviv. Even Jews who had applied for Ottoman citizenship earlier were suspect as potential traitors. Driven out of their lodgings, they crowded now onto wagons or donkeys and fled toward the Judean settlements for temporary shelter. Later the refugees were obliged to move even farther north, toward the Jewish farm colonies of Galilee. Employment and food were in desperately short supply well before this influx from the coast. The newcomers rapidly faced starvation. Many hundreds were compelled to forage for roots. Not a few Jewish girls remained alive by selling themselves to Turkish and German soldiers quartered in the Galilee.

It was in October 1917, too, that Allenby launched his invasion of Palestine. The initial phase of the campaign was successful beyond the general's highest expectations. Augmented by tens of thousands of Commonwealth troops, the Egyptian Expeditionary Force struck quickly into the interior of the country, overrunning Beersheba, capturing Jaffa on November 16, and finally taking Jerusalem three weeks later. On December 11, 1917, Allenby himself marched bareheaded into the historic capital to address a gathering of Moslem, Christian, and Jewish notables which had been convened on the steps of the Tower of David. "We have come," he declared, "not as conquerors, but as deliverers. It is our intention to open a new era of brotherhood and peace in the Holy Land." It was the anniversary of Chanukkah, commemorating the Maccabean triumph that had liberated ancient Palestine and opened a renewed era of Jewish national glory. Now, in December 1917, as menorah candles gleamed in Jerusalem and in Jewish homes throughout the world, observant Jews everywhere uttered prayers of gratitude for an astonishing coincidence.

The rejoicing was premature. With the winter rains, Allenby's campaign stalled, and Jews in northern Palestine remained hostages under Turkish military rule. Their last remnants of security were gone by then, for Ottoman troops began indiscriminately confiscating Jewish farms, and army deserters by the thousands ran amok, terrorizing Jewish settlements, looting property, even killing. It was during this final rictus of Turkish occupation in Palestine that the Yishuv endured its worst torment. By the time the British resumed their offensive in the spring, and ultimately overran the last of the enemy's forces in September 1918, the Jewish population had been reduced from its prewar figure of 85,000 to less than 55,000. Of those lost, between 8,000 and 10,000 had perished of hunger, illness, or exposure.

The Jewish Legion shared in the 1918 campaign. The moment its troops set foot in the Holy Land, Jabotinsky urgently set about recruiting younger Palestinian Jews who had escaped the exodus or the Turkish press gangs. Only a few hundred of these survivors were fit for action, but they were

SEPTEMBER 30, 1918

Damascus

MEDITERRANEAN SEA

Acre

al-Quneitra

LAKE
GALILEE

Haifa

Ezra'a

Nazareth

Dera'a

Beisan

Jordan River

Nablus

SEPTEMBER 19, 1918

es-Salt

Jaffa

Ramle

Amman

Lydda

Jericho

Iskelon

Jerusalem

OCTOBER 28,
1917

Gaza

Hebron

DEAD SEA

Rafa

Kerak

Khalasa

Beersheba

EGYPT

Wadi Araba

PALESTINE-EGYPTIAN FRONTIER

Hesa

Jurf

SINAI
PENINSULA

Ma'an

THE PALESTINE BATTLEGROUND

▬▬ British front lines   +++ Railways

ELEVATION

☐ Under 600 feet

■ Over 600 feet

0   MILES   30

GULF OF AQABA   Aqaba

among the Legion's most enthusiastic members. In the spring of 1918 the Jewish units initially were assigned to patrol the Jordan Valley against a threatened Turkish counterattack. Later, after repeated appeals by Patterson, the Legion was permitted to join Allenby's climactic autumn offensive. At this point, its ranks numbered 5,000, a sixth of the British army of occupation, and half the size of Feisal's Arab irregulars at their median strength in 1918. It was distinctly more than a token or symbolic force. In truth, its role in the conquest of Palestine eventually signified as much as the ordeal of the early Zionist pioneers, and hardly less than the Balfour Declaration itself, in reinforcing the Jews' claims to their national home. Once achieved under British patronage and the flag of liberation, that armed, self-proclaimed, and militant Jewish bridgehead would not easily be foreclosed.

CHAPTER VI THE ESTABLISHMENT OF THE MANDATE

Rarely had the fruits of military victory been as palpable as those savored by England when the fighting stopped. By December 1918, 200,000 Commonwealth troops had planted the Union Jack in Syria, western Turkey, Palestine, Mesopotamia, and lower Iran, a swath of territory encompassing all the historic land routes between the Mediterranean and the Indian Ocean. The French, to be sure, had established a civil administration of their own in the Syrian coastal littoral, even as the Hashemite Arabs managed their own political affairs in the interior. But if this occupation disposition seemed roughly to approximate the Sykes-Picot Agreement, it was an arrangement that Britain, in its incomparable bargaining position, was determined to revise. "When Clemenceau came to London after the War [in December 1918]," Lloyd George wrote later, "I drove with him to the French Embassy through cheering crowds. After we reached the Embassy he asked me what it was I specifically wanted from the French. I instantly replied that I wanted Mosul attached to Iraq, and Palestine from Dan to Beersheba under British control. Without any hesitation he agreed." Indeed, the French premier had little choice.

While rival French and Arab claims for the governance of Syria still awaited solution at the Paris Conference, there were no disagreements in principle that Syria was to be allocated to France as a special mandatory responsibility, that Iraq was to be awarded to Britain, and that Palestine, too, now would become a British mandate. The Supreme Council of the Peace Conference formally validated this understanding at San Remo on April 25, 1920. On the other hand, the one—non-Turkish—Middle Eastern boundary issue that had yet to be settled related to Palestine. Neither the British nor the Jews succeeded in achieving precisely the configuration for the Holy Land they would have chosen. On the basis of exhaustive geographic and geological surveys, Weizmann and his Zionist colleagues asked the Supreme Council for a Palestine bounded in the north by the slopes of the Lebanon range, the headwaters of the Jordan, and the crest of Mount Hermon; in the east by the Transjordan-Mesopotamian desert; and in the south by the Gulf of Aqaba. The British for their part could only favor a demand to enlarge and enrich their future mandate. Their general staff continually stressed the importance of extending the frontiers of Palestine northeastward to protect the rail routes from the Mediterranean; while Balfour, in turn, supported Zionist claims to the water resources of the upper Jordan and Litani rivers.

Yet the French hardly were prepared to accept these desiderata without qualification. Rather, they endorsed the Lebanese contention that the "historic and natural" frontiers of Greater Lebanon included the sources of the Jordan. In a meeting with Lloyd George on March 20, 1919, Foreign Minister Stéphen Pichon coldly turned down a British appeal to revise the Sykes-Picot boundaries and argued instead that the northern Galilee, with its network of Jewish settlements, must remain within the Syrian enclave. It was a literalist interpretation of the 1916 agreement that the British plainly could not accept, for their troops even then were garrisoned throughout all of Galilee as part of "Occupied Territory South." The impasse continued until February 1920.

Then, at last, in response to Britain's withdrawal of support for Feisal's demands in Syria, the new Millerand government accepted essentially the current military boundaries in Palestine. Conversely, the maximalist frontiers requested by the Zionists, and until then advocated by the British themselves, simply were ignored. Lloyd George, no less than his French counterpart, was prepared now to accept the status quo. As London saw it, buffer protection of Egypt, including the use of Haifa as a Mediterranean naval base, and the construction of a railroad and pipeline from Iraq to the sea, probably could be met within the existing Palestine borders. The Jews admittedly had been useful in fulfilling these objectives, but the broadly projected Zionist borders that would have guaranteed Palestine economic viability were of secondary importance to the British. On December 4, the two Allied prime ministers reached a final understanding on the boundary issue.

The accord represented a painful setback for the Jews. To the north and northeast, the country was deprived of its most important potential water resources, including the Litani River, a key fount of the Jordan, the spring arising from Mount Hermon, and the greater part of the Yarmuk. The boundaries similarly ignored the historic entity of Palestine—"from Dan to Beersheba"—as envisaged in the original negotiations leading to the Balfour Declaration. Moreover, by failing to approximate any natural geographic frontiers, the borders left the country perennially exposed to armed invasion. This heritage of economic and military vulnerability was to curse the Palestine mandate, and later the entire Middle East, for decades to come.

HIGH AND EARLY HOPES IN THE HOLY LAND

Notwithstanding the territorial disappointment, the Zionists had grounds for optimism on the future of the National Home. Nor were they dismayed even by the wretched physical condition of the Holy Land and its Jewish settlement. When Allenby's army occupied Palestine in 1917–18, it took possession of the single most desolated province of the Ottoman Levant. Arid, malarial, inhabited by a shrunken population of some 560,000 Arabs and 55,000 Jews near the war's end, the country had been starved by Allied blockade, ravaged and ruined by Turkish depredations. Scores of villages had been laid waste, trees and orange groves damaged, public security all but extinguished. The British thereupon gave their first and most urgent attention to food supplies, which Allenby ordered imported directly from Egypt. The American Near East Relief soon followed with shipments of clothing and medicines for the Christian and Moslem populations. The Zionist Organization and Hadassah, its women's counterpart, matched these efforts for the Jews.

The next priority clearly was to reorganize Palestine's administration and revive its economy. Under Sir Arthur Money, Allenby's military administrator in Palestine, and later, under Money's successor, Sir Louis Bols, the country was resected into districts, each under a British military governor, each operating under regulations issued by central departments of finance, justice, health, agriculture, education, and public works. British officers and civil servants held the senior administrative posts; Palestinian Arabs and Jews served in the lower echelons. The system worked well enough to become the essential pattern of the later mandatory regime (p. 131). Measures also were taken to improve the health and sanitation of Palestine, as cisterns were dug and hospitals and clinics opened. With the purchasing power of a large British army coursing through cities and towns, the nation's economic circumstances markedly improved. The atmosphere in Palestine for the time being was tranquil, even hopeful.

So, initially, were the prospects for the Zionists. For them, the Balfour Declaration was less a definitive statement than a skeleton of principles that now had to be fleshed out. To that end, the commission they prepared to dispatch to Palestine was intended to advise the military authorities in their relations with the Yishuv (p. 119). A few months later, the Zionists went so far as to draft a "constitution" under which Palestine would be reconstituted as a Jewish Commonwealth. It was evident, then, as the peace conference approached, that the Zionists intended to give the term "national home" a more vigorous, even aggressive, character, and to dispel some of its ambiguity—for which their own initial Sokolow version, written in the summer of 1917, was at least partially responsible. On November 18, 1918, they submitted their new draft proposal. It stated forthrightly that "the establishment of a National Home for the Jewish People . . . is understood to mean that the country of Palestine should be placed under such political, economic and moral conditions as will favour the increase of the Jewish population, so that in accordance with the principle of democracy it may ultimately develop into a Jewish Commonwealth, it being clearly understood . . ." (here followed the two provisos inserted into the text of the Balfour Declaration). The American Jewish Congress, meeting on December 16, 1917, adopted a similar resolution, as did Jewish congresses in Palestine, Austria-Hungary, Poland, South Africa, and elsewhere. Even the moderate Achad HaAm endorsed it. At first, too, the Foreign

Office seemed equally prepared to accept this Zionist interpretation of the original Balfour document. As shall be seen, it was not until the Churchill White Paper of 1922 that the British government felt constrained decisively to limit Zionist intentions (p. 127).

Rather, at the outset Lloyd George and Balfour made clear that they had accepted the Zionist cause as unshakable on its own merits, no less than as a *raison d'être* for a British mandate. "It is not enough that the Jews should have access to Palestine," stated Balfour in a memorandum of August 11, 1919, "but that their homeland be a viable one." As far back as December 1917 the foreign secretary had approved the departure of a Zionist Commission for Palestine to organize relief work and supervise repair of damage to the Jewish colonies. Indeed, as a special token of official approbation, Weizmann, the commission chairman, had been received by King George V on March 7, 1918. Including in its membership Zionist representatives from France and Italy, the commission embarked for Palestine later in the month. It was immediately given official status as an advisory body to the military government in all matters relating to Jews—precisely as the Zionists had demanded.

Nor were serious objections to the Zionist homeland expressed in other quarters. Although Prime Minister Millerand of France rejected British— and Zionist—claims to the headwaters of the Jordan, he did not dream of challenging the notion of a Jewish national home. Neither did the Italian government, despite its continuing resentment at a unilateral British protectorate over the Holy Land. President Wilson remained firmly committed to the Balfour Declaration throughout the Peace Conference, "and so far I have found no one who is seriously opposing the purpose which it embodies," he assured Felix Frankfurter, then a leading American Zionist. In entrusting Palestine to Britain, moreover, the Allied statesmen at San Remo incorporated into their allocation award the verbatim text of the Balfour Declaration. The basic moral support of the Western governments appeared firmly established, as a result.

For a while, too, the friendship of the Hashemite Arab leadership seemed equally beyond question. During the war, the British failed to sense any latent inconsistencies between their patronage of an Arab revolt and their encouragement of Zionist aspirations. It is recalled that in McMahon's crucial letter to Sherif Hussein, on October 24, 1915, the British high commissioner excluded from the area of Arab independence the land west of the "districts" of Damascus, Homs, Hama, and Aleppo. A controversy arose at war's end, and remained unsettled for years afterward, on the status of Palestine in this allocation. The wording here hardly was precise, for "district" was not a Turkish administrative term. Was McMahon referring to "vilayets"? Eventually that became the Arab contention. Had it been accepted, the strip of territory detached from Arab rule unquestionably would have been too narrow to include Palestine. The Jews, of course, no less than McMahon himself and the entire British government, took the opposite position, insisting that the term "district" had been used simply in a loose sense, meaning vicinity; and thus a line drawn west of the vicinities of

Damascus, Homs, Hama, and Aleppo, separating this territory from the coastal region, apparently excluded Palestine from Arab administration.

In January 1918, after the issuance of the Balfour Declaration, Commander D. H. Hogarth, research director of the Arab Bureau in Cairo, was dispatched to Jidda to clarify for Hussein the implications of the Zionist program. Reassuring the sherif that Arab freedom would be safeguarded, Hogarth added, meaningfully: "In this connection, the friendship of world Jewry to the Arab cause is equivalent to support in all states where Jews have political influence. The leaders of the movement are determined to bring about the success of Zionism by friendship and cooperation with the Arabs, and such an offer is not one to be lightly thrown aside." The hint was received with enthusiasm by Hussein. Sensing the potential financial advantages of Arab-Jewish cooperation, the sherif issued the Jews several warmly phrased invitations to return to their "sacred and beloved homeland."

For its part, the Zionist leadership was not oblivious to the need for manageable relations with the Arabs. In the summer of 1918, Weizmann conferred with a group of Syrian émigrés living in Cairo and used the fullest measure of his charm and persuasiveness to emphasize Zionist intentions of respecting Arab rights and sensibilities. The Syrians were neither charmed nor persuaded. They countered, rather, with a suggestion for the proportional representation of the Arab majority in any future Palestine government. Weizmann in turn was so unsettled by this response that he decided no time was to be lost before meeting personally with Emir Feisal, Hussein's son and leader of the Arab Revolt. To that end, the Zionist leader departed on a ten-day journey to Aqaba, at the entrance to the Red Sea. He was received cordially, even lavishly, with a sumptuous banquet prepared in his honor. Weizmann wrote afterward:

> I explained to [Feisal] . . . our desire to do everything in our power to allay Arab fears and susceptibilities, and our hope that he would lend us his powerful moral support. . . . I stressed the fact that there was a great deal of room in the country if intensive development were applied, and that the lot of the Arabs would be greatly improved through our work there. With all this I found the Emir in full agreement. . . .

Feisal promised to convey the gist of the talk to his father. "The first meeting in the desert laid the foundations of a lifelong friendship," Weizmann recalled.

It was a relationship that appeared to offer significant possibilities of cooperation. Embroiled in a diplomatic struggle with the French over the Arab role in Syria, and convinced that the Jews possessed alliance value in that battle, Feisal was prepared to reaffirm his sympathy with the Zionist movement. In December 1918, Sykes brought the two men together once more in London. Each again expressed mutual understanding and support for the other's position. It was thereupon agreed that all water and farm-boundary questions should be settled directly between the Arabs and the Jews. The atmosphere was benign. At a luncheon given in his honor by

Lord Rothschild, the emir reminded his listeners (in a draft address written by T. E. Lawrence) that "no true Arab can be suspicious or afraid of Jewish nationalism. . . . We are demanding Arab freedom, and we should show ourselves unworthy of it, if we did not now, as I do, say to the Jews—welcome back home—and cooperate with them to the limit of the Arab State."

These discussions and exchanges of courtesies ultimately were formalized in a document signed by Weizmann and Feisal, a pact envisaging a common stance at the Peace Conference. It declared:

> His Royal Highness the Emir Feisal, representing and acting on behalf of the Arab Kingdom of Hejaz, and Dr. Chaim Weizmann, representing and acting on behalf of the Zionist Organization, mindful of the racial kinship and ancient bonds existing between the Arabs and the Jewish people, and realising that the surest means of working out the consummation of their national aspirations is through the closest possible collaboration in the development of the Arab State and Palestine, and being desirous further of confirming the good understanding which exists between them, have agreed upon the following Articles. . . .

And the most important of those articles guaranteed the Jews their right of free immigration into Palestine and settlement on the land. It was accompanied by a reciprocal assurance that Arab tenant farmers would be safeguarded on their plots and assisted in their economic development. Significantly, one of the final clauses provided for British arbitration of all disputes between the two peoples—unmistakable evidence of London's role in stage-managing the agreement. The "treaty" was signed on January 4, 1919. On his own, however, Feisal attached a codicil below the signatures on the Arab version: "Provided the Arabs obtain their independence as demanded in my Memorandum dated the 4th of January, 1919, to the Foreign Office of the Government of Great Britain, I shall concur in the above article." Otherwise, the compact would be null and void, the addendum declared.

A week later, the Zionist leaders offered the Arabs a number of vital concessions, including a free zone at Haifa port and a joint Arab-Jewish free harbor on the Gulf of Aqaba. When Feisal in turn appeared before the Peace Conference on February 6 to demand Arab independence, he concurred that Palestine should be invested with its own guaranteed status as the enclave of the "Zionist Jews." As it turned out, however, Feisal expected more than a territorial quid pro quo from the Jews. He also expected Zionist diplomatic support against the French. Two weeks before, the emir's key advisers had approached the Zionist leaders with a proposal for an Arab-Jewish entente, a "Semitic" understanding in preference to the Western mandates. Together, it was suggested, the two peoples would oppose French claims to the Syrian interior. The initial Zionist reaction to this overture was noncommittal. Feisal's advisers persisted, returning to the formula continually. Embarrassed, finally, Weizmann asked his Arab friends at least not to interfere with the French regime in the Syrian "littoral."

It soon became evident that Weizmann was unwilling to act independently of his British patrons, who had made specific commitments of their own to the French. By mid-1919, as a result, Feisal terminated his public meetings with the Zionists and asked them to desist from releasing statements invoking his name. His January 4 "treaty" with Weizmann was not published, and the Zionists, respecting Feisal's wishes, withheld comment on it for many years. Increasingly disillusioned with the Zionist connection, the emir chose now to envisage the Jewish National Home as merely a subprovince within the Arab kingdom. "But when some Zionists speak about Palestine becoming as Jewish as England is English," he declared, ". . . they are really talking unreasonably." To David Yellin, a Zionist emissary who visited him in July 1919, Feisal suggested that the Jews should negotiate henceforth directly with the Palestine Arabs. It would be best, too, he warned, if the Zionists moderated their claims in Palestine and agreed instead to regard the Holy Land as an integral part of Greater Syria. In late autumn of 1919, Feisal ceased public communication with the Zionist leadership altogether. His policy of invoking Jewish cooperation for Arab diplomatic purposes in Syria manifestly had failed.

THE END OF THE MILITARY REGIME, THE REFORMULATION OF THE MANDATE

The administration of Palestine, meanwhile, began taking shape as a somewhat unimaginative collection of lower-rung professional functionaries who had been assembled hurriedly from the British army and the Egyptian civil service. Because their connections essentially were with the Arabs, most of these officials were convinced that Moslem friendship alone should be the central preoccupation of their government's policy. The Jews sensed—indeed, exaggerated—this combination of mediocrity and philo-Arabism. In an aggrieved letter to Balfour, Weizmann insisted that the government's approach was "fraught with grave danger" for the Jews. "The present system tends . . . to level down the Jew politically to the status of the native," he argued, "and in many cases the English Administration follows the convenient rule of looking on the Jews as so many natives." If the policy continued, it would "tend towards the creation of an Arab and not a Jewish Palestine." Frequently, too, Menachem Ussishkin (Weizmann's successor in 1919 as chairman of the Zionist Commission) and other—less than reticent—east European Zionists provoked British dislike by their urgent insistence upon employment for Jews in the public services, an end to restrictions on Jewish immigration and land purchases, and the immediate fulfillment of other Zionist demands. Sir Ronald Storrs commented ruefully later that "a people can be at once bitterly wronged and yet withal so maddeningly tiresome as sometimes to annihilate surprise, though never regret, for their suffering." Storrs and other British officials thereafter took refuge from this pressure by adopting a stiffly formal approach to the Zionists.

As early as June 8, 1919, Sir Arthur Money, Allenby's military administrator for Palestine, warned that "fear and distrust of Zionist aims grow daily [among the Arabs]. . . . A British mandate for Palestine on the lines of the Zionist programme will mean the indefinite retention in the country of a military force considerably greater than that now in Palestine." As if to confirm his warning, barbed Arab newspaper editorials, public Arab threats, and instances of unrest in Palestine Arab towns grew each month. In February 1920 a party of Arab raiders attacked the Jewish colonies of Metulla and Tel Chai along Palestine's northern border, in a twilight area between the British and French zones of occupation. Among those who were killed defending the outposts was Joseph Trumpeldor, wartime leader of the Zion Mule Corps. Shocked at the loss of this Zionist folk hero, and deeply alarmed for the future, Weizmann warned Money's successor, Sir Louis Bols, that far worse trouble was afoot. Bols was inclined to minimize the danger. But in March 1920 the Syrian National Congress, in a calculated gesture of repudiation toward the French, offered Feisal the throne of a united Syria, including Palestine.

More ominously yet, it was the season of Nebi Musa, a traditional Arab counterpart to Easter and Passover, when devout Moslems traveled in pilgrimage on the Jericho road to the grave of Moses (an Islamic as well as a Hebrew patriarch). The Arab revelers arrived in Jerusalem on April 4. Soon a large crowd gathered to hear a nationalist harangue by agitators, not all of them local, who extolled the name of Feisal. Their purpose clearly was to influence the Allies, who were scheduled to dispose of the mandates in San Remo within the next fortnight. The crowd became unruly, the Arab police joined in the applause, and violence began. During the next three hours, 160 Jews were wounded. Eventually British troops arrived and quelled the disturbances. The next morning, however, instigators who had been detained overnight were released, and attacks on the Jews promptly resumed. Order was not restored until the third day. A number of Jews and Arabs had been killed by then, and several hundred wounded. The aftermath of the bloodletting was as unnerving to the Zionists as the violence itself. The Arab mayor of Jerusalem was dismissed, to be sure, and two leading agitators were given stiff prison sentences. But the majority of Arab rioters received only light jail terms, while Vladimir Jabotinsky and several of his colleagues, who had organized a Jewish self-defense group during the turmoil, were sentenced by a military court to fifteen years' imprisonment.

Thereupon, in England as in the Jewish world, the reaction both to the violence and to the disparity of sentences was so uproarious that the government promptly convened an official court of inquiry. Throughout the hearings in Jerusalem, the officers of the military administration defended their conduct, insisting that Zionist provocation alone had inflamed the Arabs. The Jews in turn accused the mandatory government of complicity, of encouraging Moslem nationalist unrest. At this point, too, Colonel Richard Meinertzhagen, chief intelligence officer in Cairo, astounded his superiors by fully endorsing the Zionist accusations. So shocking was this indictment that the Palestine military administration was seriously compromised now before British public opinion. Thus, on April 29, 1920, less than a week following the Supreme Council's allocation of the Palestine mandate to Britain, London announced the imminent dismantling of the military regime in the Holy Land in favor of a provisional civil administration.

It was in San Remo, a day before the assignment of the mandates, that Herbert Samuel was informed of his selection by Lloyd George as civil high commissioner for Palestine. The choice was not illogical in view of Samuel's record as a Liberal party leader and former cabinet member. He was known, too, as a loyal Jew and Zionist, and this reputation seemingly emphasized the government's commitment to the Jewish National Home. The appointment obviously was not without its risks. Feisal regarded it as a provocation of the Arabs. So did Allenby, who warned that violence would follow. When, therefore, Samuel arrived in Jerusalem on June 30, 1920, it was deemed advisable to have him escorted from the railroad station to Government House by a sizable contingent of armored cars, and accompanied everywhere by detectives.

These misgivings and precautions soon appeared unwarranted. Most of Samuel's initial appointments aroused enthusiasm among Jews and Arabs alike. They included the able and progressive Wyndham Deedes as chief secretary; Norman Bentwich, a distinguished (Jewish) barrister as attorney general; Sir Ronald Storrs, retained as governor of Jerusalem as a symbol of impartiality; and experienced senior army officers brought over from Egypt as administrators of the Jaffa and Haifa districts. Well received, too, were Samuel's first executive directives: to ascertain landholdings by a cadastral survey; to establish credit banks; to undertake a large program of public works, including highway and railroad construction, telegraph and telephone lines, and swamp drainage. The Zionists, of course, were particularly gratified by Samuel's firm open-door policy on immigration. In the opening years of his administration, the influx of Jews surpassed all earlier waves (Chapter VII). The high commissioner's extensive connections in the British government also were Palestine's good fortune. He got what he wanted from London; his budgets generally were approved. Personally, the man all but radiated fairness and gentle courtesy. His very physical presence—tall, handsome, courtly—awed and impressed those who met him. Bentwich recalled that even Arab nationalists respected Samuel: " 'Nafsu Sharif!' they would say, 'his self is honourable.' "

But this very impartiality, as some Zionists had feared, proved to be the high commissioner's Achilles' heel. "All my life a convinced Liberal," Samuel wrote later, " . . . I was the last man to take a hand in any policy of oppression. . . . Nothing could be worse than if it were to appear that the one thing the Jewish people had learnt from the centuries of their own oppression was the way to oppress others." It was his obsession with fairness that influenced the high commissioner to appoint Ernest T. Richmond, a committed anti-Zionist, as formulator-planner of the administration's Arab policy; to withhold a large block of state land from Jewish purchase in the Beisan area; and to establish rigorous procedures for approving Arab land transfers to Jews. Far from placating Arab nationalism, however, these conciliatory gestures apparently encouraged it. Throughout 1921, Arab restiveness in Palestine grew. Some of it could be attributed to events in Syria. In July 1920 the French had brutally liquidated Feisal's self-proclaimed kingdom. As a consequence, Arab officials in Feisal's short-lived regime suddenly found themselves without employment or national-ist outlet. Palestine became their surrogate. Other, not less fundamental, reasons for local unrest, however, could be traced to the native politics of Arab Palestine itself (Chapter VIII). Renewed troubles accordingly began in Jaffa on May 1, 1921, when a ragtag group of Jewish Communists brashly marched through the center of town in the wake of a Zionist labor parade. The incident served the Arab nationalists as a useful pretext. They rioted, violence extended immediately to the countryside, and soon Petach Tikvah and other Jewish farm colonies were besieged. By the time British troops finally suppressed the last attack at the end of the week, forty-seven Jews and forty-eight Arabs had been killed and several hun-dred others of both peoples wounded. In the shocked aftermath of the bloodletting, a commission of inquiry was immediately appointed to con-duct hearings under the chairmanship of Sir Thomas Haycraft, chief justice of Palestine. Thereafter, the full spectrum of Arab grievances was ventilated, including the repugnance felt by Moslems for Zionist social ideals and the disquiet shared by all Arabs at mounting Jewish immigra-tion.

The commission's final report made little effort to veil its essential sym-pathy for Arab resentment. More alarming, from the Zionist viewpoint, was Samuel's decision temporarily to concede Arab demands by stopping Jewish immigration. The ban was lifted shortly, in July 1921, but under more rigid controls, including a guarantee of available employment. The very notion of "artificial" quotas deeply rankled the Zionists, who were certain now that the measures foreshadowed a policy of British retrench-ment on the Jewish National Home. They were not wrong. Although at London's insistence the text of the Balfour Declaration had been incor-porated directly into the San Remo mandatory award, in Britain itself by late 1921 growing reservations were being expressed at the government's pro-Zionist policy. Numerous former officials of the defunct Palestine military government, including several recently cashiered army personnel, volunteered as advisers to the Arab delegation that had arrived in London to protest the Jewish National Home. Their most useful weapon was the anxiety of the British people to demobilize their far-flung military units and to reduce imperial expenditures. A violent uprising in the Iraqi mandate in 1920, suppressed only at great cost, had aroused misgivings that were further exacerbated now by the riots in Palestine. At this point, Lord Northcliffe's influential chain of newspapers urged the government to drop the Palestine responsibility like a hot potato. The warning was echoed by Sir William Joynson-Hicks and a small group of fellow members of the House of Commons. To the Lloyd George government it was evident that a formula would have to be devised to ensure security and order in the Holy Land, lest Parliament reject the mandate altogether.

In the spring of 1921, as it happened, Colonial Secretary Winston Churchill summoned a gathering of leading military and imperial officials to Cairo to formulate a new approach to the unsettled Iraqi mandate. Churchill's visit also provided a logical occasion to explore a Palestine settlement. In late March the colonial secretary journeyed on to the Holy Land. There, to Jew and Arab alike, he firmly reiterated his support of the Jewish National Home. Yet his tour also resulted in the separation of Transjordan from Palestine, and a "reclarification" of the Balfour Declaration. Nominally within the boundaries of the Palestine mandate, Transjordan was a high plateau land—the biblical Edom—inhabited by some 300,000 Arab peasants and seminomads. With the end of the war, this entire region east of the Jordan River was included within the Arab sphere, for a vague understanding existed that it was reserved to the Arabs by the Hussein-McMahon correspondence. No attempt was made by Feisal to administer the area, however, and following his involuntary departure from Syria in the summer of 1920, Transjordan was reduced entirely to a no-man's land. Soon Bedouin attacks on the inhabited Jewish areas west of the Jordan threatened to get out of hand. To pacify the territory, Samuel received approval from London to dispatch a few officials across the river; it was hoped that they would guide the Arabs to self-government. The effort failed. Beyond the town limits of Keraq and Amman, lawlessness continued unchecked.

It was at this juncture, in the late summer of 1920, that Emir Abdullah, the sherif's oldest son, appeared on the fringes of Transjordan with his retinue. He was en route to Syria to help "restore" his brother Feisal to power. By March of 1921 Abdullah had succeeded in pushing on to Amman. Churchill's Middle East conference was under way in Cairo at the time, and news of Abdullah's presence east of the Jordan aroused dismay among the assembled officials. It was apparent that the little emir would have to be stopped before he provoked a crisis between France and England. Thereupon T. E. Lawrence and Churchill revived an idea that had been discussed between them even before this latest crisis. It was to ask Abdullah to stay in Transjordan, where he could reign (though not rule) as Britain's protégé. Churchill immediately cabled London and obtained its permission to make the offer. He and Abdullah met on May 26 and conferred for a day and a half in Jerusalem. The emir, a "cheery-faced, shrewd, genial little man," as Churchill described him, listened intently as the colonial secretary outlined the proposal. By its terms, Abdullah would withhold any further action against the French. He would establish an orderly government in Amman, recognize Transjordan as an integral part of Britain's Palestine mandate, and administer the territory in the name of the mandate. In return, Britain would provide Abdullah with a monthly subsidy, with trained advisers, and with the assurance of Transjordanian independence at some future date. After discussing the proposal with his advisers through the night of the twenty-sixth, the emir accepted the offer the next morning. Churchill then departed for home glowing with self-satisfaction.

The establishment of an Arab government east of the river was Britain's first explicit admission that Transjordan was included in the zone of Arab autonomy, as promised by McMahon to Hussein in 1915, rather than in integral Palestine. It followed logically that the Balfour Declaration could not be applied to that territory. Interestingly enough, Balfour himself had not made such an assumption. In a memorandum to Lloyd George on August 11, 1919, the foreign secretary had proposed drawing the frontier well east of the Jordan for the development of Zionist agriculture. Abdullah himself, for that matter, was astonished at the shift in Britain's position. Later he wrote: "[God] granted me success in creating the Government of Transjordan by having it separated from the Balfour Declaration which had included it since the Sykes-Picot Agreement assigned it to the British zone of influence." This major concession to the Arabs evidently registered only slowly on the Zionists. In their earlier correspondence with the British they had expressed at most a perfunctory interest in the Transjordanian area; their colonies were all to the west. Only afterward, when the mandate officially excluded the Jewish National Home east of the Jordan, did recognition of the lost bargaining point fully dawn on the Zionist leadership.

Still other restrictions were imposed on the Jewish National Home. In May 1922, Herbert Samuel returned to London to impress on the Colonial Office the need for dispelling Arab fears on the Palestine question once and for all. This could be accomplished only by a "definitive" interpretation of the Balfour Declaration, he insisted. His recommendation was accepted. A statement of policy was drafted, mainly by Samuel himself, for issuance over Churchill's signature. Known afterward as the Churchill White Paper, the document restricted the Jewish National Home to the area west of the Jordan, eschewed the notion of creating a predominantly Jewish state, and limited Jewish immigration thenceforth to the "economic capacity of the country." The statement read in part:

> Phrases have been used such as that Palestine is to become "as Jewish as England is English." His Majesty's Government regard any such expectation as impracticable and have no such aim in view. . . . When it is asked what is meant by the development of a Jewish National Home in Palestine, it may be answered that it is not the imposition of a Jewish nationality upon the inhabitants of Palestine as a whole but the further development of the existing Jewish community . . . in order that it may become a center in which the Jewish people as a whole may take . . . an interest and a pride. But in order that this community should have the best prospects of free development . . . it is essential that it should know that it is in Palestine as of right and not on sufferance.

The draft was submitted to the Zionist Organization in June. Fearful of losing British support altogether, Weizmann and the Zionist Executive reluctantly signed it. The Arab delegation, on the other hand, rejected it flatly. The mixed reception notwithstanding, the government published the Churchill White Paper on July 1, 1922, as the official interpretation of the British mandate in Palestine. On this basis, too, the mandate won swift ac-

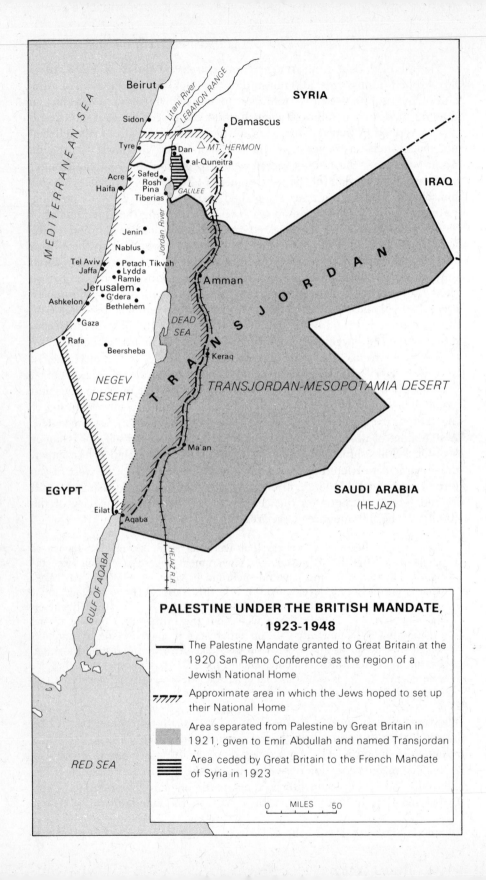

MEDITERRANEAN SEA

Beirut

Sidon

Tyre

Acre

Haifa

Safed
Rosh
Pina
Tiberias

Jenin

Nablus

Tel Aviv
Jaffa

Petach Tikvah
Lydda
Ramle

Jerusalem

G'dera
Bethlehem

Ashkelon

Gaza

Rafa

Beersheba

NEGEV
DESERT

Eilat
Aqaba

GULF OF AQABA

RED SEA

LITANI River

LEBANON RANGE

SYRIA

Damascus

Dan

MT. HERMON

al-Quneitra

L. GALILEE

Jordan River

Amman

DEAD SEA

Keraq

TRANSJORDAN

TRANSJORDAN-MESOPOTAMIA DESERT

Ma'an

IRAQ

SAUDI ARABIA
(HEJAZ)

EGYPT

HEJAZ R.R.

PALESTINE UNDER THE BRITISH MANDATE, 1923-1948

—— The Palestine Mandate granted to Great Britain at the 1920 San Remo Conference as the region of a Jewish National Home

//// Approximate area in which the Jews hoped to set up their National Home

▓ Area separated from Palestine by Great Britain in 1921, given to Emir Abdullah and named Transjordan

≡ Area ceded by Great Britain to the French Mandate of Syria in 1923

0   MILES   50

ceptance by the House of Commons five days later, and by the Council of the League of Nations on September 29.

The Zionists had suffered a reverse of sorts, but hardly a fatal one. In the preamble of its mandatory award to Britain, after all, the League Council recited the Balfour Declaration almost verbatim; alluded specifically to "the historical connection of the Jewish people with Palestine" and to the moral validity of "reconstituting their National Home in that country"; imposed on the British the obligation not simply to permit but to "secure" the Jewish National Home, to "use their best endeavours to facilitate" Jewish immigration, and to encourage Jewish settlement on the land. Hebrew was recognized as an official language. A Jewish Agency (provisionally the Zionist Organization itself) was authorized to cooperate with the mandatory in the development of natural resources and in the operation of public works and utilities. It was plain, then, from beginning to end, that the League award was framed to protect the Zionist redemptive effort. The British accordingly were invested with "full powers of legislation and administration," a provision not included for the Syrian and Iraqi mandates, in which the obligation was imposed of ensuring self-government; self-government manifestly was not intended for the Holy Land on the basis of an obvious Arab majority. It was significant, for example, that the word "Arab" did not once appear in the mandatory award, and that the Arabs and other nations in Palestine were repeatedly described merely as "non-Jews." Nor was there doubt that the British government intended to stand behind the mandate. The Bonar Law cabinet, which succeeded the Lloyd George coalition in October 1922, firmly rejected every Arab effort to alter Britain's support of Zionism and of the Jewish National Home.

THE "CONSTITUTION" OF THE MANDATE

As the legal instrument defining Britain's obligations under the mandate, the League of Nations award similarly laid down a number of general "non-Zionist" provisions. Public order, good government, and civil and religious rights were assured for all the inhabitants of the country, "irrespective of race and religion." The Administration was charged with recognizing the sacred holidays of the various communities, with guaranteeing the security of the holy places and freedom of access to them. English, Arabic, and Hebrew were recognized as official languages. By the same token, each community was authorized to maintain its own school system. To ensure, also, that these and other requirements were fulfilled, the mandatory document obligated Britain to submit an annual report of its tenure in the Holy Land to the Permanent Mandates Commission of the League of Nations. Yet, at best, the award could only set guidelines for the mandatory. It was for the British themselves to institute the operative government for Palestine. An organic law, therefore, upon which the mandatory administration based its functional activities, was signed by the king in London on August 10, 1922, and proclaimed by Sir Herbert Samuel in

Jerusalem on September 1. This was the Palestine Order in Council. Although it included the traditional provisions of freedom of worship, liberty of conscience, and Britain's responsibility to foster the Jewish National Home, the Order in Council in essence was an austerely practical document that defined the various components of the mandatory government.

Thus, the executive was designated as a high commissioner, who appointed all subsidiary administrative officials. An independent judiciary under a chief justice was empowered to protect the rights of natives and foreigners alike, and to assure solicitude for the traditions and mores of the various religious communities. To that end, the Order in Council affirmed the jurisdiction of the religious courts in matters of personal status (p. 135). One of the most important of the document's features reflected Samuel's warmest hopes for the cultivation of self-government in Palestine. It was for the election of a legislative council, subject to the powers reserved to the high commissioner to "establish such Ordinances as may be necessary for the peace, order, and good government of Palestine." The body would consist of twenty-two members, ten of them official members of government, and twelve unofficial members. The latter, citizens of Palestine themselves, would be elected through a delicately calibrated scheme of primary and secondary elections. To ensure the protected status of the Jewish and Christian minorities, the secondary electors would be organized into twelve electoral colleges according to their religious communities. The council would be debarred, too, from passing ordinances that violated the terms of the mandate—specifically, the growth of the Jewish National Home. Tax and revenue matters similarly were exempt. In any event, the high commissioner possessed the option of veto.

On the basis of this elaborately delimited format, Samuel's administration laid the groundwork for general elections. A census was taken, revealing a population of 650,000 Moslems, 87,000 Jews, and 73,000 Christians. No serious opposition to the legislative council was encountered in its earliest phase. But within a few weeks Arab nationalist leaders expressed growing misgivings about a scheme permitting Jews to share even limited consultative authority with Arabs. In the end, therefore, a majority of Arabs boycotted the primary elections, and the government was obliged to cancel the rest of the voting. Samuel reverted instead to a purely nominated body. At his request, the Palestine Order in Council was amended by a second Order in Council, this one issued on May 4, 1923. The new instrument authorized the high commissioner to establish simply an advisory, rather than a legislative, council. In Samuel's blueprint, the new body would include (besides himself) ten official members, as well as eight Moslem, two Jewish, and two Christian Palestinians—to be appointed by the government. Yet even this modification failed to placate the Arab nationalists. Once more they forced the appointed Arab representatives to withdraw from the advisory council, thereby dooming the scheme. It was evident that the opponents hoped to compel Britain to institute majority self-government, an arrangement that would entirely favor the Arabs.

Somewhat frantically, at this point, Samuel requested the Arab leaders at least to organize their own Arab Agency. The organ would serve as a counterpart to the Jewish Agency prescribed by the mandatory award and would cooperate with the government on matters relating to Arab interests in Palestine. But at a tense meeting in the high commissioner's palace, the Arab leadership rejected the proposal on the spot. Musa Kazem al-Husseini, who earlier had led an Arab delegation to England to protest the Jewish National Home (Chapter VIII), observed that his people had never recognized the status of the Jewish Agency and therefore had no desire for a similar agency of their own. Samuel accordingly was left with no choice but to accept this third rejection of Arab cooperation as final. With regret, he announced that the legislative as well as the executive functions of the government henceforth would be reserved exclusively to the high commissioner and subordinate officers of the Palestine administration.

From 1923 on, therefore, until the end of Britain's tenure in 1948, the government that functioned in Palestine was unique among League "A" mandates. Far from nurturing the local population to self-government, it was a Crown Colony in all but name. The high commissioner was all-powerful, with full rights to appoint, dismiss, or suspend anyone holding government office in Palestine, and to sell or lease any public lands. Ultimately, Samuel and his successors were restrained by no constitutional limitations whatever as far as the nation's inhabitants were concerned. The only built-in checks on the executive's authority lay in the provisions of the mandate itself and of those in the Order in Council guaranteeing freedom of conscience, worship, fair trial, and similar traditional Western liberties. Occasionally citizens of Palestine themselves appealed real or fancied injustices to London, to the Colonial Office, or if necessary beyond that to the Privy Council—even to Parliament. But the method was unwieldy, at best.

Nor did the high commissioner hesitate to use his powers of legislation extensively. Each year his office issued as many laws for Palestine as Parliament did for Britain. Indeed, the Arab press spoke derisively of this "law factory" that turned out new ordinances without rest. To a degree, the spate of legislation reflected the need for revising a host of near-medieval Ottoman legal practices, especially in the realm of criminal and commercial law. Most of the ordinances, however, were devoted to restructuring the nation's administration. With its 9,000 square miles, Palestine was divided now into three districts—north, south, and Jerusalem. The city of Jerusalem functioned both as the headquarters for its own district and as capital of the mandatory government. British commissioners governed each of these administrative units, with other British officers responsible for subdistricts. Although municipal councils were elected in 1926 (p. 136), throughout the entire period of British rule mayors were appointed by the high commissioner, who could remove them at his discretion. In effect, there were no limits to the government's centralized authority.

Neither were there any restrictions, except financial ones, on the mandatory's allocation of its budgeted funds. After the police, the public works department accounted for the bulk of government expenditures.

This was the office responsible for construction and upkeep of roads, for government buildings and transport, for harbors, public water supplies, and sewage and drainage. To finance the various projects, as well as the cost of government itself, the administration organized departments of customs, excise, and trade. These collected nearly half the revenues of the mandate. Other income producers were land taxes, urban property taxes, livestock taxes, assessments on agricultural produce, license fees, and court fees. Public communications, including railroads, mails, telegraph, and telephones, similarly earned revenues. It was only after 1929, when renewed violence broke out in the Holy Land, that substantial expenditures from Britain itself were required to underwrite the country's enlarged military and police forces. But until then, the mandate was paid for almost exclusively by the citizens of Palestine.

THE OPERATION OF THE MANDATE

What did the Arabs and Jews get for their money? As early as the mid-1920s, the answer was becoming dramatically evident. When Britain assumed responsibility for the Holy Land, it took over an economic cripple, a nation that was impoverished well beyond the ravages of war itself. Underpopulated, boasting little industry or trade and few known natural resources, Palestine was debilitated, too, by administrative chaos no less than by famine. The Turks had taken their records of land ownership with them upon withdrawal, and the enforcement of security and justice, the fulfillment even of the most elementary duties of public administration, had ceased. In addition to dispensing public relief, therefore, Britain's initial efforts in Palestine during the first two years of its occupation were devoted simply to restoring a minimal degree of law and order. The task was fulfilled impressively, despite occasional outbreaks of rioting. Shortly before the Jaffa bloodshed of 1921, Samuel's associates had been contemplating a locally recruited Palestine police force to be composed exclusively of Arabs and Jews, under British officers. This project had to be dropped temporarily, in the aftermath of the May riots, and a Palestine Gendarmerie substituted for it. While still consisting largely of Jews and Arabs, the force this time was heavily corseted with British police veterans, many of them former "Black and Tans" who had served in Ireland. By mid-1922, fortunately, violence had subsided almost completely. Thus, upon Samuel's retirement in 1926, Lord Plumer, his successor, felt confident enough to disband the Palestine Gendarmerie. In its place he established the Palestine Police Force, staffed it with about 600 men, and backed it with the Transjordanian Frontier Force, a small regular military corps of 1,200 troops that normally was assigned to patrol Palestine's eastern frontier. By general recognition, Plumer's soldierly, no-nonsense personality was itself worth a battalion.

Yet the British brought more than order to Palestine. They provided law as well. Perhaps the mandatory's single most impressive accomplishment was the establishment of an honest and efficient judiciary. Samuel's civil regime had laid down the pattern for the future, and it was not altered significantly by the Order in Council of 1922. The administration of justice was based on twenty magistrate courts, possessing civil and criminal jurisdiction in minor cases. A number of the magistrates were Arabs and Jews. More serious litigation and issues of appeal went before three-judge district courts, and afterward to courts of appeal consisting of between three and five judges. The juridical hierarchy led eventually to a supreme court, functioning as a court of appeals as well as a high court of justice, and comprising six justices—usually two Englishmen, two Moslems, one Christian, and one Jew, presided over by the chief justice. Although the jury system was not introduced into Palestine, the writ of habeas corpus was, and the courts, separated altogether from the executive, operated with efficiency and fairness. Their judges were men of known probity. In nearly all instances, the justice they dispensed was evenhanded and incorruptible. Indeed, it was applied quite frequently against the mandatory government itself.

The content, no less than the administration, of the law was similarly revolutionized. Virtually the entire Ottoman criminal and commercial code was replaced both by modern legislation and by the English Common Law and Equity. From the early 1920s on, lawyers and judges alike quoted British, Commonwealth, even American law reports, until by the end of the mandate the Common Law had become the dominant legal tradition in Palestine. The exceptions for the most part were those provisions of Ottoman law that dealt with land matters and civil law as codified in the old Turkish Mejelleh, while issues of personal status were left to the religious courts of the various religious communities (p. 135). It was essentially in this form that the legal system of Palestine was adopted in 1948–49 by the State of Israel.

The mandatory administration expended much effort and talent, as well, on fostering agriculture, a sector of the economy the Turks had ruinously neglected. The government's agricultural department established research stations for improving cultivation and livestock. With this help, the ravages of cattle plague, locusts, and fruit flies were markedly reduced. Extensive afforestation was carried out. In its first decade the government planted a million trees (the Zionists planted millions of others). Tobacco cultivation was fostered. A modern, efficient procedure was instituted for land registration. Imaginative fiscal reforms were carried out, too, in property assessment and taxation. Customs tariffs were alternately lowered on industrial goods and raised to protect citrus and other agricultural crops. By 1925 Palestine exports—largely citrus—climbed to £1,330,000, a 40 percent increase in five years.

Wide-ranging improvements in communications were accomplished by enlarging the rail network, building roads and bridges, and further modernizing and augmenting postal, telegraph, and telephone services. Air links were established with Europe and the rest of the Middle East. An international airport was constructed at Lydda. Plans were under way to enlarge the harbor at Haifa. Educational reforms also were carried out. Each village was required now to maintain a school building, while the government provided teachers, furniture, and books. By 1929, 30,000 Arab children attended these government schools. The British similarly established clinics and dispensaries in the major Arab population centers.

Unquestionably, there were also shortcomings in the government scheme of administration. The Jews complained that the mandatory had virtually abandoned its legal and moral responsibility to foster the economic growth of the Jewish National Home. For example, the Jewish share of contributions to the public revenues totaled approximately 45 percent by the end of the first decade. Nevertheless, it was the Arabs who benefited most impressively from government expenditures. The departments of agriculture, public health, and education all concentrated heavily on the Arabs. By the same token, the ratio of Jews employed in public works was far smaller than that of the Arabs. The British of course had a rationale for this imbalance. They explained that the Jews were competently providing their own social services, while the illiterate and impoverished Arabs had only the mandatory to supply their needs. This was true. Even so, the Jews resented the fact that their taxes were not being returned to them in the form of additional government help, and that the major investments in Palestine's economic growth were being supplied not by the government, surely not by the Arabs, but by Jewish public and private capital.

These weaknesses and inequities notwithstanding, it was soon evident that the improvements wrought by Samuel's administration were light-years beyond anything Palestine had ever known. The high commissioner himself completed his term of office in June 1925. In that month the Hebrew University was inaugurated on Mount Scopus in Jerusalem with the visit of distinguished figures from abroad. Allenby came from Egypt. Balfour came from England and was moved to tears by evidence of the progress he saw everywhere around him. Writing his final summary report for Parliament, Samuel could allude not merely to the organization of a civil police force, the gradual pacification of the country, the excellent legal system and public services. He could refer meaningfully, as well, to the spectacular rise of the Jewish population since 1917, from 55,000 to 103,000. Much of this Jewish growth and progress admittedly was the result of Zionist enterprise alone. Yet it benefited in measurable degree from a quality of peace, order, justice, and administrative integrity far superior to that provided by any neighboring government. This record of achievement was to continue under the forthright, soldierly administration of the new high commissioner, Herbert, Viscount Plumer.

THE ROOTS OF SELF-GOVERNMENT

If the British accomplished much in Palestine, however, the Jews matched and ultimately surpassed this progress by their own exertions. The fact was well recognized by Churchill, who observed in his White Paper of 1922:

During the last two or three generations the Jews have re-created in Palestine a community, now numbering 80,000, of whom about one-fourth are farmers or workers upon the land. This community has its own political organs; an elected assembly for the direction of its domestic concerns; elected councils in the towns; and an organization for the control of its schools. It has its elected Chief Rabbinate and Rabbinical Council for the direction of its religious affairs. Its business is conducted in Hebrew as a vernacular language, and a Hebrew press serves its needs. It has its distinctive intellectual life and displays considerable economic activity. This community, then, with its town and country population, its political, religious and social organizations, its own language, its own customs, its own life, has, in fact, "national" characteristics.

The religious identity to which Churchill alluded traced back to a period well before British rule. For several centuries it had been the Ottoman tradition to allow Palestine's religious communities virtual self-government in ecclesiastical matters, under the so-called millet system, by which communal autonomy was expressed largely through the jurisdiction of the empire's various religious courts. In this manner, for example, the individual Christian communities administered their own charitable endowments and dealt with questions of personal status—marriage, divorce, inheritance—in accordance with rules and regulations issued by hierarchical tribunals. So did the Moslems. The personnel of these institutions normally were appointed by the Ottoman government. Upon occupying the Holy Land, the British chose to continue the practice of religious autonomy; although, in the case of the Moslems, appointments to the religious courts were transferred from the mandatory government (as successor to the Turkish regime) to a Supreme Moslem Council, under the presidency of the Mufti of Jerusalem (Chapter VIII).

The Jews similarly had enjoyed religio-autonomous privileges under the Turks. Their communal leader during those years was the Sephardic chief rabbi, the Chacham Bashi, who in turn appointed the members of the Jewish religious tribunals. As in the case of the Moslems and Christians, the British maintained the practice, but enlarged and systematized it. In February 1921 they authorized the election of a Rabbinical Council by select groups of rabbis and Orthodox Jewish laymen. The Council, in turn, consisted of two chief rabbis, one Sephardic, the other Ashkenazic, together with a number of associate rabbis and lay councillors from each "ethnic" branch of the Jewish community. It was this body that appointed the members of the rabbinical courts, whose jurisdiction over Jewish law included the traditional areas of marriage, divorce, and inheritance.

The mandatory's recognition of Jewish communal identity extended into a number of secular areas, as well. We have noted that the Yishuv's prewar attempts to establish an organized Jewish representation largely had foundered (Chapter IV). Now, with hostilities over and the Turks gone, the effort was renewed. On December 18, 1918, an impressive assembly of Palestine Jews gathered in Jaffa to draft a "constitution" for the National Home. The measures adopted by this group ultimately exerted a powerful influence on future—Jewish—governmental development. For example, it was affirmed that elections should be not only direct, secret, and equal (including women), but also proportional, based on the old Zionist Congress technique of votes for separate party lists. Thereafter, elections for an Asefat HaNivcharim—a National Assembly—took place in April 1920. Some 20,000 persons, more than 70 percent of all registered Jewish voters, participated in the balloting; and afterward, the newly elected National Assembly formally opened in Jerusalem in October 1920. Its 314 members belonged to twenty different parties, and its first order of business subsequently was to elect a Va'ad Le'umi—an executive of thirty-six men and women. Samuel, meanwhile, impressed by this evidence of Zionist communal purpose, offered the National Assembly a certain functional latitude over Jewish religious, cultural, and social welfare activities.

The embryonic Jewish government functioned continually from 1920 on, meeting at least once a year and holding new elections every three to six years. For a long while it did not achieve official mandatory recognition. The delay stemmed partly from the opposition of Orthodox Jews, who resented the equal membership allowed women; and partly from British unwillingness to delegate taxation powers to the Assembly—even within this body's restricted sphere of competence. But when the Assembly's representatives submitted a complaint to the Mandates Commission of the League of Nations, the Plumer administration relented. In July 1927 the government issued an ordinance formally recognizing a single Jewish community, the Knesset Israel, with its own religious and secular organs. The religious organ, of course, was the Rabbinical Council, and it had been functioning for a number of years. In the secular area, the National Assembly and its Va'ad Le'umi now also were granted official status. More significantly, the Assembly was granted a qualified power of taxation within the Knesset Israel for education, relief of the poor, care of the sick and orphans, and the financial maintenance of the Rabbinical Council and of the Assembly itself. Similar rights of taxation were accorded to any local community encompassing a minimum of thirty Jews. For the Yishuv these measures represented a limited, but potentially important, new avenue to self-government.

Moreover, both Arabs and Jews were granted yet additional jurisdiction over their internal affairs by the Municipal Franchise Ordinance of 1926. It will be recalled that the Arabs earlier had refused to accept the 1922 Order in Council scheme for a legislative council. Such a body, they argued, would neutralize their majority advantage in Palestine. The ordinance of 1926 therefore represented a government compromise at the lower echelon of municipal government. It replaced the nominated local council with elected officials, provided for separate registries of voters (Moslem, Christian, Jewish), and allocated council seats to the various communities in proportion to the voters on their respective registries. It was by no means surprising that these features proved attractive enough to dissipate Arab, as well as Jewish, suspicions. In the largest number of Palestine towns and villages Arabs comprised a majority on the local councils, and this was sufficient inducement for them to participate. The Jews, on the other hand, not only ensured themselves of at least minority representation in the councils (and of course majority representation in Tel Aviv, inhabited by Jews alone), but were protected in "mixed" towns through the restriction of council authority to purely economic, sanitary, and other "neutral" matters that were not affected by religious or cultural differences. Nor were activities relating to Jewish schools, orphanages, and hospitals touched upon; these continued within the jurisdiction of the Knesset Israel. By providing this single, isolated opportunity for Arab-Jewish cooperation in self-government, the Municipalities Ordinance represented one of the happier accomplishments of British tutelage.

Here then, in essence, was the structure of the mandate, of its "constitution" and government. Endowed with the official imprimatur of the Peace Council, of the League of Nations, and of Parliament in London, Britain as the mandatory authority further validated its tenure in Palestine through a succession of imposing ordinances and statutory codes. Its obligation under the mandate to provide a fair and just administration was discharged in letter and spirit by an efficient, honest bureaucracy, by an incomparable legal system, by high commissioners palpably devoted to the physical and economic well-being of Palestine's inhabitants, and by a transparently sincere desire to conciliate the ethnic and religious sensibilities of both the Arab and the Jewish communities. A principal consideration, too, in all the mandatory's activities during its early tenure, and simultaneously animating and inhibiting them, was the legal commitment to foster the growth of the Jewish National Home. Indeed, it was in their determination to fulfill this responsibility—this mandate, in its most literal sense—that the British proconsuls in the Holy Land (together with the Zionists themselves) achieved some of their most notable—early—successes. What turned out to be a substantially different matter was the endeavor to reconcile the Zionist goal with the national aspirations of Palestine's Arab majority. It was here, with the passage of years, that the mandatory learned that it had embarked on a far more complicated and, in the end, an all but hopeless undertaking.

CHAPTER VII BUILDING
THE JEWISH NATIONAL HOME

THE REVIVAL OF THE ZIONIST ORGANIZATION

The establishment of the Palestine mandate offered the Zionist movement considerably more than an opportunity. It offered, as well, the challenge of an active partnership with Britain in fulfilling the Jewish National Home. The terms of the League mandatory award were explicit on this point. "The Zionist Organization," it said,

> shall be recognized as an appropriate Jewish Agency for the purpose of advising and cooperating with the Administration in matters affecting the Jewish National Home and the interests of the Jewish population in Palestine, and to assist and take part in the development of the country, and shall take steps to secure the cooperation of all Jews who are willing to assist in the establishment of the National Home.

Yet in view of Britain's rather modest efforts to develop Palestine's economy, it was soon clear that the task of building the Jewish National Home would devolve first and foremost upon the Zionist Organization itself, as a kind of senior partner in the undertaking.

The Organization, however, was a somewhat uncertain instrument in the early postwar era. Its elaborate political machinery had all but ceased operations during four and a half years of hostilities. The central Zionist offices had remained in Germany, the bulk of its membership in Russia, a "neutral" bureau in Copenhagen, and a Provisional Executive Committee for General Zionist Affairs in New York. Afterward, to be sure, Weizmann's stupendous coup in achieving the Balfour Declaration transformed London into the operative political headquarters of Zionism. It was Weizmann and his associates, therefore, who convened the first postwar meeting of the Zionist Actions Committee in February 1919, and later a special conference of Zionist leaders in London in July 1920. All this may not have been precisely constitutional, but someone had to take the initiative and no one seriously disputed the authority of the meetings, nor Weizmann's moral authority in calling them. Accordingly, the London Conference took it upon itself to elect Weizmann president of the Zionist Organization.

The July gathering was a poignant one. Here was a reunion of the great prewar figures of world Zionism: the central Europeans, Nordau, Warburg, and Hantke; the Russians, led by Weizmann, Sokolow, and Ussishkin; and, for the first time, a sizable delegation from the United States, led by Louis Brandeis. A new eleven-man presidium, organized under the chairmanship of Weizmann, assigned six of its members to Palestine under the rubric of a "Palestine Zionist Executive." It was this latter body, assuming and enlarging upon the liaison duties initially performed by the Zionist Commission (Chapter vi), that represented Zionism on the spot in all dealings with Britain. For all practical purposes, then, the Executive became the Jewish Agency itself, to be consulted by the British mandatory administration on issues relating to the Jewish National Home. As the years went by, too, the Executive in Palestine transcended the Va'ad Le'umi (the organ of the National Assembly) as the functioning quasi-government of the Jewish community. Each of its members became responsible for a specific facet of the Zionist reconstructionist effort in the Holy Land. Thus, departments were organized for political affairs, immigration, labor, colonization, education, and health. The political department, for example, remained in touch with the high commissioner in Jerusalem on major issues affecting the implementation of the Balfour Declaration. The immigration department undertook the placement of Jewish newcomers and advised the mandatory on work opportunities and labor schedules. The colonization department was responsible for the development of new Jewish agricultural villages. The public works department either collaborated with the mandatory or, from its own resources, launched projects intended to absorb unemployed immigrants. Educational matters, as has been seen, were largely the responsibility of the Va'ad Le'umi; but here, too, the Zionist Organization cooperated financially.

Yet it soon became evident that the various Zionist leaders sharply differed on the actual authority vested in the Palestine Executive. A few, like Nordau, insisted that Britain was obliged now to follow the Executive's recommendation and open the doors of Palestine for an immediate and massive resettlement of hundreds of thousands of Jews. The influx in turn would lead directly to a Jewish majority in Palestine, and thereafter to the establishment of a Jewish state. Weizmann, conversely, regarded any such maximal interpretation as sheer fantasy. Better than the others, the Zionist president appreciated that the Jews remained essentially an impoverished and scattered people. With their meager resources both in eastern Europe and in the Yishuv, they could hardly yet demand additional political concessions. What was needed first, Weizmann knew, was a more substantial Jewish demographic and economic base in Palestine itself; and for this, time was pressing. Lloyd George himself had given the Zionists a warning at the Peace Conference: "You have to take your chance now, because the political world is in the state of the Baltic Sea before it freezes. As soon as it is frozen, nothing can be moved, and one has to wait a long time until a second opportunity arises."

THE CONTEST FOR AMERICAN ZIONISM,
THE STRUGGLE FOR LAND AND FUNDS

At the London Conference, therefore, Weizmann emphasized that the priority need in building the Jewish National Home was not verbal urgency but expert knowledge, modern methods, and above all, money. The income of the Jewish National Fund, inadequate as it was, was further limited by charter to the purchase of land in Palestine. Sums of far more impressive quantity were required for other purposes, for the clothing, housing, and employment of thousands of east European immigrants who even then were pouring into the Holy Land. To that end, Weizmann and his colleagues on the Zionist Executive authorized the establishment of a Keren HaY'sod—a "Foundation Fund"—to tap the resources of Diaspora Jewry. Yet it was precisely on the issue of mass fund-raising that Weizmann found himself in direct confrontation with Louis Brandeis, the one man who approached him in reputation and moral influence throughout the Zionist world.

Born in the United States of Czech Jewish immigrant parents, Brandeis had been raised in a semiassimilated milieu. Throughout his distinguished legal career in Boston, he had maintained only peripheral Jewish interests. His conversion to Zionism was a consequence rather of several extended discussions with Jacob de Haas, editor of the Boston *Jewish Advocate*. De Haas had attended the early Zionist Congresses and had come to know and revere Herzl. He communicated something of Herzl's vision and eloquence to Brandeis, who from then on regarded de Haas as his teacher and companion in all Zionist affairs. Brandeis was influenced as well, however, by the American progressivist tradition. The connection became evident once he assumed the chairmanship of the Provisional Executive Committee for General Zionist Affairs in 1914. In Brandeis's scheme, Zionism shared precisely the ethical and democratic ideals that he regarded as the hallmark of Americanism. It absorbed, also, the philosophy of cultural pluralism that even then was being introduced in the United States by William James and Horace Kallen. Not least of all, Zionism seemed to blend integrally with the Wilsonian concept of national self-determination that was broadly accepted at the time as a legitimate Allied war aim. This thoroughly "American" version of Zionism, therefore, enhanced by Brandeis's reputation as a Supreme Court justice, made it possible for thousands of American Jews to accept Jewish nationalism even before the issuance of the Balfour Declaration. The efficiency, too, that Brandeis contributed to his administration of Zionist affairs was as distinctly American as his ideology. Uninterested in theories, he emphasized those practical features Americans could best understand: "Members! Money! Discipline!"

Brandeis visited Palestine in the summer of 1919. He was not unmoved by what he saw. Standing beside Rachel's Tomb on the Bethlehem Road at sunset, he murmured to de Haas: "I know now why all the world wanted this land and why all peoples loved it." But neither was Brandeis oblivious to the dangers that still lay ahead for the Jewish National Home. Not the least of these, surely, was the windy dogmatism of the European Zionists, a phenomenon he encountered at the London Conference of 1920. Spared the doctrinal burden that already encumbered much of Zionist thinking, his pragmatic mind was unable to make head or tail of programs submitted without any conception of budgetary factors. It was in London, too, that a fundamental ideological schism opened between Brandeis and the European Zionists. The American jurist had his own conception of the way in which the Jewish National Home was to be realized. Now that Britain had been entrusted with the implementation of the Balfour Declaration, Brandeis regarded the era of Zionist political action as over. "The work of the great Herzl was completed at San Remo," he observed in a memorandum to Weizmann. "[The nations of the world] have done all that they could do. The rest lies with us." "Us," in Brandeis's view, meant Zionists and non-Zionists alike, joined together in the Zionist Organization on an increasingly apolitical basis. Zionist political interests, on the other hand, from then on should be defended essentially by the Va'ad Le'umi in Palestine, which would undertake its own negotiations with the British high commissioner and his projected advisory council.

This attenuated conception of the Zionist goal was unacceptable to Weizmann or to other veterans of the movement. It represented to them a wholly unreal evaluation of what actually could be accomplished through the council or the Va'ad Le'umi. Worse yet, it placed its emphasis on the legal terminology of the San Remo award and ignored the much deeper, longer-range purposes of Jewish nationhood worldwide. For Weizmann and his colleagues, it was supremely the force of this latent peoplehood that had continually to be mobilized. Only repeated exhortation would launch a Zionist tidal wave powerful enough to assure survival for the Jewish National Home. As Weizmann put it in his autobiography: "[O]ur reason for wishing to keep the Zionist Organization in being as a separate body was precisely the conviction that the political work was far from finished; the Balfour Declaration and the San Remo decisions were the beginning of a new era in the political struggle, and the Zionist Organization was our instrument of political action. . . ."

This basic dichotomy in approach surfaced after the London Conference of 1920, when Brandeis criticized Weizmann's plans for launching the Keren HaY'sod as Zionism's major fund-raising instrument. The American had no objection to the collection of money for such "philanthropic" purposes as immigration, public health, or education. But he opposed the solicitation of charitable funds for public works, utilities, large-scale industrial and agricultural enterprises, or other ventures that belonged more appropriately within the realm of private investment. Such an approach, he argued, would merely duplicate the baneful old custom of Chalukkah on a larger scale. This view again was consistent with Brandeis's interpretation of the Jewish National Home as an accomplished fact, and one which henceforth had to be put on a businesslike basis. Weizmann and the Europeans, on the other hand, insisted that funds were urgently needed not merely to cope with a huge immigration but to persuade the British mandatory that Zionism was a movement to be taken with continual seriousness in its international depth of support.

With the overwhelming endorsement of the Zionist Executive, therefore, Weizmann departed for the United States in the spring of 1921 to launch the Keren HaY'sod. Whatever his misgivings, they were dispelled upon his arrival in the port of New York. Awaiting him were cheering thousands of American Jews who tendered him one of the most ecstatic receptions in the city's history. Here was an immigrant community, Weizmann sensed, that regarded itself as entirely identified with the Zionists of the Yishuv and Europe. The impression was reaffirmed in June at the Cleveland convention of the Zionist Organization of America. Once again the debate on Zionism's future was conducted between the partisans of Weizmann and those of Brandeis—"the man of Pinsk and the man of Washington"—and the voice of east European Jewry in the United States made itself heard. By a large majority, the convention voted for an open-ended interpretation of the Jewish National Home, a process rather than an accomplishment, a goal yet to be attained. Brandeis's slate of officers was repudiated, and resigned. Assured then of the backing of American Zionism, the Keren HaY'sod campaign raised $2 million by the end of December, four times the amount Brandeis had predicted.

It was significant, too, that the Zionist fund raisers continued to place their emphasis on broadening the Yishuv's agriculture. For virtually all elements within the movement, the normalization of Jewish life would be achieved only through the transformation of "rootless" European immigrants into farmers. Without a literal foothold on the soil, moreover, the Jews would never be able to defend their claims in Palestine against the Arabs, or possibly even against the British. By 1917 the Jewish National Fund already was in possession of 160,000 dunams in Palestine; and it was expected now to triple or quadruple its holdings. Yet the notion that additional soil would be acquired cheaply, that the British would cooperate in making public land reasonably available, was soon dissipated. In fact, the administration paid little heed to its obligations under the League mandatory award to "encourage . . . close settlement by Jews on the land," to "promote . . . intensive cultivation of the land." The British chose instead to leave the Jews to their own, presumably ample, resources and to devote their major efforts to the larger and more backward Arab community. Thus, of 960,000 dunams of state domain, 397,000 were turned over to Arab cultivators under the Beisan Land Agreement of 1921; only 83,000 dunams were leased to various Jewish organizations. As a result, the Zionists were obliged to buy fully 92 percent of their land from individual Arab owners, usually at exorbitant prices.

The Jewish National Fund operated under still another restriction, this one ideological. By the provisions of its charter, the tracts it leased out could be worked by Jewish hands alone. In this fashion the invidious Jewish squirearchy of the First Aliyah would not be perpetuated on Jewish soil; and through the Conquest of Labor the foundation for an authentically

"Jewish" National Home would be laid where it first belonged, on the soil itself. As Ruppin and others had learned even before 1914, the results of this directive were to encourage collective or cooperative farms. Indeed, the London Conference of 1920 now went so far as to confirm that the establishment of working-class villages henceforth should be an official aim of Zionist settlement in Palestine. It was a major concession by the Organization's essentially middle-class leadership, but probably an inevitable one, in view of the Socialist orientation of the immigrants themselves (p. 146). At London the decision similarly was reached for land to be acquired on a contiguous basis whenever possible.

One such enclave already was in the process of formation. It was in the Valley of Jezreel—the Emek—a belt of land nine miles wide extending from the Carmel range forty miles southeastward between the hills of Samaria and lower Galilee. Jewish settlement in this flat, swamp-ridden terrain had begun as early as 1911, but in ensuing years had not managed to produce a viable agriculture. Then, in 1919, an additional 80,000-dunam stretch of Emek land was put up for sale by its Arab owners. At the initiative of Weizmann and Ussishkin, the tract was purchased. With JNF help, the swamps were drained, water supplies installed, and roads built. Despite the crippling bouts of hunger and illness the settlers had to endure, twenty new collective and cooperative villages were functioning in the Emek by 1925. Most of them were founded by youthful immigrants who regarded the presence of this virgin tract as a standing and romantic challenge to their Zionism. Ultimately the Emek was transformed from a malarial waste into one of the glories of Jewish Palestine. Other farm settlements were rising on JNF land that had been purchased along the coast and in lower Galilee. At the same time, private acquisitions by the Palestine Land Development Company (Chapter IV) and by individual buyers also continued. Quantitatively, in fact, private purchases in the early 1920s still exceeded JNF tracts by three to one. Yet the ratio was steadily declining. In both Europe and America, the JNF became the very symbol of a Jew's Zionist commitment. The little blue-and-white collection boxes, silently awaiting weekly donations of shillings and quarters, were to be found in tens of thousands of Jewish homes throughout the Diaspora.

Land alone, however, would not have guaranteed survival for the wave of immigrants arriving in Palestine after the war. The newcomers had to be assured immediate food and shelter, then equipment and livestock for their farms, as well as schools and dispensaries for their families. It was to underwrite these expenditures that Weizmann in 1920 had launched the Keren HaY'sod over the objections of the "investment"-minded Brandeis. As president of the Zionist Organization, Weizmann afterward carried the major responsibility for this undertaking, and soon became Zionism's principal fund raiser—the "King of Shnorrers" (beggars), as he described himself. Over the next decade he traveled to every major Jewish community in the world, cajoling wealthy individuals in western Europe and North and South America, addressing mass rallies in Poland, Hungary, and Rumania. It was heartbreaking work. Even in the affluent United States, the Jews had not yet fully transcended their status as an immigrant population. Against the context of need, money still was raised in painfully limited quantities. In 1921 Weizmann had announced a goal of $150 million over five years. Instead, eight years were required to collect $20 million. To those who criticized him for Zionism's lack of diplomatic achievements under the mandate, Weizmann had a ready answer: "Jewish people, where are you?"

IMMIGRANTS AND IDEOLOGIES

The financial urgency could hardly have been exaggerated. Although the population of the Yishuv had fallen to 55,000 by war's end, the numbers were replenished almost immediately in 1919—at a time when Palestine was not yet open officially to immigration. This influx was to be known as the "Third Aliyah," and it was more appropriately titled than any of its predecessors, for it poured in from eastern Europe at the rate of 1,000 a month by 1920, and ultimately reached a total of 37,000 newcomers between 1919 and 1923. Most of the immigrants were simultaneously fleeing revolution, counterrevolutionary pogroms, and civil wars. Many came under the illusion that a Jewish state was about to be established. All of them, in any case, regarded postwar eastern Europe as a dead end.

They were not wrong. To be sure, the Russian Revolution of March 1917 and the overthrow of the tsarist regime initially ended all Jewish disabilities, removed the shackles on Zionist activity in Russia, and even led briefly to an unprecedented sunburst of Russian Zionist enthusiasm and growth. By early autumn the movement embraced some 1,200 local groups and a membership of 300,000. Yet if 1917 was Russian Zionism's golden opportunity, it was foreshortened by the Bolshevik Revolution in November of that year. The new Communist regime in its early stages placed few limitations on Zionist activities. Palestine emigration bureaus at first functioned without interference in the major cities, and during 1918 some 4,000 Jews managed to depart Russia for Palestine. In December, however, the Yevsektsia, the Jewish section of the Communist party, began to denounce the "counterrevolutionary essence" of Zionism, and in February 1919 Zionist offices were closed and Zionist periodicals banned. Soon a full-scale anti-Zionist crusade was unleashed in the Ukraine and in other Jewish centers. Like the vindictive Jewish Yevsektsia members themselves, the Communist leadership took the official position that Zionism denied the primacy of the social revolution, that it rejected the solution of the Jewish problem on Russian soil, and, most important, that it threatened the Communist party with an unacceptable competition for Jewish loyalties. Periods of intermittent relaxation in the anti-Zionist campaign were followed by renewed bannings, arrests, even trials and imprisonments. By 1923 Zionist organizational activity had all but expired in Russia.

Despite this Bolshevik repression, curiously enough, and parallel with it, an unusually effective Zionist emigration organization sprang up, and was allowed to function on Russian soil in the early 1920s. It was known as

HeChalutz (the Pioneer), and its formal training program in Russia itself infused the Third Aliyah with a practical dynamism unique in Zionist history. While mooted as early as 1915, the notion of advance agricultural experience was first propagandized widely by Joseph Trumpeldor. The famed one-armed officer had returned to Russia in February 1917. At the outset, his intention was to recruit a Jewish legion for the liberation of Palestine. Yet the following year, when the Bolshevik Revolution aborted this plan, Trumpeldor immediately issued another call to his admirers: "If we cannot be an army, let us be pioneers, let us sow the seeds a handful at a time, until we conquer the Land of Israel."

Trumpeldor warned his listeners and readers, however, that it was not enough simply to depart for Palestine to become workers or farmers. After all, the pioneers of the Second Aliyah had followed this course, certain that they would build a utopian society by sheer force of tenacity and willpower. They had failed. Profiting from the setback, Trumpeldor instead urged Jewish youth to equip themselves in advance for the tasks ahead. They must train while still in Russia, he declared, cultivate the soil adjacent to their own villages, learn from the farmers about them. To that end, he himself and a number of close associates traveled throughout western Russia organizing HeChalutz groups and establishing training centers in Minsk and Simferopol. Tens of thousands of young men and women joined the organization during the summer and autumn months of 1918. Enthusiastically they took up the study of agriculture on purchased or rented tracts of land, closely following the advice of Jewish, and occasional Russian, instructors. The Bolsheviks, meanwhile, tolerated this activity for a purely functional reason. It attracted badly needed American Jewish philanthropic funds.

Simultaneously, other HeChalutz groups were established in Lithuania, Rumania, Czechoslovakia, in Austria and Germany. In 1921 a World HeChalutz Organization was founded at Carlsbad, and a central office was opened in Berlin—later transferred to Warsaw. By 1925 HeChalutz membership had reached 33,000 and by 1933, 83,000. As early as 1919, however, the first HeChalutz youngsters began arriving in Palestine. Their routes often were circuitous. Those departing from eastern Europe—by far the majority—usually arrived through Turkey, Italy, or Egypt. Not a few made their way from Siberia via China and Japan. In August 1919, Trumpeldor himself returned to arrange facilities for the expected influx of chalutzim. A half year later he was killed in an Arab attack on his kibbutz, Tel Chai. Yet news of his death merely provided additional incentive to other HeChalutz members waiting to set out for Palestine. Seized by the urgency of circumstances in the Yishuv, they departed Europe in unprecedented numbers.

The mass immigration caught both the Zionist Organization and the Palestine government unprepared. The youngsters were pouring in like a tidal wave, and in their enthusiasm were almost completely indifferent to the lack of accommodations in Palestine, the certainty of hardships awaiting them. It was the Nebi Musa violence, we recall (Chapter VI), that convinced Sir Herbert Samuel that Arab disquiet could best be appeased by qualifying the principle of unlimited Jewish immigration. At that juncture, in August 1920, the mandatory government issued an ordinance restricting the number of Jewish immigrants to a maximum of 16,500 annually; and, at that, only to those for whom guaranteed employment was waiting. In the wake of the Arab riots of May 1921, Samuel went further, briefly halting all Jewish immigration. Finally in 1922, the Churchill White Paper additionally stipulated that immigration should not exceed Palestine's absorptive capacity. At this point the mandatory government adopted the system of issuing permits by categories—laborers, farmers, capitalists, and others. The restrictions imposed no severe hardship on Jewish immigration during the early years of the mandate. What was ominous to the Zionists, rather, was the precedent established for conceivably more drastic limitation in the future.

Of equal significance was the impact of these quotas upon the political coloration of the Yishuv. As it happened, the British granted the Zionist Executive effective control (within the numerical limits) over the distribution of immigration certificates. The allocation of these permits abroad, therefore, became a cause for impassioned struggle among the numerous Zionist factions. Eventually an agreement of sorts was reached among them to operate by the "party key"—that is, to distribute the certificates on the basis of the respective strengths of the various parties in the Zionist Organization. Yet, under the terms of the Organization's charter, double weight was accorded Zionist votes cast in the Yishuv, and thus the strength of the parties in Palestine itself soon became crucial. Those parties were oriented increasingly toward Labor Zionism, and by the mid-twenties, as a result, immigrants of similar affiliation in Europe were given priority.

It was in the early 1920s, then, that the political composition of the Yishuv—and with it, increasingly, of the Zionist Executive—took on its decisively leftist stance. The bulk of the newcomers was provided by HeChalutz, and although this pioneering organization was nominally apolitical, in fact it was overwhelmingly influenced by the doctrines of Labor Zionism; most of its followers in Europe were committed to one or another of the Labor Zionist parties. The largest numbers of the immigrants belonged to the Poalei Zion. A smaller proportion gave its loyalty to the Zeirei Zion, a collection of youth groups that, while not formally Socialist, expressed intense social concern and advocated the nationalization of land. After the war the Zeirei Zion split into two factions, and the more leftist branch eventually joined with the Poalei Zion in an enlarged Achdut HaAvodah, or Union of Labor (see below). By then the ideological differences between Poalei Zion and HaPoel HaZair, the party of A. D. Gordon and the "religion of labor" (Chapter IV), had narrowed considerably. At a conference of Labor Zionist groups in 1919, members of both factions began exploratory discussions on the idea of merging their organizations. These talks led to the formation of the unified Achdut HaAvodah. At the last moment, however, the leadership of HaPoel HaZair refused to join the new group. Gordonians by philosophy and moderates by temperament, they were repelled by the aggressive class activism of men like Ben-Gurion and Ben-Zvi. On the other hand, this decision to stay clear of Achdut HaAvodah led to a gradual atrophy of HaPoel HaZair's political influence within the Yishuv.

HaShomer HaZair—the Young Watchman—meanwhile took a curiously lone stance of its own, independent both of the doctrinaire socialism of Achdut HaAvodah and of the gentle Gordonianism of HaPoel HaZair. The movement had first developed in Galicia in 1915, and many of its followers subsequently came from Polish and Lithuanian middle-class families. Deeply romantic, they were influenced partly by the German Wandervogel youth movement and were in revolt, as they saw it, against the vapid and decadent Jewish bourgeoisie of the Pale. In their endless debates and theorizing, HaShomer HaZair projected a collectivist vision of the Jewish National Home more radical than anything conceived even by the Poalei Zion. For them, the kvutzah—the collective settlement—was more than an economic goal; it was an opportunity to abolish the family as a social unit, with all the tyranny of elders this organism had represented for them in the Old World. Children would even be housed separately from their parents. Inasmuch as politics was irrelevant to the utopian community envisaged by HaShomer HaZair, however, the group failed to become a political force in the Yishuv. Its impact was entirely social and, at that, limited to the kibbutz movement (p. 150).

Actually, none of the various trends and factions really considered themselves essentially political. They were all "movements" in the broadest sense, encompassing entire philosophies and societies within their ambit and including specialized youth groups—Gordonia, Dror, HeChalutz HaZair, and others. They lived and worked among themselves and organized their own clubhouses and choral and sports associations, often their own school systems. For all their dedication to a just, laboring society, they shared an equal commitment to maintain their ideological "purity." It was this relentless, doctrinaire factionalism that set the tone for the emergent political character of the Yishuv, of the Zionist Organization, and ultimately of the State of Israel itself.

A NEW UTOPIA ON THE SOIL

For the newcomers of the Third Aliyah, the initial priority clearly was to find employment. Here the mandatory administration was willing initially to offer a certain limited help, by providing scattered job opportunities in road building. Arab workers generally were hired out by their sheikhs; the Jews preferred to seek work through Achdut HaAvodah and HaPoel HaZair employment offices. Moreover, some of the youthful HeChalutz immigrants already had brought a plan with them from Europe for group employment. It was known as the G'dud HaAvodah, the Labor Battalion, and its rationale had been provided by the incomparable Trumpeldor in 1917. Trumpeldor's conception was of an austere and disciplined body, organized on collectivist lines, its members prepared to work in any region of Palestine and, if necessary, under the most trying circumstances. "We need," he declared,

people ready to serve at any cost at whatever task Palestine requires. . . .
The metal, whatever is needed to forge anything, whatever the national machine will require. Is there a wheel lacking? I am that wheel. Nails, screws, a
block? Take me. Must the land be dug? I will dig it. Is there shooting to be
done, are soldiers needed? I will enlist. Policemen, doctors, lawyers, teachers,
water-carriers? If you please, I am ready to do it all. I am not a person. I am
the pure embodiment of service, prepared for everything. I have no ties. I
know only one command: Build.

Trumpeldor himself did not live to see his scheme put into action. But in
August 1920, six months after his death, a group of his HeChalutz followers
arrived in Palestine from the Crimea, determined to breathe life into the
project. Their numbers grew from 40 to 560 by the following year. While
animated in part by the Gordonian vision of "conquering labor," the early
G'dud HaAvodah members also intended to socialize the Yishuv by force
of sheer willpower and example. Nor would they limit their efforts to
agriculture. Their plan was to introduce Jewish workers into every sphere,
including road construction, swamp drainage, and railroad building. By
acquiring strategic positions for the laboring class in the Yishuv's economy,
they intended ultimately to transform Palestine into a nationwide commune
of Jewish workers. On this basis, then, they hired themselves out for public
works projects. By 1921 "detachments" of the Battalion were found throughout Palestine, clearing swamps, building roads, living in tents, deprived
even of the most elementary facilities of accommodation or leisure. Their
work was the hardest, the most dangerous and backbreaking in the country. It was also the most egalitarian. All workers, irrespective of their labor,
turned over their income to a central committee.

Near a work camp in the Emek of Jezreel, moreover, the young workers
founded a kvutzah, Ein Charod, to provide themselves with food and
shelter. And it was on the issue of Ein Charod's future that the Labor
Battalion eventually foundered. Many of the group preferred to stay on at
the kvutzah and develop it into a model of collective farming. Others insisted that Ein Charod was merely a way-station to the broader goal of a
"nationwide commune." The vision was utopian certainly beyond the most
extravagant dreams of the earlier Labor Zionist pioneers, and it touched off
an angry dispute among the workers. Eventually, in 1929, the G'dud
HaAvodah disintegrated in acrimony and recrimination. Several dozen of
the "extremists" broke their ties with Palestine altogether, returning to the
Soviet Union. There, in the Stalinist purges of the 1930s, they were liquidated to the last man. Those who remained in Palestine, settling down to a
more "normal" life, in the end became a kind of political aristocracy. As
late as 1954 almost half the leading politicians of the Mapai party, and a
third of all senior officials in government and in the Histadrut labor federation (p. 157), could boast that in the 1920s they had been pioneer members
of the G'dud's exalted little brotherhood.

The majority of Third Aliyah immigrants in fact were not eager to work
as hired laborers at all. Their Socialist convictions ran too deep for that.
Most, rather, were intent upon founding collective villages of their own.

A tiny handful of kvutzot actually had survived the war, but their total membership of 660 was hardly impressive. The largest kvutzah, Kinneret, possessed fifty-eight members, and several of the rest fewer than a dozen. Nor did these pioneer Socialist farmers nurture a well-defined concept of their future experiment—until the early 1920s. It was the Third Aliyah that revived collective farming and provided it with an idealized image as the emergent trend of Jewish agriculture in Palestine. Once again, Arthur Ruppin was the catalyst of change. As director now of the Zionist Executive's settlement department, Ruppin viewed the task of absorbing the "sweepings of the ghetto" as a personal crusade. Moreover, he persuaded the postwar Zionist Congresses that collective farming offered the Yishuv its most substantial hope for a viable agriculture. The kvutzah required only a modest initial investment, he pointed out; it allowed greater flexibility on a smaller tract of marginal land and was more capable of defending itself in isolated and vulnerable regions of Palestine. In any case, Ruppin added, no other method of farming would have been acceptable to the impassioned new Socialist immigrants.

The G'dud HaAvodah pioneers who remained on at Ein Charod also had much to do with the emergent lineaments of collective settlement. In establishing this farm, and its sister colony, Tel Yosef, they dramatized the advantages of a large-scale collective—that is, a kibbutz—over the more intimate kvutzah. In 1921 the two villages supported a joint membership of three hundred, an unprecedented number for communal farming. The social advantages of a more variegated population were matched economically by an increased, and hence more productive, specialization of labor. It soon became clear that the large kibbutz offered a vital key to the Yishuv's agricultural growth. By 1927 Ein Charod had grown by another two hundred and had been joined by a number of smaller "satellite" kibbutzim. In that year, too, delegates from these colonies organized a federation, HaKibbutz HaMe'uchad (the United Kibbutz), which rejected the exclusivity of the smaller kvutzah settlements in favor of larger-scale immigrant absorption. The example was indeed followed with growing frequency, and in the 1930s members of HaKibbutz HaMe'uchad went so far as to permit their settlers to accept employment outside their own villages, in road gangs and quarries and on fishing and maritime assignments.

Throughout the 1920s and 1930s, nevertheless, there still remained communal settlements that insisted on guarding the highly personal, familylike character of the little kvutzah (although "kibbutz" soon became the generic term for all collective settlements, large or small). The original pioneers of Degania were among them. So were the Third Aliyah founders of Geva, Chefziba, Ginegar, and a handful of others. In 1925 these elitist communities organized an association of their own, Chever HaKvutzot (the Kvutzah Group). It appeared at first, too, as if Chever HaKvutzot were destined to become the least vigorous branch of the kibbutz movement. As other groups expanded, Degania, Kinneret, Geva and Ginegar stagnated, failing to develop economically or to absorb new immigrants. This deficiency was partially remedied in the 1930s, however, by the arrival of a

well-organized Polish Jewish youth group, Gordonia, devoted to the ideals
of its namesake, A. D. Gordon. In 1933 Chever HaKvutzot and Gordonia
merged, and the federation of smaller kibbutzim was given a new lease on
life—even as its individual communes slowly enlarged themselves. Ha-
Shomer HaZair (p. 147) similarly experienced a revival of sorts. In 1927
the four settlements established by this intensely utopianist movement organized the Kibbutz HaArtzi (National Kibbutz) federation. In subsequent
years, its collectives were to be known as the most ideologically committed
and intellectually active in Palestine. Yet, while preserving much of the old
radical idealism, Kibbutz HaArtzi also began enlarging its individual villages and gradually abandoning the older mystical notion of a familylike
commune.

In many ways, the 1920s were a crisis period in the development of the
kibbutzim. The collectives did not grow spectacularly during these years,
and their economic position remained precarious. As new settlements were
established, old ones would collapse. Deficits rose more rapidly than profits.
But in the 1930s a new wave of immigration brought additional members
and a resurgence of hope. Indeed, the reputation of the kibbutz movement
throughout Europe provided a kind of built-in dynamism. By 1939 the
newcomers of the Fifth Aliyah (Chapter VIII) had raised the kibbutz population to 25,000 living in 117 collective settlements, or 5.2 percent of the
Yishuv.

Why did so many of the immigrants choose the collectivist alternative?
As late as the 1930s, after all, kibbutz life was grim and colorless, harsh and
demanding in labor and sacrifice, in lodgings, diet, and recreation. Yet, as
we recall, collectivism was the result not simply of an ideological blueprint.
It developed rather from the concrete needs and demands of Jewish farm
life. Straitened in land and capital, isolated in remote outposts, Jews found
the technique of joint sharing the most functional method of survival, both
economically and physically. There were other advantages, too, well beyond the emotional compensation of returning to the soil. By agreement
reached in democratic village meetings, parents were spared the responsibility of family duties, from the education, even the care, of children.
Women, assigned to communal tasks—in the garden, the nursery, the
clinic, the schools—were emancipated from the drudgery of routine domestic chores. Men and women alike, for that matter, enjoyed more time for
cultural activities, for group discussions, debates, and lectures. This was a
crucial inducement; kibbutz dwellers were far from the stereotype of
lethargic peasants. Rather, in high school and youth movements, their children were reminded continually that they were nothing less than the
vanguard of Israel's redemption. The appraisal was widely shared throughout the Yishuv. It explained the disproportionate influence of kibbutz
members in the emerging Labor parties, in the Histadrut and the Va'ad
Le'umi, in the growing Jewish defense movement, and ultimately, as shall
be seen, in the government and public institutions of the State of Israel.

Even at its apogee, however, the kibbutz movement by no means
dominated Jewish agriculture. Throughout the prewar years there were

farmers, Socialists among them, who decried the collective's lack of family privacy. An initial effort to develop a somewhat less radical alternative at Merchavia failed. But afterward, in 1919, Eliezer Yoffe, himself a veteran of the Second Aliyah, outlined a plan for a "moshav ovdim," a workers' cooperative, in which farmers would settle on JNF land, buy their equipment and sell their produce cooperatively, maintain their village services cooperatively—but live with their families on their own plots and keep for themselves the income they earned with the sweat of their brows. The idea appealed to many settlers. With the help again of Ruppin, who provided a tract in the Emek of Jezreel adjacent to Nazareth, a group of nineteen veteran farmers established a moshav, Nahalal, which they operated on cooperative lines. The village eventually grew to ninety families. It was joined by other moshavim in the Emek, in the Chefer Valley, and the central Sharon plain.

The cooperative farms proved successful, by and large. For one thing, most of their members had acquired experience in earlier agricultural communities. Solid family people, they were less interested than were the kibbutz members in absorbing untrained immigrants. As a result, their village turnover was much lower than that of the collectives. In 1931, when the number of kibbutz dwellers was 4,400, the moshavim were not far behind at 3,400. In 1936, as the kibbutz population rose to 16,400 members, the cooperative villages still boasted a respectable membership of 9,000. Subsequently, in the 1930s, the kibbutzim forged ahead more dramatically. The moshav movement, less ideological, hardly bothered to recruit in Europe or to develop youth groups. As late as 1940 its federation, the T'nuat HaMoshavim, lacked a compulsory membership tax or even a loan fund. Yet the advantages of cooperative endeavor, of initiative, privacy, and family life, were in the long run to become the wave of the agricultural future—not in the Yishuv, to be sure, but later, in the State of Israel.

During this same period of kibbutz and moshav growth, the older capitalist farms, specializing increasingly in citriculture, experienced a major revival of their own. By 1927, Rishon l'Zion comprised over 1,800 inhabitants, Rehovot 1,200, and Petach Tikvah fully 6,000. Other citrus groves were purchased and became the nuclei of new villages on the Sharon plain, among them Ra'anana, Magdiel, B'nai Brak, Ramatayim, Herzlia, Pardess Channa, Tel Mond, and Netania. By 1936 the number of capitalist villages had reached forty, almost double their prewar total. The value of their output, in citrus products, grape wines, and occasional other mixed crops, exceeded that of the moshavim and kibbutzim combined. Nevertheless, their landholdings and population fell behind those of the others. Nor was their political influence even remotely as far-reaching. Both cooperative and collective settlements maintained extensive ties with political parties and with national federations. Their leftist social views animated virtually all the major institutions of Jewish Palestine. This was hardly the case for the bourgeois colonies. Their national organizations, Hitachdut HaIkkarim (the Farmers' Association), and Pardess (the Citrus Growers' Association), enjoyed neither cohesion of purpose among their highly individualistic members nor any wide degree of political sympathy among the Yishuv. As a result, by the end of the first decade of the mandate, the once powerful capitalist farmers of Petach Tikvah, Rishon l'Zion, Rehovot, and G'dera had become a fading influence in the public affairs of the Jewish National Home.

THE VOICE OF CHALUTZIUT

Nowhere was the mood of the postwar settlers more apparent than in the literature of the Third Aliyah, with its emphasis on self-sacrifice and national revival. One of the Yishuv's authentic voices in these years was Avraham Shlonsky. An east European immigrant, a member of the G'dud HaAvodah, Shlonsky had labored to drain the malarial Emek, and the ordeal of that grim crusade, its fixation with chalutziut (pioneering idealism), resonated through his poetry. So, too, did a kind of divine sanction for the feverish ecstasy of rebuilding:

> O lead me thou, Lord,
> And let me bear the measure of seed
> On the ploughed fields of spring. . . .
> O, let me bear the measure of seed
> On my little parcel of land—
> Till my last day is weaned and stands before you
> Like a slender stalk
> That has bent its head full with grain:
> "Cut me, scythe, for the time has come."

The stormy longings for a new life and country animated virtually all the important Hebrew poets of the Third Aliyah, among them Yitzchak Lamdan, Avigdor Hameiri, Uri Zvi Greenberg, and Yehuda Karni. Their Palestine was not the biblical idyll, the groves and vineyards of First and Second Aliyah poetry. It was the barren desert and lurking menace, the anguish and fanaticism of the Labor Battalion and of the early kvutzot.

In this genre, Yitzchak Lamdan's epic poem *Masada* was the distilled incarnation of postwar chalutziut. A fortress in the Judean wilderness overlooking the Dead Sea, Masada in the first century was the site of a climactic Hebrew resistance against the legions of conquering Rome. Eventually Roman power triumphed here as elsewhere in Palestine, but only after the Hebrews had devoured the cream of General Flavius Silva's army, then put themselves to the sword. Lamdan understood well the fanaticism of those ancient Hebrew warriors. He had come from the Ukraine with the Third Aliyah, and he was writing of the people he knew, the youngsters who had returned to the Holy Land on a prayer and a herring skin, with empty pockets, famished bellies, and in their hearts a dream of the secular Utopia they would create in the Jewish National Home. For Lamdan, then, the epic of Masada was the epic of the Third Aliyah.

The poem began with Lamdan's own biography, a composite of his entire generation. His mother was perishing in flight from her ruined home.

His brother lay murdered somewhere along the roads of the Ukraine. And he himself was fleeing at midnight for Masada. Others, the partisans of the Bolshevik Revolution, sought to dissuade him, warning that he was abandoning all hope of social progress on native soil for a chimera in the wilderness of Zion:

> Behold, the Red Curtain has been lowered
> Upon the stage of mighty changes,
> As an intermission between the acts;
> Be strong, comrade,
> Until the curtain be raised
> And the tempest calmed. . . .
>
> Masada will not rise!
> She will not withstand
> The storm of great battles;
> Nor will there be a resurrection
> For this host of desperate ones,
> The weak within her.

But the poet strove on, arriving at last in Palestine in 1920. There he joined a G'dud HaAvodah work gang that had been assigned to leach brome and potash from the wastes of the Dead Sea. Masada brooded above their labors in the crippling purgatorium of the Judean salt desert.

> Bear it—bear it,
> My aching back!
> A man of Israel,
> Too proud am I
> To go and seek another refuge,
> And salvation! . . .
>
> Beneath this orphaned shrub
> In the desert of refuge,
> This is not the cast-off son of the Egyptian—
> Here faints from thirst
> Isaac, seed of Abraham and Sarah!

And here, ultimately, infused with the spirit of Masada, the Third Aliyah would triumph.

The identical passion fired the writings of Lamdan's contemporary, Uri Zvi Greenberg. The son of a prosperous Galician Jewish family, Greenberg had served in the Habsburg army during the war, then in 1922 and 1923 lived briefly in Warsaw and Berlin, where he edited a Yiddish expressionist journal. He reached Palestine in 1924, where soon he achieved the reputation of "poet of the chalutzim." As a journalist in Tel Aviv, Greenberg did not physically share the sufferings of the pioneers. Yet no one captured better than he the scorched tenacity of that postwar generation. His God was remorseless, as bleak and demanding as Yahweh of old. A pall of melancholy enveloped the task of reclaiming even the most sacred of God's ancient shrines:

But to me, the body of my dismembered mother is
Jerusalem: every rock shattered or severed, and the
Blood ever dripping, invisible blood of the soul. . . .
A wall encircles your woe—a fearful ring; darkness
Covers your stones, and your silence has become a
Shriek heard by the possessed and sainted ones in their
Death.

In Lamdan's fortitude, Greenberg's vehemence, Shlonsky's harsh, granu-
lated imagery, the élan of the Third Aliyah was the spirit neither of pastoral
awakening nor of rapturous self-assurance. It was one rather of fevered
anguish, of despair mingled with a bitter and cynical hope that a new
society ultimately could be resurrected out of a desolated land and a ruined
people.

THE GROWTH OF URBAN SETTLEMENT, THE STRUGGLE FOR LABOR UNITY

The postwar immigrants of the 1920s were by no means all impassioned
Socialist pioneers. As early as 1922 and 1923 the numbers of the middle
class among them began to increase, and this trend was further augmented
in 1924 by an unexpected and sizable influx of Polish Jews. They came
essentially as economic fugitives. The Warsaw government, intensely
chauvinistic, regarded all of its non-Polish minorities with unqualified distrust. Yet it was Poland's 3 million Jews who were uniquely vulnerable to
successor-state xenophobia. A Polish senator phrased the issue succinctly:
"If the aboriginal nation reaches economic maturity, the immigrant nation
must step aside." During the 1920s, this formula was implemented by the
government's finance minister, Wladyslaw Grabski, who nationalized those
branches of industry and commerce in which Jews were most heavily represented, then dismissed Jewish employees in favor of Poles. As a result, fully
a third of the nation's Jewish merchants were driven to bankruptcy, and
emigration soon became their only hope. Between 1924 and 1928, 70,000 of
them made their way to Palestine. The arrival of this "Fourth Aliyah,"
which also included some 8,000 Jews from the Caucasus and the Middle
East, raised the Jewish population of Palestine from 84,000 in 1922 to
154,000 in 1929.

Few of the newcomers were animated by Labor Zionist or even agricultural ideals. Having rescued a few thousand zlotys from their doomed
little shops in Poland, the Fourth Aliyah immigrants generally gravitated
to the cities and towns, where they set up pathetic duplicates of the enterprises they had left behind. During Palestine's economic slump in 1927
many of these erstwhile businessmen were wiped out. Weizmann had
regarded their arrival with misgivings from the outset. In a speech of
October 13, 1924, he warned:

When one leaves the Emek and comes into the streets of Tel Aviv, the whole
picture changes. The rising stream of immigration delights me. . . . Nor do

I underrate the importance of this immigration for our work of reconstruction. Our brothers and sisters of Djika and Nalevki [typical ghetto districts of Warsaw] are flesh of our flesh and blood of our blood. But we must see to it that we direct this stream and do not allow it to deflect us from our goal. It is essential to remember that we are not building our National Home on the model of Djika and Nalevki.

If the mercantile refugees were less than pioneers, however, their contributions to Jewish Palestine were substantial. It was in fact the newcomers of the Fourth Aliyah who laid the basis for the Yishuv's urban economy. Within five years they doubled the Jewish population of Jerusalem and Haifa. By the same token, their immigration was largely responsible for making a city out of Tel Aviv. As late as 1921 barely 3,600 Jews inhabited this miniature "garden suburb" of Jaffa. The numbers tripled in April of that year when Arab riots in Jaffa emptied the port community of its last remaining Jews. But it was essentially the influx of the mid-1920s that swelled Tel Aviv's population to 16,000 in 1924 and to 46,000 five years later. From then on, growth produced its own momentum; Tel Aviv boasted 160,000 inhabitants by 1939—all Jews. The rise of this and other urban communities offered a new insight into the Yishuv's emergent demographic profile. Unquestionably the presence of 33,000 Jews on the soil by 1931 was an impressive figure. Indeed, the proportion of Jews in agriculture climbed from 14 percent in 1914 to 23 percent in 1931, and to 29 percent in 1939. As early as the 1920s, nevertheless, it became clear that the largest numbers of Jewish settlers were moving into the towns and cities.

The 1920s witnessed the beginning of Jewish industry in Palestine. In 1921 a brick factory was constructed in Tel Aviv. That same year a Russian Jewish engineer, Pinchas Rutenberg, obtained a concession from the mandatory government to build the first electric power station in Tel Aviv, and soon afterward to build power stations in Haifa and Tiberias. From 1922 on, private Jewish capital established a salt works, a large flour mill, and the Shemen oil and soap factory in the Haifa area. In 1925 the Nesher cement factory was opened near Haifa, together with several textile plants. The contribution of most Polish Jewish immigrants during the 1920s was hardly this impressive, of course. By and large their "industrial" enterprises consisted of little more than small workshops with a handful of workers. Even so, it was their arrival by the thousands that stimulated the Yishuv's single most important industry, construction. By 1927 as many as 45 percent of the workers of Tel Aviv were employed in the building trade, and the lineaments of a sizable Jewish urban working class were visible for the first time. The Labor Zionist leadership watched this development closely. It was persuaded by then that in the cities, as on the soil, labor's task was to conquer the Palestine Jewish economy and shape it altogether in its image.

In fact, rudimentary workers' organizations had appeared in the Jewish colonies as far back as the 1880s and 1890s, but the PICA directors had managed to stamp out most of them. The effort to create labor unity was

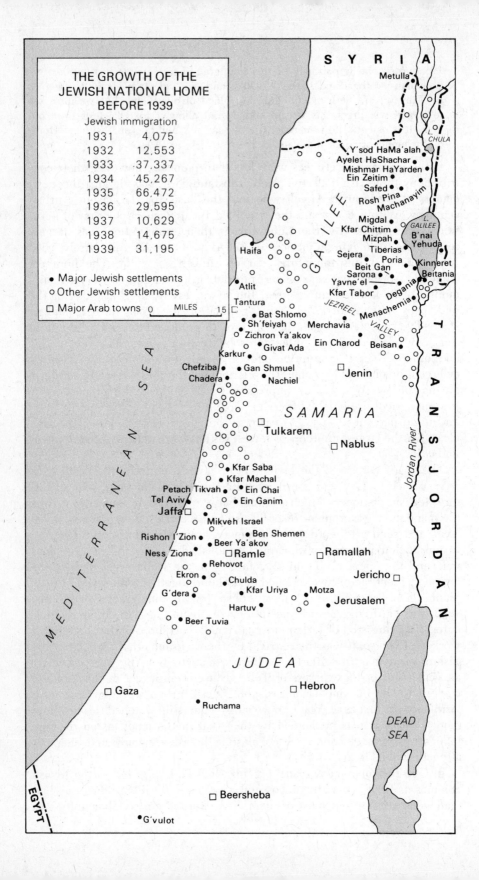

THE GROWTH OF THE JEWISH NATIONAL HOME BEFORE 1939

Jewish immigration

1931	4,075
1932	12,553
1933	37,337
1934	45,267
1935	66,472
1936	29,595
1937	10,629
1938	14,675
1939	31,195

● Major Jewish settlements
○ Other Jewish settlements
□ Major Arab towns

0   MILES   15

SYRIA

Metulla

L. CHULA

Y'sod HaMa'alah
Ayelet HaShachar
Mishmar HaYarden
Ein Zeitim
Safed
Rosh Pina
Machanayim

Migdal
Kfar Chittim
Mizpah
Sejera
Tiberias
Poria
Beit Gan
Sarona
Yavne'el
Kfar Tabor

L. GALILEE

B'nai Yehuda

Kinneret
Beitania
Degania
Menachemia

GALILEE

JEZREEL

Haifa

Atlit

Tantura

Bat Shlomo
Sh'feiyah
Zichron Ya'akov
Givat Ada
Karkur
Chefziba
Gan Shmuel
Chadera
Nachiel

Merchavia
Ein Charod
Beisan

VALLEY

Jenin

SAMARIA

Tulkarem

Nablus

Kfar Saba
Kfar Machal
Petach Tikvah
Tel Aviv
Jaffa
Ein Chai
Ein Ganim
Mikveh Israel
Rishon I'Zion
Ben Shemen
Beer Ya'akov
Ness Ziona
Ramle
Rehovot
Ekron
Chulda
G'dera
Kfar Uriya
Hartuv
Beer Tuvia

Ramallah

Jericho

Motza
Jerusalem

TRANSJORDAN

Jordan River

JUDEA

Gaza
Ruchama

Hebron

DEAD SEA

EGYPT

Beersheba

G'vulot

MEDITERRANEAN SEA

revived only in the decade before the war. Although essentially political in character, HaPoel HaZair and the Poalei Zion functioned as incipient trade unions and even supplied a certain rudimentary medical care (p. 158). During the war, food shortages led to the establishment of a consumers' cooperative, HaMashbir HaMerkazi (the Central Provisioner). In varying degrees, these struggling societies were predecessors of the Histadrut, the Jewish Labor Federation of Palestine. Yet the essential postwar impetus for the Histadrut was supplied by the two political factions, Achdut HaAvodah and HaPoel HaZair. While the latter refused to join the former in an all-embracing union of the Left (p. 146), both groups agreed that they could submerge their differences in an "apolitical," purely labor, federation. On that basis the Histadrut was founded in Haifa, in December 1920. From the outset, its membership was open to "all toilers who live by their own labor without exploiting others."

It was significant that a majority of the Histadrut's early members belonged to kibbutzim and moshavim, and that the federation placed its heaviest emphasis on creating work opportunities for Jews on the land. But while the likeliest potential jobs for new immigrants appeared for many years to be in the citrus groves of the coastal belt, as late as 1930 no more than a few hundred Jewish workers secured employment on the capitalist plantations, working cheek by jowl with several thousand Arab laborers; and this at a time when growing numbers of Jewish immigrants were camping in tents on the beaches of Tel Aviv, waiting vainly for jobs of any kind. The Histadrut accordingly began to organize strikes against planters who refused to give work priorities to Jews. Not infrequently picketers used strong-arm tactics to "induce" Arab workers to return to their homes. In resorting to these methods, the Histadrut operated on the assumption that the Arab economy was self-contained. To the newcomers from eastern Europe, on the other hand, employment in the Jewish-owned orchards was a matter of life or death. The issue eventually was resolved in favor of Jewish labor (Chapter ix). It did nothing to improve Arab-Jewish relations, however.

Nor were the planters the only Jewish capitalists in Palestine who exploited their workers. In the cities, hundreds of minor entrepreneurs recruited Jewish laborers from the streets with the promise of little more than a free lunch and a mattress for sleeping. With the bulk of Jewish manpower pouring into the cities, too, the Histadrut increasingly turned its attention to the urban areas. Indeed, it organized unions not simply among manual laborers, but among clerks, technicians, even doctors and lawyers. Labor exchanges were set up for job applicants, and collective bargaining was undertaken on their behalf. Slowly, opportunities were opened for Jewish workers in the building industry, even in the British-controlled railroads, in the post offices, and in other key sectors of the urban economy.

The Histadrut's function was by no means limited to that of a bargaining agent for workers. Its trade union purposes were combined both with the Zionist ideal of rebuilding the country and with the Socialist aim of "establishing a Jewish workers' society in Palestine." In fulfilling these goals, the

Histadrut in 1923 established a central economic corporation, the Chevrat Ovdim (Workers' Association), to serve as a holding company for a wide variety of independent undertakings Among these was HaMashbir Ha-Merkazi (p. 157), revived in the mid-1920s as a cooperative wholesale society to buy the products of the kibbutzim and moshavim and, in turn, through its chain of retail stores, to sell these farm villages foodstuffs, clothing, and industrial goods. In 1926 the Chevrat Ovdim organized a marketing outlet, Tnuva, for kibbutz and moshav dairy products; then a workers' bank (Bank HaPoalim) as its major credit instrument for the farm settlements and labor enterprises in the cities. The Chevrat Ovdim's housing company, Shikun, provided workers with flats at the lowest, nonprofit rentals; even as a wide network of cooperative endeavors—fully a thousand of them by 1939—was established in other areas, ranging from bus transportation to hotels and restaurants.

In forestalling the worst of the Yishuv's economic inequalities, however, and in minimizing cutthroat competition, one of the Histadrut's most important innovations undoubtedly was its program of universal medical coverage. Known as the Kupat Cholim (Sick Fund), it had been launched as far back as 1911, with some 2,000 participants on the eve of the war. By 1930 its membership had climbed to 15,000, a number that would double five years after that. By then, too, the Kupat Cholim maintained not only the largest registry of physicians and nurses in Palestine, but its own clinics in five cities and fifty-three rural centers, as well as two hospitals and two convalescent homes. In the absence of a compulsory medical insurance law in Palestine, the growth of Kupat Cholim was a tribute to the organizing skills of the Histadrut. So were yet other institutions of the workers' commonwealth. These included an autonomous Histadrut school network, established in 1921 and functioning under the supervision of the Va'ad Le'umi. By 1934 the 135 Histadrut schools in Palestine represented 44 percent of all schools in the Hebrew educational system (the other two networks were operated by the General Zionists and the Mizrachi). Additionally, the Histadrut sponsored a broad network of adult education courses, together with related programs in literature, art, music, and drama. In 1925 the Histadrut founded its own dramatic company, Ohel, and began publication of its newspaper, *Davar*.

Finally, to broaden the employment market by any and all means, the workers' federation launched a number of its own industrial companies. The enterprises served the dual function of offering jobs to Jews and of fulfilling the kind of Zionist public services—drainage of swamps, building of settlements—that private entrepreneurs, and certainly the British government, would not have undertaken on their own. The most important of these firms was Solel Boneh (Paving and Building), established initially as a semi-independent contracting agency for road laying and, later, public construction. Within two years, Solel Boneh was handling over P£1 million in contracts from private investors, from the Zionist Executive, even from the mandatory government. It drained swamps in the Jezreel and Chula valleys, built roads, erected housing and office buildings; and in the process it opened up thousands of new job opportunities, creating the working class whose interests it then defended. As early as 1930, then, the multitude of these activities drew into the Histadrut fold three-quarters of the Jewish working population of Palestine. Nearly all phases of a man's life, and the life of his family, were embraced by the vast canopy of the workers' organization. By the eve of World War II, the Histadrut had become much more than a powerful institution in Jewish Palestine. For a majority of the Yishuv, the Histadrut was all but synonymous with Jewish Palestine itself.

As it developed, labor unification was a political no less than an economic achievement. The federation had little alternative but to operate on two levels, for by 1929 a new series of Arab riots and the growing coolness of the mandatory regime (Chapter viii) revealed the urgent need for Jewish political consolidation within the Yishuv. The leaders of Achdut HaAvodah, Ben-Gurion and Ben-Zvi, and of HaPoel HaZair, Yosef Sprinzak and Chaim (Victor) Arlosoroff, sensed that the issues uniting the two labor factions were more important than those dividing them. In January 1930, therefore, the membership of both groups voted approval for a merger. The ensuing united party was known thenceforth as Mapai (Mifleget Poalei Eretz Israel), the Land of Israel Workers' party. In large measure the guiding spirit of the new body was Berl Katznelson, an authentic giant of the Palestine labor movement. A ruggedly built, tousle-headed man, a veteran of the Second Aliyah, Katznelson founded the newspaper *Davar* in 1925 as the organ of the Histadrut and remained its editor until his death in 1944. From the mid-1920s, the entire cultural program and doctrinal orientation of Jewish labor strongly reflected his influence. It was chiefly Katznelson's genius that steered Mapai away from the traditional theorizing complexities of Zionist politics and concentrated instead on pragmatic gains for Jewish workingmen and the Jewish National Home.

By 1933, as a result, this judicious blend of nationalist idealism and Socialist gradualism ensured Mapai control not only of the Histadrut (the reservoir of its strength in all future years), but also of the National Assembly and of the Jewish Agency's political department. From then on it was Mapai that led the Yishuv through the mandatory period, and that eventually became the largest single party in Zionist Congresses. The international situation favored Labor Zionism, as well, for the economic crisis of the 1930s popularized leftist causes everywhere. It is of interest, moreover, that despite the larger numbers and the more intensive radicalism of the Third Aliyah, the Yishuv's vast labor apparatus remained essentially in the hands of the prewar Second Aliyah: of such experienced veterans as Katznelson, Ben-Gurion, Ben-Zvi, Sprinzak, David Remez, and Yitzchak Tabenkin, most of them born in the 1880s. More than any other, this would be the group that would shape the ideology and the institutions of the Yishuv, and later of the State of Israel itself.

THE CREATION OF THE JEWISH AGENCY

If Jewish labor had achieved a form of unity in Palestine, so, in a different and more limited way, had world Jewry in its commitment to the growth of the Yishuv. It will be recalled that the League of Nations, in awarding the mandate, had recognized the Zionist Organization as the Jewish Agency authorized to cooperate with Britain in developing the Jewish National Home. Yet this recognition was at best provisional, for the Agency was required ultimately "to secure the cooperation of *all* [italics the author's] Jews who are willing to assist in the establishment of the Jewish National Home." We have noted, too, that Brandeis's prescription for mobilizing world Jewry was for Zionists and non-Zionists alike to join the Zionist Organization on an increasingly apolitical, "businesslike" basis. In the United States this approach was shot down at the Cleveland convention of 1921. Throughout the 1920s, however, it was Weizmann who pursued the hope of recruiting support from affluent non-Zionist Jews. No one knew better than he how urgent was the need for their resources, particularly those tapped by the (non-Zionist) Joint Distribution Committee in the United States on behalf of impoverished Jews in Europe. Weizmann wrote later of the American Jewish philanthropists who raised and controlled the allocation of JDC funds:

> They had done and were doing magnificent relief work for European Jewry during and after the First World War, but for one who believed that the Jewish Homeland offered the only substantial and abiding answer to the Jewish problem their faith in the ultimate restabilizing of European Jewry was a tragedy. It was heartbreaking to see them pour millions into a bottomless pit, when some of the money could have been directed to the Jewish Homeland and used for the permanent settlement of those very Jews who never had a real chance.

It was true that the Keren HaY'sod (the Foundation Fund) provided a vehicle of sorts for contributors who wished to help the Yishuv financially without committing themselves politically. But the mandate referred to a "Jewish Agency." The Fund was an instrument, not an agency.

In repeated meetings and conferences over the years, therefore, Weizmann pressed for the creation of an "extended Jewish Agency," to include Zionists and non-Zionists alike. It was hard sledding. Many of the European Zionists opposed the inclusion of wealthy American Jews, whom they considered "assimilationists." Fortunately for Weizmann, the Labor Zionists, the single most cohesive group within the Zionist Organization, supported him in his plan; and at the Thirteenth Congress in 1923, sanction was given for enlargement of the Jewish Agency beyond its purely Zionist constituency by adding representatives of other Jewish organizations. Yet even then, the opposition of non-Zionists had to be contended with. The JDC leadership feared the political objectives implicit in the Jewish National Home. It required all of Weizmann's charm and eloquence to convince these men that the National Home deserved their support on purely moral and humanitarian grounds. Eventually, after countless meetings, the Zionist president began at last to win over such prestigious American Jewish leaders as Nathan Strauss, Jacob Schiff, Samuel Untermeyer, and—most importantly—Louis Marshall. A distinguished attorney, Marshall was chairman of the nativized and highly influential American Jewish Committee, and it was he who secured the endorsement of other wealthy and prominent American Jews.

A formula acceptable to both Zionists and non-Zionists was worked out as early as the Zionist Congress of 1925. It set as the goals of a Jewish Agency: continuous increase in the volume of Jewish immigration; redemption of the land as Jewish public property; agricultural colonization based on Jewish labor; revival of the Hebrew language and of Hebrew culture. Agreement similarly was reached that the Council of the Jewish Agency would include in equal numbers representatives of the Zionist Organization and of Jewish communities in various parts of the world. Even so, four additional years of conferences, joint meetings, and semantic refinements were needed before the blueprint of an enlarged Jewish Agency won final approval by the Zionist Congress in 1929. Immediately afterward, then, in August 1929, the Constituent Assembly of the Jewish Agency met at last in Zurich.

It was a formidable gathering, almost as impressive as the early Zionist Congresses of the late 1890s. Indeed, the roll call of delegates was a pantheon of world Jewish notables. Among those present with Weizmann were Marshall, Léon Blum, Stephen Wise, Cyrus Adler, Chaim Arlosoroff, Ben-Gurion, Lord Melchett, Felix Warburg, Sir Herbert Samuel, Albert Einstein, and other renowned Jewish figures. In the last session of the four-day conference, Weizmann was elected president of the Jewish Agency, and Louis Marshall chairman of the Council. As the two men publicly embraced in a symbolic union of Jewish leadership on behalf of the National Home, Einstein was moved to tears and dashed off a note to Weizmann: "On this day the harvest of Herzl and Weizmann is wonderfully reaped." Weizmann shared this exaltation. Leaving afterward, he recalled that "I felt free from care, I anticipated confidently a future that would witness a great acceleration in the building up of the National Home."

By the end of the mandate's first decade the tangible accomplishments of the Yishuv itself seemed to bear out this expectation. More than 162,000 Jews lived by then in Palestine, 17 percent of the country's inhabitants. Of these, 37,000 lived on the soil, in 111 agricultural settlements totaling 700,-000 dunams; thirteen other Zionist agricultural schools and experimental stations also were functioning. Improved farming techniques were continually being devised. Citrus crops were growing in size and quality. The industrial development of the Yishuv showed similar promise. By 1930, 1,500 Jewish-operated factories and workshops were producing textiles, clothing, metal goods, lumber, chemicals, stone and cement, with a total capital value of about P£1 million.

The quality of life was improving, as well. The broad Kupat Cholim health network was partially responsible. So was Hadassah, the Women's Zionist Organization of America. Founded in 1912 by an American Jewess,

Henrietta Szold, Hadassah's dedicated mass membership by 1930 had established in Palestine four hospitals, a nurses' training school, fifty clinics, laboratories, and pharmacies, and an excellent maternity and child hygiene service in most of the cities and in a number of the larger villages. The Women's International Zionist Organization (WIZO) maintained three infant welfare centers in Tel Aviv. It was as a result, then, of expanding medical care, of systematic Jewish efforts to drain marshes and swamps, to provide a reasonable diet and living standard for the Yishuv altogether, that marked reduction was achieved in the incidence of tuberculosis, malaria, trachoma, and typhoid, the historic scourges of the region. The Jewish mortality rate fell from 12.6 per thousand in 1924 to 9.6 per thousand in 1930; Jewish infant mortality dropped from 105 per thousand in 1924 to 69 per thousand in 1930. Progress in education was not less impressive. In the early years of the mandate, the Va'ad Le'umi instituted compulsory school attendance on the elementary level. By 1930, 28,000 children were attending Jewish schools.

This, in sum, was the measure of the Yishuv's growth. It had developed its own quasi-government, its own largely autonomous agricultural and industrial economy, its own public and social welfare institutions. Its schools were infusing children with a spirit of Jewish national pride unprecedented either in western Europe or among the most intensely Zionist communities of eastern Europe. These qualities of self-sufficiency and national loyalty ultimately would prove decisive—more crucial even than the expansion of landholdings, financial resources, and world Jewish support—in protecting the National Home against the mounting perils of Arab hostility and British diplomatic equivocation.

THE SEEDS OF
ARAB-JEWISH CONFRONTATION

ARABS AND JEWS BEFORE THE MANDATE

In 1907 Dr. Yitzchak Epstein, a noted Zionist educator, published an article in the Hebrew journal *HaShiloach*. "Among the grave questions linked with the concept of our people's renaissance on its own soil," he wrote, "there is one question *which is more weighty than all the others combined*. This is the question of our relations with the Arabs. Our own national aspirations depend upon the correct solution of this question. . . . [Yet] it has simply been forgotten by the Zionists and is hardly referred to at all in its true form in Zionist literature." Epstein did not exaggerate. Occasional references to the Arabs appeared in the writings of such proto-Zionists as Kalischer, Lilienblum, and Levanda, but almost in passing, as if the Arab inhabitants were hardly a factor of political significance. "Outside Palestine," noted Achad HaAm in 1891, "we are accustomed to believing that the Arabs are all wild beasts of the desert, a people akin to jackasses who do not understand what is going on around them."

The early political Zionists were certain in any case that Jewish enterprise and financial investments in Palestine would be greeted with enthusiasm by the Arabs. We recall, too, that this optimism was fully shared by Herzl in *Altneuland*. Elsewhere, Herzl had not a single word to say about the Arab population, not even in his extensive diary. On one occasion, Nordau evidently was given pause. "But there are Arabs in Palestine!" he said in consternation to Herzl. "I did not know that! We are committing an injustice!" The moment of doubt passed quickly. Nor was it revived by events in Palestine itself. Violence between Arabs and Jews was rare before the turn of the century. While Arab banditry was an endless harassment to the Zionist colonies, it signified no particular nationalist animus. JNF purchases of Arab land occasionally deprived fellahin of their traditional homesteads, but the numbers of Arabs who benefited from Jewish immigration more than compensated for rare injustices. Indeed, in the Middle East, it was Palestine alone that saw Arab immigration exceeding emigration; the Jews were providing a new market for Arab food and services. As neighbors, Jews and Arabs cooperated on many occasions, and not infrequently were guests in each other's homes. The former did not hesitate to borrow from the diet, dress, even the vernacular of their "Ishmaelite cousins." They anticipated no future difficulties in relations between the two peoples.

In a deeper sense, however, the Zionists made little effort to fathom the complexity of Arab mores. The early kibbutzim, the radical political and social values of Labor Zionism, the limitation of employment to Jewish workers, the emphasis placed by immigrant pioneers on equality between the sexes—all offended the Arabs more than the Jews appreciated at the time. Epstein, in his 1907 article, was referring precisely to this lack of sensitivity when he implored his fellow Jews "to avoid a narrow, limited nationalism, which sees no farther than itself." He proposed instead "an alliance with the Arabs and a pact with them which will benefit both sides and the whole of mankind." Yet Epstein's views were rejected. Ze'ev Smilansky, a leader of the Second Aliyah, expressed the prevailing Zionist viewpoint when he accused Epstein of being "the victim of his own fantasies. . . . He is attracted to the wretched Arabs. . . . We are told by Epstein that we are not entitled to redeem the land of our forefathers with money, even if we do this in a fair and peaceful manner. . . . So we have nothing to worry about except the fate of the Palestine Arabs?" In Smilansky's view, Epstein was afflicted with a "Diaspora way of thinking," with a typical and timorous concern for "what the non-Jews say."

Perhaps the Zionists were not altogether culpable in failing to take Arab nationalism seriously. The phenomenon barely existed before 1908. In truth, nationalism developed later in the Arab communities than among any of the other subject peoples in the Ottoman empire, with the possible exception of the Albanians. Even the anti-Turkish strictures of al-Afghani, Muhammad Abdu, Rashid Rida, and other Moslem ideologues were evoked less by the oppressiveness of Turkish rule than by the sultan's manifest failure to protect the empire from the incursions of the Christian West. It was essentially this Ottoman ineptitude, nevertheless, that first evoked hostility against Constantinople among a small but articulate group of Arab writers, students, army officers, and businessmen. In the last half-decade following the Young Turk Revolution of 1908, the al-Fatat and al-Ahd parties began tentatively expressing the demand of an incipient Arab bourgeoisie for cultural and political autonomy. The appeal was echoed by several Egyptian and Syrian journalists living in Cairo, most of them former members of the (by then) defunct Ottoman "Decentralization" party. There were other, smaller opposition elements; but until the 1908 revolutionary period they occasioned little concern on the part of the Turks or of the West, and least of all of the Jews. It was not surprising, under the circumstances, that the latter identified Arab anti-Zionism with Christians like Naguib Azouri, a former Ottoman official who had founded a society called the Ligue de la Patrie Arabe in Paris. Azouri's book *Le Réveil de la nation arabe* warned of the "effort of the Jews to reconstitute on a very large scale the ancient kingdom of Israel," and asserted that Arab and Jewish nationalism represented "two contradictory principles." The fact that only small numbers of Moslems were aware of Azouri's writings persuaded the Jews that his enmity represented merely a variation of the Christian anti-Semitism that had bedeviled their lives in the Diaspora.

The Young Turk Revolution, on the other hand, gave the problem of Jewish-Arab relations a new dimension. Alerted by then to new opportunities of self-rule, Arab—Moslem—members of the Ottoman Parliament embarked for the first time on an anti-Zionist campaign. Both in debate and in the Turkish press of Constantinople, they warned that the Jews were developing nothing less than self-government in Palestine, with their own schools, national anthem, stamps, scrip, even their own illegal militia. The charge touched off repercussions among the Palestine Arabs, whose journals and newspapers similarly adopted a vigorously anti-Zionist line. In 1911 some 150 Palestine Arab notables founded an anti-Jewish association in Jaffa, telegraphed Constantinople to protest land purchases by Jews, and encouraged several—minor—demonstrations against Jews. Yet, even then, the Zionists insisted on attributing Arab opposition essentially to small numbers of Christian merchants and wealthy effendis. Dutifully professing their loyalty to the Turkish regime, moreover, the Jews were inhibited from seeking a common front with Arab nationalism; it was their hope that the Ottoman government would regard them as a barrier against Arab autonomy. As a result, this professed devotion to Constantinople merely aroused further Arab resentment. The Zionist leadership never managed to resolve the dilemma.

Neither did it effectively exploit a unique opportunity for Arab-Jewish cooperation that opened in 1913. In June of that year an Arab Congress met in Paris to formulate its autonomist demands. On the eve of the gathering, Arab leaders approached the Zionist representative in Constantinople, Victor Jacobson (who had come to Paris as an observer), to discuss a possible Arab-Jewish common front against the Turks. Jacobson in fact was one of the few Zionist spokesmen who had long sought a connection with the Arab movement, and he immediately dispatched his assistant, Sami Hochberg, to Cairo to meet with Arab spokesmen there. In subsequent discussions with the Arab committee, Hochberg intimated that the Jews might support Arab nationalism, provided the impending Congress similarly accepted Zionist claims. This the Arabs apparently were not yet willing to do "for tactical reasons." Nevertheless, the chairman of the committee, Rafik Bey al-Azm, issued a formal statement:

> The party had decided to protect Jewish national rights and not to adopt any law or resolution limiting them or placing them beyond the pale. . . . We fully understand the valuable assistance that the capital, the diligence, and the intelligence of the Jews can provide to the accelerated development of our areas, and hence we must not err by not accepting them. Certainly there might be a need for regulating immigration, both Jewish and other. . . . But there is a difference between reasonable, fair regulations and extraordinary measures, such as were introduced by the old Turkish regime and have been maintained by the new regime.

While less than overwhelmed by the declaration, Hochberg agreed to act as a mediator between the Arab Congress and the Young Turk leaders in Constantinople. At one point he managed to elicit an Ottoman assurance of sympathy for Arab demands, and a number of these demands in fact were granted before the war broke out.

Far from winning Zionist endorsement, however, Hochberg's efforts generally were denigrated. Richard Lichtheim, who once had served in the Constantinople office with Jacobson, warned later that "as long as Palestine belongs to the Turks," the Jews would be risking too much by collaboration with the Arabs. When the Arab leadership requested a meeting with their Zionist counterparts in May 1914, the Zionist Executive turned it down, fearful of provoking Constantinople. All efforts still were devoted to keep-ing "the [Ottoman] government on our side." Learning of the rejection, Nasif-al-Khalidi, spokesman of the Arab Congress, murmured gravely to Nachum Sokolow, who was in Paris at the time: "Be very careful, gentle-men of the Zionist movement. Governments come and governments go, but a people remains forever."

The warning was validated once the war broke out. Within a few years it became clear that Arab leaders in Palestine, to a far greater extent than the Hashemite dynasty in Arabia, regarded Zionism as a genuine threat. Weizmann encountered this hostility in April 1918 during his meeting with several émigré Palestinians in Cairo (Chapter VI), among them Musa Kazem al-Husseini, mayor of Jerusalem, and a number of well-known Chris-tian Arabs. By the opening days of 1919 anti-Zionist sentiment among the Palestinians was becoming increasingly vocal. Nationalist speakers, led by Aref al-Aref and Amin al-Husseini (p. 170), toured villages and towns to mobilize Arab demonstrations in advance of the arrival of the King-Crane Commission, appointed by President Wilson to sound out Arab public opin-ion in the Middle East. Again, these developments were not taken with full seriousness by the Jews. Weizmann continued to place his hopes on Feisal. "With him I hope to establish a real political entente," he had written earlier. "But with the Arabs of Palestine—in whom . . . the Sharif is little interested—only proper economic relations are necessary." Yet as matters turned out, events in the Holy Land itself ultimately proved far more mean-ingful than the brief diplomatic rapport achieved between Weizmann and the Hashemite dynasty.

Feisal, at least, sensed that unrest in Palestine was threatening his honey-moon with the Zionists. Hopeful even at this late date of maintaining a solid Arab-Jewish front, he invited Chaim Kalvarisky, a known moderate and advocate of Arab-Jewish cooperation, to attend the Syrian National Congress in July 1919. There, in Damascus, Kalvarisky submitted a draft blueprint on a future Palestine government. The document laid its emphasis on freedom of religion and self-expression for all, on the teaching of both Arabic and Hebrew in the schools of both peoples, and on the annulment of separatist arrangements of any kind for Jews, Moslems, or Christians in the nation's public institutions. The Arab leaders initially approved this proposal. Several days later, however, when Kalvarisky brought the draft to an assembly of Palestine Jews—the "Provisional Jewish Committee" that subsequently was to be expanded into the Yishuv's National Assembly—the latter repudiated the scheme as "ridiculous and dangerous." Moshe Medzini, a Palestine Jewish journalist, later commented ruefully:

> The gravest political failure of the Yishuv was in its failure to create an atmosphere of mutual understanding between Jews and Arabs. . . . Relations with the Arabs should have been the main political issue facing the Yishuv. . . . [But the] sad fact is . . . that the Yishuv showed the same lack of understanding and appreciation of this question immediately after the war that it displayed before and during the war. . . . The Yishuv as a whole was deep in economic preoccupations and internal quarrels, and paid no attention to [Kalvarisky and others like him].

Certainly the Nebi Musa riots of April 1920 (Chapter VI) should have been warning enough to the Jews that they did not yet know their neighbors.

THE ARABS OF PALESTINE

As late as 1882 the Arab population of Palestine barely reached 260,000. Yet by 1914 this number had doubled, and by 1920 it had reached 600,000. Under the mandate the figure grew even more dramatically, climbing to 840,000 by 1931, and representing 81 percent of the country's inhabitants. Approximately 75,000 of the Palestine Arabs were Christian, heavily impacted in the urban areas, comparatively literate, and widely employed at the middle and lower echelons of the mandatory administration. The Moslem Arabs—the majority—were much more backward. Fully 70 percent of them lived on the soil, mainly in the hilly northern and central regions of the country, where they raised grains, vegetables, olive oil, and tobacco. A 1922 census revealed that a third of the Arab farmers were fellahin—tenant sharecroppers—whose average plot rarely exceeded 100 dunams (25 acres). Endlessly indebted to their landlords, to whom they paid a rent of from 33 to 50 percent of their crops, they lived with their families of five or more children in mud-brick huts, possessed virtually no sanitary facilities, and suffered chronically from amoebic dysentery and bilharziasis.

Submarginal as these conditions were, they were immeasurably better than those of Moslem Arabs elsewhere in the Middle East. The statistics of Arab population growth were revealing; in Palestine the increase between 1922 and 1946 was 118 percent, a rate of almost 5 percent annually, and the highest in the Arab world except for Egypt. It was not all natural increase. During those twenty-four years approximately 100,000 Arabs entered the country from neighboring lands. The influx could be traced in some measure to the orderly government provided by the British; but far more, certainly, to the economic opportunities made possible by Jewish settlement. The rise of the Yishuv benefited Arab life indirectly, by disproportionate Jewish contributions to government revenues, and thereby to increased mandatory expenditures in the Arab sector; and directly, by opening new markets for Arab produce and (until the civil war of 1936) new employment opportunities for Arab labor. It was significant, for example, that the movement of Arabs within Palestine itself was largely to regions of Jewish concentration. Thus, Arab population increase during the 1930s was 87 percent in Haifa, 61 percent in Jaffa, 37 percent in Jerusalem. A similar growth was registered in Arab towns located near Jewish agricultural villages. The 25 percent rise of Arab participation in industry could be traced exclusively to the needs of the large Jewish immigration.

Nor were the Arabs unaware of the advantages to be reaped from Jewish settlement. Indeed, left to their own, the fellahin conceivably might not have become intensely anti-Zionist. It was simply that the 1920s and 1930s did not allow for tolerable and genial intercourse. During the military regime, Generals Allenby, Money, and Bols were openly hostile to Zionism, fearing the Jewish National Home's potentially disruptive influence among the Arabs. Until May 1920, therefore, no official British reference to the Balfour Declaration was circulated in Palestine. British officers also played a role in the founding of the Moslem-Christian Association, the first postwar Arab organization in Palestine. Even under Samuel's civilian government, a number of key officials remained inflexibly opposed to the Jewish National Home. Among these were Colonel Ernest Richmond, the assistant chief secretary of the political department. "In matters relating to the participation of the Arabs [in the legislative council then planned]," admitted Raghib Bey al-Nashashibi, in 1923, "the High Commissioner is guided by the advice of Richmond, who makes all cooperation with the Jews impossible."

On several occasions, British opposition torpedoed promising joint discussions between Jewish and Arab leaders. In the early months of 1922, for example, a series of unofficial Arab-Zionist meetings took place in Cairo. They were attended on the Arab side by prominent Syrian nationalists, including Sheikh Rashid Rida, president of the central committee of the Syrian United party, Riad al-Sulh, later to be prime minister of Lebanon, and Emile Ghori, a Palestinian editor of *al-Ahram*, the leading Egyptian newspaper. Representing the Jews were Dr. Montague David Eder, of the Zionist Executive, and Asher Sapir, a man with extensive connections in the Arab world. At each discussion the usual amenities were exchanged, the pious references to a "common Semitic revival" in the Middle East. In the initial conference on March 18, the Arabs renewed their proposals of January 1919 (p. 121). One was for the Jews to cooperate with the Arabs in evicting the French from Syria. Another was for the Zionists to repudiate the Balfour Declaration and deal with the Arabs "nation to nation." Acceptance of the first proposal clearly would have been an embarrassment to London. Acceptance of the second would have made the Jewish National Home dependent upon agreement with the Arabs rather than upon British protection. Hearing of these offers, the Colonial Office asked the Zionists to postpone all further discussions until the mandate had been ratified. The Jews acquiesced.

Further Jewish-Arab meetings were resumed in April 1922, however, and soon appeared to bear fruit. A résumé declared that each side would actively cooperate with the other. The Jews promised to supply their Arab neighbors with economic and political help, while the Arabs undertook to cease all anti-Zionist propaganda and to establish a mixed Christian-Moslem-Jewish commission in Palestine. Most important, it was agreed that future Jewish dealings with the Arabs no longer would be related to the Balfour Declaration or the mandate, while the Arabs, for their part, would not invoke their 1915 treaty (the Hussein-McMahon correspondence) in negotiations with the Jews. Nor did this modified Arab stance apparently require a Zionist repudiation of the Balfour Declaration, simply a willingness to avoid reference to the document as the major basis for Arab-Jewish cooperation. Weizmann approved the understanding in principle. The British did not. Again, the Colonial Office ordered an immediate stop to the discussions. Meetings scheduled later between Weizmann and Sa'ad Zaghlul Pasha, the Egyptian nationalist leader, and between Weizmann and Emir Abdullah of Transjordan, were summarily canceled by the British. There would be no agreement reached between Arabs and Jews independently of the mandatory power.

Yet it was by no means British obstructionism alone that undermined cooperation between Arabs and Jews. The exigencies of Palestine Arab politics were also decisive. Under the Turks, Arab political life had been quite rudimentary and had consisted largely of maneuvers for civil office among rival effendi families. No organized nationalist movement whatever came into being until after the Armistice, when Moslem-Christian Associations were founded in various Arab towns to protest the impending Jewish National Home. This opposition, too, was at first essentially a projection of Syrian nationalism; it followed the lead of Arab politicians in Damascus during the unsuccessful 1919–20 effort to establish an independent Syrian kingdom. Accordingly, the collapse of Feisal's regime in the summer of 1920, and the transfer of nationalist headquarters from Damascus to Jerusalem, played a critical role in the development of an authentic Palestine Arab nationalism. It did not escape the Arab leadership, especially those who formerly had devoted their energies to the Hashemite cause in Syria, that the Zionists, as a minority settlement, were surely more vulnerable to concerted resistance than were the French or British.

In December 1920, therefore, the Moslem-Christian Associations sponsored a convention in Haifa, a gathering that subsequently transformed itself into a Palestine Arab Congress. Here at last the demand was expressly submitted that Britain institute a national—that is, Arab—government in Palestine. The Congress afterward proceeded to elect an Arab Executive, a body that from 1921 on implacably opposed the British mandate and the Jewish National Home. While the Executive's hostility to Zionism was rooted at least partly in suspicion of Jewish free labor and collective agriculture, and the ideas these innovations might plant in the minds of the fellahin, it reflected more basically a fear of the political consequences of Jewish immigration. Centuries of exile in Europe clearly had westernized the Jews and enabled them far to exceed the Arab community in their intellectual and technological accomplishments. The Arab leaders were genuinely alarmed by the influx of these "overbearing and truculent" newcomers, and warned that the European Jews, with apparently limitless energy and financial backing, someday would engulf the whole of Palestine.

Initially, attempts by the Arab Executive to press its case in London or before the League of Nations in Geneva were rebuffed. Despite these setbacks, the Palestine Arab Congress managed to broaden its influence within the nation's Arab community at large. Its delegates were chosen by the Moslem-Christian Associations, serving as local branches of the national movement in the towns. The selection procedure even appeared likely for a while to develop into a form of representative spokesmanship—thereby matching the emergent Jewish quasi-government. If this early promise was not fulfilled, it was largely because the nationalist movement came to be the virtual monopoly of the Husseini clan. Wealthy landowners in southern Palestine, the Husseinis had provided thirteen mayors of Jerusalem between 1864 and 1920. One of them, Musa Kazem al-Husseini, who had been dismissed by the British for his role in the Nebi Musa riots, presided over the Arab Executive and the several Palestine Arab Congresses and led the Arab delegations to England. The family's influence was enhanced subsequently by its grip on the religious affairs of the Islamic community. Even before the war, the leading figure among Palestine Moslems was the Grand Mufti of Jerusalem, a jurisconsult who issued decrees on Koranic law. As it happened, the office of Mufti became vacant with the death of Kamal al-Husseini shortly after Samuel arrived in Palestine, and to the high commissioner fell the prerogative of appointing a new incumbent. In April 1921, determined to keep the honors balanced between the Husseini and Nashashibi families—traditionally competitors for nearly every public office in the country—Samuel approved the dubiously honest election of Haj Muhammad Amin al-Husseini (who in fact received less votes for this position than did three other candidates).

Born in 1893, Amin al-Husseini had been educated in a government school in Jerusalem, and at al-Azhar University in Cairo. He had served as an Ottoman officer during the war, then had returned to Jerusalem immediately after the British occupation to become politically active in Arab life. While a teacher in the Rashidiya school in Jerusalem, Haj Amin had incited the crowds during the Nebi Musa riots of 1920; upon fleeing to Transjordan, he was sentenced *in absentia* to ten years' imprisonment. Soon afterward, however, he was amnestied by Samuel, and returned to Jerusalem in 1921, where almost immediately he became Mufti. He was not the happiest choice. Although disarming in appearance and demeanor, with mild blue eyes, neatly trimmed red goatee, and gentle, ingratiating manner, Haj Amin was soon revealed as an impassioned Arab xenophobe, a preacher of venom and destruction against his nation's and his family's enemies.

The danger Haj Amin presented to the mandate actually resided less in his office of Mufti than in his far more influential presidency of the Supreme Moslem Council. In December 1921 the British had authorized the establishment of this institution to direct the religious affairs of the Palestine Moslem community; it was intended as a counterpart of the Rabbinical Council of the Jews. Yet the Moslem Council also exercised virtually unlimited rights of patronage and control over the Islamic religious hierarchy of Palestine, over Moslem schools, religious courts, and waqf (religious) trust funds. In 1922 Haj Amin was elected president of this Council by a remnant of the Moslem property owners who had voted in the last election for the Ottoman Parliament. Thereupon, exploiting to the full his triple position as religious head, national leader, and senior government official (the post of Mufti in effect was a state office), Haj Amin began to mobilize the loyalties of the Islamic population for his own highly developed personal and nationalist ambitions.

At first, during the 1920s, the Mufti's campaign against the mandate and the Zionists was only partially effective. Resentful of Husseini power and patronage, a number of disgruntled Arab mayors, gentry, and businessmen grouped themselves around Raghib Bey al-Nashashibi in the "National party," intended as a counterpoise to the Moslem-Christian Associations. For nearly five years this rivalry helped keep the nationalist movement in abeyance. So did the firm personality of Viscount Plumer, Samuel's successor as high commissioner. A tough and respected general, Plumer made it clear that he would tolerate no disorders. As a consequence of economic recession in Palestine, too, Jewish immigration declined somewhat between 1925 and 1927, and this partially allayed Arab fears of Jewish domination. Indeed, Plumer was sufficiently encouraged by the absence of unrest to disband the Palestine and British gendarmerie, even to reduce the military garrison to a single squadron of armored cars. In 1928, finally, the Seventh Palestine Arab Congress displayed an uncharacteristic moderation. Rather than present its usual demand for an outright end to the Jewish National Home, the members simply requested parliamentary institutions on the basis of democratic majorities. The new high commissioner, Sir John Chancellor, was impressed by this seeming flexibility. Before leaving for his vacation in June of 1929, he promised to consult London on the chances of reviving a "more acceptable" (to the Arabs) version of a legislative council.

A FAILURE OF PERCEPTION, A RENEWAL OF VIOLENCE

If the high commissioner was shortsighted in failing to detect the simmering volcano of Arab hostility, the Jews were hardly less obtuse. During the immediate postwar period they gave scarcely more attention to the Palestine Arabs than during all the years since the birth of Zionism. The Arab negotiations that mattered most to Weizmann were those with Feisal and the leaders of Syria and Egypt, not with the Arabs of Palestine. Once the former's goodwill was won, nothing else mattered. Typically, Ussishkin could dismiss the Palestine Arab community as a "negligible quantity." This illusion was not dispelled at first even by the Nebi Musa riots; the bloodletting was regarded as a mere transitory outburst, and provoked, at that, by British equivocation. It was the violence of 1921 that first brought the Zionists up short and offered sobering evidence of possibly grave dangers ahead. George Landauer, a German Zionist leader, pleaded with the Twelfth Zionist Congress that year for renewed efforts at Arab-Jewish accommodation. Writing from Jaffa in May 1921, Chaim Arlosoroff warned that the Arab nationalist movement would have to be taken seriously; a program of reconciliation was the only answer. But as quiet returned to the Holy Land during the mid-1920s, Zionist policy toward the Arabs remained lethargic and unimaginative. It was the prevailing view that, once Jewish immigration gained momentum, the backward native population would accept the Jewish National Home as a *fait accompli*.

For the Labor Zionists, particularly, the economic benefits of Jewish settlement appeared to be the decisive response to Arab nationalism. Berl Katznelson, otherwise an incisive and sophisticated intellect, was convinced that the fellahin, exploited by a rapacious feudal plutocracy, soon would appreciate the importance of economic solidarity with the Jews. For Ben-Gurion, "only the narrow circles of the Arab ruling strata have egotistical reasons to fear Jewish immigration and the social and economic changes caused by it." The Arab masses, at least, would understand that Jewish immigration and colonization brought prosperity. In the view of the Labor leadership, it behooved the Jewish laboring class to form an alliance with its Arab counterpart. "Can there be any doubt," asked Ya'akov Chazan, a respected leader of HaShomer HaZair, "that only the organized help of the Jewish worker can bring about the self-development of the Arab working class?" Yet if the effendis, in the Zionist scheme, were the authentic enemies of Zionism, it was significant that few of the leftist parties bestirred themselves to make common cause with Arab workers and farmers. In 1927 the Third Histadrut Convention provided for the establishment of a Confederation of Palestine Labor, a kind of roof organization for all workers of Palestine. Several common unions were in fact organized among government employees, particularly the railroad and telegraph workers. Despite its 1927 resolution, however, the Histadrut continued notably uninterested in encouraging joint Arab-Jewish unions within the broader labor sector.

Effendi dislike of Socialist practices unquestionably was a factor in Arab hostility. Yet it was one factor only, and by no means the predominant one. The living standard of Arab farmers and workers was rising, to be sure; but the Arab leadership noted only that the Jewish standard of living was rising much faster. One of the bitterest Arab complaints, moreover, related to the sale of land to the Jews, and to JNF policy in ensuring that Jewish land, once acquired, could never be resold to Arabs nor opened for non-Jewish employment. This surely was not an "effendi" complaint. On the contrary, it was from the effendis that the JNF purchased their tracts—at exorbitant prices. In fact, the "class" approach to Arab nationalism was bankrupt from the outset, as was every other effort to qualify or minimize the depth of this sentiment. Perhaps the one Zionist faction that took the Arab problem seriously from the outset was Revisionism, although the latter's solution was hardly that of appeasement or compassion (p. 186). The truth was that neither Arab resentment nor the Mufti's ambitions were likely to be placated by Zionist reassurances. The Arab Executive's seemingly mild proposal to Sir John Chancellor bespoke a change of tactics, not of purpose. By the summer of 1929, too, Jewish immigration was rising again. The establishment of the Jewish Agency in August of that year promised yet additional financial support to the Jewish National Home. While no major disturbances had erupted between Arabs and Jews since 1921, festering emotions were merely awaiting their spark.

As it happened, violence was to be ignited in an unlikely venue, the Old City of Jerusalem, where Arabs and Jewish pietists had been living in close proximity for several centuries. There, abutting the Haram es-Sharif complex of mosques, was the venerated Jewish Western Wall (often called the "Wailing Wall"), a remnant of the Hebrew Temple of antiquity. The Wall belonged to the Moslem community. By tradition extending back at least to the Middle Ages, however, the Jews enjoyed an easement to the strip of pavement facing the historic buttress and the right of prayer at the Wall itself. In 1928, shortly before the Jewish holy day of Yom Kippur, which fell on September 24, the Jewish sexton at the Wall placed a screen on the flagstones to separate men and women, according to Orthodox Jewish practice. The Arabs immediately complained that the status quo had been violated. The British authorities agreed and ordered the screen removed. The Jews remonstrated, but to no avail. Subsequently the entire Yishuv, religionists and nonobservant alike, expressed indignation at the "wanton interference" with Jewish freedom of worship. The Zionist Organization submitted protests to London and Geneva. The Arabs meanwhile appealed to the Moslem world, charging that the Jews intended to seize control of the venerated al-Aqsa Mosque, within the Haram area. At the initiative of the Mufti's Supreme Moslem Council, Arab workers set about building operations in the neighborhood of the Wall, to interfere with Jewish worship, even as an especially cacophonous Moslem religious ceremony was launched to disrupt Jewish prayers there. Months of protests and counterprotests followed. On June 11, 1929, after prolonged equivocation by the mandatory government and repeated consultations with legal officers of the Crown, the high commissioner notified the Mufti that the Jews were entitled to worship without disturbance. The building operations might continue, provided "no disturbance is caused to Jewish worshipers during the customary times of their prayer."

Neither Jews nor Moslems were satisfied with this decision. On August 16 a right-wing Jewish youth group sought permission to conduct a peaceful march on the Wall. In the absence of Chancellor, who had departed for London to submit the Arab Executive's proposal on the issue of a legislative council, the British acting high commissioner, Sir Harry Luke, acceded to the youth group's request. Immediately, then, the Moslem leadership organized a turbulent counterdemonstration near the Wall, delivering inflammatory speeches and provoking minor skirmishes. During the subsequent week Moslem agitators traveled throughout the country, exhorting the peasantry to "protect al-Aqsa against Jewish attacks." Finally, on the night of August 23 and the next morning, crowds of Arabs armed with weapons poured into Jerusalem. The newcomers gathered near the mosque courtyard to be harangued by the Mufti. Then, at noon, the mob attacked the Orthodox Jewish quarters, and violence spread rapidly to other areas of Palestine. In the late afternoon Arab bands descended on the Orthodox Jewish community of Hebron, murdering sixty and wounding fifty inhabitants. Other assaults were carried out in Haifa and Jaffa, even in Tel Aviv. Numerous Jewish agricultural villages were similarly attacked. The RAF contingent in Amman was inadequate to restore order, while the Arab police were sympathetic to the rioters. The acting high commissioner was obliged to telephone Egypt for military assistance, but the main body of troops did not reach Palestine until three days afterward, and order was not restored until August 28. By then 133 Jews had been killed, 399 wounded. The Arabs had suffered 178 casualties, 87 of them dead.

Chancellor, rushing back from England, issued a proclamation on September 1 that furiously condemned the Arab atrocities; he then proceeded to levy heavy collective fines on Arab towns and villages. But the effect of these measures was soon dissipated. No sooner had the Mufti protested Chancellor's "brutality" than the high commissioner issued a second proclamation a few days later, stating that an inquiry into the conduct of *both* sides would be held as soon as possible. Whereupon the Jews, appalled at the implication that the murderers and their victims were somehow on a common level, turned to London for redress.

THE AFTERMATH OF VIOLENCE

At this critical moment in the Yishuv's fortunes, the Zionists learned to their dismay that they no longer enjoyed the backing of a sympathetic government in England. The Baldwin cabinet had fallen in midsummer of 1929, and the Laborites under Ramsay MacDonald had returned to office. Leopold Amery, the last of the wartime group that had sponsored the Balfour Declaration, was now replaced as colonial secretary by Sidney Webb— shortly to be appointed Lord Passfield. Notwithstanding the large Jewish minority in its ranks, the Labor party had developed no affirmative views on Zionism. MacDonald had himself visited Palestine in 1922 and returned declaring that British promises to Jews and Arabs were contradictory. Weizmann soon discovered which way the wind was blowing upon reaching London. For the first time in his experience, the Zionist leader encountered a chill atmosphere in Westminster; he was unable at the outset to secure an interview with Passfield. The colonial secretary's wife, Beatrice Webb, on meeting Weizmann, commented only: "I can't understand why the Jews make such a fuss over a few dozen of their people killed in Palestine. As many are killed every week in London in traffic accidents, and no one pays any attention." When Passfield finally received Weizmann, he bluntly declared himself opposed to mass Jewish immigration into Palestine.

Other shocks were in store. The political ramifications of the violence would continue for a year and a half and encompass a torrent of controversy that threatened the very future of the Jewish National Home. In mid-September, the Colonial Office dispatched a Royal Commission to Palestine "to enquire into the immediate causes which led to the recent outbreak in Palestine and to make recommendations as to the steps necessary to avoid a recurrence." The appointed chairman was Sir Walter Shaw, a retired chief justice of the Turkish Straits Settlements. Serving with him were representatives of each of Britain's three political parties. Unlike the Haycraft investigation of 1921, the Shaw Commission sat as a public court of inquiry, with authority to summon witnesses, to take evidence on oath, and to hear counsel on behalf of the Palestine government, the Jewish Agency, and the Arab Executive.

The commission conducted its hearings over a period of five weeks and finally issued its report on March 31, 1930. The document was a bombshell. It found the Arabs responsible for the violence and apportioned "a share in the responsibility for the disturbances" to the Mufti and individual members of the Arab Executive. Yet, by a majority of two to one, the commission rejected the view that the assaults had been carefully premeditated. By the same vote, it exonerated the government and the police for apathy in handling the outbreaks. Moreover, ignoring its limited authorization to deal exclusively with the immediate cause of the riots, the commission went on to state that the fundamental cause of the tragedy was the "Arab feeling of animosity and hostility towards the Jews consequent upon the disappointment of their political and national aspirations and fear for their economic future." It noted that the government had not yet given —and therefore should provide—a more precisely worded statement on its obligations to the "non-Jewish communities." In the interval, the mandatory administration was urged to tighten its control of Jewish immigration, protect Arab tenants from eviction by Jewish land purchasers, and ensure that the Jewish Agency understood henceforth that it was in no sense empowered to share in the government of Palestine.

If the Shaw Report aroused consternation among the Zionists and jubilation among the Arabs, subsequent governmental measures intensified these reactions. On May 12, the Colonial Office instructed the mandatory to suspend the latest Jewish immigration schedule of 3,300 labor certificates. Two weeks later, in a statement presented to the League Mandates Commission, the British government declared that it viewed the Shaw recommendations favorably and was considering additional measures for suspending Jewish immigration and for protecting the Arab population. Although the League body, for its part, rejected the contention that Arab rights could best be protected by limiting Jewish immigration and land purchases, London nevertheless proceeded to explore further the recommendations outlined by the Shaw Report. That same May it dispatched Sir John Hope Simpson to Palestine. A retired Indian civil service official and an authority on agricultural economics, Hope Simpson embarked upon three months of travel-investigation and aerial surveys of landholdings. He then issued a massive 185-page report of his own on October 20, 1930.

It was Hope Simpson's conclusion that the land available to Arabs was less than previously had been believed. The Arabs, he said, gradually were being driven off the soil by Jewish land purchases and by the JNF policy of not reselling to Arabs or allowing them employment on Jewish tracts. This was a distinct breach of Article Six of the mandate. The report doubted Palestine's capacity to sustain any meaningful industrial growth. Accordingly, "the importation of large numbers of immigrants to be employed on new industries . . . whose economic success is quite problematical, might well cause a [severe] crisis. . . ." The government virtually had abdicated its control of labor certificates to the Jewish Agency and Histadrut, the report declared, and this was inexcusable. Further measures, then, should be taken to restrict both Jewish immigration and Jewish land purchases. Hope Simpson expressed his personal belief that when all development schemes were in full operation there would be room in Palestine for 20,000 additional immigrant families, about 100,000 people, and of these not more than half should be Jews.

The Zionists, shocked and angered, were not tardy in rejecting Hope Simpson's data and conclusions. The man had grossly underestimated the amount of cultivable land in Palestine, they argued, and had overestimated the quantity required either by Arabs or by Jews. His attempt to blame Jewish immigration for Arab village poverty was libelous and inflammatory. Even official statistics proved that of the 1,481,000 dunams in Jewish hands, 350,000 were swamp, and 500,000 were tracts never before cultivated. The entire Yishuv held only 6.3 percent of the land considered to be arable. All these figures, too, were less relevant than the dramatic rise in Arab living standards as a consequence of Jewish settlement in Palestine, the irrefutable evidence that Arab immigrants, no less than Jews, were flooding into the country as a result of new economic opportunities provided by the Jewish National Home.

Yet before these arguments could be marshaled, London released an official statement on the same day, October 20, that the Hope Simpson Report was published. It took the form of a twenty-three-page White Paper issued by Lord Passfield. "It must be realized once and for all," declared the White Paper, "that it is useless for Jewish leaders . . . to press His Majesty's Government to conform to their policy in regard . . . to immigration and land, to the aspirations of the more uncompromising sections of Zionist opinion. That would be to ignore the equally important duty of the Mandatory Power towards the non-Jewish inhabitants of Palestine." While observing that "it is equally useless for Arab leaders to maintain their demands for [majority rule]," the document proceeded to skewer virtually every Zionist hope for the future. "There remains no margin of land available for agricultural settlement by the new immigrants," it asserted, "with the exception of such undeveloped lands as the various Jewish agencies hold in reserve." Jewish immigration must be suspended, too, as long as extensive unemployment in Palestine continued.

The Passfield White Paper went much further than the Churchill White Paper of 1922, for it appeared to repudiate the very purpose of the Balfour

Declaration and the terms of the San Remo award. It foreshadowed serious immigration restrictions and threatened the Jews with an embargo on additional purchases of land. More significantly yet, it commented upon the work of the Jews in Palestine in disparaging terms, omitting altogether to credit the Zionists for the benefits they had conferred upon the country and all its peoples. It was little wonder that the Arabs expressed general satisfaction with the document. The Jewish reaction was quite different, of course. Outraged, Weizmann immediately resigned as president of the Jewish Agency. In his formal protest to the British government, he stated:

> If the obligation of the Mandatory is reduced to an obligation toward 170,000 people as against 700,000 people, a small minority juxtaposed to a great majority, then of course everything else can perhaps be explained. But the obligation of the Mandatory Power is toward the Jewish people, of which the 170,000 are merely the vanguard. I must take issue, as energetically as I can, with the formulation of the obligation of the Mandatory Power as an identical obligation toward both sections of the Palestine population.

Weizmann's was perhaps the most temperate Zionist reaction. The response from the Jewish world—in Palestine, Britain, and America—was altogether infuriated. Besides letters, petitions, cables of protest, and impassioned newspaper editorials, it took the form of endless individual and collective meetings with British public figures. Some of these latter, in fact, hardly needed persuasion that the British government had betrayed a solemn trust. Stanley Baldwin and the Conservatives promptly dissociated themselves from the Passfield White Paper. Leopold Amery and Winston Churchill anathematized the document in the House of Commons. In a heated parliamentary debate on November 17, Lloyd George scored MacDonald for breaking the word of England. "It was not a word we inherited," the prime minister shot back. "We inherited words, and they are not always consistent." Nevertheless, MacDonald was shaken by the intensity of the attack upon him, the schism even among his own Labor party, many of whose members were dependent upon Liberal and Jewish support. At the suggestion, therefore, of Harold Laski, the party's most respected theorist, and of his own son, Malcolm MacDonald, the prime minister invited Weizmann to lunch on November 6, several days before the parliamentary debate. Years later, Weizmann's widow published her husband's account of the meeting:

> The Prime Minister went on to say, "I understand there are errors in this White Paper." I told him there were two groups of things: infringements of the Mandate; and interpretations which cause considerable difficulties and misgivings. . . . To which the Prime Minister replied, "The errors have to be put right, and the misunderstandings to be cleared up; and any new statement which is to be issued is to be issued in agreement with you. . . . [But] we cannot simply withdraw the White Paper. . . ."

The agreed face-saving device for a policy shift took the form of a letter from the prime minister to Weizmann on February 13, 1931, significantly re-interpreting the Passfield White Paper. In effect the document was a reversal, for it said: "The obligation to facilitate Jewish immigration and make possible dense settlement of Jews on the land is still a positive obligation of the Mandate, and it can be fulfilled without jeopardizing the rights and conditions of the other part of the Palestine population." The letter admitted that the number of Arabs dispossessed was surely less than Hope Simpson had determined and required more extensive investigation. Meanwhile, it gave additional assurances that the prohibition of further land purchase by Jews was not government policy.

> His Majesty's Government does not intend to interrupt or prohibit immigrants of any of the various categories. . . . Immigrants who can expect to obtain work, even of a temporary nature, will not be excluded from immigration for the sole reason that they are not assured work for an unlimited period.

The authority of the Jewish Agency to employ Jewish labor on purely Jewish ventures was confirmed, as was the right of Jewish workers to secure a fair share of employment in the mandatory government and in public works projects. In MacDonald's summary: "The obligations laid upon the Mandatory are solemn international promises and there is no intention at present, as there was not in the past, of disregarding them."

Although the letter did not enjoy the status either of a Command Paper or of a Colonial Office announcement, MacDonald released it to the press, transmitted it as an official document to the League, and embodied it in a dispatch as instructions to the Palestine high commissioner. Weizmann rightly interpreted it as "official," and hailed it as reestablishing a basis for Zionist cooperation with Britain. It did little, however, to encourage cooperation between Arabs and Jews. Instead, the Passfield White Paper and the MacDonald letter revealed British policy at its worst, for both documents convinced first the Arabs and then the Jews that sufficient agitation and pressure could reverse the intentions of the mandatory. Certainly the Arabs did not regard the MacDonald letter as the final word. "I want to assure your Excellency," wrote Musa Kazem al-Husseini, the president of the Arab Executive, to the high commissioner on February 19, 1931, "that Prime Minister MacDonald's letter has ruined hope of a policy of cooperation between Arabs and Jews, if there existed such a hope, and has rendered the possibility of understanding between the two parties absolutely impossible."

POLARIZATION AND A FAILURE OF DEFINITION

The Arabs had reason for their intractability. For one thing, their numbers in Palestine had grown to 960,000 by 1935, an increase of 67 percent in less than two decades, and an absolute growth over the Jews of nearly 500,000. Their urban population had risen from 194,000 in 1922 to 398,000 in 1936. Additionally, the infusion of Jewish capital—in payments for land, for agricultural produce, building materials, wages, rents, and services—profoundly stimulated the Arab economy. So, to a lesser extent, did the services and construction projects furnished by the mandatory. The most dramatic change was among the Arab upper and middle classes. Their investment in citriculture quadrupled between 1918 and 1935. Arab manufacturing by then had branched out from traditional soap, olive oil, and textile cottage products to a wider variety of consumer goods. Arab funds went now into trade and transport and supported their community's first two banks. By 1935 no fewer than seven hundred Arab cooperatives were functioning. New opportunities were opening out in medicine, law, government employment, journalism, and teaching. The number of Arab children attending schools had grown from less than 2 percent in 1920 to about 13 percent in 1936.

Here, then, were the classical ingredients for a burgeoning nationalism: rising literacy, a growing middle class, larger numbers of white-collar workers and professionals. If the Arabs hardened their position in the 1930s, moreover, it was because their leadership fell increasingly into the hands of the Mufti, who was emerging as a considerably stronger figure than his relative, the aging Musa Kazem al-Husseini. Indeed, Haj Amin's prestige and patronage lent Arab nationalism an additional ingredient of religious xenophobia. Unlike earlier Arab spokesmen, the Mufti had no illusions that the British would cooperate in the suppression of the Jewish National Home. He taught his followers to regard the mandatory as an infidel tyranny in alliance with other, Jewish, nonbelievers. His influence was given political expression in the Palestine Arab party, founded in 1935 under the titular leadership of his cousin and intimate aide, Jamil al-Husseini. Associated with the Husseinis were several mayors and leaders of the Haifa and Jerusalem branches of the Palestine Arab Workers Society. The faction also organized its own paramilitary group, al-Futuwwa, and adopted a militant, unbudging posture equally against the Balfour Declaration and the mandate.

Yet the Mufti's leadership, although preeminent, was by no means unquestioned. Opposition to his dominance remained largely centered in the Nashashibi family. Adopting in 1935 the title of National Defense party, the Nashashibi clan won a certain rural backing in Galilee as well as the support of a number of Arab mayors in the coastal towns. The family was known also to have established close relations with Abdullah of Transjordan. It had political rivals of its own, of course, and these were to be found not only among the Husseini partisans but in a handful of other organizations that developed in the early 1930s. Whatever their titles— National Bloc party, Istiqlal party, Arab Youth Congress, Reform party— none was a political party in the Western sense; all were merely groupings self-interestedly attached to ambitious individual families. In order, nevertheless, to achieve political influence within the Arab national movement, each was obliged to vie with the others in the tenacity of its anti-Zionism. It was this factionalism that rendered a *modus vivendi* with the Jews increasingly unlikely by mid-decade. Yet, by the same token, the family rivalries partially immobilized any effective united action against either the Zionists or the British. Early in 1934, for example, when Musa Kazem al-Husseini died, the Nashashibis managed to block the election of Jamil al-Husseini as the new president of the Arab Executive. In the next months, followers of both groups engaged in furious recriminations, each attacking the other for cowardice, for selling land to the Jews, or for lacking Arab patriotism. Paralyzed by this internecine conflict, the Arab Executive was all but dissolved, and the Eighth Arab Congress did not convene at all in the summer of 1935.

It was the failure of Arab unity, on the other hand, that accounted in turn for the Zionists' lack of urgency in defining their own intentions in Palestine. Even the 1929 violence was not perceived as a decisive moment of truth. The rank and file of the Yishuv chose to regard the killings less as a nationalist uprising than as a religious jihad, encouraged by Haj Amin for motives of personal ambition. Increased security measures were demanded of the British, but little more appeared necessary. Informal and wide-ranging contacts between Arabs and Jews, in the marketplace, in municipal councils, even at occasional social events, all clouded rather than accentuated the need for an official formulation of the relationship the Zionists ultimately intended to establish with the Arabs.

On the nonofficial level, to be sure, a number of sentient Jewish thinkers had confronted the problem. One of these was an American-born rabbi, Judah Magnes. Ordained in the Reform tradition, Magnes had visited Palestine twice before the war, became enamored there of the dream of Jewish national revival, and settled in Jerusalem in 1922. In 1925 he became chancellor of the newly established Hebrew University. From the outset of his career in Jerusalem, Magnes expressed growing concern about the exclusivist implications of the Jewish National Home. His ideas were shared by the newly established Brith Shalom, a society of intellectuals devoted to the cause of an Arab-Jewish binational state in Palestine. The Brith Shalom's most influential members were central European Jews, among them Professors Hugo Bergmann and Gershom Scholem of the Hebrew University, Robert Weltsch, former editor of the *Jüdische Rundschau*, and, not least of all, Martin Buber, whom the members regarded as their spiritual teacher. A mystic, deeply influenced by the "spirit of the East," Buber in 1920 urged his fellow Jews to lay the foundation of a true brotherhood with the Arabs and not to rely upon the "dazed dream [of themselves] as emissaries of a West that is doomed to destruction." The events of 1929 seemed to confirm this premonition. Yet the Brith Shalom was an ideological, not a political, group. Its membership never exceeded two hundred, and in its speeches and publications it made hardly a dent on the leadership of the Yishuv. Neither did it evoke even the faintest response from the Arabs.

There were other groups, too, that in modified form similarly expressed an interest in a binational regime that would allow freedom of Jewish immigration. The most outspoken of these was the radical, utopianist Ha-Shomer HaZair. In the 1920s the movement's kibbutz federation vigorously advocated the notion of political parity in the Holy Land. It was HaShomer HaZair that in 1926 persuaded the Histadrut to explore the idea of a binational Confederation of Palestine Labor. Little came of the scheme (p. 172). Even so, HaShomer HaZair remained the most influential of the Yishuv's parties to seek a mutual accommodation between Arabs and Jews, and labored endlessly for class and political solidarity among the Jewish and Arab working classes.

However minuscule in size or impact, these apolitical or quasi-political organizations at least took a forthright position on Zionist aims in the Holy Land. But this was hardly true of the Yishuv's political leadership, and the phenomenon did not escape the Arabs. Muhammad Achtar, editor of *Falastin,* the largest Arab daily in Palestine, made the point in a speech to a group of Jews on November 26, 1930:

> Another mistake that continually surprised me was that so much money and time and paper and ink were wasted on propaganda to explain Zionism to the Western nations. If only even the thousandth part of this effort were expended to clarify Zionism to the Arabs. . . . I suspect that you will not find a single leaflet in Arabic in which Zionists explain their needs, their rights, their claims—absolutely none. You yourselves know better than I the extent to which this was explained to the Americans, the English, the French. Although they must live among Arabs, the Zionists did not care whether or not the Arabs understood. They thought it more essential for someone in Vienna or in Paris to know what Zionism desired.

As it happened, the Zionists had by no means clearly formulated their aims even to themselves. Labor Zionism presumably recognized the importance of framing a compromise goal in Palestine. Yet, except for HaShomer Ha-Zair, the moderation of the Left was one of theory more than of practice. While carefully avoiding so much as mentioning ultimate Jewish statehood, its leadership devoted little thought or effort to a rapprochement with the Arabs. In fact, no group was more intent than the Laborites in building a totally self-sufficient economy and community amid the Arab majority.

Better than most of his colleagues, Weizmann appreciated the impossibility of projecting maximalist goals for the National Home. He divined almost intuitively the misconception that animated others in the Zionist movement. Obsessed by the ideal of self-determination that was the theme of the Peace Conference and postwar years, many Zionists had developed the notion that the Jews, with their aspiration to a national existence, were to be defined as on the same level and as enjoying the same rights as the Czechs, Poles, Croats, Lithuanians, and other long-subjected European peoples. Weizmann, on the other hand, regarded this analogy as fatal to both Arab and British cooperation. He was haunted lest Arab opposition inflict the same blow on the Zionists that the Greeks had lately suffered, and the Armenians earlier, at the hands of the Turks—while the British retrenched and abandoned their patronage. Only a moderate policy could now hope to retain British goodwill and understanding. This was what Weizmann had in mind, after the shock of the Churchill White Paper, when he informed the Carlsbad Zionist Congress in 1923: "I am not ashamed to say: I have no success to produce. After the Mandate there will be no political successes for years. Those political successes which you want you will have to gain by your own work in the Emek, in the marshes and on the hills, not in the offices of Downing Street."

Even to those of his followers who understood the importance of restraint, however, Weizmann appeared to carry moderation to a fault. During a recess in the sessions of the Seventeenth Zionist Congress in 1931, he granted an interview to the Jewish Telegraphic Agency. "I have no understanding of, and no sympathy for, the demand for a Jewish majority in Palestine," he observed. "Majority does not guarantee security, majority is not necessary for the development of Jewish civilization and culture. The world will construe this demand only in the sense that we want to acquire a majority in order to drive out the Arabs." The remark created a furor among delegates of all parties. Surely, they argued, it was embracing compromise to the point of national abdication. The Congress thereupon passed a resolution of "regret" and followed it with a new, hopelessly involuted, formula of Zionist purpose. "The homeless, landless Jewish people," it declared, "eager to emigrate, desires to end its economic, spiritual, and political plight by rerooting itself in its historic homeland through continuous immigration and to revive in the Land of Israel a national life endowed with all the characteristic features of the normal life of a nation." Weizmann found even this wording provocative, and refused to accept it. Nevertheless, the motion carried, and Weizmann immediately resigned his presidency.

Curiously enough, the movement afterward seemed to bypass its official "definition" in favor of a more conciliatory goal outlined by Chaim Arlosoroff, director of the Jewish Agency's political department. It was to promote "friendly relations and [establish] a rapprochement between Jews and Arabs in Palestine, starting from the basic principle that . . . *neither of the two peoples shall dominate or be dominated by the other, regardless of what the numerical strength of each may be*" [italics the author's]. In 1933, Ben-Gurion, a leading member of the Jewish Agency and Zionist Executive, continued for a while to give lip service to this moderate view. But he soon made clear his lack of interest in defining the Yishuv's political future as long as the Jews were a minority in Palestine. As Ben-Gurion saw it, the lesson of the 1929 riots was not of the sin of obstinacy, of failure to placate the Arabs. Far from it. "We have sinned in this land, in all other lands, we have sinned for two thousand years, *the sin of weakness*. We are weak—that is our crime." For Ben-Gurion, the Zionist priority thenceforth was to strengthen Jewish self-defense in Palestine, to build the Yishuv quickly and massively, to impel the mandatory to fulfill its obligations to the Jewish National Home. In the end, accomplishment of the Zionist dream was linked inevitably with Jewish strength and size. "Can we in the future become a majority?"—that was the critical issue.

Ben-Gurion was not a hypocrite. He would not leave the Arabs, any more than the Jews, in doubt of his position. On several occasions in the 1930s, he stated his views forthrightly to those Arab leaders who would meet with him. Thus, in 1934 he conferred with Auni Abd al-Hadi, the

Istiqlal leader. "Auni asked me," Ben-Gurion recalled later, "'How many Jews do you want?' I told him: 'During a period of thirty years, four million.'" A year earlier he and Moshe Shertok conferred with Musa al-Alami, scion of a distinguished Arab family and consultant on Arab affairs to High Commissioner Sir Arthur Wauchope. Shertok opened the conversation in traditionally soothing terms, likening Palestine to a crowded hall "in which there is always room for more people," and stating that it could always accommodate the Jews who wanted to come without inflicting any vital harm on the Arabs. At this point Ben-Gurion interrupted, snapping that it was useless to talk like that to a realist like Musa al-Alami. The Jews had nowhere to go but Palestine, he insisted, whereas the Arabs had at their disposal the broad and undeveloped lands of the Arab world. What he, Ben-Gurion, and Shertok wanted to know was whether there was any possibility of the Arabs agreeing to the establishment of a Jewish state encompassing both Palestine and Transjordan, in return for Jewish support of a federation of independent Arab nations. Alami did not commit himself. Although impressed by Ben-Gurion's candor, he felt then that he had received a final lesson on the nature and aims of Zionism.

It was by no means the official Zionist version, however. Weizmann was still thinking in terms of parity. On September 19, 1936, as president once again of the Zionist Organization, he outlined what he conceived to be the movement's basic position and submitted the draft to the Foreign Office:

> Our contention is that the Jews and Arabs in Palestine must be treated as two communities, two units with absolutely equal rights: these rights being independent of numbers. We shall offer them this as a basis of an understanding and of future cooperation, and with this system of permanent parity to be placed under a permanent guarantee of the British Crown.

Shertok endorsed this statement on behalf of the Jewish Agency. Parity appeared to be the one acceptable approach to Arab and British goodwill. Until the Peel Report (Chapter IX), statehood never was openly discussed. In view of these conflicting attitudes and equivocating definitions, then, it was hardly suprising that the Jews, no less than the Arabs, were in a quandary on the ultimate Zionist purpose in the Holy Land.

THE REVISIONIST ANSWER

For some Jews, at least, as for many Arabs, a definition of intent no longer could be postponed even for the short term. Certainly for the Jews of Poland, Rumania, and Hungary, exposed as they were in the 1920s to a successor-state anti-Semitism almost as virulent as in prewar Russia, there was little time for gradualism. They required assurance that the Jewish National Home would offer immediate and unlimited sanctuary, and the opportunity for uninhibited growth. Nordau was one of those who argued that the great reservoir of European Jewry would never be safe until it was permitted, indeed encouraged, to flow into Palestine rapidly, massively, without awaiting even assurance of housing or employment. Whatever the initial hardships upon arrival, this migrated Jewry would at least have escaped the cold pogroms of Europe and have won immediate majority status for the Yishuv, with important political advantages for the future. In the 1920s, to be sure, the notion of "catastrophic" Zionism was rejected by Weizmann and by the majority of his colleagues. Yet it was never stilled, and by the 1930s it became increasingly the countertheme to the prevalent notion of "building step by step," according to plan.

By then, too, Vladimir Jabotinsky had emerged as the principal spokesman of the maximalist approach. Reared in a secular Russian Jewish home, Jabotinsky passed as a youth directly into Russian life, immersing himself in its literature and ideals. Tsarist persecution subsequently shattered his Russophilism. Like Herzl and Nordau, he detected in the vision of a Jewish state an immediate and thrilling opportunity for national freedom and self-assertion. At the age of twenty-three he attended the Sixth Zionist Congress, was overwhelmed by Herzl, and became a fiery advocate of "political Zionism." Moreover, for Jabotinsky, as for Herzl, Zionism prefigured a revolution in character as well as in status. Contemptuous of the limitations of Diaspora existence, he regarded Zionism as the instrument by which Jews would shuck off their qualities of submissiveness and timidity and become instead bold, proud, and militant. He yearned, too, for his people to become like the Gentiles on the battlefield, in the athletic world. Jabotinsky traveled widely afterward, becoming a versatile linguist. In Italy he studied and admired the works of Dante and d'Annunzio. The careers of Mazzini and Garibaldi tremendously impressed him. It was in Italy, as well, that Jabotinsky developed his forceful oratorical style, with its instinct for the theatrical. Despite his bespectacled, rather prognathous face and a distinctly authoritarian manner, he generated an extraordinary personal magnetism. Ultimately he would become the single most charismatic figure, after Herzl, in Zionist history.

It is recalled (Chapter v) that the formation of the wartime Jewish Legion was all but singlehandedly Jabotinsky's achievement. Afterward, Jabotinsky worked in close cooperation with the short-lived Zionist Commission in Palestine. From the very outset of this political apprenticeship, he scored Weizmann for the Zionist president's credulity, even naïveté, in his dealings with the British. Not a moment was to be lost, Jabotinsky argued, in pressing for large-scale Jewish immigration and an officially recognized Jewish armed force in Palestine. Thus, as founder and first commander of the Haganah, a locally organized Jewish quasi-militia, Jabotinsky personally led the resistance to the Nebi Musa riots in April 1920. For his troubles, we recall, he was arrested by the British as an "inciter to violence" and sentenced to a long prison term. Although he was soon amnestied, as the "prisoner of Acre" he cast thereafter an image unique both in the Yishuv and in the Diaspora. To wide circles of Jewish youth he became the very symbol of militant Zionism.

As a member, later, of the Zionist Executive, Jabotinsky continued to ventilate his opposition to Weizmann's gradualism. In 1922 he urged the Executive to demand of the mandatory authorities that they intensify their efforts on behalf of the Jewish National Home, remove anti-Zionist officials, and "ensure the safety of the Jewish population and the unhampered development of Zionist constructive work. . . ." There was no solution to the current deadlock, Jabotinsky insisted, other than to "have it out" with the British. One may imagine Weizmann's reaction to this less than diplomatic approach. With further cooperation precluded between the two men, Jabotinsky afterward resigned from the Zionist Executive. Later he moved to Berlin, where he joined the board of *Rassviet,* the organ of the émigré Federation of Russian Zionists. Soon he transformed the journal into his principal weapon of attack against the Zionist leadership. Little remained of Herzl's great design, Jabotinsky warned. The Zionist Organization had abdicated its political goals and had degenerated into a mere fund-raising enterprise. Philanthropy had become the ultimate rationale of Zionist effort and planning.

The last two important political figures of the Herzlian epoch, Nordau and Oskar Marmorek, both died in 1923. Contemplating this fact, Jabotinsky made the decision to found an alternative political movement on his own. During his travels in Latvia and Lithuania he had encountered groups of intense, militant youth who shared his views, and who had already organized themselves into a society, Betar (Brith Trumpeldor), devoted to a program of Zionist maximalism. He would build on this following. In 1924 he moved *Rassviet* to Paris and launched the Revisionist movement in April of the next year. Jabotinsky's inaugural address immediately struck a responsive chord in the Diaspora of the east European successor-states, among young Jews who had been disheartened by the apparent failure of Zionism to solve the crippling problems of anti-Semitism and Jewish sovereignty. Bitterly, he attacked a "laggardly and unimaginative" Zionist program that contented itself with the establishment of a Hebrew University or the absorption of a few thousand immigrants. What Revisionism demanded, he said, was "the systematic and active participation" of the mandatory in the establishment of the Jewish commonwealth. Mass colonization was not a private enterprise, nor a project for voluntary organization; it was state business requiring the active assistance of the state power. Jabotinsky's idea, in short, was to recruit Britain as a full-fledged partner in the building of the National Home—as opposed to Weizmann's policy, which regarded colonization in Palestine as essentially the task of the Jewish people.

Within a few years, this uncompromising program was surpassed by an even more far-reaching one of "gradually transforming Palestine [including Transjordan] into a self-governing commonwealth under the auspices of an established Jewish majority." Jabotinsky's notion of "gradualism" envisaged the creation of a Jewish majority in Palestine, west and east of the Jordan River. This must be Zionism's priority target, he asserted, and to that end immigration must be encouraged at the rate of 40,000 a year for the ensuing twenty-five years. It was altogether a revolutionary proposal, so much so that the Zionist Organization and its journals denounced it as "treason"; for it undermined Weizmann's repeated, diplomatic efforts to placate the British and the Arabs. Yet Jabotinsky was not oblivious to the Arab problem. It was simply that, unlike the Labor Zionists, he was fatalistic about Arab opposition. Their hostility was inevitable and had to be accepted. The Arabs had lands of their own in the Middle East, after all, but the Jews of Europe faced a lingering doom, and accordingly their moral case was the stronger. No compromise was possible.

The very clarity, the brutal straightforwardness of this program, articulated at a moment of deep Jewish frustration, conveyed something of the dramatic impact of Herzl's original *Judenstaat*. The periodic conferences of the "World Union" of the Revisionist movement attracted increasing numbers of delegates from Europe and the United States. In 1925 the Revisionists elected four delegates to the Zionist Congress. Despite the modest showing, Jabotinsky traveled widely, propagandized intensively, and won over tens of thousands of new followers. Thus, in the 1929 Congress, twenty-one Revisionist delegates were represented; in the 1931 Congress, fifty-two.

It was in this same period that Jabotinsky's disillusionment with the Zionist leadership reached its final crisis. Several factors were responsible. Over the opposition of the Revisionists (and others), the enlarged Jewish Agency was established to include non-Zionists. Soon afterward the 1929 riots erupted and the British revealed their willingness virtually to scuttle the Jewish National Home under Arab pressure. Not least of all, while deploring Weizmann's "minimalism," the Zionist Organization issued a less than forthright statement of Jewish intentions in Palestine. Exasperated by this debilitating sequence of events, Jabotinsky announced that the "policy of the Zionist Executive must now be declared bankrupt," and that the Revisionists would do better to leave the Zionist Organization altogether. The decision was hastened by the Eighteenth Zionist Congress in 1933, following the Arlosoroff murder (p. 188), when the Labor and General Zionists refused to sit on the Executive with the Revisionists. As tension between these parties and the Revisionists mounted almost unbearably, the latter decided to force the issue. Their World Union determined now to act independently of the Zionist Organization, to make their own representations to foreign governments, to provide their own funds, and in other ways to repudiate the authority of the official Zionist movement. By 1935 all efforts at rapprochement had failed. That summer, following a plebiscite among the Revisionist members, Jabotinsky announced the establishment of a "New Zionist Organization," which henceforth would cease all dealings with the older Zionist Organization. The first congress of this body took place in Vienna, its delegates elected by 713,000 Revisionist voters (as compared with 635,000 voters for the Nineteenth Zionist Congress).

Emancipated from the discipline of the Zionist Organization and its obligations to the mandatory, the Revisionists concentrated on approaching other governments directly, without reference to London. Thus, Jabotinsky took it upon himself to enlist the support of east European successor-state regimes in pressing Britain to open the gates of Palestine to "surplus" Jews. In conjunction with the reactionary Smigly-Ridz government of Poland, Jabotinsky and his colleagues worked out a "ten-year plan" for mass Jewish emigration to the Holy Land. At the same time, they organized their own program of illegal immigration, and by 1939 had managed secretly to bring over nearly 15,000 Jews. By then, too, the New Zionist Organization boasted an impressive network of subsidary associations, including students', veterans', and women's groups, a Revisionist high school society, and Nordia, a Revisionist sports club. In Palestine, the Irgun Z'vai Le'umi (National Military Organization) was formed by groups of Revisionist youth and dedicated to active reprisals against Arab marauders.

By the late 1930s, also, as younger leaders emerged within the movement, Revisionism gradually was radicalized. The source of this new orientation was the Betar youth movement; in 1938 it numbered 78,000 members in twenty-six countries. Like other Zionist youth movements, Betar prepared its European members for life in Palestine, maintained training farms, and conducted Hebrew classes. Yet it also stressed paramilitary education and discipline, mass gymnastics, uniforms, and solemn torchlike processions. While its leadership revered Jabotinsky as man and leader, the movement veered further to the right than he himself would have preferred, and at times came dangerously close to emulating the Giovanni Fascisti of Italy. Jabotinsky had no objection to militarism per se: his study of history had convinced him that all great nations were born on the field of battle. Yet he remained uneasy to the end of his life that the Betar activities might be projecting a totally erroneous impression of him as a Fascist. Interestingly enough, Mussolini encouraged the comparison, saying to Rome's Chief Rabbi David Prato in 1935: "For Zionism to succeed you need to have a Jewish state with a Jewish flag and a Jewish language. The man who really understands this is your Fascist, Jabotinsky." The truth of the matter was that Jabotinsky rejected fascism. He insisted that his models were Mazzini and Garibaldi, not Mussolini or —heaven forbid—Hitler. Indeed, he and the Betar fought Nazism by word and deed, and were the first Zionists collectively to declare a boycott against German goods.

Nevertheless, Jabotinsky hardly erased his ultrarightist image by the economic and social views he insisted on propounding. Although a Socialist in his youth, an admirer of the kibbutz and moshav movements in Palestine, he was shaken by the devastating impact of the Bolshevik Revolution on his own family and on Russian Zionism. In later years, too, he regarded Labor Zionism's preoccupation with wages, benefits, and strikes as a diversion from the national struggle against Britain and the Arabs. Authoritarian by temperament, Jabotinsky in any case had little patience with Socialist egalitarianism. He pinned his hopes rather on the emergent Jewish middle class of Palestine. "If there is a class in whose hands the future lies," he wrote editorially, ". . . it is we, the bourgeoisie, the enemies of a supreme police state, the ideologists of individualism. . . . We don't have to be ashamed, my bourgeois comrades." Nor did Jabotinsky confine his opposition to Labor Zionism to journalistic polemics. With his approval, the Betar leadership in October 1933 dispatched a secret memorandum to its followers, instructing those who wished to emigrate to Palestine to avoid doing so in collaboration with the Labor-dominated Jewish Agency, which distributed the entry permits. It would be better, the circular observed, to negotiate directly with employers in Palestine, who were entitled to invite workers from abroad. A year earlier Jabotinsky authorized the establishment in Tel Aviv of a Revisionist-sponsored National Labor Federation, a body that renounced the class struggle and operated independently of the Histadrut. These measures were unsuccessful, for the most part. Nevertheless, they infuriated the Labor Zionists. So did Betar's role as occasional strike-breaker on behalf of Jewish employers.

The hostility between the Zionist Left and Jabotinsky's emergent Right was potentially as ominous as class schisms in other, European, nations. This was revealed in an episode that occurred on the night of June 16, 1933, when Chaim Arlosoroff, director of the Jewish Agency's political department and youngest of the Labor leaders in Palestine, was shot and killed while strolling with his wife on the Tel Aviv seashore. Three days later Avraham Stavsky, a Revisionist worker, was arrested and later identified by Mrs. Arlosoroff as a companion of the man who had fired the shot. Tried before a district court, Stavsky was convicted and sentenced to be hanged. It was significant, too, that the arrest had taken place at the home of Dr. Abba Achimeir, editor of a Revisionist newspaper and the man suspected at first as the "brains" behind the killing. A leading theorist of Palestinian Revisionism, Achimeir had frequently expressed his contempt for the "Bolshevik" spirit of Labor Zionism. It subsequently emerged that he had also written in defense of political assassination.

Although the conviction of Stavsky himself eventually was quashed on appeal, the Labor Zionists in ensuing years remained convinced that he and Achimeir somehow were implicated. The evidence did not support this view. Rather, after World War II, a series of libel trials revealed that Stavsky may indeed have been innocent. In the interval, nevertheless, a lethal fratricidal hatred developed between the camps of Revisionism and Labor. Ben-Gurion pinned the label "Fascist" on Jabotinsky and often referred to him splenetically as "Vladimir Hitler." Under the pressure of events, the schism between Ben-Gurion and the Revisionists on the Arab question would narrow considerably in later years. But the unrelenting social and economic hostility between the two groups was never to be dissipated, not even in the most critical moments of national survival.

THE FIFTH ALIYAH, THE GROWTH OF THE CAPITALIST SECTOR

If Labor and its institutions consolidated their gains in the 1920s and 1930s, the growth of capitalist enterprise in the Yishuv was equally impressive during the same years. The demand for Palestine citrus remained stable. By 1931 Jewish (capitalist) planters held some 50,000 dunams of groves under cultivation, and by 1936 they owned three times that amount. Their exports rose from 2.5 million cases in 1931 to 5.9 million in 1936, and the number of their Jewish employees from 8,000 to 16,000. By 1936 Jewish industry had established itself firmly in the home market and was beginning to develop outlets in Egypt, the Levant, and South Africa. While the rest of the world lay mired in depression, Palestine, ironically, was embarked on a period of unprecedented economic growth.

Part of this success could be attributed to the new high commissioner, Sir Arthur Wauchope, a Bible-reading Scot who evinced a benevolent concern for Jewish settlement and enterprise. The principal reason, however, lay in a massive influx of Jewish immigrants. In 1932, immigration rose to 12,500; in 1933 to 37,000; in 1934 to 45,000; and in 1935 to 66,000. The annual rate declined somewhat later, as the mandatory imposed new restrictions. Yet it was significant that between 1932 and 1935 alone the Jewish population of the Yishuv doubled, from 185,000 to 375,000, the largest number of Jews immigrating into any country in the world during those years. The majority continued to arrive from eastern Europe, where the quasi-official Judeophobia of the Polish and Rumanian governments made life all but insupportable for their Jewish populations. But for the first time, too, a significant minority began to arrive from central Europe, as fugitives of Nazi anti-Semitism. Indeed, the quantity of German-speaking Jews reaching Palestine was an altogether novel phenomenon for a country built on east European lines. Until 1933 the yearly number of German, Austrian, and Czech immigrants had never exceeded 2,000—less than 2.5 percent of the annual Jewish immigration figure. Then, in 1933, their numbers reached 25 percent of the annual Jewish immigration; in 1934, 23 percent; in 1935, 13 percent; in 1936, 29 percent; in 1937, 35 percent; in 1938, 55 percent; and in 1939, 71 percent. Although still a numerical minority, this central European group, by virtue of its culture, skills, and capital imports, set its own unique imprimatur on what henceforth was to be known as the Fifth Aliyah.

Economically, the German-speaking immigrants were the most successful in the history of the Yishuv. A majority of the newcomers in fact had been Zionists in their lands of origin. Committed, educated, and reasonably affluent, they managed to get back on their feet in Palestine within a very few years. Approximately a quarter of the central Europeans settled in villages. Many of the younger ones among them, those who had belonged to Zionist groups in Europe, registered in kibbutzim. These included several thousands who had been brought over by Youth Aliyah, an organized immigration of German Jewish children; the companionship of other kibbutz youngsters now helped ease their parentless adjustment to a new life. Others, adults as well as children, similarly returned to agriculture, settling either in kibbutzim or in variations of individual and cooperative farms. Their numbers augmented the Jewish rural population, which climbed from 45,000 in 1931 to 105,000 by 1939, approximately 27 percent of the Yishuv. The agricultural sector was thriving by then. While the

Jewish Agency's research stations and modern irrigation techniques played a crucial role, an even greater stimulus was the sheer enlargement of the urban market. For the first time, Jewish agricultural villages were able to sell their goods at decent prices and in rising quantities. By 1938, all settlements—collective, cooperative, and capitalist smallholders alike—were showing a profit. Many at last began repaying their loans.

The most extensive impact of the Fifth Aliyah, however, like that of the immigration wave of the early and mid-1920s, was in the development of larger Jewish urban centers. These now underwent a complete transformation and began taking on the aspect of modern cities. Tel Aviv and its suburbs absorbed not less than half the new immigrants. Its "metropolitan" population, including Jaffa, grew from 46,000 at the end of 1931 to 135,000 in 1935. The number of Jews living in Jerusalem rose from 53,000 in 1931 to 70,000 by 1935. Haifa, Herzl's "city of the future," witnessed the opening of a modern British port in 1933 and the completion of an oil pipeline terminal from the Mosul field in 1934. The city's Jewish population nearly tripled between 1931 and 1935, from 16,000 to 40,000. Tiberias and Safed each absorbed an additional 11,000 Jews during the same period. Petach Tikvah, with a population of 18,000, was awarded the status of municipality in 1938.

Urban progress, in turn, reflected a dramatic infusion of German Jewish funds. Ironically, the Nazis themselves were not unwilling to facilitate the transfer of Jewish capital to Palestine. By an understanding reached between the German foreign ministry and the Jewish Agency, emigrating Jews were allowed to take part of their savings out of the country in the form of German goods. The chattels and other purchased items were accordingly shipped to Palestine and sold there by the immigrants for local pound currency. Together with their extensive business, industrial, and professional experience, therefore, the German Jewish newcomers brought with them fully P£63 million in imported capital. Invested in commerce and industry, these funds launched a significant economic expansion, notably in the metal trades, textiles, and chemicals. The number of industrial firms rose from 6,000 in 1930 to 14,000 in 1937, and employed a work force that grew from 19,000 to 55,000 in the same period. The tempo of growth could be measured in the sevenfold rise of electricity sold for industrial purposes by the Palestine Electric Corporation between 1931 and 1939. During the same period, the nation's other main concessionary enterprise, the Palestine Potash Company, registered a sixfold gain in the value of its Dead Sea output, from P£70,000 to P£428,000. By the mid-1930s, with trade and new sea and air routes opening in Europe and Asia, optimism for the Yishuv's economic future appeared solidly based.

THE GROWTH OF ZIONISM

The rise of capitalist enterprise in Palestine might have been expected to exert a far-reaching impact on the Yishuv's political life. Indeed, the extraordinary growth of Revisionism in the 1920s and 1930s seemingly bespoke the growing appeal of rightist ideology. Yet revulsion at the Arlosoroff murder, and suspicion of Revisionist implication in the deed, gravely undermined the movement's influence within the Yishuv itself. In the aftermath of this episode, the Socialist parties tightened their grip equally on the public institutions of the Yishuv and on the Zionist Organization. For secular non-Socialists, to be sure, another alternative to Revisionism was conceivably to be found in General Zionism. The Zionists of the Diaspora were still largely middle-class, and their votes, added to ballots cast in the Yishuv itself, elected the Congresses that in turn selected the "Zionist" members of the Jewish Agency. Moreover, by the 1930s the Jewish Agency played a far more significant role in the quasi-government of the Yishuv than did the National Assembly.

But although middle-class and middle-of-the-road, General Zionism for many decades was not really a party at all in the various Zionist Congresses; it was rather a negative definition. Without any particular commitment of its own beyond loyalty to Zionism itself, it simply embraced those members of the organization who did not belong to any specific ideological grouping—whether Mizrachi, Poalei Zion, or Revisionist. Within the fold of General Zionism, admittedly, were to be found Weizmann, Sokolow, Brandeis, and other leading figures, those who had won the great political victories of the war and postwar era, including the Balfour Declaration and the League mandate award with its proviso on the Jewish National Home. The General Zionists in fact returned 73 percent of the delegates to the Twelfth Zionist Congress in 1921, while the Labor Zionists constituted only 8 percent, and Mizrachi 19 percent. As events developed, however, the Twelfth Congress represented the apogee of General Zionist strength. During the ensuing years, Labor Zionism, Revisionism, and Religious Zionism grew in doctrine and membership. The General Zionists, on the other hand, neglected the opportunity to reorganize themselves into an aggressive party with a clearly formulated program, and the movement therefore suffered a decline in later Congresses. Thus, in 1923–25, its share fell to 60 percent, and in 1931 to 36 percent. More significantly, General Zionism failed to develop a substantial power base within the Yishuv. It satisfied itself that outside Palestine its great Jewish middle class provided the driving spirit and financial means for the Keren HaY'sod and the JNF, for the network of Zionist schools and cultural institutions in the Diaspora. Even so, its achievements in Palestine itself were meager by contrast with Labor's, and specifically because it refused to become doctrinaire.

It was the debacle of 1931 that warned the General Zionists that they no longer could afford to bask in their reputation. That year, as a result, they set about politicizing themselves by convening a World Organization of General Zionists in Basle. The effort was counterproductive. The gathering failed to agree on an ideological stance. And when the second World Conference of General Zionism in 1935 endorsed an antilabor program, the organization shortly afterward fractured into two separate bodies. The conservative wing retained the original name. The liberal wing adopted the title of Confederation of General Zionists—except in Palestine, where it was known as the General Zionist "A" party. This A faction exerted a marked appeal for the central European newcomers, who welcomed the chance to bypass Labor Zionism without opting for the "lawless" Revisionists. But as late as 1936, the total of General Zionist A membership in Palestine failed to exceed 6,000. At most, it was given a kind of honorific standing as the party of Weizmann, and three of its members were seated in the Yishuv's quasi-government, the Executive of the Jewish Agency. The second, conservative branch, the Union of General Zionists, was known in Palestine after 1935 as the General Zionists "B." Although rejecting the jingoism and right-wing economic ideology of the Revisionists, it was essentially this group that became the champion of private enterprise. Associated with it were the (capitalist) Farmers Federation and the Palestine Manufacturers Association. Yet the B faction's membership was smaller even than that of the progressive group, and it was allowed but a single delegate on the Agency Executive. None of its austere, middle-class members, either in the Zionist Congresses or in Palestine itself, displayed an instinct for the rough-and-tumble of political infighting.

There remained singularly few alternatives, then, for the Yishuv's non-Orthodox bourgeoisie. Religious Zionism, as embodied in the Mizrachi, appeared the least attractive choice of all. The movement unquestionably had grown in influence since the early twentieth century, when the first Mizrachi rabbis adopted the policy of fighting for Torah within Zionism rather than outside it. Many of the immigrant traditionalists of the 1920s and 1930s similarly became devoted followers of the venerated chief rabbi of Palestine, Avraham Kook. But while Kook himself was a man of saintly compassion no less than of rich intellect, his adherents demonstrated little of his own exemplary tolerance toward nonbelievers. Nor did they hesitate to use the public Zionist institutions in an effort to impose their traditionalist views on others. As a consequence, both in Palestine and in the Zionist Congresses the Mizrachi alienated all but a small minority of the very devout.

Politicking at least was a difficulty not faced by the Agudat Israel. These were the ultra-Orthodox pietists—most of them Chasidim—who lived impacted together in the Old City of Jerusalem, in the Mea Sh'arim neighborhoods of the New City, and in other quasi-medieval ghetto enclaves in Tel Aviv, B'nai Brak, and Petach Tikvah. As in the nineteenth and early twentieth centuries, when they subsisted on Chalukkah charity, the Agudists disdained participation in the Zionist movement. Rather, in 1927, they won mandatory recognition of their separate status outside the organized Knesset Israel (Chapter VI). Their encysted courtyards, prayer rooms, and family networks evidently were scope enough for their way of life.

The splinterization of parties was a direct consequence not only of ideological divergence, of perhaps a timeworn Jewish propensity for creedal hairsplitting, but also of the involuted mechanism of the Zionist Organization itself. Over the years a body of Congress procedures and practices had developed. The system of election became increasingly complex as a result of the worldwide dispersion of the Organization's members and the anachronistic method of voting not for separate candidates but for lists of candidates sponsored by international Zionist parties, with representation determined proportionally. The method allowed no leeway for the expression of individual views by individual candidates; the party central committees kept an iron grip equally on members' rankings on the lists and on doctrine and dogma. The lockstep of Zionist politics was additionally frozen by the double weight given votes cast by Zionists residing in Palestine itself. With the passing of the years this double representation enabled the Yishuv's party leaders virtually to dominate the proceedings of the Congresses.

Of even greater importance, party-vested interests dramatically exacerbated the Yishuv's "normal" politicization. Immigration was a case in point. It is recalled that the mandatory government determined the number of immigrants permitted under various schedules ("capitalists," "farmers," "laborers," etc.); but the Jewish Agency was empowered to disburse the certificates in Europe and elsewhere. It was this latter process, as a result, that touched off acrimonious struggles among the various parties, each of which was allocated its quota in relation to its strength in the Zionist Organization—and especially in Palestine. The factional influence on immigration affected every aspect of a potential immigrant's future. It determined not only how and when he would come, but similarly how he made his way in the Yishuv upon his arrival. For here again, the parties dominated almost every feature of communal life. Kibbutzim, moshavim, jobs in towns and cities, in the Histadrut, even in the mandatory administration, were controlled by parties, as were banks and the three major school "trends." In effect, the parties were closed societies of their own, functioning in parallel competition, and enveloping nearly every phase of a Palestine Jew's life from cradle to grave.

The National Home could ill afford this relentless politicization. In 1933, the nadir of the world Depression and the year in which Hitler came to power, the Zionist Organization was made acutely conscious of its missed opportunities. Zionism itself still remained a minority movement in the Diaspora. Money from the Keren HaY'sod and the JNF was being accumulated in unimpressive driblets. The Palestine budget adopted by the Congress—P£175,000—was the lowest since the establishment of the mandate. Weizmann's soaring hopes of 1929, that the enlarged Jewish Agency would become a powerful instrument for mobilizing the resources of world Jewry, clearly had been dashed. Within days, too, after the Agency had been established, Louis Marshall, chairman of the Agency's Council and the designated pillar of Agency strength in the United States, died suddenly. Without his guidance and prestige, the funded wealth of the Joint Distribution Committee and of the "established" American Jewish philanthropists remained largely untapped. Worse yet, the definition of a "non-Zionist" member soon came to mean anyone who was not actually an official of one or another of the Zionist parties or institutions. Under this nomenclature, the Jewish Agency, far from developing into an authentic partnership between Zionism and world Jewry, largely devolved again into the hands of ideological—if unofficial—Zionists, whose commitments and loyalties hardly required energizing.

Yet bleak as were the circumstances of organizational Zionism worldwide in the 1930s, they were not without rays of encouragement. In Europe, even in the United States, Zionist youth groups of all factions and trends were proliferating with extraordinary speed. Their members placed great stress upon emigration to Palestine, upon pioneering values, and upon the establishment of kubbutzim and other agricultural settlements. In Poland and the Baltic states, Zionism was responsible for the establishment of a network of Tarbut (Culture)—Hebrew-language—schools, thus fulfilling a hope that Ben-Yehuda had devoutly cherished. In the last analysis, moreover, the fluctuating organizational strength of the Zionist movement was less important in its impact upon world Jewry than the growth and the impressive accomplishments of the Yishuv itself. Freedom, physical and spiritual awakening, dignity, self-assurance—all were embraced in the resurgent nationalist experience. It was a *Weltanschauung* that lifted the hearts of caftaned Jews in Poland and awakened the sympathetic interest of those American Jews whose roots lay in eastern Europe. The schoolboy in Bucharest, the tailor in New York's garment district, the disillusioned intellectual in Vienna—all were moved by the vision of a bronzed new race of Jews who spoke their own Hebrew language, plowed their own fields, loaded their own rifles, sang their own anthems, and never hushed their voices or looked back in fear over their shoulders. These were the palpable accomplishments that kindled the imagination and hopes of Jews abroad, and that were reflected in a quiet, if still tentative, renaissance of Jewish folk music and drama, of Jewish art and belles-lettres, even of Jewish religious expression. By the eve of the Second World War, it began to appear as if Achad HaAm's vision of a morally galvanized Diaspora was no longer to be consigned exclusively to the distant future.

REPUDIATES THE JEWISH

NATIONAL HOME

THE INTRUSION OF THE AXIS

However unchallengeable its military strength in the Middle East since the war, Britain took with full seriousness its mandatory obligation to nurture its Arab wards to independence. Thus, in 1930, it reached treaty agreement with the Feisal government in Baghdad for Iraq to enjoy juridically sovereign status, under the proviso that British military installations remained. On the same basis, Abdullah, installed as emir of Transjordan in 1922, was allowed to preside over his own domestically autonomous government, with assurances of future sovereignty. Egypt, occupied by the British since 1882, was summarily awarded its freedom in 1922; and fourteen years later Britain curtailed its traditional military garrison rights in that country. These were not unimportant concessions, and in 1935–36 they were seemingly matched by France in treaties negotiated between Paris and the Syrian and Lebanese governments. Yet in neither instance, British or French, was imperial control relaxed simply as a response to legal obligation. The decision was extracted, rather, by a festering Arab and Egyptian nationalism that erupted intermittently in violence and that threatened not merely to undermine the Western presence in the Middle East but to become an instrument in the hands of Britain's and France's European adversaries.

One of these enemies, Italy, was obsessed by the need to rectify the "injustice" of the Paris Peace Conference by extending its imperial presence throughout the Mediterranean littoral. After 1935, moreover, that ambition seemed within range of fulfillment. With his impressive African staging bases in Libya, Ethiopia, and Italian Somaliland, Mussolini could indeed begin to look westward toward French Tunisia, and eastward toward Egypt and the Levant, the historic destinations of the merchant fleets of Venice, Genoa, and Trieste. A high-powered Italian short-wave radio station in Bari broadcast Arabic-language propaganda nightly to the Maghreb and the Middle East, striking systematically at Britain's and France's tenure in their Arab lands of occupation. Posturing as the "friend and protector of Islam," the Duce at the same time left no doubt that he regarded the Mediterranean as *mare nostrum*—our (Italy's) sea.

The Italian campaign for influence in the Moslem world was shrewdly reinforced by Nazi Germany. Hitler may have evinced little enthusiasm for projecting German territorial claims into the eastern Mediterranean; it was understood that the Middle East was Italy's sphere of expansion. But it was the Führer's intention to erode the Allied position in a region widely considered to be the very pivot of Anglo-French imperial and defensive power. By 1935, therefore, the Nazi propaganda bureau was subsidizing a wide variety of Middle Eastern courses, institutes, and journals, and spending millions of marks on the "educational" activities of German cultural and press attachés in the Islamic world. Beginning in 1938, the newly equipped German radio station at Seesen transmitted propaganda to the Middle East in all the languages of the area (except, of course, Hebrew). Combined with the broadcasts of Radio Bari and Spain's Radio Sevilla, these programs won a large and appreciative reception in the Arab world. So did the "good-will" visits to the Middle East of eminent Nazi figures, among them Dr. Hjalmar Schacht and Baldur von Shirach.

One particularly successful Axis technique of winning favor among the Arabs had its basis in ideology. German journalists and diplomats constantly drew parallels between Nazi Pan-Germanism and "the youthful power of Pan-Arab nationalism [which] is the wave of the Arab future." More significantly, the Arabs were reminded of the enemies they shared in common with the Nazis. Even in the mid-1930s, when Berlin exercised a certain restraint in ventilating its animosity against Britain and France, German diplomats evinced no hesitation whatever in publicizing the Nazi anti-Jewish campaign. Hardly a German Arabic-language newspaper or magazine appeared in the Middle East without a sharp thrust against the Jews. Reprints of these strictures were widely distributed by the Mufti's Arab Higher Committee (p. 200). Upon introducing the Nuremberg racial laws in 1935, therefore, Hitler received telegrams of congratulation and praise from all corners of the Arab world. The Palestine newspaper al-Liwa eagerly borrowed the Nazi slogan "One Country, One People, One Leader." Ahmed Hussein, leader of the "Young Egypt" movement, confided to the Lavoro Fascista that "Italy and Germany are today the only true democracies in Europe, and the others are only parliamentary plutocracies." A delegation of Iraqi sporting associations, returning from a trip to Germany in September 1937, expressed their profound admiration for "National Socialist order and discipline." During a visit to Transjordan in 1939, Carl Raswan, a noted German-born journalist, was struck by the near-unanimity of Arab opinion that only "Italy and Germany were strong, and England and the whole British Empire existed only by the grace of Mussolini and Hitler." Throughout the Arab Middle East a spate of ultra-right-wing political groupings and parties developed in conscious imitation of Nazism and Italian fascism.

THE SEEDS OF ARAB REVOLT

It was a fateful irony, therefore, that transformed Nazi Germany, self-appointed patron of the Arab world and inspiration for Arab right-wing nationalism, into an involuntary benefactor of Zionist growth and expansion in Palestine. Yet, as the tempo of persecution mounted in Germany itself, Jewish emigration to Palestine and other lands grew correspondingly. Zionist refugee and training centers were of vital importance in channeling this exodus, but the German government also played an unexpectedly helpful role. It is recalled that a unique transfer agreement permitted departing Jews to withdraw their savings in the form of German goods, which later were sold for British currency in Palestine. However bizarre in origin and purpose, the growing economic connection between Nazi Germany and Jewish Palestine proved useful to each side. Although certain foreign ministry officials in Berlin expressed dissatisfaction with this mutually accommodating relationship, the Nazi leadership continued to favor any understanding that would speed the exodus of German Jews. Thus, Adolf Eichmann, the SS officer charged with organizing Jewish emigration, dealt cordially and cooperatively with Zionist representatives from Palestine. When the Zionists sought permission to open vocational training camps for future emigrants, Eichmann willingly supplied them with housing and equipment.

Germany was hardly alone, we recall, in disgorging its Jews by the tens of thousands. Government-sponsored anti-Semitism was no less invidious a fact of life in the successor-states of eastern Europe. By 1939, therefore, as 275,000 Jews fled the "Greater Reich," approximately the same number of Polish, Hungarian, and Rumanian Jews departed their countries. Immigration quotas in other lands were severely limited and enforced; accordingly, not less than a third of these fugitives made their way to Palestine. Nor was it surprising under the circumstances that the rising tide of Jewish migration to the Holy Land during the mid- and late 1930s should have become a principal cause of renewed Arab unrest. Even the most restrained and responsible Arab spokesmen argued, by 1936, that Britain's mandatory obligation to foster the establishment of a Jewish National Home had been fulfilled. Such a home surely existed now, they observed, with nearly 400,000 Jews operating their own quasi-government, their own schools, universities, hospitals, educational centers, clubs, and associations. Was it not time, asked the Arab critics, to end the Palestine mandate altogether? Iraq, after all, had been granted its independence in 1930, as had Syria, Lebanon, and Egypt in 1936. Even Transjordan now enjoyed a semi-independent government of sorts. Why should Palestine, with its Arab majority, have less?

The resentment was given vivid expression by a new and younger group of Palestine Arab writers who had been educated in the mandatory school system. Several of these came from Nablus, a middle-sized Palestine community whose inhabitants, overwhelmingly Moslem, had been uniquely favored with jobs and industry under the Turks and as a result had produced a large and sentient middle class. In the 1930s the most prominent of the nationalist writers, Muhammad Izzat Darwazah, was a secondary school principal and later a member of the Arab Higher Committee (p. 453). Two of his associates, Muhammad Rafiq al-Tamini and Qadri Hafiz al-

Tuqan, were both Nablusis and teachers in private schools. A third, Aref al-Aref, held several minor administrative posts under the mandate. All were anti-Zionist pamphleteers of fiery intensity and considerable popular influence. The journalistic output of these and other, younger, writers—Muhammad Yusuf al-Husseini, the literary member of the Husseini clan, and Hassan Sidqi al-Dajani—was as impressive, both in range and in literary skill, as anything produced in the Arab world. The common ingredient in their writings was an appeal for uncompromising solidarity in fighting the Zionists and their British patrons, for waging nothing less than a Jihad Filastin al-Arabiyah—an Arab holy war for Palestine (the actual title of a popular book written in the late 1930s by three Moslems from Jaffa).

The unprecedented Jewish immigration of the Fifth Aliyah, then, was the fuel that stoked these subterranean fires. In an article for *International Affairs*, the Palestine Christian lawyer and journalist Emile Ghori expressed Arab resentment in its basic essentials:

> In 1918, we, the Arabs, constituted 93 percent of the population of Palestine. We have increased in number, fortunately, and in 1936 we represent 70 percent of the population. The Jews constituted 7 percent in 1918, and now they constitute 29 percent. . . . And if Jewish immigration continues, we shall be in a position of being a minority, which is contrary to Article 6 [of the League mandatory award].

Arab leaders were acutely aware of the views that had been stated publicly by a number of Zionist militants. They quoted Ussishkin. "Certainly I think it is possible for Jews and Arabs to arrive at an agreement," Ussishkin wrote in 1936, "but only when the Arabs are faced by a *fait accompli*— that is to say, when the Jews are no longer a minority in the country." Ben-Gurion expressed similar views to Musa al-Alami. Jabotinsky, of course, was a particular *bête noire* of the Arab intelligentsia, with his militantly outspoken proposals for a Jewish state of Palestine (including Transjordan). These remarks outraged even Arab moderates, who were terrified of being inundated by Jewish settlement.

Several years earlier, it is recalled, the Shaw and Hope Simpson reports of 1929 and the White Paper of 1930 had appeared to validate their misgivings. The Jews may not have owned more than 20 percent of Palestine's cultivable soil even by maximalist Arab claims (the Zionists insisted the figure was less than 5 percent). But the Arabs knew only what they saw, and what they saw was an unquestioned increase in Jewish land purchase, the growing departure of Arab fellahin to the cities, and the immeasurably greater rate of productivity of Jewish agriculture. To the typical Arab, the family plot of land had an almost mystical quality, and it was here, on the soil, that Arab tenure evidently had become fragile. Yet hatred of the Zionists was widely diffused and extended significantly beyond fear of Jewish population growth or land ownership. It was no less a reaction to the demoralizing effect of Jewish social patterns upon the traditional Arab way of life. Carl Raswan described a typical shouted response of an Arab villager:

Money is God [in Tel Aviv]. . . . Must all Palestine become one day like this, including the Holy City of Jerusalem? . . . Tel Aviv is an ulcer eating into our own country. If it is what the Jews want to make of Palestine, I wish my children dead. We do not mind poverty, but we weep when our peace is taken away. We lived a modest and contented life, but what shall we do if our children grow up to ape the noisy ways of these new people?

By 1936, inflamed by German and Italian propaganda and by the religious xenophobia of the Mufti's partisans, this fear and hatred assumed uncontrollable dimensions. The Palestine Arab press warned that the British were introducing Jews into the country "to push the Arabs into the sea and finish them," that the Zionists were being incited to kill the Arabs, to attack and torture Arab women and defile mosques.

Tension in Arab Palestine was heightened by the untimely introduction of a constitutional issue. In December 1935 Sir Arthur Wauchope, the high commissioner, ventured yet another attempt to establish a legislative council including both Arabs and Jews, this time under an impartial chairman from outside Palestine. Superficially the idea appeared reasonable; joint Arab-Jewish municipal councils had been functioning for years. But the plan was flatly rejected by the Mufti and his followers. To them, the very notion of Jewish membership in a Palestine legislature was unthinkable. Nor were the Jews enthusiastic about the scheme, detecting in it a potential Arab veto over the Jewish National Home. Weizmann and his colleagues fought the proposal in Jerusalem and London and were successful. In late winter of 1936, their objections registered in Parliament, which sharply criticized the council idea. The League Mandates Commission similarly upheld the Zionist position. Whatever their own reservations, the Arabs were outraged that Jewish protests, rather than their own, appeared invariably to find sanction in London and Geneva, that the Zionists' ability to mobilize powerful support for their cause evidently was as undiminished in 1936 as in 1930, when Prime Minister MacDonald had repudiated the Passfield White Paper. With Axis moral and ideological support, therefore, with Britain increasingly on the defensive in Europe, the Mufti's followers decided that the chance to strike back at Zionist incursions would never be more timely.

THE ARAB REVOLT BEGINS

The first acts of violence occurred in a spontaneous and unrelated way during April 1936. Arab bandits stopped a bus, killing two of its Jewish passengers. The following night two Arabs were murdered as a Jewish act of revenge. Whereupon Arab followers of the militant Sheikh Farhan al-Sa'ada began destroying Jewish property, uprooting Jewish crops, and killing occasional Jewish civilians. In response, the British administration imposed a curfew on Palestine's larger cities and issued other emergency regulations. The upsurge of violence was the Mufti's opportunity, however. Haj Amin's financial power was at its apogee, with yearly income from waqf and orphan funds totaling nearly P£115,000 in 1936. The greater part of this money was used now to subsidize his representatives and organizers, who became active in Moslem towns and villages throughout the country. On April 25, the Mufti induced several of Palestine's clan leaders to establish an Arab Higher Committee, with himself as president. It was this group that supported his call for the nonpayment of taxes after May 15, to be followed by a nationwide strike of Arab workers and businesses. The British at first chose not to punish the emerging challenge to their authority. Rather, High Commissioner Wauchope decided to engage in parleys with the Mufti and the Higher Committee.

Wauchope's restraint was wasted. Demanding that the British terminate Jewish immigration immediately, Haj Amin loosed a series of grim warnings of the "revenge of God Almighty." The initial outburst of Arab violence was then followed by a mass strike against the government's immigration policy. It was destined to endure for nearly seven months. Enforced by the Mufti's strong-arm men, the work stoppage paralyzed government and public transportation services, as well as Arab business and much of Arab agriculture. Ironically, one of its most decisive effects was to stimulate the Jewish economy. For the first time large numbers of Jewish workers supplanted cheaper Arab labor in Jewish citrus groves, and Jewish produce replaced Arab fruit and vegetables in the markets. On the other hand, the cost of the strike to the Arabs themselves became increasingly punitive.

By midsummer of 1936 the intensity of the fighting mounted as Arab irregulars poured into the hill country around Jerusalem, into Galilee and Samaria. A majority of them at first were local Palestinians recruited by Haj Amin's agents. But soon "Committees for the Defense of Palestine" were established in neighboring Arab lands. Syrian and Iraqi volunteers began arriving in Palestine at the rate of two or three hundred a month. Their leader, Fawzi al-Qawukji, played a vital role in the ensuing civil war. Born in Aleppo, he had served in the Ottoman army during the World War, then worked briefly for French intelligence in the Syrian mandate. At the outbreak of the 1925 Syrian revolt, however, Qawukji suddenly joined the rebels; when the uprising collapsed he fled the Levant, eventually accepting a commission in the Iraqi army. Now, in 1936, envisaging himself as a kind of Arab Garibaldi, Qawukji resigned his command to help organize the Palestine rebellion. He was a compact, sandy-haired man in his early forties when the civil war began, gruff, vigorous, and endowed with an unquestionable dynamism that he cultivated in open imitation of his hero, Adolf Hitler. During the summer of 1936, it was Qawukji who organized military training among the Arab nationalists, imposing a single, unified command over the disparate rebel forces and helping smuggle in Axis weapons. His guerrilla technique rarely varied. It took the form of night assaults on Jewish farms, the destruction of cattle and crops, the murder of civilians.

Yet armed rebellion soon became a tactic of desperation for the Mufti, as the strike's most crippling effects were experienced mainly by the local Arabs. By late summer the work stoppage had been going on for nearly

half a year, and the Arab middle class was already at the end of its resources. The problem for the Higher Committee was to devise a face-
saving excuse for allowing work to be resumed. The mandatory government
cooperated in this effort. It turned first to Abdullah of Transjordan as a
mediator. Unfortunately, the little Hashemite prince was compromised in
the Mufti's eyes for his known dependence on the British and his friendship
with the Zionists; at times he himself barely had escaped assassination at
the hands of the Mufti's gunmen. The British therefore looked next to the
Iraqi government. Here they were more successful. Foreign Minister Nuri
es-Saïd traveled to Jerusalem in late July 1936 and persuaded the members
of the Arab Higher Committee to negotiate an end to the uprising. Their
decision was not uninfluenced by Wauchope's hint of an impending British
military campaign. Indeed, it was not an idle threat. By then fully 20,000
British troops were stationed in Palestine, and 10,000 more were on the
way.

To sweeten the inducement, the high commissioner allowed it to be
known that if the fighting and strike came to an end, a Royal Commission
of Inquiry would be dispatched to Palestine and the Arab Higher Committee might then present its complaints in the appropriate diplomatic circles.
This information was conveyed to the Mufti via the neighboring rulers,
who urged him to rely on "the goodwill of our friend the British Government and her declared intention to fulfill justice." The offer was accepted.
On October 11, the Arab Higher Committee called off the strike. Work
resumed the next day. The guerrilla bands, already severely mauled by
the British army, were permitted to leave Palestine quietly. Fawzi al-
Qawukji departed for Transjordan. Organized violence slowly died out.
By then some 1,300 casualties had been incurred through the country,
including 197 Arabs, 80 Jews, and 28 British personnel killed. The direct
cost of the half-year's disturbances to Palestine taxpayers was nearly P£6
million.

THE PEEL COMMISSION

On November 11, 1936, the Royal Commission of Inquiry arrived. Its
instructions were to determine the fundamental causes of the unrest, to
explore Arab and Jewish grievances, and to make recommendations for
the future. All six commissioners were men of distinguished background.
The chairman, Lord Robert Peel, was the grandson of the eminent nineteenth-century prime minister, and had served as secretary of state for
India. A large, genial man of forceful personality, he was seventy years
old at the time; despite his failing health, he maintained an unshakable
equanimity throughout the hearings. The vice-chairman, Sir Horace
Rumbold, had served as British high commissioner in Constantinople and
later as ambassador to Berlin. Other members included professional diplomats and experienced jurists. The single most influential participant,
however, turned out to be the one academician of the group, Dr. Reginald

Coupland, professor of colonial history at Oxford, a tenacious advocate of unorthodox ideas.

Although the Zionists hardly were delighted that their National Home should be reevaluated by yet another Royal Commission (they had bitter memories of the earlier Shaw and Hope Simpson inquiries), they agreed to cooperate. By contrast, the Arab Higher Committee decided as a matter of strategy to boycott the proceedings. The visitors accepted this setback manfully; from the day of their arrival, they began collecting whatever evidence they could from British and Jewish witnesses. Thus, during their two-month stay in Palestine, the commissioners held thirty public and forty private hearings throughout the country. The Jewish Agency officials were well prepared, their memoranda carefully formulated. Their most eloquent witness was Weizmann himself. In his three appearances before the commissioners, the sixty-two-year-old Zionist leader described the tragedy of Jewish life in Europe, the rising specter of anti-Semitism' throughout the world. As in his many earlier briefs before statesmen and parliamentarians over the years, Weizmann traced the historic Jewish connection with Palestine and related in detail Jewish accomplishments under the mandate. He issued an impassioned plea for Britain to respect its obligation under the Balfour Declaration and the League mandatory award, and emphasized to his listeners that, "[if] a Legislative Council were now established and if the present Jewish minority were given an equal number of seats there with the Arab majority, the Jews . . . would never claim more than an equal number, whatever the future ratio between the Arabs and Jewish population might become."

This assurance was reinforced by Ben-Gurion, chairman of the Agency's Palestine Executive. It was far from the Zionist goal to transform Palestine into a Jewish state, Ben-Gurion insisted (with something less, perhaps, than full candor), or to dominate the Arab community. Yet he, too, and those who followed him, insisted upon the right of unlimited Jewish immigration and land purchase. The Zionist leaders cited economic and agronomical data to rebut the Arab claim that Palestine was land-poor and hence unable to support additional immigration. Repeatedly, the Jews laid stress on economic development as the most practicable method of reconciling Arab and Jewish interests.

Once again the Zionists grievously underestimated the depth of Arab fear and hatred. This became apparent when, at the intercession of Kings Ghazi (of Iraq) and Ibn Saud, the Mufti and his colleagues decided at the last moment to drop their boycott of the Royal Commission. In their testimony, none of the Arab spokesmen found redeeming qualities of any kind in the Jewish National Home. They denied that the British mandate or Jewish economic development had brought other than grief to their people. Their principal and repeated demand was for the establishment of an independent Palestine at a time when the Arabs still constituted a majority of the population. Only in this way could the Palestinian nation be spared the dangers of Zionist economic domination, and the anomalous position it held vis-à-vis other, independent Arab countries. On January 13,

1937, the Mufti appeared as chief witness for the Arabs. With his gentle bearing, accentuated by the delicacy of his gestures and a voice of almost musical purity, Haj Amin seemed the very incarnation of restraint and reasonableness. His arguments, like the Zionist ones, were by then familiar to the commission members. He traced the history of the Arab independence movement, the promises Britain had made the Arabs during the World War, the Wilsonian ideal that (he insisted) had animated Arab nationalism from the outset. Like his predecessors, Haj Amin emphasized that the 400,000 Jews then domiciled in Palestine were more than the country could absorb. When asked by Peel if this did not mean that in an independent Arab Palestine some Jews would have to be removed, the Mufti replied: "We must leave all this to the future." Other Arab witnesses made the same point, although rather less obliquely.

It was during Weizmann's testimony at the fifty-first meeting of the commission, held in Jerusalem on January 8, 1937, that the notion of partitioning the country was first broached. Professor Coupland said to him at the hearing: "If there were no other way out to peace, might it not be a final and peaceful settlement—to terminate the Mandate by agreement and split Palestine into two halves, the plain being an Independent Jewish State . . . and the rest of Palestine, plus Trans-Jordania, being an Independent Arab State. . . ." Weizmann was astonished at the magnitude of the proposal. At first his reaction was uncertain: "Of course, it is cutting the child in two," he said. He asked for time to consider the plan. Outside the meeting room, however, Weizmann confided to his secretary that the long toil of his life was at last crowned with success. A Jewish state was at hand. Excitedly, he began to indulge in dreams of the future, even outlining his vision of the new state's political structure.

Shortly afterward, in February, Weizmann and Coupland arranged to meet privately at the moshav of Nahalal. It was a drab winter day, and the two men conferred indoors for nearly eight hours at the girls' agricultural school. Now it was Weizmann's turn to convert the Englishman into an enthusiast for a divided Palestine. Apparently he succeeded. Years afterward Coupland described the meeting to Aubrey (later Abba) Eban. He recalled Weizmann's summary of the conditions necessary for the Jewish National Home to flourish, and decided that these conditions could never be fulfilled under the British. Coupland had said to Weizmann: "There needs to be an operation; no honest doctor will recommend aspirins and a hot-water bottle." Weizmann in turn recalled years later:

> I saw in the establishment of a Jewish State a real possibility of coming to terms with the Arabs. As long as the Mandatory policy prevails, the Arabs are afraid that we shall absorb the whole of Palestine. . . . A Jewish State with definite boundaries internationally guaranteed would be something final. . . . Instead of being a minority in Palestine, we would be a majority in our own State, and be able to deal on terms of equality with our Arab neighbors in Palestine, Egypt and Iraq.

As the two men ended their lengthy discussions at Nahalal, emerging to starlight, Weizmann had a presentiment of what might develop from his talk with Coupland. He cried out to the waiting farmers: "Comrades, to-day we laid the basis for the Jewish State!"

THE PEEL REPORT AND ITS RECEPTION

After five months of preparation, the Royal Commission Report was issued in July 1937. It filled 404 pages, contained elaborate maps and statistical indices, and ranked as one of the major documents of British foreign policy. First summarizing the views expressed by Arabs and Jews, the report then fully detailed the accomplishments of the Jewish National Home, not the least of which was an economy vigorous enough to have stimulated a 50 percent growth of Arab population since 1921. There was no question that the Arabs, fellahin and landlords alike, were enjoying unprecedented affluence in Palestine. The Arab charge that the Jews had obtained too large a proportion of the best soil could not be substantiated, for much of the citrus land originally had been sand or swamp. Upon making this point, however, the document went on to repeat the cautionary view of the earlier Shaw and Hope Simpson reports, urging an abridgment of future Jewish land purchases—although less for economic than for political reasons, to assuage Arab fears of dispossession. For the same motives of political reassurance, the document suggested a curtailment of Jewish immigration to a limit of 12,000 annually for the next five years.

The proposals at first appeared to be a grave setback for the Zionists. The commission appreciated this, and added that a flat repudiation of Zionist claims under the mandate was hardly a solution. The issue that had to be resolved was the future of the mandate itself. The plain truth was that Britain's obligations to the Arabs and Jews were essentially irreconcilable. There was no common ground between the two communities, one "predominantly Asiatic in character, the other predominantly European," and for these reasons the mandate "cannot evolve . . . into a system of self-government . . . in which both the Arabs and Jews would agree to participate." Certainly it was not Britain's intention to continue governing Palestine on the existing basis, without the consent of the local populations. But neither did the Royal Commission propose handing over 400,000 Jews to Arab domination, or nearly a million Arabs to Jewish rule. The only feasible solution, then, the report concluded, was to divide Palestine into two self-governing communities. Neither side would be fully satisfied, but both would come "to realize that the drawbacks of Partition are outweighed by its advantages. For if it offers neither party all it wants, it offers each what it wants most, namely freedom and security." The commission briefly discussed an alternative scheme for autonomous Jewish and Arab "cantons," but gave it short shrift as being too intricate and unwieldy.

Although not elaborated in detail, the report's proposal was for Palestine and Transjordan to be divided into three regions: a Jewish state comprising, essentially, the coastal plain and Galilee; a much larger Arab state embracing the rest of Palestine and Transjordan; and a permanently mandated British enclave including the Jerusalem-Bethlehem promontory, with a corridor to the sea and British bases on Lake Galilee and the Gulf of Aqaba. Evidently there was no way to divide Palestine without leaving a substantial Arab minority within Jewish borders. A plan was therefore later formulated for transferring land and exchanging populations on the Greco-Turkish model of fourteen years before. In 1937, at any rate, the notion that large irredentist minorities would remain on either side of the partition line was never envisaged, except as a consequence to be avoided.

The proposal was so revolutionary that it left most observers stunned. Even more astonishing than the plan itself, however, was the speed with which the British government accepted it. For, simultaneously with the publication of the Peel Report, on July 7, London announced its commitment to the recommendations, including the blueprint for partition as "the best and most hopeful solution of the deadlock." Actually this endorsement came rather faster than political or public support warranted. The mandatory officials by and large favored the alternative cantonal plan, certain that the existence of minorities would doom partition. They were unquestionably influenced by another factor, as well. Although Wauchope himself eventually was persuaded to endorse the report, the high commissioner did not disguise his concern for the government employees whose jobs and pensions would be eliminated with the termination of the mandate. In England the reaction to the scheme was mixed, but generally unfavorable. Zionist sympathizers in Parliament expressed reserve at the notion of confining the Jews to a state of these lilliputian dimensions. Sir Archibald Sinclair alluded to the dangers of "two racially totalitarian states side by side . . . with the Jews established along an indefensible coastal strip—congested, opulent, behind them the pressure of impoverished and persecuted World Jewry; in front of them Mount Zion." Herbert Samuel, now a member of the House of Lords, anticipated that the proposed states, within their jigsawed frontiers, would be "entwined in an inimical embrace like two fighting serpents." He regarded the scheme as economically unviable, particularly for the Arabs, who would be compelled to depart the most fertile region of their country.

The League Mandates Commission was even less enthusiastic. Nevertheless, it did not reject partition, if only because the Peel Report had fatally discredited the mandate. The commissioners urged simply that the period of apprenticeship be extended, either by provisional cantonization or by the establishment of two new mandates, but that in any case British tutelage continue for the near future. Perhaps surprisingly, Arab reaction to the report was ambivalent at first. It was rumored that the attitude of Abdullah and the Nashashibi group in Palestine was not unfavorable. Partition, after all, would have united the Arab sector of Palestine with Transjordan, thereby enlarging Abdullah's emirate. Raghib Bey al-Nashashibi may have coveted a leading position in this augmented realm, in exchange for his support. And yet, publicly, the Nashashibi faction and even Abdullah felt obliged to repudiate the Peel Report. The Arab Chris-

THE ROYAL COMMISSION (PEEL)
PLAN FOR PARTITION OF PALESTINE
1937

tians were altogether confused; they hardly relished being subjected to a Moslem-dominated government. But at least there was no ambiguity whatever in the views of the Mufti and his followers. They rejected the plan with contempt and ensured that the entire Arab Higher Committee formally turned it down. In their stand, they now mobilized the support of Arab and Moslem leaders far beyond the boundaries of Palestine itself (p. 209).

The Jewish reaction was slower in coming. The Zionist Congress assembled a month after the issuance of the Peel Report. Jabotinsky and the Revisionists, although no longer formally members of the Zionist Organization, were grimly opposed to any further attenuation of Palestine, and made their views known. They had not forgotten that only a decade and a half earlier the original Palestine mandatory award had been truncated and the country's largest hinterland transformed into the Emirate of Transjordan. Now apparently even this rump state was to be amputated and its largest portion transferred to the Arabs. The solution was an unthinkable one. The American delegates shared the Revisionist viewpoint. So did the majority of the Congress. But by the same token, the majority favored at least exploring the plan, for it offered the immeasurable advantages of a recognized Jewish state. Ben-Gurion and most of the Labor group took the initiative in advocating further talks.

For Weizmann himself, of course, even the notion of Jewish sovereignty was a vision of paradise. He had been in Paris when the Peel Report finally came out, and several days later was introduced to the visiting president of Lebanon. In a cordial chat, Weizmann informed President Émile Eddé of what was happening and observed that he, Weizmann, looked forward to enduring friendship between the Jewish state and the Lebanese republic. Whereupon Eddé was moved to shake Weizmann's hand, exclaiming: "I salute the first President of the Jewish Republic." In this somewhat euphoric mood, therefore, Weizmann reminded the Congress that the partition plan, for all its shortcomings, was a lesser evil than crystallized minority status in a hostile Arab state or federation of states; and certainly it was preferable to further mandatory restrictions on Jewish immigration. Agricultural experts reinforced Weizmann's contention by noting that there was enough cultivable soil even within the anticipated Jewish state to make possible the absorption of 100,000 immigrants annually for the next twenty years. Eventually, then, the Congress passed a resolution withholding overt approval of the Peel scheme but empowering the Jewish Agency to explore with London the precise terms upon which a Jewish state might be created.

Unspoken in this compromise approach was a private hope nourished by some of the Zionist leadership. Even before the Peel Report was issued, but when its tenor was known, Ben-Gurion exultantly wrote to Moshe Shertok, director of the Jewish Agency's political department:

> We shall smash these frontiers which are being forced upon us, and not necessarily by war. I believe an agreement between us and the Arab State could be reached in a not too distant future. And if we bring hundreds of

thousands of Jews into our State, if we can strengthen our economic and military position, then a basis would be established for an agreement on the abolition of frontiers, between ourselves and the Arab State.

In speeches before his Labor colleagues, Ben-Gurion was equally plain-spoken: "This Jewish State now being proposed to us is not the Zionist aim," he declared, "for it is impossible to solve the Jewish problem in such a territory. But this will be a decisive state in bringing about the great Zionist aims. In the shortest possible time it will build up the real Jewish strength that will carry us to our historic objective."

PARTITION IN THE BALANCE

Ben-Gurion had never lacked confidence in the possibility of reaching di-rect agreement with the Arabs. It will be recalled (Chapter VIII) that on several occasions in 1934 and 1935 he and Shertok had met with Musa al-Alami, either at the latter's village home in the Judean mountains or at Shertok's apartment in Jerusalem. The discussions were always frank—par-ticularly on Ben-Gurion's side. Later, nevertheless, when the partition plan was first mooted, Ben-Gurion requested Alami to communicate a Zionist offer to the Arab leadership. It was for substantial Jewish financial help to the proposed Arab nation in Palestine, in return for Arab acceptance of the Jewish state. Assurance was given, too, that the Jews would not object to membership by the incipient Arab state in a federation of surrounding Arab countries. Alami reported the offer to the Mufti personally. A week afterward he returned carrying an answer. Notwithstanding Haj Amin's public strictures against partition, the Mufti was favorably impressed by the Jewish proposal. Although he refused to alter his official stance of hostility to partition, he suggested through Alami that Ben-Gurion go to Geneva and present his offer there before a committee of Syrian and Palestinian Arabs. It was impossible to know how honest this response was. Even so, Ben-Gurion decided to accept it at face value. He departed in the late summer of 1937 for Switzerland. And there his meeting with the Arab leaders Sheikh Majid al-Arslan and Ihsan Jabri was altogether a failure. The two Moslem spokesmen made no effort to disguise their animus, their suspicion that "you want us to agree to . . . the Jews becom-ing a majority in Palestine. . . ." The rejection was so total, in fact, that Alami dared not meet with Ben-Gurion afterward in Palestine. On isolated occasions the Agency leaders conferred with other influential Arabs— Auni Abd al-Hadi Bey and Raghib Bey al-Nashashibi—but without mean-ingful results.

Arab-Jewish dealings were compromised not merely by the public ob-duracy of Haj Amin himself but also by the ventilation of the Palestine issue throughout the Arab world. Shortly after the Higher Committee issued its rejection of the partition plan, it appealed for support to Arab leaders elsewhere. The response was by no means unanimous. Abdullah, as has been seen, was hardly unnerved by the possibility of enlarging his realm through some sort of modified partition, although the changes he suggested to his Jewish Agency contacts, of a guaranteed autonomous status for the Jews within an Arab Palestine, were unacceptable even to the most moderate Zionists. Ibn Saud, meanwhile, had never been thrilled by Haj Amin's messianic claims to leadership of the Arab nationalist movement. The replies of the Hashemite and Saudi rulers now were cautious, even vague.

By contrast, the response of the Iraqi and Syrian governments was hostile to partition in any form. This became evident in an oblique warning to Abdullah by Iraqi Prime Minister Saïd Hikmat Suleiman: "Any person venturing to agree to act as head of such a [partitioned Arab] state," declared the prime minister, "would be regarded as an outcast throughout the Arab world, and would induce the wrath of Moslems all over the East." As it happened, Iraqi interest in Palestine had been growing steadily in recent years. Mutually advantageous economic ties between the two countries had developed following the completion of the oil pipeline from Kirkuk, the highway across the desert from Baghdad, and the free zone in Haifa harbor allotted to Iraqi trade by recent commercial agreement. Accordingly, the Baghdad government was eager to assume the leadership of anti-Zionism as a cover for these private economic accommodations, and possibly, too, as a façade for its own lack of a concerted anti-British policy.

The Syrian leaders, shielded from British reprisals by the French mandate, were equally outspoken in their denunciation of partition. In September 1937, at the invitation of the Damascus government, a Pan-Arab Congress of some five hundred delegates assembled at Bludan, Syria. The theme of the gathering was struck by the chairman, Naji Suweidi, a former Iraqi premier, who emphasized that Zionism was "a cancer," that the Jewish National Home and the Palestine mandate must be terminated immediately in favor of a sovereign Arab state. Unless Jewish immigration were halted forthwith, Suweidi warned, the Arab nations might turn their back on the Western democracies in favor of a new alliance. The implication of support for the Axis was plain. With this bargainer's approach, the Arabs already had elicited important overtures of Axis friendship. When Fawzi al-Qawukji met with Dr. Fritz von Grobba, the German minister in Baghdad, on July 6, 1937, Grobba hinted that important quantities of arms soon would be provided for the Palestine revolt. Although Berlin quickly obliged the minister to renege on his promise, the mere knowledge of Axis friendship, and the increased diplomatic leverage this support implied, convinced Arab leaders that the British were vulnerable to warnings on the Palestine question.

Before and after the Bludan Congress, too, attacks on the Peel Report increased in frequency and vehemence throughout the Arab world. The Syrian government addressed an official note to the French high commissioner, scoring the partition plan. In Egypt the Moslem Brotherhood initiated fund-raising campaigns on behalf of the Palestine Arabs. There were mass demonstrations in Baghdad, a one-day strike in Mecca and

Medina, a protest to the British consul from the Moslem Youth of Tunis, and numerous Moslem demonstrations in India. From October 7 to October 11, 1938, a "World Inter-Parliamentary Congress of Arab and Moslem Countries for the Defense of Palestine" met in Cairo. It was a much larger and more impressive conclave than the one in Bludan the year before, and it significantly prefigured later rivalries on the Palestine issue. Thus, the Syrian representatives insisted upon describing Palestine and Transjordan as amputated provinces of their own country, whereas the Egyptians regarded Palestine as an indispensable buffer for the defense of the Sinai Peninsula. The Iraqi vision was of Palestine transformed into a commercial outlet on the Mediterranean for Mosul oil. None of these ambitions, in turn, was acceptable to Ibn Saud, whose representatives laid stress on Palestine Arab independence and freedom of choice. Ultimately, the cross-purposes were papered over in a resolution that simply declared the Balfour Declaration void and rejected any further Jewish immigration to Palestine and any form of partition. Again the warning was issued, as at Bludan, that if these demands were not accepted, Arab and Moslem peoples throughout the world would regard the British and Jews as equally guilty and would turn elsewhere for political and military support.

THE ARAB REVOLT IS RENEWED

The alternative of Axis patronage was systematically encouraged by Rome and Berlin. During 1937 the Italian radio transmitter at Bari doubled its Arabic-language broadcasts to the Levant, striking vigorously at British and French imperialism, and at Zionism as a British instrument. The Nazi anti-Jewish program, of course, was animated by domestic considerations, and not primarily by any foreign-ministry scheme to encourage Arab unrest in the Middle East. Yet, once Britain released the Peel Report, the Wilhelmstrasse officials began taking their first active interest in the Palestine question. On July 1, 1937, when the general outline of the Peel Report was known, although before it was actually published, Foreign Minister Konstantin von Neurath issued special instructions to German legations in the Middle East:

> The formation of a Jewish state or a Jewish-led political structure under a British Mandate is not in Germany's interest, since a Palestinian state would not absorb world Jewry, but would create an additional position of power under international law for international Jewry, somewhat like the Vatican state for political Catholicism or Moscow for the Comintern. . . . Germany therefore has an interest in strengthening the Arab world as a counterweight against such a possible increase in power for world Jewry.

Throughout 1937 the Palestine issue opened new opportunities for Nazi activity in the Middle East. Grobba, the German minister in Baghdad, was increasingly in contact with Arab nationalists and members of the Palestine Arab Higher Committee, assuring them of German opposition to the Peel plan. In July, the Mufti visited the local German consul-general in Jerusalem to declare his own admiration for the new Germany, and to solicit German friendship in return. In September, Syrian nationalists approached Franz Seiler, the German consul in Beirut, with a request for German weapons to be shipped to the Arab rebels in Palestine. In November and December, Dr. Saïd Abd al-Fattah al-Iman, president of the Arab Club of Damascus, traveled to Berlin on behalf of the Mufti to seek German financial and military help. These appeals did not go unanswered. Admiral Wilhelm Canaris, chief of German military intelligence, allocated limited subventions to the Mufti. Quantities of weapons from the Sühl and Erfurter Gewehrfabrik works were dispatched to Palestine by way of Iraq and Saudi Arabia.

Meanwhile, the Nazi propaganda apparatus in Palestine itself was growing rapidly and was staffed by German shipping agents, commercial travelers, and businessmen, as well as by diplomats and permanent residents. The latter included the Brotherhood of Knights Templar, numbering about a thousand, and living in Jaffa, Sarona, Waldheim (in Haifa), and Jerusalem. Since the early nineteenth century these pietists had renounced German nationality to live in biblical simplicity in the Holy Land. Berlin now launched a concentrated effort to mobilize their loyalties, and won over nearly half the Templars to Nazi party membership. Additionally, the director of the German news agency in Palestine, Dr. Franz Reichert, enjoyed cordial relations with the Mufti. Arab editors borrowed freely now from Nazi and anti-Semitic clichés. "Hitlerism," wrote one Arab newspaper, "is violently but nevertheless truly symptomatic of a world which is sick to death of the materialistic civilization . . . which gave the subversive activities of Judaism the chance to develop a stranglehold on international economics." When the Prophet Muhammad's birthday was celebrated in May 1937, German and Italian flags and photographs of Hitler and Mussolini were carried prominently by Arab demonstrators in Palestine, while Arab newspapers hailed this demonstration as a "significant gesture of sympathy and respect . . . with the Nazis and Fascists in their trials at the hands of Jewish intrigues and international financial pressure. . . ."

On Sunday morning, September 26, 1937, Lewis Y. Andrews, district commissioner of Galilee and Acre and a known friend of the Zionists, started out on foot for church in Nazareth with an assistant and a police constable. As the men turned up a steep narrow lane, they were fired on at point-blank range by a group of Arabs. Andrews and the police constable were killed instantly. Four days later the mandatory government announced the most stringent emergency regulations in its history, vesting itself with authority to deport political undesirables and to dissolve any organizations conducting activities "inimical to the Mandate." Simultaneously, Haj Amin al-Husseini was removed as president of the Supreme Moslem Council, while the Council itself and the Arab Higher Committee were abolished. Shortly afterward, five of the six members of the Higher Committee were arrested, charged with "moral responsibility" for recent acts of terrorism, and deported to the Seychelle Islands. The sixth member, Jamil al-Husseini, escaped to Syria. At that point, the Mufti, accompanied by his Sudanese bodyguards, retreated into the sanctuary of the Mosque of Omar. On October 15, eluding the tightening British police cordon, Haj Amin slipped out of the mosque disguised as a beggar. Traveling by private car to Gaza, he boarded a sailboat that carried him to Lebanon. Although the French authorities confined the Mufti to a villa in the remote coastal village of al-Zug, north of Beirut, his aides could come and go at will. Through them he established contact with his exiled followers, and the outlawed Higher Committee was reconstituted in Damascus, beyond British reach.

By mid-October, violence surpassing the level of the previous year raged throughout Palestine, with attacks on Jewish settlements and buses and the murder of Jewish civilians. For the first time, British patrols also were cut down by snipers, the new airport at Lydda was burned, troop trains were derailed, and the oil line from Mosul to Haifa was badly damaged. As the killings and sabotage increased, so did British reprisals. Military courts dealt harshly with suspects. In 1938 alone, fifty-four executions were carried out. Life sentences were common. From July to November 1938, when the uprising was at its fiercest, perhaps 16,000 local and imported guerrillas were engaged in the insurrection, and they succeeded almost completely in paralyzing civil authority outside the nation's larger cities and in the Jewish agricultural areas. Railroad service from Lydda to Jerusalem was discontinued for three months. All interurban transportation was prohibited at night, as Arab infiltrators laid mines and explosives along roads and highways. By mid-October, too, the rebels virtually had taken control of the Old City of Jerusalem. This was the high point of their uprising.

In July of 1938 the British found it necessary to ship two additional infantry battalions to Haifa, together with two RAF squadrons and an armored car and cavalry unit. Construction gangs were set to work erecting huge police (Taggart) fortresses at strategic promontories and road junctions throughout Palestine (the stockades were destined to play a vital role in the country's future military history). By the end of the year some 20,000 British soldiers were launched on a campaign that was hardly less than a second military occupation of Palestine. Even these heavy troop concentrations barely managed to restore a semblance of order in the northern and central districts of the country. The Jerusalem and southern districts, meanwhile, were flooded with trained units that earlier had been kept in England during the Munich crisis.

The fighting among Jews, Arabs, and British ultimately claimed several thousand lives and inflicted tens of millions of pounds of property damage (p. 222). But for the Arabs there was another bitter assessment. Even in exile, Haj Amin was making a supreme bid to consolidate his power in Arab Palestine. At his orders, many hundreds of noted Arab leaders, among them prominent members of the (Nashashibi) National Defense party, were either murdered or terrorized into fleeing the country. Thus, Hassan

Bey Shukri, mayor of Haifa, barely escaped attempts on his life in May 1936 and January 1937. In February 1937 the mukhtar of Caesaria was shot down outside his home. In April of that year Ibrahim Yusuf, a member of the Tiberias municipal council, was assassinated. The mayor of Nablus, Suleiman Bey al-Toukan, fled the country in December 1937. The mukhtar of Majdal and his wife were slain in April 1938. So was Nasr al-Din Nasr, the mayor of Hebron, the same month. The wife and three sons of the mukhtar of Deir es-Sheikh were killed by a bomb in September 1938. Hassan Sidqi al-Dajani, a member of the Jerusalem municipal council, was shot to death in November 1938, and the remaining Arab council members fled Palestine.

Efforts by Fakhri Bey al-Nashashibi, leader of the anti-Husseini faction, to mobilize a counterassault against this terror campaign were largely unsuccessful. The Mufti's offensive grew in scope and momentum, until by the end of 1939 his victims exceeded 3,000. Egypt and Lebanon were crowded with nearly 18,000 fugitives of the terror. Yet from beginning to end Haj Amin's principal Arab target remained Fakhri Bey al-Nashashibi. The Mufti's henchman, Aref al-Razzaq, issued a "death warrant" against Fakhri Bey, calling upon every Arab "in the name of God" to shoot this "traitor" on sight. Several years passed before the warrant could be executed. But on November 9, 1941, as Fakhri Bey was walking through the streets of Baghdad, a Palestinian member of Haj Amin's organization rode past on a bicycle and gunned him down.

THE GROWTH OF JEWISH SELF-DEFENSE

Still another important consequence of the Arab uprising was its effect upon Jewish military activity. It is recalled that the tradition of self-defense went back as far as HaShomer, the Jewish Watchman's guild of the early 1900s. After the war, however, those members of the guild who had survived Turkish mistreatment were prevented by the British from bearing arms. An abortive self-defense effort was initiated by Jabotinsky during the 1920 riots, but once more was suppressed by the mandatory authorities. Yet shortly afterward the Achdut HaAvodah party appointed a special committee to establish a more widely based (if clandestine) self-defense organization called simply Haganah—defense. It was understood that the organization would be broadly based, for henceforth defense clearly required more than the protection of an outpost or an occasional settlement; the entire Yishuv would now fall within the ambit of Jewish security. Thereafter, as the Histadrut assumed responsibility for the Haganah, officers' training courses were organized, weapons were purchased illegally from Europe and smuggled in, and eventually secret armories were built for the production of light weapons.

The riots of 1929 were the critical juncture for the defense program. It was evident now that training would have to include most of the able-bodied Jewish youth of Palestine. Newer and more modern weapons would have to be secured. Ben-Gurion and Arlosoroff were determined, therefore, to give enlarged priority to Haganah activities, and in 1931 solicited the Zionist Congress for additional funds. Initially, the appeal failed, largely because the General Zionists in the Congress objected to giving Socialists a monopoly over the Yishuv's defense. The objection had some merit, actually. From the outset, except for the earliest months of Achdut HaAvodah sponsorship, the Haganah had functioned under the supervision of the Histadrut. Most of its leaders were Histadrut officials, and its membership was recruited almost exclusively from laboring ranks. Nor was this Socialist orientation to be altered, particularly after 1936, when the Zionist Congresses themselves, like the Yishuv, came to be dominated by the Labor Zionists. Even so, the ideological coloration of the Haganah rarely affected its efficiency or the loyalty it claimed from most of the nation's Jewish population. Operating out of a single room in Histadrut House in Tel Aviv, Haganah's headquarters became an embryonic ministry of defense. By 1936, too, it was receiving larger quantities of Jewish Agency funds, accumulating a number of illegal weapons, and enlarging its program of military training.

When renewed Arab violence broke out that year, the Jewish military leadership decided at first upon a policy of restraint. In practice, this meant simply that Jewish communities would be defended vigorously, but without resort to acts of retaliation against Arab villages. The decision was influenced by the need to maintain British goodwill. Nevertheless, Yitzchak Sadeh, the Haganah field commander, placed his own interpretation on the concept of restraint. Sadeh was a memorable character, a powerfully built, ebullient bull of a man, a veteran of the Red Army and a committed Marxist. He infused his own self-confidence and reckless exuberance into his young officers. These included such teenagers as Yigal Peicovitch (later Allon) and Moshe Dayan, both of whom eventually would play vital roles in the emergent army and government of Israel. In his autobiographical work *My Life with Ishmael*, Moshe Shamir, a distinguished Israeli novelist, recalled the personal devotion inspired by the young leaders:

> In the Youth Movement it was a natural growth, from the cell of ten boys and a leader only a year or two their senior. As time went by, the social framework was enlarged—and the loyalty became greater and made its leader greater. I am not ashamed of the naive expressions of that first belonging and loyalty. From the Movement it was an easy transition to the Palmach [shock troops of the Haganah]. . . . What surrounded the "old man," Yitzchak Sadeh, and after him Yigal Allon, was simply love, young love for the friend at the head.

It was Sadeh who taught his youthful commanders to plan ambushes, to organize mobile patrols, to anticipate Arab marauders by striking first.

The shift from purely defensive to preemptive tactics was made feasible, too, by an agreement newly reached with the mandatory government. Even before the worst of the Arab attacks, the British had raised no objection when the Jews accumulated a certain quantity of their own weapons for the protection of outlying farm settlements. As fighting gained in intensity throughout 1936, however, the Jewish Agency demanded additional—free, legal—equipment to protect its isolated farms, and recognized status for its own guards. Hard-pressed for military manpower, the administration decided to grant these requests. Light weapons were distributed to some 3,000 authorized "ghaffirs," uniformed Jewish auxiliary guards (whose parallel membership in the Haganah the British accepted). Even more significantly, the man appointed by the British as operating commander of the ghaffirs, Captain Orde Wingate, vigorously and imaginatively enlarged Sadeh's concept of "active defense."

Arriving in 1936 as an intelligence officer in the Fifth Division, Wingate was a cousin of the governor-general of the Sudan and was seconded to Palestine because of his fluency in Arabic and his presumed rapport with the Arab community. The authorities had not been aware of Wingate's deeply rooted Protestant millennialism. Within weeks of his arrival in the country, however, it was this biblical mysticism that transformed the young captain into a passionate adherent of the Zionist cause. "I count it my privilege to help you to fight your battle," he told David HaCohen, his closest Jewish friend. "To that purpose I want to devote my life. I believe that the very existence of mankind is justified when it is based on the moral foundations of the Bible." It was difficult at first for the Haganah leadership to trust this short, blond, intense little Scotsman, for his background appeared identical to that of hundreds of other officers and civil functionaries whose careers in Palestine generally were advanced by social and political sympathy for the Arabs. But within a short time Zionist suspicions were overcome, and Wingate became a confidant of Weizmann and of the Jewish Agency leaders.

In studying Arab tactics, Wingate noted the manner in which the guerrillas would strike and escape from heavily armed government columns. He was determined to retaliate by developing fast patrols and placing emphasis on night operations. His opportunity arose in September 1937 when General Sir Archibald Wavell was appointed commander of British forces in Palestine and authorized Wingate to organize the ghaffirs into "Special Night Squads." With official approval, then, Wingate was able to innovate a technique even more aggressive than that employed by Sadeh's semilegal Haganah units. The young Scottish officer's tactical adaptability in the field, his leadership and resourcefulness, soon evoked the admiration of his Jewish troops. So did his method of exploiting the night and every trick of decoy and feint to carry out audacious surprise raids against guerrilla hideouts—a welcome relief from the older doctrine of restraint. Indeed, Wingate's conception of "active defense" went so far as to include crossings into Lebanon and Syria and attacks on guerrilla villages there. Throughout 1938, during their scores of forays and ambushes, the Jewish Special Night Squads inflicted heavy casualties on the Mufti's rebels and kept them off balance and increasingly ineffective.

Despite these not unimpressive achievements, the Special Night Squads were sharply reduced early in 1939 and gradually assigned a minor role.

Political factors by then militated against British cooperation with the Jewish defense units (p. 218). Wingate himself was considered expendable; his pro-Zionist views were becoming an embarrassment to the government. Eventually, in the spring of 1939, he was sent back to England. His superiors wrote in his file: "A good soldier but a poor security risk. Not to be trusted. The interests of the Jews are more important to him than those of his own country. He must not be allowed to return to Palestine." Christopher Sykes notes that years later Sadeh generously observed of Wingate: "Eventually we would have done by ourselves what Wingate did, but we would have done it on a smaller scale, and without his talent. We were following parallel paths until he came and became our leader." Yet, even at their peak, the Special Night Squad operations were less than far-ranging. Their effect was primarily psychological—and not only on the Arabs. The Haganah's ability to cope with the rebellion infused a new confidence into the Jewish population. Again, Moshe Shamir has caught the spirit of those days:

> But more important than all else, a national consciousness was forged in the minds of the people, and a wave of healthy optimism arose, a surge of faith in themselves, a genuine feeling that their roots had gone deeper and that a time of organic growth had come, suckled by the land and bearing fruit. . . . [This feeling] was so organically typical of the country in those days: the night hikes or the illegal immigration, the love of the land and the dedication to pioneering in its remotest corners, the patrol-trucks and the new "stockade and tower" settlements erected overnight.

The reference to new settlements was apt. None of the existing Jewish villages was ever abandoned. Rather, from the outset of the Arab revolt in 1936 until its end in 1939, some fifty-five new Jewish farm communities were established, and largely in areas not until then penetrated by Jews. Most were kibbutzim, settled by HaShomer HaZair and HaKibbutz HaMe'uchad youth groups, and occasionally by new immigrants. The colonies were founded on new principles, as well, and these were essentially strategic rather than economic. After the issuance of the Peel Report, the Jewish Agency was convinced that the partition of Palestine was imminent. It was certain, too, that the boundaries of any future Jewish state would be determined by the practical evidence of Jewish habitation. Accordingly, land was now to be purchased on the borders of Palestine, especially in western Galilee, and matched by immediate settlement. In order to provide instant protection for the young kibbutz members, therefore, the tower-and-stockade method was devised. The emphasis here was upon prefabricated construction. What at daybreak was an empty patch of ground by nightfall would be covered with a solid encampment, protected by an outer stockade and a wooden tower with searchlight. There was little concern for economic viability in this crash program of infiltration. The most urgent priority during the late 1930s was simply to achieve a Jewish foothold, even with the barest nucleus of pioneers, in the outlying regions of the country. Other settlers would come later.

BRITAIN RETREATS FROM PARTITION

It was in reaction to the mounting Arab violence in Palestine that London announced the impending visit of another commission, this one to determine methods by which partition might be carried out and to recommend boundaries for the proposed Arab and Jewish states. The commission chairman was Sir John Woodhead, a civilian official who had served in the Anglo-Indian administration. Two of his three colleagues were similarly members of the Indian civil service. Owing to disrupted conditions in Palestine, the four men did not arrive in the Holy Land until the end of April 1938. By then the Arab boycott of the Woodhead hearings was even more effective than it had been before the Peel Commission. During their three and a half months in the country, the visiting Englishmen were limited almost exclusively to interviews with British and Jewish witnesses.

For the most part, however, the mandatory officials presented the Arab case no less effectively than would have the Arab Higher Committee itself. They were traditionally hostile to Zionism and the difficulties this movement created for what otherwise might have been a sanguine Iraq-style relationship in Palestine. For that reason, and others of social distaste, the British in Palestine maintained an arm's-length attitude toward the Jews. An English journalist living in Jerusalem, D. S. Elston, recalled:

> One had little to do with the Jews. . . . The Englishman administering the Palestine Mandate rarely went into the Jewish quarters of Jerusalem: and, unless he were a policeman, was hardly ever seen in Tel Aviv or any of the small towns. As for the collective settlements, they were no place for him. . . . There was hardly any interweaving of British and Jewish social life anywhere.

The Arab historian Albert Hourani added that "it was true that most British officials in the Middle East were opposed to the Zionist policy," but he attributed this phenomenon less to romantic pro-Arabism than to the English sense of fairness.

The hearings were taking place at a black moment in Jewish history. The Nazis had already reduced German and Austrian Jews to mendicancy, pariahdom, and increasingly to concentration camp imprisonment. At the same time the virulent anti-Semitism of Poland, Rumania, and Hungary was making Jewish life in those eastern successor-states all but intolerable. The issue of free immigration to Palestine had become quite literally one of life and death. Its urgency was further heightened by an international conference on refugees that met in July 1938 at Évian, France, with representatives of thirty-one countries. Whatever hope was entertained for an alternative solution to the Palestine asylum was soon dashed at Évian. None of the governments, with the single exception of the Dominican Republic, was prepared to modify its immigration quotas on behalf of the refugees.

During May, June, and July, meanwhile, as the Woodhead hearings continued, violence in Palestine raged on. It was only with substantial reinforcements that the British army finally broke the grip of the Arab rebels on the Old City of Jerusalem and restored a semblance of order in the nation's larger towns. During the course of the fighting, protests from neighboring Arab governments flooded into London. They came at a time when Axis blackmail diplomacy in Europe obliged Whitehall to become increasingly solicitous of Arab friendship along the Middle East lifeline. The Zionists sensed that their position was eroding, that the Cabinet was indecisive. They watched in alarm as the Chamberlain government revealed its willingness to appease Hitler and Mussolini at the expense of other, smaller nations. Weizmann was already drawing parallels for the Yishuv. It was significant that by the spring of 1938 both the high commissioner, Wauchope, who had espoused a policy of compromise, and the colonial secretary, Ormsby-Gore, who was identified with the partition scheme, had been replaced: Wauchope by Sir Harold MacMichael, formerly governor of Tanganyika, and Ormsby-Gore by Malcolm MacDonald, the former dominion secretary. MacDonald, too, left no doubt that a shift in policy was imminent by ordering the mandatory government to impose even tighter restrictions on Jewish immigration.

On November 9, 1938, the Palestine Partition Commission Report—the Woodhead Report—was submitted to Parliament. It was a bulky document, 310 pages long, elaborately supplemented with hydrographic and cadastral surveys and by maps containing alternative partition suggestions. It declared, in sum, that the Peel plan was unfeasible, and based this assertion upon the huge Arab minority that would remain within the projected Jewish state and the restricted land available there for the settlement of tens of thousands of new Jewish immigrants. In any case, while a Jewish state conceivably might become economically viable, this was unlikely to be true of a Palestine Arab state deprived of a Jewish hinterland. What, then, was the solution? The report professed to find it in a "modification" of partition by which an Arab state and a Jewish state (drastically attenuated) would be linked together in an enforced economic union, both nations to be deprived of sovereignty in all matters of economic policy. "There remain the political difficulties," the report concluded, with some understatement. "We cannot ignore the possibility that one or more of the parties may refuse to accept partition under any conditions."

Predictably, the Zionists were enraged by the Woodhead Report. They noted that, by its proposal, the Jewish state would comprise less than one-twentieth of western Palestine and less than one-hundredth of the mandated area originally awarded Britain at San Remo in 1920. Worse yet, from their viewpoint, most of the existing Jewish settlements and landholdings were excluded from the Woodhead boundaries. The Arabs, meanwhile, although less critical of the plan, rejected it on the grounds that it still envisaged Jewish sovereignty, even in diluted form. Yet by then it was doubtful if the British government was seriously interested in any version of partition. At first London officially endorsed the report. In a speech before Parliament on November 24, Colonial Secretary MacDonald paid tribute to Jewish accomplishments in Palestine, then argued that Jewish educational and technological superiority was precisely the reason the Zionists would be able to get by in a much smaller area. Concluding on a note of personal reverence, MacDonald noted that "I cannot remember a time when I was not told stories about Nazareth and Galilee, about Jerusalem and Bethlehem where was born the Prince of Peace." At the mention of the Prince of Peace, Churchill could be heard to murmur: "I always thought he was born in Birmingham"—a sharp dig at Chamberlain.

It was the cabinet's last official gesture toward partition. Two days later yet another White Paper was issued, this one formally rejecting as impracticable any notion of dividing Palestine. The statement resorted instead to the familiar observation that "the surest foundation of peace and prosperity in Palestine would be an understanding between the Jews and Arabs." To that end, the government announced its intention of inviting representatives of the Zionists, of the Palestine Arabs, and of the neighboring Arab states to a conference in London. If negotiations did not produce an agreement within a limited time, the government would make a policy decision itself and enforce it with or without Arab or Jewish cooperation. After the initial phase of the uprising, in 1936–37, London had admitted that the Palestine mandate was unworkable, a claim Arab nationalists had advanced from the start. Now the second phase of the rebellion was followed by abandonment of the partition plan, well before an effort could be made to put it into operation. The Arabs plainly had mastered a crucial lesson, that violence on behalf of their rights in the Holy Land was effective diplomacy.

THE LONDON ROUND TABLE CONFERENCE

Weeks before the London Round Table talks began in February 1939, the British were already severely curtailing Jewish immigration and land purchases. In December 1938 the mandatory government rejected a Jewish plea for the immediate rescue of 10,000 Jewish children from central Europe. An additional and more telling concession to Arab pressure was Britain's willingness to accept the Mufti's latest demand, communicated from his exile in al-Zug, Lebanon. It was for the release of the Arab Higher Committee members interned in the Seychelles and their acceptance as bona-fide representatives of the Palestine Arab delegation in London. The men were thereupon set free and transported back to the Middle East, where they conferred with Haj Amin before proceeding on to England. Although two members of the Nashashibi faction were admitted to the Palestine delegation, they were completely outnumbered now by Husseini partisans. On the other hand, representatives of the Arab governments who attended the London session were men of far greater acceptability and reputation. They included Emir Abdullah from Transjordan, Foreign Minister Nuri es-Saïd from Iraq, Prince Feisal from Saudi Arabia, and ranking parliamentarians and political figures from Egypt. The Jewish delegation was led by Weizmann, Ben-Gurion, and Ben-Zvi (the latter president of the Va'ad Le'umi in Palestine), and by two non-Palestinians, Rabbi Stephen Wise, the leading American Zionist spokesman, and Lord Reading, Anglo-Jewry's most distinguished figure and in the past a chief justice of the high court and viceroy of India.

The conference opened on February 7, 1939, at St. James Palace. When the Arabs refused to sit in the same room with the Jews, arrangements were made for the two delegations to enter the palace by separate entrances. What devolved, therefore, were essentially two parallel conferences, each continuing under this format until the "Round Table" discussions ended on March 17. As always, the Jewish case was given its most effective presentation by Weizmann. The Zionist leader recognized Arab concern that Jewish immigration would exceed Palestine's limited absorptive capacity, and again sought to dispel this fear. He implored the British not to cut off Jewish immigration and settlement in "this blackest hour of Jewish history." The Arab case was presented by Jamil al-Husseini, whose statement, like the Mufti's testimony before the Peel Commission two years earlier, was uncompromising, demanding an end to the mandate and to Jewish immigration as the quid pro quo for a treaty to safeguard reasonable British interests in Palestine.

At one point discussions threatened to stall altogether when the Arabs insisted upon reexamining the commitments Britain originally had made to Sherif Hussein during the World War. The Colonial Office eventually acceded to this demand, however, and on February 15 the authentic text of the Hussein-McMahon letters was officially published for the first time. London's increasingly pro-Arab orientation was evident not merely in its willingness to review the very premises upon which Britain occupied the Holy Land, but in its public admission that "the Arab contentions [that Palestine was not excluded from the area originally promised Hussein] . . . have greater force than has appeared hitherto. . . ." At the same time, in a private meeting with the Zionists, Colonial Secretary MacDonald asserted frankly that Britain's lifeline in the Middle East largely depended upon the sympathetic understanding of the Arab world. With war imminent, His Majesty's Government was left with no choice but to ensure that the Arab governments were not tempted to accept support from hostile powers. If it came to a choice between Arab and Jewish support, MacDonald explained, Jewish help, however valuable, represented no compensation to Britain for the loss of Arab and Moslem goodwill. The first stage of the talks ended on February 13, when MacDonald asked whether the Jews seriously contended that the Arabs must be forced to accept Jewish immigration. Weizmann sharply retorted: "Are the British in Palestine with the consent of the Arabs?"

The second stage opened on February 15, when the British pressed the Jews to accept an immigration ceiling for several years, and afterward to base additional immigration upon Arab consent. The proposal, in short, was for a moratorium on the further growth of the Jewish National Home, on the continued sanctuary Palestine offered Jewish refugees. When the Zionist delegation angrily rejected the plan, MacDonald hinted that the

British might then be forced to withdraw from Palestine and abandon the Jews to superior Arab power. "As long as the Jews have the British government behind them," he explained later, "they will never meet the Arabs halfway." It became evident, however, that Prime Minister Chamberlain and MacDonald were themselves prepared to go rather more than halfway. The key Arab demand remained unchanged; it was for termination of the mandate and the award of independence to Palestine in the form of an Arab-dominated state. The British now agreed to this demand in principle, and conversations revolved essentially around the fate of the Jewish minority. The British urged special minority provisions for the Jews, a concession that the Arabs were not willing to offer.

The final stage of the talks, then, from March 1 to March 12, consisted essentially of legalistic discussions in which the British offered a number of alternatives. These included: a federation of cantons; a bicameral system, with the lower house to be chosen by proportional representation and the upper to be based on parity; a unicameral system with reserved questions dependent upon a separate majority among both Jewish and Arab members; and other, even more exotic variations reminiscent of Habsburg constitutionalism. None of the proposals found acceptance by either side. On March 11 the colonial secretary made a last effort to win the Jews over to his approach. Ignoring diplomatic amenities, he warned the Zionists that immigration lay at the heart of Arab unrest and, for that matter, of revived anti-Semitism in Britain itself. "This was the last thing desired by the British government," he said, "who wished to remain the friend of the Jews."

In despair of achieving agreement between the parties, MacDonald revealed the contours of the government's emerging Palestine formula on March 15. He proposed that Jewish immigration be limited to 75,000 during the next five years, with further immigration to depend upon Arab consent. Land sales would similarly be curtailed. His one concession to the Zionists was temporarily to drop the idea of an independent Palestine state, with an Arab majority government. Although both sides rejected MacDonald's formula, it was quite obvious by then that the Jewish position had drastically worsened. Two months passed between the end of the London Conference, on March 17, 1939, and the announcement of British policy in the form of an official White Paper. Meanwhile, the Zionists frantically sought to prevent or delay a British statement based on the March 15 proposal. Yet no hope was offered by the British. Weizmann called on Chamberlain at 10 Downing Street on March 21. "I pleaded once more with the Prime Minister to stay his hand and not publish the White Paper," he wrote later. "I said: 'That will happen to us which has happened to Austria and Czechoslovakia. It will overwhelm a people which is not a state union, but which nevertheless is playing a great role in the world, and will continue to play one.'" The Zionist leader stressed, too, that Britain was in need of American support and emphasized the power of the American Jewish community. But the allusion to Jewish friendship in the United States proved less effective in 1939 than in 1917, when it had largely induced the British War Cabinet to issue the Balfour Declaration. There were legitimate British security interests now that could be protected only through Arab goodwill. "The Prime Minister of England sat before me like a marble statue," Weizmann recalled, "his expressionless eyes fixed on me, but he said never a word."

As it developed, the British had made the—perhaps inevitable—decision to appease the Arabs at the very moment when the rebellion in Palestine itself was guttering out. In the aftermath of the Munich settlement, the British felt less threatened in releasing troops from the home island. Their military and constabulary strength in Palestine, as we recall, reached 20,000 by the end of 1938. Systematically now, the Arab rebels were combed out of the hills and villages. At the same time, dissension arose between the Arab nationalist leaders in Palestine and members of the Arab Higher Committee in Damascus; the former accused the Committee of misappropriating Arab funds. Abd al-Rahim, the Palestine Arab commander, abandoned his post in January 1939 and was succeeded by Aref al-Razzaq. Two months later Abd al-Rahim was slain by Mufti partisans, and Razzaq fled to Damascus, where he surrendered to the French. In August 1939 the disturbances finally ended after three years of fighting. By then the toll in Palestine had reached 6,768 casualties, of whom 2,394 were Jews, 610 were British, and 3,764 were Arabs.

THE WHITE PAPER OF 1939

Early in May 1939, Weizmann was invited to visit MacDonald at the Englishman's country home. He motored down with his political secretary, Yechezkal Sacharoff, who then waited outside. Two hours later Weizmann emerged from the house, pale and trembling. He had often heard that the English were double-faced and perfidious, he told his secretary, but throughout his long experience of England and Englishmen he had never believed it until now. "He broke into strong, violent, unrestrained language against MacDonald," Sacharoff recalled. "'That he could do this!'" he exclaimed when he was more collected. "'He who made me believe he was a friend.'" During the meeting, Weizmann had received advance information of the White Paper of May 17, 1939.

When the official statement was announced in Parliament soon afterward, its opening paragraphs rehearsed the obligations of the mandatory government to safeguard the religious and civil rights of all the inhabitants of Palestine and to encourage the development of self-governing institutions. The statement admitted that the establishment of a Jewish state had never specifically been precluded by the Balfour Declaration or by the terms of the mandate, but observed that the authors of the mandate "could not have intended that Palestine should be converted into a Jewish State against the will of the Arab population of the country." Britain was unable to keep Palestine under mandatory tutelage indefinitely, the White Paper continued. In these circumstances, the government was obliged to make known its intentions forthwith.

Those intentions were to organize an independent Palestine state within ten years; gradually to transfer to the people of Palestine (within five years "from the restoration of peace and order") an increasing role in the government of their country, under British advisory officials; to assure protection for the Arab and Jewish communities, the holy places, and British strategic interests. If postponement of the Palestine state should be necessary after ten years, London would consult with each of the two peoples. But the White Paper cautioned, meanwhile, that further unlimited Jewish immigration would lead to British rule in Palestine by force, and this was inimical to the spirit of the Covenant of the League of Nations. Therefore, His Majesty's Government had decided to establish a quota of 10,000 Jewish immigrants for each of the next five years, plus another 25,000 refugees. After a period of five years (and 75,000 immigrants), no further Jewish immigration would be permitted without Arab acquiescence. The sale of land to Jews was to be prohibited immediately.

The declaration of British policy was a foreclosure of any subsequent growth for the Jewish National Home. It sealed off Palestine as a haven for all but an insignificant fraction of Jewish refugees, and this at the moment when European Jewry faced a mortal threat to its continued physical survival. Whatever their inner satisfactions, however, the Arab Higher Committee chose for tactical reasons to denounce the White Paper, insisting that the length of the transitional period favored the Jews. Only a minority of the Arab leaders, Abdullah among them, publicly admitted that Britain's concessions to Arab demands were acceptable— indeed, even more than they had dared anticipate. Yet there was no ambiguity whatever in the Zionist response. On May 18, the day after the White Paper was issued, the Jews of Palestine conducted demonstrations throughout the country, furiously denouncing the White Paper in synagogues and public meetings. Isolated riots broke out, and one policeman was killed. Ben-Gurion issued a written statement on behalf of the Jewish Agency:

> It is a policy in which the Jewish people will not acquiesce. . . . Such a regime can only be established and maintained by force. . . . It seems only too probable that the Jews will have to fight rather than submit to Arab rule. And repressing a Jewish rebellion against British policy will be as unpleasant a task as the repression of the Arab rebellion has been.

This threat, in somewhat milder form, was transmitted by letter to the high commissioner on May 31. At the same time, Jewish notables throughout Palestine were returning their British decorations. Many were convinced that the Agency's program of self-restraint had been discredited. The Revisionist paramilitary organization, the Irgun Z'vai Le'umi, bombed a number of government buildings in Jerusalem and Tel Aviv and sabotaged rail lines.

In Britain itself, the White Paper met with serious criticism on all sides. The press was almost uniformly hostile. In Parliament on May 22, Leopold Amery castigated the document as a repudiation of British pledges, and warned that the Jews of Palestine were not the passive Jewish minority of Europe, but rather a nation that had drawn the breath of freedom. They would fight, he insisted. "If the Jews of Palestine say, as I hope they will," added Colonel Josiah Wedgwood in the House of Commons the same day, "that the law is inhuman and they consider it their duty to break the law, I hope they will all unite to do so." No criticism was as acerbic, however, as Churchill's. "This pledge of a home of refugees, of an asylum, was not made to the Jews of Palestine," he emphasized, "but to the Jews outside Palestine, to that vast, unhappy mass of scattered, persecuted, wandering Jews whose intense, unchanging, unconquerable desire has been for a National Home. . . . That is the pledge which was given, and that is the pledge which we are now asked to break. . . ." Several days later, at its annual May conference in Southport, the British Labor party repudiated the White Paper, thereby endorsing the stand of its members in Parliament. When the Palestine issue reached a vote in the House of Commons at the end of the month, the Cabinet won a slim majority. But a bare 268 votes were cast in approval out of a total strength of 413, while 179 members voted against the White Paper, with an unprecedented 110 abstentions.

The Chamberlain government's stringently anti-Zionist interpretation of the mandate required the approval not only of Parliament, however, but also of the League Permanent Mandates Commission. This body gathered in June and devoted three sessions to the Palestine crisis. MacDonald appeared personally before the commissioners to defend the White Paper. He argued that his government's approach represented the only hope of settling the Arab-Jewish conflict and was a logical fulfillment of the Churchill White Paper of 1922 (the first of Britain's policy statements to limit Zionist aspirations in Palestine). In sum, the Jewish National Home was already viable enough to sustain itself without further immigration. The members of the Commission did not accept this argument. In their report to the League Council, they declared that "the policy set out in the White Paper was not in accordance with the interpretation which, in agreement with the Mandatory Power and the Council, the Commission had placed upon the Palestine Mandate."

Vindication by the world body was of little consolation to the Jews. Their mood was apparent in the Twenty-first Zionist Congress, which opened in Geneva on August 16, 1939. Basic cleavages now existed among the solid majority of delegates that traditionally had favored an accommodation with Britain. Ben-Gurion led an influential group that urged a militant policy of resistance. "The White Paper has created a vacuum which must be filled by the Jews themselves," he insisted. "The Jews should act as though they were the State in Palestine, and should so continue to act until there will be a Jewish State there." Yet even without an overtly declared policy, the Zionist tactic of resistance was beginning to take shape.

The Jewish Agency publicly sanctioned, and privately organized, clandestine immigration. The influx of illegal refugees became unusually heavy after the spring of 1939, and in July the Colonial Office retaliated by withholding the next semiannual immigration quota altogether. Agricultural settlements continued to go up under cover of darkness. The British were sufficiently incensed by these measures to order the few remaining units of ghaffirs to turn in their weapons. Haganah recruits who were discovered in training were promptly arrested. The Agency's counterresponse was to order a secret Haganah registration of all men and women between the ages of eighteen and thirty-five. Special units already were being organized to plan anti-British operations. At this point, Weizmann, always the moderate, reminded the Congress that it was not possible to assure Britain of Zionism's support, nor that of the Yishuv, against Germany in the event of war, and simultaneously to undermine British security in Palestine. "It is my duty at this solemn hour to tell England and through it the Western democracies: We have grievances. . . . But above our regret and bitterness are higher interests. What the democracies are fighting for is the minimum . . . necessary for Jewish life. Their anxiety is our anxiety; their war is our war."

This Jewish helplessness, the lack of Jewish choice, was manifestly the circumstance upon which the British depended, and it was their strategy behind the White Paper. In no way was the controversial document simply another example of political appeasement, to be deplored and execrated in the same breath with the Munich settlement. The Arabs had a solid case, after all. Their hostility to the Jews bespoke far more than the social insecurity of a few wealthy effendis or the reflected influence of Nazi or Fascist propaganda. As has been noted, resistance signified a genuine fear of being overwhelmed by rising Jewish numbers, Jewish money, Jewish brains, Jewish energy. With war now threatening, too, it appeared legitimate to Chamberlain and MacDonald that British investments and installations in the Middle East should enjoy a minimal degree of regional peace and quiet. There could be no question of allowing the Arabs to gravitate into the Nazi orbit, if only because a major part of the oil resources of the Commonwealth were in the Arab world. "To have opened a major quarrel with the Arab states," wrote Christopher Sykes, the most astute of British pro-Zionist historians, "when Europe was moving toward war, would have been an act of folly by Great Britain without precedent." For nearly twenty years Palestine had been in Britain's charge, and during that time the mandatory administration had done its honest and considerable best to deal fairly with both Arabs and Jews. Now there were British interests to be protected at a moment when national survival was in the balance. No responsible government could have ignored that obligation.

In any case, the Arabs were by no means handed a complete victory. The notion of 75,000 more Jewish immigrants within the next five years was gravely unsettling to their leadership. When the Arab National Defense party (the Nashashibi group) tentatively accepted the White Paper as a basis for negotiation, one of its members was promptly slain by a Mufti terrorist. There were other isolated acts of violence. Nevertheless, the MacDonald White Paper by and large succeeded in keeping the Arab world quiet, and this was its rationale. In the short term, the pro-Arab orientation of British policy was a defensible act of calculated self-interest. Its weakness was to be found in the long term, for it destroyed the lingering reality of Anglo-Jewish cooperation and the moral and legal basis upon which the Palestine mandate originally had been established.

The Jews were not in a position to draw emotional solace from what they regarded as the justice of their cause. They viewed the White Paper as a likely death warrant for their people in Europe and conceivably for their hopes in Palestine. Late in the evening of August 24, 1939, Weizmann bade farewell to the delegates of the Zionist Congress at Geneva. As a new European conflict threatened, the atmosphere of the final session was charged with an acute awareness of impending tragedy. The departures were painful. Weizmann said, in part: "It is with a heavy heart that I take my leave. . . . If, as I hope, we are spared in life and our work continues, who knows—perhaps a new light will shine upon us from the thick, black gloom. . . . There are some things which cannot fail to come to pass, things without which the world cannot be imagined." Deep emotion gripped the Congress. Weizmann embraced his colleagues on the platform. There were tears in many eyes. Few of the European delegates survived the war.

CHAPTER X PALESTINE

IN WORLD WAR II

AN OSCILLATION OF BRITISH FORTUNES

Nowhere did Britain enter the war more confident of early triumph than in the Middle East. With the French solidly based in North Africa and the Levant, and the British themselves in firm control of Egypt, Palestine, Transjordan, and Iraq, London had no reason to doubt the seeming invulnerability of Allied military and naval forces in the Mediterranean and the Persian Gulf. This assurance was shaken, of course, by the disaster of the Nazi blitzkrieg in Europe, by the collapse of France, and the subsequent entry of Italy into the war. Almost overnight a thousand miles of North African coast, the entire Syrian littoral, and the French Mediterranean fleet passed into an uncertain Vichy neutrality, under the supervision of German and Italian armistice commissions. Yet, even then, Britain's position was less than desperate. The Italian forces emplaced in Libya were more imposing on paper than in actual battle. This became evident in the winter of 1940–41 when a numerically inferior British army commanded by General Wavell all but annihilated Mussolini's legions in North Africa.

The respite was to be short-lived, however. In an effort to salvage his ally's faltering position, Hitler shipped two German armored divisions under a crack general, Erwin Rommel, to Tripolitania in March 1941. On the last day of that month German advance units crossed the Cyrenaican border. From then on, during the next year and a quarter, the British would be thrust on the defensive, and ultimately placed in mortal jeopardy, at the very nexus of their Mediterranean-Suez lifeline. Their gravest moment was unquestionably June 1942, when the port of Tobruk, defended by some 35,000 Commonwealth troops, fell to Rommel's Panzerarmee. During the ensuing three weeks the British Eighth Army was hurled back to the gates of Alexandria. At this point the British suddenly were threatened with the most far-reaching military disaster since the collapse of France. If Alexandria should fall, the Suez Canal would become untenable. So would Palestine and Syria. In anticipation of the impending and decisive battle, a mass evacuation of British dependents was begun. In Cairo, all east-bound trains to Palestine were jammed. A thick mist of smoke hung over the British embassy on the banks of the Nile as huge quantities of secret documents were burned.

Throughout the long and painful ordeal of retreat, moreover, Britain derived small encouragement from its Arab treaty partners. The Egyptian government refused at the outset to declare war on Italy, even when Italian bombs were falling on Alexandria. In May 1941, General Aziz Ali al-Misri, a former inspector general of the Egyptian army, left Cairo secretly for Beirut in an Egyptian air force plane. The RAF intercepted his craft, and it was subsequently revealed that the general had intended to defect to the Axis with vital data on British troop strength. Indeed, the discovery opened a window on a far more ramified Egyptian collaboration effort. A month earlier, King Farouk himself had communicated with Hitler through his ambassador in Tehran, stating that "he was filled with strong admiration for the Führer and respect for the German people, whose victory over England he desired most sincerely. . . . Now that German troops stood victorious at the Egyptian frontier the [Egyptian] people . . . long for an occupation of the country, certain that the Germans are coming as liberators. . . ." In subsequent communications, Farouk provided intelligence information on British military dispositions and offered "to come to the aid of the Axis troops at the decisive moment." In Iraq, meanwhile, a virulently anti-British government was installed under the premiership of Rashid Ali and a cabal of nationalist officers; and in April 1941 this pro-Axis cabinet solicited German "protection" against the British. Hitler immediately responded to the offer, mounting an airlift of guns and ammunition by way of Vichy Syria. It required a costly British military expedition in May to overthrow the Rashid Ali regime, and an even larger-scale invasion of Vichy Syria the following month to abort a growing Nazi presence in the Levant.

No courtship of the Axis was more avid, however, than the one carried out by the émigré Mufti of Jerusalem. Haj Amin had fled al-Zug and reached Baghdad in October 1939, where he was granted an honorific status equal to that of a government minister. From the Iraqi capital he then dispatched his protégé, Naji Shawkat, on a secret mission to Ankara. There the Arab messenger transmitted to German Ambassador Franz von Papen a personal letter from the Mufti. The message extended felicitations to Hitler

on the occasion of the great political and military triumphs which [the Führer] has just achieved through his foresight and great genius. . . . The Arab nation everywhere feels the greatest joy and deepest gratification on the occasion of these great successes. . . . The Arab people . . . confidently expect the result of your final victory will be their independence and complete liberation. . . . [T]hey will [then] be linked to your country by a treaty of friendship and collaboration.

While Berlin was mulling over this proposal, Haj Amin dispatched yet another emissary in August 1940 to reaffirm the offer of collaboration. Eventually, on October 23, 1940, Berlin and Rome issued a joint statement offering sympathy for Arab efforts to achieve independence.

For the moment the relationship was suspended on the level of generalities. But later, upon the overthrow of the Rashid Ali government in May 1941, the Mufti fled Iraq for Iran, and afterward departed for Turkey. In late July he was spirited out of Ankara in a German plane and flown to Rome. On October 27 he was received by Mussolini. By then, Axis victories in the Middle East had given Arab affairs a new importance. Following conversations between Haj Amin and the Duce, therefore, a draft pronouncement was worked out and—upon agreement with Berlin—issued jointly by Mussolini and Hitler. It committed the two Axis governments to recognize the sovereignty and independence of the Arab countries and promised Axis help in "the elimination of the Jewish National home in Palestine."

The Mufti thereupon departed Rome on November 3, 1941, for Berlin. He was received in the German capital with much ceremony and presented to Hitler on November 30. Again, the Arab leader expressed his profound gratitude to the Führer and his willingness to cooperate with Germany in every way, including the recruitment of an Arab legion. But once more, Haj Amin insisted that Arab loyalty could best be mobilized by an immediate public declaration of support for Arab independence and unity. While agreeing in principle, Hitler replied that he preferred to wait until his armies had broken through the southern exit of the Caucasus. The Reich's objective then would not be the occupation of the Arab lands (as the British had warned) but solely the destruction of Palestine Jewry. Then, too, the Führer added, the Mufti would become the official spokesman for the Arab world. Haj Amin was gratified by this assurance.

With Hitler's approval, the Mufti at once set about recruiting Arabs in Axis-occupied territory to serve in their own Arab legion. The effort failed; only a few Palestine Arab prisoners of war expressed an interest. By the summer of 1942, nevertheless, as German troops reached the gates of Alexandria and approached the Caucasus on the Soviet front, the Axis governments intensified their propaganda efforts throughout the Arab and Moslem world. The Mufti did not spare himself in this task. Broadcasting repeatedly over Germany's Radio Seesen, speaking in the "name of God and the Prophet," he urged Moslems everywhere to rise up against the Allies. To encourage that uprising, Haj Amin visited Yugoslavia to recruit units of Bosnian Tatars. Approximately 6,000 of these eventually were dispatched to fight under German command on the Russian front. The Mufti by then no longer entertained great expectations for Arabs living under German and Italian control. His plans were based, rather, upon a mass uprising of Arab peoples the moment Rommel invested the Nile Delta and crossed into Palestine. By late June 1942, those hopes appeared on the threshold of fulfillment.

A LONELY ALLY

Although sorely tried, the British were not entirely bereft of local support in the Middle East. The Jews proved loyal. Faced by a common Axis menace, they could hardly have been otherwise. Four days before the outbreak of war, Weizmann assured Chamberlain by letter of the Jews' determination to stand by Britain, of their willingness to enter into immediate arrangements for placing their manpower and technical ability at Britain's disposal. "The Jewish Agency has recently had differences in the political field with the Mandatory Power," Weizmann added, with some understatement. "We would like these differences to give way before the greater and more pressing necessities of the time. We ask you to accept this declaration in the spirit in which it is made." The prime minister's response was noncommittal. "You will not expect me to say more at this stage," he remarked, "than that your public-spirited assurances are welcome and will be kept in mind." Weizmann's promises were honored, although not without opposition. Ben-Gurion, chairman of the Jewish Agency Executive, favored a struggle to reverse the White Paper, even if this required a policy of militance and serious unrest against the British. Several meetings of the Agency Executive were held in 1940 to discuss the issue, but each time Ben-Gurion was outvoted. In any case, the Nazi blitzkrieg in Europe soon put an end to these debates, as did the appointment of Churchill as Chamberlain's successor. Acts of violence ceased, and the illegal Haganah radio station closed down.

The Jewish Agency forthwith mobilized the Yishuv's resources for wartime agricultural and industrial purposes. Soil under tillage was expanded by 70 percent. Two thousand Palestine Jewish factories were operating when the war broke out. Within the next year, four hundred new ones were built, essentially related to British military needs, and the number tripled by 1945. Indeed, the Yishuv's economy overall was progressively linked to Britain's defense effort. Among the equipment produced were antitank mines, weapons' components, tank engines and treads, light naval craft, machine tools, and uniforms. Guns, ships, and machinery were repaired; specialized scientific apparatus, optical instruments, medical supplies, and vaccines and pharmaceuticals were manufactured. By 1943, 63 percent of the total Jewish work force was employed in occupations immediately connected with defense needs. It was a supportive effort that, not incidentally, laid the basis for an expanded postwar Jewish economy in Palestine.

The Yishuv's identification with Britain's cause assumed other, equally tangible forms. In the first month of the war, the Va'ad Le'umi announced the registration of volunteers for national service. Within five days, 136,000 men and women enrolled. Their motivation was not simply an understandable desire for battle against the Nazis, but the expectation that an armed and active Jewish force would obligate Britain to reconsider the Zionist case. Additionally, military skills acquired during the war could be put to good use later. It was the Jewish Agency's hope, meanwhile, to organize these troops as a separate force under its own flag, something akin to the Jewish Legion of World War I. But from the outset, the idea was opposed by British military and civilian officials in the Middle East. General Sir Evelyn Barker, the British army commander in Palestine, warned London that the establishment of a Jewish fighting unit in the region would provoke a renewed Arab uprising. Accordingly, the war secretary, Leslie Hore-Belisha (himself a Jew), vetoed the idea of a Jewish legion "for the time being." Instructions simultaneously went out to Lord Lothian, Britain's ambassador in Washington, to avoid commitments of any kind to American Zionists. Jewish support in the war was needed, but "there must be no misunderstandings as to the possibility of rewards, whether in the form of further immigration to Palestine or otherwise."

It was the Allied collapse in Europe that raised the possibility of a more forthcoming approach. In the spring of 1940, the Chamberlain government was replaced. Winston Churchill assumed the prime ministry. Lord Lloyd succeeded Malcolm MacDonald as colonial secretary. Anthony Eden replaced Hore-Belisha at the War Office. Thereupon Weizmann again requested permission for the Jews to be trained in their own military units. With the growing Axis threat to the Middle East, he observed, it was the "elementary human right" of the Jews "to go down fighting." Lord Lloyd was impressed by this argument. So was the vice-chief of the imperial general staff, General Sir Robert Haining, who promised to authorize the training of Jewish cadres. Yet once again the Zionists faced disappointment when Lloyd, alerted by General Wavell, reconsidered the matter. For the time being, the cautionary views of the Middle East army commanders were respected.

Their misgivings were not shared by the new prime minister, as it happened. Rather, Churchill was intrigued by the idea of arming Palestine Jewry, if only to release British troops in the Holy Land for other fronts. On June 25 he complained in a memorandum to Lloyd that "the cruel penalties imposed by your predecessor [MacDonald] upon the Jews in Palestine for arming have made it necessary to tie up needless forces for their protection. Pray let me know exactly what weapons the Jews have for self-defense." Three days later he rebuked Lloyd, who had ventured to protest. "I do not at all admit that Arab feeling in the Middle East and India would be prejudiced in the manner you suggest," the prime minister insisted. On September 6, 1940, in the most critical phase of the Battle of Britain, Churchill invited Weizmann to a private luncheon and assured the Zionist leader of his full support for the Jewish army project. A memorandum was sent afterward to the chief of staff:

1. Recruitment of the greatest possible number of Jews in Palestine for the fighting services to be formed into Jewish battalions or large formations.
2. The Colonial Office insists on an approximate parity in the number of Jews and of Arabs recruited for specific Jewish and Arab units in Palestine. As Jewish recruitment in Palestine is certain to yield much larger numbers than Arab, the excess of Jews is to be sent for training to Egypt or anywhere else in the Middle East.
3. Officers' cadres, sufficient for a Jewish division in the first instance, to be picked immediately from Jews in Palestine and trained in Egypt.

The issue apparently was resolved, and a week later Eden officially informed Weizmann that "the Government have decided to proceed with the organization of a Jewish army on the same basis as the Czech and Polish armies [in exile]." Conceived initially as a force of 10,000, including 4,000 troops from Palestine, the Jewish army unit would be trained in England and then shipped back to the Middle East. Weizmann was ecstatic. "It is almost as great a day as the Balfour Declaration," he informed his friends. In February 1941 the Zionist leader was introduced to Major General Leonard A. Hawes, an officer with extensive service experience in India, who had been chosen to command the Jewish force. Plans already were being worked out for Hebrew badges and insignia.

Then, in the same month, Lord Lloyd died suddenly. He was succeeded in office by Lord Moyne. The new colonial secretary, impressed by Wavell's and Barker's objections, was determined to block the Jewish army proposal. In a series of memoranda to Churchill, he referred to delicate political conditions in the Middle East and to the lack of supplies and equipment; it appeared unfeasible to equip a new army under such circumstances. At this point, Churchill reluctantly conceded, agreeing to postpone the matter. A terse statement accordingly was sent off to Weizmann on March 4: "The Prime Minister has decided that owing to lack of equipment the project must be put off for six months. . . ." A half-year later, on October 23, 1941, Moyne announced a further postponement: "Since the Government has to give every aid to Russia it would not be possible to form a Jewish Division." In ensuing months the Zionists failed to win any satisfaction on this issue. The rigor with which mandatory officials continued to enforce the White Paper, meanwhile (p. 236), suggested that political considerations alone were now dictating British policy. Another year and a half would pass before anything came of the Jewish army concept; by then the war in the Middle East itself was over.

In the interval, the Jews found other ways of identifying themselves with the military effort. Smaller Palestinian units gradually evolved, consisting wholly of Jews, with their own Jewish junior and noncommissioned officers. Again, this development emerged out of a tangle of British red tape. At the outset of hostilities, General Barker suggested the formation of mixed Arab-Jewish companies of "Pioneers"—actually truck drivers, storekeepers, and trench diggers—to be sent to the Western Front. The Jewish Agency was offended by the proposal, but chose not to reject it. It was understood that the number of Jews to be accepted was dependent upon an equivalent number of Arab recruits. But inasmuch as Jewish volunteers exceeded their quota within a few days, while the Arab quota was never filled, the parity rule soon had to be eased. The first groups of five hundred Palestine Jews arrived in France in 1940. They were used essentially for repair and maintenance work. After the French surrender, most of them were returned temporarily to Palestine, where they served as ground personnel for the RAF. Soon afterward, upon Italy's entrance into the war, an additional 1,400 Jews were permitted to fill RAF crew openings. Several dozen of these men eventually were accepted for flight training.

By the opening of 1942, 11,000 Jews were serving with British forces in the Middle East. Nominally they were still members of the mixed Arab-

Jewish companies, the "Palestine Buffs." In fact, the units were almost entirely Jewish by then. On the basis of their predominating numbers, moreover, the Zionists demanded that the various scattered Jewish companies be organized into battalions. London ultimately gave in on this point, and by August 1942, 18,000 Palestine Jews were incorporated into purely Jewish battalions. By then, too, approximately 25 percent of them were given front-line combat positions. During the retreat of Britain's Eighth Army from North Africa in June 1942, a thousand Palestine Jews served with the Free French Brigade in defending the village of Bir Hacheim; forty-five of these troops remained alive on July 2, the day they were relieved by a Gaullist column under General Pierre Koenig.

Simultaneously with this "official" participation in the British army, there was a second, parallel, Jewish military role. It was based upon the Haganah. It is recalled that the Jewish underground had won a certain unspoken recognition from the mandatory government during the guerrilla uprising of the late 1930s. The tacit understanding broke down in May 1939, however, with the issuance of the White Paper. The Haganah determined afterward to concentrate its efforts on the secret refugee immigration. Yet the war erupted before this decision could be carried out. After several weeks of indecision, the underground command ultimately followed the Jewish Agency's lead of cooperating with the war effort; but at the same time it maintained its clandestine training activities. As a result, the British viewed Jewish professions of loyalty with skepticism. Shortly after the outbreak of hostilities in Europe, forty-three of the Haganah's best officers were arrested, among them Moshe Dayan and Moshe Carmel. They were given tough sixteen-month sentences, and it was only upon Churchill's accession as prime minister half a year later that the forty-three were released, together with two other groups that had been jailed for possessing arms.

Once the military situation turned against Britain, however, following the blitzkrieg of 1940, the government tentatively eased its policy toward the Haganah. Indeed, with France out of the war and Syria in Vichy hands, a method had to be devised to block possible avenues of German invasion into the Middle East. Senior Haganah officers thereupon were invited to collaborate with the British in preparing lists of bridges and tunnels that were vulnerable to sabotage in Lebanon, Syria, Turkey, and Iran. Other joint efforts followed. In early spring of 1941, Rommel's Panzerarmee launched its operations in the Western Desert and the Nazi infiltration of Syria became more overt. Haganah cooperation was urgently needed. Unfortunately, the Jewish defense force was still at less than full strength. Its best instructors and hundreds of its fighters had enlisted in the British armed services, and the training of its civilian reserves was restricted mainly to weekends. The "professional" soldiers at its disposal were only a few dozen veterans of Sadeh's commando groups and of Wingate's Special Night Squads, while the reserves alone would hardly have been effective in the event of a combined Arab-Axis attack. The need soon became evident for a permanently mobilized Jewish task force. Such a unit accordingly was established by the Haganah in May 1941, and classified as the Palmach (Plugot Machaz—Strike Companies). One of its purposes was the defense of the Yishuv against Arab bands that inevitably would harass Jewish towns and settlements the moment the British retreated from Palestine. More importantly, if and when Axis armies entered the country, the Palmach would be employed to attack the enemy whenever possible, disrupt his communications, sabotage his transport and airfields. The commander of the new elite force, not surprisingly, was Yitzchak Sadeh. As in the 1930s, the veteran night fighter immediately set about recruiting the Haganah's ablest young men, mainly from the kibbutzim.

Even as Sadeh and his company commanders were organizing the Palmach, the military situation suddenly worsened in the Levant. It was plain that the British had no choice but to strike across the northern frontier quickly before the Germans ensconced themselves in Syria. Yet, in advance, scout forces were urgently needed to reconnoiter the enemy terrain. It was at this point, then, that the British entered into negotiations with the Haganah leadership, and specifically with Sadeh, who agreed to provide the manpower. In early summer, 1941, nearly one hundred Palmach troops were made available for special duty. A number of these, Arabic-speaking Jews, were charged with infiltrating Syria at night and penetrating various Arab towns to gather information and to mine key bridges and crossroads. The operation was successful. A second Palmach venture was not. British intelligence recruited twenty-three of Sadeh's best men for an amphibious mission to demolish the oil refineries at the Lebanese port of Tripoli. The vessel was detected offshore and sunk with the loss of all lives.

The climactic joint effort worked perfectly, however. On the eve of the Allied invasion of Syria, June 8, 1941, Palmach volunteers were needed for a final reconnaissance of Vichy positions. Sadeh chose two companies for the task. Their officers were the commander's favorites, Moshe Dayan and Yigal (Peicovitch) Allon. The troops were divided into twelve squads. Two of these units guided the advancing Australians; others cut wires, ambushed Vichy patrols guarding bridges over the Litani River, blew culverts, and sabotaged roads. In the attack on Iskanderun, Dayan showed exceptional bravery, capturing twelve Vichy troops (later, in an exchange of fire, he lost an eye).

Elated over this accomplishment, Sadeh pressed the Haganah leadership to supply the Palmach with its own bases for additional training. The request was granted, and two camps were established at the kibbutzim of Ginnosar and Beit Oren. They were quite primitive, without tents or decent sleeping accommodations. Worse yet, funds were lacking to maintain the troops. Eventually the Palmach youths worked in the kibbutzim to "earn" the right to serve as a quasi-permanent mobilized force. From these rural bases, their availability was soon to be exploited again. Indeed, collaboration between the British and the Jews reached its peak at the most threatening phase of the Middle Eastern fighting, as Rommel bore down on Alexandria in the summer of 1942. The British set about fortifying northern Palestine and the Judean mountain range. The Zionist defense machinery in turn was rapidly enlarged, as a broadened recruitment effort was launched equally for the British army and the Haganah reserves. At the same time, British staff officers began organizing the Palmach units into a special task force to meet the developing Nazi threat.

The strategy that was devised, the "Carmel Plan," actually was worked out entirely by the Jews, by Sadeh and Dr. Yochanan Ratner, a Technion professor who served on the Haganah command. It was to establish an enclave in the Carmel Range to which the entire Yishuv could be moved if necessary, there to live out months or even years of Nazi occupation in a state of siege. The population would be governed by a Jewish military administration, supplied by RAF planes and British submarines and by its own agricultural resources. An enlarged Palmach force would defend the redoubt, using former Allied arsenals as well as a variety of its own miniature industries and workshops. Eventually the Carmel enclave would become a major guerrilla base from which attacks could be launched against the Axis occupation troops, disrupting enemy communications and supply lines. This elaborate Haganah scheme of defense plainly did not reflect the mentality of a ghettoized European Jewry, nor even of European nations already under the Nazi heel; it was rather the militant approach of a totally new Zionist community. With considerable admiration (if some doubt), then, the British approved the plan. British general staff intelligence coordinated the training operations. German-speaking and Arabic-speaking Jews were picked for selective espionage and sabotage work. As the operation gradually expanded, 725 Palmach recruits were chosen, and other Jewish underground members were allowed to work in open collaboration with British officers.

The Carmel Plan was never set into motion. In July 1942, Rommel's forces were hurled back at al-Alamein, and four months later driven out of Libya altogether by a reorganized Eighth Army under the command of Lieutenant General Bernard Montgomery. By then in any case the joint effort with the Jews was becoming a source of discomfiture to the mandatory government; Zionist spokesmen already were making pointed contrasts between the Jewish and Arab war efforts. Once the danger to Palestine ebbed in the autumn of 1942, therefore, the British closed the various Palmach training bases, allowed the "German Platoon" and the "Arabic Platoon" to dwindle, and even demanded lists containing names and addresses of Palmach members. The alliance finally ended in bad blood when the British army appropriated the weapons it had distributed earlier to the Palmach. Whereupon Palmach units broke into a government arsenal several days later and reclaimed the guns. The British in turn relegated the Haganah to its former illegal status.

Refusing dissolution, however, the Jewish defense force simply became an underground once again. Indeed, its numbers swelled to 21,000 men and women. The Palmach also remained intact in various scattered kibbutzim, training secretly, even organizing a clandestine naval program (Pal-Yam) and developing a rudimentary air arm under the façade of a tiny aviation club. By then, too, having worked closely with the British, the Haganah (and Palmach) leadership understood better the ways in which a European regular army functioned, and what its strengths and limitations were. For example, the British command structure was maintained intact, but several of its more tradition-bound procedures were discarded. Palmach section commanders were taught to rely less on orders than on their own initiative. Sadeh and his colleagues laid their emphasis on unconventional tactics—initiative, surprise, and preemptive attack. Few underground movements elsewhere managed to achieve quite this degree of military sophistication. The training and mobilization effort had served a vital wartime purpose for Jews and British alike. After the war it would serve a Zionist political and military purpose exclusively.

TRAGEDY AND RESCUE

To the Yishuv, the cause of Jewish rescue abroad was no less critical than the survival of the Jewish National Home itself. For more than a year after the issuance of the 1939 White Paper, a limited clandestine exodus to Palestine still flowed from central and eastern Europe. Inasmuch as the Germans themselves encouraged this migration at the outset (Chapter IX), the British viewed it as a fifth column, one that ideally fostered the Nazi purpose of arousing the Arabs and undermining the security of Palestine. As a result, it became the mandatory's tactics at all costs to prevent the refugees from landing and to intern them elsewhere in the British Commonwealth. The rigorous application of this policy after the war began, when the absorption of as many as 100,000 Jewish fugitives might have been accomplished without Arab knowledge, suggested an unwritten decision on the part of mandatory officials to abort the growth of the Jewish National Home. In support of this decision, Colonial Secretary MacDonald terminated all further land sales to the Jews on February 28, 1940. Soon the Jews were confined to a new Pale of Settlement embracing barely 5 percent of western Palestine.

During the spring of 1940, too, even as the question of Jewish recruitment in Palestine was being discussed, the Colonial and Foreign Offices emphasized repeatedly the importance of placating the Arabs. On May 25, the Iraqi foreign minister, Nuri es-Saïd, demanded that London issue a clear and unambiguous statement guaranteeing the Arabs self-government in Palestine once the war ended. Nuri observed that such an assurance would go far to counteract Axis propaganda in the Middle East. Accepting this view, London on June 12 submitted a draft of a public statement asserting that "the policy of His Majesty's Government for Palestine continues to be that laid down in the White Paper of May 1939," and that it was Britain's intention "when the war ended . . . [quickly to] permit the various stages of constitutional development to follow one another on the lines which the White Paper lays down." Had it not been for Churchill's personal opposition, the cabinet would have approved the draft forthwith. Instead, on July 3, 1940, a shorter declaration was issued stating only: "His Majesty's Government do not see any reason to make any change in their policy for Palestine as laid down in May 1939, and it remains unchanged." A few months afterward London decided to proceed with the next step in the White Paper program, the appointment of a number of Palestinian (that is, Arab) heads of departments. The move was cut short only at the last moment by an unforeseen development, the sinking of the refugee vessel *Patria* in Haifa harbor.

On this aging transport in November 1940, the mandatory authorities had loaded some 1,900 recently arrived, illegal Jewish immigrants. The government's intention was to carry the refugees away to Mauritius Island in the Indian Ocean, where they would be interned at least for the duration of the war. Determined to sabotage the transshipment, the Haganah in turn arranged to blow a small leak in the vessel's hull, forcing the disembarkation of the passengers. On November 25, the explosion went off, but the ship sank almost instantly, with the death of 240 Jews and a dozen British policemen. Only a month after the *Patria* tragedy, the SS *Atlantic*, another obsolescent vessel, reached Haifa with 1,600 new European refugees. In this case, the British transshipped the passengers to Mauritius without incident. A few weeks later the SS *Salvador* docked at Haifa with an additional 350 fugitive Jews—and was ordered to return to Bulgaria. The ship capsized in the Turkish Straits, leaving only seventy survivors. As the British wartime naval blockade gradually tightened, immigration by sea came to an end.

A later incident occurred, however, which became for the Yishuv the very symbol of Britain's unrelenting wartime policy toward the refugees. On December 16, 1941, the SS *Struma* entered the harbor of Istanbul and dropped anchor. It was an unseaworthy vessel of 180 tons. Several weeks before, it had departed the Rumanian port of Constanta and limped along the Black Sea coast with Palestine as its goal. Now, with its engine malfunctioning and its hull leaking badly, the *Struma* was forced to anchor for repairs. The ship was packed with 769 refugees for a voyage across the high seas. Unable to proceed farther, the Jews implored the Turkish government for sanctuary. The appeal was turned down. Barred from going forward and unwilling to return, the *Struma* passengers remained in Istanbul harbor for two months, suffering from hunger, overcrowding, and mounting panic. The Jewish Agency implored the British to allow the refugees entrance to Palestine, if only for transshipment later to Mauritius. Once this approval was forthcoming, the Turks would surely allow the Jews to disembark and entrain for the Levant. The mandatory government refused. Eventually, on February 24, 1942, the Turks ordered the *Struma* towed out of the harbor. Five miles beyond the coastline the ship foundered and sank with the loss of 428 men, 269 women, and 70 children. The horrified reaction of Palestine Jewry was at least partially echoed in other Allied countries. Even in Britain, the tragedy was angrily debated in the House of Commons. A few other isolated vessels remained to test British obduracy. One of them, the *Pencho,* was similarly lost at sea, although most of its passengers were rescued.

By then the motive for escape was not merely to avoid persecution. It was to remain alive. The first, unconfirmed reports of Nazi mass killings were made by Thomas Mann, the émigré German novelist, in a series of BBC broadcasts in December 1941 and January 1942. In August 1942, Washington received an account of the gas chambers and crematoria from the Polish government in exile. Soon other reports were forthcoming from World Jewish Congress and Jewish Agency officials, who had learned of the killings from transferred Polish war prisoners arriving in Palestine. It is of note that the State Department reacted by imposing a ban on the further transmission of such news through diplomatic channels. When funds were solicited by Jewish organizations for possible rescue efforts, the answer from both Washington and London was that the money would fall into enemy hands; or that it would relieve Germany and its partners of the legal burden of supporting all their inhabitants. In February 1943, Admiral William Leahy, President Roosevelt's chief military liaison officer, vetoed a safe-passage proposal that would have allowed some 10,000 Jewish refugees to move from occupied Europe via Spain to North Africa; ostensibly shipping could not be provided. The following month, Bulgaria sensed the shifting tide of war and attempted to disassociate itself from the "Final Solution" (Hitler's euphemism for the destruction of European Jewry); the Sofia government expressed a willingness to allow Jewish departure for Palestine. When Washington raised the question with London, however, it was Foreign Secretary Eden who blocked action. "If we do that then the Jews of the world will be wanting us to make a similar offer in Poland and Germany," Eden explained. "Hitler might well take us up on such an offer and there simply are not enough ships . . . in the world to handle them." Besides, "Hitler would be sure to sneak his agents into the group." In December 1943 the State Department finally authorized the transfer of rescue funds to Rumania and Vichy France, provided the British supplied the necessary certificates. But once more Eden objected, alluding to "difficulties of disposing of a considerable number of Jews."

The furthest either Allied government appeared willing to go was to send representatives to an international conference in Bermuda, in April 1943, to study methods of dealing with the refugee question. At the gathering, about a dozen remote islands were mentioned as possible refugee sanctuaries, among them British Guiana, Mindanao, and Sesua in the Dominican Republic. Palestine was omitted from consideration. No other government expressed a willingness to open its doors. Ultimately Bermuda proved as much an exercise in futility as the Évian Conference of 1938. In January 1944, therefore, Roosevelt authorized the establishment of a war refugee board to negotiate asylum for Nazi-persecuted minorities in Europe. Yet the board's representative, Ira Hirschmann, achieved his one limited success in persuading the British to open Palestine's doors to a few thousand Soviet Jewish refugee children who had been interned under wretched conditions in Turkey.

It was in 1944, too, in one of the most bizarre episodes of the war, that a possibly dramatic opportunity for large-scale Jewish rescue was forfeited. Until early that year Admiral Miklos Horthy, the regent of Hungary, had jealously guarded from Germany his nation's right to handle its own "Jewish problem." Then, on March 19, the Nazis occupied Hungary. The following month Joel Brand, a member of the Hungarian Jewish Rescue Committee, was summoned to a meeting with Adolf Eichmann, who had arrived in Budapest personally to supervise the "Final Solution" in Hungary. Eichmann presented Brand with an astonishing offer. He was willing, he declared, to allow Hungary's 800,000 Jews exit on condition that the Allies supply Germany with 10,000 trucks, 1,000 tons of coffee, and 1,000 tons of soap. Although shaken and incredulous, Brand discussed the proposal with his colleagues in the Rescue Committee. They, too, were skeptical. Even if the offer were sincere, the Allies would surely refuse Germany war matériel. On the other hand, it was evident that conversations with Eichmann had to be prolonged, if only to stay the Nazi executioner's hand. But Eichmann's hand was not to be stayed. Early in May he began sending off 12,000 Hungarian Jews a day for liquidation. On the thirteenth of the month, he had Joel Brand flown to Turkey in a German courier plane, with orders to make known the offer of "blood for goods" to Jewish and British representatives.

On May 14, Brand met with Jewish Agency officials in Istanbul. Learning to his dismay that these men had no authority to negotiate for Jewish lives, he immediately entrained for Palestine. He got as far as Aleppo before British detectives hustled him off the train for interrogation. Finally he was transferred to Cairo, where he was kept under virtual house arrest. On one occasion, Ira Hirschmann, the American war refugee board representative, was allowed to interview Brand. Hirschmann then carried the information back to Washington. If war matériel could not be supplied, he pleaded, at least the formalities of negotiations should be initiated with the Nazis. But if the State Department gave even limited consideration to the proposal, it was soon stopped short by London. The British released word of Eichmann's offer to the press and simultaneously repudiated the "brazen attempt to blackmail His Majesty's Government." On their own, then, two Jewish Agency emissaries, Ehud Avriel and Menachem Bader, prepared to fly to Portugal early in July to make contact with Nazi agents. The British denied permission for their trip. By this time, fully 434,000 Hungarian Jews had been shipped to Auschwitz and murdered. The remainder were saved—when the Red Army entered Hungary.

Whatever was accomplished in the way of rescue was less through British sufferance than by Jewish underground efforts. The Haganah managed to smuggle a few thousand Middle Eastern Jews into Palestine by organizing an "underground railroad" through Iraq and Transjordan. Rescue camps were established secretly along Bedouin caravan routes, with the

Arabs bribed to transport their disguised Jewish passengers. In this way, some 4,000 Persian and Iraqi Jews eventually were infiltrated into Palestine during 1942 and 1943. Still another Jewish response to Axis terror was to participate in a series of clandestine rescue operations in northern Italy and the Balkans. The project had its origins in the unexpectedly heavy losses suffered by American bombers during the 1943 raids on Rumania's Ploesti oil refineries. In light of these reverses, the British were convinced that additional intelligence information was needed on German defenses in the Balkans. Whereupon the Haganah leadership offered the British a proposal of its own. It was for Jews with connections in those lands to be parachuted into Europe, where they might serve a double function as intelligence agents and as organizers of resistance among the hostage Jewish communities. After some hesitation, the British approved the plan. Subsequently, thirty-two Palestine Jewish volunteers were accepted for the mission, three of them women. The British trained them in a special camp in Cairo.

Nine of the parachutists were dropped into Rumania, three into Hungary, two into Bulgaria, three into Italy, six into Slovakia, nine into Yugoslavia. All were natives of those countries; all spoke the languages fluently and had relatives there. Of the thirty-two, seven died with the Jews they attempted to rescue. Channa Szenes was the best-known of the agents, a Hungarian Jewish girl who had left her family to settle in Palestine as a chalutzah in 1934. Now, ten years later, she was seized by the Hungarian police within days of reaching Budapest, tortured by the Gestapo, then executed. Another woman, Chaviva Reik, helped form a Jewish underground unit in Slovakia and established a transit camp for escaping Russian war prisoners and Allied airmen. She also was caught and executed, together with two other parachutists. Enzo Sereni, the oldest member of the group, had been born and raised in Italy, where his father was personal physician to the king. An early immigrant to Palestine, Sereni was one of the first to volunteer for the parachute mission. He was dropped into Italy in May 1944, caught at once, imprisoned by the SS, and killed in Dachau. While several parachutists managed to transmit intelligence data to the British, and even arranged for the rescue of Allied fliers through Partisan territory in Yugoslavia, the mission had only limited practical success in organizing Jewish resistance in Hungary and the Balkans. But together with other Jewish wartime operations, at least, the rescue project was incorporated into Zionist folklore and nourished the longing for Jewish independence.

ANGLO-ZIONIST DIPLOMACY DURING THE WAR

Even as the Zionists mobilized their limited resources to breach the immigration blockade, their representatives in London explored methods of solving the refugee question within the framework of a larger Palestine agreement. At the beginning of the war, the Jewish Agency leadership remained committed to the original 1937 partition plan. They may have been encouraged in their demand for sovereignty by a remarkable proposal first mooted in September 1939 by the British world traveler H. S. John Philby, a friend of Ibn Saud. Philby's idea was for the whole of Palestine to be allocated to the Jews, who in turn would make £20 million available to the Saudi ruler for the purpose of resettling Palestine Arabs in his kingdom. It was expected that the hint of Ibn Saud's primacy among other Arab leaders would be a major inducement to the desert monarch. Although skeptical, the Zionists were willing to have Philby explore the idea. In January 1940 the Englishman traveled to Arabia and discussed the plan with his royal friend. Ibn Saud was cautiously interested. So was Churchill, who first learned of the scheme from Weizmann in 1940 and discussed it briefly again with the Zionist leader in March 1942. Evidently the prime minister gave the suggestion tentative approval, for Lord Moyne, later to become minister-resident in Cairo, met with Ibn Saud in December 1942 to pursue the question further. Lacking a firm Allied endorsement, however, the Saudi ruler declined to commit himself. Nor did he react favorably when approached on the subject by an American representative, Colonel Halford Hoskins, late in 1943 (p. 254).

If the Philby proposal fell through, Weizmann and his colleagues nevertheless took heart from Churchill's reaction. The prime minister clearly had lost none of his traditional sympathy for Zionism. On April 18, 1943, he vigorously endorsed Weizmann's appeal to modify the White Paper. "I cannot agree that the White Paper of 1939 is 'the firmly established policy of His Majesty's present Government,'" he said. "I have always regarded it as a gross breach of faith." Ten days later Churchill circulated a note to the cabinet challenging the right of the Arab majority to deny Jewish immigration into Palestine. At his orders, a special cabinet committee to reexamine the future of Palestine was organized on July 12, under the chairmanship of Herbert Morrison and including Oliver Stanley, Lord Cranbourne, and Leopold Amery. By October of that year the group had reached a consensus, although postponing its formal report until December 20. The Morrison Committee offered partition as the best solution to the Palestine imbroglio and suggested that the government promote an association of Levant nations, consisting of a Jewish state, a Jerusalem territory (under a British high commissioner), some three-fifths of Lebanon, and a "Greater Syria," to include Syria itself, Transjordan, southern Lebanon, and the Arab-inhabited areas of Palestine.

The plan was generous to the Jews. Churchill liked it. Although a public announcement would have to be deferred until after the war, the prime minister revealed the scheme's general outline to Weizmann at a luncheon in October 1943, at which Clement Attlee, leader of the Labor opposition, was present. "When we have crushed Hitler," Churchill said emphatically, "we shall have to establish the Jews in the position where they belong. I have an inheritance left to me by Balfour and I am not going to change. But there are dark forces working against us. Dr. Weizmann, you have some very good friends. For instance, Mr. Attlee and the Labour Party are committed on this matter." "I certainly am," Attlee agreed. A year later, on November 4, 1944, the prime minister again received Weizmann and promised unreservedly to find an acceptable Palestine solution after the war. According to Churchill, the immigration of one and a half million refugees over ten years and the immigration of 100,000 to 150,000 orphans immediately were reasonable guidelines. So was the partition plan, which he hinted would be a "good" one from the Jewish viewpoint.

Despite their grief at the unfolding tragedy in Europe, none of the Zionist leaders could doubt by then that they had in Churchill a man whose friendship warranted the fullest loyalty. Even the militant Ben-Gurion shared that judgment. Evidence of the prime minister's good intentions, moreover, was his determination to force through the issue of a Jewish brigade before the war ended. Upon the invasion of Italy in the autumn of 1943, the front line shifted north from the Arab countries. It was a much simpler matter by then to justify Zionist participation in the struggle for Europe, where millions of Jews were being exterminated by the enemy. On July 12, 1944, therefore, Churchill sent a memorandum to the war secretary, instructing him to begin organizing a Jewish army group forthwith. "I like the idea of the Jews trying to get at the murderers of their fellow countrymen in Central Europe, and I think it would give a great deal of satisfaction in the United States. . . ." In subsequent weeks, the plans were worked out in detail with the Jewish Agency, and on September 29 the prime minister himself made the announcement to the House of Commons:

> I know there is a vast number of Jews serving with our forces and the American forces throughout all the armies, but it seems to me indeed appropriate that a special Jewish unit of that race which has suffered indescribable torment from the Nazis should be represented as a distinct formation among the forces gathered for their final overthrow. I have no doubt that they will not only take part in the struggle but also in the occupation which will follow.

In October, the War Office appointed Brigadier Ernest Benjamin as commanding officer of the brigade. A Zionist banner was approved, together with a blue-and-white shoulder flash inscribed with the Shield of David. A recruiting and training program was launched, and early in 1945 the 3,400 Palestinian members of the brigade were shipped off for combat duty in Italy, where they were attached to the British Eighth Army. As it turned out, this Jewish fighting force represented the one important political accomplishment of Zionist diplomacy during the war. Equipped with its own staff services and artillery support, it became the training ground where hundreds of Palestinian officers and NCOs first·mastered logistics, organization, and tactics on a brigade scale. The experience added of course to the Haganah reservoir of trained fighting men in the event of a postwar struggle against the British or the Arabs. But in 1944, Weizmann and other moderates of Zionism preferred to regard the brigade as harbinger of a significant change in British policy toward the Yishuv.

THE RISE OF JEWISH MILITANCY

The expectation was premature. Churchill's wartime gestures of friendship were steadfastly resisted, and frequently undermined, by the traditionally pro-Arab element within the Foreign Office and the mandatory administration. On the one side, the prime minister continued to urge a reevaluation of attitude toward the Zionists, with a strong bias in favor of partition. On the other, Richard Casey, Britain's minister-resident in Cairo, transmitted a memorandum to Whitehall on June 17, 1943, giving details of Jewish secret military organizations (p. 247) and warning that London hardly could repudiate its White Paper assurances to the Arabs without turning the whole of Arab opinion against Britain. In October of the same year, moreover, Eden urged a reconsideration of the Morrison Committee's scheme of partition, and delay in resolving the Palestine issue until hostilities ended. There was no need to incur Arab wrath prematurely, he explained. The War Cabinet accepted this argument and agreed to hold off a final decision. In the meantime, Eden was reminded by his ambassadors in Cairo and Baghdad that Palestine served as an indispensable link in the British defense system, one that under no circumstances should be abandoned after the war.

At the beginning of June 1944, therefore, the Colonial Office suggested an alternative to partition. It was for the establishment of a Palestinian state under the aegis of the United Nations but "supervised" by a British high commissioner. Jewish immigration could be resumed, but fixed at a number small enough to ensure continuing Arab numerical preponderance. On September 26, 1944, unwilling yet to abandon its earlier proposals, the special cabinet committee on Palestine—the Morrison Committee—allowed minor revisions of its original report but continued to stand fast on partition. Eden and his Foreign Office colleagues, on the other hand, repeated their view that a division of Palestine would not alleviate Arab fears, particularly if the Jews encouraged large-scale immigration. And there the matter rested, frozen at dead center.

If the Zionists lacked detailed knowledge of this impasse within the British government, they were perfectly capable of judging its results. Churchill's assurances of a favorable postwar solution were gratifying, and the eventual approval of a Jewish brigade hardly less so. But in the meanwhile the gates of Palestine remained tightly closed, and the arrival of survivors from Nazi Europe had trickled to a stop. It was at the end of 1941 and the beginning of 1942 that the *Struma* tragedy occurred. Then, a few weeks later, came authoritative information on the Nazi "Final Solution." As has been seen, the response of the Allied nations to this unfolding horror was to close their doors more tightly. Visa regulations in the United States were tightened on the grounds that enemy agents might be traveling as disguised refugees. In April 1942 seven Latin American countries denied entrance altogether to fugitives from Axis-dominated Europe. Turkey, the most likely way station out of the neutral Balkans, denied all transit rights and even adopted a thinly disguised policy of internal racism. To Ben-Gurion and his colleagues in the Jewish Agency, promises and expressions of goodwill from Western governments seemed increasingly meaningless.

It is of note that as late as May 1940, Ben-Gurion, like Weizmann, had not closed his mind to various compromise solutions of the Palestine question. As chairman of the Jewish Agency Executive, he had been willing to consider a partition scheme as a framework for discussions, even a limited binational state allowing parity between Arabs and Jews. It was not the magnitude of the Jewish tragedy alone that transformed Ben-Gurion into an uncompromising advocate of Zionist sovereignty. In 1942 he visited the United States and there felt "the pulse of her great Jewry, with its five millions." The visit, his first in many years, was an apocalyptic experience. Ben-Gurion experienced at last, in depth, what he felt to be his people's latent strength. It was only after this first wartime visit to America that he began discussing with his colleagues the notion of a Jewish state in Palestine "as a means of moving millions of Jews [there] . . . after the war, at the fastest possible rate." He was convinced, too, that with the immolation of European Jewry (the full extent of which was not yet revealed), any fundamental alteration of the official—and more moderate—Zionist program would have to receive American Jewish endorsement. At Ben-Gurion's initiative, then, an emergency Zionist Conference to formulate postwar goals was convened at the Hotel Biltmore in New York from May 9 to May 11, 1942. It was attended by six hundred delegates, the majority Americans, but including also several European Zionist leaders and three members of the Agency Executive, among them Weizmann and Ben-Gurion himself. The accumulation of Jewish grievances against the British was ventilated, and a forthright resolution was passed insisting on nothing less than the establishment of Palestine "as a Jewish Commonwealth integrated in the structure of the new democratic world. . . ."

Privately, Ben-Gurion and his associates were committed to rather less than a demand for Palestine in its entirety. They were in fact quite willing to accept the territorial limitations of partition. What no longer was negotiable was Jewish self-rule, a position the Agency leadership had been unwilling to adopt earlier for fear of antagonizing the Arabs and the British. This time Ben-Gurion had achieved his purpose; he had won firm support for a maximalist program. He hinted, too, that violence would be used to achieve it if necessary. "To be ready, also, for another way, the way of armed struggle. . . . Our youth must be prepared to do everything possible when the right moment comes," he declared on May 16, 1942, in a memorandum to the Jewish Agency. In fact, it is doubtful whether the Zionist militants achieved much by announcing this unequivocal program. They erred if they assumed that the Yishuv's participation in the Allied war effort, even when contrasted with the Arab record of pro-Nazi activity, invested their movement with the extraordinary bargaining power it had briefly—and under unique circumstances—enjoyed in World War I. Regardless of the economic and political strength Ben-Gurion and others detected in American Jewry, the Zionists were considerably less than a powerful international force. The wounds of the unfolding holocaust in Europe were crippling. Friends and enemies alike regarded the Jews simply as a desperately beleaguered race. Far-ranging manifestoes appeared altogether ill-suited to their current plight.

Moreover, Ben-Gurion's interpretation of statehood was sharply at odds with that of Weizmann. The difference was not immediately apparent. During the partition debate of 1937, after all, Weizmann had been the first to advocate a state, albeit one comprising less than the whole of Palestine. "We shall have on our hands [at the end of the war] a problem of at least three million people," he wrote later, in 1941. "Even on purely financial grounds a Jewish state is essential in order to carry out a policy of such magnitude." In an article published in *Foreign Affairs* in 1942, Weizmann added that a Jewish state was also a "moral need and postulate, a decisive step towards normality and true emancipation." Repeatedly he predicted that an Arab federation and a Jewish commonwealth would emerge at the end of the war, and he anticipated intimate cooperation between them. The "Biltmore Program," therefore, hardly signified a repudiation of Weizmann's position. Indeed, the formula adopted at the emergency conference in New York actually had been devised by Meyer Weisgal, one of Weizmann's closest political aides.

Yet Weizmann regarded the program essentially as a statement of intent, with the time of its implementation left open. Unshakably gradualist, the Zionist elder statesman continued to think in terms of an uninterrupted flow of Jewish immigrants who slowly might become a majority and establish an autonomous entity in Palestine. Ben-Gurion, on the other hand, discerned in the Biltmore Program an end at last to irresolution and equivocation on the Zionist purpose. The vote in New York for him was a mandate for statehood immediately, thereby opening the gates of Palestine to hundreds of thousands of immigrants within a very short time span. Afterward, upon returning from the United States, Ben-Gurion explained his views to the Yishuv, winning broad public support for his approach, emphasizing that a maximalist demand would project Jewish claims before the council of nations at just the moment that other peoples would also be submitting their desiderata. It would be better, he insisted, to ask for too much than for too little. At its meeting of November 19, 1942, the Zionist Actions Committee accepted the Biltmore Program overwhelmingly. Weizmann meanwhile remained in New York, and was unable as a result to ensure the Yishuv's approval for his own gradualistic interpretation of the Biltmore formula. Exhausted, still crushed by the death in action of his younger son, an RAF pilot, the aging Zionist leader was becoming an increasingly remote figure to Palestine Jewry. In the developing collision of views between himself and Ben-Gurion, it was Weizmann who was losing out.

The British proved curiously sluggish in appraising this new Jewish mood. Nor did they detect the growth and strength that animated Palestine Jewry's emerging militance. In the years between the two wars, however, the Yishuv had grown from 85,000, or 10 percent of the total population of the country, to 560,000 in 1946, or about 32 percent of the total. Jewish agriculture had been dramatically expanded. From 1939 to 1947, ninety-four new villages were founded, half of them during the war, raising the total of Jewish settlements to 348, with a population of 116,000. Between 1937 and 1943 alone the number of Jewish industrial workers more than doubled, from 22,000 to 46,000. The value of Jewish industrial production increased nearly fivefold, from P£7.9 million in 1937 to P£37.5 million in 1943.

This radical alteration of the Zionist economic structure in Palestine, and its implications for Jewish self-confidence, were virtually ignored by the mandatory administration. Thus, early in 1943, Sir Harold Mac-Michael, the high commissioner, broadcast a message to the country explaining the government's postwar economic blueprint for Palestine. It stressed the nation's essentially agricultural character and the importance of weeding out the mushroom industries that had sprung up on wartime prosperity. Emphasis henceforth would be placed on raising the living standards of the Arab community, MacMichael declared. Ben-Gurion and his colleagues in the Agency were outraged by this broadcast. The Arabs had done virtually nothing for the war effort, after all; and if the economy of the Yishuv had developed, it had done so in support of the Allied cause. The Zionists also regarded the plan as a thinly disguised scheme for limiting the Yishuv's absorptive capacity. The next day Ben-Gurion gave the Agency's uncompromising response: "Our program is the maximum development of this country in agriculture, in industry, and on the sea, in order to prepare for a maximum immigration within the shortest possible period of time." He warned that the Jewish emphasis under all circumstances would be on "development," not "reconstruction."

Shortly afterward, as if to give tangible expression to Ben-Gurion's challenge, members of the Jewish underground infiltrated several British military bases and made off with quantities of light arms and ammunition. The reaction of the mandatory government was to launch police searches of increasing range and severity, bearing down on the contraband Jewish arms traffic in captured Axis weapons and sentencing Jewish smugglers to heavy prison terms. General Sir Henry Maitland Wilson recalled in his memoirs that by January 1944 the Jewish Agency

. . . was in some respects arrogating to itself the powers and status of an independent Jewish government. It no longer attempted to deny the existence of arms caches, but claimed the right not only to hold arms for self-defense but to resist any attempt on the part of lawful authority to locate them. It was, in fact, defying the Government, and to that extent rebellion could be said to exist.

Wilson did not exaggerate. Beyond control of the Jewish Agency itself there emerged a number of activist splinter groups, limited in number but fanatical in purpose, that were unwilling any longer to accept Zionist discipline at a time when Jews were being exterminated in Europe and the

British were barring the doors of Palestine to survivors. The technique adopted by these militants was violence, "the tragic, futile, un-Jewish resort to terrorism," wrote Weizmann, who encountered this phenomenon upon returning to Palestine in 1944. The most ungovernable faction in the emergent underground movement was the "Fighters for the Freedom of Israel," known simply as the Lech'i (for its Hebrew initials). Consisting of barely three hundred members, the Lech'i was one of a handful of Jewish paramilitary organizations that sprang up during or immediately following the Arab insurrection of 1936–39. Its founder, Avraham Stern, a blond, Polish-born Jew in his early thirties, a teacher and poetaster, had briefly studied classics at the University of Florence and had been decisively influenced there by what he saw of Fascist tactics and of Mussolini's intense Anglophobia. He was soon convinced that Britain's presence in the Middle East was inimical to the future development of the Jewish National Home and that henceforth all emphasis should be placed on an anti-British rebellion. No other Jewish underground group was willing yet to go that far, not even the Irgun Z'vai Le'umi (p. 265).

After the outbreak of war, however, Stern moved even further to the Right. In 1941 he attempted to make contact with Otto von Hentig, the German emissary in Vichy Syria, in the hope of striking a deal against the British in Palestine. His overtures were contemptuously ignored. Desperate for funds, Stern and the Lech'i were soon reduced to occasional bank robberies. In January 1942 a Sternist bomb attempt meant for a British intelligence officer instead killed two Jewish police inspectors. A few weeks later, Stern was shot dead by the police. Far from ending the Lech'i's militancy, these events seemed to impel its remaining members to acts of even greater desperation. Although a number of the Sternists were Oriental Jewish youngsters from the slums of Tel Aviv and Jerusalem, many were east Europeans whose families were being destroyed by the Nazis. Their hatred of the British transcended reason or control. One of the killers of Lord Moyne, for example (p. 248), Eliahu Chakim, watched the sinking of the *Patria* in Haifa harbor, and the memory of this tragedy never left him.

After 1942 the Lech'i, under its new leaders, Nathan Friedmann-Yellin and Dr. Israel Scheib, concluded that violence was the one method capable of driving the British from Palestine. Thus, extorting funds from Jewish shopkeepers, the Lech'i soon engaged in indiscriminate shootings of British police. Not infrequently, Lech'i members were themselves shot down in gun battles. The attacks mounted in intensity. So did British retaliation, with mass arrests, curfews, and the imposition of the death penalty on those carrying weapons. Still the underground campaign went on, and once included an unsuccessful murder attempt against the high commissioner, Sir Harold MacMichael, on August 8, 1944. Three months later, the Lech'i perpetrated its most audacious crime. It took place in Cairo and was directed against Lord Moyne, the British minister-resident. Walter Edward Guinness, first Baron Moyne, was a millionaire-owner of the Guinness beverage company, a gentle and widely respected man. He had briefly directed the Colonial Office after Lord Lloyd's death in 1941, and in January 1944 became minister of state for the Middle East. The Zionists regarded him as an enemy from his days as colonial secretary; and perhaps, also, for his coldly negative reaction to Eichmann's barter offer for Hungarian Jewry. On November 6, less than forty-eight hours after Weizmann's friendly and reassuring luncheon with Churchill in London, two Sternists shot Moyne fatally as he was leaving the British residence. The youths were placed on trial in Cairo on January 10, 1945, and were swiftly convicted and hanged.

With few exceptions, the Zionist community was horror-stricken by Moyne's assassination. A shaken Weizmann, in London at the time of the killing, promised Churchill that Palestine Jewry "will go to the utmost limit of its power to cut out this evil from its midst." Ben-Gurion endorsed these words by issuing a passionate appeal to the Yishuv "to cast out all members of this underground gang and deny them shelter and assistance. . . ." Thereupon the Haganah launched a full-scale attack against Etzel (Irgun) and Lech'i members alike, denouncing them to the British police. But the damage to the Zionist cause was already far-reaching. In a statement before the House of Commons ten days after the assassination, Churchill uttered a sharp warning against terrorism in Palestine. "If our dreams for Zionism are to end in the smoke of an assassin's pistol," he said, "and the labours for its future produce a new set of gangsters worthy of Nazi Germany, many like myself will have to reconsider the position we have maintained so consistently and so long in the past." For England, the Moyne assassination was a revelation of the seething bitterness within Jewish Palestine. Although the episode was repudiated by the Jews no less than by the British, it terminated the collaborative period of government promises and Jewish credulity. Jewish goodwill had come to an end. British patience was now similarly to be exhausted.

THE YISHUV

REPUDIATES THE MANDATE

Within months after hostilities in Europe ended, a tentative balance sheet could be drawn up. The statistics of the "Final Solution" numbered 2,800,000 Polish Jews, 800,000 Soviet Jews, 450,000 Hungarian Jews, 350,000 Rumanian Jews, 180,000 German Jews, 60,000 Austrian Jews, 243,000 Czechoslovakian Jews, 110,000 Dutch Jews, 25,000 Belgian Jews, 50,000 Yugoslav Jews, 80,000 Greek Jews, 65,000 French Jews, 10,000 Italian Jews —all liquidated by shooting, gassing, hanging, burning, or starvation and disease. The data of survival took longer to accumulate, for it was based upon the number of Jewish "displaced persons" who gathered in the Allied occupation sectors of Germany.

General Eisenhower's initial policy was to return these "DPs" to their countries of origin. Yet the majority were natives of eastern Europe, where they had escaped Nazi massacre in the wake of the retreating Soviet army. Eisenhower's order would have compelled them to return to the graveyards of their families, and to the less than tender mercies of the Polish, Ukrainian, and Rumanian populations. It was not until late summer of 1945 that visiting Jewish welfare teams alerted the American commanders to the anti-Semitism rampant in eastern Europe. It happened that Earl G. Harrison, dean of the University of Pennsylvania Law School, had already been appointed by Washington to make a survey of European refugee conditions. The White House therefore instructed him to pay special attention to the circumstances of the Jews. Harrison fulfilled his mission, and his later report was an indictment of military insensitivity to the plight of the Jewish DPs in the American zone. Immediately afterward, on direct orders from President Truman, the treatment of these survivors was improved, their housing augmented, their rations increased. Under no circumstances, the directive stated, were east European Jews to be turned back from refugee camps in Germany.

Spontaneously, then, refugee traffic from the East to German relocation centers gained momentum. It was still largely unorganized throughout 1945 and was carried out with the help of private German or Polish smugglers, who moved the Jews westward in return for money or goods. By the opening days of 1946, 2,000 to 3,000 Jews a day were crossing from Poland into Czechoslovakia and on to central Europe. By the summer of that year, nearly 100,000 Jewish DPs had reached Germany. Jewish living conditions in the renovated former concentration camps were not intolerable. Food, clothing, and medical attention were provided by the American army and supplemented from Jewish philanthropic resources. For the survivors, however, each additional day in the European charnel house was a psychologically intolerable ordeal. The vision of escape became their obsession.

With equal expectation, the Zionist world in turn placed its trust in Britain's new Labor government. The Agency leadership by then had written off the Conservatives as verbalizers. Until the end, as late as June 1945, Churchill had maintained the White Paper restrictions intact, cautioning the Zionists that the Palestine issue could not be "effectively considered until the victorious Allies are definitely seated at the Peace Table." By contrast, the Labor party record on Palestine was known to be sympathetic. Indeed, Labor's numerous resolutions of support for the Jewish National Home had been evoked by no American-style pressure group, but rather by a "profound conviction," in the recollection of a Laborite MP, Richard Crossman, "that the establishment of the national home was an important part of the Socialist creed. . . ." This lent a unique significance to the pro-Zionist plank adopted at the Labor party's convention in 1944. The statement went so far in its endorsement of a Jewish Palestine, actually suggesting a mass transplantation of the Arab population to neighboring lands, that it left even the Zionists gasping.

Hopes in the Yishuv revived dramatically, therefore, following Labor's stunning upset victory of July 1945. "The British workers will understand our aims," Ben-Gurion declared exultantly, upon hearing the news. There was additional reason for encouragement. The community that now demanded recognition was no longer a precarious minority settlement. By 1944, as has been seen, the Jewish population of Palestine had reached 560,000. Its economy had been profoundly stimulated by the war. Almost half its food needs could now be supplied by its own farms. Industrial production had risen dramatically. Weizmann, returning to Palestine after a five-year absence, was astonished at the magnitude of growth. He wrote later:

> The war years had knit the community into a powerful, self-conscious organism—and the great war effort, out of all proportion to the numerical strength of the Yishuv, had given the Jews of Palestine a heightened self-reliance, a justified sense of merit and achievement, a renewed claim on the democratic world, and a high degree of technical development. . . . The National Home was in fact here—unrecognized, and by that lack of recognition frustrated in the fulfillment of its task.

In this mood of suppressed exasperation at years of blocked immigration, therefore, combined with renewed confidence in the Yishuv's strength and in the pro-Zionism of British Labor, Ben-Gurion led a deputation to London within ten days of the Attlee government's accession to power.

He presented his demands to the new colonial secretary, George Hall. The list was the autonomist Biltmore Program in all its essentials except the demand for final sovereignty, coupled with a request for the immediate admittance into Palestine of 100,000 Jewish displaced persons. The very scope of the demands, not less than the aggressiveness with which Ben-Gurion presented them and the colonial secretary rejected them, turned the interview into a disaster. The outraged Hall sputtered afterward that Ben-Gurion's attitude was "different from anything which I had ever before experienced." Several weeks later, on August 25, the Colonial Office replied with a palliative offer of 2,000 immigrant certificates remaining unused from the original White Paper allotment, with a supplemental monthly quota of 1,400—provided the Arabs agreed. This response in turn dumfounded and appalled the Zionist leadership.

By then, a guideline for the entire Middle East already had been prepared by the Labor foreign secretary, Ernest Bevin. Drafted even earlier by previous British governments, it accepted as unchallengeable the importance of maintaining the friendship of the Arab world. One reason was economic. Britain in 1945 was virtually bankrupt. Its armies had engaged the Axis on five continents and had borne the weight of hostilities longer than any other Allied nation. When the bill was calculated afterward, a quarter of Britain's national wealth was found to have been expended. The domestic cupboard was bare. The nation's remaining supply of hard currency was adequate for barely 40 percent of current purchases, and this at a moment when the new Labor government was intent on carrying out an extensive, even revolutionary, program of social welfare.

One of Bevin's priority concerns during the grim postwar era, therefore, was to assure the single most important of Britain's remaining overseas resources. This was oil, the power source of the country's very industrial existence and a foreign-currency earner of near-sacred importance. Britain's vast holdings were concentrated in the Middle East, partly in Iran, but largely, too, in the vast Kirkuk field of Iraq, in Kuwait, and in Qatar. Both the production and the potential of this liquid El Dorado were calculated as immense. If there was anxiety for continued supply, it was related less to the bottomless wells of the Persian Gulf than to the pipelines crossing the frontiers of other, politically unstable, Arab lands. The growing network, traversing hundreds of miles of desert, was uniquely vulnerable to disruption and sabotage, and its security would be assured only as long as Britain could depend upon Arab political friendship and quiescence.

If a need for oil and pipeline easements was one factor in determining Bevin's Middle Eastern policy, geopolitical strategy was another. Between 1943 and 1947, the British fulfilled their long-cherished ambition of maneuvering the French out of Syria and Lebanon, and thus ended a perennial source of imperial competition in the eastern Mediterranean. During those same years, however, the Soviet Union was emerging as a potentially far more serious threat to Britain's military and economic hegemony in the Middle East. This became evident in the immediate postwar period as Soviet funds, weapons, and advisers fueled a Communist insurrection in Greece; as Moscow issued harsh and ominous territorial demands upon Turkey; and as Red Army divisions continued solidly emplaced and apparently immovable in northern Iran. Notwithstanding his comradely Socialist background, Foreign Secretary Bevin entertained no illusions whatever about the magnitude of the Soviet danger. After Potsdam, he stated his misgivings on Russian policy in Parliament, his certainty of Soviet intentions "to come right across . . . the throat of the British Commonwealth." In response to that threat, Bevin appreciated with acute urgency that Britain's sphere of influence in the Persian Gulf area, with its immense oil reserves, and in the lower Middle East, fronting the "warm waters of the Mediterranean," had to be protected at any cost.

By the same token, the foreign secretary understood how vital, and now how fragile, was his nation's complex skein of imperial relationships in the Arab world. Reduced as it was to near-insolvency, Britain scarcely was capable of assuring its relationship with the Arabs through the conventional methods of armed force or intimidation. Rather, a more promising technique had been initiated and encouraged by the Churchill government after 1942. It was to foster an Arab confederation as an instrument of regional stability under British influence. After several preliminary meetings, the Arab leaders did in fact join together in such an organization in March 1945—although the League of Arab States hardly became the extension of British policy that London had anticipated. Another method was to cultivate Arab goodwill by offering to evacuate Britain's garrisons in Egypt, the Sudan, and Iraq. It was London's expectation that, as a quid pro quo, the Egyptians and Arabs would accept treaty arrangements guaranteeing Britain the option of return to its former bases upon the event of war or the threat of war. In the end, of course, the entire concept of a new Middle Eastern relationship depended on Britain's trustworthiness in Arab eyes.

Bevin appreciated this fact. He did so, moreover, not as a babe in the woods, awkwardly dependent upon the more experienced professional staff in the Foreign Office. He was his own man. Indeed, the stamp of Bevin's own background and personality influenced every phase of the explosive Palestine negotiations for the next three years. He had been molded in a hard school. Orphaned at ten, he had spent his youth laboring at slave wages as a farmer's helper, a dishwasher, a truck driver. At times he stole for his food. Remarkably, he escaped brutalization. As a young man he diligently studied economics in night courses offered by the Social Democratic Federation. At the age of twenty-nine he became an official of the dockers' union, and eventually a member of the general council of Britain's Trades Union Congress. The lineaments of Bevin's personality were already visible by then: blunt, hard-driving, impatient of criticism, scornful of inefficiency. His prestige in the labor movement was unshakable. When the Socialists won in 1945, Clement Attlee, a mild and diffident man, recognized the need for a strong person beside him.

Bevin was unquestionably the strongest in the party, and he was chosen for the key post of foreign secretary. To the surprise of many, he brought with him solid ideas on international affairs. His position in the trade union movement and as wartime minister of labor had taken him to all parts of the world, and he had acquainted himself with the problems of other countries. Most important, Bevin was afraid of no man. Bull-like in appearance and manner, he was unwilling to tolerate intellectual intimidation from any source.

Nor was he unfamiliar with the Palestine question. At the time of the second Labor government under Ramsay MacDonald, when the Zionists were denouncing the Passfield White Paper, representatives of the Histadrut had called on Bevin as a fellow trade unionist for help. He had given it willingly. "Don't worry," he said, "I'll tell the old man." His intercession with MacDonald had played a decisive role in safeguarding the Zionist cause. Now, however, fifteen years later, Bevin was unwilling as foreign secretary to thrust himself into the Palestine question without detailed additional study. To that end he organized a new committee of cabinet ministers and Foreign Office experts. The most knowledgeable of the latter was Harold Beeley, a pronounced Arabophile and Whitehall's authority on all Palestine matters.

The committee launched into its work in August 1945 and reported back to the cabinet in the middle of September. In its deliberations, the group had been influenced by a special report completed in February 1944 by the Royal Institute of International Affairs, which emphasized again the vital strategic importance of preserving Arab friendship. The more the Laborites on the committee studied the Palestine question now, the more they were embarrassed by the visible gulf between their party commitment to Zionism before the election and the advice tendered by men like Beeley. Attlee wrote afterward: "We'd started something in the Jewish National Home after World War One without perceiving the consequences; it was done in a very thoughtless way with people of a different outlook on civilisation suddenly imported into Palestine—a wild experiment that was bound to cause trouble." For the time being, then, the committee suggested carrying on with a small monthly quota of Jewish immigration visas. Partition was deemed unacceptable, for apparently it could not be put into effect except by force against the Arabs. Whitehall's long campaign against the Churchill cabinet committee report now seemed to be paying off under the Socialist administration.

At no time, on the other hand, did Bevin give serious consideration to the use of force against the Jews. Better methods of accommodation were surely available. Certain that conciliation was the answer, and that his years of experience as a union negotiator would decide the issue, the foreign secretary went so far as to give his "personal assurance" to Barnet Janner in the House of Commons that he would "stake [his] political future" on solving the Palestine issue. Bevin's plan was to convince Washington that it must share responsibility in dealing with the refugees. The government of the United States would influence the Zionists to be reasonable. In their unlimited resources, the American people would help find sanctuary for the DPs elsewhere.

THE UNITED STATES AND THE REFUGEE QUESTION

The Roosevelt administration had earlier displayed its concern for the Jewish plight. Yet its solicitude had taken the form not of a relaxation of American immigration quotas (Chapter x), but of occasional efforts to intercede with the British to modify the White Paper. Secretary of State Cordell Hull recalled that throughout the war he had "repeatedly spoken on this matter to Ambassador Lord Halifax." In March 1944, Roosevelt assured Zionist leaders that the United States government had at no time given its approval to the White Paper, and he hoped that "full justice will be done to those who seek a Jewish National Home." Weizmann met with Roosevelt in 1942 and 1943. The Philby scheme came up for discussion in the second of the two meetings. At the suggestion of Undersecretary of State Sumner Welles, who was present, Roosevelt agreed to dispatch a representative to Arabia in an effort to win Ibn Saud to a more friendly position on the Zionist issue. The emissary he chose was Colonel Halford Hoskins, a veteran Middle East hand with important oil connections among the Persian Gulf sheikhdoms. Hoskins arrived in Riyadh in August of 1943 and conferred with Ibn Saud. In the course of discussions, the Arab ruler sensed that the United States had no intention of pressing him to accept the Philby scheme. He therefore curtly rejected the proposal, and nothing more came of it. Roosevelt meanwhile continued to express a genial interest in the Zionist cause, repeating to Jewish visitors his personal sympathy with the Jewish National Home. But the president's assurances of friendship were cautiously deprecated by American ambassadors in Arab nations, even as Roosevelt himself privately minimized their importance to congressional leaders.

By early 1945 the State Department had moved firmly to a position of anti-Zionism, from Secretary Edward Stettinius down. During the course of the year, in fact, Undersecretary Joseph Grew warned the administration that "Zionist activities in this country will remain the gravest threat to friendly relations between the United States and the countries of the Near East until solution to the problem is reached." For the previous two years a series of research studies on Palestine had been conducted by a State Department interdivisional committee, led by Gordon P. Merriam, director of the Near East desk—a division, then, of Loy Henderson's Office of Near Eastern and African Affairs. In their summary of January 1945, the committee members urged that Palestine be stipulated an international territory under United Nations trusteeship. Such an arrangement of course would permit only limited Jewish immigration and landownership. Roosevelt was not uninfluenced by this consensus. In discussing the Palestine question with Hoskins on March 5, 1945, therefore, he accepted the State

Department's view that an autonomous Jewish commonwealth would provoke a mass Arab uprising, and that an international trusteeship was far to be preferred.

The president's own ambiguity on the Palestine issue had been evident during his return trip from Yalta the previous month, when he met briefly with Ibn Saud off the Arabian coast. The meeting had been arranged by Stettinius in the hope that American oil and air landing rights on Saudi territory might be reconfirmed. But Roosevelt was optimistic at the same time that his charm and personal magnetism could win the desert ruler over to a flexible position on Zionist demands. If all else failed, the president had an additional inducement in the Lend-Lease aid Washington had been providing Saudi Arabia since 1943. Nevertheless, the king remained unimpressed with Roosevelt's plan to use Palestine as a sanctuary for Jewish refugees. He explained Arab opposition forcefully, if courteously. In the end his argument reached the mark. Roosevelt assured Ibn Saud, both on the occasion of their meeting and afterward in a letter of April 5, 1945, that he would not adopt a stance hostile to the Arabs and that Washington would not alter its basic approach toward Palestine "without full and prior consultation with both Jews and Arabs." The president told Congress afterward that of "the problems of Arabia I learned more about the whole problem, the Moslem problem, the Jewish problem, by talking with Ibn Saud for five minutes than I could have learned in an exchange of two or three dozen letters." To Judge Joseph Proskauer, president of the American Jewish Committee, Roosevelt subsequently remarked that "on account of the Arab situation, nothing could be done in Palestine." Later, he issued another perfunctory statement of reassurance to the Zionists. But the president's assistant, David K. Niles, was probably correct when he once remarked: "There are serious doubts in my mind that Israel would have come into being if Roosevelt had lived."

Harry Truman's approach was rather less equivocal. Upon assuming office, the new president was of course exposed immediately to the full force of the State Department's objections to Zionism. On the other hand, he had come to the presidency at a moment when the trauma of the displaced persons first became acute, as it had not in Roosevelt's lifetime. Without the backlog of prestige Roosevelt had enjoyed, moreover, Truman was obliged to remain sensitive to ethnic political pressures. American Zionism was not the least among these (Chapter XII). Soon it became virtually a reflexive accusation for Attlee and Bevin, in the heat of their anger toward Truman, to charge that his support of Jewish immigration into Palestine was motivated essentially by domestic politics. At best, this was an oversimplification. Truman's long history of sympathy for the underdog, in politics, economics, and religion, was a matter of record. In his account of this period, Dean Acheson recalled that "Mr. Truman held deep-seated convictions on many subjects, among them, for instance, a dislike of Franco and Catholic obscurantism in Spain." Not least of all, he had been a pro-Zionist since his early manhood. Truman wrote in his autobiography:

I had familiarized myself with the history of the question of a Jewish homeland and the position of the British and the Arabs. I was skeptical . . . about some of the views and attitudes assumed by the "striped-pants boys" in the State Department. It seemed to me that they didn't care enough about what happened to the thousands of displaced persons who were involved. It was my feeling that it would be possible for us to watch out for the long-range interests of our country while at the same time helping these unfortunate victims of persecution to find a home.

The president's instinct was to assign the broader Palestine issue to the United Nations. "For the immediate future, however," he explained, "some aid was needed for the Jews of Europe."

With this aim in mind, Truman sent Churchill a brief note on July 24, 1945, during the Potsdam Conference, expressing hope that the British government would "take steps to lift the restrictions of the White Paper into Palestine," and that the prime minister would let him have his "ideas on the settlement of the Palestine question so that we can at a later . . . date discuss the problem in concrete terms." Before a reply could be sent, Churchill was defeated in the general election. Soon afterward, it is recalled, Truman dispatched Earl G. Harrison to study the conditions of the Jewish DPs. Harrison's report not only indicted American military insensitivity but also laid out a number of uncompromising proposals for solving the refugee question. With thinly veiled indignation, Harrison described the appalling circumstances of the death camp survivors, their despair, their frantic anxiety to leave the European morgue. At least 100,000 of them, the report suggested, ought to be evacuated immediately, and "Palestine is definitely and preeminently the first choice."

Truman endorsed this proposal without qualification, despite the cautionary advice of Loy Henderson and Secretary of State James Byrnes (who had succeeded Stettinius). In a letter to Attlee of August 31, 1945, the president urged that 100,000 Jews be allowed into Palestine forthwith. "The main solution appears to lie in the quick evacuation of as many as possible of the nonrepatriable Jews, who wish it, to Palestine. If it is to be effective, such action should not be delayed." The appeal took Attlee by surprise, so much so that it required two and a half weeks until Bevin and the Foreign Office could prepare a response. Dispatched over Attlee's signature on September 16, the reply offered a clue to London's emerging approach to the Palestine question. It rejected the notion that Jewish displaced persons had suffered more than non-Jewish victims of Nazism, and then proposed that the survivors be shipped to Philippeville and Felada in North Africa, where camps existed with facilities for up to 35,000 persons. The letter continued:

In the case of Palestine, we have the Arabs to consider as well as the Jews, and there have been solemn undertakings . . . given by your predecessor, yourself and by Mr. Churchill, that before we come to a final decision and operate it, there would be consultation with the Arabs. It would be very unwise to break these solemn pledges and so set aflame the whole Middle East. . . . In addition to this problem we are engaged upon another related one and this is India. The fact that there are ninety million Moslems who are easily inflamed in that country compels us to consider the problem from this aspect also.

There is little doubt that the British government made a serious error in its refusal to accept the 100,000. London might have avoided an ugly confrontation with the United States. More important, a good deal of the stridency might have been taken out of Zionist demands. It would also have been useful if Bevin had exercised verbal restraint, rather than warn, on November 2, "that if the Jews, with all their suffering, want to get too much at the head of the queue, you have the danger of another anti-Semitic reaction through it all." This remark elicited a day of mourning in the Yishuv.

As late as the autumn of 1945, it was not the Jewish Agency's intention that Britain should abandon its ties to Palestine altogether. Yet the Zionist leadership had concluded that if Whitehall's attitude was based on the assumption of Arab strength, then Britain must be equally impressed by Jewish strength. For the first time, the Agency countenanced specific measures of physical resistance. Thus, in November 1945, the commanders of the Haganah and of the two dissident Jewish underground forces reached agreement that all future Etzel (Irgun Z'vai Le'umi) and Lech'i operations would be coordinated under Haganah direction. For the next eight months the three groups undertook systematic attacks on British installations. Arms were acquired from various sources. British soldiers occasionally were willing to sell equipment. Jewish units in the British army filched weapons from depots, scavenged for German guns on the battlefields of the Western Desert and Italy, and smuggled them back in large quantities. A number of secret Haganah munitions factories began turning out grenades, mines, and light automatic rifles. Finally, during late 1945 and early 1946, the Etzel and Lech'i embarked on a number of daring and successful raids against British armories.

With these accumulated weapons, an underground attack in October 1945 "liberated" several hundred illegal Jewish immigrants from a British detention camp. That same month a joint Haganah-Etzel operation dynamited the British rail network at two hundred different points throughout the country, effectively paralyzing British troop movements; while the Haganah destroyed three British naval launches that had been used for intercepting refugee vessels. Other acts of sabotage were carried out against British airfields, radar stations, and coastal lighthouses. Although shaken, the mandatory authorities were intent upon dealing firmly with this Jewish resistance. Military reinforcements were promptly sent in, among them the Sixth Airborne Division, veterans of the Normandy invasion. By the beginning of December 1945, four destroyers, two cruisers, and large numbers of patrol planes had similarly been added to the blockade of Palestine coastal waters. Under a new high commissioner, Lieutenant General Sir Alan Cunningham, the government's retaliatory measures became increasingly severe. Early in 1946, for example, after the Etzel successfully raided a number of arms depots in the Judea area, the British rounded up more than 14,000 civilians for a particularly harsh interrogation. Yet underground agents were rarely caught. General Barker, the commanding officer in Palestine, had to admit later that "the Jews knew all government secrets and military plans within a day of our making a decision. Their Intelligence system is uncanny." The attacks continued, hitting police, army, and naval garrisons. The British were confounded. Until the postwar period, they had been accustomed to thinking of violence in Palestine as exclusively an Arab prerogative. The force and savagery of Jewish resistance came as a shock to them. Nevertheless, Bevin's determination to solve the refugee issue and the future of Palestine in his own way was not easily to be undermined.

THE ANGLO-AMERICAN COMMITTEE OF INQUIRY

Ten weeks passed before London formulated a new compromise approach to Truman's request. On October 26, 1945, before the House of Commons, and on the following November 13, in a letter to the American president, Attlee proposed a joint Anglo-American committee to investigate the tragedy of the refugees and devise a solution to it. Unspoken in the offer was the assumption that the United States would also cooperate in putting a solution into effect. Truman accepted the challenge with alacrity, but with the qualification that Palestine alone, rather than any alternative refuge, become the focus of the inquiry. Attlee and Bevin grudgingly accepted this condition as evidently the only means of winning American participation. The foreign secretary warned, however, that His Majesty's Government could not "accept the view that the Jews should be driven out of Europe," nor that Palestine alone could solve the problem of rehabilitating European Jews.

Among the six British members of the joint investigating body the most influential were the chairman, Sir John Singleton, a judge of the high court; Herbert Morrison, one of the top Labor political tacticians; and a young Labor member of Parliament, Richard Crossman, who became the intellectual gadfly of his colleagues. Accompanying the British delegation was Harold Beeley, the Foreign Office expert on Palestine. The committee members first visited the United States to meet with their American counterparts. The latter's chairman was also a judge, Joseph Hutcheson, a seventy-year-old ultraconservative from Texas. Other leading members included Dr. Frank Aydelotte, director of the Institute for Advanced Study at Princeton; Dr. James MacDonald, a professor of government at Columbia and former League of Nations high commissioner for German refugees; and Bartley Crum, a San Francisco lawyer and would-be politico whose Zionist leanings were as undisguised as the pro-Arab bias of Beeley.

The members underwent their first briefing in Washington, then heard their first Jewish and Arab witnesses in New York. Both sides were equally uncompromising. The Arabs insisted that Jewish political intercession alone was forcing the American government's hand. The Zionists launched a scathing attack on British policy, as if England were mainly responsible for the tragedy of European Jewry. Proceeding then to London in January 1946, the committee was received by Bevin at a formal luncheon. Crossman recalled that the foreign secretary "stated slowly but emphatically that, if we achieved a unanimous report, he would personally do everything in his power to put it into effect." Bevin then devoted the rest of his remarks to an attack on "racialism" and indicated that he foresaw no solution in the establishment of "racial states in Palestine." The London hearings continued until February 1. Although a number of pro-Zionist witnesses testified, including Lord Herbert Samuel and Leopold Amery, it was in London that the committee members at last encountered the full force of bureaucratic anti-Zionism. Experts from the Colonial and Foreign Offices direly predicted a bloodbath in Palestine if thousands of additional Jews were introduced into that country.

The warning was to be echoed even more decisively by the various British officials whom the committee later interviewed in the Middle East. "They detest the [Jewish] Agency like sin," Crossman wrote, and ignored the Jewish side as "outrageously" as the Zionists in America had disregarded the Arab position. The line of continuity between Arab and British spokesmen was all but seamless. Ironically, Azzam Pasha, secretary general of the Arab League, had once counseled his fellow Arabs "to explain our case in reconciliatory terms and as people who understand the present situation." But when Azzam himself, tense and suspicious, appeared before the Anglo-American Committee in Cairo, his objections to Jewish immigration were bitterly uncompromising. The single high point of his address was an authentically moving peroration:

> The Zionist, the new Jew . . . pretends that he has got a particular civilizing mission with which he returns to a backward, degenerate race in order to put the elements of progress into an area which has no progress. Well . . . the Arabs simply stand and say "No." . . . We are a living, vitally strong nation, we are in our renaissance, we are producing as many children as any nation in the world. . . . We have a heritage of civilization and of spiritual life. We are not going to allow ourselves to be controlled either by great nations or small nations or dispersed nations.

Even more impressive was the testimony of Albert Hourani, the distinguished Lebanese scholar and Oxford don. Coldly logical, brilliant in exposition, Hourani made a formidable case for the historic Arab connection with Palestine.

But it was in the Holy Land itself that the visceral quality of Arab nationalism was at last fully gauged. The Palestine Arabs in fact were under the severest disadvantage of those testifying before the investigating group. Their community still had not recovered from the economic losses of the 1936–39 civil war. Their political leadership, outlawed by the British, had fled the country and were living in neighboring lands. Until 1945 the Arab Higher Committee had ceased to function in Palestine. From time to time efforts were made to resuscitate this body, but they were invariably blocked by the Mufti's followers, who refused to allow any challenge to his leadership. Instead, their repeated demand was that Haj Amin himself, with his aides, should be allowed first to return to Palestine. The British vetoed the request.

Eventually a compromise was reached, virtually on the eve of the Anglo-American Committee's arrival in Jerusalem. Through the intercession of the Syrian foreign minister, Jamil Mirdam Bey, the Husseini family agreed to reactivate the Higher Committee. The British in turn agreed to release the Mufti's nephew, Jamil al-Husseini, from his internment in Rhodesia as an enemy agent. Shortly afterward the Committee was reestablished. British and Arab moderates alike, however, were appalled at its composition. The chairmanship was left vacant for the Mufti. The vice-chairman now was Jamil al-Husseini, whose record of pro-Axis activity almost matched his uncle's. Other leading members equally shared pro-Axis backgrounds. Thus, Wasif Kamal had played an important role in the Iraqi rebellion of 1941, and in 1943 had flown to Italy and Germany to serve as a close associate of the Mufti. Dr. Hussein al-Khalidi similarly had participated in the Rashid Ali uprising, and afterward, in 1943, had become an announcer for the German Arabic-language radio station in Athens. Emile Ghori, the earliest of the Mufti's followers to return to Palestine (in 1941), was an organizer of the assassination squads that had disposed of the Mufti's Arab enemies in the civil disturbances of the late 1930s. It was not the most impressive body that could have been chosen to present the Arab case hardly a year after the war against the Axis.

With full self-assurance, nevertheless, the Arab Higher Committee resumed its inflexible prewar stance during its testimony in March 1946. Jamil al-Husseini cited the Arab majority in Palestine (1,300,000 to 560,000 Jews), the nation's blood relationship with the rest of the Arab world, the inability of Palestine to unite with other Arab countries that had attained or nearly attained self-government. "All these evils," the argument went, "are due entirely to the presence of the Zionists and the support given to them by certain of the Powers. . . ." Among the "positive evils" described by the Higher Committee was the economic and political imbalance already caused by Jewish immigration, which had reduced the Arab proportion of the country from 93 percent in 1918 to 65 percent in 1946, and appeared likely to transform the Arabs into a minority in Palestine. The usual warnings of Jewish land mastery were advanced. Nor did the Higher Committee hesitate to venture a noteworthy reference to Arab wartime activities, citing the "large number" of Arabs who had volunteered to serve in the Allied forces, and the loyalty of the Palestine Arab community "even when the Germans reached the borders of Alexandria. . . ." The Jews, by contrast, "in their present attitude in Palestine are nothing but the embodiment of Nazism." In any event, the *cri de coeur* with which the Higher Committee expressed its deepest fears of Zionism was palpably genuine and evoked the sympathy of the British and American visitors. "The Zionists claim further," the brief declared, that they are acting as mediators of Western civilization in the Middle East. Even if their claims were true, the services they were rendering would be incidental only; the Arab world has been in direct touch with the West for a hundred years, and has its own reawakened cultural movement, and thus it has no need of a mediator. . . . In a deeper sense the presence of the Zionists is even an obstacle to the understanding of Western civilization, insofar as it . . . is tending to induce in the Arabs an unsympathetic attitude towards the West and all its works.

The Arabs summarized their claims, then, by demanding an end to Jewish immigration, abolition of the mandate, repudiation of the Balfour Declaration, and recognition of Palestine as a sovereign state consonant with other Arab independent nations.

The basis of the Jewish case was laid even before the Anglo-American Committee reached Jerusalem. Shortly after leaving London and Vienna, in February 1946, the committee members visited the displaced persons' camps. "The abstract arguments about Zionism and the Jewish State seemed curiously remote after this experience of human degradation," Crossman wrote afterward. "We had been cut off from what had previously been reality." By then the Jewish survivors already were responding to the challenge offered them by Ben-Gurion, who had addressed a huge crowd of DPs in Landsberg, Germany, in the autumn of 1945: "Do not be afraid if you hear of new laws promulgated against us tomorrow or the day after. A Jewish power has arisen which will fight together with you for a proud, independent Palestine. I promise you that not only your children but also we, the white-haired ones, will live to see the Jewish homeland."

Early in 1946 the refugees gave their answer by holding a Congress of Jewish Displaced Persons in Munich and accepting the challenge of mobilizing large-scale immigration to Palestine. To that end, a wide-ranging program of Zionist activities was organized, including Hebrew classes, courses in Jewish history, calisthenics, even agricultural training schools. The committee members witnessed this phenomenon as they toured the displaced persons' centers. What they had heard about the Jewish survivors in Washington and London apparently was confirmed here. The visitors understood Jewish feelings better, moreover, after encountering the poisonous anti-Semitism that still lingered in central Europe even at the highest level. "They found themselves increasingly regarding Palestine as the Jews of Europe regarded it," wrote Crossman, "as a solution rather than a problem."

In Palestine itself Weizmann was the first Zionist spokesman to appear. Although over seventy and half blind, the Zionist elder statesman waxed surprisingly vigorous before the committee. He described the ineradicable nature of European Judeophobia, even after the collapse of the Nazi Reich. Resorting to classical Zionist arguments, he insisted once more on the unlikelihood of a cure for anti-Semitism as long as the Jews remained a stateless people. As in many previous appearances before earlier investigating bodies, Weizmann again found it necessary to review the diplomatic context of the Balfour Declaration, to describe the circumstances of Jewish life throughout the world and—in this instance—the contributions of Palestine Jewry to the war effort. During the intensive questioning that followed his remarks, Weizmann admitted that he had gone much further toward the statehood position than before the war, but insisted that the White Paper and the Holocaust of European Jewry now rendered Jewish sovereignty indispensable. He confessed, too, that the Palestine issue was not one between right and wrong, but between the greater and the lesser injustice.

Ben-Gurion's testimony was much tougher, although not without a certain harsh effectiveness. In fuller detail than Weizmann, the Jewish Agency chairman recounted Zionist accomplishments in Palestine, the welfare community that had been established on the basis of democratic socialism. Jewish statehood was even more central to the Zionist goal than the admission of 100,000 refugees, he insisted. "We are not going to renounce our independence, even if we have to pay the supreme price, and there are hundreds of thousands of Jews . . . both in this country and abroad who will give up their lives, if necessary, for Jewish independence —for Zion." Unlike Weizmann, Ben-Gurion was evasive about repudiating the current wave of Jewish violence in Palestine (the committee members were under constant armed protection), and less emphatic about the ideal of Anglo-Zionist cooperation.

The Jews made their strongest case in documenting Zionist achievements and plans for the future. Their graphs and statistics rebutted Arab claims of Jewish economic exploitation and suggested that the opposite was the case, that the Arab standard of living was rising uninterruptedly. A survey conducted by a team of American (Jewish) economists was cited in evidence of Palestine's capacity to absorb "between 685,000 and 1,250,000 immigrants in the next decade." A blueprint prepared by the eminent American hydrologist Dr. Walter Lowdermilk anticipated that the water to support this enlarged population could feasibly be drawn from the harnessed flow of the Jordan River. The visitors were impressed. "I had to admit," wrote Crossman, "that no Western colonists in any other country had done so little harm, or disturbed so little the life of the indigenous people [as the Jews]. . . . If Zionism in 1918 was a synthetic importation, in 1946 it had become the fighting patriotism of an existing commonwealth."

The mass of transcribed and documentary evidence was taken by the committee to Lausanne at the end of March. There, in the next month, it was boiled down to a unanimous report of less than one hundred pages, and issued on May 1, 1946. It described the unbearable physical and psychological conditions of the European Jewish survivors and the improbability of any serious revival of Jewish life on the Continent. "We know of no country to which the great majority can go in the immediate future other than Palestine," the report continued. It then recommended the immediate authorization of 100,000 immigration certificates. The suggestions for Palestine itself were more equivocal. Most of the group favored a unitary solution for the country. Accordingly, the report turned down either an Arab or a Jewish state, for "in neither case would minority guarantees afford adequate protection for the subordinate group." Without offering a detailed solution, the conclusion simply proposed a regime in which further Jewish immigration would neither be subject to an Arab veto nor be allowed to grow to such numbers as to produce a Jewish majority. During the interim, the mandate should continue to function.

Whatever the document's limitations, hardly any of the group anticipated that it would be categorically rejected, for it appeared to fulfill Bevin's principal desiderata. It was unanimous, for one thing. Moreover, it recommended (however vaguely) a unitary state. Finally, it enjoyed American moral and financial backing. London's response was frigid, nevertheless. Inundated by difficulties in Europe, Egypt, and India, the British government was unprepared to face the consequences of opening Palestine to an additional 100,000 Jews. Should such a step be taken, the mandatory government anticipated that an extra British division would be required to maintain the peace. The chancellor of the exchequer calculated the expense of these reinforcements as £40 million. He did not have the money. In any case, Whitehall was hardly eager to risk further antagonizing the Arab world—possibly the larger Moslem world—at a critical juncture of British diplomacy in Egypt and Iraq, in Iran, Turkey, and India, as well as in Palestine itself.

But if the committee members had not expected an outright rejection of the fruits of their labors, presumably London had not envisaged official endorsement from the United States government, without prior consultation, and while the ink of the report was barely dry. The State Department was known to be sympathetic to Britain's difficulties, after all, and cautious about accepting any simplistic approach to the Palestine question. On April 27, Bevin pleaded with the American government to delay release of the report until after joint discussions. The request was turned down. The text of the document was published in Washington on May 1, 1946, and that same day Truman publicly announced his approval of the recommendations for admitting 100,000 DPs into Palestine. Indeed, the president concentrated on this issue to the exclusion of the longest section of the report. E. F. Francis-Williams, Bevin's friend and biographer, wrote later that Truman's statement "threw Bevin into one of the blackest rages I ever saw him in." The foreign secretary sent an immediate protest to Washington, making clear his government's collective anger at this intervention of "unparalleled irresponsibility in a period of acute tension when British soldiers are being killed by Jewish terrorists." Attlee went further. He was determined that if the Americans wished to press Zionist claims and lecture Britain on its responsibilities, then they must help foot the bill. The prime minister thereupon cabled Truman on May 26, setting out the expenses both governments had to consider in putting the report into effect, including the costs of transporting, housing, and maintaining the immigrants, suppressing terrorism, and shouldering the additional commitments that might follow.

Somewhat reluctantly, the president accepted this challenge, confirming that American and British experts should meet. But Attlee continued to procrastinate, requesting further discussions even before working out a final plan of action. The approach was short-sighted. Even at this late juncture, had London granted the humanitarian request of admitting 100,000 Jews, the Palestine question undoubtedly would have lost much of its unendurable tension. Certainly Jewish emphasis upon territorial sovereignty would have been moderated. If rejection of Truman's appeal was a serious tactical blunder, moreover, Bevin insisted upon compounding it by the harsh insensitivity of his remarks. Thus, his irritated reaction to the president's suggestion was to declare publicly that the Americans favored the admission of 100,000 Jews into Palestine because "they did not want too many of them in New York." The outrage provoked by this statement was not limited to Jews. Sailing to the United States shortly afterward, Bevin discovered that the stevedores in the port of New York refused to handle his baggage.

JEWISH EXTREMISM INTENSIFIED

London's rejection of the committee report began one of the darkest periods of the Jewish postwar experience. The movement of DPs from eastern Europe to the American zone of Germany was picking up momentum. In the summer of 1946 it was given new urgency by the spontaneous outbreak of native pogroms against the remnant Jewish community in Poland. As a result, the survivors once again began to depart the country by the thousands. During July, August, and September, 90,000 of them arrived in the Western zone of Germany, where they all but overwhelmed American military and Jewish philanthropic resources. During the same period, another 25,000 Jews arrived from the Balkans. Ultimately, by the end of 1946, more than a quarter of a million Jews were packed into the displaced persons' camps of Western Germany.

The summer and autumn thus represented a new threshold of emergency for the Zionist leadership. Far from being impressed by the Anglo-American Committee Report, Ben-Gurion rejected it in its totality. He had always insisted on self-rule as the one sure method for acquiring control of immigration. Even the admittance of a limited installment of refugees was not inducement for him to abandon this goal. In any case, Bevin had rejected the Anglo-American proposals. The foreign secretary's obstinacy, together with the explosion of refugees from eastern Europe, made it clear that additional pressure would have to be exerted on the British. This new spirit of grim militancy was expressed in a secret Haganah broadcast of May 12, 1946:

> Present British policy . . . is based on an erroneous assumption: Britain, in evacuating Syria, Lebanon, and Egypt [sic], intends to concentrate her military bases in Palestine and is therefore concerned to strengthen her hold

over the mandate, and is using her responsibility to the Jewish people as a means to that end. But this double game will not work. . . . We would therefore warn publicly His Majesty's Government that if it does not fulfill its responsibilities under the mandate—above all with regard to the question of immigration—the Jewish Resistance Movement will make every effort to hinder the transfer of British bases to Palestine and to prevent their establishment in this country.

Even before this warning, the Jewish underground groups had been engaged in a vigorous campaign against British installations. Now, however, on the night of June 17, Haganah units launched their most daring attack thus far. They blew up ten of the eleven bridges connecting Palestine with surrounding nations, thereby isolating the country from land communications with its neighbors. Until that moment, the British had refrained from striking back at Jewish sabotage with quite the harshness they had demonstrated in their repression of Kenyan or Malaysian rebels; they were by no means impervious to the tragedy of European Jewry. But the destruction of the bridges ended the last of the mandatory's restraints. On Saturday, June 29—"Black Sabbath," as the Jews henceforth described it—the British embarked upon the most far-reaching cordon and search in Palestine history. It lasted for two weeks and was nationwide. Tel Aviv was combed block by block, its houses and buildings inspected from basement to attic. Schools and hospitals were not immune from search. Even casts were broken off patients. Many Jewish Agency officials were arrested and placed in detention camps (Ben Gurion himself was in Paris at the time). Nevertheless, the British were unsuccessful in finding the ranking underground commanders. Nor were arms caches of any importance discovered.

Yet the Jewish Agency in turn sensed that continued assaults on military bases risked even more paralyzing British countermeasures. It therefore instructed the Haganah to concentrate on illegal immigration. On the other hand, the extreme dissident groups were unwilling to accept restraints of any kind. Although badly decimated by earlier attacks on British forces and installations, the Lech'i now carried out over one hundred acts of sabotage and murder between September 1946 and May 1948. It was at this point, too, that the Etzel—the Irgun Z'vai Le'umi (National Military Organization)—which thus far had been erratic in its use of violence against British personnel, reverted to Lech'i methods of killing. And this it did with a vengeance, indeed, with more terrible effect than ever before in the history of the Yishuv. The Etzel had originated in 1931 as Haganah Bet (B), a non-Socialist faction that broke away from the "official" but Labor-dominated underground. Its rank and file consisted overwhelmingly of Betar members and of other young Revisionists, together with small groups of extreme nationalists from the capitalist farm colonies and from the Maccabi, the Jewish middle-class sports movement. The policy of the new organization was based squarely on Jabotinsky's teachings: every Jew had a right to enter Palestine; only active retaliation would deter the Arabs;

only Jewish armed force would ensure the Jewish state. The Etzel's symbol was a hand grasping a rifle over the map of Palestine—including Transjordan—with the motto "Rak Kach" (Only Thus).

From the outset, the Jewish Agency sternly denounced the Etzel, and the British countered by mass arrests of its suspected members. Shlomo Ben-Yosef, an Etzel partisan, was the first Jew to be hanged in Palestine (June 8, 1938), for an attack on an Arab bus. Until the publication of the White Paper in May 1939, however, the activities of this group generally were limited to retaliation against Arab marauders. It was only afterward that officials of the mandatory government became the Etzel's principal target. The campaign of violence might have gained serious momentum but for the outbreak of World War II. The Etzel then announced a cessation of its anti-British activities and offered its cooperation in the military effort. In May 1941 its commander, David Raziel, volunteered for a particularly hazardous mission on behalf of the British in Iraq. He was caught in Baghdad and killed by the Rashid Ali government. The loss, coupled with the death of Jabotinsky the previous year, temporarily immobilized the Etzel, and for two years it appeared unlikely that the organization would recover even its limited prewar strength of several hundred members.

Two factors accounted for its revival. One was the ebbing of the conflict in the Middle East and the possibility, therefore, of undertaking rescue and assault measures without endangering the war effort. The other was an infusion of new recruits, many of them Jewish deserters from General Wladislaw Anders's Polish Army, which was stationed temporarily in Palestine. The newcomers were consumed by recent memories of their kinsmen's fate in Nazi Europe. Trained militarily, they were intent now upon following an activist policy of resistance. Even with their enlarged membership, the Etzel's numbers rarely exceeded 2,000 during the entire period of militance from 1944 to 1948. Yet the quality of the group's leadership was altogether fanatical. Thus, Menachem Begin, a gaunt, bespectacled intellectual in his mid-thirties, who commanded the Etzel during its most violent phase, had been toughened in the school of resistance long before arriving in Palestine. A Polish Jew, he had been arrested in Soviet Lithuania for Zionist activities in 1941, and sentenced to imprisonment. Afterward, in a Siberian labor camp, he displayed exceptional physical and moral courage among his anti-Semitic fellow prisoners. A year later he was allowed to enlist in the Anders army. Upon reaching Palestine with this force, he promptly deserted, joined the Etzel, and rose to its command in December 1943.

Under Begin's leadership, the Etzel intensified its assaults on British military installations. The discipline of its members was apparently unshakable. So was their ruthlessness. They extorted funds from Jewish businessmen and occasionally "executed" Jewish informers. Their world was entirely conspiratorial. With a price on their heads, under threat of hanging or long prison terms, they adopted false names and moved from one hiding place to another. After the "Black Sabbath" of June 29, 1946, the Etzel command refused any longer to accept the authority of the joint resistance committee. Instead, Begin determined to carry out a spectacular operation that would dramatize Jewish resistance beyond the frontiers of Palestine or even Britain. He succeeded. On July 22 a group of armed Etzel members entered the kitchen of the King David Hotel in Jerusalem. An entire wing of this building was occupied by government offices, together with the headquarters of the CID, the Criminal Investigation Division. The saboteurs deposited heavy milk cans packed with gelignite in the hotel's lower quarters. Time fuses were set and the men departed. According to Begin's later account, a warning of the impending explosion was telephoned to the CID. The British subsequently denied that the warning was ever received. When the explosion went off in the hotel twenty-five minutes later, ninety-one Britishers, Arabs, and Jews were killed, forty-five injured.

This time British punitive measures were directed against the entire Jewish community. Tel Aviv and Jerusalem were placed under curfew for four days and isolated from the rest of the country. A division of British troops received orders to shoot curfew breakers on the spot. Angrily branding all Jews guilty of complicity in terrorist crimes, General Barker put the nation's Jewish homes and shops out of bounds for his troops. In fact, the Agency was no less horrified than the British government by the King David bombing. Ben-Gurion, who had never brought himself totally to disavow earlier underground raids on British installations, now furiously anathematized the Etzel and urged Palestine Jewry to turn its members in wherever they were discovered. On a later occasion, the Haganah managed to foil an Etzel scheme to blow up British police headquarters in Tel Aviv. Begin and his men were not to be that easily deterred. Rather, they intensified their attacks on military transport, destroying vehicles, paralyzing railroad traffic, occasionally killing British personnel.

Well before this new spate of violence, however, the Haganah had perfected a less sanguinary, and ultimately a far more compelling and effective, method for undermining British policy in the Holy Land.

THE ILLEGAL IMMIGRATION

Quietly, unacknowledged, and certainly unappreciated by the Zionists, the British by 1946 were disregarding the limits set by the White Paper and allowing a Jewish immigration of 18,000 a year. It was a not inconsiderable figure by prewar standards. Yet the Jews measured it against the tens of thousands of Jewish refugees still confined in the DP camps. Even before the war, we recall, the Zionist leadership (and the Revisionists) had sponsored an illegal immigration of Jews from Europe and the Middle East. Known as Aliyah Bet—Immigration B (nonofficial immigration)—the Agency-directed rescue effort was increasingly linked with the Haganah. From the inception of this program in 1938, its director was Shaul Avigur, a tough, resourceful underground veteran, still in his early thirties. When the war ended, Avigur returned to Europe to open a new office, this time in Paris, a block from Allied military headquarters. His instructions from the Jewish Agency were clear and unequivocal. They were to organize the immediate departure of Jewish DPs for Palestine. Nor was this to be a clandestine smuggling effort of a few hundred or even a few thousand refugees. What was intended, rather, was a traffic organized on a scale of far-reaching proportions, involving tens of thousands of Jews. The homelessness of these victims of Nazism was to be exploited fully, even ruthlessly, to dramatize the fate of the Jewish people and the callousness of British immigration policy in Palestine. In short, the exodus was intended as the realization of Ben-Gurion's promise to the displaced persons at Landsberg: "You are not only needy persons, you are also a political force."

During the next few months Palestine Jews, many of them veterans of the Jewish Brigade, began to appear in the DP camps and elsewhere throughout Europe, working as emissaries of the Agency. With funds supplied by Jewish philanthropy from abroad, frontier crossings were arranged, transit stations established, housing, food, and clothing secured, ships purchased and repaired in French Riviera ports. None of these activities would have been feasible, in turn, without at least the tacit approval of the French government. Often cooperation was made possible by influential French Jews, ex-members of the Maquis, the French wartime underground. A few were themselves strategically placed members of the government. Thus, André Blumel was the *chef de cabinet* in the brief postwar government of Léon Blum (who had no personal dealings with the Zionists until much later). Jules Moch served as defense minister in the cabinets of both Blum and Georges Bidault. Daniel Mayer held a succession of ministries between 1945 and 1947. These men and others were committed to the rescue of the DPs, and they secured government help from ministerial offices in Paris down to the final port authorities on the coast. Simple compassion for the Jewish victims of Nazism was unquestionably a factor in the French attitude. So was the extensive representation of Maquis veterans in the bureaucracy, men and women who shared a sense of partisan camaraderie with the Haganah. They shared another emotion, as well. This was unremitting hatred (the word was Avigur's) of the British, for having maneuvered France out of the Levant between 1943 and 1945, and perhaps even for having sunk the French fleet at Mers al-Kabir in 1940. The sense of helpless rage was compounded by the presence of British CID agents in French cities and ports liberated by Montgomery's army. It was for all these various reasons, then, of mutual sympathy and common interest that the French interior ministry, under Edouard Deprux, worked closely with Avigur in securing transit facilities for the DPs in French border and port areas, in offering political asylum to fugitive Etzel members from Palestine. Later, in 1947–48, the French army was prepared to extend itself even further to help the Zionist cause (Chapter XIII).

By autumn of 1945 the first groups of several hundred refugees were taken out of their camps in the American zone of Germany. In trucks supplied by the Jewish Brigade, they were carried to the French (and later, Austrian) borders. Here they made their way over mountain passes by foot, to be transported afterward to the French or Italian coasts. By the opening of 1946 the number of "illegals" was more than a thousand a month. A score of Palestinian agents directed the migration from one transit point to another, often helped by couriers from the DP ranks themselves. Throughout 1946 the route of travel shifted increasingly toward Italy, where long coastlines and deep-water inlets proved ideal for secret embarkations. It was in Italy that the organizational abilities of Yehuda Arazi, Avigur's principal lieutenant, were decisive.

A former officer in the Palestine police, Arazi was also a veteran Haganah gunrunner who only recently had evaded the British dragnet by fleeing to Europe. There he was immediately assigned the task of coordinating DP escape traffic from Germany to the Mediterranean. His success in exploiting the chaos of postwar Italy for this underground operation was phenomenal. Dressed as a British sergeant, Arazi found an ideal cover working through the Palestinian units of the British Army of Occupation. In this manner, he "requisitioned" vehicles for DP transportation, sequestered Italian estates for refugee camps, and obtained large quantities of food and equipment from British military stores. Well after the British ordered the Palestinian units home in late 1945, Arazi maintained the intensive pace of emigration. He forged papers, confiscated supplies, transported fuel, hired ships and sailors. At the same time, the Italian government, whose compassion for the DPs was matched by an undisguised resentment of British occupation, generally abstained from interfering with the escape effort.

The largest number of Haganah vessels were Italian coastal ships of prewar vintage. Hardly one of these obsolescent tubs was fit for a Mediterranean crossing; it appeared unthinkable to load them with hundreds of passengers. Nevertheless, hastily repaired at various Italian shipyards, they were sent to their embarkation rendezvous, usually secluded inlets near larger Tyrrhenian and Adriatic ports. Even at this last stage before departure, a battle of wits was continually being fought between the Palestinian agents and British intelligence. CID agents were everywhere on watch. Hoping to ferret out departure schedules from the refugees, a number sought to pass themselves off as Jews. Usually the Haganah detected their identity. On several occasions the CID managed to confiscate Jewish supplies in Italy and to sabotage their ships before departure time. Yet, with few exceptions, the Palestinians succeeded in obtaining new vessels and supplies and in hiring new crews.

The immigration had its counterpart in Palestine itself. Although the British naval blockade off Palestine waters was seemingly leakproof, and fully 80,000 British troops were patrolling the country by 1946–47, Haganah intelligence often secured copies of British interception plans and monitored radio messages between police and CID headquarters, and between coast guard stations and patrol launches. Ruses were used to decoy the British while the illegals landed. The initial sailings caught the British by surprise. Half a dozen ships slipped by the British coastal watch in Palestine during the late autumn and early winter of 1945–46, unloading 4,000 refugees.

Early in 1946, however, the British intensified their blockade. Their flying boats and destroyers cruised vigilantly along the Palestine shore, and this blockade was reinforced by a tight naval scrutiny of Europe's Mediterranean coast. With nearly 8,000 displaced persons sailing from Italian ports by then, interception was almost certain, usually just within Palestine territorial waters. The refugees were forcibly transferred to British vessels and carried off to Cyprus. To discourage immigration, the internment camps at Cyprus were made as forbidding as possible. The heat in the summer was infernal, water was always short, and food barely adequate. Even so, the flow of illegals continued with growing momentum; to the Jewish survivors, Cyprus was merely another stepping stone to Palestine. Not infrequently the DPs resisted British boarding parties, and deaths occurred on each side. On several occasions, Haganah underwater demolition teams sabotaged British transports assigned to deport refugees from Palestine to Cyprus. When the immigrant ship *Beauharnais* was towed into Haifa harbor, its passengers unfurled a long banner over the deck: "We survived Hitler," it proclaimed. "Death is no stranger to us. Nothing can keep us from our Jewish homeland. The blood be on your head if you fire on this unarmed ship." Photographs of this and other demonstrations appeared in many of the leading newspapers of Europe and the United States, and profoundly stirred Western sympathies. All but five of the sixty-three refugee ships were intercepted between 1945 and 1948, with the internment of 26,000 DPs on Cyprus. Yet it was precisely this message of the refugee tragedy that the Zionists were determined to convey. Its impact on world opinion and the British taxpayer turned out to be the Jews' most effective weapon.

BRITAIN'S FINAL EFFORT: THE MORRISON-GRADY PLAN AND THE LONDON DISCUSSIONS

Early in the summer of 1946 the confluence of Jewish underground violence and Aliyah Bet refugee sailings began to have its impact on British policy. The colonial undersecretary, Arthur Creech-Jones, long identified as mildly pro-Zionist, succeeded finally in persuading Bevin that the DP crisis was incapable of resolution except in relation to Palestine, that neither the Jews nor the United States government would countenance an alternative approach. The mandate itself would have to be restructured. And once this new flexibility was communicated to Washington, Truman indicated a willingness to share the task of altering Palestine's status. Three weeks after London's rejection of the Anglo-American Committee Report, the president announced the establishment of a special cabinet committee to help formulate his policy. The day-to-day work of this group was referred to a board of deputies under the chairmanship of Dr. Henry F. Grady, an assistant secretary of state. It was Grady and his associates who now entered negotiations with a parallel British committee to define a joint Anglo-American program and to allocate economic and military responsibilities between the two governments. In late June of 1946, Truman had the Grady mission flown to London in his own plane. There, during the next five weeks, the two sets of experts met under the chairmanship of Herbert Morrison. The discussions were intensive, for unrest was mounting in Palestine and reached a new peak with the Etzel bomb attack on the King David Hotel. On July 31 the fruits of the joint committee's labors were revealed to Parliament. It was evident then that Grady and his American colleagues had been won over to the British position.

Following Bevin's line, the report began by proposing "that our two Governments should seek to create conditions favourable to the resettlement of a substantial number of displaced persons in Europe itself, since it is recognized that the overwhelming majority will continue to live in Europe." Other nations were urged to participate in the relocation of those survivors who chose not to remain on the Continent. Thereupon an intricate scheme was worked out for transforming the mandate into a trusteeship and dividing the country into separate Jewish and Arab provinces, with the Negev and Jerusalem remaining under British administration. By this formula the Jewish province, the smallest, would be limited to 17 percent of the country, the most drastically attenuated offer ever made the Zionists. Although the two communities would be allowed self-rule in purely domestic affairs, the British high commissioner would reserve for himself authority over defense, foreign relations, customs, police, courts, and communications, and would similarly exercise veto power over all legislation for a transitional period of five years. The one important concession offered the Jews was the proposed admittance of 100,000 refugees during the first year after the plan went into effect. But thereafter the high commissioner would control immigration on the basis of the province's "economic absorptive capacity." Full implementation of the scheme, moreover, would depend upon its acceptance by both Arabs and Jews. The report concluded hopefully: "We believe that this plan provides as fair and reasonable a compromise between the claims of Arab and Jews as it is possible to devise, and that it offers the best prospect of reconciling the conflicting interests of the two communities."

It unquestionably reconciled British interests. In fact, its basic outlines had been formulated in advance by the Colonial Office. As one British official later summed up the plan: "It is a beautiful scheme. It treats the Arabs and the Jews on a footing of complete equality in that it gives nothing to either party, while it leaves us a free run over the whole of Palestine." With Egyptian pressure mounting in the summer of 1946 for the British to evacuate Suez, London recognized the heightened danger of abandoning its foothold in the Middle East altogether. Except for Transjordan, which was inaccessible from the Mediterranean, Palestine was the last remaining base from which Britain still exercised a reasonable freedom of action. Haifa might compensate for Alexandria. Control of the Negev would preserve British military installations on the northern flank of Suez. Newer, larger, permanent camps even then were being constructed in the Gaza area, and the decision recently had been taken in London to lay a new oil pipeline from the Kirkuk field to Haifa.

The official British reaction, then, to the Morrison-Grady Report was distinctly favorable. Whitehall emphasized that it was on the basis of these recommendations that it was inviting Jewish and Arab representatives to London on September 10, 1946, to negotiate a solution to the Palestine impasse. It was a basis that the Jews found unacceptable. The Zionist Executive, meeting in Paris at the end of July, voted for partition alone as an appropriate format for negotiations, and rejected the invitation. The Palestine Arabs meanwhile flatly refused to attend as long as the Mufti, who remained *persona non grata* to the British, was not allowed to lead their delegation. As a result, when the conference opened on September 10, participation was limited to the British and to representatives of the Arab states outside Palestine. The Arab stand in London was uncompromising. It called for the establishment of an interim Palestine government under the transitional supervision of a British high commissioner. Once in operation, the provisional government would be independent, ruling over a unitary state with its own elected legislature. Freedom of religion and guarantees for the holy places would be provided, even three Jewish ministers out of a government of ten; and Hebrew would become a second official language in districts where Jews formed an "absolute majority." But otherwise naturalization would be extended only to citizens who had lived in Palestine for a continuous period of ten years. In this fashion the DPs would be excluded.

Two days after the Arabs delivered their plan, the British suspended the conference, asking time to study the proposal. It is unlikely that they were given pause by the maximalism of the Arab stance. The Arabs at least had agreed to participate in the discussions, and this was already a clue that their governments were impressed by the Morrison-Grady proposals. Indeed, Azzam Pasha declared on the Arabs' behalf that they felt "much nearer agreement [with Britain] than we ever thought we would be." It was rather the absence of both the Palestine Arabs and the Jews, as well as the lack of American support, that appeared to undermine the usefulness of any further parleys. The Mufti himself continued to direct Palestine Arab political affairs from Cairo, where urgent meetings of the Arab Higher Committee were being held. Thus, in the midst of rising Jewish violence, special Arab measures already were being taken to boycott Jewish industrial products, to block the sale of Arab land to Jews, and to subsidize various Arab paramilitary organizations. The latter, functioning under the euphemism of youth movements, included the Najjada, founded in 1945 by a Jaffa lawyer, Muhammad Nimr al-Hawari, and the Futuwwa, the activist arm of the Husseini faction. Both groups received military equipment smuggled across from neighboring Arab lands. By 1946 their combined numbers exceeded 30,000. Needled continually by the Palestine Arab leadership to stay "honest," therefore, the Arab League Council held to its unyielding position.

On October 1, 1946, Bevin met unofficially in London with Weizmann and other Jewish Agency members and presented his own blueprint for an interim trusteeship that would lead ultimately to self-government. In a gesture of goodwill to the Zionists, the government on October 4 promoted Creech-Jones to colonial secretary. The atmosphere for a compromise appeared faintly hopeful. Referring to these gestures and discussions later in a speech before the House of Commons on February 25, 1947, Bevin recalled: "I did reach a stage . . . in meeting with the Jews separately, in which I advanced the idea of an interim arrangement, leading ultimately to self-government. . . . I said to them: 'If you will work together for three, five or ten years, it might well be that you will not want to separate. Let us try to make up the difference!' At that stage things looked more hopeful. There was a feeling . . . when they left me . . . that I had the right approach at last." Bevin underestimated the gulf that remained to be bridged. The Morrison-Grady proposal for admitting 100,000 Jews was out of date even before the London meetings. The Zionists had awakened by then to their earlier mistake of pressing for this limited number as the *summum bonum* of their demands. Bevin himself, in fact, unwittingly admitted this in the same address of February 25, 1947, even as his remarks betrayed the exceptional opportunity he had cast aside in rejecting the early Anglo-American Committee Report:

> I say this in all seriousness. If it were only a question of relieving Europe of 100,000 Jews, I believe a settlement could be found. . . . Unfortunately . . . from the Zionist point of view the 100,000 is only a beginning, and the Jewish Agency talks in terms of millions. . . . The claim made by the Arabs is a very difficult one to answer. . . . Why should an external agency, largely financed from America, determine how many people should come into Palestine, and interfere with the economy of the Arabs, who have been there for 2,000 years? That is what I have to face.

There was no meeting of minds between the British and the Zionists.

In truth, the White House was hardly more impressed by the Morrison-Grady Report than were the Zionists. Accepting the evaluation of Undersecretary of State Dean Acheson, Truman considered the scheme a ghetto, a betrayal of the Jews. "I studied the plan with care," he wrote later, "but I was unable to see that anything would come out of it except more unrest." Truman then conveyed his view to Attlee on August 7, 1946. Fending off the prime minister's entreaties, he cabled again on August 12: "The opposition in this country to the plan has become so intense that it is now clear that it would be impossible to rally in favor of it sufficient public opinion to enable this Government to give it effective support." Soon afterward, on October 4, the eve of Yom Kippur, the Jewish Day of Atonement, Truman issued the customary presidential statement of greeting to American Jewry. Acheson helped him prepare it. An advance copy was sent to Attlee on October 3. The prime minister was horrified by what he saw. He pleaded that the statement be postponed at least until he could discuss it with Bevin. Truman refused. The greeting then was issued. Officially endorsing the partition approach, it urged further that "substantial" immigration into Palestine, which "cannot wait a solution to the . . . problem," should commence immediately. Bevin, of course, was livid and attacked the statement as a blatant play for the Jewish vote at a time when congressional elections were only a month off. "I was told," he said, "that if it was not issued by Mr. Truman, a competitive statement would be issued by Mr. Dewey [the Republican leader]. In international affairs I cannot settle things if my problem is made the subject of local elections. . . ." Acheson subsequently denied the political motivation:

> When President Truman engaged in a political maneuver, he never disguised his undiluted pleasure in it. . . . About the Yom Kippur statement the president was very serious. The Day of Atonement seemed to come on a particularly dark day in Jewish history. The President chose it as a fitting occasion to announce that he would continue his efforts for the immigration of the one hundred thousand into Palestine.

Despite the setback that the British professed to see in the Truman statement, the new colonial secretary, Creech-Jones, was determined to reduce tension in Palestine itself. This, it was hoped, would induce the Zionists to join the second stage of the London Conference. At Creech-Jones's request, therefore, the mandatory government abstained from further searches of Jewish villages. General Barker, who had issued an angry anti-Semitic remark in the aftermath of the King David bombing, was replaced on October 22. Two weeks later the British released from internment the Jewish Agency leaders and more than a hundred others who had been arrested on the "Black Sabbath" of the previous June. For a while, these and other gestures removed some of the venom from the dispute. Even so, the next stage of the London Conference was delayed until early 1947, to enable the Jewish Agency leaders to refer the question of participation to the Twenty-second Zionist Congress, which was scheduled in Basle for December 1946.

The gathering was a melancholy affair. The two major groups remaining now were the Palestinians and the Americans. Between them sat only isolated representatives of European Jewry. The reservoir upon which Weizmann had depended for the two decades of his moderate leadership had vanished. The Americans, led by a fiery Cleveland rabbi, Abba Hillel Silver, were hardly less militant than Ben-Gurion and the Palestinians, and were convinced of the need to attack British authority head-on in Palestine. Weizmann issued an appeal for a final effort to seek a compromise solution, perhaps on the basis of a transitional regime that would lead to partition. He met with a cold response. It was the consensus that the Zionist movement ought not to be represented at London except on the basis of Jewish statehood. The Congress then pointedly refrained from reelecting Weizmann to his traditional presidency of the Zionist Organization.

During the four-month interval between the first and second installments of the London Conference, the views of Arabs and Jews alike had hardened. If the Agency now sent back word that it would accept nothing less than a Jewish state in Palestine, the Arab League representatives declared in advance that they insisted upon an Arab state with an even more drastically reduced Jewish membership in the government. The Palestine Arab Higher Committee this time was formally represented, and its militancy equaled the Arab League's. The Jews continued to boycott the discussions. Unofficially, however, Ben-Gurion and Shertok had gone to London for talks with Creech-Jones, who was characteristically sympathetic. He informed the Zionist spokesmen that he personally favored partition. The trouble was Bevin, said Creech-Jones, who listened to no one except Harold Beeley, the "unavoidable."

When the foreign secretary turned up for a later private session, the Zionist leaders experienced a shock. Their archenemy, Bevin, tottered into Creech-Jones's office like an exhausted man. He blinked suspiciously at Ben-Gurion, Shertok, and other Agency representatives. These were the spartan days of Britain's fuel cuts, and the large room was eerily lighted by candles. Bevin ventured a heavy joke that there was really no need for candles since they had the Israe*lites* present. The Jews smiled thinly. The foreign secretary then listened in obvious restlessness as Creech-Jones proposed a compromise: if the Jews agreed to shelve their political demands for five years, Britain in turn would not enforce the White Paper and land-purchase veto. Bevin interrupted to reject the idea. He would not prolong the original mandate under any circumstances, he emphasized, for it was unworkable, a mistake from the very beginning. Whatever happened, he was against racialism, and if the Jews would only leave him in peace he could compose their differences with the Arabs. Then, impatiently, the foreign secretary pressed the Jews to reveal their territorial demands.

At this moment Ben-Gurion suddenly asked the foreign secretary if he might see him alone. Bevin agreed, although he took Beeley with him into the other room. "Why don't you believe we are honest about our policy?" Bevin complained. "We have no selfish intentions. It's peace and stability in the Middle East we are looking for, no more." Ben-Gurion replied with equal bluntness: "Tell me frankly what you want. Perhaps we Jews would be willing to help. Perhaps our interests coincide." The interests of the two men did in fact coincide, at least partly. Ben-Gurion mentioned the possibility of British bases in the Negev, and access to Haifa harbor, of oil drilling prospects in the southern desert. Bevin reacted favorably. He intimated that he still had hopes of devising a formula that the Zionists could accept. It is possible, in the light of this exchange, that London may not have entirely discounted partition. Acheson recalled that early in 1947 he was sounded out on the idea by the British ambassador, Lord Inverchapel. Would the United States support a partition resolution in the United Nations? the Englishman asked. Acheson gave his personal opinion that his government would, and that partition appeared the most feasible of all solutions. The ambassador promised to convey this response to London. If Bevin gave serious consideration to the idea he soon abandoned it. He described his reasoning later:

> The best partition scheme, and the most favourable one that I have seen up to now, has the effect that it would leave . . . 450,000 Jews and 380,000 Arabs in that Jewish State. I put that to the Arabs quite frankly, and what was their answer? The Arabs say: "If it is wrong for the Jews to be a minority of 33½ or 40 percent in the whole country, what justification is there for putting 380,000 Arabs under the Jews. What is your answer to that?" I have no answer.

But if the foreign secretary was unwilling to swallow the partition plan, it was hardly expected that his eventual formula would be less palatable to the Zionists or Americans even than the Morrison-Grady scheme. In mid-February of 1947, however, such a proposal was submitted. Its modification of the earlier blueprint was to suggest a time limit of five years for the period of trusteeship. During the transition, the country would be progressively readied for independence as a unitary state, while the high commissioner would retain supreme legislative authority. Instead of provincial autonomy, moreover, the inhabitants of Palestine would be granted cantonal self-government in areas where Arabs or Jews constituted a majority. The Jewish Agency would be dissolved, and the Jews, like the Arabs, would be represented by delegates on an advisory council. A constituent assembly for the projected unitary state would be admitted over a period of two years, instead of one, and in the last three years of trusteeship the Arabs would be assured a voice in determining immigration policy. Elaborate and complex as it was, the scheme was wasted effort. The Arabs immediately denounced it; a postponement of majority rule was unthinkable to them. The Jews for their part were appalled by the cantonal plan and rejected it outright. Ben-Gurion insisted that it moved away from the Morrison-Grady plan in the direction of the 1939 White Paper. The Yishuv had already developed a viable quasi-government, after all, while the Arabs possessed no institutions of self-government whatever. The latest proposal offered the Arabs more than they already enjoyed and the Jews much less.

The deadlock was complete, and on February 14 Bevin announced that he was referring the entire problem to the United Nations. The decision was taken not alone for reasons of the Labor Cabinet's utter weariness and frustration on the Palestine issue. The government's economic resources by then were strained to the limit. Only six days later, Attlee appeared before Parliament to announce that the government also intended to transfer the government of India to the Indians not later than June 1948. One day after that, on February 21, Whitehall revealed that it was ending its military and financial commitments to Turkey and Greece by March 30. In the course of a single week, therefore, a series of official announcements foreshadowed the divestment of a historic sphere of influence. "If I could get back to the contribution on purely humanitarian grounds of 100,000 into Palestine," the foreign secretary remarked bitterly in his February 25 speech, "and if this political fight for a Jewish State could be put on one side, and we could develop self-government by the people resident in Palestine, without any other political issue, I would be willing to try again." But Bevin had had his chance earlier to defuse the issue by allowing the immigration of 100,000 refugees, and he had forfeited it.

It was not yet certain that London had entirely abandoned the notion of trying again. "We are not going to the United Nations to surrender the Mandate," Creech-Jones warned on February 25. "We are . . . setting out the problem and asking for their advice as to how the Mandate can be administered." This was the impression received by the new Palestine high commissioner, General Sir Alan Cunningham, upon visiting London in March 1947. Bevin and his advisers were evidently uncertain that the decision to withdraw was final, and suspected—perhaps hoped—that the United Nations would ask Britain to stay on as policeman in the Holy Land. On April 2 Bevin called for a special meeting of the UN General Assembly to discuss the Palestine mandate. Yet more than six weeks later, on May 29, the foreign secretary informed the Labor party convention that he personally would not be bound by any United Nations decision on the future of Palestine unless it were unanimous—hardly a likely development.

Events in Palestine itself gradually doomed this secret expectation of remaining on. The Etzel now intensified its coercive efforts. On March 1 it blew up the officers' club in Jerusalem, while the same day attacks elsewhere killed 18 and injured 25 Englishmen, a number of them civilians. By the end of 1947, the Lech'i boasted that it had killed 373 people, of whom 300 were civilians. Meanwhile, the scale of Jewish violence obscured the fact that the two Arab paramilitary groups were simultaneously terrorizing their own community. Most of the Arab victims allegedly had violated the land-sale boycott against the Jews; but between November 1945 and February 1947 six political opponents of the Husseinis also were murdered.

Indeed, the most significant development in Palestine throughout the eighteen months of Labor's incumbency was the virtual collapse of security. In 1947 the mandatory had stationed in the tiny country no less than 80,000 troops, in addition to units of the Transjordanian Arab Legion and 16,000 British and local police. This was a combined military-police establishment four times larger than the one of eight years earlier, at the height of the Arab revolt. Huge army and police structures had been erected throughout the country at a cost of £2 million. To pay for military transport and upkeep, British taxpayers had spent an estimated £50 million during Labor's year and a half in office, and the Palestine government another £5 million. Nothing better illustrated the bankruptcy of Labor policy in the mandate than the captivity into which British officials themselves had fallen. Despite far-reaching and elaborate security measures, conditions in the Holy Land were so tense in February 1947 that families of British civilian personnel, about 2,000 people, were evacuated and returned to England. The remaining nonmilitary employees were placed behind wire-enclosed security zones in the larger towns, and at the end of the month only eleven British civilians resided outside these enclosures. All of them lived under a dusk-to-dawn curfew and ventured forth only under armed escort.

It is not possible to draw sweeping generalizations about Jewish nationalism and its impact on the mandate. The formulation of the Biltmore Program and its endorsement by the Zionist Congress in 1946 hardly signified that the Yishuv had at last matured as a national-political organism. Only a minority of Palestine Jews had been born in the Holy Land, after all; their aspirations and claims were by no means dictated by nationalism alone. Immigration was the key. Even to a maximalist like Ben-Gurion, assurance of free immigration was more important than statehood. If, as late as 1946, Bevin had managed to devise a scheme for keeping Palestine within the Commonwealth and simultaneously assuring the unhampered flow of Jewish refugees from Europe, Ben-Gurion and the Agency Executive would have acquiesced. More than any other factor, it was London's preoccupation with Arab goodwill and, correspondingly, Bevin's agonized jntransigence on the immigration issue that provoked the maximalist Zionist demands for Jewish statehood, that ignited the terrorism, launched the illegal refugee traffic to Palestine, undermined Britain's economy, eroded its international reputation, and finally doomed the Palestine mandate itself.

CHAPTER XII THE BIRTH OF ISRAEL

THE PALESTINE ISSUE REACHES THE UNITED NATIONS

From the vantage point of the early twenty-first century, it is difficult to recapture the near-mystic hopes that were enshrined in the United Nations of the immediate postwar era. In its first decisive test of strength, the crisis provoked by the Soviet occupation of northern Iran, in 1946, the world body had shown itself an effective forum for the peaceful settlement of national rivalries. A year later, therefore, the United Nations was again chosen as the instrument to cope with a second international dilemma. The issue of Palestine admittedly was far more complex than that of Iran. This time a formula would have to be devised that would satisfy the legitimate aspirations of two bitterly hostile communities, and very probably establish a new sovereign entity to replace the British mandate. But if the task was more difficult, it was also specifically the kind of challenge the United Nations had been founded to deal with. Confrontations between the Great Powers were assumed to be outside its scope; the Security Council veto was an admission of this limitation. On the other hand, the dampening of hostility between contentious smaller peoples was ostensibly the United Nations' very *raison d'être*. In acknowledging this fact, Harry Truman was not simply being naïve in distinguishing between the humanitarian question of the refugees and the more intricate challenge of Palestine's juridical status. "My basic approach," he emphasized in his memoirs, "was that the long-range fate of Palestine was the kind of problem we had the UN for." And now, on April 2, 1947, by choosing to turn the fate of Palestine over to the world body, Britain itself seemed openly to be endorsing this approach.

But the appearance was partly illusory. In selecting the General Assembly as the organ of competence, rather than the smaller and more efficient Security Council, the Attlee cabinet betrayed its lingering hope that the United Nations, failing to provide a solution, would turn the matter back to London. In this fashion Britain presumably would enjoy a wider latitude in dealing with Zionist obstructionism. Harold Beeley said as much to David Horowitz, a Jewish Agency representative whose memoirs offer a fascinating insight into this period:

Look at the U.N. Charter and at the list of countries belonging to it. In order to obtain a favourable decision, you will need two-thirds of the votes of those countries, and you will be able to obtain it only if the Eastern bloc and the U.S. unite and support both the decision itself and the same formulation. Nothing like that ever happened, it cannot possibly happen, and will never happen.

Moreover, in bypassing the Security Council, Bevin revealed his anxiety lest the Soviet Union, as a permanent member of the smaller body, exert undue influence in dealing with Palestine and the Middle East. The concern was fully justified. When the Assembly convened on April 28, 1947, and debate opened on the membership of a proposed committee of inquiry, the Russians suggested limiting participation to the Big Five. Reacting instinctively, the American and British delegates expressed their preference for a "neutral" body with no "special interests." The Anglo-American view was upheld.

Accordingly, an eleven-nation investigative board was set up on May 13. Entitled the United Nations Special Committee on Palestine—UNSCOP— the special body consisted of the representatives of Australia, Canada, Czechoslovakia, Guatemala, India, Iran, the Netherlands, Peru, Sweden, Uruguay, and Yugoslavia. If less than neutral, it was probably as balanced a group as could have been found. India, Iran, and Yugoslavia, for example, with their own considerable Moslem populations, were likely to sympathize with the Arabs. On the other hand, Czechoslovakia had actively helped the Jewish refugee traffic from eastern Europe to Germany, while the Guatemalan and Uruguayan members had long been outspoken Zionist partisans. The Canadian, Australian, Peruvian, and Swedish delegates were genuinely uncommitted. When, therefore, the Arabs sought repeatedly to divorce the problem of the DPs from Palestine, a majority of the UNSCOP members rejected the attempt.

Under the best of circumstances, the chances of success did not appear promising. Sir Alexander Cadogan, Britain's representative in the Security Council, insisted that his government would neither abandon the mandate nor enforce a decision unless the solution were "just" and acceptable to both Arabs and Jews. It was an improbable condition. Upon learning that UNSCOP's terms of reference included—by implication—the plight of the displaced persons, the Arab states warned that they, too, would not necessarily be bound by the United Nations' recommendation. Meanwhile, the Arab Higher Committee decided that it would boycott the UNSCOP hearings altogether. It will be recalled that the Committee had originally been resuscitated in June 1946. Since then, eradicating rival Palestine Arab organizations, it had come to exert a decisive influence on the Arab League in all matters dealing with Palestine. The Committee's authority reflected in some degree the enormous personal impact of the Mufti. The mere presence of this éminence grise in Cairo overpowered the occasionally more moderate counsels of Azzam Pasha, secretary-general of the Arab League.

In the spring of 1945, ironically, as the Allied armies were driving into

Germany, Haj Amin had come within a hair's breadth of being seized as a war prisoner. He was able at the last moment to escape by plane to Switzerland, accompanied by Marshal Pétain's physician. The Swiss promptly shipped the Arab leader back to Germany, where French troops took him into custody, and Paris became the Mufti's home. His detention was brief. In December 1945, a clean-shaven "Syrian" gentleman slipped into a French military transport plane bound for the Levant. Four days later the "Syrian" entered Abdin Palace, Farouk's home in Cairo, and claimed the right of a fellow Moslem for shelter. Farouk willingly granted it. Immediately afterward, Haj Amin began issuing directives from his Egyptian exile, and did so with the same sure-handed authority as in the prewar years. His orders were followed in Palestine to the last detail. By early 1947, as a result, the Husseini party had merely to invoke the spell of the Mufti's name to restore its political machinery in every Palestine Arab town and village. By then, too, organized opposition to the Husseinis had been liquidated so completely that the British were prepared to extend full recognition to the Arab Higher Committee as the legitimate voice of Arab Palestine. It was in February, we recall, that Whitehall agreed to accept the Committee's delegates at the second phase of the London Conference. Three months later, the UN General Assembly similarly accredited the Higher Committee as the official representative of the Palestine Arabs.

With this recognition, and the threat of the revived paramilitary armies behind it, the Husseini faction adopted an increasingly uncompromising stance. From mid-June of 1947 on, when the UNSCOP group arrived in the Holy Land, the Mufti's followers staged anti-Zionist demonstrations in the larger Palestine cities. Jamil al-Husseini warned also that this unrest was merely the overture to a large-scale Arab revolt, unless the United Nations gave "full justice." It was in the interval, then, that the Higher Committee decided to boycott the UNSCOP hearings. The decision was probably a tactical blunder. Although the United Nations group managed to interview Arabs unofficially during its five-week stay in Palestine, and sample their views, this informal poll hardly compared to the elaborate and documented testimony offered by the Zionists. It was only when UNSCOP left Palestine for Beirut, on July 20, that the visitors had the opportunity of meeting with representatives, not of the Higher Committee, but of the Arab League. By then little new could be added to the evidence previously supplied the Anglo-American Committee of Inquiry. If anything, the League spokesman offended the UNSCOP group by emulating the strident, aggressive tone of the Mufti's partisans and issuing warnings of bloodshed if Palestine were divided. Even the normally urbane Azzam Pasha hinted that a decision in favor of partition risked danger not simply to the Jews of Palestine but to other Jewish communities in the Middle East, particularly to the 120,000 Jews of Iraq. "I do not think anyone could protect the Jews of the various Arab states," Azzam Pasha confided to a journalist later. These remarks achieved the opposite of their purpose. They convinced the UNSCOP members that it would be fatal to leave the Jews as a minority in Arab hands.

The Zionists for their part went through the entire series of reports and hearings during UNSCOP's five weeks in the country. The material they presented was essentially the data that had been submitted a year earlier to the Anglo-American Committee. But there was nothing routine in Zionist testimony. The Jewish Agency spokesmen recognized that if the UNSCOP report were negative, world sympathy for the Zionist cause would be dissipated, perhaps irretrievably. The tension gripping the Yishuv was well evident to the UNSCOP members. In harsh counterpoint to the sessions, Etzel and Lech'i violence reached its apogee in the midsummer of 1947. On May 4, several weeks after four of their men were hanged at Acre prison, the Etzel launched a spectacular assault against the prison building, dynamiting its walls and freeing 251 inmates. Several of the condemned prisoners were recaptured and hanged in late July. Two days after the executions, the Etzel kidnapped and hanged two British sergeants in retaliation. "We repaid our enemy in kind," boasted Menachem Begin. The horror this deed aroused in England was movingly expressed by the *Daily Mail,* which on August 1 appealed to the feelings of "American women whose dollars helped buy the rope."

Repelled as they were by the killings, and the evidence they saw everywhere around them of elaborate military precautions—barbed wire, armored car patrols, searchlight beams at night—the UNSCOP members sensed that they were witnessing in the mandate a doomed political entity. If they needed additional proof of Jewish desperation, moreover, they found it in a widely publicized episode that occurred while they were in Palestine, in mid-July. During the preceding half-year the illegal refugee traffic had been fairly well throttled. Then, early in the month, a battered little American Chesapeake Bay ferry, packed with 4,500 DPs, set out from the French port of Sète. Six British destroyers and one cruiser were waiting offshore. They immediately "escorted" the refugee ship, appropriately renamed *Exodus-1947,* across the Mediterranean. Twelve miles outside Palestine territorial waters, the British armada closed on the *Exodus* for boarding. A furious hand-to-hand struggle ensued. The DPs fought off the boarding party for several hours. Eventually the British put machine guns and gas bombs into action, killing three Jews and wounding a hundred. All the while a detailed account of the battle was radioed to Haganah headquarters in Tel Aviv, and later rebroadcast throughout the world. The crew of the *Exodus* surrendered only when the British began ramming the vessel, threatening to sink it.

Listing badly, the ferry was then towed into Haifa harbor. Under ordinary circumstances the British would have transshipped the boat's passengers to Cyprus. But in the previous twelve months some 26,000 Jews had been packed onto that island, hopelessly overcrowding its two internment camps. In this case, therefore, Bevin personally decided to "make an example" of the refugees by sending them back to their port of origin. Shortly afterward, on British transports that were essentially prison ships, the DPs were carried off to Marseilles in the full blaze of the Mediterranean summer. And there, except for a small number of the old, ill, or pregnant among them, the Jews refused to disembark. The French government offered the refugees hospitality and medical care. The offer was rejected. Notwithstanding the suffocating heat and illness, and a contagion of rashes and boils, the passengers insisted that their destination was the Land of Israel. A correspondent, Ruth Gruber, described their plight:

> Squeezed between a green toilet shed and some steel plates were hundreds and hundreds of half-naked people who looked as though they had been thrown together into a dog pound. . . . Trapped and lost, they were shouting at us in all languages, shattering each other's words. . . . The hot sun filtered through the grillwork, throwing sharp lines of light and darkness across the refugees' faces and their hot, sweaty half-naked bodies. Women were nursing their babies. Old women and men sat weeping unashamed, realizing what lay ahead.

What lay ahead was Germany. After three weeks, the French government, concerned by the possibility of epidemics, ordered the vessels to depart. At this point the British cabinet held an emergency meeting and decided that its only alternative was to ship the Jews back to Germany. Most of the refugees were thereupon returned to Hamburg. Some 1,500 of them refused to disembark at the North Sea port. As the local German inhabitants watched in incredulity, the Jews were carried off by British troops wielding clubs and hoses. Eventually the DPs were transported by rail to German internment camps at Pöppendorf and AmStau. For a month the British attempted to register them, but they elicited only one response for all questions: "Eretz Israel." The *Exodus* tragedy, prolonged over three months, was extensively reported in newspapers throughout the world. The UNSCOP members were not unaffected by the episode, as it developed. "It is the best possible evidence we can have," said the Yugoslav representative, before the group departed for Beirut on July 20. A week after that, arriving in Geneva, the members voted to dispatch a subcommittee to the refugee centers in Germany and Austria. And the visitors witnessed in the camps precisely the spectacle that Harrison and the Anglo-American Committee had encountered earlier: a community of refugee Jews, some 250,000 by this time, who measured their very existence against the hour of departure for Palestine.

THE UNSCOP REPORTS

The committee spent most of August evaluating alternatives. Moshe Shertok and David Horowitz, the Jewish Agency representatives, met endlessly with the various delegates, pleading the Zionist case. So did Richard Crossman, who had become a Zionist convert while on the Anglo-American Committee of Inquiry. The report was finished on August 31. In it, UNSCOP laid down eleven guiding principles. The most important of these stated that: the mandate should be ended and independence granted at the earliest practicable date; the political structure of the new state or states should be "basically democratic"; the economic unity of Palestine must be maintained; the security of the holy places and access to them should be assured; the General Assembly should carry out immediately an arrangement for solving the urgent problem of a quarter-million Jewish DPs in Europe. Applying these principles, then, UNSCOP divided, seven to three, into a majority (Canada, Czechoslovakia, Guatemala, the Netherlands, Peru, Sweden, and Uruguay) recommending partition, and a minority (India, Iran, and Yugoslavia) proposing federation. The delegate of Australia abstained.

In favoring partition, the majority scheme envisaged an Arab area comprising western Galilee, the hill country of central Palestine except for the Jerusalem enclave, and the coastal plain from a line south of Isdud (Ashdod) to the Egyptian border. The Jewish territory would include the rest, except for the Jerusalem-Bethlehem promontory, which would be internationalized. During a two-year interim period beginning September 1947, Britain would administer Palestine under United Nations supervision, although it was the implication of the majority report that the United States would assume a share of the responsibility. At the same time, Jewish immigration would continue at the rate of 6,250 monthly in the first two years—for a total of 150,000—and thereafter at the rate of 5,000 monthly, or 60,000 a year, if it were necessary to extend the transitional period. The economic unity of Palestine would be maintained by a ten-year customs and currency treaty between the Arab and the Jewish states. A separate board, composed of three Arabs, three Jews, and three members appointed by the United Nations, would administer the economic union, and the Jewish state would provide a limited financial subsidy to the Arab state.

The UNSCOP minority report considered all this unworkable and anti-Arab. It proposed instead the transformation of the mandate into an independent federal government of Jewish and Arab cantons, with Jerusalem as capital. Cantonal authority would apply to internal matters. Immigration, foreign relations, and national defense would belong to a central government, consisting of a bicameral legislature in which one house would function by equal representation and the other by proportional representation. A majority in both houses would be required for the enactment of all laws. The most crucial difference related to Jewish immigration. By the minority scheme, refugees were to be allowed into the Jewish cantons for three years only "in such numbers as are not to exceed . . . absorptive capacity . . . having due regard for the rights of the population then present within that state and for their anticipated natural rate of increase." The "absorptive capacity" of the Jewish areas was a matter to be decided by an international commission. Finally, under the minority plan, Jaffa and most of the Negev were allocated to the Arab state rather than, as envisaged in the majority report, to the Jews.

There was little even in the majority report, for that matter, to set the Zionists dancing in the streets. Territorially, it envisaged for both peoples asymmetrical segments that were "entwined in an inimical embrace like two fighting serpents," as Herbert Samuel had once described the Peel

Plan. The assumption was unrealistic that the Jews, after their own state was established, would agree indefinitely to subsidize the economically weaker Arab regime. Even so, the Zionists generally regarded the proposal as an improvement over the minority report, with its throwback to the Morrison-Grady cantonal scheme. It offered them at least two indispensable prerequisites: sovereignty and an uninterrupted flow of immigration for the reasonable future. The Jewish Agency therefore expressed cautious satisfaction with the majority report.

The Arabs, conversely, rejected it with passion. Indeed, both the majority and the minority plans horrified them. As soon as the contents of the reports became known, Prime Minister Salih Jabr of Iraq summoned an emergency conference of the Arab League's Political Committee. Meeting at Sofar, Lebanon, on September 16, the committee voted to impose economic reprisals (p. 299) and to supply men and weapons for the Palestine Arabs. On the following day the Arab League formally threatened war if the United Nations approved either of the two UNSCOP reports.

The Zionists were no less eager than the UNSCOP committee to break this impasse with the Arab League. They sensed that their best hope in the long run was to be found in a private understanding with their neighbors. To that end, in an effort to reach a compromise settlement, the Jewish Agency liaison officials David Horowitz and Aubrey (Abba) Eban met with Azzam Pasha in London on October 14, 1947. Horowitz later recalled that the Zionist emissaries declared their willingness to offer cast-iron guarantees against Jewish expansionism in any form, as well as arrangements for regional economic development. Azzam smiled resignedly. The issue was beyond settlement through reason or compromise, he explained. If he, or any other Arab leader, returned to Cairo or Damascus the next day bearing a peace agreement with the Zionists, he would be a dead man within hours. The secretary-general observed that he and his personal colleagues no longer represented the new Arab world. His son, and the students who burned streetcars and stoned Western embassies—these were the Arabs who now decided policy. The Middle East would have to find its own solution, Azzam commented regretfully, just as Europe had done earlier, by force.

There was apparently no room for negotiation between Arabs and Jews. The future status of Palestine rested with the members of the United Nations, and notably with the Great Powers. The General Assembly thereupon turned the Palestine question over to an *ad hoc* political committee of all member nations. In this manner fourteen meetings and an additional twenty-four days were spent in open hearings. From the outset of the sessions it became evident that any lingering hope of British cooperation was doomed. This was the period when London was negotiating a new treaty with Egypt and seeking Arab goodwill as a means of protecting British oil interests. The notion of participating in any scheme that was objectionable to the Arabs, even a plan enjoying international sanction, was unthinkable. Rather, Sir Alexander Cadogan declared that Britain accepted UNSCOP's recommendations for ending the mandate. But thereafter, Britain would limit its support to a plan on which agreement had been reached between Arabs and Jews. The statement was of course a euphemism for rejecting the UNSCOP majority report. In truth, Britain's "neutrality" served as a rationale for declining even to fix an evacuation date until the partition subcommittee had nearly finished its work. The British also rejected the suggestion of a gradual transfer of authority to a United Nations commission, or any scheme delegating authority to the projected Arab and Jewish governments.

In the alignment of blocs within the General Assembly, however, the influence of the Soviet Union proved far more decisive than Britain's. It was of interest that fully two years after the war the Kremlin still refused to give an inkling of which way it would land on the Palestine issue. The Jews had never been particularly optimistic—antipathy to Zionism had been an axiom of Soviet policy since the early 1920s (Chapter VII). To be sure, the Histadrut's wartime fund-raising efforts on behalf of the USSR had favorably impressed the Soviet leadership, and Russian visitors to Palestine during the early 1940s had expressed their goodwill. Nevertheless, Moscow's consistent support of Arab nationalism in the Levant and Egypt appeared to bode ill for the Zionist cause. It was thus all the more unexpected, near the end of the special United Nations session in mid-May 1947, when Soviet delegate Andrei Gromyko suddenly assailed the bankruptcy of the Palestine mandate and endorsed the "aspirations of the Jews to establish their own State." In his speech, Gromyko made the barbed observation that no western European country "has been able to ensure the defense of the elementary rights of the Jewish people." He added that the Soviet Union's first choice of a solution would be "the establishment of an independent, dual, democratic homogeneous Arab-Jewish State." But if such an arrangement were demonstrated to be unfeasible, his government would then be willing to support partition.

However opportunistic, the shift in the Soviet approach was not illogical. Its ultimate purposes were well summarized by Walter Bedell Smith, the United States ambassador to Moscow, in a long memorandum afterward to Washington. Bedell Smith shrewdly noted that if Russia were to fulfill its historic ambition of gaining a foothold in the Middle East, it would have to explore all avenues. Northern Iran was one. The Turkish straits and Greece were another. In both cases, Western opposition to Soviet pressure was mounting. Conceivably Palestine was a third gateway, if a vacuum could be opened in that country by an accelerated British departure. From Moscow's vantage point, then, the establishment of a modern Jewish state, imbued with a fiery nationalist spirit, was more likely to eliminate British influence than was a backward Arab regime, heavily dependent upon Britain for funds, advisers, and weapons. Moreover, even if a Jewish state did not come into existence immediately, it was likely that hard fighting would take place between Arabs and Jews once the British withdrew. The ensuing chaos would still be to Moscow's advantage, as long as British evacuation were not attended by a corresponding increase in American influence.

In the light of this incisive analysis, all subsequent Russian behavior followed a consistent pattern. On October 13, 1947, the Soviet representative to the UN Palestine Committee, Semyon Tsarapkin, officially endorsed the UNSCOP partition plan. Indeed, he did so with a vengeance, at first insisting that the Security Council itself should be responsible for administering Palestine in the transitional period. The Americans and British rejected the proposal. Still, Tsarapkin did not give up easily; he pressed Britain to dissolve the mandate forthwith and to abstain from playing any active role in a Palestine settlement thereafter. Soviet intentions in the Middle East by then were transparent. But to the Zionists, the votes were all that mattered. And by 1947 this shift in the Soviet position assured the votes of the Soviet Union itself and the Ukrainian and Byelorussian Soviet Republics, as well as those of Poland, Czechoslovakia, Bulgaria, and Rumania—possibly even of Yugoslavia. For the advocates of partition, an important hurdle evidently had been overcome.

THE UNITED STATES MAKES A COMMITMENT

Ultimately, to Arabs and Jews alike, everything hinged on the attitude of the United States, by common recognition the most powerful force in the world body. That attitude in turn was mightily influenced by several contending viewpoints within the United States government itself. American economic and strategic interests in the Middle East had grown dramatically since World War II. The area's importance as a communications center was so highly regarded that in September 1946 a representative of President Truman, George A. Brownell, was sent to the Arab capitals to negotiate air transport agreements on behalf of American airline companies. A bilateral treaty was successfully reached between the United States and Egypt, and eventually similar agreements were concluded with Lebanon and Syria. Then, in 1947, the Palestine issue suddenly obtruded, blocking a treaty with Iraq. Brownell wrote later that "public statements on the Palestine question by officials of the American government . . . so angered certain Iraqi officials that our representatives were advised that no agreement of any kind would be possible. It is difficult to exaggerate the feeling that exists on this subject throughout the Moslem nations."

Yet the concern for air rights was dwarfed by a far greater preoccupation with American oil holdings. By 1947 American petroleum corporations owned approximately 42 percent of Middle Eastern supplies, largely in Saudi Arabia, but also in Kuwait, in Bahrein, even in Iraq. During the war U.S. output and refinery capacity in the Persian Gulf had doubled. Still, the oil corporations were intent upon enlarging their holdings. James Terry Duce, executive vice-president of the Arabian American Oil Company (Aramco), was determined to assure the friendship of the Saudi government, and by the same token to increase his company's share of the Persian Gulf reserves. From the viewpoint of Duce and other oil company officials, the eruption of the Palestine issue clouded the outlook both for additional concessions and for assured pipeline rights across Arab territory. The fear that Washington's support for Zionism might endanger corporate earnings was phrased euphemistically, as a rule. In the *Petroleum Times* of June 1948, for example, Max W. Thornburg, a vice-president of the Cal-Tex Oil Company, one of the partners of the Aramco complex, expressed his dismay that Washington should have "prevailed upon [the United Nations] Assembly to declare racial and religious criteria the basis of political statehood. . . . In that one step . . . the moral prestige of America was extinguished and Arab faith in her ideals destroyed." After the United Nations vote was taken, Kermit Roosevelt, another former oil company executive, echoed this indignation: "The process by which Zionist Jews have been able to promote American support for the partition of Palestine," he wrote, "demonstrates the vital need of a foreign policy based on national rather than partisan interests."

In fact, Defense and State Department officials entirely shared the concern for American oil holdings in the Middle East. The military Joint Chiefs of Staff reminded Truman that access to Arab petroleum was a matter of critical national importance, one that would have to be evaluated in any governmental decision on the Palestine issue. "[Secretary of Defense] Forrestal spoke to me repeatedly about the danger that hostile Arabs might deny us access to the petroleum treasures of their country," the president recalled. Indeed, the issue was much on Forrestal's mind. He warned a small-businessmen's luncheon on October 9, 1947, that as a consequence of the evident depletion of American oil reserves, "we . . . have to develop reserves outside the country. The greatest field of untapped oil in the world is in the Middle East. . . . We should not be shipping a barrel of oil out of the United States to Europe. . . . [P]ipe for the Arabian pipeline should have precedence over pipe for similar projects in this country." The defense secretary's concern for adequate oil reserves was soon transformed into an obsession with Zionist pressures on the government. Repeatedly he emphasized the need for lifting the Palestine question "out of politics." His posthumous papers reveal that on several occasions he admonished J. Howard McGrath, chairman of the Democratic National Committee, that "no group in this country [i.e., the Zionists] should be permitted to influence our policy to the point where it could endanger our national security."

Forrestal's alarm at American Zionist influence was shared by James Byrnes and Loy Henderson in the State Department, and by their colleagues at the Near East Desk, Gordon Merriam, Fraser Wilkins, and Evan Wilson. In a typical memo of January 14, 1947, Wilkins cautioned Byrnes that a pro-Zionist stance would be

> . . . prejudicial to America. Arab relations in the fields of education, trade, petroleum and aviation [would be threatened]. Continued agitation and uncertainty regarding the Palestine question, by weakening the Anglo-American position in the Near East, permits a more rapid expansion of Soviet Russian objectives, and is distressing to Christians everywhere because the Christian

interest in Palestine tends to become submerged in an Arab-Jewish controversy.

Truman wrote later that the State Department personnel were "almost without exception unfriendly to the idea of a Jewish state. . . . Like most of the British diplomats, some of our diplomats also thought that the Arabs, on account of their numbers and because of the fact that they controlled such immense oil resources, should be appeased. I am sorry to say that there were some among them who were inclined to be anti-Semitic." Some in any case reflected a pro-Arab background and training, particularly those who had studied at the American University of Beirut and others who had accumulated years of consular or ministerial service in various Arab cities and capitals. Their acquaintance was limited for the most part to the Arab world and its mentality.

But there were other factors that, in their turn, exerted a markedly pro-Zionist influence on the White House and Congress. Chief among these was the importance American political leaders placed on the Jewish vote in New York, Illinois, Pennsylvania, and other states with urban Jewish populations. This influence in turn would hardly have been effective if the American Jewish community itself had not been won over to Zionism through years of cultivation. By the end of World War II, American Jewry numbered some 5 million. The revelations of the death camps and the emergent plight of the refugees effectively transformed Zionism into the dominant mood of this strategically placed minority bloc. As a result, fund-raising drives on behalf of European survivors and the Palestine sanctuary raised $100 million a year by 1947, far surpassing the philanthropic efforts of any other American charity or of any American ethnic group.

Not least of all, under the guidance of such Zionist leaders as Abba Hillel Silver and Stephen Wise, American Jewry mobilized to deluge the White House and Congress with letters and telegrams from all parts of the country. As early as 1943, an American Zionist Emergency Council had been established to orchestrate this lobbying effort. The AZEC, in fact, soon developed into one of the most formidable pressure groups of its time. With a large budget and fourteen professionally staffed departments, it was capable of obtaining mass signatures for petitions, or a flood of letters to Washington, in a matter of days. The AZEC worked through synagogues and other Jewish institutions, activated labor leaders, the press, and clergymen (through a front group, the American Christian Palestine Committee), and arranged speeches for such public service organizations as the Rotary Club, Kiwanis, and others. It issued an endless stream of memoranda, reprints, books, and directives, and planned rallies, conferences, and campaigns. It was extraordinarily effective in Congress, and hardly less so with the executive branch of government.

When Harry Truman assumed the presidency in April 1945, therefore, he was subjected instantly to the full impact of this Zionist appeal. He was annoyed by it (p. 291), but he was impressed by it as well. In addition to his own deeply felt compassion for the Jewish refugees, the president was unquestionably responsive to the counsel of several pro-Zionist liberals whose integrity he trusted. These included Eleanor Roosevelt, Governor Herbert Lehman of New York, and Colonel Jacob Arvey, chairman of Cook County's (Chicago's) Democratic Committee. Truman and his advisers were not insensitive to the American Jewish political support these figures marshaled. On September 4, 1947, for example, Robert Hannegan, newly appointed chairman of the Democratic National Committee, urged the president to issue a pro-Zionist statement on Palestine, "for such a statement would have a very great influence and great effect on the raising of funds for the Democratic National Committee." Forrestal quoted Hannegan as reporting that "very large sums were obtained a year ago from Democratic contributors and that they would be influenced in either giving or with- holding by what the President did on Palestine."

One of those who functioned most effectively behind the scenes was David K. Niles, Truman's special assistant for minority affairs. Through the office of this inconspicuous, rather dour man, the sense and fervor of American Zionism were transmitted to the president. It was Niles who persuaded Truman in July 1947 to drop the State Department officials George Wadsworth and Loy Henderson as advisers to the American delega- tion at the UN General Assembly, and to replace them with Major General John H. Hilldring, whose sympathetic treatment of the DPs during his tenure with the American military government in Germany had favorably impressed the Zionists. This was evidently as far as the president was will- ing to go, however, and as late as October 6, he turned down Hannegan's request for an official statement of intent on partition.

The State Department meanwhile remained determinedly noncommittal in its public comments. Throughout the UNSCOP hearings in the late sum- mer of 1947, Secretary George Marshall declined to take an official stance on the Palestine issue. On the other hand, he privately endorsed a group memorandum submitted in June by Henderson, by Warren Austin, the American representative in the Security Council, and by Dean Rusk, director of the State Department's Office of Special Political Affairs. The document strongly favored the concept of a unitary state under a United Nations trusteeship, with immigration not to exceed Palestine's "economic absorptive capacity." As late as July 7, moreover, the secretary of state quietly assured Bevin of American cooperation in helping suppress illegal Jewish immigration to Palestine. Marshall was also impressed enough by Henderson's urgent appeal of September 22 to refrain from supporting the UNSCOP majority report. Nevertheless, the initiative on Palestine was soon taken out of Marshall's hands.

On October 9, 1947, Truman learned that the Arab League Council had instructed its member nations to dispatch troops to the Palestine borders. Even earlier, public statements from the Arab capitals were becoming increasingly belligerent. Evidently the president's back was up. He in- structed the State Department to support the partition plan, and Marshall dutifully abandoned his personal objections. Later Truman wrote that his essential purpose was "to help bring about the redemption of the pledge of the Balfour Declaration and the rescue of at least some of the victims of Nazism. I was not committed to any particular formula of statehood in Palestine or to any particular time schedule for its accomplishment. . . . The simple fact is that our policy was an American policy rather than an Arab or Jewish policy." On October 11, Herschel V. Johnson, the representative on the General Assembly's Palestine Committee, announced the president's decision to endorse the "basic principles" of partition, subject to "certain amendments and modifications." It was a moment of bitter disappointment for the Arabs, of intense rejoicing for the Jews.

On October 21, 1947, the Palestine Committee assigned the task of refining UNSCOP's majority report to a subcommittee of nine partition supporters, including, by then, the United States and the Soviet Union. It was an imposing combination. Working together smoothly in this group, the American and Soviet delegations produced a compromise timetable for British evacuation. The Americans had briefly contemplated withdrawing most of the Negev Desert from the projected Jewish state; but Weizmann was able to meet with Truman personally, to captivate the president with a historical disquisition on Jewish links with this ancient wilderness, and to win Truman's support for the original partition boundaries.

On November 24, 1947, the minority subcommittee, composed largely of Moslem delegates, presented blueprints for a federal state to the full Palestine Committee. The latter in fact represented all the members of the General Assembly; its impending vote accordingly was crucial as a prefiguration of the General Assembly's ultimate decision. The Zionists counted on the full weight of American influence being thrown now against this—essentially pro-Arab—plan. They were disappointed. In a final, anguished memorandum, Henderson succeeded once again in staying Marshall's hand. The secretary of state instructed Herschel Johnson not to press the official American position on other delegations. This time, too, the Jews found a closed door at the White House. The president was irritated by Zionist tactics. "I do not think I ever had as much pressure and propaganda aimed at the White House as I did in this instance," he wrote. "The persistence of a few of the extreme Zionist leaders . . . disturbed and annoyed me." Undersecretary of State Robert Lovett reported later at a cabinet lunch of December 1, 1947, that he personally "had never in his life been subject to as much pressure as he had been during the last few days of the Palestine issue at the United Nations." The Arabs meanwhile warned even more intemperately of retaliation against Western oil interests, of a Middle Eastern bloodbath, should the vote go against them.

If the Zionists hoped to win over the remaining delegations, they understood now that they would have to do so on their own, without U.S. help. Meeting repeatedly with these statesmen, therefore, the Zionist emissaries— Shertok, Horowitz, Eban, Silver, Eliahu Epstein, and others—urgently reminded their listeners of the Arabs' pro-Axis record during the war, and emphasized the plight of the displaced persons. In their desperation, they were not less single-minded in exploiting American Jewish connections than the Arabs in threatening war and economic reprisals. Thus, unofficial but highly effective economic leverage was applied to the Chinese and to a group of smaller countries that had tended initially to favor the minority plan, including Haiti, Liberia, the Philippines, Ethiopia, and Greece. These six governments were deluged with wires, phone calls, letters, and visitations, many from important business customers. In the end, all of them except Greece voted against the Arab proposal. As a result, the minority scheme for a federal Palestine state was defeated by a vote of twenty-nine to twelve. On the following day, November 25, the Palestine Committee approved an amended partition plan, twenty-five to thirteen.

THE VOTE FOR PARTITION

The blueprint that was now to be submitted to the full plenary session of the General Assembly included several modifications. These had been suggested by the United States and approved by the Palestine Committee. The first was for the largely Arab-inhabited port of Jaffa to be assigned to the Arab state rather than to the Jews. The second was for two portions of the Negev, including the town of Beersheba and its hinterland, and a narrow strip of territory running from the Mediterranean along the Egyptian border halfway to the Gulf of Aqaba, to be allocated to the Arab rather than the Jewish state. Under the final plan, therefore, the Arab state would embrace 4,500 square miles, 804,000 Arabs, and 10,000 Jews. The Jewish state would encompass 5,500 square miles, 538,000 Jews, and 397,000 Arabs. Except for these changes, the UNSCOP majority report was accepted in basically unaltered form. The two states were to be linked in an economic union and to share a joint currency, joint railroads and interstate highways, as well as postal, telephone, and telegraphic services. Between 5 and 10 percent of the surplus revenue from customs and other common services was to be allocated to the City of Jerusalem; the remainder would be divided equally between the two governments. Each year the Jewish state would pay the Arab state a £4 million subsidy, reflecting the former's better citrus areas and anticipated higher technological efficiency.

The method of putting the resolution into effect was its weakest feature. After sharp debate, the Palestine Committee unenthusiastically adopted a Canadian formula. By its terms the General Assembly would name an international commission to supervise partition under the jurisdiction of the Security Council. Law and order were to be maintained by armed militias within the respective states, but the Security Council would be asked to assume responsibility "in the event of a threat to the peace." It was a meager palliative, yet no attempt was made to remedy it by providing an outside military force. One reason was the widely held expectation that Britain finally would agree to police the country on an interim basis. In any case, the United States feared that a mixed Security Council force would give the Russians a share in the administration of "peace and security" in Palestine.

On November 29 the partition resolution was submitted to the full ses-

**THE UNITED NATIONS PLAN
FOR PARTITION OF PALESTINE
NOVEMBER 29, 1947**

Allotted to Jews

Allotted to Arabs

International zone
of Jerusalem

sion of the General Assembly for the desired vote. The political maneuvering of Jews and Arabs continued to the last moment. By then, however, pressure tactics were largely gratuitous. The Americans and the Soviet bloc were committed to partition. So were Norway, Canada, and Guatemala. So, too, at last, were the five small nations whom the Zionists had succeeded in winning over. As expected, the Moslem bloc, together with India, Yugoslavia, and Greece (the latter with an important diaspora in the Arab world), continued unshakable against partition. One of the remaining question marks was France. The French had demonstrated an uncharacteristic sympathy for the Jews during the early postwar period, and an equivalent distaste for British policy and the Arabs. A Jewish state in the Middle East unquestionably would strengthen the position of the pro-French Maronites in Lebanon. Even so, the French delegation was ambivalent. Its chairman, Alexandre Parodi, was fearful of antagonizing the North African communities and of undermining a wide network of French Catholic institutions in the Moslem world. In the end, however, a transatlantic telephone call from Weizmann to Léon Blum in Paris resolved the issue. The former prime minister's influence was still considerable. Less than two hours before the final vote, the French delegation received instructions to support partition.

The General Assembly resolution was approved by a vote of thirty-three to thirteen, giving it the necessary two-thirds majority. With the exception of Cuba and Greece, all the states voting against the measure were either Moslem or Asian. The pivotal bloc of votes in favor of the resolution—not less than 40 percent of the United Nations membership—ultimately was cast by the Latin American delegations. Zionist pressure here was minimal. Nor was the intercession of the United States anywhere apparent in the Latin American stance. On the contrary, later, in April of 1948, when Washington proposed temporarily shelving partition in favor of a trusteeship (p. 303), the Latin American delegates unanimously rejected the notion. The evidence is compelling that these Latin governments, with few interests either way in the Middle East, accepted the majority report at face value. Simple compassion for the displaced persons unquestionably influenced their decision, the identical sympathy they would display the following year on behalf of Arab refugees from Palestine.

As matters developed, therefore, Jewish—or Arab—pressure tactics influenced the General Assembly vote much less than critics of partition were willing to admit. Far more important was the unexpected but impressive phenomenon of Soviet-American agreement on an international issue. Moreover, the General Assembly was offered little valid alternative to the partition plan. Both Arabs and Jews had insisted that they would not accept a federalized Palestine, while partition claimed the support of at least one of the parties in the dispute. Significantly, on the morning of the final vote the Arab delegates panicked, announcing that they would support a federal solution in principle. Yet it was clear that Jewish immigration was still unacceptable to them, and that the tragedy of the DPs would not be alleviated by the minority plan. By then, too, the supporters of partition had the necessary votes and were uninterested in further delay.

The Arab scholar Albert Hourani shrewdly evaluated the factors responsible for the partition decision. The Jews belonged mainly to the West, he observed; they were far better known than the wholly alien Arabs. Their plight, registering directly and intimately on the Western conscience, was magnified by the Western sense of guilt by inaction. It was surely not a coincidence that the nations whose doors remained closed to Jewish immigrants were precisely the ones voting in favor of the Jewish state. Hourani noted also that the order, efficiency, and social philosophy of the Zionists appealed to Western minds. "[Westerners] were attracted by the gallant little people with a great and tormented past, by the pioneers taming the wilderness, the planners using science to increase production, the collective farmers turning away from the guilt and complexity of personal life, the terrorist making his gesture in the face of authority—all images of a new world . . . hopeful, violent, and earnest." The Zionists had a simpler explanation. It was the one Weizmann had offered the Anglo-American Committee of Inquiry a year earlier, when he suggested that the decision to establish Jewish and Arab states and thus provide asylum for a nation of refugees was a choice not between right and wrong, but between the greater and the lesser injustice.

THE RESPONSE TO PARTITION

The partition formula anticipated a reasonable degree of economic cooperation between Arabs and Jews in common association. The members of the General Assembly hoped also to minimize difficulties by seeking British help on a number of crucial issues. These included the evacuation of Palestine not later than February 1, 1948, the use of a port adequate for substantial Jewish immigration, and a willingness to share the administration of the country with the appointed Palestine commission during the transitional period of British departure. To achieve these goals, a Palestine commission was appointed less than a month after the resolution was passed, consisting of delegates from Bolivia, Czechoslovakia, Denmark, Panama, and the Philippines. Like the General Assembly itself, the commissioners expected active support from Britain.

These hopes were disappointed. Sir Alexander Cadogan had warned repeatedly that his government would play neither a lone nor a leading role in effecting a plan that was not "accepted by both Arabs and Jews." Eventually Britain declined to assume any tutelary responsibility whatever, refusing so much as to fix a schedule for the evacuation of its troops until the partition subcommittee's work was nearly completed. Even then the date was finally set at August 1, 1948, well beyond the United Nations deadline, although several weeks later the British advanced the timetable to May 14. Cadogan balked, too, at the suggested gradual transfer of authority to a United Nations commission. His explanation was that this procedure would result in "confusion and disorder." On December 1, 1947,

Ben-Gurion paid a call on High Commissioner Cunningham at Government House in Jerusalem. Cunningham received the Jewish Agency chairman with reserve, offering no word of congratulation. "I suppose you are happy about the Resolution," was his only comment. Ben-Gurion attempted to discuss the future, requesting photostatic copies of land registry deeds, information about supplies of food and fuel in the country, and permission to organize a militia. Cunningham promised to reply to these requests. But no information was ever forthcoming. Indeed, the British refused to allow members of the UN commission to visit Palestine before May 1. When an advance UN party nevertheless arrived early in January 1948, British mandatory officials pointedly made the group unwelcome. The six commission members were housed in an unventilated basement opposite British headquarters in Jerusalem, where they did their courageous but futile best to represent the majesty of the world body. Under increasingly difficult and dangerous conditions, they searched for methods to develop a transitional regime in Palestine. But soon they were reduced to foraging for food and drink. They accomplished nothing.

There were tangible reasons for British noncooperation. The most obvious was London's determination to avoid provoking the Arab world at a time when Britain's foothold in the Middle East was already precarious, when oil royalty and pipeline agreements were continually under review in Arab capitals, and delicate treaty negotiations were under way with Egypt. Another was simple bitterness at the Jews. British security forces had lost 127 killed and 331 wounded at the hands of Jewish terrorists between May 1945 and October 1947. The Jewish refugee traffic and Zionist propaganda had shamed Britain before the world. Bevin personally had been harassed beyond endurance by what he considered to be Truman's politically motivated intrusiveness. An insight into the foreign secretary's mentality was provided by Richard Crossman, who met with him on August 4, 1947, and afterward described Bevin's outlook as corresponding roughly with the *Protocols of the Elders of Zion,* a notorious anti-Semitic canard of the 1920s. The main points of Bevin's discourse were, first, that the Jews had successfully organized a worldwide conspiracy against Britain and against him personally. He went on to claim that the whole Jewish "pressure" was a gigantic racket run from America. Here Crossman pointed out that the Irish Republic had also been a racket operated from America, but that Britain had been forced to concede a state. "Yes," Bevin replied, "but they did not steal half the place first." Referring to the latest Etzel outrage, the foreign secretary added that he would not be surprised if the Germans had learned their worst atrocities from Jews. From this discussion Crossman sadly concluded that Bevin was insane on the Palestine issue.

If concern for Arab goodwill and personal vindictiveness both were factors, so was London's evaluation of Palestine's future, now that the mandate was ending. The likelihood of an Arab military triumph was hardly remote. The opportunity, therefore, to return to Palestine in unofficial association with the Arabs, particularly with Britain's treaty partner, Abdullah of

Transjordan, was worth safeguarding. Years later, Edward Francis-Williams, one of the foreign secretary's closest advisers, revealed that Bevin had predicted an Arab military victory in the developing hostilities, and an appeal to the British by the Jews to intervene on their behalf, with the result being a partition of Palestine in which the Jews would control neither Haifa nor the Negev. These were the sites Britain's military general staff urgently coveted in the event of a withdrawal from Egypt; it was hoped that they could be regained afterward by treaty arrangements with Abdullah. On December 17, Bevin warned Marshall that the Jews would get their "throats cut." The foreign secretary's appraisal was entirely shared by British military leaders. In March of 1948, with hostilities now begun, Field Marshal Montgomery offered his opinion that "the Jews had bought it"—that they were unable to protect their lines of communication. The reports of British officers in Jerusalem, Amman, and Cairo sustained this view. The following month General Sir Gordon Macmillan, commander of British forces in Palestine, stated flatly that the Arab armies "would have no difficulty in taking over the whole country."

It was therefore in Britain's interest to refuse help to a scheme that in any case appeared likely to founder against Arab resistance. On the contrary, a policy of deliberate chaos would serve Whitehall as a means of returning to influence in Palestine. The British undoubtedly had this aim in mind in removing Palestine from the sterling bloc and freezing its currency balances in London, a measure that threatened to bankrupt the embryonic Jewish state at the outset. Not a penny was left in the Palestine treasury for a successor regime. In February 1948 the one financial concession that was approved for the post-mandate period was an appropriation of £300,000 for the Supreme Moslem Council, equivalent to an indirect subsidy of the Arab war effort. As the British relinquished their hold, moreover, the railroads ceased to run and the post office gradually stopped functioning; the local inhabitants of Palestine were barred from operating these facilities until the British evacuated.

The single most notable feature of mandatory noncooperation by late 1947 was Britain's undisguised partiality for the Arab military effort. The embargo on Jewish immigration and Jewish weapons acquisition was stringently maintained. The Jews were denied the right to organize a militia. Haganah members were disarmed wherever they were found. All the while, Britain continued to sell weapons to Iraq and Transjordan under its treaty relations with those states. With 50,000 troops at his disposal in Palestine, General Macmillan could have easily and swiftly throttled Arab infiltration. Yet, under orders, he limited all attempts to maintain law and security to the areas held by British troops during evacuation. Occasionally, pro-Arab bias took the form of overt support. For example, having almost completed the sale to the Jews of Sarafand, the largest army camp in Palestine, Macmillan received instructions from London that the installation must instead be sold to the Arabs. The identical procedure was followed with strategically placed fortresses and other government property up and down the country.

General Taha Hashimi, an Iraqi general charged with training Arab volunteers in Damascus, told in his *Mudhakkarat 'an al-Harb* (War Memoirs) of Arab leaders receiving detailed advance notice of Britain's schedule for evacuating the police stations of Safed and Nebi Yusha. Both these stockades were immediately occupied by Arab irregulars. In this manner, too, the fortress of Samakh and the large army camp nearby were turned over to the Arabs. By Hashimi's account, the British deputy police commander in Jerusalem alerted the Arabs to the impending military evacuation from the New City, to facilitate their occupation the moment the British departed. The Jaffa attorney Muhammad Nimr al-Hawari recalled that "members of the British Office for Arab Affairs came to me offering help, in arms and men. . . . The British were distributing arms and ammunition to our fighting men on the field and in the streets. This was a secret to no one." Christopher Sykes provides an unsparing evaluation of the British mandate in its concluding phase: "When one compares the British and French records in protectorate administration, the advantage . . . is strongly in favour of the British, but there is nothing in the French record in next-door Syria comparable in mischievous incompetence to the British record in Palestine from November 1947 to May 1948."

The initial Arab response to the Partition Resolution was to carry out their oft-repeated threat of violence. It set the pattern for the months and years ahead. In Aleppo, Syria, three hundred Jewish homes and eleven synagogues were burned to the ground, and half the city's four thousand Jews fled elsewhere. At Aden, seventy-six Jews were killed. In Palestine itself the Arab Higher Committee proclaimed a three-day general strike from December 2 to December 4, 1947. Violence began immediately with attacks on Jewish quarters in Jerusalem, Haifa, and Jaffa. Soon after, the Higher Committee began recruiting volunteers throughout Palestine Arab towns and villages. Most of the ensuing "militias" were organized around the nucleus of the Futuwwa and Najjada societies. Their opening tactics were essentially hit-and-run assaults on isolated Jewish settlements and transportation, and the pillage and destruction of Jewish property. The attacks were launched entirely by Palestine Arabs, although part of the funds and some military equipment came from neighboring Arab countries. Offensive planning at this stage was quite uncoordinated, even on a local basis. Frequently it was impeded by the lingering hostility between the Nashashibi and Husseini factions.

In the weeks immediately following the Partition Resolution, a number of moderate Arab leaders interceded with the mandatory government and with leaders of the two national communities to avoid bloodshed. One of these was Hawari, who had begun his public career as a Mufti partisan (p. 272), but who later became increasingly disenchanted with Husseini terror tactics. "The question is, was I a traitor in this struggle?" asked Hawari. "Could I incite the people of Palestine to engage in a war they could not fight?" Convinced that the spread of violence would end in disaster for his people, the Arab lawyer met frequently with Jewish authorities. "In many instances, I succeeded in avoiding clashes between Arabs and

Jews. We initiated a successful effort to convince our people that it was to our advantage to coexist peacefully with the Jewish people." Hawari did not exaggerate. Left to their own devices, Arabs and Jews for the most part continued to live together peacefully, if fearfully. The Higher Committee's violence alone would not have precipitated a full-scale war between the two peoples.

But the Palestine Arabs and Jews were not left alone. During the September 16, 1947, meeting at Sofar, Lebanon (p. 285), the Arab League Political Committee appealed for economic reprisals against Britain and the United States, and for money and weapons for the Palestine Arabs. Three weeks later the group met again in the Lebanese town of Alay, this time to organize a military committee of Arab states. At first the decision on armed intervention was put off. After the United Nations vote, however, the fiery Iraqi prime minister, Salih Jabr, took the initiative once again in calling a meeting of Arab premiers in Cairo, on December 12, 1947. By then Salih Jabr wanted no further procrastination. He insisted that the secret decisions of the Bludan conference (p. 315) be put into immediate effect, that the Arab countries now move to intervene directly in Palestine. The proposal was still too far-reaching for the Egyptian and Saudi governments. Abdullah of Transjordan disliked even the notion of volunteers. Yet a compromise plan eventually was adopted to supply the League's military committee with 10,000 rifles and other light weapons, to arrange for the passage of 3,000 Arab volunteers through Syria into Palestine, and to supply £1 million toward the cost of the "defense of Palestine."

These were the circumstances in which the "Arab Liberation Army" was organized. General Sir Ismail Safwat Pasha, an Iraqi staff officer, was appointed its commander in chief and promptly established his headquarters at a Syrian military camp on the outskirts of Damascus. Field command of this ostensibly volunteer force was invested in the redoubtable Fawzi al-Qawukji, guerrilla leader of the Palestine civil war of 1936. Following his participation in the Vichy defense of Syria in 1941, Qawukji had escaped to Germany, where he lived until the end of the war. In 1945 he was granted sanctuary in France (together with the Mufti and other Arab enemies of Britain) and eventually made his way back to Syria. Most of his "volunteers" now actually were mercenaries from Syria, combined with a scattering of Yugoslav Moslems, Circassians from the Caucasus, a few Poles from the Anders Army, some German SS veterans, and a few Spanish Falangists. In late January 1948 elements of the Liberation Army began infiltrating over the Palestine border. Soon afterward Qawukji transferred his headquarters to Tiberias, in north-central Palestine, and almost immediately set about moving larger detachments of men into the country, until by the end of February they numbered 5,000, and by the end of March, 7,000. In contrast to the Mufti's undisciplined gangs, these non-Palestinian units lent their Arab billet communities a certain protection and security.

By early spring of 1948 the guerrillas had divided Palestine into fronts.

The northern sector of the country, with 7,000 men, remained under the personal command of Qawukji and of the Syrian Adib al-Shishakli. The central sector was held by 5,000 men, the largest number of them the Higher Committee's irregulars under the command of Abd al-Qadr al-Husseini, a nephew of the Mufti. The southern "front," comprising the entire Negev, was given over to a fluctuating number of about 2,000 Moslem Brotherhood volunteers from Egypt. It was by no means a tightly organized military force. With superiority in numbers, nevertheless, Arab operations at least became more extensive by the winter and early spring of 1948. Assaults were launched against Jewish quarters in the cities, particularly in Jerusalem. There were concentrated attacks against outlying kibbutzim in the Hebron hills. Far from interfering with these Arab military activities, the British turned over their police fortresses to the guerrillas. As a result, the Arabs succeeded during this period in cutting the roads between Tel Aviv and Jerusalem, between Haifa and western Galilee, between Tiberias and eastern Galilee, and between Afula and the Beisan Valley. Jewish farm colonies in the Negev soon were isolated from the rest of Palestine.

In Jerusalem the situation of the Jews was particularly grave, as relief columns moving along the highway from the lowlands were systematically decimated by ambushes in the hills. Prohibited by the British from bringing in ammunition, from organizing their reserves and defending their communications openly, the Jews faced the grimmest period of their struggle for independence in these spring months. By the end of March 1948, as the gauntlet of Arab fusillades from the hill areas became increasingly lethal, the entire Haganah convoy system was in danger of collapse. By then, too, the three roads leading to Jerusalem were in the hands of Arab irregulars, and the Jewish population of the city faced the imminent likelihood of being starved or overrun.

The Zionists had not foreseen the speed with which they would be thrown on their own, politically or militarily. Nor, preoccupied with their campaign against the British, had they anticipated the gravity of the Arab military threat. The only Jewish forces immediately available throughout 1947 were the Palmach, a standing group of approximately 3,000 youths, some 5,000 ill-armed Etzel "troops," and a scattering of perhaps 800 to 1,000 Lech'i members. The Haganah reserves, numbering about 21,000 by March 1948, were only partially trained and quite ill-equipped. Indeed, weapons even more than manpower now became the priority for the Jewish Agency. As early as the summer of 1945, Ben-Gurion had traveled to New York to raise several million dollars for the purchase of surplus American arms machinery. The equipment was acquired, dismantled, and its 75,000 parts shipped to Palestine as "textile machinery." Yet, hidden as they were in kibbutz underground warehouses, the parts could not be assembled until the British left Palestine. Other weapons were purchased in Europe in isolated odd lots: a dozen rifles here, fifty there, three machine guns elsewhere. There was little standardization among them.

Strategic planning had also to be improvised quickly. In late 1947, once the United Nations decision for partition was assured, the Haganah leadership concentrated on two major objectives. The first was the security of the Yishuv against local Arab forces during the half-year period of British withdrawal. The second was defense of the country against a possible full-scale Arab invasion after May 15. The initial phase was the more difficult of the two. It was based on the decision taken by Ben-Gurion and the Agency Executive to hold every square mile of territory allocated to the future Jewish state. In the long term, the commitment was an inescapable one for the Zionists: withdrawal in the immediate aftermath of the UN Resolution would have been politically disastrous. But in the short run the decision was to prove exceptionally costly; for its implications were that Haganah forces would have to be dispersed in small units throughout Palestine rather than concentrated in strength. It also meant that supply convoys would be obliged to move through Arab-controlled territory, where they would run the certain risk of ambush. Galilee and the Negev, for example, were mainly Arab. So were Jaffa, Ramle, Lydda, and Acre. Haifa and Jerusalem were divided. The Jewish enclaves in this territory would somehow have to be provisioned. Initially, therefore, the Haganah command was obliged to think in terms of static defense, avoiding military action against Arab population centers even for the most compelling strategic reasons. The British would have blocked any other move.

PARTITION IN JEOPARDY

In its endorsement of the Partition Resolution, the United States government had counted on a swift, surgical division of Palestine. But now, with the escalation of hostilities, it appeared that this gamble had failed. No sooner, in fact, was the resolution approved than State Department officials began discreetly qualifying their government's pro-Zionist stance. Early in December 1947, Washington suspended the licensing of arms shipments to the Middle East. On the twenty-second of the month Loy Henderson turned down the request of Eliezer Kaplan, treasurer of the Jewish Agency, who had come from Palestine to request a $500-million American loan to help settle immigrants. Henderson's State Department colleague, Gordon Merriam, noted afterward: "It is inconceivable that Congress or the Eximbank would now provide funds for the purpose of setting up an economic and immigration regime on a shaky, indigent basis . . . to carry forward an unsuccessful investment."

Arab pressure on Washington and on American oil companies lent weight to the argument that partition must now be quietly dropped. On January 6, 1948, Secretary of Defense Forrestal met with the president of the Socony Vacuum Company. The latter regretfully declared that, as a consequence of the Palestine unrest, his company and other associated oil corporations were suspending work on the pipeline in Saudi Arabia. Forrestal's shock was compounded on February 21, when the Arab League tentatively agreed to deny American firms pipeline rights until the United

States altered its Palestine policy. Syrian Prime Minister Jamil Mirdam Bey announced his intention of visiting Riyadh in the hope of inducing Ibn Saud to take punitive steps against Aramco.

Temporarily free of White House interference, then, and assured of the tacit support of Secretary Marshall, State Department officials became increasingly evasive on the question of partition. On January 21, Undersecretary Robert Lovett showed Forrestal a document recently prepared by the State Department planning staff. It concluded that partition was unworkable, that the United States was not obliged to support this measure if it could be made to work only through force, and that the American government should now seek cancellation or, at least, postponement of the United Nations Resolution. In ensuing weeks, Henderson and his group at the Near East desk elaborated upon this theme with increasing persistence and urgency. Eventually it won the approbation of Marshall. Thus, on February 24, Warren Austin, the American ambassador to the Security Council, asked his fellow delegates to consider whether there did not exist in Palestine a threat to international peace and security. He then declared his government's willingness in principle to consider the use of armed force for the sake of restoring peace, but not to enforce partition.

The Zionist leadership, watching breathlessly for a clue to American intentions, recognized the magnitude of the policy shift here. They exerted every effort now to persuade the administration to resume its original line. But in mobilizing their supporters throughout the United States, the Zionists very nearly alienated their most dependable ally, the president himself. Truman recalled:

> The Jewish pressure on the White House did not diminish in the days following the partition vote in the U.N. Individuals and groups asked me, usually in rather quarrelsome and emotional ways, to stop the Arabs, to keep the British from supporting the Arabs, to furnish American soldiers, to do this, that, and the other. I think I can say that I kept faith in the rightness of my policy in spite of some of the Jews. . . . As the pressure mounted, I found it necessary to give instructions that I did not want to be approached by any more spokesmen for the extreme Zionist cause.

The spokesman most intent upon seeing the president at this juncture was Weizmann, who to that end had just made the 6,000-mile trip from Palestine. Truman at first was unwilling to receive him. In a somewhat incongruous episode, however, he was persuaded to change his mind through the intercession of Edward Jacobson, a Kansas City Jewish merchant who had been Truman's business partner years before. Weizmann was brought in through a side entrance of the White House on March 18. The discussion lasted nearly an hour and was cordial. Weizmann's unfailing dignity and charm, in marked contrast to the near-hysteria of the American Zionists, had their effect on the president. "I told him, as plainly as I could," Truman wrote, "why I had at first put off seeing him. He understood. I explained to him what the basis of my interest in the Jewish problem was and that my primary concern was to see justice done without bloodshed. And when he left my office I felt that he had received a full understanding of my policy and that I knew what it was he wanted."

On March 19, one day after the Truman-Weizmann "understanding," Warren Austin dropped a bombshell in the Security Council by recommending that partition be suspended. "There seems to be general agreement that the plan cannot now be implemented by peaceful means," the ambassador explained. He proposed instead that the General Assembly be convened in special session to consider the establishment of a temporary trusteeship over Palestine "without prejudice . . . to the character of the eventual settlement." This announcement horrified the Zionists. Their response to the United States was to deluge the president with wires and petitions, to organize large and angry parades of American Jewish war veterans. On March 23 the Jewish Agency Executive cabled Washington that the Zionists would oppose with all their strength any postponement of Jewish independence. Only Weizmann appeared to retain his faith in the American president. "I do not believe that President Truman knew what was going to happen in the United Nations on Friday when he talked to me the day before," he told Jacobson. This interpretation was at least partly correct. Truman had known of Austin's statement in advance. Surprised and embarrassed, however, by the timing, if not the content of the proposal, he immediately ordered Clark Clifford, a political adviser, "to find out how this could have happened. I assured Chaim Weizmann that we were for partition and would stick to it. He must think I am a plain liar."

Actually, the State Department, without being privy to Truman's conversation with Weizmann, had interpreted the president's recent silence on Palestine as approval for a gradual shift of policy. Endorsing the long-held views of Henderson, Merriam, and other Foreign Service professionals, Secretary Marshall had authorized the trusteeship proposal in an official memorandum to his United Nations delegation. When Truman learned of this development, he spoke by long-distance telephone to the secretary of state, who was in San Francisco. Marshall apparently convinced the president that a trusteeship was regarded as an interim expedient until the fighting died down, not a repudiation of partition. Yet it is doubtful by then if government officials, aside from the president himself, were contemplating simply a postponement. Dean Rusk, recently appointed chief of the State Department's United Nations division, called a news conference and vigorously defended the trusteeship plan. His language referred to the scheme as "temporary," but the overtones of cancellation were not hard to discern.

The proposal was received badly by other delegations. More than their governments, these diplomats viewed "postponement" as a serious blow to the authority of the United Nations. Trygve Lie, secretary-general of the world body, was aggrieved enough to suggest to Austin that both of them resign as a gesture of protest (the American refused). Ironically, Bevin himself was now hostile to the trusteeship plan. He suspected that Washington's *volte-face* would lead ultimately to a request for extending the mandate, and developments in Palestine had convinced him that such an extension was out of the question. Jewish underground activity had not abated. Since passage of the Partition Resolution, in fact, the Lech'i had intensified its attacks on mandatory forces and installations. Hardly a day passed without an incident of anti-British violence. It was becoming apparent, too, that Washington had no clear notion of the way a trusteeship could be put into effect. On March 29, Forrestal admitted to Lovett that American troops were unavailable, although he did not see how the United States "could avoid making an effort to contribute." Lovett then spoke to Truman, who said "he did not want to make any firm commitment to send troops into Palestine."

The lack of international enthusiasm for the American plan was increasingly evident in the United Nations. At the Security Council meeting on March 30, Austin pointedly avoided making reference any longer to a trusteeship. He spoke now merely of seeking a truce between Arabs and Jews and of the need for a special session of the General Assembly to consider an interim government for Palestine. On April 1, the Security Council approved this innocuous suggestion. When the General Assembly convened two weeks later, scarcely a month was left before the British mandate expired, and these final proceedings took on an air of unreality. "A strange lethargy overtook the United Nations," recalled Jorge Garcia Granados, the Guatemalan delegate. "War continued in Palestine but nothing seemed to move at [the United Nations]." On May 3 the sentiment of the Assembly was expressed by Creech-Jones, who proposed that the United Nations drop the American plan entirely and appoint a "neutral" authority to do what it could to maintain administrative and public services in Palestine. It was another way of saying that partition already was in effect.

THE JEWS FORCE THE ISSUE

With their military position crumbling badly, the Jews in late March 1948 embarked on a desperate effort to provision their beleaguered communities in Jerusalem and the Galilee. The rescue operation failed; the Arabs annihilated the convoys. It was accordingly at this moment that a painful decision was taken. On April 1 the Haganah commander of operations, Yigael Yadin, met with Ben-Gurion and the latter's advisers to report that the Arab guerrillas were strangling the Yishuv. It was impossible any longer, Yadin said, to rely on passive defense and isolated convoys to supply Jerusalem and the outlying Jewish settlements. The one remaining alternative was for the Haganah to go on the offensive, immediately to seize control of Palestine's interior road network, as well as the country's important heights. The operation would require the capture of all Arab towns dominating vital arteries and communications, something entirely new in the Haganah tradition. The gamble was a quite frantic one, for the danger of inadequate manpower and weapons was compounded by the likelihood of pitched battle with the British. The exodus of mandatory forces was going forward according to plan; yet there was no way of predicting General Macmillan's reaction to a full-scale Jewish military campaign. The Zionist cabinet debated the proposal for three hours. It was Ben-Gurion who forced the issue.

No decision Ben-Gurion later took, to declare the State of Israel, or even to invade Sinai in 1956, was fraught with profounder risks. His willingness to face them revealed the true dimensions of the man's tenacity and boldness. Only then, in fact, did the Jewish Agency chairman become a household name outside Palestine itself. Yet no Jew alive had been more fully identified with the Yishuv than Ben-Gurion—since the moment, in 1906, of his arrival in Jaffa harbor from Poland as a nineteen-year-old youth named David Green. From then on, every facet of his career reflected a stage in the history of the Zionist redemptive effort. In the years before 1914 he labored as a farmhand in the citrus groves. During World War I he served in the Jewish Legion. After the war he became a leader of Achdut HaAvodah (later Mapai), then a secretary-general of the Histadrut. In 1935 he was elected chairman of the Palestine Executive of the Jewish Agency and found himself thrown willy-nilly into the world of statecraft.

Ben-Gurion was no suave diplomat in the Weizmann manner. At heart he remained the tough union leader, as forceful and outspoken as Bevin, yet even more stubborn. He looked the militant role he was to play: short, stocky, his hands still callused, his face hard and weather-beaten, with a granitic chin thrusting belligerently forward. His colleagues remembered a singleminded devotion to the cause of the Jewish National Home that approached fanaticism, a total disinterest in material comforts, and a lack of personal vanity that was not to be confused with indifference to authority. Certain in his mind where the fate of the Yishuv lay, Ben-Gurion was determined to ensure his nation's security against any opposition and any odds. It was with this approach that he browbeat the members of the Jewish shadow government into approving the plan to clear the Palestine interior.

Weapons were the initial priority. Several days before, Ben-Gurion had cabled Ehud Avriel, his Haganah agent in Prague, ordering a shipment of rifles and machine guns to be flown in immediately. On the night of April 1, the first Dakota transport plane arrived from Czechoslovakia at an abandoned British airstrip in the south of Palestine. The plane's cargo was immediately unloaded and the arms distributed among neighboring farm settlements. Two days later a ship arrived secretly off a coastal inlet with additional Czech weapons, including a few hundred machine guns and additional thousands of rifles. The recruits were then sent into action to break the Arab grip on the Jerusalem road.

Even as the Jews made preparations for their offensive, they found an ally in Arab factiousness. Hawari later recalled that the purchasing agents of the Arab League's military committee bought weapons at cut-rate prices in Cairo, then sold them to the Palestinians for exorbitant profits. A number of these dealers made fortunes out of the arms traffic. Not uncommonly, too, their guns were inferior in quality (although not to Jewish weaponry) or of World War I registry. At the same time, the Mufti was determined to retain effective personal control over all Arab forces in Palestine. It was then that the rivalry between himself and Fawzi al-Qawukji, commander of the Arab Liberation Army, became noticeably acute. "Qawukji confided to me," wrote Hawari, "how the Mufti had accused him, while in Europe, of spying for Britain . . . and of drinking wine and running after women and therefore, he, Qawukji, did not deserve to be the general of the Army of Liberation." Yet the Arab rulers by and large favored Qawukji and often provided him with handsome payments and gifts. Incensed at this favoritism, Haj Amin simply undertook to operate on his own, and appointed his personal lieutenants as commanders in various parts of the country. He did a bad job of it. His officers failed to impose general conscription among the Palestine Arabs. As a result, the local defense forces were all volunteers, most of them irregulars operating without central direction or discipline. While not unsuccessful in the 1936 civil war, this rough-and-ready approach lost much of its effect when matched against growing Jewish organization.

The conflict between Qawukji and the Husseinis intensified during the early spring of 1948. The former preferred to exclude all Palestine Arabs from his ranks. "They can blow up a bridge here and there," explained one of his officers to the press, "but for military operations they simply get in the way." General Safwat Pasha, the League-appointed commander of Arab forces in Palestine, complained that the indiscipline of the Mufti's bands was undermining the entire military operation against the Jews. The earlier division of authority continued. The Liberation Army maintained responsibility in the northern part of the country, in loose cooperation with the Syrian general, Shishakli, who was assigned the Galilee front. Central Palestine, as has been seen, was reserved for the Mufti, whose nephew, Abd al-Qadr al-Husseini, was placed in command of Jerusalem and the Hebron mountains; while Hassan Salamah, another Husseini partisan, directed operations in the coastal area. Yet even with this understanding, coordination among the various groups remained poor. The Mufti's troops acted on their own, ignoring the directives of the Arab League. Mutinies and desertions, often of entire units, were not uncommon among both Qawukji's followers and the Mufti's. "One city or village may fall to the enemy while the next village stands idle and careless," wrote one participant. "Each faction operates separately and independently of the others." Safwat warned the League that "if the situation is not changed, general headquarters will become an empty farce." The factional hostility became so bitter that a tacit understanding actually was reached between Qawukji and the Haganah for the Arab Liberation Army to refrain from supporting Abd al-Qadr if the Jews attacked on the Jerusalem front. This private agreement was soon to be put into effect.

The Zionist operation to break the Arab grip on the Jerusalem highway comprised 1,500 Haganah men, much larger than any Jewish force thrown into action before. The newly arrived Czech weapons were now to be put to their first use. The offensive began with an attack on the mountain fortress of Castel, only five miles west of Jerusalem. During the vicious fighting, Abd al-Qadr telephoned Fawzi al-Qawukji for arms. Qawukji's answer (intercepted by the Haganah) was: "Ma'fish"—I have not any! In fact he had plenty, but was not about to share them. Soon afterward Abd al-Qadr was killed—in the act of surrender—and the village fell to the Jews. Enough of the road was then captured to enable the Haganah to rush three large convoys of some 250 vehicles into Jerusalem. The Arabs reimposed a stranglehold on the highway within days, but the relief supplies enabled the city's Jewish population to hold out for the next few weeks.

Toward the end of April, the British markedly increased the tempo of their evacuation. Although they continued to provide the Arabs with advance notice of their withdrawal, the Haganah by then had also succeeded in capturing its share of police fortresses and abandoned army camps. The most decisive coup in this period took place in Haifa, a city of mixed population. It was known that the British intended to leave on April 18, and both sides prepared for battle. The Arabs comprised a slight majority of the city's 150,000 inhabitants, but lacked effective leadership. On the other hand, the Jews for the first time enjoyed the strategic advantage. Their population was concentrated on the slopes of the mountain city, while the Arabs were located essentially in the lower port area. The Haganah also learned the routes of eleven arriving Arab arms convoys and ambushed nine of them. By mid-morning of the twenty-first, after a day and a half of intermittent shooting, several hundred Jewish troops descended suddenly from the Carmel heights and wrested control of Haifa's major buildings and crossroads. The Arab population of the city fled soon afterward (Chapter xiii).

The Jews' offensive tactics clearly were succeeding. Yet the Arabs maintained their advantage in the upper Galilee. As the British withdrew in the last weeks of April, twenty Jewish farm communities on the northern valley floors were exposed to mounting pressure from surrounding Arab forces in the hills. Accordingly, the Haganah operation to relieve this siege was entrusted to Yigal Allon, a twenty-nine-year-old native-born Palestinian and perhaps the ablest field commander of the Jewish defense forces. In a calculated gamble, Allon stripped all the Galilee kibbutz settlements of their arms and turned the weapons over to his troops. His force of a thousand Palmach youths then advanced on the key British police fortress and army camp near Rosh Pina, investing these sites before the Arabs could move in. Safed was the next objective. The circumstances of the 1,400 native Jews in this remote little mountain community, surrounded by 10,000 Arabs, were altogether desperate. Syrian mercenaries, operating under the command of Adib al-Shishakli, were tightening their vise on the Jewish quarter. Neighbors who had lived together in peace for decades were now furiously at each other's throats. On the night of May 9–10 Allon's troops launched their offensive, engaging in house-to-house and room-to-room fighting. The Arab military position was hardly untenable, for Shishakli's men outnumbered Allon's. But their morale cracked first under the pressure of close-quarter combat, and the irregulars fled, together with the rest of the Arab inhabitants.

The fall of Safed was a defeat of considerable magnitude for the Arabs. Over the generations the mountain fortress had been the administrative center of northeastern Palestine. Indeed, from his field headquarters in nearby Tyre, Lebanon, the Mufti had designated Safed as the capital of his future Arab state of the Galilee. Its capture now by the Jews became the signal for most of the Arabs in the surrounding area to flee to Lebanon and Syria. Communications between the Jewish settlements in eastern Galilee were restored for the first time in months. Northern Palestine was virtually cleared. So was the coastal plain. Its one remaining Arab city, Jaffa, was captured by the Jews on May 14; the local Arab population of 70,000 fled in terror (Chapter XIII). In this manner, the Haganah was freed of the responsibility of protecting isolated Jewish enclaves and was able now to concentrate on the anticipated May 15 invasion by the neighboring Arab armies.

On the evening of April 22, 1948, as the Jews consolidated their victory in Haifa, Bevin telephoned Attlee at Downing Street. The foreign secretary was in a state of panic. The newspaper reports from the Arab capitals, he said, told of the Jews massacring 23,000 Arabs in Haifa while the British had stood by and done nothing. Bevin complained that the army had "let him down" and placed him in an impossible position with the Arabs. Attlee immediately summoned Field Marshal Montgomery, then army chief of staff. Bevin arrived at the same time, as did Field Marshal Alexander, the war secretary. Montgomery wrote later that "Bevin was very worked up," and Attlee was inclined to support him. Early the next morning, the four men met again, and the foreign secretary, by Montgomery's recollection, "was even more agitated." Matters clearly were not going as Bevin had intended. In order to salvage Arab goodwill, therefore, the government began urgently reformulating its policy. On April 23, Creech-Jones proposed to the General Assembly that the United Nations now aim at a "more modest objective" than partition, without seeking to arrive at a final solution of the Arab-Jewish conflict. The British would cooperate in the effort. But it was too late by then, as Creech-Jones himself would admit only ten days later. The Jews had established a new military reality in Palestine.

They had moved far toward establishing a new political reality, as well. No one took seriously any longer Bevin's statement, issued in late March, that the British were responsible for "law and order" in Palestine until the mandate expired. "Law and order" plainly were the opposite of the mandatory's intention. In the ensuing chaos the inhabitants of Palestine experienced an almost total stoppage of public services: of law courts, post offices, telephone exchanges, rail transportation. It was to fill this administrative vacuum and to lay the groundwork for the Jewish state that, in early spring, a Jewish interparty committee appointed a provisional Zionist Council of State, under the chairmanship of Ben-Gurion. In a series of emergency meetings, the body's thirteen-member Council of Government —an embryonic cabinet—agreed that all taxes in the Jewish sector would be collected on the same basis as before, that Jewish Agency and Va'ad Le'umi officials would remain at their posts with their former quasi-official functions now transformed into ministerial responsibilities. Offices were commandeered for a temporary capital in north Tel Aviv, office equipment was foraged, and secretaries and clerks were recruited from throughout the Yishuv. A national loan was authorized, a manpower and supplies directorate organized. On April 27, the Haganah and Etzel signed an agreement of full cooperation. At the last minute a printer's shop in Tel Aviv even managed to run off a design for postage stamps, and paper currency was also printed. Actually the typical Palestine Jew did not require these legal verifications from the national administration, and did not ask for them. The habits of communal discipline, inculcated through years of Zionist settlement, remained intact.

The achievement of Jewish state-building was in marked contrast to the almost total dissolution of the Palestine Arab community. Perhaps the British had believed that chaos in Palestine would affect only the Jews and not harm the Arabs—or, at least, encourage the Arab population's hope for redemption through Abdullah of Transjordan. But in the final weeks of the mandate everything seemed to be going wrong. Administrative pandemonium was giving the Jews a decisive advantage. The Higher Committee thereupon issued a belated, rather panic-stricken appeal for all Arab civil servants in the collapsing mandatory administration to remain at their posts; supervisory jurisdiction in each district would be exercised by the Mufti's local agents. Too much precious time had elapsed for this kind of innovation, however. Nor was the Arab exodus alone responsible for aborting the plan. During the entire mandatory period, Arab leaders had refused to cooperate with the British in any scheme of national autonomy as long as the Jews were similarly included. They were now to pay for their unbudging stand. The Arabs possessed nothing comparable to the Jewish quasi-government. At no time had the Supreme Moslem Council or the Arab Higher Committee ever served as more than organs for propaganda or violence. Neither organization had provided administrative training or governmental experience. For the tradition-bound Arab community, therefore, the moment of reckoning had arrived at last. It was to be a flight of such unprecedented proportions that the Arab leadership was incapable either of organizing or of inhibiting it (Chapter XIII). Indeed, the leadership itself was the first to take refuge in neighboring lands. The Husseinis and the Nashashibis were precisely the intellectual and political elite who were absent when the Palestinians needed them most.

THE BIRTH OF ISRAEL

These developments did not go unremarked in Washington. While abandoning the ill-fated trusteeship scheme, the State Department intensified its efforts to avoid a full-blown war in the Middle East. In early May 1948, Assistant Secretary of State Dean Rusk entreated the Zionists at least to postpone their declaration of independence. If they did not, the threat was implicit that Washington might block the transfer of American Jewish philanthropic funds to the Jewish state. This veiled warning made a strong impression on Dr. Nahum Goldmann, chairman of the Agency's American section, who thereafter worked closely with State Department officials in an effort to delay the proclamation of sovereignty. Ben-Gurion and his colleagues in Jerusalem refused to be budged, however, particularly in an American election year. On May 4 they sent Rusk a cable of refusal. Four days later Moshe Shertok, foreign minister in the Jewish provisional administration, flew to Washington to meet with Marshall and Undersecretary of State Lovett. The Americans uttered no threats. Yet they predicted that the Arab regular armies would invade, and "if the Jews persisted in their course, they must not seek the help of the United States in the event of an invasion." Far from appearing intimidated, Shertok tersely scored the Americans for having failed to maintain their support of the Partition Resolution. Much of the bloodshed in Palestine could be attributed to the equivocation of the United States government, he insisted, for it had encouraged the Arabs in their belligerence. At this point Marshall terminated the conference with a warning:

> I shall remember all that you have said. I fully appreciate the weight of these considerations. It is not for me to advise you what to do. But I want to tell you as a military man: don't rely on your military advisers. They have just scored some success. What will happen if there is a prolonged invasion? It will weaken you. I have had experience in China. At first there was an easy victory. Now they've been fighting two years and they've lost Manchuria. However, if it turns out that you're right and you will establish the Jewish State, I'll be happy. But you are undertaking a grave responsibility.

In fact, Shertok took the warning seriously. With Goldmann's support, he told his Zionist colleagues in New York that Marshall's words at least deserved much thought.

The gravity of the decision was made equally plain by Yigael Yadin in Tel Aviv. The young officer gave his report on May 12, in a lengthy meeting with Ben-Gurion and other members of the national administration. Haganah troops had won control of Palestine's interior lines of communication, Yadin explained. The situation in Jerusalem nevertheless remained extremely critical, for the Arabs dominated half the city, together with all the surrounding high ground and road network, including vital stretches of the highway from the coast. At that very moment, units of Transjordan's British-trained Arab Legion were converging on Jerusalem along most of these arteries. Additionally, the Legion had just succeeded in overwhelming and capturing the Ezion bloc of kibbutz settlements between Jerusalem and Hebron. Yadin pointed out that the shortage of equipment was no less serious. Even with supplies from Czechoslovakia, no artillery whatever had yet arrived. It was known that the Arab armies possessed large quantities of British guns, some of which already were shelling Jerusalem with devastating effect. When the invasion came, the Arabs plainly would outnumber the Jews in manpower and in the quantity and quality of weapons. On the other hand, Yadin noted, the British were evacuating, and full-scale Jewish mobilization was now possible. More important, the Jews possessed the morale, the tactical ability, and the planning and military experience the Arabs lacked. Presumably manpower and weapons would be coming in after May 15. If these could be distributed and integrated swiftly, the chances of a successful defense were even. Yadin personally was inclined to be cautious, however, and wished that a truce might still be possible without sacrificing political objectives.

After discussing the pros and cons through the night, the Jewish cabinet voted six to four to reject the American proposal for a truce and to proceed with the declaration of the state. Contacted by phone in New York, Weizmann endorsed the decision: "Proclaim the State, no matter what happens," he said. Two days later the die was cast. At eight o'clock on the morning of May 14, the British lowered the Union Jack in Jerusalem. By mid-afternoon full-scale fighting had erupted throughout the country. The Jews mounted a new offensive to relieve Jerusalem, while elsewhere in Palestine bitter struggles were going on for the last evacuated Taggart fortresses. At 4:00 P.M. the Jewish population, except for Jerusalem, which was without electricity, heard the proclamation ceremonies as they were broadcast from the Tel Aviv Museum. Ben-Gurion read the Declaration of Independence of the State of Israel. It notified the world that the Land of Israel was the historic birthplace of the Jewish people, that the Zionist movement was testimony to the role Palestine had fulfilled in Jewish history and religion, that the Balfour Declaration, the United Nations Partition Resolution, the sacrifice of the Zionist pioneers, and the torment suffered by Jews in recent years—all had laid the moral and legal foundations for the new state. Israel, it was announced, would be open to all Jews who wished to enter, would extend social and political equality to all its citizens without distinction of religion, race, or sex, and would guarantee freedom of religion, conscience, education, and culture to all. On the eve of the Arab invasion, the authors of the declaration issued a final plea: "We extend our hand in peace and neighborliness to all the neighboring states and their peoples, and invite them to cooperate with the independent Jewish nation for the common good of all. The State of Israel is prepared to make its contribution to the progress of the Middle East as a whole." Immediately after adopting the Declaration of Independence, the Council of State unanimously passed an ordinance abolishing the White Paper of 1939.

Two days earlier, on May 12, a letter from Weizmann had arrived at the White House asking the United States government to recognize Israel when it came into existence shortly. The appeal reached the mark. Truman had been uneasy in recent weeks at the State Department's equivocation on partition. On April 23 he had told Judge Samuel Rosenman: "I have Dr. Weizmann on my conscience." There was a certain pathos in Truman's eagerness to regain Weizmann's respect. Now, on May 12, Truman discussed the issue with his advisers. He personally favored recognition. Marshall and Lovett did not. After lengthy discussion and further consideration, Truman eventually made up his mind on May 14 to extend de facto recognition to the State of Israel. The announcement was issued at 6:10 P.M. of the same day. "The old doctor will believe me now," the president murmured.

Political considerations unquestionably influenced Truman's gesture. There was a national election approaching, and the votes of the major urban communities could be decisive. The president must also have appreciated the importance of anticipating action by Moscow. The Soviets, whose recognition of Israel was expected momentarily (it came two days later), hardly deserved a monopoly on Jewish gratitude, after all. But at the same time there were personal qualities of tenacity and stubbornness that welled out of Truman's character. He wrote later: "I was told that to some of the career men of the State Department this announcement came as a surprise. It should not have been if these men had faithfully supported my policy. . . . I wanted to make it plain that the President of the United States, and not the second or third echelon in the State Department, is responsible for making foreign policy." The president's compassion for a beleaguered minority people, apparent earlier on the refugee issue, similarly influenced his decision to recognize the Jewish state. Ben-Gurion, who met Truman years after 1948 (although while both men were still in office), recalled in a series of taped interviews with Moshe Pearlman:

> At our last meeting, after a very interesting talk, just before he left me—it was in a New York hotel suite—I told him that as a foreigner I could not judge what would be his place in American history; but his helpfulness to us, his constant sympathy with our aims in Israel, his courageous decision to recognize our new State so quickly and his steadfast support since then had given him an immortal place in Jewish history. As I said that, tears suddenly sprang to his eyes. And his eyes were still wet when he bade me good-bye. I had rarely seen anyone so moved. I tried to hold him for a few minutes until he had become more composed, for I recalled that the hotel corridors were full of waiting journalists and photographers. He left. A little later, I too had to go out, and a correspondent came up to me to ask "Why was President Truman in tears when he left you?"

If Washington's recognition of Israel evoked Jewish gratitude, the opposite effect could have been anticipated in the Arab world. There had been no shortage of warnings that the Arab governments would retaliate against American oil interests. Yet, shortly after the birth of Israel, when the management of Aramco announced its intention of laying "Tapline" to the Mediterranean across Palestine, Egypt made a simultaneous bid for the legal easement, and the Syrian government similarly rushed to approve a license for the project. Relations between the Saudi government and Aramco continued harmonious throughout. In the summer of 1948, longstanding negotiations on the division of oil royalties were at last settled amicably between the company and Riyadh. In July of 1948, too, the sheikh of Kuwait announced that he had granted a concession to the American Independent Oil Company for exploring and developing Kuwait's undivided half-interest in the neutral zone between Kuwait and Saudi Arabia. Neither then nor for the next twenty-five years, until October 1973, was there ever to be a serious interruption in the flow of oil to the Mediterranean from American-owned wells in the Middle East.

On May 14, as Ben-Gurion was reading the independence proclamation, Sir Alan Cunningham left his official hilltop residence in Jerusalem and drove quietly down to Haifa. There he boarded the awaiting cruiser *Euryalus* and departed for Cyprus. In London several hours earlier, War Secretary Alexander rose in the House of Commons to announce briefly that Palestine was no longer part of the Commonwealth. There was an hour's listless debate. Soon afterward, the Foreign Office issued an official statement of policy for Palestine, concluding:

> Although British responsibility for Palestine has ceased, it is the earnest hope of His Majesty's Government that, as both sides come to realize the tragic consequences of attempting to conquer Palestine by force, some compromise may yet be possible which will prevent the destruction of all that has been achieved during the last thirty years and which will enable the people of Palestine to live at peace and to govern themselves. To that end His Majesty's Government are still prepared to give every assistance in their power, short of imposing by force a solution not acceptable to both peoples.

The statement was less apologia for Britain's role in the Palestine tragedy than a bid for the continued friendship of the Arab world. It was already apparent that London's posture of officious neutrality had redounded calamitously against the Palestine Arabs.

Notwithstanding the labored officialese of the document, the reference to "all that has been achieved during the last thirty years" did not ring entirely hollow. Later, when passions were cooler and wounds healed, the Jews would have occasion to remember what they owed Great Britain. They owed their first meaningful foothold on Palestine to the Balfour Declaration, after all. For three decades, until the last six months of the mandate, a kind of junior membership in the British Commonwealth had been theirs, assuring them the protection of the British fleet and the British army—against Rommel no less than against the Mufti. That membership also had brought with it the immeasurable advantage of participation in the sterling bloc of trade and finance, a virtually open market in Britain for the Yishuv's citrus products, and a free-spending area in Palestine for British military and civilian personnel. British administrative innovations in Palestine were hardly less impressive than in Egypt or Iraq, while the Common Law provided no less matchless a standard of justice here than elsewhere in the Commonwealth. The accomplishment was rich. It deserved a better epitaph than the one Bevin provided.

With few exceptions, the Arabs anticipated a renewal of security within their own zone of Palestine, and hopefully more than that if the neighboring governments fulfilled their promise to redeem the entire country. The lot that awaited the Jews, on the other hand, the invasion of their newborn republic by the armies of five Arab nations, was the last ordeal the Zionists would have anticipated a decade, or less, earlier. But for the holocaust of European Jewry and its aftermath in the displaced persons' camps, no responsible Jewish Agency leader, neither Ben-Gurion nor Weizmann, would have envisaged statehood as the irreducible minimum of Zionist demands. None would have predicted sovereignty except within the framework of the British Commonwealth, or under the active protection of the international community. It seemed a kind of ordination of fate, and one that was consistent with the central pattern of Jewish history. Nothing was to be achieved except within the matrix of immense tragedy. Jewish nationalism had been reborn at the moment when European anti-Semitism of a new and profoundly virulent nature first made its appearance in the latter part of the nineteenth century. The Jewish National Home was established in a period when Arab nationalism, the feeblest autonomist instinct among all the former member races of the Ottoman realm, belatedly sputtered into life. Afterward, the waves of immigration that transformed the Zionist experiment into a thriving and viable community consisted largely of human derelicts, the impoverished fugitives of envenomed European Judeophobia between the wars. And by the time the Jews of Europe were prepared at last to recognize Palestine as their final sanctuary, the doors to the Promised Land were closed and European Jewry itself was doomed. Even the United Nations Partition Resolution seemed at best an uncharacteristic spasm of the Western conscience, for humanitarianism did not extend so far as to offer assurance of protection to the peoples on each side of the line. The Arab nations presumably could be depended upon to take care of their own, but the Jews faced the less than remote possibility of another genocide. Nothing in the Jewish experience elsewhere, then, should have prepared them for a better fate. As it developed, the Yishuv was not a fatalistic community.

THE WAR
OF INDEPENDENCE

THE ARAB STATES PREPARE FOR INVASION

"How beautiful was this day, May 14," an Arab Legion officer said, "when the whole world held its breath anticipating the entry of seven Arab armies into Palestine to redeem it from the Zionists and the West. On this day Arab forces broke forth from all sides and stood as one man to demand justice and to please God, conscience, and the sense of duty." Lieutenant General Sir John Bagot Glubb, the British commander of the Transjordanian Arab Legion, recalled of the invasion:

> It was a sultry May day, with a haze of dust hanging over the roads. In the city of Amman and in every village along the road the people were gathered, cheering and clapping wildly as each unit drove past. The flat roofs and the windows were crowded with women and children, whose shrill cries and wavering trebles could be heard above the roar and rattle of the vehicles, and the cheering of the crowds of men beside the road. The troops themselves were in jubilation. In some trucks, the soldiers were clapping and cheering. In others, they were laughing and waving to the crowds as they passed. Many of the vehicles had been decorated with green branches or bunches of pink oleander flowers, which grew beside the road. The procession seemed more like a carnival than an army going to war.

Yet behind the excitement lay months of indecision and cross-purposes. Almost until the last week before the end of the mandate, it was not certain that the invasion of Palestine actually would take place. The possibility of armed intervention had been discussed as far back as June 9, 1946, during the conference of Arab leaders at Bludan, Syria. Abdullah of Transjordan supported the idea. So did the Iraqi prime minister, Salih Jabr, and the Mufti himself. Their aims were quite different, however.

Abdullah recently had been elevated by treaty with Britain to king in his realm, and his ambition thenceforth was primarily to extend his dynasty to the Arab sector of the Holy Land; he was willing to arrange his own deal with the Jews for the rest of the country (p. 322). The Syrians, on the other hand, were determined to seize as much as they could of northern Palestine, preempting this area from the Arab Legion. The Mufti's aims were simplest of all. They were to drive the Jews out of Palestine and rule the country. The rest—Lebanon and Iraq, Egypt and Saudi Arabia—

by and large were anti-interventionist. As a consequence of this lack of unanimity, the invasion decision had to be postponed.

Later meetings, at Sofar and Alay, Lebanon, did not effectively resolve the issue, although a military committee was organized. In early 1948, we recall, as fighting gained momentum in Palestine, the Arab League appointed an Iraqi general, Sir Ismail Safwat Pasha, to coordinate the training of "volunteers." But it was not until the Jews captured Haifa and Tiberias that the Arab League summoned its military commanders and demanded a plan for the intervention of regular Arab armies in Palestine. Even then, as the Iraqi minister of defense wrote afterward, ". . . the members of the Political Committee were convinced that a [mere] show of determination to engage in battle would suffice to prevail on the major powers to intervene on behalf of the Arabs, and that thus the Jews would be forced to comply with Arab demands."

By the end of April, a "show of determination" clearly was not going to be enough to block partition. The Jews were tightening their grip on Jaffa, the largest Arab community in Palestine. Except for the Jerusalem area, the military balance seemed to be shifting in favor of the Zionists. The Arab chiefs of staff therefore hurriedly met in Damascus to work out a united approach. As the strategy was formulated, the Syrian and Lebanese armies were to invade northern Palestine and occupy Tiberias, Safed, and Nazareth. Once these forces engaged Jewish units in the north, the principal effort would be opened by the Iraqi army and the Arab Legion south of Lake Galilee, moving west toward Haifa. The port city was scheduled to fall to a combined assault of the four Arab armies on May 21. The role of the Egyptians in this first phase was to be essentially diversionary, pinning down Jewish forces south of Tel Aviv.

The scheme was never put into operation. With ideas of his own for eastern Palestine, Abdullah was totally uninterested in a joint effort to share the division of the country. Anyway, the plan was outdated once the Haganah defeated Qawukji's Arab Liberation Army in the north. By the first week of May the Jews were in firm possession of the whole of western Galilee, with their lines of communication to Haifa well protected. Safed, intended as a base for invading Syrian forces, was captured instead by Allon's Palmach troops. As a consequence of this reversal, the elaborate Arab blueprint deteriorated into a loose understanding that the Iraqis would enter north-central Palestine on the flank of the Arab Legion, the Syrian brigade would enter southeast of Tiberias, while the far northern sector would be left to the undersized Lebanese division. The Egyptians, finally, would be responsible for investing the southern half of Palestine.

Logistics compounded the difficulties of Arab invasion. The distance from Baghdad to Haifa was fully 700 miles. The Egyptian army's line of communication extended 250 miles, mainly across desert. Even the Arab Legion required between 80 and 90 miles of travel to the Palestine front, including first a descent and then a climb of 4,000 feet in crossing the Jordan Valley. Advance knowledge of this extensive terrain was so grossly inadequate that the Syrian and Iraqi general staffs lacked even a single military map of Palestine and were obliged to rely on geographic charts used by school pupils and the advice of civilian guides. Neither was there a unified command worthy of the name. On May 14 Abdullah appointed himself commander in chief by virtue of his Legion's recognized military superiority in the Arab world. The title was purely honorific. Coordination among the various Arab armies was nonexistent. Indeed, the Hashemite ruler admitted as much to Muhammad Fadil al-Jamili, the Iraqi minister of interior, who was visiting Amman the day the war started. "At dinner the king told me that he was chosen as commander in chief of all Arab armies," Jamili recalled, "but that he did not know anything about the Arab armies and he had not been given the information he had requested."

THE JEWS FACE INVASION

The Arabs would have been considerably less hesitant to invade Palestine had they known the actual state of Jewish defenses. As late as May 12, the Haganah mobilized barely 30,000 men and women. The number itself was perhaps not much smaller than the total of Arab forces on the Palestine front, consisting of approximately 10,000 Egyptians, 4,500 Arab Legionnaires, 7,000 Syrians, 8,000 Iraqis, and 3,000 Lebanese. But the Arabs' strength, however limited, was concentrated primarily in their much greater firepower, the air forces at their disposal. At the beginning the Jews had nothing comparable. Nor, lacking defense in depth, could they afford to give ground on any of their four fronts. The Jewish general staff also remained unwieldy in its command structure. Ben-Gurion was obliged to pass his orders to senior officers through Israel Galili, a civilian intermediary. The system was a vestige of the Haganah's early ideological role as a pioneer-labor defense force.

The Jews' most important resource was to be found, rather, in the dedication and military experience of their troops. Yigael Yadin, Israel's commander of operations, was a case in point. A graduate student of archaeology in civilian life, Yadin from his earliest youth had followed a typical Haganah career of secret maneuvers and operations against both Arab guerrillas and British military installations in Palestine. Demonstrating flair and imagination in clandestine officers' training courses, he rose swiftly through the ranks of the underground, becoming chief of Haganah planning operations in the last years of the mandate. In 1948 he was called to assume acting command of the Jewish defense forces. A tall, prematurely balding man with a photographically detailed archaeological knowledge of the Palestine terrain, Yadin was thirty years old when he assumed this responsibility. None of his brigade commanders was older, or less experienced in underground operations. The task they now faced, to be sure, was more formidable than any they had previously encountered. Jewish agents and hired informers in neighboring Arab lands confirmed that a major invasion was imminent. A general plan of battle had to be put into effect immediately.

Yadin divided his forces with care. Three of his nine brigades were allocated to the north. Two were held back in the coastal plain to guard the Tel Aviv area. In the south, as a counterpoise to the Egyptians, a brigade was dispatched to the Rehovot-Isdud (Ashdod) area, and another to the northern Negev region. Finally, in the Judean hills one brigade was allocated for the defense of Jerusalem, and one to the struggle for the highway in the Jerusalem Corridor. These 30,000 troops represented the full complement of Jewish fighting strength. In ensuing weeks, additional thousands of recruits were pressed into service, but on May 14 Jewish manpower resources were still critically limited. So was the supply of weapons. Quantities of arms had been hurriedly accumulated in Europe and elsewhere during preceding months, and even carried across the Mediterranean. But the British refused to allow the unloading of these cargoes until the mandate ended. It was only now that the arms-producing machinery, formerly disguised as "textile equipment," could be assembled for the maufacture of small grease guns and grenades. By the evening of May 14, Haganah intelligence had begun piecing the military situation together. Transjordan's Arab Legion was concentrating on Jerusalem and its surrounding villages. Detachments of the Iraqi army were buttressing the Legion in the central Palestine sector. In the north, the Syrians and Lebanese were moving into Galilee, while Iraqi and other Syrian units were deploying against Jewish farm settlements in the Jordan Valley. In the southwest, meanwhile, the Egyptians were crossing Sinai with a force of two brigades.

The Lebanese army of between 3,000 and 3,500 men was the weakest threat to the newly established Jewish republic. Its officers were essentially young men of leisure from "good" families; like their government, they cared more for striking a belligerent pose than actively fighting. The government itself, for that matter, was precariously balanced between rival Moslem and Christian factions, which held divergent views of the emerging Jewish state. Two days after the end of the mandate, a thousand Lebanese troops seized the Palestine frontier post of Malkiyah, lost it to a Palmach counterattack, recaptured it on June 5, then were content to stop there for the rest of the war. In theory the Syrian army represented a weightier factor. Trained initially by General Maxime Weygand before World War II, and later by a British military mission in 1945, it reached a manpower strength of 7,000 troops by May 1948. The typical Syrian recruit demonstrated little fighting spirit, however. The army lacked a general staff, and its single effective formation was a mechanized brigade, which took the leading role in the invasion of Palestine. Actually the Syrians' major asset was their equipment. It was far superior, in tanks and artillery, to anything the Jews possessed at the beginning of the war.

Thus, shortly after May 16, a Syrian column of two hundred armored vehicles, including forty-five tanks, moved deliberately toward the southern tip of Lake Galilee. Its target was the cluster of lush, prosperous Jewish settlements on both sides of the Jordan River. Several of these were overrun. The column then proceeded to attack Degania, the oldest kibbutz in

Palestine. Without artillery, Jewish forces were helpless to block the Syrian advance. Until then the only heavy weapons that had been unloaded at Haifa were four howitzers of the type used by the French army in the Franco-Prussian War of 1870. Two of these ancient fieldpieces were promptly dismantled and rushed to Degania. The local commander, Lieutenant Colonel Moshe Dayan, had them reassembled at the very moment the first Syrian tanks rumbled through the kibbutz perimeter, and they scored a hit on the advance tank. Had the Syrians known that these two obsolete weapons represented half the arsenal of Jewish fieldguns in Palestine, they might have pressed the attack. Instead, the armored vehicles swung around in their tracks and clattered back up the mountain road. They never returned. From then on, the Syrian government and high command concentrated on a more limited strategy. The Damascus regime had inherited from the French mandatory several territorial claims against Palestine dating back to the Paris Peace Conference of 1919–20. The most important of these was the protruding finger of northeastern Galilee, giving access to additional water resources. Farther south, too, the Syrians laid claim to the eastern shore of Lake Galilee. Accordingly, their subsequent military campaign was designed to resolve these essentially local issues in their favor.

The Iraqis proved only barely more effective than the Syrians. Their contingent, stationed in Transjordan near the Palestine frontier before May 15, numbered about 8,000, of whom 3,500 were combat troops. An effort was launched to cross the Jordan River opposite Beisan the day the mandate ended. It failed. The Iraqi battle commander, General Tahir, thereafter withdrew his men from this region and stationed them in the Samarian "triangle," where they were dispersed thinly as far as Jenin and Tulkarem, only eleven miles from the Mediterranean. Qawukji's irregulars held the Mount Gilboa range and several nearby Arab villages, thus acting as a protective screen for the Iraqis. On May 28 the Jews managed to destroy this screen by clearing the northern tip of the mountains.

Five days later, however, a Jewish frontal attack on Jenin itself was driven back by Iraqi reinforcements. A second Jewish effort failed two days later. Remarkably, the Iraqis were unwilling to counterattack. From then on until the truce of June 11, they simply held their earlier positions. Had they continued their offensive in the early days of the war, they might well have cut the newborn Jewish state in half. But enthusiasm for battle was notably lacking among the Iraqi peasant-conscripts. There were instances when the Jews found dead Iraqi gunners chained to their weapons.

ISRAEL'S SURVIVAL IN THE BALANCE

The most critical battle areas of the Palestine war proved to be in the south, along the Egyptian line of invasion up the coast, and in the Judean hills, where the Arab Legion laid siege to Jerusalem. Ironically, until May 6, Egyptian army headquarters assumed that military activity would be limited to occasional volunteers or to Moslem Brotherhood irregulars in southern Palestine. When the order came to march on Palestine with two brigades, Major General Ahmad Ali al-Muawi, commander of the Egyptian expeditionary force, protested to the government that the condition of his troops was deplorable. The military staff was responsible for this, of course. The contrast between its officers and men was that of pharaohs and slaves. Nevertheless, Prime Minister Nuqrashi Pasha assured Muawi that little fighting actually would be necessary. The United Nations would surely intervene in Palestine before hostilities began. The Egyptian force gathering at al-Arish consisted of about 10,000 men, reasonably mechanized and organized into the Second and Fourth Brigades. Brigadier Muhammad Naguib commanded the Second Brigade; his principal staff officer was Major Abd al-Hakim Amir.

Naguib led his troops toward the coastal road extending to Gaza and Tel Aviv. The Fourth Brigade, under Lieutenant General Abd al-Aziz, moved inland toward the Hebron hills. On May 20, en route, Aziz's column entered the small Bedouin town of Beersheba, and then continued northward through Hebron to Bethlehem, which was handed over to the Egyptians on May 22 by the Arab Legion. Thereupon this brigade moved at once against the kibbutz of Ramat Rachel, guarding the New—Jewish—City of Jerusalem. Naguib, meanwhile, leading 5,000 troops, proceeded cautiously up the littoral road toward the Tel Aviv urban enclave. To counter this threat, Yadin ordered the 2,000 men of his southern brigade pulled from their battle stations on the Jerusalem highway. These troops had already suffered grievous losses fighting the Legion, and were exhausted and underequipped. Naguib was unaware of the actual precariousness of the Jewish situation, however. The Egyptians had just encountered unexpectedly stiff resistance from the isolated kibbutz of Yad Mordechai, which had managed to withstand five days of intensive Egyptian shelling before being evacuated. Those five days had tied up approximately half of Naguib's coastal force and mauled one of his battalions so thoroughly that it had to be deactivated temporarily. Several miles away from Yad Mordechai, another kibbutz, Negba, was blocking the Egyptian advance in a resistance of equal ferocity. Although General Naguib eventually decided to skirt the bristling farm community, Negba remained a continual threat to his flank. He moved with elaborate caution, as a result, slowing his drive barely sixteen miles from the outskirts of Tel Aviv.

With a population of a quarter-million, Tel Aviv had burgeoned spectacularly into one of the most advanced and impressive cities of the Middle East; it was now more than three times larger than New Jerusalem, the former concentration of Jewish settlement. Its fall clearly would mean the end of the war for Israel. At this point, therefore, Yadin decided to risk a tactical offensive. On May 29 he ordered reinforcements from the Jerusalem Corridor to circle Naguib's positions at night and attack the Egyptians from the rear. With a troop strength barely half that of the invaders, the relief force nevertheless found darkness and surprise no less effective than had Sadeh and Wingate in the 1930s. The Egyptians were thrown into confusion by the unexpected descent upon their flank. Yadin shrewdly exploited their disarray by calling a press conference and announcing that the Egyptian supply lines had been cut by "overwhelming concentrations" of Israeli troops. The "news" was immediately dispatched over the international wire services, and eventually reached Cairo. As Yadin had hoped, the Egyptian high command accepted the story at face value and radioed Naguib to pull up short. The bewildered commander dutifully followed these instructions.

Naguib's setback proved to be the turning point of the Egyptian invasion. Tel Aviv was never again in jeopardy. In any case, the Egyptian government and high command were not dissatisfied with their accomplishments thus far. By June 11, when the first United Nations truce came into effect (p. 327), Egyptian troops were within artillery range of Tel Aviv and encamped near the suburbs of Jerusalem. They dominated all the main roads of the Negev, as well. Conversely, the Jewish reinforcement column in the south had lost nearly 1,200 dead and wounded and urgently needed rest and new equipment. The Zionist settlements in the Negev were isolated and in danger of being starved out.

The Jewish situation in the Jerusalem area, besieged by Transjordan's Arab Legion, was even more precarious. It was the more unexpected, as well. Both the Zionists and the British had long considered Abdullah to be the most accommodating of all the Arab leaders. Indeed, the Hashemite ruler had always made clear that his interest lay exclusively in the Arab sectors of Palestine. In the spring of 1948, Transjordanian Prime Minister Tewfik Pasha, visiting London to negotiate a new treaty, informed Bevin that the Amman government had decided to send the Arab Legion across the Jordan River when the British mandate ended. Its goal would be limited to the occupation of eastern Palestine, the portion awarded the Arabs by the United Nations Partition Resolution. General Glubb, who attended this meeting, recalled: "I can to this day almost see Mr. Bevin sitting at his table in that splendid room. When I finished my translation thus far, he interrupted Taufiq Pasha's statement by saying: 'It seems the obvious thing to do.' He added later, 'but do not go and invade the areas allotted to the Jews.' 'We should not have the forces to do so, even if we so desired,' [replied the Arab prime minister]."

Abdullah did not disguise his intentions from the Arab League. At an earlier meeting with the other Arab delegations in Amman, on October 14, 1947, the king warned that he was reserving his "freedom of action" in Palestine. Under no circumstances would he countenance a Palestinian government, with or without the Mufti. He also disliked the notion of using Palestine Arabs for operations against the Jews. Two weeks before, he had explained his views to a close friend:

> The Mufti and Kuwatly [the Syrian president] want to set up an independent Arab state in Palestine with the Mufti at its head. If that were to happen I would be encircled on almost all sides by enemies. This compels me to take measures to anticipate their plans. My forces will therefore occupy every place evacuated by the British. I will not begin the attack on the Jews

and will only attack them if they first attack my forces. I will not allow massacres in Palestine. Only after quiet and order have been established will it be possible to reach an understanding with the Jews.

Such an understanding apparently was reached as early as the following month. Under British patronage, the Hashemite realm had coexisted for two and a half decades in intimate economic association with the Jews. Abdullah himself had always entertained a shrewd appreciation of Zionist dynamism and staying power, and of the advantages the Jewish redemptive effort in Palestine could offer his own impoverished little nation. Over the years he had made and cultivated numerous friendships with the Jews. He expected to be able to reach a political agreement with them. Conceivably there was leeway for minor alterations to be negotiated in the Partition Resolution—for example, granting a Transjordanian easement to Haifa harbor and an outlet for Arab agricultural produce. In November 1947, therefore, the diminutive king held a secret meeting with Mrs. Golda Meyerson (later Meir) in Rutenberg House at the Jordan River power station of Naharayim. The conversation was entirely amicable. If the United Nations decided to partition Palestine, Abdullah explained, he frankly preferred to annex the Arab sector to his kingdom. Mrs. Meyerson foresaw no difficulties, agreeing with Abdullah that "we both have a common enemy—the Mufti." She added that the Jews would themselves do nothing to breach the partition line envisaged in the United Nations Resolution, but what would happen in the Arab area was no business of theirs.

This genial exchange was typical of the understanding that had always existed not only between Abdullah and the Zionists but also, we recall, between Abdullah's late brother Feisal and the Jews—and was accordingly a source of deep suspicion throughout the rest of the Arab world. In later years continued reference would be made to the "Hashemite-Zionist partnership." "Of all the Arab leaders, King Abdullah, dean of the Hashemite family, was closest to the hearts of the Zionists," wrote the Iraqi historian Muhammad Udah. "Their most important writers considered his tenure on the Jordanian throne one of the greatest assurances for the preservation of Israel." Yet as late as Tewfik Pasha's discussion with Bevin, and Abdullah's conversation with Mrs. Meyerson, it was still by no means certain that the Arab League would authorize military intervention in Palestine. Only later, when this step became increasingly likely, did Abdullah admit to a visiting journalist on April 26: "[A]ll our efforts to find a peaceful solution to the Palestine problem have failed. The only way left for us is war. I will have the pleasure and honour to save Palestine."

Abdullah cherished no illusions of winning the entire country for his dynasty; the Legion comprised barely 4,500 men available for battle operations. Even so, he expected to do well. His troops were equipped with artillery and commanded by British officers. Two days before the British withdrawal from Palestine, moreover, the Arab League had promised Abdullah a war chest of up to £3 million, in deference to his position as commander in chief. Now that hostilities were certain in Palestine, the king was determined to exploit these advantages by stealing a march on the other Arab states. He explained his position to Mrs. Meyerson in a second secret conversation of May 11, this one in Amman. Accompanied by Ezra Danin, a veteran Sephardic native of Palestine with extensive connections among Palestinians and other Arabs, Mrs. Meyerson had disguised herself as a peasant woman to make the dangerous trip to the Transjordanian capital. Abdullah implored his visitors to postpone the declaration of the Jewish state and to accept instead an undivided Palestine with autonomous Jewish areas. Mrs. Meyerson turned down the offer. Somewhat embarrassedly, then, the king explained that he had intended to honor his original agreement not to invade Jewish territory, but now "I am one among five. I have no alternative and I cannot act otherwise."

As the discussion continued, Mrs. Meyerson warned Abdullah that the Jews were his only friends. "I know it," he replied, "and I have no illusions on that score. I know the [other Arabs] and their 'good intentions.' I firmly believe that Divine Providence has restored you, a Semite people who were banished to Europe and have benefited by its progress, to the Semite East, which needs your knowledge and initiative. . . . But the situation is grave, and we must not err through hasty action. Consequently I beg of you to be patient." Mrs. Meyerson firmly rejected the proposal of delaying Jewish statehood. "I am sorry," Abdullah replied. "I deplore the coming bloodshed and destruction. Let us hope we shall meet again and will not sever our relations. If you find it necessary to meet me during the actual fighting, do not hesitate to come and see me." On their way back to Palestine, the two Jewish visitors could see at a distance Iraqi army units moving toward the front with their heavy transport and extensive field artillery.

Abdullah's decision to engage in hostilities was influenced not merely by suspicion of his Arab neighbors but by a deeply rooted, almost visceral yearning for the city of Jerusalem, with all its Moslem historical associations. Indeed, capture of the venerated shrine community would recompense the Hashemite king for his father's loss of Mecca and Medina to the Saudi dynasty in 1925. It was for this reason, too, that Abdullah indicated his disapproval of the Arab League plan of battle, which assigned the Legion to northern Palestine and Haifa. Rather, he ordered his troops to concentrate on Jerusalem and its hinterland and on those sectors of Palestine awarded to the Arab state. It is of interest that the decision was taken over the strenuous objections of the Legion commander, General Glubb. The Englishman was fearful of bogging his army down in Jerusalem. The Jews were experts in street fighting, he pointed out, and by engaging in the enemy's kind of warfare the Legion would dissipate the advantage of its superior tactical training and mobility. "With our slender manpower and no reserves, we could not afford a slogging match," he insisted. Yet the king would not be budged. Glubb, in turn, was so unnerved at the prospect of war in Jerusalem that (he recounted later) he fell upon his knees. " 'O God,' I said, 'I am not equal to these events. I entreat Thee to grant me Thy help.' "

But if Abdullah was shortsighted in committing himself to the battle for Jerusalem, Glubb was equally ill-informed in his estimation of Jewish defenses. They were much less formidable than he imagined. The Arabs controlled every height around the city and within it. Their fighting strength by then was nearly 4,500 armed men, while the Jews, if numerically their equal, were virtually weaponless. Half the Haganah field strength was committed to protect ten or twelve beleaguered settlements around the Judean hills, and was isolated from Jerusalem and the rest of the Yishuv. A large minority of the city's Jewish population was Orthodox and quite fatalistic, unwilling to resist a major invasion. Had Glubb known, then, how desperate the enemy's circumstances were, he would have concentrated all his forces on Jerusalem immediately.

THE BATTLE FOR JERUSALEM

Thus, for the 85,000 Jews in the Holy City, already weakened by the Arab stranglehold on their lifeline from the coast, the initial weeks of the Transjordanian attack nearly proved disastrous. On May 19, Abdullah sent his first units into the Old City, that historic enclave consisting of mixed communities of Arabs, Armenians, and Greeks, with a small Jewish quarter, all surrounded by a medieval Turkish wall. Simultaneously an additional 2,000 Legionnaires, well equipped with artillery and commanded by British officers, moved on Jerusalem from the north and soon invested its outlying perimeter. Within the opening days of hostilities, they threatened a breakthrough into the Jewish inhabited area of the New City.

After ten days of savage fighting, however, the outnumbered Jewish troops finally managed to drive the Legion back from the point of its farthest advance at the Mea Sh'arim quarter. On May 28, Glubb decided to call off the attack in the northern part of the city. Some of his companies had lost fully half their effective strength, and others were unnerved by the shattering blast of homemade Jewish mortars. From this point on, the Arabs switched their offensive to Jerusalem's southern approaches. Units of the Egyptian army had already achieved a juncture with the Legion's advance lines in Bethlehem. On May 2, under cover of a heavy Transjordanian artillery bombardment, Egyptian infantrymen stormed the kibbutz of Ramat Rachel, lying astride the entrance to southern Jerusalem. What followed was the single most furious encounter of the Palestine war. The little kibbutz changed hands five times during the next four days. Soldiers pressing forward in bayonet attack often had to climb over bodies piled on top of each other. When the last attack was over, the Jews—most of them former Etzel members—remained in control. For the moment, at least, the imminent possibility of the Arabs capturing the New City had faded.

The Jewish quarter behind the Turkish wall failed to hold out, however. This congested little warren of streets and courtyards was inhabited exclusively by Orthodox pietists and defended by a single Haganah unit. On May 18 a second company of Jewish troops fought its way into the Old City and took up positions at the side of the defenders. In the following week other Jewish units made repeated attempts to break through the tightening Arab ring, but each time a Legion artillery barrage drove them off. At last, on May 28, the Jewish quarter surrendered. News of the fall of the Old City was received with profound shock by the Jewish inhabitants of Palestine. The venerable enclave had traditionally been revered as the site of the ancient Hebrew Temple, of the surviving Western Wall (Chapter VIII), and was the cynosure of Orthodox Jewry the world over. Its loss, and the subsequent desecration of its Jewish shrines, was to be lamented with unalleviated bitterness in years to come.

Yet from the purely military viewpoint, the fate of the New City and of its Jewish inhabitants had to be the principal concern of the Israeli high command. The Arabs thus far had been unable to conquer the sprawling urban complex through direct assault. By the opening of June, nevertheless, the ability of the metropolitan area to hold out was far from certain. During the three and a half weeks of fighting after May 15, the city was hit by more than 10,000 shells that destroyed some 2,000 homes and other structures and inflicted 1,200 civilian casualties. With the supply line from Tel Aviv blocked, ammunition for the New City defenders was nearly exhausted. Under a firm, efficient military governor, Bernard (Dov) Joseph, the largest numbers of the Jewish population somehow maintained their discipline, except for fainthearted elements among the Orthodox. This civilian tenacity was to prove crucial, inasmuch as the water pipeline from the coast had also long since been cut, and citizens were obliged to queue up each day for rations of drinking water. The prospect of mass starvation was also very real. In a number of the poorer, Sephardic-Oriental neighborhoods, children were foraging in the streets. During prolonged and anguished meetings with Yadin, therefore, Ben-Gurion insisted that full military priority now be given to the opening of the Jerusalem highway.

To that end, Israel's most respected field commander, Yigal Allon, was called down from the north on May 23 to assume strategic responsibility for the assault on Latrun, the Arab strongpoint controlling the road. New recruits had to be coopted to augment the Jewish forces, including hundreds of recent immigrants possessing no military experience or even basic training. They were rushed up now by bus and taxi from Tel Aviv. On May 25, under the operational command of Colonel Shlomo Shamir, the attack was launched in a blistering desert sirocco. Despite the lack of adequate reconnaissance or artillery support, the men were thrown into a direct frontal offensive. Thereupon the Arab Legion's Fourth Regiment, ensconced in the village heights, raked the attackers with mortars and artillery. The Jews were thrown back with heavy loss of life. During the next few days additional efforts were mounted, and each time with the same result. Latrun very nearly became the graveyard of Jewish hopes for breaking the siege of Jerusalem.

A single alternative remained for opening the Jewish supply line. During the previous weeks, Colonel David Marcus, an American Jewish volunteer and West Point graduate serving as area commander for the road, had been using a path south of Latrun and Bab al-Wad to infiltrate troops on foot through the hills to Jerusalem. Marcus speculated that the path might be widened to enable vehicles to pass through. With Yadin's approval, hundreds of laborers were now summoned from Tel Aviv and immediately put to work clearing boulders and dynamiting rock sidings. There was no opportunity for rest, even in the fiercest heat, for a United Nations truce was to come into effect on June 11. If the "Burma Road" were not completed before then, no further efforts would be permitted after the truce

THE INITIAL ARAB INVASION
OF PALESTINE
MAY 15 - JUNE 11, 1948

Allotted to Jews in UN partition
Allotted to Arabs in UN partition

MILES
0   30

deadline, and Jerusalem would starve. Finally, by June 9, a primitive road-bed was cut through the Jerusalem mountains. The first trucks, loaded with cans of food and water, ventured out on the pitted makeshift highway. Several hours later they entered Jerusalem, where they were greeted rapturously by the awaiting Jewish population.

THE FIRST UNITED NATIONS TRUCE

It was the British representative, Sir Alexander Cadogan, who had repeatedly voted against a truce resolution in the Security Council. Indeed, throughout the UN debates, Cadogan refused to use the word "Israel." His favorite circumlocution was to refer to the new state as "the Jewish authorities in Palestine." Maintaining a proprietary interest in the Arab war effort, then, the Englishman declined to approve a cease-fire order until the Arab armies clearly were reaching the exhaustion point. Even then he was unwilling to go further than to suggest the appointment of a United Nations mediator, with power to recommend a settlement. This minimal proposal, at least, was endorsed by the Security Council on May 20, and the chosen mediator, Count Folke Bernadotte of Sweden, arrived in the Middle East the following week. The Arabs were generally receptive to the idea of a truce, but the Jews were unprepared to accept Bernadotte's limitations on immigration during the projected month-long cease-fire. Eventually a compromise was reached. It provided for a ban to be imposed on the introduction of additional weapons, and male immigrants of military age would be gathered in camps under United Nations supervision (neither side, as it turned out, observed this restriction). All fighting would stop on June 11.

The truce descended on the exhausted armies "as dew from heaven," in the words of one Israeli commander. Both sides were at the limit of their resources. Strategically, the Arabs had gained little. The Syrians had established a bridgehead on Israeli territory, but it was a negligible one. The Arab Legion had taken the Old City, but the achievement was of questionable military importance. The Egyptians had acquired a foothold in the Negev, but this was barren desert. Whatever pretense to a united command ever existed among the Arab armies had disintegrated in the actual fighting. The Syrians, for example, had attacked at Samakh, and the Iraqis had launched an offensive six miles to the south at Gesher; neither army had attempted to coordinate its strategy with the other. During the lull in the hostilities, the Iraqi chief of staff, General Salah Saïb al-Jaburi, presented a long report to his government, warning that the Jews would come back much strengthened after the expiration of the truce, and urging that the Arabs unify their forces immediately.

Such an effort was briefly made. On their own, the Iraqis offered the post of commander in chief to General al-Muawi, who was leading the Egyptian expeditionary force. When informed of the offer, however, Abdullah promptly vetoed it. The truth was that the Hashemite king by then had lost interest in continuing the war. His casualties had been heavy, and the likelihood of further territorial gain in Palestine was minimal. Glubb recalled that when he, Glubb, asked the government for new troops, he was rebuffed. " 'There won't be any more fighting,' [Prime Minister Tewfik Pasha] said to me, shaking the first finger of his right hand to the right and left. . . . 'No more fighting! I and Nokrashy Pasha [the Egyptian prime minister] are agreed on that, and when we two are agreed we can sway the rest. No! No more fighting!' " Glubb commented sourly afterward that a month's priceless respite was wasted. In contrast, the other Arab leaders made effective use of the truce. The Iraqis increased their numbers at the front to 10,000 and added large quantities of equipment. The Syrians also carried out an extensive recruiting campaign, as did the Egyptians. By the first week in July, the number of Arab regular troops in Palestine had grown from 32,000 to some 45,000.

As the time approached for the truce to expire, the Arab League Political Committee met again in Cairo. There Tewfik Pasha argued strenuously against resuming hostilities. He was a minority of one, although most of the Arab chiefs of staff privately supported him. The decision was made by the politicians, who evidently hoped to protect their reputations by declining to renew the cease-fire; the Security Council then hopefully would impose a new truce. Nuqrashi Pasha in Egypt actually doubted that his cabinet would survive if the cease-fire were prolonged. As it turned out, by renewing the war after having given the Jews a month's respite, the Arab governments doomed their military effort in Palestine. "Those governments did not know either how to enter the battle or how to get out of it," wryly observed Musa al-Alami later.

For the Jews, the issue of continuing the struggle was much simpler. Their military position at the time of the United Nations truce was by no means assured. The invading Arab armies had been contained, but more than a third of the territory allocated to Israel—essentially the Negev—remained in Arab hands. The Syrians on the west bank of the Jordan still threatened the safety of Galilee, while the Iraqis in the central sector were ensconced only twelve miles from the Mediterranean. Not least of all, the narrow artery to Jerusalem remained vulnerable, and in the city itself the Jewish population was far from secure in its provisions of food, water, and medicine. Gravely short of manpower and weapons, the fledgling Israeli army actually was in danger of collapse on nearly every front. Troop morale was poor as a result of delayed or inadequate compensation to soldiers' families.

By the truce provisions, neither side was permitted to introduce new troops. Jerusalem was to be allowed enough food and water for a month, but not more. The Israeli high command had no intention of abiding by these conditions, however, which it regarded as suicidal. Convoys of food and medicines were rushed to Jerusalem. Mobilization was continued and increased dramatically in early July. The little armaments factory moved into full production, turning out bullets, grenades, and mortar shells. Weapons were secretly unloaded at coastal sites. By then the quantity of guns and equipment had become more substantial. Well before the end of the mandate, the Czechoslovak government had expressed a willingness to sell the Jews weapons from the great Skoda works. This decision was in part political (reflecting the Soviet line), in part humanitarian (evincing a traditional Czech compassion on the refugee issue), and in part economic (the payment was in dollars). On May 20 the Czechs turned over an entire military airfield to the Jews, which in the following months became Israel's principal base in Europe for the shuttle service of arms and planes. Eventually several Dakota transports commuted back and forth between the two nations, ferrying to Israel dismantled fighter planes, artillery pieces, armored vehicles, and lighter weapons and ammunition. Planes arrived from other countries, as well, including bombers and fighters often flown illegally by veterans of the Allied air forces out of Britain and the United States. For each plane that crashed or was interned en route, two others landed safely. Thousands of tons of ammunition, military equipment, and clothing now arrived, much of it purchased, much donated from Jewish sources throughout the world.

The French government, too, continued its support. Weapons were sold in large quantities to the Jews. Training, storage, and assemblage facilities were provided near French arms depots and at abandoned French air force landing strips. Airfields in Corsica were made available to planes refueling en route to Israel. Nor did Prime Minister Georges Bidault obstruct Etzel agents from conducting their recruiting and arms purchases on French soil. It was in this manner that the Etzel purchased an American LST vessel and sailed it to France in early May. Anchored near Marseilles, the ship was to be loaded with several hundred European and North African Jews of military age and with large quantities of French weapons. Indeed, at Bidault's intercession, these arms actually were supplied free of charge. Meanwhile General Rouen, the French army chief of staff, and Inspector-General Weibeau of the French police made embarkation facilities available to the Etzel. It was expected that the vessel, called *Altalena*, a pen name of the late Jabotinsky, would make several trips between France and Israel with additional recruits and weapons. The LST sailed on May 29 with 500 men and women aboard, and a cargo of 5,000 rifles, 450 machine guns, and millions of rounds of ammunition. It was still en route when the United Nations truce came into effect.

Ben-Gurion had consented secretly for the *Altalena* to land on June 20. Difficulties arose only when the Etzel demanded that 20 percent of the weapons go to its own units. The prime minister adamantly refused this challenge to the authority of the Israeli government. Soon shooting broke out between regular forces and the Etzel as the LST commander sought to land the vessel on a beach north of Tel Aviv. The firing continued for several hours. The *Altalena* then burst into flame; twelve of its crew were killed (one of them was Avraham Stavsky, who had been tried in 1933 for the murder of Arlosoroff), together with seventy of the recruits. Some of the cargo was lost. The incident immediately terminated all further arms shipments from France. It reopened, too, a bitter factional dispute between

the Israeli Right and the Labor government that was destined to envenom
the politics of the Jewish republic for the next generation. Yet the immediate consequence of the *Altalena* episode was the Israeli cabinet's decision
to arrest a number of Etzel leaders and to abolish remaining Etzel units
within the army.

For that matter, Ben-Gurion was determined now to impose unity and
discipline at all levels of the military effort. He announced his intention
henceforth to bypass Israel Galili, the civilian Haganah intermediary, and
to issue orders directly to the military staff. Whenever possible, too, he
appointed former officers of the British army's Palestinian units as front
commanders. These decisions, perhaps understandably, provoked a near-
mutiny within the Haganah and Palmach command, including Yadin himself. But, after intensive discussions and considerable tension, Ben-Gurion
had his way in all essentials. Uniforms became standard, and a differential
pay scale was established for commissioned officers. During the month-long
truce, new recruits were given intensive training and new weapons
were mastered. With 60,000 men in service and growing quantities of
European and American equipment at its disposal, the army was systematically transformed into a modern fighting force. Its power now emerged
as a central fact of Middle Eastern life in the months—and years—that lay
ahead.

TERRITORIAL AND DEMOGRAPHIC CHANGES

The Egyptians prepared to strike the first blow. On July 8, even before the
truce expired, General Naguib renewed the attack against Negba, the
linchpin of the Israeli defense system in the south. But Negba, too, had
been reinforced with heavy equipment during the truce, and now successfully hurled back repeated Egyptian assaults. Thereupon the Jews themselves began a limited offensive, reoccupying a number of villages in the
northwestern corner of the Negev, forcing back the main Egyptian line
in the center. It soon became evident to Yadin and his staff that the Egyptians no longer represented a serious offensive threat. They would be dealt
with at a more opportune time later.

In the north, meanwhile, the Syrians were content to dig in at the captured farm settlement of Mishmar HaYarden, where they shelled the
approach road. Their foothold in Jewish territory no longer constituted
a bridgehead. The presence of 2,000 Arab irregulars under Fawzi
al-Qawukji in the lower Galilee mountains was a more serious potential
danger. The Jews disposed of it, however, in a brutal week-long campaign,
during which they overran the Arab town of Nazareth and cleared the surrounding Arab villages. At the same time, the principal Israeli military
effort was concentrated on the Legion-occupied Lydda-Ramle area that
formed a wedge only eleven miles from Tel Aviv and threatened to cut the
nation in two. The salient also dominated Palestine's major road junctions,
north-south, east-west, including the neck of the Jerusalem Corridor, and

the country's one major airport. On July 9, therefore, Yigal Allon led two of his brigades in an attack on this Arab strongpoint. In the course of a day and night of fighting, the enemy positions were completely encircled. On the eleventh, Lydda and its international airport fell to Lieutenant Colonel Moshe Dayan's mechanized infantry. The following afternoon, Dayan led his column of jeeps into Ramle. Barreling through the main street at full speed, machine guns firing, Dayan's troops sent the Legionnaires fleeing. With this sledgehammer operation, the Jews eliminated any remaining Arab threat to the Tel Aviv area. An alternative, if precarious, route to Jerusalem was simultaneously opened, and the most important communications centers in Palestine were wrested from the Arabs. Allon's subsequent efforts to outflank Latrun failed. Yet it did not escape Glubb, the Arab Legion commander, that the Jews had been continuously on the offensive during the entire period of fighting, and the Arabs on the defensive—a precise reversal of the earlier phase of the war.

By mid-July, too, Glubb was compromised in Abdullah's eyes for having failed to save Lydda and Ramle. The moment the second truce came into effect, the king sent his English commander on leave to Europe for "rest." Like Glubb himself, Abdullah now turned entirely defensive in his thinking and concentrated exclusively on protecting his strongholds in and around Jerusalem. The Legion thenceforth ceased to be a factor in the Palestine war. In truth, the shift in military fortunes registered no less dramatically on Abdullah's patron, the British government. On the first day of renewed fighting after July 9, the Arab capitals had turned down an appeal for another cease-fire, expecting that their armies would retrieve the situation. The British shared this illusion. But on July 12 the news reached Whitehall that Lydda airport had fallen to the Jews; an Israeli "gunboat" (actually a reconverted landing craft) had shelled the Lebanese city of Tyre; three heavy "Flying Fortresses," new additions to the Israeli air force, had bombed Cairo en route from the United States to Israeli air fields. Thereupon, under urgent instructions from London, Cadogan pressed the Security Council to order an immediate truce under penalty of sanctions. The Council endorsed this proposal unanimously on July 15, with instructions for hostilities to cease three days later. Meanwhile Glubb met with Bevin in London. "The [foreign secretary] opened the conversation with bitter complaints against the Arabs," the Legion commander wrote later, "whom he had done his best to help, but who had in reply only loaded him with complaints and abuse." It was painfully evident to Bevin that by July 18 Israel occupied far more of (inhabited) Palestine than the UN Partition Resolution had allocated, while the Arabs occupied only one Jewish settlement, Mishmar HaYarden, together with an indeterminate Egyptian foothold in the Negev.

There were other unanticipated changes in the configuration of Palestine. These were demographic. In the months immediately following the Partition Resolution, approximately 30,000 Arabs decided to leave Palestine. As in the civil war of the 1930s, most of these émigrés were businessmen and their families from the larger cities. Liquidating their holdings,

they transferred their accounts to banks in Egypt and Lebanon and departed unobtrusively. No one else budged. On the contrary, with the arrival
of Arab volunteers and weapons, and the early successes of Qawukji's Arab
Liberation Army in the first two months of 1948, the morale of the Palestine Arab community was measurably strengthened.

It was afterward, we recall, in April and May of 1948, that the Jews
began to secure the upper hand in Palestine, clearing the interior road network, seizing the vital towns, and dominating the principal arteries except
for the Jerusalem highway and small pockets in the Galilee. Simultaneously, Arab public services collapsed in the pandemonium of British
evacuation. The exodus of Arab families resumed, and this time included
large numbers of communal officials, village mayors, judges, and cadis.
Thousands of fellahin and town dwellers began to accompany them. The
most dramatic episode of flight in this second phase of Arab departure
occurred in Haifa. Approximately 70,000 Arabs lived in the harbor city. The
businessmen among them began leaving directly after the Partition
Resolution. As early as February and March 1948, Archbishop George
al-Hakim, the Greek Catholic primate, arranged for the removal of large
groups of Arab children to Damascus and Beirut. By the end of March,
approximately 25,000 Arabs had already left. An additional 20,000 departed
in early April, following Qawukji's offensive and rumors that the Arab
air forces would soon bomb the Jewish quarters on Mount Carmel. Finally,
on April 21 and 22, the British garrison withdrew and the Jews captured
the city.

On the afternoon of the twenty-second, the Jewish mayor of Haifa and
his colleagues met with Arab leaders and pleaded with them to remain
in the city with their fellow townsmen. With three and half weeks remaining before the end of the mandate, and the United States no longer firmly
in support of partition, the Jews were apprehensive of the interpretation
world opinion would place on mass Arab departures. For their part, the
Arab spokesmen, including Archbishop al-Hakim, initially agreed to stay
on; they asked only for several hours to consult with the Higher Committee.
Couriers were then promptly sent off to Lebanon to hold discussions with
representatives of the Mufti and the Arab League. That same afternoon
the reply was conveyed to the mayor and his associates: the Arabs would
not live for a single day under Jewish rule; they demanded permission to
leave the city. All efforts to change their minds failed—as United States
consular reports to Washington confirmed. Within thirty-six hours the remaining Arab population of nearly 30,000 left the city and departed for
Lebanon, either overland or by sea.

Elsewhere in Palestine, too, the Arab exodus gained momentum, reaching nearly 175,000 during the last weeks of the mandate. There were
various reasons for this flight, but none of them could be traced to an
alleged appeal for evacuation by the Arab governments themselves,
ostensibly to make way for the impending invasion of Arab armies. This
was a frequently repeated Israeli claim after the war. Yet no such order
for evacuation was ever found in any release of the Arab League or in

any military communiqués of the period. Rather, the evidence in the Arab press and radio of the time was to the contrary. By and large, except for towns like Haifa, already captured by the Jews, the Arab League ordered the Palestinians to stay where they were, and stringent punitive measures were reported against Arab youths of military age who fled the country. Even Jewish broadcasts (in Hebrew) mentioned these Arab orders to remain. Azzam Pasha, Abdullah, and the various "national committees" appealed repeatedly to the Arabs not to leave their homes. The Ramallah commander of the Arab Legion threatened to confiscate the property and blow up the houses of those Arabs who left without permission. At one point the Lebanese government decided to close its frontiers to all Palestinians, except for women, children, and old people.

The most obvious reason for the mass exodus was the collapse of Palestine Arab political institutions that ensued upon the flight of the Arab leadership—at the very moment when that leadership was most needed. The departure of mukhtars, judges, and cadis from Haifa and the New City of Jerusalem, from Jaffa, Safed, and elsewhere, dealt a grave blow to the Arab population. The semifeudal character of Arab society rendered the illiterate fellah almost entirely dependent on the landlord and cadi, and once this elite was gone, the Arab peasant was terrified by the likelihood of remaining in an institutional and cultural void. Jewish victories obviously intensified the fear and accelerated departure. In many cases, too—in the battle to open the highway to Jerusalem, for example—Jews captured Arab villages, expelled the inhabitants, and blew up houses to prevent them from being used as strongholds against them. In other instances, Qawukji's men used Arab villages for their bases, provoking immediate Jewish retaliation.

The most savage of these reprisal actions took place on April 9, 1948, in the village of Deir Yassin, a community guarding the entrance to Jerusalem. The Etzel and Lech'i initiated the operation, and the ruthlessness these groups had earlier demonstrated against the British was now applied in even fuller measure against the Arabs. The village was captured, and more than two hundred Arab men, women, and children were slain, their bodies afterward mutilated and thrown into a well. Although the deed was immediately repudiated by the Haganah command, then by the Jewish government, which arrested the Etzel officers responsible, the consequences of the massacre were far-reaching. News of the outrage rapidly circulated throughout Palestine, and characteristically was embellished and soon dramatically exaggerated by the Arab population. The fellahin found these accounts wholly credible, for they knew well how their own guerrillas had stripped and mutilated Jewish civilians; photographs of the slaughter were peddled openly by Arab street vendors. Later, too, the villagers were to recall the words of Azzam Pasha on the eve of the Arab invasion, describing the coming fate of the Jews: "This will be a war of extermination and a momentous massacre which will be spoken of like the Mongolian massacre and the Crusades." It was not unnatural for the Palestine Arabs to expect the same treatment from the Jews. Arab leaders similarly gave wide publicity to authentic or rumored acts of atrocity committed by the Zionist enemy, with utter indifference to the impact these accounts would have on Arab civilian morale. In April and May, entire Arab communities were fleeing in terror even before Jewish forces overran their homes. A Swiss observer, Jacques de Reynier, described the panic among the inhabitants of Jaffa when the Jews attacked:

> Immediately everyone was consumed with terror, and soon the evacuation started. In the hospitals, the drivers of cars and ambulances took their vehicles, assembled their families, and fled in complete disregard of their responsibilities. Many of the ill, nurses, even physicians, departed the hospital wearing the clothes they had on, and fled to the countryside. For all of them the one obsession was to escape at any cost.

The arrival of the regular Arab armies after May 15 had a brief stabilizing influence on the Palestine Arab population. The friendly cooperation beween the makeshift civil administration and the local Arabs has been described in the published war memoirs of various Arab officers, including those of Nasser, Abdullah al-Tel, Kamal al-Din Hussein, and even Qawukji himself. But it was an intermittent relationship at best; the Arab armies failed to consolidate their positions. By June 11, when the first United Nations truce came into effect, some 250,000 Arabs had fled the Jewish-occupied areas of the country. Once on the offensive, moreover, Israel changed its policy toward the local Arabs. No further effort was made to persuade them to stay and share in the anticipated benefits of Jewish statehood. Rather, attacking on the central front after the truce expired, Israeli troops occupied Lydda, Ramle, and the cluster of surrounding Arab villages, and "encouraged" approximately 100,000 of the local inhabitants to flee. The method was simple. By spreading tough warnings ahead of them, the Jews ensured that most of these settlements were evacuated even before the Israeli army arrived. The number of Arab émigrés reached 300,000 by July 9 and swelled rapidly in the early autumn after the Jews launched their first Negev offensive (p. 339). By then even the most optimistic Palestine Arab recognized that the Jewish republic, far from succumbing helplessly to armed invasion, was in fact capable of waging ruthless and brutal warfare on its own.

After the hostilities ended, the United Nations placed the number of Arab fugitives from Israeli-controlled territory at approximately 720,000 (the Jews listed the number as 538,000), 70 percent of the Arab population of Palestine. Not all of those who fled their homes departed Palestine itself. Roughly 240,000 Arabs simply crossed into the Legion-occupied, eastern sector of the country. Another 55,000 to 60,000 crossed the Jordan River and entered the Hashemite Kingdom proper. There were as well 180,000 refugees who originally had encamped in the south, and who now fled toward the Gaza area, within Palestine territory, but on the edge of the Sinai Peninsula. The fate of these Gaza derelicts was to be particularly cruel. Refused employment and resettlement by Israelis and Egyptians alike for the next generation, they were destined to vegetate in a confinement even more tragic than that endured by Jewish displaced persons in Europe between 1945 and 1948. In addition to the fugitives in Gaza and Hashemite-occupied territory, nearly 100,000 Arabs sought refuge in Lebanon, another 70,000 in Syria, with smaller groups traveling on to Iraq and Egypt—and later to the Persian Gulf sheikhdoms. The descent of the Palestinians upon neighboring Arab lands at first served Israel's short-term purpose. It did away with the likelihood of fifth-column activities and similarly inundated the Arab nations with thousands of penniless families, thereby complicating their economies and obstructing their military efforts. After the war, however, the refugees ultimately would fulfill as useful a political purpose for the Arab states as the Jewish displaced persons had served initially for the Zionists.

Well before hostilities ended, the Jewish leadership made plain its approach to the refugee question. As early as April 1948, addressing his Labor Zionist colleagues, Ben-Gurion declared: "The Arabs are wrong if they think they will lose nothing in entering the war: what has happened in Haifa or Jerusalem might happen in other parts of the country." He frankly predicted a "great change in the composition of the population of the country." Later, at a cabinet meeting of June 16, the Israeli leader stated his attitude more unequivocally: "As for the return of the Arabs, not only can I not accept the opinion of encouraging their return . . . but I think that one should prevent their return. . . . War is war . . . and those who declared war upon us will have to bear the consequences after they have been defeated." In answer to Count Bernadotte's appeal to permit Arab repatriation, the Israeli prime minister made his stand official on August 1, 1948, consciously resolving a half-century-old Zionist policy dilemma on the Arabs:

> When the Arab States are ready to conclude a peace treaty with Israel this question [of refugees] will come up for constructive solution as part of the general settlement, and with due regard to our counter-claims in respect of the destruction of Jewish life and property, the long-term interest of the Jewish and Arab populations, the stability of the State of Israel and the durability of the basis of peace between it and its neighbors, the actual position and fate of the Jewish communities in the Arab countries, the responsibilities of the Arab governments for their war of aggression and their liability for reparation, will all be relevant in the question whether, to what extent, and under what conditions, the former Arab residents of the territory of Israel should be allowed to return.

For all its self-serving intent, the language bore a remarkable similarity to that used by Turkish diplomats at the Conference of Lausanne, in 1922–23, as they rejected Greek demands for repatriation following the late war between the two countries. What ensued at that time was the first great exchange of refugees in Near Eastern history. Nor were the circumstances entirely dissimilar in the Arab-Israeli war, although the plight of the Arab refugees was destined to weigh increasingly heavily on the consciences of later Israeli intellectuals. Even as Ben-Gurion was speaking, the Damoclean sword of Moslem xenophobia was descending on the large and historic Jewish communities of North Africa and the Islamic Middle East. Between 1948 and 1957, as a consequence of government pressure, economic strangulation, and physical pogroms, some 467,000 Jews would be compelled to flee their ancestral homes in Moslem lands. The largest number of them would find asylum in Israel (Chapter xv).

BERNADOTTE MAKES A PROPOSAL

With these emerging demographic changes in mind, reinforced by a growing awareness of military success, the Israeli government evaluated the possibilities of transforming the United Nations truce into a permanent peace. The world organization and its mediator in Palestine, Count Folke Bernadotte, had moved with unanticipated dispatch in effecting the second cease-fire of July 18, 1948. This had not been a negotiated but rather an imposed truce with warnings of severe economic sanctions against those refusing to comply. It was intended, moreover, to remain in force without time limit. Bernadotte now had an enlarged staff at his disposal to supervise the querulous lull in hostilities, including 310 Swedish, American, French, and Belgian military observers and enough technical personnel to man his eighteen planes, four ships, his fleet of hundreds of vehicles and radio transmitters. This was in fact an apparatus capable of supervising rather more than a limited cease-fire. The mediator intended to use it in a strenuous effort to achieve permanent peace.

Bernadotte was supremely confident of his abilities as a negotiator. Fluent in six languages, an experienced diplomat with family ties to the Swedish royal dynasty, he had served as president of the Swedish Red Cross during and after World War II. In that capacity, throughout the last weeks of the German Reich he had engaged in critical negotiations with the SS chieftain, Heinrich Himmler, in an effort to rescue surviving prisoners in Nazi death camps. At the time, Bernadotte had conducted the discussions with elaborate (and in the eyes of the Jews, unforgivable) caution and circumspection, refusing until the last moment to promise Himmler immunity from Allied retribution. Although many thousands of Jews were transferred to western Germany, where they were eventually liberated by the American and British armies, the majority of the death camp inmates still alive in April had perished by May. The Swedish count nevertheless regarded his mission as a success and was not hesitant afterward to describe the imaginative stroke by which he had rescued "his" Jews from the Nazi maw. Now, in the summer of 1948, a tall, long-jawed, vigorous extrovert in his late fifties, Bernadotte viewed the Palestine war as a dramatic challenge and was determined to transform the cease-fire into the first stage of a binding peace treaty, his personal triumph and an assured lien on the Nobel Peace Prize.

Speed and initiative were of the essence, more even than perfect justice for either side. "The experience I had during the past month," wrote Bernadotte of the first truce in June 1948, "had gradually . . . strengthened me in my view that the resolution adopted by the United Nations General Assembly on 29th November 1947 had been an unfortunate one. . . . The artificial frontiers given to the State of Israel and the solid resistance put up by the Arab world against the partition of Palestine and the creation of a separate Jewish State were bound to result in warlike complications." The mediator's proposal, therefore, completed on June 27, offered new variations on the Partition Resolution. Instead of two independent states, it provided for two independent members of a "union" in which the Arab partner would not be a Palestine Arab state at all, but an enlarged Kingdom of Transjordan. Bernadotte suggested unlimited Jewish immigration during the first two years, after which the right to decide Palestine's absorptive capacity would be transferred to the United Nations Social and Economic Council. The mediator emphasized, too, that all Palestine Arabs must be returned to their homes and have their property reinstated. Finally, it was his suggestion that the Negev be assigned to Transjordan, with western Galilee transferred to Israel. Jerusalem would be given outright to Transjordan, with assurance of full autonomy to its Jewish population. Haifa and Lydda airport would become free zones.

In one fell swoop, Bernadotte had managed: to disregard eighteen months of painstaking United Nations investigation and formulation; to outrage all the Arab states except Transjordan; and to infuriate the Jews, who had not declared and successfully defended the independence of their sector of Palestine, including the New City of Jerusalem, only to return half of it and forfeit their right to control immigration. Not surprisingly, Cadogan in the Security Council discerned in the mediator's scheme a way out of the "proved impossibility" of enforcing partition. For London, the Bernadotte plan had the obvious merit of giving over the larger part of Palestine to Abdullah, a British protégé. But the Arab League response was pithily expressed by a Syrian staff officer, Muhammad Nimr al-Khatib: "Most of these mediators are spies for the Jews anyway," he insisted. "This is a fact known to everyone." The Arab statesmen icily rejected Bernadotte's plan, and Abdullah was obliged to maintain a common front with them. The Israeli government refused even to discuss it. "From the expressions on the faces of many of those who sat nearest to me," Bernadotte wrote of a Tel Aviv conference, "I realized that they strongly disapproved both of my proposals and myself." Sobered by the hostile reception on both sides, the mediator decided not to press the issue for the time being. In the weeks following the second truce, from August 13 to September 16, he flew back first to Stockholm for rest and reflection, and then to the island of Rhodes for additional consultations with his staff. "The Jews had shown a blatant unwillingness for real co-operation," he explained, "and the Arabs had asked me to leave them in peace for a few weeks, so as to allow time for popular excitement in their countries to die down."

By the time the mediator returned to Jerusalem, the Jews had won more defensible frontiers for themselves, and Bernadotte, in turn, had decided to abandon his scheme for transferring Jerusalem to the Arabs or limiting Jewish immigration. In his final report to the Security Council, a ninety-page document that he and his colleagues prepared at Rhodes and transmitted on September 16, Bernadotte sharply modified his original proposals. He noted that the Jews had established their state and that Israel was "a living, solidly entrenched and vigorous reality." The initial conception of a political and economic union accordingly was dropped. Jerusalem no longer was envisaged as an Arab city but rather as an international community, under United Nations control. Bernadotte still anticipated giving the Negev to the Arabs, together with Lydda and Ramle (recently captured by the Jews). But the entire Galilee would be assigned to Israel as compensation. In a heartfelt warning, too, at the very outset of the report, Bernadotte emphasized that "no settlement can be just and complete if recognition is not accorded to the right of the Arab refugee to return to [his] home. . . ." Yet, for all its apparent balance and evenhandedness, the document was contemptuously rejected by both sides.

In Jerusalem, the day after the report was submitted to the United Nations and to the Arab and Israeli governments, Bernadotte and a group of colleagues started on the drive back to their headquarters at the YMCA building in the Jewish New City. Their three automobiles entered a neutral zone where Arab and Jewish snipers were known to be active. At this point a jeep suddenly pulled out of an alley and blocked off passage. The four men inside were dressed in the khaki short trousers and peaked caps of the Jewish army. Three of them jumped out and approached Bernadotte's vehicle. The first soldier immediately thrust the muzzle of a Sten gun through the driver's window and fired a burst of shots. Bernadotte and another member of the United Nations staff died almost immediately. Two days later, on September 19, the mediator's body was flown back to Sweden. Deeply shocked and mortified by the killing, the Israeli government immediately launched a wide-ranging manhunt. It was assumed that the Lech'i had perpetrated the assassination; but the murderers were later described as even more fanatical right-wingers, zealots who considered Bernadotte a secret agent. They were not found. Nevertheless, in the course of the search more than four hundred Sternists were arrested, including their leader, Nathan Friedmann-Yellin. Many of them were kept imprisoned for the remainder of the war and even after, on the accusation of "incitement to treason." Few were actually brought to trial, however, a matter that did not escape the attention of the Swedish and other Western governments.

The tragedy of Bernadotte's assassination lent further weight to his report. What initially had been intended as mere suggested lines of thought became the "political testament" of a man who had sacrificed his life for peace in the Holy Land. Bevin eagerly seized upon the document to announce in the House of Commons that "the recommendations of Count Bernadotte have the whole-hearted and unqualified support of the Government." In Washington, too, Secretary of State Marshall endorsed the report and urged the General Assembly to accept it. The Israelis followed these developments with intense concern. The mediator's scheme for amputating the Negev and internationalizing Jerusalem gave the British and Americans a convenient handle for applying pressure on the Jewish state. It was evident to Ben-Gurion and his colleagues that Israel's bargaining position would have to be strengthened by new and decisive military realities.

THE BATTLE FOR THE NEGEV

In the last days before the imposition of the second truce, on July 18, 1948, the Jews managed to recapture a number of villages in the northwestern corner of the Negev. Yet the majority of Negev settlements still remained under Egyptian blockade. As Yadin and his staff viewed it, strategic considerations alone would have dictated a future Israeli offensive in the desert. The need to abort the Bernadotte proposals now lent such a campaign a final measure of urgency. It was agreed that the Egyptian danger was potentially the greatest, and that priority henceforth should be given to a full-scale offensive in the Negev. In this southern desert region, Egyptian forces loosely controlled three long strips. The first was the coastal region from Rafa to Gaza. The second was an inland strip running south to north, from al-Auja through Beersheba and Hebron to Bethlehem. Linking the two enclaves was the third, a cross-country strip running from west to east along the road from Majdal to Beit Gubrin, through Faluja (see map, p. 344). Tactically, these holdings were extremely vulnerable, although the Egyptians had reinforced them with 15,000 new troops and large quantities of heavy weapons.

The Jewish no less than the Egyptian forces had grown impressively in troop and weapons strength since the early weeks of fighting. By the middle of October their personnel numbered 90,000 men, including some 5,000 Jewish volunteers and several hundred non-Jewish mercenaries from abroad with extensive military experience. During the same period the flow of supplies from Czechoslovakia and elsewhere continued uninterruptedly, bringing in fighter planes, tanks, artillery, thousands of cases of light weapons and ammunition, as well as machine tools for Israel's armaments industry. In preparation for the new offensive, Israeli transport planes ferried men and matériel to an airstrip carved in the northern Negev. From August until late October 1948, some 2,000 tons of equipment and 1,900 troops were carried down in this fashion. Under cover of darkness, the soldiers were infiltrated into the Negev kibbutzim, until a full Israeli brigade was operating behind Egyptian lines. During the same period, Yigal Allon slowly moved his veteran northern brigades southward. By mid-October the young commander had 30,000 troops at his disposal on a single front, plus a small air fighter squadron. He chafed impatiently to move onto the offensive.

The opportunity came on October 14. With United Nations approval, the Israelis set out to provision their settlements by conducting an unarmed convoy across the Egyptian-controlled Faluja crossroads. The moment the column drew within sight of the farms, the lead vehicles were blown to bits. In fact, undetected by United Nations observers, the Israelis themselves had dynamited the trucks. Armed with the pretext he needed, Allon went into action immediately. The speed with which he now launched his offensive was a shattering surprise for the Egyptians. Sweeping low behind enemy lines, the fledgling Israeli air force bombed and strafed Egyptian bases and supply lines in the Sinai Desert. Simultaneously, the Israeli brigade that had been operating clandestinely in the Negev destroyed the railroad line near the Egyptian supply dumps, hammered wedges between Egyptian positions, and drove steadily up the coastal road toward Beit Hanun.

It was all a feint. Allon's actual goal was the Faluja crossroads, the junction controlling the highway net into the Negev Desert. Throughout the next day, other detachments of Israeli infantry launched a major attack against the Egyptian fortifications at Iraq al-Manshiya. The battle was an exceptionally vicious one, with serious losses on both sides. The Jews took the fortress. On October 20, in another costly frontal assault lasting a day and a night, Allon's men invested Huleiqat, the heavily defended stockade anchoring the Egyptian line in the upper Negev. That line was now breached, and the major concentration of Egyptian troops in the Negev, over 35,000 men, faced the possibility of defeat or even entrapment near Faluja. There was little time for the Jews to exploit this victory, however. Chagrined by the turn of events, the British introduced a resolution in the Security Council demanding yet another Palestine cease-fire. The measure was adopted. The Jews were determined to strike quickly. Without pausing to consolidate his position, Allon sent his three brigades racing down the newly opened road to Beersheba, the sleepy little Arab "capital" of the Negev. The Egyptian garrison in Beersheba was caught off guard, and surrendered after only brief resistance. Two days later the neighboring Lachish area was occupied by fast-moving Jewish motorized columns.

During the next week of October 22, as the United Nations truce gradually settled on the desert, the Egyptians began evacuating their units from the western Negev, loading their troops on naval vessels anchored off the coast. Even here they suffered painful losses. Two of their destroyers were sunk by Israeli underwater demolition teams. One of the vessels, *Emir Farouk*, flagship of the Egyptian navy, went down off the coast of Gaza with 700 soldiers aboard. Finally, 3,000 of Egypt's elite troops, the crack Fourth Brigade, were entirely encircled and immobilized in the northwestern Faluja "pocket." Both sides chose to ignore the truce in this isolated sector. Under the command of a resourceful Sudanese brigadier, Taha Bey, the Fourth Brigade dug in and steadfastly resisted the tightening Israeli vise.

The reaction of Egypt's allies to the new military crisis was instructive. Rather than attack the Jews on another front to alleviate the pressure on Faluja, Glubb sent a Legion force down to Bethlehem and Hebron to "save" this district for the Hashemite kingdom. The Legionnaires simply moved into the area vacated by the Egyptians. On October 23, the Arab heads of government met in Amman, where once again they went through the ritual of discussing ways to help the Egyptians. The meeting was a travesty. In his memoirs, Abdullah recalled:

> Directing my words to Nokrashi Pasha [the Egyptian prime minister], I said: "Let us hear what His Excellency has to say."
>
> His reply, word for word, was "God, I have come to listen, not to talk."
>
> I answered, "I think that Your Excellency should do the talking under the present circumstances in view of the fact that Beersheba has been lost and al-Faluja is besieged."
>
> "Who says so?" he inquired. "The Egyptian forces are still holding their positions. . . . [T]he Egyptian Government has no need of anyone's assistance. But where are the royal Jordanian and Iraqi forces? And we all know that the Syrian forces are useless." This was said in the presence of Jamil Mardam Bey, who was listening.

Eventually Glubb submitted a plan for two Iraqi battalions and one Legion battalion to attack Jewish positions in the Beit Gubrin area. Meanwhile the isolated Egyptian brigade at Faluja would destroy its heavy equipment and escape along a secret trail known to one Major Lockheed, a British officer serving with the Legion who was already in contact with Taha Bey. The Egyptian military staff immediately turned down the suggestion. Aside from the risk in destroying heavy equipment, the scheme was compromised by the fact that the Englishman Glubb had proposed it.

On his own, meanwhile, the Israeli commander, Allon, decided to enter into conversations with Taha Bey. Under a flag of truce, a meeting was arranged between the generals at Kibbutz Gat, two miles east of the Faluja "pocket." The Egyptian commander was a stocky, square-jawed Negro, gentle of manner and quick to smile. He congratulated Allon on Israel's "admirable" military victories and agreed that the Egyptian position at Faluja was grave. "But one thing I shall be able to save," he insisted, "the honor of the Egyptian army. And therefore I shall fight to my last bullet and my last man." Nothing would persuade Taha Bey to change his mind, in this or two subsequent meetings. The one consequence of the discussions was to establish friendly ties between Major Yerucham Cohen, Allon's Yemenite, Arabic-speaking aide, and Taha Bey's adjutant, Major Gamal Abd al-Nasser. Nasser was fascinated by the kibbutz settlements and the evidence he saw around him of Jewish social democracy, and contrasted Israeli "progressivism" with the venality and absentee landlordism of his own country. He reserved his angriest diatribes, however, for the British. "They maneuvered us into this war," he insisted. "What is Palestine to us? It was all a British trick to divert our attention from their occupation of Egypt." Egypt's "so-called" allies were equally the target of Nasser's wrath, particularly Abdullah, who was not lifting a finger to help the trapped Egyptians. Someday the Hashemite ruler would pay for his "betrayal," Nasser declared.

The young major's comments accurately reflected the festering suspicion that had developed among the Arab states, and most notably between Egypt and the Transjordanian kingdom. The distrust eventually became

uncontainable on the issue of occupied Palestine. The Egyptians, determined to block a Hashemite annexation, paid worshipful lip service to
the "rights of the Palestinian people" and announced plans for a separate,
quasi-independent government for the Holy Land. To that end, in late
September 1948, Cairo organized an "All-Palestinian Government," with its
seat in Gaza. And on October 1 an Egyptian-sponsored "National Palestinian Council" dutifully met in Gaza to elect the Mufti as president.
Within two weeks the Gaza regime was extended formal recognition by
Syria, Lebanon, and Iraq. Yet its status as an Egyptian puppet became
entirely transparent the moment Haj Amin himself eagerly visited Gaza,
against the orders of the Cairo government. Upon being recognized, the
Mufti was immediately seized by military authorities, driven to Suez, and
placed under tight surveillance there.

Abdullah did not sit by quietly in the interval. Warning that the Gaza
"government" was unwelcome in Hashemite-occupied territory, the Transjordanian ruler swiftly organized his own hand-picked conference of
Palestinian delegates, most of them refugees. In late October the gathering
assembled in Amman, where it solemnly repudiated the Gaza regime as a
façade for de facto partition. Afterward, in Arab towns and villages on the
west bank of the Jordan, crowds demonstrated "spontaneously," entreating
Abdullah to annex the Legion-occupied sectors of Palestine. Finally, on
December 1, a ceremonial conference of Palestinian and Transjordanian
delegates assembled at Jericho and issued a resolution favoring the
joinder of Palestine and Transjordan as an indivisible "Arab Hashemite
Kingdom of Jordan." Abdullah "accepted" the resolution in principle and
appointed Sheikh Hassan Muhyi al-Din al-Jarallah as Mufti of Jerusalem,
in place of Haj Amin al-Husseini.

Abdullah's countermaneuver provoked an infuriated response from
Cairo and other Arab governments. On December 10, 1948, King Farouk
issued a statement anathematizing the Palestinians who had attended the
Jericho conference. The Egyptian army had not shed its blood to leave
the destinies of Palestine in their hands, Farouk warned; the Jericho resolution was a threat to Arab unity and would not be countenanced by the
Arab League. The next day the Grand Ulema of al-Azhar University
formally denounced the Hashemite regime for "nefarious interference
threatening to destroy Arab unity."

THE FINAL CAMPAIGN OF THE PALESTINE WAR

Even as the Egyptians and Hashemites reviled each other, the Jews were
making preparations to attack and eradicate the Egyptian army's last remaining garrison on Israeli territory. The purpose this time was to establish the irrefutable fact of Israel's sovereign power and viability and, it
was hoped, end the war altogether. The armed forces were ready. They had
successfully rationalized their structure, absorbed the last Palmach and
Etzel elements into the general rank and file, and organized clear mobiliza-

tion schedules. Their manpower surpassed 100,000 by December 1948, and their accumulated weaponry included even such heavy equipment as landing craft and frigates.

The Egyptians were deployed slightly to the north of the Sinai frontier, between their own country and Israel, and formed two prongs. The northern force, consisting of two brigades flanking Rafa and Gaza, was supported by the principal Egyptian staging base of al-Arish. The southern prong, also of two-brigade strength, extended from al-Auja to Bir Asluj and aimed upward toward Beersheba. Additionally, the Egyptian Fourth Brigade, locked in the Faluja pocket, tied down a Jewish unit of comparable size. The Egyptians defended well-fortified positions. The Israelis enjoyed the advantages of surprise and the choice of terrain best suited for the offensive—advantages that Yadin and Allon were determined to exploit to the maximum. The Egyptians presumably would expect the attack to be launched against their northern line, the detachments threatening the heavily populated coastal area. Without hesitation, therefore, the Israeli command agreed to thrust southward, driving toward al-Auja, the anchor of the Egypian position in the Negev Desert. If al-Auja fell, the Jews would be in a position to sweep upward into the Sinai Peninsula itself, toward al-Arish and the Mediterranean, breaking the back of the Egyptian military effort in one crushing offensive.

However daring the conception, it presupposed the capture of al-Auja, and the main road from Bir Asluj to al-Auja was well protected by sizable Egyptian artillery and tank units. A direct assault along the southern highway was hardly feasible except at prohibitive cost in men and equipment. Yadin grappled with the problem for nearly a week. On December 17, he discovered a possible solution in his archaeological guide to Greco-Roman Palestine. There, in the classicist's map, an alternative road was identifiable just south of al-Auja. Actually it was the barest memory of a road, a stone-knuckled Roman pathway. Allon thereupon ordered his scouts to determine whether the road still existed. Eventually it was found in the dunes above Bir Asluj. With effort it could be made usable.

During the next three days the effort was mounted. Under cover of darkness, engineers laid boards and Bailey-bridge remnants on the most difficult stretches of this ancient route of march. The work was completed in such uncanny silence that the Egyptian outposts, less than two miles away, remained completely unsuspecting. On the night of December 22 the offensive began. According to plan, Allon sent an armored column rolling ominously toward Gaza. Another brigade of infantrymen, protected by strafing aircraft, charged in the direction of the main highway between Bir Asluj and al-Auja. Both attacks were feints. They effectively convinced the Egyptians that the Israeli offensive was unfolding according to orthodox pattern. During the next few days, then, as the Egyptians braced themselves against repeated frontal assaults on their central fortifications, a powerful Israeli column of half-tracks and troop carriers was already moving slowly along the Roman road. At dawn of December 26 the Jews were within firing range of al-Auja. The mighty fortress was silent; its garrisons had taken up positions to the north. The muzzles of the Egyptian artillery faced northward, too, covering the approaches of the main highway. Now, suddenly, the vanguard of the Israeli army battered into the defenders' rear, the assault tanks and Bren carriers careening into the town square. Although stunned, the Egyptians fought back courageously. But after a full day and night of close-quarter fighting, they raised the white flag.

Isdud (Ashdod)

Iskelon (Ashkelon)
Majdal (Migdal)

Faluja
(crossroads)

Huleiqat
MEDITERRANEAN SEA

Beit Hanun
Gaza

Iraq al-Manshiyah
Beit Gubrin

I S R A E L

Hill 86

Rafa

Beersheba

al-Arish
AIRFIELD

Chalutzah   ROMAN ROAD

INTERNATIONAL BOUNDARY

Ruheibah

Bir
Asluj

ASPHALT ROAD

E G Y P T

Mishrefe

Abu Agheila

al-Auja

Abde

Bir Hamma

al-Qusseima

**THE LAST JEWISH CAMPAIGN
OF THE PALESTINE WAR**
DECEMBER 22, 1948-JANUARY 8, 1949

Attack

Raid

Israeli territory

Bir Hassana

0   MILES   20

Their colonel was still in his pajamas; the lightning attack had caught him in bed.

Allon was determined to forge ahead now without pause. In an enveloping movement, his columns overran Abu Agheila, ten miles inside Egyptian territory. From there they pressed on unhesitatingly toward the Mediterranean coast and the central Egyptian base of al-Arish. The Jews had come farther in eight months of war than the limited distance of mere geographical advance. In May their ill-armed little militia had faced Egyptian tanks only sixteen miles from Tel Aviv. In December their battle-seasoned troops, supported by armor and fighter planes, were driving into Egypt, to the very gates of al-Arish, cutting the last exit routes of the Egyptian expeditionary force. Reeling from these blows, meanwhile, Cairo undertook feverish diplomatic activity to seek military assistance from other Arab states. It was a doomed effort. The Syrians and Iraqis were exhausted. Abdullah considered the war over for his kingdom. Indeed, throughout November 1948, a series of meetings between Moshe Dayan and Transjordanian Colonel Abdullah al-Tel, the Legion commander in Jerusalem, produced an agreement for a "sincere cease-fire," which came into effect on December 1. Further talks between the two officers dealt with the passage of Jewish convoys to Mount Scopus and the relief of Israeli policemen stationed there. The discussions transcended local military issues without quite reaching the level of armistice negotiations.

Virtually bereft of support from its Arab allies, at this point, the Egyptian government soon had to face equally painful repercussions at home. By entering the Palestine war, Farouk had intended to divert national attention from the internal difficulties of his country and upstage his perennial rival, the Wafd party. For a while he appeared to have succeeded. Real and imaginary victories filled the press. In advance, the king had his "triumph" inscribed on postage stamps. With the onset of Allon's final December offensive, however, Cairo found it necessary to conceal its defeats not only from its allies but also from the Egyptian public. Ultimately the failures became known, of course. In November violent demonstrations, largely instigated by the Moslem Brotherhood, were launched against foreign-owned and Jewish business houses. Riots erupted in the streets of the larger cities. Nationalist slogans were intermingled with epithets against Nuqrashi Pasha and his government. The prime minister reacted by outlawing the Brotherhood and ordering the confiscation of its property. But before the order could be carried out, Nuqrashi himself was murdered on December 28 by a Brotherhood member. Some observers believed that Egypt was on the verge of civil war.

Help came to the distraught nation from another quarter. Under the terms of the 1936 Anglo-Egyptian Treaty, Britain was obliged to assist Egypt in the event of attack from an outside party. On December 29, as it happened, the Security Council ordered an immediate cease-fire in Palestine. Now was Britain's chance to revive its tenuous presence in Egypt—and conceivably in Palestine. In fact, by 1948 there were hardly any circumstances, not even an enemy presence on Egyptian soil, that would have persuaded the Cairo government to invoke its 1936 treaty of mutual defense with Britain. London nevertheless chose this moment to deliver a warning. Unless Israel obeyed the Security Council resolution, it declared, Britain would employ its forces in accordance with the Anglo-Egyptian Treaty. The ultimatum was a chilling one. Whatever Israel's rights under international precedent, Ben-Gurion appreciated that he dared not risk a confrontation with a Great Power. Yadin shared this view; the Israeli armed forces had won too much to gamble with their victory now. On January 2, 1949, orders reached Allon's headquarters to withdraw his men from Sinai.

At Yadin's insistence, however, Ben-Gurion permitted Allon and his troops to seize the heights above the border town of Rafa. Thus was sealed off the final escape route of the shattered Egyptian forces in the Gaza Strip. It was here again that the British made another ominous move. For several weeks RAF planes had regularly been flying with Egyptian air squadrons over the Egypt-Israel frontier. On January 7, the day the United Nations issued yet another cease-fire order, four of these British fighters were shot down by Israeli Messerschmitts. Bevin apparently was convinced now that he had found his pretext for threatening direct intervention against the Jewish state, thereby presumably limiting Israel's bargaining strength in any future Arab-Jewish negotiations. On January 8 he announced that the Jews had made "unprovoked aggressions" against Egyptian territory, but "so far" the British had not chosen to move from their Suez bases toward the Palestine frontier. Three days later the British Foreign Office informed the press that it took "an extremely serious" view of Jewish military operations.

Cairo was not hesitant in exploiting the threat of British intervention against Israel. On January 12 the Egyptians issued an ultimatum of their own. No armistice negotiations would begin unless the Jews first evacuated the Rafa heights, they warned. To the Israeli army staff, on the other hand, acceptance of this demand was unthinkable; release of the encircled enemy troops would nullify Israel's most effective bargaining weapon and leave Egypt with a contiguous strip of land well within Jewish territory. Again the decision was Ben-Gurion's to make. As the prime minister saw it, refusal of Egyptian terms would bring with it a continuation of the war on Egyptian soil and the inescapable possibility, therefore, of British intervention. On the other hand, the Jewish state was born, secured, and functioning. It had carved out an additional 600 miles of territory and had changed the demographic composition of the nation in its own favor. The other Arab nations had indicated their willingness to follow Egypt to the armistice table. Perhaps the wiser course now would be to allow the Egyptians an opportunity of saving face. Despite the urgent entreaties, then, of Allon, who rushed to Tel Aviv personally to implore the prime minister not to abandon Israel's strongest bargaining weapon, Ben-Gurion made the decision to pull back.

In the second week of January the Jews withdrew their troops from the Rafa heights. Two weeks after that (following the opening of armistice negotiations), the mauled and battered remnants of Taha Bey's brigade were permitted to depart Faluja. As the Egyptians assembled in formation, Yerucham Cohen, Allon's aide, watched the ceremonies from a hillside. Suddenly he caught sight of Major Nasser. Cohen shouted a greeting, and the two men ran toward each other, warmly shaking hands for the last time. To the strains of an Israeli army band, the Egyptians then marched off toward their encampment at al-Arish.

NEGOTIATIONS FOR AN ARMISTICE

On December 29, 1948, the Security Council, which for a half-year had confined itself to orders for cease-fire and truce, issued a call for a permanent armistice in all sectors of Palestine. Although the Egyptians and other Arab nations were exhausted by then and palpably eager to end hostilities, it was understood that no Arab state would agree to negotiate "directly" with Israel—that is, without benefit of mediation by the United Nations. When, therefore, initial discussion opened between Israel and Egypt on the island of Rhodes early in January 1949, the talks were clearly defined as United Nations negotiations. Both delegations were housed in the same hotel. This produced occasionally ludicrous complications. Walter Eytan, the foreign ministry official who led Israel's negotiating team, recalled that whenever the Egyptians spotted an Israeli approaching in the corridor downstairs "they would eye him, literally askance—demonstratively turning away their heads, although soon overcome by curiosity and turning back sufficiently to catch a glimpse." The United Nations acting mediator, Dr. Ralph Bunche, an American Negro in his early forties and Bernadotte's deputy until the Swedish diplomat's assassination, was a resourceful and imaginative negotiator. Yet even Bunche's considerable charm failed initially to persuade the Egyptians to meet with their Jewish opposite members. As a result, the mediator or his deputy held the opening conversations separately with each delegation.

After several days, however, Bunche's persistence was rewarded. The Egyptians and Israelis finally were gathered together in his suite, while he himself presided from his sofa. It was the pattern that was adopted for subsequent armistice conferences (not all of them in Rhodes) with Jordan, Lebanon, and Syria. At first, to be sure, the Egyptians insisted on addressing all their remarks to Bunche, as if the Jews were not in the room. But it was impossible to maintain an artificiality of this kind. Soon the two groups were arguing with each other directly, in English and French. Both Israelis and Egyptians assured each other that their intention was to secure permanent peace for Palestine. To that end, and as a first step, the armistice agreement was drawn on the basis of the existing military lines. The Negev accordingly would remain in Israel except for the narrow Gaza coastal strip occupied by Egyptian troops. Only the town of al-Auja and its vicinity were to be demilitarized under United Nations supervision.

Israel agreed to this arrangement as a domestic face-saving gesture for the Egyptian government, which could then inform its people that it continued to exert influence in at least one sector of Palestine, even as the Hashemites did.

Each side assumed that the armistice would be supplanted in the near future by a permanent peace treaty (see Chapter XVI). In fact, the armistice agreement itself included such phrases as: "With a view to promoting the return of permanent peace in Palestine and in recognition of the importance in this regard of mutual assurances concerning the future military operations of the parties, the following principles . . . are hereby affirmed"; and "the establishment of an armistice between the armed forces of the two Parties is accepted as an indispensable step toward the liquidation of armed conflict and the restoration of peace in Palestine." The agreement was signed on February 24, 1949. Eytan, chief of the Israeli delegation, later recalled the amiable mood in which the conversations ended:

> In the course of the six weeks we spent together at the Hotel des Roses, we became quite friendly with the Egyptians. . . . We did not meet socially much, but when Abdul Moneim Mustafa, the chief political adviser of the Egyptian delegation, fell ill, we sat at his bedside and comforted him and when the armistice agreement was finally signed, Dr. Bunche had us all to a gay party in the evening, for which the Egyptians had sent in a special plane from Cairo with delicacies from Groppi's. I well remember sitting with the head of the Egyptian delegation, as he showed me photographs of his family. . . . It was an atmosphere as different as one could imagine from that of the first day in the corridor, with its averted heads.

The precedent established at Rhodes was generally followed in subsequent negotiations between Israel and other Arab states. Once Egypt, the greatest of the Arab powers, had agreed to treat with the Jews, it was much less difficult for the others to follow. Thus, the discussions with Lebanon were conducted without incident at Rosh HaNikrah on the Israel-Lebanon frontier. By the terms of an agreement signed on March 23, 1949, the Israelis abandoned the fourteen Lebanese villages their troops had occupied during the war and restored the old international border. Except for specific territorial provisions, the language of the agreement was virtually identical with that of the Israeli-Egyptian document. It, too, stated the expectation that the end of hostilities would usher in permanent peace. The agreements with Egypt, Lebanon, and Jordan (p. 350) were all signed within less than six weeks. The Syrians alone of the signatories raised difficulties. Their intransigence was due in part to a highly inflamed nationalism—Syria was the birthplace of Arab nationalism, after all—and in part to an instinctive unwillingness to remove their forces from occupied Israeli territory. The meetings between the two delegations took place in the stifling heat of late spring and summer, in a tent pitched across the no man's land of the Tiberias-Damascus highway. Negotiations dragged on from April 5 to July 20. After endless haggling, the Syrians agreed finally to withdraw to the original frontier, but stipulated in turn that Israeli troops should not replace theirs in the evacuated areas. In this way another series of demilitarized zones were created. Otherwise, the document adopted the basic provisions of the earlier agreements.

On March 19, the Iraqi government informed Bunche that it had authorized the Jordanian delegation to negotiate in its place, and that its troops would then be withdrawn. They were. As matters turned out, Iraq was the only one of the Arab belligerents not to sign an armistice agreement directly with the Jews. This exception later permitted Baghdad to adopt a verbal hostility to Israel even more uncompromising than that of the Jewish state's immediate neighbors, without the corresponding obligation to translate words into deeds. As Nuri es-Saïd had discovered years before, the technique was a useful one for winning popularity at home and, conceivably, political leadership in the Arab world. Later the approach would be adopted by other Moslem governments even further removed from the scene of battle—by Algeria and Libya, for example.

Of all their negotiations with the Arab regimes, the Israelis found dealings with the Hashemite Kingdom to be at once the most complex and potentially the most hopeful. Talks began at Rhodes within days of the armistice agreement with Egypt. The Transjordanians were a somewhat less impressive group than their Egyptian predecessors; they looked helpless and lost, and uncertain of their instructions. Actually, no clear guidelines had been given them. Abdullah had preferred to make direct contact with the Jews through Colonel al-Tel in Jerusalem, and it was arranged that an Israeli delegation should secretly meet with the king in his winter palace at Shune, near the Dead Sea. Evidently Abdullah was not willing to devolve negotiating authority on his emissaries at Rhodes, although he agreed that the talks on the island should formally continue.

Colonel al-Tel arranged the passage into Transjordan of the Israeli delegation, identifying the visitors at checkposts as United Nations observers. The charade was not a simple one, for, in addition to Eytan, the Jews included Yadin and Dayan, whose faces were well known. The crossings were never challenged, however. Abdullah received his guests personally at Shune, and once again was as gracious a host as before the war. In the first joint meeting with the assembled Jewish and Arab negotiators, the king addressed the whole room, reviewing the events that had brought the delegates together at this strange gathering. He spoke with unusual frankness and emphasized that his own ministers must recognize that it was they, together with the Egyptians, who had forced him into a war he had not wanted. He continued in this vein—accusing his officials, berating them—for twenty minutes. When the Arabs and Jews sat down afterward to a banquet, the prime minister, Abd al-Uda, asked to be excused, complaining of a stomach ache.

Abdullah himself withdrew following the dinner, and his negotiators continued talks without him. After bargaining through the night, the Jews left in Tel's car, to reach Jerusalem before daybreak. These nocturnal journeys and talks continued for a week. All the while, to maintain pressure, the Israeli army demonstratively continued its preparations for a

large-scale offensive against the "Iron Triangle," the Jordanian-occupied
salient in eastern Palestine. The price of calling it off was Abdullah's willingness to agree to a revised border area. And in the end, a compromise
agreement was reached. The demarcation line was not drawn strictly in
accordance with the position of the armies, but several miles to the east,
favoring Israel, and ceding to Israel the Chadera-Afula highway and the
Lydda-Haifa railroad, as well as a portion of the dominating hill country.
For prestige reasons, the Jordanians kept the largest number of villages on
their side of the line, but were less interested in retaining village lands.
Many farmers were cut off from their soil, as a result. The arrangement
at best was considered temporary, pending a formal peace treaty and the
establishment of an agreed frontier. A revised, demilitarized border line
was established between the Dead Sea and Aqaba, and from the Dead
Sea northward to Beisan. On the other hand, the Jerusalem district was
exempted from these revisions. Here the status quo continued: the New
City remained in Jewish hands, the Old City in Arab hands. The Jordanians
promised the Israelis free access to the Hadassah hospital and the Hebrew
University on Mount Scopus, and to the shrines and cemeteries on the
Mount of Olives.

This was the essence of the understanding approved on both sides at
three o'clock on the morning of April 1. Immediately afterward, Dayan and
Jundi, the respective Jewish and Arab delegates, flew the agreement to
Rhodes, where it was formally signed on April 3 by the "official" Israeli
and Jordanian representatives. The Jews thereupon moved forward to
occupy the strategic hills. In August 1949 the United Nations staff remained
behind to watch over the cease-fire, but on a presumed temporary basis.
In later months Abdullah carried on secret, but detailed, conversations with
Israeli representatives, and a draft peace instrument actually was initialed
in March 1950 (Chapter xvi). For reasons of political expediency alone,
however, the king allowed the document to lie for a while. That may have
been his mistake. Had he negotiated and signed a treaty immediately, it
probably would have been accepted as a *fait accompli*. Instead, news of
the conversations leaked during the uncertain limbo of a protracted armistice period. It doomed the ablest statesman in the Arab world (p. 451).

The agreements left Israel in possession of approximately 8,000 square
miles of Palestine, or 21 percent more land than had been allotted under
the partition plan. It was assumed, nevertheless, that the frontiers were
tentative and that they would be adjusted and altered in subsequent peace
negotiations. Because they were not, the accords represented a built-in time
bomb for Israel. The demarcation line with Jordan, for example, quite
heartlessly separating many Arab farmers from their land, became a
perennial magnet for infiltrators and a source of endemic border violence
between the two countries. The convoluted nature of the Jerusalem
settlement, with its precarious easements to educational sites and holy
places, was too dependent upon Arab goodwill to be inherently workable.
The Jews were obliged to guard their hospital and university on Mount
Scopus by special police. No agreement was ever satisfactorily achieved

for access to, or proper care of, Jewish religious shrines in the Old City. This was an endless source of dismay to Jewish religionists in Israel and elsewhere.

The arrangements with Syria were equally fraught with danger. The territory adjacent to Israel's demilitarized zones along the Syrian frontier was populated by Jewish farmers. Several of Israel's major agricultural development schemes were being planned for these areas, including the drainage of Lake Chula and the realignment of the bed of the Jordan River. Intending to work the demilitarized zones themselves, the Jews cited the clause in the Syrian-Israeli Agreement of July 20, 1949, that recognized "the gradual restoration of normal civilian life in the area of the Demilitarized Zone" as a basic aim of the armistice. The Syrian government rejected this interpretation, and very quickly the region became a source of conflict. When the Jews undertook agricultural or irrigation activities along the border area, the Syrians periodically fired on them from their revetments on the Golan Heights. It was in this fashion, as shall be seen, that Syria blocked Israel's original plans for tapping the Jordan River and forced the Jews to adopt the less practicable and more expensive method of siphoning water directly from Lake Galilee. The zones remained a critical focus of danger and possible warfare (Chapters xvi, xxi).

So, also, did the Gaza Strip, where the Egyptians continued to maintain armed forces within Palestine territory. At the instigation of Cairo, the densely congested refugee zone in future years would become a major staging base for the infiltration of Arab guerrillas into Israel. The ambiguous text of the Israeli-Egyptian agreement offered a cover for these quasi-military operations. All the armistice settlements spoke of a full armistice and a moratorium on "aggressive action" by either party against the other. But one provision in the other agreements was not incorporated into the Israeli-Egyptian covenant (at the time, possibly by inadvertence). It was: "No warlike act or act of hostility shall be conducted from territory controlled by one of the Parties to this Agreement against the other Party." The Egyptian government subsequently construed this lack of reference to aggressive action as legal justification for encouraging guerrilla activity, for denying Israel access to the Suez Canal, and—before 1956, and briefly again in the spring of 1967—for proclaiming its right to bar Israel's use of the Strait of Tiran. Here, too, was an unimaginably lethal delayed-action bomb. But so remote did these dangers appear in 1949, so transitional in nature the armistice agreements themselves, that even before the final documents were signed in the summer of that year a newly appointed United Nations body, the Palestine Conciliation Commission, began to take over and enlarge upon the functions of the mediator. By the terms of the General Assembly resolution of December 11, 1948, the PCC's announced intention was to arrange nothing less than "a final settlement of all questions outstanding between [Israel and the Arabs]." This matter-of-fact statement appeared so pregnant with hope for the future that it was compensation enough to the Jews for all they had recently endured.

THE RHODES ARMISTICE
DEMARCATION LINE

0   MILES   30

Indeed, they had endured much. The war had taken 6,000 lives and five times that many wounded, an appreciable number for a nation of less than 600,000. Military expenditures alone had consumed nearly $500 million. Once again, as in the 1917–18 period, the land was desolated. Many of its most productive fields lay gutted and mined. Its citrus groves, for decades the basis of the Yishuv's economy, were largely destroyed. These grievous wounds notwithstanding, the little Jewish republic at least was alive and operating, and its statehood was an internationally accepted fact. Once the nation's elections were held in January 1949, and a functioning government and parliament given a public franchise, the countries that had extended Israel de facto recognition at the moment of its birth began to open legations and embassies in Tel Aviv and Jerusalem.

Following the Rhodes Armistice agreements, Israel's application for membership in the United Nations was approved by the Security Council on March 11, 1949, and membership itself came the following May. (In those days admission to the world body was still considered meaningful evidence of a nation's sovereign viability.) As the Israeli flag was ceremoniously hoisted in the plaza of the General Assembly building, Shertok, Eban, and other participants, together with the Jewish world at large, asked themselves whether only four years had passed since the Star of David had been identified primarily as the seal of doom worn by concentration camp inmates. The rise to independence of history's most cruelly ravaged people transcended the experience, even the powers of description, of case-hardened journalists and social scientists alike. It appeared somehow as if a new law of nature had been born.

THE GROWTH
OF THE ISRAELI REPUBLIC

THE FRAMEWORK OF GOVERNMENT

By all external signs, in May 1948, the Yishuv's leadership was rushing to sovereignty in a kind of disorganized frenzy. It was known, for example, that even the decision on a name for the new state had been put off until the last minute, and that the final typewritten version of the Declaration of Independence had been approved only an hour before it was publicly read. Appearances belied reality, however. Far from being a haphazard patchwork, the emergent government of Israel in fact was organized according to a carefully devised master blueprint. As far back as October 1947, a joint committee of the Va'ad Le'umi and Jewish Agency Executive drafted a legal code and a proposed constitution for the impending state. By the first stage of the plan, an interim functional government was established on March 1, 1948, consisting of a People's Council whose thirty-seven members—party representatives of the Va'ad Le'umi and of the Agency Executive—were selected according to their proportional political strength in the Yishuv. It was this People's Council, in turn, that three weeks later approved a meticulously structured formula for a Provisional Government, to come into effect with the end of the mandate.

The Declaration of Independence itself prescribed the transformation of the prestate to the poststate government. The legislature of the Provisional Government, entitled the Provisional Council of State, comprised the identical thirty-seven members of the People's Council that had functioned since March 1, with the identical thirteen-member executive. On the same day, May 14, the Provisional Council of State issued a proclamation formally legalizing its own authority. It was on behalf of the Council, therefore, that Ben-Gurion announced the continuance in force of all mandatory laws, except those to be amended by the Council itself. The proclamation then went on to revoke a number of the British measures most repugnant to the Jews, including the 1939 White Paper and subsequent ordinances of 1941 and 1945 that had placed additional limitations on Jewish immigration, Jewish land purchase, and freedom of movement. Stormy applause greeted these amendments and revocations.

On May 16 the Provisional Council of State elected Weizmann as its president (although not as president of the State of Israel) and launched into the task of governing in the midst of a war emergency. With few exceptions, the government ministries were transformations of departments and bureaus that had existed under the Va'ad Le'umi, the Jewish Agency, or the mandatory administration. The Va'ad Le'umi's departments of health, religious affairs, and social welfare, for example, became ministries of health, religions, and social welfare in Israel's government, while the departments of culture and education were united to form the ministry of education and culture. Similarly, the financial, immigration, labor, political, and trade and industry departments of the Jewish Agency became the new regime's ministries of finance, immigration, labor, foreign affairs, and commerce and industry. The mandatory's forty-odd departments were similarly taken over now and allocated among the government's thirteen ministries. During its tenure, from May 14, 1948, until March 10, 1949, when the first constitutional government was officially installed, the Provisional Government evoked the broadest measure of national loyalty. No one questioned either its moral or its legal authority when it established a supreme court, issued Israeli currency and postage stamps, assessed and collected taxes, and laid down directives for elections to a Constituent Assembly. The acid test of its recognition was full public acceptance of its emergency ordinances during the war period.

On the other hand, none of Israel's inhabitants had ever assumed that the wartime regime was more than its name suggested, a "Provisional Government." The UN Partition Resolution had declared that a "Constituent Assembly of each State [Arab and Jewish] shall draft a democratic constitution for its State. . . ." Indeed, the Resolution specifically listed the features to be included in the constitution. Among them were a legislature elected by universal suffrage, an executive responsible to the legislature, and guarantees of equal rights in civil, political, economic, and religious matters. These obligations subsequently were reaffirmed by Israel's Declaration of Independence, which asserted that a Constituent Assembly would be elected not later than October 1, 1948. Although the date was postponed as a result of the war, the Provisional Government eventually made good on its commitment. In July 1948, the cabinet fixed the election date as January 25, 1949, authorized a census, and specified detailed electoral procedures.

One of the most noteworthy of those procedures maintained the system of proportional party lists that had been used for decades in elections both to the Zionist Congresses and to the Yishuv's National Assembly. Another delimited the size of the forthcoming Constituent Assembly at 120 members. The voting age was set at eighteen, the franchise was extended to all "inhabitants" of Israel without distinction of race, creed, or sex. In the elections of January 25, therefore, 21 party lists vied for 120 Assembly seats. Some 440,000 individuals cast ballots, 87 percent of the eligible voting population. Following a mathematical computation of each party's share of the votes, the Labor parties were awarded 57 seats, the Center-Right parties 31, and the Religious parties 16. This ratio was essentially the voting profile that had existed in the Yishuv before the state. Of the elected delegates, 117 were Jews, 3 were Arabs.

The first session of the Constituent Assembly was opened on February 14, 1949. A speaker and deputy speakers were elected, and committees were appointed. Two days later the Assembly debated and then passed its first major bill, the terms of which actually had been worked out by party leaders well in advance of the elections. Entitled a Transition Law, the act more generally was known as the "Small Constitution," and it established a clearly defined structure of government that was intended to function until the adoption of a regular constitution, which presumably would institute additional governmental changes. Yet, as shall be seen, this "Small Constitution" was destined to remain the operative law of Israel's government ever after. It consisted of fifteen brief sections that established the nation's republican form of government, including (among its other features) a president, a cabinet, and a parliament. The moment this Transition Law was adopted, the Constituent Assembly formally elected Weizmann president of the state, at which point the Provisional Government resigned.

After consultations in the next few days with party leaders, Weizmann charged Ben-Gurion, leader of the Mapai party, which had gained a plurality of seats in the election, with the formation of the state's first regular government. Three weeks of negotiations then followed, at the end of which Ben-Gurion finally reached a coalition agreement with three other parties. These were the Mizrachi and HaPoel HaMizrachi parties (acting as a "United Religious Front"), the Progressives, and the Sephardim. Selected ministries would be distributed among them. At last, on March 8, the newly formed cabinet and its program were submitted to the resumed Assembly—now entitled the Knesset—and on March 10 Israel's first regular government was confirmed by a vote of seventy-three to forty-five.

The initial Assembly had not been elected simply to become a Knesset, however, a parliament operating along normal legislative lines. Ostensibly it had been elected to prepare a constitution. Nor was there doubt on the eve of the election of January 25, 1949, that most of the Israeli population, no less than the authors of the UN Partition Resolution and of Israel's Declaration of Independence, anticipated such an instrument. For one thing, constitutions were the rule among the nations that had gained statehood after 1945. Moreover, the Zionist Organization itself functioned by constitution. Even during the mandate, the Palestine Order in Council had served as a constitution of sorts. Finally a committee under the chairmanship of Dr. Leo Kohn, legal adviser to the Jewish Agency, had spent months preparing a draft constitution, which the expiring Provisional Government then transmitted to the Constituent Assembly. And yet, all these precedents and advance labors notwithstanding, Ben-Gurion and the Mapai leadership eventually decided to reject the draft constitution.

There were several reasons for this astonishing decision. The prime minister argued, first of all, that it would be a mistake to rush into a constricting legal straitjacket. He pointed out that even the United States had required eleven years to adopt its constitution, and then had amended it fundamentally several years later with a Bill of Rights. The British government, on the other hand, had operated quite efficiently for centuries without a formal constitution of any kind. Ben-Gurion noted, too, that Israel's population still was growing, that time was needed for absorbing immigrants and putting an end to the threat of Arab invasion. Constitutional issues therefore would only tax the Knesset's attention and energies when it had a surfeit of other problems to resolve. One of those problems, for example, was the insistence of the Orthodox partners in Ben-Gurion's coalition government that the Bible and Talmud should be the basis of Israel's fundamental law. Plainly, the last thing Ben-Gurion and Israel then needed was a *Kulturkampf* between religionists and secularists. For these and other reasons, then, the decision was taken in June 1950, after prolonged debate, to reject a formal organic law. Instead, a constitution would be allowed to develop over time through specific legislative acts that would be designated as "Fundamental Laws." Ultimately, as they evolved, these "Fundamental Laws" collectively would become the constitution.

The compromise did not work out in practice. It failed to differentiate between the methods of adopting "Fundamental Laws" and ordinary statutory laws. Indeed, during ensuing years the Knesset enacted several "Fundamental Laws" of great constitutional importance, yet these hardly could be distinguished from routine legislation in the manner of their passage. As a result, a written constitution never emerged. Rather, for all practical purposes, the Transition Law of 1949—the "Small Constitution" —determined the future contours of Israel's government. The Constituent Assembly in turn became Israel's first operating Knesset, and the Knesset's individual acts shaped the nation's subsequent political evolution.

LEGISLATURE AND EXECUTIVE

It was a development based, nevertheless, on a very substantial foundation of prestate experience. Over half the members of the first Knesset had participated in various Zionist Congresses or in the Va'ad Le'umi. Exposure to three decades of British legislative schemes under the mandate also had produced a hybrid of British parliamentary and Zionist continental practices. Thus, Israel's Knesset bore a similarity to Westminster in its powers of legislation, its supervision of the government and administration, and its review of domestic and foreign affairs. It differed from British parliamentarism by adopting, in modified form, the Zionist Congress system of a one-chamber legislature elected by ballots cast for party lists rather than for individual members representing separate constituencies. Each of the party lists, in turn, contained names of up to 120 candidates. If, for example, one of the larger parties received 50 percent of the vote, and thus won sixty seats in the Knesset, the first sixty people on the party's list took office. The order of listing was decided by the party's central committee and indicated party rank or importance as a vote-getter (Ben-Gurion accordingly was ranked first in the Mapai list). The Israeli voter had no right to strike out the name of any candidate on the list of his choice. In effect, he was voting for a party ideology rather than for individuals whose flexibility and powers of discretion he trusted.

On February 14, 1951, the government was defeated over the issue of religious education in the immigrant transit camps (p. 367). Immediately Ben-Gurion submitted the resignation of the cabinet. This created a new difficulty, inasmuch as the Knesset had not adopted procedures for holding new elections. The cabinet and Knesset thereupon drafted legislation to terminate the First Knesset and schedule elections for the Second, and set the length of office for all ensuing Knessets at four years. Such "procedural" legislation was rare, however, although occasional subsequent amendments to the Transition Law were passed. More commonly, Knesset policies and directives were adopted through evolution and by rulings of the speaker. As the technical procedures of the Knesset underwent changes over the years, many of its rules came to be adapted from the constitutional experience of other nations, particularly of Britain. Thus, each new Knesset elected its own speaker, held two sessions a year, but might also be convened for occasional extraordinary sessions. The bulk of the Knesset's work was accomplished in nine permanent standing committees, ranging from the judicial committee and finance committee to the highly important foreign affairs and national security committee. The composition of these bodies was proportionate to the strength of the various political parties in the Knesset. All draft bills followed the British tradition of three readings. Once having wended its way through debate and committee, and having achieved its third and final approval, a bill then was signed by the prime minister, by the minister responsible for its implementation, and by the president.

Opposition existed in the Knesset's political life, to be sure. Yet it did not provide an alternative "shadow" administration, as in Britain. This lacuna could be traced to the precedent established by the Zionist Congresses, most of which had been inclined to give all parties at least a minimal representation on the presidium, rather than consign them to active opposition. In the case of Israel, moreover, few of the parties that remained outside the government were united or cohesive, and accordingly they were unable to replace the government even if they succeeded in harassing or toppling it. The result was that Israel's government often functioned with only the narrowest of Knesset majorities. Legislative pressure was inconsistent, at best. For example, although parliament was reasonably vigorous and effective in maintaining its supervision over purely domestic affairs, it rarely enforced its authority over the government in such crucial matters as foreign affairs and national security, and its inquiries ordinarily were after the fact. Nevertheless, by Israel's second decade the Knesset already was enacting between sixty and ninety laws annually and had won universal respect as an effective legislative body. It was gradually acquiring a sense of discipline, and its respect for the speaker more than once saved it from gross disorder and potential violence. Initial fears of endless, windy parliamentary debate without constructive results proved groundless.

Conceivably the nation's president might have been regarded as an executive counterweight to the legislature. This was surely the role that Weizmann, with his distinguished international reputation, envisaged for himself when he arrived in Israel late in 1948 as president of the Provisional Council of State. Ben-Gurion quickly shot down that notion, however, ensuring that the Zionist elder statesman would enjoy little more than a British monarchical status. By the terms of the Transition Law, the president would not be popularly elected, but would be chosen rather by the Knesset (as indeed Weizmann swiftly was, overwhelmingly), with his term of office linked first to the duration of the parliament, then extended in 1951 to a five-year term. As head of state, the president was invested with authority to appoint diplomatic representatives, the state comptroller, justices and judges, but only on recommendation of the appropriate ministers and Knesset committees. While he was authorized to grant pardons and reprieves, even this power was qualified, for it depended upon the recommendation of the minister of justice and the endorsement of the court of appeals. Weizmann made no secret of his disappointment with his essentially honorific role. "I am a prisoner in Rehovot [the site of his private home]," he confessed to his intimates.

Nonetheless, as in most nations after World War II, the founders of Israel were determined to have strong executive leadership that would not be paralyzed by interminable governmental crises. Their intention was to combine the best of the continental system with the noblest of the British. The outcome was a powerful legislature in law, but not in practice, and a dominant cabinet in practice, although not in law. The cabinet—or, as the Transition Law described it, the government—was formed by the leader of the political party holding the largest number of Knesset seats (in February 1949, this meant Ben-Gurion as leader of Mapai). Designated prime minister, the leader selected his various ministerial colleagues —all of them the nominated choices of the respective coalition parties— either from among Knesset members or from persons outside. When organized, the government was obliged to present itself to the Knesset for a vote of confidence.

As head of government and its directing force, Israel's premier decided the agenda of cabinet meetings, and orchestrated government policies and cabinet committee activities. Technically he was merely *primus inter pares* vis-à-vis other ministers; but the threat of his resignation, an event that automatically would cause the fall of the entire government, gave him the strength to exert a decisive influence both in the cabinet and in the Knesset. On the other hand, the Israeli prime minister did not possess quite the far-reaching authority of his British counterpart. He could not dismiss a cabinet member. He could not advise the president to dissolve parliament, thereby necessitating a new and costly national election; the Knesset reserved this authority to itself. Nor did the fall of a cabinet in Israel automatically precipitate a national election. Rather, the president consulted with party leaders in the Knesset and then invited one of them to form a new government.

Yet the most significant limitation on the prime minister's authority was the nature of coalition government itself. A characteristic feature of the Israeli system was the repeated breakdown of joint cabinet responsibility. This principle of collective loyalty was outlined in the Transition Law, as well as in the government programs of 1949, 1951, and 1955—all stating that "the Government will be established on a basis of collective responsibility of all its members and all the parties which form part of it." Before joining the government, however, parties often sought to establish preconditions allowing them to disagree with certain motions of the cabinet as "exceptions" to the rule of joint responsibility. Thus, on several occasions, the Orthodox parties stipulated that they must have a free hand to vote their conscience on religious matters. Other minority members of coalitions occasionally won similar concessions. The only effective means of warding off disruptive governmental interruptions, therefore, was through hard bargaining, compromise formulas, and vigorous leadership by the prime minister himself. Certainly Ben-Gurion was decisive enough a man to assert that leadership.

When resignation nevertheless was tendered, Ben-Gurion and others at least could be assured that the government would not fall into limbo. The administration stayed in office as a "caretaker" until a new government was approved by the Knesset. The "caretaker" regime hardly was strong enough to initiate legislation, but at least it averted the void and pandemonium that followed resignations in such nations as France and Italy. Balancing up the strengths and weaknesses of the Israeli cabinet system, then, it is noteworthy that in the first decade of statehood, the government still managed thoroughly to dominate the Knesset. Through its control of parliamentary agenda, its initiation of the most important bills, the cabinet remained preeminent in the legislative process. It shaped major policies and decided virtually all crucial issues.

A BICEPHALOUS JUDICIARY

While the constitutional organs, the Knesset and the government, were established by Israeli legislation, the judicial system and the laws it administered were carried over almost intact from the mandate and were left basically untouched by the "Small Constitution." Later Knessets refined or enlarged upon the court structure but did not significantly alter it. Thus, at the lowest echelon, there functioned twenty-three magistrates' courts, six municipal courts, and eleven magistrates' courts for juveniles. The intermediate level consisted of five district courts. Finally, a supreme court presided over the judicial hierarchy as the court of final appeal (under the mandate it had been subservient to Britain's Privy Council). Separate courts and laws also were provided for the military forces and for labor disputes. Under a Knesset law of 1953, all judges were nominated in a refreshingly apolitical way: by a committee including the minister of justice, two Knesset members, three justices of the supreme court, two other ministers, and two representatives elected by the Israel Bar Association. The nominations were forwarded to the president, who made the (life) appointments, subject to Knesset confirmation. By 1956 nearly one hundred judges were serving in the various courts of the land, although, as in other countries, there were never enough of them. The growth of Israel's population jammed the courts with a huge backlog of litigation.

The basic elements of Israeli law were derived from a number of different sources. One of these was Ottoman jurisprudence, a legal compendium that related particularly to issues of land ownership. A second element was legislation originally passed by the British mandatory government. With the passing years, however, these various mandatory ordinances, regulations, and Ottoman laws were replaced increasingly by a third component, Israeli legislation itself. The fourth, and by all odds the most significant, element inherited by the Israeli legal system was the British Common Law. Indeed, this tradition of Common Law and Equity comprised the major foundation upon which Israel, by precedent or statute, built virtually its entire system of jurisprudence, both in court procedure and in criminal and civil law. Finally, in the drafting of Israeli legislation, efforts occasionally were made to draw inspiration from yet a fifth element, the biblical and talmudical sources of Jewish law.

Despite the absence of a formal constitution, the courts, no less than the Knesset and the press, ensured the growth of an impressive enclave of civil rights, largely patterned after British and American legal tradition. Trial by jury was not introduced into Israel, to be sure, as it had not been under the mandate. Nevertheless, the Anglo-Saxon habeas corpus and the presumption of innocence were maintained in Israeli judicial decisions. While the state occasionally limited freedom in the areas of public security and censorship, it did so on the basis either of various British mandatory emergency regulations that continued on the statute books or of Knesset legislation that slowly replaced or modified these emergency provisions. For example, when issues of national security came up in relation to Arab-inhabited areas of Israel (p. 384), the courts usually upheld the government more consistently than in Britain, the United States, or other, larger, more secure Western nations.

The Israeli judicial system allowed yet another departure from Anglo-Saxon norms in dealing with individual rights. This was in the area of "personal status." We recall that the millet structure of Ottoman Palestine had allowed each religious community an extensive juridical autonomy on issues such as marriage, divorce, burial, and inheritance that related to the personal status of its members. The mandate preserved the system and authorized Moslem, Jewish, and Christian religious tribunals to decide these questions on the basis of their individual religious law. Israel, then, upon achieving independence, first maintained and later enlarged upon this status quo. Ben-Gurion and his fellow Socialists surely were not eager to institutionalize the power of the Jewish religionists; yet there were other and more urgent military and economic dangers that took precedence over a confrontation with the Orthodox.

Accordingly, in successive stages of legislation during the first two Knessets, the rabbinical courts, as well as the religious courts of the Moslems and of the various Christian communities, were given significantly augmented jurisdiction. Under the mandate, participation in the Jewish community (the Knesset Israel) had been a voluntary matter. By a 1953 act of Knesset, however, rabbinical courts were invested not simply with extensive authority in matters of personal status, but their ambit was broadened to include any "Jewish national or resident of Israel." Thus, even foreign citizenship no longer removed a Jew dwelling in Israel from the jurisdiction of the rabbinical courts. More significantly yet, the Dayanim Act of 1955 transformed the judges of rabbinical courts (and of Moslem and Christian courts) into state officials. As in the case of civil judges, they were appointed by the president of the state upon the recommendation of a special committee—which for the Jews included the two chief rabbis, two rabbinical judges, and several members of government and of the Knesset. Not surprisingly, these bills caused violent debate in the Knesset at the time of their introduction and were bitterly opposed by the nation's secular majority. Nevertheless, Ben-Gurion and his Mapai coalition rammed them through. In exchange, the prime minister secured Orthodox support for other measures of decisive importance to his government. As shall be seen, the religious court system signified but the tip of an iceberg of Orthodox political power in Israel (p. 377).

CRISES OF ISRAELI DEMOCRACY

1. *An Entanglement of Parties*

It represented, as well, one of the critical weaknesses of the emerging Israeli state: a politicization not less tenacious or all-embracing than in the days of the Yishuv. It is recalled that this legacy could be traced to the non-indigenous origins of Israel's parties. They were born and nurtured in the Diaspora. Far from serving as instruments for the achievement of power in the lands of their origin, they were international organizations seeking the fulfillment of a somewhat remote ideal in an even more remote country. Nor did their activities in Palestine itself necessarily spring from local, pragmatic conditions. Rather, the parties continued to absorb ideas from abroad that subsequently were transplanted to the Yishuv, taking the form of virtually closed political societies, highly institutionalized and mutually suspicious. This European-inspired ideological commitment survived for nearly a decade after the birth of Israel, and in its relentless purism ensured that none of the various factions was willing to compromise on issues of dogma, much less on the question of self-liquidation.

Even more crucially, statehood immediately made available to the parties new and unprecedented opportunities for patronage and other material benefits. At stake now were important financial empires, most particularly employment in government ministries or in the vast sectors of Israeli society controlled or influenced by the government, among them settlements, housing, and education. After May 14, 1948, therefore, the parties competed with renewed ferocity for the nation's single most important reservoir of potential voters, the immigrants. At times party emissaries actually were dispatched abroad to organize and direct immigrant groups to party-controlled villages in Israel. In the event that immigrants arrived still politically uncommitted, the parties offered the kind of inducements newcomers could best understand: housing, jobs, and other forms of economic security. Uneducated in politics or ideologies, the Oriental Jews proved especially willing to assign their loyalty to whichever faction showed greatest efficiency in distributing food packages, money, clothes, in finding homes and jobs, in offering information, advice, welfare services, and guidance through the bureaucratic maze.

It was a measure of this devouring politicization that, in the election to the Constituent Assembly—the First Knesset—in 1949, fully twenty-one parties submitted lists of candidates and actively campaigned, that seventeen parties competed in elections to the Second Knesset in 1951, eighteen to the Third Knesset in 1955, and no fewer than twenty-six to the Fourth Knesset in 1959. The differences between them could not always be ascribed to the economic status of their constituents. On the contrary, working-class people represented the base support of nearly all parties, and in almost equal proportions. Thus, Cherut's working-class membership was no less broad than that of the Labor parties. Indeed, Cherut received much of its vote from the underprivileged Oriental population. By the same token, many non-working-class voters cast their ballots for Mapai. The differences, rather, were ideological and organizational far more than economic. By and large, the parties split into two main groupings, Labor and Conservative, with a subgrouping of the religious factions. On the Right, few internal issues divided Cherut, the General Zionists, and the Progressives. Nor were there extensive ideological differences among the three principal Labor parties. Even so, doctrinal purity and vested interest were intensified by the patronage opportunities of statehood.

Left of Mapai, for example, the Mapam (United Workers) party rigorously maintained both its principles and its factional identity. Mapam's origins traced back to 1930, the year Mapai itself was formed. It was then that the militant activists of HaShomer HaZair rejected the invitation to form one large political organization—Mapai—embracing all shades of Socialist Zionism (p. 159). Their preference instead was for a revolutionary Marxism based on the kibbutz. For the ensuing eighteen years, as a result, HaShomer HaZair continued to exert only a modest political appeal, even losing ground through its endorsement of a binational Arab-Jewish state. Then, in 1948, Achdut HaAvodah, Mapai's original left-wing faction, broke away from the mother party, accusing its former colleagues of having stultified at dead center. Thereupon HaShomer HaZair joined with Achdut HaAvodah and with remnants of the old Poalei Zion to found Mapam. The new party continued to draw its rank-and-file mainly from the kibbutzim, and its program tenaciously echoed the HaShomer HaZair litany: of a classless society under kibbutz leadership; equality for Israel's Arabs;

an end to military rule in Arab areas; and a "neutralist" stance in foreign policy—which for all practical purposes meant an orientation toward the Soviet Union.

It was indeed this doctrinaire affinity for the Soviet line that ultimately weakened and fractured Mapam. In 1951 Czech police arrested an Israeli citizen, Mordechai Oren, a respected Mapam leader who was on a party assignment in Prague, and charged him with "Zionist subversion." The trial of fourteen leading Czech Communists the following year, many of whom were Jewish and some of whom were accused of "collaboration with international Zionism," further shocked Israeli opinion, as did the Moscow Doctors' Plot in 1953. Mapam thereafter suffered a precipitous decline in elections for the Third Knesset. Yet when the party's central committee decided to adopt a more balanced approach toward the Soviet Union, a splinter element within Mapam, led by the distinguished Zionist and former Haganah commander, Dr. Moshe Sneh, broke away to form an even more radical group called the Left Socialists. Eventually this dissident faction joined the Communist party—and thus consigned itself to political oblivion. The following year Mapam's "right wing," in turn, defected to establish a reincarnated Achdut HaAvodah. As a consequence of these schisms, Mapam, which in 1949 had emerged as Israel's second-largest party, dropped to third in the 1951 elections, and to sixth in the 1955 elections. Its leadership in any case was committed to a pioneering agricultural socialism that meant virtually nothing to a huge, largely Oriental immigration that wanted security, not collectivism.

By leaving Mapam in 1954, and establishing itself as a separate party that year, the Achdut HaAvodah wing made clear its rejection of the doctrinaire Marxist approach to social and foreign policy issues. The Prague trials and Moscow Doctors' Plot had been the final straw for this Socialist "right-wing" component. On the one hand, Achdut HaAvodah continued to place a traditional Labor Zionist emphasis on the pioneering values of manual labor, both in farms and in factories. Like Mapam, it advocated an end to military rule in Arab villages. On the other hand, the party rejected Mapam's pro-Soviet orientation in international affairs and favored strict nonidentification with either world bloc. It was an attractively "progressive" stance, and Achdut HaAvodah's leaders, the former Palmach heroes Yigal Allon and Israel Galili, were universally admired figures. Yet, while Achdut HaAvodah for nearly a decade remained second only to Mapai within the Histadrut, it failed to gain ground in the Knesset. Ranking as the fifth-largest party in the 1955 elections, it dropped to sixth place in 1959.

Besides Cherut (p. 371), the leading force of the Right Center was the General Zionist party. We recall that the very name, General Zionism, had been adopted early in the century to overcome partisanship within the Zionist movement. As advocates of unity and integration, the General Zionists made little effort to develop an ideology or a program, and within the Yishuv itself they were quite ineffective after the 1920s. In 1946 the two wings of the General Zionists, "A" and "B," merged to form a United

General Zionist party. The reconciliation was very brief, and in August 1948 the A faction departed to form the Progressive party (below), leaving B to become the General Zionist Party of Israel. From then on, General Zionism described itself as the spokesman of Israel's Center. Conservative, it favored private enterprise, opposed the chronic politicization of national life, and supported a pro-Western orientation in foreign affairs. The party's electoral fortunes oscillated sharply. In 1949 it polled a meager 5 percent of the vote and won seven seats in the First Knesset. For a while afterward, however, as public discontent with rationing and economic controls mounted, the General Zionists gained new strength and in 1951 acquired fully twenty seats in the Knesset. This turned out to be the apogee of the party's fortunes. In 1955 its Knesset delegation slipped to thirteen, its political ranking fell from second to third, and in the 1959 elections to fifth.

While General Zionism's decline could be attributed in some measure to the growing vitality of Cherut, its erosion was influenced, as well, by the unexpected staying power of the original A faction, the Progressives. Modest in size, the latter nevertheless appealed strongly to those central European immigrants who had arrived in the 1930s, and reflected their cautious moderation. Under the leadership of Felix Rosenblüth (later Pinchas Rosen), the Progressives thereafter bore a certain resemblance to England's Liberal party. Although essentially middle class, they evinced greater sympathy than the rightist parties for labor and social welfare, and favored a more moderate line toward the Arabs. Indeed, in the Knesset, they ordinarily voted in support of Mapai legislation and ended up as a rather dependable partner of Mapai in coalition governments. Otherwise, however, they exerted little influence on their own. The nation's sixth-largest party in 1949, they dropped to eighth in 1951, and to ninth in 1955.

A decisive feature of this constellation of parties, surely, was the pre-eminence of Mapai among them. The election returns told the story, in the State of Israel no less than in the Yishuv. In the first Knesset of 1949 Mapai won forty-six seats; in the second election of 1951, forty-five; in 1955, forty; in 1959, forty-seven. Whatever the fluctuation, Mapai invariably received a plurality of votes. To Israeli voters of all parties it was supremely Mapai that had ensured the growth of the Histadrut, of the Haganah, and that ultimately had nurtured the Yishuv to sovereignty and to victory in the War of Independence. Mapai was the party of Ben-Gurion, not least of all, a patriarchal and heroic figure, especially in the eyes of Oriental newcomers. It was Mapai, too, finally, better than any other party, that had mastered two crucial lessons during the Yishuv. The first was to sacrifice dogma to pragmatic flexibility. Under the tutelage of Katznelson and Arlosoroff, we recall, Mapai rejected a narrow class outlook. One of its key slogans was "From Class to Nation," and it fulfilled this injunction during the state by admitting into its ranks independent craftsmen and laborers alike, even by organizing associations of Mapai doctors and lawyers.

Similarly, Mapai's emphasis on grass-roots organization was a model of its kind. Its leadership perfected the technique of winning control of other interest groups, and then, by mutual accommodation, of coordinating the latter's policies with those of the party. Thus, early on, Mapai concentrated its efforts on the quasi-government of the Histadrut and invariably won for itself the dominating role within the labor federation. In the rural sector, Mapai energetically promoted its views among Chever HaKibbutzim, the largest kibbutz federation. By the same token, the party maintained its traditional grip on the Executive of the Jewish Agency. Nor was Mapai inclined to rest on its plurality control of the government. In the late 1950s and early 1960s, for example, when the largest numbers of immigrants were taken directly from the ship and settled in development towns, Mapai ensured that absorption was guided by the party "key." Under this system, each party was allotted its traditional quota of immigrants and authorized to channel the newcomers to kibbutzim or moshavim, to villages or frontier communities, that historically had been under its own majority control. As it turned out, use of the "key" simply ensured Mapai's continuing domination.

The party oligarchs took nothing for granted, however. They organized and propagandized the immigrants to a fare-thee-well, directing them into the Histadrut, setting up women's departments for them, publishing journals and newspapers in the various languages of the ingathering. With a shrewd, even cynical, concentration on the Oriental newcomers, the party leaders established special Yemenite, North African, and Iraqi departments within Mapai, assured slots for ethnic representatives in the Histadrut bureaucracy, in controlled government ministries and local governments. On the other hand, well into the 1960s Mapai's leadership at the highest echelon remained exclusively in the hands of the older, Ashkenazic veterans of the party. It was a Europocentrism that in fact characterized virtually all the nation's parties. As shall be seen (Chapter XIX), the political processes of Israel by then had generated an organic staying power that for years inured them to fundamental change or democratization.

II. Government by Coalition

They were processes, too, that ensured the kind of government described in Herbert Samuel's memorable phrase, separate entities "entwined in an inimical embrace like fighting serpents." The "inimical embrace" of Israeli politics was that of separate and contending parties entwined in makeshift coalition governments. Throughout Israel's later political experience, it was all but unheard of for a single party to win an absolute majority in a national election. At no time did Mapai, for example, enjoy a plurality of more than 38.2 percent; while (until 1974) no other party reached so much as 20 percent. Under the circumstances, political deals in forming coalition cabinets were inevitable. This had been the tradition of the Zionist Congresses, after all, where most of the parties were represented on the executive, and where a coherent notion of an opposition and its functions had never developed.

Precoalition bargaining on the allocation of cabinet seats was tough. Agreement had to be reached not only on the number of portfolios to be awarded a coalition party, but which portfolios they would be. Ben-Gurion always insisted that the defense, foreign affairs, and treasury ministries remain within the preserve of his own Mapai party; these were never negotiable. What too often were negotiable were policies and principles. Ben-Gurion recalled:

It was my experience in all the governments I headed that small parties [that were] asked to join my coalition demanded as their price the fulfillment of their factional demands. When I used to tell them that these demands had been rejected by the majority of the voters, or otherwise they would have gained as many Knesset seats as my party, they would counter by arguing that without the few seats they could offer me I would have no coalition. To which I could reply that I would approach another of the small parties. Sometimes they would reduce their demands: sometimes, thinking I was bluffing, they would remain adamant—and I *did* go to another party.

But sometimes, too, especially in the case of the Religious parties, Ben-Gurion felt obliged to accept minority demands (p. 378). Between 1949 and 1960, Israel had nine constitutional governments. Each was formed by Mapai in coalition with several other parties. Indeed, Cherut and the Communists were the only factions that at one time or another were not included in these gyrating cabinets. As a rule, Mapai preferred to deal with the Orthodox rather than with the General Zionists, who imposed the heavier price on economic policy. But whichever the partner of the moment, the bargaining ordeal was long, devious, and brazen. At times the formation of new governments was delayed for intervals of up to three months. Worse yet, as a result of coalition pressures, the terms of office of Israel's nine governments were painfully limited, ranging from four months to twenty-six months. No government completed the maximum statutory tenure of four years, although only twice, once in the 1950s and once in the 1960s, was it necessary to dissolve a Knesset and hold new elections.

The first cabinet crisis occurred in October 1950, as differences arose over the hated ministry of supply and rationing (Chapter xv). Failing to get satisfaction on the issue, Ben-Gurion resigned. In this case, the interruption ended quickly and the prime minister formed a second government, with virtually no changes in his cabinet. In February of the next year, however, the government was defeated over the much more important issue of religious education in the ma'abarot—the immigrant transit camps —where the Religious Front demanded automatic educational jurisdiction over Yemenite children. When the demand was rejected by the Mapai leadership, the religionists promptly withdrew their support from the Ben-Gurion cabinet. This time it was plain that there was no alternative to new elections.

Voting for the Second Knesset took place in July 1951. It effected few substantial changes in the membership of the new parliament, which convened in late August. Nevertheless, another six weeks passed before

Ben-Gurion managed to forge a new coalition, Israel's third government. Ironically, the new cabinet was almost a replica of the previous, unstable one, except that the Progressives remained outside until later. Yet as the quid pro quo of their participation, the Religious parties secured four ministries instead of the former three, and won additional concessions on such matters as a ban on nonkosher food imports, and state support of religious schools. A year later, in December 1952, yet a new crisis was provoked when the Agudah religious faction withdrew from the coalition on the issue of national service for Orthodox women. Ben-Gurion accordingly reorganized the cabinet—his fourth government—by including the General Zionists and Progressives. Less than a year after that, the coalition was threatened still again by the resignation of the General Zionists, who had lost patience with the "trend" system of education and insisted on depoliticized state schools. Mapai eventually acceded to their demands, the rift was healed, and the General Zionists rejoined the coalition. By then, however, the endless political give-and-take, the continual reorganization of new governments, had quite exhausted Ben-Gurion, and he resigned as prime minister in December 1953.

For the next two years Moshe Sharett (formerly Shertok) served as head of government. His tenure was not to be an easy one. In June 1955 his cabinet was overturned by the withdrawal of the General Zionists in the wake of the Kastner trial (p. 373). Sharett remained on temporarily as prime minister of a caretaker administration, for the government had fallen only a month before scheduled elections to the Third Knesset. But after the voting, Ben-Gurion himself took over the reins of the Mapai-dominated cabinet. Three grueling months of negotiations followed before a coalition was organized; Mapam and Achdut HaAvodah ministers were substituted for the outgoing General Zionists. It was surely evident by then that the coalition system, with its game of political musical chairs, its factional alliances and divisions, was a less than ideal method of governing a nation already overwhelmed by grave economic and security problems.

The parliamentary situation was by no means entirely bleak, however. Mapai stayed on as the perennial mainstay of cabinet coalitions, reserving the key ministries for itself. Turnover in the cabinet was minor, therefore, and restricted to the less important portfolios. Similarly, until well into the 1960s, Ben-Gurion remained prime minister, except for a twenty-two-month voluntary relinquishment of office; this ensured a certain continuity of government policy. Moreover, Israel's democracy functioned competently in ways that were not always evident. Election campaigns were spirited, national interest brisk; voters turned out in high proportions. There was little electoral corruption, virtually no intimidation, scarcely any disturbance, and an honest count. Even the proportionate list system had the merit of accurately mirroring every shade of factional opinion. Had a single constituency system existed, as in Britain or the United States, for example, the weaker of the two leading parties might have polled 49.9 percent of the votes in each of the nation's constituency districts and still not have gained one seat in the Knesset.

Yet there could be little question that the shortcomings of Israel's parliamentary system in the long run outweighed its advantages. Residents of a particular town or district were offered no choice whatever between individual candidates; no Knesset member was available to represent their local interests. Instead, Knesset members looked for guidance in legislation almost exclusively to their central committee, and deviation from the committee line meant immediate eviction from the party roster in the next election. Nor was there any doubt that proportionate representation tended to fragmentize the electorate. In return for their votes in the Knesset, smaller parties succeeded in blackmailing larger ones for concessions. Conceivably even these circumstances might have been tolerable had the voters known in advance what they were getting. As Ben-Gurion recalled, however, "those who voted Mapai . . . did not know in advance which other parties I might be forced to take into my coalition and what concessions I might therefore be forced to make."

Nor did the coalition system promote efficient administration. Frequently a minister was surrounded by deputy ministers from another party or parties and was unwilling to delegate authority to them because of their known hostility to his views. Occasionally, too, ministerial lines of authority overlapped. In the Sharett government of 1954–55, for example, the Mapai minister of finance advocated tightened controls over foreign currency, while the General Zionist minister of commerce and industry urged the elimination of controls. With the disagreement at the cabinet level, the two ministers went their own ways, ignoring the need for coordination and hopelessly blurring such matters as the issuance of import licenses. Political factors similarly accounted for the existence of a ministry of development. The office initially was conceived with the specific purpose of developing the Negev, but its functions soon began overlapping those of other ministries. Nevertheless, Mapai was unwilling to abolish this essentially redundant portfolio because of its usefulness as bait in coalition forming. Neither, on the other hand, did it wish to give central policy functions to a ministry—the ministry of development—that as a rule was slated for one of the minority parties. Here ultimately was the most grievous failure of coalition government during the 1950s. It virtually closed off long-term national planning in the areas of social policy, transportation, health services, and other sectors not ordinarily earmarked for Mapai ministers. It gave the Religious parties, too, an iron grip over vital matters of private conscience and personal identity (Chapter xx). In short, coalition government awarded priority to the requirements of tactical consensus over the need for long-range solutions.

III. *The Bureaucracy*

For the private citizen, the shortcomings of Israeli democracy were first and most painfully encountered in the waiting rooms of government offices. No obstacle course of inefficiency or obstructionism was ever more difficult to navigate. Nor did politics alone account for the uniquely exasperating quality of the Israeli bureaucracy. Chutzpah (effrontery) was the civil servant's proof of his revived dignity as a Jew, no less than of his moral equality in a Socialist nation. The torpor of the Middle East and the lethargic byzantinism of the east European tradition were similarly factors in this bureaucratic pandemonium. Not least of all, the Israeli civil service was born in the chaos of British departure and Arab invasion, and it never fully recovered. The expiration of the mandate deprived the nation of its most experienced (British) public servants. In consequence, the fledgling Israeli government was obliged hastily to recruit its personnel from four sources: Jews who had served in the lower echelons of the mandatory administration; officials of the Jewish Agency and of the Va'ad Le'umi; war veterans, whatever their actual job qualifications; and, most important, functionaries of the various political parties, who normally were hired in accordance with the traditional party "key."

Two areas only, the army and the judiciary, were entirely spared the taint of politicization (although education was similarly depoliticized in later years), and then only through the herculean efforts of Ben-Gurion. But elsewhere party allegiance determined the selection of new employees. In time entire ministries became indistinguishable from party cells. The notion of a politically neutral civil service was so alien to the Israeli mentality that a civil service commission was organized only after the first great spurt of government activity had passed, in 1950. By then, however, depoliticization could affect only future openings, and at the lower echelons. In the Jewish Agency and the quasi-governmental Histadrut, depoliticization never really began; from beginning to end, job openings and entire departments of these institutions were staffed on the basis of party proportions. It was of relevance, too, that even those few civil servants who possessed training and experience often found their advice ignored by senior politicians. During the mandatory period, the Yishuv had developed a certain suspicion of "experts," particularly British "experts" who had rejected as impossible many facets of Jewish pioneering settlement and growth. This attitude prevailed even after the birth of the state. Political leaders, after all, not technicians, had brought Israel into existence; and the former, accustomed to—often brilliant—emergency improvisation, disdained the long-range blueprints or statistical recommendations of professional functionaries.

There were in any case few enough of these officials whose recommendations were worthy of serious attention. The available supply of trained personnel, party or otherwise, was rapidly exhausted. Only the smallest minority of the new immigrants had acquired public training in their countries of origin, and fewer yet had received a higher academic education. Moreover, the handful of genuinely able people discerned little financial inducement for civil service careers. In the mandatory administration the salaries of leading officials were ten times higher than of those in the lower ranks. In Socialist Israel, by contrast, top officials earned only three times the salaries of those in the lower grades, and inflation and sharply graded income taxes later narrowed this ratio from 3 to 1 to 1.3 to 1. Anyway, the sheer physical limitations of government service were grim enough. In the early years of statehood, two-thirds of the ministries were located in ancient, ramshackle buildings or barracks, and office accommodations were painfully constricted. Few ministry canteens offered hot lunches. For many years, then, office hours were concentrated into a single 7:30 A.M. to 2:30 P.M. time span, with only a brief tea interval at mid-morning. It was a rare employee who performed his work energetically or courteously under these circumstances.

Whatever limited facilities existed for government employees were acquired the hard way, by the workers themselves. During the early months of statehood the vacuum of responsible leadership in the civil service was filled by the Histadrut. Committees of employees began laying the ground rules for working conditions, and in some measure these reflected Jewish Agency and Histadrut procedures that had become entrenched during the mandate. Relieved that the task was being assumed by others, the government in late 1948 actually signed a contract with the Histadrut, promising that all changes in rules of civil service employment would first be negotiated with the workers' committees themselves. From the moment this authority over jobs was abdicated, it became all but impossible for a ministry to dismiss inefficient or insolent employees. The manner in which civil servants thereafter carried out their duties reflected their sense of invulnerability.

But for the future there was a glimmer of hope. A civil service commission was established in 1950. After a shaky start, it gradually developed a workable set of procedures. The tradition of indiscriminately drawing middle-level and lower-rank staff from the parties gradually was abandoned. Job candidates were obliged increasingly to pass competitive examinations. Within each ministry a training division was established, providing courses in administration and routine office management. Finally, the state comptroller, operating on behalf of the Knesset as a combination of public accounting officer and national ombudsman, scrutinized the performance of all government ministries and public corporations, and more than occasionally issued withering reports that brought swift correctional action. As late as the 1970s, administrative performance levels remained woefully below those of Britain or the United States. By east European or Mediterranean standards, they were, perhaps, barely tolerable.

IV. *Demagoguery*

In the early years of Israeli statehood, the nation was made aware of a hard core of implacable, even venomous, hostility to the Mapai-dominated administration. It was an enmity that threatened not only the cabinet coalition but the traditions of restraint and moderation upon which functioning democracy itself rested. A principal source of this animus was the Cherut party. Tracing its origins back to the Revisionist movement and the Irgun Z'vai Le'umi, Cherut remained fully as uncompromising in its demands after 1948 as in the prestate Jabotinsky era. Its platform stated that Israel must expand to its full "historical" borders on both sides of the Jordan River, adopt a straightforward Western orientation in foreign affairs and a vigorous capitalist approach in its domestic policy. Mass immigration was to be encouraged, and a written constitution adopted to guarantee the nation's future political stability.

At first, Cherut's strength lay primarily among the east European middle class of Israel's larger cities. But in the early 1950s, the party concentrated increasingly on the urban underprivileged, particularly the Oriental immigrants who were closed out of the Ashkenazic establishment, and who tended to identify emotionally with Cherut's vigorous anti-Arab stance. Tough and uncompromising, then, in its appeal to these disparate elements, Cherut rapidly became the single most important reservoir of opposition to the Mapai-controlled governments. Its appeal fluctuated. In the 1949 elections it achieved the impressive status of the nation's third-largest party, with fourteen seats in the Knesset. In the 1951 elections, losing strength to the General Zionists, it dropped back to eight seats in the Knesset and to fifth place among the parties. It was this latest setback that committed the Cherut leadership, under Menachem Begin, the former Etzel commander, to a policy of intensified militancy against the Labor regime.

One of Cherut's early opportunities came shortly after the elections to the Second Knesset, in 1951. By then the nation was in desperate financial straits, and Ben-Gurion the year before had made the agonizing decision to seek financial reparations from the West German government. Bonn had agreed in principle to negotiate on this issue (Chapter XVI). Great pains were taken to make clear that the money was to be regarded exclusively as a financial infusion to help Israel absorb hundreds of thousands of survivors of the Nazi terror. Under no circumstances was it intended as "compensation" for millions of liquidated Jews. Despite this scrupulously qualified interpretation, the notion of taking "blood money" from Germany rocked Israeli public opinion. By December 1951, preliminary discussions with Bonn were concluded, and on January 7, 1952, the Knesset was summoned to approve wider-scale negotiations. The ensuing debate was unprecedented in its violence. Bitter opposition to dealings with Germany was expressed by every shade of the political spectrum, including the General Zionists, Mapam, and the Communists. Yet the Cherut bloc was by far the most uninhibited in its attack. For Menachem Begin, German reparations signified "the ultimate abomination, the like of which we have not known since we became a nation." The Cherut leader ensured, too, that his followers transmitted his meaning in its widest implications. On the morning of January 7 he addressed a crowd of 15,000 in Jerusalem's Zion Square. "When they fired on us with their cannon, I gave the order—No!" he shouted, referring to the *Altalena* episode in the War of Independence. "Today I give the order—Yes! This will be a war of life or death." In anticipation of disorders, the government ringed the parliament building with barbed wire, and five hundred police were on hand to cope with violence. The precautions proved inadequate.

Lines of demonstrators began marching on the Knesset, forcing their way through the police cordon, setting fire to automobiles, and hurling rocks and brickbats at the Knesset building. Inside, Begin launched a furious verbal attack on Ben-Gurion from the Knesset dais, excoriating the prime minister as "a Fascist and a hooligan." The crowd meanwhile surged forward, grappled with police reinforcements, and threatened to batter its way into the Knesset Chamber. At this point the speaker ordered a recess. Ben-Gurion went further. He called in the army, and shortly afterward troops arrived to disperse the mob and restore order. Yet by then the windows of the Knesset had been smashed and more than one hundred police had been injured. Would the unrest lead to civil war? Begin hinted at this possibility when the Knesset reconvened later in the day. He warned the legislators:

> There are things in life that are worse than death. This is one of them. For this we will give our lives. We will leave our families. We will say goodbye to our children, but there will be no negotiations with Germany. . . . Today you have arrested hundreds. Perhaps you will arrest thousands. We will sit together with them. If necessary we will die together with them, but there will be no reparations from Germany.

The Cherut leader added that he and his supporters no longer would promise to respect the immunity of the Knesset members themselves. The threat of physical assault was perfectly clear.

The next day Ben-Gurion broadcast to the nation: "Yesterday, the hand of evil was raised against the sovereignty of the Parliament, and the first steps were taken to destroy democracy in Israel. . . . I want to reassure the nation—all necessary measures have been taken to safeguard democratic institutions, and law and order. . . ." The prime minister's energy and calm had great effect. On January 9, 1952, the Knesset gave him a vote of confidence by the solid margin of sixty-one to fifty. Begin promptly wilted and called off further demonstrations. Indeed, he accepted without demurrer a Knesset resolution to deny him his parliamentary seat for fifteen months. It appeared for the while the Cherut had decided to reject incitement as a political technique.

The moratorium was a short one. On January 1, 1954, a historic trial opened in the Jerusalem district court. The defendant, Malkiel Greenwald, a Hungarian-born Jew of seventy-two, was accused of having committed criminal libel against a member of the government. Greenwald had emigrated to Palestine in 1938, where he joined the Mizrachi party. Ten years later he began issuing a newsletter that specialized in rumors of corruption among the Mapai leadership. The vocation was hardly a new one for him; as a youth in Hungary he had edited a similar letter and once had been convicted of criminal libel. In Jerusalem, in 1944, a British magistrate had fined him for slander. Unfazed by his previous convictions, however, Greenwald pressed on in his irascible and somewhat unbalanced campaign for "moral regeneration" in high places. In 1953 one of his circulars attacked Dr. Rudolf Kastner, a fellow Hungarian then employed as public relations director for the Israeli ministry of commerce and industry. "For three years I have been waiting for the moment to unmask this careerist who grew fat on Hitler's lootings and murders," the paper stated. "Because of his criminal machinations and collaborations with the Nazis I consider him implicated in the murder of our beloved brothers. . . ." At this point the Mapai minister of commerce and industry, Dov Joseph, decided to make an example of Greenwald by instituting criminal proceedings against him.

A lawyer in his native Hungary, Kastner had served as chairman of the Jewish Rescue Committee in Budapest during the war. On April 24, 1944, his associate on the committee, Joel Brand, was summoned to a meeting with Adolf Eichmann in Budapest's Majestic Hotel. During the course of the interview, the SS officer proposed his "blood for goods" deal, the trade of 800,000 Hungarian Jews for vast quantities of Allied war matériel (p. 239). Brand, it will be recalled, was flown to Turkey on May 13 to transmit the proposal to Allied and Jewish Agency representatives. Meanwhile, the mass deportations of Hungarian Jews had begun, 12,000 a day. Kastner, meanwhile, unaware that Brand had been interned by the British in Syria, desperately bargained for time with Eichmann. He got nowhere. Yet on one occasion Kastner came up with a proposal that the German found acceptable. It was for Eichmann to offer a "token" of his sincerity by permitting a limited number of Jews to emigrate to Switzerland. Thereupon Kastner himself was given the task of providing the SS with a list of two hundred families—in effect, a list of who was to be chosen for life. Kastner came up with the names of 1,685 Jews. Eichmann in turn kept his promise and allowed the departure of these fortunates for Switzerland on two special trains. They were saved. During the ensuing months, until the Red Army entered Hungary, an additional 434,000 Jews were shipped to Auschwitz and murdered. Kastner himself survived.

Now, in Jerusalem in January 1954, during interrogation by Greenwald's lawyer, Shmuel Tamir, Kastner admitted that he had testified at Nuremburg on behalf of one of the Nazi officials with whom he had dealt in the Budapest negotiations. Cross-examination on this point was unusually fierce. Tamir was a former Jerusalem commander of the Etzel, and later an active member of Cherut—although recently he had left the party. Determined now to place the onus of the Hungarian Jewish tragedy where he was convinced it belonged, on Kastner and Kastner's "allies"—that is, the Mapai officials who had directed the Jewish Agency during the war and who currently played leading roles in the government—Tamir went after Kastner with a vengeance. Why, he asked, had Hungarian Jews passively allowed themselves to be rounded up and deported to Auschwitz? Why had Kastner not warned them? Kastner's lame answer was that he had not dared jeopardize his negotiations with Eichmann. Then Tamir revealed that of the 1,685 rescued Jews, 388 came from Cluj, Kastner's hometown, and that every one of these 388 was either his relative or a friend. The government in turn produced witnesses who corroborated Kastner's account and who indicated that Kastner himself, far from profiting from his

negotiations, had arrived in Israel a virtual pauper. These and other prosecution witnesses were sharply interrogated by Tamir, who accused them
repeatedly of protecting a government "clique," of collaborating with
Kastner in the "betrayal" of Hungarian Jewry.

By the end of August 1954, the trial at last neared its conclusion. It had
already consumed eighty sessions and two thousand pages of testimony,
more than any other case in Palestine legal history. Indeed, the Kastner
affair had become Israel's *cause célèbre*. For more than six months the
tension it had aroused in the nation had made calm discussion of the proceedings all but impossible. Perhaps the facts of the Eichmann-Kastner
negotiations alone would have been enough to transfix the public. But the
unprecedented bitterness with which Tamir—himself a man widely respected for his patriotism, courage, and integrity—and the Cherut press
attacked Kastner and the Mapai–Jewish Agency leaders for their wartime
roles carried far wider political implications. Hundreds of thousands of
survivors of the Nazi inferno were living in Israel, after all, and these
were the people who now were being infected with the cancerous suspicion
that they had been betrayed by their own kind, by individuals who occupied eminent positions in the Mapai party and public life. There was little
doubt, actually, that men formerly venerated as national heroes, including
Ehud Avriel and Menachem Bader, the Jewish Agency officials who had
been in touch with Joel Brand in 1944, had faltered and contradicted themselves on the witness stand. Moreover, the conspiratorial theory of the
Holocaust exerted a certain natural fascination. It averted the necessity
of coming to grips with a far less palatable reality: that the great majority
of the Holocaust's victims had gone to their doom like sheep.

Judge Benyamin Halevi chose to issue his judgment on June 22, 1955,
one month before the scheduled Knesset elections. It was a three-hundred-
page opinion, and it was a bombshell. Halevi declared that Kastner in fact
had done nothing to alert Hungarian Jews to their impending fate, to urge
them to go into hiding. On the contrary, Kastner had allowed tranquilizing
rumors to be circulated, and it was therefore less than coincidental that his
role in the deception enabled him to save his family and friends in Cluj.
When Kastner accepted the task of allocating permits for the two freedom
trains, said the judge, he "sold his soul to the devil." Kastner's actions were
"collaboration in the fullest sense of the word," and according to Jewish
law, by sparing oneself at the expense of others, "a man forfeits his right
to life." Judge Halevi then declared Greenwald innocent of the major
charges of libel. The shock generated by this verdict reached directly into
the government. The following day, June 23, the cabinet met in emergency
session and decided to appeal the ruling to the supreme court. In the
Knesset, meanwhile, four days later, Cherut submitted a motion of nonconfidence in the government for its "reprehensible" behavior in appealing
the Kastner decision. The motion was rejected; but one coalition partner,
the General Zionists, abstained from the vote, and this abstention was
equivalent to withdrawal from the coalition. Immediately, then, Prime
Minister Sharett resigned, having thus failed to maintain the principle of

collective governmental responsibility. He remained on simply as care-taker, until the scheduled elections of the following month.

During the campaign, Cherut exploited the Kastner verdict for all it was worth, even demanding Kastner's arrest as a Nazi collaborator. Was the government's willingness to employ him, asked the Cherut press, not of a piece with its equally odious decision to accept German reparations? If the Mapai-dominated cabinet was unable to put a stop to Arab terror raids, if it was willing passively to accept disappointment and tragedy as the normal course of events, could this weakness not be imputed to the same Mapai figures in the Jewish Agency of eleven years earlier, in their reaction, then, to the Nazi liquidation program? Cherut's charges registered dramatically, and in the subsequent elections it nearly doubled its Knesset membership, which rose from eight seats to fifteen, and thereby became the nation's second-largest party.

There seemed at this time to be a genuine danger that the Cherut op-position—which, for all its animus to the Labor government, nevertheless remained for the most part within the bounds of parliamentary responsi-bility—might be intensified and exploited by overtly Fascist, even psychotic, elements. This possibility, however, was decisively averted by the events of the following two years.

In March 1957, Kastner was ambushed outside his home and shot at close range by three young men. The assailants were captured. Upon in-terrogation, they were revealed to be admirers of the outlawed Lech'i. One of them indeed had belonged to the Lech'i and had served as a police agent. Further investigations divulged large arms caches with which the young criminals and their henchmen intended to fulfill a paranoid right-wing vision of an Israeli empire extending from "the Mediterranean to the Tigris and Euphrates." The public, including Cherut and most of the other non-Socialist parties, was appalled by the hitherto unrecognized threat of demagoguery gone wild. It was given further pause when Kastner died of his wounds, and when the supreme court, in January 1958, reversed the original district court verdict. Of more decisive importance yet, the gov-ernment in October 1956 launched its military invasion of Sinai. Within a hundred hours Egypt's shadow over Israel was lifted (Chapter XVII). The evidence of their own unity and power was more than reassuring to the citizens of the Jewish state. All the doubts and anxieties of the previous months dropped away. What had occurred in Europe belonged to Eu-ropean history, not Israeli history. It was a Labor government, after all, that had put the world on notice that the Jews were a sovereign nation and were not about to be blown away. The bitterest nationalist diatribes of the Right at last were muted. Years would pass before they would be revived with quite the same intensity.

v. Religion and State

There remained one sector of Israeli life, nevertheless, where passions con-tinued to run high and vocal. This was in the area of institutionalized religion. We have seen that assurances of freedom of religion were incorporated both in the UN Partition Resolution and in Israel's own Declaration of Independence. In order to guarantee these commitments the government adopted a practice familiar to central and eastern Europe: it established a ministry of religions, with special departments for Jewish, Moslem, Christian, and (later) Druze religious affairs. The ministry assumed the task of protecting, even subsidizing, the communities' houses of worship and shrines, and confirmed the appointment of their ecclesiastical personnel, including their religious judges. The department for Jewish religious affairs was understandably the ministry's largest, as well as the most extensive in its activities. It organized facilities for religious life in immigrant settlements, built and maintained synagogues and yeshivot (rabbinical seminaries), issued directives for the religious courts and for elections to the chief rabbinate and religious councils. It cooperated with the rabbinate on the supervision of dietary laws. After 1953, too, it paid the salaries of virtually all Jewish religious functionaries (as well as those of the other communities).

In the case of the Jews, however, the prerogatives of this far-reaching clerical establishment were guaranteed less by administrative blueprint than by political muscle. The ministry of religions, the chief rabbinate, the religious courts, the rabbinical council, even the local religious councils— all diligently maintained their (religious) party affiliations, and from beginning to end these parties tightly supervised and monitored every expression of institutionalized Judaism in Israel. Originally there were four such parties: Mizrachi, HaPoel HaMizrachi (Mizrachi Workers), Agudat Israel, and Poalei Agudat Israel (Agudat Israel Workers). The former two, it is remembered, grew and developed within the Zionist movement. The latter two rejected Zionism. In any case, the leadership of both blocs— Zionist and non-Zionist—remained in the hands of the Europeans even during the subsequent years of Oriental immigration.

The Mizrachi was the oldest and largest of the religious parties. While consisting largely of urban, middle-class, east European Jews, its central committee had formulated no sharply defined social program and was largely unconcerned with economic matters. As a rule, then, it was prepared to support Mapai in return for concessions on religious issues. Until 1974, Mizrachi was part of every one of Israel's coalition governments. HaPoel HaMizrachi, with its somewhat more dynamic program of agricultural settlement and (non-Socialist) trade unionism, found even less difficulty than the mother party in working closely with Mapai. In 1955, Mizrachi and HaPoel HaMizrachi submitted a joint electoral list, which attracted 9 percent of the vote and won eleven Knesset seats. In 1956 the two factions merged officially into the National Religious party.

The Agudat Israel, on the other hand, remained far more conservative and aggressively Orthodox than either of the Mizrachi partners. Its approach was devoid of any pioneering idealism whatever, and concentrated largely upon building yeshivot and fostering Orthodox education. We recall that, under the mandate, the Agudah had sternly refused to identify with the "Knesset Israel." Its grudging decision to participate in Israel's political life after 1948 was influenced almost exclusively by the desire to share in the patronage opportunities of statehood; otherwise, the party remained unchanged in its fundamentalism. A subsidiary movement, the Poalei Agudat Israel, was rather more tolerant of secular activity. By 1955 it had established some fifteen rural villages and an agricultural school, and its members occasionally participated in (non-Histadrut) trade union activities. Nonetheless they still sent their children to the Agudah schools, and generally followed the Agudah voting line. Finally, with the two parties barely exceeding the voting strength even of the tiny Progressive and Communist factions, they, too, like the Mizrachi partners, combined their lists for the 1955 elections and a year later formally united as the Torah Religious Front. The new grouping derived its importance less from its parliamentary participation—six seats in the Third Knesset—than from the loyalty it evoked from a devoted hard core of supporters, particularly in Jerusalem.

In 1949, the four religious parties joined in a temporary coalition for the First Knesset elections. Their combined vote then was 12 percent, and by 1955 it had risen to 13.8 percent. This was a small, but hardly negligible, factor in Knesset politics. Moreover, the very limitation of their ambitions rendered the Orthodox useful for coalition purposes. They were prepared to barter their support to Labor, on condition that Labor, in turn, met their —essentially religious—demands. For its part, Mapai found the understanding generally more useful than an alternative deal with the rightist parties, whose economic views struck at the very heart of Labor Zionist ideology, and in any case represented more of a threat to Labor patronage. There was little doubt, in fact, that Mapai's choice of the Orthodox as coalition partners accounted for the astonishing stability of Labor domination.

This Labor-Orthodox *mariage de convenance* affected numerous areas of Israel's public life, as it had to a lesser degree under the mandate. Municipal Sabbath laws were enforced in all the larger Jewish cities except Haifa. Shops, theaters, offices, and public transportation were closed for the day. Throughout the country, too, on Saturdays and religious holidays, communications ceased to operate except on a skeletal, emergency basis. A tacit agreement between the government and the religionists virtually banned the importation of nonkosher meat, except for the Christian population. It was similarly under Orthodox pressure that the Knesset in 1954 passed a law allowing municipal councils to forbid the breeding of pigs and the sale of pork products. In an interview years later, Ben-Gurion explained these concessions:

> Any government leader must prescribe for himself priorities, must decide on first things first. . . . [W]here there was agreement on what was urgent to me, I was prepared to make concessions on what was urgent to others. . . . When I wanted to introduce national service conscription, the religious parties said they would of course support it but they insisted that all army kitchens be kosher. Kosher kitchens to them were of paramount importance; to me they were of subsidiary interest. It was a price I was prepared to pay for

their full-fledged support on a vital defense measure. . . . In the same way
I agreed not to change the *status quo* on religious authority for matters of
personal status. I know it was hard on some individuals. But I felt, again in
the national interest, that it was wise to . . . pay the comparatively small
price of religious *status quo*.

The price was not always small. The Orthodox played a key role in
torpedoing Dr. Leo Kohn's superb written constitution. The rabbinical
courts system, operative during the mandate, not only was preserved under
the status quo understanding of the immediate prestate period, but later
enlarged under the Rabbinical Courts Jurisdiction Law of 1953 to affect all
Jewish residents of Israel, irrespective of their citizenship. The archaisms
enforced by the rabbinical courts were galling enough to Israel's own
citizens, for that matter. As examples, the religious judges might order a
husband to divorce his wife, a wife to accept a divorce, or a childless
widow to abstain from remarrying if she failed to receive the prior consent
of her brother-in-law—who under the ancient law of chalizah could marry
her himself, to carry on the family bloodline. Despite the protests of
the secular majority, however, the Mapai coalition repeatedly bent over
backward to accommodate the Orthodox. It was only when the basic question arose of the future character of the state itself that tension between
the religious and secular parties erupted in a succession of paralyzing
cabinet crises.

The first of these confrontations occurred late in 1949 over the issue
of religious education in immigrant camps. We recall that the trend system
of education, permitting separate Histadrut, General Zionist, and Mizrachi
school systems, had operated throughout the entire period of the mandate
(p. 158). Hardly one year after Israel's independence, moreover, the
anachronism was given renewed life by a Compulsory Education Act,
which all but ensured that interparty competition for schoolchildren would
go on. It was this competition that now threatened the Mapai alliance less
than ten months into Israel's first government. The Orthodox, who regarded the children of the traditionally devout Yemenites as specifically
within their fold, argued that these youngsters should not be exposed to
the bewildering problem of choosing between school trends once they
arrived in the immigrant camps. Predictably, Mapai capitulated: Yemenite
children were assigned automatically to the Mizrachi schools. But this
time the accommodation survived only until February 1951, when a new
crisis arose over schooling in the ma'abarot, the transit camps that represented a second stage beyond the initial immigrant reception centers. For
the secularists, the ma'abara dweller no longer was a confused and
hapless immigrant, but rather an apprentice Israeli; whether Yemenite or
of any other ethnic group, he should be allowed henceforth to make a free
choice on the school trend he wished for his children. In short, the "surrender" of the immigrant camps would not be repeated in the ma'abarot.

Angered, the Religious bloc warned that if the ruling were put into
effect, its members would leave the coalition government. For once Mapai
stood firm. Thereupon the Orthodox fulfilled their threat and the coalition

dissolved; Ben-Gurion immediately handed in his cabinet's resignation. Exasperated in any case by the thankless task of governing in alliance with the religionists, the prime minister seized on this issue for new elections. Both religionists and secularists then mobilized the full panoply of their weapons and followers during the election battle for the Second Knesset. Obviously many issues, economic even more than religious, were at play in the furious, invective-ridden campaign. But none aroused passions quite as bitterly as did the *Kulturkampf*. None, too, apparently remained as insoluble, for Mapai's hopes of emerging as a solid majority party were not fulfilled. Attempts to negotiate a coalition with the General Zionists similarly foundered on economic issues. To his intense chagrin, therefore, Ben-Gurion recognized that he would have to seek a deal with the religionists once again. Eventually, after lengthy haggling, a bargain of sorts was reached in October 1951. By its terms, Labor won Orthodox approval for ending the baneful trend-school system. Yet, for its part, Mapai conceded that religious schools would share equal status with secular schools as part of an "official" state education program. Following additional interparty discussions over the next year and a half, this understanding eventually was translated into the State Education Law of 1953.

As anticipated, the bill provided for two new categories of educational institutions, to be known as state schools and state religious schools. A common secular curriculum would encompass 75 percent of the instruction for both school networks; but in the state religious schools, the remaining 25 percent of the curriculum would be devoted exclusively to religious subjects. The "compromise" was more than a little one-sided. For example, the state religious schools, although legally vested in the ministry of education and culture, devolved in practice into the hands of an (essentially) Orthodox council, reserving to itself final authority on instruction and choice of staff. Wherever two-thirds of the parents demanded, moreover, the government was obliged to grant equal status to "recognized schools." This was a euphemism for the autonomist Agudah school system, which now was allowed to continue—often with the financial support of local municipalities. By 1955, as a result, 17,000 pupils were enrolled in the Agudah "recognized schools." Their education remained uncompromisingly Orthodox, and pitiably inadequate by any secular criterion.

The Defense Service Law, introduced into the Knesset in 1952, represented no less flagrant a capitulation to the Orthodox. The original law, issued in 1949, had rendered young women liable to conscription for a year's military service. Inasmuch, however, as the rabbis contended that army duty would "threaten the morals" of Orthodox daughters, girls from religious homes by and large were allowed to secure exemptions. And while later amendments to the act extended the conscription period of men and women alike, the status of Orthodox girls remained unaffected. Public dissatisfaction with this inequity soon became acute. Early in 1951, therefore, the cabinet submitted yet another bill to the Knesset, one authorizing the government to call Orthodox girls to "national" rather than military service. This qualification meant that they would function as replacements for civilian personnel in offices, hospitals, or communal kitchens. They would not live in barracks but would go home at night, they would not be in uniform, their activities would be limited essentially to teaching or nursing, and mainly in immigrant settlements. In short, every possible effort was made to forestall the religionists' objections.

But conciliatory gestures were unavailing. When the bill was reintroduced in late 1952 (intervening elections had blocked its consideration), the Agudists launched an enraged hue and cry. In Mea Sh'arim, Jerusalem's Orthodox stronghold, placards and banners called on families to protect their daughters from "infamy" and "defilement." Crowds of pietists marched on the Knesset, flailing hysterically at police lines. Indeed, the Agudah's campaign extended well beyond the frontiers of Israel. Demonstrations were mounted in New York's Chasidic enclaves of Brownsville and Williamsburg. Even Israel's Chief Rabbi Yitzchak Herzog, ordinarily a mild and tolerant man, was chivvied into joining the denunciation. After many weeks of this upheaval the protests eventually were called off; it developed that yet another "compromise" had been worked out. In a meeting with Rabbi Herzog, Ben-Gurion privately gave assurances that if the (presumably more tractable) Mizrachi parties would drop their opposition to the bill, the national service obligations of religious girls would be interpreted with great flexibility. On that basis the amendment was passed. And, as it turned out in practice, large numbers of Orthodox girls simply were not conscripted for any kind of national service at all.

It should be noted, too, that the religionists' grip on the legislative jugular, impressive as it was, generally was tightened even further within the municipality of Jerusalem. In this case, the intensity of Orthodox pressure was dictated by the transformed status of the city. Under the mandate, the British had ensured that Jerusalem's mayor invariably was an Arab. Once the municipal administration passed into the hands of the Jews, however, the Agudists, largely concentrated in Jerusalem, sensed their unique opportunity to win control of the city's public life and to share in its patronage. Whatever the changes taking place elsewhere in Israel, in Jerusalem at least—where the Orthodox community represented a third of the Jewish population in 1948—the old way of life, and its vested interests in the courtyards of Mea Sh'arim, its Bikur Cholim (Orthodox) hospital, its loan societies and Agudist school system, would all be defended tooth and nail.

The first municipal elections took place concurrently with those of the First Knesset. The Agudists knew by then that they no longer comprised the majority even of religious Jews, most of whom belonged to the Mizrachi parties. Yet they offered to support a Poalei Mizrachi mayoral candidate for Jerusalem in return for the usual tough quid pro quo of shared authority and patronage. The Mizrachi acquiesced, fearing the even more dangerous consequences of secularist domination. The partnership was effective enough to win the election. For nearly seven years afterward, the municipal government of Jerusalem remained in the hands of the religionists, with the Mizrachi politicians serving as a front for the militant Agudists. The latter were not timorous in claiming their rewards. Their "special school" system, intensely parochial and pedagogically backward, now received virtually 100 percent subsidization from the municipal treasury. Their share of local patronage was hardly less than engorged. Moreover, the Agudah was able to win "tax relief" for many thousands of its followers, on the frequently questionable grounds of destitution or neardestitution. Not least of all, the Agudists pushed their views vigorously in municipal legislation, ensuring the passage of dietary and Sabbath blue laws for Jerusalem that were unprecedented in their severity and in the rigorousness of their enforcement.

As it turned out, the Orthodox were more proficient in enforcing the blue laws, and in winning patronage and subsidies, than in managing the complicated administrative affairs of a city of 150,000 souls (by 1955). Neither of the first two Poalei Mizrachi mayors had an inkling of how these distasteful "secular" functions were to be performed. Street lighting continually failed, garbage frequently went uncollected, taxes rarely arrived on time, and months often passed before municipal employees received their salaries. By 1955 the situation had become intolerable. Many of the city's veteran residents were departing for Tel Aviv and other communities. Eventually the ministry of the interior was obliged to dissolve the Jerusalem municipal council and fire the mayor, Kariv. During the next four months, the city was governed by an appointed committee. And then, in the ensuing municipal elections, Mapai at last won its first working plurality, seven out of twenty-one councilors. Biting nails, the religionists were obliged to accept a secularist mayor, Gershon Agron (Agronsky), former editor of the English-language *Palestine Post*. Even then, however, they had by no means given up the struggle. Out of power, unburdened by the responsibilities of office, the Agudists generated an implacability of opposition that in later years pushed the *Kulturkampf* in both the city and the country at large to the outer limits of civic toleration (Chapter xx).

vi. *The Arab Minority: Citizenship and Military Government*

In their testimony before the UNSCOP in the summer of 1947, the Zionists had been explicit and emphatic in their assurances that the Arab minority of a projected Jewish state would enjoy full civil, national, and cultural rights. Later the UN Partition Resolution itself elaborated upon these rights, even as Israel's Declaration of Independence contained its own specific guarantees. In the early years of statehood, nevertheless, these various assurances and provisions were considerably mitigated by two unanticipated developments. One was the magnitude of Arab flight and demographic change within the newborn Jewish republic. The other was the impact of invasion by neighboring Arab countries and the remorselessness of Arab hostility in the aftermath of the war.

With the fighting ended, an estimated 156,000 Arabs remained within

Israel's borders, a number that would nearly quadruple in subsequent years. They continued to make their homes essentially in a hundred towns and villages of their own, and in five mixed towns—Acre, Haifa, Jaffa, Ramle, and Jerusalem—with large Jewish majorities. Approximately 60 percent of the Arab population lived in the Galilee, another 20 percent in the "Little Triangle" of farm villages abutting the Jordanian frontier; while two smaller enclaves, each encompassing about 7 percent of the Arab population, remained in the Haifa area and in the Negev. All these Arab population centers, in any case, were quite near Israel's land borders, and it was this very proximity to nations intent upon the destruction of the Jewish state that conditioned and qualified many of Israel's prewar assurances of equal citizenship. As shall be seen, the Arabs enjoyed every right to vote and sit in the Knesset, to organize their own political parties, to criticize the government, to publish their own journals, to send their children to Arabic-language schools. They had access to Israel's public services and to Israel's courts. In addition, like all the other religious communities, the Moslem population (the overwhelming majority of the Arabs) was granted broad juridical autonomy in matters of personal status. Moslem cadis, like the dayanim of the rabbinical courts, were salaried officials of the state. Their waqfs—religious trust funds—no longer were administered by their own muftis; but Israel's ministry of religions performed this function scrupulously and generously on their behalf. In one vital area, too, that of military conscription, Arabs were exempted from all national service obligations.

And yet it was precisely this exemption that revealed most dramatically the onus of suspicion that attached to Israel's Arab inhabitants. They were known to maintain close ties with the hundreds of thousands of their kinsmen who had fled as refugees to neighborhood lands. It was assumed, therefore, that the remnant Israeli Arab community would experience grave psychological problems of divided loyalty at best, and at worst an unquenchable antipathy to the new Jewish regime. This assumption similarly explained the government's delay in enacting nationality legislation until April 1952. During the intervening four years of early statehood, Israel remained in law a country without citizens, either native-born or naturalized. It was true, of course, that the First Knesset passed a Law of Return in July 1950, investing Jews everywhere with the legal right of immigration to Israel. Even so, Ben-Gurion's interpretation of this measure could not have been reassuring to the Arab minority. The Law of Return confirmed, in his words, that "this is not only a Jewish state, where the majority of the inhabitants are Jews, but a state for all Jews, wherever they are, and for every Jew who wants to be here. . . . This right is inherent in being a Jew." For all its impressive rhetoric, the Law of Return granted citizenship neither to Jew nor to Arab. Thus, voting in the elections to the First and Second Knessets was based on residence, not on nationality. There was no mystery to the postponement. A "legal" method had to be found to delimit the status of a large and profoundly distrusted Arab minority. Eventually, therefore, after much debate, and without specifically mentioning Arabs or Jews, the Knesset in 1952 passed a Nationality Law that accomplished this purpose in a highly functional manner.

Under the 1952 bill, Israeli nationality might be acquired in four ways: by immigration, birth, residence, or naturalization. Nationality by immigration was granted to all those who entered the country officially as immigrants either before or after statehood, or who later expressed their desire, under the Law of Return, to settle permanently in Israel. Manifestly, only Jews fell under these categories. The remaining three provisions affected Arabs far more than Jews. Thus, nationality could be extended to persons born in the country before or after statehood, provided one of his parents was an Israeli citizen. Nationality by residence was granted to persons not born in the country but nevertheless Palestinian citizens, provided they were registered on March 1, 1952, as inhabitants of Israel, resided in Israel on July 14, 1952 (when the law came into effect), and legally had been resident in Israel since independence (these qualifications eliminated most of the Arab refugees). Last of all, nationality by naturalization could be acquired by those who: lived in Israel, had resided in Israel for at least three years, were entitled to settle permanently, had some knowledge of Hebrew, and had renounced their former nationality.

The conditions that required an Arab to prove his citizenship by "residence" were obviously, and intentionally, very difficult to fulfill. Large numbers of fellahin had no proof of Palestine citizenship; under the mandate, thousands of them simply had crossed over the frontier from neighboring Arab lands and had settled in Palestine without official permits. This was equally true, after the 1948 War of Independence, of at least 50,000 Arab returnees from adjacent countries. None of these people qualified for citizenship—in palpable violation of the UN Partition Resolution, which stated that Arabs and Jews alike "residing in Palestine shall become citizens of the state in which they are resident upon recognition of independence." It was hardly surprising that the law evoked intense resentment among the Arab community. Nor were Jewish critics of the act lacking, both in and out of the Knesset. The measure was not applied rigorously, to be sure. Indeed, the overwhelming majority of Arab residents in Israel eventually acquired Israeli nationality, and within the next five years. It was the legal basis for discrimination, rather, that embittered the Arab population.

Other measures were destined to inflict far greater practical hardship on the nation's Arabs. The Provisional Government's "Law and Administration Ordinance" empowered the minister of defense to invoke the Defense Emergency Regulations—originally passed by the British in 1945 to cope with Jewish subversion—for the purpose of establishing "defense areas" under the rule of military government. The ordinance was immediately put into effect in the strategic border regions, where the majority of Israel's Arabs lived. There the army co-opted governmental authority, and did not relinquish it once the 1948 war ended. Instead, in the atmosphere of siege engendered by hostile Arab states and by mounting Arab guerrilla raids from across Israel's borders, the earlier, impressive Zionist pronouncements on Arab equality in a Jewish state were considerably diluted. As a case in point, the most tightly restricted sectors within the "defense areas" were known as "security zones." These were small and very specific enclaves, abutting the frontiers, that were notorious magnets for Arab infiltration from Syria and Jordan. Arabs living here were cleared out on a bare four days' notice. Several Negev Bedouin tribes and the inhabitants of the border villages of Sha'ab, al-Birwah, Um al-Faraj, and Majdal (Migdal) were peremptorily expelled by the army. The evicted Christian villagers of Ikrit in western Galilee were assured that their removal was only for two weeks. It stretched on for years, and became permanent. In 1951, moreover, the army destroyed every house in the village, sparing not even the church.

While hardly more than 1,500 individuals were ever affected in the critically located "security zones," the border "defense areas" encompassed the majority of Israel's Arabs; and it was over this heavily impacted Arab population that the military governorates were established, and authorized to use "all force necessary" to maintain security. Thus, military courts in the defense areas were invested with broad jurisdiction to try offenses against the emergency regulations, and the trials frequently were held in closed session. Police and military personnel were empowered to search any home or business suspected of being used for activities "inimical to public safety. . . ." Individuals in the military areas could be detained or searched, limited in their movements or employment, or deported. "In the interest of public safety," too, district commissioners were authorized to take possession of any land and requisition any chattel. Police or troops could be billeted among the inhabitants at the latter's expense. Road movements could be prohibited or limited, curfews established, mail, telephones, and other public communications suspended.

Actually, few of these regulations were implemented except in periods of dire military crisis. By and large, the military administration operated with flexibility and understanding—and certainly with far greater compassion than evinced by Arab military administrations across the borders in the treatment of Jewish minorities. In fact, only one of Israel's emergency regulations was applied uninterruptedly over a period of many years. This was the restriction on movement between towns and villages. The Nazareth Arab, for example, who wished to visit a relative in Jaffa had to apply for a military permit to leave his town. He was required to fill out application forms, bring them to the military government headquarters, and wait in line, sometimes for hours. An unemployed Arab from a village like Shafa Am'r, seeking work in Haifa, was obliged to follow the same procedure and take the same chance of refusal. Refusal was not common, as it happened, but the process of application was time-consuming and humiliating.

The government explained that the regulations were instituted for purposes of security alone. It noted that the Arab minority was exposed to continual radio propaganda from neighboring Arab lands and covertly or otherwise maintained relations with family members across the borders. The explanation was valid as far as it went, but it was a question whether the hardships and humiliations did not exceed the dangers. This was the suspicion of Jewish and Arab critics alike, and the issue was raised on numerous occasions in the press and Knesset. Responding to these charges in December 1955, Ben-Gurion appointed a blue-ribbon commission to investigate the possibility of eliminating or restricting the military government. But after extensive hearings, the commission reported in March 1956 that the time had not yet come for a significant alleviation of the emergency measures; the borders were still too insecure. The report was a great disappointment to the Arabs, and it was followed by several dignified Arab protest meetings and much Arab and Jewish left-wing press censure.

Unofficially, however, there were already signs of a gradual relaxation of emergency rule by the mid-1950s. Travel restrictions within the Arab "defense area" were slowly eased. The courts, too, for the first time began calling the military to task for occasional abuse of power. Deportations of Arab civilians, even in proved instances of subversion, frequently were reversed by the supreme court acting as the high court of justice. While the relationship between the high court of justice and the military tribunals had not yet been clearly defined by 1956, the trend appeared to be increasingly in favor of civilian review. For that matter, the spirit of the Common Law was beginning to pervade even the decrees of the army courts, and it offered hope of a possible further modification of emergency rule.

VII. *The Arab Minority: Land and Economy*

The humiliation of that rule was compounded for the Arabs by an additional and appalling economic blow. It was struck as a consequence not merely of the war, but of Israeli land policy. The language of the UN Partition Resolution, clear and unequivocal, might have been expected to stay the government's hand. "No expropriation of land owned by an Arab in the Jewish state shall be allowed except for public purposes," the document had stated. "In all cases of expropriation, full compensation as fixed by the Supreme Court shall be paid previous to dispossession." But omens of impending tragedy surfaced as early as December 1948, when the Israeli Provisional Government issued its first absentee property regulations. The effect of these decrees was to forestall the return of any émigré Arabs, including those who were citizens of Israel, to property abandoned during or immediately after the war. Initially the provisions seemed to apply only to that great Arab majority which had fled as refugees across the battle lines to neighboring Arab lands. This evidently was the intention, too, of the absentee property statute passed by the First Knesset in 1950, authorizing the Custodian of Absentee Property to sell former Arab lands and buildings to a Development Authority. Working through related institutions, the Development Authority in turn was empowered to lease the land and other real property to various Jewish kibbutzim and moshavim—or, in the case of city property, to individual Israelis (Chapter xvi).

But within two years of the establishment of the state, it developed that the "absentee property" regulations similarly authorized the confiscation of nearly 40 percent of the land belonging to legal Arab residents of Israel. The victims of this policy fell into two categories. The first and smallest group were those Arabs who were expelled from the highly sensitive "security zones." As has been noted, approximately 1,500 individuals, most of them farmers, were affected by the evacuation policy. Those who applied for redress were told to wait. Soon, they were promised, they would receive alternative plots elsewhere. Eventually they did, but often not until several years had passed; and in the interval the farmers were obliged to accept shelter and meager employment opportunities in the households of kinsmen. A far larger category of expropriatees were some 30,000 Palestine Arabs who had left their towns or villages after the Partition Resolution without actually intending to flee the Jewish area of the country, but who soon found themselves classified as "absentees" under the December 1948 regulations. All Arabs who held property in the New City of Acre, for example, even those who may never have traveled farther than the several hundred yards to the Old City, were listed as absentees. Similar instances occurred in other parts of the country, notably in Lydda, Ramle, and Jerusalem. The aggregate holdings of these "internal refugees," in land alone, totaled nearly 300,000 dunams. It was now all fair game for the Custodian of Absentee Property.

Jewish critics of this injustice were not absent. Writing in *HuAretz* in November 1949, Moshe Smilansky, a respected Mapai member, warned that "someday we will have to account for [this] theft and spoliation not only to our consciences but also to the law." Under mounting pressure, therefore, the government appointed a committee to deal with Arab demands for redress. A few gestures were made. Sixty-seven Arab residents of Jaffa, Haifa, and Jerusalem, who had never left the country, received all or part of their property. Between thirty and forty farms were released to their Arab cultivators. In all, however, the Custodian issued a mere 209 certificates returning lands to their original owners. The meagerness of this response evoked an outpouring of shame and condemnation from Knesset members of all parties. Responding to it, the government in 1950 agreed to make certain additional changes. It obliged the Custodian for the first time to reveal the source of his information concerning the status of the absentees. It narrowed the definition of an absentee, excluding Arabs who remained in areas controlled by Jewish forces on November 29, 1947 (the date of the Partition Resolution). But inasmuch as only a small area of current Israel had been in Jewish hands in November 1947, the number of Arabs who benefited from the change was insignificant. Other, equally minor, alterations limited the Custodian's right to take over businesses. For example, he could do so only when all Arab partners, shareholders, directors, or managers, rather than merely 50 percent of them, no longer were present. Except for these provisions, the status of absentee property was hardly affected.

Defending government policy in the Knesset, Finance Minister Eliezer Kaplan emphasized that absentee property belonging to Israeli Arabs was a "delicate matter" involving "national security." Although he personally favored equality of rights, "how," he asked, "[can] we disregard the fact that we are still surrounded by enemy countries who have repeatedly declared that they intend to open a second round? We must take precautions." In Kaplan's view, security, not "business or commercial considerations," should be decisive in matters relating to absentee property. Shortly before the 1951 Knesset elections, the government countenanced a few additional, essentially minor, amendments to the regulations. Yet by then Israeli Arabs were drawing attention to a curious anomaly: most of the 300,000 dunams of Arab land that already had been requisitioned for Jewish villages still remained uncultivated. For reasons of Israel's economic self-interest, if not of law and decency, the Arabs argued, should the land not be returned to its original owners for cultivation? The point registered on the government. In 1952 the Custodian began at last to release larger quantities of absentee property. Within two years some 100,000 dunams were "leased" to 5,000 "absentee" families in one hundred villages.

Finally, in 1953, reflecting the nation's gradual economic stabilization as well as the response to domestic and international criticism, the government passed an impressive Land Acquisition Law. The measure in effect offered compensation for the 300,000 dunams of land taken from Arab citizens of Israel and included redress for soil or chattels acquired for purposes of "vital development or security" between May 4, 1948, and April 1, 1952. Landless farmers, the majority, were entitled to choose between financial remuneration and the lease of an alternative plot sufficient to maintain them. All cash payments were based on the value of the land in January 1950.

It was this latter provision that the resident "absentees" most bitterly criticized. Each year since 1948 the mounting inflation had robbed the Israeli pound of its purchasing power. The dunam that had been worth 25 pounds in 1950, for example, was worth 150 pounds in 1954, and 170 pounds in 1955. The government responded to this criticism by observing that it was Jewish settlement and endeavor, after all, that had augmented the value of the land, and the Arabs ought not to be reimbursed for that. Nevertheless, after several months of tense negotiations with Arab claimants and their lawyers (many of whom were Jews), the government finally offered yet another "compromise." By its terms, the committee that determined the land's worth would add 3 percent a year to the 1950 value of the requisitioned property. It was still a pitiably inadequate formula. Many Arabs refused it, preferring to fight their claims through the courts. Others reluctantly took payment as a means of ending an intolerable limbo in their status. By 1956, the Development Authority reported that about a third of the 3,076 outstanding claims had been settled by payment of money or award of land. The process was moving very slowly. Two more years would pass before a final and more acceptable solution could be worked out (Chapter XVIII). Until it was, the tragedy of Israel's "absentees" remained in harsh contrast to the nation's vaunted pretensions of equal law and justice for all its citizens.

The Arabs were not without other economic grievances. During the late 1940s and early 1950s, the narrowing of the land base of the Arab village, and its arrested growth, compelled many younger men to seek work elsewhere. Upon reaching the cities, however, they soon learned that decent jobs were unavailable to them. The Jews distrusted them. The Histadrut, founded on Zionist as well as Labor premises, was unwilling for many years to bestir itself in support of Arab job equality. Arab workers therefore turned to marginal employment. Their wages and social benefits invariably were meager. Often they lost much time and money commuting between their villages and their jobs; landlords in Haifa or Tel Aviv were unwilling to rent to them. Their social life was negligible. To be sure, Arab economic circumstances would improve dramatically in the mid- and late 1950s (Chapter XVIII). But the intervening years often were as financially painful and debilitating for Arab wage-earners and landowners as they were for impoverished Jewish immigrants from Moslem countries.

COMMUNAL STRUCTURE IN AN ALIEN SOCIETY

Israel's apparent lack of decisive policy toward its Arab minority was both the cause and the consequence of overlapping governmental approaches. Three separate administrations, the ministries of police and defense, and the Arab affairs section of the prime minister's office, were preoccupied mainly with security factors. Others, including the ministries of agriculture, religions, interior, labor, and education and culture, were concerned primarily with improving and uplifting the quality of Arab life. Yet the efforts even of these latter often foundered on the difficulties of coping with a large, sensitive, and unassimilable minority.

Typical was the quandary of the ministry of education and culture. Israel's Compulsory Education Law was intended for Arab as well as Jewish children. For the first time, schools were constructed in every Arab village, and as a result the number of Arab primary schools was increased from 59 in 1948 to 114 in 1956, the number of teachers from 250 to 846, the number of pupils from 10,000 to 26,500—and all this among a far smaller Arab population than in the mandatory years. The proportion of Arab girls attending school, for example, rose from less than 2 percent in 1949 to 40 percent in 1956. Veteran Arab teachers attended government refresher courses, and new ones were trained in an Arab teachers' seminar. At the same time, the ministry of education went to great lengths to respect Arab cultural sensibilities. Arabic was retained as the language of instruction, with Hebrew taught as a second language only. The teaching materials in literature and history classes related almost exclusively to the Arab cultural heritage. Indeed, very little information on Jewish subjects was injected into the course program at all, except for the barest facts of Israeli civics. Nothing approaching Zionist propaganda ever made its appearance in an Arab textbook. Notwithstanding these palpably sincere and high-minded Israeli efforts, however, it did not escape Arab teachers that if little attention was devoted to Zionist history, even less was devoted to the Arab nationalist movements of Palestine and of neighboring Arab lands. The writings of Arab novelists or essayists, some of them major figures in the Arab literary world, were deliberately scanted if their themes touched on Pan-Arabism.

The process, too, by which schools and other local facilities were maintained often was resented by Arab villagers. Under the mandate, the British government generally had supplied Arab communal services at its own expense. The Israeli government, on the other hand, now expected Arab local governments to do precisely what the Jews themselves were doing—that is, finance village services, including teachers' salaries and school equipment, by imposing local taxes. When local Arab authorities more than occasionally refused to accept this burden, the government was obliged to institute its own poll tax and enforce collection. At times local resistance took the form of strikes, and there were instances when police had to be called in to suppress unrest. What often underlay these disputes between Arab local authorities and the Israeli government, in fact, was a quiet struggle for political authority within the Arab community itself. For several years after Israeli statehood, leadership in the Arab villages continued to be the prerogative of the heads of hamoulas—family clans. As a rule, these elders were the only individuals in their communities who could afford the expense of an electoral contest. Yet patriarchal domination of local affairs frequently was resented by younger village members, many of whom chafed to inaugurate overdue social reforms. Their helplessness, then, to make so much as a dent in this traditional control often vented over into mounting bitterness at Israeli rule, which in youthful Arab minds was identified with the local status quo.

Surely one of the worst frustrations for Arab nationalists was the lack of political outlet for their complaints. The best-known spokesmen of the Palestine Arab community—the Husseinis and the Nashashibis, among others—had been the first to depart in 1948. Early attempts by Israeli Arabs to establish new parties on their own failed repeatedly. For one thing, the sheer mechanics of political organization in an authentically representative government were beyond the Arab experience. More important, Israel's Arabs were deprived both of seasoned advice from veteran leadership and of financial help from established party coffers. Their own aspiring politicians were unable to count on the support of the armed forces, as in neighboring Arab lands, or upon influential business circles, as in Lebanon. Rather, in a strange twist, the Arabs now found themselves largely dependent upon the Jews for political guidance. An initial example of this curious relationship was the vigorous role suddenly adopted by Maki, Israel's Communist party. Devoid of influence or even visibility under the mandate, the Communists now boasted that theirs was the only party in Israel whose ideology was not Zionist; as a result, they alone had the true interests of the Arabs at heart. Avoiding discussions of Marxist theories, the Maki leadership—Jews and Arabs together—concentrated instead on attacking the military government, the national land policy, and other grievances suffered under Israeli rule. At first, the party even ventured to advocate independence for Israel's Arabs; but after a few years it shifted its emphasis to autonomy within Israel. As shall be noted, however, Maki's ability to attract substantial Arab votes was quite limited.

The record of Mapam was equally unimpressive. Early in 1949 this left-wing workers' party, highly idealistic and traditionally sentient to Arab rights, organized and helped underwrite an associated slate of Arab candidates for elections to the First Knesset. But when the "Arab Popular Bloc" failed to win even one parliamentary seat, Mapam established its own Arab affairs section, and in 1951 went so far as to include an Arab candidate high on its party list, thus ensuring his election. Mapam leaders conducted strenuous activity among the Arabs. Their kibbutzim extended themselves in offering aid and friendship to neighboring Arab villages. On the Arabs' behalf, too, Mapam organized agricultural schools, vocational training programs, and transportation cooperatives, published reprints of Arab literature, and arranged meetings and discussions among Arab and Jewish teachers and intellectuals. Yet Mapam hardly could go as far as the Communists in its program for Arab rights; nor, on the other hand, could it offer the material inducements of the ruling Mapai group. Its campaign efforts accordingly aroused little enthusiasm among the Arab population.

It was ironic, then, that the most important political factor in the Arab community should be Mapai itself, the party chiefly responsible for the basic Arab grievances. The Arab electoral lists sponsored by this dominant labor faction bore impressive titles: for example, the Democratic List of the Arabs of Israel (Nazareth and Galilee), the Agriculture and Development party (Western Galilee and the Druze), and occasionally one or two others. By whatever name, however, they were all Arabs hand-picked for the Mapai cause, and were shrewdly balanced with Moslem, Christian, and Druze personalities. The lists also took into account the competing interests of eminent hamoulas, and their most prominent candidates usually were affluent notables. A number of these Mapai clients unquestionably were opportunists plain and simple, concerned mainly with prestige or individual advancement. More commonly, they demonstrated a shrewd Arab appraisal of where the power lay, and thereby the source of material help for their own communities. After all, the other parties could only protest; it was Mapai alone that could, if it chose, perform. To ensure Mapai goodwill and support, therefore, the Arab candidates were mild and tractable in their demands, generally focusing on local and communal programs. Their constituents by and large understood this restraint, and what could be achieved by it.

Moreover, once overcoming the shock of war and their altered status in a Jewish state, the Arabs learned rapidly to participate in the national elections. Except for the 1949 Knesset balloting, when few Israeli parties made serious efforts to campaign among them, Arab voter turnout actually was heavier proportionately than that of the Jews. Even in 1949, 79.3 percent of registered Arab voters cast their ballots. That early, too, the lineaments of their voting patterns began to emerge. It confirmed that the Arabs' instinct for the main chance bore little relationship to their deeper nationalist frustrations. Thus, 51.7 percent of all Arab ballots were cast for the four Arab Labor lists, of which all but one were sponsored by Mapai, the other by Mapam. Additionally, 22.2 percent voted for Maki (the Communists), 11.4 percent voted for the Party of Oriental Jews (soon to be defunct); while 9.6 voted for Mapai directly. Together, in short, Mapai and the Mapai lists received 61.3 percent of the Arab vote, an absolute majority. In later elections this affinity for Mapai was preserved, even occasionally strengthened. It was evident that the Arabs were gravitating to the nation's "sadat"—its established chieftains, the fount of all bounty.

Most of the seven or eight Arab members of the Knesset were prosperous landowners, occasionally interspersed with a journalist or two, even one architect. Whatever their background, the Arab MKs rarely spoke up in parliament on general matters. They concentrated rather on topics of special interest to the Arab minority, appealed gently and repeatedly for peace in the Middle East, expressed the discreet hope that the military administration might be relaxed, that separated Arab families might be reunited. More specifically, however, they continued to press for an improvement in Arab living standards, asked larger budgets for roads, clinics, and schools, and wider employment opportunities for young Arab intellectuals. But whether or not their requests were answered, the Arab MKs continued dutifully to follow the (generally Mapai) party line in Knesset voting.

This obsequiousness, on the other hand, by no means reflected Arab adaptation to the circumstances of Israeli rule. Indeed, all along the Jordanian "bulge" the frontier remained psychologically unreal. Crossings and visits with kinsmen on the other side of the armistice zone went on uninterruptedly. The impact of radio and later television broadcasts from neighboring lands reinforced Israeli Arab identification with the wider Arab hinterland. As Arab economic opportunities in Israel began dramatically to rise, so too, in the classical manner, did Arab impatience with second-class citizenship. Among the Jews, the common view in the mid-1950s was that "the position of the Arabs in Israel is better than ever before and incomparably better than that of the Arab countries." This surely was true. Yet the Arabs themselves did not assume that, but for Israel, they would have remained static in their progress. Exposed continually to pious talk of democracy and civic equality, witnessing the realization of these values in the Jewish sector, the Israeli Arabs preferred to compare their own fortunes not with those of Arabs living across the borders, but with those of their Jewish neighbors in Israel. The seeds of loyalty that the ministries of agriculture, public welfare, health, and education attempted to cultivate through a plenitude of good works were neutralized in large degree by the policies of the military government and the Custodian of Absentee Property. Comprising more than 10 percent of the Israeli population, the Arab minority was awarded not a single cabinet or other senior government post. "What is the use of opening the university to Arab youths," wrote Ze'ev Schiff in an article in *HaAretz*, "if . . . the military governor can delay for months the permit of a youth studying in Jerusalem and prevent him from leaving his village because his father quarreled with the government?"

For years, nevertheless, the status of the Arabs in Israel was either consciously or unconsciously ignored by public opinion. By 1953 this anomaly had become painful enough for a Moslem cadi of Nazareth, Sheikh Tahir al-Tabari, to write the president of Israel. With the Jews convinced that the Arabs were a fifth column, Sheikh Tahir noted, his people feared that their situation would become increasingly vulnerable as relations between Israel and the Arab nations worsened. For this reason, he suggested that any Israeli Arab desiring to emigrate and join his people across the border should be allowed to liquidate his property and do so. The letter received front-page coverage in Israeli newspapers and evoked much public discussion. Responding to Sheikh Tahir in the press, Foreign Minister Sharett reminded his correspondent, and the nation at large, that Israel's Arabs "remain connected by ties of blood and common national consciousness with the Arab people outside Israel, the declared position of which is that it is still at war with Israel. . . ." The threat of subversion accordingly would have to remain the government's central preoccupation "as long as there is no peace." The implication was plain. The welfare of the country's Arabs ultimately would be influenced less by the guarantees upon which the state was founded than by the effectiveness with which the state could be defended.

If the fate of the Arab minority represented less than perfect justice, however, it was surely not alone among the nation's inequities and imperfections. The legal issue that affected Jews exclusively among Israel's citizens, for example—the impact of the rabbinate and Orthodox law upon personal status—was destined to remain a far more bedeviling anachronism. By contrast, in the years after 1956, Arab juridical status, not to mention Arab economic circumstances, would be transformed more beneficently and dramatically than any other single facet of Israeli public life. Many other features of republican government would experience a similar improvement. Thus, with time, multiparty coalition government gradually refined itself. By 1955, out of eighteen party lists, only twelve survived in the polls. A year later, the process of amalgamation evolved functionally, along Western lines, and tended to unite the various Labor and Conservative parties into more widely based "alignments" (Chapter xix). Even the bureaucracy was moving almost imperceptibly toward a certain creaking professionalism. Of perhaps greater consequence yet than improvement in specific mechanisms of government was the growing viability of the democratic "tradition." For with each passing year the authority of republican institutions was impressively transcending the challenges of military crises, political demagoguery, and the overwhelming economic and sociological burdens of the ingathering. Beleaguered as the nation was, somehow its elections were honestly conducted, its legislation debated and passed, its taxes collected, its court edicts upheld, its laws obeyed, its public order maintained. Evaluated against the record of other nations founded since World War II, Israel's political accomplishment was more than remarkable. With few if any exceptions, it was unmatched.

CHAPTER XV INGATHERING AND THE STRUGGLE FOR ECONOMIC SURVIVAL

THE GATES OPEN

In the eighteen months following the Declaration of Independence, 340,-000 Jews arrived in Israel. They came by passenger liner, by rickety dormitory steamer, by plane, and in some instances by clandestine land routes. Even as war still raged and the little state faced possible destruction or bankruptcy, the newcomers continued to pour in. During the mandate, the rate of immigration had averaged 18,000 a year. During the first three years of statehood, the average reached 18,000 a month, and in some months the figure exceeded 30,000. Between May 15, 1948, and June 30, 1953, the Jewish population of the country doubled. No influx like it had been witnessed in modern times. It was an "Open Door" from which older and vastly wealthier nations would have recoiled in dismay. Emotionally, the policy was dictated by the most fundamental of Zionist tenets, extending back to biblical promises and forward to the commitment in the Declaration of Independence that Israel "will be open to the immigration of Jews from all countries of their dispersion." Indeed, the very *raison d'être* of statehood, as the 1950 Law of Return made clear, was to provide a homeland for all who wished to forsake the Diaspora and "come home."

But there was another, no less valid, explanation for the unprecedented ingathering. It was the government's acute recognition of the need for an instant population: for inhabitants to deepen the nation's military manpower reservoir, to preempt the vulnerable empty spaces in the land, to garrison the new agricultural colonies and the border settlements girdling the exposed frontiers, and to create the modernized economy that was indispensable for achieving a Western standard of living. Although never stressed in public, it was essentially this military and economic factor that persuaded Israel's leaders to run the risks of virtually uncontrolled mass immigration. Moreover, the decision to swing open the gates was all the more unchallengeable as dispersed communities of Jews in Europe, Asia, and Africa launched a rising clamor for transportation to safety in Israel. No sooner was one crisis of "repatriation" met and resolved than it was overtaken by a fresh one.

Upon the establishment of the state, therefore, the first priority for the Israeli government and the Jewish Agency was to empty the displaced persons' camps in Germany, Austria, and Italy. Thereupon, between Septemper 1948 and August 1949, fifty-two refugee centers were closed in Europe and their inhabitants shipped on to Israel via Marseilles and Bari; even as 25,000 internees similarly were removed from the Cyprus detention camps. At almost the same time, a full-scale transfer of Bulgarian Jewry was set in motion, paralleled by the immigration of large numbers of Yugoslav and Turkish Jews. Between spring of 1948 and autumn of 1950, meanwhile, the Communist regimes of Poland and Rumania allowed a sizable, if intermittent, Jewish departure. Eventually, under Soviet pressure, Warsaw closed off further Jewish emigration in September 1950; while Bucharest denied additional permits in February 1952. Yet by then fully 100,000 Polish and 120,000 Rumanian immigrants were already in Israel. During the next four years their numbers would be augmented by another 48,000 Jews from eastern and western Europe.

The tidal wave of immigration was by no means animated by pioneering élan. In truth, the newcomers had undergone little scrutiny or screening. The aged and the infirm, the weary and the disillusioned, flooded in indiscriminately, seeking peace and security, not creative adventure. Most of the Europeans among them had lived through war, many had survived death camps and crematoria. They had little stomach for the rugged challenge of frontier agricultural outposts, and even less for the grim economic and bureaucratic obstacles that confronted them upon arrival in Israel. Their misgivings were compounded, too, not alone by the circumstances of immigration and transit camp life, but by their encounter with a simultaneous avalanche of Jews from Moslem nations whose frequent lack of commitment to a progressive, dynamic Zionism infected even the idealistic minority among the "Westerners."

THE ORIENTAL IMMIGRATION

The arrival of these Oriental Jews was for the Europeans a belated reminder of a "world passed by" in the Jewish hinterland. That world was an ancient one, as it happened, and in many cases older than the Ashkenazic Diaspora. Not a few of the Orientals had settled in Babylon and the Levant in preexilic times. Others had made their way to the Arabian Peninsula and North Africa as refugees during the early centuries of the Common Era. By far the largest numbers of them, however, had journeyed through the Near and Middle East in the wake of the Arab expansion, settling in lands conquered by the armies of the Prophet. From the seventh century on, then, until the rise of European imperialism in the nineteenth century, Oriental Jews experienced virtually no first-hand contact with Western peoples or cultures. Their outlook and cultural surroundings were almost entirely "Eastern," and as the Islamic Renaissance faded in the late Middle Ages, they became increasingly attuned to the passivity and torpor of the Middle East.

The numbers of Jews living in Islamic countries reached 1,700,000 by 1939. At a time when the Ashkenazim totaled some 15,000,000, this figure represented barely 11 percent of the world Jewish population. Moreover, with the power centers of Jewish life concentrated in the Western world, it was hardly surprising that the ideologues and pioneers of Zionism gave only fleeting attention to the remote and impoverished Oriental hinterland, or even to the driblets of Sephardic and Oriental Jews who had been attracted to Palestine throughout the centuries for reasons of economic compulsion or religious messianism. As late as the outbreak of World War II, European Jews comprised the bulk of the Yishuv, approximately 77 percent. In the end, of course, it was the Nazi Holocaust that revolutionized the demographic basis of Jewish life in Palestine, as elsewhere. Within a period of five years, the Final Solution in Europe nearly doubled the Sephardic and Oriental component of world Jewry, and increased it to 45 percent of the reservoir of likely immigrants to Israel. Only then did the Zionist leadership awaken belatedly to the role to be fulfilled by the denizens of these Eastern backwaters in populating and building the Jewish state.

The Yemenites were the first to reinforce their numbers in Israel. The Imamate of Yemen, lying at the southwestern tip of the Arabian Peninsula, could hardly have been more veiled from Western eyes than the Tibetan fastnesses of the Himalayas. At the beginning of the twentieth century some 30,000 Jews lived there, and by 1945 nearly 50,000. Concentrated in and around the capital city of Tsan'a, they traced their presence to the mass dispersion from the Holy Land after the Roman suppression. Their status as dhimmis—that is, as a barely tolerated minority—was the result of the Moslem conquest in the seventh century. Thereafter, under the narrowest of legal protection, the Jews were restricted to their own ghetto quarters, and earned a meager livelihood as artisans for the Arab peasantry. As late as the twentieth century they paid special Jewish taxes, wore distinctive garb, and were forbidden to ride horses or camels or to leave their neighborhoods after dark. It was the more remarkable, under these galling limitations, that the little Arabized group somehow held fast to its Jewish traditions and continued to live in an unshakable, if touchingly naïve, expectation of the arrival of the Messiah, who would surely lead God's People back to the Land of Israel.

In 1880 the vision of Return suddenly assumed tangible contours. By ship and caravan, accounts reached the Imamate that large numbers of European Jews had settled in Palestine to lay claim to an ancient dream. Perhaps the tales were exaggerated, but even the slightest hope of redemption dared not be overlooked. In the grip of a messianic delirium, a hundred families from Tsan'a promptly disposed of their homes and set out for the Holy Land. Making their way on foot to the ports of Hudeida and Jidda, they traveled up the Red Sea by dhow to Suez, from there by land to Alexandria, then by ship to Jaffa, and once again by land to Jerusalem. Fully a third of them perished en route. Nevertheless, the survivors were joined each year by additional hundreds of their kinsmen, until by 1914 no fewer than 7,400 Yemenites had arrived in Palestine. Three decades later, swollen by immigration and natural increase, their population in the country totaled nearly 40,000. They were poor, among the poorest of all the Yishuv's inhabitants. A few labored in the citrus groves. Some were artisans. Most lived in slums, and did the hardest and least rewarding work in the Jewish community. Their wives hired themselves out as maids. Few of them complained. They were in Zion.

Then, with Israel's independence in 1948, Zion was the only world that mattered. Nor was it a question now of messianic portents alone. Life in Yemen suddenly had become physically precarious. Chagrined at the defeat of Arab forces on the battlefields of Palestine, and aroused by the opportunity of loot, bands of Moslems swarmed through the Jewish quarters of Tsan'a and other towns, plundering and burning. Departure now became a matter of survival. The Imam put few obstacles in the way—not as long as the Jews left all their property to the Crown. The Jewish Agency in turn reached an understanding with the sheikhs whose territories lay between the Imamate and the British Crown Colony of Aden. For an agreed sum, the rulers consented to let the Jews pass through their domains. Across this bleak and rugged terrain, then, the largest numbers of Yemenites made their way on foot southward to the coast. By the time they reached the Joint Distribution Committee camp in Hashed, adjoining Aden, most of them were reduced to walking skeletons.

Transportation across the Red Sea no longer was possible once Egypt closed the Suez Canal to Israel-bound shipping. Instead, by contract with a group of chartered American air transport firms, the JDC swiftly organized an alternate method of departure—"Operation Magic Carpet." The emaciated little Yemenites, some adults weighing barely eighty pounds, were loaded on the American DC-4s, up to two hundred at a time. At the peak of the airlift, planes were flying round-the-clock schedules to Israel, seven and eight flights a day. Their route crossed Yemen but skirted the other Arab countries, flying a narrow corridor with uncertain instruments at night, and deprived of radio guidance. Forced landing anywhere would have meant disaster. Remarkably, no mishaps occurred. By the time the airlift ended in September 1950, 47,000 people, the bulk of Yemen's Jewish population, had been carried to Israel, together with some 3,000 Aden Jews.

The emigration from Yemen was soon followed, and ultimately surpassed, by a massive airlift of Jews from Iraq. Here was the largest, oldest, and most distinguished of all Eastern Jewish communities. Numbering approximately 130,000 in 1948, its inhabitants traced their origins to the famed preexilic Jewish settlement of Babylon. In ancient and medieval times, this was a Jewry unsurpassed in wealth and culture. Baghdad was the seat of the Exilarch, the Prince of the Captivity, and of the venerated academies of Sura and Pumpedita. From the middle of the eleventh century, however, successive invasions of Mongols and Turks ravaged Iraq's economy, undermining the security of Jews and Arabs alike. The next several hundred years were precarious ones. During the latter Ottoman period the Jews finally managed once again to resume a quiet, if stagnant, life; a few of them even achieved a certain prosperity. Yet their major recovery awaited the end of World War I. It was then at last, under the British-sponsored Feisal government, that Iraqi Jewry experienced its most dramatic revival. Indeed, its members soon played a key role in the largest business establishments of the nation, and not a few of them occupied important positions in government service.

The first intimations of change for the worse came with the penetration of German agents in the 1930s and a rising swell of Arab right-wing nationalism. The xenophobia first crested in 1941, during the Rashid Ali uprising, when mobs attacked Jewish homes and shops, inflicting hundreds of casualties. Although the pro-German regime was soon overthrown by an invading British army, the Jews were shaken by the evidence of their new vulnerability. A small number of departures for Palestine followed and continued intermittently until the birth of Israel. It was in 1948–49, however, during the Palestine war, that Iraqi Jewry entered its darkest hour. Under the cloak of martial law, the Baghdad government subjected the nation's Jewish citizens to organized persecution. Jewish homes were searched, often pillaged. Hundreds of Jews were arrested and imprisoned under charges of treason. Jews were expelled from government, Jewish doctors and pharmacists barred from practice, Jewish students expelled from the university, Jewish banks ordered closed, Jewish merchants denied their import licenses. The community faced economic ruin.

Since the outbreak of fighting in Palestine, emigration to Israel had been declared a capital offense. Nevertheless, the government was soon intrigued by the prospect of inheriting large quantities of abandoned Jewish property. In March of 1950, therefore, the Iraqi parliament gave official sanction to Jewish emigration, on condition that Jews applying for exit permits relinquish their Iraqi citizenship. As an inducement for departure, the government assured prospective emigrants that the homes, businesses, and bank accounts they left behind would be disposed of legally, and that eventually they would receive the proceeds. Yet on March 10, 1951, one day following the deadline for exit registration, the government suddenly announced that the property and bank accounts of emigrating Jews henceforth were forfeited to the government.

By then, in any case, Iraq's Jews had applied for emigration by the tens of thousands. Their immediate problem was transportation. The Jewish Agency's original plans had been to send them by ship from Basra to Eilat. These soon had to be abandoned due to Iraq's continuing state of war with Israel and the tightening Egyptian blockade of the Strait of Tiran. Nor was overland travel possible through Syria and Lebanon. Eventually the Baghdad regime granted permission for air transport. Its condition was simply that the planes should not fly directly to Israel, but rather land first in neutral Cyprus. On that basis the great airlift transfer, known in Israel as "Operation Ali Baba," was launched in May 1950. By the time it ended in December 1951, 113,000 passengers had been flown to the Jewish state. Afterward, smaller numbers of Jews reached Israel via Iran, bringing the total Iraqi immigration to 121,000. In 1955, the number of Jews remaining in Iraq was estimated at less than 4,000.

Even the Yemenite and Iraqi airlifts, however, did not exhaust the wave of Jewish emigration from Moslem lands. Libyan Jewry soon joined the exodus. This was an indigenous community, extending back to Berber tribes that had been proselytized by Jewish traders and refugees in Carthaginian times. While not a prosperous or a notably cultured minority, the Jews of Libya had enjoyed a reasonable dhimmi security under both Arabs and Turks, even under the Italians, who protected them from physical persecution. Numbering 23,000 by 1945, they earned their livelihoods as merchants and artisans in Tripoli, Benghazi, and other, smaller communities; while yet another 7,000 Jews lived a primitive, Berber-like existence in the desert interior. In 1945, too—ironically, under British occupation—an eruption of anti-Jewish riots left several hundred Jews dead and wounded and destroyed over a thousand Jewish homes and shops. The outburst was linked to the emergent Libyan nationalist movement; the Palestine issue simply exacerbated the unrest. In June 1948, a renewal of violence inflicted additional Jewish casualties. By then few Libyan Jews believed that it was possible to remain on in the country. Fortunately for them, in 1949 the Jewish Agency succeeded in organizing direct sailings from Benghazi to Haifa. By the summer of 1951, as a result, virtually the entire Libyan Jewish community had sold its property at distress prices and embarked for Israel. The newcomers arrived in a state of destitution.

If the Jewish minority of Syria-Lebanon was as old as Libya's, it was considerably more advanced and affluent. For centuries, under Arabs and Turks alike, Jewish traders in the littoral cities had played a decisive role in the Mediterranean import-export trade. Under the French mandate, too, Jews had occupied eminent positions in the civil service, and even the brief Vichy interregnum did not threaten their essential physical security. By 1943 approximately 20,000 Jews lived in Damascus, Aleppo, Beirut, and other cities, practicing their trades and maintaining their Jewish religious and cultural traditions. Yet in the Levant, more than other Middle Eastern nations, the pattern of emigration for both Christians and Jews had been established long before the rise of Israel. Throughout the twentieth century, until 1945, not less than 40,000 Syrians and Lebanese had departed for Europe, for North and South America, and for Egypt and Palestine. In the case of the Jews, the birth of sovereign Arab regimes after World War II merely intensified the emigrationist pressure. Thus, in Syria, independence was accompanied by the gradual eviction of Jewish employees from the civil services and banks, and by outbreaks of mob rioting against Jewish homes and businesses. It was the UN Partition Resolution, however, that ultimately signified the beginning of the end for Syrian Jewry, as for Jews elsewhere in the Arab world. After 1948, the Damascus authorities froze Jewish accounts, blocked the liquidation of Jewish property, and eventually subjected Jewish residential neighborhoods to nightly curfews. Large numbers of Jews fortunately managed to cross the border to Lebanon, and from there (with the unofficial acquiescence of the Beirut government) proceeded on to Israel. Between November 1947 and February 1949, 14,000 Syrian and Lebanese Jews reached Israeli soil. The 3,000 of their kinsmen who remained behind in Syria, a cowed and impoverished minority, lived from day to day in tremulous uncertainty even of physical survival (Chapter XXIII).

Egyptian Jewry, by contrast, was distinguished from other Middle Eastern communities in the brevity of its history and in the more prolonged agony of its dissolution. Nearly all of the 75,000 Jews registered on the Egyptian census in 1948 considered themselves "Europeans," integral members of that elite social and economic circle that included 350,000 Greeks, 200,000 Italians, and 40,000 English, French, and Armenians. Except for a minuscule group that traced its lineage to the Alexandrian community of antiquity, and a scattering of refugees from the Ottoman Levant, the country's Jewish population had been almost negligible before the end of World War I. The largest migration wave of Jews arrived in the 1920s and 1930s, most of them Near Eastern in origin, and drawn to Egypt specifically to shed their Asian inheritance. The country offered Jewish newcomers the cherished opportunity of European status under the protection of Western consuls. By 1939, as a result, perhaps 80 percent of the Jews residing in Egypt were foreigners who nevertheless enjoyed European consular solicitude.

With the outbreak of World War II, the Egyptian government lost no time in ending this capitulatory relationship. At first, to be sure, the change created few problems. As loyal "subjects," if not citizens, Egypt's Jews continued to enjoy full legal protection in their individual and business activities without the corresponding responsibilities of citizenship. And they prospered mightily. Belonging almost exclusively to the middle class, they served as the leading business executives, cotton brokers, bankers, financiers, and professionals of Egypt. Rarely if ever did they encounter prejudice. The first indications of native animus surfaced only after 1945, as Egyptian nationalism burgeoned—against the British, and later against the other minorities that dominated Egyptian economic life. In the case of Jews, of course, local resentment was exacerbated soon afterward by the Palestine issue. Thus, following the birth of Israel, a number of leading Egyptian Jewish companies were sequestered. Egyptian nationality later was required for the practice of medicine and for membership on the cotton exchange. The cumulative effect of these measures was gradually to undermine the structure of Jewish economic life in Egypt.

For many thousands of Egyptian Jews the logical solution was emigration. Yet the decision was not lightly carried out. Although the government lifted its ban on departure in August 1949, it imposed penalties that ultimately inflicted the kind of financial loss suffered by Jews in Iraq, Syria, and elsewhere in the Middle East. Homes, chattels, businesses, all had to be disposed of on a distress basis, and in a majority of instances property reverted to the state. The 20,000 Jews who managed to flee in November 1949 left as declassed relics of a once affluent bourgeoisie. Many remained in Europe to begin anew, but in 1950 approximately 7,000 of them proceeded on to Israel. For a while at least, this appeared to be the crest of the Egyptian aliyah. Later that year a new Wafdist government in Cairo eased the harshest of the restrictions, canceled the sequestration measures, even handed back a portion of the confiscated property. The exodus slowed, as the remaining Jewish population of 55,000 anticipated a gradual return to normalcy. They were wrong. Their attempts to recoup their fortunes soon collided head-on with the emergent chauvinism of the Nasser government. By then, the fate of Egyptian Jewry was sealed (Chapter XVIII).

The emigration of Jews from Turkey and Iran shared less of the draconian compulsion of other Middle Eastern nations. In 1948, 82,000 Jews lived in Turkey's principal cities. A tolerated, even favored, millet under the old Ottoman regime, they did not experience the cutting edge of Turkish nationalism until the early Kemalist republican period of the 1920s. Pressure then intensified for Jews and other minorities to adopt the Turkish language and Turkish names, to enroll their children in Turkish schools, to hire Turkish business partners. During World War II, as the Ankara government maintained a circumspect friendship with Nazi Germany, national policy toward the Jews approached a thinly veiled anti-Semitism. The harsh capital levy that was imposed upon all the nation's minority peoples represented nothing less than an economic disaster for Turkish Jewry. Uncomfortable in any case within this tough Moslem warrior nation, many thousands of Jews greeted the birth of the Zionist state in 1948 with urgent petitions for departure. The government interposed no serious obstacles. By 1950 fully 33,000 Turkish Jews had arrived in Israel. Most came from the poorer strata, and of these, thousands were the ruined victims of Ankara's wartime taxation laws. In the early years after their arrival, they shared with other immigrants the cruelest ordeal of settlement in Israel, and in their poverty added to the nation's economic woes.

This was essentially the pattern, too, of the Iranian exodus. Like the Jews of Iraq, those of Persia represented one of the most venerable of the Middle Eastern minority communities, dating back to the preexilic era. Yet no Jewry in Asia or Africa was ever more wretchedly impoverished. Numbering close to 80,000 in 1945, the largest numbers of them were impacted into the fetid mellahs of Tehran and Isfahan, where they barely subsisted as petty traders and hucksters. Indeed, of the 25,000 Jews residing in Tehran at the end of World War II, fully half were supported by Western Jewish charities. There were, as well, some 18,000 Jews dwelling in Iranian Azerbaijan and Kurdistan whose backwardness was comparable to the most primitive of their Moslem neighbors. In their lifetime, they had experienced not only economic duress but the chauvinism of the Reza Shah Pahlavi regime and assaults and pillage carried out with the tacit connivance of the government.

Several thousand Iranian Jews had fled to Palestine as early as the turn of the century. Most, however, preferred to wait until they could be assured subsidized transportation and welfare guarantees. Israel was prepared to offer those opportunities, even as the Tehran government was frankly relieved to have the Jews depart. Between May 1948 and October 1956, therefore, the number of Iranian Jews reaching Israel mounted to 39,000—nearly half the Jewish population of Iran. Not all arrived as mendicants; there were a few businessmen among them with capital to invest. But the majority, like the majority of immigrant Jews from other Islamic communities—from North Africa and Iraq, from Turkey and the Levant, from Yemen and smaller, forgotten Jewish enclaves in Afghanistan, the Caucasus, and Cochin—poured into Israel on a wave of destitution. Even more than the hostility of the neighboring Arab states, it was the influx of these rudderless derelicts that threatened to engulf and overwhelm the Jewish republic from the very moment of its birth.

The demographic impact of the immigration was profound. Fully 7 percent of the entire Diaspora arrived in Israel between 1948 and 1953 alone. The number of Israel's Jewish inhabitants accordingly rose from 6 percent of world Jewry at the founding of the state to 13 percent by the end of 1953. During its initial four and a half years, Israel's population doubled. By the end of 1956 its population had nearly tripled, reaching 1,667,-000. By then, too, the ingathering had slowed, although it would soon regain momentum. As events developed, immigration, far more than natural reproduction, accounted for the largest share of Israel's population increase. And the growth would become increasingly Oriental. In 1948 Jews from Moslem lands accounted for 14 percent of the immigration, in 1949 for 47 percent, in 1950 for 71 percent, in 1952 for 71 percent, in 1953 for 75 percent, in 1954 for 88 percent, in 1955 for 92 percent, and in 1956 for 87 percent. In 1948 Jews of European ancestry comprised 75 percent of Israel's Jewish inhabitants; by 1961; the ratio had fallen to 55 percent, and it would continue to decline in later years. This constituted an ethnic revolution for the Zionist state, one that none of its leaders had anticipated even after the Holocaust, nor as late as 1948. Far from serving as an outpost of the West in Asia, Israel itself appeared to be undergoing orientalization, both in its human resources and to some degree in its way of life.

THE SHOCK OF ABSORPTION

The little nation was ill-equipped to provide shelter for this avalanche of refugees. At the very outset, many of the newcomers proceeded to follow their own well-honed instincts for survival by taking over abandoned Arab dwellings in Haifa, Jerusalem, and Jaffa, in Safed, Ramle, and Lydda, and in smaller towns and villages. Ultimately 200,000 Jewish immigrants preempted some 80,000 Arab rooms (Chapter XVI). But soon every derelict Arab village and neighborhood was full. The immigration continued, and other shelter was urgently needed. The Jewish Agency then imported thousands of prefabricated huts of Scandinavian design. At the same time, a national corporation, Amidar, was established to build permanent immigrant housing by every known contrivance of inexpensive and accelerated construction, including homes of precast cement blocks manufactured on the spot. Most of these units were painfully functional. A family of four was entitled to one room plus a small alcove for washing, cooking, and storage. By the end of 1949, 25,000 such dwellings had been erected; a year after that, there were twice as many. But it was taking much too long. In the interval, the largest majority of newcomers had to be sheltered by other means. The camp was the obvious solution. During the last years of the mandate, the Jewish Agency had housed immigrants in temporary barracks near Haifa and Chadera. These were supplemented early in 1948 by makeshift shelters in Ra'anana and Rehovot. While the facilities accommodated up to 5,000 people at a time, they were woefully inadequate for the immigration that followed the birth of the state. Ordinarily it would have been possible to use the network of barracks recently abandoned by the British army. Following orders from London, however, the British had systematically destroyed furniture, windows, and doors before leaving; only the shells of the buildings remained. Yet even these were temporarily repaired and instantly packed with Jews arriving from the Cyprus internment compounds.

Thus it was that the tent cities went up. At first, they were erected close to Haifa. But soon this port community was filled to bursting, and the Jewish Agency was obliged to lay out immigrant camps elsewhere: by the other coastal cities, in the Jerusalem Corridor, in the Galilee, in the approaches to the northern Negev. By early 1951, 17,000 tents in fifty-three camps housed 97,000 men, women, and children—fully one-tenth of the population of Israel. The circumstances were identical in each tent village: food from a central kitchen, clothing from a Jewish Agency warehouse, makeshift schools provided by the Israeli government. And, above all, unemployment. For with the end of the Palestine war, the demobilized Israeli soldiers returned to their former jobs, and for some two years few opportunities were left for the immigrants, who were instructed now to await their resettlement outside the camps before seeking employment.

It was a grim ordeal for the newcomers. They subsisted on the dole month after month, waking and sleeping each day in unalleviated squalor. Their shacks or tents leaked in winter and roasted in summer. School facilities for their children were poor. Worse yet, the immigrants were cut off from their normal social environment, often from their families and friends. The intermixture of peoples from Europe, Asia, and North Africa, many of them thrust together in the same tents, was an agonizing experience. A mood of endless anomie prevailed, a lack of norms, structure, and certainty. By 1952 nearly 40,000 of the newcomers, embittered and exhausted, had given up the attempt to create a new life for themselves in the Jewish state. With the help of relatives abroad, they departed the country for western Europe, North or South America, or the British Commonwealth. Few of them returned.

Even earlier, the Israeli government and the Jewish Agency had sensed that the problem of absorption was psychological as much as economic. If poverty was debilitating, so was enforced idleness. Years might pass before living conditions improved and the necessary full-time employment opportunities were generated. In the meanwhile the immigrants could hardly be permitted to wander about aimlessly as mendicants. In the autumn of 1950 it occurred to Levi Eshkol, director of the Jewish Agency's land settlement department, that few of the original reception camps had been located near employment opportunities. Now that the army veterans were at work again, perhaps the imbalance could be rectified if "mushroom" villages were erected on the outskirts of urban and other industrial development zones, where part-time jobs were available. It was worth a try.

The first of these transit camps—ma'abarot—were located outside Tel Aviv. Physically, there was little enough to distinguish them from the original immigration depots. Indeed, life in the ma'abarot was hardly less austere than in the reception centers. Shelter still was an aluminum or galvanized iron shack. Flooded by winter rains, exposed to summer heat, deprived even of the basic amenities, the shantytowns represented a physical improvement only over the most primitive Iranian or North African ghettos. And yet the differences between the transit communities and the immigration centers, although subtle, were crucial. There were occasional part-time jobs to be found nearby. In lieu of food and clothing, each family received a modest supplementary income from the Jewish Agency. In each ma'abara, the immigrants bought their own provisions and did their own cooking on cheap gas burners. For all their deprivation, then, the newcomers enjoyed privacy at last, and freedom of movement. To those who had endured the shiftlessness and despair of the immigrant camp, the ma'abara represented a tangible step toward self-improvement.

Encouraged by the success of the experiment, the Jewish Agency now proceeded to dismantle the reception depots altogether in favor of the transit camps. By November 1951, not less than 127 ma'abarot were functioning outside the country's urban centers. A year after that, fully 223,000 immigrants were "settled" there. In the interval, the government provided these makeshift communities with schools, kindergartens, children's homes, synagogues, and clubs, while the immigrants themselves were encouraged to elect their own municipal councils and to assume a larger share in the public life of their settlements. Many of the newcomers in fact responded eagerly to the challenge. Whatever their economic privations—these were hardly less severe than before—the immigrants accepted the ma'abara in its literal meaning, as a temporary way station to full employment and decent shelter. No one expected to remain there beyond one or two months. As it turned out, the period of transition more commonly approached one or two years, and occasionally even longer.

EFFORTS TO DISPERSE AND FEED A POPULATION

The fate of the immigrants depended less upon their own negligible resources, in funds or family connections in Israel, than upon the policy decisions of the nation's authorities. Those authorities were by no means limited exclusively to the government, however. It was understood, of course, from the outset of independence, that a sovereign nation should be entirely responsible for the conduct of its domestic and international affairs, and that most of the functions hitherto exercised by the Jewish Agency would have to be transferred to the government. Yet it was equally plain that a beleaguered and overworked administration could not by itself deal adequately with the immense task of absorbing and settling hundreds of thousands of immigrants. The reasons were not only financial but moral. The burden of the immigration should hardly have been Israel's alone; rather, it deserved to be shared at least in some measure by Jews through-out the world. During the period of mass influx in the early years of the state, therefore, the Jewish Agency, which since 1929 had been the historic conduit of overseas funds, remained primarily responsible for transporting immigrants to Israel and for supplying their immediate needs. Even perma-nent absorption became a joint undertaking, with the Agency and the government sharing the burden of housing and agricultural settlement. The arrangement was made reasonably workable in 1951–52, when Levi Eshkol served both as minister of agriculture and as director of the Agency's land settlement department. By the same token, the Jewish Agency shared re-sponsibility with the prime minister's office and with the ministries of housing and interior in dispersing the immigrants throughout the country.

The task of population dispersal in fact became urgent from the moment of Israel's birth. For one thing, the concentration of Jews in the three major urban centers of Tel Aviv, Haifa, and Jerusalem—60 percent of the Yishuv by May 1948—was an economic and social anomaly that had to be rectified. More important, there was no time to be lost in settling the under-populated areas of the country in the Negev and in the Galilee hills. Only a chain of predominantly Jewish settlements was capable of filling the vacuum opened by Arab departure and of blocking Arab infiltration from across the armistice lines. Not least of all, Israel was critically short of food, and its agricultural sector required immediate development. It is of interest that the traditional Zionist vision of a "healthy" agricultural popu-lation base lingered on well after statehood. Thus, if the choice in building a cooperative commonwealth were to lie between industry and an en-larged agriculture, Israel's labor leadership in the early 1950s still was inclined toward the latter.

For the confluence of these economic, social, and security reasons, then, the initial development scheme formulated in 1950 by Eshkol's committee for joint agricultural planning included a four-year program for agricul-tural self-sufficiency. Some of its basic assumptions surely were unrealistic. The plan overestimated the number of farm settlements and farm workers that actually would be needed, and the quantity of water available for agriculture. Indeed, by 1958, after 35 percent of the nation's gross invest-ment had been devoted to agricultural and irrigation purposes, many of these early assumptions were reevaluated, and there was better under-standing that self-sufficiency was not necessarily good economics. It would have been more rational to narrow the trade gap by increasing such ex-ports as citrus and light industrial goods, for example, in which Israel enjoyed a competitive advantage. Nevertheless, in the immediate post-inde-pendence years, the obsession with Arab infiltration, and with the dangers of a critical food shortage and an imbalanced urban society, all militated for intensive agricultural settlement.

Land, at least, presented no difficulty, as it had in the prestate years. Together with abandoned Arab tracts, the bulk of Israel's unoccupied soil was taken ultimately under the joint authority of the government and the Jewish National Fund. Here, too, the Zionist leadership adhered rigorously to the principles that had built the nation's hundreds of kibbutzim and moshavim—that is, of exclusively Jewish possession of the land and of physical cultivation of the soil by the (Jewish) occupants themselves. The financial terms of allocation remained as liberal as before 1948. Rent was nominal and was not imposed at all until a new farmer was well settled and his tract producing. Rarely did settlers have a better inducement. The availability of practically free land was a crucial factor in drawing newcomers to the soil, particularly to areas that were isolated and climatically oppressive.

Lack of alternative was another inducement, however, and ultimately an even more compelling one. During the first three years of Israel's independence, barely 1 percent of the immigrants were professionally trained. More than 50 percent were entirely unskilled in any craft or trade whatever. The Europeans, to be sure, generally resisted the pressure toward agriculture. The DP camps had stripped them of their resilience and often of their ideals; many had grown hard and brutal, and others remained indifferent to the Zionist pioneering challenges of an agricultural life. It was surely significant that, of the immigrants who turned to agriculture in the postindependence years, by far the largest numbers were Oriental Jews. For example, while less than half the newcomers between 1947 and 1951 arrived from Moslem countries, fully 136 of the 231 immigrant settlements established during this period were founded by "Easterners," and only 95 by Ashkenazim (67 additional settlements were founded by veteran Israelis).

The lacunae in immigrant pioneering values were reflected as well in the statistics of kibbutz and moshav development. In 1947 the Yishuv encompassed 176 kibbutzim and 58 moshavim. By 1959 the balance had shifted to 229 kibbutzim and 264 moshavim. The numbers of villages alone did not tell the entire story. In the prestate era, two-thirds of the Jewish agricultural population were to be found in the kibbutzim and only one-third in the moshavim. By the opening of 1960 this ratio had nearly been reversed. The kibbutz population may have doubled by then, but the moshav population had quintupled. It was obvious that the collective settlement, widely regarded as the very paradigm of Zionist national and social accomplishment, now was experiencing an important proportionate loss. Even in the mandatory period, we recall, the kibbutz had failed to attract substantial numbers of families; recruitment then concentrated on unattached persons. Now, after 1948, the Orientals arrived for the most part in family groups, and without Zionist indoctrination at that. The pioneering significance of the kibbutz was lost on them. If they were to be hustled onto the soil, only the tangible advantages of privacy and profit would keep them there.

The initial circumstances of their settlement were harsh enough, in any case. Like the kibbutzim, most of the cooperative farms established after 1948 were located on or near the sites of abandoned Arab villages, and the narrow coastal plain therefore was the first region to be blanketed with large numbers of Jewish farm communities. Afterward came the hills of the Jerusalem Corridor, and finally the northern and southern regions of Israel. Tiny cement-block houses and small plots of land were awaiting the newcomers in these new villages. The blueprint devised by the Agency's land settlement department called for each moshav family to be given one cow, some fifty laying hens, and ten to fifteen dunams of soil, with irrigation facilities provided to encourage mixed farming. In practice, however, many communities were founded with little economic planning at all. Two or more years might pass before irrigation was provided, or a connecting road laid out between a moshav and its nearest highway. During the rainy season villages were cut off from their supplies. Often electricity was lacking. During the peak years of the immigration, not a few of the moshavim were congested with over a hundred families, and arable land rarely exceeded eight or ten dunams for each family unit. The shortages inevitably produced factionalism. As a result, several villages were divided and reconstituted as two or three moshavim.

Plainly, the settlers were not without help and advice. Their initial investment money for seed, fertilizer, and tractor services was advanced by the Jewish Agency. The Agency similarly helped determine what and when the newcomers would plant, while their produce was marketed later by Tnuva, an arm of the Histadrut (Chapter VII). In the early years, immigrants were provided with such quick-ripening crops as tomatoes, tobacco, or others that would show immediate income and encourage the farmers to hang on. Supplementary employment also was made available in JNF reclamation and afforestation projects. But despite these quite substantial economic and moral assurances, a combination of inadequate equipment and occasional crop failures, together with the sheer physical hardships of work, climate, and Arab depredation, took their toll. Not a few of the more backward Orientals resorted to eating their laying hens or selling their equipment. They were often uncomfortable, too, about being thrust into a village cheek by jowl with immigrants from other nations and cultures. Iraqis quarreled with Moroccans, and Bulgarians with Yemenites. Many of these in turn suspected the European madrich—the agricultural adviser— of deluding or even cheating them. Occasionally entire villages rocked with scandal. It was not uncommon, as a result, for immigrants simply to desert their moshavim for the urban slums, leaving their property neglected and debts on the Jewish Agency books. Between 1948 and 1958, 35 percent of the newcomers who had been settled in cooperative farm communities abandoned their villages and disappeared into the cities.

These setbacks notwithstanding, the agricultural crash program and the effort to decentralize the population were by no means a failure. It was true that Tel Aviv, Haifa, and Jerusalem continued to burgeon into sizable metropolitan communities. Yet the percentage of Israel's inhabitants in the three major cities declined from 52 percent in 1948 to 31 percent in 1957. While the proportional growth of the Jewish agricultural community —from 18 percent in 1948 to 22 percent by the end of 1957—may have been less than spectacular (indeed, the figure would drop later), nevertheless, the Jewish rural population, 116,000 in 1948, had climbed to 325,000 by 1959, and this was impressive absolute, if not proportional, growth. In 1948 land cultivated by Jews totaled 1,600,000 dunams; ten years later the amount was 3,900,000 dunams. By 1958 the value of Jewish agricultural production in Israel had risen to I£675.7 million. Most importantly, by the end of its first decade, the nation was feeding itself in the key staples of dairy products, poultry, vegetables, and fruit.

THE CRISIS OF THE ISRAELI ECONOMY

Hopeful as this progress was, Israel's economic infrastructure in the early years of statehood remained woefully underdeveloped at a time when the country's population was doubling and its enemies were still under arms. The Arab market, representing 15 percent of Palestine's export trade before 1948, was foreclosed by the continuing state of war. Moreover, the war damage sustained by the Dead Sea (potash) Works, the enforced idleness of the Haifa oil refineries, and the preoccupation of domestic industry with the needs of the army and of the growing local market, all deprived the little nation of vital sources of export earnings. With many of the best groves laid waste during the war, citrus output, traditionally the backbone of the Palestine economy, remained far below its prewar level. It was ironic, too, that Israel's very military success in the War of Independence eased the pressure on Jewish sympathizers abroad to match their unprecedented donations of 1948. A $100 million loan from the United States Export-Import Bank provided some hope of relief, but it was hardly adequate to raise the nation's standard of living.

One important opportunity presented itself to the young state, but it was decisively missed. This was the visit of hundreds of Jewish businessmen from abroad who, in their enthusiasm for Israel, offered to establish factories and private companies. Most Israelis were convinced, however, that if American and other Jews had shown themselves extraordinarily generous with gifts, they would demonstrate even greater magnanimity when it came to investment. It was not foreseen that the visitors would raise the issue of costs and profits when they dealt with Israel as a business proposition rather than as an object of charity. When this fact belatedly registered, the Knesset in March 1950 passed a Law for the Encouragement of Capital Investments, and later added other tax-exemption inducements in the hope of making foreign loans progressively more attractive. But the measures lured no gold rush. Some investments did come, to be sure, including the General Tire Company, the Rogosin textile mills, and a few

shoe, radio, and plastics factories. They were not enough. Foreign businessmen had learned by then that productivity in Israel was considerably lower
than in Western, industrialized countries. Workers often lacked respect for
their jobs, for machines and materials, to say nothing of their employers
and the ultimate consumers—who, after all, were only Jews like themselves.
They resisted new techniques, fearing expendability or a swifter work
tempo. The Histadrut, meanwhile, protected all but the newest or most
totally inept employees. Nor was the government blameless. The high taxes
it enacted dulled incentive for increased production.

By mid-1949 the balance of payments crisis became sufficiently acute for
the minister of finance to ask public institutions and private importers to
tap foreign sources of credit against long-term government guarantees.
Modest loans obtained by the Jewish Agency from Scandinavia, Belgium,
Switzerland, and elsewhere were linked to the import of goods from those
countries. The indefatigable David Horowitz (p. 291) traveled to England early in 1950 and succeeded at last in unfreezing Israel's sterling accounts there. These various efforts brought some relief, but in November
1950 circumstances still were critical enough for the government to requisition all foreign securities for sale against hard currency. Since 1949, too,
the threat of inflation had become all but unmanageable, and in April of
that year Ben-Gurion chose Dov Joseph to inaugurate rigorous austerity
measures. Joseph, the tough and respected former military governor of
Jerusalem, was the right man for this thankless task. He immediately
launched a tight, uncompromising program of rationing and cost and wage
control. The effort was not without impact. Between April 1949 and July
1950, it succeeded partially in reducing the cost-of-living index. By the
same token, however, the deflationary measures imposed a painful sacrifice
on the Israeli people. The supply of food to consumers was lowered to the
barest minimum, with one small portion of meat and two eggs a week as
the standard fare. Virtually all essential foodstuffs, clothing, and other consumer goods were rationed at set prices. Life became drab and gray. Serious
shortages developed, and long lines of consumers waited outside groceries
and shops for rationed goods that often expired before they could be
distributed fully. While the austerity program of 1949–50 checked what
otherwise would have been a ruinous inflation, and enabled the nation to
function on a minimum diet, it also accumulated a large supply of
unspent, progressively cheaper money that began to find its outlet in the
black market.

The quality of daily life became all but unsupportable in the winter of
1950–51, when Joseph imposed total rationing on clothing. Outraged,
private merchants immediately closed their shops; and when Joseph pressed
on, cutting food rations more drastically yet, exasperation led to spontaneous protest marches by workers and housewives. Eventually Joseph
was relieved of his post. If the crisis of shortages and black-marketeering
was deferred, however, it was not solved. Agriculture thus far was providing only about a quarter of the nation's food requirements. Industrial production was even lower. Imports were exceeding exports by five times—

although even the slightest reduction in the overseas purchase of meat and grains would have led to famine. Early in 1951, too, there were prolonged work stoppages in factories for lack of raw materials and electricity. Newspapers were on half format for lack of newsprint. The Israeli pound was collapsing, as the treasury frantically sought to back its notes with long-term "government land bonds" rather than hard currency. By then black-market prices almost completely dominated the economy. Even comparatively affluent citizens were becoming dependent on food parcels sent by relatives overseas. The army was set to work growing vegetables.

Eventually, as a measure of desperation, the government in February 1952 inaugurated a "New Economic Policy." Ben-Gurion announced that inflationary credit expansion would end. Further sales of treasury bills and land bonds were stopped, and the currency was selectively devalued. A forced loan of 10 percent was imposed on all bank deposits. In the autumn of that year, the General Zionists entered the new coalition government, and one of their preconditions was the abolition of rationing on clothing and food. Consequently, as restrictions ended, the black market slowly disappeared, inducements were restored for manufacturing, and a sound investment opportunity was opened at last for bond purchases and private investments. With the introduction of the freer market a second, no less important, government policy change was adopted. In recognition that unlimited immigration was breaking the country's back, the unspoken decision was taken to limit entry for the while only to Jews in gravest physical peril of their lives abroad. As a result of these measures, the economy by 1953 very gradually began to stabilize. Soon afterward, as a consequence of German reparations, and of United States governmental and overseas Jewish financial infusions, the economy began to grow (p. 424).

THE ROLE OF THE PUBLIC SECTOR

It was in the early years of mass immigration and near-bankruptcy, too, that the heavily weighted impact of the economy's public sector began to be felt. In a way, the development was but an enlargement of the public responsibilities fulfilled during the Yishuv by the Jewish national institutions. These latter included the Jewish National Fund and the Keren Ha-Y'sod (their monies distributed by the Jewish Agency), the Histadrut, the Va'ad Le'umi, and the municipalities. After 1948, however, ideology was reinforced by necessity. There was simply no local capital available for dealing with mass immigration and national economic development. If, then, overseas loans and grants were raised primarily by the government, by the Histadrut, and by other public and semipublic agencies, these same authorities logically insisted afterward on playing a key role in allocating the funds. Indeed, by 1954, the government budget accounted for 50.2 percent of national income and for over a quarter of the nation's total resources.

In the immediate poststate years, half this budget was allocated to housing, with defense the second principal expenditure. Additionally, however, government grants and loans to public sector ventures embraced almost every facet of the nation's economy, including all public communications and government corporations in mining, handicrafts, water, and power. By 1960 the public sector—the government, municipalities, the Histadrut, and the Jewish national institutions—directly employed 60 percent of Israel's wage earners; while indirect government action in the form of subsidies, loans, tax reductions, and part ownership also extensively shaped the activities of most of the larger private enterprises in Israel. By then, in fact, Israel was exerting more governmental and quasi-governmental influence on the national economy than any other democratic state in the world, with the exception of Sweden.

It was the Histadrut, too, not less than the government, that projected the decisive impact on Israel's economic development. During the mandatory period, we recall, the labor federation had become far more than simply a collection of unions. Through its subsidiary, Chevrat Ovdim, the Histadrut organized the cooperative sector of Israel's society, including the largest kibbutz and moshav federations, and the principal marketing and consumer cooperatives. Numbered among the Histadrut enterprises were Israel's largest building firm, Solel Boneh, the Koor network of industries, the Workers' Bank, local savings and credit banks, and the nation's largest insurance company. As early as 1954, moreover, the Histadrut was the nation's single largest industrial employer, with a total work force of over 100,000 men and women. There was virtually no economic or social activity in which the labor federation was not represented. Its interests ranged from publishing newspapers and books to manufacturing pipes, importing drugs, operating hotels, cement factories, convalescent homes, kindergartens, even airplanes and a fishing fleet.

The Histadrut's sheer size gave it important advantages. Its complex of interlocking functions and properties allowed it to operate virtually as an autonomous economy within the national economy. Thus, Solel Boneh controlled so large a supply of building materials that it became a huge trust, able to freeze out private builders, and for that reason to achieve a near-monopoly of public works contracts. The labor federation similarly was awarded the prize tracts of abandoned Arab property, often without competitive bidding, and well below market cost. Even where a private firm was able to stand its ground in the market, strikes by its Histadrut-organized employees occasionally drove the company later to accept a Histadrut purchasing bid. There were instances, too, during the early years of the state, in which a local or foreign entrepreneur discovered that if he sold the Histadrut a 51 percent share in a partnership or corporation, his business led an easier life and received currency allocations or import licenses from the government with less difficulty.

Yet the Histadrut's impact on the economy and sociology of Israel was not simply that of a producing and employing conglomerate, but even more that of guardian of the "Labor Zionist Workers' Community." For example, as a consequence of the Oriental immigration, the educational level of Israeli workers by 1954 had declined markedly over the prestate period. It was the view of the Histadrut leadership, nevertheless, that un-skilled, even illiterate, employees with large families deserved as much protection as skilled European veterans. Yosef Almogi, a Histadrut and Mapai leader, put the issue succinctly:

> Don't forget that our only hope of avoiding disastrous social problems, espe-cially among the [Oriental] immigrants, is to offer them a high standard of social services. Some countries are wealthy enough not to have to worry about this. For example, Germany can afford to keep its wages comparatively low. But those wages, low as they are, will still assure a German worker com-fort and security. Here it isn't the same. Israel is a poor country. And pre-cisely because we are poor we must have a certain minimum standard of living—unless we're prepared to drop to the level of our Arab neighbors. And that we are not willing to do. . . . We . . . believe that in the long run a progressive community such as ours will achieve—will be forced to achieve—productivity high enough to maintain its services. On the other hand, a so-cially backward community would fail to develop Israel's economy. And . . . otherwise we probably wouldn't be able to maintain ourselves at all. . . . [E]ven our military superiority over the Arabs comes from our technical skills and our advanced system of education, our better diet, the superior environment we're able to provide our children. We can't give all that up. If we did, we might go under.

As immigration gained momentum, therefore, and as the number of factories signing "closed shop" agreements increased, workers recognized that their economic survival depended quite literally upon membership in the Histadrut. Indeed, for a decade after 1948, the federation actually controlled the labor exchanges. With newcomers joining the Histadrut by the tens of thousands, the federation's registered membership by 1955 climbed to 35 percent of the nation's work force. Including wives and children, the figure approached 75 percent of the population.

The demands of a local workers' council or of an industrial union were so compelling in Israel's early years, too, that no sane employer was likely to resist for long. Wages rose steadily during the nation's first decade. But wages alone were not the test of labor's gains. The workingman measured his progress, rather, in cost-of-living increases, in bonuses, family and seniority allowances, and pension and sickness benefits. Moreover, as employers were obliged to match their employees' contributions, the network of benefits was extensively enlarged to include Mish'an, a social organization providing help for the chronically ill; sick leave insurance; suitable homes for children with family problems; Dor l'Dor, a fund for elderly members requiring help over and above old-age pensions. In all, the benefits included seven principal funds and a number of smaller ones.

It is recalled, too, that even during the Yishuv the most important of those funds by far was Kupat Cholim. The care provided by this medical insurance was exceptionally far-ranging, if often erratic in quality. It included treatment by a physician either in clinics or at home; full hospitalization in institutions belonging to Kupat Cholim itself or, when necessary, in government, municipal, or Hadassah hospitals; free medicines in Kupat Cholim pharmacies and dispensaries, as well as artificial limbs, hearing aids, and other prosthetic devices; convalescent care; payment for sick leave; mother-and-child preventive health care; medical treatment in case of accidents at work; and, finally, treatment of the chronically ill. All these services were available for the seven or eight pounds the typical Israeli paid monthly (in the 1950s) for his Kupat Cholim dues. Together, then, with Kupat Cholim and other pension advantages and fringe benefits, the value of a worker's paycheck was augmented by as much as 50 percent.

Yet it is of interest that several of the most tangible employee benefits were achieved less through collective bargaining than through national legislation. The Mapai leadership in government and in the Histadrut were comrades-in-arms, after all, and occasionally interchangeable in their responsibilities. Together, they regarded the enactment of social welfare and labor legislation as one of the nation's priorities. Thus, a Fundamental Law was passed in March 1949 assuring workers their right to organize and strike. The National Insurance Law of 1954 provided old age, disability, unemployment, and retirement insurance, as well as maternity, orphan, and dependent insurance (the burden of premiums to be shared by workers and employers alike). Other measures included an Hours of Work and Rest Law, establishing a forty-seven-hour work week with a pay rate 25 percent higher for overtime; an Annual Holidays Law, guaranteeing two weeks of paid leave; a Night-Shift Work in Bakeries Law; a Youth Employment Law, prohibiting child labor up to the age of fourteen and restricting the work hours until the age of nineteen; an Apprenticeship Law; an Employment of Women Law, disallowing night-shift work for women; a Leave of Absence Law for expectant mothers; a General Sanitary Law; a Severance Pay Law, providing for dismissal compensation equivalent to a month's salary for each year of employment; a Labor Exchange Law, requiring employers to hire workers through official labor exchanges. It was a vast, remarkably all-embracing canopy of labor legislation. As a projection of the classic Labor Zionist vision, it appeared to offer the basic conditions for an authentic welfare state. And so it was traditionally described by Western observers.

In fact, those conditions were still preliminary. In a welfare state literally defined, the major burden of social expenditure is covered by the government and financed by a progressive income tax. In Israel, by contrast, primary education alone was underwritten by the government, while the expense of health and social insurance was borne on a voluntary, negotiated basis by employees and employers themselves. In England most of the national health service was financed by the treasury. In Sweden the government and municipalities underwrote hospitalization costs, the single largest expenditure item in health services. Old-age pensions in Sweden and in England also were subsidized principally by the taxpayers. Measured against the achievements of Britain and the Scandinavian countries, then, Israel was rather less than a fulfilled welfare state. Its employees and employers still assumed a heavier direct responsibility for their pensions and insurance benefits than did their counterparts in Sweden, England, or Denmark. As a consequence of its more limited resources, and also, perhaps, of the Histadrut's vested interest in retaining the largest enclave of social services under its own jurisdiction, Israel preferred to move cautiously, if deliberately, toward the goal of authentic social welfare.

THE IMMIGRATION RESUMES, THE ROOTS OF SOCIAL CRISIS

In 1952 and 1953 immigration dropped to a small fraction of the previous four years, with less than 36,000 newcomers arriving in this two-year period. Large numbers of European Jews were denied exit permits for Israel. Rumania, for example, shut its gates in 1952, and from then until 1956 the barest trickle of Jews managed to leave. The early 1950s represented the first, authentically virulent period of Communist anti-Zionism (Chapter XVII), and large numbers of Jews were imprisoned by the Bucharest regime for their actual or suspected "antiparty" conduct. Poland similarly closed off Jewish departure in 1950. In Israel itself, meanwhile, the nation's parlous economic straits compelled the government and Jewish Agency for the first time to limit immigration exclusively to Jews facing serious physical danger abroad. Whenever room could be spared for others, priority was assigned younger, more vigorous, or better-trained workers and their families. The policy was never official, but it operated in fact.

Afterward, however, as the economy stabilized, immigration gradually regained its former momentum, climbing to 18,000 in 1954, 37,000 in 1955, 56,000 in 1956, and 72,000 in 1957. This time the renewed influx came principally from North Africa. In 1954, for example, Jews from the Maghreb comprised 67 percent of the total immigration; in 1955, 87 percent; in 1956, 80 percent. By May 1958 fully 160,000 North African Jews had arrived in the course of Israel's first decade, exceeding even the Yemenite and Iraqi immigration waves. The figure revealed a seismic upheaval in a part of the world that had been largely overlooked by Western Jewry until then. Few Israelis appreciated that the Maghreb refugees were lineal descendants of one of the most ancient (pre-Carthaginian) and productive civilizations in Jewish history. Yet, during the Islamic renaissance between the ninth and thirteenth centuries, this community fully rivaled Spanish Jewry in its affluence and literacy; while after the fifteenth century its ranks were augmented by some 40,000 Sephardic newcomers, fugitives of the Inquisition and the Spanish expulsion decree. From the medieval to the early modern era, therefore, the galaxy of Maghreb Jews included such distinguished figures as the religious philosopher Moses Maimonides, the poet Yehuda ibn-Abbas, the mathematician Yusuf ibn-Aknin, the merchant prince Samuel Pallash, ambassador of Morocco to the Netherlands, and others renowned in scholarship, science, and literature.

Then, in the eighteenth century, during an interval of acute Moslem religious reaction, a blight suddenly descended on the Maghreb. Dhimmi
taxes were tripled. Jews were transformed into the serfs of their local
Moslem sayed, virtually locked into their mellahs, and forbidden to travel.
Within the space of a century, too, the great majority of North African
Jews forgot how to read or write. It awaited the appearance of the French
in Algeria (1830), Tunisia (1881), and Morocco (1912) to ease the worst
of these legal restrictions and to permit a certain uneven cultural revival.
In Algeria, the earliest French bridgehead, Jews were granted French
citizenship from 1870 on, and full civil equality. They began to flourish
and prosper, as a result, adopted French as their language, and regained
their earlier intellectual acuity. By the same token, with Algeria the most
tranquil of Maghreb countries under imperial rule, few of that nation's
130,000 Jews gave serious thought to emigration. The numbers departing
for Israel in the 1950s were minimal.

The status of Tunisia's 105,000 Jews was far less assured. As late as 1951,
the majority of Tunisian Jewry were lower-middle-class tradesmen congested in the slum-ghetto neighborhoods of Tunis, Bizerte, Sfax, and other
cities. One-third were French citizens, the rest subject to Tunisian civil
jurisdiction. While physically safe enough in the urban littoral area, Jews
living in the isolated mountainous interior were beyond the pale, despised,
insulted, often beaten, occasionally murdered. With the upsurge of Neo-
Destour nationalism in the early 1950s, moreover, Tunisian Jews everywhere quailed at their imminent vulnerability upon French departure. The
danger was evidently realized in 1956, when the nation achieved full independence. At first, to be sure, President Habib Bourguiba offered assurances of friendship to the Jews, and even included several Jews in his
government. But soon afterward an official program of "Tunisification"
abolished the special corporative status of all religious communities, including the millet of the Jews. It was in anticipation of these and even more
ominous developments that growing numbers of Jews picked up stakes
and emigrated well before the final establishment of Tunisian independence. Between 1950 and 1958, 22,000 of them arrived in Israel, and another
15,000 in France. But if the migration represented fully 35 percent of the
Tunisian Jewish population, it did not necessarily include the most creative
elements. Rather, those who settled in Israel were generally the least affluent and least literate members of their community, often from the Tunisian
interior. Few brought capital or skills with them.

The largest single component in the North African immigration arrived
from Morocco. There, some 225,000 Jews lived as an island in a Moslem
ocean of 8 million Berbers. For centuries before the establishment of the
French protectorate in 1912, the Jews had been tolerated in Morocco as
dhimmis but cribbed with innumerable and humiliating restrictions. Their
economic life was marginal, their cultural vitality almost completely atrophied. Although a certain improvement in their legal status was effected
under the French protectorate, they remained impacted in the fetid mellahs
of Casablanca and of the smaller, urban centers, and quarantined from

both the Islamic majority and the French colonial administration. They were extremely poor. For many years before and after the rise of Israel, American Joint Distribution Committee funds literally saved tens of thousands of Moroccan Jews from starvation.

To compound the difficulties of Jewish existence, the rising Istiqlal nationalist movement of the early 1950s brought Moroccan Berbers and French settlers to the verge of civil war. Not until 1956, after a protracted and bloody series of clashes, was agreement eventually reached to award Morocco independence within the French Community. Throughout this struggle, the Jews had remained publicly uncommitted but privately in support of the French occupation. In truth, they had good reason to fear Berber nationalism; by the summer of 1955 Jewish shops and homes already were being pillaged throughout the country's smaller towns. During the 1950s, as a result, Israeli "aliyah centers" were established in Morocco. Working through the Moroccan Zionist Organization, these agencies painted a glowing picture of life in the Jewish state. At first, the response to the propaganda was less than uniform. The skilled and affluent minority, those whom the Israelis hoped to attract, for the most part kept aloof from the Zionist campaign. It was rather the small shopkeepers, the artisans, and working-class elements that proved somewhat more receptive. In several cases entire Jewish villages applied for emigration. Between 1952 and 1955, nevertheless, the annual departure figure rarely exceeded 5,000. We recall that, during the austerity period, the Israeli government in effect imposed a moratorium on the large-scale immigration of unskilled or semiliterate Jews.

A more substantial influx developed in 1955 as the Istiqlal nationalist uprising gained momentum. During the next few years the Jewish Agency allocated the major part of its budget to "saving" Moroccan Jewry—the skilled and the unskilled alike. Soon tens of thousands of Jews were applying for rescue. At the outset, too, the newly established Istiqlal regime showed little interest in blocking this departure. It was only later, witnessing the loss of a significant proportion of the nation's bourgeoisie, that the authorities became increasingly concerned. In 1957, therefore, restrictions were imposed on the transfer of funds. Two years later, in deference to the Middle Eastern Arab countries, the Rabat government severed postal communications with Israel. And finally, in 1960, the Moroccans ceased issuing passports to Jews suspected of planning departure for Israel. As a result, the emigration, frozen in mid-stampede, dropped from 36,000 in 1956 to 9,000 in 1957, and to 2,000 in 1958. But by then some 120,000 Moroccan Jews had left for Israel.

The newcomers were virtually paupers, having sold their belongings at desperation prices for a few weeks' subsistence money in the Jewish state. Their educational level was among the lowest of the immigrant Jewries (p. 420). Some were totally illiterate. Although a number of Maghreb Jews were leatherworkers, shoemakers, or silversmiths, more commonly they were hucksters, greengrocers, fruit salesmen, sidewalk vendors of imitation jewelry and knickknacks, porters, or dealers in secondhand clothing. Their vocations were nearly all marginal. Like the tens of thousands of Oriental Jews who had preceded them, they were an economic liability to the state. Nevertheless, they had to be absorbed somehow and put to work.

By 1954, as the Moroccan influx grew in scope, the Jewish Agency adopted a daring "ship-to-village" program intended to bypass the squalid limbo of the ma'abarot transit camps. It was understood that the newcomers should under no circumstances be allowed to gravitate back to the urban slums that were their normal surroundings. Rather, they would be assigned forthwith to moshavim and development towns. As it worked out, then, 83 percent of the Moroccans who had arrived since 1954 were sent directly to these new communities, several of them in the far north, but the majority in the south, on the fringes of the Negev Desert. In the latter area thirty-one moshavim were hastily established, twenty-seven to be inhabited by North Africans. This time, too, the worst mistakes of the initial crash period of immigration were avoided. To ensure viability for the cooperative farms, a new technique of regional settlement was adopted. No longer were the moshavim carved out of frontier areas on an isolated, patchwork basis. Instead, they were laid down now in grouped clusters of three to five villages. Comprising eighty to one hundred farm units, each moshav was built immediately adjacent to the others. A common service center provided the cooperative villages with such shared institutions as marketing facilities, stores, a clinic, a tractor station, a movie theater, a bank, a school, a post office, and other government, Jewish Agency, and municipal offices.

From the outset, the regional technique avoided the economic vulnerability that characterized the earlier and more isolated moshav communities. It fulfilled a social purpose, as well. On the one hand, it permitted each village to be settled with a single homogeneous ethnic group. On the other, it promoted more relaxed and leisurely contacts between different immigrant communities in the joint institutions of the regional centers. In the regional cluster of Lachish, for example, north of Beersheba, the villagers of Moshav Ozem, who were Moroccans, lived close by Moshav Shachar, a settlement of Tunisians; while the neighboring community, Nir Onen, was inhabited by native-born Israelis. These three moshavim, together with Noga, also settled by Moroccans, and Zohar, a village of Rumanians, shared the facilities of the regional center. Here their children learned together in school, and here villagers met for shopping, to attend a movie or a sports event. Once having proved its essential functionalism in Lachish, the village cluster system later was adopted in Adullam in the Jerusalem Corridor and in the Zanach area near the Emek of Jezreel. By 1965 some forty-five regional centers were operating, and another sixteen were planned.

Yet the moshav cluster was hardly the exclusive settlement model for the North African immigrants. Development towns were going up in the outlying regions of the country (Chapter XVIII). And here, too, reception camps and ma'abarot were bypassed. Upon arriving in these skeletal communities in the mid- and latter 1950s, the Moroccans found housing units awaiting them. Each cinderblock unit was equipped with simple furniture, basic kitchenware, and other functional items. The newcomers were given the opportunity to buy their homes at cost, with long-term mortgages provided at low interest rates. Social workers again were at hand to counsel the North Africans and others in their adjustment to the new life. The full spectrum of Histadrut facilities, including Kupat Cholim medical care, was instantly available. Schools, synagogues, playgrounds, and clubs were organized. Every possible inducement was offered from the limited resources of the government and Jewish Agency to ensure that the immigrants stayed where they were settled.

The program was neither a failure nor an overwhelming success. By 1959 a bare majority of the North African Jews, 52 percent, remained in the development towns. Another 24.8 percent were living in agricultural villages. In fact, of the 206 moshavim established in the first decade of statehood, 82 were settled originally by North Africans. This percentage was deceptive, however. Only 10 percent of the Maghreb immigrants stayed on in the farm communities. Worse yet, as late as 1959, 6,000 North African families comprised the largest single group among the 19,000 hard-core families—essentially social misfits—that refused to be budged from the dilapidated ma'abarot transit towns into productive communities and livelihoods.

THE NORTH AFRICAN MALAISE

While the difficulties encountered by the Maghreb immigrants were in some degree common to all Oriental newcomers, not all Orientals were problem children. The 43,000 Jews from Iran and Afghanistan, for example, adjusted to Israeli life reasonably quietly and inconspicuously. So, by and large, did the 35,000 Turkish Jews, the 23,000 Libyan Jews, the 36,000 Egyptian Jews, and the 14,000 Syrian and Lebanese Jews. More than any others, too, the Yemenite immigrants of 1948–50 proved astonishingly tractable and docile. Envisaging any livelihood in the Holy Land as a blessing, these diminutive newcomers responded willingly to the challenges and hardships of agricultural life. Thus, comprising less than 8 percent of the total immigration up to the summer of 1951, the Yemenites provided the human material for 57 out of the 206 new moshavim (over 25 percent) by the end of Israel's first decade. Their farms were models of diligence and thrift. Their contribution to Israel's handicrafts was outstanding. In consequence, the Yemenites evoked an almost universal, if paternalistic, affection from the nation at large.

The Iraqi community of 121,000, on the other hand, approached its new life in Israel with much less equanimity. Rather, with their background as the educated elite of Baghdad and Basra, the Iraqis regarded themselves as aristocrats, in many ways superior to Western Jews. With all their strength, then, they resisted the initial effort to hustle them into

moshavim or development communities. A bare 3 percent of them became farmers. Angered by the impersonality of government and Jewish
Agency bureaucrats, the Iraqis became vocal, even strident, in their complaints of ethnic bias. In July 1951, they mounted a large-scale demonstration in Tel Aviv against "race discrimination in the Jewish state"—the first
(but by no means the last) display of its kind. They protested their transformation into "second-class" citizens. If once they had held high positions
in an Arab land, they insisted, should they not be qualified for similar
employment in a Jewish state? By protest and persistence, the Iraqis
ultimately succeeded in finding their place in Israel's economy. It was
the place they wanted, however, not the one chosen for them by the authorities. They settled in the urban areas. By 1951, 33 percent of their
breadwinners had managed to resume their former vocations as merchants;
42 percent found well-paying employment as skilled manual workers;
while another 21 percent served as professionals, clerical workers, or members of the police force. At the same time the Iraqis produced a hard core
of 5,000 families—many of them backward Kurds—who remained in the
ma'abarot as late as 1959, a group second only to the Moroccans in their
obdurate resistance to directed transplantation.

There was little question that many of the Oriental immigrants faced
serious problems of absorption and acculturation. For one thing, not less
than 68 percent of them were children (Oriental families were very
large), old people, widows, disabled, chronically ill, or simply unemployable misfits. They had to be provided for. Yet the vocational background
even of the able-bodied was hardly more encouraging. In the first decade
of Israel's statehood, a mere 37 percent of immigrant males from Moslem
countries were former artisans or industrial workers. The rest were divided among clerks, low-echelon office workers, small merchants, peddlers,
and other unskilled livelihoods. Israel effected no vocational revolution
among these newcomers—surely nothing comparable to the first waves of
Zionist immigration in the early twentieth century. While more than half
the Oriental immigrants initially were put to work in agricultural or semi-
skilled manual occupations, fully 30 percent of the rest gravitated back to
part-time unskilled labor, to petty trade, huckstering, or even less productive activities. It was an occupational profile that substantially reflected
the newcomers' lack of educational background. In 1954 only 5 percent had
completed elementary school, and only 1 percent had received a secondary
education (nor did the figures exclude the more literate Iraqis). The impact
of this tragic legacy was reflected directly in earning power. It was
found in 1957–58 that the bottom tenth of Jewish urban families, virtually
all of them Oriental, received a meager 1.6 percent of the nation's total
personal income. The upper tenth, nearly all Europeans, received 24.2
percent. While taxes and Histadrut benefits ordinarily modified these extremes, as late as 1957 Oriental immigrants still earned 27 percent less than
European immigrants.

As a result, one of the government's most concerted efforts in dealing
with the Oriental newcomers was to educate their children. With free,

compulsory schooling available in Israel through the age of fourteen, the tens of thousands of Oriental youngsters who fell within this age bracket presumably would have seized upon an unprecedented opportunity. Throughout the 1950s, nevertheless, Israel's school program remained critically limited. The shortage of qualified teachers was very grave. Most of the new schools in the immigrant and transit camps, in the moshavim and development towns, had to be staffed with unqualified personnel, not a few of them recruited from among the immigrants themselves, others co-opted from among eighteen-year-old army girls. And these were precisely the teachers who faced the difficult task not only of imparting information but of enforcing the most elementary rules of hygiene, discipline, punctuality, and appropriate relations between the sexes.

In the classrooms, too, no less than in society at large, a kind of de facto segregation emerged between the Europeans and the Orientals. School zoning, after all, followed the distribution of the population, and the better areas were European, the slum areas Oriental. Congested among their own, Oriental children experienced great difficulty in learning even to read. Their overcrowded dwellings were ill-suited to effective homework, and obviously their immigrant parents were incapable of helping them. It was not remarkable, under the circumstances, that the Oriental pupil often became deeply frustrated, suffered an inferiority complex, and failed to attend classes. The inclination to avoid high school was particularly strong, for here tuition had to be paid, and it was a rare Oriental family that was willing to meet this expense. In 1958, therefore, of 100,000 primary graduates who registered for secondary schools the following year, only 4,000 were Orientals; and the great majority of these departed before completing high school, often at the insistence of parents who needed their earnings.

The school dropouts headed as a rule for the youth labor exchanges. A 1958 survey revealed that of 2,000 young people registering for work in Haifa, virtually all were Orientals, and 1,800 were North Africans. Few of them possessed skills. If they secured employment, it was poorly paid. Many in any case did not find jobs, and among these youngsters the delinquency rate was high. In 1958, for example, 80 percent of Haifa's delinquent children came from the Oriental communities; over half of them were Moroccans. The crime rate among the Oriental group was eight times higher than among the Ashkenazim in that year, and the North African rate eleven times higher. But in fact antisocial behavior among the North Africans was no monopoly of the youth. During the immigrant-camp period in the early post-independence years, the Maghreb newcomers had all proved obstreperous wards. In dismay, one (Ashkenazic) observer wrote in *HaAretz* in 1950:

> They are completely ruled by primitive and wild passions. How many obstacles have to be overcome in educating the Africans—to stand in line for food in the dining room and not to cause a general disturbance. When one Bulgarian Jew argued with them about standing in line, an African immediately pulled out a knife and cut off his nose. It happened several times that

they attacked the official of the Jewish Agency and beat him up. The workers in the camps do their jobs in constant terror of such attacks. In the living quarters of the Africans in the camps you will find dirt, card games for money, drunkenness and fornication. . . . Nothing is safe in the face of this asocial element, and no lock can keep them out from anywhere. . . . In several parts of Jerusalem it is again unsafe for a girl, and even for a young man, to go out alone in the street after dark. And this was the situation even before the young Africans were demobilized from the army. By the way, these soldiers promised us more than once: "When we finish the war with the Arabs, we will go out to fight the Ashkenazim!" . . . Has it been considered what will happen to this country if this will be its population?

Several years passed before the European population finally identified the critical ingredient in the North Africans' malaise. The Moroccans were slowly choking of pent-up rage.

The discovery could be dated quite precisely: July 9, 1959. It emerged from a sordid barroom brawl in Wadi Salib, one of the shabbier slums of the formerly Arab section of Haifa. With its ramshackle tenements and narrow winding alleys, its overcrowded one- and two-room apartments opening onto dilapidated courtyards, Wadi Salib bore all the lineaments of a classical Near Eastern mellah. Nearly all of its 15,000 inhabitants were Orientals, and a third of these were Moroccans. As the brawl developed, police were called to the scene. In the ensuing melee a drunken Moroccan was shot and wounded resisting arrest. He was taken immediately to a hospital, where his condition was described as serious but not dangerous. Nevertheless, the rumor quickly circulated that he had died, the victim of "police brutality."

Early the next morning a large crowd of Moroccan immigrants surrounded the Wadi Salib police station, demanding "revenge." At first the police allowed the demonstration, but unrest continued sporadically throughout the day. Shortly before 6:00 P.M., therefore, a police task force stormed and dispersed the crowd. By then thirteen policemen and two civilians were injured, most of them by stones thrown from roofs. Thirty-two persons were arrested. Extensive damage was caused to property in the lower slum areas of the city. Parked cars were burned, twenty shops and cafés wrecked; a Mapai club and the Histadrut club were completely gutted. An account of the riots appeared on the front pages of all of Israel's newspapers. It was quite apparent that some sort of mass protest was being registered by the Oriental community, with implications far deeper than a barroom fracas.

Several days later the government appointed a nonparty committee to evaluate the more fundamental causes of the Wadi Salib uprising. Witnesses were called. One of them, David Ben-Haroush, offered a typically grim account of individual and collective discrimination. He had arrived in Palestine from Morocco in 1947, he explained, and had served in the Israeli army during the war. After being demobilized, he set about finding a home for himself. But he promptly discovered that the government and Jewish Agency had allocated the better lodgings to European immigrants.

He was obliged to settle for a shanty in Wadi Salib. Later he found employment in the police department. Together with other Oriental patrolmen, however, his duties were confined to routine guard assignments. Eventually Ben-Haroush left his job and opened a small cafe in Haifa. It was patronized exclusively by North Africans. "You ask if there is prejudice in this country," Ben-Haroush cried. "A North African is always down at the bottom of the list wherever he applies—whether in the development authority, the city administration, the welfare organization for the aged, or the Jewish Agency. It's always the European immigrants who get the most favored treatment."

Ben-Haroush's vehemence was not atypical. Other North African witnesses insisted that schooling appeared to be exclusively a European prerogative. The meager ratio of Orientals in high schools was cited, and the shocking dropout rates. Nor was there evidence that the situation would become anything but worse. The pressure of a mounting population forced high school authorities to become increasingly selective in admitting pupils. Those of lower cultural background or lower IQ ratings were the first to be turned down—nearly always the Orientals. These facts were known to the Orientals themselves, and not least of all to the North Africans. But lacking newspapers of their own, lacking so much as a single North African representative in the Knesset or any effective means of public expression, they had brooded in impotent silence. Until Wadi Salib.

The commission report was issued in August. In some ways it was innocuous. It failed to dwell at any length either on the limitations the Moroccans themselves had brought with them or on the fact that the exchange officials rarely seemed willing to give the North Africans an even chance. Perhaps the bureaucrats had been jaded by their experience with the newcomers. But it was not unlikely, too, that the employment officials had been affected, as had so many other Israelis, by the steady attrition of prestate idealism. Since 1948, housing, food, and employment increasingly were secured through patronage and political connections. The Ashkenazim possessed those connections. The Orientals did not. Frequently the latter were assigned to jobs that minimized their potential competition with the European group.

On the other hand, the report shrewdly noted that from the moment of their arrival in Israel, the North Africans were exposed to a series of grave psychological shocks. In the immigrant camps they encountered an almost complete apartheid between European and Maghreb Jews, even as later they discovered a similar wall in the nation at large. The Europeans plainly were obsessed by the danger of levantinization. By their standards, the backward Easterners had to be "reformed"—"purified of the cross of Orientalism," as *Davar*, the Histadrut newspaper, had put it in September 1950. The idea of "reforming the primitives," of transforming them along the European model, had been the dominant trend of Israel's acculturation effort from the onset of the poststate immigration (Chapter xviii). The Orientals resented it. An Indian Jew, writing the press in 1959, noted: "The belief that Western culture and civilization are . . . superior to the 'lethargic' and 'drowsy' civilizations of the East . . . is still accepted by many thinking Israelis. . . . Apparently European culture itself constitutes the 'melting pot,' and all other cultural forces are expected to dissolve in it."

The commission report touched upon a last, and even more fundamental, grievance. The illness of a split personality had been eating away at the Moroccans throughout all the decades of French occupation in North Africa. In the Maghreb, Jews had encountered Gallic culture firsthand and had adopted many at least of its superficial features. They had ventured even to aspire to influential positions in the French administration and in French society. It had been a vain hope; the *colons* wanted no part of the Jews. In Israel, then, the Maghreb immigrants searched for the recognition that had been denied them at home. Instead, they discovered that most of the positions they had expected, but failed, to win in Morocco, and which they had anticipated winning in a Jewish land, now were reserved for the Ashkenazim. Nor was their self-esteem restored as they were hustled from city to countryside—precisely the opposite of the Jewish migrational tradition in Morocco—and instructed to perform farm labor ordinarily reserved for "Berber riffraff" in North Africa. Unsure which of the two component parts, the Oriental or the European, represented their authentic character, snubbed in Morocco by the French and in Israel by the Ashkenazic guardians of the new, Western order, the Maghreb Jews found their *amour-propre* irretrievably shattered. Thus it was, in antisocial acts in Wadi Salib and elsewhere, that they gave vent to their agony.

In making this incisive observation, the commission report drew no elaborate social blueprint for the future. But the implication was plain that more than civic goodwill was needed, more even perhaps than an increase in government welfare and educational allotments to the North Africans and other Oriental newcomers. The Wadi Salib episode had opened a window into the little republic's soul. Almost imperceptibly during the previous decade, two Israels evidently had materialized within one Jewish society. The authorities now recognized their urgent obligation swiftly to make peace between Jacob and Esau, if Israel were to remain viable, or perhaps even to survive at all.

THE ECONOMY REVIVES

Much of this incipient social lesion was disguised in the mid- and latter 1950s by an impressive upturn of the nation's economy. In some degree, the "New Economic Policy" of 1952 was responsible. Production was rising, the balance of payments was improving, and the surging wave of inflation was being held to a manageable 7 percent a year. Of much greater significance, however, was the dramatic infusion of new foreign capital. Indeed, in few other countries was such intensive effort devoted to the acquisition of resources from abroad. The task consumed a large part of the energy of

the minister of finance, of the minister ·of trade and industry, and of
senior officials in the political ministries. Thousands of additional man-
hours similarly were dedicated to this purpose by each faction within the
Zionist movement, each sector (agricultural, industrial, commercial, cultural) of the Histadrut, every local government, and virtually all ambitious private enterprises.

A number of Israeli economists viewed this campaign with skepticism
and warned of a sharp decline in an economy based less upon the nation's earning capacity than upon an uncertain reservoir of overseas
goodwill. Advocating a stringent retrenchment both in consumption levels
and in programs of intended investment, these critics urged the nation to
live within its means in order to build up reserves against the lean years.
It was the orthodox view, in short, that economic growth, even the rate of
immigration, should be slowed to accommodate the conventional economic laws. A leading advocate of this cautionary viewpoint, Don Patinkin,
an economist teaching at the Hebrew University, warned in his survey-
history of the nation's economy that the lack of careful savings "must be
considered the major failure of Israeli economic policy. . . . The failure to
reduce the import surplus, and the decision instead to increase the foreign
debt significantly in every year since 1954 . . . represents the government's
refusal to face up fully to the inflationary problems of the economy."

But the orthodox approach was rejected. Even if Israel's government
planners, led by the well-beloved finance minister, Eliezer Kaplan, had
been able to stomach the often dogmatic manner with which Patinkin
and the academicians pressed their case, they understood that the state
could not be guided by economic considerations alone in dealing with its
major priorities of national defense, absorption of immigrants, development
or restoration of natural resources, and expansion of education. The plight
of the newcomers was so acute that only a quantum improvement in their
standard of living would transform them into a committed citizenry. These
goals were unprecedented in their magnitude. They required more, not
less, spending; more, not less, aid from overseas. To maintain the infusions
from abroad, therefore, the government exploited all opportunities of help
from the Western countries, particularly from the United States. Economic
assistance from Washington took many forms: grants, soft-currency loans,
Export-Import Bank loans, as well as technical assistance. From 1950 on,
net receipts from this source varied between $40 million and $60 million
annually.

In the long run, however, financial assistance from world Jewry proved
even more substantial than American government contributions and loans.
In the immediate post-independence years, help from the Diaspora took
the form essentially of private transfers—that is, charitable contributions.
Prominent among these were institutional gifts to the Hebrew University,
the Technion, the Weizmann Institute, the Hadassah hospital, and scores
of smaller institutions. The contributions exceeded $750 million be-
tween 1949 and 1961. Impressive as the sum was, it was matched and
ultimately exceeded by proceeds from two other Jewish sources. The first,

income from (American Jewry's) United Israel Appeal and from its counterpart outside the United States, the Keren HaY'sod, totaled between $60 million and $100 million annually in Israel's first decade (Chapter XXIII); while the second, State of Israel Bond sales abroad, reached a yearly level of between $40 million and $60 million in the 1950s and climbed even more sharply in the 1960s.

Of nearly equal importance were unilateral transfers from West Germany, funds that included both reparations to the Israeli government and restitutions to individual Israeli survivors of Hitler. The Reparations Treaty, better known in Israel as the Shilumim Agreement, was signed in the autumn of 1952. Under its terms, the West German government allocated to the Israeli government, and to a selected group of Jewish institutions, the equivalent of $820 million over a twelve-year period, with the largest share of the payment forthcoming in German goods. The financial aid was used imaginatively. An interministerial Shilumim Corporation channeled the German counterpart funds into priority growth sectors of Israel's economy, with special attention devoted to the modernization of electrical generating capacity and railroads, to the expansion of ports and agricultural irrigation, the exploitation of Negev minerals, and the acquisition of a merchant marine (Chapter XVI). The role of these vital supplies—ships, machinery, equipment, fuel, and raw materials—in developing Israel's economy could hardly be overstated. In 1953–54, for example, one-quarter of the government's entire development budget was provided by Shilumim counterpart funds. The next year, the percentage rose to 47 percent. Thereafter the ratio declined. Yet for the period as a whole, between 1953 and 1966, not less than 20 percent of the development budget was supplied by Shilumim.

In the course of Israel's first decade, then, only one-twelfth of the nation's foreign currency expenditures were paid through "earned" income. The rest derived from American, German, and other overseas sources. During the 1950s, world Jewry covered 59 percent of the balance-of-payments deficit, the United States government 12 percent, and West Germany 29 percent. Quite literally, these funds sustained Israel's economy, gave the nation breathing room in the unprecedented task of tripling, feeding, housing, and employing its population and defending its borders. Moreover, with the stimulus of foreign aid, Israel generated an impressive increase in its own domestic resources, which reached an annual growth rate of 8.7 percent by the mid-1950s. Notwithstanding the backbreaking pressures of the ingathering, and academic criticism of "transfusion economics," Israel's per capita resources in its first decade grew by 74 percent.

To the typical Israeli, the improvement was measured in the quality of life. The nation was feeding itself increasingly from its own resources by the latter 1950s (p. 409). Its "real" income was climbing uninterruptedly. The average family income of urban Jewish wage earners, for example, was I£936 in 1951. In 1957 the figure rose to I£3,290, an increase of 252 percent. This was less than net gain, to be sure, for the cost-of-living index rose by 173 percent during the same period. Nevertheless, improvement was registered not merely by a growth in real wages, but by a wider income distribution—through graduated taxes, fringe and Histadrut benefits —than anywhere else in the free world outside the Scandinavian countries. One particularly tangible indicator of national welfare was life expectancy. By 1956, it reached 70 years for men and 73 years for women, 8 percent above the 1949 figures. Another indication was the average housing density of Israel's Jewish population. By 1955 it was down to 2.3 persons per room, a major improvement over 1951. In 1960, 81 percent of the nation's Jewish families had access to electricity and 94 percent to running water. Several years later, improvement would be even more dramatic (Chapter XVIII). By 1960, too, all but the smallest pockets of ma'abarot had been eradicated from the countryside. Occasional isolated shantytowns served essentially as a reminder of the nation's ordeal in the direst acceleration period of its immigration. By 1961 the Jewish population had climbed to 1,938,000. Broad belts of villages and towns had gone up in the Jerusalem Corridor and the coastal plain, throughout the Galilee and even the northern Negev. By far the largest numbers of Israelis were sheltered, eating adequately, and working. While the circumstances of life unquestionably remained drab, by the end of the 1950s they no longer were grim.

Few of Israel's Jewish citizens were blind to the progress they had made. Yet, by the same token, few were insensitive to the price they had paid. The scars of the awesome ordeal of immigration were less physical than psychological. They were borne not merely by the Orientals, whose status expectations had been rudely shattered, but by native Israelis, as well. For several years, the influx of hundreds of thousands of semimendicants threatened to extinguish the idealism even of Israel's veteran European population. Many of these "Westerners" plainly were shaken by the apparent levantinization of their Zionist Utopia, and for the first time began to question their own traditionally spartan values. Thus, in growing numbers, Israel's sabras—members of the Palestinian-born generation—turned their backs on the kibbutz and the frontier outpost. Joining the migration to the Tel Aviv metropolitan area, they vied with the refugees in seeking out the easier life and the main chance.

Nor did they regard their move as evidence of waning patriotism. Indeed, they had always prided themselves on their love of country, on their willingness to defend the nation's borders, to share the burdens of housing and feeding impoverished fellow Jews who had returned for sanctuary and a new life in the Land of Israel. But now, with independence, that responsibility evidently no longer required the same kind of personal commitment. A government and bureaucracy existed for the first time to care for the immigrants, to educate the youth in their civic duties, to provide farm settlements and factories with salaried instructors. In a regularized society of legal sanctions and official directives, of concentrated political power and widening differentiation between the "establishment" and the general population, of palpable suspicion, even elementary lack of communication, between "backward" Oriental and "modern" European, the selfless and spontaneous emotional commitment of the pre-1948 era appeared increasingly out of date. The old idealism, then, was the most lamented casualty of Israel's post-independence era. While not yet altogether moribund, it would revive henceforth less amid the prosaic interludes of domestic routine than in the adrenalizing crises of war.

THE SEARCH

FOR PEACE AND SECURITY

THE REALITIES OF ISRAEL'S FOREIGN POLICY

The preambles of the Rhodes armistice agreements made impressive and encouraging reading. Each stated that it was designed to facilitate the transition from truce to permanent peace. Each endorsed the Security Council injunction against the use of force and affirmed Israel's and the Arab nations' rights to security and freedom from attack. For Israeli statesmen, nevertheless, future policy was to be dictated not by the sonorous verbalization of international documents but by an acute awareness of the nation's physical and diplomatic vulnerability. To begin with, Israel's geographic position was a strategist's nightmare. The newborn republic comprised less than 8,000 square miles. Its 600 miles of land frontier provided virtually no defense in territorial depth. Thus, three-quarters of its population was impacted into the coastal plain between Haifa and Tel Aviv and along the narrow corridor leading to Jerusalem. Except for scattered outposts in the Negev Desert, no town or farm settlement lay more than 18 miles from an Arab border. Israel's "waist" measured scarcely 9 miles from the Transjordanian bulge to the Mediterranean. At points, the Jerusalem Corridor narrowed to a width of 10 miles, and the Israeli sector of the Holy City was flanked on three sides by Hashemite artillery. From the Golan Heights, Syrian guns were capable of wreaking havoc on the Jewish farm communities of eastern Galilee. Finally, access to Eilat, Israel's southern gateway to Asia and Africa, was vulnerable to Egyptian maritime blockade. The entire country, in short, was a frontier, the only non-island in the world that could be reached by sea alone (or by air over sea).

The nation's human resources were equally limited. The surrounding Arab populations outnumbered Israel's population by forty to one, their standing armies by eight to one. Even within the framework of the armistice agreements, the Israeli government was suspicious of future understandings with neighbors that were traditionally volatile and mercurial. It was significant that during the first two decades of Israeli independence, the Arab nations underwent some twenty political revolutions, nearly all of them precipitated by army juntas. None of the successor military regimes dared adopt less than a hostile policy toward Israel for fear of losing popular support. It was a unique kind of hostility, moreover. It was not confined to one particular area of Israel's life or territory. It was not directed toward a specific portion of Israel's land, water, or mineral resources. As the Israelis saw it, the Arab purpose was single-minded and all-absorptive. It was flatly committed to the destruction of Israel as an independent state.

In girding its strength against this danger, too, the Jewish republic was limited by more than a paucity of territory, weapons, or citizens. It was deprived equally of friends and patrons. For Israel alone in the Middle East belonged to no defensive pact or political alliance whatever. Even the funds and diplomatic manpower it had available to explore and establish ties abroad were painfully meager. To be sure, Israel's first foreign minister, Moshe Sharett (formerly Shertok), a colleague of Ben-Gurion's since Second Aliyah days, was a man of uncommon brilliance and charm, and endowed with almost superhuman linguistic and negotiating skills. His closest associates, Reuven Shiloach and Walter Eytan, were similarly persons of unique dedication and imagination. But their personnel were under strength. As late as 1968, after twenty years of independence, only eight of Israel's missions abroad possessed staffs of ten or more, while twelve missions were staffed by one person only, and the rest by three or fewer representatives.

The perception of national vulnerability, then, remained the obsession of Israel's leadership. Its one advantage for the government was political. National isolation ensured that at least in foreign policy the government enjoyed a reasonable freedom of action. In fact, the Knesset played no direct role in foreign affairs at all, not even in the ratification of treaties. Parliamentary debates on international policy were useful mainly in their contribution to public education, but these discussions rarely took place more than once a year. Although the foreign affairs committee met weekly, hearing testimony from ministers, diplomats, and army leaders, its sessions were executive, and those attending were pledged to secrecy. The committee's membership unquestionably was of high quality, and this enabled it to exert a certain intangible influence on foreign policy. Yet initiative and virtually complete freedom of decision in this area remained the prerogative of the cabinet.

THE PALESTINE CONCILIATION COMMISSION, THE STATUS OF JERUSALEM

The armistice agreements, meanwhile, were but one phase of a twofold effort under United Nations auspices to end the Arab-Israeli conflict. By the terms of the General Assembly Resolution of December 11, 1948 (Chapter XIII), a Palestine Conciliation Commission was established and charged with three major tasks: the accomplishment of a binding peace settlement between Israel and its Arab enemies; the facilitation of measures to repatriate and resettle the Palestine refugees; and the formulation of a plan to organize a permanent international regime in Jerusalem. As matters developed, the PCC failed to achieve any of these goals. More distressingly yet, by its ineptitude it hastened the destruction of whatever chances for peace still existed. It would surely have been useful, for example, had the Israelis and the representatives of individual Arab states been pushed into direct negotiations immediately. Instead, the three members of the PCC, appointees of Turkey, France, and the United States, operated with a deliberation that amounted to near-lethargy. Spending three months in a leisurely, disorganized tour of Middle Eastern nations, the commission members did not journey on to the permanent site of their discussions, Lausanne, until April 1949. Once in the Swiss city, moreover, the PCC made the disastrous mistake of allowing the various Arab representatives to participate in the discussions as a bloc, rather than separately. Under this format, no individual Arab dared take the initiative in expressing moderation. Instead, on the rare occasions when efforts were made to bring the two sides together, the Arabs repudiated the pattern of the early armistice negotiations and declined to sit in the same room with the Jews (Chapter XIII).

As for the members of the PCC themselves, they agreed on one point only, that an Arab-Israeli settlement must not harm the interests of their own countries. France's purpose, for example, was to limit the influence of Abdullah, a British client. Thus, during the early stages of the Lausanne Conference, the Frenchman Claude de Boissanger openly sided with the Syrian delegation. The Turkish delegate, Hussein Calkit Yalcin, sharing his government's fear of Soviet imperialism, and intent upon establishing some sort of military alliance with the Arab nations, made no secret of his pro-Arab bias. Mark Ethridge, representing the United States, strongly endorsed the official Arab League policy on Jerusalem and the refugees, and urged the Israelis to make far-reaching concessions. It was an approach that undermined the position both of the Israelis and of the more moderate Arabs.

There were serious enough differences to be resolved between Arabs and Jews, in any case, without Great Power intrusion. This became apparent even in the PCC's single, debatable accomplishment at Lausanne. Shuttling back and forth between the parties, the commissioners managed to hammer out a series of protocols that both sides eventually accepted on May 12, 1949. The key statement declared:

> The United Nations Conciliation Commission for Palestine, anxious to achieve as quickly as possible the objectives of the General Assembly Resolution of 11 December 1948, regarding refugees, the respect for their rights and the preservation of their property, as well as territorial and other questions, has proposed to the Delegations of the Arab States and to the Delegation of Israel that the working document attached hereto be taken as a basis for discussions with the Commission.

The "working document" alluded to was the original UN Partition map of November 1947. In fact, the protocols represented not a covenant between Israel and the Arab states, but merely an agreement to discuss, to negotiate. The 1947 partition map was attached "as a basis for discussions with the Commission." At the time the protocols were signed, this was the only

official United Nations map available; as late as May 12, 1949, the armistice
agreement between Israel and Syria had not yet been worked out. Nevertheless, when the Commission failed to bridge the gap between rival Arab
and Israeli claims, the Arabs subsequently demanded a return to the boundaries of the 1947 Partition Resolution as their terms for a settlement. In so
doing, they usually referred to the Lausanne protocols as "a commitment"
by Israel to accept these frontiers. The Israelis emphatically rejected the
interpretation, declaring that their armistice agreements with the Arabs
superseded the territorial boundaries of the Partition Resolution.

A more complicated, if no less basic, disagreement was encountered
on the question of Jerusalem. The PCC regarded it as its function to devise
the kind of permanent trusteeship regime for the Holy City envisaged in
the 1947 Resolution. Well before the mandate ended, however, it became
clear as fighting raged in Jerusalem that internationalization would not
succeed. The day before the British finally evacuated Palestine, in fact,
the General Assembly itself rejected a trusteeship for the city as unworkable. During the hostilities of ensuing weeks, the world body preferred
to assign the problem of Jerusalem's status to Count Folke Bernadotte.
Yet by the time the United Nations mediator reached the scene, on May
28, the Arab Legion had occupied all the Old City, while most of New
Jerusalem was in Israeli hands. And when the first truce soon afterward came into operation, Bernadotte decided that a *corpus separatum*
for Jerusalem no longer was realistic. We recall (Chapter xiii) that the
mediator proposed instead to assign the entire city to Transjordan. The
other members of the Arab League understandably rejected this scheme;
the Old City by then was in Hashemite possession, and the Arab governments were not interested in giving Abdullah the entire prize. Neither
were the Israelis. They had endured a grim siege and had tenaciously held
on to their New City. The notion of abandoning it now to Transjordan
was unthinkable.

As the war resumed in July 1948, Bernadotte himself finally recognized
the altered situation and offered a stopgap proposal that would have demilitarized the city but left its administration to the respective occupying
forces. It was a suggestion that Israel and Transjordan were prepared at
least to discuss. The other Arab nations were not. On July 29, therefore, the
UN Trusteeship Council decided to postpone indefinitely all considerations
of a statute for Jerusalem. Whereupon, that same day, Israel's Foreign
Minister Sharett declared that Arab aggression in Palestine had ended
his government's obligations to carry out the terms of the UN Partition
Resolution. Sharett implied that he would soon demand the New City
for the Jewish state. The implication became quite explicit on February 2,
1949, when Ben-Gurion officially announced that Israeli-held Jerusalem
was no longer to be considered "occupied territory." Military rule in the
New City was accordingly abolished. On March 1, the Transjordanians and
Israelis signed an agreement on the demarcation of armistice lines in
Jerusalem, and that same day the Hashemite government replaced military
rule in its own section of the city with a civil administration.

The other Arab nations watched this development in alarm. To counteract it, their governments informed the PCC that they were prepared now to accept internationalization for Jerusalem. Bemused by the sudden show of Arab moderation, Ben-Gurion in turn genially declared his willingness to establish a *corpus separatum*—not for the Jewish New City, however, but for the holy places. Even this gesture was less than far-reaching. Of the thirty principal holy places designated in the UN Partition map, only two Christian sites and two Moslem mosques were in the New City; all the others were in the Old City and its environs, including nearby Bethlehem. Failing, then, to overcome the intransigence either of the Israelis or of the Jordanians, the PCC adopted a compromise plan on September 1, 1949. It envisaged a permanent international regime for the Jerusalem area, with the city itself to be divided into two zones, one Arab and one Jewish, corresponding with the Transjordanian and Israeli sectors. In each zone the local authorities would be responsible for the administration of municipal affairs, while a United Nations commissioner would both ensure the protection of the holy places and disallow any immigration that "might alter the present demographic equilibrium of the area of Jerusalem."

The reaction of Jews and Arabs alike was splenetic. The Israelis refused even to discuss the scheme. Abdullah warned that Jerusalem would be internationalized only over his dead body. Indeed, by the time the General Assembly opened discussions on the plan in late November, Abdullah's representatives were already secretly negotiating with Israel for a de facto partition of the city. What developed in ensuing months, therefore, was an almost surrealistic counterpoint of debate on Jerusalem's status in the UN General Assembly, on the one hand; and pragmatic, operative decisions on the city's future reached by the Israelis and Jordanians, on the other. In the world body, the Catholic nations generally followed the lead of the Vatican in endorsing territorial internationalization. The Holy See had been indifferent to the political regime in Jerusalem as long as it appeared likely that the city would be merged in an Islamic state. But once the New City became part and the future capital of a Jewish republic, the papal authorities declared themselves inclined toward a *corpus separatum*. An extensive propaganda against Israel was launched throughout the Catholic world. In this campaign, Transjordan was ignored, although Abdullah's forces controlled the great majority of Jerusalem's holy places.

The Vatican's position conceivably reflected apprehension about the way the mystical genius of Jerusalem would evolve under Israeli rule. In Jewish hands, too, the city was hardly likely to attract a Christian population large enough to foster papal interests in the Near East. Nor was an internationalization limited to the shrines, as Israel suggested, appealing to the Vatican. For centuries an intense rivalry had festered between Orthodox and Latins in the Holy City. Generally, the Latins had been outnumbered there by Eastern and other non-Latin Christian groups. In the United Nations, on the other hand, the non-Catholic elements possessed no spokesmen at all, while the Latins were represented by a substantial bloc of delegations. With this diplomatic influence available to widen their bridgehead in the city, the Catholics understood that it was no time for minimalism in defining the United Nations' role in a *corpus separatum.* These were the considerations Pope Pius XII had in mind when he issued his second encyclical on Palestine, *Redemptoris Nostri,* on April 15, 1949, urging the faithful to exert every effort on behalf of Jerusalem's full territorial internationalization.

When the matter came to a vote on December 9, 1949, a majority of the General Assembly rejected a Swedish resolution advocating "functional" internationalization—in other words, United Nations control limited to the holy places—and instead voted for the entire city to be transformed into a *corpus separatum* as envisaged by the original Partition Resolution. It was an irony that the Soviet bloc joined with the Catholic delegations in supporting the plan; their aim was to embarrass Abdullah (and his British patrons). Israel's reaction to the vote was swift and emphatic. On December 13 the Knesset unanimously approved Ben-Gurion's proposal that the legislature be moved to Jerusalem; and on January 1, 1950, the entire Israeli government was transferred to the New City, except for the ministries of defense, police, and foreign affairs (the latter two were transferred later). That same day, across the border, Abdullah issued a decree conferring Transjordanian citizenship on the population of the West Bank, including the inhabitants of Arab Jerusalem. The following April he went so far as to rename his kingdom Jordan (p. 451). Several months later, Moscow archly declared that it was withdrawing its support for the internationalization scheme on the ground that neither the Jewish nor the Arab population would accept it. By then the Soviets had accomplished their purpose of setting Jordan and Britain at odds with the rest of the General Assembly. In later sessions of the United Nations body, alternative proposals of territorial and "functional" internationalization repeatedly failed to win majority support. Rather, from then on, the Jerusalem issue slowly faded out as a topic of diplomatic controversy.

In the interval, the Israeli government did more than simply transfer itself to Jerusalem. On January 23, 1950, the Knesset solemnly proclaimed that the Holy City had "always" been the capital of the Jewish nation. Three and a half years later, in July 1953, the foreign ministry declared that henceforth it would require foreign envoys to present their credentials in Jerusalem. After some hesitation, the British and American ambassadors accepted the condition and submitted their letters of credence to the Israeli president at his official Jerusalem mansion. Other nations followed in train. By 1957, nearly 40 percent of the fifty-four diplomatic establishments in Israel maintained their offices in Jerusalem (it was noteworthy that the largest number were Latin American embassies). Even as the Israeli government was pouring millions of pounds into the city, meanwhile, and settling tens of thousands of immigrants there, it scrupulously honored its promises to respect the holy places. No one was ever denied free access to Christian or Moslem shrines. The edifices were kept in full repair and under close guard. On the Jordanian side of the line, Christian shrines

PARTITIONED JERUSALEM, 1948-1967

0   MILE   1

SANHEDRIA

ISRAEL
DEMILITARIZED
■ HADASSAH HOSPITAL
ZONE

TEL ARZA

■ HEBREW
UNIVERSITY

MT. SCOPUS

NO
MAN'S
LAND

J

NO MAN'S LAND

MANDELBAUM GATE

JAFFA ROAD

+ AUGUSTA
VICTORIA
CHURCH

O

MEA
SH'ARIM

JORDAN
DEMILITARIZED
ZONE

I
S
R
A
E
L

QUARTER
VIA
DOLOROSA

LION'S GATE

R

MOSLEM QUARTER
WESTERN WALL
HARAM-ES-SHARIF

CHRISTIAN
QUARTER

MOSQUE
OF OMAR

RECHAVIA

JAFFA GATE

JEWISH
QUARTER

D

MT. OF OLIVES

ARMENIAN
QUARTER

OLD
CITY

← NEW
HEBREW UNIVERSITY

ZION GATE

JERICHO ROAD

JERUSALEM

GAZA ROAD

TALBIYA

MT. ZION

SILWAN

A

HILL OF
EVIL COUNSEL

ABU TUR

N

E
L

GOVERNMENT HOUSE
(U.N. HEADQUARTERS)

NO MAN'S LAND

TALPIOT

enjoyed similar protection and care. Not so the Jewish holy places under Arab control, however. The Israeli-Transjordanian armistice agreement had provided for unlimited Jewish access to the Western Wall. Nevertheless, the Hashemite authorities refused to observe this provision. In later years, a road was cut through the Jewish cemetery on the Mount of Olives, and the headstones of Jewish graves there were used for building purposes, some of them in footpaths to army latrines.

THE ARAB REFUGEES: THE FATE OF ABANDONED PROPERTY

One of the most significant provisions of the General Assembly Resolution of December 11, 1948, was to be found in Paragraph Eleven. It stated that "refugees wishing to return to their homes and live at peace with their neighbors" should be allowed to do so, and that "compensation should be paid for the property of those choosing not to return and for loss of or damage of property which . . . should be made good by the Governments or authorities responsible." The paragraph took cognizance of the single most poignant tragedy of the recent war, the fate of the refugee Palestine Arabs. Estimates of their numbers varied. The Israelis set the total at 539,000. Initial United Nations appraisals in 1950 placed the figure some 100,000 higher. It was generally agreed, in any case, that 100,000 had fled to Lebanon, 80,000 to Syria, perhaps 5,000 to 10,000 to Iraq, 115,000 to 150,000 to the Gaza Strip, and between 250,000 and 325,000 to the eastern, Hashemite, sector of Palestine. Their plight at the outset was one of unspeakable wretchedness. Kenneth Bilby, reporter for the New York *Herald-Tribune,* described his visit to a refugee settlement in the Jordanian West Bank:

> The tent camp in the Jordan Valley on the approach to Jericho had perhaps 20,000 inhabitants. . . . I looked at their filthy habitations—brush for mattresses, a torn blanket or two, a larder empty except for a pinch of meal, a pat or two of lard. The camp was talking about an Arab businessman from Haifa. The day before he had taken his two sons from behind the tent, shot them through the head, and turned the gun on himself. . . . [T]he [Jews had taken] his home and business, and refused to allow his return even to liquidate. He was penniless and couldn't stand watching his children's bellies bloat. The tent camp at Ramallah was even worse. Icy winds off the Judean hills whipped through the torn flaps. The widow from Ramle wore an old flour sack, and her legs were blue with cold. Her five children emitted a monotonous wail; she was on the move perpetually, swabbing their runny noses. Her husband, a Ramle carpenter, had been killed in the war. . . . Agonized, she asked me what happened to her home. I could have told her it was probably occupied by a family from Bulgaria or Poland, but I stalled with a don't know answer.

As early as July 1948, Bernadotte, the United Nations mediator, persuaded the world body to enlist the help of international welfare organizations in supplying the refugees with emergency relief. The General Assembly thereupon appointed Sir Raphael Cilento of Australia to coordinate the work of these bodies. The latter included the International Refugee Organization, which cared for displaced Arabs in the Israeli-occupied and Transjordanian-occupied sectors of Palestine; the Red Cross, which assumed this responsibility in Lebanon, Syria, and Transjordan east of the river; while the American Friends Service Committee ministered to refugees in the Gaza Strip. To support the work of the various agencies, the General Assembly in November and December 1949 voted the sum of $34,500,000. Yet financial aid of this sort could hardly be more than a short-term palliative. A more fundamental solution had to be found, and quickly. Paragraph Eleven of the December 11 Resolution suggested an apparently logical answer.

It was not logical to the Jews. The departure of the Arab majority in the Israeli sector of Palestine had solved a number of crucial problems for the new republic. One was economic. More than 60 percent of Israel's total land area consisted of tracts abandoned by former Arab proprietors or squatters. To be sure, much of this terrain was waterless, marginal, unclaimed, or wasteland, and the Israelis subsequently estimated that not more than 5,793,000 cultivable dunams in fact had been abandoned by legitimate Arab proprietors. The Israeli figure was disputed equally by the Arab League and the United Nations, which calculated abandoned Arab land at closer to 10 million dunams. Yet, by any estimates, the sheer extent of newly available farm soil was at least four times that possessed by the Jews when they embarked upon statehood. In addition to agricultural domain, moreover, the Arabs had left behind entire cities, including Jaffa, Acre, Lydda, Ramle, Beisan, and Majdal (Migdal), as well as 388 towns, villages, and large parts of 94 other cities and towns, containing nearly a quarter of all the buildings in Israel, some 100,000 dwellings and 10,000 shops, businesses, and stores. In 1951 the PCC calculated the value of abandoned Arab property as I£120 million (by 1947 values).

The Israelis regarded this émigré property as a windfall of the first magnitude. Even as the war progressed and the departure of Arab families gained momentum, the Provisional Government issued its first Abandoned Areas Ordinance on June 30, 1948. It defined an "abandoned area" as any place conquered by the Israeli armed forces or deserted by all or part of its inhabitants. Under this ordinance Israel's first Custodian of Abandoned Property was appointed two weeks later, on July 15. And when, gradually, the Custodian moved into an area, taking possession of Arab land and housing, he found much of the disposable property already in the hands of individual Jews or Jewish farm settlements. He decided therefore simply to legalize its "use" by designating "temporary" (Jewish) cultivators and proprietors. In December, the government made its long-range intentions for the property even more explicit by issuing a series of Absentee Property Regulations. The practical effect of these measures, we recall (Chapter XIV), was to disallow the return of Arabs, including those who were citizens of Israel, to any property abandoned during or immediately after the war. The Custodian—now entitled the Custodian of Absentee Property—was empowered to take over Arab land, homes, or businesses merely by certifying that any person or body of persons was "absentee" (later these features were modified somewhat).

During the first year of statehood, in any case, most of this property was simply occupied by Jews, veterans and immigrants alike. Even before the future of the Arab areas was determined, the Jewish Agency and the army were directing the movement of Jewish newcomers toward the vacant land and lodgings. It was the view of the Israeli authorities that hundreds of thousands of immigrants should not be confined indefinitely to their tents and shanties. Better simply to let them find their own accommodations at the expense of the Arabs. Once begun, therefore, the stampede could not be halted. By 1951 nearly all abandoned Arab property had been coopted. The Jewish squatters, in turn, tens of thousands of whom were themselves victims of confiscatory measures in Moslem lands, left no doubt that any suggestion of relinquishing this shelter to Arab returnees would be met with force if necessary. They would not allow themselves to be expropriated twice.

The government had no intention of forcing them out. In September 1951 the Knesset passed a new bill to legalize the occupation of Arab holdings. Its most important provision dealt the Arab absentees a bitter and decisive blow. The Custodian was authorized thenceforth not simply to control, operate, or lease the vacant property, but in fact to sell it. The purchaser would be a Development Authority—a legal fiction to avoid the onus of governmental confiscation—which afterward would sell the land to the state or, more commonly, to the Jewish National Fund. The latter finally would lease out the property to the identical persons or settlements that had been there from the outset. Quickly, then, it was all disposed of, all placed in Jewish hands, and it became obvious to the Arabs that there remained nothing to which they could return. Of 370 Jewish settlements founded between 1948 and 1953, 350 were on absentee property. In 1954 more than a third of Israel's Jewish population lived on absentee property, and nearly a third (350,000) of the new immigrants were settled in towns and villages abandoned by the Arabs.

In response to queries from the PCC, Israel gave assurance that the funds received from the sale of absentee Arab land would be credited to the refugees for future disposal. On the other hand, there could be no question of compensation until the opening of final peace talks with the Arab governments, as envisaged in the December 11, 1948, General Assembly Resolution. And even then, Foreign Minister Sharett emphasized, compensation would be applied exclusively to a fund to resettle the refugees elsewhere, not to repatriate them. Moreover, when the tally was calculated, account would have to be taken of Israel's counterclaims for the sequestration of Jewish property in Arab lands. On several occasions, the foreign minister reminded the United Nations that between 1948 and 1953 some 400,000 Jews had arrived in Israel as refugees from Moslem xenophobia, departing as paupers, stripped by the Arab governments of most of their belongings, and reduced to complete dependency upon the Jewish welfare organizations in Israel. Sharett added, finally, that his government's ability to pay compensation was necessarily limited by the economic impact of continuing Arab boycott and blockade. These, too, would have to be lifted. The Israeli stance was tough, and apparently unshakable.

THE ARAB REFUGEES: REPATRIATION VERSUS RESETTLEMENT

The provision of the General Assembly Resolution of December 11, 1948, calling upon the Arab states and Israel to begin peace negotiations without delay and to allow the refugees to return to their homes "at the earliest practicable date," was seemingly humane and reasonable. Yet both the Arab and the Jewish response to it were less than encouraging. The Arabs insisted that they expected the refugee question to be fully resolved before they would so much as consider peace negotiations. The Israelis rejected this approach. The truth was, however, that until then the Jews had neglected to formulate their own views clearly, even to themselves. James D. McDonald, the first United States ambassador to Israel, recalled:

> I doubt that during this first hectic year of Israel the top officials ever took the time to concentrate on the refugee problem. I had the distinct impression that this was being left primarily to the technicians. No one of the big three —Weizmann, Ben-Gurion, or Sharett—seemed to have thought through the implications of the tragedy or of Israel's lack of concrete helpfulness. . . . No responsible Zionist leader had anticipated such a "miraculous" clearing of the land. Dr. Weizmann, despite his ingrained rationalism, spoke to me emotionally of this "miraculous simplification of Israel's task," and cited the vaster tragedy of six million Jews murdered during World War II. He would ask, "What did the world do to prevent this genocide? Why should there be such excitement in the UN and the Western capitals about the . . . Arab refugees?"

As late as January 1949, the Ben-Gurion cabinet took the position that return of the refugees was dependent upon the establishment of formal peace; otherwise the repatriated Arabs would pose a threat to Israel's security. But within weeks, public and government opinion alike hardened against the very notion of repatriation. Even if a peace agreement were signed, the Israelis warned, a "fundamental solution" of the refugee issue would have to be based upon the resettlement of émigré Palestinians in neighboring Arab countries. As the months passed, Israel's growing intransigence on this matter became a source of concern to friends of the Jewish state. In a sharp note to Ben-Gurion on May 29, 1949, Harry Truman expressed his "deep disappointment" at Israel's failure to evince flexibility on the refugee question. The president then warned that unless "tangible refugee concessions" were forthcoming, "the United States would reconsider its attitude toward Israel." Ben-Gurion did not flinch. "The United States is a powerful country," he declared in the Knesset.

"Israel is a small and weak one. We can be crushed, but we will not commit suicide."

Nevertheless, when the second phase of the Lausanne Conference opened in late July 1949, the Israelis agreed to discuss the refugee question, even to contemplate taking back as many as 100,000 Palestine Arabs, with the understanding that repatriation would be linked with meaningful peace negotiations. It was a shrewd test of Arab intentions. At first, nevertheless, it evoked a howl of rage in Israel itself, and not only from Cherut but from Mapam and from large numbers of Mapai members who broke party discipline on this issue. Yet, as events turned out, even this expedient Israeli gesture did not materialize. Throughout the summer months, as peace discussions failed to develop, the Ben-Gurion cabinet narrowed its interpretation of eligible returnees to wives and minor children of "Arab breadwinners lawfully resident in Israel" and to occasional other "compassionate cases. . . ." The practical effects of the concession were unimpressive. By 1956, the total number of Arab family members reunited under the scheme amounted to barely 35,000.

By early 1950, Israel's position on the refugees had hardened irretrievably. In the General Assembly debate on the issue, Abba Eban, the Israeli ambassador to the United Nations, formally repudiated the Lausanne offer of the previous year—to accept back 100,000 Palestinians—with or without a peace treaty. It was the Arab governments, Eban insisted, by their belligerency and blockade, that had killed any chance of repatriation. In a later speech, he elaborated upon this argument:

> Cut off from all land contacts, intercepted illicitly in two of its three maritime channels, subjected to blockade and boycott, the object of an official proclaimed state of war and the target of a monstrous rearmament campaign—this is the picture of Israel's security. . . . Can the mind conceive anything more fantastic than the idea that we can add to these perils by the influx from hostile territory, large or small, of people steeped in the hatred of our very statehood? I do not believe that any responsible conscience will sustain such an idea. There could be no greater unkindness to an Arab himself than to expose him to such an invidious role, perhaps reproducing the very circumstances which first made him a refugee.

In Israel, meanwhile, Foreign Minister Sharett stressed that the tragedy of refugees was in no way unique to Palestine. He noted that there were 60 million refugees in the free world. Beside this number, even the officially cited United Nations figure of 700,000 Palestinians comprised a mere 1.25 percent of the total. There were no historical precedents for the return of such large numbers of fugitives, Sharett observed, particularly if the émigré Arabs in effect represented a population "exchanged" for Jewish refugees from Moslem lands. In the early 1920s, for example, nearly 2 million displaced war victims were resettled in a population transfer between Turkey and Greece. Following World War II, 900,000 Germans were forcibly transferred to Germany from Czechoslovakia, Poland, Hungary, and Yugoslavia; while an exchange of populations between Poland and

Soviet Russia affected 2,520,000 Poles, Ukrainians, White Russians, and Lithuanians. In the wake of the partition of India, in 1947, an immense, two-way migration of Hindus and Moslems uprooted nearly 13 million people. Exchanges of population were not reversible, Sharett insisted. Far better to accept the exodus of Arabs from Israel and of Jews from Moslem lands as a *fait accompli,* and to encourage their resettlement among their kinsmen.

In March of 1950 the General Assembly reached essentially the same conclusion and terminated Cilento's ad hoc relief committee. In its stead a United Nations Refugee Works Administration was established with a budget of $54 million. Unlike its predecessor agencies, UNRWA was not charged with the task of supplying the Palestinians with relief, but with employing them on relocation projects in their Arab lands of sanctuary. Within eighteen months, so it was estimated, most of these fugitives would be as self-supporting as their Arab neighbors, and relief handouts could be ended once and for all. The illusion was rapidly dispelled. From the moment UNRWA officials initiated talks with the Arab governments, they encountered an uncompromising refusal to cooperate with any plan designed for economic integration. "Paragraph Eleven of the General Assembly Resolution of December 1948 guarantees the refugees the right to return to their homes," the argument went. "We cannot participate in any scheme that might compromise such a right." In fact, the Arab nations themselves had voted unanimously against the resolution, for it had envisaged peace negotiations with Israel. The refugee issue accordingly served as a useful obstacle to future discussions and as an effective lien on the world's conscience. The Arab governments were not about to drop it. By the end of 1950, as a result, the date the United Nations had fixed for ending relief, no more than 10,000 of the 650,000 or 700,000 refugees were employed. The rest were confined to their tents and ration lines.

Some of the Palestinians were formulating their own solution by then. In 1952 UNRWA observed that in recent years not a few of the Arab émigrés were finding homes and livelihoods in neighboring countries, in Iraq and the Persian Gulf states. At least 280,000 refugees had established themselves in Jordanian Palestine and by their own efforts had become an integral part of that nation's economy. Moreover, their presence in the Hashemite kingdom transformed Amman from a placid country town of 50,000 in 1948 to a bustling, reasonably modern city of 150,000 by the end of the 1950s. In 1954, too, a study committee of the Royal Institute of International Affairs noted that

> the better informed and more realistic among the refugees . . . would, in fact, not dream of trying to live in Israel. They believe that an Arab minority in Israel would if anything be more insecure in the future than it is today, when primary consideration is naturally given for employment, land, and house room, to immigrant Jews, not to the depressed Arabs. . . . It would have been much better if the realities of the situation had been honestly faced, and if every effort had been devoted to showing the Arab refugees how and

why their chances for repatriation were limited, and to providing an immediate alternative by which the disappointed majority of the refugees could hope for an improved life elsewhere.

In January 1951 a "Committee of Palestine Refugees" in Lebanon wrote the Arab League political committee, observing that a return to their homes was less than imminent for most of the Palestinians. Until a political solution was found they could hardly be left to rot in the Arab countryside without decent food, shelter, or means of livelihood. The letter suggested that the Arab states should at least provide those refugees willing to settle outside Palestine the opportunity to do so. Yet the one affirmative response to this appeal was Abdullah's decision to confer Jordanian citizenship on the 200,000-odd refugees on the West Bank. Of these, it is recalled, some 100,000 found employment; the rest continued to live in camps on the UNRWA dole. By contrast, the Gaza Strip refugees were confined virtually as prisoners in their tiny zone. With the exception of perhaps 20,000 fugitives who managed to secure jobs in Iraq and the Persian Gulf area by 1951, they were denied employment or citizenship in Egypt itself. Their status was one of unalleviated misery.

From time to time, meanwhile, the UNRWA directors came up with specific and well-funded employment programs for the émigrés in neighboring Arab lands. The Arab governments immediately shot these proposals down, allowing the money to be spent on relief, nothing more. In truth, their opposition to anything smacking of resettlement was no longer exclusively one of principle. They suspected that the refugees were not capable of being absorbed that easily. In 1949 only about 20 percent of the adult males among them possessed useful skills or training (and these quickly became self-supporting). The other 80 percent were either farmers or untrained workers living in areas already saturated with fellahin and laborers. In addition, political instability in most of the Arab nations and friction between Arab governments compounded the problems of refugee absorption. Thus, having won the sympathy and support of the Arab masses, the Palestinians frequently applied effective pressure on the various national regimes, notably in Jordan, where they comprised a third of the population, and in Lebanon, where they represented a tenth of the population. As the refugees settled in other parts of the Arab world, moreover, they tended to impart their intense feelings of bitterness and frustration to the established citizenry. Under the circumstances, the Arab governments were not eager to add to their political and economic difficulties.

For the Palestinians themselves, the "advantages" of refugee status were not altogether negligible once the relief programs were instituted and regularized. They had access to health services. The incidence of sickness and deaths accordingly was lower among them, and their birth rate higher, than among the surrounding Arab populations. Some 45 percent of their children of school age received free education. While their rations were meager—about 1,600 calories of flour, pulses, sugar, and rice per day—they did not suffer from malnutrition. By the end of 1956 only 39 percent of the registered fugitives actually lived in UNRWA camps; yet nearly all of them drew UN rations. What was unsalvageable was not their existence but their morale. Vegetating helplessly in the squalor of their UNRWA shantytowns, they experienced tensions so acute that their perodic outbursts occasionally imperiled the regimes of their host countries. If, then, the ordeal of these hundreds of thousands of embittered exiles was complicating the task of peace in the Middle East, the unrest it threatened was not between Israel and the Arab countries alone, but among the Arab nations themselves.

A FLICKERING OF BORDER VIOLENCE

Inevitably this frustrated and seething refugee presence made its impact along the Arab-Israeli frontiers and activated one of the most critical provisions of the four armistice agreements. It is recalled that these accords were intended to provide a transitional period in which resentments would cool, hopefully creating an atmosphere favorable to peace negotiations. To that end, machinery was established to lessen the danger of violence along the borders. It consisted of two elements. One was the Mixed Armistice Commissions (MACs), established by the armistice agreements themselves. The other was the United Nations Truce Supervision Organization (UNTSO), which had been established earlier, during the Palestine war, and which therefore drew its authority and personnel from the world organization. Both elements were functionally intertwined, and the plan to reduce the threat of conflict depended upon their close cooperation. Thus, each MAC (for each of Israel's four frontiers) was composed of an equal number of Israeli and Arab delegates and presided over by the UNTSO chief of staff. The purpose of these mixed bodies was to determine if an armistice violation had occurred, and then to encourage the parties to resolve the dispute. In investigating evidence of violations, the MAC chairman was authorized to cast the decisive vote.

However impressive in conception, this machinery depended for its effectiveness upon the willingness of the Arabs and Israelis themselves to take seriously the preamble to the armistice agreements—that is, not merely to avoid resort to force but to agree "that the establishment of the armistice is an indispensable step toward the restoration of peace in Palestine." When the agreements were signed, in 1949, none of the parties expected that more than an additional few months would be required to conclude final and binding peace treaties. Because the momentum generated at Rhodes was not sustained, however, the rot set in almost at once. The armistice machinery was not equipped to serve as a permanent substitute for peace. The configuration of the Rhodes boundaries, too, was yet another source of difficulty. The frontiers had been intended simply as temporary lines, and made no concession to civilian needs. Between Israel and Jordan they cut off Arab villages from their fields and wells. Almost nowhere was the frontier clearly marked. At once, therefore, local Arabs on the Hashemite side began crossing the artificial boundary to reclaim their possessions. Some even attempted to harvest their old fields. Large numbers of refugees moved into Israel to rejoin their families, or simply because they did not know the precise demarcation of the armistice line.

The Israeli government regarded the infiltration with much concern, for it was damaging the morale of the border settlers, most of whom were new immigrants. At first the MAC was at least partially effective in dealing with the pilferage of crops and chattels. By late 1951 and early 1952, however, the theft or vandalism of farm property became particularly acute, and the Israeli response increasingly emphatic. Infiltrators who offered resistance were shot by Israeli border police each week almost as a matter of routine. In 1952 alone 394 Arabs were killed, 227 wounded, and 2,595 captured. Not all Israelis approved of this policy of toughness. The poet Natan Alterman, writing in *Davar,* exclaimed indignantly: "Oh, you Knesset members, you former passport forgers, you infiltrators, grandchildren of infiltrators, how quickly you have learned the new morality of militarism!" But hesitation vanished after 1952 when Arab thefts and sabotage were compounded by murder and arson. Hardly a week passed without the slaying or wounding of Israeli civilians by Arab marauders. If the raids ordinarily were not initiated by the Hashemite government, they were nevertheless generally tolerated by lower-echelon Arab officials and the Jordanian police. What fellow Arab could have prevented the refugees from striking back, after all? Complicity was difficult to prove, even when the infiltrators' tracks led back to the police fortresses. Even so, the Israelis chose to attribute responsibility to the Arab governments, and they retaliated with increasing harshness. Thus, from June 1949 until October 1954, Israel claimed that Jordan had violated the armistice agreement 1,612 times. Jordan, in turn, accused Israel of 1,348 violations. The MAC verified that Jordan was answerable for 34 of 124 Israelis killed, and that 127 of the 256 slain Jordanians—infiltrators and soldiers alike—were Israel's responsibility.

The violence reached a crescendo of sorts in 1953. On October 13 of that year, a grenade was thrown into a house at Tirat Yehuda, well inside the Israeli frontier, killing a mother and two children. The Israel-Jordan MAC was summoned, and concluded that Jordanian terrorists had perpetrated the act. Choosing not to wait, however, for Amman to fulfill its promise "of discovering and punishing the guilty," the Israeli cabinet decided to strike back hard at known Jordanian murder bases. One of these was the village of Qibya, facing Tirat Yehuda across the border. Plans were laid for the army to attack and destroy about fifty homes there. During the course of the Israeli raid, sixty-nine Jordanians, half of them women and children, were killed within the demolished homes; they had hidden there and gone unnoticed. Shocked and embarrassed, Ben-Gurion dissembled by insisting that the action was not a military operation but rather an act of revenge by civilian victims of Arab attacks. The MAC swiftly exposed the lie and condemned the action. So did the Security Council. Privately, Sharett and Eban had growing misgivings about the strategy of retaliation, concerned that it was undermining Israel's diplomatic position.

The policy remained in effect, however. General Moshe Dayan, Israel's

new chief of staff, warned that retaliatory operations against known guerrilla sites and even army posts would continue. On March 17, 1954, a
Jewish holiday bus was ambushed at Scorpion's Pass in the Negev; eleven
passengers were killed and two wounded. When the MAC refused to condemn the Jordanian government, stating that the murder was the work of
private Arab criminals, Israel angrily withdrew its delegates from the
armistice commission. Powerful army raids then followed against suspected
Jordanian guerrilla bases. Nor was the strategy of reprisal by any means a
failure. Taking note of the growing harshness of these Israeli expeditions,
Amman sought urgently to restrict further infiltration. In 1954, as a result,
the number of Israelis killed by infiltrators declined to thirty-three, and in
1955 to twenty-four. Yet the most serious casualty was the Israel-Jordan
MAC itself. By mid-decade it had ceased to function. The "armistice" line
on Israel's eastern frontier was no man's land again.

DEMILITARIZED ZONES AND FEDAYEEN

Still another chain reaction of violence erupted in the demilitarized zones
between Israel and its Arab neighbors. The armistice agreements established four such zones: one (divided into two sections) in the north on
the former Palestine-Syria border; a second encircling the Hebrew University and Hadassah hospital buildings on Mount Scopus in Jerusalem;
a third on Jebel al-Mukabbir in Jerusalem, comprising the old high commissioner's palace; and a fourth, diamond-shaped area around al-Auja on
the Egyptian border. It was the Mount Scopus zone that became the initial
focus of rivalry. Commanding a general view of Jerusalem, and dominating the city's eastern and northern approaches, the entire promontory lay
within Hashemite lines. The Israel-Jordan armistice agreement had placed
the enclave under United Nations protection, however, and off limits to
the armed forces of either side, although not to Arab and Israeli civilian
police. Despite this provision, both Jordanians and Israelis violated the
understanding almost from the outset. The Arab Legion openly posted
troops at the Augusta Victoria Church. The Israeli "policemen" stationed
at the Hebrew University and Hadassah hospital were in fact soldiers. To
ensure that their outpost on Mount Scopus could hold out in the event of
attack, the Israelis periodically smuggled weapons and ammunition in
"food" convoys and stashed them in the basements of university and
hospital buildings.

A far more volatile zone was the one established between Israel and
Syria as a "compromise" solution to the prolonged and grudging armistice
negotiations of 1949. At first, the Syrians had refused to abandon their
limited foothold in Israel. As an inducement for withdrawal, however,
the Israelis agreed for the evacuated bridgehead to be transformed into
a demilitarized zone, consisting essentially of two noncontiguous strips of
40 square miles. The first, central strip ran from the southern half of Lake
Chula along the Jordan River to the mouth of Lake Galilee. The other

strip extended along the southeastern shore of Lake Galilee, with a tail projecting eastward for about 3 miles. Both sectors lay entirely within Palestine. It was understood in both Jerusalem and Damascus that even limited control over the DMZ would enable the Syrians to obstruct crucial Israeli development projects; for only within this zone could Israel undertake the work necessary to drain the Chula swamps, to build hydroelectric power stations, and to channel water to the Negev. Indeed, of all Israel's neighbors, Syria was the most favorably located, and temperamentally and politically the most eager, to cripple the Jewish nation's economic growth. To prevent any further confrontation on the issue of Israel's development, therefore, Ralph Bunche, the United Nations acting mediator, assured Israel during the 1949 armistice negotiations that normal civilian life could be resumed in the demilitarized zone. Conversely, it was Syria's understanding that the DMZ would not be regarded as sovereign Israeli territory.

The UNTSO representative, functioning as chairman of the Syria-Israel Mixed Armistice Commission, was invested with responsibility for the "gradual restoration of normal civilian life" in the DMZ, without prejudice to a final settlement. Initially, it appeared to this officer that Israel's Chula drainage scheme, intended to release about 45,000 acres for cultivation, was permissible under Bunche's format. The swamps lay entirely outside the demilitarized zone. Nevertheless, once work began in January 1951, it was discovered that a road would have to be built affecting 100 acres of Arab-owned land in the DMZ. The Israelis accordingly sought to negotiate with the landowners, and at one point tentative agreement was reached on compensation. Then, at the last moment, the Arab farmers were called to Damascus and persuaded to reject all offers. Thereupon the Israelis expropriated the land, and on February 14 Syria lodged a complaint with the MAC. On March 7, 1951, the UNTSO chief of staff, General William Riley, an American marine officer, endorsed the Syrian claim that some Arab land was affected against the wishes of the owners, thus interfering with the "restoration of normal civilian life," and hence violating the armistice provisions. No party was sovereign in the DMZ, Riley declared, and the right of compulsory acquisition therefore could not be exercised.

Stung by the decision, the Israelis on March 25 overrode Riley's protests and launched into work on the enterprise. Immediately the Syrians began firing on the civilian engineers. The Israelis in turn evacuated 630 Arabs —whom they described as a potential fifth column—from the central sector of the DMZ and flattened their villages. When Syrian troops moved into the zone, Israel on April 5 bombed the garrison village of al-Hamma at the tip of the DMZ. Armed units were then rushed into both sides of the zone, and on May 2 heavy fighting began. Hostilities continued for twelve days until the Security Council forced through a cease-fire. The matter was discussed in the United Nations body, and Israel was ordered to return the evacuated Arabs forthwith and to cease work on Arab lands. The Israelis reluctantly acquiesced. Ultimately, too, they devised a means of completing the project without using Arab land, and the tension gradually subsided. In 1953 the canal was finished and the drainage of the swamps proceeded quietly.

Other crises subsequently arose in demilitarized territory. One, an effort to construct a hydroelectric power plant at the B'not Ya'akov bridge, just north of Lake Galilee, involved the building of a water diversion canal in the DMZ that would have affected the flow of the Jordan River in Syrian territory. Although the Israelis were prepared to guarantee the Syrians their allocated share of water under the impending Johnston irrigation scheme (p. 457), the Damascus government took the issue to the United Nations, and there it was upheld. The Israelis consequently dropped their work on the project. By then, too, a potentially even more explosive issue had arisen over fishing rights on Lake Galilee. This placid little water body lay entirely within Israeli territory, although in places the Syrian border reached to within 10 meters of the eastern bank. Israeli fishing boats approaching the northeastern shore often were fired upon. In August 1951, Israel agreed to reduce tension by keeping the boats at least 250 meters from the shore. But in December of that year, Syrian regular army units shot and killed several Israeli fishermen close to the eastern bank. Immediately afterward Damascus announced that Israelis would not be permitted closer than 400 meters from the water's edge. Israel rejected this delimitation, incidents of violence continued during the next few years, and occasionally the Syrians shelled Israeli boats.

In October 1955 five Israeli soldiers were captured inside Syria as they repaired a wiretap. When the Arabs refused to release the prisoners, two Israeli platoons crossed the DMZ on Lake Galilee's northern shore, destroyed a Syrian military convoy, and took five soldiers as hostages for their own imprisoned men. Renewed efforts to negotiate an exchange failed, and the Syrians continued to fire on Israeli vessels. Whereupon the Israeli army launched a powerful retaliation raid on the night of December 11, hitting a series of Syrian military positions along the northeastern shore, killing twenty-six soldiers and twelve civilians and taking thirty Syrian prisoners. After evaluating a report from the Israel-Syrian MAC on January 12, 1956, the Security Council denounced the Israeli attack and warned of firm United Nations measures if the raids were not halted. The Israelis were sobered by the threat. For the time being they exercised restraint. The number of Syrian shootings also declined. The storm between Israel and Syria was postponed.

During the interval, however, in the 1950s, it was the southern line of confrontation, in the demilitarized zone of al-Auja and particularly the Egyptian-ruled Gaza Strip, that was transformed into the single most lethal battleground between Israel and its enemies. The al-Auja DMZ, evacuated by the Egyptians in return for assurances of tactical sterilization, lay roughly diamond-shaped for a distance of 22 miles along the former Palestine-Egypt Sinai border. Virtually from the outset of the armistice, the Israelis made repeated efforts to establish a military camp in the area under the guise of a kibbutz—thereby circumventing the de-

ISRAEL–SYRIA
DEMILITARIZED ZONES

- — ·· — International frontier
- — — — Armistice demarcation line
- ⊠ Demilitarized zone
- ✕ Syrian position

0   MILES   5

militarization provision of the Rhodes Agreement. To manage this, it was necessary first to evict 6,000 Bedouin and deprive others of their traditional water sources. The Israelis carried out the expulsion in two operations, in September 1950 and May 1951, burning the Arabs' tents, crops, and possessions and killing thirteen Bedouin who resisted. Some of these unfortunate nomads may indeed have been Egyptian agents, as the Israelis claimed, and others potential saboteurs and thieves; but most were peaceful inhabitants grazing their camels on ancestral tracts.

Finally, in September 1953, the Israelis established their first settlement in the al-Auja area. It was a Nachal kibbutz—that is, a village operated by soldier-farmers. Soon afterward, an Egyptian checkpoint was also discovered within the demilitarized zone. The Israelis demanded its removal, but the Egyptians refused to budge until the Nachal forces were out of the area. Several clashes erupted during late 1954 and early 1955, with casualties on both sides. The zone became increasingly tense. Finally, in October 1955, the Israelis wiped out an Egyptian army post at al-Quntilla, far to the south, killing five Egyptian soldiers and taking twenty-three prisoners. When nevertheless the Egyptians insisted upon clinging to their few meters of the DMZ, Israeli troops moved in force against the Egyptian position on November 2. About fifty Egyptians were killed and over forty captured in the attack. The UN Security Council censured Israel for this action, but the Jews did not relinquish their hold on al-Auja.

In fact, Israel's determination to emplace its troops in the DMZ was influenced by more than a perverse need to assert its sovereignty. The zone was a vital flank guarantee against rising Arab infiltration from the Gaza Strip, a penetration that by 1955 had become more critical even than the volatile developments along Lake Galilee or the uncertain Jordanian frontier. This modest wedge of Palestine coastal land, about 4 miles wide and 30 miles long, was allotted to Egypt at the end of the 1948–49 war; it became the focal area of some 120,000 Arab refugees (the number would swell to over 200,000 within a decade) in addition to the 50,000 regular inhabitants. Tightly circumscribed under Egyptian military rule, denied the right of employment in Egypt proper, the Gaza refugees generated a hatred against Israel more unremitting than that of any other émigré concentration elsewhere on Israel's borders. Indeed, their bitterness and rage made infiltration and armed raids into Israel nothing less than a patriotic duty. At first, the Egyptian authorities did little to encourage or even to cooperate with the refugee crossings. The armistice agreement worked reasonably well here. It was the advent of the Nasser regime, together in some degree with Israel's own irascible border policy and the subsequent deterioration of Egyptian-Israeli relations (Chapter XVII), that eroded this restraint. Egyptian surveillance later was relaxed sufficiently to allow the passage of marauding bands into Israel. What ensued was a mounting cycle of attacks and reprisals.

By United Nations reports, Israel launched more than seventeen military raids in one form or another on Egyptian-held territory between 1949 and 1956, and a total of thirty-one attacks against Arab towns or military forces during these seven years. Virtually all of these were condemned by the Egypt-Israel MAC or censured by the Security Council—as, occasionally, were Arab provocations. It was Israel's apparent failure to win the under- standing of the world body that convinced Abba Eban, Israeli ambassador to the United Nations, that retaliation was a dead end. In the aftermath of a unanimous Security Council condemnation, following Israel's Gaza raid of spring 1955 (p. 481), Eban wrote a friend: "Retaliation is just finished as a policy, and our people should become used to obeying the same rules, even under provocation, as other governments when provoked."

Living abroad during those years, Eban perhaps failed to appreciate the intensity of his nation's exasperation. He himself cited to the Security Council the figures of Israeli casualties in the 1950s, the victims of Arab infiltrators and trained marauders. Through shellings, military assaults, and hit-and-run tactics of fedayeen—trained "suicide" forces—the Arabs inflicted 1,300 Israeli casualties between 1949 and 1956. Four-fifths of those losses were civilian (two-thirds of the Arab casualties were military), and they included many women and children. Each death, too, was measured against the context of unremitting Arab hostility toward Israel, a juridical and emotional state of war that utilized yet additional techniques —quarantine, blockade, and propaganda—designed to capsize Israel's economy, sap its powers of resistance, and ultimately efface the Jewish republic from the community of nations.

THE DYNAMICS OF ARAB BELLIGERENCY

As we recall, little of this militancy could have been prophesied from the armistice agreements of 1949. The documents manifestly had been intended as transitional steps toward permanent peace. For that matter, the Arab governments no less than Israel were known to have vested interests in a policy of mutual recognition. Presumably they had urgent problems that required solution, among them arbitrary and volatile frontiers based on immediate military necessities; the demilitarized zones; the need for an outlet on the Israeli Mediterranean coast, for Egyptian-Hashemite access through the Negev, and for a defined status for Jerusalem. It developed, also, that Abdullah was intensely eager for a compromise agreement that would placate the tens of thousands of restive Palestine Arabs living on the west bank of the Jordan. If he succeeded in winning meaningful con- cessions from the Jews, the refugees might regard him as a savior rather than as a scapegoat. Confident, too, of his negotiating skills, Abdullah decided to risk the ire of his fellow Arab rulers and the possible misunder- standing of his subjects. He renewed his secret contacts with Lieutenant Colonel Moshe Dayan, the Israeli military commander in Jerusalem.

At first the Israelis responded to Abdullah's feelers somewhat re- luctantly. It was felt that a prior agreement with Egypt would secure broader territorial concessions from the Hashemite ruler. Nor were Abdullah's initial demands modest. He wanted access to the Mediter-

ranean through Beersheba and Gaza, the return of the Arab quarters of
New Jerusalem, passage along the Jerusalem-Bethlehem road, and a free
port in Haifa. In return, he offered Israel access to the potash works on
the north shore of the Dead Sea and a free port on the Gulf of Aqaba, a
quid pro quo implying that at least a portion of the southern Negev would
be returned to Transjordan. The Israeli government had no objection to
the inclusion of Gaza within Hashemite territory—this was a purely Arab
matter—and was willing even to concede Transjordan access to the sea.
Yet the Jews were by no means eager to permit an easement through the
south, for the danger was greater of fracturing their country in this comparatively empty terrain. What Ben-Gurion had in mind was a corridor
yards wide. Abdullah was thinking in terms of a corridor miles wide.
No agreement seemed possible at first.

Meanwhile, accounts of the secret talks reached the Arab press. Egypt
retaliated by appealing to the United Nations to endorse the territorial
internationalization of Jerusalem; and this effort, it is recalled, succeeded
in December 1949. It was the setback on Jerusalem, in turn, that revitalized
Israeli-Hashemite negotiations. This time the discussions bore fruit. A
formal agreement was reached early in 1950. By its provisions, the
frontiers between Transjordan and Israel would remain unchanged for
five years. Certain unresolved problems would be assigned to various
joint committees, but in the meanwhile normal trade and travel would
proceed between the two countries. Transjordan would enjoy a free port
zone in Haifa, linked by a narrow corridor across the more densely
inhabited part of northern Israel. Finally, both peoples would be guaranteed mutual access to their holy places in both parts of Jerusalem. In March
1950 the draft treaty was initialed by the Israeli and Transjordanian
representatives.

The moment news of the agreement leaked to the rest of the Arab
world, a storm broke over Abdullah's head. He faced a crisis within his
own cabinet. The West Bank refugee population seethed. Warnings and
accusations poured into Amman. Syria threatened to close its Transjordanian frontier. When the Arab League met in Cairo several days
later, Egypt and Saudi Arabia proposed expelling Transjordan from the
organization. The measure was averted at the last moment, but only at the
price of Transjordanian acceptance of a resolution barring separate
agreements with Israel. Privately, the Hashemite king sent reassurance
to the Israelis: "Abdullah, the son of Hussein, does not break his word."
The little monarch anticipated that the impending election in Transjordan
would vindicate his policy, and that it would be safe then to ignore
Egypt. Instead, the election returned candidates flatly hostile to the
notion of peace with Israel. From then on, Abdullah decided to move
cautiously vis-à-vis the Jews. On January 1, 1950, he annexed all of Arab
Palestine, and on April 25 entitled his realm the Hashemite Kingdom of
Jordan. The Arab League protested, but did nothing. The king decided he
had gone far enough at the moment; he would not risk publication of his
treaty with Israel. Indeed, he had already gone too far. On July 30, 1951,

an assassin in the pay of Egypt shot Abdullah dead on the steps of the Mosque of Omar in Jerusalem.

To the Israelis, the hardening of Arab opposition was apparent as early as the stalemated PCC negotiations in Lausanne. The truth was that the Arab states had not really experienced the cost of the war in a physical or territorial sense. Except for the Palestinians, they had suffered almost no property destruction and had abandoned no territory. Militarily, their losses were negligible in relation to their populations. Their entire war expenditures had come to roughly $300 million, a trifling sum. Their price levels continued relatively stable afterward, and hunger among their fellahin was no greater than ordinary. Nor did the burden of the refugees fall on them; they simply refused to accept it. After the Rhodes armistices, in fact, the Arab governments—with the possible exceptions of Jordan and, intermittently, Lebanon—saw little to gain and much to lose by making peace. The restoration of land communications between Egypt and the other Arab countries was of marginal importance; little trade passed over these routes. Territorial concessions to be gained through peace were of small value to any country except Jordan. Rather, a formal end of the war would have obliged Lebanon to share its transit and oil pipeline outlets with Haifa. An Israel at peace with its neighbors, exploiting its advanced economic and technological position, was likely to prove a strong competitor for Middle Eastern markets.

By the same token, fear of potential Israeli expansion was very real in the Arab world. "The Arabs are keenly aware," said an article in *al-Hayat* of May, 1954, "that the population growth in Israel's now narrow territory will undoubtedly lead her to seek ways of expanding her living space. And it is clear that she will not achieve this except at the expense of her neighbors, the Arab states on her borders." Politically, too, it would have been dangerous and conceivably fatal for the Arab leadership to make peace with Israel. Egyptian Prime Minister Nuqrashi Pasha was assassinated by a Moslem Brotherhood gunman merely for having accepted a cease-fire, even before Egypt had signed the Rhodes armistice agreement. As punishment both for losing the war and for signing the armistice accord, the entire Syrian regime was overthrown by a military coup. Prime Minister Riad al-Suhl of Lebanon was assassinated for displaying moderation, although his country had played only a minor part in the hostilities. And Abdullah was murdered for negotiating peace. Whenever inter-Arab relations reached a point of crisis, moreover, enmity toward Israel was usefully invoked for Pan-Arab purposes. Through the years since 1948, a boycott of Israel and other expressions of hostility proved to be the one dependable integument among contending governments and factions in the Arab world.

Psychologically, most important of all, the Arabs simply could not bring themselves to admit defeat at the hands of the "Zionist gangs." The Moslem tradition of jihad—of unceasing warfare against infidel interlopers—played a role here. Pride and self-esteem were equally critical factors, however. Once signed, the peace treaties would have been admission that the game was over. Azzam Pasha put the matter forthrightly: "We have a secret weapon which we can use better than guns and machine guns, and this is time. As long as we do not make peace with the Zionists, the war is not over; and as long as the war is not over, there is neither victor nor vanquished." Even Arabs formerly known for their moderation burned with resentment at Israel's 1948 victory. Kay Antonius, widow of the distinguished Arab historian George Antonius, expressed this bitterness: "Before . . . the Jewish state I knew many Jews in Jerusalem and enjoyed good relations with them socially. Now I will slap the face of any Arab friend of mine who tries to trade with a Jew. We lost the first round; we haven't lost the war." The Zionists were also equated, in this regard, with the medieval Crusaders and with modern imperialism, and the history of the Arab world characteristically was described as a prolonged resistance to European invasion and domination (Chapter XXI). The venom and gall directed by the Arab press and even Arab scholars against Zionism and Israel, against the Jews as a "treacherous race" and Judaism as a "vipers' nest of cunning," gained momentum in the 1950s, as it had not in the pre-Israel period. It was a measure of this animus that Egypt's most respected writer, the former Palestinian Muhammad Izzat Darwazah, could indict Jews for their "historical" malice, treachery, and selfishness. "How extraordinary it is," he wrote, "that we realize that their characteristics today, although they live in various places, are exactly as they were described by the Koran. . . . Time does not add to their qualities, but makes them more deeply rooted. . . . The vices pass on from fathers to sons."

THE MECHANICS OF ARAB BELLIGERENCY

As the Arabs moved almost imperceptibly toward a policy of heightened belligerence, the likelihood of peace treaties correspondingly diminished in the early 1950s. For the while, the techniques of revenge were essentially nonmilitary. Their purpose henceforth was to isolate, harass, and eventually strangle Israel through political pressure, boycott, blockade, propaganda, and border violence. In this effort, the Arab rationale was that the armistice agreements had not yet transcended the juridical state of war.

One of the most effective Arab maneuvers was diplomatic quarantine. All borders with Israel were closed, except for a tiny crevice at Rosh HaNikrah, at the Lebanese frontier, which was open to foreign diplomats, and the Mandelbaum Gate in Jerusalem, which was limited to non-Jews passing to and from the Jewish sector. All postal, telephone, and telegraph facilities between the Arab nations and Israel, all sea, air, road, and rail communications, were severed. Moreover, no person whose passport bore an Israeli visa was given entry into any Arab state; neutral travelers were obliged to carry two passports. The Arab governments were relentless, too, in their attempts to dissuade other nations from establishing diplomatic relations with Israel. The campaign was particularly effective among the newly liberated states of Asia, most of which accepted the contention that Israel was an imperialist puppet rather than an emerging nation like themselves. The larger of those nations—Indonesia, Pakistan, Iran, India —were Moslem or part Moslem, and others possessed substantial expatriate colonies throughout the Arab world. Although Turkey, Iran, and India established consular links with the Jewish state, they declined Israeli overtures for political or economic relations. The Israelis in turn regarded the Arab diplomatic vendetta with mounting gravity. They had anticipated that their socialism and technology would establish a common interest and common bond with the Asian nations. That hope now appeared dashed. The Bandung Conference of Afro-Asian countries, meeting in the spring of 1955, refused to invite Israel. The affront seemingly climaxed Arab efforts to isolate Israel from the emerging bloc of "neutral" states.

It was the Arab economic boycott, however, that inflicted an even more painful and crippling blow. In January 1950, the Arab League officially drew up a far-reaching plan to deter other nations and companies from entering into business relations with Israel. The following year, a central boycott office was established in Damascus, with branches throughout the Arab world. One by one, the Arab states enacted stiff controls with harsh penalties for violators. These were applied to companies in Europe, the United States, or elsewhere that maintained branch factories, plants, or agencies in Israel; even to firms that sold Israeli patents, copyrights, or trademarks, or that purchased shares in Israeli enterprises. Intensive efforts similarly were launched to persuade neutral countries to observe the boycott as a matter of diplomatic policy. These attempts were unsuccessful, for the most part. Nor did Western governments appear to suffer for their resistance to Arab pressure. On a national basis, for example, West Germany paid reparations to Israel annually beginning in 1953, and each year thereafter the value of West German exports to Arab countries rose steadily.

Nevertheless, violating the longstanding Western tradition of open commercial patterns with friendly nations, many individual companies unquestionably acquiesced to the Arab boycott—to Israel's severe loss. The major American and British petroleum corporations halted the flow of oil from Iraq to Haifa in 1948, and it was not resumed. For many years the Haifa refinery, formerly owned and operated jointly by the Royal Dutch Shell group and the Iraq Petroleum Company, worked at only one-third capacity. Many important air and maritime companies were dissuaded from serving Israel. Under the boycott, vessels found it impossible to call at Israeli and Arab ports on the same run. Thus, the American Export Lines ran a second, expensive and time-consuming, Middle Eastern service to Haifa. In the 1950s alone more than 120 ships of foreign registry were blacklisted for sailing to Israel. While the Arab nations were not powerful enough to deter the major international airlines from offering service to and from Israel, they ensured at least that no plane touching down in Israel could so much as fly over Arab territory.

Not a single flight to Asia originated in Israel, as a result, and Europe-Israel-Asia routes proved unfeasible. Israel soon became a minor side stop of world tourism rather than an international crossroads.

Perhaps even more constrictive was the Egyptian blockade of Israel's international waterways. When the Rhodes armistice agreement was signed, the likelihood of a blockade had not occurred to the Israelis, for the document contained a flat injunction against "aggressive action" by either party. It was taken for granted that the wartime maritime block-ade of the Suez Canal and the Gulf of Aqaba would promptly end. This was the understanding of Dr. Bunche, who reported to the Security Council on July 26, 1949: "There should be free movement for legitimate shipping and no vestiges of the wartime blockade should be allowed to remain, as they are inconsistent with both the letter and spirit of the Armistice Agreement." Additionally, the Constantinople Convention of 1888, to which Egypt was a signatory, guaranteed free passage through the Suez Canal to all vessels of all nations in peace or war. The Egyptian reaction to these injunctions, nevertheless, was simply to continue to deny Israeli shipping the right of passage through Suez. Although at first Cairo moved somewhat more obliquely against neutral shipping bound for Israel through the waterway, an Egyptian government decree of February 1950 published an extended list of "strategic" goods that might not be transported to Israel. The banned items included oil, pharmaceuticals, chemicals, ships, and automobiles. Cairo's purpose obviously was to deny use of the Canal for Israel's most important traffic. In November 1953 the list was enlarged to include foodstuffs and similar consumer goods.

As early as July 1950, moreover, Egypt strengthened its blockade by issuing regulations designed to prevent transshipments to Israel via third countries. Ship captains were required to submit declarations counter-signed by Egyptian consuls in the ports of origin, guaranteeing that their cargoes actually had been discharged and were intended exclusively for local consumption. Other, even more onerous restrictions were imposed later. Israel angrily protested these measures in the Security Council. In August 1951 Eban noted that if the armistice agreement freed Egypt to purchase arms, then Israel was entitled to traverse the Suez Canal and Gulf of Aqaba; the two advantages were "contingent and reciprocal." Impressed by the argument, the Security Council in September ordered Egypt to end its restrictions on the passage of international shipping. For several months afterward the Egyptians deemed it expedient to relax their blockade. In 1952, however, the ban was gradually reimposed. Indeed, it was accepted as an international *fait accompli* in July 1954, when Britain and Egypt reached agreement on the evacuation of British forces from Suez. Israel protested that the treaty ignored Egypt's illegal closure of the waterway to Israeli shipping. There was little international reaction. Subsequently, an Israeli freighter, the *Bat Galim*, tested the Egyptian blockade. The vessel was seized and its cargo confiscated. By then the threat of a Soviet veto inhibited the Security Council from acting on the blockade. Few shipping companies henceforth would agree to test the closure against Israel.

The second of Israel's intended routes to Africa and Asia, the Red Sea outlet, was similarly interdicted by the Egyptians. The 230-mile coastline of the Gulf of Aqaba, Israel's main avenue to the Red Sea, was shared in fact by four countries: Saudi Arabia, Jordan, Egypt, and Israel. Two uninhabited Arabian islands, Tiran and Sanafir, located at the southern end of the Gulf, restricted the navigable area between the Gulf itself and the main body of the Red Sea to a three-mile channel, the Strait of Tiran. At the end of 1949, by agreement with Saudi Arabia, Egypt installed heavy military equipment on Tiran and Sanafir, as well as on Ras Nasrani, at the tip of the Sinai coast facing the two islands. Thereafter the Egyptians closed the Strait of Tiran to all shipping bound for the Israeli port of Eilat. The move represented a contravention not only of the armistice agreements but of international legal precedents for gulfs and bays flanked by the territories of more than one littoral state.

The issue of the Strait of Tiran was particularly urgent to Israel. Although traffic to and from Eilat would have been quite meager in any case during the 1950s, the principle of unilateral closure imperiled the Jewish state's future trade with the Orient and East Africa. Yet when the Israelis appealed to the Security Council in 1954, they faced the near-certainty of a Soviet veto. Accordingly, no anti-Egyptian resolution was passed. With both the Canal and the Red Sea cut off, Israel was blocked from all its potential Eastern markets. Nor was there any real likelihood of forcing a change in Egyptian policy through normal diplomatic channels. To be sure, the confluence of Arab pressures—boycott, blockade, diplomatic isolation, border violence—had not yet strangled Israel's capacity to survive, or even to grow. By the mid-1950s, however, as the Jewish state gradually absorbed its first waves of immigration, it recognized that its opportunities for both physical and economic viability were being painfully, even intolerably, limited.

Perhaps the most dramatic example of this inhibition was in the one area most crucial to the nation's economic future, that of water development. In the early 1950s it was the conviction of John Foster Dulles, the United States secretary of state, that Arab hostility toward Israel could be defused, and the plight of the refugees mitigated, by an economic scheme that required the joint commitment of Arabs and Israelis alike. The plan Dulles had in mind was a Jordan Valley Authority, to exploit and allocate the waters of the Jordan River system among all the neighboring riparian states. The idea in fact had been advocated by the Jews for years and had been endorsed on numerous occasions by UNRWA specialists.

The Jordan River descended from headwaters in Lebanon, Syria, and Israel, proceeded down through the Jordan Valley, and finally ended its sluggish crawl in the Dead Sea. One of the river's tributaries, the Yarmuk, passed through Hashemite Jordan; the other, the Litani, flowed through Lebanon. If this water system could be tapped, not less than a million and a quarter dunams of arid land in Israel, Jordan, and Syria could be reclaimed, and 170 million kilowatt hours of turboelectricity generated. Most important of all, from Washington's viewpoint, at least 160,000 Arab refugees would earn a livelihood on soil made fertile by the Jordan Valley scheme, another 60,000 to 70,000 would find work in the construction project itself, while perhaps 140,000 would be employed simply in meeting the needs of the farming population. The cost of such an undertaking was estimated at between $100 million and $110 million. The United States was prepared to cover much of it.

In the autumn of 1953 Dulles assigned the task of "selling" the plan to Eric Johnston, a genial and dynamic public servant with years of successful negotiating experience in business and government. Johnston encountered a surprisingly friendly response in the Arab capitals, particularly in Amman. Possibly Jordanian anxiety over refugee unemployment and bitterness was a factor. The American emissary shrewdly exploited this concern, therefore, by hinting that the United Nations (i.e., the United States) would not fund the refugee camps indefinitely, and that if some wide-ranging irrigation program were not soon adopted, the Israelis would launch an undertaking of their own. Faced with these alternatives, Jordan and the other Arab regimes agreed to discussions. Unspoken in Johnston's efforts, of course, was the prayerful hope that a joint irrigation scheme would establish an economic basis for later, political, Arab-Israeli cooperation. His conversations with the various governments did not always go easily. The original plan was for Israel to receive about 35 percent of the water, with Syria and Jordan dividing the rest between them. But the Israelis insisted on 60 percent, and the right to pipe their water out of the Jordan Valley into the Negev Desert. The Arabs for their part argued that Israel was entitled to only 20 percent of the water and obliged to use it exclusively within the Jordan Valley Basin.

During the next two and a half years, Johnston made five trips to the Middle East. With uncommon tenacity and imagination, he succeeded finally in working out a compromise formula between the parties. By tentative agreement reached in August 1955, Israel's share of the water allocation was set at 40 percent, while the Arabs consented to Israel's using its portion of the water in the Negev, the intended site of the Jewish nation's industrial and agricultural development. The understanding was a remarkable feat for Johnston, all the more so in that it was achieved at a time of mounting border violence between Israel and the Arabs, when the Israeli raid at Gaza early in 1955 badly shook the prestige of the Egyptian government (Chapter XVII). Elated, the American negotiator expressed "not the slightest doubt that Israel and her Arab neighbors . . . now recognize the Jordan Valley Plan as the only logical and equitable approach to the problem of developing a river system which belongs, in some part, to all of them. . . . They believe the remaining minor differences can readily be reconciled. I am sure that they can be."

Johnston's optimism was premature. When the Arab League met in October to debate the scheme, they decided to "postpone" it—thereby avoiding the diplomatic onus of an outright rejection. In later months the Arabs blamed Israel for the collapse of negotiations, asserting that the Israelis refused United Nations supervision of the project. They argued, too, that in the light of Israel's raid at Gaza the Arabs manifestly could not trust the Jews to carry out a water agreement in good faith. But the authentic explanation was simpler. Cooperation with Israel, even on a purely technical level, implied Arab recognition of the Jewish state. Worse yet, from the Arab viewpoint, the Jordan Valley project would have fostered Israel's growth and development. Against the background of Arab suspicion and hatred, and the mounting crescendo of raids and re- taliations, it was altogether extraordinary that Johnston's efforts had progressed even beyond the first exploratory discussions with the Arab governments.

ISRAEL LOOKS TO THE WEST

For the while, then, Israel's best hope of coping with the hostility of its neighbors plainly was to seek allies elsewhere. The decision was not easily made. In the autumn of 1948 the government had decided originally upon a foreign policy of nonidentification. "We have friends both in the East and in the West," Ben-Gurion explained to the Provisional Council of State. "We could not have conducted the war without the important help we received from several states of East and West. . . . The interests of the Jewish people are not identical with those of any state or any bloc in the world. . . ." The theme was given formal status in the Basic Principles of Government program announced on March 8, 1949; while Sharett used the phrase "the principle of nonidentification" on numerous occasions in public addresses and statements. In adopting this stance, the Israeli government was influenced first by the need to obtain weapons from all nations, and second by concern for large elements of the Jewish people both in the West and in Communist eastern Europe. Domestic party pressures were also a factor. In the 1949 elections, for example, Mapam emerged as Israel's second-largest party, and this leftist faction traditionally had endorsed a policy of friendship with the Soviet Union. It had not forgotten Russian support during the previous two years.

Even so, it was the West that took the first decisive action to restore stability in the Middle East and thus block Soviet penetration of the region. In May 1950, with the Lausanne peace conference a shambles, the United States, Britain, and France issued a Tripartite Declaration. "Should the three Governments," it warned, "find that any one of these states [Israel or its Arab neighbors] contemplates violating the frontiers of armistice lines, they will . . . act both within and without the framework of the United Nations in order to prevent such a violation." Weapons would be rationed out to the Middle Eastern nations only for legitimate purposes of self-defense and to "permit them to play their part in the defense of the area as a whole." While this gesture reflected Western self-interest, it was nevertheless gratefully welcomed by most Israelis.

Indeed, the possibility of building on that support was mutually explored by Israel and Britain early in 1951, when General Sir Brian Robertson, commander of British Middle Eastern forces, paid an official visit to Tel Aviv. Robertson did not conceal the potential advantages of defense relations between Britain and its former mandatory ward. He had in mind a pact that would give British air and naval squadrons access to Israeli bases and harbors. Robertson indicated, too, that he would favor Israeli construction of the arsenals and repair workshops to be used by his forces. Negotiations developed in a friendly spirit. Soon afterward, Herbert Morrison, Bevin's successor as foreign secretary, wrote Ben-Gurion of his desire to achieve a close understanding between their two governments. The Israeli prime minister replied in a similar vein. "I think our entry into the Commonwealth is out of the question," he admitted, "but we would like to establish relations with you on the lines of those between you and New Zealand." The ambassadors on both sides then got down to details, and it appeared momentarily that Israel would indeed become Britain's ally, thus assuring the Jewish nation's security as well as enlarging its economic resources.

The illusion was soon shattered. The British election of autumn 1951 returned a Conservative government. Anthony Eden, a traditional patron of the Arabs, resumed his earlier position as foreign secretary and once again evinced his customary reserve toward the Zionists. Military negotiations with Israel were dropped. By then, too, other plans were afoot for a Middle Eastern defense system. Egypt was invited to join the projected organization. Israel, conversely, was asked to stand aside at least until the other Arab states agreed to participate. Ben-Gurion and his colleagues regarded this development with intense anxiety. In the event the Arab nations joined the defense pact, Israel's enemies would have access once more to Western arms, equipment that could be used later against the Jewish state. In fact, one of the most critical problems Israel faced in the 1950s was that of ensuring its own supply of modern weapons. The hodgepodge of obsolescent matériel accumulated during the 1948 war clearly was useless in an age of electronics and jet planes. Yet the industrialized nations manufacturing this equipment kept tight control over its disposal. The most Britain was prepared to sell Israel were very limited supplies of outdated Meteor jets. The French, despite their earlier record of help, were chronically suspicious of Israel as a member of the sterling bloc—even as a close association with Israel might endanger whatever remained of French influence in the Levant states. For the immediate future, then, there appeared little hope of acquiring substantial quantities of modern arms from western Europe.

Of all the democratic nations, it was the United States that remained incomparably the most valuable of Israel's potential allies. By 1950, however, Washington's attitude toward the Jewish state was dictated less by the emotional and political pressure of 1947–48 than by a forthright strategic need to counter Soviet imperialism in the Middle East. One method of achieving this was to co-sponsor the Tripartite Declaration guaranteeing the integrity of Arab and Israeli frontiers. Moreover, by acquiescing in the Great Power declaration, Israel revealed the obvious limitations of nonidentification. In 1950 the Israeli economy was faltering critically. The United States government and, particularly, American Jewry were the only important likely sources of economic help. In that year Israel was awarded a $100 million loan from Washington, and from then on the Israeli cabinet exerted itself to secure a much wider measure of American friendship and generosity. Thus, in 1951, it won permission to launch a State of Israel Bonds campaign in the United States. Other substantial infusions of American capital, both governmental and private (Jewish), were forthcoming. By then even Israel's most committed Socialists recognized which side of the ocean their bread was buttered on.

Washington imposed a price for its friendship. This soon became evident when the Korean War began in June 1950, and the United States insisted that friendly nations "stand up and be counted." After several days of intense soul-searching, the Ben-Gurion government voted to endorse the Security Council resolution condemning North Korean aggression. From then on, Sharett and Eban all but dropped their earlier policy of nonidentification and instead advocated support of the "free world." Indeed, this approach now represented a conscious bid for a United States guarantee or treaty of alliance. It was a goal that virtually obsessed the Israeli foreign ministry from 1951 to 1955, and the zeal with which it was pursued was in direct ratio to mounting Soviet hostility against the Jewish state (p. 462).

Yet the returns of this pro-American orientation, while economically impressive, did not produce a formal security guarantee. Intent upon ringing the Soviet Union with Middle Eastern air bases, Secretary of State John Foster Dulles in 1953 won assurances of cooperation from Turkey, Iran, Pakistan, and Iraq. His policy thereafter, in tandem with Eden's, was to seek a new Middle Eastern alliance oriented primarily toward these Islamic "northern tier" countries. The efforts of the Western diplomats were crowned two years later with the signing of the Baghdad Pact. Inasmuch, however, as this multilateral treaty included not merely Britain (and obliquely, the United States), but also Iraq among the four Moslem signatories, the complications of the Arab-Israel issue were unavoidable. The Israelis were deeply concerned lest Iraq's adherence evoke broadened Western military assistance to an enemy nation. The American government in turn sought to reassure Jerusalem, observing that the Arab states would prove less dangerous within a Western alliance than outside. But the Israelis were not reassured; they urgently sought a treaty relationship of their own, either with NATO or, bilaterally, with Washington itself. It was a hopeless quest. The Eisenhower administration was in no sense prepared to enter an alliance capable of jeopardizing relations with the

Arabs. Instead, the president rejected the notion even of selling Israel planes and tanks. Quite aside from its efforts to woo the Arab nations into a collective Middle Eastern security organization, Washington maintained close ties with Saudi Arabia and Libya. These provided air bases and oil sources in the Arab world that Eisenhower and Dulles were not prepared to forfeit. For the while, then, Israel had to satisfy itself essentially with American financial largess.

THE QUEST FOR SOVIET FRIENDSHIP

In August 1948 a Soviet legation was opened in Tel Aviv, and in September of that year Mrs. Golda Meir (formerly Meyerson), Israel's first minister to the Soviet Union, arrived in Moscow. Mrs. Meir's welcome by Soviet officials was cordial. Her reception by Soviet Jewry was something far more; it was rapturous. Attending the central synagogue or visiting the Jewish theater, she was cheered ecstatically by milling thousands of Russian Jews. These demonstrations in turn came as something of a shock to the Soviet government. It was astonished that the Jews, who had the good fortune of living in the Great Communist State where "a Jewish question did not exist," should hold Israel in such intense affection. As retribution, the authorities closed a leading Yiddish journal, then dissolved the Jewish Anti-Fascist Committee and arrested its members. The Kremlin nevertheless anticipated that friendly relations with Israel somehow could be fostered, even in tandem with a culturally repressive policy toward the Soviet Union's own Jewish population. In the United Nations, the Russians continued to support Israel's appeal for direct Arab-Israeli negotiations.

Early in 1949, however, the Soviet leadership displayed increasing concern about Israel's relations with the United States. Consequently, before returning home in April, Mrs. Meir found it necessary to reassure Deputy Foreign Minister Andrei Vishinsky that her government would never be induced to join an anti-Soviet alliance, nor to give military bases to Western nations. But Vishinsky was not reassured, and the Soviets continued to raise the matter of Israel's attitude toward the West. At approximately this time—late 1949 and early 1950—the circumstances of east European Jewry began to deteriorate. The Jewish theater was closed in Moscow. Jewish emigration from Poland and Rumania was slowed and eventually stopped. On the diplomatic level, meanwhile, the Soviet government warned repeatedly that its friendship with the Jewish state was conditional upon the latter not "working for Anglo-American interests." The message registered, and the Ben-Gurion government went to considerable lengths to maintain its posture of nonidentification. The Israeli delegation in the United Nations remained silent even during the vote of October 22, 1949, on the observance of human rights and fundamental freedoms in Bulgaria, Hungary, and Rumania.

Yet Israel's economic dependence on the United States was growing with each passing, near-bankrupt month. Additionally, the Tripartite Declaration of May 1950 seemed to offer the little republic a territorial guarantee that no other power, not even the Soviet Union, could match. Then in June the Korean War broke out, and with it Israel's agonized decision to yield to American pressure in condemning North Korean aggression. Despite Sharett's repeated assurances to Moscow that his government would not join any extension of NATO in the Mediterranean —even if the world crisis spread to that area—Israel was now hopelessly compromised in Soviet eyes. Between October 20 and November 17, 1950, the Security Council discussed six complaints relating to the operation of the armistice agreements between Israel and its neighbors. For the first time, the Russians abstained from voting. Clearly they were adopting a new line, one of passive neutrality. In October 1951, shortly after Turkey joined NATO, the three Western powers made known their decision to establish an Allied Middle East Command, and added that "countries able and willing to contribute to the defense of the area should participate." We recall that Israel was not invited to join. Nevertheless, it was inconceivable to Moscow that the close relations between Israel and the United States should not ultimately find expression in such a pact.

Throughout 1952 the Soviets continued to refrain from voting on Arab-Israel issues in the United Nations. Their silence was ominous. When the storm finally broke, moreover, it did so in unexpected fashion. In November 1952, the world was shocked by the Prague show trial. Of the fourteen top Communist officials accused of "treason"—actually, of disloyalty to the Stalinist line—eleven were Jews. The trial was not only anti-Jewish; it was also explicitly anti-Israel. Much was made of the role played by Israeli "spies" in the alleged conspiracy of Rudolf Slansky, the Czech (Jewish) Communist leader, and his group (p. 364). The accusations were reported prominently by *Pravda* and *Izvestia,* and without reference to the Israeli government's outraged denials. But in fact the Czech trial was merely a prelude to the most violent tempest of anti-Semitism— outside the Arab world—since Hitler, and this time within the Soviet Union itself. In December 1952, the Soviet press reported the first in a series of trials of "economic criminals." Nearly all the names published were of Jews. On January 1953, too, Moscow astonished even its enemies and confounded its friends in the West by announcing the "discovery" of a "conspiracy of doctors" planning to liquidate Soviet political and military leaders. Again, the accused were primarily Jews, who were described as agents simultaneously of American intelligence and of the Zionist Organization. Ignoring Israel's vehement protests, the Soviet media launched their own onslaught against Israel as "the chief instigator of anti-Soviet feelings throughout the world." On February 5 the Israeli minister in Prague was declared *persona non grata.* So, two days later, was Israel's emissary in Warsaw. On February 9, in what was possibly a deliberate *cause provocative,* an explosive charge went off in the garden of the Soviet legation in Ramat Gan, Israel. The damage was slight, and the Israeli government promptly condemned the incident. But four days later the USSR severed diplomatic relations with Israel.

There were a number of reasons for this furiously anti-Jewish and anti-Israel policy. One related to the fear of heterodoxy that had plagued Stalin since his rupture with Yugoslav Marshal Tito in 1948. As a minority group with extensive connections abroad, particularly in the West, the Jews, like the Titoists, appeared to present a "deviationist" threat to the Soviet ruler. They were known, too, as a repository of the old, idealistic Trotskyite socialism that Stalin had feared and execrated since the 1920s. Plain and simple anti-Semitism as a distraction from internal economic failures may also have been a factor. If so, it was infinitely exacerbated by the notorious paranoia of Stalin himself in his last years. And surely of critical importance between 1950 and 1953 was growing suspicion of Israel as a potential ally of any Western attack launched from the Middle East.

The diatribes against Israel—and the West—eased somewhat in the months immediately following Stalin's death in March 1953; and during the ensuing "thaw" Moscow resumed diplomatic relations with Israel. The respite did not endure, however. Israel had assured the Soviets that it would never join an aggressive pact against the Communist bloc. Yet its method of protecting itself against the Middle East Defense Organization was, first, to request admission into NATO; and, failing that, to seek a bilateral defensive treaty with the United States. The Russians were deeply angered. It was from this point that they began to concentrate exclusively upon securing Arab favor. Between March and December 1954 questions relating to the Arab-Israel conflict were brought before the Security Council eight times. In each instance the Soviet delegate led the attack against Israel, and this pro-Arab policy was reinforced in 1955. From the Soviet viewpoint, the events of 1954–55 provided additional justification for the diplomatic shift. On the one hand, Washington and London were intensifying their efforts to forge a chain of anti-Soviet treaties in the Middle East, culminating in the Baghdad Pact. On the other hand, left-wing regimes were consolidating their power in Egypt and Syria, and adopting a strenuously anticolonialist line in doctrine and orientation. Moscow was not laggard in sensing the opportunity to use these "liberationist" movements for its own purposes (Chapter xviii).

The corollary of growing Soviet friendship with the "progressive" Arab nations was a further deterioration of relations with Israel. It took the form of virulent press attacks against the Jewish state for its role as an "agent" of Western imperialism, and condemnation of Israel's raids across Arab borders. In August 1955, three members of the Israeli embassy in Moscow were declared *personae non gratae*. Finding itself confronted now both by a chain of Western-sponsored defense alliances in the Middle East —with its promised infusion of sophisticated weapons into the hands of the Arab enemy—and by the palpable and growing truculence of the Soviet bloc, Israel recognized that it was being driven into a strategic isolation as ominous as it had ever faced in its short history.

A CRISIS OF CONSCIENCE:
TO NEGOTIATE WITH GERMANY

In its earliest years, the nation's diplomatic problems were intimately related to the parlous state of its economy. By late 1950 the crisis of immigration had become so acute that the treasury had all but exhausted its foreign exchange reserves. It was at this juncture that the issue of compensation negotiations with West Germany suddenly assumed a new urgency. The entire question of German financial payments in fact extended back at least a decade. It was first mooted in 1941 by Dr. Nahum Goldmann, president of the World Jewish Congress. Subsequently the idea was further developed by a number of German Jewish refugees, preeminent among them Siegfried Moses, the future comptroller-general of Israel. In December 1944, Dr. Moses organized a "Council for the Protection of the Rights and Interests of German Jews." The influence of this group was far-reaching. Eight years before the Luxembourg Treaty (p. 467), its members already had outlined the basic components of future German reparations: individual claims, Jewish institutional claims, and the collective claims of the Jewish people, with the proceeds of the latter category to be used for building the Jewish National Home in Palestine. The approach was refined after the war in a study prepared by Dr. Jacob Robinson, legal counselor of the World Jewish Congress, and in a letter from Weizmann to the victorious Allied Powers on September 20, 1945.

The idea of reparations was hardly novel to the Allied leaders. At the Yalta and Potsdam conferences they themselves had agreed to impose a reparations figure of $20 billion on defeated Germany. Yet the Paris Reparations Conference in late 1945 disregarded all Jewish claims except for a maximum of $25 million in German assets deposited in neutral countries, representing the assets of Jewish victims of the Nazis who had died without heirs. Subsequently, too, in the late 1940s, the German Federal Republic authorized a certain limited indemnification. Jewish restitution organizations were authorized to file claims on behalf of survivors and their heirs. Unfortunately, this process required the submission of individual applications, each of which ultimately had to be approved by separate German Länder (states). By 1953, 110,000 applications had been filed, and a niggardly $83 million had been paid out by the states for "loss of liberty, limb, or occupation."

Quietly, however, in 1949 and 1950, Dr. Noah Barou, vice-president of the British section of the World Jewish Congress, was discussing with West German officials alternative means of securing meaningful compensation. Barou made some forty trips to Bonn on this mission, and in March of 1950 finally won confirmation from the West German foreign ministry that the principle of collective indemnification was valid, and could serve as a basis for negotiations. In January 1951, Israel made its first move. Its government sent notes to the four Allies, announcing a Jewish claim for reparations upon the new Germany in the amount of $1.5 billion. The

sum was calculated on the basis of Israel's role in absorbing nearly half
a million Jewish victims of the Nazis at a per capita expense of $3,000
for their economic rehabilitation. The Soviet Union did not bother to
answer the Israeli note ($500 million of the claim was upon East Ger-
many). The Western Allies acknowledged Israel's moral justification, but
observed that there was no way to force West Germany to meet the claim.
They advised Israel instead to negotiate directly with Bonn. Here, at last,
the explosive issue of dealings with the Germans no longer could be
evaded by the Ben-Gurion government.

The Israeli leaders were in a quandary. No diplomatic issue—whether
of Jerusalem, of the Arab refugees, or of national alignment in the Cold
War—raised profounder complications for the Jewish state. Within the
country, emotions ran high against negotiations, indeed, against contact
of any sort with Germany. Yosef Sprinzak, speaker of the Knesset, declared that "the honor of the Jewish people precludes any acceptance
of restitution from Germany even if it were voluntarily and spontaneously
offered." Other objections, particularly from the right-wing Cherut, were
even more emphatic (p. 372). Ben-Gurion pressed ahead, however. In
July 1951 his foreign ministry established a special department, the Claims
Office of the Jewish People Against Germany, under the direction of
Dr. Felix Shinnar (himself a refugee from Germany). Barou meanwhile
informed West German officials that Ben-Gurion had agreed to request
Knesset authority to negotiate with Bonn, but that this step could be
taken only after Chancellor Konrad Adenauer himself had solemnly acknowledged before the West German Bundestag his nation's responsibility
for the Holocaust.

Adenauer accepted these terms. As a matter of personal conscience
no less than of political leadership, the aged chancellor regarded atonement to the Jews as one of his foremost objectives. At his instructions,
legal officials in the Bonn foreign ministry prepared the first draft of the
statement in July 1951. Yet it required almost three months of further
negotiations in Israel, London, New York, and Bonn before agreement
was reached on a text that satisfied Jewish demands. Finally, on September
27, 1951, Adenauer delivered his long-awaited Bundestag address. He
emphasized that Bonn would do everything possible to make amends for
Hitler, inasmuch as the Nazi crimes, if not committed by all Germans,
had been committed in the name of all Germans. He stressed that his
government felt obliged to do penance in the form of material payments
to Israel and the Jews at large. The chancellor also committed himself
to the relentless prosecution of all those who might still be disseminating
anti-Semitic hatred. The speech won the Bundestag's near-unanimous
approval; its members rose to their feet afterward in silent approbation.
The event represented as well an official invitation to the Israeli government for direct conversations.

The next initiative on the Jewish side was taken by Nahum Goldmann
in his capacity as president of the World Jewish Congress and chairman
of the Jewish Agency. Born and educated in Germany, Goldmann was

a man of unusual linguistic and diplomatic virtuosity. He brought his considerable personal dynamism and negotiating skills to bear now in establishing a "central address" for the Jewish people. Organizing some twenty-two world Jewish organizations into a Conference on Jewish Material Claims against Germany, Goldmann won the endorsement of that body for negotiations with Bonn. Similarly, he was requested by Jerusalem to conduct the initial personal discussions with Adenauer on Israel's behalf, to lay the basis for Israeli-German agreement. In December 1951, therefore, the meeting between Goldmann and Adenauer took place secretly in London, where the chancellor was on an official visit. The interview was extended and cordial. After presenting the Jewish demands of $1.5 billion, Goldmann asked the chancellor to confirm the sum in writing as a basis for forthcoming talks with Israel and world Jewry. Adenauer agreed. Goldmann then prepared a text, and that same afternoon Adenauer returned the document signed.

Ben-Gurion waited no longer. He scheduled the question of negotiations with Germany to be laid before the Knesset on January 7, 1952. It will be recalled that the ensuing debate, in and out of the parliament, became perhaps the single gravest crisis of Israeli democracy (Chapter XIV). As Ben-Gurion asked the Knesset for permission to begin formal talks with Bonn, he reminded the members that if the request were not granted, Israel would forfeit more than a billion dollars' worth of heirless Jewish property. "Let not the murderers of our people be also their heirs!" he cried. And despite the violence outside—the surging crowds, the wail of sirens, the explosion of gas grenades—and the fury of Cherut accusations within, the prime minister held his Mapai party in line. At the end of the debate on January 10, the measure passed. Thereupon the Israeli government and the Jewish Claims Conference mapped a common strategy for the impending negotiations. Talks with the Germans subsequently began on the "neutral" Dutch territory of Wassenaar, near The Hague, on March 21, 1952.

THE TREATY OF LUXEMBOURG AND SHILUMIM

Three parties sat at the conference table in Wassenaar's ancient ducal castle. The German delegation was led by Professor Franz Böhm, the Israeli delegation by Dr. Giora Josephthal and Dr. Felix Shinnar, and the Jewish Claims Conference by Moses Leavitt and Alex Easterman. Böhm, the first postwar dean of Johann Wolfgang Goethe University in Frankfurt, was known for his unblemished anti-Nazi record. Josephthal, German-born and possessing a doctorate from Heidelberg, was treasurer of the Jewish Agency and director of the Agency's absorption department. Leavitt, an American Jew, served as European director of the Joint Distribution Committee. Talks between these men and their associates began in a chilly atmosphere, with no handshakes, and care taken to avoid using the German tongue. English was spoken.

The Israelis related their claim for a billion dollars to the expense of integrating half a million refugees. The Claims Conference asked $500 million for the welfare and rehabilitation of Jewish victims dwelling outside Israel. The German negotiators accepted in principle the obligation to pay, but rejected the Israeli demand on the terms of payment—a third in hard currency and two-thirds in goods, to be dispensed over a period of five to six years. Böhm and his colleagues noted that the London Debt Conference had imposed upon West Germany the obligation of paying off its heavy postwar debts, and accordingly a compromise would have to be found between Israeli and Jewish claims, on the one hand, and Germany's "limited ability to pay," on the other. Affronted by this coldly businesslike response, Shinnar and Josephthal rejected any connection between Israeli demands and outstanding German financial obligations. An impasse soon developed on the issue. As news of the difficulties leaked, reaction in Israel was immediate and bitter. Some 40,000 demonstrators gathered in Tel Aviv to roar their opposition to any further negotiations. The mayor of Tel Aviv announced his readiness to go on a hunger strike. The early hopes of the Ben-Gurion government appeared shattered. Bonn was aware of these developments, of course, and instructed its negotiators to offer both Israel and the Claims Conference a total payment of DM3 billion, approximately $750 million, payable in goods. The amount was half the sum demanded by the Jews, but it was felt that Israel's desperate financial position would compel it to accept. The assumption was wrong. The Israelis walked out of the conference on March 31, and the Germans departed for home.

At this point Adenauer intervened personally. He cabled Goldmann, inviting the Jewish leader to West Germany for a personal conference. The two men met on April 20, and Goldmann reminded the chancellor that the payment was a debt of honor, not a matter for financial horse-trading. Adenauer agreed and promised to find an acceptable method of resuming the Wassenaar discussions. He kept his word by the simple device of threatening his Christian Democratic party with resignation if Germany failed to respect its moral obligation to the Jews. The German cabinet immediately agreed to revise its negotiating approach. Subsequently Böhm met with Goldmann in Paris on May 23, and also later with the Israeli representatives. He sounded out their reaction to a more generous compromise offer to Israel of DM3 billion, this time in addition to payments to the Claims Conference. The offer was accepted in principle. And finally, on June 8, Adenauer called the Jewish and Israeli representatives directly to Bonn. During the next two days, conversations between both sides resolved all other outstanding issues.

The signing of the various agreements took place on September 10, 1952, in the Luxembourg City Hall, a site dictated by Adenauer's presence that day to initial the pact establishing the European Coal and Steel Community. The ceremony was secret; Jewish terrorists had made threats of assassination. It was quiet, as well, with scarcely a word spoken; no public handshaking took place, although the men exchanged handshakes privately later. The Luxembourg Treaty consisted of four related but separate agreements. The first, between Israel and the Federal Republic of Germany, was the Shilumim, or reparations, agreement. Under its terms Bonn would pay DM3 billion in goods to Israel, in annual allotments over fourteen years. The second was an agreement with the Jewish Claims Conference for Bonn to initiate new legislation providing individual compensation (restitutions) to victims of Nazi persecution (p. 469). The third agreement, also with the Claims Conference, called for the payment of DM450 million to the Conference—through Israel—for the rehabilitation of Nazi victims living outside Israel. Thus, in all, the sum of DM3.45 billion ($820 million) would be paid to Israel, with DM450 million ($107 million) of these funds to be transferred by Israel to the Claims Conferenec in New York. The fourth agreement, a minor one, obliged Israel to refund the value of German property, most of it belonging to the Knights Templar, that had been confiscated in Palestine. The schedule of delivery payments to Israel included four categories of goods: ferrous and nonferrous metals, manufactured products of the steel and metalworking industries, chemicals, and agricultural goods. The Israel Purchasing Mission in Cologne would act on behalf of Israel and would enjoy quasi-diplomatic status and immunity.

Before the Luxembourg Treaty could go into effect, however, it had to secure the ratification of the German and Israeli parliaments, and in Bonn this was to prove as stormy as the negotiations at Wassenaar. The Arab League warned that if the treaty were confirmed, no Arab state would grant import licenses to German firms. Shaken by the threat, a number of German politicians opposed ratification, including Franz-Josef Strauss, leader of the Christian Democratic Union. Fully six months went by before the pact could be approved. But in the end the Arab nations were placated by substantial West German grants for their own economic development. With the support of the Social Democrats, then, the treaty was ratified by both houses of Parliament on March 19 and March 20, 1953. The Israeli government ratified the treaty on March 22.

Ironically, Ben-Gurion himself greeted the ratification with skepticism. "This is a great day," he observed wryly, "but the Germans will never pay." After the exhausting negotiations of the past year, he was convinced that the Shilumim would suffer the fate of the Versailles Treaty after World War I. But the prime minister underestimated his German counterpart. A devout Catholic, believing with all his heart in sin and atonement, Adenauer was profoundly gratified that the first international treaty to be signed by his government should be with the Jews. Under his stern tutelage, the Germans were destined to carry out the terms of the agreement punctiliously. On July 30, 1953, the Israeli freighter *Haifa* took aboard its first German consignment of iron in Bremen. The process would continue without interruption for twelve years.

Upon the agreement coming into force, a mixed German-Israeli commission was established to fix delivery schedules. It worked with remarkable smoothness. The German members displayed understanding and flexibility in permitting Israel to move from annual orders to long-range orders for development projects. At the same time, the Israel Purchasing Mission in Cologne rarely encountered difficulty in securing approval for its commodity requests. By the time the Shilumim payments were completed in 1965, some 1,450,000 tons of goods had been shipped to Israel.

Not all the deliveries, it is true, proved of equal value. For example, too many ships were ordered on a concentrated basis, and at inflated prices. Between 1953 and 1964, Shilumim-financed ship purchases amounted to $137.3 million out of a total of $751.3 million; yet shipping ultimately contributed but 1 percent of Israel's national income (the decision to acquire ships was influenced by important strategic and political considerations, as well). On the other hand, nearly 10 percent of Shilumim capital goods went toward the electricity-generating and -transmitting grid, and this laid the basis of the nation's industry. Oil was desperately needed, and the Shilumim arrangement provided that, too. A tremendous flow of matériel for harbor improvements, railroads, and telecommunications paid off spectacularly, as did heavy machinery, factory, and refining equipment. There was virtually no area of Israel's economy that was not transformed by these capital infusions.

Aside from Shilumim, Germany provided another vital stimulus to Israel's economy. This related to Bonn's Federal Indemnity Law of 1954, with its closely linked Federal Restitution Law. The measures were enacted specifically on behalf of individuals who had been oppressed by the Nazis for "racial, religious, or political reasons." Legally, hundreds of thousands of Jews of many different European countries, nations invaded and despoiled by Germany, were entitled to indemnification. Yet the largest single group of Jewish survivors were those who had escaped from Germany and central Europe before the outbreak of World War II. By 1954 over half of them were settled in Israel, and these were the principal beneficiaries of the statute. The law established four categories of indemnification: loss of property, loss of freedom, loss of health, and loss of "economic realization." Different schedules of payment were attached to each category, but all were fair and generous. And once the claims were validated, the restitution commissioners paid immediately, even to the heirs of deceased relatives. Although all claims were not fully processed until the mid-1960s, it became evident long before then that restitutions ultimately would amount to many hundreds of millions of marks. Indeed, by the end of 1964, no less than DM7 billion in restitutions had been paid to survivors in Israel alone; and this was exclusive of the DM3 billion provided Israel in Shilumim.

Adenauer had always intended that the reparations and restitutions agreements should serve as the merest beginning of a unique and enduring relationship with Israel. This was a matter close to his heart. So it was also to Ben-Gurion's. Almost from the outset of independence, the Israeli prime minister had recognized that Germany represented for his beleaguered nation a key to Europe, and a vital potential ally in Israel's efforts to seek associate membership in the emerging Common Market, possibly even in NATO. By the mid- and later 1950s, moreover, the notion of a relationship with Germany was no longer unthinkable to a majority of Israelis. The Germans were scrupulously fulfilling their reparations and restitutions obligations. German ships were unloading without incident in Haifa. In Ben-Gurion's view, the moment should be seized.

Difficulties already were surfacing, however. To inhibit other countries from recognizing East Germany—the Deutsche Demokratische Republik— Bonn's undersecretary of state, Dr. Walter Hallstein, enunciated a policy in September 1955 that was destined to guide his nation's foreign relations for the next decade. The "Hallstein Doctrine" was an open warning to other countries that the establishment of diplomatic relations with the Pankow regime would be regarded as "an unfriendly act [toward Bonn] calculated to aggravate the division of Germany." The Arab states accepted the doctrine. Yet their own price for not recognizing the DDR was West Germany's promise to abstain from establishing diplomatic relations with Israel. The quid pro quo was acutely embarrassing to Bonn, particularly in view of Foreign Minister von Brentano's recent decision to exchange consuls with Israel. With a heavy heart, therefore, Brentano terminated arrangements that would have led eventually to diplomatic relations. It was a stunning blow to Israel. After the protracted negotiations of recent years, there had seemed a growing likelihood that West Germany—of all nations—was to pioneer Israel's acceptance as an integral member of the Western community. But now it appeared that history would not be reversed quite that swiftly or dramatically.

THE BALANCE SHEET

If the setback was painful, the record, nevertheless, of Israel's diplomatic links by the mid-1950s was far from unimpressive. It encompassed a virtually total presence in North and South America, in western and eastern Europe, and in parts of Africa and Asia. Where breakthroughs did not occur, Arab hostility remained the major obstacle. Yet at least some of Israel's reverses probably could be traced to a lack of imagination in Jerusalem itself. The delicate wire-balancing act between East and West was a case in point. Sharett's and Eban's effusive protestations of loyalty to the "free world" during the General Assembly debates in 1950 and 1951 hardly were necessary to assure American financial and diplomatic support. Other nations in Africa and Asia went much less far, and were still able to maintain a certain bargaining leverage between the Great Power blocs. The only consequence of this overt partisanship in the 1950s was to exacerbate Soviet suspicions—irretrievably, as it turned out.

Israel's inability to win recognition from the "Third World" in Asia, to receive credit for its emancipation from colonial tutelage, was probably the nation's most grievous diplomatic failure. The Asians remained ill-informed about Jewish nationalism, which they conceived to be alien. Nehru, for example, regarded Zionism as an accomplice of British imperialism. To be sure, Arab political and economic influence was a factor here. But the Israelis themselves were partly responsible for this lack of understanding; they had concentrated their Zionist activities for decades in Europe and America. Even afterward, too, Israel's leaders might have interpreted Jewish statehood as the expression of a national liberation movement, something every former colonial people would have understood. The term was scarcely mentioned, however, in the addresses and writings of Ben-Gurion, Sharett, or Eban. Rather, the Israeli statesmen chose to discern a profounder explanation for the "miracle" of rebirth in the historical and theological roots of the Jewish people. As Michael Brecher—a shrewd analyst of Israel's foreign policy—observed, this was a false analogy and unimaginative diplomacy. Had greater insight been shown, it is conceivable that Israel's overtures of friendship might have evoked something more than a resentful Asian indifference.

Other lapses of imagination were evident in Israel's policy toward China. In 1955 Jerusalem rejected Peking's bid to establish formal ties. The Israelis argued later that they dared not forfeit American support. But that support was hardly impressive during the Eisenhower-Dulles period. More important, there were no Sino-Arab links at the time. Relations with China might have exerted a beneficent influence on India's attitude to Israel, for that was the period of Sino-Indian friendship. It might have won Israel an invitation to the first Afro-Asian Conference at Bandung in 1955. Instead, Arab threats to boycott the conference precluded an invitation to Israel. Had the Chinese been friendly, moreover, and certainly if India had been more temperate, the Arab bluff might easily have been called. This was a turning point in Israel's diplomacy. It foreclosed the Jewish republic's last, best chance of acceptance in Asia. The fatal error was attributable in part to unfamiliarity with Asia in general, and with China in particular. Sharett, Eban, Shiloach, and others responsible for the miscalculation were Europeans by background, outlook, and affinity. The world east of Iran claimed only their marginal attention.

Since its birth, then, Israel was one of only a very few countries that did not belong to any pact, bloc, alliance, or regional organization whatever. Neither did it possess a security guarantee of any kind by a Great Power. Nor, finally, did it share so much as a community of culture or language with other nations—except, ironically, with the Arabs. The links with its fellow Jews overseas surely were as unbreakable as they were indispensable; but in every other respect the new state was alone. This was not a heartening basis for security at a time, 1955, when Israel's political and military circumstances were unexpectedly transformed from lonely, unwelcome, and partial diplomatic isolation into an acute and imminent strategic vulnerability.

SINAI AND SUEZ

NASSER CASTS A SHADOW

For the better part of two decades, from the summer of 1952 until the autumn of 1970, the history of the Arab world was largely dominated by Gamal Abd al-Nasser, the most charismatic personality to appear in the Middle East since Mehemet Ali, a century and a quarter before. A tall, hawk-faced colonel, thirty-four years old in 1952, Nasser was the son of a post office employee in upper Egypt. Since his early youth he had been active in anti-British causes, and had belonged to the neo-Fascist Green Shirts. In World War II he had participated in an abortive effort to collaborate with the Nazis. The indignity of British rule was compounded six years later, moreover, by military defeat in Palestine at the hands of the Jews. For Nasser, as for other officers of his generation, the Palestine debacle could be attributed less to Jewish steadfastness and courage than to the ineptitude and corruption of the Farouk regime. Decisive and far-ranging political change appeared the only solution to the nation's woes. Returning to Egypt, Nasser and his fellow conspirators—Anwar al-Sadat, Abd al-Hakim Amir, Salah Salim, Zakariyya Muhyi al-Din, among others—broadened their following within the officer corps, and on July 23, 1952, seized control of the government in a bloodless coup. At the last moment, Major General Muhammad Naguib was invited to assume titular leadership of the uprising.

Thereupon Farouk was hustled off into exile, and a promising social revolution was launched. The titles of "bey" and "pasha" were abolished. Landed estates of more than 200 acres were expropriated (a decree honored more on paper than in fact). Corrupt and dishonest officials were purged from office. In June 1953, Egypt was proclaimed a republic. It was only in subsequent months that the officers embarked on a more radical, and ultimately more repressive, program. The constitution was abrogated, the parties dissolved, and political arrests became more frequent. During the subsequent year and a half, too, an internal struggle continued between Naguib and Nasser, until in March of 1954 Nasser finally outmaneuvered and replaced Naguib as premier. Later he would assume the presidency.

The priority goals on Nasser's agenda henceforth, aside from keeping himself in office, were to liquidate the British occupation and to redirect Egyptian energies to the struggle against poverty and social stagnation. By then conciliation was the mood on both the British and the Egyptian side. Negotiations on Suez and the Sudan were resumed, and full agreement was reached in July 1954 for British evacuation of the Canal area, a process to be completed within the ensuing twenty months. The evacuation treaty was received with jubilation throughout Egypt, indeed throughout the entire Arab world; it appeared as if the government's principal foreign policy objective had been achieved. By early 1955, however, failing to solve his nation's almost insurmountable domestic problems, Nasser shifted his emphasis away from traditional Egyptian anticolonialism. Even as he imposed an increasingly burdensome police regime upon his nation, on the one hand, on the other he offered his people the compensation and diversion of a militant new program of world influence. Egypt's destiny, Nasser announced in a series of public addresses, was to lead the struggle against imperialism everywhere in the Middle East at the head of a Pan-Arab federation of nations. The decision was given cutting edge, moreover, when Iraq entered the Baghdad Pact, an updated version of the Middle East Defense Organization that had been rejected by Egypt in 1951. With Britain as a co-signatory, and the United States later a member of the pact's military committee, it seemed evident to Nasser that the Western Powers, having just recently evacuated the Middle East, were returning through a northern "back door." Worse yet, Nasser's cherished role as leader of the Arab world was now being threatened.

The young colonel accepted the challenge with imagination and ruthlessness. All the resources of Egyptian bribery, diplomacy, subversion, and Nasser's personal magnetism were thrown into the campaign to rally Arab nationalist sentiment against the envisaged defense organization. It was in the course of this battle, too, that the Egyptian ruler determined to augment his influence as champion of Pan-Arabism by securing arms, concluding a series of treaties with other Arab nations, undermining Western influence in the Mediterranean through propaganda and sabotage, and orchestrating a new guerrilla campaign against Israel. Yet at the outset, Nasser failed to acquire modern weapons from either the United States, Britain, or France, who still were bent on preserving the Middle East arms freeze contemplated under the 1950 Tripartite Declaration. Opportunity opened elsewhere. Nasser flew to the Bandung Conference of Afro-Asian nations in April 1955. There he found that prestige and influence could be achieved by bargaining in the emergent "neutralist" world. Accordingly, at the suggestion of China's Prime Minister Chou En-lai, Nasser began exploring the possibilities of obtaining military equipment from the Soviet bloc.

Moscow was entirely receptive. Challenged by the Baghdad Pact, it was prepared to exploit any opening to undermine Western influence in the Middle East. These were the circumstances, then, in August 1955, under which a historic arms transaction was consummated. Nasser was allowed to purchase some $320 million worth of modern weapons from Czechoslovakia. Payments on an interest-free basis would be spaced out over twelve years in shipments of Egyptian cotton. The quantity of war matériel involved was unprecedented by Middle Eastern standards. It included 200 tanks, 150 artillery pieces, 120 MiG jet fighters, 50 jet bombers, 20 transport planes, 2 destroyers, 2 submarines, 15 minesweepers, plus hundreds of vehicles and thousands of modern rifles and machine guns. Deliveries were to commence immediately. In a parallel treaty, Syria, Egypt's partner in an emergent defense alliance, contracted with the Soviet bloc to purchase an additional 100 tanks, 100 MiG jet fighters, and hundreds of artillery pieces and armored vehicles. Soviet and Czech instructors would be made available to train the Egyptian and Syrian armed forces in the use of the weaponry. There is evidence that, in providing these arms, the Soviets had intended simply to encourage Egypt to decline membership in the Baghdad Pact. But in fact they accomplished more than that. The sudden disequilibrium in the regional balance of power was destined shortly to edge the Western Powers out of the Middle East altogether.

Reinforced in power and reputation, Nasser now moved ahead in his Pan-Arabist campaign. In October 1955, he signed a mutual defense treaty with Damascus. By April of the following year, Saudi Arabia and Yemen similarly concluded a five-year trilateral military alliance with Egypt. What Nasser could not accomplish by formal signatory agreements, moreover, he achieved through subversion. When Jordan's King Hussein appeared willing to enter the Baghdad Pact, pro-Nasserist rioters forced the resignation of the entire Jordanian cabinet in December 1955. Two months later Hussein was obliged summarily to dismiss General Glubb, commander of the Arab Legion, and order him out of the country. Determined also to erode British influence in Africa, Nasser embarked upon intensified propaganda broadcasts to the Mau Mau rebels in Kenya and to the Islamic minorities of Eritrea and Ethiopian Somalia. Nor was the French Maghreb empire neglected in this campaign of incitement. By late 1955 Egyptian funds and transshipments of Soviet weapons were being disbursed to the FLN nationalists in Algeria.

Israel, too, not least of all, was singled out as a target of Nasser's ambitions. Ironically, only three weeks after the Colonels' Revolution in July 1952, Ben-Gurion had extended the "hand of friendship" to the new regime, declaring in a Knesset speech that Israel wished to see a "free, independent, and progressive Egypt." Privately, he offered Cairo economic and political assistance. And in fact the Egyptian junta initially responded to these overtures. In March 1953 a set of Egyptian proposals was accepted as a basis for discussions. Cairo asked for £120 million as refugee compensation, for certain adjustments of the Israeli-Egyptian border, and for a land link to Jordan through the southern Negev. For their part, the Israelis agreed to negotiate on these terms, provided the Arab boycott and blockade ended. Contact between the two governments was maintained through intermediaries, including the future American treasury secretary Robert Anderson and British MPs and journalists. Nevertheless, by the spring of 1954, Nasser's imperialist vision for his regime precluded further communications with the Jews, and in December of that year Salah Salim, the Egyptian minister of national guidance, announced that Egypt would never make peace with Israel, not even if the Jews agreed to observe all the General Assembly resolutions on partition and refugees. These developments took place at a time of widespread German—ex-Nazi—participation in the Nasser government, and as a new campaign of Egyptian-organized sabotage was launched against Israel.

Until then, Hashemite Jordan had served as the principal base for marauding attacks over Israel's frontiers. But in 1954 leadership in the guerrilla campaign passed to Egypt. Between May and July of that year, Israel issued nearly four hundred complaints to the Israel-Egypt Mixed Armistice Commission of intensified assaults from Gaza. By October, fedayun squads, trained and equipped by Egyptian army units, were penetrating deep into Israel. Roads, bridges, and water pipes were mined, large quantities of equipment and livestock stolen. Soon the entire development program in Israel's southern desert was threatened, and many of the settlers there were leaving. In February 1955 alone, forty-five incidents occurred, and Israel's retaliatory raid into Gaza of February 28 (p. 481) was mounted as a response to this violence. After only a brief pause, the fedayun attacks were resumed, extending to the very outskirts of Tel Aviv and inflicting dozens of civilian casualties each month. General E. L. M. Burns, the Canadian officer who served as the UNTSO chief of staff, traveled back and forth between Cairo and Tel Aviv, urgently seeking methods of improving border control. It was wasted effort. By the summer of 1955 the Egyptian armed forces were integrating their first shipments of Czech weapons, and Nasser openly boasted that at last an Arab country possessed the capacity to destroy Israel. It was in anticipation of that final moment of truth, moreover, that the Arab League announced on October 11 that it was "deferring" acceptance of the Eric Johnston plan for the allocation of Jordan River waters.

ISRAEL IN ISOLATION

The Israelis had reason enough for concern as early as 1953, as London and Washington intensified their efforts to win Arab participation in a Middle East defense pact. Far from inviting Israel to join, Secretary of State Dulles issued a call on June 1 for a repatriation of specific numbers of Arab refugees to "the area presently controlled by Israel." The phrase was interpreted by Jerusalem as a thinly veiled denigration of Israel's current territorial frontiers. Other alarming developments in the second half of 1953 included Washington's hint of future arms sales to the Arab states and repeated American condemnation of Israel's retaliatory attacks against fedayun bases. The Johnston Plan brought an element of constructive cooperation into United States–Israel relations in early 1954. But the Israelis were shaken again in April and May of that year by the speeches of Assistant Secretary of State Henry Byroade, who proposed limits on Jewish immigration as a gesture of reassurance to the Arabs. All that remained was the negative effect on Israel of the emerging Baghdad Pact. This ambitious structure, linking the states of the Middle East with the Western democracies, clearly was being forged on the assumption that one nation alone must be excluded, precisely the most vulnerable state in the region.

As if the growing weapons imbalance and treaty isolation were not cause enough for apprehension, London and Washington decided to press Israel once again for territorial concessions as a method of forestalling the Egyptian arms transaction with the Soviet bloc. In a major policy speech of August 1955, Dulles stressed that the Rhodes Armistice lines of 1949 were not designed to be permanent frontiers. "The difficulty is increased by the fact that even territory which is barren has acquired a sentimental significance," the secretary added, plainly alluding to the Negev Desert. On November 9, 1955, in language even more plainspoken than Dulles's, Prime Minister Eden appealed for a "compromise" between the boundaries of the 1947 United Nations Resolution and the 1949 armistice lines. Eden admitted later that the timing of his speech may have been a mistake. "Once Russian arms had begun to flow into Egypt," he wrote in his memoirs, "it was unwise to raise the issue of frontiers."

In fact, Israel's unsettled relations with Britain and the United States occurred at the identical period when the Soviet Union was enlarging its military and diplomatic support of Egypt and Syria. In an address before the Supreme Soviet on December 29, 1955, Prime Minister Nikita Khrushchev loosed a particularly tough blast against Israel:

> Deserving condemnation are the activities of the State of Israel, which from its very first days began to threaten its Arab neighbors and to behave in an unfriendly way toward them. It is clear that . . . behind those who are pursuing such a policy, there are imperialistic states known to everybody. They are trying to use Israel as their own weapon against Arab nations.

Israel's indignant protest was rejected. Moscow made no effort thereafter to disguise its hostility, repeatedly condemning the Jewish state in the Security Council and accusing Ben-Gurion of preparing war against the Arabs. Manifestly, there was no hope for Jerusalem here.

Neither, apparently, was there in Washington or London. Both governments were retreating from the Tripartite Declaration of 1950. In the early winter of 1956, Eden and Eisenhower issued a joint communiqué referring to "[mutual] discussions as to the nature of action to be taken [in the Middle East] if the contingency arises." The original guarantee of frontiers now was palpably diluted. In February, Anthony Nutting, Britain's minister of state in the Foreign Office, declared his frank opposition to territorial commitments for borders "that are not agreed upon. . . ." The tripartite commitment received its *coup de grâce* in April 1956, when Washington announced that, in the event of a new Arab-Israeli war, it would place its major emphasis on action through the United Nations. The approach plainly would have exposed future enforcement measures to a Soviet veto in the Security Council.

Under these bleak circumstances, then, the Israelis were reminded that the nation's security depended ultimately upon its own resources. Here the role of the military was to prove crucial. Fortunately for the Jewish state, political disarray in the Arab world after the 1948 war allowed Israel five precious years in which to build its population and economy, and not least of all to augment its defense forces. Once the 1949 armistices were signed, it was possible to make objective, long-range decisions about a peacetime army. The nation's limited resources clearly dictated a military force based essentially upon reserves. Yigael Yadin, operational commander during the War of Independence, happened to be vacationing in Switzerland in 1949 before accepting his new appointment as chief of staff. He was particularly impressed by what he saw of the Swiss mobilization system. Thus, upon returning home, Yadin persuaded the cabinet to adapt the Swiss approach to Israel's needs, borrowing as well from Haganah, British, continental, and American practices. In September 1949, finally, the Knesset enacted a comprehensive Defense Service Law that established the legal foundation of Israel's citizen army.

By the provisions of the legislation, the armed forces were divided essentially into a regular service and a reserve. The former consisted of a limited number of commissioned and noncommissioned officers, as well as conscripts. The conscripts included all men and women who had reached the age of eighteen. Men were obliged to serve for twenty-six months, women for twenty. The former were assigned to combat training, the latter to duty as clerks, typists, drivers, signalers, even as teachers and social workers, particularly in immigrant villages. Upon completion of their terms, the draftees entered the reserve service, composed of all able-bodied men under forty-five and unmarried women under thirty-five. Men under forty were called up for an uninterrupted month of refresher training each year, older men for two weeks of training. Each age group also reported for duty the equivalent of one day a month; reserve officers served an additional week each year. By a law passed in June 1953, all men between the ages of forty-five and forty-nine constituted the civil defense, with training obligations of its own. In later years the periods of both conscript and reserve service would be lengthened even further. But as early as the 1950s mobilization already had become an integral part of Israel's everyday life. The child saw his father putting on his uniform to go to the army for a day every month, and for a month every year. His older brother or sister would either be in the regular army at the age of eighteen or else be performing reserve service. If the child lived in one of the new development settlements, his teacher would be a girl soldier doing her military service in the classroom; others, members of the military agricultural (Nachal) corps, would be fulfilling part of their responsibilities as club instructors, youth leaders, or cultural workers. In short, virtually every Israeli was a soldier on either active or reserve status.

From the outset of independence, the ministry of defense was held by Ben-Gurion himself, and it was uniquely the stamp of his forceful, single-minded character that was placed upon the growth and development of the armed forces. Israel's state of siege gave Ben-Gurion leeway to act freely and vigorously, to make basic decisions, informing the cabinet and the Knesset only afterward. And his purpose was nothing less than the transformation of Israel's voluntary—and still highly politicized—defense branches into a unified, compulsory, professional, and apolitical military machine. As premier and defense minister from 1947 to 1963 (with only a year and a half interruption between 1953 and 1955), Ben-Gurion accomplished the task in its essence. It is recalled (Chapter XIII) that he began by disallowing political groups within the defense forces and by replacing the political "key" system that operated in other government institutions with a merit system for all appointments and promotions. This was a more notable accomplishment than was generally realized, for the Palmach, like a majority of the Yishuv's institutions, was essentially Socialist, and highly motivated ideologically; its leaders were seeded throughout the officer corps. Only the extraordinary force of Ben-Gurion's personality could have brought these men to heel, compelled them to accept the dissolution of the Palmach, and inhibited them from launching a political revolt. The armed forces thereupon became the first of Israel's institutions to be nationalized and formalized.

On the other hand, Ben-Gurion was by no means willing to discard the apparatus of traditional ideology. Rather, he found ways of keeping the best of those values alive within the armed forces, particularly the Palmach's egalitarianism, its state-strengthening qualities. "The primary function of the defense forces," he wrote in 1949,

> has been to safeguard the state. However, this is not its sole function. The army must also serve as *an educational and pioneering center* for Israel youth—for both those born here and newcomers. It is the duty of the army to educate a pioneer generation, healthy in body and spirit, courageous and loyal, which will unite the broken tribes and diasporas to prepare themselves to fulfill the historic tasks of the State of Israel through self-realization.

The prophecy was vindicated. The defense forces were transformed into a citizens' academy, the inculcator of public spirit. For example, in order to narrow the educational gap between officers and conscripts—by the 1950s a majority of the latter were Orientals—the armed forces provided special schools to teach Hebrew and related subjects to newcomers. Members of Nachal carried on the Palmach's tradition of farmer-soldiers, working in border kibbutzim, often founding kibbutzim of their own while serving in the army. Like the former Palmach members, in fact, Nachal recruits consisted largely of volunteers from existing kibbutzim and moshavim, and from the pioneer Socialist youth movements in the cities. Their ideals of self-sacrifice and nation-building were inculcated well before the age of formal conscription. In addition to the youth movements, all high school students belonged to Gadna, a paramilitary organization that laid much emphasis on sports, physical training, manual crafts and hobbies, on seamanship, signals, and marksmanship. As a result, by the time the youngsters were conscripted, they were usually well oriented in the direction of national service.

DAYAN CREATES A FIGHTING FORCE

Following the armistice agreements of 1949, nevertheless, the quality of army personnel deteriorated for several years. The decline was essentially a consequence of the vast immigration, the cultural backwardness of Oriental youths, and the lack of knowledge of Hebrew among all new-comers. Moreover, with instruction manuals and all technical literature written in Hebrew, conscripts who knew the language or who were quick-est to learn it were ordinarily taken by the technical services; the fighting units received only the leftovers. By the time Moshe Dayan was appointed chief of staff in December 1953, the army was in the doldrums. Quickly ap-praising this deterioration, the vigorous one-eyed commander immediately revised the system, ordering the best men, the more intelligent and better educated, into the fighting units; the specialized services would take the rest. As a next step, Dayan instituted a toughening-up program for all members of the general staff; he led the way himself by completing a parachute and commando course. Officers were ordered thenceforth to lead personally in combat. By 1956 the new activist policy began to show dra-matic results, and the army once again became a hard-hitting, aggressive force. It was significant that the proportion of combatants to noncomba-tants, 50 percent, was by far the highest in the world. Unlike other armies, requiring large, self-contained expeditionary forces with many support units, Israel's armed forces operated on short interior lines and were struc-tured for short, intensive bursts of warfare.

For Dayan, the emphasis throughout was on striking power. The weak-ness of Israel's economy, the nation's limited size and narrow width, dic-tated a strategy of attack—on enemy terrain. All planning was geared to the surprise preemptive blow, the hard-driving, even reckless, offensive aimed at breaking the enemy's morale. It was a strategy ideally suited to Dayan's temperament, as well. In contrast even to his tough and dynamic prime minister, who had been born in Poland and was influenced by the experience of the Holocaust, Dayan, a native-born sabra, had nothing but confidence in the spirit and quality of Israeli troops. His own memories were of "Arabs scattering like birds at one bang on a can." The possible annihilation of Israeli Jewry was inconceivable to him. Years later he would even refer to the Six-Day War of 1967 as an expression of the na-tion's yearning for the land of its forefathers, rather than as a war of survival. With or without allies, Israel would manage. Dayan put his philosophy of aggressive retaliation to work almost immediately. With Ben-Gurion, he was determined to prove to the Arab states that the cost of marauding and killing Israelis was prohibitive. In the mid-1950s, then, the government's approach was to launch a series of triphammer punitive expeditions against Arab villages harboring infiltrators, and occasionally against Arab military strongpoints. The raids did much for army morale and training. For a while, too, they exerted a certain inhibiting effect upon the Jordanians, even upon the Syrians. Yet it is recalled that the cost in world opinion and in repeated United Nations censure was high.

Then, in November 1953, exhausted by the pressures of recent years, Ben-Gurion stepped down from office. In his place as defense minister, he appointed Pinchas Lavon, a brilliant Mapai theoretician and orator in his early fifties. Although Lavon had been little connected with defense matters, he was a dedicated Ben-Gurionite. Indeed, he embarked upon his tenure as defense minister as an activist, seeking even to outdo his predecessor in the vigor of his response to the Arab enemy. The policy of retaliation was intensified. Lavon added a new dimension, however, by asserting his personal authority at the military-command level. This was his mistake. Within a matter of weeks, relations between Dayan and the defense minister became strained. Thus, at the chief of staff's orders, the intelligence branch now began holding back details of impending operations. It is uncertain whether Lavon would have approved or vetoed the plans, but his lack of information in any case prevented a review of the one crucial scheme that ended in disaster for Israeli intelligence in Egypt.

The project actually had begun three years earlier, in 1951, when an Israeli intelligence officer, Avram Dar, arrived in Cairo under a British alias. There he made contact with a group of young Egyptian Jews who had been engaged secretly in emigration activities, and recruited several of them for undercover training. By 1954 the skills of this little group were urgently needed. It was the year Britain announced its intention to evacuate Suez upon completion of a treaty with Egypt. The Israelis were alarmed at the news, for until then the British had exerted a certain restraining influence on Egyptian adventures in the Middle East. At this point, therefore, Colonel Benyamin Gibli, chief of army intelligence, devised a plot calculated to forestall an early British evacuation. The plan was to dynamite a number of American and British buildings in Egypt, thus seeming to demonstrate the "irresponsibility" of the Nasserist regime and, it was hoped, persuading the British to remain on. Orders were now sent back to the Jewish network to begin operations in Alexandria and Cairo.

Throughout July of 1954, as a result, homemade bombs exploded in post office buildings, public checkrooms, movie theaters, and United States information centers and consulates in Cairo and Alexandria. Damage was slight and there were no injuries. A weapon ignited accidentally, however, in the pocket of one of the Jewish spies. The wounded saboteur was arrested, his living quarters raided, and much incriminating evidence was found, including names. Other members of the network were immediately seized and put on trial. In Israel, Prime Minister Sharett expressed outrage at the "despicable slanders designed to harass the Jews in Egypt"—until he was discreetly alerted to the facts by Israeli army intelligence. The trial in Cairo rapidly unfolded in the full glare of Egyptian publicity. By the time it ended, on January 27, 1955, one of the accused had committed suicide, two others had been sentenced to death and were later hanged, and all but two of the remaining defendants had received sentences varying from seven years to life imprisonment. The episode damaged more than Israel's intelligence underground in Egypt. It blemished the Jewish state's reputation for credibility in the eyes of Britain and the United States.

Not least of all, the failure produced an embittered internecine struggle between Lavon and his colleagues. The moment the plot backfired, Prime Minister Sharett questioned Lavon, who angrily disclaimed any advance knowledge of the operation. He was, however, contradicted by Colonel Gibli, who insisted that the plan had been cleared in advance by the defense minister. Sharett thereupon appointed an impartial commission of inquiry consisting of Supreme Court Justice Yitzchak Olshan and Technion President Ya'akov Dori. But after extensive interrogation, the two men were unable to produce conclusive findings that Lavon had authorized Gibli to carry out the operation. In the interval, Lavon sought to dismiss Shimon Peres, director-general of his ministry, and Gibli, who had issued the order for the Egyptian operation; these men were guilty of insubordination at the least, Lavon insisted, and of criminal negligence at the worst. Yet if Sharett had agreed at this point to uphold the defense minister, he would have lost several of the army's highest-ranking officers. Consequently he chose to support Peres. Lavon promptly tendered his resignation in February 1955. As events developed, Lavon's burning sense of grievance was destined years later to effect a tumultuous upheaval in Israel's political life (Chapter xix).

Upon Lavon's resignation, meanwhile, Ben-Gurion himself returned from his desert retirement to assume his former position as defense minister. The "old man" by then was no longer prepared to tolerate repeated acts of Egyptian belligerence, including the closure of Suez to Israeli-bound shipping, the ongoing blockade of the Gulf of Aqaba, and particularly the mounting cycle of Egyptian-directed fedayun raids. On February 28, therefore, only six days after Ben-Gurion's return to office, the Israeli army launched a reprisal of brigade strength against Egyptian military headquarters at Gaza, blowing up a number of buildings, killing thirty-eight Egyptian troops and wounding twenty-four. Although the raid was described as a response to a succession of major Egyptian provocations, it was also intended to make plain to Cairo Israel's decisive military superiority. For Nasser, on the other hand, the attack served as an ideal pretext for the Czech arms deal. "February 28, 1955, was the turning point," he declared later. "This disaster was the alarm bell. We at once started to examine the significance of peace and the balance of power in the area." General Burns, the UNTSO chief of staff, endorsed this view. So did a number of Israelis, including Eban, who afterward stated: "I don't believe [Gaza] was the only reason but at least the excuse was there." It was only the excuse, for the policy of blockade and organized fedayun operations had considerably predated the Gaza raid, as had Nasser's decision to secure a major arsenal for undermining the Baghdad Pact.

By mid-1955 the Egyptian-directed guerrilla campaign had moved into high gear. Burns admitted later that "what the Egyptians were doing in sending in these men . . . with the mission to attack men, women, and children indiscriminately was a war crime." In reaction to the intensified violence, Ben-Gurion and Dayan authorized a series of harsh retaliatory raids against the Egyptian garrison of Khan Yunis, against al-Auja, against even the city of Gaza, as well as against Jordanian fedayun bases. By the spring of 1956 UN observers were speculating that Israel was preparing a major preemptive strike before the Egyptian army could assimilate its huge quantities of Soviet equipment. The speculation was not farfetched. The blockade of the Gulf of Aqaba was known to be particularly galling to the Jews. Since 1953 the Egyptian coast guard unit at Ras Nasrani had closed off Israeli shipping through the Strait of Tiran, and in September 1955 the Egyptians similarly turned back the vessels of other nations bound for Israel's port of Eilat. El Al flights to South Africa that had routinely overflown the strait were now foreclosed.

His patience exhausted, Ben-Gurion on October 22 ordered Dayan to make preparations for capturing the Strait of Tiran, including Sharm es-Sheikh, Ras Nasrani, and the islands of Tiran and Sanafir. The chief of staff immediately set about organizing an elite task force of paratroopers and infantry under the command of Colonel Chaim Bar-Lev. At a cabinet meeting soon afterward, Ben-Gurion (who in November also had resumed office as prime minister) formally raised the issue of a preemptive campaign. His ministerial colleagues rejected it. Dayan protested the decision. Time was working against Israel, the general insisted; the infusion of Soviet weaponry into Egypt was drastically shifting the Middle Eastern balance of power. Ben-Gurion endorsed this warning. The Israeli assault would have to be launched sooner or later. The one missing ingredient was adequate equipment.

THE SEARCH FOR AN ALLY

In late 1955 the first shipments of Soviet bloc arms began to reach Egypt, and the astonishing scale of this weaponry evoked a "backs to the wall" psychology in Israel. Tens of thousands of volunteers, young and old, took up picks and shovels and set about digging trenches and preparing fieldworks. Citizens contributed money, even jewelry, for the weapons fund. Schoolchildren gave their lunch money. The arsenals remained inadequately stocked. Over the years, the Israelis had strained themselves to the limit to build their defenses. Between 1950 and 1956, the nation's military expenditures represented at least a third of total government consumption. Averaging 7.2 percent of the GNP, the disbursements in fact were proportionately heavier than those of all the Arab states combined.

Nor were the results of this effort negligible. By 1955, Israel managed not only to organize its defense establishment, but also to acquire some 200 tanks and 200 planes. On the other hand, most of these were obsolescent British and American equipment and insufficient in both quantity and quality. The Czech arms deal threatened to give the Arabs a weapons superiority of six to one.

Israel's quest for modern arms was hardly more productive than its search for territorial guarantees. The United States had no intention of matching the Czechoslovakian supplies that were going to Egypt. The December 11 raid against Syria (Chapter XVI) had not raised Israel's stock in Washington, while Dulles in any case professed to see no immediate danger to the Jewish republic. On February 7, 1956, the secretary of state informed a group of congressmen that Israel would invariably lose an arms race against the Arabs. Its population was less than 2 million, he explained, and its security would be better assured by reliance upon the United Nations. Fully endorsing this view, President Eisenhower remarked to French Prime Minister Guy Mollet that there was no point in selling arms to Israel inasmuch as 1,700,000 Jews could not possibly defend themselves against 40 million Arabs.

Whatever Mollet's response to this observation, it was in France, nevertheless, that Israel's search for weapons at last began to bear fruit. The French government would still have preferred to ensure Moslem goodwill in North Africa and the Levant. Even so, Israel knew that it could depend here upon certain traditional sources of understanding. The French Left maintained a pro-Jewish sympathy extending back to the Dreyfus affair and forward to the Socialist regimes that governed in both countries. The French Right, too, shared with Israel a common fear of rising Arab nationalism. French-Israeli scientific contacts had begun as early as 1949, when it was learned that an Israeli physicist, Dr. Israel Dostrovski, had invented a technique for producing heavy water. Acquiring the process in 1953, France secretly opened many of its own nuclear installations to Israeli scientists. The following year, the French ministry of defense invited Dayan for a visit. The dashing Israeli general made a great impression in Paris and was inducted into the Legion of Honor "in recognition of his heroism during the Syrian expedition of 1941." By autumn of 1954, too, relations between Paris and Cairo were deteriorating alarmingly, as the Egyptian radio broadcast effusive assurances of support to the rebel Algerian FLN. In December, finally, the French government approved an Israeli order for twelve Ouragon jet fighters.

It was at this point that Ben-Gurion returned to the Israeli defense ministry and accepted the contention of Shimon Peres, the ministry's director-general, that all efforts now should be exerted to developing a relationship with Paris, rather than with Washington. Polish-born, only thirty-two years old at the time, Peres was revolutionizing the defense ministry, bringing under its jurisdiction Israel's armaments industry, expanding the production of local weapons, fostering nuclear research and development. An imaginative, articulate man, Peres demonstrated uncommon skill in negotiating on Israel's behalf with French defense officials. So, too, during this period, did Israel's ambassador in Paris, the eloquent, Sorbonne-educated Ya'akov Tsur. In January 1955, when the Mendès-France government was succeeded by the cabinet of Edgar Faure, Tsur encouraged Peres to visit France to establish personal contact there with defense ministry officials. The suggestion was followed, with good results. Peres, and later Dayan and other Israeli officers, found a growing understanding among their French counterparts. If the Soviet-Egyptian arms pact lent renewed urgency to Franco-Israeli discussions, so did Nasser's intensified campaign of support for the Algerian rebels. "I've always been a friend of Israel," Faure assured Prime Minister Sharett, who visited Paris on October 25, 1955, "but now it is not a question of friendship. It is for reasons of political realism that France is called upon to help you. . . ." Thereupon arrangements were made for the shipment of twelve additional Ouragons and—for the first time—twelve of the new Mystère-4 fighters, considered the equal of the MiG-17s the Egyptians were receiving.

The shipment of Mystères, as it turned out, almost immediately became bogged down in complications with the United States. The NATO command in Europe enjoyed first priority on these jet interceptors, and Dulles was unwilling to see them diverted to Israel. At his insistence, fighters loaded with arms for Israel were immobilized in the ports of Marseilles and Toulon. Yet at this critical juncture Peres had a stroke of good fortune. He met and became warm friends with Maurice Bourgès-Maunoury, the French minister of the interior, and with Abel Thomas, the ministry's director-general. Veterans of the Maquis, the French wartime underground, Bourgès-Maunoury and Thomas evinced a sympathetic interest in Israel that considerably predated their common antipathy to Nasser. Moreover, in January 1956 the French elections returned a new Socialist government under the leadership of Guy Mollet, a protégé of Léon Blum and an ardent admirer of Socialist Israel. One of the prime minister's first moves was to transfer Bourgès-Maunoury and Thomas to the ministry of defense. "Now you will see that I will not be a Bevin," Mollet assured Peres and Tsur. Determined to resist Nasser's burgeoning power by any and all means, Mollet informed Washington that the Mystères would be sent off to Israel, with or without American approval. Henceforth, as far as Mollet was concerned, the best means of sustaining French influence in the Middle East was through help to the Israelis. While this mutual interest played a role, and increasingly so as Egyptian weapons were transshipped to the Algerian FLN, the basis of Franco-Israeli friendship developed into something more romantic. The French people experienced a certain moral uplift by helping "courageous little Israel." The French government, too, in adopting this course, projected a younger and more vigorous image—and notably by contrast to the rival Communist party.

In March 1956 a contingent of Israeli pilots arrived in France to receive instruction in operating the Mystères. Several weeks later, the twelve jets landed at an Israeli military airfield, where they were met personally by Ben-Gurion and Dayan (the euphoric prime minister insisted on drinking tea with the young pilots). It was the merest beginning of Western support for Israel's needs. By April, Dulles himself was becoming increasingly alarmed at the shifting power balance in the Middle East. Although determined not to involve the United States directly in the provisioning of Israel, the secretary of state relinquished NATO's claim on further Mystère shipments to the Israelis. Indeed, he went further, requesting the Canadian government to provide Israel with a squadron of American-licensed jets. France remained the principal supplier, however. On July 4, Foreign Minister Christian Pineau informed Ambassador Tsur that all former limitations on weapons delivery to Israel were now ended, irrespective of American or British policy. Paris would reserve its own liberty of action in supplying France's "true friends."

NASSER ISSUES A CHALLENGE

In February 1956, British Foreign Secretary Selwyn Lloyd arrived in Cairo, hopeful at the last moment of reaching an understanding with the Egyptian president. Notwithstanding the Arab shift away from the West, Lloyd warned Nasser on March 1 that "we still have Glubb and the [Arab] Legion." Thereupon Nasser archly informed his visitor that King Hussein had just exiled Glubb from Jordan. Lloyd returned to England furious at this palpable evidence of Egyptian subversion. On March 14, French Foreign Minister Pineau similarly visited Cairo in a bid to normalize Franco-Egyptian relations. During their meeting, Nasser assured his visitor that Egypt henceforth would refrain from supporting the Algerian FLN. The promise was belied the very next day when an Egyptian vessel was intercepted off the Algerian coast loaded to the gunwales with Soviet-manufactured weapons.

Ironically, the West's final break with Cairo was precipitated by a matter related entirely to local Egyptian economic development. Nasser's most cherished domestic project for his nation was the Aswan High Dam on the Nile. The cost of the undertaking was estimated at $1 billion. On February 9, 1956, the World Bank agreed to lend Cairo $200 million of the sum, contingent upon an American loan of $56 million and a British loan of $14 million, as well as upon a commitment by Egypt itself for $700 million. Yet by then the United States had moved close to participation in the Baghdad Pact. In response, Nasser mortgaged a further $200 million of unplanted cotton for additional Soviet bloc arms, and on May 5 reached agreement to coordinate the armies of Egypt and Jordan. With the polarization of the Middle East well dramatized, and Iraq partially outflanked, the British and American governments took an increasingly jaundiced view of Nasser and the Aswan project. Their suspicions were compounded on May 16, when the Egyptian foreign ministry announced its recognition of Communist China. The following month Soviet Foreign Minister Dimitri Shepilov appeared in Cairo to offer an interest-free loan of $120 million. This sequence of events was too much for Washington; Nasser clearly was playing one side against the other. It was in any case doubtful whether Egypt, with its expensive new arms purchases, would be able to repay the interest and capital on a sizable loan. On July 19, therefore, Dulles formally notified the Egyptian ambassador that Washington was retracting its offer of funds. The United States would not submit to blackmail. Two days later, London similarly withdrew its own offer, and the World Bank loan in turn was dropped.

In fact, Nasser had cards of his own up his sleeve. He had anticipated the Western reaction, and intended to use cancellation of the loan as his pretext for nationalizing the Suez Canal. The move had been under consideration since 1954, although it was not until June 1956, with the evacuation of the last British troops, that the chance existed for swift and painless action. By then, too, the international balance in the Middle East had shifted, thanks to the advent of the Soviets. Accordingly, on July 26, as part of the week-long celebration commemorating the fourth anniversary of the Colonels' Revolution, Nasser addressed a huge crowd in Alexandria. After describing the negotiations with Britain and the United States, and urging the Americans to "go choke on your fury," Nasser proceeded to drop his bombshell: the Suez Canal Company was being nationalized, and its future revenues henceforth would be applied to the construction of the Aswan Dam. That night there was delirium throughout Egypt. Nasser was hailed as a national hero. His domestic position had never been more secure, nor his reputation in the Arab world higher.

Upon receiving word of this development, Eden called an emergency meeting of his cabinet. Of all Western nations, it was Britain that was most directly affected by the sequestration. Its government owned a controlling interest in the company's shares. Nearly a quarter of British imports passed through the Canal, and a third of the ships using the waterway were British. At stake, too, was Britain's general prestige in the Arab world. Eden was in no position to accept this latest affront. The pressures on him to adopt a tough attitude were compelling, and emanated not only from his own party but from many Laborites. The prime minister in any event hardly needed a reminder of the fruits of appeasement. Neither did Mollet, whose anti-Munich reflex was as strong as Eden's, and who had frequently characterized Nasser as the "Hitler of the Nile." Socialists, Gaullists, and Radicals alike in Mollet's cabinet detested "Nasserism" and all its implications for the Maghreb. At this point, then, both the French and British governments ordered their civilians evacuated from Egypt.

In the United States, on the other hand, it was an election year. Eisenhower was campaigning as the Prince of Peace. American dependence on Suez hardly matched that of the Western allies. Only 15 percent of United States oil imports passed through the Canal, while American investments in the Canal Company were negligible. Moreover, the vindictive temper of London and Paris quite appalled Eisenhower, who shared Dulles's view that there was no legal case for force. Thus, at the president's instructions, the secretary of state immediately departed for London on August 1, with a mandate to prevent armed intervention at all costs. Reluctantly, Eden and Mollet acceded to Dulles's request for an urgent conference of maritime powers. And during the conference itself, which began in London on August 16, majority agreement was reached in less than a week. The participants issued a declaration recognizing Egypt's sovereign right to a fair return on the use of the Canal, but insisting on international control of the waterway. It was an exercise in futility. On September 9, Nasser rejected the London Declaration.

Anglo-French military preparations thereafter gained momentum. As early as August 5, a joint team of staff officers had begun work on a plan for landings in Egypt. A combined headquarters was established in London with branches in Paris, Malta, and Cyprus. The impending operation was eventually dubbed "Musketeer." Its assigned commander was General Sir Charles Keightley, with French Vice-Admiral d'Escarde Barjot as his deputy. The plans were for Britain to contribute the bomber force and part of the fighter force, as well as 50,000 men. The French in turn would contribute several fighter squadrons and 30,000 men. A combined naval armada was envisaged of over 100 British warships, 30 French vessels, and hundreds of landing craft. Not less than 7 aircraft carriers were to be gathered, as well as approximately 20,000 vehicles. While several thousand airborne troops would be used for initial, tactical landings, it was estimated that the bulk of the expeditionary force would reach Egypt by sea on September 15. Following thirty-six hours of air bombardment, British and French paratroopers would then drop to the south of Alexandria. Other seaborne divisions would be unloaded on the beaches. Once having captured Alexandria, the joint Allied force would advance on the main Egyptian army and on Cairo. Planning for the vast operation was almost as intricate as for the Normandy invasion of 1944. Indeed, the French saw little reason for these elaborate preparations. Their troops had fought in Indochina, their equipment had been adapted in recent wars, and they much preferred a quick, simple knockout of Nasser. Although for the time being the British had their way, the French later would return to their own approach.

News soon filtered through to Washington of what was happening. Gravely concerned, Eisenhower dispatched a stern letter to Eden on September 2, warning against the use of force. Eden replied vigorously, comparing Nasser to Hitler and stating that "it would be an ignoble end to our long history if we accepted to perish by degrees." Washington persisted, and two days later Dulles transmitted to the Allies a scheme for a Suez Canal Users' Association that would at least partially "manage" the waterway. Despite his skepticism, Eden persuaded his own cabinet and the French at least to explore the idea. It soon became clear, however, that Dulles had no intention of exerting more than verbal pressure to induce Egypt to accept the plan. Eden was now certain that Dulles, that "terrible man," had consciously deceived him. Worse yet, the Egyptian government by then was using both its own and hired foreign pilots to direct ships through the Canal, and they managed the job efficiently. Exasperated, but constrained by American pressure to hold off a military offensive, Eden and Mollet put their case before the Security Council on September 23. The move failed; the Soviets vetoed any meaningful resolution of censure against Egypt. As far as the two Western prime ministers were concerned, then, all peaceful recourse was exhausted. D-Day was now tentatively set for October 8. The one change in strategy was to abandon the Alexandria plan, to shift the objective to Port Saïd, and to place greater reliance upon air bombardment before the paratroop and amphibious landings. It was precisely this alteration, in turn, that opened up the opportunity of collaboration with Israel (p. 489).

Meanwhile, Nasser's self-assurance in dealing with the British and French was fully equaled in his intensified campaign against Israel. As far back as March 1956, another cycle of infiltration and retaliation had begun along the Gaza demarcation zone. On March 22, eleven Israeli settlers were wounded near G'vulot, opposite the Strip. On April 3 an Israeli soldier was killed and three were wounded during a clash in the Nirim area. On April 4, three Israeli soldiers were killed near Kisufim. Following a day of heavy mortar exchanges, an Israeli shelling of Gaza on April 5 killed fifty-six of the town's inhabitants. A few days later, yet a new series of fedayun raids took place, and by April 11 nearly a dozen Israeli civilians had been killed and more injured; among the victims were five children in a religious boarding school near Ramle. All the while, the Egyptian press hailed the fedayeen in extravagant terms, acclaiming them as "heroes back from the battlefield."

On June 19, Nasser made his intentions toward Israel clear in a public speech: "We must be strong in order to regain the rights of the Palestinians by force." Abd al-Hakim Amer, commander in chief of the Egyptian army, informed his troops on July 5: "The hour is approaching when [we] . . . will stand in the front ranks of the battle against imperialism and its Zionist ally." Earlier, Shukri al-Quwatli, president of Syria and Nasser's ally, declared: "The present situation demands the mobilization of all Arab strength to liquidate the state that has arisen in our region." On July 26, Hussein of Jordan wired Nasser: "We look forward to the future when the Arab flag will fly over our great stolen country." Nasser was at the apogee of his strength. Only the destruction of Israel remained to clinch his position as a modern Saladin. Between July 29 and September 25, therefore, Egyptian-trained fedayeen assaulted Israel from bases in Gaza, Jordan, and Syria, killing another nineteen Israelis and wounding twenty-eight.

By then, too, a final confrontation had taken place between Ben-Gurion and his foreign minister, Moshe Sharett. The latter remained a principled advocate of moderation, essentially a genteel diplomat of the old school, conscious of the limitations of small-state diplomacy, and mortally fearful that large-scale reprisals would antagonize public opinion in the West. After the Lake Galilee operation against Syria (Chapter xvi), Sharett protested that Israel's overreaction had defeated his efforts to acquire arms from the United States. It was nevertheless the view of the foreign minister's critics—Ben-Gurion, Dayan, large elements within Mapai, as well as the entire Cherut party—that all earlier and repeated efforts at moderation had accomplished nothing except to intensify Nasser's belligerence. When Ben-Gurion privately mooted his intentions sooner or later to break the Egyptian blockade of Aqaba, Sharett sensed that his days as foreign minister were numbered. And indeed, on June 18, 1956, Ben-Gurion asked for his old comrade's resignation and replaced him with Mrs. Golda Meir, the former minister of labor. The groundwork was laid for vigorous action against Israel's principal enemy. The elections of 1955, almost doubling Cherut's representation in the Knesset, had made evident the way Israeli public opinion was veering. Ben-Gurion now searched only for the decisive moment to act.

ISRAEL IS BROUGHT INTO THE PICTURE

France supplied the opportunity. In his memoirs of the Suez episode, General André Beaufré, the French air commander, explained later: "Actually our commitment to Israel originated from the spell that Israeli dynamism—compared to the hesitant attitude of the British—cast over the officers whom we dispatched there *en mission.*" In early August 1956, Bourgès-Maunoury sent for Peres, who had been shuttling on supply missions between Tel Aviv and Paris, and asked: "If we make war on Egypt, would Israel be prepared to fight alongside us?" Instantly, Peres said yes. Nothing further was said for the time being, but the conversation was Peres's first intimation that extraordinary new possibilities were developing. Ten days later he was cautiously informed that an Anglo-French attack was indeed being prepared against Egypt. Finally, early in September, Bourgès-Maunoury asked Peres straight out if Israel would attack Egypt on October 20 in conjunction with the French and British. It was evident by then that the French leadership was interested not only in a pretext for Allied invasion, but in a carefully structured, two-pronged offensive against Nasser. An Israeli ground attack through Sinai would enable the British and French to shift their emphasis from an extensive amphibious operation to more limited paratroop assaults on the Canal Zone.

Peres immediately referred the matter to Ben-Gurion. He cabled Jerusalem twice, but received no answer. Flying back to Israel several days later, he and Dayan discussed the matter with Ben-Gurion personally. Still the prime minister made no comment. Finally, in mid-September, Bourgès-Maunoury and his staff began to press Colonel Nishri, the Israeli military attaché in Paris, warning that the price of French support was nothing less than Israel's collaboration in the impending operation, and at a time close to the American elections, when Eisenhower, it was hoped, would be unable to react. On September 23, Ben-Gurion cabled Peres, who had returned to Paris: "Tell them that their dates suit us," the wire said. The commitment was made.

Upon informing Bourgès-Maunoury, however, Peres coupled Ben-Gurion's acquiescence with a demand for immediate and larger shipments of French supplies. On September 29, Dayan and Golda Meir flew to Paris on a French bomber, bringing their shopping list with them. In addition to the weapons and jet planes already on order, the Israeli requirements included 100 medium tanks, 300 half-tracks, 50 tank transporters, 300 trucks, 1,000 recoilless rifles, and a squadron of Nord-Atlas transport planes. General Paul Ely, the French chief of staff, accepted this list on the spot. The shipments began at once, and although they took place in secrecy, a general awareness of renewed French support invigorated the entire Israeli nation. The poet Natan Alterman was allowed to witness the nocturnal unloading of a French LST and described it in veiled but exultant terms:

> Perhaps this is a night of dreams, but wide awake, and
>   What it saw was the melting away of the terror gap
> Between us and the forces of destruction. Iron comes
>   On steadily and the bowels of the earth tremble. . . .

On October 2, Dayan revealed to his senior staff what was afoot. The purpose of the impending campaign, he explained, was to wipe out the Egyptian army in Sinai, to destroy the fedayun bases in Gaza, and to open up the Strait of Tiran. Only eighteen days were left for preparations before the target date of the twentieth. Elsewhere, in civilian circles, all was silence.

The question preying on Ben-Gurion's mind was the attitude of the British in the event of hostilities. His concern was justified. When news of the emergent Franco-Israeli collaboration was transmitted from Paris to London on September 24, Eden was incredulous. He disliked the scheme intensely, fearing that it would strain Britain's relations with other Arab countries. Moreover, until then, dealings between Britain and Israel had been less than encouraging. Nor did they appear likely to improve with Israel launching reprisal raids against Britain's treaty partner, Jordan. On September 11, for example, in retaliation for a guerrilla attack that had killed six Israeli soldiers, the Israeli army struck hard at the Jordanian post at Qariya, killing sixteen Arab Legionnaires. In the wake of subsequent fedayun attacks from Hashemite territory, a brigade of Israeli troops assaulted Jordanian positions at Husan on September 25, inflicting several dozen casualties. Other raids and counterraids followed, reaching their apogee on the night of October 11, when Israel launched a massive retaliation against the Jordanian police fortress of Qalqilia. Tanks, artillery, and eventually planes were used in a savage battle that approached full-scale warfare.

By then Hussein was sufficiently shaken to demand invocation of the Anglo-Jordanian defense treaty. On October 12, therefore, the British chargé d'affaires in Tel Aviv informed Ben-Gurion that an Iraqi division was about to enter Jordan to "protect" the smaller country. In the event Israel took military action, Britain would be obliged to come to Jordan's aid under both the Anglo-Jordanian Treaty of 1948 and the Tripartite Declaration of 1950. The prime minister did not flinch. Israel would reserve its freedom of action, he replied. Privately, however, Ben-Gurion was astonished by London's attitude at a moment when Israel, with French assistance, was preparing an offensive against Britain's enemy, Nasser. Dayan, for his part, was utterly exasperated. "I must confess to the feeling," he noted in his diary of the Sinai Campaign, "that, save for the Almighty, only the British are capable of complicating affairs to such a degree." Eventually, on October 16, Eden and Lloyd met with Mollet and Pineau in Paris, and in a five-hour conference reached extensive understanding at last on the desirability of Israeli military collaboration against Nasser. Hereupon the British statesmen finally shifted gears and called off their Jordanian plans. Pineau sent a reassuring cable to Ben-Gurion: "You can have complete trust in the British." It was at that moment that the Israeli premier suddenly chose to push the date of attack back from October 20.

Ben-Gurion was concerned, first of all, with the need for air cover. An Israeli attack in Sinai would risk heavy Egyptian bombing attacks against Israeli cities. Indeed, Operation Musketeer might never begin at all, leaving Israel exposed in Sinai with Egypt controlling the air. As it was, the Allies already had hinted to Israel that they were changing their plans—on the assumption of an Israeli invasion—from a broad-front amphibious landing to a more limited plan for paratroop landings along the Canal. Who knew how much further the Allies might attenuate their own participation? Certainly the role Britain was proposing for Israel (via Paris) was unacceptable to Ben-Gurion and Dayan. That was for the Israeli army to advance in great strength and on a broad front in Sinai and to mount a heavy attack that would threaten Cairo. It would be a real war, and the Allied forces thereby could intervene as saviors of the peace. Selwyn Lloyd, the foreign secretary, had even proposed an indiscriminate air bombardment of Israeli and Egyptian armies on either side of the Canal, thus demonstrating to the world that the British were concerned only with safeguarding the waterway. Either of these schemes was out of the question for Ben-Gurion, of course. His aim was simply to clear the Egyptians from the Gaza Strip and end their blockade of the Strait of Tiran. An advance on the Canal, let alone Cairo, was the last thing the Israeli prime minister had in mind. Clarifications were urgently necessary.

On October 22, shortly before dawn, a French air force plane carrying Ben-Gurion, Dayan, and Peres touched down on a little-used airstrip at Villa Coublay, southwest of Paris. The Israelis were immediately driven to nearby Sèvres, where a small, inconspicuous house had been placed at their disposal. Later in the day Pineau arrived, accompanied by Bourgès-Maunoury and Thomas. The following morning, Mollet arrived at the villa. In an emotion-packed meeting, Ben-Gurion outlined to the French statesmen the mortal danger facing his country, the importance of destroying the fedayun bases and breaking Nasser's stranglehold on Israel's economy. If Israel were to run the awesome risk of invading Sinai, its cities had to be protected. "Monsieur Mollet," said Ben-Gurion, "you are a member of the Resistance, a Socialist, and a democrat. You cannot allow us to perish." Originally it had not been Mollet's intention to commit France beyond its participation in Operation Musketeer. Appalled, however, at the prospect of another mass Jewish extermination, the French leader instinctively reassured Ben-Gurion: "I shall not allow these things to happen." By lunchtime the two prime ministers had reached formal agreement that the French air force would provide cover for Israel's major cities and that French warships would guard the Israeli coast. Israel would mobilize on October 26, just three days away; French Mystère squadrons would arrive in Israel throughout October 27 and October 28, and French warships would reach their positions off the Israeli coast by October 29, the date Ben-Gurion now set for the attack on Sinai. Abel Thomas also undertook to have French planes, operating from Cyprus, drop supplies to Israeli armored columns as they advanced across the peninsula.

But the Israeli leaders had arrived in Paris to secure yet additional assurances. These were certainty of British involvement and a more modest scheme contrived for Israel. Eventually it was Dayan who proposed his government's compromise formula. Israel would carry out a limited offensive—"more than a raid, less than a war"—an operation that would be interpreted as threatening the Canal and justifying Allied intervention to safeguard it. During the next two hours Ben-Gurion began to reap the benefits of his stubbornness. The French liked Dayan's idea, and it was the pretext suggested to Selwyn Lloyd when the British foreign secretary arrived at Sèvres that afternoon—the twenty-third—accompanied by Patrick Dean, the Foreign Office official charged with Middle Eastern affairs. Both men accepted the Israeli plan.

By evening, when the session closed, the main lines of action had been agreed upon. Israel would strike first on October 29, dropping paratroops east of the Canal area, and would announce the operation over the radio. Britain and France would then address a joint ultimatum to Israel and Egypt to cease military activity. Israel would accept, but would not be obliged actually to observe the cease-fire until its troops advanced to a line 10 miles east of the Canal. In fact, the Israelis would have twelve hours to reach this point. Egypt meanwhile would almost certainly reject the discriminatory Allied conditions. At that point the RAF and the French air force would attack Egyptian airfields, destroying Nasser's planes on the ground, thus removing all fear of Israeli cities being bombed, and of course eliminating a threat against the prospective Anglo-French landings. Finally, Allied troops would land along the Canal and seize the waterway. The earlier French agreement, to supply air and naval protection to Israeli cities and to parachute supplies to Israeli units in Sinai, was not revealed to the British. The next day, October 24, the draft of this tripartite "Treaty of Sèvres" was completed. It included political features as well as military. France would defend Israel's interests at the United Nations. Britain would not, lest its influence among the other Arab states be compromised irretrievably. Even so, Britain would exert private influence on Israel's behalf and would be friendly to Israel's territorial claims should the United Nations press for a general peace settlement. The document was signed by

Pineau, Patrick Dean, and Ben-Gurion, with the understanding that it should never be published. The participants then dispersed.

Returning to Israel on October 25, Dayan issued his staff a revised schedule of orders for "Operation Kadesh." Emphasis now would be laid on posing a threat to the Suez Canal; only afterward would the underlying purpose of the campaign develop—that is, Israeli capture of Sharm es-Sheikh (thus opening the Strait of Tiran), destruction of the fedayun bases, and defeat of the Egyptian forces. Two days later, on October 27, French LSTs were discharging additional heavy equipment at Israeli ports, and a French naval flotilla was approaching Israeli waters. That evening, too, a squadron of French Nord-Atlas transport planes arrived from Cyprus with equipment and technicians. Finally, two squadrons of French-piloted Mystères and Thunderstreaks, withdrawn from French NATO forces, landed at Israeli military airfields to assure protection for Israel's cities. They were not tactically linked to the sixty Mystères provided Israel's air force earlier. It is of interest, too, that Israel's own Mystère squadrons were never fully operational. The Israelis managed to fly only sixteen of the planes during the war, and French pilots operated twenty others. Dayan was not exaggerating when he wrote later: "Had it not been for the Anglo-French operation, it is doubtful whether Israel would have launched her campaign." At most, an offensive would have been limited specifically to breaking the Egyptian grip on Israel's southern shipping route from Eilat.

OPERATION KADESH IS LAUNCHED

Until the last moment, the Israeli government skillfully disguised its intentions. As the fedayun attacks gained in momentum, and as Nasser absorbed his vast quantities of new Soviet weapons, Ben-Gurion steadfastly resisted Cherut appeals for a preemptive war. In late August the prime minister assured a Mapai congress that "the first principle of our policy is to maintain the peace—even a bad peace, to the extent that this depends upon us." In a seventieth-birthday interview on September 21, Ben-Gurion told a reporter: "As long as it is for me to decide, we shall make no war. . . . I will never make war. Never." In any case, by October the most volatile of the nation's frontiers was still regarded as the one shared with Jordan. Israel's heaviest reprisal actions were taking place along this sawtoothed eastern boundary. On October 3, the foreign ministry announced that it was withdrawing its representatives from the Israel-Jordanian Mixed Armistice Commission. On October 11, the massive retaliatory raid against Qalqilia seemed to portend even more far-reaching hostilities, and, it is recalled, evoked the British warning of October 12. Additionally, in late October, as plans for the Sinai campaign—Operation Kadesh—gained momentum, Israeli intelligence circulated rumors of impending war against Jordan. The accounts were given credibility on October 24, when a tripartite military agreement was signed among Egypt, Syria, and Jordan. With the chain tightening around Israel, there appeared a certain logic in a preemptive attack against its weakest link. Taking the threat with full gravity, the Hashemite state feverishly reinforced its defenses. When it became evident on October 27 that the Israeli defense forces were mobilizing, General Burns and his UNTSO staff were similarly convinced that Jordan was the intended target.

That day, too, Eisenhower personally cabled Ben-Gurion, expressing urgent concern. Two days later the president cabled again, emphasizing that United States intelligence sources had found no evidence of "Iraqi troops entering Jordan" and requesting "that there be no forcible initiative on the part of your Government which would endanger the peace and the growing friendship between our two countries." Yet by then the outbreak of the Hungarian Revolution, and its suppression by invading Soviet forces, had claimed world attention, and Ben-Gurion was convinced that the tumultuous events in eastern Europe would totally absorb the diplomatic efforts of both Washington and the Security Council. There would never be a more opportune moment for Israel to attack. On October 27, therefore, the prime minister at last revealed the plan for Operation Kadesh to his cabinet colleagues and secured their approval. Ben-Gurion admitted to the ministers:

> I do not know what will be the fate of Sinai. What we are primarily interested in is the coast around Eilat and the Gulf. I imagine that there will be Powers who will force us to withdraw. There is America, there is Russia, and there are the United Nations, Nehru, Asia, Africa; and I must say that I fear America most of all. America may compel us to withdraw from positions we will occupy—but the important point is freedom of shipping.

Operation Kadesh had to allow for a number of military and diplomatic contingencies. Even as Dayan prepared to fulfill his obligations under the Treaty of Sèvres by creating a "threat" to the Suez Canal—thus opening the door to Anglo-French intervention—he knew that he would have to act circumspectly, lest the Egyptians commit their air force and the bulk of their armor. As a result, he evolved what was less a detailed operational plan than an anticipated series of fluid movements along east-west axes. He gambled that speed and daring would compensate for tactical obstacles. Those obstacles surely existed. One was the awesome expanse of the Sinai itself. The peninsula was 24,000 square miles of desolation, inhabited by perhaps 40,000 nomadic Bedouin and possessing no settled life or communications to speak of. A few small villages—al-Thamd, al-Qusseima, Nakhl—subsisted at the junction of camel tracks, but little more. In the north, the terrain at best was pure desert and rolling sand dunes, and at worst, in the south, it consisted of almost impassable mountain ranges, some peaks climbing to 9,000 feet. Only one ridge of high ground, traversing Sinai from north to south, and through it the Mitla and Gidi passes, offered passage to and from the Canal and integral Egypt.

Taking this bleak terrain into account, Dayan's plan for the first night at dusk, October 29, was to drop a battalion of paratroops near the Mitla Pass, 40 miles from the Canal and 180 miles overland from the Israeli border. Other battalions of the brigade would move along the southern axis of the peninsula and link up with the paratroops within thirty-six hours. At one stroke, then, the Israelis would "threaten" the Canal, triggering the Anglo-French expedition to eliminate the Egyptian air force and at the same time confusing the Egyptians. With a brigade loose in central Sinai and paratroops at Mitla, the Egyptian command would have to decide whether or not the Israelis were serious. Dayan was optimistic that their reaction would be sluggish and uncertain. But if things went badly for Israel in Sinai, or on the international scene, the whole brigade could be pulled back and Operation Kadesh passed off as a retaliatory raid.

The second stage of the offensive was only slightly more orthodox. After a pause of twenty-four hours, a second, larger Israeli force would move out of the Negev and push west toward Ismailia on the Canal. The final stage of the operation, farther to the north, was comparatively straightforward. It would be reminiscent of Allon's final campaign in the War of Independence (Chapter XIII), a swift hook into Rafa to amputate the Egyptian coastal strip. Once Rafa had fallen, another brigade would clean out the Gaza Strip. Simultaneously, a brigade would move down the uninhabited eastern shore of Sinai toward Sharm es-Sheikh, at the tip of the Gulf of Aqaba. By then, it was hoped, the Egyptians would be paralyzed and incapable of response. The morale and prestige of their army would have been shattered, the fedayun menace ended at Gaza, and the Gulf of Aqaba opened.

The second major obstacle beyond the terrain of the Sinai itself was the newly equipped Egyptian army and air force. Dayan was not inclined to overrate this threat. The poor quality of Egyptian pilots and maintenance staffs was notorious. There was little doubt that the mobilized strength of the regular Egyptian army had grown impressively by 1956. It came to nearly 100,000 men, most of them equipped with first-rate weapons. Yet even in the "new" Egyptian army the identical class divisions of the old Farouk era lingered between officers and men. It was known, too, that the fellah recruit still tended to panic and flee if caught by surprise. Nor did it escape the Israeli general staff that the enemy's deployment in Sinai was extremely vulnerable. The Egyptian army's professional German advisers had urged a defensive position along the north-south line in the middle of Sinai. But Nasser was uninterested in defense. He intended for his glittering new army to loom large on the Israeli border, and to be positioned to guard and supply the fedayun bases in the Gaza Strip. Rather than secure a line deep in Sinai, therefore, the Egyptian command deployed the bulk of the Sinai army along the al-Arish–Rafa–Gaza area on the coast, and around Abu Agheila close to the border farther south. For defense against a surprise Israeli attack, these dispositions were shockingly inadequate. Tied down to static coastal hedgehogs at the end of a long and vulnerable supply line, the Egyptian army was a mailed fist on an exposed and feeble arm. Additionally, once the Suez crisis broke in late

July 1956, the Egyptian high command pulled its best divisions out of Sinai to guard the Canal against an Anglo-French invasion. The remainder of the Egyptian army in Sinai and the Gaza Strip, therefore, consisted of two understrength infantry divisions, units of the marginal National Guard and Frontier Constabulary. At no time did their forces in Sinai exceed 40,000 men.

Israel's own manpower resources were seemingly even less impressive. The standing army was hardly more than skeletal, and the entire nation virtually had to be mobilized out of its civilian routine. Even so, the system worked effectively. When the emergency code method was used on October 25, men rushed to their units, even those who had not received their orders. Fully 90 percent of the 100,000 civilians slated for mobilization turned up, considerably more than were expected or could be equipped. Indeed, there were insufficient helmets or boots even for the 32,000 troops assigned to the Sinai offensive. The call went out for 13,000 civilian vehicles to transport the attack army to the Negev, but only 60 percent of the requisitioned trucks and vans were in running shape. The belated arrival of several hundred French personnel carriers almost literally saved the day. Upon reaching their units, moreover, the reservists, large numbers of them in their thirties, had to spend the next three days undergoing a crash training in the new French equipment. Until the last moment, preparations were nip-and-tuck. Until the last day, too, the troops were convinced that they were going into action on the Jordanian front.

At 3:30 P.M. on October 29 a squadron of Israeli transport planes crossed the Negev frontier and skimmed at a 500-foot altitude over Sinai under the enemy radar screen. The Dakotas and Nords then climbed to 1,500 feet at "Parker's Monument," an identification point less than six miles from the Mitla Pass, and there the paratroop battalion jumped. By 7:30 that evening the Israelis had reached their assigned positions a mile from the eastern approaches of Mitla. Dayan had given the men orders to dig in at this spot, to avoid provoking the Egyptians into air action; the Pass was a bare two minutes' flying time from Egyptian fields. Meanwhile, the greater body of the 202nd Paratroop Brigade under Colonel Ariel Sharon had moved into Sinai. Its objective was to link up overland with the units at Mitla. Many of the brigade's vehicles and most of its artillery became bogged down in the sand. Sharon left them behind. No time could be spared to await reinforcements; the main goal was to barrel through to the drop zone within twenty-four hours. The first two objectives, the villages of al-Quntilla and al-Thamd, were stormed without difficulty. But Sharon's pared-down column was already behind schedule.

Even by midnight of October 29–30 it was too early for Nasser's officers to gauge the situation accurately. They were puzzled by the air drop near Mitla, less than 40 miles from the Canal. Nevertheless, they were still inclined to regard it as a long-distance sabotage raid, and assumed that after inflicting some damage the Israelis would make their way back to their own country. When the attack developed in depth, however, following Sharon's crossing into Sinai, Nasser began to appreciate what was happening and ordered reinforcements moved across the Canal. By midnight an armored brigade had traversed the waterway at Ismailia and headed straight for Mitla. At the same time Nasser called upon the other Arab states to make war on Israel. It was a less than realistic appeal. Syria and Jordan could engage in some shelling, but hardly in an all-out war within twenty-four hours. Even so, time now became increasingly vital to the Israelis. Sharon raced on toward Mitla at full speed. His column took Nakhl without losing a man, and finally reached the Pass without incident at 10:30 P.M. of the thirtieth. There it was greeted joyously by the awaiting battalion. Hours later, French transport planes reprovisioned Sharon's men by parachute.

As Operation Kadesh unfolded, the Israeli government was obliged to lift its veil of secrecy. From his bed, where influenza had prostrated him with a 103-degree temperature, Ben-Gurion approved the deceptive announcement early on October 30 that "Israeli defense forces entered and engaged fedayun units in Ras en-Nakeb and Quntilla, and seized positions west of the Nakhl crossroads in the vicinity of the Suez Canal. This action follows the Egyptian assaults on Israeli transport on land and sea destined to cause destruction and the denial of peaceful life to Israel's citizens." Just enough had been revealed to enable the British and French governments now to fulfill their part of the scenario.

"THE SEPARATION OF COMBATANTS"

Immediately following the Israeli announcement, Mollet and Pineau flew to London, and on the afternoon of October 30 Pineau and Sir Ivone Kirkpatrick at the Foreign Office handed notes to the Israeli and Egyptian ambassadors demanding that their forces "withdraw," respectively, to points 10 miles east and west of the Canal. The ultimatum to Egypt read:

> The Governments of the United Kingdom and France have taken note of the outbreak of hostilities between Israel and Egypt. This event threatens to disrupt the freedom of navigation through the Suez Canal, on which the economic life of many nations depends. The Governments of the United Kingdom and France . . . accordingly request the Government of Egypt:
> a.) to stop all warlike action on land, sea and air forthwith;
> b.) to withdraw all Egyptian forces to a distance of ten miles from the Canal; and
> c.) in order to guarantee freedom of transit through the Canal by the ships of all nations and in order to separate the combatants, to accept the temporary occupation by Anglo-French forces of key positions at Port Saïd, Ismailia, and Suez.
>
> The United Kingdom and French Governments request an answer to this communication within twelve hours. If at the expiration of that time one or both Governments have not undertaken to comply with the above requirements, United Kingdom and French forces will intervene in whatever strength may be necessary to secure compliance.

The ultimatum plainly was a fake in its alleged purpose of separating the combatants, for the Western governments were ordering the victim (Egypt) to withdraw from Sinai to the west bank of the Canal, and allowing the invader (Israel) to advance to a distance 10 miles east of the Canal. Nor did the Allied rationale, "protection of the Canal," impress the other governments. The Afro-Asian world regarded it as a throwback to gunboat diplomacy. Washington viewed the Anglo-French intercession as a betrayal of the special Atlantic relationship. Moreover, the Americans suffered an additional shock when, for the first time, the British and French used their veto in the UN Security Council to kill a resolution appealing for restraint in the Middle East.

At midnight on October 30, Foreign Minister Golda Meir transmitted Israel's reply to London and Paris. It accepted the Anglo-French ultimatum, but added: "In giving this undertaking it is assumed . . . that a positive response will have been forthcoming also from the Egyptian side." The assumption could not have been serious. From Cairo, the response was precisely the one Israel and the Western Allies had anticipated. Despite the panic-stricken entreaties of his generals, Nasser rejected the Allied demand. At first, indeed, the Egyptian ruler was convinced that it was a ruse to help Israel achieve an easy victory in Sinai by luring Egyptian forces away to the Canal. Accordingly, he ordered the immediate return to Sinai of numerous units he had withdrawn only three months earlier.

Throughout the thirtieth, Egyptian air action against Israeli advance units was minimal. Lack of air force training was one factor. The performance of Egyptian fliers was unimpressive; in air-to-air combat over the battle zone not a single Israeli fighter was shot down. For the time being, Israeli planes concentrated on ground support, strafing Egyptian armored columns approaching from the west. During the late afternoon, nevertheless, the Israeli command tensely awaited the promised Anglo-French air bombardment against Egyptian fields. The source of Dayan's concern was his paratroop units at Mitla. The Pass, he knew, was a sideshow to his larger purpose of breaking the Egyptian grip on Sharm es-Sheikh. As it happened, the men of the 202nd did not wish to be a sideshow, and the brigade commander, Colonel Sharon, wangled permission from Dayan to send a reconnaissance column into the Mitla defile. Sharon interpreted this permission liberally, however, stiffening the "reconnaissance" force with enough troops and equipment to transform it into a combat team. Under the command of Major Mordechai Gur, the unit was sent into the Pass—and there fell into a lethal trap. The vehicles were knocked out by the heavy fire of Egyptian troops ensconced in caves and makeshift bunkers along the ravine walls. Hours passed before Sharon's infantry could move in, foot by foot, clearing the Egyptians from their defenses and finally investing the Pass. The unfortunate "reconnaissance" had cost the brigade heavily in killed and wounded. Thus, after departing Mitla, the chastened paratroops withdrew and continued to position themselves at the eastern entrance to the defile. There they awaited orders to move south toward Sharm es-Sheikh. This decision, in turn, was facilitated by Anglo-French operations against the Canal.

At 7:00 P.M. on October 31, Allied jet squadrons at last began their bombardment of Egyptian airfields near Suez. Ultimately, 200 British and French fighter-bombers, operating from carriers and from bases in Malta and Cyprus, swept back and forth over the Delta and Canal fields, destroying the largest part of the Egyptian air force on the ground. Even as Nasser was contemplating the wreckage of his expensive fleet of Soviet planes, a message arrived from Khrushchev, bluntly informing him that the Soviet Union could not risk a possible third world war for the sake of the Canal. Moscow would provide Egypt with all necessary moral support, but otherwise Nasser was advised to make his peace with Britain and France as soon as possible. The response of Egypt's Arab partners was hardly more encouraging. Both the Jordanian and the Syrian governments rejected Nasser's appeal for military support. As a result, the Egyptian president was now forced into a major shift of strategy. On the night of October 31 he ordered a general withdrawal from Sinai. Further air operations were canceled, and pilots were ordered to make their escape to bases up the Nile, even to other Arab states. All defenses were to be concentrated henceforth on the impending Allied invasion. For the Israelis, this switch in Egyptian priorities now opened up a unique opportunity to fulfill Dayan's maximum plan of operations.

OPERATION KADESH IS COMPLETED

On the afternoon of October 30, Israel's southern front commander, Brigadier Assaf Simchoni, dispatched his Seventh Armored Brigade across the central axis of Sinai. Immediately the tank column began grinding its way toward the massive Egyptian defensive positions at Um Cataf, blocking the approaches to Abu Agheila (see map, p. 502). Capture of the fortified hedgehog at Abu Agheila would clear the entire central access route and produce an alternate Israeli line into Mitla. But while Um Cataf was reached at dawn of the thirty-first, Simchoni's attack on the fortifications was thrown back with heavy tank losses. For the while, then, the general risked leaving the great bastion intact at his rear. Colonel Uri Ben-Ari's armored column was ordered simply to bypass the fortress and push out on an alternative central axis. The gamble paid off. Nasser had ordered a general withdrawal from Sinai, and Ben-Ari's hard-driving tanks subsequently invested the Egyptian bases of Bir Hassana and Bir Gafgafa. Soon, in fact, the colonel's advance units were engaged in a high-speed, hit-and-run battle, attempting to gobble up the "tail" of the Egyptian column fleeing Bir Gafgafa. Eventually Ben-Ari called a halt only 10 miles short of the Canal. At the Abu Agheila hedgehog, meanwhile, the Egyptians similarly decided to pull out; they were outflanked and exhausting their water supplies. The Egyptian commander simply informed his 3,000 troops that it was now every man for himself, and he urged them to make their way across the sand sea to al-Arish, 52 miles away. It was an insane plan. By dawn of November 1, as Israeli tank columns probed the hedgehog, they discovered that the Egyptians had "escaped" to a wretched fate in the desert, their throats cut and their bodies stripped by Bedouin.

Finally, in the north, Brigadier Chaim Laskov was given responsibility for the most straightforward operation of the campaign. This was the attack on Rafa, key to the al-Arish highway supplying the Gaza Strip. Rafa was strongly fortified and manned by the crack Fifth Egyptian Brigade, possessing extensive artillery and antitank support. There was little opportunity for surprise or mobility here; a frontal attack was inevitable. It began on the night of October 30. Heavy losses were suffered on both sides. The Egyptians still held out on the morning of October 31, and a naval and air bombardment was necessary to overcome further resistance. But by 7:30 A.M. the Rafa complex was an occupied shambles, and Israeli armor at last began moving along the al-Arish road. Egyptian defenses along the way put up little fight. By noon of November 1, Cairo's general withdrawal order was in effect everywhere. When Laskov's armor reached the town of al-Arish itself at 6:00 A.M. of the next day, the defenders were gone.

At this point Brigadier Chaim Bar-Lev's tank column moved along an open coastal road to Suez. After 10 miles the advance was halted, not by Egyptian resistance but by a rich windfall of some 385 vehicles, including 40 heavy Soviet-made tanks that had been abandoned by Egyptian troops under Israeli air strafing. Thousands of Egyptian troops were making their way from the dunes to the road just as Bar-Lev's brigade arrived, and they walked directly into the bag. The prisoners were sent back to internment compounds. The Israeli tanks then continued their blitzkrieg down the coastal highway. By 5:00 that afternoon they had passed through Rumani, within sight of the Canal, 20 miles away. It was approximately at the same moment that Ben-Ari's tanks completed the 80-mile distance to the Canal on the central axis. The roadsides were littered with abandoned Egyptian equipment, and Egyptian troops wandered about forlornly seeking their captors and food and water. Once the complex at Rafa was broken open, moreover, the Egyptian forces to the north and in the Gaza Strip were also trapped. When Israeli armor broke into the city of Gaza, the defenders immediately surrendered. The northeastern sector of the Gaza Strip was mopped up by the Israeli "Home Guard"—kibbutz members from the Yad Mordechai area. By nightfall November 2, the Israeli army was in full possession of the three lines of communication extending through the peninsula from east to west and was systematically destroying the fedayun bases. The guerrillas themselves were rounded up from prepared lists and shot on the spot.

For Ben-Gurion and Dayan, however, the most crucial phase of the Sinai offensive lay deep at the southeastern tip of the peninsula. In some ways this was the most extraordinary operation of the campaign. The overland march from the east to the bottom of the Sinai wedge was assigned to the 1,800 farmer-reservists of Colonel Avraham Yoffe's Ninth Brigade. Theirs was an uncommonly difficult expedition, for southern Sinai was a lunar surface of jagged peaks, impassable ridges, and rock-strewn slopes. Yoffe was compelled to scale down his brigade, discarding tanks and artillery in favor of trucks, weapons carriers, and jeeps. At dawn on October 31, the brigade moved out through al-Quntilla (already taken by the 202nd paratroops) into Sinai. By noon of November 2, it had reached Ein al-Furtaga, 12 miles inland from the Gulf of Aqaba. Grim as the trek had been until then, progress became even tougher over a hideous ganglion of boulders, many of which had to be dynamited. Trucks and command cars were literally manhandled over part of the route. With Yoffe falling behind his three-day timetable, Dayan decided to parachute one of the 202nd's companies at al-Tur, two-thirds of the stretch from Mitla down the western coast of Sinai. From there the paratroops pushed overland toward Sharm es-Sheikh, thus reinforcing Yoffe's brigade, moving along the eastern Sinai coast.

The Ninth Brigade continued to inch its way down. Egyptian resistance was encountered at Dahab on November 4, but was quickly overcome. Soon the road became clearer. The vehicles then rolled on to within sight of Ras Nasrani, the heavily fortified Egyptian base commanding the narrow channel between the Sinai coast and Tiran Island. It was abandoned. The Egyptian commander, astounded that a battle force should have descended upon him over a hazardous land barrier, a natural and unapproachable defense, had pulled his troops back to Sharm es-Sheikh itself. And there they resisted. Yoffe halted, awaited fighter-plane cover, then advanced again. By 9:30 P.M. of the fourth, all the Egyptian posts had been steamrollered. The commander of Sharm es-Sheikh surrendered. Almost immediately afterward, Yoffe's men were demobilized and returned home in time to harvest the winter crops. Within the space of less than a week, they had traveled 1,400 miles to Sharm es-Sheikh and back.

The Sinai war was over. In its initial stages, the opposing forces had been roughly of equal size. But the quality of Israeli manpower on all levels was far higher. The officers had led imaginatively and bravely—and had suffered half the army's casualties. They had allowed nothing to stop their advance. At a cost of 180 men killed and 4 captured, of 20 planes and some 2,000 worn-out vehicles, Israel in essentially a hundred-hour campaign had occupied the whole of the Sinai Peninsula and the Gaza Strip, had shattered 3 Egyptian divisions, killed 2,000 of the enemy, and taken nearly 6,000 prisoners (a number that could have been far higher). Similarly, Israeli forces had captured war matériel valued at over $50 million, including 7,000 tons of ammunition, half a million gallons of fuel, 100 Bren carriers, 200 artillery pieces, 100 tanks, over 1,000 other vehicles, and an Egyptian frigate that had been trapped off Haifa by a French destroyer, then rocketed into surrender by Israeli planes.

**THE SINAI CAMPAIGN,
OCTOBER 29–NOVEMBER 5, 1956**

Israel 1948–1967

Principal Israeli advances
October 29–November 5, 1956

Paratroop landings

0   MILES   50

MEDITERRANEAN SEA

Tel-Aviv

ISRAEL

Jerusalem

Jordan River

*DEAD
SEA*

Gaza

Khan Yunis
Rafa

Beersheba

Port Said

al-Arish

NEGEV DESERT

al-Qantara

Suez Canal

Abu Agheila

Ismailia

al-Qusseima

*BITTER
LAKES*

E G Y P T

Bir Gafgafa   Bir Hassana

GIDI PASS

Suez

MITLA PASS

Nakhl

al-Quntilla

JORDAN

Ras Sudr

al-Thamd

Eilat   Aqaba

SINAI PENINSULA

GULF OF SUEZ

Abu Zeneima

GULF OF AQABA

MT. SINAI △

Dahab

SAUDI ARABIA

al-Tur

Nabek

TIRAN ISLAND

Sharm es-Sheikh

STRAIT OF TIRAN

RED SEA

A WORLD IN OUTRAGE

Whatever the Israelis' thrilled relief at the annihilation of the Egyptian enemy, the reaction elsewhere, even among Israel's traditional sympathizers, was markedly different. In New York, the angered members of the United Nations bypassed Anglo-French vetoes in the Security Council by transferring the Middle East crisis to the General Assembly. In Washington, Eisenhower was furious at having been "double-crossed" by his two oldest NATO partners only a week before the American elections. On October 30 the president reached Eden by transatlantic telephone and expressed his outrage in barracks-room language. The following day he sent word to Ben-Gurion that "despite the present, temporary interests that Israel has in common with France and Britain, you ought not to forget that the strength of Israel and her future are bound up with the United States. I expect a prompt reply." He got it through Eban, who visited Dulles on the morning of November 1, in advance of the forthcoming emergency meeting of the General Assembly. The ambassador described the magnitude of Israel's victory in Sinai. "As a result of what Israel has done," he pointed out, "Nasser is going to lose all his credit. A more moderate government will replace his. Possibly Israel and other countries will be able to make peace at last in the Middle East. Another thing: Russia's influence in Egypt will be reduced. The victory might cause a total change in the map of political power." Dulles paced his office for several minutes. Finally he replied:

> Look, I'm terribly torn. No one could be happier than I am that Nasser has been beaten. Since spring I've had only too good cause to detest him. . . . Yet, can we accept this good end when it is achieved by means that violate the Charter? . . . [I]f we did that, the United Nations would collapse. So I am forced to turn back to support international law and the Charter.

On November 2, then, by an overwhelming vote of sixty-four to five, the General Assembly approved the United States resolution for an immediate cease-fire and withdrawal of all occupying forces from Egyptian territory. If the situation was awkward for the Israelis, it was far more so for the British and French. By the following day, November 3, Dayan's army had all but cleared Sinai. But Operation Musketeer was still hanging fire, with the armada of one hundred ships still 500 miles off the Egyptian coast and airborne troops waiting in Cyprus. In the United Nations, frantic efforts were being mounted to devise a solution before the Western Allies landed their amphibious forces. The atmosphere was heavy with crisis. In Hungary, Soviet troops were sending tanks into Budapest, and Moscow's intention of creating a diversion in the Middle East was palpable. The statesmen in New York felt themselves teetering on the brink of an atomic cataclysm. On November 4, therefore, the General Assembly voted in overwhelming numbers to create a United Nations Emergency Force that would anticipate Britain and France in "separating the combatants" along the Suez Canal and elsewhere in Sinai. Ensnared by their own declared rationale for

Operation Musketeer, the Allies hardly could oppose an international effort to carry out this purpose.

On the eve of the General Assembly vote, Pineau flew to London to urge that paratroops be dispatched to the Canal immediately. He suggested that the Israelis could provide flank support during the three-day interval before the amphibious force reached Egypt. The idea had been broached to Dayan the day before. With Ben-Gurion's approval, the Israeli commander had agreed to seize al-Qantara on the east bank of the Canal, to protect the designated area of the French paratroop landing. It was London that now vetoed the idea. Such an operation would give the lie to the pretext of "separating the combatants." Its offer declined, then, the Israeli government on November 4 announced its willingness to accept the General Assembly cease-fire resolution "provided a similar answer is forthcoming from Egypt." Immediately the Allies protested to Jerusalem. What justification existed for their intervention at the Canal, they asked, if a cease-fire came into effect? Paris then implored Ben-Gurion to retract the announcement. Uncomfortable as he was at the notion of further dramatizing Israel's belligerency, the prime minister nevertheless agreed to help. Later the same day Eban informed the General Assembly that his nation's acceptance in fact was conditional on Egypt's declared willingness: to accept a cease-fire; to end the state of war with Israel; to terminate all guerrilla operations; to enter into immediate peace negotiations with Israel; and to cease the economic boycott and lift the blockade against Israeli shipping. Thereupon the British demonstrated their gratitude with yet another backhanded swipe. At their instigation, the Allied response to the General Assembly Resolution of November 4 contained the sentence:

> The two Governments continue to believe that it is necessary to interpose an international force to prevent the continuance of hostilities between Egypt and Israel, to secure the speedy withdrawal of Israeli forces, to take the necessary measures to remove obstructions through the Suez Canal, and to promote a settlement of the problems in the area.

The Israelis were appalled.

Finally, at dawn on November 5, a wave of British and French paratroops dropped outside Port Saïd. A second wave descended in the early afternoon. Throughout the night, the first ships of the Allied flotilla arrived off Port Saïd, and at dawn on November 6 they began their shelling. At 4:50 A.M. British and French commandos landed amphibiously without incident. The town surrendered in the late afternoon. Immediately afterward an armored column set off for Suez City. British patrols were only 25 miles short of this southern exit of the Canal when, at 6:00 P.M., London suddenly announced that it was accepting the United Nations demand for a cease-fire, to come into effect at midnight.

By its collapse at the very threshold of success, the British government was reacting in part to the warning issued by the Soviet Union. Actually it was the Israelis who were the initial targets of Soviet fury when Operation Kadesh was launched on October 29. By then the Russians already had their hands full with the Hungarian uprising. In ensuing days, therefore, the enraged Soviet press and radio campaign against Israel—and later against Britain and France—became a useful smoke screen for the humiliating developments in Budapest. On November 4, Moscow dispatched a scorching note to Jerusalem, accusing the Israeli government of

> . . . playing with the fate of the whole world, with the fate of its own people. It is sowing hatred of the State of Israel among the peoples of the East. Its actions are putting a question mark on the very existence of Israel as a State. . . . We suggest that the Government of Israel should weigh its action as long as there is still time, and stop all military movements against Egypt.

Ben-Gurion's response was astonishingly firm. "Our foreign policy is dictated by our vital interests," it concluded, "and by our desire to live in peace, and no foreign factor determines it or will determine it in the future."

But with the opening of the Allied air assault, the Russians proved even more brutal in their warnings to the British and French. On the evening of November 5, as paratroops descended on Port Saïd and Port Fuad, Soviet Prime Minister Nikolai Bulganin dispatched notes of unusual violence to Eden and Mollet, emphasizing that the Soviet Union was prepared to crush the "warmongers" by using "every kind of modern destructive weapon." Both the Soviet Union and Red China were said to be registering "volunteers" for service in the Middle East. Indeed, Allied headquarters suspected that Communist bloc personnel already were operating in the area. A British Canberra was brilliantly intercepted by MiGs 45,000 feet above Damascus, and crippled; an efficient radar system plainly was operating from Syria. NATO headquarters reported, too, that the volume of military electronic communications traffic across the Warsaw Pact nations had tripled.

Yet it was not Soviet pressure alone that cracked Britain's resolve to fulfill Operation Musketeer. On November 6 Eden was informed by Washington that Britain's urgent loan application for $1 billion from the International Monetary Fund was contingent on a cease-fire. A very sick man by then, the prime minister became completely unnerved. He phoned Mollet: "I am cornered. I can't hang on. I'm being deserted by everybody. My loyal associate [Anthony] Nutting has resigned as minister of state. I can't even rely on unanimity among the Conservatives. . . . Everybody is against me! The Commonwealth threatens to break up. Nehru says he will break the ties. Eisenhower phoned me. I can't go it alone without the United States. . . . No, it is not possible." Mollet pleaded for only a little more time to complete the seizure of the Canal. Eden agreed finally to delay the cease-fire until midnight, November 6. But it soon became evident that the French were incapable of salvaging the operation on their own; it was too intimately combined under British leadership at every level. Frustrated and bitter, sensing that victory at the Canal had been lost by only a few hours, Paris agreed to act jointly with the British. The Suez adventure would end at midnight.

The Israelis were unshaken. They had accomplished their own purpose, at least. On November 7, in the first flush of victory, Ben-Gurion intimated to the Knesset that he was giving serious thought to annexing Sinai. "After all, Sinai has never been part of Egypt," he mused. Sharing in this exultation, a majority of Israelis regarded Ben-Gurion's notion as distinctly less than farfetched. One of the participants in Operation Kadesh, Shlomo Barer, recalled:

> Groups began climbing Mount Sinai. Piper Cubs landed there. Within days of the fighting, Israeli geographers, geologists, archaeologists, pre-historians, philologists and scholars of the Bible descended on the wilderness and began scouring it for traces of the Exodus route which the Tribes of Israel had followed out of Egypt. Botanists looked for, and found, a plant species which might be the Biblical manna. And from every camp and bivouac in the Peninsula the resting troops began trekking in by scores and hundreds, in dusty jeeps and command cars, across whirling sand plains, through dry wadis and pink canyons . . . to see the mythical Mountain of God in its resuscitated aura and the Israeli flag fluttering briefly from a wooden pole. . . . [T]he whole nation so recently returned to the Promised Land was being suddenly confronted with the cradle of its birth at the beginning of civilization.

But the prime minister enjoyed only one sweet day of uncompromised triumph. Crossing his speech was a letter from Eisenhower, referring ominously to a possible cessation of "friendly cooperation between our two countries." Nahum Goldmann cautioned Ben-Gurion that even American Jewry might not support Israel if its troops held fast to the conquered territory. The prime minister then changed his tone. Responding to Eisenhower the following day, he gave assurance that Israel would evacuate western Sinai the moment a United Nations force entered the Canal region. The president was not appeased. In yet a second dispatch, he warned that in the event of a Soviet-assisted attack on Israel, the Israeli government should not count upon American help.

To Ben-Gurion's dismay, Britain now chose to back away even further. On November 8, Foreign Secretary Lloyd privately urged an Israeli withdrawal in return for certain "assurances." These included a peace treaty guaranteed by the Allied Powers, a defensible frontier, and free passage through the Suez Canal and the Gulf of Aqaba. In making this proposal to the Israeli ambassador, Lloyd clearly hoped to accommodate Nuri es-Saïd in Iraq, thus salvaging the already shaken partnership of the Baghdad Pact. It was the confluence of these pressures, then, that forced an agonized reappraisal in the Israeli cabinet. Even France now was an uncertain reed. Pineau informed Israel's Ambassador Tsur that "France will share all she has with Israel. But our combined means are not sufficient against the Soviet menace. In the circumstances, we can only advise you to withdraw."

Israel enjoyed a certain degree of borrowed time, nevertheless, in its army's new Sinai emplacement. During November and early December the main United Nations efforts were concentrated on evicting British and

French troops from Egypt and opening the Canal again to the flow of Arab oil. But by November 20, 700 UN troops from "neutral" countries already were operating under the command of General Burns in Egypt and 3,000 more were on the way. Consequently, on November 22, Britain's acting prime minister, R. A. Butler (Eden had departed for convalescence in Jamaica), announced that British withdrawal was about to begin. It had been delayed this long at the request of Paris, and essentially to give the Israelis an added margin for carrying off their booty of Czech and Soviet weapons. Finally on December 22, the last British and French troops left Port Saïd. For the Allies, the Suez episode was finished.

ISRAEL HOLDS OUT FOR SAFEGUARDS

In its determination to effect a withdrawal of invading forces from Egypt, the United Nations had included Israel among the aggressors. Yet the Western countries were by no means oblivious to the provocations Israel had endured. Counting in turn on this residue of sympathy and understanding, the Israeli government now fought for time, hoping that its case would gradually win international support as world panic subsided. In his personal history of Israel, Ben-Gurion recalled:

> The longer the time at our disposal, the longer the time we were in effective control of the western shore of the Strait [of Tiran], and the greater the number of ships that sailed through the Red Sea and the planes that flew over it, the better our chances for demonstrating to the world the value and importance of the Strait. If we could also lay a pipeline from Eilat to Haifa . . . our case would be strengthened. Only if we succeeded in convincing the nations that this was vital for them as well as for us was there any prospect that we might have free navigation through the Strait.

This political campaign, in the United Nations and elsewhere, lasted from the beginning of November 1956 to early March 1957.

Its first stage, until February 11, was a continual uphill struggle. The General Assembly had committed itself overwhelmingly to the evacuation of all occupying troops, and in favor of a United Nations Expeditionary Force. Dag Hammarskjöld, the secretary-general, was adamant on this point. Indeed, he refused even to discuss Israel's demands for security guarantees until Israeli forces withdrew from Sinai and Gaza behind the Rhodes armistice line. This view was shared, although less for moralistic than political reasons, by the Afro-Asian bloc, which detested "imperialism" in any form. It was endorsed, too, by most of the Western nations, whose economies were critically dependent upon the passage of oil through the Suez Canal; Nasser shrewdly refused to allow clearing operations in the blocked waterway until the Israelis departed. When, therefore, a new General Assembly resolution of January 7, 1957, again demanded instant Israeli evacuation, the margin this time was seventy-four to two. Only France still loyally voted with Israel.

The Israelis pulled back grudgingly. On December 3, 1956, their forces withdrew a distance of 30 miles from the Suez area. The UNEF immediately took up its positions along the Canal. On January 8, 1957, Israeli troops retreated still farther, this time to the al-Arish line in eastern Sinai. On January 15, 1957, Ben-Gurion finally announced his government's decision to evacuate Sinai completely by January 22, with the crucial exception of the Sharm es-Sheikh area. The Gaza Strip, an integral part of Palestine, would similarly remain under Israeli control. Mrs. Meir, recently arrived from Israel, explained this stand before the General Assembly:

> It is inconceivable to my government that the nightmare of the previous eight years should be reestablished in Gaza with international sanction. Shall Egypt be allowed once more to organize murder and sabotage in this strip? Shall Egypt be allowed to condemn the local population to permanent impoverishment and to block any solution of the refugee problem? . . . [I]t must be admitted that any international force would be powerless to prevent . . . the recrudescence of fedayun activities. Nor is it possible to maintain an area such as the Gaza Strip almost entirely devoid of economic resources in a state of economic isolation from any adjoining territory.

The Israeli foreign minister was equally graphic in her description of years of Egyptian blockade from Sharm es-Sheikh, Ras Nasrani, and the neighboring islands of the Tiran Strait. "The mere entry into this area of the United Nations Emergency Force, even with the specific aim of preventing belligerency, would not in itself be a solution," she insisted. More effective international guarantees of free navigation were required.

These arguments did not fail to register on the United Nations, particularly as the threat of a world conflagration receded. On February 2, 1957, the General Assembly adopted two resolutions. The first again simply required Israel to complete its evacuation without delay. But the second recognized that withdrawal must be followed by action to guarantee the establishment of peaceful conditions. This spirit of flexibility was not matched in Washington—not at the outset. There were long-term American interests in the Arab world that could not be forfeited. One of them was the United States air base in Dharan, Saudi Arabia. The Saudi monarch was prepared to allow the Americans use of this facility for another five years; but his condition was successful American pressure on Israel to evacuate the remaining territory in Gaza and Sinai. By late December 1956 Washington's frustration with the Israelis boiled over. Henry Cabot Lodge, the American ambassador in the United Nations, declared angrily in the Security Council that "I cannot predict the consequences if Israel fails to comply with the resolution." Dulles warned again in an open press conference that Israel must withdraw "forthwith," or American-Israeli relations would have to be seriously reexamined. Eisenhower himself was altogether hostile to Israel's stance. With his near-mystical view of the United Nations as the last best hope for mankind, the president regarded Israel's defiance of the world organization as brazen and unconscionable. "Continued disregard for . . . the U.N. resolutions," he wrote Ben-Gurion on February 4, "will almost certainly . . . seriously damage relations between Israel and U.N. members, including the United States." The message foreshadowed the possibility of sanctions against Israel, a threat Dulles later made explicit. Ben-Gurion's lengthy reply to Eisenhower, describing once again the ordeal endured by Israel as a consequence of Arab and Egyptian hostility, failed utterly to move the president.

Dulles, on the other hand, was made increasingly aware of the need for some gesture to Israel's security needs, if only to assure Senate endorsement of the government's Middle East policy. By January 1957 both the press and congressional friends of Israel drew attention to the double standard of international morality: the Soviet Union had not been punished for Hungary, but Israel, with its legitimate security grievances, was to be punished for Sinai. The development of this pro-Israel consensus marked the beginning of a second, and more effective, phase of Ben-Gurion's "holding action." Lyndon Johnson, Democratic leader in the Senate, telephoned Eban every few days to express indignation at the administration's tactics. "They're not going to get a goddam thing here [from Congress] until they [treat you fairly]," Johnson assured the Israeli ambassador. Other political leaders were equally sympathetic.

Early in February, Dulles hinted at last at a possible accommodation. To that end, on the eleventh of the month, he and Eban formulated a compromise *aide-mémoire* on Aqaba and Gaza. Expressing awareness that Gaza had been the source of armed infiltration into Israel, the document stated Washington's belief that the UN secretary-general should invite the United Nations Emergency Force to move into the strip and occupy the boundary between that danger zone and Israel itself. On behalf of his government, the secretary of state further asserted his belief that the Gulf of Aqaba constituted an international waterway and that no nation had the right to prevent free and innocent passage in the Gulf and through the Strait of Tiran. The United States was "prepared to exercise the right of free and innocent passage and to join with others to secure general recognition of this right."

When the *aide-mémoire* was relayed to Jerusalem, the cabinet noted that mere recognition of Israel's free right of passage through the Gulf did not in itself guarantee this right; earlier United Nations resolutions on the Suez Canal had made that much clear. It was vital, the ministers insisted, that the UNEF remain on at Sharm es-Sheikh without time limit, until the conclusion of a peace treaty. The identical condition was laid down for the Gaza Strip. This Israeli reply was conveyed not only to Dulles but (shrewdly) to political leaders in Congress. Thus, at the behest of Lyndon Johnson, the Democratic Policy Committee on February 19 unanimously expressed its opposition to the threat of sanctions against Israel. Eisenhower was taken aback by the emerging political confrontation. The following day he cut short his vacation to discuss the Middle Eastern emergency with twenty-six congressional leaders.

In the three-hour meeting, the president emphasized that his demand for unconditional withdrawal actually was issued "for Israel's own good." Israel soon would be in a dangerous financial crisis, he explained, and would require United States government loans. These would be forth-coming only if the "brawls" between Israel and Egypt came to an end. The congressional leaders were not impressed by this argument. That evening the president described his chosen course in a speech on nation-wide radio and television. He insisted again that Israel must withdraw unconditionally, relying upon the United Nations and the United States to assure it the two conditions it required—afterwards. Israel, Eisenhower noted, was seeking "firm guarantees" as a condition of withdrawal. Could a nation that had used force demand guarantees? he asked rhetorically. Again, the speech was not well received by congressional leaders, and still less by American Jewish leaders, who met with Dulles the next day to express their resentment.

A FORMULA IS DEVISED

In fact, Ben-Gurion himself had detected some flexibility in Eisenhower's address. On the morning of February 21, 1957, he discussed it with his cabinet. Eban, who had flown back from the United States, offered his view that this was probably the furthest Washington would go. Accord-ingly, Ben-Gurion and Mrs. Meir sent Eban back to Washington with a list of questions that had been carefully prepared by the foreign ministry. The ambassador submitted the list to Dulles on February 23. It asked first what action the United States would take if Egyptian guns barred American ships from innocent entry to the Gulf of Aqaba. Sensing the thrust of Eban's approach, Dulles answered immediately: "Mr. Ambassador, it is the policy of the United States to defend its shipping rights anywhere in the world." With this understanding, the two men then brought in their respective advisers, and during the next day and a half engaged in intensive discussions. On the afternoon of the twenty-fourth, much to Dulles's jubilation, a consensus finally was reached. In writing, a series of American answers had been given to Eban's questions:

1. Will the United States send a ship through Aqaba and will you react if stopped? Answer: Yes.
2. Will you support the idea that the UNEF should stay at Sharm es-Sheikh for a long time? Answer: Yes.
3. Will you send a ship with the UNEF flag through the Gulf of Aqaba? An-swer: This depends on [Security-General] Hammarskjöld's assent.
4. Will you open an oil route for us from Iran—that is, through the Red Sea and the Gulf of Aqaba? Answer: Yes.
5. Will Gaza be a UN-administered enclave? Answer: We will try our hardest to persuade the UN and Hammarskjöld to make such an ar-rangement.

The obstacle to a final understanding was no longer Dulles, but rather Hammarskjöld. The secretary-general refused to send a ship through Aqaba bearing the United Nations flag; this was not the *agent provocateur* role he envisaged for the world body. He made clear, too, that he opposed the notion of a specifically UN regime in the Gaza Strip, for the United Nations was a peacekeeper, not a sovereign government. Both Dulles and Eban reacted in exasperation to the secretary-general's unbudging legalism. In the effort to break the impasse, however, the Canadian ambassador to the United Nations, Lester Pearson, now offered a compromise proposal of his own. He had discussed his plan several weeks earlier, and only lately had refined it in discussions with Mollet, Pineau, and Hammarskjöld. By its provisions, the United States, France, Britain, and other maritime nations would assert every country's right to freedom of navigation in the Strait of Tiran, and their recognition specifically of Israel's right, under Article 51 of the Charter, to safeguard this freedom against any aggression. Thus, while Israel's right could not be safeguarded *by* a two-thirds majority of the UN General Assembly (given the stance of the Communist bloc and the "neutralist" Afro-Asian bloc), it could be meaningfully asserted *within* the General Assembly by that forum's most influential maritime members.

The solution for Gaza was even more convoluted, but not less hopeful. At Pearson's suggestion, Hammarskjöld in mid-February 1957 had privately discussed the Canadian's proposal with Egyptian Foreign Minister Mahmud Fawzi. The formula was swiftly appraised as a possible face-saving blueprint for Nasser and, indeed, for the United Nations itself. It was agreed, first of all, that the Gaza Strip provided an ideal location for UNEF command headquarters and for UNEF units assigned to patrol the demarcation lines. Inasmuch as the area was desperately overcrowded with refugees, hardly enough space existed in this little enclave for both the Egyptian army and the UNEF. On the other hand, if the UNEF actually established its bases inside the Strip, there would be no further necessity for the Egyptian army to take up positions there. Rather than being formalized by written agreement, the arrangement should be allowed simply to develop into a pragmatic ongoing situation.

Hammarskjöld liked the idea. It offered the best method for enabling the UNEF to maintain "peace and order" after Israeli withdrawal. The secretary-general thereupon added Sharm es-Sheikh to the plan. Dulles endorsed the formula with equal enthusiasm and offered to sell it to the Israelis as the best compromise for their evacuation without clear-cut guarantees (something the United Nations would never approve). Presenting the scheme to Eban, he urged the ambassador to rely on the good faith of the United Nations and the United States. Eban, for his part, was sufficiently impressed to transmit the plan to Jerusalem. It was approved. Meanwhile, Fawzi similarly accepted it as a compromise that avoided any public derogation of Egyptian authority over Gaza or Sharm es-Sheikh. As he put it to Hammarskjöld in reference to the Israelis: "If they would keep their mouths shut, we would keep our eyes shut." Within the next few days, therefore, as other members were consulted, it became clear that Hammarskjöld had a General Assembly consensus, rather than a formal "resolution," for sending the UNEF into both Gaza and Sharm es-Sheikh.

The Israelis were cautiously pleased. Yet they were still concerned that the UNEF might be precipitously withdrawn, that shipping might again be obstructed and hostilities renewed. Consequently, they sought an undertaking from Hammarskjöld that any proposal to evacuate the UNEF from Sharm es-Sheikh or Gaza must first be submitted to a special committee of the General Assembly; the procedure would ensure that no hasty steps were taken that might lead to hostilities. Hammarskjöld confirmed the understanding on February 26 in a memorandum, and Dulles also endorsed it in writing. These two assurances, from Dulles and Hammarskjöld, placated the Israelis, and most notably Golda Meir, who by this time had returned to Washington and was now supervising Israel's negotiations each step of the way. In consultation with Dulles and his staff, the foreign minister and her own advisers prepared the draft for the address she was scheduled to give at the General Assembly meeting of March 1.

Mrs. Meir delivered her speech at 3:00 that afternoon, informing the General Assembly that Israel would now evacuate its forces from the Gaza Strip and Sharm es-Sheikh. The withdrawal, however, was conditional on certain "expectations and assumptions," which she detailed. These included assurance that the two sites henceforth would be garrisoned exclusively by the UNEF; that the UNEF would safeguard life and property in the two areas and develop specific plans for coping with the refugee problem; that the UNEF would remain at Gaza and Sharm es-Sheikh for whatever length of time was required to achieve a permanent settlement between Egypt and Israel. The foreign minister warned, too, that if conditions arose in the Gaza Strip indicating a repetition of disturbances, Israel would reserve its freedom to act in defense of its rights. It was similarly Israel's understanding, she added, that freedom of passage would be ensured in the Strait of Tiran, and to that end Israel would reserve the right to defend its freedom of passage in this waterway—if necessary by force. Finally, Mrs. Meir stated her government's expectation that any proposal for removing the UNEF from the Gulf of Aqaba area would first be referred to the Advisory Committee of the General Assembly, to ensure that "no precipitate changes are made which would have the effect of increasing the possibility of belligerent acts. . . ."

By prearrangement, Mrs. Meir's interpretation of the conditions of Israel's withdrawal from Sharm es-Sheikh was endorsed in the next few days by the principal maritime members of the General Assembly—sixteen nations in all—and including, most importantly, the United States. "The main objective has been reached," Ben-Gurion pointed out to his cabinet: "Freedom of navigation in the Strait of Tiran, through the Red Sea, and into the Indian Ocean, and the introduction of a United Nations force outside our territory to guard this freedom of navigation and quiet in the Gaza Strip." On March 4, as Israeli soldiers pulled out of their encampments, General Burns and six battalions of blue-helmeted United Nations troops moved into Gaza and Sharm es-Sheikh. At this point, in gratitude to Israel for having ended an intolerable diplomatic impasse, the United States immediately approved a generous loan from the World Bank, and other loans soon followed. On April 7 an American tanker anchored in Eilat. Washington circulated notices to shipping companies that the United States government specifically upheld the principle of free navigation in the Gulf of Aqaba and the Strait of Tiran.

Had Operation Kadesh been worthwhile for Israel, then? Reporting to the Knesset on March 7, Ben-Gurion admitted that there could be no certainty that the Egyptians would not return to the Gaza Strip. Indeed, the prime minister's misgivings were confirmed even sooner than he predicted. Only two days following the departure of Israeli troops from Gaza and the arrival of UNEF soldiers, the local Palestinians issued "vehement demands" for the return of an Egyptian administration. For reasons of prestige, Nasser decided to take the risk of Israeli retaliation and to meet these "demands." He then appointed and dispatched a civil governor to the Gaza Strip with an appropriate staff. No troops accompanied them, however. The Israeli government immediately protested, but agreed with Dulles that Nasser's act was not worth another military confrontation. By then, in any case, it was evident that one of Israel's most devoutly cherished hopes for Operation Kadesh would remain unrealized. This was the fall of Nasser himself. The Egyptian dictator had emerged from his battlefield disaster with his prestige reasonably intact. He had managed to camouflage the awesome shellacking his army had suffered at Israeli hands under the palpable evidence of Anglo-French bombardment and landings. By diplomatic if not by military means, too, he had secured the evacuation of every last invading soldier. Neither had he been compelled to give a permanent undertaking that his government might not someday choose to return Egyptian troops to Gaza or even interdict Israeli shipping to and from Eilat. On the contrary, he asserted the rights of a belligerent in deed as well as theory by maintaining the ban on Israeli shipping through the Suez Canal.

Operation Kadesh imposed other penalties as well. For the Afro-Asian bloc, Israel was identified at first as a partner in the heaviest-handed kind of Western imperialism. Within Israel itself, for that matter, a number of spokesmen afterward expressed misgivings at having collaborated with the British and French. Moshe Sharett shared this concern, and in his diary tersely scored "the belief that it is impossible to reach peace through coercion." Years later, in a collaborative biography of himself with the journalist Robert St. John, Abba Eban offered his own evaluation of Operation Kadesh:

> The Sinai campaign was politically the most unplanned war in history. It was based on a complete lack of political appraisal. Exaggerated importance was attached to France and Britain. We appeared before the whole world as tools of the imperialists. We should have avoided the Franco-British collusion and been satisfied with their political support. If we were going to break through and free ourselves of the fedayeen and clear the Gulf of Aqaba, it should have been a completely Israeli operation and we should have done it after the American election. . . . It was not necessary to get the violent UN and American reactions we did get.

In this account, Eban did not speculate on the additional casualties the Israelis would surely have sustained had they invaded Sinai deprived of French air support and an Allied bombardment of the Egyptian air force.

On the other hand, there could be little question that the hundred-hour campaign fulfilled its principal goal of advancing Israel's security. For one thing, it profoundly enhanced the morale of the Israeli people themselves. It liberated them from their uncertainties and self-doubts and convinced them, veterans and immigrants alike, that they could overcome all their shortcomings in physical resources, population, and territory through the intangibles of élan, organization, and technical and combat skills. The military lessons of the campaign, with its demonstrated advantages of pre-emptive attack, were themselves invaluable (Chapter xxi). Not less important, the stubbornness with which Israel resisted an evacuation deprived of guarantees ended all further efforts by the Powers, notably Britain and the United States, to impose a political settlement inimical to Israel's security. There would be no further speeches in Washington or London proposing an attenuation of Israeli territory. The Sinai Campaign had not brought Israel formal peace, to be sure. Yet in his Knesset speech of March 7, Ben-Gurion made it clear that "we did not wage war to seize Sinai or to force peace on Nasser, and after the Sinai Campaign I had no hopes for an early peace." He cautioned his listeners that enduring peace in the Gaza Strip was in any case unlikely as long as tens of thousands of unsettled refugees were impacted there. While the arrangements that had been worked out for Gaza and Sharm es-Sheikh were essentially makeshift, they were also the best that could be achieved for the time being, and Ben-Gurion regarded their value as considerable.

The prime minister was not wrong. Fedayun activity from Gaza virtually ended. Israelis in the outlying border settlements now could work and sleep in peace for the first time in seven years. The Gulf of Aqaba was open and stayed open for eleven years. Unquestionably, the accomplishment was less than the officially recognized freedom of passage Ben-Gurion had sought for his nation. But those eleven years were all that were needed to establish Israel's trade relationships with the Orient, to inaugurate a series of pipelines that transformed the little republic into one of the major oil entrepôts between Iran and Europe, and to develop an industrial infrastructure that launched Israel on the period of its most impressive economic growth and diplomatic influence. From November 1956 on, by universal recognition, the Jewish state had established itself at last as a factor to be reckoned with, indeed, as a sovereign entity to be treated with circumspection and respect in the councils of nations.

CHAPTER XVIII YEARS OF ECONOMIC AND SOCIAL GROWTH

THE EMERGENCE OF A NATION

Until the Sinai Campaign, Israel had been regarded less as a state in many diplomatic circles than as a kind of besieged refugee camp, frantically striving to organize itself in an arid and impoverished land and confronting in the process awesome economic, social, internal, and military obstacles. After 1956 all this became history. The nation's frontiers were reasonably secure. The Israeli army, hobbled until 1953 by problems of organization and command, had since been transformed into an efficient military machine, as well as into the country's most socially unifying force. In a sense, Operation Kadesh represented the crowning achievement of Israel's herculean efforts at integration. The reclamation of extensive land areas, the full utilization of abandoned (or sequestered) Arab properties, the rise in economic aid from America, Germany, and world Jewry —all now at last were bearing fruit. Israel, in short, no longer faced the question of survival, but rather of choosing between alternative ways of life.

One of the most palpable consequences of victory was a sudden and dramatic upsurge of immigration. The figures for 1956 and 1957 alone were 55,000 and 70,000, respectively. At first the majority of newcomers came from North Africa and Egypt. The former were Jews who had been inhibited in their departure until late 1956 by accounts of fedayun incursions and of Nasser's tightening garrot around Israel. All that, too, apparently was in the past. The choice between Islamic xenophobia in Morocco and assured physical security in a Jewish state was clear-cut once again. So it was for Egyptian Jewry. Nasser's government, mortified by its battlefield losses, imposed a new series of decrees against the jobs, homes, even the personal safety of "foreigners." As the most vulnerable of the nation's minorities, some 25,000 Jews fled during the winter of 1956–57, "paying" for their passage to Europe by the simple expedient of leaving behind everything they owned. Two-thirds of these fugitives subsequently were transported to Israel by the Jewish Agency. Fluent in languages and experienced in business, they settled mainly in the coastal cities, often finding employment in tourist offices, hotels, and banks.

North African Jews were not the only ones subject to political convulsions; Jews living in Communist lands were similarly affected. Some 40,000

European immigrants reached Israel in 1957, most of them from Poland and Hungary. Between 1958 and 1960 an additional 43,000 east Europeans arrived, this time from Communist Rumania. For the most part the newcomers were refugees from the Polish and Hungarian uprisings of 1956, and from the revulsion against Stalinism that followed soon afterward in Rumania. In each of these lands, upheaval brought with it a revived and spontaneous public anti-Semitism that the Communist governments were prepared to alleviate through a tolerated Jewish emigration. Many of the east Europeans were well educated, often in the professions. They had remained on under Communist rule after the war precisely because their skills were needed and rewarded. Now, supplanted by a new generation of educated "natives," they brought their administrative and professional experience with them to Israel.

The Jewish Agency had not been prepared for an immigration of this scope. Nevertheless, it reacted swiftly. Agency officials organized transportation, set up transit camps in Europe, and in Israel provided temporary facilities in hostels and rented rooms. This time there was no question of sheltering the new arrivals in ma'abarot. Neither was there a doctrinaire effort to apply the earlier ship-to-village scheme. Better trained than their predecessors, the east Europeans were granted special treatment. Decent housing at low interest rates was provided for them in Tel Aviv and in other cities. Many of the newcomers were enrolled at public expense in five-month ulpanim, intensive Hebrew-language courses. Afterward, far-reaching efforts were made to secure them employment befitting their training and cultural level. The Agency's solicitude in no way represented conscious or unconscious discrimination against the Orientals, but rather an awareness that immigration from the Iron Curtain nations—where the economic circumstances of Jewish life, after all, were still tolerable—had to be encouraged at almost any cost. For Israel, Communist Europe represented virtually the last important source of trained and educated potential citizens.

Between 1961 and 1964, another influx added fully 194,000 Jews to Israel's population. Although many of these, too, were east Europeans, the largest majority arrived from Islamic communities: from Iran and North Africa, and particularly from Morocco, which by then, under French influence, had agreed to allow the departure of the last remnants of its Jewish community. Included among the Maghreb newcomers were an additional 15,000 Algerian Jews, members of the French colonial population that was departing in the aftermath of de Gaulle's award of independence to that nation. Their arrival was greeted with mixed emotions by the Israeli government, which noted anxiously that the largest numbers of Algerian Jews, some 130,000 souls, had opted to depart for France. It was a shocking revelation to the Zionist leadership that distraught Jewish communities overseas, particularly in the Maghreb, would gravitate elsewhere than to Israel. Yet the circumstances of the Algerians were not to be equated with those of Moroccan Jewry. Possessing the rights of other Frenchmen, the Algerians considered themselves in the same category as west European or

American Jews, few of whom until then had evinced much desire to leave the protection of large and benevolent democracies. Thus, during the recession period of 1965–67, the Algerian aliyah seemed rather more impressive in the context of a modest total yearly immigration to Israel of 25,000.

With all its annual fluctuations, however, Israel's Jewish population was maintaining a steady upward curve, rising from 1,667,000 in 1956 to 2,384,000 by the end of 1967. Within this citizenry, too, important "ethnic" changes were taking place. By 1965, for the first time, the numbers of Orientals and Europeans were equal, and three years later the Orientals comprised a Jewish majority of 55.5 percent. Moreover, the shift in favor of the Easterners was likely to increase, for this group was producing nearly twice the number of children born to European families. The implications for Israel's cultural future were significant (p. 539). Of more immediate interest to the government, nevertheless, was the sheer uninterrupted growth of the nation's human resources. The increase was reflected not merely in the continuing diversification of the economy, but in the very physical configuration of the land and its growing defensibility in depth. Population dispersion had improved significantly. In 1948, 18 percent of Israel's Jews lived in rural areas, 52 percent in the three major cities, and 30 percent in other towns. Twenty years later, although the proportion in rural areas had actually declined (to 11.3 percent), Jews living in the three main cities represented less than 35 percent of the Jewish population, while 54 percent lived in other, smaller towns—a few of them satellites of the big cities, to be sure, but many of them new development communities. Thus it was, in the years after Operation Kadesh, that Israel "fleshed out" its demographic lineaments no less effectively than it had built its political institutions, augmented its economy, and defended its sovereign independence.

THE CONQUEST OF LAND AND WATER

The Jews consolidated, even broadened, their grip on the soil in the second decade of their independence. At the end of 1966 they inhabited 729 of the country's 834 rural settlements and comprised a rural population of 340,000 (out of 616,000 Arabs and Jews). Indeed, Jewish agricultural villages employed 13 percent of the nation's Jewish labor force and cultivated nearly 4.5 million dunams of land. Their farms were meeting Israel's staple food needs, even producing a surplus in vegetables, eggs, and milk. By the mid-1960s, as a result, export production, formerly limited mainly to citrus, was expanded to include cotton, peanuts, and the more exotic winter vegetables and fruit. In 1964 agricultural shipments, including citrus, represented a third of Israel's total exports and 10 percent of the national income.

Except for the citrus groves, the principal source of agricultural output remained the moshavim and kibbutzim. The balance established between these two pioneering farm models did not alter appreciably in the next decade. By 1965 the nation's 229 kibbutzim supported a population of 78,000; its 336 moshavim, a population of 120,000. There were as well 64 ordinary capitalist farm villages and a score of other mixed farms. It is recalled that regional settlement had charted the way for the moshav future. That future continued to bear hope of promise, both economically and sociologically. And despite its loss of proportional strength in the countryside, the kibbutz, too, was dramatically improving its productivity and profitability. Mechanization, improved marketing techniques, broadened experience, and the secular dynamism of its—largely European—inhabitants transformed the collective settlement into as efficient an agricultural unit as any in the world, and a model for the developing countries. While its expenditures for municipal services were considerable, the rewards for these disbursements were high. Thus, with secondary schooling freely available to all its children, the range (if not always the quality) of kibbutz education was greater than anywhere else in Israel. So were the cultural opportunities for its adults. They shared in lectures, choirs, drama, and orchestra circles. The three national kibbutz federations maintained seminaries that operated as training centers for affiliated villages, and fostered publishing houses that issued literary quarterlies. Talented kibbutz youths were given time off for artistic or musical work, and particularly gifted members were allowed to attend university at kibbutz expense. The collective settlement accordingly produced some of the nation's best writers and artists (Chapter xx).

In some degree, also, the kibbutz maintained its tradition of public leadership. By 1967, 30 percent of the air force pilots and 22 percent of the army officers were its products. Among the representatives of the three Labor parties in the Knesset, 25 percent (sixteen of sixty-three) were kibbutz members. Yet the ratios were slowly declining by the 1960s and early 1970s. Preoccupied with new opportunities for such creature comforts as television sets, beauty parlors, and swimming pools, the kibbutz membership increasingly reflected in its own outlook the emergent class differentiation of Israeli society at large. In Israel, as in Europe, belief in socialism was weakening by then. The revival of the capitalist nations, the trend toward a welfare statism that appeared to resolve social problems within the framework of a capitalist economy, the revived anti-Semitism and anti-Israel posture of the Soviet Union—all these weakened many of the collective's original Socialist premises. The government and army, too, were now performing many of the tasks that kibbutz settlers once had fulfilled on a voluntaristic basis. As a result, the collective, this former showpiece of Zionist idealism, was increasingly tinctured by the materialism and the status-seeking that everywhere were beginning to afflict Israeli life (p. 597 and Chapter xxiv).

The dilemma of growing affluence was hardly an unpleasant one. The land was revealing its abundance in ways no earlier pioneer had ever dared imagine. Nor was individual sacrifice alone unlocking its riches. Water was flowing at last. From the earliest days of Jewish settlement in Palestine, no one had doubted that irrigation was the indispensable key to economic survival and growth. Rain fell only in the winter, and largely in the northern part of the country. Elsewhere annual precipitation dropped from some forty inches in Galilee to less than one inch in the southern Negev. The Jewish Agency had been studying the possibilities of irrigation throughout the mandatory period. Under its auspices, Dr. Walter Lowdermilk, a distinguished American soil conservationist, prepared a report in 1944 that laid the basis for all subsequent water planning in Israel. Lowdermilk asserted that the harnessed flow of the Jordan River, combined with the exploitation of ground water, would enable the Holy Land to support a population of at least 5 million in the ensuing decades. This appraisal was later endorsed and refined by other authorities, particularly by the American engineers James Hayes and John Cotton. By 1960, therefore, Mekorot, Israel's water planning authority, had laid out the working blueprint for a national irrigation scheme. Mekorot's list of priorities included: intensive utilization of ground water; reclamation of flood overflow and sewage; tapping the Yarkon and Kishon rivers; and, finally, the mighty Jordan Valley Project itself.

The budget for the entire undertaking came to over $175 million. No Knesset committee ever questioned it, for the Israelis regarded water as no less sacrosanct than defense. Moreover, German reparations, American loans, and State of Israel Bonds were increasingly available to fund the venture. Available, too, were the skills of hundreds of trained engineers and technicians, many of them immigrants. The results of the combined effort were impressive. In 1948, for example, Israel was utilizing 240 million cubic meters of ground water annually. By 1963 the annual rate approached 850 million cubic meters, nearly two-thirds of the nation's entire known water supply. Additionally, sewage treatment plants reclaimed 90 million cubic meters each year and constituted another 5 percent of Israel's total water resources. The purification of sewage was then followed by the Yarkon-Negev and Kishon Valley projects. The Yarkon was a runty little stream that wended its way along the suburbs of Tel Aviv. With dams, pumping stations, and pipes, 100 million cubic meters of the Yarkon's flow were rechanneled southward to the Negev and distributed among the desert's sixty-five agricultural colonies—although not without occasional damage to the ecology. The Kishon Valley Project, in turn, used catch basins and pipes to trap the rivulets and streams of the Galilee hills and direct them to the Emek of Jezreel. In this fashion, some 160 million cubic meters of water were made available by 1957.

The last phase of the master plan, the Jordan Valley Project itself, was aimed singlemindedly at the broad and undulating plains of the northern Negev Desert. It was here, in the somewhat mystical view of Ben-Gurion, that there was to be found the vital living space for Israel's future immigrant population and for its anticipated factories and towns. Again, water would have to come from the Galilee rain area. Inasmuch as the largest proportion of this surplus flowed into the Jordan, the river would have to be tapped, its reserve extended by pipe and conduit through the Emek to the coastal plain, and from there to the Negev. The task was an immense one. The Jordan River system was unique. As noted earlier, it did not flow westward to the Mediterranean, but rather southward, emptying into the Dead Sea. Unlike Israel's other streams, moreover, the Jordan was a confluence of three tributaries and two rivers, not all originating within Israel. Its headwaters rose from a kind of delta, consisting of the Chazbani in Lebanon, the Litani, originating in Israel a short distance from the Syrian border, and the Banias, arising in Syria. All of these converged in the Jordan a few miles to the north of the Chula Canal. From there a single river, constituting the border between Israel and the Hashemite Kingdom, proceeded for another 10 miles, descending 820 feet into Lake Galilee, then continuing its descent through Hashemite terrain into the Dead Sea.

For Israel, all attention focused on the upper stretch of the river, the portion emptying into Lake Galilee. Here the engineers laid their elaborate plans. Here, too, unfortunately, any diversion of the river's upper waters would affect the flow that subsequently reached Hashemite territory, and the Arabs warned that they would block this. Eric Johnston's efforts over the years to negotiate an agreement were frustrated at the last moment, when the Arab nations in 1955 "postponed" a decision (Chapter XVI). Incensed, the Israelis declared that they would move ahead on their own. By the terms of the abortive Johnston Plan, the Israeli water project formed an independent unit, based on the master blueprint worked out by Hayes, Cotton, and local Israeli engineers. From the purely technical viewpoint, it could be executed with or without Arab cooperation. The Israeli government therefore launched into immediate construction. When periodically the Syrians mounted tentative efforts to dam the sources of the Jordan, Israeli artillery and planes flattened the Arab bulldozers (p. 618). The work never ceased.

Its first phase was the building of an enormous conduit, traversing two-thirds the length of the country, absorbing local water surpluses and replenishing local shortages en route. Lake Galilee, the mouth of the conduit, functioned as a seminatural reservoir and was tapped during the warm season. Although the sealing of the lake's brackish underground salt springs on occasion reduced the water level drastically, enough flow remained to be sluiced into a tunnel extending westward to the lower Galilee hills. Subsequently a huge concrete pressure pipe funneled the water on through the Emek of Jezreel, boring through the hills south of the Carmel range in a four-mile tunnel, then extending along the coast to the threshold of the Negev. Thereafter, large distribution lines circulated water throughout the upper quadrants of the desert as far south as Beersheba. Completed in 1964, the "National Carrier" henceforth supplied the nation with an additional 320 million cubic meters of water annually. It was a 25 percent increase in supply (and 75 percent for the Negev) that revolutionized the possibilities for agricultural and industrial development in the northern sector of the desert. The communities of Ashdod, Ashkelon, Kiryat Gat, Beersheba, and Dimona for the first time were able

INTEGRATED NATIONAL
WATER DISTRIBUTION SYSTEM

0   MILES   25

LEBANON

SYRIA

L. CHULA

Chazbani R.

Safed

Rosh Pina

Acre

PUMPING STARTS HERE

Haifa

L. GALILEE

Tiberias

Nazareth

MEDITERRANEAN SEA

Jenin

Netania

JORDAN CONDUIT

SECOND STAGE OF JORDAN PROJECT STARTS HERE

Jordan River

Tel Aviv-Jaffa

WESTERN YARKON LINE

J O R D A N

Ashdod

Jerusalem

Ashkelon

Hebron

DEAD SEA

Gaza

EGYPT

Beersheba

to meet the growing water requirements of new factories and municipal services. For Israel as a whole, the completed Jordan Valley Project opened up assurances of employment for an intended population of at least 5 million.

THE DESERT UNLOCKED, THE SEAS OPENED

The anticipated site of much of this habitation, the Negev Desert, was largely *terra incognita* at the inception of Israel's statehood. A British geologist, S. H. Shaw, had begun preliminary investigations there during the latter years of the mandate. As the British withdrew, Shaw disregarded his orders and smuggled his material to the Haganah. The Jews, in turn, were unwilling to await the end of hostilities before measuring Shaw's data against further exploration. The United Nations mediator, Count Folke Bernadotte, was applying pressure on Israel to forfeit at least part of the Negev; no time could be lost, therefore, in determining what these 6,500 square miles, 60 percent of the country's land surface, actually were worth. Accordingly, in December 1948, a geological expedition led by Dr. Ya'akov Ben-Tor of the Hebrew University departed for the south. It remained there for thirteen months under harsh physical circumstances, suffering even the murder of one of the geologists at the hands of Bedouin, before finally completing its task in January 1950.

The results were not initially encouraging. Even along the Negev's attenuated coast the "soil" was 80 percent sand. The rest consisted of marl, salt, and loess (rock dust). Without water, prospects for farming were bleak. Without an open harbor at Eilat, the possibility of industrial and commercial growth was even more negligible. A handful of kibbutzim had subsisted along the coastal strip and northern Negev plateau even before 1948, but these outposts were less farms than staked Jewish claims to the wilderness. Development of the region's agriculture awaited completion of the great irrigation scheme. Then, in 1964, once the water pipeline reached the desert, impressive changes at last began to take place. By 1967, not less than fifty-seven kibbutzim and moshavim were supporting a rural population of 55,000 people, and in the process sealing off the western corner of the Negev against Arab penetration. By then, too, 140,-000 acres of Negev wasteland were under cultivation, and the region was self-sufficient in vegetables, dairy products, and fruit.

Agriculture had never been regarded as the Negev's future, however, no more here than for the rest of Israel. It was assumed from the beginning that minerals and industry offered the key to regional development in the south. The exploitation of raw materials, on the other hand, remained critically dependent upon access to world markets. Fortunately, the Sinai Campaign ended the blockade of the Gulf of Aqaba, and the importance of an opened water route soon became almost mathematically discernible. In the first year after Operation Kadesh thirty ships arrived at the port of Eilat, carrying 24,000 tons of import commodities; twenty-eight ships departed with 20,000 tons of export goods. In 1967, with the improvement of Eilat's anchorage facilities and the growth of Negev-based industries, the number of freighters arriving was sixty-six, and the same number embarked with Israeli products for Africa and the Orient. Within the Negev itself, communications were dramatically improved. A highway was completed from Beersheba to Eilat, and later from the Dead Sea Works at Sodom to Eilat. The railroad from Beersheba to Dimona was completed. Here at last were facilities to mine and market the Negev's wealth.

Among the desert's resources, copper ore was available at the Timna mines near Eilat, and by 1967 half a million tons was being extracted annually. Potash, a key ingredient in fertilizers, was manufactured at the Dead Sea Works at the rate of 600,000 tons a year; and this industrial plant similarly turned out extensive quantities of bromine compounds, magnesium chlorides, and common salt. Flint clay deposits from the central Negev crater of Machtesh Ramon supplied 600,000 tons of kaolite. Quartz and gypsum were also mined; dolomite and limestone were quarried in small but promising quantities. In 1965, oil was discovered in the southern coastal plain and later in the northern Chelez fields, and for the next few years the annual petroleum output of 188,000 tons sufficed for approximately 10 percent of Israel's local needs. By then, too, good quantities of methane gas were being tapped in the Zohar fields of the northern Negev. In their enthusiasm, government economists noted that the products of the Dead Sea and the surrounding desert soon would provide Israel with as much foreign currency as its annual citrus crops. Perhaps this was true. But the added—net foreign currency earning—value of the Negev's resources did not exceed 15 percent for many years (the added value of citrus exports, for example, was 80 percent). The desert was by no means a Yukon or a Klondike for Israel. Until the market for potash and phosphates opened up briefly after 1972, the products of Israel's southern wilderness supplied a bare 7 percent of the nation's total income.

Rather, the Negev's usefulness was augmented in other ways. One was as an access route for international trade. A second was as a land canal for oil—other nations' oil. For this purpose, pipelines were laid, at first of eight-inch, then of sixteen-inch, eventually of forty-two-inch diameter, to funnel petroleum from oilers docking at Eilat to storage tanks or oilers waiting at the Mediterranean coastal town of Ashkelon. Of equal importance, the Negev was the vast, spacious terrain on which a quarter of a million new immigrants were settled and a wide complex of industrial projects established to employ them. Not less than 40 percent of those industries were based on the resources of the Negev itself. The rest—textiles, chemicals, armaments—were transplanted to the south from alternative sites elsewhere.

It was supremely the influx of new manpower that gave the development communities their character. In the initial phase of immigration, between 1949 and 1953, security considerations and the grave housing shortage led originally to the resettlement of older, mixed towns. Most of these were in the north, where Jews and Arabs had lived together until 1948. At this early stage, then, neighborhoods abandoned by Arabs in Lydda, Ramle, Migdal Ashkelon, Beersheba, Acre, Beit Sh'an, Safed, and Tiberias were simply preempted by Jewish immigrants, and in later years supplementary residential quarters were built and industrial projects established in these communities. In the second phase, from 1953 to 1958, new towns were constructed in previously uninhabited areas in both the northern and southern parts of Israel. Settlements here included Kiryat Shmonah, Chazor, Sh'lomi, Ma'alot, Migdal HaEmek, Or Akiva, Beit Shemesh, Kiryat Gat, Dimona, and Mizpeh Ramon. Their purpose was to meet security, population dispersal, and immigrant-absorption needs; at first no special emphasis was placed on industry as the economic mainstay. With the third and last phase, however, the orientation became increasingly industrial and increasingly southward—to Israel's "future."

By the opening of the 1960s an impressive necklace of pioneering towns had arisen along the fringes of the desert. Most of these communities were very small. N'tivot and Yerucham, for example, did not exceed 5,000 souls, and many of their inhabitants were semitransient members of drilling or quarry gangs. With Kiryat Malachi, Sh'derot, and Ofakim —each about 7,000 in population—they shared certain characteristics with the larger townships rising on the edges of the Negev. The majority of their inhabitants, 65 percent by 1964, were Orientals. Indeed, by then fully 37 percent of Israel's entire Oriental population were living in development towns and settlements. Hardly any of them had come southward of their own volition; they had been moved "from ship to town" precisely as earlier immigrant groups had been taken directly to the moshavim, although later their needs were met with considerably greater solicitude. All these communities, moreover, were planned, supervised, and guided to a degree never experienced by Israel's older settlements. Interministerial committees laid out the town blueprints and organized elaborate housing, employment, educational, health, and other social services. Years often passed before authority was handed over to locally elected councils.

The most impressive example of the new development community was Beersheba. Although the town had functioned as scarcely more than a Bedouin caravansary until 1948, the Israeli government instantly sensed the little outpost's potential importance. Straddling the Negev communications network, Beersheba logically would become the desert's administrative center once trade and industry were organized in the south. So it happened. Wherever mines or factories were opened in the desert, the central offices invariably remained in Beersheba. The city became the southern headquarters as well for the government, the army, the Jewish Agency. Its growth was explosive, approaching 100,000 by the end of the 1960s and boasting the highest employment rate in Israel. On a smaller scale, Beersheba's success was paralleled by that of Kiryat Gat, regional center of the Lachish plan (Chapter xv). By 1967, Kiryat Gat had grown to a population of 18,000 and boasted housing, schools, and cultural opportunities not inferior to those of Beersheba itself.

Ashdod, too, 11 miles north of Ashkelon, became one of the success stories of the nation, and Israel's most dramatic example of a totally planned community. Laid out in the mid-1950s as Israel's "port of the future," Ashdod from the beginning was the object of intense and elaborate government attention and of substantially more expenditure—$120 million in harbor facilities alone—than was devoted to any other of the country's new cities. Progress was faster even than expected. The first stage of the port was already functioning in 1965, and hundreds of thousands of tons of Negev minerals were being trucked in to waiting vessels. Two years later the population had reached 20,000 and its anticipated expansion for the next twenty-five years was revised—somewhat optimistically—from 150,000 to 350,000. Meanwhile, Eilat, at the southern tip of the Negev, also shared in the development boom. An overgrown fishing village as late as 1956, Eilat came into its own after the Sinai Campaign with the opening of the African and Far Eastern trade. By 1967 this little port community was handling 700,000 tons of cargo annually, much of it Negev exports of potash, bromine, magnesium phosphates, and copper cement; while among Eilat's imports were hundreds of millions of tons of oil from Iran, fuel that then was pumped by pipeline to Ashkelon for reloading or directly on to the Haifa refineries for use in Israel. Doubling as a major tourist attraction, Eilat swelled from a town of less than 2,000 to 17,000 by 1967, and government experts—again, perhaps overoptimistically—projected it as a city of 50,000 within two decades. Dimona, too, consisting almost entirely of immigrants from India and Morocco, had reached a population of 18,000 by 1967. While a number of these settlers worked in the Dead Sea plant at nearby Sodom, most were employed in locally operated textile factories. Several miles away, Arad, with a population of 5,000 (in 1970), was rising as the site of an impressive new petrochemical industry based upon Negev gas deposits and Dead Sea chlorine and bromine.

There was every expectation, in fact, that these planned townships would grow virtually without limit. Shortage of space, a key factor limiting expansion in other small communities, was no problem in Israel's development towns; land here was public, cheap, and specifically allocated for urban growth. Care was taken to ensure ample width for streets and plazas and extensive park and garden space. Each neighborhood was provided with its own communal center, its own attractive commercial and recreational facilities. Ashkelon and Arad, for example, often were cited by other developing countries as classic models for town planning. In any case, the problems of architecture, of functionalism, even of ethnic homogeneity, turned out to be more manageable than those of cultural isolation. For with the exception of Kiryat Gat, Arad, and—occasionally—Beersheba, the development towns remained essentially a cultural no man's land. Throughout most of the 1960s and early 1970s they were visited mainly by the smaller, second-rate acting companies and orchestras, and infrequently at that. Blame for this artistic

ISRAEL'S SOUTHERN HINTERLAND

Oil pipe lines

0   MILES   20

DEAD SEA

ZOHAR GAS FIELDS

Beersheba

Arad

Ein Boqeq

R'vivim

Dimona

Sodom

Kfar Yerucham

HAMACHTESH HAGADOL

Oron

Sde Boker

Chazeva

THE WILDERNESS OF ZIN

N E G E V

Mizpeh Ramon

Ein Yahav

MT. HEMET

MACHTESH RAMON

MT. RAMON

MT. LOTS

MT. ARIF

D E S E R T

Beer Menuchah

MT. SAGI

MT. KARKOM

E G Y P T

SINAI PENINSULA

J O R D A N

E D O M

Yotvata

COPPER MINES

Timna

Beer Ora

Eilat

Aqaba

GULF OF AQABA

SAUDI ARABIA

impoverishment could not be imputed to the nation's cultural authorities alone. By and large, Orientals still comprised the majority in the new development towns, and their intellectual threshold remained low. For them, the crises of cultural isolation and social anomie were far more serious, even in the Negev, than those of climate, employment, or physical danger. The psychological challenge implicit here remained among Israel's most urgent unconquered frontiers.

Ironically, the area of the nation's most dramatic growth beyond the arid Negev was on the high seas. It was a development that hardly could have been anticipated during the mandate, when Jewish-owned vessels were limited to a scattering of tuna fishing boats and harbor ferries. The British did not permit more. It was essentially the great postwar rescue effort that laid the initial basis for Israel's merchant marine. At the outset, to be sure, this "fleet" consisted of a rickety, jerry-built force of obsolete European tramp steamers. Yet no one doubted afterward that a strong commercial navy would enjoy a high priority in the government's planning. The country was small and poor, with limited agricultural and industrial potential. Its one frontier unrestricted either by space or (as in the Negev) by natural resources was the sea itself. Political and military factors similarly dictated the need for a merchant marine. With its borders sealed by the Arabs, Israel possessed no overland trade routes. If physical links were to be maintained with the rest of the world, the sea would have to be the principal outlet.

The decision to build a merchant marine was facilitated in 1952 by the signing of the Shilumim Agreement with Bonn. Immediately the government placed extensive orders with West German shipbuilding firms for cargo and passenger vessels (other orders later were placed elsewhere). Eventually, by the end of 1967, the Israeli maritime fleet grew to 105 vessels of various sizes and types, with a gross tonnage of 1.4 million. The ships' average age was four years, thus providing Israel not only with the fastest-growing merchant navy in the world but also the most modern. By then, too, Israel boasted the fourth-largest commercial fleet among the Mediterranean nations. It was larger than Spain's, for example. In 1948 less than 1 percent of the nation's seaborne trade was carried by Israeli vessels. By 1967 the figure reached 45 percent, and 73 percent between Israel and other Mediterranean countries. Yet even earlier, Israeli vessels were anchoring regularly in hundreds of ports on all five continents.

Progress was not uninterrupted. Israeli maritime companies faced increasing difficulty in recruiting personnel. Family-oriented, Jews disliked being away from their homes for weeks and months at a time. The quality of sailors declined, as a result, and ships were manned increasingly by fly-by-night types. Indeed, by 1967, 40 percent of the help employed on Israeli vessels were foreigners, and the ratio would climb in subsequent years. The crisis that struck passenger shipping elsewhere inevitably affected Israel, and so drastically that in the end its companies were obliged to dispose of all their passenger liners, even those used on the once profitable Atlantic run. Notwithstanding these weaknesses and setbacks, the gleaming new merchant marine at least fulfilled Israel's intended purpose of sustaining the nation's trade arteries and asserting a tangible sovereign presence in the harbors of the world.

THE "TAKEOFF" POINT

The economic picture improved markedly in the years following Sinai. The nation was moving out of its period of austerity to one of abundance, even of relative prosperity. By 1965 Israel's GNP had increased two and a half times since 1952. The average per capita GNP increase for this period was 6.3 percent, ranking Israel midway among the world's thirty most affluent states. In 1950 Israel imported more than half its foodstuffs. By 1967, with a far higher standard of living, it was producing 85 percent of its food needs and, as has been seen, exporting surpluses of eggs, vegetables, dairy produce, and fruit. Nevertheless, well before 1967, it was industrialization, not agriculture—not even citriculture—that emerged as the wave of Israel's economic future. It was significant, too, that this industrial growth was based not upon the traditional components of ample raw materials and cheap labor, but rather upon the consumer demand of a burgeoning immigrant population. In the decade after Sinai, industry worked overtime to meet the nation's domestic needs, and in the process absorbed over 90,000 new workers, bringing its total labor force to 260,-000 and industry's share of the working population to 25.4 percent. The figures would continue to rise. Between 1950 and 1969 industrial output quintupled. Its gross foreign currency earnings jumped from $18 million to $552 million, an increase of 20 percent a year. These achievements were registered, too, despite shortages of natural and energy resources, and with the disadvantages of undersized plants, fragmented production, and a distance from "natural" markets extensive enough to impose heavy transport and insurance costs.

While much of the growth was accomplished through massive infusions of foreign capital (p. 427), much of it was also the result of growing sophistication in government planning. By the late 1950s the civil service had become increasingly professionalized, and competent young economists at last began exerting a certain limited influence on the political elite. Techniques of fostering economic growth became more refined. In the next decade, as a result, the government was imaginatively orchestrating a program that included low-interest loans from the development budget, reductions in direct and indirect taxes, government-sponsored industrial enterprises in Negev minerals, industry-wide subsidies, partial cartelization in vital industries, and a number of efficiency-training programs. More emphasis was placed, too, upon stimulating industrial competitiveness in the world market by gradually abandoning import quotas and lowering tariffs.

With government encouragement and guidance, industrial export development followed three principal courses: production on the basis of raw materials locally available, such as Dead Sea minerals, other Negev products, and cotton and cotton products; production based on skill, including electronics, pharmaceuticals, precision instruments, and fashion goods; and production using such raw materials as furs and diamonds, which were physically small and light, thus minimizing transport costs. It was the latter two categories that ultimately became the most profitable, especially finished diamonds. Indeed, in 1966 alone finished diamonds earned $164.7 million in foreign currency, 35.5 percent of the nation's total export income. The amount, if not the "added value," actually exceeded the currency earned by citrus. Specialized skills made the difference here. The diamond-finishing industry dated back to 1939, when Jewish refugees from the Netherlands and Belgium brought their experience in diamond cutting and diamond marketing to Palestine, and then remained on after the war. With three hundred polishing factories, sawing works, and disk-turning workshops, Israel by 1968 ranked second only to Belgium as the world's largest manufacturer of polished diamonds, and accounted for 30 percent of the world output.

The "invisible" exports of transportation and tourism also became substantial foreign currency earners, and largely as a result of the nation's expanding merchant marine and air services. Foreign currency income from transportation rose from $35 million in 1948 to $115 million in 1965. Receipts from tourism increased rapidly after the Sinai victory, climbing to $56 million in 1966. By 1967, as a result of the Six-Day War, tourism actually ranked second to citrus as Israel's leading "added value" currency earner, and ahead of polished diamonds in that category. Ultimately the nation's exports in all fields—transportation, tourism, agricultural and industrial shipments—exceeded $1 billion in 1967. This was substantial progress for a beleaguered and arid little country endowed with few natural resources beyond skilled manpower and intelligent leadership.

Even as the ratio between imports and exports continued to narrow, however, Israel's trade deficit in absolute figures was steadily increasing. From 1957 to 1960 the import surplus remained comparatively stable at around $330 million. But as the nation's tastes and buying power subsequently expanded, the trade deficit, compounded by defense burdens, widened to $570 million in 1964, to nearly $1 billion in the years immediately following 1967, and to over $3.5 billion following the Yom Kippur War (Chapters XXIII, XXIV). Fortunately for Israel's standard of living, which continued to rise uninterruptedly until 1973, this payments gap was made good by a steady inflow of capital transfers. Of the $6 billion import surplus between 1949 and 1965, for example, world Jewry covered not less than 59 percent, largely through United Israel Appeal contributions and bond purchases. Additionally, West German reparation and restitution payments to Israel comprised $1.73 billion from 1953 to 1965, equivalent to 36 percent of Israel's balance-of-payments gap. Third in importance, behind Jewish and German transfers, was United States government aid in the form of grants, hard- and soft-currency loans, and technical assistance, reaching nearly $850 million between 1949 and 1965—and compensating for about one-seventh of Israel's trade deficit. No other independent state in the world received quite as large a per-capita infusion of help from abroad. But neither did any other nation use foreign aid more intelligently or efficiently in absorbing mass immigration and expanding productive capacity.

Israel's most serious economic failure was less in reducing the payments gap than in coping with its own inflationary pressures. Hardly a year passed without rising, and at times steeply escalating, prices. A number of factors contributed to this spiral. Among them were full employment, the influx of financial transfers from abroad, government conversion of foreign exchange receipts, and borrowing from the banking system. The rise of labor costs also far exceeded worker productivity. Yet it was difficult to correct this imbalance as long as the Histadrut blocked all efforts either to freeze wages or to dismiss redundant employees. As in many European countries, a spate of walkouts added to the inflationary pressure. The worst of them, ironically, were triggered not by blue-collar Socialists but by members of the liberal professions, beginning with government-employed doctors in 1954, continuing with government lawyers the following year, then secondary school teachers after that, and leading finally to a work stoppage by government engineers in 1962. These strikes by the nation's professional elite bespoke a deep resentment at the equalization of their wages with those of lesser-skilled employees. The walkouts similarly released an avalanche of public expenditures, as the government became entrapped in the demands of many competing groups.

The single most exacerbating factor in the inflation, however, was the continual rise in the military burden. Annual defense expenditures in Israel multiplied by sixteen times between 1952 and 1966 and accounted (officially) for about 11 percent of total resources. In fact, the real cost to the economy was higher, for it included production lost to annual reserve duty, the expense to employers and the nation of sustaining families during reserve training periods, and the cost of border settlements established on the basis of national security rather than of economic feasibility. As a consequence of all these inflationary factors, then, the price level ascended so rapidly between 1962 and 1965—18 percent a year and climbing—that it became evident that drastic economic surgery was needed if Israel's output were not to be priced out of the world market and foreign currency reserves exhausted. Levi Eshkol, by then prime minister, warned the Knesset in the spring of 1965 that the time had come for a moderation of growth and development, and an emphasis instead on consolidation. A policy of mitun—restraint—was thereupon put into effect by various measures, among them reduced government spending, credit restriction, freezing of a proportion of German restitution payments, attempts to hold the wage-price line, and a curb on building activity.

Restraint was assisted, too, by the completion of such major building ventures as the Jordan Valley (irrigation) Project and the harbors of Ashdod and Eilat, and by the sharp decline of immigration, which subsequently reduced demand in the nation's vital housing industry. Together, then, restraint and "spontaneous" economic developments gradually checked the inflationary spiral. The balance of payments noticeably improved between 1965 and 1967, as the trade deficit fell by 30 percent, the rate of per-capita consumption dropped, personal savings rose, and the Israeli pound slowly gained strength. Witnessing these events from his retirement, Ben-Gurion had to admit that "the recession is having the effect of a blast of fresh air in sobering people up and making them see things with open eyes."

Yet the price of restraint was heavy. It cut GNP growth to a dangerous 1 percent by 1966, and resulted in widespread unemployment, variously estimated at between 40,000 and 100,000. In several development towns the unemployment rate reached 20 percent, and the blow fell heaviest on the Oriental majority, for these were the families with the largest numbers of children. But the recession affected the European and native-born, as well. Many young Israelis, particularly doctors, engineers, and scientists, began to emigrate. In 1966, as a result, emigration exceeded immigration for only the second time in the nation's history.

Nevertheless, the growth moratorium hardly represented the full picture of Israel's economic development, and in any case it was destined to be quite short (Chapter xxi). Over the years since the Sinai Campaign the quality of Israeli life by and large was taking on distinctive and encouraging lineaments. In 1965 Israel's per capita income of $1,135 was already in the range of such west European countries as Austria, Italy, and Ireland. By then 93 percent of Israel's Jewish families were supplied with electricity, and 97 percent with running water. Housing density had fallen to 2.1 persons per room. The share of expenditures allocated to food, beverages, and tobacco declined from 41 percent in 1953 to 30 percent in 1965. The number of Jewish families owning refrigerators climbed from 37 percent in 1958 to 84 percent in 1965; the number of those owning gas ranges and cooking stoves, from 38 to 90 percent; and of those owning washing machines, from 10 to 31 percent.

Conditions in Israel were by no means luxurious yet, or even moderately affluent. The working day generally began at 7:30. The work week stood at forty-seven hours. Clothes remained a heavy investment, and most Israelis dressed shoddily. Furniture, even of the poorest quality, was very expensive. Foreign travel was punitively taxed. Lack of air conditioning in an inclement climate lent a harassed, nerve-frazzled quality to the daily routine. If the amenities of life were improving, moreover, they were no longer as evenly distributed as in the prestate period. In 1948 Israel was still largely an egalitarian society. By 1961, after the mass immigration of the 1950s, the bottom 20 percent of the population was earning approximately 5 percent of the national income, and the upper 20 percent was earning more than 40 percent. In 1966 a report published by an investigative committee under the chairmanship of David Horowitz, governor of the Bank of Israel, revealed that the gap between the rich and the poor was widening. By then in fact 400,000 people, a sixth of the total population, were subsisting below the poverty line. If affluent neighborhoods were growing, so were slums.

Curiously, Israel's leadership for many years avoided facing this emerging social polarization. In a country long obsessed with defense problems, issues of social welfare tended to be rated low on the scale of national priorities. Anyway, it was taken for granted that poverty was far worse elsewhere in the Middle East, that Israel's position was quite mild by comparison with the Arab nations. There was a wide and perhaps naïve assumption, too, that once the task of immigrant absorption was completed, the problem of economic survival gradually would disappear. And, as has been seen, it did vanish for a majority of the nation. "We have done everything possible, considering that our state is less than two decades old"—so went the refrain. But self-congratulation was not enough. The hard-core pockets of destitution, the widening gulf between rich and poor, were under no circumstances rendered palatable to those at the lower rungs by facile comparisons with earlier times or other lands (p. 540).

THE ARAB MINORITY

There were the non-Jews to be considered as well, and their self-image and state of mind were no less crucial for the nation's growth and stability. When the Palestine war ended, we recall, some 156,000 Arabs continued to live within the borders of Israel. By 1966, as a consequence of natural reproduction and of declining infant mortality, the Arab community reached 301,000 (and by 1975 the figure would rise to 411,000). It was an increase that lifted the Arab ratio to 12 percent of the entire Israeli population, and this notwithstanding succeeding waves of Jewish immigration. Approximately 75 percent of the Arabs remained dispersed in 101 rural villages in the Galilee, on the Carmel range, and in the "Little Triangle," close by the Jordanian border. The rest lived in towns and cities, essentially in Nazareth, Shfar'am, and six mixed urban enclaves.

There was a certain irony in the fact that the most rural and backward element of this Arab minority, the 30,000 Druze who were scattered in inaccessible and poverty-stricken villages in the Galilee and Carmel range, should have been the favored wards of the Jews. Traditionally the persecuted victims of Moslem Arabs, the Druze accepted their new Israeli rulers with gratitude and assurances of ironclad loyalty. Israel, in turn, cultivated that friendship by granting the Druze the status of an official religious community, with their own religious council and courts, by allowing Druze breadwinners freedom of travel throughout the land, and by supplying their villages with a generous measure of roads, water pipelines, and agricultural credit and guidance. The Druze additionally received permission to serve in the Israeli armed forces, where they distinguished themselves in later years as border guards and scouts. After fully two decades of Israeli solicitude, nevertheless, this inbred little sect-nation remained by choice an isolated and parochial backwater among the state's minority peoples.

The largest numbers of Israel's Arabs, even the Moslem "majority" among them, fared considerably better in their economic achievements. The agricultural working force was beginning to recover from the trauma of war and sequestration. In the aftermath of the Sinai triumph, as the nation's military and economic prospects improved dramatically, the government could afford to deal more generously with its Arab minority. In 1958, therefore, a substantially more equitable and acceptable compensation agreement finally was worked out for Arab farmers who had been expropriated in the "security" zones. More important yet, the Custodian of Absentee Property was systematically undermining the old semifeudal Arab landholding pattern. By 1960 the Custodian's office had leased 100,000 dunams of choice soil to smaller Arab farmers, thereby providing 30,000 fellahin in nearly 100 villages with yearly leases of 20 dunams or more. The social metamorphosis represented here was but one of many crucial transformations. Throughout the 1950s and 1960s, the Israeli government enlarged its efforts to improve the living standards of Arab towns and villages. Public investments exceeding I£120 million financed irrigation and land reclamation schemes and introduced progressive, mechanized farming techniques. By 1967, as a result, Arab agricultural productivity had climbed sixfold over 1949 and had achieved by far the highest per-capita farm output in the Arab Middle East. The improvements were particularly evident in the quality of Arab town and village life. By 1967, electric lighting was available to 80 percent of Israel's Arab population, most of the villages possessed access roads linking them to the national highways, and inside the villages paved streets increasingly replaced narrow, muddy lanes. At the same time, new mosques and churches were constructed and old ones renovated, and the majority of Arab villages boasted youth and cultural facilities, sports teams, clinics, even shopping centers.

Two decades of Israeli rule produced other, equally far-reaching changes in the Arab way of life, however, and not all of them positive. Before the exodus of 1948, 65 to 70 percent of the Arab working population had tilled the soil. But during the ensuing nineteen years, the area of cultivable Arab land, if far more equitably divided, was nevertheless markedly reduced. Thus, by 1967, only 35 percent of the Arab working population earned their livelihoods directly from the soil; the rest consisted essentially of wage earners, with a small minority of independently employed businessmen and professionals. Several factors accounted for this vocational shift. One was Israel's early post-independence policy of expropriation, which was never fully reversed or made good. The introduction of agricultural technology similarly made thousands of farm workers redundant. So did Arab inheritance laws that fractionated holdings below working value. As a result, thousands of young Arab men were forced to look for employment outside their villages, a search that opened grave new social and political difficulties. In Jewish enterprises, for example,

Arab wage laborers ordinarily toiled at harder and less remunerative tasks and frequently suffered discrimination in wages and social benefits. They also lost much time and money in their journey to work. Those who chose to rent rooms in their place of employment, such as Haifa, Afula, or Rehovot, found themselves generally confined to the slum areas of town. Cut off from home for long periods, they lacked an adequate social or recreational life. The results were especially painful for unmarried men.

The Histadrut was not insensitive to this dilemma. In fact, Arab workers had been admitted to Kupat Cholim as early as 1953 and encouraged to use the labor federation's mutual aid institutions. But it was not until 1959 that the Histadrut leadership finally chose to reinterpret their original ideological premises ("the Jewish Federation of Labor") and to admit Arabs to full membership. From then on, the organization's Arab department, staffed with employees from both peoples, helped guide confused Arabs through the labyrinth of the Israeli bureaucracy. Labor councils were established in Arab villages, school equipment was provided, cultural activities were encouraged and occasionally financed. Yet the federation's major contribution was to establish some 125 cooperative societies in the Arab sector by 1967, most of them providing water services. To many Israeli Arabs, therefore, the Histadrut membership card provided the first significant opportunity to move from alienation in the Jewish republic to at least a more comfortable economic citizenship.

Education may well have been the most far-reaching single influence in the process of communal change. In no area of Arab life, it is recalled, did Israel's local and central authorities invest quite as much effort, for here alone the government was obliged to start from scratch. Hardly any qualified Arab teachers whatever remained in the aftermath of the 1948 war (Chapter xiv). By 1956, nevertheless, a two-year Arab teachers' training college was established. The number of Arabic-language instructors was significantly increased with the arrival of well-educated Jewish immigrants from Iraq, some of them with extensive teaching experience. Thus, by 1963, approximately 1,500 reasonably qualified elementary teachers were available for Arab schools. When Arab local or municipal councils proved unwilling to tax themselves to build school buildings, the national government itself often supplied the funds in the guise of educational "loans." As a consequence of these efforts, the number of Arab elementary school pupils reached 70,000 by 1967. This represented an 80 percent attendance rate for boys and 50 percent for girls—figures unmatched elsewhere in the Arab Middle East.

On the other hand, schooling without a focused communal goal would hardly have been effective in reducing tensions between the two peoples. For the Israeli authorities, particularly, the ultimate success of Arab education depended on extensive and meaningful contacts between Arabs and Jews. Yet these were minimal at first, due to geographic and linguistic barriers. Accordingly, several Mapam and Achdut HaAvodah kibbutzim included Arabic in their school curricula and regularly organized exchange visits with Arab schools. At one of the kibbutzim, Lehavat Chaviva, an

"Institute for Arab-Jewish Relations" was established, a one-year course attended jointly by Arab and Jewish students. On the initiative, too, of Mayor Abba Choushi, long an advocate of Arab-Jewish cooperation, the municipality of Haifa founded a program of shared activities. Later a mixed high school was opened with special Arabic-language classes. In Acre a joint children's center and playground operated. The N'urim young people's village, sponsored by Youth Aliyah, held classes for Arab students from neighboring villages, even as one of N'urim's own (Jewish) schools fostered a parallel Hebrew-language class in a neighboring Arab secondary school and invited Arab students to Sabbath assemblies and sports gatherings. There were other examples of Arab-Jewish cooperation, almost all of them on the local level. Nevertheless, these isolated efforts clearly were less than adequate to dissipate suspicions between the two peoples.

Where education had its most dramatic impact, perhaps, was upon the women of the Arab community. Exposure to schooling, indeed, to sheer literacy, could hardly fail to raise their social awareness and expectations. Legal and political change also played a role. The status of Arab women before 1949 had been altogether wretched. Possessing no legal rights whatever, they could be sold into marriage, often on a polygamous basis, and divorced without so much as being consulted. In addition to providing education, then, the Israeli government set about improving the legal and social circumstances of Arab—and Jewish—women by passing the Equal Rights Act of 1951, assuring women full juridical equality of status before the law. Bigamy was prohibited, as were child marriages. No woman might be married or divorced without her consent. Political rights, of course, had been extended to women from the very outset of the state. Assurance now of legal protection, together with the example of social freedom enjoyed by their Jewish counterparts, were all factors in offering Arab women new opportunities of status and dignity in Israel. However theoretical these advantages for the immediate future—given the deeply conservative nature of Arab society—the opportunities at least would be protected now by law.

The growing number of literate Arabs, men and women alike, provided a mixture of both hope and concern. Secondary and even primary school graduates increasingly found employment as clerks in government offices (in Arab areas), as well as in other public institutions. A few of them worked for enterprises financed jointly by Jewish and Arab capital, including the Israel-Arab Bank and several canning factories. Yet there were large numbers of Arab high school graduates, even graduates of teachers' seminaries and universities, who remained unemployed because they did not wish to become clerks or teachers, or because they were not offered any other job they considered suitable. The truth was that mass education at all levels in Israel was producing a new generation of Arab "intelligentsia," dissatisfied with its condition and increasingly uninhibited in criticizing the state and its government. Here, then, was to be found the single most restive and volatile element in the Arab community (Chapter XXI). It did not lack for nationalist grievances.

Few could efface the memory of the Kafr Qasim shooting, for example.

On October 29, 1956, the day the Sinai Campaign was launched, a curfew was imposed from dusk to dawn on Arab villages lying along the Israeli border with Jordan, where an attack was anticipated. Late that afternoon, forty-three inhabitants of the village of Kafr Qasim returned from work in the fields after the curfew had begun, either unaware that it had been enforced or innocently breaking it. They were immediately shot and killed by members of an Israeli patrol. The press expressed the nation's shock and dismay. Those responsible for the killing, two officers and six men (four of them marginally educated immigrants from Moslem countries), were put on trial before a military court. The officers were given long prison sentences. Later, however, the sentences were considerably reduced, and Kafr Qasim subsequently became a rallying cry for Arab opponents of the government. Their resentment continued intense and vocal for years afterward (p. 537).

At the same time, the demographic growth of the Arab minority enhanced its sense of unity. By 1967, more than half the Arabs in Israel had been born after the establishment of the state. Together with thousands of other young Israelis of all backgrounds, they had no recollection of the mandate, and their political behavior was largely conditioned by the dynamics of life in Israel. Inevitably, then, they contrasted their own circumstances not with the way things were under the British, but with the advantages of full citizenship currently enjoyed by the Jews. Their sense of grievance was further strengthened by compact residence in Galilee and the "Little Triangle," and their exposure to Arab broadcasts and telecasts from Amman, Ramallah, Damascus, Beirut, and Cairo. Israeli radio was no match for this avalanche of enemy propaganda. A number of young Arabs, frustrated by minority status and exhorted by neighboring governments, were tempted to escape across the border. More than a hundred such escapes occurred in 1956 alone. The émigrés were then often persuaded to return to Israel as spies; and when they did, they were usually caught or killed by Israeli border patrols. Such episodes did nothing to assuage Arab feelings.

This bitterness was taken into account, in August 1959, when the government decided to ease somewhat further the restrictions of military government. The case for the military administration had long rested on a vicious circle; it fed the resentment that became its justification. For years, as a result, Mapam, Maki (the Israel Communist party), even several leading Mapai members, had favored a complete abolition of the martial regime in Arab areas. It was in response to their pressure that the cabinet eliminated the majority of off-limits areas in the north and ended all Arab application requirements for work and business travel to Jewish areas. At Ben-Gurion's insistence, military government still remained legally in effect. In 1963, however, Levi Eshkol succeeded Ben-Gurion as prime minister. In an effort to woo Achdut HaAvodah back into a common Labor bloc, Eshkol agreed to eliminate the single most onerous feature of the Emergency Regulations, the lingering restriction on Arab movements —except for individuals considered "security risks" and Arab villages located directly on the border. In 1966, finally, the Knesset took the decision to abolish military government altogether. The Emergency Regulations remained in effect, but the apparatus of military rule, for years a continual and galling reminder of unique Arab status in Israel, at least was no longer visible.

The sources of Arab frustration were not that easily eradicated, of course, particularly when momentous changes in the Arab world tended to overshadow developments in Israel itself. In 1958 the establishment of the "United Arab Republic" of Egypt and Syria invested the Communists with unprecedented popularity among Israeli Arabs. To meet this challenge, Mapai was obliged to promise Arab voters a vastly enlarged program of social services for their villages. But this time the inducement no longer exerted its old magic. In the 1959 Knesset elections Mapai dropped from 62.4 percent of the Arab vote (in 1955) to 52 percent. Less than two years later, in the elections to the Fifth Knesset, Mapai and its associated Arab lists together received a bare 50.8 percent of the Arab vote. Maki, on the other hand, benefiting from the restored ties between Nasser and the Soviet Union, climbed to second rank in the Arab community, with 4.1 percent.

During the four years before the Sixth Knesset elections in 1965, the Israeli party system changed substantially (Chapter xix). Maki underwent its own transformation, splitting into two factions, Maki and Rakach. The former denounced Moscow's anti-Israel policy; the latter favored it and declared itself henceforth as Israel's first truly Arab party. Indeed, Rakach campaigned with a vigor unknown until then in the Arab sector, and its achievement was quite remarkable. Mapai and its allied Arab lists this time polled only 50.1 percent of the Arab vote. Maki, with a pitiable 0.4 percent, was erased altogether as a factor in the Arab community. Rakach, conversely, won an unprecedented 22.6 percent of the Arab ballots. It should be noted that this success hardly represented an ideological affinity for communism among Israeli Arabs. In part it was a response to Cairo Radio's endorsement of Rakach. More significantly, the abolition of military government shortly before the elections encouraged Arabs to vote their true inclinations, without fear of possible reprisals. Not least of all, Rakach offered the Arabs their first political opportunity, under the guise of communism, to repudiate Israel's very right to exist. The shift plainly was a significant one in favor of rising nationalism. As late as 1965, to be sure, most of the Arab Knesset members, even the two Rakach spokesmen, carefully avoided issues of foreign policy and addressed themselves instead to matters relating to their own towns and villages. But no one doubted by then that their mood was increasingly militant. As they responded emotionally to the charisma and grandiose declarations of Nasser, their political yardstick was increasingly the national and social liberation movements flourishing elsewhere in the Arab world—rather than their own, admittedly substantial, material progress in Israel.

The truth was that for nearly twenty years the Israelis, consciously or unconsciously, had sought to isolate their Arab population from the Middle East, and in their first decade of statehood even to isolate the Arabs from Israeli society at large. At no time had the government succeeded in defining any clear, long-term policy toward the Arab minority. Did the Israeli leadership wish the Arabs to stay or leave? Should the Jews sympathize with the Arabs or quietly tolerate them? There were as many policies during Israel's first two decades as there were officials. In the state's early years, one ministry expropriated Arab lands and offered the landowners preposterously low rates of compensation; while another ministry worked with Arab farmers to improve their crops. One ministry invested funds to modernize the school system in the Arab sector, but other ministries refused to employ Arabs, even those who were graduates of Israeli universities. On the one hand, the government preferred that the Arabs remain in their own villages rather than flock to Tel Aviv or Jerusalem; accordingly, it discouraged the construction of Arab workers' flats in the major cities. On the other hand, the economic ministries by and large continued uninterested in fostering industry in the Arab villages, which would have provided stable employment and reduced the migration of Arab workers. The result of this ambivalence was to lock the Arabs in a state of weightlessness, victims of the Israelis' own feelings of insecurity and confusion, and of the government's less than adequate understanding of the Arab human condition. Under the circumstances, the Arab minority demonstrated a quite remarkable patience with its Jewish overlords. It was significant that, shortly after the 1967 war, as he outlined his policy for coexistence in the occupied territories (Chapter xxii), Moshe Dayan felt impelled to warn: "We must not repeat the mistakes we have made in handling the Arabs in Israel."

ISRAELI JEWRY'S "OTHER HALF"

If Israel had other stepchildren, they were to be found less among its minority than among its majority. By 1967, it is recalled, Jews from Moslem lands outnumbered those of European background and constituted 55 percent of the nation's Jewish population. Nurturing deeply rooted grievances, acutely aware of their higher birth rate and growing numerical preponderance, they meant to be heard from; the Wadi Salib incident of July 1959 attested to that (Chapter xv). After the special Knesset committee hearings, many of the Orientals chose to press their case through an extremist-populist Organization of North African Immigrants. Although small in size, and never really an effective political force, the organization was intensely militant, and like the "Black Panthers" of the 1970s (Chapter xxiv), it ventilated its claims in public protest meetings, newspaper interviews, and appeals to the Knesset. By then, in any case, the Ashkenazic "establishment" was well apprised of the problem of a divided community. This awareness led to important policy innovations in the economic and educational spheres.

Education was a matter of particularly intense concern for the nation. Despite the government's formidable efforts in the 1950s, schooling in the development towns remained scandalously inadequate. As late as 1959, the dropout rate from elementary schools reached 10 percent in the largely Oriental, immigrant moshavim and new towns. Worse yet, barely 28 percent of the students in the outlying communities reached the second year of high school. Deeply alarmed, therefore, the ministry of education in 1962 established a Center for Educational Institutions in Need of Special Care. The title plainly alluded to schools in slum or development areas—indeed, in any predominantly Oriental neighborhood. Schools designated as "in need of special care" received preferential treatment—for example, grants for books and audiovisual equipment, funds for extended school days and prolonged school years, loans (often convertible into grants) to experienced and highly qualified teachers who agreed to work in development areas.

Financially, these efforts were matched by the local governments in a coordinated program of "graded fees" under which qualified students were admitted to high school at reduced rates, or even free, depending upon the income of their parents. By 1965, 45,000 pupils were attending secondary school under the graded-fee program. The number would have been larger but for the Oriental family tradition of putting children to work the moment they finished their elementary schooling. Yet even here, in the hope of encouraging gifted youngsters to continue their education, the government began selectively paying family stipends for the loss of children's earnings. In 1965 plans were similarly being considered for the phased introduction of another year of free, compulsory schooling. All these efforts, too, were in addition to a developing program ·of adult education carried out through the ministry of education, the Jewish Agency, and the Israel defense forces. As early as 1963, in fact, Israel was spending 7 percent of its GNP on education. The corresponding figure for Britain was 4.5 percent, and for the United States about 5 percent. The ministry of education's expenditure that year was 12 percent of the national budget, second only to the outlay for defense.

The results of this educational crash program were not altogether unimpressive. In 1951–52 only 42.8 percent of the fourteen-to-seventeen age group continued on to secondary school. By 1964–65 the ratio was 63 percent. Yet of this figure only 16 percent passed the matriculation examination that qualified high school graduates for university education. Predictably, the wastage was far higher among Oriental children, only 8 percent of whom finished high school altogether. By 1966, Oriental youngsters constituted 51 percent of Israel's college-age youth, but only 13 percent of the nation's university undergraduates. Perhaps the best that could be said for the government's strenuous educational effort in the 1960s was that it stabilized the gap between European and Oriental youngsters, and even showed some faint signs of beginning to narrow it.

Economically, too, a certain progress was becoming evident. At the government's initiative, jobs were made available—even artificially created

—for unskilled Orientals in public projects, especially in development areas. For the first time, limited numbers of Jews from the Eastern communities, particularly from Egypt and Iraq, reached middle-level administrative positions. Although no Orientals yet attained top commands in the armed forces, by 1971 they comprised almost half the noncommissioned officers and were increasingly represented up through the rank of captain. More significantly, the economic gulf between Oriental and Ashkenazic families apparently was beginning to stabilize. The former still averaged only 70 percent of the income of the latter, but real income in the lowest decile of the population rose by 35 percent as compared with an overall rise of 26 percent.

These hopeful figures told only part of the story, of course. While Oriental workers comprised 34 percent of the labor force, they still represented (by 1969) only 16 percent of the nation's professionals and 19 percent of its white-collar workers. Their families were far larger than those of the Europeans; their paychecks were stretched much thinner, as a result. The chasm between the two groups was particularly evident in housing. By 1967, 120,000 families, or 20 percent of the Jewish population, lived in substandard, even slum housing. Fully 83 percent of these families were Oriental. Two years before, awakened to the critical social danger of urban blight, the Knesset had enacted a Rehabilitation Area Clearance Law, with the purpose of razing the slums of Israel's three major cities and offering displaced families alternative housing or compensation. Yet the program had hardly begun before the Six-Day War, and rising defense expenditures afterward slowed its progress markedly. Thus, in 1969, 83 percent of the Westerners enjoyed an average density of less than two people per room. Among the Orientals, only 49 percent achieved this ratio.

The fact, then, that the gulf between the two communities, although narrowed in certain areas, had not appreciably been eliminated remained a source of continuing bitterness among the Easterners. By 1967, a majority of them had lived in Israel some fifteen years. They could hardly be described as newcomers or novices any longer. Like the Arabs, they measured what they had by the achievements of others—in this case, the Ashkenazim. Failing to attain the same levels, they were persuaded that social discrimination was as responsible for their plight in the 1960s as in the 1950s. Nor were they entirely wrong. Even the nation's leading figures occasionally betrayed this lingering ethnic prejudice. As minister of education, Abba Eban could state in an address that "one-half of our population comes from countries which, since the decline of Islamic culture, have had no educational history or environment." "Shall we be able to elevate these immigrants to a suitable level of civilization?" Golda Meir once publicly asked. President Ben-Zvi, a scholar of Oriental Jewish history, could refer in his book *The Exiled and the Redeemed* to "these lost and forlorn tribes." The Westerners' lingering distaste for the Easterners occasionally took the psychological form of "projection." Thus Kalman Katznelson, in his neo-Fascist book *HaMahapechah HaAskhenazit* (The

Ashkenazic Revolution), written in 1964, ventured the observation that the "Sephardo-Orientals" hated the Ashkenazic Jews and often expressed their regret that Hitler did not finish them off. Until the mid-1960s, the Israeli school syllabus emphasized the Ashkenazic heritage, with extensive courses in European Jewish history and literature.

It was only belatedly that the country's educators and sociologists recognized that integration through the earlier, shopworn technique of "merging the communities"—a euphemism for the assimilation of the Oriental Jews to the Europeans—was a dead end. In 1965 this approach finally was dropped by government and Jewish Agency leaders in favor of "cultural pluralism." Zalman Aranne, an exceptionally able minister of education, laid it down as a pedagogic guideline that Israeli culture was no longer to be envisaged monolithically, but rather as the sum total of numerous subcultures, Eastern and Western alike, each with its own dignity and tradition. As the Orientals became the nation's majority, the Ashkenazic leadership conceded that they were entitled to a decent image of themselves and to a greater voice in the country's affairs.

In one area, certainly, the Orientals no longer awaited the dispensations of the Westerners. It was the sphere in which demographic majorities counted most of all, that of politics. By the early 1960s, the various party leaders had recognized the importance of attracting non-European votes by placing Orientals on the Knesset lists—usually in "safe places," near the bottom. The number of Oriental deputies accordingly doubled between the Fifth and Sixth Knessets. As late as 1965 the Easterners may not have constituted more than 12 percent of the total parliamentary membership, with a single Sephardic minister in the cabinet. But if this representation in the national government was less than impressive, the achievements of the Orientals in local politics were considerably more striking.

The evidence of their new political impact was visible as early as 1963, when a nationwide movement of Easterners was organized by several affluent Iraqis living in Ramat Gan and Jerusalem. The new group concentrated first upon supporting the local "ethnic"—that is, Oriental—electoral list in Beersheba. Sensing the implications of this movement, the Mapai leaders in Beersheba hurriedly searched for an appropriate Oriental candidate of their own. They found their man in Judge Eliahu Navi, an Iraqi Jew who had come to Palestine at the age of thirteen and had made his way up from a working-class background. The election results in Beersheba produced a Mapai-dominated coalition headed by Navi and by several Oriental municipal councilors. A week before, elections had taken place in the port community of Ashdod, where a majority of the 16,000 inhabitants were North Africans. Here the victorious Mapai coalition ticket was led by an Egyptian immigrant, Robert Haim, with Albert Boskiliah, a North African, as deputy mayor. The trend was unmistakable. In 1950, only 13 percent of the members in Jewish local governments were Orientals. Thereafter the figure climbed impressively: to 24 percent in 1955, 37.5 percent in 1959, and 44 percent in 1965 and 1969. By 1970 there were Oriental mayors in 30 percent of the country's Jewish municipalities, and Oriental deputy mayors in 39 percent. It was certain that this mounting political influence eventually would make itself felt in the national government. Deputy ministerial positions, for example, were likely to be filled by increasing numbers of Easterners.

If politics was one sphere in which the Orientals had at last discovered a great equalizer for themselves, there was a no less vital augury of change in yet another sector, that of intermarriage. It was dramatically symbolic of the "new" Israel, for example, that Beersheba's recently elected Mayor Navi, son of an Arabic-speaking, turban-wearing Iraqi who had lived simultaneously with two wives in the old country, was married to the daughter of a former Prussian Jewish army officer. To be sure, as late as the 1960s, a high degree of endogamy characterized not only the Ashkenazic and Oriental communities, but, by the same token, individual ethnic strains within each. Among the Easterners, Iraqis tended to marry Iraqis, Moroccans to marry Moroccans, and so on. Nevertheless, by 1969 the ratio of intermarriage between Orientals and Europeans rose to 17.4 percent of all Jewish marriages in Israel. Here, ultimately, then, in the "mingling of the tribes," lay the one decisive assurance of single Jewish nationhood within a multinational and pluralistic Israeli republic.

CHAPTER XIX A DECADE OF POLITICAL AND DIPLOMATIC ACHIEVEMENT

THE CRISIS OF THE POLITICAL
ESTABLISHMENT: THE LAVON AFFAIR

Israel's political configuration remained seemingly unchanged in the years immediately following Operation Kadesh. To all appearances, the brilliant military victory strengthened the grip of the Mapai-led coalition on the central organs of power. This became evident in the 1959 elections to the Fifth Knesset, when the dominant Labor faction achieved an impressive plurality of forty-seven seats. Earlier, misgivings had been expressed that the party's aging veterans were clinging to office too long. Ben-Gurion now shrewdly blunted the criticism by placing newer, younger figures high on the electoral list, including Abba Eban, Moshe Dayan, and Shimon Peres. Eban eventually became minister of education, Peres was appointed minister of defense, while Dayan remained minister of agriculture, a post he had held since 1958. Notwithstanding these innovations, however, and the solid Mapai victory, the life of the 1959 Knesset was destined to be nasty, brutish, and short. As events developed, it was Ben-Gurion himself who cut it short.

The instrument of this unwilling act was Pinchas Lavon, the former minister of defense, who had resigned under a shadow at the time of the Cairo spy debacle (Chapter XVII). Although honorably ensconced since 1955 in the influential office of secretary-general of the Histadrut, Lavon remembered the painful circumstances of his departure from government, and he brooded. As the years passed, he watched helplessly as the most influential ministries faded beyond his reach. It was apparent that Ben-Gurion was grooming a number of younger protégés as his successors, especially Dayan and Peres, the men Lavon had cause to recall with undiminished bitterness. These officials and other, lesser-known technocrats were assuming policymaking roles in the army, in the government, and not infrequently in Mapai itself.

Indeed, for a number of years a quiet revolt had been brewing within Mapai against the party's veteran oligarchs, the mandarins of the Second and Third Aliyot. Since his entry into politics in 1958, it was Dayan who had become associated with the "Young Guard" and who was regarded increasingly as their unofficial leader; most of his political statements were made in their forums. Yet Dayan soon shifted the focus of the Young Guard's criticism from intraparty affairs to the general sphere of Israeli society. Questioning many of Labor's traditionally sacred values, he aimed his sharpest barbs at the Histadrut's collective bargaining methods, its protection of inefficient workers. With his friend and ally Shimon Peres, Dayan then coined a phrase destined to have far-reaching impact in public discussions. He asked for a shift in emphasis from chalutziut (pioneering) to mamlachtiut (state efficiency). Technocracy and meritocracy, he argued, not seniority and ideology, should hence-forth be the guiding principles of modern administration. Peres, Dayan, and their group thereafter associated themselves with the transformation of the prestate voluntary institutions into "official" government agencies. Ben-Gurion himself, perhaps unconsciously following the line once ad-vocated by Jabotinsky, had shown the way by establishing a unified army and school system. Now, the Young Guard pressed for the identical mamlachtiut in transforming Kupat Cholim, Histadrut's medical insurance, into state socialized medicine, in nationalizing bus transportation and a wide variety of cultural activities that lay within the guarded preserve of the labor federation. A policy of austerity once again should be adopted, the critics insisted, with a freeze on living standards in order to develop export industries and the Negev. All these proposals were at variance with the traditional Histadrut position.

In fact, Lavon and his associates were not blind to the needs of the time. They had frequently demonstrated restraint in the wage raises they had sought for their constituents. Between 1955 and 1959 the secretary-general personally had introduced a number of far-reaching changes in Histadrut's structure, including the decentralization of Solel Boneh (the Histadrut's labor contracting arm), the professionalization of staff, and new regulations for bus cooperatives. But he drew the line specifically on the issue of Kupat Cholim. Health insurance was the Histadrut's most effective inducement for membership, and a key source of Lavon's own power. In 1958, resentful of Dayan's growing popularity and influence, the secretary-general began firing back, accusing Dayan and his friends of "careerism" and warning that the traditional Socialist Zionist elite of pioneers and laborers must continue its leading role if Israel were to remain a "chosen society." Lavon's broadsides failed to check the growing appeal of the younger men, however; the latter enjoyed the vital, if discreet, patronage of Ben-Gurion himself.

Then, in April 1960, a crucial bit of information unexpectedly offered Lavon a new lease on his political future. An intelligence officer, Yosef Harel, was examining the minutes of the 1954–55 Olshan-Dori hearings on the Egyptian spy mishap when he noted two incongruities in the testimony of Colonel Benyamin Gibli, the former intelligence chief. Harel called these to Lavon's attention. Gibli had declared that Lavon personally had issued the order for the Cairo cinema bombing at a meeting in his, Lavon's, home. Yet the meeting actually took place a week after the failure of the intelligence operation. A second inconsistency was the copy of Gibli's letter to Dayan, containing the phrase "according to the orders of the minister of defense." The original of the letter was now in the files, and it did not include this vital clause; evidently the copy that had been presented to the Olshan-Dori committee was a forgery. The following month Lavon revealed his new evidence to the prime minister and demanded exoneration of all responsibility for the Egyptian debacle. Promising to investigate the matter immediately, Ben-Gurion appointed a committee of inquiry under the chairmanship of Chaim Cohen, a supreme court justice.

Shortly after the Cohen committee began its deliberations, it was presented with other, even more astonishing information. Half a year earlier, in November 1959, Paul Frank, the intelligence bureau's former European contact man, had been placed on trial in Jerusalem. The charge, heard *in camera*, was treason. Apparently Frank had been a double agent, escaping detention in Egypt by betraying his comrades there. During his testimony before the district court, Frank warned that he would not go down alone. He revealed that he had committed perjury before the Olshan-Dori committee. He had declared in 1955 that he had not been coached by his superiors. But in fact Gibli's assistant had provided Frank with a detailed account of the Olshan-Dori hearings and had advised him on his testimony against Lavon. At that time Frank had followed instructions. Now, in Jerusalem, facing a sentence of twelve years (he was convicted), he was taking his revenge. The evidence of this perjury reached Lavon and astounded him. In September 1960, returning from a vacation abroad, the secretary-general hinted darkly to the press that he had been "framed" years earlier for political reasons. He demanded, and received, a special meeting with the Knesset foreign affairs and security committee.

Throughout the next few weeks a dramatic series of hearings ensued. Although they were held in closed sessions, extracts of each day's testimony somehow found their way into the press. Thereupon, in response to Lavon's accusations of slander and perjury, defense officials struck back with leaked accounts of the secretary-general's alleged incompetence as minister of defense in 1954 and 1955. The public was mystified. The spy events of 1954 and their aftermath were still top-secret. As late as 1960, the government censor permitted only the vague information to appear that years before an "unfortunate mishap" had occurred in the defense ministry, that Lavon had been held responsible for it and had left office under a cloud, and that now at last, five years after the fact, new evidence had come to light which Lavon was resolved to exploit, and that a major schism was opening between distinguished officials of the government and of Mapai. A vague feeling of restiveness swept through the country. Was Lavon another Dreyfus?

In October 1960 the Cohen committee issued its report. It concluded that perjury had indeed taken place in the 1955 Olshan-Dori hearings, enough to render them invalid. Even so, the report observed, no subsequent prosecution appropriately could be initiated in view of the unofficial nature of the Olshan-Dori committee, and the long period of time that had since elapsed. Armed with this report, then, Levi Eshkol, Mapai's most respected intermediary, visited Sharett, who had been prime minister in 1955, and the two men devised a compromise formula intended to resolve the impasse. Sharett issued a statement in mid-October declaring that if he had known in 1955 of the evidence now available, he would have regarded it as a "weighty confirmation" of Lavon's version of the facts, although he would still have accepted Lavon's resignation rather than consent to the dismissal of Peres. With this statement, it was hoped, both Lavon and his rivals, Peres and Dayan, would be placated. They were. Lavon eventually declared himself satisfied that the "slur" on his "personal integrity" was expunged. The "Lavon Affair" apparently had come to an end.

It was not to be that easy. Ben-Gurion was infuriated by the Sharett statement. He regarded it as a slander against his beloved army and, worse yet, as a threat leveled by Lavon and the Mapai Old Guard against his younger protégés. At this point, then, the prime minister openly repudiated the "so-called finality" both of the Cohen report and of the Sharett statement and called instead for a legal commission to reevaluate the case. Although shocked by the unexpected outburst, the cabinet nevertheless appointed an investigative commission from among its own members, under the chairmanship of Minister of Justice Pinchas Rosen, to review once again all the facts of the "Affair." On December 21 the ministerial committee pronounced its unanimous decision: Lavon had not given the direct order for the security mishap. The committee then declared the matter resolved once and for all.

It was wishful thinking. The outraged Ben-Gurion insisted now that only a legal inquiry was capable of probing the evidence objectively. When the Mapai central committee hesitated at first, the prime minister threatened to resign. Not everyone was impressed by the ultimatum. In January 1961 an "Intellectual Committee" of Hebrew University professors released a statement to the press, excoriating Ben-Gurion's "dictatorial" methods and branding them a threat to the republic. Various student groups then followed their teachers' example by organizing a "Committee for the Defense of Democracy" and by voicing their concern in public addresses and through the press. The newspapers of course debated the issue vigorously, most of them supporting Lavon. Now, too, the non-Mapai members of the cabinet—Mapam, Achdut HaAvodah, and the Progressives —notified the Knesset that they were "supporting the . . . government because it had stood up against the prime minister. . . ." The extraordinarily involuted statement in fact represented a vote of confidence in a government without Ben-Gurion.

The next day Ben-Gurion astounded his colleagues by submitting his resignation. In shock, pleading with him to reconsider, the Mapai central committee on February 4, 1961, expelled Lavon as a member of the group and as secretary-general of the Histadrut. It was a serious mistake. Whatever their private views about the importance of younger leadership and mamlachtiut—state efficiency—several of Mapai's ablest spokesmen were appalled at the peremptory dismissal. Under the leadership of the "Intellectual Committee," they organized an ideological faction known as Min HaY'sod (From the Foundation), demanding, in curiously Dayan- and Peres-like language, the democratization of the party. Failing to overrule Lavon's dismissal, this group eventually left Mapai. By mid-February, too, the other coalition parties formally ended their association with Mapai, as long as Ben-Gurion remained the Mapai candidate for premier. After weeks of protracted interparty discussion failed, new elections were scheduled for the following August—less than two years after Mapai's impressive victory of 1959.

Campaigning began listlessly, with Mapai emphasizing its record of peace, security, and prosperity. The response was apathetic this time. The "Affair" had reduced Ben-Gurion's popularity to its lowest ebb. The election consequently produced a major setback for Mapai: a loss of five seats, from forty-seven to forty-two. Two months went by until a patchwork coalition could be formed. Although Ben-Gurion stayed on, this time his government partnership was much narrower, for the Liberals and Mapam remained outside the coalition. Operating on a smaller base, the "old man" found his liberty of action far more seriously restricted than in earlier cabinets. In truth, he would never recover from the acrimony and spleen of the Lavon Affair.

THE AFTERMATH: A RECONSTRUCTION OF PARTIES

Others were not laggard in exploiting Mapai's disarray. In the spring of 1961 negotiations were opened between the General Zionists and the Progressives with a view to a merger. Both parties sensed that the time was ripe for a vigorous assault on Mapai's traditional domination. In April, therefore, after swift and businesslike discussions that reflected the central European mentality of leaders on both sides, the two groups united in a Liberal party. Announcing their platform for elections to the impending Fifth Knesset, the Liberals favored a transference of all social services from the Histadrut to the state, equality of recognition for private initiative, limitation of government intervention in economic affairs, and renewed emphasis on the preservation of individual liberties. In the 1961 elections the new party won seventeen seats in the Knesset.

The number was matched by Cherut, also in opposition. Plainly neither group had managed on its own to undermine Labor's dominance. Early in 1964, therefore, spontaneous appeals arose among centrists and rightists of all factions for a joint parliamentary bloc. A majority both of Cherut and of the Liberals quickly approved the scheme. Yet seven of the Liberals' seventeen Knesset members, representing almost the whole of the Progressive wing, declined to join the new alignment; Cherut was too militant for their tastes. Rather, they formed the Independent Liberal party, the last redoubt of central European moderation in Israel. Undeterred by this defection, Cherut and the majority wing of the Liberals moved with dispatch, confirming their agreement for a joint parliamentary bloc to be known as Gachal. Yet their platform was virtually identical with that of the Liberal party in the 1961 voting; and in the subsequent joint campaign effort, Gachal emerged from the 1965 Knesset elections with an unspectacular twenty-six seats.

No far-reaching changes were portended by Mapai itself in the interval, once it resumed its—somewhat shaken and attenuated—control of government in 1961. The party appeared initially to have weathered the Lavon Affair. Even so, Ben-Gurion's own position became steadily weaker, for he now led a cabinet that had been formed by someone else, Levi Eshkol. Nor was the prime minister unaffected by the growing opposition to his leadership among the members of the "Bloc," the influential cadre of Old Guard veterans in the central committee, grouped around Golda Meir, Shraga Netzer, and Zalman Aranne. The rift between Ben-Gurion's protégés in the Young Guard and the Bloc had not been mended. The former continued to press for a new spirit of efficiency and technocracy in government. The latter, in unofficial alliance with the Lavonists, criticized the notion of mamlachtiut as lacking in traditional Labor Zionist values and made plain that ideology was not an expendable factor in Mapai's vision of Israeli society. As the months passed, the gulf between these two wings of the party apparently remained unbridgeable. In June 1963, therefore, worn out by factional strife, Ben-Gurion unexpectedly resigned. Retiring to his Negev kibbutz of Sde Boker, the old warrior let it be known that his departure from national leadership was final. During the course of a lifetime in the Zionist cause, he had guided his nation to independence and sovereignty. Except for one brief interregnum, he had dominated Israel's public life for fifteen years. Now, at the age of seventy-six, returning like Cincinnatus to a life of agricultural simplicity, he would be content to pass the reins of government to others. His departure accordingly was a moment for public reflection. Whatever "B-G's" crotchets and irascibilities of late, even his political enemies admitted that no other of his contemporaries had embodied the vision of the reborn People of Israel more gallantly or singlemindedly. The nation would not see his like again.

Ben-Gurion's hand-picked successor, Levi Eshkol, assumed office as a self-professed healer of wounds. Born in 1895 in the Ukraine, Levi Shkolnik (he changed his name in 1948) had emigrated to Palestine in 1914, in the waning days of the Second Aliyah. There, laboring in Petach Tikvah and afterward in the vineyards of Rishon l'Zion, he became a devoted follower of A. D. Gordon and of Gordon's "religion of labor." A hard-working, patient, modest man of great organizing ability, Eshkol fulfilled a wide variety of assignments during the Yishuv. He participated in the Jewish Legion and helped found Kibbutz Degania B immediately after World War I. Later he served briefly as an arms procurer for the Haganah, as a founder-member of the Histadrut, as director of the Jewish Agency's settlement department in Berlin, and as secretary-general of the Tel Aviv labor council. Upon the establishment of the state, Eshkol was immediately coopted by Ben-Gurion as director-general of the ministry of defense.

Yet Eshkol's most fulfilling and productive role after independence was as director of the Jewish Agency's land settlement department from 1949 to 1953; and simultaneously, from 1950 to 1952, as minister of agriculture. In that dual capacity he brilliantly orchestrated the massive absorption of immigrants. From 1952 to 1963, too, he held the key portfolio of minister of finance, thereby exercising ultimate authority over the economy as a whole. Moreover, his talents as negotiator and conciliator ranged over the entire field of government; as a result, no one questioned his accession as Ben-Gurion's logical successor in 1963. A huskily built, broad-featured man of practical and mundane interests, Eshkol differed strikingly from his predecessor. He possessed neither Ben-Gurion's charisma nor his intellectual depth. Rather, he was the born committee member, a careful planner with a special gift for getting on with people. Tireless in discussion, he won over his colleagues by solid and patient persuasion. Israel never had a better-liked politician, down-to-earth, kindly, and tolerant.

Eshkol inherited a volcano, however, that would have tested the mettle of even greater leaders. Within a short period after Ben-Gurion's resignation, it became clear that the "old man" had never ceased to brood about the Lavon Affair. During the aftermath of the Knesset elections of 1961, two years earlier, he had asked a journalist from *Davar*, Hagai Eshed, to pull together all available material on the Cairo "security mishap" of 1954. Eshed's report was completed on June 14, 1963. It was two days later that Ben-Gurion left office, determined now to reactivate the Lavon Affair from the freedom of private life. In October 1964, he sent on the dossier of materials relating to the Affair to the attorney general, to secure the latter's opinion. This opinion in fact was given to the cabinet in December, and amounted to a detailed criticism of virtually every phase of the handling of the Affair, and in particular of the work performed by the ministerial "committee of seven" (the Rosen committee), Ben-Gurion's archenemy. The statement was Ben-Gurion's testament of vindication—for himself, for his beloved army, for his protégés.

In the months following Ben-Gurion's retirement, too, an acrimonious struggle began for his political mantle. Until then he himself had been the balance between the two groups. But now Eshkol, who had been picked by Ben-Gurion as a "neutral" and thus as a mutually acceptable figure, leaned increasingly toward the older veterans of the "Bloc." Ben-Gurion's protégés—Peres, Dayan, Eban, Yosef Almogi—soon found themselves excluded from major policy decisions. In 1964 and 1965, moreover, Eshkol and the veterans concentrated on broadening their political alliances. Wanting neither the Young Guard nor the Orientals, they turned rather to an alternative reservoir of Labor Zionist strength. This was the Achdut HaAvodah party, once members of Mapai, but for the previous twenty years a small, left-wing splinter faction. Its leadership, including Yigal

Allon and Israel Galili, was nationally respected and could be depended on to stay clear of the Mapai Young Guard, with the latter's technocratic principles and disdain for Socialist theorizing. By 1965, tentative arrangements were concluded for a joint electoral and parliamentary list between the two parties, to be known as the Alignment. To achieve this *mariage de convenance,* each party compromised on some of its ideological platform. But the largest concession was forthcoming from Mapai, which agreed now to abstain from its longstanding struggle on behalf of electoral reform—that is, the substitution of a constituency for a party list system. It was essentially a commitment to refrain from further efforts to undermine the "constitutional" basis of the smaller Labor parties. On the other hand, recognizing that they would face a stiff battle with Ben-Gurion and his disciples in the Alignment, Eshkol and his close circle of veteran leaders immediately set about protecting their flank by inviting Lavon and his followers to return to active party work.

Predictably, Ben-Gurion was enraged by this maneuver. For the first time he openly mounted a campaign against Eshkol and the Bloc, demanding a supreme court inquiry into the 1960 handling of the Lavon Affair and furiously attacking the abandonment of Mapai's long-held goal of constituency elections. Unfazed, Eshkol and the Bloc pushed a vote through the Mapai executive committee in favor of the Alignment and against reopening the Lavon Affair. At this, Dayan resigned from the cabinet, and subsequently Eshkol forced out Peres and Almogi, the last remaining Ben-Gurion supporters. In February 1965, at the annual conference of the party in Tel Aviv, the Mapai-Histadrut Old Guard launched a decisive counterattack against Ben-Gurion and his followers. Even the dying Sharett was brought from his hospital bed to accuse the man who had expelled him from power in 1956. Golda Meir, too, vented her scorn on the former prime minister. The party then gave final and formal approval to the Alignment with Achdut HaAvodah and the decision to bury the Lavon Affair.

Yet even afterward the struggle between Ben-Gurion and Eshkol partisans continued within Mapai and the Histadrut. The former exerted all their remaining leverage in an attempt to nominate Ben-Gurion as the party's candidate for the impending elections to the Sixth Knesset. Instead, the party executive committee voted decisively in favor of Eshkol. Thereupon Ben-Gurion (and Dayan, Peres, and other Ben-Gurionites) resigned from Mapai altogether. They founded a new electoral party, Rafi (The Workers' List of Israel), which claimed to represent Israel's dynamic younger generation and described itself as the forerunner of modernization in the nation. Mapai now was confronted with its most serious political challenge since the birth of the state. Its old idealism seemingly had faded, and socialism's enemies were organized at last into a joint bloc.

The 1965 elections were the longest, the bitterest, the dirtiest, and the most expensive in the state's history. Indeed, they were made so in large measure by the near-paranoid virulence of Ben-Gurion's attack on Eshkol and his followers. The former prime minister described the entire Mapai establishment as stale and sterile, as a caucus of party hacks and position-seekers. As an alternative, he and his Rafi followers promised a new look, new ideals, more technocracy, and electoral reform. The campaign failed. Although Rafi cracked the Mapai-Achdut HaAvodah Alignment in several municipal elections, including Jerusalem and Haifa, the Alignment held on to forty-five seats in the Knesset. It is recalled, too, that Gachal, the Cherut-Liberal bloc, returned twenty-six members. Rafi, however, under the leadership of Ben-Gurion, elected only ten members to Parliament. The "old man" and his closest associates thereafter declined into a small party, one that apparently was spent as an influence in the Labor movement and the country. In truth, the election had not really presented the choice Ben-Gurion thought he was offering between young Mapai and old Mapai, between a new generation of pragmatic economists, scientists, and managers, on the one hand, and a tradition-bound group of septuagenarian dogmatists on the other. Eshkol's decisive victory signified, first of all, a repudiation of the once revered Ben-Gurion, who evidently had lost all balance and perspective in his fixation with the unsavory Lavon Affair. But after that it was a vote for Eshkol's different and more relaxed style of political leadership, for a government that, it was hoped, would make fewer demands upon the ideals and self-sacrifice of a people that was tired of living in endless crisis.

As soon as the returns were in and a new coalition cabinet formed, Eshkol proceeded to strengthen the partnership between Mapai and Achdut HaAvodah. Here the genial politician and conciliator showed himself at his best. Party lines between the two groups were increasingly blurred. Even the break with Rafi, if not with Ben-Gurion himself, slowly was overcome. On one side, Dayan, Peres, Almogi, and Abba Choushi (the powerful mayor of Haifa) recognized that they were going nowhere in quarantine. On the other, as Eshkol's prestige slumped during the economic recession, the Mapai leadership was prepared to make certain compromises of its own. Dayan, after all, remained the nation's most popular figure, and that popularity was significantly enhanced by his role as defense minister in the 1967 war (Chapter XXI). Once Dayan ensconced himself at the center of power, therefore, Achdut HaAvodah could not allow itself to be outflanked. In 1968, after protracted negotiations, the three factions agreed to join in a combined Israel Labor party, with a united leadership. Ministerial portfolios were allocated to members of all three groups.

In his eighties by then, watching from the sidelines, Ben-Gurion interposed no further objections as his protégés entered a united Labor party. It did not escape him that Labor had moved appreciably closer to his cherished vision of a single monolithic political force. Mapam's accession was only a matter of time; in fact, the Mapam leaders already had consented to enter a parliamentary alignment with Labor. Even more acutely, however, the "old man" sensed that his followers were not returning to Mapai, but rather to an entirely new party, one that offered increasing hospitality to fresh and pragmatic views. Dayan and Peres, holding crucial ministries, would make their weight felt. If constituency elections had to be postponed, at least one of the results Ben-Gurion had intended to achieve through electoral reform already was within sight. This was the transformation of a congeries of hairsplitting Zionist parties into two or three major Israeli parliamentary blocs. The accomplishment was no mean one. It represented a giant step forward toward the goal of political modernization.

THE EICHMANN TRIAL

On May 23, 1960, Prime Minister Ben-Gurion made an electrifying announcement in the Knesset:

> I have to inform the Knesset that a short while ago the Israeli Security Services captured one of the greatest Nazi criminals, Adolf Eichmann, who together with the Nazi leaders was responsible for what was termed "the Final Solution to the Jewish problem," that is, the destruction of six million European Jews. Eichmann is already in detention in Israel and will soon be put on trial here under the Nazi and Nazi Collaborators Punishment Law, 1950.

These words were received in incredulous silence. Several moments passed before the listeners grasped the full import of Ben-Gurion's words. Then, slowly, the members rose to their feet in a sustained ovation of applause and cheering. The announcement culminated one of the most extraordinary manhunts in recent history, the search for the SS officer who had directed the Jewish Section of Nazi Germany's Reich Main Security Office and who in that capacity had presided over a major phase of the Final Solution. After the war, nearly all of Hitler's closest associates had been seized, tried at Nuremberg or elsewhere, and most were either hanged or sentenced to long prison terms. A few, like Himmler and Göring, like Goebbels and indeed Hitler himself, were suicides. One way or another, the more notorious of the mass murderers were accounted for. There were only a few exceptions. Adolf Eichmann was one of them.

In April 1945, Eichmann paid a farewell visit to his wife and children in Linz, Austria, then fled into the Alps and waited there as Germany surrendered. Afterward he returned under a fake name and surrendered to the Americans. He was kept in a prison camp, his identity unsuspected. He was there the following year when his name initially came up in testimony at the Nuremberg Trials. He decided to escape again. With forged papers, he departed the American sector and entered the eastern, Soviet, zone of Germany. There Eichmann and a handful of fugitives ran a small chicken farm for four years. Soon, however, his name was being mentioned with greater frequency in the postwar trials as the arch exterminator of Jews. It was at this point that ODESSA (Organisation der SS Angehörigen—Association of Former SS Members) smuggled Eichmann out to Austria, and from there to Italy. Eventually a Franciscan monk in Genoa provided him with a refugee passport bearing the name of

Ricardo Klement. On July 14, 1950, Eichmann obtained an Argentine visa; a month later he arrived in Buenos Aires. There he secured employment as a labor organizer for a construction company in the province of Tucumán, which sheltered many ex-Nazis. In 1952 he felt confident enough to send for his family. The children, who had been small when their father left them years earlier and who had been informed that he was dead, were told that he was "Uncle Ricardo." Subsequently, Eichmann "married" their mother, and she became "Mrs. Klement."

During the ensuing years Eichmann held various jobs, but finally joined the automobile firm of Mercedes-Benz, to which he was openly introduced and openly recommended as "SS Lieutenant Colonel Adolf Eichmann, in retirement." He was sure by then that the search for him was ended. Nor was he entirely wrong. The official pursuit was indeed over, once the West began courting Federal Germany. But there were other hunters. These were survivors of the Nazi death camps. One of them, Simon Wiesenthal, had founded a documentation center in Vienna immediately after the war and made it his life's purpose to track down Nazi criminals. It was Wiesenthal who managed finally to secure a rare picture of Eichmann. With the help of other Jewish deathcamp survivors, a maid was planted in Frau Eichmann's household in Linz. As it happened, Eichmann never contacted his wife at the time he knew she was bound to be watched, and only later arranged for her to bring their children to Argentina. Wiesenthal, however, and Tuvia Friedmann, who ran a documentation center of his own in Vienna (later in Haifa), continued to pursue every scrap of information. They received the more than perfunctory support of the Jewish Agency. All leads were investigated. Few revealed anything. Then, at last, in 1960, Wiesenthal noticed that the obituary announcing the death of Eichmann's father on February 5 of that year was signed, among other mourners, by Vera Eichmann, née Liebl. This proved that her reported "second marriage" in Argentina was a fake; she still called herself Eichmann.

Just at that time the Israeli Shin Bet (a branch of the secret service) was already pursuing a clue transmitted to Dr. Felix Shinnar in Bonn from a reliable source, Dr. Fritz Bauer, the attorney general of Hesse province, and himself a Jew. It stated that Eichmann was living in Buenos Aires. One of the Shin Bet's ablest investigators flew immediately to Argentina. He swiftly loca..d the house where the Klement family lived. The vital question now was the actual identity of Vera Eichmann's husband. The Israeli managed at last to snap a long-range telephoto of Klement. It was sent back to Israel, where experts tentatively reconciled it with the old photograph of Eichmann. In early March 1960 four additional Israeli agents arrived in Buenos Aires. They watched Klement closely. And in late March their vigil finally was rewarded by decisive evidence. Klement returned home with a bouquet of flowers. It was a day of no meaning if he were the second husband of his wife. But the day commemorated the original anniversary, March 21, 1935, of the Eichmanns' marriage in Austria.

There was no alternative now but for Eichmann—it was surely he—to be kidnapped and brought to Israel. The Argentine government hardly would have been interested in arresting or trying him; it had taken no action in the case of other revealed Nazis on its territory. Nor was the government under legal obligation to permit Eichmann's extradition to Israel. Fortunately, a chartered El Al jet-prop transport would be in Argentina in mid-May, bringing Abba Eban on a speaking trip. During Eban's stay, the plane would be available for an unscheduled round trip to Israel. Thus, on the evening of May 11, two cars waited near Eichmann's bus stop. Eichmann returned from work and emerged from the bus at his customary time, proceeding toward his home. He was accosted by two of the Israelis, wrestled to the ground, and hustled into a car, which carried him away to an isolated villa that had been rented in advance. There Eichmann confessed his identity. "I am in the hands of Israelis," he added. No reply was given, but he was asked in German whether he consented to proceed to Israel to be tried for his deeds. Fearful of being liquidated on the spot, Eichmann agreed, and signed a prepared declaration to that effect. On the evening of his departure, May 14, he was drugged, then taken to the airport in a large, expensive car befitting a "wealthy but sick traveler." He was carried to the plane on a stretcher. The four-engined transport took off at once for Israel. The trip was smooth. At Lydda airport, Eichmann was disembarked at a special apron, carried into an ambulance, and followed by police cars. On the afternoon of May 23, Ben-Gurion notified first the cabinet, then the Knesset.

On the very day the announcement was made, Eichmann was arraigned before a magistrate in Jaffa. There he was charged with crimes against the Jewish people, war crimes against humanity, and membership in criminal organizations. He had nothing to say at the moment, but observed that at the appropriate time he would defend himself. Eichmann was thereupon returned to Ramle Prison, an old police building where elaborate security precautions were taken, including antiaircraft batteries. A light bulb was kept continually burning in his cell, and a guard was never absent from a peephole at the door. A special bureau to deal with the Eichmann case was organized by the police under Commander Avraham Selinger, with a staff of other German-speaking officers and men. When Eichmann was asked if he would describe his role in the Third Reich, he agreed. Thus began an investigation that continued for eight months. Eichmann's statement was recorded and transcribed on 3,564 typewritten pages. The prisoner displayed an incredible memory, recalling the smallest trivialities about people, places, books, meals, prices. It was only when asked about Jewish matters that he lapsed into forgetfulness. He could not seem to remember, for example, either then or at the trial, what he had seen at the death camps. From beginning to end, too, he insisted that he had merely been following orders, and he felt that he had done no wrong. He obfuscated, engaged in generalizations, and, as it later developed, consciously fabricated.

Yet even as Eichmann was being questioned, Selinger's bureau was engaged in an intensive effort to assemble and organize masses of documents from seventeen countries. These revealed Eichmann's activities during the last ten years of his career in Germany. Among the material were tons of German foreign ministry documents captured by the American army, as well as similar evidence from England, France, West Germany, Poland, Czechoslovakia, and elsewhere. In nearly every instance, Selinger, who personally visited these documentation centers, received full cooperation. The Soviets alone refused assistance. Otherwise, the research compilation was an extraordinary achievement.

Meanwhile, other reactions began to come in from abroad. One was from the Argentine government, which, after a week of shocked silence following news of Eichmann's capture, transmitted an official protest to Israel and demanded the prisoner's immediate return to Argentina. Ben-Gurion himself responded in a long, apologetic, and conciliatory letter to President Arturo Frondizi. The Argentine foreign ministry was unbudging, however, and insisted that Israel accept responsibility for violating Argentine sovereignty and hand Eichmann back. When private negotiations through mediators broke down, the Argentine representatives in the United Nations called for a meeting of the Security Council. The debate began on June 22, 1960. The moment was an embarrassing one for most of the other ambassadors, whose sympathies were palpably with Israel. Conscious of this, the Argentine delegate asked simply that Israel punish the abductors and "make appropriate reparation for violations of territorial sovereignty committed by its nationals abroad." It was significant that by then there was no more talk of returning Eichmann. Throughout the ensuing discussions, the American, British, and French delegates sought to devise a formula by which Israel's apology to Argentina might be regarded as "appropriate reparation." Indeed, on this basis the Security Council voted the next day, June 23, to condemn Israel. Still, the Argentinians remained unsatisfied, and at this point declared the Israeli ambassador in Buenos Aires *persona non grata*—without going so far as to break off formal relations with Israel. Thereupon Ben-Gurion dispatched Shabtai Rosenne, legal counselor of the Israeli foreign ministry, to Buenos Aires in search of a compromise. Finally, on August 3, 1960, the impasse was terminated by a joint communiqué:

> The Governments of Israel and of the Republic of Argentina, animated by the wish to comply with the resolution of the Security Council of June 23, 1960, in which the hope was expressed that the traditionally friendly relations between the two countries will be advanced, have decided to regard as closed the episode that arose out of the action taken by Israeli nationals that infringed fundamental rights of the State of Argentina.

Yet censure of Israel's deed and of Israel's claims to jurisdiction over Eichmann was not limited to Argentina. Jurists of international standing in many different countries fell out over the issue. It was noteworthy, too, that the liberal press in the United States and Britain joined in expressing misgivings about Israel's behavior. The reaction was in striking contrast to the general approval with which Western journalists had greeted the trials of Marshal Pétain and Pierre Laval in France in late 1945, proceedings that were virtually kangaroo courts. It was in contrast, as well, to the broadly favorable liberal response to the Nuremberg trials, when a court of victors applied laws that had not been invoked previously in international concourse. In 1960, to be sure, criticism of Israel was based not on anti-Semitism, but on its opposite, on friendship and philo-Semitism. Never was the point raised, as it had been raised in all the hate literature of the nineteenth and twentieth centuries, that nothing better could have been expected from the Jews. Rather, it was evident that the liberals expected something much better from the Jews, something maximal, indeed the austerest standards of human behavior—which by their lights had been betrayed. The reaction verified once again Hannah Arendt's shrewd observation on the philo-Semites of the eighteenth-century Enlightenment: that they expected *their* Jews to be not merely exception-Jews, but exceptional specimens of humanity. Yet whatever the mixed intellectual response to Israel's deed, no other country (except for Argentina), neither West Germany nor East Germany, neither the Soviet Union nor other European nations that had been victims of Eichmann's wartime activities, officially demanded the prisoner's extradition. In one way or another, all expressed their conviction that Israel would handle the Eichmann case fairly and justly.

This expectation was fulfilled to a degree that surprised even the prisoner. The Israeli authorities allowed him to choose his own counsel from any nation of his preference. At the suggestion of his family, therefore, he picked Dr. Robert Servatius, a distinguished sixty-five-year-old lawyer of the Cologne bar who had acquired experience in defending war criminals at the Nuremberg trials. Servatius was allowed to bring an assistant counsel with him. The Israeli government paid all their fees and expenses.

At last the trial began on April 11, 1961, at Beit HaAm, a large public auditorium in Jerusalem. Intensive precautions were in effect. Hundreds of police surrounded the building. Visitors to the trial were obliged to obtain special passes from the minister of justice. Those admitted included no fewer than 600 foreign correspondents. Their first view of Eichmann was of a slight, balding, rather nondescript man in spectacles, attired in a dark suit. He was seated in a prisoner's dock enclosed by bulletproof glass. The three judges of the special session were all members of the supreme court, and two of them, Moshe Landau and Dr. Yitzchak Raveh, had been born and educated in Germany. The prosecutor was Israel's attorney general, Gideon Hausner. When the trial began, the principal elements of the charges came under the heading of Crimes against the Jewish People. Eichmann was accused of having caused the death of millions of Jews in his role as a leading administrator of the Final Solution; of having secured the annihilation of Jews in concentration, labor, and death camps, and by SS killer teams in the Soviet Union. Servatius then offered two preliminary demurrers: the judges should be disqualified by reason of their preconceived opinions; the court had no jurisdiction over Eichmann inasmuch as he had been taken from Argentina by force, and because Israel's Nazi and Nazi Collaborators Law had been enacted *post factum*.

Hausner's answer was that judges were obliged to be fair, but hardly to be neutral; otherwise no decent citizen would ever be able to try a criminal. As for Eichmann's abduction, the manner in which a defendant was brought within the jurisdiction of a given state had no bearing on the state's competence to try him. Hausner similarly rejected the *post factum* defense, observing that humanity had no alternative but to invoke retroactive laws against crimes of this nature, precisely as the Nuremberg trials had done years before. The crimes had been perpetrated before Israel was established, to be sure; but all the Great Powers had since recognized Israel not only as the legal successor to the British mandate but as the successor to murdered Jewry. After deliberating on these arguments for several days, the court announced on April 17 that it was competent to try Eichmann. Observers at the trial were understandably fatigued by the length of the procedural battle, as it went on dryly, exhaustively, day after day, with precedents and documentation elaborately trotted out by both sides. But foreign lawyers and historians were impressed by Israel's lengthy citations of precedent, especially from British and American decisions. Gradually legal opinion began to shift Israel's way.

Attorney General Gideon Hausner then launched into his prosecution. Polish-born, a middle-sized, balding man of forty-six, Hausner had enjoyed a distinguished career before the Israeli bar and later was to become an eminent member of the Independent Liberal party, which, after 1965, he would represent in the Knesset and in the government coalition. Now, on April 17, 1961, his introductory address was high drama at last. It lasted eight hours and three sessions, tracing the course of Nazi anti-Semitism and wartime massacres throughout Europe, and Eichmann's role in the killings. "As I stand before you, Judges of Israel," Hausner declared, thrusting an accusatory finger at the prisoner behind the bulletproof glass, ". . . I do not stand alone. With me, in this place and at this hour, stand six million accusers." Many in the courtroom felt hackles on their spines. Following the opening peroration, Eichmann's entire statement, recorded in prison, six volumes of it, was offered in evidence. The prosecution cross-examined, submitted vast quantities of its own documentation, then presented innumerable Jewish (and occasional non-Jewish) witnesses to testify on their ordeal and that of the Jewish people during the Holocaust. The audience listened in horror, many at times breaking into tears, some fainting. In his defense, Eichmann continued endlessly to minimize his role. Servatius presented twenty charts of the various Reich organizations that dealt with Jewish affairs, all intended to show that the main lines of authority did not pass through Eichmann's office. Hausner, in turn, did not contradict the wide diffusion of guilt; but he would not allow Eichmann to fade away in the process. He kept the prisoner under cross-examination for two weeks, and in that time Eichmann's image as a "victim of orders" was thoroughly demolished.

On August 14, 1961, after 114 sessions, the main proceedings came to an end. The court then adjourned for four months and reassembled on December 11 to pronounce judgment. Eichmann was convicted on all fifteen counts of the specific indictment. "Together with others," he had committed crimes "against the Jewish people": by "causing the killing of millions of Jews"; by placing "millions of Jews under conditions that were likely to lead to their physical destruction"; by "causing serious bodily and mental harm" to them; by "directing that births be banned and pregnancies interrupted among Jewish women" in Theresienstadt. On December 15 Eichmann was sentenced to death.

Public exposure to the trial itself had been constant and unrelenting. For more than a year Israeli newspapers, and much of the world press, had been filled with it almost daily; many of the sessions had been broadcast. The proceedings had their impact on all generations. For example, the memory of the Holocaust was vivid in the consciousness of every Israeli on the eve of the Six-Day War. Research later by government and university sociologists revealed the profound impact of the trial on the minds of Israeli youth. Asked what lesson they derived from the Holocaust, students responded by emphasizing the dangers inherent in the position of a Jewish minority living among non-Jewish majorities, the need for an "ingathering of Jews" from all parts of the world in a homeland of their own. These reactions were not the least of Ben-Gurion's purpose in conducting the trial. Indeed, he never pretended otherwise. During a break in the court sessions on Israel's thirteenth Independence Day, the prime minister referred to the trial in a speech:

> Here, for the first time in Jewish history, historical justice is being done by the sovereign Jewish people. For many generations it was we who suffered, who were tortured, were killed—and were judged. . . . For the first time Israel is judging the murderers of the Jewish people. . . . And let us bear in mind that only the independence of Israel could create the necessary conditions for this historic act of justice.

The lesson was not for Jews alone. It was for the nations that had allowed catastrophe to befall the Jewish people, and who as a result had incurred a unique moral obligation to ensure Israel's survival.

Eichmann appealed the verdict, and his case reached the supreme court in March 1962. The issues that had been argued before the special tribunal earlier were covered again, if more briefly. This time the hearings were completed in six sessions. On May 29 the lower court verdict was sustained. Eichmann then appealed to the president of Israel. "I abhor the atrocities committed on the Jews as the greatest crime," he stated in his plea, "and consider it just that the people responsible should be brought to justice. . . . But a line should be drawn between leaders and tools like myself." At 8:00 P.M. the following day, May 31, Eichmann was informed that his petition for mercy had been refused, and that the execution would take place at midnight. At the gallows, he refused the black hood and sent his greetings to Germany, Austria, and Argentina, to his wife and family. "I had to obey the rules of war and my flag," he declared, just before the trap was sprung. Eichmann's body was cremated, and in the small hours of June 1 his ashes were carried aboard a police launch. When the vessel crossed the territorial three-mile limit, the prisons commissioner dropped the ashes overboard.

THE COURTSHIP OF GERMANY

In no nation outside Israel did the capture and trial of Adolf Eichmann evoke as powerful a reaction as in Germany. The early postwar trials of Nazi criminals on German soil had long since faded into memory. Whatever their disapproval of the kidnapping, therefore, most Germans were certain that they did not want Eichmann tried in Germany, with the appalling psychic wound that would be reopened there. Adenauer solved the question on a technicality, by observing that "Eichmann is no German citizen and we have no obligation toward Eichmann." But the chancellor also quietly reminded the Israelis of West Germany's extensive financial help, and added that "goodwill must be mutual." It was an obvious appeal to dissociate postwar Germany from the Hitler epoch, and perhaps also to distract attention from the many ex-Nazis employed in the West German administration. The chancellor finally requested his "friend," Ben-Gurion, to show continuing generosity in his evaluation of the German people. The Israeli prime minister's response was favorable. Publicly he indicated again that he distinguished between Eichmann and the current free Germany. "My views about present-day Germany are unchanged," Ben-Gurion said. "There is no Nazi Germany anymore." Adenauer was grateful. So were the German people. Afterward, Eichmann's conviction and execution were disputed by hardly anyone. The three major West German parties were unanimous in their assertion that justice had been done.

For the youth of Germany, particularly, the trial was a horrifying revelation. It supplied answers their parents had never given them. As they followed the court sessions in the press or on television, they sensed the truth at last of what their nation had done. Deeply penitent, thousands of them wrote the Israeli government, imploring to be allowed to atone by working in Israel. For older Germans, too, it was suddenly much easier to talk about Israel, even to meet Israelis, than to face individual Jewish survivors in Germany with whom they, the Germans, had to live side by side. It became the fashion to admire Israel, to laud its achievements, to urge the rising generation to visit it. And the young people did go, fully 20,000 of them between 1961 and 1967. Some traveled in youth groups, some on their own. Not a few arrived to work in kibbutzim or in development projects. All of them were eager to witness the spirit that had made this Jewish nation victorious against its more numerous enemies, and that had enabled it to capture Eichmann. It was ironic, then, that the Eichmann trial played a major role in fostering a new understanding between Germans and Israelis.

The process of rapprochement between the two governments had begun much earlier, of course, with the Shilumim (Reparations) Agreement. At Ben-Gurion's instigation, efforts subsequently were made to raise the financial agreement to the level of diplomatic relations. The "Hallstein Doctrine" blocked that (p. 470). Yet Ben-Gurion was unprepared to give up. Somehow Israel had to fight its way out of international isolation. The Sinai Campaign and its aftermath had revealed how unwise it was to rely for help on the United States, or on any individual country, even on France. In Washington, Eban had asked Dulles to use his influence with Adenauer on behalf of a diplomatic exchange. Dulles agreed, but his efforts were unavailing. The Arab ambassadors had warned that their governments would retaliate against any West German–Israeli accord by establishing diplomatic ties with the Pankow regime of East Germany. For the time being, then, the Hallstein Doctrine stood. At this point Ben-Gurion listened more attentively to Peres and others who urged that efforts henceforth should be directed toward "practical" cooperation with Germany, notably in the economic sphere, where German strength already was much greater than that of France.

To achieve even this "practical" relationship, then, Ben-Gurion sought an early meeting with Adenauer. Both men in fact were eager to know each other; each held the other in great respect. The chancellor's impending visit to the United States, in March 1960, finally provided the opportunity to meet on neutral ground. Arrangements were easily made for Ben-Gurion to receive an honorary degree at Brandeis University. From there he would proceed to his meeting with Adenauer in New York. The groundwork was laid in extensive negotiations in Jerusalem and Bonn. Preliminary agreement was reached that Adenauer should be asked for a loan of $250 million over ten years, but that the more sensitive question of diplomatic relations between the countries should not be raised.

Adenauer in his own way needed a meeting as badly as the Israeli prime minister. A photographed handshake with Ben-Gurion could make all the difference in the chancellor's reception in the United States; for that single gesture of Jewish reconciliation, the sum of $250 million was ridiculously low. Only a few minutes before the interview in New York's Waldorf-Astoria Hotel, however, Ben-Gurion's advisers entreated him to ask for $1 billion. The prime minister resisted, but finally compromised on $500 million. Then the private meeting took place in Adenauer's suite. After a cautious exchange of amenities, Ben-Gurion explained that the loss of European Jewry had retarded Israel's development and security; that the presence of millions of additional Western Jews in Israel would vastly have accelerated the nation's growth. He proceeded to ask Adenauer to participate in the task of developing Israel by lending its government $50 million annually over a span of ten years. The chancellor immediately agreed. "We will help you for moral reasons and for reasons of practical politics," he assured Ben-Gurion. He did not discuss the figure that had been suggested, but he did not reject it. In the same spirit, the Israeli prime minister emphasized—and later repeated to the press—that he made a vital distinction between Germany under Hitler and Germany now. Adenauer was moved and grateful. Photographers were then admitted, and the two statesmen parted in great cordiality.

If political reaction to the meeting was less than favorable in Israel, Ben-Gurion had other reasons for concern. He and his advisers were sure after the Waldorf-Astoria interview that the half-billion-dollar loan was already in their pockets—a sum that dwarfed earlier credits provided by France, Israel's closest ally, or even by the United States. But when one of the prime minister's aides released the news in London, West German spokesmen immediately denied it. Adenauer himself probably had been sincere in his agreement, but failed to mention that the Bundestag normally had to approve foreign loans exceeding $35,700,000 annually. The original sum of $250 million over a ten-year period had been devised to avoid this complication. Thus, after subsequent discussions in Brussels between West German Finance Minister Ludwig Erhard and his Israeli counterpart, Levi Eshkol, a "gentleman's agreement" emerged in the form of an exchange of letters between the heads of government. The understanding was for ten annual payments of $35,700,000. Each "installment" would be earmarked for a certain project to be proposed each year by Israel, and to be considered on an ad hoc basis by Germany. The arrangement worked well. With few exceptions, the projects suggested by the Israelis were accepted by the German government without qualification, or even close investigation. These dealt principally with the construction of urban centers in the Negev: first Arad, then Mizpeh Ramon, later Eilat, and others. For Israel the loan conditions were excellent. Annual interest rates were 3.6 percent, and repayment time could be stretched to between twelve and twenty years. The agreement seemed to confirm Ben-Gurion's long-held belief that Germany, not France, was Israel's most likely potential European source of economic development.

German-Israeli economic relations in fact were expanding in every sphere. As a consequence of the Shilumim agreement, German business automatically obtained a market in Israel; by the 1960s, Israel's purchases from West Germany amounted to $25 million annually. On the other hand, Israel's own exports never caught up with this figure, except for reparations. Rather, the trade imbalance was further unsettled by the impact of the European Economic Community, to which West Germany belonged, and the customs barriers this Common Market was raising against imports from abroad. By the end of 1962, for example, it was all but impossible any longer to sell Israeli eggs and oils in Germany. Bonn sympathized with Israel's predicament and conscientiously supported Israel's request at least for associate membership in the EEC. But the application was repeatedly barred by the French and Italians, who were intent upon protecting their own citriculture and agriculture from competition.

To assist Israel economically, therefore, individual German companies and German institutions (with active government encouragement) purchased large quantities of State of Israel Bonds. Banks and insurance companies, as well as hundreds of German municipalities, were among the largest subscribers. The Trade Union Bank of Frankfurt in 1961 bought substantial shares of Koor, the Histadrut's iron and steel complex. The German government and the Volkswagen Foundation underwrote specific research projects carried out by the Technion and the Weizmann Institute. German universities and technical institutes provided scholarships for Israeli students.

WEAPONS AND DIPLOMACY

In the sphere of "practical cooperation," Israel regarded German weapons as hardly less important than German funds. Ben-Gurion appreciated that Israel dared not rely exclusively upon one or two sources of supply, essentially France and Britain. Political uncertainties in France later strengthened that conviction (p. 569). In September 1957, therefore, Shimon Peres, director-general of the defense ministry, succeeded in arranging an interview with the West German defense minister, Franz-Josef Strauss. A consummate politician, Strauss needed no reminder that an understanding with Israel would dispel liberal misgivings about him and his highly nationalist party, Bavaria's Christian Democratic Union. More objectively, Strauss appreciated that a defensible Israel would remain an effective bulwark against Soviet penetration in the Middle East. He and other NATO defense ministers had received from Israel samples of captured Russian equipment following the Sinai Campaign, and had been alarmed. Accordingly, in conversation with Peres, the German promised to do all in his power to secure the necessary military help. He reconfirmed this promise in a second discussion, four months later, when Peres and Israeli military officials brought him an extensive list of required military hardware. Adenauer himself then approved the list, but imposed the condition that the arrangements would not be committed to writing, that secrecy would be guarded carefully on both sides. It was also understood that the matériel would be supplied gratis, or near-gratis.

On this basis, then, German weapons began flowing to Israel early in 1959, usually via French ports, where they were less likely to draw attention (Chapter xxi). By the end of 1961 the shipments grew in quantity and diversity. They included fifty planes, among them transports, helicopters, and trainers manufactured in Germany under French license, as well as trucks, ambulances, antiaircraft guns, howitzers, and antitank rockets. With the arrangements secret, the arms deliveries not infrequently took on the character of smuggling. Bills of lading attached to the shipments often were disguised or fake. Occasionally weapons were purchased by Germany for Israel in other countries—for example, helicopters in France, antiaircraft guns in Sweden, even two submarines in Britain— with the invoices sent to Bonn. The practice developed of shipping the cargo to another country first, where it would be unloaded at once and readdressed to Israel. When Strauss was forced to resign his post in November 1962, as a consequence of a political upheaval, his successor, Kai-Uwe von Hassel, quietly maintained the Israeli relationship. The opposition parties, too, learned of the secret arms pact, but tacitly acquiesced in it.

The second phase of the German weapons deal, beginning in summer 1964, was the result of American initiative. A year before, Washington had approved the delivery of antiaircraft missiles to Israel. Learning of this, however, the Arab states protested so vigorously that the Johnson administration hesitated to meet Prime Minister Eshkol's newest request for additional equipment. When, therefore, Chancellor Ludwig Erhard (who had recently succeeded Adenauer) visited the United States in June 1964, he was asked to deliver to Israel some of the obsolescent American arms in his nation's possession, particularly 150 American medium tanks stored in German arsenals. Erhard was uncertain. The shipment would constitute the largest bulk delivery of its kind to Israel, and secrecy would be harder to guarantee. At this point, Peres arrived in Bonn with an ingenious scheme for Germany to deliver empty tank bodies to Italy; there, they could be refitted with new American guns, engines, and electronic equipment, and after six months the tanks could be shipped to Israel without their origin being divulged. Erhard agreed to the proposal.

Yet by then the entire issue of German-Israeli rapprochement had been placed under a shadow by other developments. It is recalled that the Hallstein Doctrine, promulgated in 1956, was regarded in Jerusalem as merely a temporary obstacle to an eventual diplomatic relationship with Bonn. The Eichmann trial had produced a renewed and intensified German commitment to Israel's survival and growth. In the late 1950s and early 1960s, exchange visits increased among Histadrut, Mapai, and German Social Democratic and trade union leaders. Franz-Josef Strauss and his Bavarian Christian Democratic Union untiringly championed Israel's cause among German nationalist circles. Nevertheless, in March 1962, when Eshkol and Erhard—both then still the finance ministers of their nations—met for the second time in Brussels, it immediately became clear that Erhard was unable actively to support Israel's request for associate membership in the Common Market. The Arabs had threatened a boycott of German goods.

It was a difficult moment. German reparations were tapering off. The Israeli Mission staff in Cologne was being sharply reduced, and with it the only quasi-diplomatic relationship between the two countries. Accordingly, Ben-Gurion decided to pin his hopes on Adenauer himself, before the old chancellor carried out his plan to retire. And, indeed, Adenauer reassured Jerusalem that he was determined to end his career by forcing through the issue of diplomatic relations. In August 1963, however, West German Foreign Minister Gerhard Schroeder urgently requested the chancellor to postpone further discussion of the question; there was a strong danger that the Arab governments would strike back immediately by recognizing East Germany. The warning was endorsed by American Secretary of State Dean Rusk, who observed that it would also be in the United States' interest for Bonn to retain its links with the Arabs. Sobered by these appeals, Adenauer backed away from the issue. Shortly afterward, he retired in favor of Erhard. The latter similarly abstained from diplomatic relations "for the time being."

In the meantime, other issues had arisen to complicate the emergent Bonn-Jerusalem relationship. One of these was the role played by German scientists in developing Egypt's warmaking capacity. As far back as 1950, German technicians and engineers, many of them former Wehrmacht officers, had been hired to serve as instructors for the Egyptian army and to organize an Egyptian arms industry. Willi Messerschmitt, the famous pioneer of Hitler's aviation program, sold Egypt manufacturing rights to his supersonic jet fighter, the HA-200, developed in Spain. Eventually 200 Austrians and Germans were supervising the construction of airplane assembly plants in Helwan, while German factories supplied the parts. Most of this personnel, and much of the equipment, were obtained through the efforts of one Hassan Saïd Kamal, an Egyptian-Swiss engineer living in Zurich. Moreover, in 1960 a "National Research Center" was established in Cairo, ostensibly to develop a "space research rocket for meteorological purposes." And among the scientists recruited by Kamal was Germany's leading rocket expert, Dr. Eugene Sänger, and Sänger's deputy, Professor Wolfgang Pilz, both of whom had been active in the Nazi V-rocket program during the war. Their staff included a number of colleagues from Germany's postwar Stuttgart Rocket Institute.

Israeli intelligence learned of this development at its outset and did not hesitate to call Bonn's attention to it. The embarrassed Federal Government promised to take immediate action; and it did in fact ensure that scientists connected with the Egyptian enterprise were promptly dismissed from the Stuttgart Institute. Sänger himself returned to Germany. But Pilz and the others remained in Egypt. Finally, on July 23, 1962, Egypt's first locally manufactured missiles were paraded through the boulevards of Cairo, to the ecstatic cheers of hundreds of thousands of spectators. The first rocket, al-Kahir, possessed an alleged range of 200 miles; the second, al-Safir, a range of 165 miles. Both easily could reach Israel. Appalled, the Israeli government registered its protest with Bonn. Yet, while the latter was entirely sympathetic to Israel's concern, it had no notion of what steps could be taken in a democracy to prevent its citizens from working wherever they chose. The West German cabinet hardly wished to revert to Nazi police state methods.

Thereupon the Israeli secret service took matters into its own hands. In July 1962, Kamal's German wife was killed by a bomb that exploded in her plane over Germany (Kamal himself had postponed his trip at the last moment). In September of that year, Dr. Heinz Krug, director of Kamal's procurement firm, disappeared under mysterious circumstances. In November an air-mail parcel addressed to Pilz exploded when opened in his office in Cairo, blinding and mutilating his German secretary. The series of "accidents" continued, reaching their denouement in March 1963 when Israeli agents sought to persuade Professor Paul Görke's daughter and son, both in their twenties, that it would be safer for their father to abandon his work in Cairo. The daughter was induced to come to Switzerland, where it was "suggested" that she transmit the warning to her father. Instead, she alerted the Swiss police, who promptly arrested the two Israeli agents on charges of attempted coercion. During their widely publicized trial, the agents in turn exhibited documented evidence that Egypt was preparing missile weapons against Israel, with nuclear warheads of cobalt 60. The impact of these revelations was profound. On June 11, the Swiss court found the two Israelis guilty but imposed only a nominal sentence upon them, then released them altogether after a prison term of several months. In Israel itself, meanwhile, bitterness against the West German government was intense, even among moderate politicians who had been prepared for an accord with Bonn. The Knesset passed a resolution insisting that "it is the duty of the German government to put a stop to these activities at once. . . ." Again, the Bonn ministry of justice insisted that it had no legal recourse.

Ben-Gurion was gravely concerned by the furor. He had received private word from Franz-Josef Strauss that Israel's violent anti-German campaign might endanger the secret arms deal between the two governments. In March 1963, therefore, the prime minister instructed his security chief, Iser Harel, to terminate all secret service activities against the German scientists. Harel resigned instead. When Ben-Gurion then asked the Knesset to withdraw its resolution of protest to Bonn, he immediately touched off a storm of recriminations. Worn out by this—and other issues —the "old man" himself resigned on June 16. On the other hand, the West German government was increasingly successful by then in luring German scientists back from Egypt with offers of higher pay and better jobs at home. Eventually most of the engineers and technicians returned to Germany. But the episode left a residue of distrust in Israel.

There was yet another issue, meanwhile, that further exacerbated relations between the two countries and similarly threatened progress toward a diplomatic normalization. This related to German legal procedures in dealing with Nazi war criminals. Throughout the 1950s, the West German judicial system had been lax in dealing with Nazi atrocities. It was the Eichmann trial that suddenly revived arrests and prosecution in the Federal Republic. Within months German courts were flooded again with war crimes trials. But inasmuch as charges of murder carried a twenty-year statute of limitations, war criminals could be prosecuted only until 1965 at the latest. The restriction aroused protests in Israel and elsewhere. Nevertheless, with the 1965 national elections approaching, Bonn was unwilling to change the situation. Indeed, the cabinet overruled Chancellor Erhard himself and voted to let the statute of limitations expire on schedule in May of that year. Jerusalem accordingly expressed its "disappointment and indignation." Israel's resentment was compounded, too, when the Pankow East German government shrewdly released documented information of Nazi criminals still at large in the Federal Republic. Eventually, on April

13, 1965, the West German cabinet approved a bill extending the statute of limitations another four years. The "compromise" aroused only disgust in Israel.

Even as these issues widened the gulf between the two nations, final arrangements were being made for the transfer to Israel of the 150 American tanks stored in West German depots. Then, in October 1964, news of the deal suddenly broke in two German newspapers. Chagrined at having been kept in the dark for the past years on the arms transactions, the press all but unanimously condemned military—as distinguished from economic—aid to Israel. In January 1965 the Social Democrats and Free Democrats belatedly joined the condemnation. Chancellor Erhard and his associates were in a quandary. They knew that Walter Ulbricht, the Communist party chief of East Germany, had just been invited to Egypt. His invitation there was a less than veiled warning by Nasser that diplomatic relations between Cairo and Pankow would follow if West German arms deliveries to Israel continued. On the other hand, if weapons shipments were stopped, there was general recognition that Bonn would be morally obliged to compensate Israel somehow—and in a way that would not provoke Arab recognition of the East German regime. Immediately, then, Jerusalem let it be known that the only compensation it regarded as acceptable was the establishment of diplomatic relations.

Without committing itself, the Federal Government took the preliminary step on February 10 of announcing the termination of further weapons deliveries to countries outside of NATO. The blow was a grave one for Israel. Eshkol summoned his cabinet into urgent session. The Knesset in turn passed a resolution expressing "astonishment and indignation" at the German decision. At the same time, Bonn was issuing a tough ultimatum of its own to Egypt, declaring that a visit by Ulbricht would be regarded as a hostile act. The warning was of no avail. On February 21, Ulbricht arrived in Cairo at the head of a large mission and was given a tremendous reception. Although Nasser stopped short of recognizing East Germany, the Bonn government concluded that the Hallstein Doctrine had been breached and that the only effective countermeasure was to seek the exchange of ambassadors with Israel. In fact, German public opinion by then strongly favored the move. Without it, warned Rainer Barzel, a leader of the Christian Democratic Union, "we shall lose everything, our prestige, our honor." Erhard then made the crucial decision on his own and announced in the Bundestag that the Federal Republic intended now to enter into diplomatic relations with Israel.

The chancellor picked a close friend, Dr. Kurt Birrenbach, to fly to Israel and negotiate with the Eshkol government. Birrenbach was obliged to inform the Israelis at the outset that there would be no compromise on the matter of arms shipments, which could not be resumed. On this issue discussions in Jerusalem were blunt, even harsh. But eventually a compromise was reached. The Americans would be asked to provide the matériel that Israel had expected to receive from Germany; Bonn would pay for it. Birrenbach also hinted of future long-term loans to Israel at modest interest rates and reassured the Israelis that all German scientists soon would be out of Egypt and that legal action would be taken against any person who sought to recruit Germans for military purposes abroad. On March 9, the Israeli cabinet voted to accept this package, and several days later the government's decision was approved by the Knesset. On May 12 diplomatic negotiations were formally opened with an exchange of letters between Erhard and Eshkol. That same evening, too, Iraq, Egypt, Sudan, Syria, Lebanon, Saudi Arabia, Jordan, Kuwait, Yemen, and Algeria severed connections with the Federal Republic.

On August 19, 1965, the first West German ambassador, Dr. Rolf Pauls, arrived in Jerusalem to submit his credentials to President Zalman Shazar. Shouting and rioting erupted in the streets of the Israeli capital; stones and bottles were thrown at the emissary's automobile. But in the presidential mansion, at least, Pauls was received correctly by Shazar, Eshkol, Golda Meir, and other officials. No one smiled. The ambassador then read a moving speech (in English) in which he informed his listeners that "the new Germany looked back on the horrible crimes of the National Socialist regime with grief and disgust. . . ." An Israeli military band played the national anthems of both countries, and the German and Israeli flags were raised. Five days later, in Bonn, Israel's first ambassador, Asher Ben-Natan, presented his credentials to the German chief of state. Once the formalities were over, Ben-Natan departed to attend a memorial service at the Cologne synagogue for the victims of the Holocaust. After this solemn overture, however, dealings between Germany and Israel proceeded in a cooperative spirit. In 1966 financial negotiations were consummated successfully for a DM160 million loan; the following year another loan of the same amount was provided. It was in 1966, too, that Konrad Adenauer visited Israel to accept an honorary doctorate from the Weizmann Institute. The former chancellor was greeted with respect and dignity. And when he was taken by helicopter to Sde Boker, Ben-Gurion's desert kibbutz, his reception by the former prime minister was more than respectful. The two old men embraced, tears in their eyes. A bitter chapter in both Jewish and German history had ended.

ISRAEL, FRANCE, AND THE EUROPEAN ECONOMIC COMMUNITY

Between Israel and France, conversely, a new and somewhat more equivocal chapter was opening. At first, to be sure, in the immediate aftermath of the Sinai Campaign, the two nations remained linked together in a friendship so tight and mutually supportive that it appeared virtually ineradicable. In Israel, gratitude toward "our one great friend" was spontaneous enough to evoke a renaissance of interest in French culture, to encourage the widespread introduction of French-language courses in Israeli schools, the establishment of chairs of French literature in Israeli universities, the opening of handsome new French libraries and bookstores

in Israel's leading cities. Diplomatically, too, Israel appeared entirely willing to be guided by France in its other international relations, particularly
the decision to accept a more European, rather than a purely American,
orientation in foreign affairs. The Israelis also agreed to minimize
border retaliation against Syria, lest this prejudice France's efforts to reestablish its influence in the Levant.

For their part, the French appeared no less committed to maintaining
the recent battlefield partnership with "gallant little Israel." Between 1956
and 1958, certainly, no other Great Power appeared as committed to Israel's
survival and growth. Friendship for the Jewish state was dramatized by
the emergence of an influential pro-Israel bloc in the Chamber of Deputies,
a group of parliamentarians that spoke warmly and often on behalf of
French-Israeli collaboration. The Alliance France-Israël, organized even
before the 1956 campaign, flourished in the latter 1950s and early 1960s
and included among its ranks the nation's most respected political and
cultural leaders. Other manifestations of sympathy and joint interest were
even more tangible. Shortly after Sinai, for example, a French consortium
reaffirmed its decision to invest $15 million in the projected new sixteen-
inch oil pipeline from Eilat to Ashkelon. With French governmental approval, this was a diplomatic, even more than an economic, gesture of
support for freedom of shipping along Israel's southern waterway.

Military collaboration, too, remained for a while as intimate as during
the wartime alliance. So long as the Algerian insurrection continued, French
defense and military officials regarded Israel as the key to Middle Eastern
stability. Thus, after 1956, a joint French-Israeli strategic planning committee met regularly to explore ways of protecting both nations' interests
in the Mediterranean and the Red Sea. In 1958 the French government
invited Israel to participate in joint naval maneuvers. Israeli destroyer
crews subsequently received training in antisubmarine warfare at a time
when the Egyptians were taking possession of their first Russian-built
submarines. The air forces of Israel and France also shared in joint training
programs; even as the French and Israeli secret services worked closely together, sharing vital information on Middle Eastern developments. At one
point France assisted Israel's manpower recruiting efforts by supplying
false papers to Jewish emigrants from Morocco and Rumania.

In the ensuing decade, not least of all, France remained the principal
source of military equipment for Israel. Indeed, weapons sales continued
at the accelerated pre-1956 level, and one branch of Israel's defense forces,
the air arm, was almost entirely dependent on French equipment, particularly the new generation of Mirage jets. The usefulness of these shipments was by no means one-sided. Except for the French air force itself,
Israel was the single most important market for France's lagging aircraft
industry. Israel similarly was a proving ground and advertisement for
French jets, the only nation in which French equipment was being tested
in combat against Soviet-made planes. Moreover, Israel's numerous suggestions for technical improvements were quickly and profitably adopted
by the French manufacturers.

For these reasons, then, of mutual strategic and economic self-interest, the commerce in aircraft and other weapons survived as the most enduring ingredient in the French-Israeli relationship, and well beyond the change in the political climate between the two nations. Until the mid-1960s, over the objections of Foreign Minister Maurice Couve de Murville, the French defense establishment and air industry convinced President de Gaulle that the economic, technological, and research value to France of Israeli military purchases was indispensable. As early as 1957, in fact, Israel was allowed to produce the French Fouga Magister jet trainer under license. From then on, Israel's aircraft industry grew in size, expertise, and ultimately in its ability to design and manufacture its own planes. In 1959, Israel was allowed to invest in the Dassault Company, one of France's largest plane manufacturers, to assist in research projects of special value to Israeli defense needs. The development of the French Matra air-to-air missile was essentially a joint French-Israeli project. So, in 1961, was the production of the two-stage solid fuel "meteorological" rocket, Shavit II, which received its first, unpublicized launching tests in the French Sahara. Joint research extended to the nuclear field, as well. Here the pooling of information went back as far as 1949 (Chapter XVI). In 1957, however, an agreement was signed enabling French private industry to assist Israel in constructing a nuclear reactor at Dimona. There was little doubt that the accord was a political decision with military implications for Israel. At a cost of $75 million, the reactor plainly was intended for more than civilian research.

But if the sale of military equipment continued into the mid-1960s, the French-Israeli political honeymoon endured barely two years in its fullest intensity. Several factors accounted for the gradual, almost imperceptible, change. By 1960, two years after de Gaulle's accession to power, France's leading military staff officers were purged for their role in the Algerian colonialist insurrection. Their successors had developed few earlier contacts with the Israelis. Nor were they encouraged thereafter to do so, upon the liquidation of the Algerian question; for by 1960 the Gaullist regime was embarked upon a basic reassessment of the nation's foreign policy. The decision soon was reached to extend new political and economic overtures to the Islamic world, both in the Maghreb and in the Middle East. Influence in the Mediterranean henceforth would be achieved through friendship, rather than through occupation. Inevitably this new approach required a more cautious stance on the Arab-Israeli question. Ministers in the cabinet were instructed to sever their ties with the Alliance France-Israël.

The new departure produced no sudden chill in French-Israel relations. Its effects at first were oblique. In French Africa, Israel's emissaries began to encounter difficulty in securing permission to open consulates. Until 1960, French naval and air forces at Djibouti had maintained patrols against Egyptian interference with Israeli shipping in the Red Sea. But thereafter surveillance no longer was consistent, and when Israel suggested a joint French-Israeli strategy in the Red Sea, Paris expressed little interest.

In the United Nations, too, the former partners slowly diverged. Thus, in 1962, the French delegate to the General Assembly supported a formula calling for the repatriation of Arab refugees to Israel, with resettlement offered merely as a voluntary alternative. Israel in turn felt obliged to vote with the United States and against France on a number of international questions, among them disarmament, Germany, and the Congo crisis. In June 1960 de Gaulle received Ben-Gurion cordially at the Élysée Palace, and in a toast to his visitor described Israel as France's "friend and ally." But the statement may have been intended as ambiguously as de Gaulle's celebrated remark to the Algerians in 1958, "Je vous ai compris"; for the visit took place only after two years of repeated solicitations by the Israeli foreign ministry. And when Eshkol succeeded Ben-Gurion as prime minister, visiting de Gaulle on his own in 1964, he sensed the growing unreliability of this French "friend and ally." Thereafter, over Shimon Peres's objections, Eshkol began diversifying Israel's arms purchases, turning increasingly to the United States.

Except for weapons acquisitions, moreover, trade between Israel and France had not developed extensively. While imports from France climbed from $22.7 million in 1959 to $46.9 million in 1961, Israeli exports in return grew from a meager $4.2 million to $4.7 million during the same period. It had never been assumed that France could match the potential, for example, of West Germany as an investor in Israel's development or as a market for Israeli goods. Nor, unlike Germany, was France inclined to offer Israel meaningful help in securing access to the Common Market. In 1963 de Gaulle agreed to help ease slightly a range of Common Market tariff items against Israeli goods. But thereafter Paris opposed Israel's applications to the EEC (p. 571). As the diplomatic relationship between the two countries gradually waned, military collaboration and even joint scientific projects were similarly affected. By the mid-1960s, leaders in both nations were willing for the first time to admit that the once ardent relationship at last was over. Dayan put it succinctly in 1965: "Israel's position today . . . is established by various international organizations, such as the North Atlantic Treaty Organization and the Common Market, and not by the Suez-Sinai alliance [with France], which is now seen as no more than a passing episode."

In all its dealings with Bonn and Paris, the Israeli government kept sharply in focus these nations'—particularly Germany's—long-range importance as an avenue to Europe, and specifically to the Common Market group of nations. The EEC was an entrepôt of great potential. Its six members embraced an aggregate population of 180 million, whose 1967 output totaled $400 billion. In the mid-1960s, 30 percent of Israel's exports went to the Common Market countries, and the latter in turn supplied 28 percent of Israel's imports. Although the trade gap between the two sides was narrower than with any other of Israel's partners, it was still wide; the dollar value of Common Market exports to Israel was far higher than Israel's to the EEC. Accordingly, it was a matter of urgent importance for Jerusalem to bridge this gulf; no alternative outlets were as promising as western Europe. Britain's share of Israel's exports, for example, had declined from a third in 1950 to less than an eighth by 1968. Transportation factors offset any meaningful profits from North America. Nor was trade with the Soviet bloc likely to increase. The Common Market was the one best hope. Yet broadened access to the EEC was no simple matter in view of the unified tariff barrier being erected against outsiders. Indeed, this obstacle placed Israel at a disadvantage not only vis-à-vis the EEC members, but also in relation to the North African nations, to Greece, Spain, and Turkey, all of which had achieved associate membership and preferential status with the Common Market.

As a result of persistent Israeli efforts, nevertheless, an agreement of sorts was reached with the EEC nations in 1960. Under its provisions, limited quantities of Israeli industrial products were offered a 20 percent tariff concession. Unfortunately, no concessions at all were extended for several of Israel's major hard currency earners—citrus, eggs, tires, and plywood. The agreement was renewed for another five years in 1967, but only with minor modifications. One of the principal objections to accommodating Israel was the EEC's desire to maintain its European character, and with it a political and economic infrastructure that some of its members regarded as the basis for a future United States of Europe. An additional, even sharper, objection was registered by several of the Common Market's Mediterranean and associate members—Italy, France, Spain, Greece, and the Maghreb nations—whose citrus products competed with those of Israel. Finally, in view of the Arab boycott, and Israel's lack of success in developing meaningful trade relations with other parts of the world, the potential of the Israeli market for EEC members did not appear convincing. In spite of the best efforts of West Germany and the Netherlands, therefore, who strongly advocated Israel's case, the latter's struggle to gain a foothold in the Common Market got nowhere for the time being.

But if integration with western Europe did not appear likely through diplomacy, several of Israel's leaders conceived of more imaginative approaches. In his volume *Kelah David* (David's Sling), for example, published in 1970, Shimon Peres recommended instead that Israel seek an association not with European governments but with European companies operating inside the framework of the EEC. The relationship could be established by purchasing shares in individual firms, Peres explained, or by gearing Israel's production to European corporations and becoming in this fashion a subcontractor for specific components.

As an illustration, Peres noted that in 1969, 13 percent of Israeli families owned private automobiles. Although the percentage undoubtedly would continue to rise (to 24 percent by 1973), the nation's growth rate still did not justify automobile production locally. A better solution, Peres observed, would be to seek agreement with one of the large automobile companies of Europe, to acquire a portion both of its shares and of its production. Rather than manufacture complete vehicles for a limited market, Israel would be turning out vehicle parts for a much wider buying public. By entering into mass production, too, Israel would significantly reduce the product's final cost. A similar components approach would be useful not only for automobiles, but also for television sets, radios, washing machines, electronic equipment, and other products that Israel with its trained man-power was well capable of manufacturing. The nation's resources admit-tedly were modest. Yet Israel might profit from the operational methods of the giant American companies in Europe. The latter had also found the political gates of the Common Market closed to them, and therefore had entered by special trade arrangements. In a limited way, Israel could bor-row from this example. Peres's views were increasingly shared. Well before 1970, in fact, joint stock sharing, licensing, and manufacturing contracts were drawn up between individual Israeli and European corporations in fields as varied as aircraft, electronics, and weapons. And, meanwhile, ne-gotiations with the EEC continually were being pressed (Chapter xxv).

ISRAEL AND THE DEVELOPING NATIONS

Despite Israel's failure to overcome the Common Market barrier, the little nation's progress and vitality were becoming an increasingly recognized fact of the Western state system. It happened, too, in the 1950s and 1960s, that a new force was surfacing in the council of nations, one that appeared to offer Israel a major opportunity for transcending the Arab diplomatic and political quarantine. It was the "Third World" of emerging African, Asian, and Latin American countries. Jerusalem's initial overtures to the Afro-Asian group, we recall, had not been encouraging. Indeed, Israel's ex-clusion from the Bandung Conference of 1955 marked the lowest point of its international isolation. None of these developing nations possessed tra-ditional links with the Jewish republic. On the contrary, Zionism for them was identified largely with the West, and more particularly with Western imperialism. The Suez-Sinai episode of autumn 1956 plainly strengthened this impression.

Yet there was another side to the picture. The opening of the Gulf of Aqaba at last provided Israel with a maritime outlet to Asia and Africa and facilitated contacts there with the newly independent countries. In exploring these communications, moreover, Israel was able to draw on two resources with which it was far better endowed than many other new states. These were trained manpower and recent—successful—experience in development. Thus, in 1950, several Burmese delegates to an interna-tional trade unions congress in Belgrade stopped off in Israel and were impressed by what they saw of Israeli labor achievements. Further discus-sions between Burmese and Israeli representatives at an Asian Socialist conference in Rangoon in 1953 led to the establishment of diplomatic rela-tions between the two countries. Subsequently, David HaCohen, an eminent Mapai leader, was appointed ambassador to Burma and brought with him a rich experience as a former director of Solel Boneh, the Histadrut contracting company. At HaCohen's suggestion, the Burmese government in 1954 dispatched a military mission to Israel, and arrangements were made for Israeli experts to train Burmese air force ground crews and army technicians. The following year Prime Minister U Nu demonstrated his interest in the new relationship by visiting Israel, where he was greeted by the Jewish state's beleaguered citizens with paroxysms of joy. U Nu's visit soon led to even warmer cooperation between the two nations and included Israeli help in planning large-scale Burmese agricultural programs. At this point, too, Jerusalem sensed that it had found its most promising avenue to the newly emancipated nations. The attempt to exploit the opening was launched initially by Foreign Minister Sharett, but was considerably expanded under Golda Meir, who succeeded him in 1956.

In embarking upon its aid program, Israel drew to some extent on help its government had received from other countries, notably from the United States. Yet most of the 4,000 Israeli advisers, scientists, and technicians abroad in the Third World since 1958 concentrated upon areas in which Israel had developed a unique expertise in building its own state and society: in agriculture and irrigation, rural planning and development, the formation of pioneer and youth movements, medical, academic, and vocational education, and community development. By the same token, a majority of the visitors who studied in Israel after 1958 trained in these and other, related fields. New agricultural techniques, for example, proved to be one of Israel's most sustained contributions to the developing nations. Israeli moshav and kibbutz methods were particularly appealing to the Africans. The regional development schemes, especially the Lachish project, aroused great interest in South America as well as in eastern Mediterranean countries and Asia. Thus, in 1962, with the help of Israeli advisers, Venezuela utilized the Lachish approach in settling a thousand families in its own Majaguas region. A variation of the Lachish plan was successfully carried out in the Nawalpur region of Nepal, again with Israeli advisers. Israel's pioneering youth movements, Gadna and Nachal (Chapter XVII), were highly attractive to a large number of African and South American nations. Israeli experts consequently were invited to establish similar programs in eighteen countries, most of them African, but including also Bolivia, Ecuador, Costa Rica, and Singapore.

Short-term study courses, seminars, and foreign visitors' conferences similarly promoted Israel's image as an international training center for the Third World. Perhaps the most widely publicized of the colloquia was the Rehovot Conference on Science in the Advancement of New States, sponsored by the Israeli government and the Weizmann Institute. The gathering attracted some 120 representatives from thirty-nine nations, who shared in twelve days of lectures and discussions. Later conferences in Rehovot were attended by Asian, African, and Latin American ministers, by planning officials, economists, sociologists, and agronomists. In 1965 a permanent Settlement Study Center was founded in Rehovot; each year delegates participated in an extended course of seminars on science in the Third World. Other programs were conducted by Israel's Latin American Productivity Institute and the Afro-Asian Institute for Labor Studies and Cooperation—the latter founded by the Histadrut. The foreign training department of Israel's agricultural extension service offered courses ranging from poultry husbandry to irrigation. In 1962 the Mount Carmel International Center for Community Services was established to offer women from developing countries training in health, nutrition, adult education, and home economics. By 1966, then, sixty-nine various short-term courses and seminars were operating in Israel. The Israelis also conducted several longer-term academic and vocational training programs, notably in medicine, nursing, agricultural engineering, comprehensive rural planning, and vocational education. Thus, during 1964, 420 students from developing countries were pursuing extended studies in Israel (together with 2,000 participants in shorter programs). The courses generally were offered in English or French.

As its venture in foreign training burgeoned—indeed, much more rapidly than Israel had anticipated—the government decided eventually to coordinate these numerous operations in a special department of international cooperation under the foreign ministry. By 1967 the department's budget had risen to $4.5 million annually, a sum that would have been far greater had the partner governments not covered the largest share of the bill. In later years, too, a number of Israeli programs were funded by such international organizations as UNESCO, FAO, UNICEF, and the International Atomic Energy Agency. The Organization of American States underwrote much of the cost of Latin Americans studying in Israel and of Israeli teams providing training in Latin America. Certainly Israel's expenditure was negligible in return for the goodwill it reaped (p. 579).

The nation's main investment was less in money than in people. By the mid-1960s, in fact, Israel had more experts working abroad in relation to its population than all the western European nations combined. It was precisely the quality of this manpower, too, instructing and advising in the developing countries, that accounted for Israel's remarkable success overseas. The typical emissary was the madrich, usually a young man who had acquired experience at home as a leader and a teacher of youth groups and immigrants during the formative period of Israel's own early statehood. In Africa and Asia, as in Israel, the madrich demonstrated not only enthusiasm and patience but a unique instinct for the human touch. Frequently he was less interested than the European expert in comfortable offices and lodgings. He trained his students by working at their side, and more than occasionally by living among them. Untouched by color consciousness, he rarely patronized—as he had not with backward Moroccan or Kurdish immigrants in Israel. And this egalitarianism ultimately created a bond of trust and affection, especially between African and Israeli, that survived until the painful diplomatic vicissitudes of the 1970s (Chapter xxv).

THE ISRAELI-AFRICAN HONEYMOON

The Israeli government made no secret of the pragmatic goals it hoped to achieve through its investment in the underdeveloped world. Most important by far was the opportunity to avoid the political isolation it had experienced at the Bandung Conference in 1955 and at the New Delhi Asian-Socialist Conference in 1956. Thus, the program of technical cooperation soon became a useful technique of circumventing diplomatic quarantine and of erasing the Jewish state's former Western, "imperialist" image. In Israel's favor were its demonstrated abilities and achievements in self-development. The technologically backward nations saw in Israel an economy that had reached the "takeoff" point in less than a generation. It was noted that the Israelis had gained valuable experience in dealings with individuals of varied backgrounds from all cultural levels, including hundreds of thousands of relatively untutored Oriental immigrants, and in quickly training them to master a variety of necessary skills. These feats had been accomplished through hard work, through a social value system that attached prestige to manual occupations and to the technical professions. The scale of Israel's enterprises, moreover, was regarded as better suited for many African and Latin American countries than the large plants available to the industrialized nations. Suspicious of the Europeans, the Africans, particularly, felt reassured by Israel's small size, and not least of all by the Jews' common history of racial suffering.

Nowhere, then, were the exertions and rewards of Israel's calculated gamble in the Third World seemingly as dramatic as in Black Africa. The emergence of these former protectorates and dependencies to independence coincided with the aftermath of Israel's 1956 Sinai victory. As has been seen, the end of the Egyptian blockade also freed the maritime outlet from Eilat to East Africa, and Israel's trade routes with the African nations were the first to be opened. Direct communications soon overcame lingering African suspicions of Israel's role in the Suez-Sinai episode. The earliest contacts were with Ghana, and were established not only in trade but in meetings between Ghanaian and Israeli leaders at various international Socialist conferences. In anticipation of a possibly useful relationship, an Israeli consul was appointed to Accra in 1956, fully a year before Ghana achieved its independence. When the two nations exchanged ambassadors in 1957, the man chosen for the Accra post was Ehud Avriel, one of Israel's most respected public servants, the organizer of the military airlift from Czechoslovakia in 1948. Through Avriel's initiative, a broad series of Israeli technological and economic projects was launched, including agricultural, medical, financial, and educational advisers to the Ghanan government, joint shipping and construction ventures, and the organization of Ghanaian military and aviation training programs. News of Israel's accomplishments in Ghana spread rapidly through the African continent. Soon Israel was receiving a flow of visitors from other African lands, intent upon observing the young nation's economic progress. It was to accommodate that interest that the Histadrut organized its first Afro-Asian Seminar in 1958. The program's success, in turn, led to the expansion of Israel's foreign training activities both in trade unionism and in economic cooperatives. In 1960 the Afro-Asian Institute for Labor Studies and Cooperation was accepting hundreds of African students annually for four- and eight-week training programs.

Among Israel's leaders, it was Foreign Minister Golda Meir who laid greatest emphasis on cultivating relations with the African nations. Mrs. Meir's encounters with Asia had not been productive. On the personal level, she had failed to establish a rapport with Asian statesmen, who embodied ancient and complex civilizations. The basic human and political needs of the young African peoples, on the other hand, appealed to the foreign minister's innate simplicity. Her approach—unquestionably a sincere one—was to identify Israel's own experience of persecution with the Africans' long colonial bondage, with their recent attainment of independence, and their future aspirations. But at the same time she reminded the Knesset in 1960 that "our aid to the new countries is not a matter of philanthropy. We are no less in need of the fraternity and friendship of the new nations than they are of our assistance."

Under Mrs. Meir, then, and the brilliant young director of the foreign ministry's African department, Netanel Lorch, the effort in this former colonial terrain was vigorously enlarged. Of 3,948 Israeli experts serving abroad from 1958 to 1970, 3,483 were in Africa. Of 13,790 foreign students in Israel during the same period, nearly half were African. Projects carried out in Africa under Israeli supervision were extensive and diverse. They included, among many others, a pilot venture for the irrigation of cotton in Tanzania; a training school for rural social workers in Kenya; a Histadrut advisory team to develop the Kenyan Federation of Labor; medical teams sent out to Burundi, Ethiopia, Ghana, Liberia, Malawi, Mali, the Republic of Congo (Brazzaville), Ruanda, Tanzania, and Upper Volta. In Ethiopia, Israelis occupied key positions in the national medical sector, including chief pharmacist, director of the Asmara Hospital, Eritrea district health officer, and department heads in government hospitals. Perhaps Israel's most dramatic medical welfare contribution was its special program in the treatment of eye diseases and education of the blind, a field in which it had acquired vast experience during its own Oriental immigration. In 1960, Israeli physicians organized a thirty-bed hospital in Monrovia and staffed it with two Israeli ophthalmologists and Israeli-trained Liberian nurses. Related programs, as well as schools for the blind, were established by Israeli doctors in Tanzania, Ethiopia, and Ruanda.

In science, education, and administration generally, Israel was deluged with requests. Fourteen Israelis served on the faculty of Ethiopia's Haile Selassie I University in 1963, including three deans. Israelis similarly organized the Ethiopian postal and telegraph services. Ghana was a prime example of the sheer diversity of Israel's contributions. There, Israeli experts organized a shipping company for the Accra government, sent medical and pharmaceutical teams to work in Ghanaian hospitals, and participated in such varied enterprises as the establishment of a philharmonic orchestra, a meteorological service, a standards institute, a nautical college, an academy of science, a development bank—all these in addition to Israeli projects in agriculture, industry, and vocational education.

The Nachal movement was particularly attractive to the African countries, most of which urgently required training and employment opportunities for their youth and a variety of national development schemes for their economies. In supplying its help, Israel developed Nachal-like organizations in the Ivory Coast, in the Central African Republic, in Dahomey, Cameroun, Senegal, and Togo. The paramilitary function performed by these youth groups turned out to be equally valuable. In January 1964, for example, when Tanzania's regular army disintegrated after an unsuccessful insurrection, the Nachal-style national service units, led and trained by Israelis, remained disciplined and loyal. Impressed by the fact, President Julius Nyerere asked the Israeli government to train a thousand picked men on an emergency basis to serve as the core of a national army. Israel accepted the challenge. Even earlier, other African nations displayed interest in Israel's military prowess. Shortly after winning independence, Ghana requested Israel's help in establishing a flying school, as did Uganda some years later. A veil of secrecy surrounded Israeli military aid. It was known, however, that Shimon Peres advocated the military approach and in fact was the architect of Israel's military aid program to the new states from 1958 onward. In Peres's words, one of Israel's key policy goals was "to build a 'second Egypt' in Africa, that is, to help convert Ethiopia's economic and military strength into a counterforce to Egypt, thereby giving Africans another focus." There was general awareness that Israeli instructors played a vital role in Ethiopian officers' schools, that Zaire, Uganda, Ghana, and other nations were frequent recipients of Israeli military instruction and weapons. The future presidents of Congo and Uganda, Joseph Mobutu and Idi Amin, won their paratroopers' wings in Israel (Chapter xxi). Ugandan pilots flew Israeli-manufactured Fouga trainers.

Despite its modest resources, Israel shrewdly combined investment aid and technical assistance to African nations in such joint economic ventures as hotels, shipping lines, and construction companies. These were usually capitalized at between $300,000 and $500,000, with the Israeli partners holding 49 percent of the shares and the host government investing the balance. The partnership normally was established for five years. In the interim, the Israelis supplied key managerial personnel and trained local staff, and afterward sold off their shares to the African government. It was on this basis, for example, that Israel and Ghana organized the Ghana National Construction Company and the Black Star Shipping Line. Similar partnerships were established in the Ivory Coast, Sierra Leone, and Nigeria. The joint enterprises benefited Israel in various ways. Young Israeli engineers and technicians gained valuable experience, even as the financial returns were often quite impressive. Profits similarly were earned from a number of commercial and semicommercial ventures, including Israel's construction of the parliament building in Sierra Leone, the university campus in West Nigeria, and four hotels in Nigeria. Israeli companies managed hotels in Ibadan, Monrovia, Abidjan, and Dar es-Salaam.

The political consequences of this elaborate interchange were far-reaching. Within five years Israel had established diplomatic relations with all but one of the African countries south of the Sahara. In 1961 President Maurice Yaméogo of Upper Volta opened the long list of African heads of state who, after years of participating in the Afro-Asian diplomatic quarantine, agreed to set foot officially on Israeli territory. By 1968 most of the presidents of these nations had visited Israel, some of them twice. Indeed, hardly a month passed without the visit of a senior African minister. Israeli leaders—President Ben-Zvi, Prime Minister Eshkol, Foreign Ministers Meir and Eban, and various individual ministers—toured Africa in the 1960s. Rarely, too, before 1973, did the developing nations allow Arab pressures to obstruct their bilateral relations with the Jewish state. President Nyerere of Tanzania spoke for the majority of them: "We are not going to let our friends determine who our enemies shall be." The Arabs, of course, persisted in their efforts to "chase Israel out of Africa" (in Nasser's words). Except for Somalia and Mauritania, however, with their large Moslem populations, the campaign failed for many years. The Israeli government meanwhile was willing to take political risks of its own to ensure African goodwill. Thus, it faithfully supported General Assembly resolutions "deploring" or "condemning" South Africa's policy of apartheid, and this notwithstanding Jerusalem's deep sense of obligation to the South African government, and to the wealthy and generous South African Jewish community, for their crucial support over the years.

Israel continued to suffer occasional rebuffs in Africa, to be sure. As early as mid-1958 there was evidence of Egyptian influence on Ghana. A communiqué issued by Presidents Nasser and Kwame Nkrumah in Cairo urged a "just solution" to the Palestine problem and expressed anti-Israel sentiments. A year later, Israel was the only country not invited to the "African Day" celebration at the United Nations. Again, at the end of 1959, Israel was the one United Nations member excluded from an African reception honoring President Sékou Touré of Guinea. Plainly there was a gap between the relationships individual African governments expected to establish with the Jewish state and their dealings with Israel as an African bloc (or as an Afro-Asian bloc). This dichotomy was emphasized by the Casablanca Declaration of January 1961, in which the presidents of Egypt, Ghana, Guinea, and Mali branded Israel as "an instrument of imperialism and neocolonialism." Not infrequently the very governments maintaining strong bilateral and technical cooperation links with Israel were those voting, under Arab influence, for anti-Israel resolutions.

These setbacks notwithstanding, Israel's reputation in Africa seemed likely for a while to bear fruit even on the international scene. Thus, for many years, a key goal of Israeli foreign policy was to secure a General Assembly resolution calling for direct talks between the Arabs and Israel. Invariably, the effort was defeated by a combination of Arab and Communist votes. Neither did the resolution pass in 1963. Yet it was sponsored that year by an unprecedented nineteen delegations, and ten of these were African. For that matter, even when the Africans chose to vote against Israel in the General Assembly, or to adopt anti-Israel positions in other international settings, their governments often advised the Israelis after the fact to disregard the vote. And in June 1967, during the General Assembly debate on the Six-Day War, forty-two developing nations, including Ghana and Ethiopia, voted for a resolution that would have linked Israeli withdrawal from captured territories with Arab abandonment of belligerency against Israel. Had it not been for its far-reaching program of cooperation in the Third World, Israel unquestionably would have suffered a far more extensive and painful diplomatic isolation. As it was, by 1967 the country's network of ties in western Europe, Africa, and North and South America offered impressive evidence of how far Israel apparently had surmounted the Arab quarantine since Operation Kadesh, and of the considerable degree to which the Jewish republic had become an established and seemingly unchallengeable fact of life in the international community.

CULTURAL AND IDEOLOGICAL CURRENTS

THE RISE OF AN ARAB INTELLIGENTSIA

The contours of Israel's growth were to be charted not only in statistical tables but along the less tangible lines of intellectual accomplishment. In this area, however, the gap between Arabs and Jews remained wider for many years than in any other sector of Israeli life. The majority of Palestine's Arab intellectuals fled to neighboring lands during the 1948 war, and those who remained were divorced thenceforth from the mainstream of Arab cultural activity. Thus, virtually the whole of the post-independence Arab intelligentsia was educated in the new Israeli state. It was a not altogether insignificant group, to be sure. Each year Israel turned out a new and larger crop of Arab high school and even university graduates. By 1975, some 300 Arab youths were enrolled at the Hebrew University (a dozen of them women), nearly 500 at the University of Haifa, and between 200 and 300 at other Israeli higher institutions. Hundreds of Israeli Arabs pursued their studies in Europe and the United States, as well, many with the assistance of church and missionary groups, others with grants from the Israeli government and various international organizations. In all, the educated Arab minority numbered about 4,000 by 1975.

Playing only a marginal role in the nation's affairs, this small elite group was intensely self-absorbed and bitterly conscious of real or fancied discrimination. In some degree, its members had themselves to blame for their limited influence even on the life of their own community. Although settled mainly in rural areas, they contributed little to village integration; rather, they openly despised the backwardness of their surroundings. For many years their literary output was unimpressive. Until 1958 not one Arabic full-length novel was printed in Israel. Barely fifteen slim volumes of poetry appeared, usually published by the authors themselves, and the quality of this work was not high. Indeed, their publishing houses had to be established after the birth of the state, most of them founded or subsidized by the Christian communities, by the Histadrut, or by the Mapam and Maki (Communist) parties.

It was the establishment of Michael Hadad's journal, *al-Mujtama* (Society), in 1954, that finally offered writers and poets a common forum and nurtured a certain initial growth of Israeli Arabic literature. An energetic young teacher and editor, Hadad threw open the columns of his magazine to Moslem and Christian writers alike, founded a poets' association, and edited a volume of contributions by its members. Equally important roles in fostering literary activity were played by the Hebrew University Library, which circulated a large number of Arabic books, and by the Arabic program of the Israel Broadcasting Service. In 1958, to mark Israel's tenth anniversary, the Histadrut published an anthology of Arabic stories and poems. That year, too, the Orthodox Youth Club of Ibillin underwrote the publication of several Arabic volumes of poetry and prose. Although the output remained meager until 1958, Arabic publishing expanded somewhat in later years. The Arab Book Society, founded by Mapam in 1958, published seventeen volumes in the next decade, mainly novels. Three new Arabic commercial presses also began turning out novels and volumes of history. In the mid-1960s an Arabic-language theater group was functioning successfully in Haifa, together with an Arab popular theater in Nazareth. Both received grants from their municipalities and from the government.

By and large, poetry continued to be the most popular literary form in Arabic, although the standard of verse was quite mediocre. It was significant, too, that poetry remained "safely" apolitical in the early years, devoted essentially to love themes and ignoring the political and social problems of the Arab minority. Whenever, occasionally, an attitude toward the Jews was expressed at all, it usually took the form of obsequious appeals for mutual goodwill and practical cooperation. The Arabic short story, on the other hand, while less developed even than poetry, strove at least for realism and concentrated on Arab society and the hardships and aspirations of the fellahin. Samir Marid was a leading writer in this genre, dealing mainly with the life of the poor. Adib al-Kass and Jamil Musa explored similar themes. Mrs. Maja Qa'war-Farah was distinguished for her penetrating studies of human emotions; an established writer since the 1940s, she published two volumes of short stories, *Abiru al-Tariq* (Wayfarers) and *Durub wa-Masabih* (Roads and Lamps), as well as four volumes of essays. In prose, at least, criticism was not lacking of the backwardness of Arab life. Favorite themes were the lessons to be learned from Jewish progressivism, and the importance of education and modernism. Thus, the stories of Rashid Hussein were marked equally by their graphic and colorful style and by their vigorous denunciation of polygamy and *mohar* (wife purchase), both widespread practices in the Moslem community.

It was not until the 1960s that Arabic literature began to confront the deeper issue of national antagonisms. By then, mass education was producing a larger group of Arab high school and university graduates. Resentful at being consigned to teaching, despising physical work of any kind, many of these young men preferred to express their criticism of the state and its government in increasingly nationalist or Communist terms. With only the dimmest recollections of cultural and economic backwardness under the mandate, they preferred to contrast their situation with that of the Jewish majority; and the gulf between the two peoples was hardly encouraging. Uncertain, too, whether they were Israeli Arabs or Arabs in Israel, they veered increasingly toward political protest. Sympathy for Nasser and the Pan-Arab cause was universal among them. The Arab Students Committee of the Hebrew University, for example, became exceptionally aggressive in the mid-1960s, sponsoring "literary" evenings that frequently became occasions for nationalist incitement. The students in any event were continually being exhorted by Cairo and Damascus Radio to "prove" their Arabism by taking an anti-Israel stand.

More than the other media, it was the press that reflected the politicization of the Arab intelligentsia. Indeed, by the 1960s, Israeli Arabs were using the newspapers and political journals as their primary literary vehicle. As in the case of their Jewish counterparts, Arabic-language periodicals remained under the sponsorship of either the parties, the Histadrut, or the religious communities. Thus, for many years Israel's one Arabic-language daily, and hence the most widely read newspaper in the Arab community, was *al-Yawm* (The Day), financially supported by the Histadrut. The polemical journals were more influential yet, if more limited in circulation. Perhaps the best-known of these was *al-Ittihad* (Unity), an ably edited Communist biweekly that followed a stridently Nasserist line. But even the literary journals of the Arab Christian communities—the most important of them was *al-Rabita* (The Bond), organ of Greek Catholic Archbishop George al-Hakim—adopted a vigorous nationalist tone that ensured their popularity among Israeli Arabs.

Not all Arabic literature in Israel was political, of course. In the 1960s as in the late 1950s, lyrical poems continued to appear, as well as poetry and prose dealing with changes in mores and traditions, with the status of women and of the fellahin. But what was true of newspapers was essentially true of belles-lêttres. After 1958 even the poets steadily became more outspoken. Isam al-Abassi, Sami al-Qasim, Hanna Ibrahim, and Mahmud Darwish sang the praises of the Arab nationalist movement, and with such vigor and persistence that Rashid Hussein, in an article published in the journal *al-Ra'id*, felt compelled to object: "I do not deny that our poets should write political poetry, but does that mean that everything they write must be political?" Apparently it did. The new determination to enshrine in verse political and other essentially topical themes lent a superficial, journalistic quality to much of later Arabic poetry.

In marked contrast to the early post-independence years, then, nearly all Arab writers of whatever genre or merit evinced hostility toward the state and a willingness to incite against it. Presenting the Jews as strangers, infidels, as fanatical haters of all Arabs, the short-story writer Faraj Nur-Suleiman openly upbraided the village mukhtars for collaborating with them. In Tawfiz Mu'ammar's stories, the Arab was depicted, typically, as a naïve, goodhearted bumpkin, and the Jew as an avaricious speculator. The ordeal of the Arab refugees, a favored subject of virtually all Arab writers, was characteristically portrayed through the tragedy of divided families yearning for lost homes and land. Alienation, too, was a recurrent theme. In Mu'ammar's collection *Bit'un* (Never Mind), the Israeli government was described as a tough cabal of opportunists, whose persecution of the Arab minority was shrewdly calculated to provoke the Arab states into retaliating against their own Jews, thereby touching off further Jewish emigration to Israel. It was significant that the full plenitude of Israel's accomplishments on behalf of its Arab citizens—good roads, irrigation, electricity, social welfare, broadened education, economic prosperity —was scorned as nothing better than the last meal offered a condemned man.

Nor was there a qualitative distinction in the attitude toward Israel of the state's Moslem and Christian Arabs. Religion neither inflamed nor tempered their attitude. Neither community was particularly devout any longer. While Moslem peasants still held fast to ancient customs, painting their houses blue, emblazoning hands on their doors as protection against the Evil Eye, Islam no longer exerted a meaningful creedal influence in their lives. Rather, Arab nationalism, and Nasser as its champion, became a kind of surrogate object of worship. Certainly religion was of little help in enabling Moslems to cope with their transformed status in a Jewish nation. That deep-rooted emotional malaise continued, and no religious or intellectual formula appeared likely to resolve it. In the end, a political solution involving the neighboring Arab states—in short, a formal termination of the Arab-Israeli war—appeared to offer the one remaining hope for ending at least the psychological anomaly of Arab minority status.

THE GROWTH OF A MAJORITY CULTURE: EDUCATION AND SCIENCE

The rising curve of Jewish economic progress was fully matched in the Jewish intellectual arena. For one thing, the increase of secondary schooling opportunities produced a larger number of high school graduates who qualified for universities. As in Europe and the United States, moreover, demand for educated personnel was steadily reinforced by the advance of science and technology, by the development of industry, commerce, and communications, and by the needs of an expanding government and defense infrastructure. Thus, a year after independence, 1,600 students were attending the nation's two universities. By 1975 enrollment in Israel's seven academic institutions had reached 47,000 students, the overwhelming majority of them Jews. This growth in higher education was proportional as well as absolute. By 1975, academically trained persons (not all of them educated in Israel) comprised 15 percent of the nation's work force, one of the highest such ratios in the world.

In the early years of the state, the Haifa Technion and the Hebrew University of Jerusalem maintained their exclusive position in higher learning. The former offered training in fields as diverse as chemical engineering, nuclear physics, aeronautical engineering, and computer sciences. By 1975 the Technion's handsome new campus on Mount Carmel included fifty major buildings, a student enrollment of nearly 10,000, and a faculty of

1,300. Fully matching this progress, the Hebrew University boasted an impressive spectrum of undergraduate and graduate schools that eventually included the natural sciences, agriculture, medicine, dentistry, pharmacy, law, education, library science, and social work. By 1975 the student body of the Jerusalem institution had climbed to 17,000, its academic staff to 2,200. Moreover, the university's senior status in all educational fields except technology generated a certain academic imperialism, and as early as 1949 it took over the formerly autonomous Tel Aviv School of Law and Economics as the "Tel Aviv Branch of the Hebrew University."

The municipality of Tel Aviv did not countenance this incursion for long. In 1956 it founded its own university. For a number of years the school grew cautiously, even unimpressively. Then, in 1963, a dynamic American, Dr. George Wise, became its president and immediately launched the university upon an era of spectacular growth. Within ten years, as a result, the student enrollment of the new institution had reached 10,000 and its academic staff 2,000. Its course offerings were dispersed among thirteen faculties, including medical, music, and engineering schools; while twenty-eight institutes conducted research in fields as varied as criminology, urban and regional studies, and Middle Eastern studies. In the modernity both of its administration and of its academic orientation, the University of Tel Aviv in some respects was beginning to outstrip the older Hebrew University as the nation's outstanding liberal arts institution. Both of these schools, in turn, shared their academic prestige with the Weizmann Institute of Science. Founded in Rehovot by Weizmann himself in 1934, and guided afterward during its most impressive growth by a hard-driving American impresario, Meyer Weisgal, the Weizmann Institute achieved a reputation as one of the world's outstanding research centers in the natural sciences. By 1975, it operated nineteen departments, including applied mathematics, nuclear physics, isotopes, X-ray crystallography, spectroscopy, organic chemistry, polymers, biophysics, microbiology, and genetics. By then, too, it had launched a graduate school offering a Ph.D. program for some 200 students.

Not yet in the first rank, but growing rapidly, was a series of newer colleges and universities. Among them was Bar Ilan University, a school founded by the Mizrachi movement in 1955 and endowed with a specifically Orthodox religious character. Located at Ramat Gan, a suburb of Tel Aviv, Bar Ilan listed a student enrollment of 4,000 in 1975, a faculty of 900, and course offerings in a reasonably wide diversity of arts and sciences. Elsewhere, in Haifa and Beersheba, "university institutes" were organized initially under the academic supervision of the Hebrew University, and by the early 1970s acquired autonomous status as the University of Haifa and the Ben-Gurion University of the Negev. Their student enrollments and faculties were small, their plant still limited; but their growth seemed as assured as the expanding population of their hinterlands.

For all Israel's universities, in fact, the number of applicants greatly exceeded the institutions' absorptive capacity. Shortages ordinarily were less in facilities than in staff; it was qualified faculty that was difficult to find. This lack of personnel could by no means be ascribed to inadequate working conditions. Well paid, professors taught only half a year, frequently begrudged the time they gave their students, and enjoyed innumerable opportunities for study and research, for consultations, and for travel grants abroad. They protected themselves unconscionably, determining the terms of their own employment and promotion by electing university rectors answerable to their every whim. Rather, the shortage of faculty could be attributed simply to an inadequate number of Ph.D.'s in Israel. As late as 1975 barely 140 doctorates were being awarded annually, at a time when the minimum number required to meet expanding higher educational needs (quite aside from competing industrial, government, and other demands) was at least five times higher. Israel still had to rely heavily, then, on graduates who completed their doctoral studies abroad and on academically trained immigrants. This latter category was becoming increasingly important in the 1960s. For example, of 1,650 new scientists and engineers who were added to the state's professional manpower in 1964, 44 percent were post-1948 immigrants who had been educated in their countries of origin.

It was the widening reservoir of trained men and women that similarly accounted for Israel's astonishing technological breakthrough in the late 1950s and early 1960s. A particularly dramatic example of scientific achievement was in the field of atomic energy. Shortly after Israel's independence, Ben-Gurion assigned his country's scientists the urgent task of exploiting atomic energy as a source of power; the nation was virtually devoid of conventional fuel resources. In 1956 the decision was taken to establish a nuclear reactor of the "swimming pool" type at Nachal Sorek. This facility went critical in June 1960 and became a major center of research and teaching, utilized by all the scientific institutions of the country and particularly by the Weizmann Institute. A second experimental reactor, based on natural uranium and heavy water, went operational in the northern Negev near Dimona, late in 1964. Surrounded by well-equipped laboratories, it too became a major research center. It was likely, however, that research both for civilian and for defense purposes (p. 569) would continue to be the major value of the reactors; for as late as the 1970s, nuclear-supplied electric power stations were not considered economically feasible.

The nation's cultural appetite was by no means purely functional, of course. If archaeologists were trained to evaluate an ancient civilization through its residual tels, anthropologists and sociologists presumably could gain insight into a contemporary society through its museums. Israel abounded in them. Jerusalem's magnificent Israel Museum, for example, consisted of a biblical and archaeological museum, a national art museum, a wing housing the Dead Sea Scrolls and Bar Kochba finds (p. 588), and an art garden exhibiting an impressive collection of neoclassical and modern sculpture. Tel Aviv, Haifa, Cholon, Netania, Petach Tikvah, Bat Yam, even Beersheba, Rehovot, and Eilat, all supported municipal art museums. The dazzling new Tel Aviv Museum possessed an excellent collection not only of Israeli and Jewish painters but of many international exhibits on loan. Additionally, Tel Aviv boasted a number of specialized museums dealing in glass, coins, alphabets, ethnology and folklore, weapons, pottery, and other antiquities. Haifa possessed a nautical museum and a large ethnological museum devoted to ceremonial objects of the various Diaspora communities. Several agricultural villages established museums of their own, among them the Kibbutz Ein Charod art museum, the Kibbutz Sha'ar HaGolan collection of neolithic finds, and Kibbutz Lochamei HaGhettaot's museum of the Holocaust.

Extensive museum and gallery space would have been required for the output of the nation's artists alone. A few veteran painters—Herman Struck, Nachum Gutman, Reuven Rubin, Ludwig Blum, Abel Pann, and Moshe Castel—had been turning out paintings since the early years of the mandate. In the 1930s, too, large numbers of refugee artists arrived in Palestine, representing almost every artistic trend then current in Europe. Joseph Budko was appointed director of the Bezalel School (subsequently Israel's national art academy), and later was joined by the woodcut master Jacob Steinhardt. Mordechai Ardon came fresh from the Bauhaus to teach painting, while David Gumbel and Ludwig Wolpert served as instructors in the Bezalel's metalwork courses. Other refugee artists found their places in kibbutzim, where they taught and continued to paint. The burst of activity involved hundreds of painters, from Marcel Janco to Yankel Adler, from Joseph Zaritzky to Anna Ticho. Although World War II and Israel's War of Independence interrupted meaningful contacts with artistic developments overseas, in the 1950s Israeli artists quickly renewed their ties with Europe and the United States. By then, in fact, there were nearly 4,000 working artists in the country. Few went hungry. Public interest in their work extended far beyond the confines of Israel itself, and Jewish tourists from abroad could be relied upon to snap up their works at continually rising prices. In 1966 alone, a dozen new galleries opened in Tel Aviv; in 1972, twice that many. Art colonies, classes, and summer courses generally were packed with students and visitors.

The national enthusiasm for art was fully matched by Israel's passion for music. As far back as 1936 the Palestine Orchestra (later the Israel Philharmonic) had given its first concert under the visiting conductorship of Arturo Toscanini. Augmented later by refugee and native talent alike, the orchestra rose into the first ranks of the world's performing bodies. From the mid-1950s on, it was housed in an elegant, modern auditorium in Tel Aviv. Jerusalem and Haifa maintained smaller but good-quality symphony orchestras and provided them with first-rate auditoriums. Ramat Gan was the home of the widely admired Israel Chamber Orchestra. All these ensembles performed before capacity audiences. On several occasions the Israel National Youth Symphony Orchestra won first prize in international competition. The leading music schools—the Rubin Academies of Jerusalem and Tel Aviv, the Israel Academy of Music, the Dunya Weizmann School in Haifa—all had record enrollments.

There was in fact hardly any field of cultural activity that was not energized by the devoted patronage and participation of this nation of Jews. Theater was yet another example. It was a medium that for many years was all but synonymous with Habima, the state's best-known company. Founded in Moscow and reestablished in Tel Aviv in 1931, the versatile repertory group was officially recognized as the National Theater of Israel in 1958 and housed in its own modern auditorium; after 1969 the government assumed responsibility for its operating costs. Fully the equal of Habima in talent and facilities, and possibly exceeding it in reputation, the Cameri (Chamber) Theater was founded in Tel Aviv in 1944 by Yosef Millo with a vanguard policy of offering "relevant" contemporary plays. In 1961 the Cameri moved into spacious, handsome facilities, and eight years later was designated Tel Aviv's municipal theater. Semiofficial— that is, Histadrut—funding was also provided for Ohel, the Israel Labor Theater, founded in 1925 and reorganized shortly after the birth of the state (although performing only irregularly after 1973). Besides these three major repertory companies, there were innumerable smaller independent revue troups located in theater clubs, nightclubs, and music halls. A healthy decentralization away from Tel Aviv began in the 1960s with the opening of impressive new theaters in Haifa, Jerusalem, and Beersheba. Nearly all of Israel's larger performing companies, too, were tax exempt and received government, municipality, Histadrut, or Jewish Agency funds. But, in any case, public support was overwhelming. UNESCO statistics in 1965 ranked Israel as first in the world in per capita theater attendance and annual number of performances.

The most telling evidence of the nation's intellectual sophistication may have been the sheer prevalence of the written word among its Jewish majority. By 1975 Israel published twenty-four daily newspapers, thirteen in Hebrew, eleven in foreign languages. Notwithstanding their various political affiliations, the quality of these journals was generally high; all were noted for their zest and readability. In addition to newspapers, more than 400 Israeli periodicals were issued, 300 of them in Hebrew. The country ranked second in the world by then in the per capita number of titles published—fully 2,000 books each year, including translations. Approximately seventy publishing firms helped meet the nation's cultural needs. So did Israel's more than 1,000 libraries, containing 9 million books by 1975. However unevenly based among European and Oriental Jews, this cultural foundation was a marvel of amplitude. Some of its breadth reflected the nation's growing prosperity, some a historic Jewish affinity for culture as a substitute for other deprivations. In Israel, to be sure, those lacunae no longer were agricultural or political. They were the deprivations, rather, of quarantine in an arid little state, far distant from the traditional ambiance of Europe, from the opportunities of travel, observation, of plain and simple leisure and material comforts. As a result, the Israelis were obliged to generate their cultural accomplishments and satisfactions largely from within.

THE SEARCH FOR IDENTITY AND STYLE

They were impelled to define themselves, as well. Actually, it was doubtful if the citizens of any other land were quite as fixated by the need to understand their status against the matrix of historical perspective. "Who are we?" "What is an Israeli?" "What is our role in the Middle East?" No thoughtful Israeli could escape these obsessive questions. In large measure, their preoccupation with roots explained the extraordinary appeal of archaeology as both science and pastime in Israel. Nowhere else in the world, surely, did the passion for historical recovery, the search for forgotten sites and ancient memorabilia, approach so closely a national vocation. Archaeological exhibits, lectures, debates, even contests and quizzes, aroused a near-fanatical response from all segments of the Jewish population. It was common on weekends for dozens of Israeli hiking groups, knapsacks on their backs, to forage hopefully in fields and dusty wadis for shards or clay figurines. Occasionally these amateurs even turned up important finds, among them inscriptions from the Gilgamesh Epic, synagogues dating back to Byzantine times, and relics of the neolithic age. Although the discoveries more commonly were of ancient Roman, Greek, and Hebrew coins and pottery, the Israelis nevertheless valued their relics highly enough to exhibit them in homemade museums. Nearly every farm village and school maintained one, as did most of the cities and towns in Israel. A number of these communities supported lively archaeological societies.

The major discoveries obviously were the accomplishment of professional archaeologists, the largest number of them working under the supervision of the department of antiquities, the Society for the Exploration of the Land of Israel, or—most important—the department of archaeology of the Hebrew University. Without exception, their finds were matters of national interest. The recovery of additional Dead Sea Scrolls in the early 1950s, for example, was front-page news in the country's press. Lectures on the subject delivered by biblical scholars attracted record audiences. Two plays and three films were produced dealing with the Scrolls. Between 1955 and 1959 Professor Yigael Yadin's excavation of Tel Chazor, the ancient Canaanite city of upper Galilee, was followed with almost breathless public excitement. Late in 1959, Yadin's even more spectacular discovery, near the Dead Sea, of letters written by Bar Kochba, military commander of the Jewish uprising against Rome in the second century, became a choice school topic of essays and pageants for months afterward. By then, too, the earth was providing Israel's Jews, immigrants and native-born alike, with a far richer sense of identity than mere history lessons or Zionist propaganda. A calcified potsherd bearing Hebrew inscriptions from the era of King Ahab, a brick disinterred from Jerusalem's ancient wall, a slag heap unearthed from King Solomon's copper mines, a pillar restored in a Byzantine synagogue, a parchment scroll recovered in a Dead Sea cave—each was a tangible link with Israel's past.

It was specifically this theme of ancestral rootedness that was emphasized in almost every field of Israeli expression, not excluding music and art. To be sure, the artistic trends flourishing in Palestine and Israel were diverse and eclectic. In the 1920s, Reuven Rubin, born in Rumania and among the first and best-known of Palestine Jewish painters, established an appealing genre of romantic pastoral landscapes, of coruscating trees, farms, and orchards. Romantic nostalgia similarly animated the works of Nachum Gutman, the painter of Jaffa in the 1920s, of "little Tel Aviv," with its horses, carts, veiled Arab women, and semi-Oriental architecture. The superbly executed canvases of Mordechai Ardon were endlessly interlaced with biblical symbols. In the same vein, Moshe Castel, descendant of a Sephardic family living in Palestine for five centuries, re-created biblical symbols and medieval Cabalistic themes in an evolving succession of styles; the latest of Castel's "periods" delved so far back into the Holy Land's antiquity that it was less painting than friezes of ancient Semitic script, resembling both Arabic and Hebrew. Nevertheless, it was increasingly difficult over the course of the years to perceive in the works of others of Israel's leading artists—among them Marcel Janco, Yosef Zaritsky, Avigdor Stematzky—anything specifically "Hebraic." The young country actually produced such an *embarras* of talent, churning out works in all genres for a seemingly endless international market, that it became far more difficult in painting and sculpture to identify the kind of self-definition that characterized music and literature.

There was little doubt that Palestine's Jewish composers tended at first to reflect the styles of their countries of origin. Yet with the growth of an Oriental, and particularly a Yemenite, immigration in the decades before the state, a number of composers became increasingly fascinated by Eastern music. In the 1940s Joseph Tal, Paul Ben-Chaim, Odon Partos, and Alexander Boscovitch were among the earliest to incorporate something of the Middle Eastern–Mediterranean flavor. The effort was not unsuccessful. Their works for orchestra and choral groups, all characterized by florid melodies, varied rhythms, and a rich palette of sounds, became standard in the repertoires of musicians in Israel and occasionally elsewhere. A new generation of Israeli composers subsequently came into its own in the early 1950s. Roman Haubenstock-Ramati, who lived in Israel only seven years, was a major inspiration for the younger composers, a number of whom became his students. In a more complex and sophisticated fashion than his predecessors, Ramati managed to link traditional Oriental music with Western serial techniques. Among his protégés, Yitzchak Sadai, Abel Ehrlich, and Ben-Zion Orgad created impressive examples of music shaped by Hebrew rhythmic and melodic inflection. Similarly, Hebrew cantillation and Near Eastern tonality formed the basis of Ami Ma'ayani's lavishly praised works. In the midst of a varied outpouring of styles, European and Oriental alike, these composers set out the main trends of a "native," "authentic" Israeli music. Their efforts were never more than tentative and experimental, and occasionally they were submerged in a familiar neo-classicism or neopopularism. But they offered the potential, at least, for an increasingly distinctive cultural identity.

LITERATURE OF THE SOUL:
THE "JEWISH" GENERATION

We recall that, as far back as the 1920s, Hebrew literature had become a remarkably sophisticated and influential medium of national expression. As it happened, many of its most eminent practitioners were still alive in the post-independence years. These included such widely revered figures as Avraham Shlonsky, Yitzchak Lamdan, Shin Shalom, Natan Alterman, Leah Goldberg, Uri Zvi Greenberg, Chaim Hazaz, and S. Y. Agnon. As a result, the major literary triumphs of Israel's early years were those of the older writers. The tribunes of exhortation to great tasks, Alterman, Lamdan, and Greenberg (Chapter VIII), continued their epic incantations of heroism and sacrifice. The lyric romantic tradition survived, too, in the writing of Leah Goldberg, perhaps the most widely read of Israel's poets.

Born in Kovno in 1911, Leah Goldberg was one of the first Jewesses of her time to be educated in a secular Hebrew gymnasium. Afterward she continued her philological studies at the University of Bonn, where eventually she received a doctorate in Semitics. In 1935 she settled in Tel Aviv, bringing with her a knowledge of European literature that was unique among the Hebrew writers of her generation. Her initial fame accordingly was as a brilliant critic of European writers and a peerless translator into Hebrew from six languages. It was Goldberg's poetry, however, that became the special delight of her audiences. Her verses were forthright, lucid, almost deceptively simple in form, and in marked contrast to the older Hebrew poetry, with its heavily freighted allusion and biblical allegorization. Although Goldberg's imagery, like that of many of her contemporaries, was romantic, evoking the Holy Land's pastoral beauty, her style was lean and exquisitely understated. She was loved as no other writer of her time. It was significant that the major poet of the Israeli younger generation, Yehuda Amichai, recalled on Leah Goldberg's death that in the midst of the Negev campaign of 1948 he had taken with him everywhere in his battle pack a dog-eared pamphlet edition of her classic *MiBeiti HaYashan* (From My Old Home).

If the traditions of exhortation and lyricism survived into the 1950s, so did an older, uniquely "Jewish" tradition of sensitive regard for Diaspora mores and values—even those that Zionism apparently had rejected. The writing of Shmuel Yosef Agnon (Czaczkes), for example, who was born in Galicia in 1888, resonated with an intense atmosphere both of southern Chasidism and of central European *Weltschmerz*. Living in Palestine only briefly early in the century, Agnon did not settle in the Holy Land until after World War I. It was then, in the 1920s, that he turned out some of his best works, most of them pietistic idylls of Chasidic life in nineteenth-century Galicia. From his home in Jerusalem, Agnon in ensuing years produced a number of full-length novels. *Hachnasat Kallah* (The Bridal Canopy), written in 1931, was perhaps his most famous. A picaresque account of the wanderings of Rabbi Yudel Chasid, the novel was a rich canvas of Jewish life in eastern Europe before the impact of modern times. In style, too, *Hachnasat Kallah* was extensively interwoven with pious allusions to the whole of Jewish religious literature—Bible, Talmud, Midrash, and Cabalistic lore. Unfortunately, this quality of rich allusiveness, the trademark of Agnon's writings, rendered his work notoriously difficult in translation. Yet for those who knew their Jewish sources and were capable of penetrating his imagery, the experience of reading Agnon offered rewards unsurpassed in contemporary Hebrew literature. Indeed, the Nobel committee accepted this evaluation on trust in awarding Agnon its prize for literature in 1966.

The ellipse of Agnon's work moved increasingly between two poles after the 1930s, the world of his native Polish Jewry and that of the new Yishuv in Palestine. Many of his stories continued to be legends of the Jewish past and often approached the Kafkaesque in their dreamlike atmosphere. As the writer's career in Jerusalem lengthened, however, the east European aura gradually faded. His work took on a Palestinian-Israeli locale, although at the same time becoming notoriously obscure in its mysticism, suffused by a dense atmosphere of personal symbolism. Manifestly, Agnon was now increasingly obsessed with the confrontation between the dynamic Zionist redemptive effort in Palestine and the fate of Jewish religious tradition in the emerging Yishuv. The tension between these approaches was brought to life in *T'mol Shilshom* (Yesterday and the Day Before), Agnon's masterpiece. Unable to find his place in Palestine, Kummer, the hero, moves between two societies, the old Orthodox community in Jerusalem and the new Zionist Yishuv of Tel Aviv and the agricultural settlements. Eventually, his search for belonging ends in failure and tragedy. This was the theme of all Agnon's later work. For him, Zionism was basically a noble failure; even as the old life, with all its past grandeur, offered no way back.

Some of this ambivalence between Diaspora "Jewishness" and the Zionist renaissance surfaced as well in the writings of Chaim Hazaz, eleven years younger than Agnon but in every respect his literary peer. Born in a small Ukrainian town in 1898, Hazaz escaped from Russia after the Denikin pogroms in 1921, lived in Constantinople and Paris, then settled in Jerusalem in 1932. He was still in Europe when his first stories began to appear in the well-known Hebrew periodicals of the 1920s, and his first novel, *B'Yishuvo shel Ya'ar* (In the Forest Dwelling), was published in 1930. It was only after extended residence in the Yishuv, however, and publication in the early 1940s of the first volumes of his collected writings, that Hazaz emerged as one of Palestine's most widely read and influential masters of Hebrew fiction.

An apocalyptic mood informed all Hazaz's works, whether describing in the 1920s the small Ukrainian town during the revolution, in the 1930s the phenomenon of Jewish exile and return to Palestine, or in the 1940s the Yemenite communities in Tsan'a and Jerusalem. Every act of his protagonists seemed charged with cosmic import. The truth was that, for Hazaz, every utopianist movement—communism, religious messianism, even Zionism—was seeded with potential tragedy. The author's *Weltanschauung* became particularly evident in his exploration of the Yemenite and Oriental communities. Emotionally incapable of discussing the slaughter of European Jewry, Hazaz turned instead to the Yemenites as carriers of his historical vision. Surprisingly enough, this exotic, Arabized little community provided him with an ideal milieu; for, like his beloved and doomed east Europeans, it was integrated, steeped in Jewish lore and tradition, in the first stages of modernization, and hence of internal disintegration. Accordingly, his two Yemenite novels, *HaYoshevet BaGanim* (Who Sitteth in the Gardens), published in 1944, and *Ya'ish*, published serially between 1947 and 1952, were the most structured and richly textured of all his writings.

In *HaYoshevet BaGanim*, Hazaz traced the metamorphosis of a single Yemenite family in Jerusalem over three generations. The elder of the clan, Mori Sa'id, is a dreamer sunk in messianic visions of the End of Days. Despite his preposterously disjointed view of the world about him, Mori Sa'id remains intact as a figure of nobility and piety. In counterpoint, his children are drawn into the gross materialism of the new society. Redemption comes only in the third generation, when a granddaughter escapes moral bankruptcy by settling on a kibbutz with the husband of her choice. *Ya'ish* traces the Yemenite chronicle back to its source, to Tsan'a, capital of the Yemen. There, Hazaz follows his hero (Ya'ish) from childhood through old age, a richly human figure oscillating between earthly desires and mystic visions. The ambivalence ends only when Ya'ish reaches Palestine. It was evidently Hazaz's implication that anchorage in the Holy Land offered the one, meaningful solution to personal and spiritual crisis.

In his last novel, however, *B'Kolar Echad* (With One Noose), published in 1963, Hazaz qualified this simplistic view. His two heroes are prisoners, young terrorists captured by the British and awaiting their execution during the final, doomed phase of the mandate. One boy is an Ashkenazi, the other a Sephardi. Both are fated to be hanged with "one noose," and in their last days they discuss Zionism and the Jewish future in terms familiar to Hazaz's readers, expressing the writer's profound concern lest the state abandon its messianic ideal ("Without the Messiah there is no Land of Israel"). Bitter scorn is heaped upon those who reject this dream, who live only for the present. Although more optimistic toward Zionism than Agnon, Hazaz in the end similarly linked his conception of Israeli statehood to the fuller totality of Jewish peoplehood. For both of these two giants of modern Hebrew literature, severance of the nexus of that peoplehood, with all its philosophical and historical connotations, was unthinkable.

"THE PALMACH GENERATION"—AND AFTER

The younger generation of Israeli intellectuals, those who participated in the War of Independence and who afterward found themselves struggling for economic survival during the postwar austerity years, bore little resemblance to the writers and thinkers of the earlier Yishuv. Their predecessors of the 1930s and 1940s were characterized by a near-fanatical interest in the "meaning of life," by a very Jewish quest for absolute truth, the large system, the laws governing history. Typically Jewish, also, was the belief of the pioneer Zionist settlers that there existed only one ideological path—Labor, Revisionist, Orthodox—to the redemption of the Jewish people. By contrast, the harassed Israeli students or writers of the postwar era, often holding down two jobs at once to make ends meet, were impelled by economic circumstances toward a more practical, utilitarian, and narrowly functional stance. They exhibited little curiosity about subjects other than their own, and tended by and large to regard ideologies as nonsense. Their attitude toward the Diaspora was new, as well. Lacking attachment or commitment to Jewish history and fate, the younger Israelis seemed altogether unrelated, for example, to the generation of Agnon and Hazaz. In contrast to their fathers, they were uninterested in either affirming or rejecting the Diaspora. They were simply indifferent.

It was true that the new Israelis were Jews as a matter of course. But it was equally apparent that they were Israeli Jews only. This fact exercised a perceptibly constricting influence upon every phase of their artistic and intellectual activity. For them, the birth of the state had decisively resolved the historical problems of Jewish existence. They no longer had the time or patience, as a result, for their forebears' agonized involvement in these questions. Perhaps the most unequivocal rejection of the Diaspora appeared even before the 1948 war in the form of the Canaanite movement. It consisted of a handful of cynical rebels who parodied their separation from Jews outside Israel by declaring themselves an indigenous Middle Eastern race ("Canaanites"), and by lavishing ridicule on the Diaspora Jewishness and synagogue Judaism of their fathers. They went to the extreme of affecting the jawline beards that they fancied were worn by the original Canaanites.

The rejection of the past was expressed in less caricatured form by the literary spokesmen of the emergent postwar generation, the first for whom Hebrew was the mother tongue and Israel the natural habitat. Known loosely as Dor HaPalmach (the Palmach generation), these writers included Yizhar Smilansky, Moshe Shamir, Aharon Meged, Yigal Mossinson, and Natan Shacham. Among the poets, the best-known were Yehuda Amichai, Amir Gilboa, Yitzchak Shalev, Abba Kovner, Chaim Guri, Tuvya Riber, Carmi Tcharny, and Hillel Omer. Their break with the older writers was immediately apparent, even in matters of style. Amichai, the most influential of the younger poets, employed free verse in low-keyed, conversational tone. With Gilboa, Shalev, and the others, he rejected the lush and often florid style of the earlier Shlonsky-Alterman tradition. Sharing in this departure was the new generation of novelists, with their lean, straightforward prose and their casual use of Arabisms.

What characterized the literature of the Palmach generation even more fundamentally, however, were new themes. For the younger writers, Israel no longer was a purpose of Jewish history but rather an accomplished fact. They made this point against the experience of the War of Independence. Indeed, their literature originally came to life on May 31, 1948, in the very midst of the war, with the Cameri Theater presentation of *Hu Halach BaSadot* (He Walked Through the Fields), a dramatized version of a novel by the twenty-seven-year-old Moshe Shamir. It was the story of a kibbutz boy, Uri, the son of divorced parents. A typical sabra (native-born Israeli), Uri tersely masks his feelings as he takes up with a newly arrived Polish refugee girl, who herself has endured harrowing experiences before reaching the kibbutz. At the hour of need, as the boy abruptly departs to join his Palmach unit, he gruffly rejects the girl's appeal to stay on a few days longer; nor does he wait to hear that she is pregnant by him. Shortly afterward he is killed in a daring volunteer action. The play was not without structural weaknesses. Yet its overriding merit was the insight with which it presented the new sabra type, his outlook on life, his manners and morals. Immigrant parents, with their European, ghetto-bred mentality, saw their offspring for the first time larger than life: strong, crude, brave, disdaining parental authority, and above all looking down on all that smacked of the Diaspora and sharply rejecting all appeals to "Zionut"—that is, Zionism in its emotional, epical connotations. Pragmatic, functional action seemed to be the motif of the new Israeli generation.

Shamir's play signaled the beginning of a trend in Hebrew writing. It was followed by a number of others in which the war, far from being glorified, was described in its prosaic and unsparing brutality. Shamir himself in 1954 created a historical romance, *Melech Basar v'Dam* (King of Flesh and Blood), in which Uri was transmuted into the image of Alexander Jannaeus, one of the last Hasmonean rulers. Alexander strives for absolute power. He extends the frontiers of Israel, but drowns all opposition in rivers of blood. Here the author appeared to warn that the positive qualities of the sabra could become negative within a certain context, and that national values could lead to moral disaster if not influenced by a fundamental humanism. With variations, it was a theme that reappeared in the works of other sabra writers, notably Yigal Mossinson and Natan Shacham, who drew a painful contrast between the humanistic Zionist ideal and the frequently debased reality of Israeli behavior.

Yizhar Smilansky, born in Palestine in 1916, pressed this theme to its outermost limits in questioning earlier styles and earlier Zionist values. In *Y'mei Ziklag* (Days of Ziklag), his greatest novel, published in 1958, Yizhar described in two thick volumes a week in the life of a unit battling for a strategic point in the Negev during the War of Independence. Here the stream-of-consciousness technique, first introduced in Israel by Uri Gneisen, enabled Yizhar to penetrate the inner world of his characters, to detail minutely the endless collision between private dreams and duty to the group. Yizhar's soldiers behave like soldiers anywhere, eagerly anticipating their furloughs, complaining about their duties, and occasionally trying to dodge them. Few seem inspired by the glories of the national undertaking. Rather, they are skeptical of their own worth, the values of the young state, disappointed with the circumstances that have transformed the country, the gulf between ideals and realization. Yizhar's heroes mock the "proud flag" and complain that Zionist rhetoric is "like a millstone around your neck." The book accurately voiced the Palmach generation's unsparing mood of iconoclasm, its impatience with cant, its remorseless self-appraisal.

THE CRISIS OF CONSCIENCE

Nowhere did the postwar generation deal more fearlessly with the gulf between Zionist sloganeering and Israeli fact than in its own confrontation with the Arab question. One event, we recall, that brutally punctured Israel's egalitarian claims was the Kafr Qasim massacre on the eve of the Sinai Campaign, when forty-three Arab civilians were shot dead by Israeli troops for innocently breaking a curfew (Chapter xviii). The government attempted to hush up the affair, but a campaign in the press and Knesset led to an eventual court-martial. Three officers were sentenced to extended prison terms. On appeal, however, the supreme military court declared the sentences "harsh" and reduced them sharply. The chief of staff then further lowered the sentences, as did the president of Israel in a "partial pardon." Afterward the Committee for the Release of the Prisoners succeeded in winning a remission of a third of all the sentences; and in 1960, hardly three years after the massacre, all the convicted officers were released outright. "Our integrity, our humanity and our courage have been put to the test," wrote the editor of the literary journal *Ner* in outrage, "and have been found wanting. . . ." Yizhar Smilansky blamed equally the press and the religious and academic leadership for their conspiracy of silence on the outrage.

In truth, few of Israel's leading writers managed to avoid either the burning issue of Kafr Qasim or the earlier injustices to the Arabs of Palestine. Most of them were willing to grapple with the plight of the Arabs in the deepest recesses of their artistic consciences. In his *Sipur Chirbat Chan* (The Tale of Khirbat Khan), for example, Yizhar laid bare Israel's profound moral responsibility for the fate of the refugees. It was a harrowing narrative, perhaps the most guilt-ridden single piece in contemporary Israeli literature. When its sequel, *HaShavui* (The Captive), appeared in 1949, the military authorities made a brief, unsuccessful attempt to forbid its circulation under the emergency regulations. Moshe Shamir, in his autobiographical *Chayai im Ishmael* (My Life with Ishmael), insisted that "we did not make the absorption of a million Jews [sic] from Arab countries conditional upon the ejection of *a single Arab* from within the borders of Israel." Shamir added: "The truth is that an Arab presence in the Land of Israel has always been accepted by us as a natural element of the uniqueness of the country, an element with which we must—and can—live amicably. . . ." He quoted with approval Dayan's 1956 eulogy of a boy killed by Arab guerrillas at Nachal Oz: "Let us not today hurl accusations at the killers," Dayan had said. "Why should we condemn their hatred toward us? For eight years they have been sitting in the Gaza refugee camps, while before their very eyes we have been taking possession of the land and villages where they and their forefathers lived."

It was in any case easier for young Israelis than for their parents to understand the Arabs. They had grown up among them. They had not brought from Europe elaborate tautologies that explained away Arab nationalist opposition as nonexistent or artificially inspired. Consequently, their own feelings of guilt and ambivalence were remorseless and ineradicable. Smilansky, Meged, Shamir, and their generation refused to envisage the struggle with the Arabs as one of right against wrong. In *Makom Acher* (Elsewhere), the first novel (1966) of Amos Oz, a young kibbutz member, the Arab enemy was completely assimilated into the book's mythic landscape, and in a sense was fused with it. Oz plainly was writing about much more than one kibbutz's physical state of siege. He had in mind no less an Israeli's nightmare of life in a garrison state, surrounded by an aggrieved majority whose presence could never be obliterated or ignored. In a spectacularly successful later novel, *Michael Sheli* (My Michael), Oz wrote incisively of the wife of a university graduate student, a girl obsessed by the memory of Arab twins with whom she had played as a child in Jerusalem before 1948. The twins return now in her fantasies to break into her home, violate, and kill her. By weaving Arab terrorism into the warp of a mythic confrontation, Oz again projected his generation's intense, if unconscious, awareness that death awaiting from without was implacable; retribution was as elemental a force of the Middle Eastern landscape as the Arabs themselves.

The guilt simply could not be exorcised. Avraham Yehoshua, a native-born contemporary of Oz, wrote a somewhat more understated fiction. In the title story of his immensely popular collection, *Mul HaYa'arot* (Opposite the Forests), the protagonist, a graduate student, accepts a job as fire watchman at a JNF forest to enjoy the solitude necessary for writing a thesis on the Crusades (a subtle reference here to the frequent Arab analogy between Israelis and Crusaders). The man-made forest has been planted over the site of an Arab village razed in the 1948 fighting. One of the villagers, however, an old mute, has stayed on as caretaker of the ranger station. At first the student-watchman strains every nerve keeping his lookout. Yet, imperceptibly, it becomes clear that he unconsciously expects, even desires, the fire to break out. When therefore the Arab mute eventually puts the forest to the torch, the student is a passive accomplice, exhilarated by the vision of the long-destroyed village he sees rising in the flames. The post-1948 generation manifestly did not intend, perhaps could not allow, the flaw in their past to be erased.

Nor could they accept without commentary the aberrant materialism with which Israelis sought increasingly to transcend their arid, petit-bourgeois environment. The land was small, the accommodations still meager. Fear of military conquest and the burden of austerity may have been lifted by the end of the 1950s, but Israel's life-style remained provincial in scope and ambition (Amos Oz marvelously distilled its shabbiness and constricted heroism in *Michael Sheli*). After the Sinai Campaign, it was an increasingly claustrophobic and joyless existence, as well. The country's ideological climate, as V. D. Segre shrewdly observed, was that of the "morning after." The nation found itself ensconced, perhaps physically more secure, but by the same token possessed of greater opportunity to contemplate the workaday aridity of its fate. In truth, the people of Israel were enervated by the Oriental influx, the bureaucratization of society, the erosion of idealism, and most of all by their own lack of additional challenge.

It was ironic, then, that the mood of affluent Israel in the mid-1960s was far gloomier than the mood of the still impoverished Israel of 1956. In 1964, for example, Shmuel Eisenstadt, a leading sociologist, was convinced that the real challenge to the country henceforth would be that of devising a new system of guidelines, of inducing the political parties to abandon their competing patronage empires, and somehow of developing a new ideology. Moshe Shamir was blunter, writing that "behind the fence of material prosperity we face spiritual catastrophe." Although plainly outgrowing its earlier slogans, values, institutions, and ideals, the nation had failed thus far to generate an effective replacement. With a Jewish refuge now apparently well established, how much idealism could be traded for security, how much Jewish universalism for Israeli nationalism? Here was a state that had been founded to revolutionize and even utopianize Jewish life, but which, far from attracting Jews, was losing them at a considerable rate in the mid-1960s. It was not Algerian Jewry alone that failed to take advantage of the Israeli sanctuary; in 1966 there was actually more emigration from Israel than immigration.

The literature of the late 1950s and 1960s reflected this malaise. Again and again its "heroes" evinced an unwillingness any longer to dedicate their lives to an ideal that appeared to be failing; they preferred to seek out the main chance. The shift in values was reflected in the nation's increasing materialism, in the startling collapse of its business ethics, the harsh aggressiveness of its interpersonal relations, and, not least, in the erosion of its family integrity. The fiction of the Palmach generation was increasingly obsessed with this lack of moral anchorage. Shamir, Meged, and Yizhar treated the flagrant consumptionism, the seething, barely contained ethnic antagonisms, of the later years in a series of plays and stories dealing with the unhinged affluence of German restitution recipients, the transformation of dedicated kibbutz members into careerists, the frustration and anomie of rudderless Orientals. In *Chedva v'Ani* (Chedva and I), for example, Aharon Meged traced the Don-Quixote-like odyssey of a simple kibbutz member, Shlomik, dragged by his wife into the city, the root of all evil, where slick bureaucrats and party bosses render his life a misery.

Shamir's play *Bayit b'Mazav Tov* (A Well-ordered Household) similarly portrayed the corroding impact of the new materialism upon a formerly austere and dedicated army family.

Convulsed by this dilemma, and shaken, too, perhaps by the Eichmann trial, which enlarged the nation's feelings of obligation to survivors of the Holocaust, Israeli-born writers began to take their spiritual bearings by embarking upon a new appraisal of their Jewish roots. Yehuda Amichai's book *Lo MiAchshav, Lo MiCan* (Not of This Time, Not of This Place), contrasted his life in Israel with an almost preconscious Jewish past in Germany. *Pitzei Bagrut* (Adolescent Pimples), by Hanoch Bartov, described the agonizing emotional encounter between troops of the Jewish Brigade in Europe and the survivors of the death camps. A reconstruction of the death camp experience was similarly the theme of the poet Chaim Guri's *Iskat HaShokolada* (The Chocolate Transaction). These works, and others by Yoram Kaniuk and Aharon Apelfeld, revealed a mounting and insistent obligation to absorb, to know, and to understand the totality of recent Jewish experience. It was a fixation that scarcely had been typical of the Palmach Generation of the early and mid-1950s.

THE CONFRONTATION WITH ORTHODOXY IN ISRAEL

For that matter, even the most pragmatic of sabras was by no means indifferent to Jewry's spiritual heritage. Israel, after all, was the only country in the world in which a daily Bible reading and commentary were broadcast during prime listening time, in which an annual Bible Contest was attended by hundreds of scholars and laymen from throughout the world. An Israel Society for Biblical Research conducted study circles and regional seminars. Numerous Bible study groups met weekly or monthly in the cities and even in kibbutzim. A Bible study circle of eminent Israeli intellectuals gathered regularly at the president's mansion. Extensively staffed departments of biblical studies attracted Israeli and foreign students to the nation's leading universities. The demand for books and albums describing and illustrating life in biblical Palestine was almost insatiable. Hardly a facet of popular culture remained untouched by interest in this supreme fount of Hebraic civilization.

The national passion similarly bespoke a consensus, shared by all the state's political factions—Orthodox, centrist, and Mapam alike—that the Bible must remain the bedrock of Jewish education and culture in Israel. Thus, in the teaching of Jewish history and literature, even Israel's nonreligious school systems were prepared to award the Bible a central position in their curricula. Nor was there effective protest in the late 1950s when the ministry of education added to the secular school curriculum a limited instruction in religious tradition, including the blessings, customs, and holidays. The introduction of this program in "Jewish consciousness" reflected a broad, if tacit, understanding that Judaism had served as an instrument of survival throughout nineteen hundred years of Jewish exile, and might continue to fulfill an identical purpose in the years ahead. Virtually every Israeli agreed that a certain minimal exposure to Jewish tradition did not necessarily imply commitment to religion in the theological sense.

Nor could public acceptance of these measures by any stretch of the imagination be equated with a widely diffused Jewish religiosity. In a 1963 survey, a bare 30 percent of the Israelis interviewed claimed to adhere strictly to traditional practices. At the other extreme, 24 percent described themselves as completely nonobservant, while in the middle area about half the population responded that they kept the tradition "to a certain extent." Five years later, in a survey of Jewish high school students carried out by Professor Simon Herman of the Hebrew University, a majority of the teenagers expressed innocence not only of any cosmic religious vision but of any serious concern for the Diaspora. Few of these young Israelis disavowed their Jewishness; they simply ignored it. Actually, the discrepancy between an almost universal Bible culture, on the one hand, and a growing indifference to Judaism as an organized religion, on the other, was not difficult to fathom. Religion was identified in Israel not with adherence to the tenets and spiritual values of the Jewish faith but with membership in the Orthodox political parties. And these parties traditionally were concerned with government enforcement both of their religious ideals and of specific, very material Orthodox perquisites. In short, it was the politicization of religion that antagonized the nation's most sentient and dynamic elements.

As early as 1956, for example, it was clear that the Agudists would not tolerate even the minutest compromise between Orthodox fundamentalism and public convenience. This became evident in May of that year, when Dr. Nelson Glueck, a well-known archaeologist and president of the Hebrew Union College, a seminary for Reform rabbis in the United States, filed a building application with the municipality of Jerusalem. It was Glueck's intention to construct a school of archaeology on a plot of ground near the King David Hotel, in the southeast section of the city. The project seemed respectable enough. In fact, the tract had been granted by the Israeli government. The building licenses committee promptly approved the application, subject to the ratification of the entire municipal council late in the summer. At this point, however, certain "ominous" information leaked out. It was learned that the blueprint for the school included a small annex to be used for religious services—presumably Reform services. Immediately, the Orthodox newspapers unleashed a furious attack on Glueck's "heretical" scheme. *HaZofe*, the Mizrachi daily, and *HaModia*, organ of the Agudah, blasted the proposed annex as "an attempt to introduce Reform worship in Jerusalem, an abomination, an obscenity in the eyes of the Lord." The Orthodox members of the council brought pressure to bear on Gershon Agron, the Mapai mayor, insisting that he remove the license application from the agenda of the July meeting. Agron refused. When the issue reached a vote in the council, late in July, the license was approved over the enraged opposition of the Orthodox, whose press and followers had maintained their hue-and-cry in the intervening weeks. At this point the religionists decided simply to announce their resignation from the municipal coalition.

From then on, Orthodox hostility, bitter and implacable, merely awaited the next provocation. It came less than a year later. At issue was a public swimming pool for Jerusalem. One Chaim Schiff, owner of the local President Hotel, had raised funds to build the city's first public swimming facility. With the encouragement of Mayor Agron, Schiff leased a site in the former German Colony, then submitted his plans to the city council for approval. The Religious bloc expressed no objection to the venture, provided (a) no bathing took place on the Sabbath, and (b) no mixed bathing, whether of men and women, or of boys and girls, took place at any time. Both conditions were overruled by the building and license committee, which then submitted the application to the full council meeting, scheduled for January 1958. Thereupon a storm of protest broke loose.

All factions among the religionists, including the Mizrachi, joined forces in opposing the pool. The religious newspapers issued editorial denunciations of those who wished to "besmirch" and "defile" the sacred character of Jerusalem. A vast correspondence campaign was organized against mixed bathing, and its advocates reviled Agron and Schiff in vituperative, even pornographic terms, some actually threatening assassination. Rabbi Amram Blau, leader of an almost surrealistically Orthodox splinter group, the Neturei Karta, chivvied other, less fundamentalist religionists into mass demonstrations. These took place not only throughout Israel, but also in Western countries. Thus, in the United States, Chasidim from the Williamsburg section of Brooklyn picketed the White House in June 1958, denouncing American support of "oppressive" Israel. Eventually the protest movement failed. Although Schiff himself was forced to sell out his shares in the pool (the chief rabbinate falsely refused to authenticate his hotel kitchen as kosher), a group of kibbutzim bought his stock. The Jerusalem municipal council approved the building license, and the pool opened on schedule.

The Orthodox were not through. In 1964, following an acrimonious political debate that lasted two years, the National Religious party eventually compelled the government to surrender on the issue of the Shalom, the gleaming new flagship of the Zim line and Israel's proudest entry on the Atlantic run. The Zim management had made provisions for two kitchens, one nonkosher for the majority of its intended passengers, and one kosher for those who required such facilities. The religionists insisted, however, that a ship bearing the Israeli flag must under no circumstances commit the "sacrilege" of offering nonkosher food at all; kitchen service must remain under the scrutiny of an Orthodox staff of ritual inspectors. This time, the religionists had their way. Predictably, the Shalom failed to attract an international clientele or to become profitable. In the end it had to be sold. Indeed, the Orthodox parties traditionally ensured that the whole sector of food-processing and inspection remained one of the most dependable sources of livelihood and patronage for their constituents. To that end, the chief rabbinate blocked the government's plans to open its recently constructed, modern slaughterhouse in Kiryat Malachi, an abbatoir that would have serviced the butcher shops of the entire country. At issue were hundreds of small, unhygienic abbatoirs operated by local municipalities, all of them under the direction of ritual slaughterers and supervisors intent upon keeping their jobs. Eventually the threat of court action produced a "compromise" by which meat packed in the new abbatoir could be sold in Tel Aviv, but not in Jerusalem.

If Israel's citizens faced economic intimidation at the hands of the religionists, they also suffered an Orthodox encroachment upon civil rights that at times jeopardized public safety and individual security. Autopsies were a case in point. Until well after the establishment of Israel, the nation's medical schools were forbidden to dissect bodies, in accordance with the Orthodox injunction against postmortems. Finally, in 1951, Chief Rabbi Yitzchak Herzog agreed to the dissection of bodies on condition that: they had formally been donated by their owners for scientific research; there were no objections from next of kin; and all the dissected parts eventually were buried with traditional ceremony and respect. This rabbinical dictum subsequently was incorporated into a Law of Anatomy and Pathology that was passed by the Knesset in 1953. The legislation also affirmed that corpses might be dissected "in order to establish the cause of death," provided three authorized physicians signed the necessary certificate.

Not long afterward, however, the Orthodox began circulating the allegation that corpses were subjected to indignity, that autopsies were becoming a matter of routine, not simply of medical necessity. By 1962 incidents of protest had escalated into violent clashes between religionists and police at hospital gates. Alarmed at the unrest, the government requested a select panel of physicians, rabbis, and jurists to produce a new formula. After three years, the committee submitted an amendment to the 1953 law that clearly reflected interparty bargaining. By its terms, a patient's opposition in writing, or that of his kin during a compulsory five-hour period from the announcement of his death, would suffice to prevent an autopsy, except in cases "where the public interest overrides the will of the family." It was explicitly stated, too, in the accompanying explanation (but not in the text), that "dissection for the sake of removing a limb from the deceased in order to heal another person shall not be allowed in the event of opposition." The "compromise" hardly appeased the Orthodox. Bands of yeshivah students intensified their protests, demonstrating outside hospitals, harassing individual physicians, breaking windows in their homes, painting swastikas on their doors, even physically assaulting them at times. Police protection of doctors was increased, but legal measures against the Orthodox assailants were rare.

Notwithstanding their alleged solicitude for the rights of the deceased, the Orthodox plainly were much less concerned about the rights and freedom of the living—those who did not happen to share their fundamentalist views. This was revealed dramatically several years earlier in the course of the "Yossele" affair. An elderly Russian Jew, Nachman Shtarkes, after years

of confinement in Siberian prison camps, was allowed to depart for Israel
in 1957 with his wife. Afterward the Shtarkeses were joined by several of
their grown sons and daughters. Most of the family were religious. One
daughter and her husband, the Schumachers, were not. Nevertheless, the
Schumachers entrusted the elderly couple with two of their small children
to enable the mother to continue working. In 1959, Mrs. Schumacher took
back the girl, who by then had reached her teens. The boy, Joseph Schumacher, called Yossele, seven years old at the time, remained with his
grandparents, who provided him with an intensive religious upbringing.
When finally the parents asked for Yossele's return as well, the grandfather
refused. Instead, Nachman Shtarkes consulted several ultra-Orthodox
rabbis in Jerusalem (two of them members of the fanatical Neturei Karta
sect), who urged that under no circumstances should the boy be allowed to
return to a secularist home environment. Whereupon Yossele was spirited
away to places unknown.

A sensational court trial followed, initiated by the Schumachers. When
Shtarkes declined to return the boy, the judge in February 1960 sentenced
the old man to prison for contempt of court. The religious press uniformly
hailed Shtarkes as a martyr, and yeshivah students, evincing little sympathy
for the distraught parents, conducted public demonstrations on his behalf.
Repelled in turn by these Orthodox tactics, a secularist committee early
in 1961 launched a vigorous antireligious campaign, with press conferences,
interpellations in the Knesset, and the distribution of pamphlets. Acrimony
between the religionists and the non-Orthodox majority by then had become more heated than ever before in the nation's developing *Kulturkampf*. Fearing, too, the danger of indiscriminate counterviolence against
all religionists, the National Religious party became increasingly hesitant
to defend Nachman Shtarkes. Orthodox Jews dared not raise an issue in
the Knesset or in public demonstrations without being greeted by shouts of
"Where's Yossele?" and "Kidnappers!" Finally, in April 1962, the Israeli
secret service located the child in New York, where he had been kept in
hiding. He was returned to his parents, Shtarkes was released, and all further proceedings against the grandfather and his accomplices were
dropped. But the episode rankled among the nation's secularist majority.
Together with innumerable other restrictions on freedom of conscience and
activity, the Yossele affair projected a stereotype of Orthodoxy that even
the richest biblical associations and archaeological expeditions failed to
modify.

WHO IS A JEW?

The problem of Jewish identity in Israel was rendered unusually complex
by three overlapping jurisdictional issues. The first was that of citizenship
itself. Israel's citizens obviously included Jews, Christians, Moslems, Armenians, Druze, Circassians, and others. All were equal under the law,
all entitled to the same rights and, with one qualification, obligated to the

same duties. The qualification was service in the armed forces: Arabs were exempt. Here the second issue, that of nationality—that is, of ethnic identification—as distinct from citizenship, became crucial. For the question of nationality affected the way in which citizenship was acquired. Israel was a Jewish state. In practice, this meant that its gates were open to all national (ethnic) Jews, but only to Jews, who decided to make Israel their home; the Law of Return made this clear.

The third issue, of religious affiliation, was determined in turn by the autonomous religious community—essentially the modern version of the old Ottoman millet. Again there was little doubt that this inherited millet system operated fairly at the corporate level. For example, the Jewish religious community enjoyed no special privileges whatever in relation to the Moslem or various Christian communities. On the individual level, however, questions of marriage, divorce, burial, and several other intimate matters of personal status were consigned to religious law, and thereby to the frequently less than benign discretion of the religious authorities within each community. In the case of the Jews, moreover, certain archaisms that were reserved to the interpretation of the rabbinical hierarchy approached the barbaric, among them levirate marriage and prohibitions against cohanim (descendants of the ancient priestly caste) marrying divorced women (p. 361). To be sure, these anachronisms were still applied to relatively few individuals. But one very serious problem related to intermarriage; and this was a matter that, by affecting the question of one's *national* Jewishness, infinitely bedeviled the *religious* rights of Israeli Jews.

As an example, a local rabbinical council refused to grant permission to a young Falasha, an Ethiopian Jew, to marry a Jewish woman unless he consented to undergo Orthodox conversion. The Falashas, it appeared, were suspected by the rabbinate of having intermarried in Ethiopia generations before; and therefore, conceivably not being Jewish by *nationality* (ethnic identification), they were not entitled to Jewish *religious* rights. The problem of the B'nai Israel was even more sensitive. This community of Jews from India, 8,000 of whom had recently settled in Israel, had lived for centuries isolated from the mainstream of Jewry. Although they had stubbornly adhered to their Jewish traditions, they had done so without benefit of rabbinical guidance. Hence doubts arose on the validity of their marriages and divorces; and some rabbis now declined to sanction unions between members of B'nai Israel and members of other Jewish communities. To its credit, the chief rabbinate at least devoted intensive research to the problem. Finally, in 1961, it decided that the B'nai Israel were to be regarded as Jews, but that in the case of an impending marriage between one of their group and a member of another (Jewish) community, inquiries were to be made as far back as possible into the ancestry of the B'nai Israel partner. Understandably, the B'nai Israel resented being singled out for this humiliating investigation. Early in 1963, therefore, a score of their families camped opposite the Jewish Agency offices in Jerusalem and demanded either the repeal of the rabbinical directive or repatriation to India. For weeks, dozens of men, women, and children squatted on the pavements in the heart of the capital, sheltering at night under improvised tents, demanding justice. Eventually, under Knesset pressure, and with the intercession of Prime Minister Eshkol, the rabbinate accepted a compromise formula under which all cases of doubtful pedigree would be investigated, without mentioning B'nai Israel as such. Had it not been for the obstinacy and courage of these simple people, it is unlikely that the rabbinate would have backed down.

The most serious problems, then, of rabbinical limitations on Jewish religious rights traced back to the ultimate question of Jewish nationality. The Law of Return had failed to define the term "Jew" in its national (ethnic) sense. Yet until this term was given official interpretation, the rabbinate would continue to deny suspected non-Jews the full religious rights and privileges—including marriage, divorce, and burial—permitted to members of the national (ethnic) Jewish community (except for authorized converts to Judaism). The supreme court accordingly made its first effort to define this national term in the Rufeisen case of 1958. Oswald Rufeisen was a Polish Jew who had taken refuge in a Polish monastery during the war, became converted, and took orders as a Carmelite monk. Adopting the name of Brother Daniel, Rufeisen still felt himself Jewish enough to emigrate to Israel to live and work. He claimed the right of entry under the Law of Return—that is, as a recognized Jew by nationality. When the authorities refused him entry under this category, he appealed to the courts. According to the Halachah—the Jewish Orthodox law— Rufeisen was indeed a national (ethnic) Jew, for he was born of a Jewish mother. But the supreme court ruled that the national term "Jew," while ordinarily applied to many who did not practice Judaism, could not "in the language of men" be applied to anyone who voluntarily adopted another faith. In effect, then, halachic—Orthodox—law was required to give way before the people's current idea of its own identity. The decision was a startling one, for it intimated that for civil purposes, at least, the state, not the rabbinate, could decide who was Jewish by nationality. Nevertheless, the Orthodox acquiesced in the decision, presumably because the question was one of excluding a dubious Jew rather than of including one.

The implications of the judgment became dramatically apparent on March 10, 1958, however, when the Achdut HaAvodah minister of the interior, Israel Bar-Yehuda, decided to systematize the hitherto inconsistent practices of officials registering the country's Jewish inhabitants. The problem resulted from a growing immigration of east European Jews, many of whom brought with them Gentile spouses and their children. In order to spare these mixed couples complications and embarrassment, Bar-Yehuda issued a directive on the method henceforth to be used for registering identity data. Israeli identity cards included two related items, religion and nationality. Some Israelis had argued earlier for the removal of the nationality category, fearing that it might be used to discriminate against Arab citizens. But the government maintained that the category was necessary because it distinguished between Arabs and Jews for security purposes. Bar-Yehuda now authorized his officials simply to record whatever nationality information the immigrant supplied the registrar: "Any person declaring in good faith that he is a Jew [by nationality] shall be registered as a Jew, and no additional proof shall be required." If both members of a married couple declared that their child was Jewish, the registering official could accept the statement at face value, without worrying about halachic law, which ascribed to the child of an intermarried couple the status of his mother. To the minister, religious law was for religious purposes, but for the purpose of state registration the individual's personal conviction and his own declaration of nationality would be the relevant guiding factor. Anyway, the rabbis were always free later to investigate a person's nationality for marriage or divorce; these were essentially religious questions.

But no sooner was the new directive issued than the religionists were up in arms. The state might designate who was a citizen, they warned, but not who was a Jew; Orthodox law alone must be followed in determining this matter—and followed according to the immutable halachic criteria which declared that an authentic Jew must be born of a Jewish mother and, if male, ritually circumcised, or that the person must be converted to Judaism by Orthodox procedure. At the intercession of the two religious ministers, the cabinet immediately began urgent discussions on the controversial directive. A ministerial committee was appointed to study the legal aspects of the question and report back. The underlying issue here plainly was whether Jewish nationality could be separated from Jewish religion. Historically, it never was in the Diaspora; the rules and traditions of the latter determined the identity of the former. For Bar-Yehuda and his Labor associates, however, the establishment of a Jewish state liberated from any official connection with religion was integral to their Socialist Zionism. If the Knesset could not determine who was to be regarded as of Jewish nationality for purely secular and security purposes, and if the criteria of Orthdox law were to apply, then Zionism would have failed to disengage Jewish nationhood from the traditional bonds of religion.

The majority of the committee upheld Bar-Yehuda's directive, with the one qualification (influenced by the Rufeisen case) that the person who declared himself of Jewish nationality must not profess any other religion. Outraged, the two ministers of the National Religious party immediately resigned from the coalition. Ben-Gurion was unsettled. The last thing he needed was a crisis with his dependable religious partners, especially when the Cherut, General Zionist, and Progressive factions were eager to support the Orthodox on this issue. Adopting his most conciliatory manner, therefore, the prime minister assured the veteran religious leader Rabbi Yehuda Maimon that the government had no intention of laying down religious law. But he pointed out that in the Declaration of Independence the government had announced freedom of religion and conscience and had not proclaimed that the Jewish state should be governed by religious law. Anyway, Ben-Gurion observed, in questions of ritual, marriage, and divorce, the government's decision would not be binding on the rabbinate. Maimon and the Orthodox parties were unimpressed by this argument.

Rather, they called upon Jews throughout the world to protest the action of the Israeli cabinet. In turn, the Labor parties solidified behind Ben-Gurion. The question now was less of who was a Jew than of who would govern Israel—the Knesset or the rabbinical council.

At this point the NRP ministers resigned from the cabinet, and on July 15 the religionists supported a motion of no-confidence, introduced in the Knesset by Cherut. The ensuing Knesset debate continued for two weeks. Finally, in despair, Ben-Gurion introduced a resolution to appoint a special committee that would invite the opinions of Jewish sages both in Israel and abroad on this question. Registration directives would be formulated afterward on the basis of an international scholarly consensus; until then, Bar-Yehuda's instructions would simply be held in abeyance. The compromise was accepted. Subsequently the committee referred the issue to forty-three scholars in Israel and elsewhere for their comment. Over the months the replies slowly accumulated. They made clear that a large majority of the sages endorsed the religionist view; the state could not infringe on the traditional halachic interpretation of Jewish nationality. The NRP meanwhile had rejoined the government, and one of its members, Chaim Shapiro, had become minister of the interior. On the basis, then, of the scholarly consensus, which Ben-Gurion had felt obliged to accept, Shapiro proceeded to issue new regulations in 1960. By their terms, a person could be registered as a Jew by nationality or religion only if he fulfilled the criteria of the Halachah: namely, if he were born of a Jewish mother and did not belong to another religion; or if he had been converted to Judaism according to Orthodox procedure. The religionists had won an unequivocal triumph.

This Orthodox interpretation of nationality thereafter remained the administrative law of the land until January 1970, when the supreme court handed down a judgment in yet another historic case. It happened that one Benyamin Shalit, a career officer in the Israeli navy, had married a Scottish Gentile woman in Europe and settled with her in Haifa. There she bore him two children. Although the mother had never converted to Judaism, both children, as natives, were automatically Israeli citizens. The question that arose now related not to their citizenship but to their nationality. Benyamin and Ann Shalit, both atheists, had filled out the entry for religion in their children's papers with the word "none." They insisted, however, that the nationality entry read "Jew." Even so, the local registrar, following the 1960 directive, wrote "no registration" under the nationality category. Shalit immediately filed a legal protest, which eventually came before the supreme court. There the young naval officer insisted that his children were being raised with a strong sense of participation in the national-historical community of Jews; they were regarded as Jews by other Israelis; and accordingly they had the right to be listed as of Jewish nationality on their identity cards.

On January 23, 1970, after an eighteen-month interval, the supreme court decided five to four on behalf of Shalit. Each of the nine justices felt called upon to render a detailed individual opinion, with the collected opinions running to a book of 180 pages. The majority justices emphasized that they were not considering the general question of who was a Jew, but simply the limited technical issue of who might be listed as a Jew under the nationality category of an identity card. Inasmuch as the Law of Registration of Inhabitants was a civil law meant for civil administration purposes only, the term "Jew" need not be interpreted in accordance with the Halachah. Despite this elaborate qualification, however, the Orthodox press shrieked in black headlines, "Court Ruling Murderous to Survival of People." The NRP warned that it would leave the government coalition if the Knesset did not immediately pass a law to amend the effect of the supreme court decision. The threat registered. However reluctantly, Golda Meir's government soon capitulated to the NRP ultimatum, and in a matter of days rushed through the Knesset an amendment to the Registration of Inhabitants Law that allayed the theological terrors of the religionists and kept them in the coalition. Shalit was allowed to register the nationality of his children as he wished. But, for the future, the law enjoined registration officials against listing a Jewish nationality for the children of mixed marriages where the mother was a Gentile.

The religionists' victory was less than complete. As compensation to the secularists, the Law of the Return was amended to grant automatic citizenship rights to Gentile spouses, to the children of mixed marriages, even to the adult descendants of mixed marriages. This was a not unimportant achievement. Citizenship, after all, carried important civil and fiscal advantages, and therefore spared Gentile wives and their immigrating children much inconvenience, even if it did not change its possessor's status under the religious law. If and when Moscow allowed a substantial departure of Soviet Jews, their entry no longer would be impeded by Israel on religious grounds as long as they either were married to Jews or had evidence of Jewish blood. Yet another concession was offered the secularists. It provided that a Jew by nationality should be defined not only as a person born of a Jewish mother, but as one who had been converted to Judaism. Significantly, the manner of the conversion was not defined. This implied that the state would recognize the validity of conversions performed by non-Orthodox rabbis abroad.

But if the secularists detected some gain in this last provision, it was an uncertain one. Subsequent court decisions revealed that no flexibility whatever could be expected on the issue of conversions performed in Israel; these still had to be carried out under Orthodox auspices. Moreover, the rabbinate continued to reserve to itself the purely religious questions of marriage and divorce. It could still refuse to recognize as Jewish, for the purpose of marriage, a convert whose nationality had been registered by the government as Jewish. Nor, in any case, were the Orthodox willing to regard the entire package of emergency "compromise" legislation as more than a temporary setback. Their next step would be to secure an amendment that would deny registration as a Jew to any convert who had failed to go through Orthodox procedures abroad, no less than in Israel. While there was little immediate likelihood that such legislation would be pushed through the Knesset, the religionists nevertheless bided their time, awaiting the next moment of Labor vulnerability when they might exert their bargaining strength anew (Chapter xxv).

In view of the tremendous uproar provoked by the registration crisis, it is worth recalling the assumption of the classical Zionist thinkers that the "normalization" of their people's lives in a sovereign Jewish state would put an end to this troubled confusion of Jewish identity. That assumption clearly had been premature. It now became evident that partisans on both sides of the nationality question took for granted that Israel was not a state like other states, but rather the sovereign arm and territorial focal point of a Jewish people dispersed extensively throughout the world. The tendency of both the Orthodox and the secularists to exaggerate the ramifications of an internal registration dispute suggested that Israel was still intimately and profoundly enmeshed in the fate of Diaspora communities everywhere. Within Israel, meanwhile, it was plain that distinctions continued to exist between two types of Israeli citizens, each with Jewish links. On one side there were Jews whose ethnic qualifications fulfilled the halachic profile of Jewish nationality. On the other there were non-Jews married to Jews, children of mixed marriages, and Gentiles converted in other lands through non-Orthodox auspices. Someday they would have to face, or see their children face, agonizing personal difficulties as a consequence of the rabbinate's unshaken monopoly over marriage and divorce, and the government's inability to frustrate that monopoly by breaking the political status quo.

THE STRUGGLE FOR FLEXIBILITY
WITHIN ORTHODOXY

In the wake of the government's surrender following the Shalit case, public revulsion against the Orthodox establishment became almost uncontainable. There was widespread identification with an open letter written to Prime Minister Golda Meir by Chanan Frank, who had immigrated to Israel from the Netherlands in 1968 with a Dutch mother and a Jewish father. Serving in the army, he had lost both legs to an Egyptian mine. In his letter, Frank asked if he was not now to be considered a Jew by nationality according to the new amendment. He himself was religious, but presumably would not be accepted as a "national" Jew unless his mother were converted by Orthodox procedure in Israel, a step she refused to take. For years it had been Orthodox practice in Israel to make conversion of non-Jewish women extremely difficult. Indeed, applicants were denied more often than accepted. Not infrequently local rabbis turned down women simply because they belonged to kibbutzim that were not affiliated with the National Religious party. The secularists asked how much longer this kind of medievalism was to paralyze an otherwise free society.

By the early 1970s there were faint indications that the rabbinate was becoming at least somewhat less obstructive, if only in response to mounting public outrage and the threat of Knesset action against Orthodox dominance in the sphere of marriage and divorce. In March 1971, the rabbinical council, presided over by Chief Ashkenazic Rabbi I. Y. Untermann, decided to offer a minor concession on the conversion issue. It was to waive the one-year "test of intention" waiting period for immigrants arriving from east European countries. The process of conversion would be carried out in a "shorter time." Both unrest and auguries of change reached a denouement of sorts in yet another legal case—this one, however, before the rabbinical rather than the secular courts. At issue was the desire of a brother and sister, Chanoch and Miriam Langer, to marry the partners of their choice. Their mother had been married some decades earlier, to a Gentile Pole, Abraham Borkovsky, who had been converted to Judaism before the marriage. After the establishment of Israel, Borkovsky's wife fell in love with a Jew, Langer, and departed with him for Israel, where she had two children by him, Chanoch and Miriam. Only afterward did she seek and receive a divorce from Borkovsky at the hands of an Israeli rabbinical council. The children reached adulthood, then applied to the Petach Tikvah rabbinical court to marry. They were turned down because they were mamzerim.

The term "mamzer" was by no means synonymous with "bastard." A bastard was one born out of wedlock, and under religious law suffered only minor legal and moral obloquy. A mamzer, on the other hand, as defined by the Halachah, was a child born of an adulterous or incestuous relationship —and exclusively between a married woman and someone other than her husband. The only restrictions, too, imposed even against a mamzer in Orthodox law were marital ones; in all other respects there were no penalties. But in the Langer case, at least, the marital limitations were painful enough. It was hardly consolation when the rabbinate advised the young people that they were permitted to marry other mamzerim. Each time, then, that the unfortunate brother and sister applied to the Petach Tikvah rabbinical court, their appeal to marry was rejected. The Jerusalem rabbinical court was loath to hear the case. Sephardic Chief Rabbi Yitzchak Nissim personally was not unwilling to review it, but his good intentions foundered on the opposition of Ashkenazic Chief Rabbi Untermann.

Exasperated, but assured of support by considerable numbers of Labor and Liberal Knesset members—who were prepared to introduce legislation authorizing secular marriage in Israel—Chanoch and Miriam Langer, together with their lawyers and fiancés, met with Prime Minister Golda Meir on August 19, 1971. They asked the prime minister's intercession with the chief rabbinate to establish a special bet din—a religious court—that would give their case a new hearing. Mrs. Meir intimated that if the young people would only exercise patience a bit longer, and desist from opening the religious question again in the Knesset, their problem might well be solved. She was clearly referring here to the elections for the chief rabbinate. These were scheduled for the next year, and conceivably might effect an important change in personnel. The Langers agreed to wait a reasonable time. In the interval the case hung on, mired in technicalities, while in the press and in public debate warnings came thick and fast that the issue could be resolved only by a Knesset law against rabbinical jurisdiction in matters of personal status. Otherwise, it was stated, archaic religious legalisms would produce in Israel a caste of "untouchables."

In the autumn of 1972 rabbinical elections were held. The aged Untermann (eighty-seven years old) campaigned once again among the religious councils, heading a bloc to stop the "liberal" threat posed by his major opponent for the Ashkenazic chief rabbinate, Shlomo Goren. It was known that a group of moderates in the NRP was supporting Rabbi Goren as a reformer, the kind of man who would dampen the *Kulturkampf* before it flared altogether out of control. This hope was seemingly well placed. For nearly twenty years Goren had been the chief chaplain of the armed forces and was respected there by secularist and religionist alike for his toleration and flexibility. Upon leaving the army, Goren (with the influential support of Moshe Dayan) had been elected chief rabbi of Tel Aviv. In this capacity, he had maintained his liberal stance. The process of conversion rarely took long under his jurisdiction. Within a year (again with Dayan's encouragement), Goren had announced that he would campaign for the post of Ashkenazic Chief Rabbi. It was an open secret that he demanded of his followers their acceptance of his known intention of resolving the Langer case in a fair and humane manner.

Goren in fact was elected, and thereupon became ex officio president of the high rabbinical court. On the other hand, Yosef Ovadia, the Sephardic Chief Rabbi, elected at the same time, was an unbudging traditionalist, and Goren knew well that Ovadia (also an ex officio president of the council) would create difficulty in the Langer matter. The situation demanded a military-style blitzkrieg operation. Striking fast, therefore, Goren was able to muster nine rabbinical judges from the district court of Tel Aviv to hear the Langer case. Ovadia had not been alerted to this maneuver, and therefore was not present. The proceedings consumed less than an hour, and from them emerged a ruling that the conversion to Judaism years before of Mrs. Langer's first husband, Borkovsky, was "questionable." As Goren explained it, the man had never taken the ritual seriously and purportedly could not so much as recite the basic Hebrew prayers. As a result, Mrs. Langer's original marriage to him could not be considered halachically valid; and from the religious viewpoint, then, her children were not the products of an adulterous liaison. The very day this ruling was handed down, in another move worthy of the best Israeli military tradition, Goren presided over the double marriage of Chanoch and Miriam Langer and their betrothed. Dayan himself attended the wedding. In Jerusalem, the next day, the Independent Liberals temporarily suspended their efforts to force a vote on civil marriage. It was the quid pro quo of a tacit agreement under which numerous pending issues of Orthodox law would now be resolved more speedily and fairly under Goren's aegis.

There were additional faint omens of hope. Within the NRP certain moderate elements, belonging to the party's Poalei Mizrachi faction, indicated a willingness to detach themselves from the policies of the rabbinate and even to criticize them openly. Their most respected national effort had been to develop a semipioneering youth group, B'nai Akiva, and the Religious Kibbutz movement. The atmosphere of these superb religious kibbutzim, like the gracious manners of their young people, displayed a liberality of thought, an openness toward secular learning, and a tone of almost purposeful mildness. Although their members accepted the *ex cathedra* pronouncements of the rabbinate when these clearly involved halachic principles, they resisted its ban on the military conscription of girls. Not infrequently, too, they turned for guidance on particular issues of Orthodox law not to the chief rabbinate but to more flexible rabbis of their own selection. Here, seemingly, was to be found at least one path toward a reconciliation of Orthodox and secular ideals.

There were other voices raised within Orthodoxy that advocated a sharper break with tradition, nothing less than a complete or partial religious disestablishment. One of these spokesmen was Pinchas Rosenblutt, director of religious education at the famous Mikveh Israel agricultural school. Rosenblutt campaigned for a more active effort by Orthodox leaders to reach out to the community to establish a discourse, to explain the significance of religion in an affirmative way rather than simply as a grillwork of limitations. In 1966 Professor Zvi Urbach of the Hebrew University, an Orthodox Jew, founded a "Movement for Judaism of the Torah" that aimed at dissociating religion entirely from politics, thereby freeing it to relate the Halachah more significantly to contemporary life. Nor was there a more vigorous critic of the Orthodox establishment than Dr. Yeshayahu Leibowitz, a sharp-tongued professor of chemistry at the Hebrew University. Scrupulously Orthodox himself, Leibowitz excoriated the nation's rabbinical leadership for its militance and xenophobia. Indeed, he advocated separation of religion and state with a fury that would have done credit to a Mapam editorialist.

Yet those who regarded occasional moderate elements within the Orthodox camp as the nucleus of an Israeli variety of Liberal Judaism were doomed to disappointment. Urbach, Leibowitz, Rosenblutt, and the religious kibbutz leaders were still agreed that what God wrote, man dared not change—except by the procedure ordained in the divinely inspired writings. For them, Liberal or Conservative Judaism was less to be desired than no Judaism at all, for each "sanctified the errors of the people." It was of interest, too, that even Chief Rabbi Goren, reviled and execrated by the ultra-Orthodox for his decision on the Langer case, made overtures again to the Right and posed as a strict constructionist on the issue of "Who is a Jew?"

THE QUEST FOR SPIRITUAL ALTERNATIVES

Whatever their disenchantment with politicized Orthodoxy, few Israelis had illusions that religious movements imported from abroad were meaningful alternatives to the fare offered by the rabbinate. American Orthodoxy was uninterested in changing Israel's status quo. American Reform and Conservative Judaism were waging an uphill, all but hopeless, battle to gain a foothold in the Jewish state. To be sure, the Hebrew Union College School in Jerusalem conducted a Reform religious service on the Sabbath and holiday mornings. Similarly, the World Union for Progressive Judaism maintained ten Reform congregations in Jerusalem, Tel Aviv, Haifa, and other cities and towns, and paid the salaries of their American rabbis. Conservative Judaism funded three synagogues, the Schocken Library, and a student dormitory for Conservative rabbinical students at the Hebrew University, and dispatched young rabbis to assist the staff of Mosad Ahavah, a youth village in Haifa for disturbed children. Both the Conservative and the Reform movements sponsored high schools, retreats, tours, and occasional conferences for adults and youth in various parts of Israel. To disarm their critics, meanwhile, both Reform and Conservative leaders proclaimed their intention simply of adapting their movements in Israel, rather than of importing them whole.

Yet whatever their disclaimers, Reform and Conservatism were seeking in fact to establish a "presence" that was doomed virtually from the outset. Their institutions and activities at best were symbolic, operated by remote control from abroad. Indeed, their failure was not merely an inability to win official authorization to perform marriages and burials, but a similar inability to make popular headway. It was true that Orthodoxy also depended on government financial support for its influence. Nevertheless, Israel's Orthodox Jews at least demonstrated a keen desire to protect and maintain the institutions they built. No such claim could be made for non-Orthodox Israelis. Few of them evinced a desire to pray in synagogues of any kind. The American rabbis were notably unsuccessful in offering the Israeli public, and especially its youth, a meaningful alternative to the extremes of Orthodoxy or secularism. Even Reform, with its great American tradition of social justice, had little to say in Israel that was not being said far more cogently by secular Israelis, thousands of whom were translating the values of equality, responsibility, cooperation, and love into new human contexts—for example, the nation's welfare institutions, Youth Aliyah villages, and kibbutzim.

What was keenly, even desperately, felt by growing numbers of non-Orthodox Israelis was the need for articulating these values somehow in universalist terms. In 1952, for example, a group of spiritually restless intellectuals launched a magazine, *Prozdor* (Corridor) optimistically described as a bimonthly, to be devoted to religious thought. In its introductory editorial, *Prozdor* declared that

> the manner in which our official religion bears itself in public is not likely to enhance its prestige. Our youth is growing up without knowing at all what religion is. Our wide public discussions of religion deal mainly with practical matters, like problems of matrimony, chalizah [restrictions on a widow's right to remarry], or mixed bathing of men and women in a swimming pool. . . . But religious thought as such has no place with us. . . . In problems

of theology and religion, the level of our discussions and deliberations is absolutely childish.

For some five years the journal published articles, often by distinguished authors, on metaphysics and theology, on the perennial secular-religious question in Israel, on education, and other general cultural subjects. Occasionally suggestions appeared for restoring Jewish life and values. One writer would establish handsome, modern synagogues to replace existing, shabby, unaesthetic ones; build decent schools to replace existing poor-quality religious state schools and outdated Talmud Torahs and yeshivot. Another would organize small groups to create a new Jewish way of life in kibbutzim, moshavim, and towns, a life of simplicity and modesty, bringing up to date traditional prayers and rituals.

After the Six-Day War, *Prozdor* was obliged to close for lack of funds. Yet by then the modest, experimental groups it had envisaged already were beginning to emerge—often under Western influences. Thus, a society calling itself Amanah (Covenant), founded and led by the British-born Joseph Bentwich, a professor of education at the Hebrew University, devoted itself to methods of transforming religion in Israel into a vital force. The eminent philosophers Professors Hugo Bergmann and Martin Buber were frequent speakers at Amanah, as well as several other former members of the Ichud (Chapter VIII). A rather more influential group was established by Dr. Jack Cohen, an American Conservative rabbi, who directed the Hillel Foundation at the Hebrew University. An erudite and compassionate man, Cohen for a number of years had detected among kibbutz members a certain groping, inchoate attempt to express spiritual values, an effort that seemed to him far more relevant than the theological philosophizing of the university professors. His ambition was to find a method of reconciling both approaches.

In 1961 Cohen organized a "Gathering of Seekers for a [True] Way." The group's first meeting included approximately seventy respected national personalities, among them kibbutz members, intellectuals, and army officers. Their response to the challenge of finding spiritual alternatives was enthusiastic. During the next few years the participants gathered annually, their numbers supplemented by other creative and articulate individuals. As Cohen hoped, the members returned to their own communities to establish local discussion societies. The most important of these, in Jerusalem, systematically explored the writings of A. D. Gordon, Mordecai Kaplan, Chaim Greenberg, and other figures whose careers were devoted to a meaningful spiritual life beyond the jurisdiction of Orthodoxy or even of organized religion. The Jerusalem group conducted its own Sabbath services. These were attended each week by seventy to eighty people, among them Mrs. Rachel Ben-Zvi, wife of Israel's second president, several distinguished academicians, and other intellectuals who ordinarily would never have been found in a synagogue. The beginning was a modest one, yet not without promise.

In the interval, too, other events obtruded, preeminent among them the Six-Day War and the recapture of the Old City of Jerusalem. The recovery of the ancient Temple Mount, seismic as it was in its impact upon every level of the Jewish population, opened yet another dimension in the quest for spiritual alternatives. In a famous collection of taped interviews with kibbutz members who had fought in the 1967 war, *Siach Lochamim* (Warriors' Dialogue), two themes emerged. Repeatedly these young secularists insisted that they had not been drawn to religion; but they admitted, too, that they had suddenly realized that they were Jews. "No, I am not religious . . . but the Wall spoke to me. . . . When I heard about the conquest of Jerusalem on the transistor there was no one in my unit who did not shed tears. . . . I felt for the first time not the Israeli side, but the Jewish side of my people." The dialogues were resumed a year later in a HaShomer HaZair kibbutz, and this time the participants described their leftist faith even more outspokenly. "The truth is," said one, in a typical interview, "that there is today a slow but uninterrupted return to tradition. . . . You can call it reactionary, you can say it's no good . . . but in my opinion . . . we are now in a period of return to the tradition, toward the Jewish people and our connection with it. . . ."

The religious establishment was unable to channel this new identity. It offered no message, no word, not even a new prayer to capture the public imagination. The need was met in part, rather, by several of the nation's most respected non-Orthodox intellectuals. Writing for the journal *P'tachim* (Portals), founded essentially as a successor to *Prozdor*, many contributors discerned in the war a thrilling spiritual challenge that might lead toward the fulfillment of Israel's humane "mission." Some of their vision surely tinctured the Land of Israel movement that developed in the aftermath of hostilities (Chapter xxii). It was expressed by the movement's founder, the eminent Labor secularist Eliezer Livneh, in the July 1967 issue of the literary journal *Moznayim* (Scales). The title of the article, "The Hidden Face Breaks Forth," was a reference to the passage in Ezekiel describing the sudden appearance of God. To Livneh there was a parallel in the miraculous deliverance of 1967. Detecting in the liberation of Jerusalem unprecedented opportunities for both material and spiritual fulfillment, Livneh concluded his article with a plea to the faithful and unbelieving alike to join in a blessing to the God of Israel. In a spasm of collective gratitude, that prayer was openly or silently acknowledged by hundreds of thousands of Israelis of every background.

THE SIX-DAY WAR

A FLUCTUATION OF NASSER'S FORTUNES

If Israel by 1967 had entered a seemingly permanent orbit in the Middle Eastern firmament, its new luster could be traced to a decade of almost uninterrupted economic and political achievement. Neither, from without, did there appear to be serious obstacles any longer to renewed and continual progress. Shaken and humiliated by Operation Kadesh, Nasser for the while appeared unwilling to give more than lip service to the perennial Arab dream of eradicating the Jewish republic. Syria, to be sure, may have been governed by an endlessly gyrating cabal of ultranationalist army officers, but this nation of 6 million was hardly in a class with Egypt as a military danger to Israel. Still less was Jordan, relatively quiet under the moderate Hussein. In the Gulf of Aqaba and the Red Sea, meanwhile, Israeli ships sailed without hindrance, their freedom of navigation assured by public and explicit international support.

But if Israel's growth and strength were increasingly a fact of Middle Eastern life, so, by the same token, was Arab hatred. The shame of defeat at Jewish hands did not remain vivid only for Palestinian refugees, brooding over the loss of their homes and soil; it was no less mortal a wound to the self-esteem of Arab peoples everywhere, and to the cherished vision of Pan-Arab unity. Whatever the rationale of "justice" or "revenge," the proffered solution never varied—the liquidation of Israel, nothing less. The demand was uttered by statesmen and scholars alike. Not infrequently it was framed in terms of religious jihad. The analogy of Israel and the Crusades was a favored one. So was the equation of Zionism with Western imperialism.

Nasser himself was not reticent in loosing pronunciamentos on the subject. Thus, in his address before the UN General Assembly in September 1960, the Egyptian ruler stated his view of the issue quite explicitly: "The only solution to Palestine is that matters should return to the condition prevailing before the error was committed—i.e., the annulment of Israel's existence." And in 1964 he repeated: "We swear to God that we shall not rest until we restore the Arab nation to Palestine and Palestine to the Arab nation. There is no room for imperialism and there is no room for Britain in our country, just as there is no room for Israel within the Arab nation." Nor was the method by which Israel's existence was to be obliterated left in doubt. "We shall not enter Palestine with its soil covered in sand," Nasser asserted in March 1965. "We shall enter it with its soil saturated in blood."

Declarations were less easily translated into facts, of course, or even into meaningful plans. It was true that Nasser had emerged from the Sinai Campaign with his power intact. The British, French, and Israelis were out of Egypt, after all. In February 1958, too, Damascus and Cairo jointly proclaimed the merger of their nations in a United Arab Republic. Disjointed as this political hybrid was, it appeared unchallengeable as the major political bloc in the Arab world. Indeed, subsequent Iraqi and Jordanian attempts to counterbalance the UAR, by announcing a federation of their own, endured less than six months. In July 1958 the officers of Iraq's army revolted, murdered King Feisal and Prime Minister Nuri es-Saïd, and supplanted them with an ostensibly pro-Egyptian military junta. Nasser was riding high by then: "sayid" of the Arab world, standard-bearer of Pan-Arabism, a respected spokesman for the Third World of Afro-Asian nations, courted by East and West.

The following year, nevertheless, the tide shifted against the Egyptian president. Amid mutual recriminations, Syria chose to withdraw from the UAR. In 1962 civil violence erupted in the Yemen between Nasserist and proroyalist factions, the latter supported by Saudi Arabia. Compulsively intervening in the hostilities, Nasser was obliged eventually to dispatch 60,000 of his troops to the quagmire of a ferocious and inconclusive war. In Iraq, too, the regime of Abd al-Karim al-Qasim proclaimed its own alternative road to Arab unity, in opposition to Nasser's "faulty and egotistical" path. Soon the revolutionary governments of Cairo and Baghdad were engaged in open ideological battle. Jordan and Saudi Arabia had long been fearful of Nasser's ambitions, even as the Tunisian and Moroccan governments belatedly awoke to Nasser's imperialist designs on their own lands. Moreover, the Third World by then was slowly tilting away from the Left, and Nasser's closest friends—Nehru, Ben Bella, Nkrumah, Sukarno—were passing from the scene. To compound the Egyptian ruler's difficulties, his nation's economy was on the verge of bankruptcy by the early 1960s. The government's investment effort, its purchases of vast quantities of industrial equipment abroad, the costs of the debilitating war in Yemen, all seriously drained Egypt's foreign reserves. Unemployment was rising, and an immense mass of destitute subproletariat was engorging the slums of Cairo.

With Nasser's problems metastasizing at home and elsewhere in the Arab world, Israel for its part appeared simply too formidable to tackle, both in its own military power and in its growing network of international support. It is recalled that a major example of this cooperation was in Africa, where the Israelis had launched highly successful programs of economic and technological help. In fact, Nasser got his bloodiest nose in Africa almost directly at Israeli hands. Unnoticed at the time, Israeli intercession helped prevent the Egyptians, and the Soviets behind them, from taking over the former Belgian Congo in 1963, the largest and potentially the richest new state in Africa. At Brazzaville, it was known that the Egyptian embassy was distributing arms clandestinely to rebel forces led by the pro-Communist Antoine Gizenga. And in Cairo, followers of Gizenga announced the creation of a "People's Republic of the Congo." To deal with this incipient civil war, Lieutenant General Joseph Mobutu, commander of the Congolese army (and later his nation's president), sought help from the Israeli embassy, which in turn summoned a panel of Israeli military advisers. The latter recommended the creation of an elite corps of paratroops as a mobile force to scotch the uprising. Thereupon Mobutu picked 250 officers and men and departed with them to Israel for an intensive course in paratroop jumping and tactics. On his return to the Congo, the general dispatched other trainees to Israel, until in 1964 he had accumulated a crack brigade of 2,000. At that point Mobutu's army, spearheaded by the Israeli-trained paratroops and commanded by white mercenaries, effectively put the rebels to flight.

With a realistic appraisal, then, of his own weaknesses and of his enemy's strength, Nasser ignored Hashemite taunts to renew the blockade of the Strait of Tiran, and Syrian appeals to obstruct Israel's irrigation project at the headwaters of the Jordan. Somewhat lamely, he explained that war with Israel would have to be delayed until the Arabs were ready. In his memoirs, Ahram Maurani, the Syrian vice-president, recalled his talk with Nasser on November 29, 1963, when Maurani proposed the use of force to block Israel's water development plans. Nasser replied: "Ahram, my brother, and what will happen if Israel bombs Damascus?" The implication was plain that the Syrians should not then look to Cairo.

A SYRIAN TIGER IS LOOSED

Despite this pained admission of Egyptian helplessness, by 1965 the Syrian regime had allowed its 47-mile frontier with Israel to become the Middle East's single most explosive boundary. There were a number of ingredients in the Syrian-Israeli tinderbox. One was Israel's irrigation project. It is recalled that in 1959, four years after the breakdown of the Johnston negotiations, Israel made the decision to embark on its own phase of the regional water plan. To avoid any further controversies on the status of the northern DMZ, the Israelis modified their original irrigation blueprint in favor of pumping water directly from Lake Galilee. Yet no sooner had construction of a pumping station begun at the northwestern corner of the lake than Damascus lodged a complaint with the Security Council. Jerusalem's response was forthright: the undertaking did not prejudice the rights of Israel's neighbors, and an independent nation could not be denied the right to pursue its vital water development needs.

When the United Nations declined to take action on the Syrian protest, foreign ministers of eleven Arab governments met in Cairo in December 1963 and there reached agreement on their next step. They would divert those tributaries of the Jordan River essentially the Chazbani and the

Banias—that arose on the Arab side of the line, and in this fashion prevent their waters from reaching Israeli territory. To that end, in February 1964, Syrian and Lebanese engineering teams began the construction of diversion canals several miles within their own frontiers. They did not get far. Israeli artillery promptly shelled and destroyed their bulldozers. When the operation was resumed in the summer of 1965, it was bombed and strafed by Israeli planes. By then, in any case, the Syrians had completed only about 1 percent of the necessary diversion.

Even more incendiary in Israeli-Syrian relations was the acute state of tension along the demilitarized zones (Chapter XVI). Nowhere were Israeli citizens more vulnerable to attack; for along the main DMZ area Syrian gun positions in the Golan Heights dominated the Chula stretch of the frontier. It became virtually impossible for Israeli farmers to secure advance approval from the Mixed Armistice Commission to work the land; the MAC's Syrian representative withheld his consent. Disputes over cultivation rights arose essentially in the southern and central demilitarized zones (see map, p. 448), where the land was approximately half Arab and half Israeli, divided into narrow parallel strips. All efforts to reach a delimitation agreement foundered, and incidents erupted with growing frequency throughout 1962 and 1963. Firing from the Golan ultimately became so persistent that the Israelis used armored tractors as standard equipment. During an especially heavy clash in the Almagor region, in August 1963, several Israeli drivers were killed. The UNTSO promptly confirmed Syria's guilt. When the Security Council upheld Israel's complaint, however, and endorsed a draft resolution of censure against Syria, the Soviet representative vetoed it. Repeated exchanges of fire in the Almagor sector caused additional Israeli deaths. The Russian veto blocked all Security Council action.

By then, the confrontation along the Israeli-Syrian frontier was escalating into prolonged artillery duels and even aerial dogfights. Nor was it confined to the DMZ areas. Indeed, the violence no longer could be related simply to territorial claims and counterclaims. Much of it reflected the unique nature of the Syrian Ba'ath regime. The Ba'ath (Renaissance) party had been founded originally in the 1940s by two Syrian intellectuals, Michel Aflaq and Salah al-Din al-Bitar. Their political ideology was a unique mixture of Leninism and Pan-Arabism, although with increasing emphasis on the latter. Eventually, in 1962, an uprising of army colonels brought the Ba'athists to power in Damascus. The new government's essential achievement henceforth was the militarization of Syrian public life and an intensification of public hostility toward the "imperialist" West and Israel. At first the country's new strong man, Colonel Amin al-Hafez, ruled through the original Ba'ath leadership of Aflaq and Bitar. This group was soon challenged, however, by another army junta led by Colonel Salah Jadid, who in turn demanded a more "Socialist-nationalist" policy on every front—against Israel, the United States, and the West—and closer collaboration with the Soviet Union, China, and the local Communists. The political conflict was by no means limited to ideology, however. It was also a rivalry between sectarian groups. Hafez was a member of the majority Sunni Moslem population. Jadid belonged to the Alawite Moslem minority. During 1965, a tug-of-war ensued between the two sides. Eventually, in February 1966, a coup brought Colonel Jadid to power; the old leadership was deposed, a number of its members imprisoned, and several executed.

The Jadid regime soon became the most grimly chauvinist in the Middle East. Its diatribes on behalf of the Viet Cong, the Maoists, and the Guevarists, and against the United States and Israel, were violent and at times psychotic. The truth was that the government enjoyed little popular support, and barely survived two armed revolts in September 1966 and February 1967. Under the circumstances, it was not the strength of the Alawite cabal that frightened outside observers, but rather its vulnerability. For this very weakness was propelling Jadid and his colleagues into a militant stance on the one issue that was universally popular—a war of liberation against Israel.

In its anti-Israel campaign, the Syrian government was determined as well to make active use of the Palestine refugees. Actually, the decision had been made as early as the Arab summit meeting of January 1964, when the Palestinians were formally authorized "to carry out their role in liberating their homeland and determining their destiny." Several months later, an assembly of Palestine Arabs was convened in Hashemite Jerusalem, and from its proceedings emerged the Palestine Liberation Organization. The PLO goal, baldly stated, was "to attain the objective of liquidating Israel," and for that purpose to establish a "Palestine Liberation Army." To ensure his own tight control, then, over this potentially volatile movement, Nasser placed the Sinai and the Gaza Strip at the PLO's "disposal." The "Liberation Army" thereupon recruited its troops from Palestinians scattered throughout the various Arab countries, although mainly from the Gaza Strip, while its budget was financed by contributions from Arab governments and by a tax levied on the Palestinians themselves. Notwithstanding this ostensible breadth of support, the PLO's elected chairman, Ahmed Shukeiry, a former Acre lawyer, drew his principal backing from the Socialist states of Egypt and Syria and launched a campaign of vilification against the "reactionary" governments of Jordan, Saudi Arabia, and Tunisia. The latter in turn encouraged conspiracies against Shukeiry, and in February 1967 the PLO leader was wounded in an assassination attempt. For the while, as a result, the organization was at least partially immobilized by factional intrigues.

Not so a rival, and even more radical, Palestinian group in Syria, the Fatah (Arab Liberation Movement), organized several years earlier by veterans of the Mufti's former Arab Higher Committee. Disillusioned with the official Arab governments and the windy resolutions on Palestine issued each year by the Arab League, the Fatah leadership spoke in terms of immediate, direct military action to regain the usurped homeland. After 1965, too, the Fatah gravitated increasingly into the orbit of Syria's militant Ba'ath regime. From the DMZ area it began striking occasionally into Israel, and from the Syrian army it received its weapons and a limited military training. In the wake of the Jadid coup of 1966, moreover, the Damascus government undertook to back a considerably larger scale of Fatah operations. The latter's raids against Israel, particularly in the Almagor DMZ area, became more ambitious. Even as Syrian troops, ensconced on the Golan, shelled and mortared Israeli farm settlements on the Chula Valley floor, Fatah guerrillas were laying repeated ambushes for Israeli army patrols and inflicting numerous casualties. The Syrian prime minister, Yusuf Zayen, virtually admitted his government's complicity in these attacks, declaring in a broadcast: "We are not the protectors of Israel. We shall never restrain the revolution of the Palestinian people who are seeking to liberate their homeland." The Syrian president, Nureddin al-Atassi, went further, appealing for a "people's war" of resistance, sabotage, and terror. "We want a policy of scorched earth for Palestine," he declared.

Nasser, on the other hand, regarded the mounting campaign of Ba'athist and Fatah violence with a distinct lack of enthusiasm. Not having extricated himself entirely from the Yemeni war, the Egyptian ruler was less than certain of his ability to defeat Israel if he were sucked into a full-scale confrontation. Accordingly, his 1964 defense treaty with Syria was proved a dead letter on April 7, 1967, when an incident on the Israeli-Syrian frontier developed into a major air battle. A flight of Israeli jets penetrated Syrian air space and downed six MiGs before circling freely over Damascus. The Egyptian army did not budge. In an effort, rather, to dampen Syrian militance, Nasser sent his prime minister to Damascus on May 5. The latter issued a stern warning that "our agreement for mutual defense will apply only in the event of a general attack on Syria by Israel. No merely local incident will cause us to intervene."

MOSCOW RIDES THE TIGER

It was the intercession not of Syria, but of the Soviet Union, that forced Nasser's hand. No basic policy change had occurred in the Soviet approach to the Middle East following the Suez-Sinai war. Relations between Moscow and Jerusalem had all but lapsed. The Russians continued to provide unlimited diplomatic support for Egypt's Suez blockade against Israeli ships, for Syrian efforts to divert the headwaters of the Jordan, and for Syrian attacks along the DMZ. Soviet newspaper and radio propaganda was unceasing in its campaign against Israel as an "outpost of American imperialism." Yet the perceptible intensification of Soviet efforts on behalf of the Arabs, and notably on behalf of Egypt and Syria, reflected in part Moscow's acute concern for the demise of Socialist regimes elsewhere. It was in this period, after all, that the downfall of Ben Bella in Algeria was followed by the overthrow of Sukarno in Indonesia and of Nkrumah in Ghana. In the Congo rightist elements had assumed power. In Greece the military regime was stamping out leftist opposition. In Syria unrest was mounting against the Ba'athist government. To the Kremlin it appeared, then, that Washington was manipulating events behind the scenes. More ominously yet, Communist Chinese representatives were descending upon Arab capitals with offers of weapons, specialists, and economic aid. Caught between these two fires, the Russians envisaged only one solution. It was to continue to outbid all others in support of the Arab "national liberation" movement. No other force offered as likely a vehicle for Soviet penetration into the Middle East.

Nasser was prepared to encourage this Soviet hope. In 1965, when Russia's Marshal Andrei Gretchko visited Cairo, the Egyptian president expressed his warm gratitude for Soviet military and financial help. After earlier periods of strain, the Russians once again had become for Nasser "our true and selfless friends"; while the Americans, conversely, were the "bloodsuckers of the people, the arch criminals of the twentieth century, the savage barbarians." In 1966, Nasser and Grétchko signed a new defense agreement. Under its terms, the Russians were extended naval facilities at the Mediterranean ports of Mersa Matruh and Sidi Barani, at the Red Sea port of Quseir, and at three Red Sea fishing villages. Three airports were placed at the Soviets' disposal. In return, Moscow undertook to increase its shipments of arms and technicians. On May 15, 1966, Prime Minister Alexei Kosygin arrived in Cairo to pledge his government's backing for Egypt's "struggle against imperialism."

That year, too, a series of windfalls appeared likely to transform Russia's cautious infiltration of the Middle East into a galloping conquest. The first was London's announcement that Britain intended to withdraw its military forces from Aden by 1968. Inasmuch as the Egyptians already were ensconced in southern Yemen, the way now appeared open for a Soviet move into the Persian Gulf area following British departure. The second decisive shift occurred in February 1966 when the Jadid faction of the Ba'ath party seized office in Damascus. Prodded by its Russian benefactors, the new Syrian regime included two Communists in the government, dispatched their younger leaders to Moscow for training in "leadership," and nationalized a great many of the country's larger business enterprises. With Syria evidently in the process of becoming the first Communist state in the Arab world, the Soviets were certain that they had access to a Mediterranean base even more dependable than Egypt. Their technicians immediately began operating Syrian electronic and monitoring equipment, and within half a year transformed this Arab nation into an intelligence clearinghouse and relay center for Soviet military personnel and diplomats on both ends of the Mediterranean—and as far east as the Persian Gulf.

Determined at all costs to preserve their Middle Eastern foothold, the Russians began loosing a tough series of hints to Israel about the "possible consequences" of further military action against Syria. On April 21, 1967, two weeks after the Israeli-Syrian aerial battle, Deputy Foreign Minister Jacob Malik bluntly warned the Israelis that they were endangering "the very fate of their state." It was the most ominous threat since the Sinai Campaign of 1956. Yet there could be little question by then that the deteriorating border situation was electric with danger. Fatah infiltration raiders were crossing over with greater frequency, each time accompanied by larger numbers of Syrian regular army troops. As early as January 1967, after a particularly violent series of firefights along the DMZ, Prime Minister Eshkol issued an open warning to the Syrians: "I cannot exclude the possibility that we may have no other recourse but deterrent measures." The air action of April 7 seemed an omen of even graver retaliatory moves. In a panic, the Syrians trundled heavy artillery directly into the DMZ, and the Israelis responded with a concentration of their own troops and weapons. On May 11, finally, Jerusalem notified the Security Council that unless Syrian provocations ended, the Israeli government regarded "itself as fully entitled to act in self-defense." At that point, deeply alarmed for the security of their favored Arab protégé, the Russians took their most calamitous misstep since the beginning of their intrusion into the Near East.

NASSER RETURNS TO GAZA AND SHARM ES-SHEIKH

As early as mid-April 1967, Leonid Chuvakhin, the Soviet ambassador in Israel, had complained to Prime Minister Eshkol about "heavy concentrations of Israeli forces on the Syrian border." Eshkol promptly offered to drive Chuvakhin to the border, to enable the Russian to see for himself that his information was false. It was questionable if Chuvakhin seriously believed that the Jews intended to attack Syria's formidable topographical defenses. Anyway, Israel's Independence Day celebrations were in the offing, and this was hardly the time for a large-scale military operation. But to the Soviets the very accusation of Israeli troop movements could fulfill a useful diplomatic purpose. If the Jews subsequently failed to move, their inaction could be attributed to Russian support for the Ba'ath regime—thus reinforcing the pro-Soviet government in Damascus. On May 12, therefore, Dimitri Podyedyeev, the Soviet ambassador in Cairo, wired Moscow: "Today we passed on to the Egyptian authorities information concerning the massing of Israeli troops on the northern frontier for a surprise attack on Syria. We have advised the UAR government to take the necessary steps."

Nasser in turn agreed to dispatch a series of military missions to Syria. Upon being taken to the southern frontier line with Israel, however, the Egyptian visitors were less than impressed by the evidence they found of Israeli "concentrations." In his testimony at the "conspiracy" trial in Cairo on February 24, 1968, one of the accused, Shams Badran, the former Egyptian war minister, said: "General Mahmud Fawzi [the Egyptian commander in chief] . . . found these assumptions [of an imminent Israeli attack] without foundation." Nasser's decision to allow the crisis to escalate was based, rather, on other factors. Ironically, one of these was his country's desperate financial plight. In 1966, Washington had informed the Cairo government that American wheat shipments would be terminated unless Egypt abandoned its quest for long-range missiles and reduced its armed forces. Nasser refused, and American agricultural help promptly ended. So did loans from Western commercial banks and the International Monetary Fund; Egypt was spending more than it earned. Almost immediately, then, food shortages and growing unemployment exacerbated public unrest and threatened Nasser's regime. In earlier years these factors might have inhibited a policy of adventurism. Now they seemed to offer an inducement for a diversion against Israel. Moreover, Nasser was being systematically taunted by the Hashemite and Saudi governments for his "cowardice" in reducing border friction with Israel, and in tolerating United Nations forces on his soil. Somehow the wind had to be taken out of his rivals' sails. Not least of all, the Egyptian ruler appreciated the extent of his economic and military dependence on the Soviet Union. If the Russians asked him to make a gesture to shore up the Ba'athist cabal in Syria, he could hardly ignore their request.

The question related simply to the form a military gesture would take. During their visits in April and May of 1967, the Egyptian military missions were shocked by the condition of the Syrian army, the low caliber of its officers. The disarray should not have been surprising, actually, for each of the numerous Syrian revolutions had liquidated a full echelon of commanders. Yet an attempt now to dispatch forces to Syrian soil would take far too long. Nasser decided instead to concentrate the bulk of his army in the Sinai Peninsula, a move that would relieve any potential Israeli threat against Syria, gratify the Russians, nonplus the Americans, and perhaps once and for all disarm his Arab critics. On May 15, therefore, Cairo announced a state of military emergency and sent two armored divisions moving ostentatiously through the boulevards of Cairo, and then crossing over the Suez into Sinai. May 15, by no coincidence, was Israel's Independence Day, and major units of the Israeli army were parading through Jerusalem. Indeed, news of the Egyptian deployment was brought to Israel's commander in chief, Lieutenant General Yitzchak Rabin, at the very moment he was reviewing his own troops along the Jerusalem route of march. Although Rabin immediately ordered a tank brigade dispatched toward the Gaza Strip, he regarded the Egyptian maneuver as essentially bluff. The Israeli government, meanwhile, took pains to assure the Great Powers that its reaction was entirely defensive. But at the same time, it asked Washington and Moscow to persuade the Egyptian dictator to rescind his troop concentrations.

Then, on the night of May 16, Nasser suddenly gave orders for the 3,400-man UNEF force near Gaza to redeploy in encampments within the Strip itself. Learning of this Egyptian demand, U Thant, the Burmese secretary-general of the United Nations, called an urgent meeting with his deputy, Ralph Bunche, and with the Egyptian delegate at the world body, Muhammad Awad al-Kony. At Bunche's suggestion, the secretary-general informed al-Kony that the United Nations would accept no "half measures"; either the UNEF accomplished its mission without reservation, or it would be withdrawn altogether from Egypt. The two United Nations officials were certain that Nasser was uninterested in having these troops evacuated and that he would back down. Unknowingly, however, U Thant had just dislodged the stone that loosed the avalanche. For on the afternoon of May 17, after a series of lengthy cabinet meetings, the Egyptian government called the secretary-general's hand. It notified him that it was ordering a complete UNEF evacuation from Egyptian territory and from the Gaza Strip.

In the aftermath of the 1956 Sinai Campaign, we recall, the duration of the UNEF presence in Sinai and Gaza had intentionally not been limited. On the contrary, the United States, Britain, France, and many other UN delegates had later specifically interpreted the General Assembly Resolution of November 4, 1956, as meaning that the UNEF could *not* be withdrawn without the consent of the General Assembly; and this interpretation had been verified in February 1957 by Dag Hammarskjöld, following a lengthy personal conference with Nasser. On May 18, 1967, therefore, U Thant met urgently with delegates of the seven countries whose troops served in the United Nations forces. It was then that the secretary-general learned to his dismay that these representatives, following the lead of India and Yugoslavia, were determined to recall their soldiers at any cost; under no circumstances would their governments risk the lives of their troops in the Middle East. Persuaded that further discussions would be useless, U Thant henceforth remained oblivious to appeals from the United States and Israel not to capitulate to Nasser's demand. Late that day the blue-helmeted UNEF garrisons evacuated their positions at al-Quntilla and Jebel al-Hamra. Egyptian troops and heavy equipment immediately moved in. Then, more alarmingly yet, an Egyptian task force suddenly ordered the evacuation of the tiny UNEF company at Sharm es-Sheikh, guarding the Strait of Tiran. As a result, then, of U Thant's unwillingness to invoke the full range of United Nations procedures, the UNEF collapsed like a house of cards. With it collapsed the world body's most impressive peacekeeping achievement.

Three Egyptian divisions and more than 600 tanks began fanning out through the Sinai Peninsula. At the same time, the Damascus regime mobilized fifty cadet battalions, and Iraqi brigades moved out toward the frontier of Jordan. The governments of Kuwait, Yemen, and Algeria announced their readiness to dispatch troops and planes to Syria and Egypt. As it developed, the afternoon of May 17 was the turning point of the Middle Eastern crisis. Until then, retreat without loss of face might still have been possible for Nasser. Having satisfied himself with a show of strength, the Egyptian president then could have ordered his divisions back to Cairo, leaving the impression that they had forestalled a Zionist attack. But his government's response to U Thant, and the latter's instant capitulation, signified the point of no return. To his own astonishment, Nasser had won a brilliant victory scarcely by raising his little finger. Once again he was on the threshold of becoming the unchallenged leader of the Arab world. Now he would have to act the part.

By May 19 Egyptian units were reinforcing their former garrisons in

Sharm es-Sheikh, while in Gaza, Ahmed Shukeiry's Palestinian army, consisting mainly of refugees, was readying to occupy the border encampments that until then had been manned by the UNEF. At the same time, Cairo Radio announced military preparations for "retaliatory" attacks on key Israeli cities and bases. Other Arab governments were openly broadcasting their intentions to "cut the Jews' throats." Up to this point Rabin and Prime Minister Eshkol had interpreted Nasser's moves as a technique to deter Israel from attacking Syria. No longer. On May 20 a general Israeli mobilization was proclaimed. Yet even at this late date, the government preferred to rely on diplomacy. Through its ambassador in Paris, it requested de Gaulle's intercession with the Soviets. No response was forthcoming. In Washington, Israeli officials entreated the State Department to give teeth to Eisenhower's declaration of March 1, 1957—stating that the United States endorsed the right of "free and innocent" passage through the Strait of Tiran—by dispatching an American warship through the Gulf of Aqaba to Eilat. But here, too, Undersecretary of State Eugene Rostow, the official who dealt most closely with Mediterranean affairs, preferred to act within the framework of the United Nations.

Nor did Israel find reason for optimism elsewhere. In London, Prime Minister Harold Wilson assured the Israeli ambassador that his government would support any United Nations measures for the protection of free shipping through the Strait of Tiran. Having given with one hand, Wilson then took with the other. He cautioned Eshkol to reconsider his unwillingness to admit the UNEF to Israeli territory; otherwise Nasser possessed a legal handle for evicting the UNEF from Egypt. The Canadian government sent Israel an identical request. Sobered and shaken by the equivocation of the Western Powers, Eshkol then addressed the Knesset in words that were conciliatory to the point of timidity:

> I wish to repeat to the Arab countries, especially to Egypt and Syria, that we do not contemplate any military action. . . . We have contemplated no intervention in their internal affairs. We ask only from these states the application of these same principles toward us as an act of reciprocity. . . . We shall follow with interest the progress of the visit of [U Thant] to the Middle East, and we will study the results of it.

There was little in these developments to give Nasser pause.

A BLOCKADE REIMPOSED

Late on the night of May 21, acceding to the request of his cabinet and of the other Arab governments, Nasser made a fateful decision. At daybreak two Egyptian submarines, a destroyer, and four missile-launcher boats passed through the Suez Canal and headed for the Red Sea. The next day Nasser made a chilling announcement: "The Strait of Tiran is part of our territorial waters. No Israeli ship will ever navigate it again. We also forbid the shipment of strategic materials to Israel on non-Israeli vessels." The threat to Israel was mortal. Tiran and the Gulf of Aqaba represented Israel's gateway to Africa and Asia. In 1966 Eilat had accommodated over a million tons of cargo, fully 30 percent of Israel's mineral exports, and was rapidly becoming an important Middle Eastern trading entrepôt. In fact, it was already Israel's key oil port, and an expanded oil pipeline was being laid from Eilat to Ashkelon, on the Mediterranean. Nasser understood well, moreover, that his act was not subject to alternative legal interpretations—not since the 1957 affirmation by the maritime nations that the Gulf of Aqaba was an international waterway. Little wonder that in Moscow there was astonishment that Nasser was risking war by violating a clear-cut legal precedent. While the Russians dutifully proclaimed their support for the Arab cause, there was evidence (later) that they were angered that Nasser had taken his step without consultations. The Soviet foreign ministry immediately began seeking a replacement for Ambassador Podyedyeev in Cairo, who had allowed this development to occur.

By noon of May 23, mobilization in Israel had become total. Bus transportation was halted as all available vehicles were commandeered for military transport. Public meetings were canceled. The streets were increasingly deserted; coffeehouses and theaters were half empty. School hours were reduced to enable pupils to work as mailmen. Throughout the nation private citizens were hurriedly digging shelters. Civil defense authorities published instructions on methods of stocking communal shelters, preparing first-aid kits, and handling fire equipment. Thousands of Israelis suddenly paid their taxes in advance, aware that the government needed money. Gifts of all kinds, from cash to wedding rings, flooded into the defense ministry. Visiting Prime Minister Raphael Passio of Finland was politely asked to shorten his stay in Israel, and he departed after two days of an official visit. Foreign embassies requested their nationals to leave. El Al canceled group flights, and other airlines dispatched special planes to Lydda to evacuate thousands of tourists.

In Jerusalem, meanwhile, the cabinet was holding urgent, round-the-clock sessions. Chief of Staff Rabin assured the ministers that Israel could win a war, but that losses would be heavy. Eban in turn warned his colleagues that the government must under all circumstances avoid the mistake of 1956, when both the United States and the Soviet Union voted against Israel in the United Nations. The foreign minister was referring specifically to an appeal from Washington of the day before, May 22, not to react yet to the Egyptian blockade, and to send no ship through the Strait of Tiran for the next forty-eight hours, while the United States attempted to find a solution. Thus far, Eban was encouraged by the growing firmness of the American reaction. He was informed of the emergency message the State Department had just sent off to Moscow. "The United States," it said, "will regard any impingement of freedom of navigation in the Strait of Tiran, whether under the Israeli flag or another, as an act of aggression, against which Israel, in the opinion of the United States, is justified in taking defensive measures." Actually, the vigor of this response signified less the attitude of the State Department than of President Lyndon Johnson himself, who on May 23 sent Nasser a personal warning in the identical uncompromising language.

Britain, too, appeared to be reacting more straightforwardly now to the closure of the Strait than to the earlier expulsion of the UNEF. Prime Minister Wilson cabled Johnson, proposing immediate international action to reopen the Gulf of Aqaba, and then dispatched Foreign Undersecretary George Thomson and Admiral E. L. T. Henderson to Washington to confer with the American leaders. These moves reinforced Eban's conviction that a swift diplomatic tour of the Western capitals was warranted to learn if anything could be achieved through diplomacy. The cabinet eventually agreed, despite the preference of at least one of the ministers to send Golda Meir, who was regarded as tougher and less likely to be swayed by American pressure. When the affronted Eban threatened to resign on the spot, however, all objections were dropped; and early on May 24 he flew out of Lydda, en route to Paris and London, then to Washington.

Actually none even of the foreign minister's critics doubted his intellectual virtuosity. Born in South Africa of Lithuanian immigrants, Eban had achieved a brilliant record at Cambridge as a student of Oriental languages. During the war he had served in Palestine as a British liaison officer to the Haganah, and subsequently entered the political department of the Jewish Agency. From 1947 to 1959, then, he defended the Zionist cause in the United Nations with formidable eloquence, doubling in the last ten of those years as Israel's ambassador both to the world body and to Washington. Subsequently, in 1966, after a rather undistinguished interlude in the Israeli Knesset and cabinet, Eban acceded to the foreign ministry, his first and principal interest. A heavyset, bespectacled individual, austere in manner, with a well-developed taste for both personal luxury and personal publicity, Eban did not come across favorably to many Israelis. Their lack of comfort with him could be traced only partly to his undisguised social snobbery. It appeared, too, that Eban's conception of foreign policy was out of step with the older and much-admired Ben-Gurionist approach. He laid what frequently seemed to be undue emphasis upon the approbation of the Western nations, and particularly of the United States. The experience of isolation after the Sinai Campaign plainly had been traumatic for him, and he was resolved at all costs to avoid a similar quarantine now.

The danger became especially acute during the subsequent two weeks. By the time Eban landed at Paris an emergency weapons airlift was under way from France to Israel. Among the French military leadership and civilian population alike, the wave of sympathy for Israel exceeded even the community of interest of 1956. Each request for vital military supplies was immediately approved by phone. The defense ministry gave priority clearance for airport runways, and French soldiers were detailed to load the equipment on planes. Nevertheless, this initial show of official warmth no longer reflected government policy. The two nations had diverged too far in recent years. Although French arms shipments to Israel had continued unabated in recent wars, it was evident, by the mid-1960s, that de Gaulle was increasingly preoccupied with France's need to assume a vigorous role in Mediterranean affairs and with the importance of regaining the friendship of the Moslem world (Chapter XIX). Similarly, he hoped to deny the United States and the Soviet Union a monopoly of influence in the Near East. Thus far, no dramatic shift had occurred in the French leader's posture, but until 1967 no crisis had arisen to test it.

By the time Eban's plane touched down in Paris early on May 24, de Gaulle, briefed by Foreign Minister Couve de Murville, had decided that Egypt's blockade of the Strait of Tiran offered no justification for hostilities. More important, he envisaged the crisis as an opportunity to convene a Four-Power conference rather than a purely Soviet-American summit, which would impose a solution. Receiving Eban at noon, then, de Gaulle began the interview with a warning: "Do not make war! Do not make war! In any event, do not be the first to fire!" When the Israeli foreign minister sought to review the origins of the new emergency, de Gaulle interrupted: "Don't rush into things. The Four Powers must act together. I will take care of that. Together we will find a way to get the ships through the Strait." Eban reminded the president of France's 1957 pledge on free navigation, but de Gaulle countered: "True, but that was in 1957, and this is 1967. It is up to the four Great Powers." At this point Eban made possibly a serious mistake. Rather than allude to vigorous future Israeli countermeasures, thereby giving his own nation a certain bargaining room as a "spoiler," the foreign minister politely took his leave, thanking de Gaulle "for all France has done and . . . is still doing . . . [by] enhancing our morale and our military strength." The reference to military help gave de Gaulle pause. Nine days later, when Reuters commented on this flow of military assistance to Israel, the president ordered the shipments stopped.

Upon departing Paris in the early afternoon of May 24, Eban found somewhat greater understanding in London, where he was received by Prime Minister Wilson at 5:00 p.m. that same day. The British leader assured his visitor that he would fully support international action to uphold the right of unrestricted passage in the Strait of Tiran. Indeed, he had already sent his representatives to Washington to discuss "nuts and bolts" methods of opening the waterway.

DIPLOMATIC AGONY, POLITICAL CRISIS

The next morning, May 25, Eban flew on to New York. He arrived to learn that his government's evident powerlessness had influenced even Hussein of Jordan. The Hashemite king now declared that he was authorizing Iraqi troops to enter his territory and take up positions along the Israeli frontier. Others of Nasser's former enemies, including Feisal of

Saudi Arabia, agreed now to revive the long-moribund "Arab united command." Algeria, Iraq, and Kuwait similarly announced that they were putting troops at Egypt's disposal (p. 633), while in the Gaza Strip, Shukeiry's Palestinian division was unloading its first heavy equipment. These were the circumstances under which Nasser agreed to receive U Thant, on May 25, and to inform the secretary-general that he would not back down an inch. "The closing of the Strait," he observed with satisfaction, "wipes out the last smears of the triple aggression in 1956." In a single gesture of conciliation, however, Nasser observed that he was prepared to revive the Mixed Armistice Commission between Egypt and Israel, even to accept the return of UNEF troops, provided they were stationed exclusively on Israeli soil. U Thant was impressed by these "concessions," and particularly by Nasser's willingness to allow ships through the Strait to Israel so long as they were not Israeli vessels and were not carrying "strategic" materials—essentially a reversion to pre-1956 conditions. Hurrying back to New York, the little Burmese proposed a new formula to the Security Council. It was for a two-week truce period in the Strait of Tiran, during which Israel would refrain from sending ships to Eilat and Egypt would abstain from blocking the passage of non-Israeli vessels. The "compromise" would have been precisely the victory Nasser had in mind; two weeks was ample time to consolidate his forces in Sinai.

Meanwhile, British Foreign Undersecretary Thomson and Admiral Henderson were conferring in Washington with Secretary of State Dean Rusk and Undersecretary Rostow. The visitors proposed the establishment of an international maritime flotilla to run the blockade under naval escort. The State Department and the White House initially accepted the plan. It was rather the Senate Foreign Relations Committee which preferred that all decisions be taken exclusively within the framework of the UN Security Council. Firm measures under these auspices were hardly a likely development, of course, in view of the Soviet veto. Indeed, by then three "nonaligned" members of the Security Council declared that they would oppose even placing the blockade issue on the agenda; while the French representative announced that his government, too, wished to postpone debate indefinitely.

On the night of May 25, Lyndon Johnson finally received Eban in the Oval Office of the White House. Once again the foreign minister explained Israel's position and reminded the president of Eisenhower's commitment in 1957. Johnson in turn rejected the assumption that Nasser had either the intention or the strength to attack Israel. The basic problem, he said, was to induce Egypt to end its blockade of the Strait. He thought this could be done, but he could not move without authority from Congress at a time when he was mired in the Vietnam war. He urged instead that the Security Council first be given a chance to grapple with the issue. If nothing happened there, then he, the president, would vigorously explore other measures—possibly an international maritime force. "I must emphasize the necessity for Israel not to make itself responsible for the initiation of hostilities," Johnson warned. "Israel will not be alone unless it decides to go alone." Eban expressed his thanks for the president's understanding and took his leave. After the interview, Johnson commented to one of his advisers: "I was ready for heavy bargaining, but I found myself up against a lightweight, and I could get away with niceties."

Eban, on the other hand, flying back to Israel on the night of the twenty-sixth, was convinced that he had won meaningful international support. Later he described his accomplishment as securing vital "time" for Israel to rearm by assuring American political understanding. In fact, he was buying time as much for the Egyptians and the other Arabs to consolidate and strengthen their positions. His essential goal was at all costs to avoid offending Washington. Arriving in Israel on the morning of May 27, the foreign minister went directly to a cabinet meeting in Tel Aviv. He found the military leadership advocating an immediate preemptive strike. Eban then urgently stressed the importance of waiting until American political understanding could be assured. He was buttressed in this argument by a cable that had just arrived for Eshkol from Johnson. "As your friend," it said, "I repeat even more strongly what I said yesterday to Mr. Eban: Israel just must not take preemptive military action and thereby make itself responsible for the initiation of hostilities." The president assured Eshkol that the United States and Britain were consulting urgently on an international naval escort plan and "other nations are responding vigorously to the idea." On the basis of these assurances, the cabinet voted to postpone military action.

It is of interest that the one source to which none of the ministers looked with even the faintest of illusions was the United Nations. On May 26 U Thant flew back from Cairo to present his report to the Security Council and to appeal for "all the parties concerned to exercise special restraint. . . ." Thereafter, from May 29 to June 4, the avoidance of hostilities became the central theme of the Council's deliberations. Only Arthur Goldberg, the United States delegate, coupled the appeal for restraint with a demand for an immediate end to the Egyptian blockade. But the Arab representatives promptly countered that the Gulf of Aqaba was an inland waterway "subject to absolute Arab sovereignty." Except for this one exchange, Israel and Egypt dominated the Council proceedings with argument and counterargument. It was not until May 31 that the UN body specifically proposed that the Arabs and Israelis use "international diplomacy" to resolve their dispute. The appeal was Goldberg's and, pallid as it was, it was rejected by Egypt, India, and the Soviet Union—who were convinced that Israel was now altogether helpless. To heighten the mood of surrealism, the Security Council voted to adjourn for two days, and in fact did not meet again until June 3. Even then, few members spoke directly about the possibilities of a resolution. Ignoring the palpable explosiveness of the Middle Eastern crisis, the delegates voted at 3:20 p.m. to reconvene on the afternoon of June 5. From beginning to end, the Security Council meetings were a bankrupt exercise in indecision and irresolution.

Johnson's promise of decisive American action on a multinational flotilla was soon revealed as equally hollow. On June 2 Prime Minister Wilson flew to Washington and admitted, not without embarrassment, that his government would be unable to join such a venture if force were contemplated. Lester Pearson of Canada also backed down. In a friendly but regretful letter, therefore, Johnson now repeated to Eshkol that the United States could not act without congressional approval, and in any case, "our leadership is unanimous that the United States should not act alone." Eban plainly had given an inaccurate impression of his visit to Washington. Nothing more could be secured from the United States. The American assurance of 1957 had been proved worthless in its first test, only ten years later.

Israel meanwhile was preparing for war. The thoroughfares were empty, the highways almost free of civilian traffic, the towns silent at night. Tel Aviv's great agricultural exposition, Agr-Expo, on which a fortune in time and money had been lavished, was now closed. Automobile headlights were painted blue. Families cemented the windows of their children's rooms as protection against shrapnel. Parks were consigned as emergency cemeteries and sanctified by rabbis. Corpse identification and burial instructions were mimeographed by civil defense offices. Nylon sheeting for the wrapping of bodies was stockpiled, funds allocated for coffins and gravestones, death certificates prepared.

If a grim mood had enveloped the country, it was one not of despair but of impatience and frustration. The interregnum unquestionably was giving Israel's armed forces time to complete their preparations. Even so, the long waiting period was taking its psychological toll. Worse yet, an apparent crisis of leadership had developed. On the evening of May 28 Eshkol was scheduled to broadcast to the nation. The entire country was waiting for a lead, civilians at home and in cafes, troops listening to pocket radios in their messes or their tents. Eshkol's performance was a disaster. The prime minister hurried to the microphones directly from a cabinet meeting, with no opportunity to read through the draft of his speech in advance. He began his remarks by describing Egypt's aggression, but then declared somewhat innocuously that the government had decided to wait, "to insist that the international institutions take measures to secure free passage for ships of all nations through the Strait of Tiran." With one phrase unclear to him, the prime minister stammered briefly in confusion before finishing. At that moment the listening audience was thrown into shock, for it appeared that Eshkol was in a quandary and the government powerless. In truth, the situation was even graver than the public knew. On May 23, after Nasser closed the Strait, General Rabin was overcome with despair at the government's indecision and suffered a nervous breakdown. The army medical officer prescribed rest for two or three days until the chief of staff recovered from his collapse, which was officially attributed to "nicotine poisoning." In effect, then, the nation and its armed forces were bereft of decisive leadership at one of the gravest moments—perhaps the very gravest—of Israel's existence.

Under the circumstances, a fierce public demand was launched during the last week of May to introduce changes in the cabinet. The need was universally acknowledged for a "wall-to-wall" government of national unity, including the opposition parties, and for a new minister of defense (Eshkol held this portfolio). Although the two main opposition parties, Gachal and Rafi, together represented only a quarter of the Knesset, Rafi's parliamentary delegation included three nationally admired figures—Ben-Gurion, Dayan, and Peres. On May 29, therefore, the leader of the Gachal faction, Menachem Begin, called on Eshkol to turn over the premiership and ministry of defense to Ben-Gurion. It was an unprecedented gesture, coming from a fire-eater like Begin, a man who for years had been Ben-Gurion's sworn political enemy. But now, belatedly, the Gachal leader was acknowledging the unifying strength of his old foe. Eshkol was hurt and angered. Ben-Gurion himself, who scrupulously held his peace during the crisis, expressed no interest in resuming office. The suggestion was turned down. The following day, however, in a gathering of Mapai leaders, one speaker after another implored Eshkol at least to give up the defense post—if not to Ben-Gurion, then to Dayan. The prime minister had few defenders at the meeting.

The growing clamor for Dayan was a strange twist in the ex-chief of staff's political career. At the age of fifty he had been until this moment a man seemingly without a political future. His womanizing and questionable dealings in antiquities had become something of a national scandal. And yet now Dayan's image as the victorious general of Sinai, a tough, ruthless leader, wrought a miraculous change in his status. The obstacle to his return no longer was public sentiment but rather Eshkol himself. The prime minister was unprepared to turn over the defense ministry to a charismatic political rival. Sparring for time, Eshkol came up with the alternative suggestion that Yigal Allon, the Palmach hero of 1948, should accept the defense portfolio. The offer was shot down by the other parties, even by Mapai itself. At last, on June 1, Eshkol wearily consented to give the ministry to Dayan. Thereupon the Government of National Unity coalesced. Popular trust in the famed, one-eyed general was overwhelming. News of his appointment immediately restored the confidence of the armed forces and of the nation at large.

A MASSING OF ARAB STRENGTH

The garrot meanwhile was rapidly tightening around Israel. The Egyptian armed forces would have been prepossessing enough, but they were joined now by military elements from other Arab states. It was a development that hardly could have been foretold only weeks, even days, earlier. As late as May 28, Radio Cairo had described Hussein as a "Hashemite whore," a "British agent," a "moral chameleon," and exhorted the Jordanian people to assassinate him. The Syrian press echoed this denunciation, and on May 23, in the very heart of the Middle Eastern crisis, a Syrian bomb exploded in a Jordanian village, killing fourteen civilians; the Amman government promptly broke off relations with Damascus. And then, astonishingly, on May 30, Hussein flew to Cairo to sign a mutual defense pact with Egypt, treating photographers to the spectacle of himself and Nasser embracing in fraternal amity. The little Hashemite monarch clearly dared not abstain from an undertaking that was sweeping the entire Arab world into its vortex, and that seemed likely at last to annihilate the Zionist enemy. The mutual defense pact he signed now with Nasser was based on the treaty worked out shortly before between Egypt and Syria; in the event of hostilities, the Egyptian commander in chief would assume military authority for both countries. The following day, May 31, Egyptian General Abd al-Moneim Riad flew to Amman to work out a common strategy with Hussein. The plan anticipated a Jordanian defensive posture along a limited front until the arrival of Iraqi and Saudi reinforcements, when an offensive gradually would be launched toward Jerusalem and several key Israeli air bases.

On June 3, Iraq also joined the military pact, and the following night an Iraqi motorized brigade crossed into Jordan, while the Iraqi air force concentrated its planes at the Habbaniyah base near the Jordanian frontier. Syria meanwhile deployed four infantry brigades along the Israeli border and two more along a second, interior line of defense. King Hassan of Morocco similarly deemed it expedient to offer Nasser assistance. Tunisia's President Bourguiba, known ordinarily for his moderation on Israel, now invited the Algerian army to use his nation's communications en route to the Israeli front. Feisal of Saudi Arabia promised troops, observing that "every Arab who does not participate in this conflict will seal his fate." By then, too, Nasser and his fellow Arabs were no longer speaking of a blockade of Israeli shipping, nor of defensive positions in the event of Israeli military action. Euphoric in the revived adulation of the Arab world, Nasser addressed the Egyptian parliament on May 25: "The problem presently before the Arab countries," he declared, "is not whether the port of Eilat should be blockaded or how to blockade it—but how totally to exterminate the State of Israel for all time."

Indeed, by the end of the month giant posters were calling upon Arabs everywhere to participate in the jihad against Israel. Flags were unfurled bearing the skull and crossbones of the Palestine Liberation Organization. On June 3, General Mohsin Murtagi, the Egyptian commander in Sinai, reminded his officers that "the eyes of the whole world are on you. . . . Reconquer the stolen land with God's help and the power of justice and with the strength of your arms and your united faith." On June 2, Iraq's President Aref exhorted the officers of his air force: "Brethren and sons, this is the day of the battle to avenge . . . 1948. . . . We shall, God willing, meet in Tel Aviv and Haifa." Not to be outdone, the PLO's Ahmed Shukeiry informed a press conference that the Arabs were prepared for the "march to liberate the country—our country." What would happen to the Israelis, he was asked, if the Arab attack succeeded? "Those who survive," he replied, "will remain in Palestine. I estimate that none of them will survive." These remarks of the Arab leaders, the bloodthirsty slogans, the thinly veiled intimations of genocide, were widely publicized throughout the world. Nothing could more effectively have assured Western sympathy for Israel.

There appeared a certain justification for Arab self-confidence this time. The sheer extent of armed Egyptian manpower in June 1967 was impressive. Seven highly trained divisions, nearly 120,000 regular troops—twice the size of Israel's forces in the south—were packed into the Sinai close to Israel's borders. Altogether this host disposed of more than 1,000 guns, 9,000 antitank guns, and nearly 2,000 tanks. If, then, Nasser taunted Rabin to strike out of the constricting Arab vise, he was waiting not merely with troops but with an elaborate and formidable network of trenches, pillboxes, minefields, barbed wire, and machine gun nests. In the decade since Operation Kadesh, the Egyptians had transformed the northeastern corner of Sinai into a military barrier capable of resisting the heaviest attack and of serving as the launching base for a powerful offensive. The roads that existed in this desert wilderness before 1956 had been significantly improved, and new ones had been laid. A vast Egyptian Maginot Line blocked the key Nitzana-Ismailia highway, the single narrow opening through which Israeli armor could move into the heartland of Sinai.

At the eastern approaches of the Nitzana-Ismailia passage, 18 miles from the Israeli border, lay the Abu Agheila crossroads that dominated not only the main highway to Sinai but the arteries connecting the central route with other roads traversing the peninsula from east to west. The Egyptians accordingly had chosen Abu Agheila as the heart of their defensive position in eastern Sinai and had invested considerable effort and money to fortify the location. In the 1950s, the Abu Agheila defense line had been planned by German military experts. Israeli forces had battled for its possession in 1956, but failed to take it; eventually they bypassed it, leaving it to hold out until the end of the campaign. Since then, the fortifications had been reinforced even more impressively, this time to correspond with the Soviet doctrine, and under no circumstances could they safely be bypassed any longer as a "pocket."

Moreover, the linchpin of the Abu Agheila network, Um Cataf, was an interlocked system of fortresses, guarded by pillboxes, defense trenches, and natural ridges, with the entire locality surrounded by minefields and guarded by heavy tanks. Deep inside the mighty enclave, between Um Cataf and Um Shihan, the Egyptians distributed scores of large-caliber guns and hundreds of mortars. To the west, a mobile "armored first" of tanks and tank destroyers was held in reserve for striking counterblows. The Egyptians intended essentially to use the Um Cataf positions as an anvil on which to hammer the Israeli armor to death. They concentrated a tank division just south of Abu Agheila itself, and another not far behind. If, as expected, Israeli forces battered themselves against the Um Cataf redoubt, both Egyptian divisions would swing north toward the Negev, maneuver behind the Israelis, and annihilate them. This accomplished,

Egyptian tanks would move north along the coastal road toward undefended Tel Aviv. It was a somber picture for Israel.

THE SOURCES OF ISRAELI MILITARY POWER

It was not the entire picture, however. When Rabin became chief of staff in 1964, he testified before the Knesset security and foreign affairs committee that any future war would have to be won in four days. It could not take substantially longer for economic reasons. The implications were that Israel should attack preemptively. Yet, to avoid alienating world opinion, the nation was left with no recourse but to allow the enemy to mobilize, gather on Israel's borders, proclaim to the world that this time the Jews would be liquidated—then to strike out at the enemy with an "anticipatory counteroffensive" at the last possible moment. A scenario of this complexity obviously required a precise understanding of the enemy's intentions. Under the civilian roof structure of the secret service, therefore, directed for many years by the brilliant Iser Harel, Israel's various information-gathering agencies orchestrated a uniquely effective intelligence program.

The most dangerous part of this undercover work was espionage in Arab countries. Some of it was carried out by Arab and foreign agents, who provided vital data on Egyptian military and political activities. Not a few of the informers were caught and subsequently died on the gallows. One who did not was a young Egyptian communications officer, fanatically anti-Nasserist, known only as Suleiman. From May 17, 1967, when Cairo ordered its armed forces to take up battle positions in Sinai, Suleiman radioed Israel coded information on Egyptian troop movements, battle plans, even the location of antiaircraft missiles. Following the Israeli air strike (p. 639), Suleiman transmitted full details on Egyptian losses. On the last day of the war, Israeli planes inadvertently bombed Suleiman's radio post near the Mitla Pass. When hostilities ended on the night of June 7, an Israeli parachute unit dropped at Mitla to search for him. His body was found. A saddened escort of Israeli officers gathered to bury him with honor.

Occasionally Israelis themselves infiltrated Arab territory, posing as Europeans or even as Arabs. One of the most successful of these was Wolfgang Lutz, son of a Jewish father and a German mother. Arriving in Egypt in 1961 as a "German businessman," Lutz spent the next three and a half years ferreting out information on the Egyptian (German-staffed) rocket program, which he transmitted to Israel. Eventually he was caught and sentenced to life imprisonment; however, in 1968, a year after the war, he was exchanged for nine captured Egyptian generals. An even more dramatic coup for Israeli intelligence was its success, in 1960, in placing an agent high in the echelons of Syria's ruling Ba'ath party. This was Eli Cohen, an Egyptian-born Jew, who posed as the son of Syrian parents living in Brazil. In Damascus, Cohen set himself up as a free-spending "importer" and became an intimate friend of the Syrian commander's nephew. With this contact, he became privy to developments in the government and the Syrian high command and was eventually allowed to inspect the highly restricted military emplacements atop the Golan Heights. For five years, through Eli Cohen, Israeli intelligence was tuned in to the most important military and political events in Syria. In 1965, Cohen was finally unmasked, tortured, and hanged.

A number of Israel's most gifted analysts were also occupied with the study of the Arab mind and temperament. Thus, General Yehoshafat Harkabi, chief of the military intelligence branch of the general staff, collated data suggesting that the Arab was a loner, distrustful of his fellows, unwilling to involve himself in collective team efforts that required sacrifice in the group's interest. This evidence was confirmed in the June War when Egyptian officers abandoned their men in the Sinai, in some instances taking their soldiers' water and food with them. Aware, too, of the Arab tendency to plummet from euphoria to despair when things went wrong, the Israelis resolved to hit the enemy with all their strength at the outset, to shift the fortunes of war immediately. The Arab tendency to camouflage unpleasant facts in fantasy was similarly exploited. Thus, anticipating enemy victory claims, Dayan ordered a blackout of war bulletins during the first day of war. When the Egyptians thereafter claimed destruction of the Israeli armed forces, the Russians stalled United Nations moves for a cease-fire. By the time the Soviets discovered what actually had happened, too much time had elapsed to salvage Egyptian fortunes. It was also too late for Hussein to retrieve his fatal blunder of entering the war.

Not least of all, intelligence was the key to determining "pure" military strategy. After 1961 Israel learned that the Russians were reorganizing the Egyptian army according to classical Soviet methods. The "Moscow Doctrine" employed vast troop concentrations and relied on heavy fortifications. With high-altitude planes, the Israeli air force minutely photographed the defensive positions being constructed in Sinai. Supplementing this information with data transmitted by informers and agents, intelligence then prepared a book on the Moscow Doctrine with scale drawings of the newly built Egyptian defenses. The prize exhibit of course was Um Cataf. Rabin staked out a wide area in the Negev and had army engineers build a model of the Um Cataf complex down to the last detail. Thenceforth the "Russian positions" in the Negev became the major concern of Israel's defense forces. Officers' schools, armor and infantry seminars, all prepared their own manuals for breaking the "Russian positions," and to that end vast maneuvers were carried out. By the time of the June War, the Israelis could have found their way blindfolded through Um Cataf.

In addition to intelligence, every branch of Israel's defense establishment was powerfully augmented under Rabin. Unlike his predecessor, Ben-Gurion, Prime Minister Eshkol was no military expert. With few exceptions, he was prepared to accept Rabin's advice and to support the general's request for expensive new weapons. Large quantities of this equipment, it is recalled, were secured from West Germany and the United States. Moreover, Israeli factories were themselves turning out considerable numbers of light and medium arms. By 1967 the government admitted to spending 11 percent of its GNP for external and domestic security, but the true figure probably was closer to 14 percent, or even higher. By then, Israel's standing armed forces comprised about 50,000 men and women in all branches, with mobilizable reserves of over 250,000. The army was reasonably well equipped, possessing some 900 tanks, both American and British, approximately 160 French self-propelled guns, and nearly 1,000 American armored personnel carriers. The air force numbered 8,000 men, and between 500 and 550 planes of all types. The navy was the smallest of the military branches, consisting of several frigates and torpedo boats and two submarines. In determining its equipment priorities, moreover, Israel decided after the experience of the Sinai Campaign to place much greater emphasis on the armored corps. Under a resourceful commander, the diminutive Brigadier Israel Tal, the proficiencies of tank warfare were vastly expanded. The army exploited every prewar incident, especially along the Syrian border, to improve and adapt its combat techniques.

But in the end, the most decisive factor in the efficiency of Israel's armed forces was the quality of its manpower. The Sinai war had proved that modern armored warfare required more skill, even more physical courage, than in the pretechnology era. Israeli tank commanders were trained to stand exposed in the cupolas of their vehicles, to direct their attacks personally. In no instance was a crippled tank to be abandoned as long as its firing apparatus was intact. Unlike their Egyptian counterparts, too, the Israelis stressed flexibility and initiative in field command. It was an emphasis that assumed a highly resilient mentality. But of course adaptability and dynamism were precisely the characteristics of a people that had been trained in the quick-motion methods of social and economic development, that had effectively built a nation under the impact of siege and boycott.

The military's top commanders were a case in point. Most of the leading army generals—Rabin, Gavish, Tal, Sharon, Elazar, Yoffe, Bar-Lev—were of Labor stock, with roots deep in the nation's pioneering cadres and long experience in adapting defense techniques to Israel's special needs. Rabin himself, a quiet, sandy-haired man in his mid-forties, set the tone. Jerusalem-born, a veteran Palmach commander and career officer, he brought to his task a lifetime of service in each of the army branches. He knew his men and based his strategy on the certain knowledge that the largest numbers of them shared his commitment to initiative. This was no less true even of the Oriental youngsters, who were developing into substantially better combat troops than in earlier days. Although still lagging behind their Ashkenazic comrades in their grasp of technology, the Orientals experienced fewer problems of adaptability or motivation than had their older brothers or fathers in 1956. And in June 1967, all Israeli civilians and soldiers, Europeans and Orientals alike, shared a commitment that was reinforced with each propaganda broadside of the Arab enemy, with each Arab boast that Israel was facing national liquidation. As Jews, together, they were fighting once again for the literal survival of their families and people.

THE DECISION TO ATTACK

On June 1 Eban informed Eshkol and the cabinet that there was no fore-seeable possibility any longer of Washington resolving the crisis. The White House had admitted that plans for a multinational naval force had collapsed. On the other hand, the foreign minister's weeks of patient diplomacy at least had assured that if Israel chose to move, it would not be opposed by a united and angry world, as in the Sinai Campaign. No further political purpose would be served in delaying military action, Eban conceded. The prime minister accepted this evaluation with a certain relief. The next morning the cabinet met again to hear Rabin and Dayan press for immediate military action. This time the generals encountered little argument. The following day, June 3, holding his first press con-ference as defense minister, Dayan veiled the government's intention in a shrewdly ambiguous comment: "At this moment, we are more or less in a position of being a bit too late and a bit too early: too late to react with force to the closing of the Strait of Tiran, and too early to come to any final conclusions about the diplomatic efforts applied to this matter." In the Arab countries the remark was interpreted to mean that Israel was unprepared for war. In Tel Aviv, Ambassador Chuvakhin cabled Moscow that Israel would not start anything for at least two weeks. Foreign cor-respondents began returning to their various countries. At a final cabinet meeting that ran for seven hours through the night of June 3–4, all the ministers voted for war except the two Mapam representatives, and they, too, concurred later in the day. Dayan secretly notified Ben-Gurion of the impending attack. The old man gave it his blessing.

Dayan as minister of defense was no longer the headlong, precipitous general he had been as chief of staff in 1956. This time he directed his war with great sensitivity to world opinion and a remarkable caution in all his military moves. His new restraint was apparent even before the outbreak of fighting, when he imposed a number of firm guidelines on his commanders. For one thing, troops on the Syrian and Jordanian fronts were to maintain an exclusively defensive posture, even if the enemy attacked first. As for Sinai, Dayan warned that it was political madness even to contemplate going beyond the Mitla and Gidi passes to the Suez Canal. A blockade of the waterway would generate unacceptable inter-national pressures. Anyway, the Canal was vital to Nasser's prestige and economy, and also was crucial to the Soviets. "If we reach the Canal," Dayan warned, "Nasser will never agree to a cease-fire and the war will go on for years."

The operational plans had been worked out by Rabin and his staff. In the Negev, facing the Egyptian border town of al-Quntilla, scores of dummy tanks were positioned to lure additional enemy forces to the south, on the assumption that the Israelis were planning another thrust down the coast to Sharm es-Sheikh, as in 1956. Yet Rabin understood that there was no possibility of repeating the strategy of Operation Kadesh now. In 1956 Israeli forces had pulled off their dash southward only because the Egyptian army to the north was weak; most of it had been deployed against the Anglo-French invasion near Cairo and Suez. In 1967 Rabin knew—if Nasser did not—that he would have to break the Egyptians at the line of their greatest strength, in the north. If this were accomplished, Sharm es-Sheikh would be rendered untenable in any case and the Gulf of Aqaba would be opened automatically. Facing seven Egyptian divisions in the Sinai was General Yesheyahu Gavish's southern front army, consisting of three divisions under Brigadiers Tal, Yoffe, and Sharon. Gavish, a forty-two-year-old native-born Israeli, was convinced that he had found the right strategy for "blowing the locks" off the Sinai. It was to crack through Egyptian defenses at Rafa and Abu Agheila; then to send an armored division leaping forward to the Mitla Pass, blocking the Egyptian escape routes; and finally to destroy the entire trapped Egyptian army.

Tal, charged with the task of breaking the Rafa line at the southern end of the Gaza Strip, had at his disposal 300 tanks, representing the elite of Israel's armored corps. His initial objective was to force a corridor by way of Khan Yunis 30 miles westward, through heavy Egyptian fortifications and a powerful enemy infantry division, to al-Arish on the coast. Here lay the Egyptians' main logistical base in Sinai. By applying Gavish's "steel fist" approach, Tal hoped to breach the al-Arish line so rapidly that he could leave his flanks temporarily exposed. But everything depended upon a crushing blow at the first impact. In turn, Sharon's division of armor and mechanized infantry was given the awesome task of breaching and conquering the Abu Agheila fortifications system. Sharon intended to meet this challenge by striking to both the front and the rear of the defense network. Before the two prongs met, the infantry would attack enemy fortifications from the flank, including the Um Cataf bastion. Finally, Brigadier Avraham Yoffe, that veteran trekker of Operation Kadesh (Chapter XVII), was assigned the responsibility of infiltrating a division of reservists between Tal's and Sharon's brigades over exceptionally difficult, seemingly impassable dunes, until it arrived deep in the enemy's rear at the Mitla and other mountain passes. There it would block the last Egyptian escape routes.

AN AERIAL THUNDERBOLT, A MAILED FIST

At 7:10 a.m. of June 5, Major General Mordechai Hod, commander of Israel's air force, radioed the attack order from the operations room of the defense ministry in Tel Aviv. Thereupon one of the world's most skilled air arms was launched into action. Israeli pilots and ground crews were considered the equal of any in the world. Thanks also to near-perfect intelligence, the Israeli command had pinpointed the location of virtually all Egyptian planes, all antiaircraft batteries, even wooden dummy planes. It knew, too, when Egyptian pilots flew their morning patrols, when they landed for their morning coffee break. All had been studied, prepared, and rehearsed innumerable times before D-Day. Now, the first Israeli planes took off at staggered intervals for Egypt's key air bases in the Sinai Peninsula, Suez rectangle, and Nile Valley. The two-engined Vautour light bombers were assigned the farthest target, Luxor on the Nile, almost twice the distance to Cairo. The single-engined Mirages headed for the nearest fields at al-Arish and others in the Sinai. All were scheduled to arrive over their targets at the identical moment, 7:45 a.m. Israel time. The pilots were ordered first to destroy the Egyptian bombers and interceptors, then devastate the air bases.

Taking off over the Mediterranean, the planes hooked back over Egypt at near ground level to avoid enemy radar. Reaching their eleven separate targets at the appointed time, the Israelis climbed high, then dived to 200 feet as they proceeded to attack the Tupolovs and MiGs. The Egyptian fighters were taxiing to a halt after returning from their morning patrol. The antiaircraft crews similarly were caught away from their positions. The Israelis accordingly made four passes over their targets, consuming their allotted seven minutes to destroy the enemy planes, then to rocket-bomb the Egyptian fields. Ten minutes after the first attack wave came the second, and ten minutes after that the third. As the Israelis streaked for home, they managed to evade a number of surface-to-air missiles that climbed after them. In 170 minutes Israel's pilots had smashed Egypt's best-equipped air bases and had turned 300 of Nasser's 340 combat planes into flaming wrecks. Another 20 Egyptian planes were shot down in the air. When the returning Israeli jets touched down and their pilots debriefed, the news of their success was received with incredulity. Hod admitted later that "in my wildest dreams I would never have thought this kind of record possible. I reckoned on at least half a day [to complete the job], maybe even a whole day or a day and a night." The Egyptian air force, the largest in the Middle East, was in ruins.

Now the Israelis were free at the very outset to concentrate on the Egyptian ground armies. Indeed, throughout the next few days the air force roamed at will over Sinai, destroying entire convoys of armor and other vehicles fleeing to the Canal. During the first day, too, as Egypt's allies began probing offensives (p. 642), Israeli planes were released to attack Jordanian and Syrian airfields, even the great Habbaniyah base in Iraq. In the course of these attacks, the entire Jordanian air force of twenty Hunter jets was destroyed, as well as fifty Syrian MiGs—two-thirds of the Syrian combat air force. At the Iraqi base, nine fighters were destroyed. Conversely, every Arab plane that entered Israeli air space was shot down, as well as planes caught in other sectors. By nightfall of June 6, Israel had destroyed 416 planes, 393 on the ground. It had lost 26 planes during that time, all to antiaircraft fire.

Meanwhile, at 8:15 a.m. on June 5, Israeli ground forces attacked.

Against heavy resistance, Tal's northern armored brigade reached the Palestinian defenses outside Khan Yunis and overwhelmed them. Bursting into the village itself, the tanks proceeded in line down the road toward Rafa, avoiding the enemy minefield. A second brigade of Tal's armor swung behind the Egyptian entrenchments and minefields leading south from Rafa. After heavy combat, this force succeeded in outflanking the Egyptian lines and investing the town. The fall of Rafa, in turn, opened the way to al-Arish, administrative capital of Sinai and northeastern gateway to the entire Egyptian defense network in the peninsula. Tal's armor then pushed on six miles to the east in the next few hours, shelling and ultimately destroying a series of extensive Egyptian fortifications. By dawn of June 6, the roads to al-Arish were cleared and Israeli supply columns followed in. After resupplying and regrouping, Tal's advance units reached al-Arish by midnight. A brutal slugging match then developed against Egyptian tanks, antitank guns, and artillery. With strafing and bombing support from the air force, however, resistance was overcome. The last phase of the operation at al-Arish consisted of liquidating the remnants of the Egyptian Seventh Division. A by-product of success here was Dayan's order to occupy the Gaza Strip, where the artillery of the Palestinian Division had loosed a heavy bombardment on nearby Israeli kibbutzim. One of Tal's brigades entered the southern end of the Strip, advancing northeastward to the outskirts of Gaza, clearing out the Palestinian defenses en route. The town fell in the early afternoon of June 7.

Meanwhile, Sharon's division had the formidable task of blasting open the other gateway to Sinai, the powerful Abu Agheila network of defenses across the Nitzana-Ismailia axis. At the western extremity of this gateway, of course, lay the death trap of Um Cataf. Sharon's forces, comprising a single undersized infantry division of regulars and reserves, a brigade of armor, and a few supplementary units, hardly matched the Egyptians' numerical strength. Planning a night attack, moreover, the Israeli commander would be deprived of vital air support. Worse yet, all parts of the entire Abu Agheila defense complex would have to be taken: if one remained, the consequences could be fatal. Yet these fearsome risks did not discourage the cocky, barrel-chested Sharon. The youngest brigadier in the army at the age of thirty-eight, the builder of Israel's elite paratroop corps, and the commander of the Mitla Pass operation in 1956, Ariel "Arik" Sharon had never doubted that imagination and spirit could overcome even the toughest of Egyptian defenses. Moreover, his plan for capturing Um Cataf brilliantly precluded the need for frontal attack. The operation was extraordinarily complicated, to be sure, requiring the synchronization of half a dozen individual assignments in darkness over a 20-square-mile area. Nevertheless, Sharon was positive that he had found the answers for all contingencies, and he was right.

The attack began at dusk on June 5, with a long, painful infantry march behind Um Cataf through the sand. At the same time a battalion of paratroops was lifted by helicopters to another point in the desert three miles behind the fortifications. The infantry, many of them re-servists, slogged through the dunes, appearing at the Egyptian flanks just as darkness fell. Running along the lip of the trenchworks, they cut down the Egyptian defenders with their automatic weapons. The heli-copter-borne troops, who also had made their way through the desert, now simultaneously attacked Egyptian gun batteries from the rear. After several minutes of close-quarter combat, a massive Israeli artillery barrage descended on the Egyptian positions. Searchlights were used only after hand-to-hand fighting had cleared the rear, permitting additional Israeli infantry and tanks to enfilade the trenches. The fighting was heavy, but the entire attack went like clockwork. By 3:00 a.m. on June 6, Um Cataf was in Sharon's hands. All that remained was the destruction of surviving Egyptian tanks, and this was accomplished three hours later, as Israeli armor moved through the rear of Um Cataf to encircle enemy pockets. The operation was to become known as a classic of tactics, and in ensuing years would be studied in military academies throughout the world.

With breakthroughs achieved at Rafa-al-Arish and at the Abu Agheila complex, the Israelis had blown open the locks to the Sinai. Yoffe's brigade meanwhile confounded the Egyptians in the afternoon of June 5 by moving through an "impassable" sector, the wastes lying between the two gate-ways. At the road junction of Bir Lahfan, the Israeli tanks fought a thirteen-hour battle against reinforcing Egyptian armor. By noon of June 6 the enemy was turned back. Yoffe's brigade then raced on toward Jebel Libni, a key military installation astride the central axis. Here the Egyptians had concentrated nearly an entire infantry division supported by tanks. But this force, too, now crumpled under Yoffe's battering ram, and Jebel Libni was taken after heavy fighting. Thus, by the end of the second day of war, after thirty-five hours of uninterrupted battle, the first and most difficult phase of the Israeli operational plan had been completed. Egyp-tian fortifications had been penetrated and bypassed, Sinai was opened wide before Israeli armor, and the roads to the west and south were clear.

A CONFUSION OF ARAB PURPOSES

Throughout the first day of the Sinai offensive, the Israeli government refrained from issuing announcements on the magnitude of its victories. The cloak of silence represented official policy (p. 636). The only military communiqués that went out over the airwaves were broadcast by Cairo; and during the first twenty-four hours these releases spoke of un-precedented Egyptian breakthroughs, of Israel's army and air force de-stroyed, of Egyptian mechanized columns driving on Tel Aviv. The "news" was accepted unquestioningly elsewhere in the Arab world, and it influenced the precipitous decisions of Syria, Jordan, and Iraq to enter the fighting. Once again, however, as in two earlier wars with Israel, the Syrians forfeited their best opportunity for an offensive. Before June, their military staff had formulated plans to move down from the Golan with two divisions, capture eastern Galilee, then proceed on toward Haifa. Yet when hostilities began on June 5, the Syrians at the last minute adopted a wait-and-see attitude and preferred simply to shell the Galilee town of Rosh Pina and its neighboring border settlements. Israeli kibbutz members accordingly went down into their shelters, in some places remaining there under enemy bombardment as long as eleven hours at a time.

Despite its topographical disadvantages, meanwhile, Israeli artillery kept up a vigorous reply to the Syrian barrage. So, too, by the late afternoon of June 5 and on succeeding days, did the Israeli air force. Indeed, by the night of the fifth, as ferocious Israeli bombing all but eradicated the Syrian air arm, it was apparent to Damascus that it had been misinformed as to the extent of Egyptian "victories." Deprived by then of the opportunity to embark on a major offensive, the Ba'ath regime made its second mistake in continuing hostilities on a local scale. On June 6 a Syrian infantry and armored company launched two attacks on Tel Dan and one on Kibbutz Sha'ar Yashuv. These were repelled by Israeli tank and air units. A similar limited offensive against Ashmura was thrown back. The Syrians were to pay bitterly for this miscalculation.

The Jordanian blunder was even more catastrophic. On the morning of June 5 Cairo informed Amman that 75 percent of Israel's planes had been destroyed and that Egyptian armored units were fighting deep inside Israeli territory. With rare candor, Hussein admitted later (in *My "War" with Israel*) that "we were misinformed about what had happened in Egypt when the Israelis attacked the UAR bases. . . . These reports—fantastic to say the least—had much to do with our confusion and false interpretation of the situation." Hussein thereafter gave sympathetic ear to the request of General Riad, the Egyptian officer commanding Hashemite forces, for Jordanian troops to launch an attack against Israeli Jerusalem and to shell Israeli towns and air bases. Even as the king deliberated this proposal, he received an urgent message from Eshkol, transmitted through General Odd Bull, the UNTSO commander. Appealing to Hussein to refrain from entering the war, the Israeli leader promised that his own government would not initiate hostilities along the eastern front. Eshkol's appeal was disregarded. "Throughout the first day," Hussein wrote later, "our batteries of long-range 155's kept pounding at the outskirts of Tel Aviv, its concentration of military targets, and the airport at Lydda."

Yet it was Israeli–New–Jerusalem that was destined to be Hussein's most compelling target. The city's Jewish population of 190,000 was immediately exposed to Arab attack from the surrounding mountain ridges. Particularly vulnerable, too, was the Israeli enclave on Mount Scopus on the Jordanian side of the city, for here were located the pre-1948 Hadassah hospital and Hebrew University, isolated in a demilitarized zone well within Hashemite territory and guarded only by a force of eighty-five

Israeli police. Indeed, of the entire central front, an area stretching from Haifa to Beersheba, Mount Scopus was the object of gravest Israeli concern. The front commander, Brigadier Uzi Narkiss, had no doubt that the local Jerusalem Brigade would manage to repel any attack on the city or its corridor to the sea. But if the Arabs overran Scopus he feared that a United Nations cease-fire might be imposed before the Israelis could retake the enclave. As Narkiss saw it, his one hope lay in a vigorous counterattack by the mechanized unit—the Harel Brigade—located near Ramle. For that matter, even the Harel tankers would be hard-pressed to counter the Arab Legion's armored brigade deployed on the plain east of Jerusalem. In the event of a contest between these two forces, starting out on opposite sides of the Judean hills, the Jordanian Patton tanks were faster than the Harel's Super-Shermans and four hours closer to Jerusalem. During that four-hour difference, too, the Israeli police garrison on Mount Scopus would be compelled to hold out with its limited (and secretly hidden) antitank guns, and whatever artillery support Narkiss could provide. The situation was not promising. In the last week before the June War, the Israeli garrison at Scopus heard Arab cadis exhorting their flock from nearby mosques to "slaughter and kill."

Narkiss's fears evidently were realized as shooting from Jordanian positions at the southern end of the city line broke out at mid-morning on June 5. Firing soon intensified, and enemy shells began hitting populated areas. Within a few hours, 250 Israeli civilians were wounded and 20 killed. Despite his instincts to strike back quickly, Narkiss remained under orders to hold tight unless a major Jordanian invasion attempt were launched. Even when Arab shelling grew heavier, Dayan's instructions to the central front commander were to "grit your teeth, and don't ask for more troops from GHQ." The Jordanians, it was hoped, were interested simply in making a gesture to remain in Nasser's good graces. To ensure, too, that they entertained no serious ambitions, the Israeli air force commenced its bombing runs on the Amman and Mafraq airfields at 12:30 p.m., liquidating the entire Hashemite fighter fleet.

Thereupon, at 1:00 p.m., either by prearrangement or in a counter-retaliatory spasm, Arab Legion forces crossed the Jerusalem armistice lines and occupied UNTSO headquarters on the Hill of Evil Counsel. This building, formerly the British Government House, overlooked some of the most densely inhabited neighborhoods of Israeli Jerusalem. Capture of its facilities and of its excellent artillery sites posed a real threat to the Jews. The Arab shift to ground attack similarly undermined the position of the tiny Israeli garrison on Scopus, which even then had come under Jordanian artillery bombardment. Yet, from the larger military viewpoint, seizure of the Hill of Evil Counsel was Hussein's gravest error. He failed to detect in the unchallengeable power of Israeli air squadrons over Amman, at a time when Cairo was boasting that virtually all Israel's planes had been destroyed, the clue to what actually was happening in the Middle Eastern war. "It was an open invitation to the Israelis to move in," wrote Evan

Wilson, the United States minister-consul in Jerusalem, who witnessed these events, "and it provided the latter with an essential base of operations to take the Old City."

THE WORLD IN SHOCK

Hussein was not alone in his miscalculation. Throughout most of June 5 Nasser studied the transmitted reports of Egyptian "victories." None of his commanders gave him the actual facts. It was only at 4:00 p.m. that a headquarters officer arrived with straight information: "I have come to tell you that we no longer have an air force." Regaining his composure, the Egyptian president soon manufactured an ingenious explanation for the air disaster. At 4:30 a.m. on June 6 the Israeli signal corps intercepted a radio-telephone exchange between Cairo and Amman. Nasser was speaking directly to Hussein. "Shall we say that the United States is fighting on Israel's side?" Nasser asked. "Shall we say the United States and England or only the United States?" "The United States and England," Hussein replied. Three hours later Cairo Radio, and then other Arab stations, began releasing the "information" that carrier-based American and British fighter-bombers were providing air support for Israeli ground forces. Throughout the Arab world, then, violent demonstrations were mounted against Britain and the United States, with attacks on American consulates and information centers. Egypt and Syria promptly severed diplomatic relations with the United States. Sudan, Algeria, Yemen, and Iraq quickly followed. Jordan refrained from taking this step, and a week later Hussein issued an apology for the canard.

In Washington, meanwhile, Lyndon Johnson was awakened at 3:00 a.m. on June 5 and informed of the hostilities. Immediately he cabled Moscow, appealing for restraint on both sides. Four hours later, the president received a phone call from Kosygin on the "hot line." The Soviet prime minister evidently had been taken in by Egyptian victory claims and chose now to delay United Nations action. Acknowledging receipt of Johnson's cable, he blamed Israel for the war and asked the president to use his influence on the Israeli government to withdraw its forces. Both Great Powers should stay out of the fighting, Kosygin emphasized. Johnson concurred, and proposed that Moscow and Washington now strive together to obtain an immediate cease-fire through the Security Council. But shortly afterward, as news of heavy Egyptian losses belatedly reached Moscow, the Soviet leadership decided that a tougher warning was in order. About noon, Washington time, a second message arrived from Kosygin emphasizing that the Soviet Union could not remain indifferent to Israel's "criminal aggression," and that if Israeli troops did not withdraw, the Soviet armed forces would use appropriate means to end the "Zionist adventure."

Johnson and his advisers had learned by then of Israel's spectacular military victories. Their reaction was one of quiet gratification that the Israelis themselves were successfully liquidating an agonizing world crisis, and inflicting a massive diplomatic defeat on the Soviets in the process. The president would not countenance Soviet bullying to reverse the situation. Accordingly, he ordered the United States Sixth Fleet to proceed toward the fighting zone. Within minutes the huge armada was moving under full steam in the direction of the Sinai coast. It was an awesome display of American power, and one that was soon visible on the radar of Soviet vessels in the area. Johnson followed this gesture with another message to Kosygin, reminding the Soviet prime minister of numerous American commitments to safeguard the integrity and independence of Israel. The Russian leadership appreciated the veiled warning; the president's unflinching reaction put an end to any further notion of Soviet military interference.

Instead, the Soviets now countered with a Security Council resolution for all belligerents to withdraw from occupied territories. Thereupon Goldberg, the American delegate, proposed a straightforward cease-fire without reference to evacuation. To outraged Arab and Soviet objections, Goldberg blandly observed that if a *status quo ante* were desired, then it must be restored to the circumstances obtaining before the crisis developed, namely, freedom of navigation in the Gulf of Aqaba and a return of the UNEF to Sinai and Sharm es-Sheikh. The Arabs rejected the linked proposal. Visibly confused, Nikolai Federenko, the Soviet delegate, finally requested that the Council simply postpone further deliberations until the next day, June 6. This was a serious blunder, for every passing hour added to Israel's military victories. Indeed, by the morning of June 6 Moscow had a clearer picture of what was happening, and was aghast at the destruction of Egyptian forces. It was evident now that time was working against the Arab nations. Ignoring Nasser's and Hussein's claims of Western air intervention, therefore, Kosygin dispatched yet another message to Washington, urging once more that Johnson endorse a Security Council resolution for a cease-fire and a withdrawal of troops. But the president, in turn, emphasized that the resolution must include freedom of navigation in the Strait of Tiran and restoration of the UNEF.

The other Security Council members by and large endorsed the American approach. When the UN body finally convened at 6:30 p.m. on June 6, the Council's president, Hans Tabor of Denmark, announced that consultations among the members had produced a draft resolution calling for a cease-fire "as a first step." The formula was unanimously accepted by the Security Council, even by the Soviet delegate. At this point, however, in a surprise move that anticipated the later course of United Nations negotiations, a majority of the Council voted for parallel efforts to achieve a "just and permanent settlement" of the Middle Eastern crisis. Unlike 1956, the diplomatic climate was now noticeably favorable to Israel. It was further enhanced later that evening by an electrifying address delivered by Eban—who had just flown in from Israel—describing the mortal danger his country had recently faced and now at last was overcoming. By the next day even the Egyptians sensed that a plain and simple cease-fire was the best they could get.

ISRAEL CONQUERS SINAI

At dusk on June 6 a helicopter landed at Jebel Libni, and General Gavish, the Israeli southern front commander, rushed up to Brigadier Tal, leading the armored corps. "The Egyptian high command has just ordered its troops to fall back to the second line of defense," he said. "We've got to go after them at once." It was then decided that Tal's forces should take the more northerly axis through Bir Gafgafa to block the roads leading to Ismailia, while Yoffe's forces would advance in a more southerly direction to the Mitla Pass, thus closing Egypt's final escape routes. At the same time the commanders agreed to launch a coordinated attack at dawn (June 7) on the remaining Egyptian secondary defenses, with Tal striking at the positions near Bir Hamma, 10 miles to the west, and Yoffe's men simultaneously engaging the Egyptians in Bir Hassana.

In the ensuing armored battles on this flat terrain, the highly skilled Israeli tankers all but annihilated their opponents. By nightfall of June 7, the Israeli vanguard had reached its objectives. In the north it had overrun Rumani on the coastal road about 10 miles from the Canal. In the center it held the road extending to the Canal from Bir Gafgafa, 30 miles from Ismailia. In the south the Israelis blocked the passageway through Mitla. Three Israeli divisions now were moving in for the kill: Tal and Yoffe blocked the passes; Sharon was driving the fleeing Egyptians into the trap. After a brief rest, Sharon's column moved out again at dawn, inflicting a fearful havoc on the retreating Egyptian armor. In one encounter alone two Egyptian regiments, fifty tanks, and three hundred vehicles were destroyed. As Egyptian mechanized forces attempted to break through south of Bir Gafgafa, Tal's men liquidated another of their brigades. Meanwhile a continuous stream of Egyptian troops and vehicles poured headlong from eastern and central Sinai toward Yoffe's force at Mitla, with no idea that the pass had been blocked two days earlier by an Israeli air strike. As the enemy converged from all directions, Israeli planes strafed and bombed them mercilessly. Yoffe's armored brigade completed the slaughter. In the end more than eight hundred Egyptian tanks were knocked out or captured. Devastation on this scale exceeded even the massive destruction of Nazi armor at al-Alamein twenty-five years earlier.

At the same time, another conquest proved surprisingly easy for the Israelis. On June 7, Sharm es-Sheikh, the Egyptian coastal fortress overlooking the Strait of Tiran, fell without resistance; the Egyptians fled even before Israeli paratroops could be dropped, or the first amphibious units disembarked from LSTs. Thus, elements of the battalions that had been landed at Sharm es-Sheikh subsequently were flown by helicopter to al-Tur, whence they continued northward along the shores of the Gulf of Suez. On June 8 they linked up with Israeli units coming down the Gulf

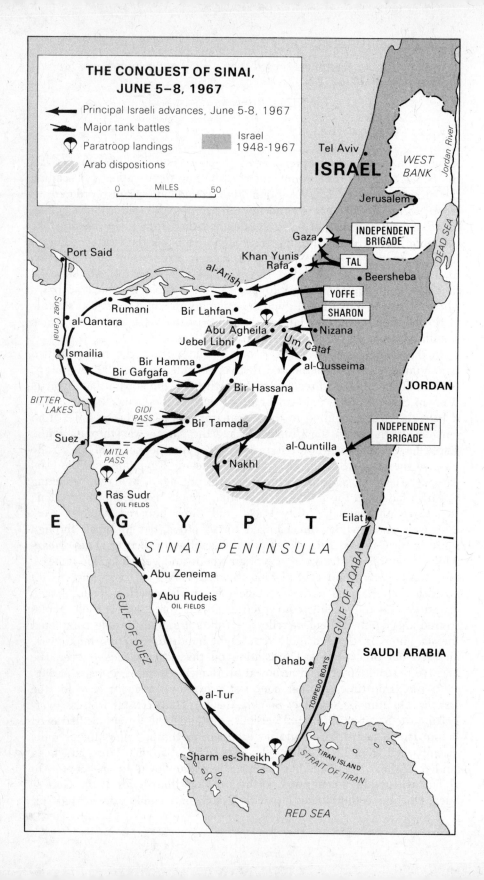

THE CONQUEST OF SINAI, JUNE 5–8, 1967

- → Principal Israeli advances, June 5-8, 1967
- Major tank battles
- ☂ Paratroop landings
- Arab dispositions
- Israel 1948-1967

0 —— MILES —— 50

ISRAEL
Tel Aviv
WEST BANK
Jordan River
Jerusalem

Gaza
INDEPENDENT BRIGADE
Khan Yunis
Rafa
TAL
al-Arish
Beersheba

Port Said
YOFFE
Rumani
SHARON
al-Qantara
Bir Lahfan
Abu Agheila
Nizana
Suez Canal
Jebel Libni
Um Cataf
Ismailia
Bir Hamma
al-Qusseima
Bir Gafgafa
JORDAN
BITTER LAKES
Bir Hassana
GIDI PASS
Bir Tamada
Suez
al-Quntilla
INDEPENDENT BRIGADE
MITLA PASS
Nakhl
Ras Sudr
OIL FIELDS
Eilat

E G Y P T
S I N A I   P E N I N S U L A

Abu Zeneima
GULF OF SUEZ
Abu Rudeis
OIL FIELDS
GULF OF AQABA
SAUDI ARABIA
Dahab
TORPEDO BOATS
al-Tur
Sharm es-Sheikh
TIRAN ISLAND
STRAIT OF TIRAN
DEAD SEA

RED SEA

coast from Ras Sudr in the north. The entire Sinai now was ringed by Israeli forces. Only one strip of unguarded territory remained. This was the Canal itself. With the greater part of the Egyptian army smashed in the desert behind them, Tal and Yoffe ordered their columns to press ahead to the waterway.

Ironically, only the day before, Dayan had observed in a Tel Aviv press conference that Israel had achieved its political and military objectives. This was, essentially, the reopening of the Strait of Tiran to international navigation. "The Israeli army can reach the Canal without difficulty," he said, "but that is not our objective. What is important for us is Sharm es-Sheikh. So why should we push on to Suez and get ourselves involved in international problems?" Then, on the morning of June 8, Dayan suddenly was informed that Israeli troops had reached al-Qantara, had destroyed the remaining Egyptian armor there, and finally had proceeded to the banks of the Canal itself. The defense minister was annoyed. Nevertheless, when he learned afterward that other Israeli tank units were advancing toward the Canal from the Mitla Pass and Bir Gafgafa, he issued instructions for the occupation of the entire eastern length of Suez. Although later he would describe the Canal as "the best antitank ditch in the world," his initial reservations were confirmed in the years ahead (Chapters xxii, xxiv). The victory was a staggering one, in any event. Seven Egyptian divisions totaling 100,000 men had been crushed in less than four days.

If the war was over for the Egyptians, the question remained whether they, and their Soviet patrons, were prepared to admit the fact. In the Security Council, Federenko launched a series of furious blasts at the Israelis, accusing them of marching in "the bloody footsteps of Hitler's executioners." Despite the anguish and rage with which Moscow contemplated the Egyptian defeat, however, and the loss of at least $2 billion in Soviet equipment, it was evident from the first day of the war that the Russians were not prepared to intercede in the fighting. Nor were they capable even of mobilizing support for a resolution demanding Israeli withdrawal. A cease-fire was the one, rather forlorn, alternative left. Accordingly, at 1:00 p.m. on June 8, Federenko submitted his proposal for a cease-fire. This time he no longer attached to it the condition of evacuation, but demanded simply an 8:00 p.m. time limit for the cessation of hostilities. The resolution was passed unanimously. Eban thereupon declared that Israel would abide by its terms, provided the Arab states indicated their agreement.

That same day, informed that his army was virtually eradicated, that no troops were left to defend Cairo, Nasser sent instructions to his UN ambassador in New York, Muhammad al-Kony, to accept the resolution. On the other hand, in Egypt itself the cease-fire was not announced until 11:30 p.m., when most of the population was asleep. At general staff headquarters in Heliopolis, Marshal Abd al-Hakim Amer attempted to commit suicide, but was revived by his friends. The following day Cairo was in sullen mourning. Armed soldiers were stationed throughout the capital to protect its main institutions. Staff officers and cabinet ministers openly accused Nasser of having brought the nation to ruin. That night the Egyptian president, haggard and pale, appeared on television to offer his resignation. Immediately, by prearrangement, thousands of demonstrators poured into Cairo's central square, carrying banners and placards, imploring Nasser to remain on. Three hours later, much to Israel's cynical bemusement, their archenemy declared that he had "reconsidered" and would stay on.

"JERUSALEM THE GOLDEN"

By the evening of June 8, Hussein's acceptance of a cease-fire had reached the United Nations almost simultaneously with Nasser's. Thereby ended the gamble that began when Jordanian troops occupied Government House on the afternoon of June 5 and proceeded to shell the small Israeli detachment on Mount Scopus. At that point, with Dayan's approval, Rabin finally issued the orders to General Narkiss: "Retake Government House, link up with Scopus, and protect the Jerusalem high ground by any means." Much relieved, Narkiss promptly assigned the task of capturing Government House to the local Jerusalem garrison. A company of troops set about ascending the Hill of Evil Counsel, and by mid-afternoon the operation was completed with the loss of eight dead. Simultaneously, a paratroop brigade under the command of Colonel Mordechai Gur was reassigned from its intended Sinai destination and ordered transported by bus from Tel Aviv to Jerusalem. Gur's instructions were to attack Jordanian fortifications on the perimeter of the Arab City, then move against the Legionnaires atop the heights near Mount Scopus.

At the same time, Narkiss ordered the commander of the Harel armored brigade, Colonel Uri Ben-Ari, to bring his force up from the encampment in the Jerusalem Corridor and push through to the ridges between Jerusalem and Ramallah. Word had arrived that the Arab Legion was dispatching heavy reinforcements from the West Bank to the Jerusalem promontory; speed was vital in wresting control of the high ground. Ben-Ari accomplished this feat by moving on half a dozen approaches at once, from the direction of Kiryat Anavim, Ma'aleh HaChamishah, and Motza, among others. Although each route was studded with nests of Jordanian bunkers, trenches, and minefields, the brigade's armor —covered by devastating tactical air support—penetrated almost everywhere. By the morning of the sixth, Ben-Ari's men controlled the Jerusalem mountain ridges.

Inside the New City, meanwhile, the arrival of Gur's paratroopers was a vital windfall for Narkiss. During the late afternoon of June 5, the thirty-seven-year-old Gur sketched out a blueprint for a three-pronged attack against the powerful Jordanian forces ensconced within the Arab City. Reconnoitering was carried out in the final two hours of daylight, and the offensive was scheduled for nightfall. At 7:45 p.m., then, search-

THE CAPTURE OF THE WEST BANK,
JUNE 5–7, 1967

ISRAELI ATTACKS
- June 5
- June 6
- June 7

✹ Israeli areas shelled by Arabs

Arab dispositions

0   MILES   15

LAKE
GALILEE

Degania

Afula

MEDITERRANEAN
SEA

Jenin

Netania

Tulkarem

Jordan River

Qalqilia

Nablus

Jiftliq

DAMIA
BRIDGE

Tel Aviv-Jaffa

J O R D A N

Rehovot

WEST BANK

Ramallah

Jericho

ALLENBY BRIDGE

ABDULLAH BRIDGE

Jerusalem

I S R A E L

Bethlehem

Hebron

DEAD SEA

lights went on atop the Histadrut building and focused their beams on Jordanian artillery and machine gun positions. The Israelis then shelled the illuminated targets. At the same moment the Jerusalem Brigade's ancient Sherman tanks were rolled out of their camouflaged shed and set moving toward the Jordanian bunkers. Their role was to stun the Legionnaires long enough to permit Gur's men to close on the enemy trenches. The attack began at 2:20 a.m. on June 6. Following a half-hour artillery and mortar barrage against Jordanian gun sites on Ammunition Hill and the Police Training School Compound, two battalions of paratroops charged, dynamiting the Legion's machine gun nests. Resistance at the Police Training School collapsed rapidly; but at Ammunition Hill the Legionnaires fought heroically, and the positions had to be stormed, trench by trench, in a fierce and costly battle.

The second prong of the attack was launched from the Mea Sh'arim quarter directly against the Mandelbaum Gate. Once more the fighting was intense, raging from street to street and house to house. With the support of the tanks, nevertheless, the paratroops completed the action by dawn, blasting through from Sheikh Jarrah to the American Colony, where resistance ceased. In the afternoon the final remaining height within the city, Abu Tur, was taken. Mount Scopus now was entirely in Israeli possession, and with it the old Hebrew University campus and Hadassah hospital. By then the walled Old City alone remained in Arab hands, awaiting the third prong of Gur's attack.

Dayan's restraining influence in the war was nowhere more evident than here. His first order to Narkiss on the Old City was: "We'll surround it if necessary, but will not enter." Yet Dayan's was not the last word. After the prodigious victory in Sinai, the other ministers excitedly demanded that the Old City be "liberated." On the night of June 5, even before the Jerusalem offensive was well launched, Eshkol adjourned the cabinet meeting by insisting that "the Old City must be taken, to avert the danger of incessant bombardment [on Jewish Jerusalem]." It was at least in part a rationalization; the vision of the Holy City restored to Jewish hands was all but overwhelming now. Still Dayan held back, not relishing the cost of a frontal assault. At midnight Eshkol pressed him again: "The government wants the Old City." The defense minister continued to procrastinate, hoping rather to invest the surrounding area and ultimately choke off Arab resistance.

Exactly as Dayan anticipated, the outcome of the fighting for the Jerusalem hinterland throughout the rest of the day (June 6) largely sealed the fate of the Old City. Indeed, control of the Jerusalem heights was already determining the future of the entire Jordanian West Bank, for the mountain range looked down on the region's most important towns: Jenin, Nablus, Ramallah, Bethelehem, Hebron, and Jericho, as well as Jerusalem itself. Problems still faced the Israeli commanders, to be sure, even in their descent to lower terrain. The region was thickly settled with villages and towns inhabited by hundreds of thousands of Arab civilians. Additionally, Jordanian regular troops, disciplined, well

THE CAPTURE OF JERUSALEM
JUNE 5–7, 1967
ISRAELI ATTACKS

⟵ June 5
⟵ June 6
⟵ June 7

RADAR HILL

Biddu

Ma'aleh HaChamishah

Beit Iqsa

Tel al-Ful

J O R D A N

ARMORED BRIGADE

MT. SCOPUS

AUGUSTA VICTORIA CHURCH

OLD CITY

I S R A E L   J E R U S A L E M

MT. ZION

GOVERNMENT HOUSE

0   MILES   2

Hadassah Hospital

MT. SCOPUS

DEMILITARIZED ZONE

SHEIKH JARRAH

HEBREW UNIVERSITY

AMERICAN COLONY

AMMUNITION HILL

PARATROOP BRIGADE

MANDELBAUM GATE

AUGUSTA VICTORIA CHURCH

MOSLEM QUARTER

OLD CITY

LION'S GATE

VIA DOLOROSA

MT. OF OLIVES

I S R A E L

CHRISTIAN QUARTER

WESTERN WALL

MOSQUE OF OMAR

HARAM-ES-SHARIF

JAFFA GATE

ARMENIAN QUARTER

JEWISH QUARTER

J O R D A N

MT. ZION

HILL OF EVIL COUNSEL

ABU TUR

JERUSALEM BRIGADE

GOVERNMENT HOUSE (U.N. HEADQUARTERS)

1   MILE   ½

trained, and fully equal in numbers to the Israeli reservists moving toward them, were entrenched in heavily fortified positions. Yet these advantages were powerfully overshadowed not only by Israel's command of the high ground after June 6, but by total Israeli domination of the air. Rabin therefore ordered his generals to launch a coordinated pincers movement through the West Bank. Brigadier David Elazar, the northern front commander, was instructed to sweep southward from Jenin toward Nablus, while Colonel Ben-Ari would descend from the Jerusalem area toward Hebron in the south. And, in fact, the operation was carried out with almost mathematical precision. By late morning of June 7, ravaged by the aerial strafing and bombing, Jordan's Twenty-fifth Infantry and Fortieth Armored brigades collapsed as fighting units. All the major cities of the West Bank were in Israel's hands. Elazar's and Ben-Ari's columns stopped at the Jordan River.

It was on the night of the sixth that Dayan bowed at last to the cabinet's pressure. Word had come that a United Nations cease-fire was imminent; if the Old City were to be taken, it would have to be seized before hostilities ended. The defense minister's one restriction was on artillery or air support, lest the holy places be damaged. Accordingly, at 8:30 a.m. on June 7, Gur ordered an infantry attack against the final remaining Jordanian high point overlooking Jerusalem. It was the Augusta Victoria Church, and it fell easily. Immediately afterward, the paratroops launched a tank and infantry frontal assault against the Lion's Gate, one of the principal entranceways to the walled Old City. Rolling up the narrow Via Dolorosa, the column made directly for the ancient Temple Mount. There the paratroops dashed for the Western Wall to clear it of snipers. They suffered casualties in the process, but within minutes the last firing stopped. The Wall, the Moslem holy places—the Dome of the Rock and the al-Aqsa Mosque—all were in Jewish hands. Arab resistance in Jerusalem ceased.

Hussein had paid bitterly for his gamble. He had lost over 15,000 troops in dead, wounded, and missing, as well as his entire air force and half his armor. He also had been stripped of half his kingdom, its richest agricultural lands, and the tourist revenues from East Jerusalem and Bethlehem that had accounted for 40 percent of his nation's income. And he had forfeited as well the last Hashemite claim on Islam's holy places. His great-grandfather had lost Mecca and Medina to the Saudi dynasty. Now, with the Israeli conquest of al-Aqsa and the Dome of the Rock, the little monarch's heritage as keeper of the Prophetic tradition was all but eradicated. But he had made the Israelis pay, too. The truth was that the Jews had paid a heavier price here than in Sinai: 1,756 casualties against 1,075. No less than a quarter of Israel's losses on the Jordanian front were taken in the battle for Jerusalem, and specifically for the Old City.

Few Israelis begrudged the cost. The firing had not yet stopped around the Western Wall before Rabbi Shlomo Goren, chief chaplain of the Israeli army, rushed to the holy site to loose a triumphant blast on his ram's horn. Dayan, Rabin, and Eshkol soon followed, dazed and awestruck by the talisman they had recovered. Touching the flagstones of the ancient wall, even hardened veterans wept. That same morning of June 7, Naomi Shemer, composer of a newly released ballad, "Jerusalem the Golden," was at al-Arish to sing for the troops. When the news flashed on the radio that the Old City was in Israel's hands, she immediately altered certain of the lyrics, then was deluged with cheers as she sang her haunting new version:

> We have come back to the deep wells
> To the marketplace again.
> The trumpet sounds on the Mount of the Temple
> In the Old City.
> In the caverns of the cliff
> Glitter a thousand suns.
> We shall go down to the Dead Sea again
> By the road to Jericho.

Taken up exultantly by the entire population, "Jerusalem the Golden" instantly became the anthem of the Six-Day War.

RETRIBUTION ON THE GOLAN HEIGHTS

The final decision awaiting the government was the action to be taken against Syria. It seemed a perversion of justice that the most implacable of Israel's enemies, a nation whose border incendiarism in large measure had precipitated the current war, should now be spared retribution or allowed to keep the strategic advantage of the Golan. All the more so as Syrian gunners on the heights continued to rain tons of shells on Galilee's northernmost settlements. Dayan, to be sure, fearful of provoking the Russians, still counseled restraint. But again, as in the case of the Old City, the defense minister's reservations were not shared by other members of the cabinet or by the army. Neither were they shared by the inhabitants of the northern Galilee villages, and these were the citizens who ultimately resolved the issue. On the evening of June 8, as the war ended on other fronts, the chairman of the upper Galilee local council and other Galilee representatives drove to Jerusalem, where they were received by Eshkol. Moved by their appeal for an offensive, the prime minister took the unprecedented step of bringing his visitors into a cabinet meeting, where they stated their views. The response was instantaneous; the other ministers unanimously demanded an offensive against the Golan. Events on the battlefield in any case were developing their own momentum. General Elazar, the northern front commander, had five brigades at his disposal, and these troops were chafing for action. Indeed, desire for revenge against the Syrians was uncontrollable by then. Volunteers were pouring into the northern units, among them men from other, recently demobilized brigades.

At 3:00 a.m. on June 9 Dayan was informed that the Egyptian and Jordanian cease-fires had come into effect. It was at this point, at last, that he decided to move against the northern enemy. Unable to locate Rabin, he called Elazar directly at 7:00 a.m. and issued the orders to attack. Still the defense minister was cautious, and instructed Elazar to concentrate exclusively on the northern sector of the Golan, in the Banias area, and not to go beyond the demilitarized zone. For that matter, even a limited sector offensive appeared a grim prospect. The Syrian plateau towered between 400 and 1,700 feet above Israel's Chula Valley settlements. Elazar's troops were restricted to an approach from the west, and it was on the west that the Syrians awaited them with the most fearsome defense complex in the Middle East. Running more than 10 miles deep, the fortifications comprised level upon level of steel-and-concrete emplacements, underground tunnels, dug-in tanks, heavy guns, antitank weapons, and rocket launchers. Moreover, the Syrians had assigned three brigades to these defense works, and six additional brigades in close reserve, half of them armored.

To solve the problem of cracking this horror, Elazar made the audacious decision to risk a breakthrough on the Golan's best fortified sector, one that was exceptionally difficult for motorized transport, but which at least had the advantage of being very short. It was the Banias area he had in mind, where the Quneitra road was only two and a half miles from the Israeli border. "I chose a narrow frontal assault," Elazar later explained. "It's the most risky. . . . But its advantage is that if you do succeed, you soon have your troops in the enemy's rear. This is very important when you're fighting the Arabs. Psychologically, they break easily." Elazar had chosen a route so angular, so densely strewn with boulders, that the enemy had positioned a mere 200 men on the ridges above. The number seemed adequate, for the likelihood of attack was apparently precluded by the Golan's fortifications. These included two strongpoints that precisely dominated Elazar's chosen route of ascent. The first was a hill 900 feet up, Tel Azaziat—known to the Israelis as "the dragon of the heights." The next, 700 feet higher, was Tel Faq'r. The troops picked for the advance against these emplacements were members of the crack Golani Brigade and were themselves largely drawn from the upper Galilee; most had grown up under the shadow of the Syrian guns. Now, at high noon of June 9, in the glare of the burning sun, the Israelis set out to ascend the heights, with bulldozers clearing the rocks, followed by the aging Sherman tanks, and infantrymen bringing up the rear.

Confounded by Elazar's route of attack, the Syrians initially regarded it a feint. They were unable in any case to call up reinforcements. For two days the Israeli air force had been raining bombs and napalm on the Syrian ridges. Dug in under tons of concrete, the Arabs held their ground under the paralyzing bombardment, but not a man could get through to another position. No ammunition could be moved in, not even water. The Syrians concentrated simply on firing back with all they had. What they had was considerable, and they inflicted heavy losses, among them the

Israeli battle commander, then his second in command, then his third in command. The buried Syrian tanks finally were knocked out of action by infantry crawling up the hill and dropping in grenades. Tel Faq'r offered the toughest resistance. The first wave of Israeli infantry reached the barbed-wire defenses, but many of the attackers were cut down. A few dozen troops of the second wave penetrated the wire and minefield, and the third wave finally reached the entrenchments. The struggle was an inferno. After three hours of fighting, however, much of it with fists, knives, and rifle butts, the positions were taken. Few Arabs survived the onslaught. The Israelis were uninterested in taking prisoners.

Even as the battle raged, Elazar's two diversionary attacks farther to the south began to make progress on their own. By darkness, the Israelis had two bridgeheads on the heights. Consolidating their positions, they rested during the night. The following morning, June 10, they embarked on the next stage of their attack. With heavy air support, they advanced toward al-Quneitra, a town of 80,000 that served as administrative-military capital of the Golan. At noon of June 10, too, while the Syrian army in the north reeled under these hammer blows, Brigadier Elad Peled's division of paratroopers and infantry launched an attack on the communications network atop the forbidding ridge stretching from Tawafiq through Kafr Harib to El Al. The heights commanded the entire northeastern Galilee area and were all but inaccessible from the Israeli side. After a heavy artillery and air bombardment, Peled's supporting tanks moved out at 2:00 p.m. Despite the harsh, angular climb, the Israelis reached the top and advanced rapidly toward Tawafiq. At 3:30 the paratroops entered the town. It had been abandoned.

Indeed, the Syrians appeared to have deserted the entire area. A paratroop unit was then swiftly airlifted by helicopter to Kafr Harib. Here again virtually no resistance was encountered. Once more the troops were airborne, this time east to the village of El Al, which also surrendered almost immediately. From then on the heliborne troops continued advancing in leaps, encountering only isolated pockets of Syrian forces, before going on to their next stop. Elazar's strategy had been proved right: crack the main fortifications, move onto the roads behind the Syrians, and the enemy will panic. Thus, by early afternoon on June 10, Quneitra also was taken without a fight. The morale of the Syrian army was shattered irretrievably, its troops were fleeing for their lives, many of them abandoning tanks with motors running. Radio Damascus hysterically exhorted the army to mount a last effort to save the nation's capital, but these appeals simply created additional panic among the men. The officers now were the first to bolt. "The black ones are running away," a voice, in Russian, contemptuously remarked over a Syrian army wavelength.

At 5:30 p.m. on June 9, the Syrian representative in the Security Council announced that his government had ordered an end to fighting in compliance with the United Nations cease-fire resolution. Within a half hour, then, Israel's delegate, Gideon Rafael, assured the Council that similar orders had gone out to Israeli armed forces on the northern front. But in fact the Jews were maintaining their drive with the intention now of seizing the entire Golan. The Soviets discerned this purpose, and were alarmed by the likelihood not only that Quneitra would fall, but conceivably even Damascus. Federenko thereupon warned the Security Council that "other measures" would be taken unless Israel halted its advance immediately. At the defense ministry in Tel Aviv, tension was growing as the Golan offensive raced the United Nations cease-fire deadline. By then Rabin personally was directing Elazar's battle plan, his timetable altered from hour to hour by Dayan, who in turn was kept informed on developments in Washington and New York.

At 8:00 a.m. Washington time on June 10, Kosygin telephoned Johnson over the "hot line," demanding that the Israelis be stopped forthwith. Johnson soothingly replied that Israel had given every assurance that its forces would not attack Damascus. Later in the morning, however, two more direct phone messages arrived from Kosygin, and their tone was increasingly ominous. In the White House there was genuine concern now that the Soviets might intervene. Johnson accordingly made a crucial decision. He ordered the Sixth Fleet, 400 miles from the Golan battle zone, to dispatch three task forces in the direction of the Syrian coast. Immediately the aircraft carriers *Saratoga* and *America* headed east with their destroyer escorts and 200 planes. But at the same time, "in the strongest possible terms," Secretary of State Rusk urged Israeli Ambassador Avraham Harman to accept a cease-fire. The Israeli pincers in any event had closed on the Golan by then, and Dayan was working out the arrangements for a cease-fire through General Odd Bull. The Six-Day War ended officially at 6:30 p.m., Israel time, on June 10.

It had been a catastrophic defeat for the Syrians. In twenty-seven hours of battle they had lost 2,500 killed and 5,000 wounded, a third of their tanks, half their artillery, while 80,000 of their soldiers and civilians had fled the Golan. Israel lost 115 killed and 306 wounded, as well as 2 civilians killed and 16 wounded from the Syrian artillery bombardments against the Galilee settlements. The entire Golan plateau was now in Israel's hands; the long nightmare of Syrian bombardment was over. So, almost at the very moment, was the last Arab pretension to a blockade of Israel's waterways. At Sharm es-Sheikh, Israeli troops welcomed a chartered Zim freighter that had steamed uneventfully through the Strait of Tiran en route to Eilat. That same day, too, the government printing office in Cairo began turning out the first issues of a new Egyptian postage stamp that had been designed three days before the war began. It displayed a genial, confident Nasser acknowledging the cheers of a huge throng. In the stamp's lower right corner Israel appeared in flames.

Israel lost 759 troops killed in the war, and approximately three times that many wounded. The nation's equipment losses were 40 planes and 80 tanks. The Arabs may have suffered up to 30,000 casualties, at least 450 planes and 1,000 tanks destroyed or captured, as well as vast quantities of supplementary equipment. More important, a new military-geographic reality had been created in the Middle East. Before the war, the main

THE CONQUEST OF THE GOLAN HEIGHTS,
JUNE 9–10, 1967

LEBANON

Metulla

Banias

Dan

Dafna

Kiryat Shmonah

△ TEL AZAZIAT

Damascus

CHULA VALLEY

al-Quneitra

Ashmura

G'dot

ISRAEL

S Y R I A

B'NOT YA'AKOV BRIDGE

GOLAN HEIGHTS

Safed

Butunia

Rosh Pina

Jordan River

Almagor

LAKE GALILEE

El Al

Tiberias

Ein Gev

Fiq

Kafr Harib

Yarmuk River

Ha'On

Degania

Tawafiq

J O R D A N

al-Hamma

THE CONQUEST OF THE GOLAN HEIGHTS, JUNE 9–10, 1967

⟶ June 9 major Israeli advance

⟶ June 9 secondary advance

⟶ June 10

⛱ Paratroop landings

Arab forces

✴ Areas shelled by Arabs

0   MILES   10

Israeli population center had lain within four minutes' flying time of the nearest Arab air base. Any Arab land offensive into Israel, except in the southern Negev, would have affected thickly inhabited areas. Much of Israel's narrow waistline had fallen within Arab artillery range, as had Jewish Jerusalem and the northern Galilee settlements. Now, after the war, the situation was reversed. It was Israeli planes and troops that were within close striking distance of Amman, Damascus, and Cairo. Jewish Jerusalem no longer was on the firing line, nor was the Galilee, nor any other Israeli population center. In the south, the 200-mile frontier between the Sinai and the Negev deserts, with its threatening spike of the Gaza Strip into Israel, was replaced by the 110-mile barrier of the Suez Canal. In the east, Israel had pushed the long and involuted Israeli-Hashemite border to the comparatively straight north-south line of the River Jordan and the Dead Sea.

What accounted for this earthquake? The explanation hardly could be attributed to superiority in weapons; the equipment advantage was entirely the Arabs'. Rather, as in earlier Arab-Israeli wars, the decisive factor was the human element. The literacy gap between the Arab and Israeli common soldier was one factor in this equation. Leadership was another. The Egyptian staff officers were guilty of astonishing overconfidence and lack of organization. At no time did they make a serious effort to develop an integrated battle plan with their Syrian and Jordanian counterparts. It was this lack of coordination that produced the decisive Arab blunder of allowing the Israelis to fight three separate and consecutive wars: against Egypt; then, at Israel's initiative, against Jordan; and finally against Syria. The force of personal example was vital, as well. At almost every echelon, Arab staff and operations officers panicked once the Jews achieved their initial breakthroughs. It was revealing in this regard that Egyptian officers comprised less than 15 percent of their nation's total casualties; the ratio in the Israeli armed forces was twice as high. In the end, however, it was more than literacy and commitment that tipped the balance in Israel's favor. It was the courage born of desperation—and at all levels. Awarded an honorary doctorate from the Hebrew University three weeks after the war, Rabin did not embellish the facts in his speech before an audience—an entire nation—ecstatic in its miraculous deliverance:

> Our airmen, who struck the enemies' planes so accurately that no one in the world understands how it was done and people seek technological explanations or secret weapons; our armored troops who beat the enemy even when their equipment was inferior to his; our soldiers in all other branches . . . who overcame our enemies everywhere, despite the latter's superior numbers and fortifications—all these revealed not only coolness and courage in battle but . . . an understanding that only their personal stand against the greatest dangers would achieve victory for their country and for their families, and that if victory was not theirs the alternative was annihilation.

This evaluation of Israel's moral case was widely shared throughout the world. The blood-curdling threats loosed by the Arab nations in the weeks before the war, the quiet discipline of Israeli soldiers and civilians, touched the hearts of common men everywhere. In western Europe there were mass parades in support of Israel during the last days before fighting erupted, and Jewish and non-Jewish volunteers formed in long lines outside Israeli embassies to offer their services. Political figures, artists, and intellectuals were among those who signed petitions affirming Israel's right to exist. In Stockholm members of Parliament discussed resigning in order to fight in Israel. In Dutch churches prayers were offered for Israel's survival. And after hostilities broke out, the Western response to Israel's underdog victory was one of almost uncontrollable joy; although in the United States, this delight may have been compounded by relief that American troops had not been obliged once again to participate in a Vietnam-style rescue effort.

It was notable, too, that the reaction even of the Communist world was by no means unanimously hostile to Israel. Although most of western Europe's Communist parties officially supported the Arabs, their rank-and-file were undisguisedly pro-Israeli. In eastern Europe, moreover, government pro-Arab policy for the first time encountered active popular opposition. In Poland spontaneous demonstrations were mounted in favor of Israel, and numerous high Polish officials, even some ministers, were unwilling to sign petitions branding Israel the aggressor. In Czechoslovakia editorial writers declined to publish articles against Israel. The Rumanian government flatly refused to take an anti-Israel position. More generally, of course, public opinion was not allowed to influence official party doctrine. On June 9 the Communist bloc leaders gathered in Moscow, where seven of them issued a long declaration of solidarity with the Arab cause, promising help to the Arab nations should Israel continue its "aggression." Within the next few days all the Communist governments, except for Rumania, severed diplomatic relations with Israel.

A DIPLOMATIC CONSOLIDATION

On the afternoon of June 13, following confirmation of the cease-fires, Federenko in the Security Council made plain his government's intention to retrieve by diplomacy what the Arabs had failed to accomplish by war. Cease-fire agreements alone were not enough, the Russian insisted; Israel must be condemned, and ordered to withdraw unconditionally to the 1949 armistice lines. Federenko warned, too, that inaction by the Security Council would make it "necessary to seek other ways and means to see to it that the United Nations does its duty under the Charter." This was by far Federenko's toughest speech. Yet it hardly unsettled the representatives of the other Great Powers; if the Russians had not intervened during the actual fighting, it seemed unlikely that they would take military steps once hostilities had ended. The Americans, particularly, were determined that their support of Israel, which had been embarrassingly ineffectual in the critical weeks before the war, should at least not be found wanting after Israel had resolved an agonizing international crisis and defended its security by its own efforts and blood. "If ever there were a prescription for renewed hostilities," insisted Goldberg, "the Soviet draft resolution is that prescription." The United States delegate went on to argue that the one feasible solution was encouragement of "agreements between the parties" themselves, and for this the Council had "an urgent obligation to facilitate [such agreements] and to help build an atmosphere in which fruitful discussions will be possible." From the outset, then, the line between the Soviet and the American views was drawn.

On June 14 only four delegations supported Federenko's proposal to condemn Israel. The rest abstained. The next paragraph of the Soviet resolution, urging withdrawal from occupied territory, gained only six votes. In its final meeting that same afternoon, the Council achieved its one show of unanimity on a rather pallid resolution asking observance of the Geneva Convention toward war prisoners on both sides, the exchange of war refugees, and humane treatment of conquered populations. Whereupon, angered by his lack of success, Federenko tried a new approach. He requested U Thant to order the General Assembly into special session. The precedent of bypassing the Security Council in favor of the larger body actually had been set in the Korean War of 1950, and was later used in resolving the Hungarian and Suez crises of 1956. In 1950, ironically, it was the United States that had initiated the technique in order to circumvent the Soviet veto. Now it was to be invoked by the Soviet Union, and over the protests of the United States, in an apparent effort to mobilize the Afro-Asian bloc against Israel.

The Assembly convened on June 19. To emphasize the importance Moscow attached to the proceedings, Kosygin himself arrived to deliver his government's first statement. In some respects, the prime minister's opening speech was milder than had been anticipated. At no time did he threaten to take the issue of Israeli "aggression" out of the world body. He acknowledged Israel's right to exist and even ventured the hope "that the General Assembly will take an effective decision ensuring . . . the restoration and consolidation of peace and security in the Middle East." The remark implied awareness that the United Nations would have to come up with more than a limited restoration of the status quo of June 4, 1967. But then, shifting to the offensive, Kosygin accused the United States and Britain of moral complicity with Israel in the recent Middle Eastern war and asked once again for a condemnation of Israel, for total Israeli withdrawal from occupied Arab territory, and for financial restitution to the Arab countries.

The Arab delegates of course supported the proposal unanimously. So did most of the other Moslem ambassadors, together with those of the Communist bloc. The representatives of Denmark, Britain, Italy, and Belgium urged acceptance of the principle of Israeli withdrawal but linked it with international guarantees for the existence of all Middle Eastern states. The compromise did not impress the Americans. Once more Goldberg argued that a stable and durable peace could be achieved only through negotiated arrangements; and those arrangements, he declared, must encompass recognized boundaries and other provisions, "including disengagement and withdrawal of forces, that will give [the nations] security against terror, destruction and war." As the Israelis gratefully noted, the American formulation declined to specify the configuration of the recognized boundaries or to assert that withdrawal necessarily required an evacuation of Israeli forces to the 1949 armistice lines.

Few diplomats expected that either the Soviet or the American resolutions would achieve two-thirds majority approval in a General Assembly fractured by competing political interests. The best that could be anticipated was a compromise formula. The Latin American bloc came up with one, on June 26. It placed its initial emphasis on the need for universal recognition of Israel and on the full right of Israeli passage through international waterways. But the draft also asserted that the problem of refugees had to be confronted, together with a recognition that alteration of boundaries by force was inadmissible. In contrast, the "nonaligned" nations, including Yugoslavia, India, and many African and Asian states, favored a text that essentially supported the Arab and Soviet demand for Israeli withdrawal and restitution. France, by then adopting an undisguised pro-Arab stance, endorsed the "nonaligned" draft. All efforts to bridge the gap between the two versions failed. On July 4, therefore, first the nonaligned, then the Latin American, draft was submitted for vote. Neither won the necessary two-thirds majority. During a week's reprieve in the General Assembly session, between July 5 and 12, the search for a compromise formula went on against a backdrop of entrenched Arab hostility to an accommodation with Israel and an equally intransigent Israeli refusal to contemplate even partial withdrawal except through direct peace negotiations with the Arabs. The prognosis for a settlement was not encouraging. Following another week of aimless discussions, the special session adjourned.

By the time the regular session convened, on September 19, Goldberg had abandoned his former insistence upon direct negotiations between Arabs and Israelis, and envisaged the possibility instead of third-party mediation. It was at this point that Lord Caradon (Hugh Foote), the British delegate, emerged as the key negotiator between the various alignments. A former governor of Cyprus, widely experienced in dealings with the volatile Greek and Turkish communities, Caradon brought an incisive imagination and almost superhuman patience to his discussions with the Latin American and nonaligned representatives. His aim was to seek out a consensus that would incorporate the two vital principles of Israeli withdrawal and the unambiguous right of Israel—and other Middle Eastern nations—to coexist in full and equal sovereignty. At first, little flexibility was registered among partisans of either side. But then, suddenly, events in the Middle East itself took a critical new turn. On October 21 Egyptian missiles sank the Israeli destroyer *Eilat;* and on October 24 the

Israelis retaliated by shelling the major oil installations in the Egyptian port town of Suez. Thereupon, in response to both Israeli and Egyptian appeals, the Security Council urgently intensified its peace-seeking efforts.

In mid-November, Caradon's strenuous diplomacy at last began to bear fruit. A formula was hammered out acceptable to a majority of the Security Council representatives, although it was a good deal less than either the Arabs or the Israelis would have preferred. On November 22 the Englishman's version was accepted unanimously as Security Council Resolution 242. On several points the text was deliberately ambiguous. It stated:

> The Security Council . . . [e]mphasizing the inadmissibility of the acquisition of territory by war and the need to work for a just and lasting peace in which every State in the area can live in security. . . .
>
> 1.) Affirms that the fulfillment of Charter principles requires the establishment of a just and lasting peace in the Middle East which should include the application of both the following principles:
>   i. Withdrawal of Israeli armed forces from territories occupied in the recent conflict;
>   ii. Termination of all claims or states of belligerency and respect for and acknowledgment of the sovereignty, territorial integrity and political independence of every State in the area and their right to live in peace within secure and recognized boundaries free from threats or acts of force;
> 2.) Affirms further the necessity
>   i. For guaranteeing freedom of navigation through international waterways in the area;
>   ii. For achieving a just settlement of the refugee problem;
>   iii. For guaranteeing the territorial inviolability and political independence of every State in the area, through measures including the establishment of demilitarized zones;
> 3.) Requests of the Secretary-General to designate a Special Representative to proceed to the Middle East to . . . promote agreement and assist efforts to achieve a peaceful and accepted settlement in accordance with the provisions and principles in this resolution. . . .

The Arabs put their own interpretation and emphasis on the resolution: withdrawal, and settlement of the refugee question. Israel, conversely, placed its stress on the absence of the word "the" before "territories," implying, in its view (and in that of the United States), a commitment to less than full withdrawal; on the recognition of sovereign integrity and renunciation of force in the Middle East; on guaranteed freedom of passage through international waters; on a special representative to "promote agreement and assist efforts to achieve a peaceful and accepted settlement" —meaning (as Israel saw it) a final negotiated settlement. It appeared to be a not unencouraging valedictory to what was, after all, an offensive military campaign; and the more so by contrast with the universal censure that had greeted Israel's Sinai victory in 1956. This time, too, a majority of the United Nations representatives appeared to reflect the new atmosphere of mild but purposeful optimism. "Resolution 242 of the Security

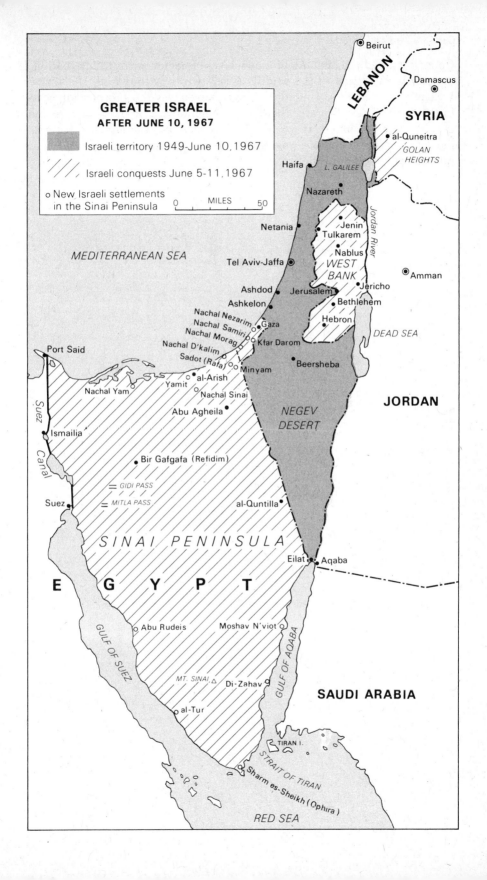

GREATER ISRAEL
AFTER JUNE 10, 1967

Israeli territory 1949-June 10, 1967

Israeli conquests June 5-11, 1967

o New Israeli settlements
in the Sinai Peninsula

0   MILES   50

Beirut

LEBANON

Damascus

SYRIA

al-Quneitra

GOLAN
HEIGHTS

Haifa   L. GALILEE

Nazareth

Netania   Jenin
Tulkarem

Nablus

WEST
BANK

Jordan River

Amman

MEDITERRANEAN SEA

Tel Aviv-Jaffa

Ashdod   Jerusalem   Jericho

Ashkelon   Bethlehem

Nachal Nezarim   Hebron

Nachal Samiri   Gaza

Nachal Morag   Kfar Darom

Nachal D'kalim

Sadot (Rafa)   DEAD SEA

Port Said   Minyam

Nachal Yam   Yamit   al-Arish   Beersheba

Nachal Sinai

Abu Agheila

Ismailia   NEGEV
DESERT

JORDAN

Suez Canal

Bir Gafgafa (Refidim)

= GIDI PASS

Suez   = MITLA PASS   al-Quntilla

S I N A I   P E N I N S U L A

E   G   Y   P   T

Eilat   Aqaba

GULF OF SUEZ

Abu Rudeis   Moshav N'viot

GULF OF AQABA

SAUDI ARABIA

MT. SINAI   Di-Zahav

al-Tur

TIRAN I.

STRAIT OF TIRAN

Sharm es-Sheikh (Ophira)

RED SEA

Council marked the opening of a new level of achievement in international diplomacy in regard to the Middle East," wrote Arthur Lall, the former Indian delegate to the United Nations. "Never was the prospect of peace in the Middle East brighter than at the beginning of 1968." Lall's evaluation was widely shared. It was neither the least nor the last of diplomatic illusions on the apparent susceptibility of the Arab-Israeli crisis to a rational, negotiated solution.

ISRAEL AS EMPIRE

A REGIME OF IMPROVISATION: JERUSALEM

The Israeli people stepped from darkness into light. Even the bereaved among them were shaken by the overpowering relief of collective deliverance, by the unimaginable scope of their triumph, and by the crowning miracle of Jerusalem restored. Yet the impact of the June victory was to be discerned not alone in the euphoria of the Israelis, but in the stunned and fearful bewilderment of the captured Arab population. Throughout the occupied territories, as white handkerchiefs fluttered poignantly from the window ledges of each shuttered little stone house, the Arab inhabitants within sat drawn and mute in the shock of defeat, of alien rule imposed, of employment and markets jeopardized, of currency and savings in limbo. No fewer than a million of these instant "subjects" remained in the 28,000 square miles of terrain that had fallen dramatically and unexpectedly into Israel's possession. Their numbers included 670,000 Arabs on the West Bank and East Jerusalem, 356,000 in the Gaza Strip, 33,000 in Sinai, and 6,000 (mainly Druze) on the Golan Heights.

Those with first claim on Israel's attention plainly were the Arabs nearest at hand, the families who lived on the other side of the barriers that had divided Jerusalem for nineteen years. Teddy Kollek, the chunky, energetic mayor of Israeli Jerusalem, now found himself responsible for a metropolitan area over twice the size of the Jewish New City, with an Arab population of 67,000 souls. Quite literally, the Arab Jerusalemites were fellow townsmen. Their legal status may not yet have been clear. Neither were Israel's duties to them under international law—particularly when Jewish shrines and cemeteries recovered from the Arab-occupied zones were found to have been despoiled and desecrated, in palpable Jordanian violation of the Rhodes armistice agreement. From the outset, nevertheless, it was the decision of the Israeli cabinet that all of Jerusalem's inhabitants, Jews and Arabs alike, were entitled to law and order, to freedom of religious worship, and to efficient and humane public services. Thus, even before the announcement of the cease-fire, municipal employees from the New City were crossing into East Jerusalem to repair broken water pipes and severed electrical wires, to dismantle wall-barriers, roadblocks, and barbed wire, and to cart away debris. The electrical grid and telephone systems of the Arab and Jewish municipalities were unified. Chronically water-short, Arab Jerusalem was linked to the plentiful West Jerusalem reservoirs. As a consequence of these efforts, the—physical—quality of life in Arab Jerusalem, a sprawling, underdeveloped Jordanian regional community, soon was improved beyond measure over its prewar level.

Yet the Israelis plainly were inspired by more than humanitarian considerations in restoring and augmenting this network of services. They were making clear, too, that they had returned to a reunited city to stay. Their purpose was apparent not only in the enthusiasm with which Mayor Kollek shared his staff's talents with Jerusalem's Arab citizens and absorbed hundreds of Arab municipal workers and inspectors in a combined and enlarged administration. It was emphasized, as well, in the removal of scores of Arab householders from the Old City's former Jewish quarter and from the bedraggled warren of flats opposite the Western Wall—thus enabling Israeli engineers to clear a plaza for Jewish worshippers. While compensation and alternative housing were offered, these measures were brutally straightforward in their implications for the city's future. For that matter, the implications swiftly enough became quite explicit. On June 27, 1967, the Knesset passed three laws that had been drafted by the cabinet within days after Israeli troops had entered the Old City.

The first bill, an amendment to the Law and Administration Ordinance of 1948, declared: "The law, jurisdiction, and administration of the State shall extend to any area of the Land of Israel designated by the Government by order." The provision was accompanied by a simultaneous order designating East Jerusalem and its environs as henceforth under this Israeli "law, jurisdiction and administration." For all practical purposes, the announcement incorporated metropolitan Jerusalem into the State of Israel. The Knesset then immediately passed a second bill authorizing the minister of the interior, "at his discretion and without an enquiry," to "enlarge, by proclamation, the area of a particular municipality by the inclusion of a [designated] area" under the Law and Administration Ordinance of 1948. The interior minister acted at once, therefore, enlarging the Municipality of Jerusalem to include the city's surrounding hinterland. Finally, in an effort to disarm any world outcry against its legislation, the Knesset enacted a third statute protecting the holy places "from desecration . . . and from anything likely to violate the freedom of access of the members of the different religions to the places sacred to them or their feelings with regard to them."

Israel's official position later was that the annexation of East Jerusalem, including its Old City, had not formally occurred—that is, that the newly incorporated areas still were neither legally nor juridically part of Israel. The explanation for this ingratiating sophistry became clear shortly afterward in the reaction of the United Nations. On July 4, 1967, the General Assembly by a vote of 99 to 0 adopted a resolution declaring that it considered the changed status of Jerusalem as invalid, and calling upon Israel to rescind its measures. In answer to this, and to a later, similar resolution, Eban insisted that the "term [annexation] . . . is out of place. The measures adopted relate to the integration of Jerusalem in the administration and municipal spheres, and furnish a legal basis for the protection of the Holy Places in Jerusalem." The rationalization was gratuitous. What Abdullah had captured in 1948, not by international law but by war, and had incorporated into his kingdom, now had been taken back by Israel as an act of self-defense. This was an argument the world would better have understood and respected.

As it was, from the moment the gates of East Jerusalem were opened to free traffic only days after the cease-fire, the local Arabs found themselves Hashemite citizens in an Israeli city. As residents of Jerusalem, they shared the privileges and obligations enjoyed by others of the city's inhabitants. They simply did not become Israeli citizens. Nor did this bicephalous status appear to perturb the Jerusalem Arabs unduly, once they had absorbed the fact of Israeli conquest. Rather, the populations of the eastern and western cities began mingling freely for the first time in nineteen years. Old acquaintances were renewed, Arabs visited homes they had abandoned two decades previously, and Mayor Kollek attended prayer services at the Haram es-Sharif on Friday, June 30. Unquestionably, the new relationship was less than a bed of roses for Arab Jerusalemites. For months they were hopelessly confused by the enlarged municipal bureaucracy and by the notorious peremptoriness of Israel's civil employees. But neither were they oblivious to their essential physical security, nor to the palpable improvement of their communal services. These included, by December 1967: 15 miles of streets newly paved, 1,200 new street lamps, thousands of new saplings planted in city gardens, new waste-removal equipment, and an average of fifty Arab houses connected to the municipal water system each week. Indeed, Kollek tripled the municipal budget for East Jerusalem. Beyond these improvements, too, hundreds of thousands of Israelis were flooding into the Old City, curious, mildly friendly, and buying with hard cash virtually everything Arab shopkeepers and artisans had on display. If Israeli rule was less than a psychological comfort, neither was it the hell of brutality that Arab governments had warned their peoples to expect.

THE WEST BANK

Of the approximately one million Arabs who fell into Israeli hands throughout the captured territories, at least 340,000 were refugees from the original 1948 fighting. These included 220,000 packed into the squalid camps of Gaza and another 120,000 living on the West Bank as Jordanian citizens. In the course of the 1967 war and its immediate aftermath, moreover, some 150,000 West Bank Arabs fled to the East Bank or to Syria, and among these were to be found not only veteran inhabitants of the area but nearly 80,000 occupants of West Bank refugee encampments. Most of these 1967 fugitives departed voluntarily; no attempts were made to influence them to leave. To be sure, Israeli law, passed by the Knesset in the early 1950s to deal with the refugees of the 1948 war (Chapter XVI), barred their return.

In this case, nevertheless, heavy United Nations pressure was exerted on Israel immediately after June 1967 to reverse the decision. Thereupon the Eshkol cabinet agreed to an initial repatriation of 40,000 Arabs. Given this agreement, it is probable that the émigrés would have hurried back within a matter of days. Yet they were blocked from doing so by the ineptitude of the Jordanian authorities themselves, who rejected the questionnaire form that bore the stamp of the Israeli government. When finally a joint insignia was approved, the Jordanians still appeared loath to encourage any meaningful return. By the end of August, as a result, only 14,000 West Bank Arabs had crossed back, and the Jews then temporarily suspended the entire repatriation. Even so, the Israelis were hesitant to appear dogmatic on the issue, and in the next six years an additional 40,000 refugees gradually were permitted to return. Their homes, land, and other property at all times were maintained intact.

In the interim, the Arabs of the occupied territories encountered a military government that had been organized swiftly and pragmatically within days after the end of the war. It was Dayan, as minister of defense, who laid down the guidelines for this regime, and who did so with a breadth of imagination that equaled any of his earlier military achievements. He insisted, first of all, on speaking directly with hundreds of mukhtars and other Arab notables, in an effort to persuade them that cooperation with the Israelis was the only alternative to a breakdown of vital public services. The appraisal was hardly an exaggeration. The Arab population was isolated from its traditional administrative centers east of the river. The banking system was paralyzed. Agriculture and industry were deprived of their usual markets, and tourism had all but ceased. "We do not ask you to love us," Dayan explained to the anxious mukhtars. "We ask only that you care for your own people and work with us in restoring the normalcy of their lives."

For his part, the general was determined that Israeli occupation should be as mild and unobtrusive as possible. It had long been his conviction, anyway, that Ben-Gurion in earlier years had been too hard on the Arabs of Israel. That mistake would not be repeated in the captured territories. Accordingly, Dayan now ordered all military command centers to be located discreetly away from principal thoroughfares. The policy of non-visibility worked better in theory than in practice. While the troop presence in East Jerusalem indeed remained minimal, the revival of the fedayun movement in the West Bank (p. 683) ultimately led to sterner Israeli measures. By 1969 entire Israeli military camps had been transferred to the occupied areas, and teams of gun-carrying Israeli soldiers were to be seen moving continually and warily through the streets of Nablus, Ramallah, Jericho, and others of the West Bank's principal towns. At Dayan's suggestion, nevertheless, the cabinet agreed that Jordanian law would remain operative throughout the West Bank, that it would continue to be enforced largely by the prewar Arab administration, and that in the Gaza enclave civil government would also be directed mainly by resident Arab officials. Ultimately, fewer than 220 Israeli army and civilian personnel oversaw these local regimes. It became the hope of the military government that Arab citizens in the occupied areas should be able to carry on their activities without so much as setting eyes on an Israeli official, if not an Israeli soldier. This discreet supervision was of course facilitated by Israel's obvious proximity to the "administered" territories (as the Jews described them). Indeed, Israel's major cities actually were closer to the West Bank and Gaza than to the central Negev. Within weeks, therefore, an Israeli government committee devised an arrangement for each military command center (in Judea, Samaria, Gaza, Sinai, and the Golan) to be staffed with representatives from the ministries of agriculture, health, justice, education, and others—all cooperating unobtrusively with the Arab civil service. If existing local taxes or Jordanian subsidies (p. 672) occasionally were inadequate to finance municipal and other budgets, the Israeli West Bank Command itself made up the necessary difference. Except for the initial transfer of army camps to the West Bank, the cost rarely exceeded $35 million annually, and it was a modest price to pay for Arab aquiescence.

Other measures were taken almost immediately to ensure the flow of goods and services in the territories. In August 1967 the Israeli pound was made legal tender on the West Bank, coequally with the Jordanian dinar. In the Gaza Strip and the Golan, local monies were accepted at the Zurich exchange rate, although the pound alone was declared official currency. Once these financial directives were issued, banking activity was restored and remittances again began to pour in from abroad. More than any other innovation, however, it was freedom of movement that revived the economy of the occupied lands. The policy was instituted first in the West Bank itself, where Dayan eliminated all road barriers and restrictions only days after the fighting ended, then soon afterward did away with curfews. In August, too, the last remaining prohibitions on Israeli travel were canceled and free crossing was allowed from Jewish territory to the West Bank and Gaza Strip. The response to this cancellation was an avalanche of Israeli tourism in the bazaars of Arab cities and towns. But free movement eventually worked both ways, for several months later the government began issuing permits to citizens of the West Bank and Gaza for daily trips to Israel. And finally, in the summer of 1970, Dayan eliminated permit requirements altogether, and West Bankers were allowed complete liberty of travel throughout Israel. Tens of thousands of Arabs immediately surged across the "Green Line"—the old 1949 armistice frontier—visiting Israeli cities, beaches, and resorts. The impact of this free movement became particularly evident in the labor sector. East Jerusalemites were offered work opportunities in the Jewish New City almost from the moment the war ended. Subsequently, employment was opened elsewhere in Israel for other West Bank and Gaza Arabs. Their numbers reached 15,000 by June 1968 and soon afterward climbed dramatically (p. 688).

Yet it was freedom of movement in another direction, between the West Bank and the Hashemite East Bank, that ultimately ensured the viability of the territories. With the Arab economy based overwhelmingly on agriculture, any interruption in access to the traditional East Bank market would have been disastrous for the local population. Two days after the end of the war, therefore, Lieutenant Colonel Israel Eytan, the newly appointed military governor of Samaria, decided on his own initiative that Arab farmers should be allowed to drive their trucks across the river and sell their produce on the East Bank. Dayan learned of the decision only afterward, but immediately approved it. The Hashemite government similarly concurred, throwing Bailey bridges across the Jordan. The cooperation of both governments saved the West Bank crop. Subsequently, with the consent of the Jerusalem and Amman governments, the open-bridges policy gradually was extended to the two-way movement of all goods—agricultural and industrial—between the West and East Banks, and this understanding was later followed by the peaceful crossings of thousands, and then tens of thousands, of West Bank Arabs to integral Jordan. The climactic triumph of the open-bridges policy was the growing summer influx of East Bank Arabs, and Arabs outside Jordan altogether, to the West Bank, Jerusalem, the Gaza Strip, and ultimately to Israel itself, for periods of up to three months (p. 706).

Although Arab governments elsewhere for several years pressed the Jordanian regime to minimize this traffic, Hussein invariably turned down their appeals. His reasons were political no less than humanitarian; he dared not abandon his connection with his former subjects. Israel similarly discerned a political usefulness in the two-way movement. Traffic would ensure that the "administered" population should not be quarantined from the rest of the Arab world, as Israel's own ghettoized Arab minority had been for nineteen years. Moreover, Dayan and others appreciated that the West Bank offered Israel its first tangible hope of wider communication, however oblique, with the surrounding enemy nations. In the meanwhile, the "administered" inhabitants continued as earlier to listen to the radio and television stations of the Arab states, to buy Arab books and newspapers from across the border. Their children even studied at Arab universities. They were entirely free to discuss their status and their political future without restraint or censorship, as long as they did not incite to violence. Nothing stopped them from crossing the bridges to meet with Hussein and members of his government. A majority of their notables in fact continued to receive their salaries in dinars from the Hashemite government, even as others shared at least indirectly in the political life of Jordan. Yet others maintained contact with Nasser, with the Ba'ath regime in Syria, and with a variety of Arab parties, institutions, and organizations in the neighboring countries.

Religious freedom for the inhabitants of the occupied territories was absolute, of course. So was freedom of education. The one alteration required in textbooks was the excision of inflammatory references to Israel, the one change in the curriculum the addition of Hebrew as a compulsory, foreign, language. Manifestly, there were psychological and occasional physical hardships to be endured under Israeli administration. But if the largest numbers of West Bank and Gaza citizens accepted this state of affairs, it was not merely because their governor was Dayan, a sayid—a chieftain—whose rule imposed no loss of face. Rather, the emerging material advantages of cooperation were far greater than the Arab population ever had known or imagined (p. 706). Nor were those benefits diluted, as in the case of the Israeli Arabs, by cultural or social anomie.

ISRAEL WAITS FOR A "PHONE CALL"

For the Israelis, the significance of the June victory transcended even the miracle of deliverance. It represented, as well, an unprecedented opportunity for concluding a final, negotiated settlement with the Arabs. On June 12, Eshkol addressed the Knesset and made plain that his nation's enemies no longer were dealing with the straitened little Israel of June 5:

> Let this be said—there should be no illusion that Israel is prepared to return to the conditions that existed a week ago. . . . We have fought alone for our existence and our security, and we are therefore justified in deciding for ourselves what are the genuine and indispensable interests of our State, and how to guarantee its future.

The Israeli government was determined, too, not simply to achieve direct negotiations with the Arabs, to hold fast to the land it had conquered until peace was guaranteed, but to inform the world at the outset that certain territories lay beyond the realm of negotiations altogether. "The Armistice Agreements of 1949 are no sacred law," Dayan warned shortly after the war. "Those agreements and the armistice relations provided by them—not peace but armistice—and the borders and all other provisions . . . were the result of the war of 1948. Today's conditions are the result of the war of 1967. Nothing confers on the results of the 1948 war any priority over the results of the last war. We are no longer bound by what happened in 1948."

The reunification of Jerusalem, for example, clearly was no longer to be a matter for bargaining. When Dayan entered the Old City in the wake of its capture, he had not found it necessary even to consult the government before announcing: "We have returned to all that is holy in our land. We have returned never to be parted from it again." Eshkol himself arrived later in the day to confirm Dayan's words: "I see myself as a representative of the entire nation and of many past generations whose souls yearned for Jerusalem and its holiness." These statements were given immediate emphasis by the three Knesset laws that linked Jerusalem "administratively" to Israel. Soon afterward, Israeli work crews began vigorously rebuilding and enlarging the abandoned Hebrew University campus on Mount Scopus and constructing new Jewish housing units along the ridges dominating East Jerusalem. On the West Bank of the Jordan, moreover, lay the biblical heartland of the Children of Israel: Samaria and Sh'chem (Nablus), Hebron and Jericho; and the Israeli government implied that these Jewish historical links had now to be taken into account. It was in any case unthinkable that the Judean mountain range should ever again become the site of Hashemite artillery, with the lethal danger this had represented to Jewish villages and cities extending as far west as the coastal plain.

On September 24, therefore, Eshkol announced plans for Israeli resettlement of the Ezion bloc, the four prestate Jewish farm communities in the Bethlehem-Hebron area (p. 310). Three days later a group of Nachal youths arrived as an Israeli vanguard, many of them children of Kfar Ezion settlers who had been killed in the 1948 fighting. Even earlier, the prime minister had revealed that Israel would establish kibbutzim in the northern sector of the captured Golan Heights, adjoining Banias; and soon Nachal units moved into this area to begin construction. Finally, Israeli bulldozers were set to work clearing the ground for "tourist" installations at Sharm es-Sheikh, the former Egyptian base in eastern Sinai that dominated passage through the Strait of Tiran. Even as colonization proceeded, too, Eshkol issued repeated appeals for large-scale Jewish immigration from overseas, to help populate a "greater Israel." On August 3, during a ceremony on the Mount of Olives for the reinterment of soldiers who had died in the Jerusalem fighting of 1948, Dayan stated meaningfully:

> Our brothers who fell in the War of Independence: We have not abandoned your dream, nor forgotten the lesson you taught us. We have returned to the Mount, to the cradle of our nation's history, to the land of our forefathers, to the land of the Judges, and to the fortress of David's dynasty. We have returned to Hebron, to Sh'chem, to Bethlehem and Anatoth, to Jericho and the fords over the Jordan. . . . Our brothers, we bear your lesson with us. . . . We know that to give life to Jerusalem we must station the soldiers and armor of [the defense forces] in the Sh'chem mountains and on the bridges over the Jordan.

These declarations and settlement efforts appeared at least partly at variance with Eban's repeated assurances that, through face-to-face discussions with the Arabs, "everything is negotiable," and "we are prepared to be unbelievably generous in working out peace terms."

Israel's essential desiderata for peace had been outlined to the Knesset, to the United Nations, and to foreign statesmen and correspondents on many occasions since the end of the war. By their terms: peace should be achieved through direct negotiations and a formal treaty; Israeli ships should be allowed free passage through the Suez Canal and the Strait of Tiran; the refugee problem should be settled within the framework of peace and regional cooperation in the Middle East. On this basis, too, the Israeli government had agreed to enter into discussions with Dr. Gunnar Jarring, Sweden's ambassador to Moscow, who had been appointed U Thant's envoy to the Middle East under the mandate of Security Council Resolution 242 (Chapter XXI). Jarring began his mission with visits to Lebanon, Israel, Jordan, and Egypt in November and December 1967. Much now depended upon the response of the Arab nations to Israel's overtures. Even as the Israelis awaited a "phone call" from their defeated enemies, however, the Arab governments already were making other, less than conciliatory, decisions of their own.

Jordan presumably would have been the likeliest of the Arab candidates for Dr. Jarring's intermediary efforts. Of all the belligerents, the little Hashemite kingdom had suffered by far the most grievous losses. Its territory had been halved; it had been stripped of East Jerusalem and three-quarters of the holy places and virtually all its tourist revenues. As early as June 18, 1967, therefore, Hussein entreated his Arab peers to accept defeat as a turning point for the better. In the hope of retrieving his losses, he intimated that he had changed his stance on Israel and was prepared to accept its right to exist within the framework of a comprehensive Middle East peace settlement. But Hussein was a weak candidate for negotiations. As a transplanted Hashemite dynast, he lacked the status and authority of a popularly elected representative of his nation. Most of the Palestinians in Jordan, and some of the leaders in his own government, gave more attention to the "Voice of Cairo" than to the "Voice of Amman." On any matter concerning relations with Israel he required the approval, or at least the silence, of Nasser. It was significant in this regard that Nasser had warned the Hashemite king that "Jerusalem is not a purely Jordanian matter but one for all Arabs and all Moslems." More ominously yet, other Arab nations coveted Hashemite territory. Iraq maintained a division of troops on Jordanian soil. The Syrians concentrated large numbers of troops along Jordan's northern border. It was not possible, as a result, for Hussein to ignore the reaction of these hostile, left-wing governments. As long as Egypt and Syria regarded themselves as in a state of war with Israel, an Israeli treaty with Jordan alone would guarantee peace neither for Jordan nor for Israel.

Damascus, meanwhile, evinced less interest in a peace settlement than any other of Israel's foes. Notwithstanding the murderous beating they had taken at Israel's hands, the Syrians were far from regarding themselves as irretrievably crippled. The Golan Heights were in Israel's hands, to be sure, and some 80,000 Arab settlers there had fled inland. But the economic—as distinguished from the strategic—value of the Golan had never been very great. For years the Syrian army had transformed it principally into a vast military camp at the expense of the region's agriculture. Moreover, virtually all elements in Syrian public life remained as impassioned in their loyalty to the Arab cause as in the post-World War I gestation-years of Arab nationalism. Israel's very presence constituted a standing affront for them. As a result, the Ba'ath party, clinging to office by the skin of its teeth, dared not make public acknowledgment either of Israel's victory or of Israel's right to exist. President Atassi and his colleagues declined even to receive Gunnar Jarring, the United Nations mediator, in the course of his December visit to the Middle East.

Of all the Arab leaders, Nasser was the man for whom defeat at the hands of the Israelis had been the gravest humiliation and whose individual prestige had been most seriously undermined. Nor were his material reverses negligible. The loss of Sinai may not have inflicted a crippling economic blow, even with that desert's potential oil resources. But the closure of Suez was far more painful. Reacting nihilistically, the Egyptians had sunk ships of every kind in the Canal and denied exit to the foreign vessels immured there in the Great Bitter Lake. The blockage of the waterway was costing Egypt more than $30 million a month, an important slice of the nation's income. Even so, Nasser's talent for political survival was extraordinary. Thus, after some deliberation, he managed to persuade the oil-rich Persian Gulf nations to supply Egypt with annual subsidies of $225 million—essentially tribute for Nasser's agreement to cease his intervention in their affairs. Militarily, too, the Egyptian dictator was able to count upon a revival of sorts. Determined to retrieve its influence from the debris of the Six-Day War, Moscow in late June embarked upon an unprecedented airlift to Egypt and Syria. Throughout July, Soviet transport planes and ships arrived with vast quantities of new weapons.

Regaining a measure of his self-confidence, then, Nasser on July 23, the anniversary of the Colonels' Revolution, announced that he was preparing his armed forces to continue the battle against Israel. "We shall never surrender and shall not accept any peace that means surrender," he assured his shaken people. "We shall preserve the rights of the Palestinians." Earlier, on June 17, the foreign ministers of thirteen Arab countries had met in Kuwait to map a joint political strategy. Agreement was reached to condemn "Israeli aggression," and to "restore Arab honor"—this latter a key proviso that Israel and other nations seriously underestimated at the time. On July 15, a conference of five Arab presidents issued another communiqué of agreement "on the necessary effective steps to eliminate the consequences of imperialist Israeli aggression on the Arab homeland." And, finally, the leaders of thirteen Arab states gathered at a summit conference in Khartoum from August 29 to September 1 to pledge a continued nonmilitary struggle against Israel. Under Nasser's influence, their conditions were quite specific: no peace with Israel, no negotiations with Israel, no recognition of Israel, and "maintenance of the rights of the Palestinian people in their nation." The Khartoum Declaration was the first serious warning to the Israelis that their expectation of an imminent "phone call" from the Arab world might be a pipe dream.

The premonition was strengthened by the fate of Jarring's visit to the Middle East in November and December 1967. As has been seen, Damascus refused to associate itself with his mission from the outset. Moreover, in Jarring's first round of talks in the other Middle Eastern capitals, these Arab governments declined to commit themselves. The Swedish diplomat then made his headquarters in Cyprus, intending to bring Arab and Israeli representatives together there. It was wasted effort. A few months later Jarring raised the possibility of encouraging bilateral Israeli-Arab talks in New York, where all countries had delegations to the United Nations. Again the Arabs rejected the proposal. Toward the end of 1968, Jarring offered a "next-door-rooms" formula. Egypt scotched the plan. Eban, meanwhile, let it be known that Israel would consider the reopening of the Suez Canal if this were agreed upon in face-to-face talks with Egypt. Nasser turned down the idea.

While Arab hostility continued as the most serious of Israel's external problems, the notorious instability of the Arab world did not rank far behind. Domestic chaos represented more than an inability to wage war. It signified also an inability to make peace. The specter of revolution loomed over every Arab ruler in the Middle East. In July 1968, the Aref government in Iraq was overthrown by the bloodthirsty Abu Baqr. A year and a half later the Hafez-Atassi regime in Damascus was overthrown by a group of army and air force officers under the leadership of General Hafez al-Assad, and based upon an even more uncertain power base of ultra-left-wing Alawite militants. Jordan, in turn, was convulsed by Palestinian guerrilla movements that formed virtually a state within a state. Even Nasser's hegemony in Egypt was increasingly being questioned by factious student elements and by left-wingers within his own government led by Vice-President Ali Sabri. The consequence of this Arab intransigence and unrest was to harden Israeli public opinion. Growing numbers of Israelis were convinced that the only remaining alternative to security was to hold tight at all cease-fire lines and consolidate behind them. A Labor party declaration published on August 3, 1969, stated that the district of Merchav Shlomo (the Region of Solomon)—the entire southeastern coast of the Sinai Peninsula—should be "linked contiguously to Israel." This declaration was signed not only by Dayan and by Israel Galili, both known hawks (p. 710), but even by the more moderate Eban.

ISRAEL TIGHTENS ITS GRIP

As early as 1968, then, it was significant that few of the officials in Israel's military governments any longer regarded their operations as temporary. In April of that year the armed forces commander, General Chaim Bar-Lev, stated in an interview that "during the coming year we shall continue settlement in all the territories. This is very important from the viewpoint of our current security, and of our security along the borders. . . ." Later a map was handed delegates of the Zionist Congress in Jerusalem, revealing thirty-five new or projected settlements in Israel and the territories. Of these, three were in Sinai, four in the West Bank, and nine on the Golan. The Golan outposts were essentially Nachal groups, but details leaked of a master plan to found at least twenty-five communities on this high land, each to begin with a settlement of about 500 soldier-farmers. And by 1969, in fact, much of the Golan had been planted with wheat, and several thousand head of livestock had been transported to the heights for upland grazing. Nor, from the outset, had there been the faintest doubt of Israel's intentions regarding East Jerusalem.

In the West Bank, meanwhile, the Israelis encountered an Arab population whose economic and political development had been systematically aborted for years by the distrustful Hashemite government. Citizens living west of the river had been refused even the mildest degree of administrative autonomy. There had been no higher West Bank governmental authority of any kind. All major Jordanian government offices and public projects had been shifted to the east, and Amman had governed the three districts of Hebron, Jerusalem, and Samaria individually. When, therefore, Israel instituted a military regime in the West Bank, it launched something entirely new, the first authentically Palestinian administration the local Arabs had ever known. Under Israeli auspices, departments were established for West Bank agriculture, education, posts and telegraphs, commerce and industry. As they operated these departments, the Israelis dealt exclusively with local civil servants, mostly Jordanian appointees, and a few locally elected mayors. The army command simply rubbed the Hashemite imprimatur from administrative regulations and substituted for it "Israel Military Command on the West Bank."

By the same token, the occupation government represented for Israel a unique opportunity to explore a separate peace settlement, if not with the other Arab states, then at least with the West Bank Palestinians. The latter comprised a not unimportant segment of the Arab world, after all. Peace might take various forms: an agreement with a West Bank still linked with Amman; a federation of Israel and the West Bank; or, least likely, a bilateral agreement between Israel and an independent Palestinian state. Accordingly, in July 1967, Eshkol embarked on an attempt to open discussions with various Palestinian notables. His first explorations were carried out through a small interministerial committee, then afterward through Moshe Sasson, a respected foreign ministry official and a Sephardi with important prewar Arab connections. Much to the prime minister's dismay, however, it soon became evident that the various Arab sheikhs, officials, and effendis were unprepared to discuss their area's future. They left no doubt that they remembered the experience of the Gaza Strip leaders in 1957, who similarly had inclined toward cooperation with Israel, then had been harshly punished by the returning Egyptians when the Israeli army withdrew. Rather, the West Bankers preferred now to let the Israeli government first make a straightforward declaration of its own intentions. From the outset, however, it was precisely this kind of declaration that Eshkol's government was inhibited from making. The Israelis, as it happened, were simultaneously attempting to reach a treaty understanding with Hussein. Directly, through a secret meeting with Eban in London, and later indirectly, through Arab intermediaries, they notified the Hashemite king that they were prepared to withdraw their forces from the largest area of the occupied territory. Their quid pro quo was retention of East Jerusalem and of a narrow belt of land, its perimeter still to be defined, along the Jordan River (p. 680).

These parallel negotiations in fact were less ambivalent than they appeared. It would have been virtually impossible for the West Bank Arabs to negotiate with Israel without the consent of Hussein. Admittedly, few of them had reason to be grateful for the discriminatory treatment the

West Bank had suffered at his hands. Even so, after nineteen years of
Jordanian rule the majority of West Bank citizens sustained a kind of un-
enthusiastic loyalty to the Hashemite ruler. Whatever his shortcomings,
he had been loyal to Egypt during the recent war, and at disastrous cost.
Although the West Bankers ideally would have preferred a separate and
autonomous West Bank canton under the Hashemite flag, most of them
still were unwilling to abandon Hussein altogether. It was this lingering
allegiance, moreover, that accounted for a brief upsurge of Arab resistance
to Israeli rule during the late summers of 1967 and 1968. It began when
eight former West Bank judges, their salaries still paid by Amman, declined to serve under the occupation regime. Their intransigence promptly
touched off a flurry of Arab teachers' strikes in East Jerusalem. These were
followed by strikes of Arab students, then of merchants in Jerusalem and
elsewhere. Outside Jerusalem, episodes of violence included exchanges
of gunfire with Israeli troops, the dynamiting of Israeli apartments in
Chadera, Omez, Givat Chabiba—later even in the New City of Jerusalem.
In reprisal, the Israeli army leveled 800 buildings in the West Bank village of Jiftliq, a base for Arab guerrillas. Dozens of Arab suspects were
arrested, some jailed, and a few deported to the East Bank. By 1969 the
worst of the unrest finally had ended; obstructionism had become counterproductive for the local Arabs. More important, by then Israel's discreet
and benign administration had generated a material prosperity unprecedented in Arab experience. Violence henceforth remained the monopoly
of imported fedayun groups (p. 683).

It had become evident, meanwhile, that Cairo and Damascus were inhibiting Hussein from reaching a private accommodation with the Jews.
As a result, the seemingly obvious alternative for Israel was to turn entirely to local leadership. Yet by 1969 it was equally plain to Eshkol and
his advisers that an understanding no longer could take the form of a
separate, autonomous Palestinian entity. To begin with, there simply was
no "Palestinian entity." Under Hashemite rule, the West Bank had been
divided into separate districts. One revolved around conservative Hebron
in the south, a community so intensely traditionalist that it remained even
without a movie theater. The second was metropolitan Jerusalem in the
center, exposed to the European influences of the foreign consulates and
missionaries. Finally, there was radical-nationalist Nablus in the north
(p. 197), its citizens devoted admirers of Nasser. Very little mutuality of
outlook existed among these sectors, or between the older, more moderate
Palestinian notables and the younger generation, who returned from universities in Egypt or elsewhere with new and varied outlooks. So thoroughly, in fact, was the Palestine question dominated by other Arab
governments that Israeli efforts to find an authentically Palestinian leadership were doomed from the outset. At best there were individual local
figures, among them Sheikh Jabari, the mayor of Hebron, and Mayor
Hamdi Can'aan of Nablus, and one or two men of rather lesser stature.
And while Jabari favored the idea of a Palestinian entity, Can'aan im-

placably rejected the notion of separating the West Bank from Jordan. In August 1967 eighty-two West Bank notables signed an open manifesto berating as ludicrous the attempts to create a Palestinian entity.

Accordingly, within three years after the war's end, the Israeli government had decided that any notion of an independent Palestinian state was unrealistic, and in the long run probably would create turmoil in the occupied areas. The entity would be unviable not only for reasons of political fragmentation and economic limitation, but as a consequence of strategic realities. The West Bank was landlocked and dependent for an outlet on Jordan or Israel. If its statehood were established in the teeth of Hashemite opposition, Hussein might well retaliate by prohibiting contacts between its citizens and their kinsmen in other Arab lands, with disastrous economic and social results. Under these circumstances, the West Bank regime would be left with no alternative but to rely upon Israel as its sole market and maritime outlet, thereby further isolating it from the Arab world.

For the time being, then, it was Israel's approach not to insist upon permanent political arrangements, but simply to minimize intervention in the life of the territories and to allow every opportunity for a growing "natural" relationship between Arabs and Jews. On August 20, 1971, Dayan made his own position clear in an address to the army staff college, when he stated bluntly that Israel should envisage its role in the occupied territories as that of a permanent government, "to plan and implement whatever can be done without worrying about the day of peace, which might be far away." The government must "create facts," Dayan emphasized, "and not confine development programs to Israel proper. . . . [I]f the Arabs refuse to make peace, we cannot stand still. If we are denied their cooperation, let us act on our own." These remarks set off shock waves throughout the Middle East, and not least of all in Israel. Dayan evidently was talking about functional annexation at last. Interrogated in the Knesset, the defense minister refused to acknowledge that this was his purpose. But there was nothing to be gained, he argued, in awaiting the chimera of final peace before creating facts, and those facts included Jewish settlements throughout the occupied territories.

Actually, none even of the most moderate Israeli leaders had denied the importance of establishing "facts"—either in the Golan, the West Bank, or Sinai. In the immediate aftermath of the war, for example, Yigal Allon, who had long enjoyed a close rapport with Israel's own Arab population, had been the first to outline a scheme by which Israel would establish a dense belt of Jewish villages along the Jordan River. Under this plan Israel would protect its security against a return of Jordanian (or Iraqi) armed forces to the West Bank, yet avoid intruding a flagrant Israeli presence on the encircled majority of the West Bank Arabs. The idea appealed to the cabinet, and particularly to Eshkol and to his successor, Golda Meir. Indeed, the Allon Plan soon gained practical momentum when eleven Nachal kibbutzim were organized along the western length of the river (see map, opposite). But the implications of Dayan's proposal were

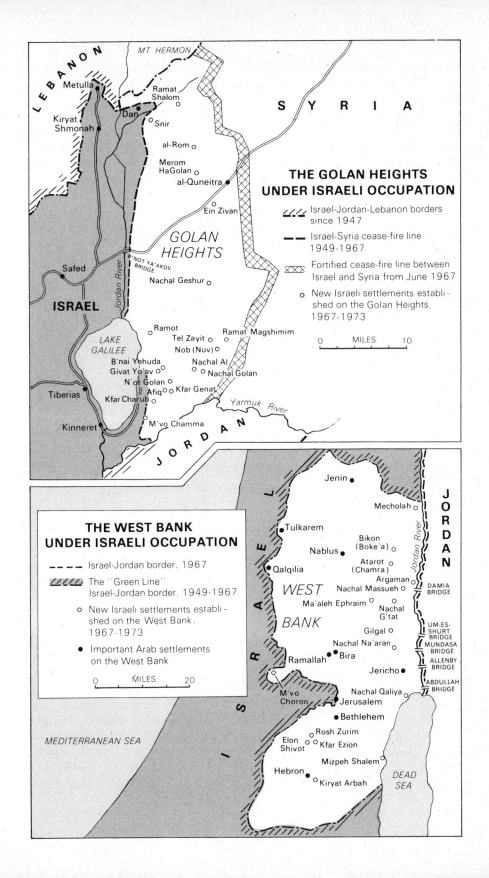

THE GOLAN HEIGHTS
UNDER ISRAELI OCCUPATION

- ///// Israel-Jordan-Lebanon borders since 1947
- – – – Israel-Syria cease-fire line 1949-1967
- ⧓⧓⧓ Fortified cease-fire line between Israel and Syria from June 1967
- o New Israeli settlements established on the Golan Heights, 1967-1973

0 MILES 10

MT. HERMON

LEBANON

Metulla
Ramat Shalom
Kiryat Shmonah
Dan
Snir
al-Rom
Merom HaGolan
al-Quneitra

S Y R I A

Ein Zivan

GOLAN HEIGHTS

Safed
B'NOT YA'AKOV BRIDGE
Nachal Geshur

ISRAEL

LAKE GALILEE

Ramot
Tel Zayit
Ramat Magshimim
Nob (Nuv)
B'nai Yehuda
Givat Yo'av
Nachal Al
N'ot Golan
Nachal Golan
Tiberias
Afiq
Kfar Genat
Kfar Charub

Kinneret
M'vo Chamma

Yarmuk River

J O R D A N

Jordan River

THE WEST BANK
UNDER ISRAELI OCCUPATION

- – – – Israel-Jordan border, 1967
- ///// The ''Green Line'' Israel-Jordan border, 1949-1967
- o New Israeli settlements established on the West Bank, 1967-1973
- ● Important Arab settlements on the West Bank

0 MILES 20

Jenin
Mecholah
Tulkarem
Bikon (Boke'a)
Nablus
Atarot (Chamra)
Qalqilia
Argaman
WEST
Nachal Massueh
DAMIA BRIDGE
Ma'aleh Ephraim
Nachal G'tat
BANK
Gilgal
UM-ES-SHURT BRIDGE
Nachal Na'aran
MUNDASA BRIDGE
Ramallah
Bira
ALLENBY BRIDGE
Jericho
M'vo Choron
Nachal Qaliya
ABDULLAH BRIDGE
Jerusalem
Bethlehem
Rosh Zurim
Elon Shivot
Kfar Ezion
Mizpeh Shalem
Hebron
Kiryat Arbah

I S R A E L

J O R D A N

Jordan River

MEDITERRANEAN SEA

DEAD SEA

even more far-reaching. And, willy-nilly, the defense minister's conception of "facts" similarly began to take shape almost independent of any government policy.

Jerusalem was the most dramatic case in point. As has been seen, the eastern half of the city had simply been incorporated into the capital and enlarged far beyond its original limits. Latrun, too, for all practical purposes was absorbed into Israel, thereby shortening by thirty minutes the driving time between Tel Aviv and Jerusalem. Hebron was yet another example. The town was revered by Jews and Moslems alike as the alleged burial place of Abraham, Isaac, and Jacob, and their wives. Moslems commemorated the sacred gravesite with the Ibrahimi Mosque; the Jews knew the resting place as the Machpelah Cave. Early in 1968 numbers of Israeli religionists began forcing their way into the cave and praying there. After some hesitation, the government decided again not to risk a confrontation with the Orthodox; it simply declared Machpelah to be an official Jewish place of worship, and apportioned prayer times between Jews and Moslems. Predictably, the Islamic world was outraged. Even worse, from the Moslem viewpoint, was Israel's policy of encouraging Jewish settlements at and near Hebron, and brazenly confiscating land in the vicinity. Thus, Kiryat Arba became a Jewish settlement directly adjacent to Hebron itself. "It is illegal," protested the mayor, Sheikh Jabari, with some justification, "and contradicts every moral and international law and code." It may have violated "law" and "code," but it hardly violated the time-honored procedures of other conquerors in other lands. Under whatever guise or justification, in the absence of treaties with its neighbors Israel was doing precisely what Dayan recommended, creating "facts."

THE RISE OF ARAB GUERRILLA RESISTANCE

Some Palestine Arabs devised their own response to these "facts." As has been seen, Arab guerrilla infiltration was by no means exclusively a post-1967 phenomenon (Chapter xxi). Before the war, a growing campaign of border violence had been mounted by the tightly knit al-Fatah organization. Now, after the June debacle, it was once again this cabal of irregulars that revived its activities, and indeed did so with explosive force and burgeoning political influence throughout the Arab world. Leadership for the renewed guerrilla upsurge was provided by one Yasser Arafat, a short, balding, heavyset man in his late thirties, perennially camouflaged by a stubble of beard, dark glasses, and a kaffiyah—a "disguise" that in fact later became his trademark. Admittedly, there were reasons for this initial passion for secrecy, for the veil that obscured the circumstances of Arafat's background. The Fatah leader's actual name was Abd al-Rahman abd al-Rauf Arafat al-Qud al-Husseini. He shortened it to obscure his kinship with the discredited ex-Mufti of Jerusalem, Haj Muhammad Amin al-Husseini.

Born in Cairo of Palestinian parents, Arafat embarked on his political career in 1951 while a student at Fuad I University. Living virtually as an ascetic, he concentrated his efforts on organizing the university's Palestinian students into a militant anti-Israel society. He received his own guerrilla initiation in 1953, joining Egyptian fedayun operations against the British in the Suez Canal Zone. Following his departure (or expulsion) from Egypt in 1957, Arafat and his colleagues took up residence in Syria, where they pioneered the Fatah movement on the basis of: an independent role for the Palestinians; noninvolvement in the internal affairs of Arab states; and commitment to the ideology of violence developed by the Algerian psychiatrist Frantz Fanon. From 1956 to 1966 the Fatah enjoyed the near-total support of the Syrian Ba'ath party and of the Syrian army, which trained and equipped the guerrillas in their raids against Israel. It was the Fatah, too, we recall, inflaming the Syrian-Israeli border, that began the chain of events leading to the Six-Day War.

Moreover, by annihilating the regular Arab armies, the June War doomed Palestinian faith in the official Arab governments as likely instruments of restoration. It similarly discredited the leadership of Ahmed Shukeiry and the Egyptian-dominated Palestine Liberation Organization. Even the Fatah, for that matter, was paralyzed temporarily by the shock of defeat. Only belatedly did Arafat awaken to the unique situation that had emerged, as new territories with large Arab population centers came under Israel's military control. It appeared suddenly that the classical pattern of a revolutionary uprising from within could now be applied. Indeed, Arafat and his followers were convinced that the Israeli occupation regime on the West Bank and Gaza, like the French regime in Vietnam and Algeria, ultimately would prove vulnerable to guerrilla operations. In September 1967, therefore, the first in a series of Fatah operations was launched and directed mainly at towns on the West Bank. Grenades were thrown at Israeli patrols. To intimidate Arabs commuting to Jewish work projects, explosives were detonated variously in town squares, marketplaces, and bus terminals. From February 1968 on, too, as West Bank and Gaza Arabs began to accept employment in integral Israel, episodes of Fatah sabotage in Jewish territory mounted. Before long they were averaging thirty a month, with grenades and dynamite charges set off in Israeli town and city centers. The worst of the explosions that year killed eleven and injured fifty-five Israeli civilians in Jerusalem.

Dramatic as these episodes were, Arafat and his followers recognized by late 1968 that they had failed in their major purpose—to ignite a war of "national liberation" among the occupied Arab territories. Within months after their June victory, Israel's security forces were effectively countering every attempt to touch off a popular armed rising on the West Bank. Reprisals occasionally were brutal. Throughout October and November 1967, Israeli troops killed substantial numbers of guerrillas in exchanges of fire. In the last fortnight of November, we recall, the Israeli army leveled all 800 houses in the West Bank village of Jiftliq. The procedure of dynamiting homes was similarly followed elsewhere (usually without a hearing, a trial, or compensation to the innocent). By the end of 1968, as a result, 1,400 Fatah members had been captured in the West Bank alone. Once the largest numbers of his followers in the West Bank were killed or imprisoned, Arafat himself was also obliged to flee his secret headquarters in Nablus and take refuge across the Jordan.

The initial effectiveness of this Israeli suppression was due partly to the guerrillas' own lack of tenacity and fiber. Whenever caught, they surrendered immediately, knowing that Israel would not impose the death sentence on them. As a rule, they collaborated afterward by informing on their fellow members; this led in turn to the wholesale roundup of Fatah groups everywhere on the West Bank. Yet the principal reason for Fatah's lack of success was the unwillingness of the West Bankers themselves to cooperate with subversion in any form. Fear of Israeli punishment and reprisal was a factor, of course. But so, too, was the West Bankers' instinctive appreciation that if the combined Arab armies had not managed to defeat Israel, surely the guerrillas could not. Not least of all, Fatah's demands on the allegiance of the West Bank population conflicted with the traditional structure of local leadership. The mayors wanted no part of the guerrillas, and the Israelis sensed this. By using a give-and-take approach toward the local mayors and village mukhtars, therefore, the Israeli occupation regime kept track of incipient unrest.

With the network inside the West Bank all but liquidated by mid-1968, the Fatah was thrown back to its pattern of the mid-sixties. It was limited to short forays across the Jordan, the harassment of Jewish settlements in the Beit Sh'an and Jordan valleys south of Lake Galilee, where the terrain was undulating and semitropical. In some cases fedayun groups launched Katyusha rockets from deep within Jordan. But while Jewish kibbutz and town dwellers frequently were driven to underground shelters, none of their communities was ever deserted. On the other side of the Jordan, conversely, thousands of Arab villagers fled Israel's reprisal shellings, joining the refugee camps inside the East Bank. Fatah bases similarly had to be transferred well inside Hashemite territory as Israeli border police refined their techniques of sealing off the Jordan Valley, through patrols, ambushes, and electrified fences. Even as the guerrillas took up new positions inland, moreover, they were unable to escape the reach of Israel's air force. In June 1968 an air strike at the principal Fatah headquarters at es-Salt killed more than seventy of Arafat's commandos and wreaked extensive physical damage. So heavy was the blow that the fedayeen were obliged to disperse over a large area in small, well-hidden caves, even in forests. There, however, deprived of convenient access to the borders, they sustained even heavier losses during their intermittent forays.

In one region only did the guerrillas achieve a limited initial success. This was the Gaza Strip, where 220,000 refugees nurtured a hatred of the Israelis that was probably unmatched elsewhere in the Arab world. Deprived of significant employment opportunities, indigent for nineteen years before the June War, the Gaza refugees were uniquely vulnerable to

Fatah propaganda. The very "logistics" of their displacement well suited the Fatah cause. Thousands of their huts in the eight camps were grouped tightly around narrow lanes that made access difficult for Israeli military vehicles and offered the fedayeen convenient hiding places. Most of the guerrilla attacks in any case were directed against Arabs and their families who sought work in Israeli enterprises. Thus, in the first year after the June War, over a thousand Arab men, women, and children were wounded by guerrilla assaults, and 219 were killed. Arafat boasted: "The Israelis may rule Gaza by day. I rule by night." His rule endured barely four years. Early in 1971 the problem of security was turned over to General "Arik" Sharon. The flamboyant paratroop commander handled the matter in his typically straightforward way, ordering engineers to bulldoze roads even through the most densely inhabited refugee camps. Once armored cars and jeeps moved freely among these warrens, the incidents of violence declined markedly.

From 1968 onward, meanwhile, Fatah and other guerrillas began to ensconce themselves deeply in Jordanian refugee camps and villages. Here they soon posed a far greater threat to Hussein than to the Israelis. Indeed, the fedayeen rapidly established a virtual substate of their own, boasting immunity to Hashemite laws and claiming extraterritorial rights. By 1969 they moved arrogantly through Jordan, wearing their own uniforms, flaunting guerrilla insignia and license plates on their vehicles, assessing and collecting their own taxes among refugees and Jordanian citizens alike, even soliciting Jordanian youths to enlist in the guerrilla forces rather than in the Hashemite army. At first Hussein was too circumspect to meet this challenge head on. Following a number of skirmishes, his government preferred instead to sign a "compact" with the guerrillas, delimiting respective spheres of activity. It was the first of many accords that would be broken. The power of the fedayeen grew daily. Some of the more leftist among them, especially George Habash's Popular Front for the Liberation of Palestine (p. 698), began openly questioning the need for a Hashemite dynasty altogether. With tension mounting, the king in February 1970 forbade dissident groups to carry weapons within Amman's city limits. The ensuing demonstrations forced Hussein to rescind the order. The guerrillas promptly broadened their demands, however, insisting upon the removal of several antifedayun members of the Jordanian cabinet. In June, when a number of Habash's PFLP followers were jailed, rampaging mobs of guerrillas seized hotels in downtown Amman, held the European guests as hostages, abducted and murdered the United States military attaché, raped several American women, and wounded a French diplomat. Again Hussein capitulated, even bowing to a guerrilla ultimatum for veto rights over cabinet appointments.

Then, in August 1970, the Egyptian and Israeli governments jointly accepted a United States peace initiative. A cease-fire was negotiated on the Suez Canal, and the Jarring talks resumed (p. 695). Friction immediately developed between Egypt and the guerrillas over the question of a political settlement, and the Nasser regime angrily shut down the Fatah radio station in Cairo. If Hussein ever intended to move against the fedayeen, clearly this was the moment. Accordingly, in the wake of an assassination attempt against him, and the hijacking of four international airliners by the PFLP on September 6, the king launched his forces against the guerrilla strongholds in the refugee camps. During the ensuing ten-day civil war—it was hardly less—nearly 2,000 fedayeen were killed, together with many additional thousands of innocent refugees. Soon the battle of "Black September," as it was later to be memorialized by the guerrillas, took on aspects of an international crisis. An Iraqi division had remained encamped on Hashemite territory since the June War, and the Baghdad government now threatened to send it against Amman. With Russian encouragement, the Syrians were also persuaded to dispatch an armored column across the Jordanian border. Once again Hussein confounded his enemies. In the ensuing battle, his forces proved more than the equal of the invaders; his tanks and jets mauled the Syrians badly. Yet, had the little monarch failed, the United States and Israel were quietly prepared to take coordinated action on their own. An informal understanding called for Israeli land and air attacks against Syrian tanks, with the United States Sixth Fleet functioning as a barrier against possible Russian intervention in the Canal area. The tacit agreement was never put into operation. As matters developed, Israel's well-publicized troop concentration near the Jordanian frontier, buttressed by American warnings to Moscow, effectively persuaded the Syrians to withdraw their task force and the Iraqis to hold back their division (p. 769).

Once the Syrian threat ebbed in late September 1970, Hussein moved to consolidate his power against the remaining fedayeen. Strengthened by $30 million in American military aid, the Jordanian army pressed its offensive during the winter months of 1970–71, bottling up the surviving guerrillas in the northwestern hill country. At last, in July 1971, Hussein's troops launched a decisive attack, shelling fedayun encampments, attacking survivors with tanks and infantry, rounding up some 2,000 prisoners, and killing hundreds of them. Demoralized and seemingly shattered as a political and military force, the guerrillas no longer appeared capable of mounting a threat to Hussein's rule or of sustaining even the most nominal infiltration effort across Israel's longest frontier. Thereafter they shifted their bases of operation entirely to Lebanon and Syria.

THE ECONOMIC IMPACT OF ISRAELI OCCUPATION

If absence of local cooperation was one of the factors undermining Arafat's efforts in the occupied territories, it was the result in no small degree of material prosperity under Israeli rule. This was particularly evident in the Gaza Strip. Of all the 1948 fugitives, we recall, the Palestinians of Gaza were incomparably the most wretched and embittered. At first, too,

Israeli rule following the June War appeared likely to exacerbate their situation. The local smuggling market was eliminated. So was the purchasing power of the Egyptian army, together with the services of Egyptian teachers, doctors, and administrators. It was hardly surprising, then, during the early years of Israeli occupation, that the Gaza refugees who accepted Fatah money to throw grenades at army patrols and Arab "collaborators" felt they had little to lose.

Yet as early as 1968, several thousand of these Palestinians were given their first jobs in Israel, and public transportation was organized for them. Eventually, by the autumn of 1973, 25,000 refugees were commuting from Gaza to work in Jewish enterprises. Their wages impressively buoyed the Gaza economy. So did the income of the 27,000 Arabs who were employed in the Strip itself, most of them in fisheries and canneries established or partly financed by Israeli capital. In addition, several hundred Gaza workshops were receiving subcontracting orders from Israeli industry. By 1973, as a result, employment in the formerly moribund Gaza Strip had reached the unprecedented figure of 98 percent. In 1969, Israel established the Economic Development and Refugee Rehabilitation Trust, a fund that disbursed millions of pounds to improve conditions inside the camps, to provide new sewage systems and street lights, and finally to make credit available for refugee housing. By the end of 1973, 36,000 refugees had been moved into new or enlarged homes. The shift was not always voluntary, to be sure; but hesitation vanished once the Palestinians were assured that they would lose neither their refugee status nor their UNRWA rations. Slowly but systematically, the Israelis proceeded to thin out the camps. Their technique resembled the one applied to Jewish immigrants during the 1950s and 1960s. It was to encourage departure from the shanties by "seeding" refugees elsewhere, in this case among the new factory areas both in Gaza and in the West Bank. By 1973 the migration to the West Bank was well launched with the initial transplantation of 12,000 Palestinian families.

None of this achievement in Gaza would have been possible, on the other hand, had it not been for the Israeli military government's quite dramatic success in resolving the economic challenges of the West Bank. The governor's staff went to great pains to demonstrate the material advantages of cooperation. Farmers on the West Bank were given access not only to the markets of the East Bank but to Israeli markets as well, even to Israeli overseas export facilities. They received low-interest credits and subsidies for certain branches of agriculture, and extensive technological advice in farming. Soon the range of Jewish agricultural services came to include guided study tours of Israeli villages, the establishment of research stations in the West Bank, of demonstration plots in most of the West Bank villages, of lectures by Israeli instructors. Under Israeli influence, too, Arab agriculture was fundamentally restructured. Farmers were encouraged to reduce their cultivation of low-priced products—melons, for example—and to increase the acreage of such labor-intensive crops as flax, tobacco, and sesame. The impact of this tutelage was easily gauged. By January 1972, the annual value of West Bank farm products had doubled since 1968, from I £ 135 million to I £ 280 million.

A similar rate of progress was achieved in industry and commerce. During nineteen years of Jordanian rule, Palestinian artisans and businessmen had been forbidden to expand their operations beyond the scale of cottage industry; Hussein had preferred to keep all major enterprises on the East Bank. Under the circumstances, employment opportunities had remained modest and had led ultimately to a sizable migration of Palestinians to the East Bank and other Arab countries. Israel now reversed this policy by encouraging local industry. Loans and technical assistance were provided for West Bank workshops and tourist facilities. Israeli entrepreneurs subcontracted orders in textiles, furniture, rubber, and shoe manufacturing. The military government itself often advanced credit to Arab subcontractors, authorizing them to expand their plant and work force. In 1969, as a result, some twenty new workshops were opened in the West Bank and twenty-four others were enlarged. In 1973 the combined figure was 200. By then, too, sixty-five of these workshops were entirely Israeli-owned. The number of West Bank Arabs employed in industry and crafts rose from 1,500 to 8,000, and from 800 to 6,000 in the Gaza Strip.

Indeed, after the June War the problem of surplus Arab labor was resolved not only by an extraordinary upsurge of local opportunities but by a developing shortage of manpower within Israel itself. In September 1967 Israel's labor ministry opened its first employment bureaus in the West Bank and Gaza. Seven years later, the number of West Bank and Gaza Arabs employed inside Israel was listed officially as 65,000, but the actual figure was much higher, perhaps 130,000 or 140,000. Arabs commuting from Gaza and the West Bank took over many of the least skilled and (for Jews) least desirable tasks in Israel's cities—window-washing, street-cleaning, garbage-collecting. In Jerusalem the (Jewish) construction boom was almost entirely dependent upon Arab workers. On Israeli farms, Arab agricultural laborers similarly assumed many of the heaviest chores in the field. Much of this labor was black-market and below official Israeli pay rates. Over the years, nevertheless, the Arabs demanded and received increasingly higher wages. In mid-1971, too, the Israeli government moved to equalize social benefits between Arabs working in Israel and their Jewish counterparts. Fringe advantages included sick and holiday pay, pension-fund membership, and eventually free medical treatment for accidents suffered in Israel.

The sum of these opportunities dramatically reduced unemployment in the West Bank and raised the area's per capita income by 80 percent between 1967 and 1973 alone. The GNP was growing by 15 percent a year. Television sets and refrigerators at last came within the reach of tens of thousands of West Bank families. In light of this unprecedented affluence, and of the comparatively painless impact of Israeli occupation overall, it was by no means remarkable that the largest majority of the "administered"

Arab population should have evinced meager interest in violence or sub-version of any kind.

THE WAR OF ATTRITION

The Egyptian government was inhibited by no similar concern for the wel-fare of the occupied areas. Except for scattered Bedouin tribes, none of its citizens was under Israeli rule. When, therefore, at the Khartoum Con-ference of August–September 1967, Nasser led the assembled chiefs of state in refusal to countenance negotiations with Israel, he understood shrewdly that he faced no imminent danger of Israeli reprisal against a hostage Egyptian population. It appeared, rather, that he had more to gain politically by salvaging his reputation on the battlefield. Evidence of domestic unrest already was beginning to surface in the aftermath of de-feat, and in October of 1968 riots erupted, led by a combination of students, the Moslem Brotherhood, and extreme left-wing groups. As Nas-ser saw it, vindication by war was the one sure method of strengthening his hand within his own country.

In fact, his hand already was being strengthened by the Russians, who viewed Israel's pulverizing victory in the Six-Day War as an intolerable challenge to their own, no less than to Egypt's, hegemony in the Middle East. The Kremlin was by no means resigned to an attrition of its ex-pensively won influence and prestige in the Arab world. It was well aware that certain intellectual factions in eastern Europe already regarded the June conflict as proof that Moscow could be defied with impunity. From the moment the cease-fire came into effect, therefore, the Soviets proceeded to reinstate large-scale arms deliveries to the Middle East. Within two weeks, over two hundred crated MiG fighter planes were airlifted to Egypt and Syria, and throughout the rest of the summer and autumn between two and three ships a week docked at Alexandria harbor carrying replacement weapons. Fifteen months after the war, Egypt's tank strength had been increased from 250 to 470, and the air force had received 400 new planes. This dramatic reprovisionment was matched by a burgeoning new Soviet physical presence in the Middle East. By 1969 3,000 Russian military ad-visers and technicians were seconded to the Egyptian armed forces, and an additional 1,000 to the Syrian armed forces. In the next year these figures were quadrupled (p. 694). As early as 1968, too, it became known that Russian crews in TU-16 bombers with Egyptian markings were pro-viding land-based reconnaissance for an impressive Soviet naval armada gathering off the coasts of Egypt and Syria.

Notwithstanding the extensive infusion of Soviet weapons and advisers, as well as the new Soviet naval and air presence, it seemed unlikely at first that the Egyptians were capable of launching a major counteroffensive against Israel. Before June 1967, flight time from airfields in the northern Sinai to Tel Aviv had been eight minutes. After the cease-fire, flight time was pushed back to at least twenty minutes even from the most advanced Egyptian bases. Israel, on the other hand, was capable now of sending its own planes into Egypt in far less time and with much heavier ordnance than before the war. The possibility of Egyptian ground assault meanwhile appeared even less realistic than aerial bombardment. While the Suez Canal traversed 110 miles of dunes and intermittent lakes, nowhere did it appear to be suited to crossings in strength. Indeed, the Sinai itself was formidable enough an obstacle, with its mountain barrier and limited road network; even as the peninsula's Mediterranean shore was bordered with extensive salt marshes. Nor did suitable terrain exist for large amphibious operations along the gulfs of Suez and Aqaba.

The pattern of violence along the Canal accordingly developed in erratic sequences. The initial phase, from the end of the war until April 1969, was characterized by sporadic outbursts that grew in intensity and frequency as the Egyptians recovered from their 1967 disaster. Each Egyptian probe from the West Bank of the Canal evoked a tough counterblow from the Israelis. One particular heavy artillery exchange in late summer of 1967 forced the evacuation of tens of thousands of civilians from Suez City and Ismailia. On October 21, an Egyptian missile ship sank the Israeli destroyer *Eilat* off the Sinai coast; the Israelis retaliated three days later by shelling major Egyptian oil installations at Suez City and destroying 80 percent of their output. Egyptian infantry raids across the Canal similarly provoked Israeli helicopter-borne counterattacks against targets deep in the Egyptian interior.

But if Israel's retaliatory actions inflicted heavy damage on the Egyptian economy, they failed to deter the Egyptians from renewed shellings and commando attacks. The Canal may have offered Israel a first-rate defensive barrier, but it served an identical purpose for Egypt; and the slashing offensive war Israel had conducted in June 1967 manifestly was out of the question afterward. By the autumn of 1968, therefore, a military stand-off had developed, with both sides consolidating their positions and seeking new options. As it turned out, October 1968 marked a turning point in the rising crescendo of Suez fighting. In a single Saturday afternoon a massive Egyptian artillery barrage killed fifteen Israelis and demonstrated that Egypt had accumulated a vast superiority of men and equipment on the west bank of the Canal. From then until late summer of 1969, the intensity of Egyptian shelling steadily mounted. The revived hostilities swiftly developed into an overt Egyptian "war of attrition." On April 23, 1969, Cairo announced that henceforth it would regard the June 1967 cease-fire agreement as void due to "Israel's refusal to implement the Security Council Resolution [242] of November 1967." A week later Nasser declared that Egypt now considered itself justified in attacking Israeli civilian targets. His goal, clearly, was to prevent the transformation of the Canal into a de facto border, and to accomplish this by inflicting such heavy casualties that the Israelis would be forced back into Sinai or compelled to accept a political solution on Arab terms. These objectives were considered feasible now in the light of Egyptian superiority in artillery and of Israel's modest population and economic resources, its inability to resume an offensive into the Egyptian heartland.

Nasser's approach was not without logic. Counting on mobile reserves to throw back hostile forays, the Israeli general staff originally had deployed only two brigades, each of 10,000 men, to hold the east bank of the Canal. Nor had the troops been provided with effective cover against heavy shelling. The lethal Egyptian bombardment of October 1968 now plainly dictated a modification of approach. To that end, the Israelis began digging into hardened concrete and steel-reinforced bunkers and fortified positions. These were known subsequently as the Bar-Lev Line, after Israel's then chief of staff, General Chaim Bar-Lev. With the completion of the fortifications in March 1969, the Israeli general staff expected to be able to withstand the developing war of attrition (Chapter XXIV). The Egyptians quickly put Israel's defenses to the test by launching isolated frontal attacks across the Canal, supported by prolonged and heavy shelling of the Bar-Lev Line. Although these exploratory crossings invariably were repulsed by the Israeli brigades, the weight of Egyptian manpower and artillery took its toll. The Israeli casualty rate reached seventy a month by July 1969, and supply efforts to the forward units were becoming increasingly hazardous. Nasser's Russian advisers in turn were hopeful that they had succeeded at last in compelling Israel to fight their kind of war. Again, their optimism was premature. To reverse the heavy casualty trends, Israel in late July 1969 launched a sustained air bombardment of Egyptian guns on the west bank of the Canal. For the next three months Israeli planes battered away at the enemy emplacements. Gradually Egyptian positions along the waterway were silenced. Israeli losses dropped markedly.

This climactic demonstration of Israeli military superiority was accompanied by a new hardening of Israel's diplomatic position. The government of course had emphasized repeatedly that the pre-1967 armistice lines would never again be reimposed, that areas such as Jerusalem and the Golan Heights were not negotiable. Despite these assertions, however, and the program of creeping annexation along the Jordan Valley, Israel's leaders after the war had made a great point of their willingness, in Eban's words, to be "unbelievably generous" in direct negotiations with the Arabs. A similar flexibility was conveyed directly to Hussein in the autumn of 1970, in the immediate aftermath of the Jordanian victory over the guerrilla organizations and the Syrian armored column. In October of that year a secret meeting took place in the Jordan Valley between the king and Yigal Allon, Israel's deputy prime minister. The two men exchanged compliments, with Allon praising Hussein's bravery and congratulating him on his victory, and the latter thanking Israel for concentrating troops on the border as a deterrent to the Syrians. Appealing, then, to the Hashemite king to negotiate a separate treaty with Israel, Allon went on to describe his plan for the West Bank and the string of fortified Israeli settlements along the river. In return for this limited Israeli military presence, the deputy prime minister offered Hussein a corridor to Gaza and the

Mediterranean. For his part, the Hashemite monarch repeated his earlier assertion (to Eban in 1967) that he would never relinquish Arab land. Yet he offered some hope for future negotiations. The meeting ended cordially, if inconclusively. Nor was this warmth altogether superficial. Earlier, in an address before Washington's National Press Club in April 1969, Hussein had outlined a plan that envisaged Arab willingness to recognize Israel, even to grant Israel freedom of navigation through the Suez Canal. In return, of course, Hussein expected that Israel would evacuate all territory —including Arab Jerusalem—occupied during the 1967 war. Despite its rejection of territorial change, the spirit of Hussein's proposal surely was light-years from the belligerency of the Khartoum Conference.

But Hussein's spirit was not Nasser's spirit. The king's plan was instantly repudiated by Cairo, which foreclosed all possibilities of negotiations unless and until the Israelis first evacuated Egyptian soil. Under these circumstances, and with Israel's planes dominating the air over the Canal, the Eshkol government stated bluntly that any notion of intermediate agreements, of phased withdrawals from Arab territory in advance of a final peace settlement, was out of the question. These were the mutual positions elicited, too, by the United Nations negotiator, Gunnar Jarring, during the Swedish diplomat's visits to Middle Eastern capitals in 1968 and 1969. With intransigence the mood in both Cairo and Jerusalem, there was small likelihood of productive mediation.

The Israelis drew some assurance not only from their military strength but from the absence of the kind of international pressures they had experienced following the 1956 Sinai Campaign. Moscow was irredeemably hostile, of course. On the other hand, the majority of Western governments understood that Israel could not be bullied any longer into a unilateral evacuation of the occupied territories. Even Britain's new Conservative government, sensitive as it was to the need of placating the Arab oil regimes, maintained its trade and diplomatic links with Israel and continued the sale to Israel of tanks and other ordnance. The one major setback to Jerusalem's relations with western Europe was at the hands of France, an old and cherished ally. Intent now upon restoring French influence in the Arab world, de Gaulle tightened the ban on military shipments to Israel, including the delivery of fifty Mirage V jets for which Israel had contracted and paid before the war. After January 1969, even the delivery of spare parts was closed off. Nor did de Gaulle's resignation in the spring of 1969 produce an improvement in relations. His successor, Georges Pompidou, moved even further in the quest for Arab goodwill, selling one hundred Mirage V planes to Libya—a near-certain guarantee of their eventual transshipment to Egypt.

Yet the shock generated by the loss of the French alliance was at least partially mitigated for Israel by a strengthened relationship with the United States. After the 1967 war, the Johnson government categorically supported Israel's insistence on direct negotiations between the belligerents and on a formal peace treaty assuring the Jewish nation secure and defensible boundaries. In 1969 the newly elected Nixon administration reaffirmed this policy. But if Washington continued to endorse Israel's crucial security demands, and to provide Israel with substantial military and economic help, there were nevertheless periods of growing tactical divergence between the two governments. As the winter of 1969 passed with Egypt and Israel still far apart and the threshold of violence lowering ominously along the Canal, Washington and Moscow reached agreement on the format for a Big Four conference on the Middle East. Notwithstanding State Department assurances that the talks were merely a "catalyst" for the purpose of "developing a substantive framework in which parties directly concerned can develop a dialogue," the Israelis feared that the American approach was veering toward a Great Power–imposed solution.

Nor were they encouraged by the blueprint presented to the Big Four negotiations by Secretary of State William Rogers. Under the terms of the "Rogers Plan," Israel would evacuate all occupied Arab lands in return for an Arab pledge of a binding peace treaty with Israel; Israel would be guaranteed freedom of passage through international waterways; the Palestine refugees would be allowed to choose between repatriation and compensation; Jordan and Israel would seek direct agreement on the future of Jerusalem; even as the issues of Sharm es-Sheikh and Gaza would be reserved for future negotiations between Egypt and Israel. All of this, the United States suggested, should be worked out in negotiations based on the Rhodes formula. The use of this "formula," which initially had been proposed by Dr. Jarring, was designed, actually, to blur the issue of whether Arabs and Israelis were talking face to face. The Israelis in any event expressed their alarm at Washington's retreat from the *sine qua non* of direct negotiations—for Israel the acid test of Arab sincerity and trustworthiness. It was to Jerusalem's considerable relief, therefore, that Nasser rebuffed the Rogers scheme in December 1969, describing the American proposals as "one-sided and pro-Israeli." And once the Egyptians rejected the plan, the Soviets felt obliged to renege as well. From then on, the State Department dropped its exploratory notion of an imposed solution.

THE SOVIETS ENLARGE THEIR PRESENCE

One of the factors that chilled Washington's efforts to devise a Great Power blueprint was a harshly aggressive new Soviet posture in the Egyptian war of attrition. On January 22, 1970, Nasser paid an urgent visit to Moscow. He informed the Soviet leadership that the Israelis, in an effort to relieve pressure on their Bar-Lev Line, were now bombing Egyptian artillery emplacements west of the Canal and targets deep in the Nile Valley. A consequence of this far-reaching aerial activity was the evacuation of some half a million Egyptian civilians from the Canal Zone, and the exposure of the Egyptian interior to Israeli incursions that were both militarily damaging and politically humiliating. A third of the Egyptian fighter force already had been shot down by enemy planes, Nasser admitted, and the morale of his troops had virtually collapsed. The Egyptian president asked then for long-range planes and Soviet pilots; these would be used for retaliatory attacks against Israeli cities.

The Russians turned down this appeal; they were unwilling to risk a confrontation with the United States. On the other hand, they agreed to participate more actively in defending Egyptian military and civilian targets. By mid-February, therefore, the Soviet airlift traffic to Egypt had increased four times above its ordinarily high level. Within six months the Russians had between 10,000 and 14,000 of their own "instructors" and "advisers" in Egypt, as well as an impressive naval flotilla of sixty vessels off the Egyptian coast—an armada that matched the United States Sixth Fleet in tonnage and surface firepower. Additionally, Soviet pilots were flying reconnaissance missions from Egyptian bases, others were on interception alert at Egyptian fields, while Soviet units manned SAM-3 anti-aircraft missile sites. The vast infusion of weaponry and manpower represented an unprecedented and clearly ominous Soviet physical presence in the Middle East.

For Israel, the most crucial development was intelligence information that Soviet pilots were assuming responsibility for air defense over the Nile Valley. Accordingly, in April 1970, the Israelis suspended their deep penetration raids. The Egyptians in turn began moving new SAM missile and artillery batteries toward the Canal. Thereafter Israeli air attacks on this equipment rapidly approached the scale and devastation of American raids in Indochina. They failed to slow the Egyptian encroachment. With each Israeli bombing raid, moreover, the Soviets expanded the perimeters of their defensive responsibilities, until at the end of June 1970 Soviet aviators were flying combat patrols on both the northern and the southern outlets of the Canal, and only 50 miles from the central Canal Zone itself. The Egyptian-Soviet defense system was further thickened (it was already the densest in the world except for the Moscow area) with the introduction of SAM-4 and SAM-6 missiles. Before these new rockets were detected on June 30, they managed to shoot down two Israeli Phantom jets. Early in July they brought down an additional five Phantoms over the west bank of the Canal. As the Israelis encountered these Soviet ripple-fire tactics and a seemingly inexhaustible supply of enemy missile batteries, they recognized that they were facing their gravest military crisis since the weeks immediately preceding the 1967 war. The Soviet Union itself clearly was laying its prestige on the line, and the battle on the Canal's west bank had become almost overnight a Soviet-Israeli confrontation. Prime Minister Golda Meir expressed the anguished mood of her country when she declared on July 7 that "today, and I mean literally today, Israel is facing a struggle more critical than we have ever had to face before." By the end of July, Israel had suffered more than 3,000 casualties since the 1967 war. If Russian fighters should now intervene directly over Suez, those losses would mount even more catastrophically.

There was another side to the picture. The Egyptians had taken a fearful battering of their own. Since April 1970 alone, they had lost over

10,000 casualties to Israeli air and artillery action. Indeed, the Soviets were well aware of the limits of Egypt's defensive capacities. The weaponry they shipped their Egyptian protégé would not by itself guarantee the success of major amphibious landings across the Canal or enable the Egyptian air force to win superiority over the waterway. On July 25, too, the first aerial contacts occurred between Soviet and Israeli planes when Soviet MiGs jumped two Israeli light bombers attacking an Egyptian position. The Israelis escaped. But several days later, on July 30, the Israelis intentionally baited Soviet pilots by feigning an attack on the Nile Valley, then ambushing the scrambled MiGs over the Gulf of Suez. Four Soviet planes were immediately shot down and the rest fled. This was Jerusalem's warning that it did not consider the Russians invincible, and that Israel was prepared to create a Vietnam for the Soviets, if the latter wanted to risk it.

The Soviets did not. As it happened, on June 19, 1970, Washington had proposed a "breathing space" for the Middle East. The plan (the "second Rogers Plan") envisaged a ninety-day cease-fire during which indirect talks between Egypt and Israel would be conducted through the mediation of Dr. Jarring. On June 29, Nasser flew to Moscow for an emergency conference. There, acknowledging the crippling effects of the war of attrition on his armed forces and their morale, he won Soviet support for acceptance of the American proposal. On July 23, Cairo made its decision public. Israel, conversely, was fearful that Egypt would exploit the cease-fire to augment its missile strength along the waterway. Eventually Jerusalem accepted the plan, but only upon receiving Egyptian and Soviet assurances, through Rogers, of a missile "standstill" in the Canal area. The cease-fire thereupon came into effect on August 7. Immediately afterward, however, new Soviet missiles were redeployed within the cease-fire zone, and first Israeli and then—belatedly—American intelligence confirmed this violation.

By then, too, the influx of Soviet military equipment and "advisers," together with the astonishing growth of the Russian naval armada in the Mediterranean, had convinced Washington that the Kremlin intended to use Egypt as a permanent base for surveillance of the United States Sixth Fleet. This sense of joint betrayal and anxiety laid the groundwork for a much closer American-Israeli understanding. During ensuing months, the United States shipped Israel substantial quantities of planes and other advanced weaponry. And once assured of broadened American support, the Israelis in turn evinced a new diplomatic flexibility. They were further influenced in this approach by Nasser's death (of a heart attack) in September 1970. The accession of Anwar al-Sadat (Chapter xxiv) allowed Jerusalem for the first time to anticipate a new and possibly more moderate stance.

Yet when indirect talks between Israel and Egypt began under Jarring's sponsorship early in 1971, they foundered almost at the outset. The Sadat government expressed its willingness to enter into peace negotiations with Israel, provided Israel committed itself in advance to a deadline for the

. . . withdrawal of its armed forces from Sinai and the Gaza Strip; achievement of a just settlement of the refugee problem in accordance with United Nations resolutions; . . . the establishment of demilitarized zones astride the borders in equal distances; the establishment of a United Nations peacekeeping force in which the four permanent members of the Security Council [i.e., including the Soviets] would participate; . . . withdrawal . . . from all the territories occupied.

These Egyptian terms were entirely unacceptable to Prime Minister Golda Meir and her advisers. The Israelis were prepared to compromise on territorial matters, but only upon the understanding that their armed forces would withdraw "to secure, recognized and agreed boundaries to be established [within the context of a] peace agreement." When the counteroffer proved unacceptable to Egypt, the Jarring mission swiftly lapsed.

Privately, however, Dayan hinted at his government's readiness to discuss a mutual interim withdrawal from the Canal of some 20 miles on each side. An Israeli pullback would enable the Egyptians to open the waterway, at the same time deescalating the conflict by making Egyptian traffic and the Suez cities hostages to an armistice. For both parties, such an arrangement would foster the kind of restraint that would encourage later negotiations. Sadat liked the idea. He accepted it on condition that Israel would regard the mutual thinning out of troops as the first stage toward "the implementation of the remaining clauses of Security Council Resolution 242." But once again, Israel rejected the notion of an advance commitment without the give-and-take of direct peace negotiations. Despite the persistent exploratory efforts of Rogers and of the chief of his Near East desk, Dr. Joseph Sisco, no basis could be found even for an interim agreement.

Whatever American impatience with Israel, it was considerably mitigated on May 27, 1971, by the revelation of a new and wide-ranging treaty between Egypt and the Soviet Union. Under its provisions, the Russians agreed to train the Egyptian armed forces in the use of the new Soviet weapons. Egypt in turn undertook to coordinate its diplomatic moves and positions with the Soviet Union. The treaty was ominous from the American viewpoint, no less than from Israel's, for it seemingly institutionalized Moscow's control of Egyptian foreign policy. Indeed, Article Two defined Egypt as a country that had "set for itself the aim of reconstructing society along Socialist lines." With no apparent likelihood of replacing Soviet influence in the near future, Washington limited its Middle Eastern efforts thenceforth to reinforcing Israel's deterrent strength and foreclosing Egypt's war option. Early in 1972, agreement was reached on a continued supply to Israel of American Phantom jets and of other sophisticated electronic equipment. By the spring of that year, as a result, the Israeli air force evidently had assured itself superiority not only over its Egyptian counterpart but over the Egyptian-Soviet defense network.

The fact registered on Cairo. It accounted for the mounting frustration of the Egyptian government, and eventually for a crisis in relations between

Sadat and the Kremlin leadership. The Egyptians urgently wanted a Soviet commitment to help drive the Israelis back from the Canal and to force them to accept Egyptian terms for a settlement. Moscow's goal, on the other hand, was limited to the establishment of what it hoped would become a permanent military base in Egypt, to be used for its own strategic and regional purposes. The May 1971 pact said nothing about direct Soviet military involvement in the conflict with Israel. Leonid Brezhnev and Alexei Kosygin plainly were not interested in falling into their own Middle Eastern Vietnam, nor in provoking a confrontation with the United States. Sadat was angered, therefore, that the nation's relations with the Soviet Union had become apparently a one-way street. He retaliated on July 13, 1972, by issuing an ultimatum through Prime Minister Aziz Sidqi, whom he sent to Moscow, for the Soviets to withdraw their advisers and instructors. Whereupon, much to the astonishment of both Washington and Jerusalem, the Russians in fact set about evacuating the largest numbers of their personnel from Egypt. For the watching Israelis, the schism between Cairo and Moscow appeared at last to validate their determination to hold firm, resisting both Egyptian artillery bombardment along the Canal and repeated Egyptian warnings of even larger-scale conflict in the future.

THE MUTATION OF ARAB GUERRILLA RESISTANCE

The collapse, almost simultaneously, of the war of attrition and of the guerrilla movement on Hashemite soil virtually traumatized the Fatah leadership. No fedayun activity whatever occurred any longer on either side of the Jordan River; while in the Gaza Strip the back of the underground movement was entirely broken. Evidently the one alternative left, then, was to shift the site of operations to Lebanon. Yet at first this peaceful little trading nation, with its mixed Christian-Moslem population, seemed an unlikely base for extensive guerrilla activities. Few of its citizens evinced interest in military or paramilitary adventures. Neither did the country offer as long or as permeable a frontier as the Jordan River line. In fact, however, Lebanon's potential for a guerrilla campaign was more extensive than at first appeared. The nation's southern border was contiguous with Israel. No fewer than 100,000 Palestinians were impacted into Lebanon's refugee camps, and many of these unquestionably were future recruits. Not least of all, the unstable Lebanese government, intimidated by the neighboring Syrian army, was all but helpless to impose restrictions on fedayun movement and activity.

By April 1970, as a result, the Arab irregulars were sufficiently ensconced to begin Katyusha rocket firings from Lebanese territory against Israeli border communities. On May 2, they ambushed an Israeli school bus passing close by the Lebanese frontier, killing twelve children and teachers and severely injuring others. This deed in turn so shocked the Jews that the government launched a particularly stern retaliation, a day-long army sweep into "Fatahland," the Palestinian refugee and guerrilla enclaves clustered along the Lebanese base of Mount Hermon and other heights. The operation not merely cleaned out Fatah nests, but established Israel's standing military presence in the hilly Lebanese border region. Afterward, too, the Israelis bulldozed roads and took up fortified positions at Lebanese observation stations. With a security belt two miles deep carved out along the frontier, quiet was restored for the time being. Even after the reappearance in Lebanon of hundreds of guerrillas expelled from Jordan in 1970, Israeli patrols and Druze scouts on Lebanese soil made infiltration difficult. If their presence flagrantly violated Lebanon's sovereignty, the arrangement was tolerated not only by many Lebanese-Christian border villagers, who openly informed on the guerrillas to their Israeli contacts, but also, tacitly, by the Lebanese government itself. Fatah rocket attacks did not cease altogether. In the ensuing three years, nevertheless, fedayun penetration of Israeli territory was almost as constricted as it had become from Jordanian soil.

By then, too, the splinterization of the guerrilla ranks largely dictated the altered nature of their offensive against Israel. Nominally, most of them belonged to an umbrella coordinating federation, the Palestine Liberation Organization. Yet this prewar, Egyptian-dominated group had been seriously crippled by the June debacle, and its leader, Ahmed Shukeiry, had been forced into retirement. Since then, the PLO had experienced less a revival than a total reincarnation of membership and purpose under the leadership of Yasser Arafat. Consisting ostensibly of representatives of all guerrilla organizations, the PLO in its resurrected form was almost entirely Fatah-dominated, and Arafat himself served as president of its executive. In this capacity he was invited to attend meetings of the Arab League, and won extensive subsidies from the oil-rich governments of Saudi Arabia, Kuwait, and the sheikhdoms of the Persian Gulf.

From the outset, as has been seen, the Fatah's reputation depended largely upon the success of its Moslem traditionalist approach of jihad against Israel, and upon conventional infiltration methods. It is also recalled that even before "Black September" of 1970—the climactic guerrilla defeat in Jordan—Fatah units already had been mauled severely by Israeli border police. In the meantime, other fedayun groups contended for influence. The most important of these "dissident" organizations was the Popular Front for the Liberation of Palestine. Its leader was George Habash, a physician by training, born in Palestine of Christian parents and a man whose pro-Nasserist activities in Lebanon before 1967 gave way after the June War to an avowed Marxist stance. The newly established PFLP at first attracted only a few hundred intellectual activists, most of them, like Habash, drawn from the Christian Palestinian middle class, and sharing for the most part Habash's goal of liberating not only Palestine from Israel but also the Arab masses from "reactionary imperialism." Yet, within months of its founding, even the PFLP splintered over personal and ideological disagreements. A smaller faction, known as the PFLP General Command, was based in Syria under the leadership of Ahmed Jibril, a former Habash lieutenant. In mid-1969 still another former Habash disciple, Ahmed Zahrur, broke with Jibril to form the Arab Movement for the Liberation of Palestine. There were other, even smaller groups by then. The only common ideological purpose among them was their determination to sabotage any likely peace agreement between Israel and the Arab governments, and ultimately to eradicate Israel altogether. Their literature exalted violence and borrowed heavily from the writings of Frantz Fanon.

Whatever their organizational divergences, too, the various guerrilla factions increasingly shared a common technique, one devised by Habash. If traditional methods of subversion against Israel had failed, the PFLP leader argued, then the fedayeen should be prepared to strike at Israelis elsewhere—outside the Jewish state or even outside the Middle East itself. The smaller dissident elements accepted this premise. Indeed, as they turned to new modes of warfare, it became clear that they were obsessed above all with the advantages to be derived from casting a shadow in the world, from drawing attention to Palestine Arab identity. To that end, no tactic was too unconventional or too brutal. Aerial piracy was one such. In the first of these efforts, on July 18, 1968, several (disguised) members of the PFLP forced an El Al transport en route from Rome to Israel to land in Algeria, where it was promptly interned. A month of negotiations followed, until Israel consented to release several imprisoned Arab guerrillas, and the passengers eventually were allowed to go free. The fedayeen regarded the hijacking as a spectacular coup. Israel's Achilles' heel apparently had been found; nothing was as vulnerable as an airborne passenger plane. More important, the abduction of planes and passengers revealed that the free world was unwilling to retaliate by severing transportation links with Arab nations harboring, even lionizing, air pirates.

The Algerian incident triggered a chain reaction of fedayun assaults on El Al, and later on other airlines with service to Israel, and ultimately on Israeli civilians in other lands. In December 1968 an El Al plane on the runway at Athens airport was machine-gunned by two Palestine Arab youths, and an Israeli passenger was killed. The fedayeen were seized by the Greek authorities; but later, under Arab diplomatic pressure, the Athens government imposed exceptionally light sentences on them, and ultimately colluded in their "escape." This time Israel reacted vigorously. In the cases of both the Algerian and the Athens episode, Lebanon was the country in which the guerrillas had been recruited and trained. On December 28, therefore, the Israelis launched a helicopter-borne raid on Beirut airport, destroying fourteen planes of Lebanon's Middle East Airways and other Arab lines. Three days later the Security Council condemned the Israeli action, and France extended its anti-Israel embargo to all military equipment and spare parts. Once again, the Arab guerrilla organizations seemingly had come off best in the exchange.

The result was a quick succession of new fedayun episodes. In February 1969 an El Al plane was attacked at Zurich airport and two crew members were wounded, one fatally. In August a TWA flight en route to Israel was hijacked to Damascus, where the plane's four male Israeli passengers were imprisoned, and released only four months later in exchange for Syrian prisoners in Israel. In November of the same year, a fedayun band threw grenades at the El Al office in Athens, injuring fourteen people, mostly Greeks, and killing a Greek infant. The Athens government later freed the killers, ostensibly to secure the release of a "hijacked" Olympic Airlines jet. Shortly afterward, three Arab guerrillas fired at passengers waiting to board an El Al flight at Munich airport. An Israeli was killed, and Channa Meron, one of Israel's most respected actresses, lost a leg in the attack. In February 1970, Ahmed Jibril's guerrillas planted a bomb aboard a Swissair plane headed for Tel Aviv. The jet blew up in midair; sixteen Israelis were among the victims. On the same day, a bomb hidden in a pouch of Israel-bound mail exploded in an Austrian Airlines plane en route to Vienna from Frankfurt. The pilot managed to land safely.

The most spectacular of the guerrilla episodes occurred on September 6, 1970, when members of the PFLP hijacked four planes belonging to Swissair, PanAm, TWA, and BOAC. In one fell swoop, 310 civilian hostages, including a number of Jews and Israelis, were brought to a remote landing strip in the Jordanian desert. There they waited anxiously for international bargaining to determine their fate (the hijackings of September, we recall, were a precipitating factor in the civil war between the Jordanian army and the guerrillas). Eventually the passengers were allowed to depart, but not until the governments of Britain, West Germany, and Switzerland agreed to release Palestinians convicted for earlier airport assaults on Israelis. In subsequent years it developed that the West German airline, Lufthansa, was paying blackmail money to a number of Arab guerrilla organizations to ensure the safety of its flights; while Paris, in return for a similar fedayun commitment, entered into a "gentleman's agreement" to maintain its anti-Israel diplomatic stance.

Yet plane hijacking and airport shootings were but one facet of the guerrillas' campaign of terrorism for export. In Buenos Aires, the Israeli exhibit at a trade fair was razed. In London, a bomb was planted in a Zim branch office (it was defused in time). In Asunción, Paraguay, two fedayeen killed a woman employee at the Israeli embassy. Bombs were set off in the Israeli embassies at The Hague and Bonn. In Brussels, grenades were thrown at an El Al office, injuring four Belgians. A letter bomb killed the Israeli agricultural attaché in London. The Israeli air attaché in Washington was shot dead outside his home. Guerrilla attacks similarly were directed at Jewish communal and private institutions in various parts of the world. In Buenos Aires a Jewish school was burned, in Prague a synagogue was set afire, in Cologne several elderly Jews died in the flames of their old-age home. In each instance, the PFLP claimed responsibility.

Nor did the PFLP and other, even smaller groups rely exclusively on their own members for these actions. A recruitment program turned up international adventurers, convicted criminals, and anti-Israel leftists. In May 1970 the PFLP hired Rolf Svenson, a Swede, to kill Ben-Gurion in South Africa during the former prime minister's stopover on an international lecture tour; the plot was exposed at the last moment by Israeli security. The following month, Bruno Bargit, a Swiss citizen, was arrested in Haifa carrying explosives and other sabotage equipment. In July of that year, an American, Patrick Arguello, was killed by an Israeli security man while attempting to hijack an El Al plane. A month after that, two French sisters and an elderly French couple were caught attempting to smuggle explosive devices into Israel. Several other Europeans were duped by Arabs into carrying "presents" to Israel on El Al flights—bombs timed to go off in the air. The fedayeen were notably successful, too, in establishing ties with radical terrorist organizations in other parts of the world. Attracted by the prospect of weapons, funds, and training, groups as varied as the Japanese "Red Army," the "Turkish Liberation Army," and the Uruguayan Tupamaros coordinated their activities with the Palestinians. Thus, in late May 1972, in the single most fearsome guerrilla coup to date, three members of the Japanese Red Army disembarked at Lydda Airport, pulled automatic weapons and grenades from their luggage, and coolly slaughtered twenty-six people and wounded seventy-two others in the passenger terminal.

What particularly alarmed the Israelis in this terrorist campaign was their vulnerability abroad. In a sense, they became living targets wherever they ventured outside their native homeland beyond the protection of their highly efficient army and border police. Worse yet, no government anywhere seemed prepared to deter murder attempts by inflicting heavy punishment on convicted Arab killers. The sense of moral confidence that Israel had infused into its citizens following the establishment of independence was at least partially stripped away. Israelis apparently were as vulnerable again as Jews had ever been. Nowhere was this more evident than in the 1972 Munich Olympics, when eleven Israeli athletes were captured and shot dead by Arab guerrillas, members of the Black September Organization (essentially the Fatah). The Olympics were allowed to continue. Indeed, those Arab murderers who survived the exchange of police fire were later permitted to go free by the Willi Brandt government, ostensibly in exchange for a hijacked Lufthansa plane.

In terms of Israeli policy, the only real accomplishment of these killings was to harden the nation's opposition to a rapprochement with the Palestinians. Their effect on the rest of the world was less certain. In Europe, the radical Left sympathetically equated fedayun violence with other Third World struggles. In several French and British universities, the Fatah replaced the Viet Cong as the most popular of the various liberation groups, and student revolutionaries joined with Fatah members in organizing Palestine solidarity campaigns. In the United States, not least of all, the influence of Arab propaganda upon the emergent New Left was altogether astonishing, and notably among black university students. Thus, the Student Nonviolent Coordinating Committee, the most militant of American campus organizations, warmly endorsed the Arab cause. The "New Politics" (that is, New Left) convention, meeting in Chicago in the summer of 1967 and attended by 3,500 delegates and observers, demanded freedom not only for blacks in the United States and Africa, but for Arabs against the "imperialist Zionist war." The *National Guardian,* largest of the New Left weeklies, editorially supported the "de-Zionization of Israel." As among the students, it was the radical black elements who were particularly vigorous and emphatic in their anti-Israel bias. But so, in a more restrained and "objective" manner, were American university professors of Middle Eastern studies. In many instances, their orientation reflected a sincere respect for the legitimacy of the Arab national cause; not infrequently, however, it signified a sharply reactive and self-conscious assertion of academic immunity to local Zionist pressures.

In addition to their resourceful propaganda effort on campuses and among the New Left, the Arabs devoted special attention to organized American Christianity. They were not unsuccessful. Several leading Christian clergymen were genuinely moved by the plight of the Arab refugees. Others experienced theological difficulties in coping with the Jews as a sovereign and triumphant nation rather than as a race of perennial martyrs. Thus, among Catholics and Protestants alike, pro-Arab sympathizers managed to foster anti-Israel resolutions at church councils and assemblies, even to organize boycotts of Holy Land tours. The American Friends Service Committee, a respected Quaker philanthropic group, publicly criticized Israel for insisting on direct negotiations with the Arabs and for denying repatriation to the Palestine refugees. By the autumn of 1973, as a result, Israel's image as a gallant and beleaguered democracy had been subtly altered into that of an implacable, if less than tyrannical, ruler of other lands and other peoples. In their persistence and dynamism, no less than in their ruthlessness, the guerrilla organizations had played a decisive role in molding that image.

THE PRICE OF PROSPERITY

Economically, the Israel that emerged from the Six-Day War bore little resemblance to the recession-plagued nation of 1965–67. Mobilization and battle expenditures had taken their toll, of course, devouring half a billion dollars of the country's resources. Nevertheless, by late summer of 1967 Israel had moved into a phase of rising affluence quite unprecedented in the state's short history. The war, as it turned out, provided a crucial stimulus to the economy. Unemployment was mopped up overnight. Even as imports mounted, foreign exchange reserves increased still faster, by an unparalleled 75 percent, approaching $840 million by the end of the year. During 1968, production rose by 10 percent, exports by 17 percent, and capital investments by 25 percent.

Ironically, one of the factors that produced this upswing was a far higher level of military expenditure, to keep pace at least in some degree with the huge Soviet shipments of weaponry to Egypt and Syria. The cost unquestionably was severe. Indeed, arms purchases overseas accounted for fully half the balance-of-payments deficit in 1967. In 1969–70 the defense budget topped $1 billion, a sum that included the cost of building military settlements in the occupied territories and the extension of male conscription from thirty to thirty-six months. In 1971 the defense budget reached $1.5 billion, equivalent to 23 percent of the country's GNP. By then, the Israelis were spending $470 per capita for defense, eleven times the rate of their Arab neighbors—and in subsequent years the figure would climb much higher (Chapter xxv). But in the immediate post-1967 era, at least, this military outlay served the purpose of tremendously energizing local industry, which poured out guns and ammunition, sophisticated electronic devices, rocket propellants, even jet trainers and spare parts for a large variety of weapons. At the same time, the armed forces increased their local orders for vehicles, processed foods, clothing, pharmaceuticals, and other matériel. By 1970 these contracts exceeded three times their prewar level; and, as a result, military expenditures alone were sufficient to wipe out the nation's lingering unemployment. Research spending by the defense ministry also provided a certain amount of "fallout" benefit in the civilian economy, notably in the precision, electronics, and metal industries.

Other factors also played a role in the postwar boom. Earlier investments in Israel's southern hinterland began to pay off dramatically after 1967. Among these were the expanded capacity of the Arad petrochemical complex, the Dead Sea Works, and Eilat harbor. A highway was completed in record speed from Eilat to Ashdod. Moreover, the blockage of the Suez Canal provided unexpected transit advantages for the Jewish state. East African and Asian cargoes now could be loaded on trucks in Eilat, transported to Ashdod, and reloaded on ships destined for Mediterranean ports. Early in 1970 this "land bridge" was operating at a rate of 900 tons a month. In late 1969, too, Israel completed a new oil pipeline from Eilat to Ashkelon. A huge $62 million investment, it represented merely the initial phase of a program that by 1975 was scheduled to increase piping capacity to 60 million tons annually, equivalent to a third of the oil transported through the Suez Canal in 1966. These postwar investments significantly broadened Israel's employment opportunities, even as it was anticipated that future income would enlarge the nation's revenues.

It is recalled, also, that the economic benefits provided by the occupied territories well exceeded their administrative cost. For example, the acquisition of the Sinai oil wells of Abu Rudeis saved Israel $60 million in hard-currency expenditures by 1970. The removal of Syria's heavy weaponry along the Golan enabled Israel to channel the Jordan's northern floodwaters into Lake Galilee, thereby increasing the water supply by about a third and permitting the reclamation of 12,000 additional acres in the Chula Valley. The June victory produced still other windfalls. Tourism was one of them. Thus, 328,000 visitors arrived in 1967, 432,000 in 1968, and 650,000 in 1970. The money they spent, nearly $100 million in 1968 alone, in turn launched an investment boom in new hotel construction as well as in other related tourist services. The growing proportion of Jews among these visitors, too, from 38 percent in 1966 to 53 percent in 1968, represented but the tip of an iceberg of worldwide Jewish commitment to Israel. The financial contributions and bond purchases of Diaspora Jewry in the six months following the June War reached an unprecedented $600 million, a vital factor in the upsurge of postwar affluence (Chapter XXIII).

No less decisive was the stimulus provided by rising immigration. The influx had steadily declined in the prewar years, to an annual figure of 18,000 by June 1967. In the ensuing year and a half, however, 43,000 Jewish newcomers settled in Israel, almost 40 percent of them from Western countries. In 1969 another 40,000 arrived, among them for the first time large numbers of Soviet Jews (Chapter XXIII). Not least of all, the boom induced many émigré Israelis to return, particularly as the growth of industry created a new demand for scientists and engineers. Immigrants and returnees alike at once created and profited from new employment opportunities. Few of the new arrivals had to wait long for decent jobs, as in earlier immigration waves. By 1970 unemployment was reduced to less than 3 percent.

The confluence of these factors, then, buoyed Israel's GNP by annual 7 percent increases in 1970 and 1971. Industrial and agricultural output in those years rose by 12 percent. In 1971 the export of goods and services totaled $1.8 billion, a 32 percent increase over 1970 and a 100 percent increase in the four years since the war. But if exports were increasing, so were imports—and much faster. They reached $3 billion in 1971. Much of this represented public expenditure, notably for defense. Yet private consumption also increased by 10 percent in both 1969 and 1970, and accounted for a major share of the import surplus. By 1971, as a result, the payments deficit in Israel climbed to $1.2 billion. The widening gulf soon was reflected in a dangerous inflation cycle. The cost-of-living index mounted ominously, by 12 percent in 1971 alone. On August 2 of that year, following the American devaluation, Israel similarly devalued its pound, from 3.50 to 4.20 to the dollar. Still the payments gap continued to widen, together with the inflation, and the two worked in vicious tandem. Well before the Yom Kippur War of 1973, therefore, the escalating price rises gave warning that the postwar boom could not sustain itself indefinitely, that more difficult times were coming, that the bill for the postwar splurge of imports and consumption eventually would have to be paid.

ISRAEL'S ADMINISTERED "COMMON MARKET"

Notwithstanding its lack of success in winning associate membership in the European Common Market (Chapter XIX), Israel found that its economic relations with "foreign" countries were broadened unexpectedly in the aftermath of the 1967 victory. In fact, those relations were with the occupied areas themselves. We recall that the pattern of trade and labor mobility between the Israelis and the West Bank and Gaza Arabs developed without reference to any master blueprint—the new arrangements were intended as strictly temporary, until peace came. Yet, almost inexorably, they produced a growing de facto economic integration. For example, before 1967 the West Bank had served as a kind of central hot-house for the shipment of fruits and vegetables to Jordan and other Arab countries. Now, after the June victory, as a consequence of Dayan's extemporized policy of open bridges, the West Bank gained an additional market, Israel, without losing the others (although West Bank goods continued to find their principal outlet in neighboring Arab lands).

More significantly, Israel gradually became the principal supplier of light industrial goods for the West Bank, even became the main source of the West Bank's agricultural equipment, including chemical fertilizers, agricultural tools, irrigation equipment, seedlings, and new breeds of cows and poultry. By 1970, as a result, the "administered" areas were spending ten times more for Israeli products than for Jordanian products. For that matter, the balance of trade between Israel and the West Bank itself was growing steadily in Israel's favor. In 1972, I£507 million in Israeli goods were "exported" to the occupied areas; the flow of goods back was I£157 million. Purchasing 8 percent of Israel's industrial "export" that year, the West Bank and Gaza became the Jewish state's closest and most natural markets. The new economic relationship was even more impressive in the sector of labor mobility. The influx of Arab workers to Israel gained momentum as the Israeli economy itself approached full employment in 1968, and as a rising share of Israel's own work force served in the army or was employed by military industries. It was a development that not only relieved manpower shortages in Israel but also spectacularly reduced the problem of Arab unemployment in the territories themselves.

Nevertheless, the issue of labor migration opened up a serious policy dispute within the Israeli cabinet. Dayan was inclined to welcome the employment of Arab workers in Israel. Not so Eban and Finance Minister Pinchas Sapir, who regarded this innovation as a threat to the nation's Jewish and pioneering character (p. 710). Accordingly, in a compromise measure of July 1968, the government specifically linked the employment of West Bank and Gaza workers to the fluctuations of Israel's own labor shortage and established a basis of equal pay for equal work. Under the new arrangement, it was expected that the ingress of Arabs would not exceed 4,000. We recall, however, that as the Israeli boom and labor shortage continued, the number of Arab workers officially employed in Israel reached some 65,000 and perhaps twice that number unofficially by 1973.

Thus, reassessing the situation as early as July 1969, a cabinet committee urged that the government ease the problem of Arab unemployment by fostering the economic development of the occupied Arab territories themselves. One major proposal was to encourage Israeli industrial subcontracting to Arab factories and workshops in Gaza and the West Bank, even to underwrite the construction of new workshops there. Another was to embark on a major revitalization of Arab agriculture. In this manner, the living standards of both peoples could be improved, and an "honorable coexistence" preserved between two national identities. The committee's recommendations were swiftly implemented, and with the spectacular results that have been noted (p. 688). The movement of Arab labor into

Israel was never reduced, to be sure. Indeed, it continued to rise. But so, in tandem, did per capita Arab income in the occupied territories themselves. Not less important than this augmented income was the unmistakable evidence of a developing Israeli-Palestinian Common Market. All the elements were there: free trade, interchangeable use of the Israeli pound, large-scale movement of labor, substantial Israeli capital investment, and a certain amount of two-way tourism. Whatever the political future of the territories, then, the patterns of economic interdependence may well have become irreversible within less than half a decade after the June War.

So, too, conceivably, were the patterns of mutual contact and discourse between the two nations. It is recalled that, from the very outset, Dayan's open-bridges policy allowed inhabitants of the West Bank to visit the East Bank. Yet in the same period of 1967–68, the decision was reached to allow Jordanian (East Bank) Arabs to cross over to the West Bank. Although these visits were confined at first to the summers, after 1972 the East Bankers were permitted to come in any season and to remain for up to three months. In 1972–73, therefore, the number of visitors reached 153,000. Their ranks included more than Jordanian citizens living on the East Bank. Some 40 percent of these "tourists" actually came from other Arab countries; relatives or friends on the West Bank had secured visiting permission for them from the Israeli military authorities. If there was something uncanny about the ease with which citizens of nations at war with Israel were given virtually free access to Israeli-administered territory, even more surrealistic was the visit of West Bank (and later other) Arabs to Israel itself. At first, official Israeli approval was required for this privilege; but, as has been seen, after July 1970 West Bankers could and did enter Israel at will. Subsequently, there was hardly a West Bank inhabitant who did not travel to Israel at least once or even many times, visiting friends and relatives in the Israeli Arab communities, on summer days even touring the beach front at Naharia, Tel Aviv, or Jaffa. Again, as in trips to the West Bank, non-Jordanian Arabs similarly were allowed to visit integral Israel upon receiving permits. As of 1973, nearly 20,000 such "outsiders" had availed themselves of the opportunity.

The arrival of these ostensible enemies into Israel was a two-way trauma, for the Israeli Arabs who hosted the visitors no less than for the visitors themselves. The former were reminded of how much they had missed in their quarantine from the surrounding Arab world, deprived of participation in the historic events of Arab nationalism. Many of the Israeli Arab intelligentsia complained that the schools were better on "the other side," that university graduates could find higher-paying jobs more easily throughout the Arab Middle East. But there were many, too, who argued that the economic, even the political, advantages of Israeli citizenship ultimately outweighed the psychic losses of isolation on the fringe of the Arab world. "Not one village on the West Bank has drinking water installed in their houses, not one cooperative society," wrote an Israeli Arab journalist, "and they did not know what chemical fertilizer was good for until we showed them." "They don't know what freedom is," remarked a member of the local (Israeli Arab) village council of J'at. "If anyone over there dared to say one word against Hussein, they would throw him in prison. They don't believe that I can go to Dizengoff Square and shout at the top of my voice against Golda Meir without anything happening to me."

For the West Bank Arabs, personal contact with Israeli Jews and Arabs evoked an even more deeply rooted crisis of recognition. In the aftermath of the 1936 civil "disturbances," and most notably since 1948, the one solution to the Palestine imbroglio conceivable to a majority of neighboring Arabs was simply the liquidation of Zionism and Israel altogether. After 1967, however, new viewpoints began to surface. The West Bankers continued ideologically as anti-Israel as before; but they now acquired a more thorough and sober understanding firsthand of Israeli efficiency and staying power. The impact of this discovery was compounded by a growing disillusionment with the Hashemite regime. As the West Bankers contrasted what they had suffered under Jordanian rule with the more benign fate of the Israeli Arabs, and indeed with the surprising liberalism of Israeli policy in the "administered" territories, they were less willing to be consigned once again to the repressive Amman government. Many, in fact, took to describing the Hashemite administration as "that tribal regime . . . which paved the way for defeat and which has gone as far as trying to annihilate our relatives and nation." In the spring of 1971 the Lebanese weekly *al-Hawadith* conducted an inquiry among West Bankers visiting Beirut and quoted many of them as insisting that "there is nothing at all that can persuade us to return to Jordanian rule and if necessary we will resist return by force."

The response to the *al-Hawadith* poll may not yet have reflected a majority view (p. 679), but the suppression of the Fatah movement in Palestine and the death of Nasser in 1970 apparently ended all hope of military liberation from Israeli rule and certainly any notion of eradicating Israel. The seeming lack of an alternative to Israeli occupation was expressed as early as September 1971 in a book, *La salam bi-ghaya dawlah Filastiniyah hurrah* (No Peace Without a Free Palestinian State), written by a Palestinian journalist, Muhammad Abu Shalbayah. Calling openly for a drastic reorientation of attitude toward the Jewish state, Abu Shalbayah asserted:

> All the Palestinians today carry olive branches. They stretch their hands out in peace to the Jewish people in Israel on the basis of mutual recognition and the establishment of two independent states, Israel and a Palestine state. We don't want to liberate Palestine, neither do we wish to throw the Jews into the sea. . . . We want that our sons and their sons, instead of killing each other, join hands in hoisting the flag of a just peace over this part of the world.

Within weeks of its publication, this book became the most heatedly discussed volume in the Arab world.

In fact, Abu Shalbayah had come close to the mark. Everywhere in the occupied areas the traditional pattern of mutual quarantine slowly was being eroded by daily contacts. Although occasional demonstrations still took place, even isolated instances of grenade-throwing in Nablus and Hebron, Jews and Arabs alike were learning the benefits of a growing, interwoven economy. It was significant that between January 1969 and November 1971, 18,000 Arabs living in Jordan and elsewhere applied to Israel for permission to settle in the occupied area; and 4,000 of them were allowed to do so. The tacit, if expedient, acceptance of Israeli rule was palpable in the West Bank local elections of 1972, the first to be conducted since before the June War. Despite harsh warnings issued by Jordanians, Egyptians, and fedayeen alike, votes were cast by 84 percent of the eligible voters in Samaria; while in a number of Judean towns the balloting was as high as 93 percent. The elections represented a sharp political shift for the West Bank. Of 23 elected mayors, 14 were newcomers. Similarly, of 192 elected councilmen, 102 held office for the first time. Many of the new officials were avowed moderates, who insisted that tolerable relations with Israel represented the wave of the future in the Middle East. It was this newer, younger, more temperate element, no less than the West Bank majority that had elected them, that apparently had staked a vested interest in a regime of two-way cooperation. Before 1973, in any case, few West Bankers discerned an effective alternative to mutual accommodation.

CONFLICTING VISIONS
OF ISRAEL'S TERRITORIAL FUTURE

Ironically, the very quiescence of the occupied territories may have proved a dangerous soporific for the Jews. It forestalled any serious additional efforts by the Israeli government to introduce an autonomist regime in the West Bank and Gaza. Ideas for such a regime had never been lacking, in fact. There were individual Israelis aplenty since 1967 who had developed a number of thoughtful and provocative schemes for the future of these captured lands. Their views represented so wide a spectrum of alternatives, however, that they defied not only consensus but even political categorization. The most extreme annexationist version among them undoubtedly was the "Promised Land Concept." Its adherents derived their inspiration from the Bible and from various divine promises, such as, "Unto thy seed I give the land, from the river of Egypt unto the great river, the River Euphrates" (Genesis 15:18). The poet Uri Zvi Greenberg and the right-wing journalist Dr. Israel Eldad (Chapter XIV) were the best-known members of this chauvinist group, together with a few of the ultra-Orthodox.

Only a fraction less extravagant in its claims was the Land of Israel movement, which included an unlikely cross-section of intellectuals and party members from virtually every sector of national life. Publishing their manifesto in September 1967, the Land of Israel leaders argued that no Israeli government had the "right" to hand back land won in battle, and that the economic development of the conquered territories should begin at once. Even as Jewish New Nazareth had been constructed next door to

Arab Nazareth, they declared, so new Jewish twin cities should be erected beside Nablus, Hebron, Jericho, and other Arab centers of the West Bank. By the same token, the wastelands of Sinai and the Golan Heights should once more be brought under cultivation, as in the days of King Solomon. The Land of Israel movement also drew heavily upon the Orthodox, with some intermingling between its followers and those of the Promised Land group. One of the most articulate of its religious spokesmen, for example, Dr. Harold Fisch, rector of the (Orthodox) Bar-Ilan University, wrote that "there is only one nation to whom the land belongs in trust and by covenant, and that is the Jewish people. No temporary demographic changes can alter this basic fact which is one of the principles of our faith. Just as one wife does not have two husbands, so one land does not have two sovereign nations in possession of it."

The Gachal faction adopted a view closely resembling that of the Land of Israel movement, although the bloc's Liberal members generally were not hawks at all, but simply were dragged along on this issue by their Cherut partners. Menachem Begin and Shmuel Tamir, the most ardent of the maximalists, found their position shared by Ben-Gurion's vestigial State List party, though without Ben-Gurion's adherence. Yet advocates of expansionism were not lacking on the Center-Left, among members of the Israel Labor party and even of Mapam. Indeed, the founder of the Land of Israel movement was Eliezer Livneh, one of the most veteran and respected theorists of Mapai. Livneh's conception hardly was influenced by pietistic tradition, or by any sense of historical mission. Rather, his views were based on the hard-boiled premise that security would be guaranteed only by Israel's new territorial defense in depth, and not by peace treaties that the Arabs were notoriously constrained to violate, even among themselves. It was a view propounded, as well, by the eminent novelist and Mapam member Moshe Shamir. "My present views don't fit in with those I held formerly," he admitted in 1973, with some understatement, "but 1967 was a shock for me." Annexation for Shamir represented a shortcut to peace, "the only way to convince the Arabs they need peace." Shamir, Begin, Tamir, Livneh, and other advocates of a greater Land of Israel refrained from stating explicitly that the demographic peril of annexing Arab Palestine eventually would have to be solved by large-scale Arab departure for neighboring lands. But the idea was implicit.

Of all Israel's expansionists, however, it was surely Moshe Dayan who was least influenced by religious and historical visions. Pragmatism was the key to the defense minister's ideas. As military governor of the occupied territories, he alone made the policies that later he defined. It was under his aegis that an economic "common market" was developing between the two halves of Palestine. Dayan soon made plain, too, that he conceived of an entity in which geographic and demographic frontiers gradually would be blurred. To that end, he proposed that the government establish four Jewish cities along the mountain ridge extending from Hebron and Nablus, in this way creating Jewish shoals and islands in the surrounding Arab hinterland. The Hebron-Beersheba area, in Dayan's view, could be turned appropriately into a single economic-administrative region. Another integrated sector, in the north, might include Afula and Jenin. In August 1971, Dayan clarified his position in his celebrated address to the staff college. It was then that he outlined Israel's function in the administered territories as that of a permanent government, "to plan and implement whatever can be done, without leaving options open for the day of peace, which may be far away." Israel must "create facts," he emphasized.

The furor raised by Dayan's plainspokenness obscured an even more straightforward, if less drastic, approach to the territories that was introduced within a month after the end of the Six-Day War. Its author was Yigal Allon, former Palmach hero, Achdut HaAvodah leader, and subsequently deputy prime minister in the newly organized Labor Coalition cabinet. Before 1967, Allon's approach to security questions in many ways had been as uncompromising as Dayan's. Even after the June War, he continued to press his hard line with renewed vigor. The famous "Allon Plan," we recall, mooted before the cabinet shortly after the war, called for paramilitary (Nachal) settlements on the hilly terrain overlooking the Jordan River, a kind of permanent Israeli crescent encircling the occupied West Bank and guarding Israel's security along a "natural" defense frontier. "We prefer secure borders that are not agreed to, to agreed borders which are not secure," Allon insisted. Yet there was a second, often overlooked ingredient in Allon's approach that was somewhat more conciliatory. Raised among the Arabs, fluent in their language, Allon had long evinced understanding and sympathy for Arab traditions and the Arab sense of honor. It was this tone of cautious moderation that also surfaced after 1967, and by no coincidence as the emerging political rivalry between Allon and Dayan intensified within the Israel Labor party. On numerous occasions the deputy prime minister expressed a willingness to recognize the legitimacy of a Palestinian nation. If such an entity should choose to organize its own state on the West Bank, he declared, or some other political autonomy within the framework of a Jordanian confederation, Israel ought to be willing to accept it. Allon remained firm on the need for an Israeli security border along the Jordan River; but, unlike Dayan, he opposed additional measures of "creeping annexation." His views succeeded essentially in angering both doves and hawks.

A more temperate stance yet was adopted by Pinchas Sapir, the energetic and widely respected minister of finance. Alarmed at Dayan's program of "establishing facts" in the West Bank and Gaza, Sapir in 1968 forcefully objected to the integration of the territories, or their inhabitants, into Israel's economy. He warned that the joinder of a million "administered" Arabs to some 400,000 Israeli Arabs, with the former's incomparably higher birth rate, sooner or later would transform the Jewish republic into an Arab country. By returning the territories, on the other hand, Israel would be surrendering nothing of value, but rather would be "freeing itself from a burden." Sapir expressed these views on numerous occasions during the next few years and insisted, as well, that "[Dayan's] plans for establishing 'facts' would tie our hands once we reached the negotiating table." Although the debate on the territories was suspended in February 1969 with the death of Eshkol, it was resumed throughout the summer in heated debates within the enlarged Alignment (including Mapam). At issue were the Alignment's foreign policy and security planks for the impending elections to the Seventh Knesset; and it was here that Eban, more even than Sapir, became the advocate of the moderate, anti-annexationist group. The foreign minister warned that a brazenly expansionist program would lose Israel support abroad, particularly in the United States. Ideologically, too, a state engorged with hundreds of thousands of new Arab citizens plainly would find it difficult, if not impossible, to sustain Israel's traditional Zionist values. Eban's views were heartily endorsed by the Mapam leadership, and by the Knesset's perennial gadflies, Uri Avneri and Shalom Cohen. Confronted, therefore, by a far-reaching schism on the Left, and aware that negotiations with any Arab government or Palestinian group were far from imminent as it was, the Golda Meir cabinet chose to procrastinate. The decision was taken simply not to decide.

It was an approach that proved uniquely congenial to the new prime minister. Like Ben-Gurion and many other veterans of the early waves of immigration, Mrs. Meir had her own personal view of the Arabs as implacably hostile to Israel; she was unimpressed by appeals to placate them with conciliatory gestures. Reared in the United States, Golda Mabovitch Meyerson had come to Palestine with her husband in 1921. Almost from the outset of her arrival, she had hurled herself into Labor Zionist politics. During the 1930s, her career in the Histadrut and Mapai executives paralleled those of Ben-Gurion and Eshkol. It was in the last years before independence, too, serving as acting director of the Jewish Agency political department, that Mrs. Meir acquired a detailed knowledge of Arab politics. She was not constrained, even then, to adopt the placative course—as Abdullah learned to his regret during the clandestine meetings of 1947 and 1948 (Chapter XIII). Afterward, as Israel's first minister to the Soviet Union, later as minister of labor, and then subsequently as foreign minister and executive secretary of the Mapai party, Mrs. Meir consistently adopted a plainspoken, bluntly straightforward approach in her dealings with Israelis and non-Israelis alike.

A stocky, heavy-featured woman, a seventy-one-year-old grandmother at the time she assumed the prime ministry in March 1969, following Eshkol's death, Mrs. Meir was incapable either by temperament or by age of modifying her views of the Arabs as perennial enemies, with whom one dealt not in trust but out of strength. Nevertheless, as an experienced political tactician, she adopted a compromise stance, endorsing Allon's formula of maintaining a "security frontier" on the Jordan River. This position left the government the option either of returning or (as seemed increasingly likely) of annexing most of the West Bank. For the time being, Mrs. Meir quietly encouraged Jewish settlement in the Jordan Valley, in the Hebron area, in the Gaza Strip, in the Rafa corridor, in the northern Sinai Peninsula, along the Red Sea littoral between Eilat and Sharm es-Sheikh, and on the Golan Heights. The economy and manpower of the occupied territories gradually were integrated with those of Israel. In this manner, then, the *faits accomplis* of the post-1967 years were emerging, bold and incontrovertible.

Those facts became a source of heartache to a number of Israel's most sentient public figures and intellectuals. Arieh Eliav, a former secretary-general of Mapai, discerned the issue within a broader context than that of national security, and he expressed this movingly in a widely read volume, *Eretz HaZvi* (Land of the Deer), published in 1970. Taking care to avoid any denigration of Israel's rights in the occupied territories, Eliav observed simply that the rights of the Arabs were no less compelling: "Whatever [the Arabs] did or did not do for the upbuilding of their country is their business, not ours (and they did in fact create a great culture and a large community there for 1,300 years). We must stick to the same principles we offered in 1936–37, in 1947–49, all the way up to 1967. We must assert once again that there is room in Palestine for the State of Israel and a Palestinian-Jordanian Arab state. In exchange for a full and permanent peace we shall waive implementing part of our historic rights in this Arab state." Eliav urged the government to declare this principle of mutual accommodation immediately, even before the Palestine Arabs expressed their own willingness to negotiate or reached agreement on a spokesman:

> No one to talk to? This is due to the fact that we are not clearly stating any principles concerning the problem of the Palestine Arabs and their and our national-historic rights. If we were to discuss it we might stir the Arabs into discussing it among themselves and with us. If on the other hand, we do not give any answers to questions of principle, and on the other hand we continue—with crass pragmatism—to create reality in western Eretz Israel by settlement, it is no wonder that we arouse suspicion and that the Palestine Arabs can also tell themselves: "There is no one to talk to. . . ." If we are proud of what Israel has done in the territories, this pride can have only one justification: that whatever we are doing there is being done on the premise of open options in the future for the inhabitants of the area. Otherwise, all the bounty we are lavishing on the inhabitants of the areas will turn into a cause for suspicion that what we are doing is really building deluxe reservations for ourselves.

Others shared Eliav's heartfelt concern. Some, like Amos Kenan, a former (but repentant) member of the Lech'i, even dared question the icon of a unified Jerusalem. He noted that "it occurred to no one to ask the annexed Arabs for their views on the fate of Jerusalem, on the plastic surgery committed on the Old City, on the way we shaved the square that faces the Wailing Wall. The city was reunified, but not united." Kenan scoffed at Dayan's allusion to Hebron, Shiloach, and Anatoth as "precious" to Israel, as sites that were integral to the Land of the Bible. "No one has thought of these [holy] places for the past nineteen years," wrote Kenan. "We got along without them just fine; the [Orthodox] champions of these communities were too busy fighting the income tax man." The brilliant

young novelist Amos Oz conveyed the tragedy of the "administered" population, of Israel's and the Arabs' dilemma, in an article written for the moderate *New Outlook:*

> This is our country; it is their country. Right clashes with right. "To be a free
> people in our own land" is a right that is universally valid, or not valid at
> all. . . . I believe in a Zionism that . . . sees the Jewish past as a lesson,
> but neither as a mystical imperative nor as a malignant dream; that sees the
> Palestinian Arabs as Palestinian Arabs, and neither as the camouflaged rein-
> carnation of the ancient tribes of Canaan, nor as a shapeless mass of humanity
> waiting for us to form it as we see fit.

The sense of moral anguish was well captured by the historian Ya'akov
Talmon, one of Israel's most admired scholars, and a man often described
as the intellectual conscience of his nation. In a sternly prophetic article
entitled "Is Force an Answer to Everything?" Talmon skewered the "creation of facts" as a predatory notion reminiscent of Mussolini's "sacro ego-
ismo," of earlier European dreams of "special missions" and "historic boundaries." All these earlier "missions" were similarly based on ancient claims,
Talmon observed, and all ended in disaster, for they ignored the bald
fact that other peoples lived in the coveted areas. For Talmon, too, as for
Sapir and Eban, there were social and moral dangers in "creeping annexation" fully as grave for Israel as the peril of outraged Arab nationalism. He
wrote:

> Better men than I have enlarged on the grim paradox that threatens the Zion-
> ist vision, the social and moral failure of that vision, which are to be expected
> from the transformation of the Jews into employers, managers and supervisors
> of Arab hewers of wood and drawers of water, and all of it plus the slogan
> of "Integration." . . . There is an inescapable process in a population that
> is divided into two peoples, one dominant, the other dominated. No! The
> State of Israel will not be such a monstrosity. It was not for this that we
> have prayed two thousand years.

Talmon's article was published in the summer of 1973.

Six years earlier, in the immediate aftermath of the June victory, the
historian's prophecy had been anticipated by an unlikely eminence.
Throughout his long career, David Ben-Gurion had been regarded as the
incarnation of grim Israeli militancy. Now, however, interviewed in his
desert retirement at Sde Boker, the former prime minister shocked reporters by quietly advocating withdrawal from all captured territory except
Jerusalem and the Golan Heights. The rest would become an albatross
around Israel's neck, he insisted, and a standing provocation to the entire
Arab world. At the time, Ben-Gurion's warning evoked a mixture of deri-
sion and sadness. Indeed, the public response was all but uniform: "The
old lion has finally gone soft."

ISRAEL

AND WORLD JEWRY

A MOBILIZATION OF THE DIASPORA

If the Israelis were swept up in a euphoria of deliverance immediately following the Six-Day War, their reaction was altogether paralleled among Jewish communities overseas. It soon became apparent, in fact, that Israel's new territorial amplitude was entirely matched abroad by an unprecedented demographic defense in depth. The revelation occurred in June and July of 1967, when a tidal wave of moral and financial support began cascading in from the Jewish hinterland of North and South America, from western Europe, South Africa, and elsewhere. Manifestly, this Diaspora population had undergone a trauma of conscience and identity during the summer crisis. Its response to Israel's needs was no longer essentially philanthropic, but this time something far more visceral. Until the last days preceding the war, only a minority of Western Jews had appreciated how vital the existence of a Jewish state had become to their own security and self-respect. The rest had unthinkingly grown accustomed to the "normalcy" characteristic of other ethnic groups. Each year of Israel's independence and consolidating strength had blurred the memory of refugees adrift on the seas like Flying Dutchmen; of Jewish intermediaries, hats in hand, waiting in foreign consulates for the revision of a visa quota; even of the *numerus clausus* that once had excluded Jewish students from good universities and professional schools. The memory had all but faded —until May 1967. Then, in the ensuing tension-wracked days, the ground suddenly opened under the feet of the Jewish people in their worldwide dispersion, and they glimpsed beneath them again the terrifying void of their former Exile. Israel's battlefield victory was no less their redemption than that of the citizens of Tel Aviv or Jerusalem.

The ecstatic response, then, of the overseas community, the hundreds of thousands of savings accounts that were instantly and gratefully emptied, the purchase of tens of millions of dollars of State of Israel Bonds, the influx of Jewish visitors from abroad, the upsurge of immigration, all evoked more than thrilled surprise among the Israelis. It was an apocalypse. In the aftermath of the war, Israeli newspaper accounts of this Western Jewish reaction shared front-page space with reports of diplomatic negotiations in the United Nations and of political maneuvers in the Arab world. Troops returning from the front experienced a renewed moral

jubilation upon learning of the Diaspora's near-fanatical commitment to
Israel's survival. Later reverses—the French arms embargo, the mounting
virulence of Soviet hostility—could not temper the joy of this discovery.
It was evident now that the peoples of Israel, on the ancestral soil and in
the overseas hinterland alike, were rapidly being fused into a single people.
Before the unity of that enlarged population, no future challenge appeared insurmountable.

The renaissance of the Diaspora manifested itself even in the most
broadly acculturated of Jewish communities. Zionism had grown only
slowly in France, for example, and the Fédération Sioniste had not become entirely respectable among the nation's 300,000 Jews until the birth
of Israel. Yet, while most of France's leading Jewish organizations and institutions were pro-Israel by the 1960s, it was the crisis of 1967 that galvanized them into unprecedented Zionist activism. On May 26, 1967, a
Comité de Coordination des Organisations Juives en France was hurriedly
assembled, led by Guy de Rothschild and dedicated to an emergency fund-
raising program on Israel's behalf. Within three weeks 20 million francs
were raised, an unheard-of sum by French Jewish standards. Emigration to
Israel picked up substantially for the first time, too, averaging 7,000 annually for the next three years. If most of these emigrants were themselves
newcomers to France from Algeria, they were French citizens nevertheless,
and their departure now for Israel unquestionably was stimulated by the
June War.

The intensification of commitment was similarly evident in Latin
America, whose 740,000 Jews (460,000 in Argentina, 155,000 in Brazil, with
smaller numbers in Mexico, Uruguay, and Chile) were only barely less
acculturated than those of France. In the 1948 war, approximately 500 of
them served in Machal, Israel's brigade of foreign volunteers; but few
remained on. While later, between 1961 and 1965, aliyah from Latin
America reached 13,000, this was mainly a consequence of anti-Semitic
riots in Buenos Aires and Montevideo. The level in any case was not sustained after 1965, as conditions improved again in Argentina and Uruguay.
As in France, it was the Six-Day War that provided the renewed catalyst.
During the subsequent five years, emigration for Israel averaged nearly
2,000 annually, and by 1970 there were approximately 25,000 South American Jews living in Israel, a third in kibbutzim, the rest making their homes
in the cities, with a disproportionately large element of physicians and
pharmacists among them.

Unlike France or Latin America, on the other hand, there was nothing
belated in the response of "Anglo-Saxon" Jewry. We recall that Zionism
had been a powerful force in England since 1917. Thus, in 1929 the entire
Board of Deputies of British Jewry chose to affiliate with the newly
formed Jewish Agency, and afterward only Zionists were permitted to hold
office in this organization. Britain's Zionist Federation maintained a network of eleven day-schools, offering a fully developed Hebraic curriculum.
During the 1967 crisis, virtually the whole of Anglo-Jewry was mobilized.
The Joint Israel Appeal raised an emergency fund of £17 million, and

2,000 young men and women departed for volunteer service in Israel. Indeed, aliyah had always enjoyed high priority in British Zionism. By 1967 the Anglo-Jewish population in Israel exceeded 10,000 (and subsequently grew by an additional 3,000); most of them had arrived after the establishment of the state. Approximately 500 British Jews served as Machal volunteers during the 1948 War of Independence. Twice that many settled on kibbutzim, and three of the most respected collective farms in the land, Kfar Blum, Kfar HaNasi, and Beit HaEmek, were founded by British Jews, with eleven others predominantly Anglo-Jewish in membership. To be sure, most of the British newcomers preferred to resume their former middle-class occupations. Several thousand entered business and professional life, while perhaps a sixth of the entire British immigration found employment in Israel's public services as government, Jewish Agency, bank, and insurance officials. On a smaller scale, they duplicated the role performed by the central European immigration wave of the 1930s, bringing order, efficiency, discipline, and thoroughness to their tasks.

Anglo-Jewry's Zionist commitment in some respects may even have been exceeded by the 118,000 Jews of South Africa. The fact was that there was no Diaspora Jewry anywhere quite as intensely Israel-oriented as the South Africans. Their Zionist membership per capita was by far the world's largest. Their contribution to Zionist funds was second only to American Jewry's, and proportionately three times larger. During the 1948 War of Independence, South Africa contributed 700 Machal members. By 1967 nearly 4,000 South Africans had settled in Israel, and by 1975, 6,000—again, the highest proportion of aliyah in the world. This unprecedented Zionist activism derived in part from the warm Jewish loyalties of a common Lithuanian ancestry, and in part from a sense of ethnic insecurity amid South Africa's racial tensions. Either way, Israel was the beneficiary.

A fourth of the South African immigration settled on the land, establishing a chain of kibbutzim and moshavim and joining other collective farms in large numbers. Many hundreds of South Africans resumed their medical and dental practices in Israel. A large minority entered the diplomatic and military services. Two South Africans were members of the cabinet, another a member of the Knesset; two were mayors. Most were businessmen, however. Indeed, a number of Israel's most important companies owed their growth and development to South African capital and leadership, among them El Al, the national airline; Ata, a leading clothing manufacturer; as well as a variety of dress factories, banks, mortgage and insurance companies, and scores of other middle-sized businesses, ranging from cold-storage plants to foundries. Perhaps the most visually impressive South African contribution was the Mediterranean resort of Ashkelon, founded in 1953 by private investors in partnership with the South African Zionist Federation and the Israeli government. Within ten years the results of this enterprise could be seen in a handsome garden city of 15,000 inhabitants, one of the showpieces of Israel, and a vivid talisman of Diaspora loyalty.

While the intensity of South African devotion probably was unmatched by any other Jewish community abroad, it was the settlement of American and Canadian Jews in Palestine that dated back furthest of any "emancipated" Jewry. By 1900 over a thousand North Americans had arrived in the Holy Land. With few exceptions, these newcomers were European-born, many Orthodox pietists, others fugitives from tsarist persecution who regarded America essentially as a way station to Zion. During World War I, 2,000 Americans and Canadians served with the Jewish Legion, and a third of these remained in Palestine to become citrus farmers, pioneers of the moshav movement, as well as founders of the communities of Ra'anana and Herzlia. Approximately 3,000 American small businessmen took up residence in the Yishuv during the mid-1920s, and nearly 1,000 others in the years before World War II. Afterward, in the period of Underground rescue between 1945 and 1948, American and Canadian Jews manned ten refugee vessels and helped transport 40 percent of the "illegals" to Palestine. During the 1948 war, too, approximately 2,000 North Americans served in Machal, and a number of army units and a large part of the air force were made up almost entirely of these volunteers.

Yet the principal growth of the American and Canadian immigration awaited the "normalcy" of statehood. Thus, between 1947 and 1967, North American settlement grew to 15,000. Its members founded sixteen kibbutzim, and hundreds joined existing collective and communal settlements. As in the case of other "Anglo-Saxons," however, the majority resumed their former middle-class vocations. Among the newcomers were several hundred teachers, doctors, dentists, engineers, chemists, agronomists, botanists, and skilled technicians. Nearly a thousand others found employment in the public institutions—the Jewish Agency, the Jewish National Fund, State of Israel Bonds, and the government. Among the latter, one eventually became prime minister, two served as cabinet ministers, one was elected mayor of Jerusalem, and two were appointed justices of the supreme court. Others worked in banks, travel agencies, insurance, and various commercial offices on an administrative level.

Their numbers were dramatically augmented by the 1967 war. Nearly 10,000 came to serve in the emergency, and half of these remained. Afterward, from 1967 to 1973, immigration from the United States and Canada averaged 5,000 annually, enlarging the North American and Canadian settlement to over 40,000 by 1973. With few exceptions, these Westerners were intensely motivated in their Jewish and Zionist loyalties. Several thousand of them were products of well-organized Zionist youth groups. Like the Chovevei Zion of the early Russian immigration waves, their commitment to Jewish nationhood was deeply rooted and intellectually buttressed. Those arriving from Canada, for example, like those from South Africa, were products of a tightly integrated Jewish communal "family" embracing a network of Zionist parties, day schools, and summer camps. Their clearly focused and precisely articulated goal in Israel was to live "whole" Jewish lives in a sovereign Jewish nation.

ISRAEL REFORMULATES ZIONISM

It was the view of Ben-Gurion and other Israelis, moreover, that these were the only Jews who had the right henceforth to call themselves Zionists. Initially, in the first year of statehood, the role of Zionism appeared to be almost exclusively functional—that is, oriented to the defense and interpretation of the state before world opinion and to the fund-raising effort on Israel's behalf worldwide. But shortly afterward, the issue of Zionist definition suddenly erupted into prolonged debate between the Israeli government and the American Zionist leadership. One source of the quarrel lay in a characteristic Israeli attitude toward the Diaspora overall. It seemed to many who had fought in the War of Independence that the overseas community was inhabited by half-men, or at least by an inferior breed of half-Jews, who preferred the comforts of life abroad to the challenges and dangers of life in Israel. This impatience was reinforced by the "Palmach generation's" contempt for any ideology that was not based on tangible sacrifice and accomplishment. For many young Israelis, the very term "Zionist," in its purely ideological connotation, signified a kind of officious, outdated windiness.

Ben-Gurion himself took the lead in rejecting the notion that Zionism could have any further validity without immigration to Israel. He had only contempt for the Achad HaAmist vision of a Jewish nation spiritually enriching a large and permanent Diaspora. Jewish life elsewhere was bankrupt in his eyes. "I don't know how long it will take," the prime minister declared in a symposium in Jerusalem, "—whether ten years or fifty years—but, in time, America will be a unitary nation, just like any other nation." When that happened, Jewish identity in the New World would be lost. "It is entirely different with Jews in Israel," he boasted. "The roads in this country are Jewish roads; they were built by Jews. . . . The houses that you see here were built by Jews. The trees are Jewish trees; they were planted by Jews. The railway is a Jewish railway; it is conducted by Jewish workers, by Jewish engineers. The papers are Jewish. We do not live a group life. Here we are living a national life."

In his uncompromising identification of Zionism with settlement in Israel, however, Ben-Gurion revealed another, more practical and political, consideration. "There is another difference between Israeli Jewry and Diaspora Jewry," he explained. "We are also an independent factor in international life. We appear like any other free people at the United Nations. We meet with representatives of large and small states on an equal footing. We don't need shtadlanim [intercessors] any more." The prime minister's anxiety lest Zionist leaders overseas presume any longer to speak for Israel was more than a phantom of his imagination. There was a mutual recognition, to be sure, that world Jewry would continue to bear a heavy financial burden for the ingathering. Indeed, it was for this reason that the Zionist Council in August 1948 decided that the Jewish Agency—most of its departments transferred by then to the Israeli government—should nevertheless be maintained as an independent body, to continue with its historic mission of transporting and settling refugees. Similarly, the Agency was charged with the task of quickening the interest of world Jewry in Israel, of fostering spiritual and cultural ties between the Diaspora and Israel, and of distributing information on Israel's achievements and aspirations.

Ben-Gurion had little objection to these various "inspirational" roles. But the allocation of major fund-raising responsibilities to the Agency, and thereby to its parent body, the Zionist Organization, with the latter's heavily weighted American membership, was a different matter. Hardly had the state been established, in fact, than Nahum Goldmann, president of the Zionist Organization, made it clear that his colleagues would demand some degree of shared partnership in Israel's future and destiny. Thereupon Ben-Gurion, prime minister of an independent Jewish government, emphatically rejected the very notion of shared authority. In his opposition, too, he had a point that even Goldmann was forced to concede. The partnership advocated by the Diaspora Zionist leadership was not simply one of ideology or moral union. It was political, as well. Even after 1948 the Zionist Organization continued to function on the basis of its traditional international party structure. What was prolonged, therefore, was the rather extraordinary anachronism of biennial Zionist Congresses, their delegates elected by parties—Mapai, General Zionist, Mizrachi, and others—in the United States, South Africa, Brazil, and elsewhere, determining in turn the membership of the Jewish Agency Executive, including the latter's department heads and money-disbursing personnel in Israel. Ben-Gurion, who had labored all his adult life to achieve sovereignty for a Jewish state, was flatly unwilling to share that independence now even with Jews and devoted Zionists living abroad.

It was the prime minister's view, moreover, that financial support of Israel was by no means the responsibility of the Zionist Organization alone, but rather of all Jewish fund-raising agencies throughout the world. On this point, he encountered opposition within months of Israel's independence. Emanuel Neumann, president of the Zionist Organization of America, and Abba Hillel Silver, chairman of the American section of the Jewish Agency—both of them leading officers of the Zionist Organization— warned that Ben-Gurion's approach threatened to undermine the very existence of Zionism in the United States. The basic priority for them was to embark on a vigorous Zionist educational and public relations effort. Without such an undertaking, they contended, American Jews would not be persuaded to enlarge their financial support of Israel. When, therefore, in 1949, Ben-Gurion and his Zionist allies in Jerusalem rejected this contention, Neumann and Silver resigned from the Agency. The prime minister was unfazed. In May 1951 he visited the United States to launch the Israel Bonds drive. Throughout his tour he studiously avoided all reference to Zionism, emphasizing by implication his view that only those Jews who settled in Israel were true Zionists, and that in any case fund-raising on behalf of Israel was a responsibility common to the entire Jewish people.

Ben-Gurion's adamancy was a source of much heartache to veterans of the Zionist movement, and not only to those perennial officeholders for whom a seat on a dais was both an ego-necessity and a rationale for continuing to live in the Diaspora. The most prestigious spokesman of world Zionism outside Israel, for example, Nahum Goldmann, asserted repeatedly that Zionism had never proclaimed as one of its goals the emptying of the Diaspora, but rather its strengthening. It was a myth, anyway, to assume that Israel could be developed by Israelis alone; Israel would always be "hopelessly" dependent on world Jewry for economic sustenance. In his autobiographical credo, Goldmann ventured to suggest that close ties with world Jewry were not less indispensable even to Israel's cultural development:

> Israel is in great danger of becoming a small nation in the cultural sense, of falling victim to provincialism and relinquishing everything the country stands for to Jews all over the world and to mankind as a whole. Only through psychological and spiritual closeness to world Jewry, only through the mutual enrichment of the Diaspora by Israel and of Israel by the Diaspora, which has a share in many of the cultures of the world, can Israel become . . . a "great nation."

But the process of mutual enrichment required more than an ordinary sentimental partnership, the Zionist statesman insisted. The Diaspora was entitled to a voice in shaping policy.

Goldmann's arguments were persuasive enough for Mapai and the Knesset majority finally to concede a special legal role to the Zionist Organization, one that would transcend the Zionist Council resolution of 1948 (p. 718). This took the form, in 1952, of the Law on the Status of the World Zionist Organization—Jewish Agency, and of a "Covenant" signed in 1954 by the Israeli government and the Executive of the Zionist Organization. The measures decreed simply that the immigration of Jews and their absorption in Israel remained the specific responsibility of the Zionist Organization and of its instrument, the Jewish Agency. In fact, the agreement signified more than a conciliatory gesture to the *amour-propre* of the Zionist leadership. By investing the Agency with the purely humanitarian, nongovernmental, task of rescue and relief, it ensured that the Agency's fund-raising efforts enjoyed a tax-exempt status in the United States (and in several other Western nations), thus enhancing the effectiveness of these financial appeals.

Even so, it was a question whether the Agency would not have been more successful in this role had it been independent of the Zionist Organization and of the residual political influence of Zionist parties whose constituents lived abroad. The truth was that the latter continued to place their men in key positions on the Agency Executive and to give favored treatment and patronage to absorption projects in Israel sponsored by one or another of the various parties. Ben-Gurion had known it would come to this. As a result, he bypassed the Agency whenever possible in launching the major development projects of the nation. Bonds, investment funds, German reparations, private gifts to universities—these henceforth became his major interest, and over them the Agency had no control. More important, he scrupulously refrained from involving the Agency leadership in major policy decisions of state. The more Israel grew in vigor and assertiveness, therefore, the more the Agency as a policymaking body (in distinction to a fund-raising organization) shriveled into a kind of honorific retirement home for the Diaspora's veteran Zionist politicians and publicists.

It is of interest, too, that in the aftermath of the 1967 war Ben-Gurion's grimly austere definition of the Zionist "partnership" was given renewed philosophical, even spiritual, emphasis by Israelis of widely differing backgrounds. Confronted with an urgent need for immigrants to protect the enlarged frontiers of the nation, Israeli leaders spoke increasingly of aliyah as a moral obligation upon Zionists in every land. Thus, at the Twenty-seventh Zionist Congress, meeting in Jerusalem in the winter of 1971, the Israeli delegates and their supporters forced through a resolution obliging the leaders of overseas member organizations to accept personally the imperative of aliyah to Israel. Aghast at this maximalism, several of the American delegates, representatives of Hadassah and others, warned of a fracture in the Zionist movement unless the resolution were dropped. Eventually the dispute was papered over, but the underlying pressures for immigration, although usually phrased in ideological terms, were clearly mounting. Indeed, since the capture of Jerusalem, Israel's religious spokesmen professed to regard the messianic age as at hand, with all its sacred obligations for a mass ingathering of Jewry worldwide. The aggressiveness, even stridency, with which these claims were projected did not fail to evoke a reaction abroad.

THE CRISIS OF AMERICAN ZIONISM

It was under these circumstances, then, as Ben-Gurion and other Israelis sternly reformulated their relationship to world Zionism, that Diaspora Jewry, and most particularly the Jews of the United States, found it necessary to redefine their own attitude toward Israel. In fact, a number of American Jewish communal and intellectual spokesmen were quite prepared to accept Ben-Gurion's evaluation of the Jewish future outside Israel. Arthur Hertzberg, for example, a New Jersey rabbi and historian of Zionism, and a leader of the American Jewish Congress, took an altogether bleak view of the possibilities for Jewish "normalcy" amid a non-Jewish majority. In a series of incisive articles, Hertzberg observed that the Jewish "establishment" historically had operated on the assumption that Jewish identity could survive and even flourish within a pluralistic, democratic order. But the facts appeared to belie the theory, in his view. "The Jew cannot settle down in freedom to be himself, 'just like everybody else,'" Hertzberg contended. "When in his own inner consciousness he begins to approach a real feeling of at-homeness within the larger society, what remains of his Jewish identity is too little and too personalized to sustain a community." Hertzberg insisted that the logical solution to this anomaly, "and of its quiet dangers to our own Jewish identities," was to "start thinking seriously . . . of aliyah; at the very least, the aliyah of our children."

At the other end of the spectrum there were American Jews who rejected not merely the obligation of aliyah to Israel (a rejection shared by
the majority of American Jewry), but of the validity of Jewish statehood
altogether within the context of the Prophetic experience. This anti-Zionist
faction was identified essentially with a tiny, vestigial group known as
the American Council for Judaism; since the 1940s, the Council had tenaciously rejected the nationalist component in Jewish history and religion.
More recently, the 1960s witnessed the participation of a small but articulate group of Jewish university students in the New Left, a movement
that in its doctrinaire anti-imperialism regarded Israel's very existence as
an affront to the emerging "Third World."

Yet anti-Zionists and New Leftists were hardly typical of those who
expressed the most penetrating criticism of American Jewry's overwhelming
Zionist bias. Rather, there were others, sensitive Jewish intellectuals, themselves fully committed to Israel's well-being, who questioned whether a
political state could appropriately fulfill its emergent role as the touchstone
of American Jewish communal life. Among these critics, Jacob Petuchowski, a Reform rabbi, and Jacob Agus, a Conservative rabbi, both eminent
scholars of Judaism, rejected the notion that an impassioned concern for
Israel and its welfare could offer a *raison d'être* for meaningful Jewishness
in the Diaspora. As Petuchowski saw it, Zionism's potential danger to
American Judaism was that it functioned as a kind of surrogate religion.
Indeed, Zionism flourished precisely because the classical religion it had
come to replace was weak and ineffectual; even as it similarly failed on its
own to meet American Jewry's more deeply rooted spiritual needs. Jacob
Neusner, a widely respected professor of classical Judaism, put the matter
succinctly: "The *State* of Israel is just that, contingent, useful, serving
valuable ends. The *people of Israel* is uncontingent, absolute, more than
merely useful. The State is the means to an end. The end is determined by
the Jewish people"—in the Diaspora as well as in the State of Israel.

Petuchowski, Agus, and Neusner wasted little time in disposing of Ben-
Gurion's claim that American Jewry, or any free Diaspora Jewry, was
living "in exile." They found suspect even the Pinsker argument that a
Jewish state would "normalize" Jewish life in the Diaspora. Israel surely
had not yet performed this function in the United States, they observed,
either economically or vocationally. Rather, in some ways, Israel's existence
actually disrupted American Jewish life. It forced American Jews to be
nationalists about Israel, when Jews traditionally disliked nationalism or
flag-waving of any kind. Was Israel performing a "mission" for Diaspora
Jewry? these critics asked. Was it fulfilling the Prophetic role of social
justice in its own country? How did the Israelis treat their own minorities?
To what extent did ethics and morality influence Israel's Orthodox establishment, or that nation's political and business life? The answers were
not always encouraging.

There was no doubt, admitted Judah Shapiro, an able and experienced
Jewish communal executive, that Zionism had made a significant contribu-

tion to American Jewish ideology. It had Hebraized Reform Judaism, energized Jewish education, united within its ambit a wide range of Jewish social orientations from the working classes to the Orthodox. Even so, noted Shapiro, Zionism as an ideological movement had lost much of its *élan* after the birth of Israel. Since 1948 the physical and financial demands of a state had taken priority in American Jewish life over the moral and ethical implications of Zionist philosophy; and Israel had related itself thereafter to the nonideological forces in the Diaspora, the fund-raising instrumentalities. The price American Jewry paid for this antiseptic, nonideological relationship was an overcommitment to pro-Israel philanthropies at the expense of legitimate American Jewish cultural needs. In a May 1969 article in the *Jewish Frontier*, Shapiro warned:

> Only if there is a cultural life among Jews in this country, is there any prospect for a genuine relationship between Israel and American Jewry. Thus, to encourage intensity in Jewish life here, however irrelevant to current fund-raising centrality, holds greater promise for the future than blandness and consensus for the protection of the annual [pro-Israel] campaign. In any event, the American-Jewish community cannot dance at the end of a puppet string manipulated in Israel. The real objective is for American Jewry to be so concerned with the continuity of Jewish life for itself that it will naturally be related to the great Jewish community of Israel in an inseparable alliance.

Actually, few American Jews, and surely not the Zionist majority among them, regarded the Diaspora as the puppet of Israel. At the least, they envisaged the two communities as partners in a common Jewish destiny. Yet, if misunderstandings existed among American and Israeli Zionists, perhaps both would have been well advised to exert an effort at redefinition. Such an attempt in fact was proposed by Mordecai Kaplan, the most distinguished of American Jewish philosophers, in his appeal for a "new Zionism" that would become in effect "contemporary Judaism in action." For the Zionist movement to renew itself, Kaplan wrote, it "should henceforth treat the establishment of the State of Israel only as the first indispensable step in the salvaging of the Jewish people and the regeneration of its spirit." To that end, Kaplan proposed nothing less than a World Jewish Conference that would proclaim Jewry an international people and that would be consecrated to a religious civilization of which the acknowledged center would be Israel. Kaplan's "new Zionism," in short, sought to convert a historic nationalist movement into a general Jewish platform. It was admittedly a rather cosmic scheme. At the least, it would have provoked and angered a number of vested religious groups, particularly the Orthodox.

In recognition of this limitation, Ben Halpern, a leading sociologist of Labor Zionism, preferred simply to regard Zionism as a method of enhancing a revitalized secular Jewish culture in America. The new identity could be sustained, on the one hand, without offering lip service to a religion that had largely forfeited its appeal in a materialistic society; and, on the other, without sentimentalizing American Jewry's largely outworn east European folkways. Zionism alone, then, was equipped to fill a Jewish cultural void with a loyalty that was both solidly and secularly ethnic.

With the largest numbers of Jews certain to remain in the Diaspora, only an ideology that recognized their essentially ethnic character would preserve them from cultural disintegration. More than any other *Weltanschauung*, Zionism was that ideology.

It seemed a fair evaluation of the role Zionism pragmatically was beginning to fulfill in Western Jewish life. The emergent music, drama, poetry, and prose of Western Jews, even the religious expression of those Jews who attended synagogue, all laid increasing emphasis on ethnic Jewishness, on Jewish peoplehood in its widest contours. The identification may have communicated little in the way of a universally "spiritual" lesson, as Kaplan would have preferred. It surely was no substitute for Prophetic ethics, as Petuchowski, Agus, and Neusner observed. By Ben-Gurion's standards, it generated a totally inadequate emigration to Israel; while, by the criteria of American and other Western Jewish communal leaders, it failed to produce a decent appreciation of Jewish religiohistory. There was little doubt, nevertheless, that pride in the accomplishments of Israel's builders and soldiers, and commitment to Israel's survival, had energized and revitalized the Diaspora as no other force in the modern history of the Jewish people. As a single example, American Jewish university students, many of them "graduates" of Hebrew camps and of summer visits to Israel, were pressing by the thousands for academic courses in Jewish studies. In their relaxed, "Western" manner, they comfortably identified themselves with a rejuvenated people, whose survival they were now quietly determined to ensure.

THE DIASPORA PAYS ITS DUES

In truth, the Jews of the United States and of other Western nations were committed to exerting every effort and utilizing every available technique to guarantee the source of their renewed security. Through the intercession of a plethora of Western Jewish organizations, ranging from the mass-membership B'nai Brith and Hadassah to a tightly structured pro-Israel lobbying group, the American-Israel Public Affairs Committee, operating under the resourceful direction of I. L. Kenen American Jewry ensured that elected officials understood precisely what was expected of them when Middle Eastern issues were debated in government. Few senators or congressmen, particularly those representing states and districts with large Jewish urban constituencies, were deprived of continual and detailed exposure to Israel's case. Indeed, no ethnic or special interest group in the United States was ever more effective in registering its partisan views. Yet it is doubtful whether congressional support for Israel was influenced exclusively by political opportunism. Goodwill for the Jewish state continued by and large to reflect national sentiment and executive policy. The basic sympathy of the American people, in turn, was mobilized far more effectively by the unassuming courage of the Israelis themselves than by the aggressiveness, occasionally even the tasteless hysteria, with which

American Zionist groups mounted public demonstrations and sponsored full-page newspaper advertisements.

Where Diaspora Jewry ultimately made its most enduring contribution to Israel's welfare was less in the realm of propaganda than in the undramatic but altogether vital area of financial support. The affluent among this overseas community provided hundreds of millions of dollars for special educational and scientific institutions in Israel, for university buildings, clinics, and cultural and recreation centers. *En bloc,* they paid membership dues to a wide range of Israel-oriented societies: to the "Friends" of the Hebrew University, of Tel Aviv University, of the Technion; to "Committees" for Bar-Ilan University, the Weizmann Institute, the America-Israel Cultural Foundation; and to broadly based organizations such as Hadassah (WIZO, outside the United States) and various Labor Zionist and Orthodox Zionist fellowships, each with its special projects in Israel. Of critical importance in Israel's ambitious Negev development undertakings was the large-scale purchase of State of Israel Bonds. First issued in 1951, these securities found an immediate market. By June 1967, $922 million had been sold, 85 percent of them in the United States. In 1967 alone, sales totaled $175 million. It was essentially bond money, together with German reparations and loans, that financed the growth of Israel's southern industrial towns and factories, of the Jordan Valley Water Carrier, the ports of Eilat and Ashdod, the oil pipelines from the Gulf of Aqaba to the Mediterranean—as well as a host of other development projects, including the enlarged Dead Sea Works and the Arad petrochemical complex (Chapter xviii).

By far the single largest reservoir of overseas financial aid, however, was the United Israel Appeal—the UIA. The origins of this remarkable philanthropy traced back to the Keren HaY'sod—the Foundation Fund—of the 1920s (Chapter vii). In fact, the Keren HaY'sod was the name by which it was still known in Diaspora communities outside the United States. For the Americans, on the other hand, the conduit through which over $3 billion was raised for the UIA between 1948 and 1973 was the United Jewish Appeal. Fund-raising was by no means an experimental venture for the American Jewish community. Jewish federations had been operating in American cities for decades, although earlier in the century they were oriented primarily to local and a few national Jewish communal needs. Then, during World War I and the postwar years, welfare funds were devoted increasingly to such overseas needs as the National Refugee Service, the Joint Distribution Committee, and finally the United Palestine Appeal. Later, too, as the Nazi horror began to unfold in the 1930s, the decision was taken to integrate the campaigns for these overseas philanthropies into a single fund-raising organization, to be known thenceforth as the United Jewish Appeal. Even as late as World War II, however, the Joint Distribution Committee remained the principal beneficiary of the combined effort; the United Palestine Appeal was regarded as of secondary importance. Competition persisted, as well, between the local federation drives and the United Jewish Appeal, with the former generally surpassing the latter in fund-raising success. The imbalance remained even when both groups began joining forces in a single campaign—known in various cities as the Combined Jewish Appeal, or the Allied Jewish Appeal, or the Jewish Welfare Federation Drive.

But as the European tragedy and the plight of the displaced persons afterward began to loom larger, greater attention and support were devoted to the cause of Palestine. The shift similarly was influenced by the emergence of a unique group of professional fund raisers, men whose dynamism and sheer bulldog aggressiveness revolutionized the entire conception of Jewish philanthropy. The first of these was an unforgettable impresario, Henry Montor. Originally a Reform rabbinical student, then a publicist for the United Palestine Appeal during its earlier, independent life, Montor was appointed the first executive director of the newly founded United Jewish Appeal in 1939. By the end of World War II, Montor had succeeded in enlarging dramatically the share of funds allocated to the United Palestine Appeal within the UJA and in raising altogether the level of American Jewish giving to the joint Federation-UJA campaigns. It was Montor who devised the technique of establishing national "goals" each year at annual conferences of Jewish leaders. In December 1945, for example, he persuaded his constituents to set a UJA goal of $100 million for the coming year. In fact, the UJA raised $102 million in 1946, an unprecedented sum in American philanthropy, Jewish or non-Jewish. Montor gave his lay workers no rest. In 1947 and 1948 he drove them into a vast effort of individual solicitation, placed advertisements in the general press, engaged celebrities to address UJA audiences. The outpouring of generosity from American Jews was full-hearted, even astonishing in its magnitude. It was a response not simply to promotional techniques, of course, but rather to the immensity of the Jewish tragedy, and above all else to the thrilling apocalypse that followed, the birth of the State of Israel.

Nevertheless, except for the incomparable South African Jewish community, the record level of this giving could hardly be sustained year in and year out, once the drama of Israel's War of Independence was followed by a lull of prosaic refugee absorption and state building. In the United States, Montor himself resigned from the UJA in 1951. His successor for the next four years, Dr. Joseph Schwartz, was the widely respected former executive director of the Joint Distribution Committee. Yet even Schwartz, with all the personal trust he inspired, was unable to match the unparalleled fund-raising campaigns of the late 1940s. A renewed upsurge came only in the mid-1950s, under the leadership of a youthful rabbi, Herbert Friedman, whose aggressiveness and impresarial skills fully matched those of Montor. Thus, in 1955, when the crisis of large-scale Moroccan immigration to Israel developed, Friedman persuaded American Jewish leaders that the urgency of the need warranted a UJA "Special Emergency Fund," the money to come off the top of all collections from the Jewish community. Because Friedman had a knack for dramatizing "special crises" virtually every year, the Special Emergency Fund became an integral part of the Jewish philanthropic landscape. By the same token, the much-disputed ratio between local and overseas allocations was now resolved decisively in favor of Israel. Other innovations included a Young Leadership Cabinet of men and women under forty who were trained in Israel's needs and in the art of solicitation, and a special Israel Education Fund that generated an additional $40 million from 1965 to 1973 for a wide complex of high schools and educational centers throughout Israel. Friedman's successor in 1971, Irving Bernstein, less flamboyant but in no sense less capable or respected, went so far as to devise a presolicitation technique of "rating" a donor's gift, then presenting the contributor with what was in effect a tax bill. The method was not unsuccessful. By 1973 there were thirteen annual "rated" gifts in the seven-figure category out of total UJA contributions that year of $827 million.

From the 1950s on, even as the largest allocation in the UJA went to the United Israel Appeal (formerly the United Palestine Appeal), the latter was obliged to show circumspection in distributing its money—through the Jewish Agency—within Israel itself. The U.S. Internal Revenue Service disallowed tax deductions for contributions abroad if the funds were expended on activities that properly belonged within the jurisdiction of a foreign government—for example, the Israeli defense effort, primary education, even housing for established Israeli citizens. In the first years of the state, therefore, the Jewish Agency disbursed UIA funds exclusively for the transportation, feeding, clothing, housing, and employment of new immigrants. Afterward, as the influx slowed, UIA funds were shifted to special educational projects that were not traditionally covered by the Israeli government, including prekindergartens, vocational and special high schools, even universities. In the end, however, the balance sheet of Diaspora philanthropy revealed an accomplishment that was greater than the sum of its individual parts. It was nothing less than the settlement of a million and a half refugees—the largest majority of Israel's population—and the transformation of a race of penniless mendicants into a self-supporting citizenry.

It is of interest, too, that the impact of the philanthropic campaign was no less profound on overseas Jewry itself. This was dramatically evident in the United States. Without doubt, there were critics of the UJA, most of them American Jewish communal leaders responsible for local or national causes, who objected to the growing emphasis on fund-raising for Israel. In their view, Israel was being assigned a rather dubious surrogate status in Jewish life, that of performing the "dirty work" of absorbing Jewish refugees and restoring Jewish dignity abroad, leaving American Jews merely the antiseptic task of picking up the check. Moreover, it was distasteful to these observers that philanthropism on behalf of Israel was growing (as they saw it) at the expense of American Jewish cultural, religious, and educational needs, and that wealthy UJA donors were increasingly being accepted as the leaders of the American Jewish community, rather than the scholars, educators, and rabbis who traditionally had fulfilled that role.

In some degree, nevertheless, the critics of Israel-oriented philanthropism may have been attacking a straw man. There was considerable evidence that the UJA itself was becoming an important educational factor in American Jewish affairs. Through its widening program of institutes, lectures, and workshops, the UJA was reviewing for its participants the totality of Jewish history and contemporary Jewish life. By the 1970s, for example, it was the "graduates" of Young Leadership institutes who were emerging by and large as the most forceful advocates in their communities of broadened Hebrew education. Additionally, the process of indoctrinating American Jews to "tax" themselves each year on behalf of their people represented a moral discipline, a kind of secularized Judaism that was not less meaningful in its human values than the rite and ritual advocated by religious traditionalists. Was there truth, anyway, to the complaint that American Jewish cultural and educational causes were being penalized by the diversion of vast sums to Israel? The opposite appeared to be the case. Precisely because UJA drives were combined with those of local federations, the enlarged scale of giving in a single campaign benefited each of the component organizations. It was equally significant that individual campaigns for specifically American Jewish institutions—universities, seminaries, hospitals—raised funds approximately in the same proportion to those contributed to the United Jewish Appeal. The evidence was overwhelming, then, that the United Jewish Appeal had taught American Jewry to support all Jewish causes; or, more fundamentally, that the sunburst of identification and creativity awakened by Israel was energizing virtually every facet of Jewish life in the United States, as in other Diaspora communities.

THE RECONSTRUCTION OF THE JEWISH AGENCY

In promoting the 1952 Law on the Status of the World Zionist Organization–Jewish Agency, and the ensuing "Covenant" of 1954 (p. 720), the Zionist leadership abroad had taken for granted that the funds disbursed in Israel by the Jewish Agency would also presumably be collected in the Diaspora by the Jewish Agency's parent body, the Zionist Organization. This assumption was rapidly dispelled, of course. We have seen that in the United States, fund-raising for Israel was in the hands of combined UJA-federations that had no official connection whatever with the Zionist Organization. To be sure, once the funds arrived in Israel, they were channeled immediately to the Jewish Agency, which administered the settlement projects and distributed the money for that purpose. Yet here, too, after a period of years, the Agency—as the arm of the Zionist Organization—gradually began to lose its exclusive right of allocation.

To understand this process of erosion, it is necessary to go back to the original format on which the Jewish Agency was established in 1929. In the 1920s, we recall, Weizmann and his followers had decided that the Zionist Organization could no longer appropriately serve as the exclusive instrument for building the Jewish National Home. The essence of the 1929 Jewish Agency reorganization was agreement that enlarged authority would be shared between Zionists and non-Zionists throughout the world (Chapter VII). For all meaningful purposes, however, the arrangement soon became inoperative. While Zionist delegates to the Agency were elected by the Zionist Organization, neither Europe nor America possessed machinery for electing bona-fide non-Zionist representatives. In practice, therefore, the Agency soon evolved into the operative arm of the Zionist Organization. Indeed, when the partition issue was revived after the war, the Zionist case was officially presented to the United Nations by members of the Jewish Agency Executive. And when the last "non-Zionist" member of the Agency Executive, Werner Senator, resigned in 1948, the Executives of the Jewish Agency and of the Zionist Organization once again became identical, as in the years before 1929. The Knesset Law of 1952 simply placed a legal imprimatur on an established fact. Ironically, once the government of Israel was established, and enforced its claim to exclusive jurisdiction in the political sphere, the Agency was left in charge mainly of philanthropic responsibilities, which the non-Zionist partners all along had regarded as its proper concern. But by then the partnership had ceased by default, and the role of the non-Zionists now consisted exclusively of providing funds for the Jewish Agency to spend in Israel.

It was this disproportionate financial burden, on the other hand, that in ensuing years persuaded the non-Zionists (rather than the Zionists, as in 1929) to take the initiative in advocating a broadened Jewish Agency. The pressure was applied mainly by the leaders of the American Jewish federations, whom the UJA had been chivvying year in and year out for increasingly larger allocations for Israeli purposes. Their first breakthrough occurred in 1960. To comply with American government regulations on tax-deductible gifts to charitable organizations, a new body was created in the United States. Its purpose was not to raise UJA funds for Jewish Agency disbursement but to supervise the allocation of those funds in Israel itself. After a period of initial semantic confusion, the new group in 1966 finally adopted the title of United Israel Appeal, Inc. (the "Inc." presumably distinguished it from the exclusively fund-raising body, the United Israel Appeal). Its representatives in Jerusalem henceforth monitored the Jewish Agency's distribution of American philanthropic funds. Here, then, was a prefiguration of a future Zionist–non-Zionist partnership; for the United Israel Appeal, Inc. was endowed with a board of trustees of 210 members, of whom half were drawn from the federations and welfare funds and half from the American Zionist organizations.

Several events provide the impetus for moving from the plane of the United Israel Appeal, Inc. to that of a reconstituted Jewish Agency. One was the Six-Day War, which provided the Jewish Agency with a tidal wave of Diaspora funds, not less than $346 million in the space of half a year. Even this unprecedented financial response was but the tip of an iceberg of international Jewish support opened up by the war. In April 1968, for example, Prime Minister Eshkol convened an International Economic Con-

ference in Jerusalem, bringing together 500 Jewish industrialists and businessmen from throughout the world. Its aim was to devise joint projects
for promoting Israel's economic development and foreign trade. One of
the gathering's most far-reaching decisions was to organize a company,
the Israel Corporation, that would mobilize $100 million to be invested
in Israeli enterprises. (Launched with high hopes, the project collapsed in
scandal a few years later [p. 743].) This meeting was followed shortly
afterward by another, a Conference on Human Needs, convened under the
sponsorship of the Jewish Agency. Some two hundred delegates from the
UJA and the Council of Jewish Federations and Welfare Funds in the
United States, and from Keren HaY'sod bodies in other lands, gathered in
Jerusalem to devise long-range programs that would meet Israel's urgent
requirements in immigration and absorption, in agricultural settlement
and development towns, as well as in social welfare, health, education,
and culture.

The spirit of Jewish unity exhibited in these conferences reinforced the
determination of Louis Pincus, the South African–born chairman of the
Jewish Agency Executive, to reconstitute and broaden the Jewish Agency.
At his initiative, therefore, the Zionist Congress in 1968 authorized the
Agency Executive to open negotiations with "fund-raising instruments for
Israel, [and to] establish a direct relationship between the Jewish Agency
and such bodies." During the next two years the principles of the enlargement were worked out in those negotiations. In August 1970 an "Agreement on the Reconstitution of the Jewish Agency" was initialed, and on
June 21, 1971, it was signed. Thereby was fulfilled Weizmann's dream of
forty-two years before, when the original Jewish Agency had been established. The reconstituted Agency called for the formation of three bodies:
an assembly, a board of governors, and an executive. In the spirit, too, if
not the detail of the original 1929 constitution, 50 percent of the members
of these governing organs were to be designated by the Zionist Organization, 30 percent by the United Israel Appeal, Inc.—that is, by the various
American federations and welfare funds—and 20 percent by Diaspora communities outside the United States. The 50-30-20 ratio applied both to the
Zionist–non-Zionist relationship and to geographical diversity. Thus, seated
on the board were twenty Zionists, twelve American non-Zionists, and
eight non-Zionists from other countries.

Yet this ratio was as misleading as it had been in the case of the original
Agency. It was true that the Zionist Organization and the Jewish Agency
once more were independent and separate bodies, with the former liberated thenceforth (except for its appointees on the Agency) from all money-
raising responsibilities and free to concentrate exclusively on Zionist
informational and cultural activities in the Diaspora. But the Agency Executive, operating as the body's day-to-day administrative organ, not only
would continue under the chairmanship of Louis Pincus (later, upon Pincus's death, of Pinchas Sapir, and upon the latter's death, of Yosef Almogi)
—that is, of officials of the Zionist Organization living in Jerusalem—but its
various department heads plainly would also have to be Israelis or Jews

living in Israel. Of even greater significance was the fact that the enlarged Agency represented at most a division between appointees chosen by the Zionist Organization, on the one hand, and those designated by organizations not formally part of the Zionist Organization, on the other. The latter, however, could by no stretch of the imagination be described as non-Zionist—and not because, as in 1929, machinery was lacking for the election of bona-fide non-Zionists; rather, because there *were* no non-Zionists in the traditional sense any longer. Even the American Jewish organizations that had opposed the idea of a Jewish state in the 1930s and 1940s—the American Jewish Committee and the Joint Distribution Committee, among them—had since undergone a profound change of heart and were committed to the survival of Israel. This was even truer of the various American federations and welfare funds whose representatives sat on the Agency's governing bodies. The new arrangement simply blurred former ideological differences altogether. In a sense, it vindicated Ben-Gurion's long-held thesis that in the Diaspora "there are no Zionists [or non-Zionists], there are only Jews."

THE "JEWS OF SILENCE"

Yet hardly all Jews, whether "Zionist" or "non-Zionist," were in the enviable position of being able to determine freely the role they wished to play in Israel's growth and welfare. Several million of them continued as the objects, rather, of Israel's anxiety and solicitude. Their numbers included approximately 100,000 scattered in isolated and vulnerable enclaves throughout the Arabic-speaking countries. Among them, barely 30,000 remained in Morocco in 1967 and another 8,000 in Tunisia. Theoretically equal before the law, these remnant Jewries in fact lived under conditions of acute apprehension and insecurity amid hostile Moslem majorities. Elsewhere in Arab lands, Jewish circumstances, precarious long before 1967, deteriorated even more alarmingly after the Six-Day War. It was known, for example, that barely 1,000 Jews survived in Egypt, and of these at least 200 were imprisoned in the Thora concentration camp near Cairo. In Syria, the circumstances of the country's 3,500 remaining Jews were an unalleviated nightmare. Even as a tight ban was imposed on their emigration, it was the habit of the Damascus regime arbitrarily to seize groups of Jews on any pretext, imprison them for a time, and release them again at whim. Their identity cards were stamped "Jew," and they were forbidden to travel more than three miles from their homes. Their economic and sheer physical survival remained acutely uncertain. In 1973 and 1974 there were episodes of Jewish girls raped and murdered at the hands of Syrian police.

By 1973, less than 3,000 Jews remained in Iraq. After the 1967 war, a boycott of Jewish tradesmen was proclaimed and a hundred leading members of the Jewish community were arrested and detained for varying periods. As in Egypt and Syria, Iraqi Jews were exposed to systematic government vilification and deprived of police protection in the frequent event of attack. "We can neither eat nor sleep," wrote one Iraqi Jew, in a letter smuggled out in August 1967.

> Day and night the fear has been constant of their coming to arrest us or search the house. . . . Some of us have been tied with chains, beaten at random with sticks, and slapped. . . . Each day we hear something different: first they are going to deport us, then they are going to kill us. . . . Those whom they fetch by car are told they will be burnt alive, shot one by one, or thrown into the desert. The Red Cross is not allowed to investigate, and even if they should come, nobody would dare to talk.

On January 27, 1969, nine Jews were among fourteen prisoners hanged as "spies" in Baghdad's Liberation Square; crowds estimated at 200,000 marched past the dangling corpses, as the onlookers were treated to a running loudspeaker commentary on Jewish "treason."

Libyan Jewry shared in this intensified persecution. Following the June War, hundreds of Jewish shops were burned again, as in 1945. Mercifully, the ban on emigration was dropped at least, with the result that two-thirds of the country's remaining 4,000 Jews fled to Europe, the rest to Israel.

Elsewhere beyond the limits of the free world, nearly 100,000 Jews stayed on in Rumania. For many years, the Bucharest government imposed no serious restrictions on those who wished to emigrate. But Rumanian Jewry was an aging population. Few of its members felt constrained to leave a nation that, though less than democratic, at least granted them equality in legal status, and even substantial opportunities for religious and cultural expression. Polish Jewry and Hungarian Jewry were rather smaller in numbers, approximately 30,000 comprising the former, and 45,000 the latter, in 1967. While the Hungarians included Jews of all ages, those of Poland, like those of Rumania, were aging, and quite fossilized in their Jewish interests. Throughout most of the 1960s, in any event, Polish Jewry had been denied exit visas for Israel. Ironically, it was in the aftermath of the June War, as a thinly veiled, semiofficial anti-Semitism revived once again, that the Gomulka regime decided to permit a limited emigration of "surplus" Jews. From July 1967 through May 1969, therefore, some 5,000 Jews departed, among them a considerable number of intellectuals and government officials. Even afterward, as the Warsaw government announced the end of its liberal emigration policy, a quiet, unofficial exodus of Polish Jews continued, with the number reaching 11,000 between mid-1967 and mid-1972. Approximately 40 percent of them settled in Israel.

Whatever the insecurity experienced by Polish Jews, their lot at least was far preferable to that of Soviet Jewry. On the basis of government registration figures, the Soviet Jewish population in 1969 was estimated at 2,268,000, although their numbers in fact may have been closer to 3 million. They were a literate, generally well-educated group, and despite restrictions against them (p. 733), they played a disproportionately active role in the intellectual and scientific life of their country. Indeed, for a number of years after World War II they were permitted a rather substantial Jewish cultural life of their own. With 22 percent of Soviet Jews listing Yiddish as their mother tongue (as late as 1959), they maintained their own Yiddish publishing houses, a variety of Yiddish literary journals, several excellent Yiddish repertory theaters, and a network of Yiddish-language schools.

These institutions were all closed abruptly in 1948, however, with the onset of an especially grim Stalinist period of oppression. Unsettled by his recent altercation with Marshal Tito that year, and increasingly fearful of disloyalty among his own subjects, the Communist ruler launched into a virulent witch hunt against "deviationist" elements within the Soviet empire. As we recall (Chapter xvi), the Jews were suspect even more than others of the minority races: and not only for classical Byzantinist reasons of anti-Semitism (to which Stalin personally was susceptible), nor for their wide-ranging role in Soviet cultural life. The essential factor was the Jews' status as the one Soviet nationality a majority of whose population lived outside the Soviet Union—and in Western, non-Socialist nations at that. Worse yet, the emerging Western orientation of Israel intensified Communist suspicion of Soviet Jews as "Zionist-imperialist" agents. The last five years of Stalin's paranoia, as a result, culminating in the notorious Doctors' Plot of 1953, were recalled by Soviet Jewry afterward as the grimmest experience of their life under Communist rule.

The harshest phase of the terror unquestionably ended with Stalin's death in 1953. Yet the nation's Jews failed afterward to regain their earlier security or self-assurance. Official discrimination was established henceforth as a permanent fact of Soviet Jewish life. In its cultural form, this oppression stripped Jews of the basic rights of linguistic and cultural self-expression—in schools, theaters, and newspapers and journals—traditionally accorded other national groups in the Communist empire. While all religions in the Soviet Union endured antireligious propaganda of one kind or another, the Jews suffered more than their share of restrictions. By the late 1960s less than seventy synagogues remained throughout the country, most of them in disrepair, and all denied licenses for refurbishment. Other Soviet religious communities—Orthodox, Baptists, Moslems—enjoyed the privilege of maintaining ties with coreligionists abroad. Not the Jews. Throughout the years, Jewish appeals to be allowed to bake substantial quantities of Passover matzot (unleavened bread) were rejected. Anti-Semitism also took on its more "characteristic" features of discrimination in employment, education, and other sectors of public life. Although talent and literacy ensured that Jews continued to occupy positions in the middle ranks of professional, cultural, and economic life, they faced grave obstacles in the "security-sensitive" areas—the diplomatic service, the army, the Communist party—and a tough *numerus clausus* at the universities. Soviet policy, then, placed Jews in a tragic vise. They were allowed neither to assimilate, to live a full Jewish life, nor (in common with other Soviet citizens) to emigrate.

Notwithstanding this grillwork of restrictions, and a considerable inter-marriage rate, Jewish ethnocentrism was not easily suppressed. Indeed, in several areas of the Soviet Union it remained extraordinarily tenacious. In Soviet Georgia, for example, a Jewish community of nearly 80,000 traced its roots back to the Byzantine period. Remote from governmental centers, surrounded by Caucasian peoples to whom anti-Semitism was alien, Georgian Jews maintained a highly inbred skein of folk loyalties. Their children studied Hebrew. Their synagogues were well attended. Almost without exception, too, Georgian Jews were devotedly, fanatically Zionist. But, for that matter, the birth of Israel was hardly less dramatic in its impact on Jews living in European Russia. It was perhaps inevitable that the kind of ecstatic Jewish reception tendered Golda Meir, Israel's first minister to the Soviet Union, was not repeated in later years, as Soviet anti-Israel policy hardened. Even so, news of Israel and books and news-papers about the Jewish state were avidly sought. The observance of religio-national holidays also proved a useful means of displaying loyalty to Israel and the Jewish people. In 1964 the writer Elie Wiesel witnessed a Simchat Torah (religious) celebration in which 30,000 young Jews danced the hora excitedly outside the Moscow synagogue, sang Yiddish and Hebrew songs, then marched through the streets in a torchlight parade.

Although the Soviet government's opposition to the emigration of any of its citizens was of long standing, there were occasional instances dur-ing the late 1950s and 1960s when the Kremlin was prepared to tolerate a limited Jewish departure for Israel. The emigrants generally were older people, those no longer capable of useful work; their numbers in any case rarely exceeded 1,500 or 2,000 annually. During the mid-1960s a number of younger professional men and women similarly were allowed to emi-grate for "family reunions" in Israel, but only those whose positions were coveted, and could be filled, by non-Jews (as in the case of Poland). For its part, the Israeli government observed a "gentleman's agreement" with the Soviets not to reveal this intermittent departure (lest the Arabs ask Moscow embarrassing questions). In late 1966, however, the "pact of silence" was jeopardized unexpectedly as Jewish groups in Israel and the United States began speaking out more frequently on behalf of Soviet Jewry, criticizing Moscow's policy of discrimination and the official ban on emigration. The Israeli government scrupulously refrained from endors-ing these protests; yet as a functioning democracy it could hardly forbid or censor them. Judging the criticism by its own methods of operation, on the other hand, the Soviet regime held Jerusalem responsible. Thus, in September 1966, Moscow angrily canceled a planned exchange visit of the Israel Philharmonic Orchestra and the Moscow State Orchestra. Several months later the Kremlin once again tightened its restrictions on "family reunions." Under normal conditions, the Israeli government might still have remained silent. But the circumstances of 1967 and afterward were by no means normal, even within the context of increasingly acrimonious Soviet-Israeli relations.

THE UPHEAVAL OF SOVIET JEWRY

As has been seen, Israel's victory in the Six-Day War was a disaster of almost unparalleled magnitude for Soviet foreign policy. Enraged at its helplessness to reverse the course of events in the Middle East, the Soviet government launched upon an anti-Zionist campaign of authentically Stalinist virulence within its own borders. By 1969, in fact, hatred of Israel and of Zionism had become a more dominant theme in the Soviet press than the issues of China, Vietnam, Berlin, or the problems of international arms control. Nor was the crescendo of propaganda left to government media alone. Under official pressure, eminent Soviet Jews were trotted out before foreign correspondents to announce their support of the government's anti-Zionist policies. At times the campaign of defamation assumed a near-Nazi intensity. For example, Yuri Ivanov's widely heralded book *Caution: Zionism*, first published in 1969, asserted that the "Jew Rothschilds" were "parasites in the economies of many countries," that the Israelis—through the Rothschilds—were financing the Czech "counterrevolution," that a new anti-Soviet conspiracy revealed "the alliance between the Catholic and Judaic churches." Anti-Semitic novels were published, with Jews invariably described as hucksters, lechers, or (most commonly) Zionist traitors.

This astonishing outburst could be attributed in part to blind rage over Soviet humiliation in the Middle East, and in part to a desire to distract public attention from problems and shortcomings in the Soviet economy through a classic diversionary technique. But another reason, surely, was the government's genuine embarrassment and alarm at the upsurge of Soviet Jewish identification with Israel following the June War. As one Russian Jew, Anatoly Dekatov, described it in an article published outside the Soviet Union in the Jerusalem *Post* in 1970:

> The [1967] victory of the tiny Jewish state over the hosts of the Arab enemies sent a thrill through the hearts of the Jews in Russia, as it did, I suppose, for Jews all over the world. The feeling of deep anxiety for the fate of Israel with which Soviet Jewry followed the events was succeeded by boundless joy and an overpowering pride in our people. Many, and especially the young, realized their Jewish identity for the first time. . . . The anti-Israel campaign in the Soviet mass media served only to spread further Zionist feeling among the Jews.

Accompanying this identification and pride, moreover, was an unprecedented rise in applications for exit permits to Israel. An émigré Jew from Riga wrote afterward: "Whenever Jews meet in the Soviet Union today they ask each other a question that has become a Jewish saying: 'Are you still here?' There is not a town or village with Jews in which at least some of them do not want to come."

Yet from the moment a Soviet Jew applied for an emigration permit, he faced an ordeal by comparison with which his earlier insecurity was a garden of delight. The documents he was obliged to submit to the visa section of the ministry of the interior included: an affidavit of invitation from his relatives in Israel; a reference from the housing administration giving the address and number of people living in his apartment; a curriculum vitae and a detailed list of all close relatives, together with their places of residence and employment. Most ominous of all was the stipulation that "employment and social character" references be presented. The moment employees in public institutions applied for these documents, they were demoted or compelled to resign. Applicants working in technical professions—engineers, technicians, even clerks—were dismissed from their jobs. Students whose families applied for visas were immediately expelled from their universities. Afterward they were promptly inducted for three years of military service, thereby precluding reapplication for emigration until five years had elapsed after their army discharge. In short, the very application for departure branded a Jew an enemy of the Soviet Union. The great majority of applications were turned down, in any case. And even the meager numbers of those who "qualified" for emigration were obliged to pay the equivalent of $2,500 for their visas, and to leave most of their possessions in the Soviet Union.

Remarkably, these and other attendant dangers failed to inhibit the rush for exit visas after 1967. The clamor was heaviest among the traditionally ethnocentric Jews of Georgia. Electrified by the June War, they applied by the thousands—as many as 40,000, by some accounts. Those who were denied permits often went on hunger strikes, sit-down strikes, even traveled in groups to Moscow to launch public demonstrations and face near-certain arrest. Yet tens of thousands of applications were filed in European Russia as well, particularly in the Baltic regions and the Ukraine, where Jewish loyalties were strong and anti-Semitism historically acute. Encountering the usual stiff obstacles, the Europeans borrowed from the Georgian example by demonstrating, fasting, petitioning, sending letters to the highest authorities in Moscow and cables to Israel. The Soviet government, meanwhile, though taken aback by this astonishing display of folk solidarity, instituted few meaningful changes in its emigration policy. Between 1967 and 1970, 4,675 Soviet Jews were allowed to leave. This was an increase over earlier years, but hardly a significant one.

The most spectacular episode of attempted departure was the planned abduction of a Soviet airliner by a group of nine young Leningrad Jews, together with two non-Jewish Russians. The transport was to be landed in Sweden, where its crew and passengers were to be picked up and returned. The plan leaked, however, and the group was arrested and charged with high treason. At the trial, the prosecution made much of the "machinations of international Zionism." One of the accused, Leib Hanoch, denounced the government's anti-Jewish policy and issued a moving appeal to be allowed to live as a Jew. The other prisoners similarly demanded the "elementary Jewish right" to live in Israel. Their defiance enraged the authorities. In December 1970 the judge sentenced two of the eleven to death, the rest to hard labor for periods ranging from four to fifteen years. But the uproar elicited by the verdict (none of the defendants had so much as boarded the plane) resulted in an unanticipated propaganda setback for Moscow. It touched off demonstrations by Jews in Israel, Europe, and the United States, and shocked protests from distinguished figures in Western nations. The State Department also quietly sought to intercede. In the end, given pause by the intensity of world reaction, the Soviet government commuted the death sentences to life imprisonment.

This avalanche of protests in turn signified a dramatic shift in tactics by Jews outside the Soviet Union, and particularly by the government of Israel. Addressing the Knesset in November 1967, Prime Minister Eshkol for the first time made public the earlier clandestine immigration of Soviet Jewry, and Moscow's recent decision evidently to close off any significant additional Jewish departures. In the light of recent Soviet behavior toward Israel and toward its own Jews, Eshkol had reached the conclusion that apparently nothing further was to be gained by maintaining the cover of secrecy. His decision was widely applauded. Indeed, two years later, Eshkol's successor, Mrs. Meir, informed the Knesset that her government henceforth would continue to press for the free emigration of all Soviet Jews who wished to depart for Israel. She kept her word. From then on, lashing back at Soviet policy with every resource of public disclosure, the Meir cabinet helped orchestrate the campaign on behalf of Russian Jewry, utilizing American Jewish organizations, international committees of scientists, musicians, and other professionals, appealing to the United Nations, to political and even Communist leaders in other lands. Special prayer services for Soviet Jewry were conducted at the Western Wall. Highly publicized demonstrations and vigils were mounted outside Soviet embassies in Washington and other Western capitals. No channel of communication was neglected to arouse public opinion in the free world.

Nor was there ever doubt that Israel's purpose in this campaign was less to improve the status of Soviet Jews than to revive their Jewish identity, kindle their hopes of emigration to Israel, and ultimately to acquire their presence and talents for the growth of the Jewish state. This vested interest became apparent in late December 1971 when Nahum Goldmann, who presumably had won certain assurances from the Soviet government, declared his intention of calling for a reversal of priorities at the impending meeting of the World Jewish Congress. Henceforth, he argued, emphasis should be placed less on aliyah from the Soviet Union than on protection of Jewish rights within that land; a majority of Jews would always be living in the Diaspora, he pointed out, and accordingly should enjoy equal rights there. Whereupon, incensed by the statement, the Zionist leadership of the World Jewish Congress promptly canceled Goldmann's invitation to address the gathering. Louis Pincus, chairman of the Jewish Agency Executive, expressed the Israeli view when he argued that the priority for the 1970s was no longer the battle for civil or national rights in the Diaspora, but rather the struggle for emigration to Israel, and from every Jewish community in the world. To facilitate that emigration, moreover, the Knesset several months before had legislated an amendment to the Nationality Law which provided that citizenship might be granted to any Jew who expressed his "desire" to settle in Israel, but who was barred from doing so. It was a potentially dangerous measure, with its implication of automatic Israeli citizenship for Jews still under Soviet rule, and indeed it was applied only sparingly afterward. But the warning was clear that Israel was determined if necessary to provoke an international *cause célèbre* for the sake of an augmented nationhood.

The Kremlin was not indifferent to this campaign. Whatever its outrage at Israel's—and Jewry's—"insolent interference in Soviet domestic and foreign policy," it was embarrassed by its repressionist image at a time when it was seeking a certain limited détente with the United States. Evidently the Soviet leadership reasoned, too, that the departure of selected Jewish activists would at least minimize Jewish unrest and liberal criticism abroad. Thus, from 1971 on, Moscow rather gingerly and discriminately began easing its ban on Jewish emigration. Its official rationale was the lack of a Jewish homeland among the Soviet Union's own constellation of ethnic republics. In 1971, as a result, 13,000 Soviet Jews were allowed to depart for Israel; in 1972, 31,000; in 1973, 32,000. In anticipation, too, of winning most-favored-nation trading opportunities from the United States, the Soviet government obliquely assured Washington in 1974 that it was prepared to relax even further its emigration quotas and its special "education tax" on those possessing university backgrounds, allowing the departure of as many as 60,000 Jews. Yet even before the Soviet-American trade agreement fell through, in January 1975, the Communist authorities knew well that other measures remained at their disposal for inhibiting a major Jewish exodus to Israel (Chapter xxiv). They bided their time. Meanwhile, nearly half of the 80,000 Jews who departed for Israel after 1967 were Georgian Jews. Few of these possessed academic education or sophisticated skills. Many were old or ill. Among the rest, however, there were several thousand trained professional people, a number of them outstanding figures in Soviet science and technology.

Jewish Agency representatives awaited them in Vienna, upon their initial arrival by train. Within days the newcomers were loaded on El Al jets and flown directly to Israel. There they were lodged in a network of eighty-two absorption centers until they could be assigned to permanent housing and employment. By 1974 the Jewish Agency and Israeli government were spending $250 million annually on the Soviet immigration, a far higher figure than had been disbursed for much larger waves in earlier years. The discrepancy could hardly be traced to inflation alone, nor to the taxes waived for goods brought in and initial salaries earned. The explanation related instead to the unique character of this latest influx. Reasonably well off in the Soviet Union, the newcomers from European Russia were accustomed to a decent livelihood in urban surroundings, to housing and employment opportunities commensurate with their training. They expected the same advantages in Israel, together with the best in high school and university opportunities for their children.

The Israeli government and the Jewish Agency in turn were determined to meet these expectations. They sensed that they dared not lose the new-comers, nor discourage the influx of equally talented and valuable immi-grants. As a result, they provided the Soviet Jews with comparatively spa-cious apartments, usually in the nation's larger cities. Well-paying job opportunities were offered—often artificially created—to ensure that scien-tific and technological skills were not wasted. Costly educational scholar-ships were made available for the immigrants' children. These expenditures represented a heavy burden for the nation. Indeed, in the eyes of veteran Oriental families still dwelling in crowded flats, eking out marginal salaries in city slums or in development communities, both the distribution of favors and the weight of the burden were inequitable. Their resentment was becoming increasingly vocal (Chapter xix).

For the Israeli government, on the other hand, values and priorities had changed by the 1970s. The neighboring Arab countries were growing in population no less than in belligerency. The reproduction rate of Israel's local and "administered" Arabs posed a long-range threat to the state's Jewish character. Thousands of sabras were departing for greater personal security and comfort in the West. Faced with overwhelming demographic and military perils, therefore, the Israelis regarded the sheer survivability of a Jewish island in an Arab ocean as the one critical, burning issue for the years ahead. To resolve that issue, the state's policy planners and the world Zionist leadership had arrived at a consensus that brooked no qualification even from Jewish well-wishers in the Diaspora. Funds, tech-nology, and moral and ideological support were not enough. As in the earliest and most parlous years of the Yishuv, an uninterrupted aliyah from abroad was the indispensable plasma of the nation's future. Many other factors and influences would shape the character of the little Zionist republic. But nothing else and nothing less than a swelling Jewish physical presence would guarantee its tenuous existence.

THE WAR

OF THE DAY OF JUDGMENT

THE POLITICS OF COMPLACENCY

THE BAR-LEV LINE. There is peace on the banks of the Canal, in the Sinai Desert, the Gaza Strip, the West Bank, Judea, Samaria, and on the Golan. The lines are safe. The bridges are open. Jerusalem is united. New settlements have been established and our political position is stable. This is the result of a balanced, bold, and far-sighted policy. . . . You know that only the [Labor] Alignment could have accomplished this.

In anticipation of elections to the Eighth Knesset, scheduled for October 31, 1973, these bold-faced and self-congratulatory Labor placards greeted citizens from kiosks and wall boards in every town and city of Israel. Their far-reaching claims actually reflected more than simply the usual political acquisitiveness. Rather, they expressed a quite genuine public mood of national security. For the most part, the borders were indeed quiet. The Arab guerrilla struggle continued, even intensified; but it was carried out essentially in foreign countries, not on Israel's soil. If the military burden was heavy, the nation seemed prosperous enough to bear it. Nor was the Labor Alignment to be outbid in its stance of tough intransigence on defense issues. Over Eban's and Sapir's objections, the Labor Central Committee in August 1973 had adopted a "compromise" program, drafted by Israel Galili, that in fact represented a decided shift toward the "hawks." Under the Galili plan, one and a quarter billion pounds was to be allocated for the development of the West Bank and Gaza, and for the integration with Israel's own economy of Arab agriculture and industry in those regions. Tax relief and government loans, similar to those offered foreign investors in Israel itself, were to be extended now to Israeli businessmen who established industrial plants in the territories.

More explicitly yet, the plan envisaged new Jewish settlements arising in the occupied areas, including a Golan Heights industrial center, a regional commercial-industrial center in the Jordan Valley, another factory complex in northeastern Sinai adjacent to Rafa, as well as new industrial zones outside East Jerusalem, Nebi Samwil, Qalkilia, and Tulkarem. For the first time, too, Jews would be entitled to purchase Arab lands and property in the West Bank and Gaza "on condition that the purchases are transacted for constructive and not for speculative purposes." Under this format, Labor's platform for the territories differed little from that of the religionists and of the right-wing Gachal bloc. Perhaps the one major point of departure was Gachal's demand for outright annexation of the West Bank and Golan, and of at least part of Sinai; while the religious parties based an identical demand upon the need to preserve the "historic Land of Israel." Otherwise, the practical implications of the Galili plan were imperialist. The Alignment leadership had recognized by then that there was to be no temporizing on the question of frontiers. The Left had suffered a mild attrition in both the 1965 and the 1969 Knesset elections, and assumed that the setbacks had resulted in some measure from equivocation on foreign policy issues. The mistake would not be repeated.

Gachal was faced now with a serious dilemma, as a result. The Galili plan had taken the wind out of its sails. While this Right-Center federation had performed creditably enough in 1969, winning 26 seats, the number hardly was sufficient to threaten Labor's domination. Rather, it appeared now that Gachal's best chance might lie in further political *mariages de convenance*. The religionists were excluded from this scheme, of course; they had always been Labor's faithful partners. On the other hand, the Independent Liberals, the Free Center, and the State List totaled 7.5 percent of the 1969 vote and held 10 Knesset seats. Although a Gachal joinder with these factions would not by itself overtake the Labor Alignment's 56 seats, at least it would represent a move in that direction.

The problem was to induce these smaller groups to enter a bloc dominated by a hard-liner like Menachem Begin. Shmuel Tamir, leader of the Free Center, was a personal enemy of Begin's. The State List, composed of dissident ex-Rafi members, was Labor-oriented. The Independent Liberals were rather "dovish." Nevertheless, stranger bedfellows had joined forces in earlier coalitions; what was essentially lacking here was a catalyst. In late summer 1973, however, the missing ingredient was supplied in the figure of General "Arik" Sharon, the burly, charismatic paratroop commander who had smashed the "Russian defenses" in the June War. A maverick, highly individualistic and abrasive in his dealings with colleagues and superiors, Sharon recently had been informed that he would be passed over for appointment as chief of staff. Angrily resigning his southern front command, therefore, Sharon informed a press conference that he might now be willing to play an active role in politics, on behalf of the Right-Center. His terms were simply that the Right-Center parties overcome their factional disarray and unite. It was a formidable condition. Even so, the opportunity to win the accession of this popular hero was highly compelling to the anti-Alignment factions. Meetings began immediately among their leaders. For a while, negotiations were nip and tuck; but by early September a new united Right-Center bloc was patched together, with only the Independent Liberals staying clear. The new entity was entitled Likud (Unity). Gachal and the other members henceforth would retain their individual party structures but would present a joint list for the impending elections. In fact, there were nearly as many "hawks" as "doves," as many Laborites and technocrats, among Likud as among the Labor Alignment. Yet as Israel gained in political experience and in toleration of diverse viewpoints, it was evident that both leading coalitions were drawing closer to the American model of accommodation for the sake of patronage—if not for the sake of principle.

In any case, during the waning period before the elections there seemed little that the Right could accomplish to undermine the government's record in defense and foreign affairs. Its one thin hope lay in the area of domestic policy, where Labor appeared to be somewhat more vulnerable. In recent years, for example, groups of Oriental youths from the impoverished Musrara quarter of Jerusalem had launched occasional public outbursts against the "system." In conscious imitation of similar demonstrators in the United States, the protesters called themselves "Black Panthers." Their circumstances, of broken homes, low education, often of juvenile criminal records, were atypical even for Israel's Oriental population (whose standard of living, we recall, was markedly improving overall). Nevertheless, the inequities attacked by the Black Panthers were worth taking seriously. The demonstrators were bitter that the government, in its preoccupation with attracting immigrants, continued to offer the most liberal housing and job opportunities to newcomers, most of them Soviet and Western Jews. It was noted that immigrants were allowed to buy cars and appliances without having to pay the crippling sales taxes borne by the rest of the population. Neither did they pay income taxes during their first years in the country, nor travel taxes when going abroad during their initial "apprenticeship" in Israel. Above all, the newcomers were able to secure larger and cheaper mortgages for their homes—a matter of critical importance to growing families. Veteran Israelis of all backgrounds experienced this identical double standard, of course. Yet it was the Black Panthers, in their stridency and unruliness, who dramatically focused public attention on it.

Indeed, their protests reminded the nation that in the last seven years more time had been consumed debating the touchy issue of Jewish settlement in the occupied territories than upgrading the quality of life of tens of thousands of Jews already in Israel. Under the aegis, meanwhile, of Finance Minister Pinchas Sapir, the boom that had enveloped Israel after 1967 was now beginning to reveal its seamier side. Many of the well-publicized egalitarian achievements of Israel's social democracy in fact were becoming eroded, and a class of *nouveaux riches,* many grown wealthy on public subsidies, infused Israeli life with a vulgar consumptionist quality. All strata shared in the economic upswing, to be sure, not excluding the Orientals. But the gap between richer and poorer continued to widen, even as some 70,000 families remained below the poverty line. Worse yet, it was the Labor government itself that appeared to be expropriating public funds for the enrichment of the few. Yitzchak Ben-Aharon, the Histadrut secretary-general, observed that although 95 percent of the nation's land was publicly owned, the remaining 5 percent—

essentially urban land in the big cities—was the object of a flagrant speculation that continued to drive up housing costs insupportably. Accusing the government of a silent partnership in this unsavory business, Ben-Aharon excoriated the shameful "protekzia"—influence peddling—that had developed among Labor officials, enabling them to acquire the most luxurious villas, drive the most costly automobiles, secure the choicest travel and expense-account opportunities. With the exceptions of Golda Meir and one or two others, few of the top Labor officials could resist the temptation to live well on either party or government funds. What had happened, Ben-Aharon asked, to the exalted idealism of A. D. Gordon and Berl Katznelson, of David Ben-Gurion and Yitzchak Ben-Zvi? For his trouble, the secretary-general lost his position after the Histadrut election of September 11, 1973.

The social lesion would not be wished away. It was visible not only in growing financial corruption, in the tendency of Israelis of all backgrounds to evade the nation's—admittedly painful—grillwork of taxes, but even in instances of bribery and embezzlement at the highest level of corporate and government enterprise: in the exploitation of the Abu Rudeis oil wells; in Mekorot, the National Water Corporation; in the bankruptcy of Autocars, Ltd., the nation's largest automobile manufacturer. One of the most notorious of the scandals involved the embezzlement of tens of millions of pounds from the Israel Corporation, established in April 1968 by the Eshkol government and funded by Jewish investors from throughout the world. By 1974 the project lay in ruins, its absconded capital dissipated in failed European investments. The press had a field day with these outrages, and ensured that they were well ventilated during the electoral campaign. Thus, as foreign policy gradually ceased to be a major bone of contention between the rival blocs, the 1973 elections for the first time in years devolved largely around questions of internal policy. Even so, there was meager chance that Likud would succeed in exploiting these issues. Granted that Labor had become flaccid and corrupt; but what solution did the opposition have? It was hardly Begin's or Sharon's policy to revive a Labor Zionist Utopia, after all. Promises of better management and tighter efficiency came with ill grace from the Right, when building contractors were reaping enormous profits, and cases of tax evasion by entrepreneurs, lawyers, and physicians were backlogged in the dockets of Israel's courts.

Moreover, public opinion polls indicated that Golda Meir had achieved an overwhelming 76 percent credibility rating, and that Dayan remained the nation's single most admired figure. Popularity of this magnitude hardly could be attributed to Labor's uncompromising stance on foreign affairs alone. The truth was that the average voter was by no means uncomfortable with the nation's domestic course. In the autumn of 1973, Israel's economy sustained its upward momentum, the GNP continued to grow at an annual rate of 10 percent, and employment opportunities were so widespread that even 130,000 Arab workers commuting from the "administered" territories did not take up the slack. Evidence of the boom was everywhere to be seen: in high-rise apartment buildings, luxurious new villas, a forest of television antennas, crowded shops, roads and highways choked with fully 370,000 private vehicles (in 1973), in a population of less than 3 million. And all this in addition to unprecedented security at home. Little wonder that the electoral campaign was taking place in an atmosphere so devoid of survivalist urgency as to border on complacency.

A REEVALUATION OF MILITARY POSTURE

By the same token, self-assurance both reflected and influenced Israel's military posture. The nation luxuriated in the defense in depth afforded by the captured territories, and most notably by the occupied Sinai. Even if the enemy were to strike first next time, war hardly was considered likely to threaten Israel's own population centers. Rather, hostilities would bring massive retaliation on the Egyptian Canal cities, on Damascus and Amman. The obverse of this defensive posture admittedly was somewhat less comforting; for in the south, Egyptian and Israeli forces were "eyeball to eyeball" along the Canal, and Israel as a result had lost its crucial early warning time. Under the circumstances, the general staff was faced after 1967 with the choice either of withdrawing its troops eastward in the desert or of reinforcing its Sinai defenses. The issue was decided as much by political as by military consensus; the nation was in no mood for tactical retreats. And so, the ministry of defense embarked upon the construction of an elaborate series of fortified defensive positions based on armor and artillery and supported by a network of roads, maintenance depots, air bases, and rear command posts.

At the direction, meanwhile, of General Chaim Bar-Lev, the chief of staff, a line of forward bunkers was established directly along the Sinai bank of the Canal itself. Under no circumstances was this "Bar-Lev Line" conceived of as a barrier against full-scale invasion. Its initial purpose was to serve merely as a trip-wire that would activate reinforcements from the bases and roads deeper in Sinai. Nevertheless, during the war of attrition between 1968 and 1970, the high command reached the decision to strengthen these outposts against the mounting weight of Egyptian artillery salvos. To that end, more than one hundred tractors were brought down to the Sinai, as well as several thousand troops of the engineering corps. The roofs of the Bar-Lev fortifications were covered by additional layers of concrete and interlaid with railroad tracks that had been pulled from the Egyptian rail lines in the Sinai. Communications centers, war rooms, even underground hospitals were constructed into the bunkers. At the expense of more than I£2 billion, some thirty major strongholds ultimately were built along the Canal at irregularly spaced intervals.

The establishment of the Bar-Lev fortifications, however, was sharply criticized by several respected army commanders. Among them were Generals Israel Tal and "Arik" Sharon, who admitted that the bunkers had been effective during the war of attrition but observed that their very existence was a standing temptation to Egyptian artillery. More dangerous yet, they would engender in the army and in Israel at large a "Maginot Line" psychology of fixed defense, something alien to the nation's traditions of mobility and retaliatory attack. Never before had such elaborate fortifications been constructed even to protect integral Israel. The air force chief, General Benyamin Peled, noted also that the money expended on the strongholds could have purchased another 1,500 tanks or 100 planes. Responding to this criticism, Bar-Lev and his supporters argued that an Israeli presence along the waterway was indispensable, if only to prevent the Egyptians in smaller or greater numbers from infiltrating across the Canal. Should these crossings occur, Soviet troops might be tempted to accompany them, a development that would lead almost inevitably to a disastrous Soviet-Israeli confrontation. The argument was not stilled. Thus, when General David Elazar was appointed chief of staff in January 1973, one of his first priorities was to seek a compromise on the Bar-Lev Line. Eventually he found it simply by reducing the number of fortifications and troops along the Canal. Of twenty-six major fortifications, ten were closed. In some instances the numbers of troops in the remaining bunkers were lowered to twenty, or even less. As a result of this "compromise," the dividing line between the Bar-Lev outposts as a warning system and as an early defense line gradually was blurred. It was the subsequent lack of clarity, then, with its mixture of fixed-defense and trip-wire concepts, that was to exact its toll in the first hours of October 6, 1973.

The uncertainty of strategic posture was reinforced by the configuration of the armed forces themselves. The Israeli general staff emerged from the Six-Day War convinced of its ability to wage future battles through the identical techniques of a skilled, well-equipped air force and armored corps—the workhorses of Israel's spectacular 1967 victory. In later years, accordingly, the military command placed unwonted emphasis upon armor and air, at the expense of infantry. It appeared unlikely to the general staff, even during the last days of the war of attrition, that the Egyptians would succeed in neutralizing an air force by surface-to-air missiles. Artillery, too, was neglected, as was infrared equipment, thereby forfeiting Israel's much admired infantry traditions of night attack and surprise. Even mobilization techniques were allowed to ossify. The army's manpower staff devised no economically practicable method for limited call-ups along the various fronts.

The confusion of purposes reached directly into the civilian command of the armed forces. When Dayan was appointed minister of defense in June 1967, the government promptly was cut off from direct involvement with national security issues, as it had not been under Eshkol. The famed commander took these matters entirely into his own hands, and his prestige was such that the cabinet and Knesset made no attempt thereafter to control or even to understand military thought and policy. Yet, in the following years, Dayan devoted most of his time to the administration of the occupied territories and paid little attention to the actual status of the defense infrastructure. Matters of "housekeeping" bored him, and he left these to his subordinates.

As a consequence of Dayan's neglect, moreover, the virus of politicization was allowed to infect the officer corps. Since the 1967 victory, generals had become Israel's new heroes, and the objects increasingly of an emergent personality cult. The focus of unrestrained adulation, they became natural vote-catchers for political parties. Indeed, those who resigned from the armed forces often moved directly into political life with virtually no interim apprenticeship. Thus, Bar-Lev was appointed a cabinet minister almost immediately. So was Aharon Yariv, and later Rabin. Ezer Weizmann, the former air force commander, became a Gachal minister during the National Coalition Government, and now Sharon was preparing to fulfill the same role on behalf of the newly formed Likud. Soon entire units had commanders identified with various parties. In this fashion, the barriers to political influence that Ben-Gurion had painstakingly erected throughout his years as defense minister were allowed to collapse. So were the austere ethical standards that traditionally had characterized the armed forces. The moral sclerosis that afflicted Israeli life following the 1967 war did not spare the army. Flattered, wined and dined, generals began taking liberties with their rank, eating at the best restaurants on the defense ministry's expense account, cultivating newly expensive tastes in clothes and automobiles, allowing their soldier-chauffeurs to serve their families. Dayan did not halt this process, as Ben-Gurion would have. Rather, he himself set the pace.

Soon the laxity began to taint all facets of the defense structure. Officers occasionally conspired with contractors to cheat the army. Military property was stolen. When war broke out in October 1973, it was found that entire tank battalions were missing their binoculars. Large quantities of army blankets had disappeared. These were extreme cases, to be sure. More common was an erosion of discipline since 1967, which was revealed most flagrantly during the alert called only hours before the outbreak of the Yom Kippur War. Arriving at their units, reservists were met by a startling lack of organization. Often vehicular equipment had not been properly maintained and could not be started. Orders to reinforce battle positions frequently were not carried out. Soldiers went into action improperly dressed. Dayan had not bothered to concern himself with these matters. In any case, no irreparable harm was anticipated from a certain laxness. The Arabs surely would not be so precipitous as to risk full-scale war again. And if they did, the 1967 war had proved that they could be dealt with—handily.

SADAT REACHES A DECISION

Israeli self-assurance plainly was not weakened by the death of Nasser in September 1970, and even less by the choice of Vice-President Anwar al-Sadat as his successor. A fellow officer, Sadat had shared Nasser's conspiracies on behalf of the Germans during World War II and had been a participant in the Colonels' Revolution of 1952. Subsequently, as judge of a revolutionary tribunal, he had demonstrated a certain flair for sending "traitors" to the gallows and prison. But thereafter Sadat was known essentially as Nasser's obsequious lackey, a "yes-man" who filled a number of honorific roles with little color or real influence. In truth, he was picked as Nasser's successor mainly for his lack of active enemies and his widely recognized talent for compromise and congeniality. A dark-skinned half-Sudanese, fifty-one years old upon assuming the presidency, Sadat made a great show of warmth and traditionalism. He was much photographed, for example, with a prayer-spot on his forehead, often wearing the peasant's djellabah. If this comfortable manner went far to answer the nation's desire for a more benign, Egypt-oriented leader, so too did Sadat's political complaisance. He gratified his nation's urban middle classes, for example, by dropping much of Nasser's bureaucratic centralism, lifting a number of import restrictions, and permitting a more generous influx of consumer goods. The shift to economic moderation, the lack of enthusiasm for Nasser's putative socialism, was evident as well in the new president's announced ten-year development plan to encourage European and American investors.

Sadat's relaxed approach, then, his lack of interest in Pan-Arabist adventures, and his involvement in essentially domestic concerns, seemingly augured well for peace in the Middle East. Yet for all his geniality and benevolence, the new president was laying the groundwork for a confrontation with Israel from the very onset of his incumbency. For one thing, Egypt's economic needs, its population explosion, dictated the vital importance of opening the Suez Canal and rebuilding the Canal cities. Additionally, the maintenance of a war economy without a war, the long conscription service for thousands of military graduates without either foreseeable activity or demobilization, created growing pressures for liberating the occupied Sinai. Still lacking a firm political base, Sadat knew that his most dependable source of alternate support was the army; he would respond to its pressure. Thus, as early as October 1971, Sadat instructed his military command to prepare for crossing the Canal before the year's end. As it happened, he was obliged to "postpone" this plan a bare two months later due to Soviet involvement in the India-Pakistan War. Nothing daunted, however, the president warned his countrymen the following May Day of 1972 that a showdown with Israel was inevitable and that he was prepared to "sacrifice a million men" in the forthcoming war.

Few in Israel gave heed to Sadat's warnings, particularly after July 1972, when he ordered the removal of Soviet advisers from Egypt. It escaped Israeli and Western observers that the Egyptian armed forces, after all, remained—together with vast quantities of Soviet weaponry. Moreover, the Russian departure liberated the Egyptian president from Soviet restraining influences. Goaded intolerably afterward by Colonel Muammar Qadafi of Libya, Sadat launched a widely proclaimed "final diplomatic effort" to secure Israel's withdrawal from the Canal. In February 1973 he dispatched his national security adviser, General Hafez Ismail, to Washington. Nixon received Ismail on the twenty-third of the month. The meeting was cordial but inconclusive. The American president made no commitment to lean on the Israelis. Furious at this rebuff, Sadat advised a *Newsweek* editor in March that the peaceful approach manifestly had failed and that a resumption of warfare was now inevitable. "Everyone has fallen asleep over the Middle East," he observed bitterly. "But they will soon wake up."

By then Sadat was well embarked on building a common strategy within the Arab camp. He had little difficulty with President Hafez al-Assad in Syria. The loss of the Golan Heights represented a permanent challenge to the Ba'ath junta, whose avowed objective was not simply the "liquidation of all traces of Zionist aggression" but a "total, ultimate solution of the Palestine question." It was a maximalist stance, but typical of the overheated nationalism that had characterized Syrian politics well before the advent of the Ba'ath. In the early years after 1967, to be sure, the Damascus government was hardly in a position to think seriously of renewed warfare with Israel. By a curious irony, it was the expulsion of Soviet advisers from Egypt in July 1972 that in the end strengthened Assad's hand. As a rebuke to Sadat, and in an effort to consolidate their position elsewhere in the Middle East, the Soviets decided to ship unprecedented quantities of military equipment to Syria, including some 300 new tanks, 300 MiG-21 fighter planes, and hundreds of late-model SAM-6 missiles. Indeed, Syria now became the most heavily armed nation per capita in the Arab world. In March 1973, therefore, when Sadat sent emissaries to Damascus to propose joint military action against Israel, the Egyptians were eagerly welcomed. Without equivocation, Assad declared now that he was prepared for war. Immediately afterward, a series of joint meetings were convened between the Egyptian and Syrian chiefs of staff. Extensive plans were laid for a two-pronged attack under Egyptian strategic command. Sadat himself visited Damascus in May and June to confirm these arrangements.

At the same time, the Egyptian president set about wooing other allies, particularly Feisal of Saudi Arabia, who had never disguised his hostility to the late Nasser's "Socialist" imperialism. To dissipate Feisal's misgivings, Sadat visited Riyadh personally in August 1973, greeted the Saudi monarch with elaborate deference, reassured him that the Pan-Arabist adventurism of Nasser no longer was a feature of Egyptian policy, and succeeded in winning assurance of a Saudi oil embargo against the West in the event renewed fighting against the Israelis went badly. Thereafter Sadat proceeded to mend his fences with Hussein of Jordan. This was a rather more difficult task, for the Hashemite king's animus toward his Arab neighbors had been inflamed by the Syrian invasion of three years earlier and by the recent murder in Cairo of his prime minister at the hands of Palestinian guerrillas. Throughout June and July, nevertheless, Sadat conducted secret political discussions with representatives of the Hashemite government, and he finally dispelled Hussein's misgivings. On September 10, Hussein and Assad arrived in Cairo, and tactical agreement was reached for the impending offensive. Hussein for his part admitted his inability to conduct full-scale warfare, but consented at least to pose the threat of attack across the Jordan, thereby tying down Israeli forces on the West Bank. On this basis, the agreement was sealed.

It remained later only to win assurance of Soviet military backing. That support was by no means to be taken for granted. Following their expulsion of the year before, the Russians were wary of major new commitments to the Sadat regime; nor was there any certainty that the Egyptians were a more potent military force now than in 1967. On the other hand, the Soviet leaders evidently calculated that, with the proper technical and military advice, there existed at least a chance that the Egyptians might win a foothold across the Canal, that the Syrians might push the Israelis back a limited distance in the Golan. If the military impasse could be broken, this conceivably might lead to a political solution. One additional possible gain, too, would be the opportunity to inflict a severe military and economic blow on Israel, which for all its small size was becoming a major impediment to Soviet political and foreign policy. The Kremlin leaders were infuriated by the groundswell of Soviet Jewish demonstrations for emigration to Israel. The danger was not only the example this Jewish activism could provoke among other restive elements within the Soviet realm, but the threat it posed to the cherished Soviet goal of most-favored-nation trading privileges with the United States. Under the leadership of Senator Henry Jackson, a congressional amendment already had been offered to the Trade Reform Act of 1973 that would have linked those privileges with a relaxation of the Soviet emigration ban. At the least, a renewed Arab-Israeli war might cripple the Zionist state economically, in this fashion rendering more difficult Israel's task of absorbing large quantities of Soviet Jews.

Throughout the summer, therefore, the Soviets accelerated their arms shipments to Syria, and in the early fall embarked upon a massive new delivery program to Egypt. The shipments included substantial quantities of the latest antiaircraft missiles, ranging from the highly mobile SAM-6s to shoulder-carried SAM-7s (Strelas), as well as limited numbers of SCUD and Frog ground-to-ground missiles, for attack against Israel's population centers. Plans also were made for a wartime airlift. In the week before October 6, the Soviets launched five new Cosmos satellites into orbit to photograph Israeli defenses in the north and south. By then, too, a Soviet electronics intelligence ship was sailing toward Egypt, and the families of Soviet advisers in Egypt and Syria were being hastily evacuated.

SADAT COMPLETES HIS PREPARATIONS

Although Sadat and Assad had reached agreement in March 1973 for a joint offensive, they had yet to decide on their precise timetable. At first, the Egyptian president was inclined to launch the operation in May, but moved the date back upon learning that a Nixon-Brezhnev conference was scheduled for that month; he did not wish to embarrass his Soviet patrons. Eventually, October 6 was decided upon. The water table of the Canal would be low then, the moon high for night crossings. Politically and diplomatically, also, the time would never be more opportune. Israel's position had weakened in Africa (p. 789), Europe was less than forthright in its own leadership, and the Nixon administration was bedeviled by the Watergate scandal. The Israelis would be preoccupied with their own election campaign, they would be worshipping and fasting on their holy day of Yom Kippur, and in any case they would hardly expect an attack during the Moslem festival of Ramadan.

In the interval, Egypt's military commanders, the able and respected war minister, General Ahmed Ismail Ali, and the highly popular chief of staff, General Sa'ad Shazli, were cautiously optimistic that they could pull off an offensive this time. They had carefully studied the errors of the Six-Day War—helped in no small degree by Israel's detailed accounts of its own battle tactics in that earlier struggle—and had taken appropriate corrective measures. Ismail and Shazli understood, too, that their best hope was to concentrate on a limited objective. This envisaged a crossing of Suez and the emplacement of infantry and armored forces on the east bank, without an immediate attempt to launch sweeping envelopments in Sinai beyond Egyptian missile protection. Such an operational plan would exploit the best qualities of Egyptian troops, their stolid courage when executing modest, thoroughly rehearsed assignments, and fighting later from established positions. To that end, in recent years, a simple but exhaustive training program had been carried out under Soviet guidance. Detailed models of Israeli fortifications had been built, and endless rehearsals conducted for storming them. Thus, one unit had done nothing since 1971 but train in passing a fuel hose across a water barrier. Infantry units assigned to attack tanks with Sagger rockets were drilled endlessly in this task, until every move became a reflex action.

While the Egyptians and Syrians between them would have approximately 750,000 men under arms (three times the numbers of fully mobilized Israeli forces), their commanders knew that the Jews were relying on air power to neutralize this quantitative advantage. The Egyptians for their part had a substantial air fleet of 550 front-line planes, and the Syrians 310, against Israel's 480; and it was not unlikely that Jordanian, Libyan, and Iraqi planes also would be available for combat. But even this ratio was inadequate against Israel's superb pilots. Following the Soviet doctrine, therefore, the Egyptians would count less on planes than on missiles to blunt Israeli air power. SAM rockets already had proved their value during the last days of the war of attrition. They would be exploited even more fully now. Afterward, ground battle would tell the story. And here, in addition to their vast numerical superiority in manpower, the Egyptians possessed fully 2,000 tanks of the latest Soviet model, the Syrians 1,200. The Israeli armored force consisted of 1,700 tanks, a number of them obsolete Super-Shermans. Between them, the Egyptians and Syrians also disposed of 3,300 guns of all varieties, four times the quantity of Israeli artillery. With this agglomeration of manpower and equipment, then, operating from short interior lines, the Arab leadership regarded the prognosis for victory as not unfavorable.

But everything depended upon simultaneous initiative and surprise. The Israelis had had these advantages in 1967. Sadat and Assad were determined now that the situation should be reversed. In the late spring of 1973 only Sadat and General Ismail knew the exact date, October 6, set for the offensive. Thereafter Assad and the Egyptian and Syrian chiefs of staff were let in on the secret; but it was not until October 2 that Ismail flew to Damascus to inform Assad that Zero Hour would be 2:00 p.m. on the sixth. Otherwise, all officers and men were informed that their immense training operations were simply exercises. These "exercises" were conducted daily up to October 6, with Egyptian brigades coming down to the waterline of the Canal each day in full view of the Israelis, then apparently returning each night. In fact, selected brigade units remained on after darkness, hidden behind the ramparts along the Canal. The Israelis were by no means oblivious to the scope of these maneuvers, nor to the fact that large quantities of men and equipment were being accumulated along the waterway. Neither did it escape them that, in the north, the Syrians were methodically augmenting their tank and artillery forces in the triple lines of defense that had been constructed across the Golan plain to the outskirts of Damascus. But for the time being the Israeli general staff persuaded itself that these maneuvers and reinforcements were essentially defensive (p. 754). In the south, they were interpreted as yet another gambit in Sadat's annual war of nerves. In the north, the Syrian show of force was regarded as Assad's response to an air battle of September 13, when Israeli jets had shot down thirteen Syrian MiGs near the port of Latakia, with the loss of only one Israeli plane.

Sadat and his advisers did much to foster this illusion. For one thing, the Egyptian president had been announcing the "moment of decision" with such frequency during the past two years that it was difficult to take seriously any of his latest warnings. Now, in the last months before October, Sadat intensified his campaign of deception. He allowed reports to be circulated of growing "tensions" between Egypt and the Soviet Union, of Soviet unwillingness to provide Egypt with new weaponry following the July 1972 expulsion of Russian advisers. Israel believed these reports. As Abd al-Satar al-Tawila, military correspondent of *Rus al-Yusuf*, later described the president's strategy:

> The brilliant plan of political camouflage was based on large-scale diplomatic activity. From time to time several emissaries would fly, as Sadat's representatives, all over the world: to Washington, London, Moscow, New Delhi, Peking and Africa. The Arabic press would print large headlines referring to what were termed diplomatic, or political, activities. Reports would appear on the travels of the former foreign ministers, Dr. Murad Ghaleb and Dr. Muhammad Hassan al-Zayat, of the former special adviser for national

security, Hafez Ismail, and of other political personages such as Hassan Sabri al-Houli, Ashraf Mawran, and others.

In this campaign, for example, Arab foreign ministers attending the UN General Assembly session in New York gathered with Secretary of State Kissinger on September 25 for "relaxed and cordial" discussions. Without themselves knowing of the impending offensive, the ministers were instructed to schedule a later meeting with Kissinger—the time to be fixed after the Israeli elections—to thrash out "a course of procedures" leading to substantive negotiations on the Middle East. The diplomatic approach was confirmed as late as October 5 in a private meeting between Kissinger and the then Egyptian foreign minister, Muhammad al-Zayat. Only a few days earlier, Egypt had hired an American company to lay an oil pipeline adjacent to the Suez Canal, extending from the Red Sea to the Mediterranean.

In these last days before the offensive, moreover, information was leaked to *al-Ahram* that Egyptian officers were about to make a Ramadan pilgrimage to Mecca and that the Rumanian defense minister was scheduled to visit Cairo on October 8. As late as October 3 the Egyptian cabinet held its weekly meeting, its discussions largely revolving around the moribund issue of an Egyptian-Libyan union. No martial atmosphere prevailed in Damascus or Cairo. Lights remained on. Civilian routine continued as normal. Thirty minutes before the scheduled offensive, Egyptian soldiers strolled along the Canal banks, without weapons or helmets.

A FAILURE OF ISRAELI INTELLIGENCE

The Israeli general staff had not failed to respond vigorously to earlier threatened crises, particularly in September 1970, in December 1972, and in May 1973. On the latter occasion, civil war in Lebanon appeared likely to provoke a Syrian move into Lebanese territory. In response, a substantial Israeli mobilization was ordered, and Israeli troops were deployed conspicuously along the Golan. It was a false alarm, and one that cost the nation's economy some I£11 million. Indeed, the cost element would weigh heavily in Israel's reluctance to mobilize again now in the autumn of 1973. Moreover, as the Egyptian and Syrian commands steadily reinforced their front lines throughout September and early October, conducting large-scale exercises and trundling heavy equipment forward, the Israeli general staff deliberately refrained from issuing a public warning. Press references to Arab military movements were censored. The Israeli-occupied Golan was left open to tourists. In short, every effort was taken to avoid outward signs of crisis, lest these provoke Arab retaliatory measures. Perhaps the government's restraint was influenced by another factor, too. Israel was in the midst of its election campaign, and it is recalled that Labor's proudest boast was of the tranquility and security obtaining along the borders.

The nation in any case was preoccupied with other security issues, mainly Arab terrorism against Israelis and Jews overseas. Lately, Israel had experienced a painful reverse in its struggle against this guerrilla campaign. In Czechoslovakia, on September 28, three armed Arabs slipped aboard a Soviet train carrying Soviet Jewish émigrés to Vienna. As the train entered Austrian territory, the guerrillas seized five Jews and a customs official as hostages, then demanded free passage to an Arab capital. To their own astonishment, the fedayeen got more than they asked for. Fearful lest his country become a battleground for the Arab-Israeli vendetta, Austrian Chancellor Bruno Kreisky (himself a Jew) announced that he would now close Schonau Castle outside Vienna, the transit center used by the Jewish Agency for classifying Soviet Jewish emigrants before transshipping them to Israel. At this point Prime Minister Meir rushed to Vienna in a last-minute effort to change Kreisky's mind. She failed. Upon returning to Israel, Mrs. Meir summoned a cabinet meeting on October 3. Its main order of business was to discuss the Kreisky episode—not the gathering of Arab armed forces on the borders. Nevertheless, a few hours before the regular cabinet session, the prime minister held a "kitchen cabinet" meeting with Dayan, Yigal Allon, Israel Galili, and the military commanders, and at that time the Egyptian and Syrian troop concentrations were discussed. The group agreed unanimously that war was not imminent.

In fact, Israeli intelligence had all the necessary data on Arab preparations and deployments. Its failure was in evaluation. Part of the difficulty lay in the structure of the intelligence organization itself. The largest number of Israel's senior intelligence-gathering branches was grouped in the Mossad, the Institution for Intelligence and Special Tasks, under the prime minister's office. Although widely respected for its dramatic coups, among them the abduction of Adolf Eichmann and of German scientists working for Egypt, Mossad's reputation also hid a string of failures. The Lydda airport massacre of May 1972 revealed a shocking lapse of Israeli security. So did the Munich Olympics tragedy. Security precautions were also shamefully negligent in Thailand, when a Black September group in December 1972 managed to take Israeli hostages from the embassy in Bangkok. In July 1973, Israeli agents in Lillehammer, Norway, killed the wrong man in their hunt for an Arab terrorist. In Madrid and Brussels, Israeli officials were lured into traps and murdered. The Arab kidnapping of Jewish hostages on the Russian train to Austria in September 1973 was yet another in this list of blunders.

Even so, the failures were largely obscured by the spectacular record of the military general staff's intelligence branch during the Six-Day War. After 1967, therefore, it was the military that gradually usurped the senior position in the Mossad itself, and that afterward paid only fleeting attention to information turned up by the Mossad's other agencies. In autumn of 1972, Major General Eliahu Zeira assumed command of this branch. Zeira was an able, even a brilliant officer, but new to intelligence, and in October 1973 he had been on the job only one year. His deputy,

Brigadier Arieh Shalev, responsible for intelligence on the Egyptian front, was similarly new at his post. Both men relied heavily on military electronic data provided by technicians. That information surely was not lacking. To monitor Egyptian preparations, for example, the defense intelligence had its own highly sophisticated listening devices in Sinai, many of them operated by former members of the United States Security Agency now working for Israel under contract. This information in turn was supplemented by the United States' own electronic surveillance, much of it provided by SAMOS satellites and by high-flying reconnaissance planes. Their photographs ordinarily were shared with Israel. Nevertheless, modern electronic equipment could not replace scholarly, analytical appraisals of the Arab mentality, and here Zeira and Shalev paid only meager attention to the research carried out by other institutions working under the Mossad umbrella. The intelligence chiefs had made up their minds that Sadat and Assad would surely understand, as Israel understood, that a far-reaching offensive operation was unthinkable without dominant air power; and the Arabs were unlikely to have an effective bomber force for several years. This was the "Conception" that inhibited a broader and more imaginative understanding of Arab frustration and vindictiveness.

Reaction to the Arab concentration of forces came belatedly, therefore —indeed, not until October 5, the eve of Yom Kippur. It was then only, faced with overwhelming evidence of large-scale Arab preparations, that the general staff agreed to declare a "C" alert. Even this fell short of mobilization, and represented essentially a warning to the standing army. Further action was left to the initiative of the various commanders. Several of these reacted decisively. General Peled, the air force commander, ordered all pilots to remain on base. General Avraham Mendler, chief of armor in the Sinai, canceled all Yom Kippur leaves for his men. Otherwise, Headquarters staff shared the prevailing view that the enemy would not attack without convincing air superiority. Then, at 4:00 a.m. the next day, Zeira was awakened by a phone call from his deputies. Israeli and American monitors had intercepted the unmistakable radio signals of final Arab war preparations. Immediately Dayan and General Elazar, the chief of staff, were notified, and informed that Zero Hour evidently would be 6:00 p.m. Upon being awakened, the prime minister in turn called an emergency meeting of her "kitchen cabinet" for 8:00 a.m. Yet as early as 5:00 that morning, the general staff commanders were meeting at the defense ministry in Tel Aviv. Elazar requested a full, immediate mobilization and a preemptive air strike. Dayan turned him down, although he consented finally to recommend the mobilization of the armored corps reserve. Even this step would depend on the prime minister's approval.

At 8:00 a.m. Dayan and Elazar reached the prime minister's Tel Aviv office. Again Elazar requested a preemptive strike, and again was decisively overruled, this time by Mrs. Meir, Allon, and Galili. Israel could not risk a diplomatic quarantine, they warned; it would have to absorb the first blow and rely upon defense in depth. The debate on mobilization was lengthier and more acrimonious. Elazar pressed for a total call-up. Dayan argued that even a limited mobilization would prove unnecessarily costly. Eventually the prime minister and the others reached a "compromise" decision: the armored reserves would be ordered to their units without delay. As the meeting convened, Mrs. Meir summoned United States Ambassador Kenneth Keating, explained the situation, and asked Washington to restrain the Arabs from a catastrophic misstep. Keating immediately notified Kissinger, who sent urgent messages to Sadat and Assad. His appeal to Mrs. Meir was firm and unequivocal: "Don't preempt." She had already made this decision on her own, of course.

In Israel the operation was begun of mobilizing 100,000 armored corps personnel. Fortunately, on Yom Kippur, it was possible to contact the largest numbers of the reservists at their homes or in synagogues. The roads also were clear of traffic. Even then, more than twenty-four hours would pass before all men reached their units. Meanwhile, General Shmuel Gonen, the southern front commander, phoned Mendler in the Sinai, informing him that the attack would begin at 6:00 p.m. Mendler was directed to have his troops stand by the fortifications on the Canal, but to allow no tank deployment before 4:00 p.m. "I don't want the Egyptians to see any movement before time," Gonen explained, "so they don't start earlier." It was a disastrous error. Against his better instincts, Mendler was obliged simply to order the men at the Bar-Lev fortifications to withdraw into their bunkers and to keep alert. This they did, in a leisurely fashion, refusing to take seriously the notion of a major attack. Many of the troops were inexperienced young reservists. Large numbers of trained regulars had been given leave for Yom Kippur—another lethal blunder.

From his headquarters in Nazareth, General Yitzchak Hofi, the northern front commander, similarly issued orders for an alert. Yet he, too, was denied authority to move his standing tank brigade forward, lest the Syrians regard this as a provocation. Again, the alert was observed laxly, reflecting the erosion of military discipline since 1967. Even the key surveillance post on Mount Hermon was not reinforced with experienced combat troops. It was evident that the commanders had not grasped that impending hostilities would mean a full-scale assault on two fronts. The men on the Golan anticipated at most perhaps a day of battle, the kind they had had in the past. On the Canal, the Israelis thought in terms of minor Egyptian commando crossings. Attention in any case was directed forward to the early evening. Then, at 2:00 p.m., as the Israeli cabinet was gathered in emergency session, a military aide suddenly entered the conference room and whispered urgently to Mrs. Meir. The enemy onslaught had begun.

AVALANCHE OUT OF THE NORTH

It had begun with a vengeance, with thousands of shells and bombs exploding along the eastern bank of the Canal and along the entire cease-fire line of the Golan Heights. Enemy planes roared overhead, strafing deep behind Israeli forward positions—in the Sinai as far as Sharm es-Sheikh.

In the north, helicopter-borne Syrian commandos appeared out of the smoke and mist, advancing toward Israel's "eyes"—the radar-surveillance fortification 6,000 feet atop Mount Hermon. Those Israeli troops who survived the bombardment on the Hermon retreated into the concrete and steel bunker, assuming it to be impregnable. But Syrian intelligence had learned of an escape exit, and blew it in; the remaining defenders were either killed or captured. It was the Syrians who now overlooked the Golan plateau. What lay before them was a modest Israeli picket of seventeen fortifications, each occupied by fifteen or twenty soldiers and backed by a single platoon of tanks, two infantry battalions, and four artillery batteries. The main armored brigade of some 150 tanks lay much farther in the rear. Had there been advance warning, the tank brigade would have been in forward position and stiffened with thousands of infantry reservists. But Israeli intelligence had failed: most of the armor and reserve infantry were well back, the largest numbers of them not even mobilized when the Syrian attack began.

It was an earthquake of an assault. After a fifty-five-minute artillery barrage, two Syrian armored divisions of 800 tanks and three infantry divisions in personnel carriers began rumbling across the cease-fire line. The tanks bypassed the advance Israeli bunkers, pouring through gaps in the defenses and smashing relentlessly through Israel's Golan settlements (the civilians had been hastily evacuated). The Israeli front was cracked in two sectors. In the north, on the approaches to al-Quneitra, 200 tanks burst through in the first wave. In the central-south sector, by Rafid, an even larger breakthrough came in two prongs. One Syrian division seized the Rafid junction, then probed toward the Nafach base camp where the Golan commander, General Rafael "Raful" Eytan, had his headquarters. The Syrians clearly were aiming here at the B'not Ya'akov bridge over the Jordan, leading down to integral Israel. The second column turned south toward Ramat Magshimim and El Al, and from there moved toward the Jordan estuary and Arik bridge. Fully 600 tanks were engaged in this sector. Throughout the remaining hours of daylight the Syrians forged ahead.

Neither were their infrared-equipped tanks slowed by darkness. By dawn they battered headlong into the final Israel defenses on the southeastern Golan. Although hopelessly outnumbered, the single remaining Israeli tank company fought as if berserk, inflicting heavy losses on the enemy. From the Nafach bunker General Eytan grimly orchestrated his meager resources, deploying isolated tank units at breakthrough points, struggling with every resource of determination and cunning to block the Arab tidal wave until reserve units arrived. But already Syrian columns were approaching within gunnery range of the B'not Ya'akov bridge and the main pumping station of Israel's National Water Carrier north of Kibbutz Ginossar. Syrian shells and SCUD missiles were exploding along the west bank of Lake Galilee. At the foot of the Golan, in the Chula and Jordan valleys, kibbutzim were hastily evacuating their wives and children, preparing to resist the enemy with light arms—exactly as they had in 1948.

In the forenoon of October 7 Dayan helicoptered to Eytan's command

THE SYRIAN OFFENSIVE
OCTOBER 6–10, 1973

- Syrian advance
- Limit of Syrian advance
- 1967 Cease-fire lines
- ▲▲ Tank traps   × Minefields
- ○ New Israeli settlements on the Golan Heights

0   MILES   10

post, where he was briefed. He had learned already that the air force, dispersed between the Golan and Suez, was being macerated equally by SAM rockets and conventional antiaircraft fire. Returning to headquarters, then, Dayan agreed with Elazar that every available plane would have to be thrown into the northern battle—and at whatever cost. "The fate of the Third Temple [the reestablished nation of Israel] is at stake," he informed Peled, the air force commander. The defense minister then phoned Mrs. Meir to suggest bleakly that the army be allowed to cut its losses, to pull its shattered forces out of the central Golan, and to establish a line just forward of the escarpment overlooking the Jordan Valley. Appalled by Dayan's breaking nerve, the prime minister said nothing, neither accepting nor rejecting the suggestion.

In the northern sector of the Golan, adjacent to Quneitra, the battle still hung in the balance. Here the badly outnumbered Israeli Seventh Armored Brigade, under Colonel Avigdor Ben-Gal, managed to knock out scores of enemy vehicles in the valley between Hermonit and Masada. Indeed, by early light of October 8, the battered Israeli force looked down on 130 destroyed Syrian tanks and larger numbers of demolished personnel carriers. The Syrians nevertheless continued pouring in fresh armor throughout the day, including the latest-model Soviet T-62 tanks. By then Ben-Gal and his men had been fighting uninterruptedly for two days and two nights. No more than forty tanks were left; hardly a single tank commander remained alive or unwounded. Each enemy attack appeared to surpass its predecessor.

It was on the evening of the eighth that the Syrians unleashed yet another devastating artillery barrage, and a new force of 600 heavy tanks emerged from the smoke, followed by even larger waves of armored personnel carriers. The Israelis fired back, but soon were virtually liquidated themselves. Ben-Gal, attempting to regroup, observed to his horror that only six of his original tanks remained in fighting condition—six between the enemy and northern Israel. At this point the nerveless Eytan, following the battle by radio, decided to risk everything on a final gamble. He ordered Ben-Gal to counterattack and take the high ground. The brigade commander followed orders, and his last surviving vehicles reached the crest of the hillocks. There they were joined by isolated tanks straggling in from other decimated units, raising their numbers to fifteen. This ravaged little band was quickly enveloped in a nightmare of enemy fire as the Syrian tanks closed in now for a decisive breakthrough. Ben-Gal sent word to Eytan that his exhausted remnant was unable to fight on any longer. Immediately the Golan commander radioed back, pleading with Ben-Gal to hold out only a half-hour more. The appeal reflected psychology more than tactics. There was no assurance that reinforcements would be arriving in a half-hour or three hours. The shadow of a new Holocaust descended upon Israel.

A TIDAL WAVE ACROSS THE CANAL

Approximately 230 miles to the southwest, during these same grim hours of October 6–7, the Israelis were tasting the power of one of the largest standing armies in the world. Positioned along the Canal were five Egyptian infantry divisions, three mixed infantry and tank divisions, and twenty-two independent infantry, commando, and paratroop brigades. With the air force, the enemy constituted not less than 600,000 men, 2,000 tanks, 2,300 artillery pieces, 160 SAM missile batteries, and 550 combat planes. Facing this war machine in the Sinai along the 110 miles of Canal were precisely 436 Israeli soldiers in a series of bunkers seven to ten miles apart, together with three tanks and seven artillery batteries. General Mendler, the southern armored force commander, had 177 tanks at his disposal, but most of these were five miles behind the line, along the parallel "artillery road." Some 20 miles to the rear, guarding the Mitla and Gidi passes, was a full Israeli armored division. It was General Gonen's intention to bring up the reserve armor the moment enemy forces proceeded across the waterway toward the trip-wire of the Canal fortifications. The Egyptians, however, in the scope and brilliance of their operation, disrupted this tidy plan.

At 2:00 p.m. on October 6, as Sadat's planes attacked air bases and radar stations behind the Israeli lines, the full weight of Egyptian artillery opened up along the entire front, including volleys of long-range Frog missiles. For the next fifty-three minutes the skeletal Israeli contingents in the east bank fortifications endured the murderous shelling. When the barrage reached its crescendo, the first wave of 8,000 Egyptian infantry moved across the waterway in fiberglass boats. With his standing orders for a preemptive bombing attack now aborted, General Peled instead loosed his planes indiscriminately against the amphibious forces. But the crossings were taking place simultaneously along the entire length of Suez, and Peled's fliers were obliged to disperse to meet this wide-flung operation. Dozens of planes also were shot down by missile salvos.

There was little that the shell-shocked Israeli reservists in the fortifications could do to halt the crossings. As the Egyptians reached the east bank, some laid explosive charges under the bunkers and directed flame-throwers at Israeli firing ports. Most, however, simply flooded on between and behind the Bar-Lev positions. By nightfall no fewer than 30,000 Egyptian infantrymen had attained a foothold throughout the eastern length of the Canal; some units had pushed forward to a depth of three miles. Meanwhile, other enemy troops with powerful Russian-made water pumps blew gaps in the sand embankments, clearing the way for armor. That night, eleven pontoon bridges went up across the water, and tanks began moving over. The Israeli air force, where it was not mauled by SAMs or blinded by smoke screens, registered occasional hits on these bridges, but to no permanent effect; the latter were easily repaired. Within twenty-four hours of the initial offensive, five Egyptian infantry and armored divisions had taken up positions three miles east of the Canal, entirely outflanking the Bar-Lev Line, which they anticipated taking at their convenience. It was a remarkable achievement. General Shazli had expected his army to suffer as many as 10,000 casualties. Instead, Egyptian dead in the first stage totaled 180 men.

When it became evident within the first ninety minutes of hostilities that the Egyptians were crossing in strength, Mendler's tanks were rushed forward to protect the strongholds at the water's edge. But they encountered a shocking surprise. While yet several hundred yards from the embankment, the tanks were hit—not by Egyptian armor, which thus far was held in reserve on the western bank, but by Egyptian infantry teams carrying lethal portable Sagger rockets. Lying in ambush, the Egyptians fired hundreds of these missiles, decimating Israeli tank reinforcements, wiping out entire crews with each blast. By morning of October 7 scarcely thirty of Mendler's tanks were operable. By then, too, as the Egyptians broadened their foothold along the east bank, it became clear that their main effort was south of the Great Bitter Lake, where General Abd al-Moneim al-Bassel's Third Army was deployed. Under the Russian system, the Egyptians would require several days to consolidate their front, bringing in and organizing their heavy armor; afterward, their goal would be the Israeli roads linking up with the key Mitla and Gidi arterials. Meanwhile, the Egyptian Second Army under General Sa'ad Mamoun was tightening its grip along the central sector, in the Ismailia district, while smaller units were penetrating the al-Qantara area to the north.

During these first thirty-six hours of combat, General Gonen, Israel's southern front commander, was hurriedly attempting to reinforce his defenses at the Gidi and Mitla passes. But if the mobilization effort lagged on the Golan front, much closer to Israel, it was even more gravely obstructed in the distant Sinai. Days passed before reserve armored units could reach the southern peninsula. With insufficient transport vehicles available, many of the tanks had to cover up to 150 miles of desert on their own motors and treads. Artillery units reached Sinai fully three days after war began, as the southward flow of convoys packed the roads. Israel's classic operational plan had called for the standing army to block all enemy advances until the reserves arrived. These latter, organized into formations, would move swiftly and efficiently into a counteroffensive. Taken now by surprise, however, the southern command had to throw reservists into immediate delaying actions on a piecemeal basis, and often inadequately equipped. It was emergency fire fighting rather than strategic warfare, with understrength and loosely coordinated Israeli units often knocked out individually by Egyptian Sagger rockets.

Until his manpower could be fully organized, therefore, Gonen tried simultaneously to buy time without losing territory. Throughout the day of October 7 he ordered his single armored division west of the passes to fight a holding action. But as the situation worsened, and the plight of the surviving troops in the fortifications became desperate, Gonen was obliged to abandon this approach. Instead, he ordered General Avraham Adan's division of 250 tanks directly forward to the Canal in

THE EGYPTIAN OFFENSIVE, OCTOBER 6–12, 1973

⟵ Initial Egyptian bridgeheads

╌╌▶ Egyptian positions after linkup of bridgeheads

★ Israeli (Bar-Lev) fortifications

0   MILES   25

MEDITERRANEAN SEA

Port Said

Baluza   Rumani

ARTILLERY ROAD

al-Qantara

SUEZ CANAL

ISRAELI COUNTERATTACK
OCT. 8-9

SINAI   PENINSULA

Ismailia

LAKE TIMSAH

Tasa

E
G
Y
P
T

Bir Gafgafa
(Refidim)

*GREAT
BITTER LAKE*

EGYPTIANS
LINK UP
BRIDGEHEADS
OCT. 9-12

*LITTLE
BITTER LAKE*

GIDI PASS

ISRAELI COUNTERATTACK
OCT. 8-9

MITLA PASS

Suez

Abadiye

GULF OF SUEZ

the central sector, a distance of nearly 30 miles, with instructions to liberate the besieged strongpoints. Once completing its mission, Adan's force, underequipped as it was, should seek to cross one of the Egyptian bridges and move over to the west bank. It was hoped that this limited tactical offensive would throw the Egyptians off balance and compel them at least to pull back some of their manpower. It was a hasty, ill-conceived gamble, designed essentially for two conflicting objectives—one of rescue, the other of offensive. Nevertheless, Adan set out with his armor on the morning of October 8. Almost immediately he encountered the full fury of Egyptian missiles and artillery. Slowly, as the day passed, the Israeli tank crews were ravaged. By nightfall not one of the fortifications had been relieved, no progress had been made in seizing a bridge, and casualties among the tankers were fearful. Everywhere deputies had assumed the posts of slain commanders. One crew lost three officers in succession and thereafter refused to fight. Indeed, this was Israel's first war in which doctors treated numerous shock cases. The entire operation soon was frittered away piecemeal. At midday of October 9, Gonen ordered the remaining tanks pulled back.

As the Israelis withdrew, the Egyptians at last turned their attention to the remnants of the Bar-Lev fortifications. Five had been overrun at the outset; six had been evacuated, their troops enduring harrowing adventures as they made their way through the surrounding Egyptian forces to Israeli lines. Only nine bunkers continued to hold out. The plight of their defenders was critical. Inside, the radio operators transmitted a running account of their ordeal, as shells exploded on their positions and the wounded slowly bled to death. At Gonen's headquarters, staff officers wept, aware that all rescue efforts now would be futile. The defenders were given permission to surrender. All but one of them did (the position at Port Fuad held out until the end of the war). Egyptian and European news photographers were treated to the spectacle of Israeli troops marching out, gaunt and bloodstained, a few of them holding Torah scrolls, others carrying their wounded, then being marched off to prison compounds. Gonen had little choice now but to regroup his lines some nine miles east of Suez. Dayan, meanwhile, tersely informed a press conference on the evening of October 9 that the Sinai army might be compelled to retreat even farther, to a second line of defense 20 or 25 miles away. Although Elazar in turn flatly rejected any such move, the Israeli public was shocked to its depths.

A REEVALUATION OF PRIORITIES

At the outset, the most important of Egypt's victories was less over the Bar-Lev Line than over fear, an inhibition that Israel under Ben-Gurion and Dayan had fostered systematically through years of tough retaliatory raids and occasional major offenses. Few in Israel would have predicted this revival of Arab nerve. Since the 1967 blitzkrieg, the country's leadership had denigrated the very notion that pride ultimately would transcend Arab terror of renewed warfare against the Jews. Yet the Egyptians made no secret that the quest for avenged honor was a vital ingredient of their renewed offensive on October 6. Thus, on October 8, at the height of Egyptian successes, Chief of Staff Shazli could declare in an order of the day to his troops: "The war has retrieved Arab honor. Even if we will be defeated now, no one can say that the Egyptian soldier is not a superior fighter." In contrast to 1967, moreover, there were few initial boasts of epic victories. Despite the brilliantly executed crossing of the Canal, the Egyptian people were warned that they faced a hard and protracted war (in fact, an extended campaign of attrition was fundamental to Egypt's strategy). The mood both in Egypt and in Syria was subdued. It was only after the first week, as Israel turned the tide of fighting, that public announcements from Cairo and Damascus revived the hysterical victory claims that had typified their earlier wars with the Zionists.

Israel, on the other hand, entered the war in a miasma of confusion and deception. The Meir government's first reaction, that of concealment, was intended at once to disguise its own blunders, to sustain the nation's morale, and—it was hoped—to erode the enemy's fighting spirit. On the afternoon of October 6, the defense ministry released only the cryptic announcement that hostilities had begun. In the early evening, Mrs. Meir addressed the country on television and radio:

> Citizens of Israel: At around 14:00 today the armies of Egypt and Syria launched an offensive against Israel. . . . The Israel Defense Forces are fighting back and repulsing the attack. The enemy has suffered serious losses. . . . They hoped to surprise the citizens of Israel on the Day of Atonement while many were praying in the synagogues. . . . But we were not surprised. . . . Our forces were deployed as necessary to meet the danger. We have no doubt about our victory, but we consider the resumption of the Egyptian-Syrian aggression as tantamount to an act of madness.

Dayan spoke shortly afterward, radiating confidence: "We shall smite the Egyptians hip and thigh. . . . We have had losses, but, relatively speaking this was what we estimated to be [likely in] the first day of fighting—which will end with victory in the coming few days. Thank you." The next morning, Dayan again proclaimed that Israel would destroy the enemy quickly. Gonen on October 7 similarly announced that the Egyptians had failed to achieve their objectives along the entire front. Mendler in his order of the day promised that within a few hours the enemy would be "utterly routed." As late as October 8, Elazar informed a press conference that the turning point was just ahead. "Our aim is to teach [the Arabs] a lesson and to win a decisive and significant victory, in short, to break all their bones."

This florid and altogether atypical braggadocio made little impression on the Israeli population and even less on world opinion. If its purpose was to influence the enemy, it failed. The Arabs had their own news sources, and in the beginning these were more accurate than Israel's. Indeed, it was from live pictures on Jordanian television that Israelis first learned that the Egyptians were on the Bar-Lev Line and had set up their flags on Israeli bunkers. It was from Syrian photographs released in Western newspapers that Israel discovered that the Mount Hermon position had been captured on the first day of the war. Not until October 9 did the Israeli government belatedly adopt a more forthcoming information policy. That evening General Yariv, the former intelligence chief, took over the news briefings from the defense minister and stated frankly that Israel had evacuated most of the Canal fortifications, that a hard struggle lay ahead, and that no "soaring visions should be nurtured of elegant and rapid conquest."

With a discipline born of long practice, meanwhile, the Israeli population turned hurriedly to its wartime routine. Blackouts came into force. Buses stopped at 6:00 p.m. Blood donors lined up. Strikes were canceled. The elections were postponed. Schools were closed on October 7 and 8 but reopened the day after. There was much volunteering for every kind of routine. Two ex-generals drove garbage trucks in Tel Aviv, and famed scientists sorted the mail in Jerusalem. While other airlines halted their service to Israel, El Al remarkably maintained its scheduled flights. Volunteers arrived from abroad. The Arabs in Israel remained quiet. After a week of confusion, civilian life in Israel returned to a kind of stoic normalcy.

By noon of October 9, after nearly three days of fighting, the general staff reached a critical decision: to shift most of the reserves originally allocated for Sinai to the Golan front. This was a reversal of the strategy adopted in previous wars (except for 1948). While the imminent prospect of a breakthrough of Syrian armor into Israel was a determining factor here, so was the failure by then of the Israeli counterattack on the Egyptian front. Victory in the south, at all events, would take much longer; the Arabs hardly would be constrained to accept a cease-fire before they took heavy losses, and this was less predictable in Sinai than in the north. It was known, too, that Hussein was under mounting pressure to open a third front, and he would hesitate only if there were visible evidence that the tide was turning against the Arabs. Finally, when news arrived that an Iraqi division of 16,000 men and 200 tanks was approaching Syria, it was even plainer that the Israelis must win a swift, conclusive victory on the Golan. The decision was largely Elazar's, and it was the right one.

David Elazar, Israel's first Sephardic chief of staff, had immigrated to Palestine from Yugoslavia in 1940, at the age of fifteen. Kibbutz-educated, he had served in the Palmach and had acquitted himself gallantly in each of Israel's earlier conflicts. It was he in 1967 who had led the conquest of the Golan Heights. Not a flamboyant tactician in the manner of Sharon, Elazar was widely respected for his sound thinking and his courage (with his square jaw and thin slit of a mouth, he looked the bulldog fighter he was). His mistakes in not anticipating the Yom Kippur attack would cost him dearly after the war (p. 803); but now, in the heat of battle, his tenacity of purpose and magisterial grasp of strategic priorities never showed to better advantage.

As early as the second day of hostilities, in fact, after the Syrians began launching SCUD missiles at Israeli towns and villages, Elazar won the cabinet's approval for an air offensive against the Syrian civilian economy. Immediately, then, Peled's fliers set about their assignment with deliberation and relentless thoroughness. The Syrian defense ministry, the radio station in Damascus, the Homs power stations and fuel reservoir, the key oil terminal outlet at Banias, the major Syrian electric grids—all were destroyed or crippled. The losses in Israeli planes and pilots were heavy. Nevertheless, the raids had the effect gradually of levering the Syrian missile system back from the front, and this withdrawal in turn opened up new possibilities for tactial air cover over the Golan.

From two and a half days, it is recalled, Israel's Seventh Armored Brigade at the central sector of the Golan had been conducting a frenzied rear-guard battle against a Syrian offensive that threatened to engulf the entire plateau, and to sweep down to the Chula and Jordan valleys below. Despite General Eytan's entreaties, it did not appear that Ben-Gal's men could hold on. All but devoured by the enemy onslaught, they were reduced to a pitiable six tanks, and the end seemed near. By dawn of the ninth, however, individual tanks from other units, mainly from the Barak Brigade to the south, began to augment Ben-Gal's shattered remnant. Soon additional reinforcements began to make their way up from Israel. It then developed that the Syrians, in this last, herculean effort, had shot their bolt. Their supply convoys, mauled by pinpoint Israeli gunnery, suddenly began turning in their tracks and withdrawing. Astonished by the miraculous reprieve, Ben-Gal shook off his exhaustion, rounded up some twenty tanks, and immediately began pursuing the Syrians. His crews now had little difficulty in making mincemeat of the fleeing enemy armor and personnel carriers. Within hours, the Quneitra-Masada road, Israel's last major artery in the central Golan, was opened again. At this point Eytan radioed Ben-Gal a succinct but heartfelt message: "You have saved the people of Israel!" It was hardly an exaggeration. By their Leonidean courage, a handful of dazed and flagellated youngsters in a scattering of battered tanks had lifted the shadow of certain catastrophe from the nation.

Even the day before, as the southern sector of the heights came within a hair's breadth of being overrun, Mrs. Meir asked Chaim Bar-Lev, the former chief of staff (and currently a government minister), to visit the Golan and evaluate Dayan's urgent suggestion of withdrawal. Bar-Lev immediately toured the battle zones, bringing his characteristic imperturbability and self-assurance with him. That night, with the concurrence of Elazar and of Hofi, the northern front commander, Bar-Lev reported that withdrawal was out of the question. On the contrary, the Israelis themselves would launch an attack the next morning in the Rafid sector. It was anticipated that by then General "Musa" Peled's reserve armored division would be organized and deployed for action. So it happened. Even though many of the brigades' tanks continued arriving at irregular intervals, some on their own tracks, Peled's force was approaching fighting strength. It was immediately ordered to push back toward the Rafid junction.

Thus, early on October 9, the counterattack in the southern sector began, moving along the El Al–Rafid route. It was slow, grinding work against heavy Syrian defenses, both of tanks and of artillery. Many old Super-Shermans had to be used against the latest Soviet T-62s. Once more, however, Israeli aggressiveness and gunnery decided the issue. Although taking heavy losses, Peled drove steadily northward, his forces replenished by convoys of troops and armored equipment moving up from Israel. Soon another Israeli division, commanded by General Dan Laner, reached the Golan and took up positions along Peled's flank. By the evening of the ninth, Laner's tankers and mechanized infantry had cut the supply lines of the largest Syrian concentration at Husniyah. Peled's armor then closed the trap. Initially thrown into battle hit-or-miss, Israeli forces now were resuming their traditional coordination and flair. Even the most battle-weary troops sensed the shift of events in the north.

By dawn of the tenth, Peled forced his offensive and gradually, against a still-powerful and disciplined Syrian enemy, managed to win control of the Husniyah-Rafid road. Among the regained ground was the city of Quneitra itself, capital of the Golan. It had been lost in the first twenty-four hours of the war—unknown to Israel's citizenry. As Peled's men rested and regrouped, Laner's division took up the slack. By early afternoon, precisely four days after the Syrians had launched their avalanche against Israel, not a single one of their tanks in fighting condition remained within the "Purple Line"—the 1967 cease-fire zone. Strewn along the route of Israeli advance were 867 destroyed enemy tanks, over 3,000 personnel carriers, hundreds of antitank guns, and vast piles of other military equipment. The Syrians had thrown all they had into the offensive, with every advantage of numbers, surprise, and equipment—and now the pride of their army lay smoking and ruined on the Golan.

A COMPETITION OF PATRONS

The Egyptian campaign far transcended the Suez battlefield. Indeed, it extended over a thousand miles from Suez, to the Bab al-Mandeb Strait, lying between the eastern bulge of Africa and the southwestern corner of the Arabian peninsula. This narrow estuary was the link between the Red Sea and the Indian Ocean. It was here that the Egyptians had leased the island of Perim from the People's Democratic Republic of Yemen, and now were using it as Nasser had used Sharm es-Sheikh in 1967, to blockade the traffic of vessels to Israel's Negev port of Eilat. Cut off, then, from their southern—Iranian—oil route, and with the transport of oil from the Abu Rudeis wells too risky, the Israelis were obliged to fall back on their emergency reserves and to order all tankers around the Cape of

Good Hope into the Mediterranean. The potential risk to Israel's economic survival was grave.

At the moment, however, the struggle on the Suez and Golan battlefields was critical enough in its international implications to require decisive Great Power action. The United States was prepared to do its share. Within two hours of the Arab attack, Washington was calling for a cease-fire and a return to the original pre-October 6 lines. On the other hand, Secretary of State Kissinger had few expectations that the Egyptians or Syrians, in their initial victories, would be constrained to accept a cease-fire linked to withdrawal. This was made quite plain by Sadat himself, in a conference that evening with the British ambassador in Cairo. The only cease-fire he would consider, the Egyptian president emphasized, was one based on implementation of Resolution 242 (in accordance with the Arab interpretation of that 1967 document). If the Arabs were interested in a United Nations meeting at all, it was of the General Assembly, which presumably would take time to convene, and which then would be heavily weighted in favor of the Afro-Asian bloc.

Yet the truth was that the Egyptians and Syrians had little to fear even from the Security Council. At the request of the United States, the smaller body met for less than an hour on October 8, adjourned without taking action, then reconvened the next day for an aimless and unproductive session. The American representative, John Scali, dutifully requested a cease-fire based upon an immediate return of forces to the October 6 lines. It was an exercise in futility, as Kissinger had anticipated. The French and British, pandering openly to the Arabs (p. 790), called only for a cease-fire in place. The Soviet delegate, Jacob Malik, went much further, vigorously endorsing Arab terms for a cease-fire—that is, a full Israeli withdrawal to the pre-1967 frontiers. With his customary lack of ambiguity, Malik excoriated the "filthy hands and barbarism" of Israel's leaders and characterized the Israeli government as a nest of "murderous gangsters." Thereupon the Security Council dispersed. Paralyzed by the Soviet-American impasse, it did not meet again between October 12 and October 21. For the time being, Moscow and the Arabs were not dissatisfied with this immobility. Time was working against Israel, they believed.

Thus, as the battle lines stabilized by October 10, with Israel finally holding its own on the Golan and the Egyptians temporarily digging in east of the Canal, Kissinger changed his tack and sought to persuade Israel to accept a cease-fire in place. At first the notion was angrily rejected. But two days later the Israelis were issuing an anguished plea for weapons (p. 769), and Kissinger was reasonably confident that he could force his proposal through. The following night, in fact, on Israeli television, Mrs. Meir went out of her way to signal Israel's willingness to talk, should the Arabs offer any kind of cease-fire. The Soviets for their part began to entertain doubts of their own, in this case of the Syrians' ability to hang on and of Egypt's capacity to push much farther in the

Sinai. As Kissinger hoped, then, Soviet Ambassador Anatoly Dobrynin in Washington intimated that Sadat (with Moscow's endorsement) might after all respond to a call for a cease-fire in place. But the Egyptian leader did not. He was still riding the crest of his early successes. As a result, the first week of fighting ended with Sadat unwittingly having thrown away an impressive military victory.

Whatever the course of diplomacy, meanwhile, the Soviets were determined that the Arabs should not have to forfeit their early gains on the battlefield. When President Houari Boumedienne of Algeria visited Moscow on October 9, the Soviet defense minister, Marshal Andrei Gretchko, publicly urged all Arab nations to supply troops and transport facilities to Egypt and Syria. Gretchko went so far as to suggest that the Arab armies need not stop at Israel's pre-1967 frontiers. At the same time *Pravda* called on the Arabs to make full use of the oil blockade, even to withdraw their multibillion-dollar deposits from Western banks. Yet Soviet help far transcended diplomatic and moral support. Protected by an impressive surface fleet in the east Mediterranean, a relay of Soviet vessels, dispatched well in advance of the anticipated Egyptian-Syrian offensive, was unloading thousands of tons of weapons at Alexandria and Latakia harbors. As early as October 9, too, the Soviets launched a massive airlift to the Arabs. From Hungarian bases, a succession of giant Antonov-12 transports carried tanks, guns, and dismantled fighter planes to the military airfield near Palmyra, northwest of Damascus. Longer-range Antonov-22s flew into Cairo. By October 12, traffic had reached its peak, with eighteen planes landing each hour. Between October 9 and October 22, Soviet flights averaged thirty a day.

Both the flagrancy and the magnitude of this Soviet intercession were a grave shock to Secretary of State Kissinger. The former Harvard professor had won a reputation as the architect of détente, as the man who had secured Russian cooperation in ending the Vietnam war, who had negotiated the SALT I disarmament agreement, and who ostensibly had laid the foundation for a "new and constructive relationship" with Moscow and Peking. Overrated at the time, these achievements were placed in clearer perspective now, as the Soviets actively fanned the flames of the Middle Eastern war. The Kremlin plainly was determined that if Sadat and Assad chose to fight on after October 12, there would be no further military disasters at the hands of the Israelis. Moscow's credibility and prestige were at stake.

No less were Washington's. With the president enmeshed in the Watergate scandal, much depended now on Kissinger's reaction. In earlier years, serving as the president's national security adviser, Kissinger initially had adopted a low profile on Middle Eastern affairs. Conscious of his vulnerability as a Jew, he had preferred to leave the Arab-Israel issue to the State Department. On the other hand, he never disguised his belief that the United States had a "historic commitment" to Israel, and that the preservation of Israel was in the United States' interest. Ultimately it was he, more than Secretary of State Rogers, who persuaded Nixon in 1970 to sell Phantom jets to Israel. It was in September 1970, too, during the Syrian invasion of Jordan, that Kissinger again proved to be more of an activist than Rogers. On that occasion he asked General Yitzchak Rabin, then Israel's ambassador in Washington, if the Meir government would provide air cover for the Jordanians. The reply was affirmative. As part of the silent bargain, the Israelis began conducting tank exercises directly adjacent to the Jordanian frontier, and the United States Sixth Fleet then meaningfully took up positions in the east Mediterranean. Stiffened by this display of American-Israeli power, Hussein immediately launched a vigorous counterattack against the Syrians. His tank corps and air force mauled the Syrian armor, driving the invaders back across the frontier (p. 686). The crisis ebbed. Kissinger and Rabin shook hands. Thereafter, the Israelis trusted Kissinger.

That confidence was to be put to its acid test in the Yom Kippur War. By October 8, informed of the alarming developments on the battlefield, Israel's Ambassador Simcha Dinitz pressed Kissinger for military aid. He reminded the secretary of Mrs. Meir's decision not to launch a preemptive attack against the Arabs, and what this forbearance had cost Israel in manpower losses and destroyed equipment; his country now was desperately short of fighter planes, of artillery ammunition and tanks. Kissinger was sympathetic but cautious. He was not eager to provoke the Russians or the Arab oil-producing states. He knew, too, that the American people wanted no further involvement overseas. Moreover, Joseph Sisco and other professionals at the Near East desk favored a standoff in the Sinai; Egypt was the key to peace and should not be humiliated once it had reclaimed its honor. Kissinger appreciated this logic.

But at the same time the secretary was kept informed of Israel's acute supply problems, among them the heavy losses inflicted on the Israeli air force by SAM-6 missiles. As early as October 8, in fact, Kissinger had authorized El Al planes to pick up ammunition and spare parts at United States air bases. The next day, he and the president approved the replacement of Israeli aircraft losses. Shortly afterward, information began to arrive of the Russian sea lift—and worse. On October 9, United States electronic monitors on Cyprus reported the developing Soviet air shuttle to Syria. News came, too, of Soviet incitement for other Arab nations to enter the war. Accordingly, on October 11, Kissinger reached a major decision. The Soviets had to be blocked, not simply for Israel's sake but to demonstrate American power in the Middle East. A substantial infusion of American weapons would help Israel turn the tide, would restore the military balance, and thus provide Washington with diplomatic leverage to shape the postwar negotiations. It was vital for the Arabs to be convinced they could never win a victory with Soviet arms alone.

Nixon himself, then, late on the evening of October 12, gave the Pentagon specific orders for an emergency American military airlift to Israel. Whatever its earlier hesitation, the Department of Defense this time responded immediately and cooperatively. The next morning Phantom jets began flying to Israel via the Azores. From military airfields in New

Jersey and Delaware, giant C-130 and C-5 cargo planes, loaded with tanks, bombs, shells, helicopters, spare transmissions, electronic jamming equipment, and other matériel, began a round-the-clock airlift. As the first American planes taxied to a stop at Lydda airport on October 14, their pilots were greeted by Israeli girl soldiers, bearing flowers. The arriving ordnance was unloaded and rushed immediately to the fronts. In this manner, between October 14 and November 14, the United States transported 22,000 tons of equipment in 566 flights. Much also came later by sea. Ultimately, American shipments were valued at $825 million, exclusive of the cost of transport. On October 19, Nixon asked Congress for $2.2 billion in appropriations to cover this and subsequent military aid for Israel, "to maintain a balance of forces and thus achieve stability in the Middle East." The reference to a "balance" was apt. The infusion by then had saved Israel's war effort.

STABILIZATION AND COUNTERATTACK

Full if belated mobilization had its effect even sooner on the northern front. By October 9–10, Israel had forced the Syrians back to the initial cease-fire lines. Nevertheless, Elazar recognized that the Syrian army could not be allowed to recover and absorb equipment pouring in from the Soviet Union, nor could the chance be forfeited of striking the enemy a crippling blow in the north. On the evening of the tenth, therefore, the general staff agreed that it was necessary to penetrate at least 12 miles beyond the "Purple Line"; only then could the Syrians be neutralized as a factor in the war. The war cabinet endorsed the decision. Moving quickly, General Hofi decided now to attack in the northernmost sector of the Golan, where the line of advance to Damascus was shortest. Laner's division would proceed along the main Quneitra-Damascus highway from the south, with Ben-Gal's forces leading the break-in. H-Hour was set for 11:00 a.m. the next day.

Meanwhile, Israeli ordnance teams were hurriedly repairing tanks. New armor and other reinforcements were pouring into the line. Entire brigades were rebuilt, including the Barak Brigade, which had lost 90 percent of its original platoon commanders and the largest part of its equipment. As the strength and morale of their units visibly and dramatically revived, many officers wept in the emotion of the moment. The priority task now was to hammer through the hilly wooded areas, through dense Syrian minefields. The Seventh Armored moved out on schedule. A brigade of Moroccan tanks offered the first resistance, but was easily scattered. The Syrians were tougher, but Laner's combined armor and infantry succeeded in driving a wedge along the main Damascus road, and in pushing ahead. Within less than twenty-four hours, as a result, the Syrians showed signs of breaking. Their command issued frantic appeals for help to all parts of the Arab world.

The threats emanating from Moscow betrayed Russian panic, as well.

"The Soviet Union cannot remain indifferent to the criminal acts of the Israeli army," ran the warning. On October 12, Ambassador Dobrynin in Washington informed Kissinger that two Soviet airborne divisions were on standing alert to move to the protection of Damascus. (In fact, Israeli intelligence had reported that a Soviet divisional staff already was housed in a wing of the Syrian military headquarters building.) The American response was firm. On the one hand, additional naval units immediately were dispatched to join the Sixth Fleet. On the other, Kissinger sharply cautioned Israel's Ambassador Dinitz that the Israelis must not proceed farther. The warning was superfluous, as it happened. Mrs. Meir and her advisers already had decided not to risk moving on the Syrian capital; the city in any case possessed little military value. Instead, Laner advanced his division over stiff resistance to wrest control of the main Damascus road network—and in the process liquidated two Iraqi armored brigades. Uncertain of Israel's intentions, the Ba'ath regime continued broadcasting agonized calls for help elsewhere. They got it, after a fashion, from Jordan.

The precise timing of the war had caught Hussein by surprise. Yet the Hashemite ruler dared not enter as a full-fledged belligerent, lest the Israelis cross the river or bomb his cities. Ironically, Israel this time was virtually defenseless along its eastern frontier, as it had not been in 1967. Unaware of this, however, Hussein decided on October 13 to enter the fray in an oblique and highly qualified manner. Rather than move directly against Israel, he dispatched his Fortieth Armored Brigade northward, to reinforce Arab units on the Syrian front. Three days later this force saw its first action, but took heavy losses to the superior Israeli tankers. The next day the Jordanians tried again, in conjunction with an Iraqi outflanking attack. Once more they underwent a severe mauling. For their part, the Israelis reported nothing of these confrontations. They understood the reluctance with which Hussein had entered the war, and his influence for moderation. They would not undermine him. Indeed, between the East and West Banks peace and quiet still reigned. Traffic proceeded as usual in both directions across the Jordan River.

By October 18, Peled's division commanded the flat terrain extending to the outskirts of Damascus, only 22 miles away. The suburbs of the city even then lay within Israeli artillery range. It was a good place to consolidate. Although Arab counterattacks were mounted each day thereafter against the Israeli wedge, the Jews launched no further offensive action against the Syrian capital. On the night of October 20, rather, Hofi issued orders to recapture the heights on Mount Hermon. Paratroop units were to be helicoptered to the ridge for the assault on the Syrian positions, while elements of the Golani Brigade would move up by land to take the Israeli radar observation outpost that had fallen in the early hours of the war. The paratroops lifted off at 2:00 a.m. on October 21. Their advance along the mountain's ledge proceeded through five miles of enemy artillery and air attacks. Eventually the Syrians broke, and by dawn of October 22 their crest on Mount Hermon was in

Israeli hands. The Golani forces meanwhile continued up arduously along three routes, led by five tanks. They faced well-entrenched Syrian commandos equipped with night-vision equipment, and took painful losses. One by one, nevertheless, the enemy was driven from their sangars. By 10:00 a.m. the former radar site was again in Israel's possession, at the cost to the Golani Brigade of 41 killed and 100 wounded. The "eyes" of Israel were restored.

The Israelis could take satisfaction from other accomplishments as well. Their air force was fully mobilized and alerted when war broke out. To be sure, its battle plan had not envisaged a stopgap tactical defense against wide-flung Egyptian crossings. Nor had its pilots been warned of the awesome density and range of the enemy missile systems. Thus, before the fighting ended, Israel had lost 114 of its planes—some 20 percent of its fighter-bombers, and more than twice the number destroyed in the Six-Day War. The attrition was proportionately smaller than in 1967, however, for this time Israeli pilots flew many more sorties. And despite its losses, the air force kept Israel—even most of Sinai and the Golan— sealed tightly against enemy air forays. Not less than 450 Arab planes were shot down in dogfights, another 48 by antiaircraft fire. Israel's losses to aerial combat were twenty planes. There were days near the end of the war when the Syrians and Egyptians hurled virtually all their remaining air power into battle, losing the equivalent of entire squadrons. Most of the Arab planes were destroyed with their pilots and navigators (unlike 1967), and the loss of these trained crews would be felt for years to come.

The Israeli navy acquitted itself particularly well during the October fighting. In 1967 its equipment had been inadequate, and its performance marginal. Yet it was as a consequence of that lackluster record that the navy became the single branch of the Israeli defense forces to prepare for the next war uninfluenced by the earlier one. Concentrating thenceforth on electronic weaponry and tactical maneuverability, the naval branch from 1967 on set about developing an entirely new "fleet" based on swift attack ships. Most of these vessels were constructed in France (and spirited away from that country despite the post-1967 French embargo); but in later years several were built in Israel itself, and all were fitted out with Israeli-engineered Gabriel missiles. Like the air force, the navy was fully mobilized and prepared for action in October 1973; by the morning of the sixth, Rear Admiral Benyamin Telem had sent his entire flotilla to sea. Once hostilities began, a task force of five missile boats was dispatched immediately toward the Syrian coast. There, off the port of Latakia, these units engaged three Syrian missile ships during the first night of October 6–7. Both sides fired volleys, and within a half-hour the three enemy vessels were sunk. It became evident then that the Israelis after 1967 had perfected their technique for jamming the Soviet-built Styx rocket on its ballistic curve. By contrast, the shorter-range Israeli Gabriel missile was devised as a sea skimmer, and the clutter of the waves disrupted the Russian jamming system.

That same night, too, a second force of missile boats approached Port

Saïd, blowing an Egyptian missile ship out of the water and sending two other ships to flight. The following evening of October 8–9, six Israeli missile boats shelled Egyptian coastal installations. Engaged by four Egyptian attack vessels, the Israelis closed swiftly, sinking three of the enemy within a half-hour. From then on, Israel's sailors harassed Arab

ISRAELI COUNTERATTACK ON NORTHERN FRONT
UNTIL CEASE-FIRES OF OCTOBER 22–24, 1973

Israeli counterattack
Farthest Israeli advance
XXXXX 1967 Cease-fire lines

o New Israeli settlements
on the Golan Heights

0   MILES   10

coastal installations with growing audacity and virtually complete impunity. Their patrol and missile boats attacked Syrian wharves and oil
farms, blasted Syrian and Egyptian coastal batteries, even Syrian air
strips, and destroyed additional enemy vessels. On October 21 three
Israeli Reshef-class ships sailed boldly into the Nile delta close by Alexandria, sinking two Egyptian radar pickets. The enemy naval forces were
altogether demoralized by then, and hesitated even to leave the shelter
of their ports. Moreover, while the Egyptians blockaded the Bab al-
Mandeb Strait, the Israelis promptly launched their own counterblockade
in the Gulf of Suez, interdicting the shipment of Egypt-bound oil. By
war's end, as a result, the fast, compact Israeli navy had succeeded not
only in keeping the northern shipping lanes to Israel open, but had ravaged
the Syrian and Egyptian coasts, and sunk nineteen Arab vessels, including
ten missile boats, without a loss.

A REVERSAL OF FORTUNES IN THE SOUTH

On October 11, the day Israel's armored brigades cracked the Syrian
defenses, Elazar and the general staff agreed that thenceforth the principal
military effort could safely be transferred to the Egyptian theater. By then
fully 70,000 enemy troops had crossed the waterway and had established
an unbroken front six miles in depth; while the Israeli attempt to destroy
their foothold on October 8–9 had been thrown back with heavy losses.
According to the Soviet doctrine the Egyptians would prepare now for
a major second-stage breakthrough. The question was one of timing.
Egyptian Chief of Staff Shazli favored an immediate transfer of armor
from the west bank and a two-column thrust into Sinai and down the
Gulf of Suez. War Minister Ismail was inclined to caution, however.
Preferring still to broaden his front, he ordered Shazli for the time being
to reinforce his armor and artillery. Later there would be opportunity to
consider a new offensive.

At the same time, in a mirror image of Egyptian strategy, Israel's
General Gonen had decided after October 9 to fight a war of containment
in the Sinai, to block any serious enemy advance toward the key passes.
The next few days were not wasted. Accelerating their mobilization, the
Israelis reprovisioned their troops and repaired their damaged equipment.
Between October 9 and October 13, Adan's division, which had carried
the heaviest brunt of the ill-fated counterattack of October 8–9, was
completely reinforced. Long columns of tanks and personnel carriers
began arriving now from the Golan front and Israel. The wall of armor
before the Mitla and Gidi passes was solidly buttressed.

Yet it was not the general staff's purpose to become enmeshed in a
static war of attrition. All military plans since 1968 had anticipated a
swift counterattack across the Canal that would take the fight to the
Egyptian heartland. During that earlier period, Sharon was the southern
front commander, and it was he who orchestrated those preparations. At

his direction, fording equipment was constructed, and a number of appropriate staging locations chosen. The most promising site was the juncture of the Canal and the northern end of the Great Bitter Lake. The lake offered protection for the southern flank of an amphibious force; and there, as a result, Sharon had two roads bulldozed along the eastern Canal bank. At that spot, too, he ordered the ground leveled for an extensive parking lot, 150 by 400 yards, surrounded by a high earthen rampart. The area was to be known thenceforth as the Compound, the staging point for the crossover. On the Canal-side embankment, one section was built quite thinly, and Sharon personally marked his intended embarkation site with red bricks.

Little could be done to activate the plan in the first critical days of the war. But on the morning of October 6, Sharon was called back from retirement to assume command of a hastily mobilized reserve division. When hostilities began, he was placed in charge of the Ismailia sector of the front, and on October 8–9 shared with Adan the abortive counterattack against the Egyptian bridgehead. It was during this otherwise costly and unsuccessful effort, moreover, that a battalion of Sharon's division happened to reach a crossroads near the junction of the Great Bitter Lake and the Canal. Although the unit did not get through to the water's edge, its intelligence team discovered something of great importance. Entirely by coincidence, a "seam" had opened between the Egyptian Second Army to the north and General Bassel's Third Army to the south—directly at the spot where the Compound had been prepared several years before.

That same night of October 9 Sharon reported his discovery to headquarters and asked permission to organize his division for an immediate crossing. Gonen turned him down. If Sharon's force were decimated (as was Adan's that same day), nothing would remain to block a further Egyptian advance in the Sinai. It was known also that the Egyptians were holding two tank divisions in reserve on the west bank, and this force would have to be destroyed before an attempted crossing. Gonen was equally emphatic that the Egyptian reserves should not be attacked west of Suez, but rather induced across the Canal, beyond their artillery and missile protection. There they could be counterattacked in a direct slugging match. Sharon disputed this approach vigorously. In any case, he was unwilling to accept a veto from Gonen, who had actually been his subordinate less than three months earlier. The clash of personalities and attitudes was not resolved until the night of October 10, when Bar-Lev arrived on the southern front as Elazar's special "representative"—that is, to become the operational commander in Sinai. Seconded by Elazar, Bar-Lev now endorsed the decision to postpone the crossing. Even then, contentious to the point of insubordination, Sharon was on the verge of appealing the matter directly to Dayan. The next day, however, the Egyptians resolved the issue themselves.

Responding to Assad's frantic appeal for help in easing the pressure on the crumbling Golan front, War Minister Ismail on the morning of October 11 transferred his remaining 500 tanks from the west bank to

Sinai. At once, the Israeli command agreed that the impending invasion would have to be met head on; in fact, the Egyptians should be given every encouragement to pull their armor far forward of their missile cover. Precisely as Elazar, Bar-Lev, and Gonen had hoped, then, the Egyptians during the next two days continued moving troops and tanks eastward across the pontoon bridges in preparation for the second stage of their breakthrough at the Sinai passes. The Israelis meanwhile feverishly reinforced their own strength by deploying 430 tanks west of the Gidi and Mitla passes. Soon nearly a thousand tanks were crowded into the western Sinai, more armor than had participated in the battle of al-Alamein thirty-one years before. Finally, at dawn on October 14, preceded by a ninety-minute artillery bombardment, the Egyptians launched their full strength eastward. The Israelis saw a huge cloud of dust moving toward them, as the principal attack developed toward the Gidi Pass. The battle lasted half a day, and it was a slaughter; over 250 Egyptian tanks were destroyed within the first two hours of combat. When the Egyptians attempted to bring infantry forward with their armor, hundreds of their personnel carriers were similarly liquidated. The expert Israeli tankers then cut off the retreat of the Egyptian stragglers, knocking out another 55 tanks without a single loss of their own. The firing gradually died by 3:00 p.m. Israel had won an armored victory that exceeded even Montgomery's triumph over Rommel in 1942.

Now, at last, Bar-Lev turned his full attention to Sharon's plan for a crossing. On the evening of October 14 the issue was discussed with the cabinet. That night, too, the first giant American C-5 arrived, and soon the United States airlift moved into full gear. Kissinger at the same time was pressing a cease-fire on the Russians, who in turn followed Cairo's lead in awaiting the outcome of battle. Reacting to these developments, the Israelis sensed that no further time should be wasted in moving to the offensive. By 10:00 p.m. Elazar and Bar-Lev had authorized a crossing for the next evening, while Sharon was instructed to work out the operational details. Gratified, the burly paratroop commander knew what had to be done. As he explained it, Adan's forces would gain the staging area at the waterway by attacking to the north of the Compound, mounting a diversion at the same time. Sharon's battalions then would cross first, to be followed by the bulk of Adan's armor. The scheme was approved. At 5:00 p.m. on the fifteenth, then, the infantry and engineering units began rolling out of Tasa toward the Canal. Simultaneously, one of Adan's tank columns launched a diversionary attack northward toward Ismailia. Hard fought, the battle gradually pulled the main weight of the Egyptian Twenty-first Armored Division toward the axis of the Tasa-Ismailia road.

In the deepening twilight, meanwhile, Sharon's troops headed southwest, then westward, pushing through sand dunes toward the Great Bitter Lake. There they moved for the "seam" between the Egyptian Second and Third armies. And there, suddenly, a few thousand yards to the north of the Great Bitter Lake, the largest part of Sharon's task force was struck by heavy Egyptian fire. A furious tank battle immediately erupted. It was destined to continue for the next two days. Although one of Sharon's columns managed to outflank the Egyptians on the Tasa road, breaking through to the Compound at the water's edge, most of the fording units had failed to keep up with Sharon's advance elements; in the darkness, traffic had become hopelessly snarled. Sharon decided then not to wait for the portable bridge. He would rely initially on rubber rafts and small pontoons. By 9:00 p.m. 200 paratroops had begun silently crossing over, undetected. They reached the west bank uneventfully.

The worst difficulties were encountered not on the west bank but on the east. For it was here that the operation's staging zone, the location at which the main bridges were to be assembled, had to be cleared and broadened as a reliable supply corridor. Unfortunately, the Egyptians were well ensconced throughout the area, and most particularly two miles behind the crossing site in a former Japanese-operated agricultural station known to the Israelis as the "Chinese Farm." Dug in with substantial armor and artillery, the Egyptians at the Chinese Farm launched a hell of fire that blocked Sharon's men from the road junction. With the first light of dawn on the sixteenth, Egyptian artillery zeroed in on the flatbed trucks carrying the bridging equipment. Denied pontoons, the Israeli engineers were compelled instead to lash tanks onto barges and send them chugging across the water slowly. By 9:00 a.m. a mere 30 tanks and 2,000 men had reached the west bank. Since dawn, moreover, the two Israeli armored brigades originally committed to the operation had been engaged in savage fighting along the intended corridor area. Tanks fought tanks at ranges of ten yards. Egyptian rockets from the Chinese Farm scoured Israeli reinforcements. Incredibly, the Egyptians failed to discern Israel's amphibious operation at the Compound; they assumed that the Jews simply were counterattacking their—Egyptian—bridgehead. Yet by any conventional military standards, Sharon's attempt to establish a foothold on the west bank had failed. Starting with a brigade, he had managed after fifteen hours to get less than a battalion across the Canal, together with some modest armor. Not one bridge was up. Had any number of Egyptian tanks attacked the Compound directly, it would have been all over for the Israelis.

All the while, Sharon radiated optimism. Crossing personally to the west bank, he learned from his men that Egyptian troops in the area were in a state of confusion and disarray; none had anticipated this kind of Israeli operation. Egyptian staff headquarters, informed by then that a number of their tanks and missile batteries had been put out of action on the west bank, assumed only that a small Israeli raiding party was roaming loose. Sadat accepted his generals' assurances that there was no cause for alarm. Indeed, the Egyptian president was occupied at the time with a distinguished, if unexpected, guest. It was Soviet Prime Minister Kosygin. Suspecting that the war had reached its turning point after Israel's victory on the Golan and the Egyptian tank disaster of October 14, the Soviet leadership had dispatched Kosygin to Cairo on October 15 to make his own assessment of the military situation. Even with their extensive advisers and surveillance teams in the Middle East, however, the Russians failed to learn of the Israeli crossings.

Sharon decided at this point to exploit Cairo's lack of reaction. He would bring over additional men and supplies, on rafts, on dinghies, on anything that could float, without pausing to enlarge the staging zone on the east bank or to get bridges across. Fortunately, by the next day, October 17, the murderous struggle for the corridor on the east bank had begun shifting in Israel's favor. At heavy cost, battling for every yard, Adan's tanks gradually levered the Egyptians away from the roads north of the Great Bitter Lake. The redoubt at the Chinese Farm was slowly being overcome. By 8:00 that morning, tanks had fought their way through to the water's edge, towing the bridge's first pontoon. In the next hours more pontoons arrived. The partially assembled bridge took a heavy shelling, and Israeli engineers laboring in the midst of the bombardment suffered extensive casualties. Nevertheless, they managed to repair and complete the structure. At noon, an Egyptian brigade attempted to pierce the corridor, but was turned back. So were later attacks. Adan's tanks began to rumble over.

By then Cairo had awakened to the fact that the Israeli crossing was far more than a raid. The danger was real. Egyptian forces on the west bank were limited to a single mechanized division and one paratroop brigade near the capital. General Shazli thereupon asked Sadat's immediate permission to withdraw 200 tanks from Sinai and rush them back across the Canal. The president vacillated, however, allowing fully thirty-six hours to pass before agreeing to this humiliation. In the meanwhile, Shazli had ordered the Egyptian Second and Third armies to converge on the Israeli east bank staging area. Yet it was now too late to retrieve the situation—either on the east or on the west bank. On the former, Israeli reinforcements were strengthening and widening the corridor. On the latter, Adan had 150 tanks of his own across by nightfall of October 18. There, his armor was systematically destroying Egyptian missile batteries, tearing great holes in enemy air defenses. Israeli planes moved into the vacuum to launch a devastating tactical ground support operation on both sides of the waterway. By 11:00 p.m. of October 18, a second bridge had been completed. Long supply columns now rolled across. Two brigades of Sharon's armor followed. Soon Israeli tanks were pushing south through the rich agricultural terrain of the Canal's west bank, knocking out missiles and occasional Egyptian tanks, and battering through makeshift Egyptian defenses.

THE SOVIETS IN PANIC

For more than a week, the Soviets had been watching Middle Eastern developments with growing concern. On October 12 Moscow began issuing its first warnings and provoking American naval countermaneuvers (p. 771). As has been seen, it was on October 15 that Kosygin flew into

Cairo for urgent high-level discussions. Continuing through the evening of October 18, five extended sessions were held between the Soviet prime minister and Sadat. According to a knowledgeable Yugoslav news agency, Tanjug, Kosygin outlined for the Egyptian leader a four-point plan to end hostilities. By its terms, there would be a cease-fire in place; an Israeli withdrawal to the pre-1967 boundaries, with only minor changes; an international peace conference at which a final Middle Eastern agreement would be negotiated; and, most important, a "guarantee" of the entire agreement, including the cease-fire, by the Soviet Union and the United States.

Yet if Moscow now belatedly sought an end to the fighting, the Israelis were hardly likely to accept a cease-fire once they had seized the initiative. For that matter, Sadat himself was recalcitrant during the initial conversations with Kosygin; the gravity of the Egyptian position still had not dawned on him. In the interval, the Israeli offensive gained momentum. A third division under General Kalman Magen already was 16 miles into Egypt. It was not until October 18, as this counterattack developed, that Sadat began to recognize its full implications. He then raised a vital question with Kosygin: What would happen if Cairo agreed to a cease-fire and Israel did not? Kosygin assured the Egyptian president that Moscow stood ready to enforce the cease-fire—alone, if necessary. At this point, Sadat endorsed the Soviet proposal. Two hours later Kosygin departed Cairo. His government's next move was to secure American cooperation.

That same night of the eighteenth, Dobrynin in Washington presented Kissinger with a Soviet cease-fire proposal based on a total Israeli withdrawal from "all" occupied lands, including Jerusalem. It was an obvious nonstarter, and Kissinger rejected it. The next morning, however, Dobrynin transmitted Brezhnev's invitation for the secretary to fly immediately to Moscow for "urgent consultations." The veiled threat of unilateral Soviet action in the Middle East was too palpable to ignore. Indeed, it was "murderously dangerous," Kissinger admitted to the president. With Nixon's approval, then, the secretary consented to make the trip the next morning. Departing for Russia before sunrise on October 20, the secretary brought with him from Nixon a "power of attorney" to sign any agreement in the president's name. It is of note, too, that by going to Moscow, rather than by accepting a Soviet offer for Gromyko to come to Washington, Kissinger purchased an additional seventy-two hours for Israel to widen its bridgehead in Egypt.

The secretary's plane landed in the Soviet capital at 7:30 that night. Ninety minutes later, Kissinger was escorted into Brezhnev's office. During the course of an extended meeting, the American visitor revealed his terms for a cease-fire (p. 780). Brezhnev seemed conciliatory, and the two men and their advisers gathered again the next morning, the twenty-first, for another lengthy session. Meanwhile, the Israelis were not idle. They sensed that only a day or two remained before the introduction of a cease-fire resolution in the Security Council. Accordingly, Magen's and Adan's divisions ground ahead at full tilt through the Egyptian Third Army's west bank supply lines, moving across excellent armored terrain. A third bridge was up by then, access to integral Egypt was quick and convenient, and the Israelis already had transferred more than half their armored strength there. It was Elazar's and Bar-Lev's intention to seize control of the entire western length of the Canal by the time of a cease-fire, in this fashion levering the Egyptians out of Sinai altogether.

Thus, in Moscow, with both Russians and Americans fully apprised of the battlefield situation, Kissinger hammered out details for a cease-fire that would assure the *sine qua non* of direct talks between Arabs and Israelis. The Soviets met his terms. The results of their agreement were immediately conveyed, via Washington, in a personal letter from Nixon to Mrs. Meir. It reached the Israeli prime minister at midnight of October 21, during an emergency cabinet session. In his message, the president cordially but firmly urged the Israeli government to accept the terms of the Kissinger-Brezhnev understanding, which expressed the American viewpoint on all key issues. He noted that the agreement would endorse a Security Council request for a cease-fire in place, and therefore could be accepted by Israel from a position of strength; the battlefield situation, after all, had been substantially rectified in Israel's favor. Meanwhile, American weapons shipments to Israel would continue, even after Israel had accepted a cease-fire. Nixon observed, finally, that the Soviets for the first time had endorsed the principle of direct negotiations between the two sides, as had Sadat. The deal was a good one for Israel, the president emphasized. Following extended debate in the cabinet, therefore, Mrs. Meir sent back word of her government's acceptance. Immediately, Kissinger radioed his staff in Washington to call for an emergency meeting of the Security Council. This was done, and the Soviets co-sponsored the request.

The United Nations body met early on the morning of October 22. With only China abstaining, it unanimously approved the Soviet and American appeal for a cease-fire in place, to go into effect within twelve hours. The resolution—Security Council Resolution 338—called for the parties "to start immediately after the cease-fire the implementation of Security Council Resolution 242 [of 1967] in all of its parts." It further stipulated that, "immediately and concurrently" with the cease-fire, negotiations should start between Egypt and Israel under "appropriate auspices" with the aim of establishing a "just and durable peace" in the Middle East. The Israelis in fact disliked the reference to the ambiguous Resolution 242, but had no objection to the succeeding paragraph, which represented Kissinger's major contribution on their behalf. Privately, too, both the United States and the Soviet Union made known that they favored an exchange of prisoners of war, a matter of intense importance to Israel.

Thus, while the resolution barred the Israelis from completing the destruction of the Egyptian armies, it nevertheless reflected their military predominance. Israel consequently accepted the cease-fire the same day.

So did Egypt and Jordan. Secure in their distance from the battlefield, Iraq and Libya, both of them marginal belligerents in any case, rejected the appeal. Syria chose simply to ignore the request for two days; and when, finally, the Ba'ath regime cabled its acceptance of a cease-fire on October 24, it stressed that its decision was linked to the "complete withdrawal of Israeli forces from all territories occupied in June 1967 and after." Israel disdained even to take note of the qualification.

It was the Israeli general staff that was particularly incensed by the cease-fire decision. The army was on the verge of inflicting a crushing defeat on the Egyptians, perhaps the most overwhelming in the four wars between the two nations. Time now became vital, to spring the trap on the Canal's west bank before the cease-fire came into effect at 6:50 p.m. Israel time, on October 22. To the north, Sharon's division encountered heavy resistance as it moved up the key Ismailia-Suez road. Adan and Magen were having better luck in the south, however, driving forward in a pincers movement toward the confluence of the Little Bitter Lake and the Canal, then thrusting down toward Suez City. Although Israel's armored columns did not quite reach the Gulf of Suez, the cease-fire deadline found the Egyptian Third Army with its main supply lines cut, large numbers of its troops fleeing in disorder, 8,000 of them already prisoners in Israel's hands, with entire formations and units blocked in the west bank, and the main force of 20,000 men on the east bank in mortal danger.

Under these circumstances, Egyptian commando and infantry teams on the east bank's southern sector ignored the cease-fire and shortly before midnight of October 22–23 struck repeatedly at Israeli tank laagers in a frenzied effort to open a corridor to the Third Army. At once, Gonen ordered Adan and Magen to continue their drive southward, and to tighten the noose. The orders were followed with alacrity. Opening its final offensive on the afternoon of the twenty-third, Adan's brigade slashed through pockets of Egyptian armor in the southwest, moving directly to gain control of Suez City's access roads. Magen's reservists pushed on, too, battering through isolated Egyptian defenses and a newly arrived Moroccan unit, and reaching the port of Adabiye, the southernmost outlet of the west bank. In the early afternoon Adabiye's garrison surrendered. By then the Egyptian Third Army was indeed hopelessly trapped, and Israeli forces were solidly emplaced on the Gulf of Suez.

Throughout the early morning of October 23, meanwhile, Sadat was issuing panic-stricken appeals to his countrymen to rise up in arms, to fight "to the death" to save Cairo. A rather more likely hope was Soviet intercession, which the Egyptian leader now requested frantically. The Russians complied. On the same morning of the twenty-third, after only a few hours' sleep following his return from Moscow and Tel Aviv (where he had stopped for a hurried three-hour meeting with Israeli leaders), Kissinger was awakened in Washington by a call from Dobrynin. The Russian ambassador complained of massive Israeli violations of the cease-fire. Unless the Israelis withdrew immediately to the October 22 cease-fire line,

ISRAELI COUNTERATTACK ON SOUTHERN FRONT
UNTIL CEASE−FIRES OF OCTOBER 22−24, 1973

Israeli attacks
Israeli bridgehead at first cease-fire Oct. 22.
Israeli bridgehead at second cease-fire Oct. 23-24
Egyptian bridgehead at end of war

0   MILES   25

Port Said

Baluza   Rumani

al-Qantara

E

SUEZ CANAL

SINAI PENINSULA

G

Ismailia

LAKE TIMSAH   Tasa

GREAT BITTER LAKE   Bir Gafgafa
(Refidim)

Y

LITTLE BITTER LAKE

GIDI PASS

P

SUPPLIES TO
THIRD ARMY

Kilometer 101

TRAPPED
THIRD
ARMY
(EGYPT)

T   MITLA PASS

Suez

Abadiye

GULF OF SUEZ

Dobrynin warned, the Soviet Union would inflict "the most serious consequences" upon them. Actually no one could be sure where that line had
been, and which side first had violated it. Nevertheless, the secretary immediately contacted Israeli Ambassador Dinitz and emphasized that the
United States expected Israel to observe the terms of the cease-fire
"scrupulously." He sensed in fact that more than a truce was at issue.
If the beleaguered Egyptians were denied a supply corridor, and their
army disintegrated, the kind of military stalemate that would ensure
productive negotiations afterward would collapse with it. So would Kissinger's credibility as a mediator between the warring Middle Eastern
factions.

At dusk on October 23 Kissinger and Dobrynin together formulated
the text for a new cease-fire proposal. The resolution—Number 339—won
Security Council approval late that evening, and demanded that Egypt
and Israel end hostilities forthwith, returning to positions occupied at the
October 22 deadline. This time, too, the Council authorized the immediate dispatch of UN observers to monitor the truce. Still, the problem
remained of identifying the original cease-fire line. Nor did fighting end
along the Canal's southern sector. On the morning of October 24 a Red
Cross convoy en route to the Third Army was turned back by Israeli troops
just as it reached Suez City. Thoroughly unnerved by then, Sadat cabled
emergency appeals to Moscow and Washington, imploring the Soviets
and Americans to organize a joint force to police a Suez cease-fire. Thus it
was, for the third time in less than two decades, that the Arab-Israeli crisis
brought the United States and the Soviet Union to the threshold of confrontation.

Determined as always to keep Soviet troops out of the Middle East,
Kissinger flatly refused Sadat's appeal. At 7:00 p.m. on October 24, however, Dobrynin phoned the secretary to inform him that Moscow now
favored such a Great Power "police force." Once more, Kissinger rejected
the notion. But at 9:25 p.m. Dobrynin called the secretary yet again, this
time with a bombshell. The ambassador had just received an urgent
message from Brezhnev to Nixon. It was a tough four-paragraph statement, accusing Israel of "brazenly challenging both the Soviet Union and
the United States," of "drastically" violating the cease-fire. Demanding
that Soviet and American contingents be flown immediately to Egypt,
Brezhnev then added: "I will say it straight, that if you find it impossible
to act together with us in this matter, we should be faced with the necessity urgently to consider the question of taking appropriate steps unilaterally. Israel cannot be allowed to get away with the violations." Implicit
in this threat was the likelihood of a full-scale Soviet rescue effort of the
Third Army. If that 20,000-man force were liquidated, the Sadat regime
would fall, and with it conceivably all remaining Soviet influence in the
largest of the Arab nations.

Kissinger reacted vigorously. He telephoned Nixon, recommending an
immediate military alert. The president concurred. So did the National
Security Council, its panel of experts agreeing that there was "a high

probability" of some form of unilateral Soviet move. At 11:30 p.m. on October 24, therefore, all United States military commands throughout the world were placed on "Defcom B"—just below acute alert. An additional aircraft carrier was dispatched toward the Mediterranean. Sixty heavy bombers were ordered from Guam to the United States, and the Eighty-second Airborne Division at Fort Bragg, North Carolina, was made ready for departure. Kissinger said nothing of these measures to Dobrynin; he knew Soviet intelligence monitoring stations would pick them up. They did, and at that point the crisis was resolved almost instantly. At 1:00 p.m. on October 25, Brezhnev instructed Malik at the United Nations to drop the appeal for a Soviet-American peacekeeping expedition. Thereafter the Russians accepted the American formulation of a United Nations force, to exclude troops of the Big Five members. So did the Security Council on the afternoon of the twenty-fifth. In Washington a collective sigh of relief was heaved.

The next day Secretary-General Kurt Waldheim proposed a 7,000-man UNEF for a half-year and revealed that the first contingents, taken from the Austrian, Finnish, and Swedish units among the United Nations peace-keeping forces in Cyprus, already had reached Egypt. The troops were dispatched to patrol an anomalous, jigsawed series of battle zones along the Suez front. The Israelis meanwhile had fought up to the last moment before the second cease-fire of October 24, in an attempt to capture Suez City (a gratuitous effort, resulting in heavy casualties). When the fighting stopped, then, Adan's, Magen's, and Sharon's divisions had penetrated from the Canal 25 miles into Egypt, dominating the west bank front between Ismailia and the Gulf of Suez. On the east bank, Egyptian forces were deployed along the Bar-Lev Line to a depth of 3 to 5 miles, apart from an extensive Israeli corridor northeast of the Great Bitter Lake.

ISRAEL CEDES A CORRIDOR

Although Nixon asked Congress on October 19 for a $2.2 billion appropriation in military aid to Israel, the reason he adduced, "to maintain a balance of forces and thus achieve stability," was warning to the Israelis that the president was aiming for the kind of military standoff that would lead to diplomatic compromise in the Middle East. In ensuing days, too, Nixon and Kissinger made plain that the initial accommodation they expected from Israel was a supply route to Egypt's Third Army, which since October 21 had been cut off from food and medical provisions. Sadat understood that the fate of these troops was essentially in American hands, and indeed Kissinger had given a commitment that they would not be allowed to perish. Immediately, then, the secretary began dunning Israel to allow the transfer of food and medicines to the beleaguered Egyptians.

The Israelis had their own priorities. One was to let Sadat taste the "full flavor of his defeat," in Mrs. Meir's words. More important, they insisted upon the return of their own prisoners of war. Kissinger in his brief stopover in Tel Aviv had assured his hosts that POWs would be exchanged within seventy-two hours of a cease-fire. Aware, however, that Israel had tightened its cordon around the Egyptians after the initial cease-fire deadline of October 22, the American secretary now supported the Egyptian demand that the Third Army had first to be reprovisioned. In truth, he had little choice. Cairo refused so much as to discuss a prisoner exchange unless a convoy were allowed through. For the most part, the Israelis from the outset of the war had supplied the Red Cross with details of Arab prisoners captured. The Egyptians had reported only a few, the Syrians none. Less sensitive to human life than the outnumbered Israelis, the Arabs recognized that they could exploit the Jews' vulnerability on the prisoners issue. The Jerusalem government in fact numbered at least 400 of its troops missing, nearly half of them on the Syrian front. It was aware, too, of the atrocities the Syrians had committed on the Golan. The bodies of Israeli soldiers had been recovered there, blindfolded, manacled, and shot. Jerusalem dared not speculate about the fate of its men in Egyptian hands. It was prepared to bargain to assure their safety.

Meanwhile, on October 26, the Egyptian Third Army made a last despairing effort to improve its position. Under heavy artillery cover, its tanks mounted attacks on Israeli pontoon bridges south of the Little Bitter Lake. Following a three-hour battle, the armor was thrown back. Demoralized, many of the Egyptians now attempted to surrender—but were shot down by their own comrades on the west bank of the Canal. At this point Kissinger communicated with Israeli and Egyptian representatives directly and, after four hours of triangular negotiations, devised a formula by which a single Red Cross convoy of medical and food supplies would be allowed through Israeli lines. To work out the details, officers of both sides met under United Nations auspices early on October 27 at a milestone on the Suez-Cairo highway, 63 miles from Cairo. This was Kilometer 101, inside Israeli-occupied territory west of the Canal. The Egyptian representative was General Abd al-Ghani al-Gamazi, commander of the Suez front; while General Aharon Yariv, the former intelligence chief, negotiated for Israel. Discussions between the two men were crisp and businesslike. On the morning of October 28, the first vehicles of a 100-truck convoy, operated by UN personnel, were inspected by Israeli troops and subsequently allowed to pass through to Egyptian lines. It was clear by then that the Third Army would not be allowed to perish. Neither would Israeli prisoners in Egypt. Nor, finally, would hostilities be resumed between Egypt and Israel.

It was at that point, too, that a tentative balance sheet could be drawn on the military lessons and consequences of the Yom Kippur War. Blunders plainly had compounded Israel's sacrifices in manpower and matériel. The most far-reaching miscalculation, of course, had been the assumption that territorial depth would take the place of early warning. As has been seen, this error led directly to critical lapses of intelligence evaluation. And when, at the last moment, warning had come of enemy intentions, the thin picket of reservists along the 1967 cease-fire lines was not reinforced by full-scale mobilization. In any event, all of Israel's military preparations had been oriented to a swift counterpunch. No one had foreseen prolonged blocking battles. No emergency plans had been made for rushing armor to the front, nor was there enough of this equipment.

The war also had taught Israel that its ground forces no longer could function effectively by placing disproportionate reliance upon the air force and armor. The enemy had learned at least partially to neutralize these branches with missiles and antitank rockets. Lacking full diversification, then, Israeli tanks had stormed enemy positions without benefit of infantry and mortar support, often in wasteful battles. Worse yet, the infantry's weapons had been no match for those provided the Arabs by the Soviets. Deprived of night-fighting equipment, Israel had made hardly any use of its superb paratroops and commandos. Only once, during the recapture of the Mount Hermon position, had its manpower been exploited to its full capacities. Many of these shortcomings could be traced not simply to an atrophy of discipline in the armed forces, but to the absence of the right people at the highest echelon. After 1967, rotation of senior commanders had become almost an end in itself, and not a few highly experienced officers at the peak of their ability were replaced at a time when their guidance would have proved crucial.

The other side of the coin was the outstanding moral courage and ability demonstrated by officers and men at all levels, once the fighting began. Ultimately, those qualities more than compensated for blunders in intelligence and preparation; for, in the last analysis, the Israeli armed forces had won the most striking victory in their history. It is worth recalling that the combined Arab forces actually had launched their offensive with more troops and weapons than those available to NATO in Europe—and this against a small country with a population unready and an army unmobilized. The Soviet airlift, within the space of ten days, had provided an additional 8,000 tons of weaponry for the Arabs, the largest airlift of military equipment in history, until it was belatedly surpassed by the Americans. The sheer scale of the battles themselves was immense. The Sinai tank battle of October 12–14, for example, was exceeded in the quantity of deployed armor only by the German-Russian battle of Kursk during World War II. And despite the fury of the war, the surprise attack on two fronts, the incomparable advantages in Arab manpower and—by and large—in army matériel, Israel had held out, and eventually its forces had penetrated well beyond the original Golan "Purple Line" in Syria; even as its bridgehead on the west bank of the Canal had more than neutralized the Egyptian capture of the Bar-Lev Line. The Egyptians had suffered 7,700 combat dead, the Syrians 3,500. The Israelis held 9,000 POWs, of whom over 8,000 were Egyptian. The combined Arab forces had lost some 2,000 tanks and over 500 planes, compared with Israel's loss of 804 tanks and 114 planes.

But if there was a clear perception of victory in Israel, there was a similar understanding of the bitter cost. The nation had lost 2,552 dead and over 3,000 wounded in the eighteen days of fighting, with a high proportion of officers among the casualties. This was a painful attrition for a tiny nation; and the losses would rise even higher in ensuing months, until the final Syrian-Israeli disengagement (p. 798). Atop the Hermon position, Colonel Avraham Ayalon, veteran of the Givati Brigade in the 1948 war, found the body of his eldest son. In the dead of night, Major General Amos Horev dragged the body of his son-in-law from a trench near the lines of the Egyptian Third Army. In the midst of a briefing session, General Chaim Bar-Lev was informed that his nephew had been killed in action. And on and on, some families losing more than one son, many suffering losses well beyond those of the 1967 war. It was a war of fathers and sons. As for the economic costs, these were only beginning to be felt. The expenditure of equipment and damaged property alone reached $4 billion. If one added to this the decline in production and exports as a result of manpower mobilization, the cost soared to $7 billion— the equivalent of Israel's GNP for an entire year.

It was a victory, in short, that provided little savor for a nation grown accustomed to quick, spectacular knockouts. Painful questions were being asked, often in shaken whispers. Four violent and brutal wars had taken place within the state's short history—indeed, within the memory of a single generation. What, then, did peace look like? How much longer could this endless hemorrhage in lives and material resources be sustained? Could even temporary victory be achieved again, for that matter, now that the Soviets had made clear that they no longer would permit the Arabs to suffer a decisive defeat on the battlefield? The implications for the future were devastating. Thus, even as the firing died down in the last week of October, and negotiations were begun for opening a supply route to the Egyptian Third Army, the Israeli people well understood that a threshold had been crossed between two eras. In a sense, the transition was marked early in November, when the eighty-seven-year-old David Ben-Gurion was stricken by a cerebral hemorrhage at his desert kibbutz of Sde Boker. The former prime minister was rushed to Hadassah hospital in Jerusalem. After lingering for two and a half weeks, he died on December 1. The vast and heartfelt outpouring at the funeral, the largest of its kind in the nation's history, manifestly was evoked by more than the passing of the old lion alone.

AFTERMATH OF AN EARTHQUAKE

ISRAEL IN ISOLATION AGAIN

And so the familiar ritual was to begin once more: the protracted diplomatic stalemate, the quest for at least an intermediate security in the wake of a dearly achieved military triumph. Under American pressure, Israel reluctantly had allowed a Red Cross supply convoy to pass through its lines to the beleaguered Egyptian Third Army. But thereafter the Meir government was unprepared to offer further concessions until the Egyptians made available a list of Israeli prisoners of war. Nor could there be any question of Israeli forces returning to their October 22 positions on the west bank of the Canal, as the Egyptians demanded. Concessions had to be mutual, Mrs. Meir insisted. As it turned out, the prime minister's difficulties henceforth were to be less with the Arabs than with the Americans. On October 27, Secretary of State Kissinger was visited in Washington by Ismail Fahmi, a genial and resourceful Egyptian diplomat who was shortly to become his country's foreign minister. Kissinger was impressed by the Egyptian's seeming moderation, his professed wish for renewed ties with the United States, and his avowed interest in peace. The secretary therefore assured Fahmi that he would do his utmost not merely to negotiate a permanent supply corridor to the Third Army—in effect, to secure Israeli withdrawal to the October 22 cease-fire line—but to persuade Israel gradually to evacuate the Sinai altogether in return for a stable peace treaty. As the initial step in fulfillment of this pledge, Kissinger requested Jerusalem to evince "flexibility" on the supply corridor.

By then, Mrs. Meir recognized that there was no further time to be lost in achieving clarification with the Americans. On October 31 she flew to Washington to meet personally with Kissinger and Nixon. In her discussions with the secretary, the prime minister expressed her government's basic reservations. By what moral obligation, she asked, was Israel to pay a higher price than Egypt for accommodation, since the Egyptians had launched the war and had failed subsequently to win it? Kissinger appreciated Mrs. Meir's reasoning. Yet his own arguments were not less compelling. It was true that Israel had won the war on the battlefield. Its army had penetrated deep into Arab territory and its casualties were less than one-fifth of those sustained by the Arabs. But the secretary knew, too, that the victory had left the Israelis with ashes in their mouths. The cost in blood and treasure had been far too high. Moreover, Israel now found itself in a state of virtual diplomatic isolation. Support for the Arab cause had been expressed not alone by the Communist nations but by nearly the entire Third World, including—in Asia—India, Pakistan, Ceylon and Burma, Turkey and Iran, even Japan.

It was in Africa, particularly, the site of Israel's most impressive diplomatic achievements in the 1960s, that the special relationship the Jewish nation had built through years of patient effort now appeared to have gone by the board. In fact, this former colonial hinterland's relations with Jerusalem had been cooling for several years. The chill to some degree reflected a rather widespread Black African disenchantment with the West altogether, for having provided too little aid to salvage the ramshackle African economies. Israel's own technical aid program had shared lately in this general decline, for the 1967 victory had opened alternative challenges for Israeli advisers and technicians in the captured Arab territories. Those madrichim (advisers) who were sent to Africa were drawn increasingly from second-rate personnel. Not a few of them projected an image of the "ugly Israeli."

More critical yet in the developing freeze was Arab intercession with the African nations. In some instances, the pressure was exerted financially. Through oil subsidies, for example, Libya's President Muammar Qadafi literally bought Uganda's and Chad's diplomatic rupture with Jerusalem. But ordinarily the intercession was not economic. A case in point was Ethiopia, one of Israel's closest friends. The Addis Ababa government had long been plagued by the dual problems of Eritrean separatism and Somali territorialism. Shrewdly, then, the Arabs promised Emperor Haile Selassie to restrain the Eritrean Liberation Front and the warlike Somalis, if the emperor in turn agreed to break with Israel. After considerable hesitation during the Yom Kippur War, Haile Selassie finally succumbed to the inducement. At the same time, the growing participation of Moslem African nations in the Organization of African Unity had its impact as well. Thus, the need for African solidarity through the OAU persuaded the black Africans to maintain a common front with the Moslem states on the Israel issue and to endorse resolutions demanding unconditional Israeli withdrawal from the occupied areas. Other inducements were somewhat more blatant—among them, Arab threats to assassinate the presidents of Liberia and the Ivory Coast.

More decisive even than Arab influence, however, was the change in Israel's image since the 1967 war. The Jewish state appeared to have become an imperialist power, and in that context was increasingly equated by the Africans with Rhodesia, South Africa, and Portugal. Indeed, for the Africans, the "inadmissibility of the acquisition of territory by force"—as Security Council Resolution 242 had phrased it—was more than a platitude. Many of the African borders had been carved indiscriminately out of desert or jungle by European rulers, without regard for demographic or even topographic considerations. Inheriting these frontiers, the newly independent states were keenly sensitive afterward to any precedent of changing borders by force. And when, finally, in the Yom Kippur War Israel crossed the Suez Canal into African Egypt, it shattered its last tenuous foothold on African affections. A wave of diplomatic ruptures followed, led by Tanzania, the Malagasy Republic, Dahomey, Upper Volta, Cameroun, and Equatorial Africa. Even such good friends as the Ivory Coast and Kenya joined in the quarantine. In all, the thirty-two nations that had maintained close relations with Israel over the years now severed their ties. The diplomatic defeat was shattering.

Yet it was the erosion of European support that proved even more traumatic for the Israelis—and the Americans. Public opinion in Europe during the war may have been generally pro-Israel, but this had little effect on foreign policy. Soon after hostilities broke out, Michel Jobert, the French foreign minister, defined his government's approach with the caustic observation: "Can you call it unexpected aggression for someone to try to repossess his own land?" Meanwhile London imposed an embargo on the spare tank parts it had contracted to sell Israel, even prohibited the shipment of drugs purchased by British Jews for wounded Israeli soldiers. Defending his policy in the House of Commons, Foreign Secretary Sir Alec Douglas-Home somewhat embarrassedly assured his critics that the government would reconsider its embargo should "the existence of Israel be at stake." In Bonn, it was Chancellor Willi Brandt's firm intention to avoid jeopardizing his new *Ostpolitik*, his quest for an accommodation with eastern Europe—the patrons of the Arabs. From the outset, then, the West German government refrained from expressing partisanship in the Arab-Israeli conflict.

Determined, moreover, to achieve a relaxation of tensions with the Soviets, nearly all the west European governments were sharply reducing their armed forces. They wanted no more international crises. Their foreign ministers tended as a result to regard American help to Israel as a nuisance, based exclusively upon the special status of the Jews in American life. It was in this atmosphere of détente at almost any price that NATO solidarity collapsed like a house of cards during the rival Soviet and American airlifts to the Middle East. Ankara permitted Soviet planes en route to Syria to violate Turkish air space for many days; while Britain's Prime Minister Edward Heath rejected a personal appeal from Nixon for American landing rights in Cyprus. Greece barred American planes altogether. Bonn initially allowed the United States use of Bremerhaven harbor for the shipment of American ordnance stored in West Germany, but, at Arab insistence, later withdrew this permission. Lisbon ultimately granted the Americans airlift landing rights at Portuguese fields in the Azores—but only in return for Washington's help in staving off United Nations criticism of Portugal's African policy. Inhibited by these limited refueling opportunities, eighteen Phantom fighter-bombers en route to Israel had to be supplied over the Atlantic from tanker craft.

Yet the foundering of America's European allies hardly could be attributed to détente politics alone. Even more basic was abject terror of the Arab's single most potent weapon, the oil embargo. Western Europe imported almost 85 percent of its petroleum from the Middle East (Japan fully 90 percent), in contrast to the United States, which until then depended upon Arab countries for a bare 7 percent of its oil imports. This Western economic vulnerability was now to be exploited during the Yom Kippur War. As a consequence of Sadat's shrewd advance diplomacy, the Arab oil-producing nations swiftly closed ranks behind Cairo and Damascus. Their petroleum ministers gathered at the Kuwait Sheraton Hotel on October 17, 1973, and within hours decided to cut export production by 5 percent, and in succeeding months further to reduce their output, "depending on the Middle Eastern situation." Indeed, the ministers soon established various categories among the European nations, upgrading or reducing the latter's oil quotas in direct relation to their support of the Arab cause against Israel. Once the American airlift began, moreover, the Arab Persian Gulf states, even such traditionally good friends as Saudi Arabia, declared a total ban on oil shipments to the United States. Soon afterward the Netherlands also found itself included in this embargo; The Hague had made an indiscreet statement of sympathy for the Israelis. It was under the façade of the war crisis, too, that the Arabs seized the opportunity to launch a drastic escalation of prices. Libya announced on October 18 that the cost of its oil would go up 28 percent—irrespective of the war and of Israel's misdeeds. Iraq thereupon declared a 70 percent price rise. Kuwait matched this latter figure. The competition in Arab acquisitiveness soon was emulated by other, non-Arab, oil-producing nations.

It was doubtful, in fact, if even the most committed Arab nationalist regime had anticipated the effectiveness of the oil weapon. Reacting to the depleted shipments and price rises with near-hysteria, the British, French, Italians, and Belgians immediately introduced tight controls on oil use. Eventually Britain reduced its factory work schedule to four days a week. Italy's ocean liners were kept in port for lack of fuel. The Netherlands, meanwhile, hardest hit of all by a total boycott, was obliged to appeal to its Common Market partners for emergency aid. On November 6 the EEC foreign ministers gathered in Brussels to discuss the problem. No public action whatever was taken to help the Dutch, however, for fear of offending the Arabs, who had threatened retaliation. On the contrary, the ministers released a statement intended to placate the Arab world, declaring that Israel must return all Arab territories occupied since 1967 and take into account "the rights of the Palestinians." If they were gratified, the Arabs were by no means fully appeased. The oil reductions continued, the agony in western Europe mounted, and with it Israel's sense of diplomatic isolation. Apparently reliance could be placed on the United States alone.

These were the circumstances under which Kissinger sought, and achieved, a more flexible Israeli bargaining position from Mrs. Meir. The secretary then pursued the opportunity for a Middle East accommodation in a five-nation swing through the Arab capitals between November 5 and 9, while en route to the Far East. He was well received by the Arab leaders as a "messenger of peace," the only man, after all, who could persuade the Israelis to disgorge occupied land. In a cordial meeting with Sadat on

November 7, Kissinger persuaded the Egyptian leader to modify his demand for an immediate Israeli withdrawal to the October 22 cease-fire line, and instead to put this narrow issue into the broader context of a general disengagement of Israeli and Egyptian troops. Both sides, in any event, recognized that the current cease-fire lines were too precariously entwined to survive. Kissinger meanwhile assured Sadat that, at a peace conference later, he, the secretary, would exert his influence on the Israelis to achieve a more generous withdrawal in the Sinai.

Israel would have to make certain concessions even now, however, principally on the issue of a supply corridor. To ensure the cooperation of the Meir government, Assistant Secretary of State Joseph Sisco flew out of Cairo to handle the discussions simultaneously in Tel Aviv. Sisco found the bargaining hard; but after many hours of detailed negotiations a compromise was reached, and later endorsed by the Egyptians. It provided that both nations would observe the cease-fire "scrupulously"; that they would immediately begin talks on the question of a return to the October 22 positions "in the framework of agreement on the disengagement and separation of forces under the auspices of the United Nations"; that Suez City and the Third Army on the east bank would receive daily supplies of food, water, and medicines; and that as soon as Israeli checkpoints were functioning along the Cairo-Suez road there would be an exchange of POWs. Not specified in the agreement, but included in a private understanding, was assurance that the blockade of Bab al-Mandeb would be lifted. In essence, then, the Israelis had given the Egyptians their corridor; while the Egyptians in turn had indicated their readiness for a peace conference with the Israelis at Geneva. On November 15, as the first scheduled convoys began rolling into Suez City and across the waterway to the Third Army, Egypt released 238 Israeli prisoners of war, and Israel returned some 8,000 Egyptians.

SHUTTLE DIPLOMACY
AND FIRST-STAGE DISENGAGEMENT

At the same time, during the interim before the impending peace conference, Israeli General Yariv, Egyptian General Gamazi, and their respective staffs continued to meet at Kilometer 101 on the Suez-Cairo highway (p. 785). Their hope was to negotiate a possible further military disengagement of the two armies, each ensconced precariously behind the lines of the other. The discussions, if brittle and occasionally even harsh, nevertheless were direct, for the first time since the Mixed Armistice Commissions of nearly twenty years before. Gamazi demanded an extensive Israeli withdrawal deep into Sinai. Yariv initially pressed for a territorial exchange, with at least a partial Egyptian retreat to the west bank. By early December it was plain that agreement was not in sight, and the Kilometer 101 talks were suspended.

Thus, on December 8, Kissinger packed his bags for another Middle

Eastern swing; he was determined at all costs to sustain the diplomatic momentum, to nudge the belligerents into a Geneva peace conference later in the month. (If the United States was pinning its hopes on this gathering, moreover, so was western Europe, frantic to achieve an end to the oil cutback.) During the course of his trip, Kissinger had also to persuade the Israelis to begin a phased withdrawal from Arab territory, if only through a transitional process of disengagement. After initial stopovers in Europe and North Africa, then, the secretary reached Cairo on December 13. A series of long conferences with Sadat that night and the next morning won important concessions from the Egyptian president. Sadat confirmed that Egyptian representatives would indeed take part in a Geneva peace conference, even sit in the same room with the Israelis— although this should not be construed as direct negotiations with Israel.

Heartened by his progress, Kissinger later flew on to Damascus. There he engaged in an exhaustive, six-hour conversation with President Hafez al-Assad. It was wasted effort. From the outset, the Syrian leader insisted that the one basis for discussion was Israel's advance commitment to a full withdrawal from the Golan. Assad's stance on the prisoners-of-war issue was even more unbudging. He would not so much as furnish a list of the POWs, nor permit Red Cross visitations or exchanges of wounded, until the Israelis pledged total evacuation. When Jerusalem flatly turned down this precondition, Assad on December 18 announced his decision to boycott the Geneva conference. By then Kissinger was philosophical; the chances for productive discussions might well be improved by the absence of the Syrians. Within the next eighteen hours, the secretary flew on to Jordon, Lebanon, and Israel. His achievements here, at least, were considerable. Hussein agreed to send his foreign minister to the conference. The Israelis also agreed to participate, upon being reassured that the United Nations' role in the conference would be purely formal, that no members of the PLO would participate, and that Arab-Israeli discussions would be "face to face." It was understood that disengagement envisaged substantial Israeli withdrawals; but Kissinger persuaded Mrs. Meir and her advisers to take the risk for the sake of the unprecedented opportunity of a final peace agreement.

Thus, on December 22, the foreign ministers of Egypt, Jordan, Israel, the United States, and the Soviet Union gathered at Geneva's Palais des Nations. Under the nominal chairmanship of Secretary-General Waldheim, the sessions were conducted with a minimum of pomp and a maximum of security. The atmosphere was cold. Arab and Israeli ministers did indeed sit in the same room, but the delegations entered by separate doors, and there was a forty-five-minute delay to ensure that neither party actually was seated next to the other. When the proceedings began, too, there was an immediate outburst of propaganda, as Fahmi launched into a harsh attack upon the Israelis, their presence on Arab territory, and their obligation to clear out promptly. Eban answered in the same uncompromising spirit. But once the representatives went into executive session, communications became somewhat more productive. The following day, by prearrangement, the conference "temporarily" adjourned, with the understanding that Egypt and Israel would begin talks at the military level for a disengagement of forces as the next stage toward peace. It had been a short "conference," and one uniquely limited in its agenda. Nevertheless, it represented the first direct meeting of Arab and Israeli statesmen since the Rhodes armistice conference of 1949, and there appeared every likelihood that discussions would resume later at Geneva. Kissinger's achievement unquestionably was a major one.

The next phase witnessed Generals Yariv and Gamazi again carrying the burden of negotations at Kilometer 101. The prognosis was unclear even for this limited "first step" toward peace. Israel was in the midst of its delayed election campaign. By then the Labor party had recognized that its maximalist pre-October stance on the Galili document (p. 740) was out of date. The realities of the costly war, Israel's losses of life and treasure, its diplomatic isolation, precluded any chance of too hard a line. Rather, the Alignment's electoral platform, issued after heated argument on November 28, almost explicitly put its trust in the sincerity of Sadat's desire for peace. While it undertook to seek at Geneva "defensible borders that will ensure Israel's ability to protect herself effectively," it offered hope, as well, for a peace based on "territorial compromise."

Ironically, the Arab summit meeting in Algiers, which published its agreed communiqué the same day, breathed no matching spirit of accommodation. Its "two paramount and unchangeable" conditions for a peace agreement were total Israeli evacuation of Arab territories, including Jerusalem, and the "reestablishment of full national rights for the Palestinian people." Even so, the rest of the Arab world did not dictate Sadat's policy. He was his own man now, his political base dramatically widened following the capture of the Bar-Lev Line. By a show of flexibility, moreover, he had a unique opportunity to achieve through Kissinger's intercession what his generals had failed to win on the battlefield. As Foreign Minister Fahmi put it: "What other country [but the United States] can force Israel to withdraw?"

Thus, despite the subsequent failure of Israeli and Egyptian military negotiating teams to reach a disengagement agreement on their own, neither Jerusalem nor Cairo despaired that all opportunity for compromise had been exhausted. At the suggestion of both governments, rather, Kissinger departed Washington on January 10, 1974, for yet a third effort at shuttle diplomacy. His first step was Aswan, along the temperate Upper Nile, where Sadat was recuperating from bronchitis. Discussions between the two men continued through the twelfth. Kissinger reviewed Israel's proposals for disengagement—these had been submitted to him in Washington by Dayan—and Sadat's response convinced him that the two parties finally were inching toward an understanding. Late on January 12, therefore, the secretary flew directly from Aswan to Tel Aviv, and from there proceeded through a snowstorm to Jerusalem for a working dinner with Israeli leaders.

It was during this evening meeting that the context of Middle Eastern negotiations dramatically shifted. Kissinger informed his hosts that Sadat had offered an immediate disengagement agreement, a pact to be mediated by the secretary himself, as an alternative to continuation of the Kilometer 101 talks. Proposals raised by either side, in any event, could be debated later at a reconvened Geneva conference. The Israelis were faced now with a crucial choice: whether or not to substitute indirect for direct diplomacy. On the one hand, the opportunity for face-to-face negotiations had been a major inducement for Israel's original acceptance of a cease-fire, and subsequently its willingness to open a corridor to the trapped Egyptian Third Army. Yet perhaps even more attractive was the chance now, through Kissinger's good offices, to defuse the threat of a new explosion between the intertwined armies. Little progress had been made through direct negotiations, after all. Even less could be expected at a renewed peace conference attended by hostile Soviet representatives and a full phalanx of Arab foreign ministers. On the spot, then, the Israelis made the choice for indirect negotiations; they preferred not to risk an additional loss of life. And, as they hoped, their decision soon produced tangible results. Shuttling in his huge presidential jet transport between Aswan and Tel Aviv, occasionally bringing with him compromise proposals of his own, Kissinger swiftly bridged the gap between the two sides. On January 17 he cabled Nixon that agreement on troop disengagement had been reached; the following day Generals Elazar and Gamazi would sign the document at Kilometer 101.

The opening and key feature of the accord clearly reflected American and world pressure on Israel. It was for the Israelis to withdraw both from the west bank of the Canal and from their advance positions on the east bank to a distance of between six and seven miles into Sinai, or approximately fifteen miles from the Canal. Although the pullback represented no essential weakening of Israel's defensive position—the Gidi and Mitla passes would not be given up—it did represent a unilateral move by one side. The withdrawal was qualified, however, by Sadat's agreement to reduce the Egyptian military presence on the east bank to a mere 7,000 troops, 36 artillery pieces, and 30 tanks in a limited geographical zone. Egyptian missile emplacements on the west bank would be exclusively defensive. A middle—buffer—zone would be occupied by United Nations troops, while a third zone would be held by the Israelis, under the same constraints imposed on the Egyptians due east of the Canal. In addition to the official bilateral agreement, eight of a series of eleven "private" letters from Nixon to Sadat and Mrs. Meir were countersigned by both Middle Eastern leaders, thus representing Egypt's and Israel's commitment not to each other but to a third party, the United States. The most important of the "private" communications transmitted Sadat's assurances that his government would set about clearing the waterway and rebuilding the Canal cities, thereby in effect making the Suez area a hostage to peace; and that nonmilitary cargoes destined to or from Israel would be allowed passage through the Canal, though not in Israeli vessels. Additionally, the United States would supply aerial reconnaissance of the disengagement area, and would "be fully responsive on a continuing and long-term basis to Israel's military equipment requirements." The accord was by no means an intolerable one for Israel.

Neither had all direct negotiations been foreclosed by Kissinger's shuttle diplomacy. Detailed plans for implementing the agreement had yet to be worked out by Generals Yariv and Gamazi at Kilometer 101. Throughout the next week and a half the two officers clarified the stages of disengagement, and the mutual extrication of forces was accomplished thereafter with little difficulty. Both sides honored their commitments. It was of significance, too, that in the four and a half months since negotiations on provisioning Egypt's Third Army had begun at Kilometer 101, in late October 1973, until the final withdrawal of Israeli troops to the new disengagement line in March 1974, Israeli and Egyptian officers and men had been in daily contact with each other, and tensions between them gradually had relaxed into a certain camaraderie, with photograph-taking, backslapping, and mutual assurances of personal visits in the future. Many in both armies clearly were taking seriously the final codicil of the disengagement pact: "This agreement is not regarded by Egypt and Israel as a final peace agreement. It constitutes a first step toward a final, just, and durable peace according to the provisions of Security Council Resolution 338 and within the framework of the Geneva Conference."

By then also, Kissinger was known in both Egypt and Israel as a "miracle man." It was indeed his success in mediating the disengagement, and his promise to undertake a similar effort between Israel and Syria, that persuaded the Arab oil-producing nations on March 18 to end their embargo, although not their continuing price hikes. Factories in Europe and the United States gradually resumed production; traffic began to move freely again. The atmosphere seemingly was conducive for a parallel Syrian-Israeli disengagement. Both Sadat and Feisal of Saudi Arabia were appealing now to Damascus to rely on Kissinger's good offices. Admittedly, the task of negotiating an accord on the Golan would not be easy. The Syrians had earned a reputation as the most uncompromising nationalists in the Arab world. Their hostility toward Israel was more deeply rooted and implacable than that of any other Arab people. Worse yet, the Assad government remained a minority cabal, largely Alawite in membership, and widely distrusted by the public at large; it enjoyed little political elbow-room for compromise. Nor were matters helped by the personality of Assad himself. Kissinger's conversations with the forty-eight-year-old ex-air force general proved to be the most exasperating of his diplomatic career. The man was apparently immovable, Kissinger confided to intimates, and given to disconcerting intervals of crooning in the midst of negotiations. Not least of all, the Assad regime was receiving powerful encouragement from Moscow to hold firm. Fearful of losing Syria altogether to American influence, the Soviets were determined to coalesce a hard-line Syrian-Iraqi-Libyan-Palestinian "rejection front." With Soviet

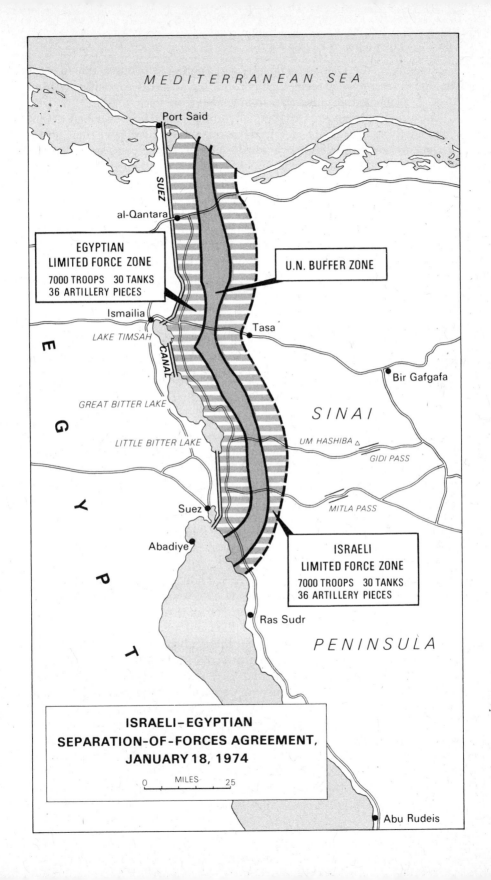

MEDITERRANEAN SEA

Port Said

SUEZ

al-Qantara

EGYPTIAN
LIMITED FORCE ZONE
7000 TROOPS   30 TANKS
36 ARTILLERY PIECES

U.N. BUFFER ZONE

Ismailia

LAKE TIMSAH

CANAL

Tasa

Bir Gafgafa

GREAT BITTER LAKE

SINAI

LITTLE BITTER LAKE

UM HASHIBA

GIDI PASS

MITLA PASS

Suez

ISRAELI
LIMITED FORCE ZONE
7000 TROOPS   30 TANKS
36 ARTILLERY PIECES

Abadiye

E G Y P T

Ras Sudr

PENINSULA

**ISRAELI–EGYPTIAN
SEPARATION-OF-FORCES AGREEMENT,
JANUARY 18, 1974**

0   MILES   25

Abu Rudeis

backing, then, the Damascus government continued to insist that part of the Golan be returned immediately, with an advance commitment from Israel to evacuate the entire plateau in final negotiations.

The Israelis at first appeared equally unbudging. If the war had taught them anything, it was not merely the incorrigible brutality of their northern enemy, but the absence of territorial leeway for concessions on the Golan. From the western edge of this highland, it was a descent of only 60 miles to the Haifa-Acre enclave, the industrial heartland of the Jewish state; and the Israelis had learned the hard way that without at least a substantial foothold on the Golan, including the "eyes" of the Mount Hermon range, their warning time and defense buffer area were critically reduced. Nevertheless, the Meir cabinet understood that some small accommodation would have to be offered even on this northern front. American pressure was not the only factor here. The Syrians evidently intended to maintain the state of tension along the cease-fire line. Throughout March and April they fired repeated artillery salvos at Israeli emplacements and launched occasional commando raids behind the Israeli front lines. The rising scale of violence imposed a daily attrition that the nation was no longer prepared to endure. In the new round of fighting between March and May 1974, the Israelis suffered an additional 37 soldiers killed and 158 wounded.

Even more decisive in altering the government's stance was the issue of prisoners of war. The Israelis counted over 200 troops missing on the northern front, and possessed no way of determining how many of these were alive; Damascus refused to supply a list of Israeli POWs or to allow Red Cross inspection. From the trussed and bullet-riddled Israeli corpses retrieved on the Golan, however, little imagination was needed to assess the fate of those troops remaining in Syrian hands. Each additional day of their captivity was a nightmare for the Israeli people. The families of missing troops already were demonstrating before the Knesset and the prime minister's office. If the Syrians could be persuaded to display even the meagerest evidence of flexibility, Israel would respond.

Kissinger had his own, not ineffective, method of selling a disengagement to Assad. The Russians could offer Syria only weapons and more fighting, without assurance of returned territory. The United States could do better: it could provide help in the form of dollars and advanced technology. The Syrian president was not unmindful of these advantages. In mid-February 1974, therefore, he finally agreed in principle to turn over a list of sixty-five Israeli POWs, on condition that Kissinger, "the miracle man," consented to preside over the triangular negotiations. The secretary agreed, and returned to the Middle East the next week. In the meantime, the Red Cross was permitted to visit the prisoners (it was discovered that at least forty-two of them had been murdered outright on the Golan, and eleven more allowed to die in captivity). A series of quick visits to Damascus and Tel Aviv persuaded Kissinger that there was room for maneuver between the two governments. Returning to Washington, he continued separate negotiations between representatives of the parties, in this case Dayan of Israel and Syria's chief of intelligence, Brigadier Hikmat Shehabi. The differences were steadily narrowed.

Finally, in late April, Kissinger departed again for the Middle East— his sixth visit since the previous October. Continuing without interruption for the next thirty-two days, this last shuttle was the longest and by far the most arduous of his experience. The distrust on both sides was so palpable that on two occasions the exasperated secretary threatened to return to the United States. At last, however, on May 31, an agreement was signed in Geneva (the façade of an ongoing peace conference was deliberately sustained) by Major General Herzl Shafir of Israel and General Adnan Wajih Tayara of Syria. After eighty-one days of almost uninterrupted firing, the guns on the Golan fell silent at last. By and large, the accord followed the guidelines of the earlier Israeli-Egyptian pact. It included the document signed at Geneva, a protocol on the status of the United Nations force, and a number of "private" American letters to Israel and Syria outlining Nixon's and Kissinger's assurances and interpretations on specific issues.

The agreement established a new cease-fire, with Israel and Syria consenting "to refrain from all military action against the other." Israeli forces would withdraw to positions slightly west of the pre-October "Purple Line," with Syrian forces advancing to a line east of that earlier frontier. Al-Quneitra would be returned to the Syrians, together with a cluster of nearby villages; but Israel would retain control of the adjacent strategic hills and of the key positions on Mount Hermon. As along the Suez Canal, the retreat effected no serious weakening in Israel's defensive posture. A demilitarized buffer zone, one to four miles wide, was established between the two armies, with two equal and parallel "areas of limitation in armament and forces" on each side. The buffer area itself was to be patrolled by 1,250 United Nations "observers." The Security Council approved the establishment of this force on May 31 for a half-year period, its mandate to be renewed every six months, upon agreement.

In the 1949 Israeli-Syrian armistice agreement, both parties had agreed that no "paramilitary forces" would be allowed to commit any "warlike or hostile" act against the other. This time Damascus refused to make a similar commitment: it would not publicly disown activities by the various guerrilla organizations. On the other hand, the United States reassured Israel. "Raids by armed groups or individuals across the demarcation line are contrary to the cease-fire," said Kissinger's letter. "Israel, in the exercise of its rights of self-defense, may act to prevent such actions by all available means." Presumably the veiled warning would inhibit fedayun attacks directly from the Syrian territory (for several years it did). On this basis the Israeli Knesset voted to approve the agreement, 73 to 35. Almost immediately afterward prisoners of war were exchanged; many of the Israelis among them were human wrecks. In the next three weeks the troop disengagement was carried out on schedule. Although the Syrians ominously took no steps to rebuild or repopulate al-Quneitra—flattened by Israel as a

L E B A N O N

MT. HERMON

Damascus

U.N. BUFFER ZONE

FARTHEST ISRAELI ADVANCE
OCT. 1973

● Saasa

Banias ●

CHULA VALLEY

● al-Quneitra

S Y R I A N
F O R C E S

G O L A N

Jordan River

Husniyah ●

B'NOT YA'AKOV
BRIDGE

H E I G H T S

ISRAELI **FORCES**

Rafid ●

LAKE GALILEE

El Al ●

Yarmuk River

J O R D A N

**ISRAELI–SYRIAN
SEPARATION-OF-FORCES AGREEMENT,
MAY 31, 1974**

ISRAEL AND SYRIA

6,000 troops 75 tanks 36 short range cannon

Unlimited troops 450 tanks

0   MILES   15

"precautionary measure" before withdrawal—it appeared nevertheless that the likelihood of renewed hostilities in the north had faded for the time being.

A POLITICAL CHANGING OF THE GUARD

Meanwhile, the elections for Israel's Eighth Knesset, postponed for two months due to the war and afterward rescheduled for December 31, were held under the shadow of the nation's heavy manpower losses and the perennial threat of renewed fighting. The Labor Alignment undoubtedly would have suffered a limited erosion in any case as a result of scandals in government and class inequities in society (Chapter xxiv). But in the wake of the recent conflict, military-territorial issues were to take precedence once more. The fall of the Bar-Lev Line and the pulverizing Syrian offensive had thrown the nation into shock. Whatever the complaints against the Alignment, no one had ever doubted that a regime headed by Golda Meir and Moshe Dayan could be relied on to maintain the invincibility of the near-sacred defense forces. Now that assurance had been undermined. So had confidence in the nation's security altogether. Israel's first three wars had not ended in peace treaties; but they had at least produced extended interludes of comparative stability. No longer, evidently. In 1973–74, Soviet pressure, with American acquiescence, had compelled the army to halt short of final victory and of logical strategic goals. The implications for the future were grave.

The trauma of the war, the specter of possibly bloodier and even more open-ended conflicts, profoundly altered national attitudes toward the occupied territories as well. On November 12–13, a poll conducted by the Israel Institute of Social Research found that three-fourths of the citizens interviewed were prepared, in exchange for peace, to give up all or nearly all of the land taken in 1967. This attitude in turn forced a certain revision of party platforms for the impending elections. As we recall, the Labor Alignment on November 28 sharply modified the original Galili plan, and implied compromise on the "administered" areas. Likud took a more adamant stance, insisting on "direct negotiations" with the Arabs. To be sure, rather than express unqualified opposition to withdrawal Likud simply demanded a "rejection of withdrawals that would endanger the peace and security of the nation." Yet in the case of Begin, Sharon, and other rightist leaders, the alteration in language effected no change in image. While many citizens would vote for Likud to punish the Meir government for the blunders of the recent war, the majority of the nation was not prepared to swing to the Right. Few Israelis believed that Likud's hard-line spokesmen could be trusted to explore all opportunities for peace.

In some respects, therefore, the December elections left the political constellation essentially unchanged. Likud gained eight seats, but most of these represented the accession of the new factions: the Free Center, the State List, and a few Land of Israel adherents. Begin's was still a minority bloc, one that owed its gains primarily to the unique circumstances of an indecisive war. Most political observers suspected that it had reached the crest of its influence and popularity. The Labor-Mapam Alignment in turn lost six seats, and therefore was duly "punished." Even so, accounting for 51 out of 120 members, it still remained the dominant factor in the Knesset. However weakened, and driven by its losses into an undignified wrangle with its traditional partners, the NRP and Independent Liberals, the Alignment managed once again to patch up a coalition cabinet, which Mrs. Meir submitted to the Knesset on March 10. Following a ten-hour debate, it secured a 62–46 vote of confidence, with 9 abstaining. Soon afterward, the prime minister won solid endorsement for the disengagement with Egypt.

As it turned out, the new government was destined to enjoy the shortest life-span in Israel's history, foundering only three weeks after its induction. It was torpedoed by an "official report" on the recent war. As early as October 29, 1973, in the immediate aftermath of the cease-fire, the press and members of all political parties had demanded to know how Israel's armed forces could have suffered such grievous initial reverses. Responding to this clamor, the government on November 18 appointed a commission to investigate the intelligence breakdown before the enemy attack, and the army's lack of preparedness for the offensive. The designated chairman of the commission was Dr. Shimon Agranat, the American-born president of Israel's supreme court. Agranat in turn appointed the commission's other members. All of them were nonpolitical figures of recognized stature. They included Moshe Landau, a supreme court justice; Dr. Yitzchak Nebenzahl, the state comptroller; Professor Yigael Yadin, the eminent archaeologist; and General Chaim Laskov, ombudsman of the armed forces and, like Yadin, a former military chief of staff.

By early April, the commission had held 140 meetings, heard 58 witnesses —all *in camera*—and taken much evidence in writing. Yet when it became evident that the investigation would not be completed for at least another half-year, Agranat and his colleagues decided to issue a partial report in early spring. The deliberations already had consumed many months, after all, and were likely to require many more until the last remaining security issues were clarified. In the interval, continuing public debate over the October war was developing into an unmanageable furor. What the Agranat Commission submitted to the government on April 2, therefore, and released to the public the following day, was an "interim" report concerning (1) intelligence data and its assessment before the war; and (2) the disposition of the armed forces up to Zero Hour at 2:00 p.m. on October 6. The remaining issues, dealing with the general preparedness of the armed forces and the conduct of the war until the enemy offensives were halted, would be covered in a later, final report. That completed report in fact was published in January 1975, but by then seemed anticlimactic, and of much less political importance in any event. The interim report was the bombshell.

Agranat and his colleagues found that the information available to the defense forces had offered more than sufficient warning that the Syrians and Egyptians were about to attack; but that, nevertheless, it was not until the morning of October 6 that the director of military intelligence had warned that hostilities actually were about to break out—and at 6:00 p.m., at that. This mistaken evaluation of the facts was due, the commission found, to an obdurate and doctrinaire adherence to the "Conception," according to which Egypt's air power was insufficient to enable that nation to resort to full-scale war, and Syria would not attack without Egypt. Even the previous morning, the intelligence branch had assured the general staff that the probability of war was "lower than low." Painful as it was, the commission accordingly recommended the dismissal of General Zeira, the intelligence chief, and of his three deputies (the recommendation was accepted and immediately carried out). The commission also observed that no defense plan had been formulated for the eventuality of a surprise attack, that a partial mobilization should have been requested at least a week before the war, and that the armored corps had not been properly deployed even after the alert of Yom Kippur morning. Holding Chief of Staff Elazar accountable for the first of these two errors, Agranat and his colleagues sorrowfully recommended his dismissal, as well as the suspension of General Gonen, the southern front commander, who had failed to deploy his tanks in advance.

It was on the issue of personal accountability at the government level that the commission's findings were less decisive. The report limited its comments only to the direct responsibility of Mrs. Meir and Dayan for their actions. "We did not consider it to be our task to express an opinion as to the implications of . . . parliamentary responsibility," it said. Under this arbitrarily delimited format, Agranat and the others refused even to speculate on the delicate question of "whether the special qualifications or personal experience of any minister—in this case Moshe Dayan, minister of defense—who had such qualifications and experience by virtue of having himself served as chief of staff . . . should lead that minister to arrive at a conclusion . . . opposed to what was unanimously presented to him" by the military staff. Declaring that the issue "falls outside the scope of this inquiry," the commission observed simply that "by the criterion of reasonable conduct . . . the minister of defense was not obliged to order additional precautionary measures other than those recommended to him by the general staff. . . ." Mrs. Meir, too, was absolved of direct personal blame, although she was gently rebuked for not having provided information at the extraordinary cabinet session of October 3, when she gave an account of her trip to see Kreisky in Vienna.

On April 2, the day the report was submitted to the government, Elazar formally resigned. In a tense meeting before the full cabinet, however, at which Dayan was present, the chief of staff expressed his sense of being treated unjustly, and implied that the minister of defense at least shared responsibility for events leading up to the war. One cabinet member later observed regretfully that Dayan had always been willing enough to take credit for success, as in 1967, but apparently not for failure. And indeed, the next day and afterward, this criticism was ventilated far more emphatically by the press and public at large. The major reaction was one of outrage that punishment was being meted out to career officers, while Dayan was being absolved of responsibility for the shortcomings of the defense forces, which had been under his personal control. News already had leaked of the defense minister's failure of nerve during the war itself (although this did not relate directly to the interim report). Now, as a result, after April 3, demobilized soldiers began organizing public meetings calling for Dayan's resignation, and similar appeals were heard within the Labor party. Even *Davar*, the Histadrut newspaper, charged the commission with flagrant discrimination in its respective treatment of Dayan and Elazar. Students, academicians, writers, and artists published their views in newspaper advertisements, insisting that Dayan step down. Likud meanwhile requested an extraordinary session of the Knesset to debate a motion of nonconfidence in the government.

In anticipation of that debate, which was fixed for April 11, tensions within the Labor party itself soon reached the breaking point. The truth was that, for several years even before the new crisis, Labor politics had become dominated increasingly by competition between Rafi and Achdut HaAvodah for Mapai's legacy. The rivalry continued well after both factions were merged in the Labor party. If there was a growing conviction within the party now that Dayan should resign, many of the defense minister's Rafi supporters argued that Mrs. Meir and her Achdut HaAvodah confidants, Galili and Allon, should also step down. The debate gained in acrimony, with neither side budging. Thus, as April 11 approached, Labor found itself split more painfully than at any time since the Lavon Affair of the early 1960s. It was by no means certain any longer that the party's members in the Knesset would close ranks to support the government on the nonconfidence motion. Exasperated and exhausted, Mrs. Meir decided not to risk the vote. Instead, she submitted her resignation, thereby causing the fall of her cabinet (although she would stay on as leader of a caretaker administration).

Labor's most urgent task at this point was to find a successor to the redoubtable old woman. The choice was not to be simple. Until the recent war, it had been assumed that Mrs. Meir's political heir would be either Dayan or Allon. But Dayan's reputation was now damaged, and Allon was in questionable health. Conceivably, Pinchas Sapir might have been acceptable to the Mapai center, which still accounted for almost 60 percent of Labor's membership. Sapir was tired, however, and determined to leave the government altogether. Under the circumstances, the best Mapai could come up with was Abba Eban, a chilly mandarin with little following in the nation at large; and Eban's candidacy fell flat almost at the outset. The major contest, then, devolved between Ben-Gurion's former protégé, the able and highly respected Shimon Peres, currently serving as minister of information, and Yitzchak Rabin, chief of staff during the Six-Day War, later ambassador to Washington, and most recently minister of labor. Peres was the candidate of the Rafi wing, but also of many other admirers within Mapai. Rabin, conversely, while of Palmach–Achdut Ha-Avodah background, had never played an active role in this leftist faction, and in truth had not joined any political organization until the Israel Labor party emerged as a united entity. It was with these essentially apolitical credentials, as well as those of a military hero and of a man untainted by the setbacks of the recent war, that Rabin gradually emerged as the most acceptable bridge between Labor's wings. Eventually, on April 22, he was chosen by Labor's central committee in a tight election.

What developed afterward represented a new era in Israeli politics, one that aroused mingled feelings of hope and apprehension. On the one hand, a smooth transfer of power was now anticipated from the generation of the founding fathers (and mothers)—the generation of Ben-Gurion, Sharett, Eshkol, and Golda Meir—to a younger sabra, or near-sabra, generation. Rabin, the first native-born prime minister in Israel's history, was fifty-one; Peres, awarded the defense ministry, was the same age; Allon, the Palmach hero who now became foreign minister, was fifty-six; Aharon Yariv, minister of information, was fifty-four; Aharon Yadlin, minister of information, was fifty-eight; Avraham Ofer, minister of housing, was forty-seven; Gad Ya'acobi, minister of transportation, was thirty-nine. The shift to newer and younger leadership was widely acclaimed. Nevertheless, the changes did not fail to arouse serious questions. These related not only to Rabin's lack of political experience, nor even to the fulsome lecture honoraria he had accumulated during his ambassadorship in Washington (Eban had set a precedent for this earlier). There was growing concern, rather, that both Labor and Likud were turning increasingly to military heroes for their most glamorous leadership (p. 746), to men like Bar-Lev and Rabin, to Ezer Weizmann, Shlomo Lahat (the Likud mayor of Tel Aviv), and the flamboyant and arrogant "Arik" Sharon. It was noteworthy, for example, that during the December 1973 election campaign, Sharon, the hero of the Suez counterattack, was greeted ecstatically at Likud party rallies, often in Oriental neighborhoods, with the mass chant: "Arik, Melech Yisrael"—Arik, King of Israel.

Yet, as events unfolded, Rabin himself turned out to be anything but a political *naïf*. This became evident as he faced the challenge of organizing a new coalition and almost immediately was tested by those masters of political opportunism, the religionists. The emergence of a newcomer as premier-designate seemed an ideal chance for the NRP to flex its muscles. The Orthodox leadership decided now against rejoining the government unless Rabin agreed to repudiate the formula worked out in 1970 on the conversion issue (p. 607). Henceforth, the NRP insisted, only Orthodox conversions performed abroad should be accepted in Israel. Under younger and increasingly aggressive leadership, the religionists took an even more adamant stand on the question of the occupied territories, particularly Samaria and Judea. These historic regions, with all their biblical associations, must never be allowed to revert to non-Jewish hands, they warned. On the other hand, the Orthodox bloc intimated to Rabin that there might yet be room for "compromise," provided a National Unity coalition were formed, including the Likud; under those circumstances, the religionists might be willing to postpone dealing with the conversion issue. Much to the astonishment of the NRP spokesmen, however, Rabin flatly rejected the "compromise." He recognized that such a coalition, with its Likud-NRP swing vote, would have sabotaged any opportunities for peace. For the time being, the premier-designate chose instead to leave the NRP out of his cabinet. He counted upon its leaders' willingness to return to office sooner or later, once their desire for patronage became uncontrollable. It was an astute gamble, and within a year it paid off.

In the meantime, Rabin fleshed out his bare majority by turning to the moderate and companionable Independent Liberals, and afterward to a new and even smaller faction, the Civil Rights Movement. This latter was one of the surprises of the recent election. It had been formed almost literally on election eve by a forty-four-year-old lawyer and mother of three, Mrs. Shulamit Aloni, to advocate separation of church and state, individual constituency elections, equal rights for women, and other forthright liberal reforms. Mildly dovish in foreign policy, the list astonished the nation by winning three seats in the Knesset and thereafter, virtually at the moment of its birth, receiving an invitation to join Rabin's government. When Mrs. Aloni accepted her ministerial portfolio, the cabinet had its majority, and on June 3 Rabin became Israel's fifth prime minister.

Although commanding a bare sixty-one seats in the Knesset, the new government's potential strength was far from negligible. Mrs. Meir had just completed the disengagement agreements with Egypt and Syria, and thus Rabin entered office with the acrimonious security debate behind him. The painful decisions to be confronted at a renewed Geneva conference were still months off. Additionally, if numbers of government supporters rejected a territorial accommodation with the Arabs, not a few opposition members were with Rabin on this issue. There was an excellent possibility, for example, that the Liberal members of Likud might vote with the prime minister if there were a chance for real peace with the neighboring countries. It was for the achievement of that objective, more than any other, that Rabin had been given his mandate.

THE COSTS OF AN INDETERMINATE VICTORY

Nowhere did the new prime minister apparently demonstrate his mettle to better effect than in his initial support of Yehoshua Rabinowitz, the quietly competent former mayor of Tel Aviv, who had been assigned the portfolio of finance minister. Both men recognized that the need for a strong, austere economic policy was hardly less than desperate. As has been seen, the loss of matériel and income during the October war totaled approximately $7 billion, equivalent to the nation's entire GNP for 1973. The loss in production alone was estimated at $400 million in 1973, a figure likely to double in 1974 as the nation's manpower was committed to additional reserve duty. It was the escalation of defense costs that manifestly imposed the single most onerous burden upon the nation's economy. Before 1973, the consensus was that Israel, with its muscular economic infrastructure, somehow would hold its own in any Middle Eastern arms race. But that expectation changed once the Persian Gulf nations made unprecedented sums of oil money available to Egypt and Syria. In the first eighteen months alone since the Yom Kippur War, nearly $3 billion in Soviet and French weaponry flowed into Egypt and Syria, most of it underwritten by Saudi Arabia, Kuwait, Qatar, and the United Arab Emirates. By a ratio of at least one to three, Israel had to match these acquisitions. The Middle East arms race thereafter took a quantum leap forward. Even before the war, as late as 1972, Israel's defense expenditures had totaled $1.5 billion, representing 21 percent of the nation's GNP. Subsequently, in 1974, confronting an apparently unending accumulation of Arab military equipment, Israel's defense budget rose to $3.6 billion, or a staggering 33 percent of the GNP. Worse yet, the largest quantities of Israel's weaponry had to be purchased abroad in foreign currency.

There were other items, too, that required hard currency payment, among them fuel, wheat, sugar, seeds, and meat products, all soaring in cost as a result of the world inflation. It is of note that in its first quarter-century, Israel's exports rose some eighty times, while imports grew only twelvefold. After the Yom Kippur War, mainly as a result of defense expenditures, this trend was dramatically reversed. The gap between imports and exports, about $1 billion in 1972, reached $3.5 billion in 1974. Where and how, then, could the difference be made up? Foreign aid was one traditional source. Indeed, in 1974, the United States government for the first time underwrote Israel's military purchases to the extent of $1.5 billion and supplied an additional $300 million in supplementary economic aid. The United Israel Appeal and Keren HaY'sod provided another $600 million. But impressive as these unilateral transfers were, they hardly made a dent in the payments imbalance. By the first quarter of 1974, Israel's foreign currency reserves declined to $1 billion, the "red line" danger mark. Foreign loans accordingly had also to be exploited for all they were worth. The government continued borrowing heavily overseas, accumulating $700 million in United States credits and approximately half that amount from Israel bond sales abroad. Yet the result was that, by September 1974, Israel already was carrying a debt load of $5.5 billion, on which accumulated interest payments exceeded $1 billion, the equivalent of almost half the nation's net exports. The sheer cost of servicing the foreign debt, as well as paying for imports with shrinking foreign reserves, contributed heavily to Israel's skyrocketing inflation. The price level jumped 56 percent in 1974 alone, an increase unprecedented in the state's history.

It was to excise this inflationary cancer that the government resorted to the harshest fiscal measures since the early austerity period of 1949–53. Even before the war ended, fuel taxes were raised and a billion-pound compulsory loan imposed. Afterward, in January 1974, the government sharply reduced its subsidies on fourteen staple items, ranging from petroleum products to foodstuffs. It was a bitter decision for a Socialist regime, and almost immediately bread jumped in price by 80 percent, milk and cheeses by 70 percent, eggs by 50 percent, margarine by 100 percent —and the bill soon would climb far higher. Six months later, as the government continued to pare its domestic budget to the bone, a moratorium was imposed on public construction, and taxes again were raised. In November 1974 the Israeli pound was devalued, from I£4.20 to the dollar to I£6.00 to the dollar. In February 1975, to meet a record $9.4 billion budget, the government instituted still another tax increase, this one of 7.4 percent on one-third of consumer goods, and of 7.5 percent on employers' payrolls. Tax loopholes were plugged by a major reform act of July 1975 (p. 835). Then, early the next year, a "value added" tax imposed new assessments on every component of every product sold throughout Israel. Even by mid-1975, however, Israelis were paying an average tax rate of about 65 percent, incomparably the highest in the world. The burden was compounded soon afterward, as the pound was devalued once again, this time on a "creeping peg" basis of about 2 percent a month. When the adjustment proved insufficient, the government devalued the currency yet again, in September 1975, by an additional 10 percent.

If these measures were almost unbearably rigorous, they were not ineffective. By April 1975 foreign-currency reserves had climbed to $1.3 billion, enough at least to cover Israel's import needs for about two months. Inevitably, though, the new austerity had its effect on Jewish morale, both within and outside Israel. A chain reaction of strikes erupted in various sectors of the economy, although few of the walkouts initially enjoyed Histadrut backing. At the same time, immigration dropped sharply. Some of this decline undoubtedly could be attributed to Soviet policy in reducing Jewish exit quotas. For a while, it had appeared that the proposed Jackson-Vanik amendment to the United States Trade Reform Act (p. 749) would induce the Kremlin to ease its restrictions on Jewish departure. In October 1974 a quiet "gentleman's agreement" between Washington and Moscow set a bench mark of 60,000 Jewish emigrants annually. But when, afterward, Congress refused to lift the ceiling on extended credits to the Soviet Union, the Russians themselves angrily declined to implement the trade pact. Jewish emigration immediately became the first casualty of this failure.

Yet it is doubtful whether Israel itself would have been able to cope with an influx of 60,000 annually, faced as it was with the back-breaking economic burdens that followed the 1973 war. Nor, in view of Israeli austerity and the danger of a renewed Middle Eastern outbreak, were Russian Jews clamoring for departure as urgently as in former years. There were numerous instances in which Soviet Jews, having formerly managed to win exit permits, now decided to bypass Israel altogether and seek entry into western Europe or the United States. A decline of enthusiasm for aliyah similarly characterized Western Jewry. Throughout American cities, Israel's aliyah centers began closing. Among veteran Israelis, too, for that matter, emigration to Western countries became far more pronounced in 1974 and 1975 (p. 834).

The impact of Egypt's and Syria's early victories in the Yom Kippur War was no less evident among Israeli and other Palestinian Arabs. Thus, in the December 31 elections, the Arabs of Israel cast an unprecedented 32 percent of their votes for Rakach, giving this Communist (that is, Arab nationalist) faction an additional, fourth, Knesset seat. In Nazareth, Rakach actually captured 59 percent of the vote. The shift to nationalist activism was even more overt in the "administered" territories. It had been an Israeli illusion, for example, that the Arabs of East Jerusalem were beginning to accept their absorption into Israel; that they would turn out in large numbers for the election, in which, as Israeli residents, if not citizens, they were entitled to vote for local candidates. But while in 1969 a modest 22 percent of Jerusalem's Arabs had voted, this time only 11 percent cast their ballots. The abstentions clearly were meant as a sign of protest.

In the West Bank and Gaza, moreover, an upsurge of bombing attacks occurred against Israeli installations for the first time in nearly four years. As in Jerusalem, the Jews appeared much less formidable, their occupation regime considerably less permanent, than before the Yom Kippur War. The military authorities retaliated by expelling selected nationalist leaders to Jordan, including the mukhtar of al-Bira and a member of the Moslem Council. Immediately, protest demonstrations were mounted in East Jerusalem and in several West Bank towns, and renewed outbursts took place in the spring and autumn of 1974. (In later years the violence would become much more severe.) The unrest in fact was directed as much against Hashemite claims as against Israeli rule. For Hussein's strongest argument over the years, that only he could win back the lost territories, appeared increasingly empty after the October war. To growing numbers of younger men and women among the West Bank Arabs, the recent struggle confirmed the belief that force, not Jordanian-Israeli negotiations, was the only viable method of removing the Israeli presence. As the nationalists viewed it, too, Yasser Arafat and the PLO once again seemed to embody that alternative.

To the Israelis, conversely, the very notion of dealing with Arafat as the "representative" of the Palestinian people, 75 percent of whom lived under Israeli or Hashemite rule, was as unthinkable after the Yom Kippur War as in all the years since 1967. And because it was understood that the PLO leader would muscle himself into the leadership of a West Bank state, it was the near-unanimous Israeli conviction that an independent Palestinian regime should be opposed at almost any cost. Arafat's intention for the West Bank hardly envisaged statehood in peaceful conjunction with Israel, after all. If there had been any doubt of this, moreover, it was dispelled by the PLO itself in June 1974, when the Palestine National Council, meeting in Cairo, emphasized its unalterable opposition to Security Council Resolution 242. That 1967 document had expressed the unthinkable, peace between Israel and its neighbors.

It was with full understanding of the PLO stance, too, that the Algiers Arab summit conference of November 1973 voted unanimously to recognize the PLO as "the sole representative of the Palestinian people." In late February 1974, the Islamic Conference at Lahore published an identical resolution. So did a later Arab summit conference in Rabat in October 1974. By then Arafat and his Fatah colleagues had somewhat refined their public image, and declared as the PLO objective the establishment of a "democratic, secular Palestinian state." In interviews with the Western press, this genial aspiration was deliberately left vague and undefined. Not so in the Arabic press, where it was made clear that such a nation would include only those Jews who had lived in Palestine "before the beginning of the Zionist invasion." Additionally, by endorsing the "rights of the Palestinians," the Arab states had devised for themselves yet another convenient slogan. Like the "plight of the Arab refugees" in the 1950s and 1960s, "the rights of the Palestinians" in the 1970s became a kind of multifunctional barrier to permanent peace with Israel. Recognizing that this was its purpose, moreover, the Soviet government, which for years had avoided contact with the guerrilla organizations, but which now feared a solution of the Middle Eastern crisis exclusively under Kissinger's auspices, decided to give Arafat its blessing, to welcome him to Moscow, and to encourage his participation in any future Geneva negotiations.

The Israelis, at least, understood precisely what the guerrilla organizations had in mind. After the October war, they lived with the fedayun program on a revived and continual basis. Thus, on April 11, 1974, in an effort to disrupt Kissinger's shuttle negotiations, three members of the PFLP General Command infiltrated across the Lebanese border and made their way to the Israeli frontier community of Kiryat Shmonah. There they burst into an apartment house, indiscriminately machine-gunned its inhabitants, and killed eighteen men, women, and children before themselves being slain by an Israeli army unit. A few weeks later, in mid-May, three armed guerrillas of the PFLP again crossed the Lebanese frontier, this time entering the northern Israeli village of Ma'alot. Breaking into a school, the Arabs took some 120 children hostage, then threatened to dynamite the buildings unless Israel released 26 imprisoned Arab guerrillas. Troops were ordered to charge the school. In the ensuing melee, which took the lives of the three fedayeen and one Israeli soldier, twenty teen-age schoolchildren died, most of them girls. On June 19, 1974, several members of the PFLP attacked Kibbutz Shamir in the Upper Galilee, killing three women. A week later, three Palestinian guerrillas slipped down the coast by boat, where they broke into an apartment house in Naharia, killing a mother, her two children, and an Israeli soldier, and wounding eight other Israelis before finally being shot themselves. On November 18 of that year, three other guerrillas shot their way into an apartment building in Beit Sh'an, killing four civilians and wounding twenty-three others.

The violence continued almost without respite. In March 1975 a group of eight Fatah members again sailed down the Israeli coast, this time disembarking in a rubber dinghy off the Tel Aviv shoreline. Entering a shabby seafront hotel, the raiders murdered eight hostages and wounded eight others (three of the Israeli soldiers who led the rescue effort were also killed, as were seven of the fedayeen). Two months later, on May 4, a bomb exploded in a Jerusalem apartment building, killing one Israeli and wounding three others. On June 15 three members of a family living in the northern Israeli town of Kfar Yuval were slain by Palestinian infiltrators; six others were wounded. On July 4, 1975, a fedayun bomb hidden in a refrigerator was set off by a timing signal in downtown New Jerusalem, killing fourteen people and injuring seventy-five. Four months later, on November 13, the first anniversary of Arafat's appearance before the United Nations (p. 812), another bomb exploded on the same street, this time killing six teenagers and wounding thirty other citizens. A mood of acute tension seized the country, as Israeli civilians, many of them parents of small children, took up guard duty outside schools and playgrounds.

At the same time, the government did not accept the continuing bloodshed without reaction. On several occasions it launched air bombardments of its own against guerrilla bases in southern Lebanon, most of them located in or near refugee camps. Scores of Arabs were killed—many of these, too, innocent civilians. Israeli army task forces crossed into Lebanon repeatedly, scouring "Fatahland," blowing up houses, abducting suspected guerrilla collaborators. Such preemptive measures unquestionably inhibited an even more extensive rash of fedayun violence. They did nothing for Israel's image in the West, however. No more, indeed, than the mounting scope of the guerrilla offensive altered a prevailing Western assumption that Arafat and his associates had moderated their stand, that their principal interest was now in a state of their own on the West Bank, and that once this nation was established, the Palestine question ("the essence of the Arab-Israel issue") would be solved. The full implications of the PLO slogan—"a democratic, secular Palestinian state"—curiously were missed. By 1975 the PLO was recognized in one form or another by more than a hundred governments, not all of them Communist or "neutralist." Arafat himself was granted interviews by numerous Western statesmen.

In late October 1974 the PLO achieved its most spectacular diplomatic coup. It was then that the Communist-Afro-Asian majority in the UN General Assembly voted to disregard the provisions of the Charter itself and to invite Arafat, the representative of a nongovernmental organization, to address the world body. The decision by and large won editorial approval in the West. What ensued thereafter was a decisive contest of Arab and Jewish propaganda. Each side botched its opportunity. Failing to sense the drift of Western opinion, which invested the fedayun cause with the identical aura of tragic nobility the Zionists themselves had projected twenty-seven years earlier, a number of American Jewish communal organizations sponsored large newspaper advertisements and mass rallies to protest the invitation extended a "murderer of women and children." By their ill-conceived outburst, the American Jewish leadership revived precisely the image that a sovereign Jewish nation had been established to dissipate: of a Jewish conspiracy attempting to exert unwonted influence upon the national consensus—and in this instance against a spokesman for homeless refugees. But Arafat, for his part, similarly dispelled a favored notion of Western liberals: that he was a "peacemaker," a man willing to live compliantly with the Israelis, if only his people were given a home of their own on the West Bank. Escorted, beaming, to the rostrum of the General Assembly on November 13, a pistol visible in his belt, the Fatah leader immediately made clear that he was demanding a state for all of Palestine and that the very existence of the Israeli republic had no place in his scheme. In the United States, thereafter, little more was heard on the PLO's behalf by chagrined editorialists and television commentators.

The significance of Arafat's appearance before the United Nations far transcended any initial Western sympathy or disapproval, however. It represented a potentially suicidal development within the international organization itself. The Fatah leader had been invited by the overwhelming vote of the Communist and Afro-Asian blocs. It was a very different United Nations from the manageable and generally restrained assemblage of the 1940s and 1950s. Fully 138 countries were now members. Most were poor and underdeveloped members of the Third World. With few exceptions, they were prepared in return for favors to support the Arab cause, whatever the rights or wrongs of the Arab-Israeli dispute (p. 789). A case in point was UNESCO's decision, on November 20, 1974, to withhold funds from Israel. The reason ostensibly was Israel's violation of "[previous] resolutions . . . [with regard] to preserving the cultural heritage of the City of Jerusalem. . . ." During their archaeological excavations in East Jerusalem, the Israelis in fact had taken great pains to leave undamaged and unblemished all historical and cultural sites—investigations by UNESCO officials had formally attested to this. But the "neutralists" were uninterested in official reports. Their bias was exposed conclusively in the summer of 1975 when, following the Arab lead, they came within a hair's breadth of voting to deprive Israel of its UN membership altogether. Only the sternest of American warnings averted this step. The episode was yet another reminder to the Israelis of their terrifying new diplomatic isolation. The comparatively benign era of the 1950s and 1960s, when the little Jewish state had luxuriated in the approbation of the Western international community, now seemed light-years distant. It appeared at last as if there were only one Great Power upon whose friendship and support the Israelis realistically could depend.

A CRISIS OF SHUTTLE DIPLOMACY

As it assessed its Middle Eastern options, however, the United States plainly had other matters to consider beyond Israel's welfare. Oil was Kissinger's fixation. For months he had been working strenuously, if without visible achievement, to reverse the debilitating price escalation launched by the OPEC governments. In the forefront of the secretary's mind, too, was the gnawing and persistent fear that a new outbreak of

Arab-Israeli hostilities would instantly revive the Arab oil embargo. To avoid that disaster at any cost, Kissinger in the spring of 1975 had been sounding out Cairo and Jerusalem on the possibility of renewed—indirect—negotiations for an additional disengagement.

The response was affirmative. Sadat by then was less than eager to return to Geneva. A reconvened conference would have opened up the explosive issue of PLO participation; and the Israelis had warned, then, that they would not attend. The Russians meanwhile would have ensured a common Arab stance of noncompromise, thereby dooming any possibility of further Israeli withdrawal in Sinai. Kissinger's mediation seemed a better alternative. The Rabin government concurred. It was a gamble for Israel, to be sure. We recall that one of Mrs. Meir's principal reasons for accepting the cease-fire of October 22, 1973, had been Kissinger's assurance, embodied in Security Council Resolution 338, that the belligerent parties would enter into negotiations leading to "a just and durable peace in the Middle East." The diplomatic opportunity appeared to be a spectacular one. Yet from the opening of the attenuated conference in December 1973, it had become evident that "negotiations" were devolving into little more than mutual exchanges of propaganda. In any case, the Egyptians argued that they were negotiating exclusively with UN Secretary-General Waldheim, who chaired the meeting, rather than with representatives of Israel. These were the circumstances under which the Israelis had consented afterward to the Kissinger shuttle approach in securing an initial disengagement of forces. They prepared now to go that route again.

The decision did not go unchallenged. Abba Eban, who had been rather inelegantly evicted from office upon the formation of the Rabin government, and who thereafter had departed the country in a sulk, issued a broadside from New York, warning that Israel must avoid a second-stage withdrawal agreement and instead return to Geneva for an omnibus settlement. Anything less than a peace treaty, he warned, was "salami tactics," with the slices to come from Israel. In Eban's view, moreover, even a failure at Geneva would have its compensations. At the least, it would expose decisively Arab claims of peaceful intent, and the unwillingness of their governments to accept the simple fact of Israel's existence. The latter argument reflected the basic orientation of Eban's own career as foreign minister, when his effectiveness in defending Israel's position had been displayed less in pragmatic negotiations than in soaring oratory before audiences of statesmen and philanthropists.

In fact, it was all too likely that the Arabs would mount a public display of obduracy at Geneva. But four wars and the likelihood of another were a heavy price for winning propaganda points. Rabin, a soldier, now wanted tangible results that would dampen the likelihood of renewed fighting. Triangular diplomacy offered the best hope for that. In any case, if by some miracle a treaty should emerge from Geneva, such a document alone hardly would offer a guarantee of peace. The Arabs had formulated treaties enough among themselves over the years, after all, and had notoriously broken them. The initial goal Rabin and his foreign minister, Yigal Allon, had in mind was something less than a peace treaty, but credible enough to establish an atmosphere of mutual trust in which peaceful conditions might then gradually emerge over the years. The concept he and Allon had worked out was for the extent of a Sinai withdrawal to be determined by the range of meaningful Egyptian political concessions: in short, "a piece of territory for a piece of peace." It would be carefully calibrated, but carefully protected, each step of the way.

The territory at stake here, first and foremost, was the Mitla and Gidi passes. Between 20 and 28 miles from the Canal, the two defiles represented the only practicable access routes to eastern Sinai. They also guarded Israel's huge military air base at Refidim (Bir Gafgafa) and dominated passage to the Abu Rudeis oil field. In possession of Gidi and Mitla, Israel could defend itself with relatively small forces. For this reason, shortly after the 1967 victory, Israeli military engineers had elaborately fortified the passes with a network of trenches, miniforts, caves, and tank laagers. Since the Yom Kippur War alone, Israel had spent an additional $150 million on roads, minefields, communications, and outposts to reinforce the Mitla-Gidi defense line. The cost of reconstructing that line deeper in Sinai, where there existed no comparable strongpoints before Israel itself, would run far higher.

The passes offered the Israelis yet another advantage. They provided an incomparable listening post from which radar and other electronic equipment could detect the movement of Egyptian forces eastward. At the summit of Um Hashiba, a 2,500-foot peak at the western entrance of the Gidi Pass, Israel since 1969 had constructed a multimillion-dollar DEW (Distant Early Warning) line. From this vantage point, a complex of elaborate monitoring devices scanned the desert, the Canal, even Egyptian bases a hundred miles away, for signs of hostile activity. Mounted on towers, for example, heat and acoustic sensors could detect the blast of a jet engine on a runway well inside Egypt. Seismic detection gear buried in the ground picked up vibrations from marching troops or rolling vehicles. Much of this equipment worked automatically, and fewer than 200 men were required to operate it from a control post several miles to the rear of the DEW line. It was a remarkable system.

For the appropriate political concessions, the Rabin government was prepared to give it all up. Indeed, Rabin, Allon, and Peres were equally prepared to withdraw from the Abu Rudeis oil field, and the smaller oil facilities at Ras Sudr—from wells that supplied the Jewish nation with more than half its energy supplies—and from key bases and road junctions in Sinai. They asked in return simply a meaningful Egyptian commitment to nonbelligerency. Kissinger knew well by then that Sadat was not prepared to make that commitment; nevertheless, buoyed by his earlier successes, the secretary of state felt confident enough to depart on a renewed effort of shuttle diplomacy. He arrived in Aswan on March 8, 1975, and proceeded immediately to discussions with the president and foreign minister. As the pattern of negotiations unfolded, Kissinger would confer with Sadat and Fahmi, then emplane for Tel Aviv, sometimes remaining less than a day before flying back to Aswan—with occasional side trips to Amman and Damascus to keep neighboring Arab regimes in the picture. At the outset, the negotiating lines were drawn sharply by both sides. The Israelis were pressing Sadat hard for a clear and irrevocable declaration of nonbelligerency. Such a declaration not only would preclude resort to force; it would render illegal any further blockades of international waterways, including the Suez Canal, and would provide the framework for liquidating economic and even propaganda warfare against Israel.

Sadat's demands, on the other hand, were essentially territorial. He and his advisers presented a map that would have given Egypt much more than the passes. They had in mind, rather, approximately 40 percent of the Sinai, extending two-thirds of the way to al-Arish, and the entire distance to al-Tur, halfway down the Suez coastline from the Abu Rudeis wells. This was considerably more than Israel had bargained for at the outset. Nevertheless, once the passes were abandoned, a few extra miles would not prove crucial, and there would still be room for negotiation. Other difficulties remained, to be sure. The Egyptians opposed a total demilitarization of the area evacuated by Israel, including the passes; they demanded instead the right to move their army forward as the Israelis withdrew. Yet because Kissinger sympathized with the Israeli position here, a narrowing of viewpoints on this issue was also conceivable. Where the Egyptians remained adamant was on the question of nonbelligerency—as Kissinger earlier had warned Rabin they would be. A state of nonbelligerency, Sadat insisted, was conceivable only after Israel had withdrawn from all occupied territories on the three fronts: Egyptian, Syrian, and Jordanian.

The best Sadat would offer, and this only after arduous negotiations, was a vague military formula about the "non-use of force" within the context of an ongoing state of war. In essence, the proposal was a repetition of the undertaking Egypt had given in the January 1974 disengagement agreement, a commitment to refrain from military and paramilitary action against Israel. It was a temptation for the Israelis to break off negotiations at this point. On the basis of his own recent dealings with Red China, however, Kissinger emphasized that it was the substance, not the terminology, of nonbelligerency that mattered; and the Israelis would have to find a way to adjust to a different formula. Rabin and Allon then consented to forgo a public renunciation of belligerency by Egypt, but insisted that at least the practical elements of nonbelligerency be forthcoming.

The Israelis were quite specific on those elements. They wanted assurance of navigation through the Canal, if not for Israeli ships, then at least for Israeli cargoes (Sadat actually had made this concession in the initial disengagement agreement a year earlier). The Israelis similarly expected to be allowed passage of mixed Israeli and other crews on non-Israeli ships. Direct third-party tourism should be permitted between Egypt and Israel, with direct (foreign) airline travel between the two countries. Additionally, the Egyptians were to disavow by word and deed all terrorist methods and organizations aimed at Israel's security. Not least of all, the

Israelis wanted time, an assurance that the UNEF force in the buffer zone would not be challenged in six months or so, or its mandate overturned by Great Power veto. Finally, Rabin demanded mixed Israeli-Egyptian patrols for the buffer zone. If only on the military level, there might then be established those human contacts that were forfeited by not resuming a Geneva peace conference.

On none of these points did the Israelis win satisfaction. Sadat was emphatic that there would be no mixed crews through the Canal. He was prepared to remove from the Egyptian blacklist a meager total of four American and European companies doing business in Israel. He rejected the proposal for third-country tourism and airline routes between Israel and Egypt. Nor was he ready yet to give a commitment for muting propaganda warfare against the Jewish state. His formula on the deployment of UN forces would allow their continued presence for one year instead of six months; after that time, the Soviets could veto a renewal of their mandate. As for Egyptian-Israeli contacts, Sadat envisaged at best a committee of army officers that would meet intermittently, in the fashion of the defunct Mixed Armistice Commission, but nothing resembling sustained Egyptian-Israeli patrols.

In his unyielding stance, the Egyptian president counted on American backing. For the most part, he got it. Kissinger was exerting all his eloquence and leverage in Jerusalem to secure Israeli "flexibility." Under this pressure, Rabin consented finally to abandon his demands for Abu Rudeis oil and for mixed crews through the Canal, even for joint army patrols. But he would not compromise elsewhere. At Kissinger's behest, then, President Gerald Ford, who the previous August had replaced Nixon at the White House, sent Rabin an urgent personal cable. If the Israelis were not more forthcoming, Ford warned, the United States would be obliged to "reappraise" its Middle Eastern policy. On the other hand, the president indicated that his government was willing to offer the kind of open-ended military aid that would compensate the Israelis for any territory they abandoned in Sinai. Yet it was a bad time for Washington to ask a little nation to rely exclusively on American support. Even as Kissinger's shuttle negotiations reached their denouement in the Middle East, another painful struggle was reaching its climax in the Far East. The Republic of South Vietnam was entering its final rictus, as the North Vietnamese Communist army swept decisively southward. The Saigon government turned again to Washington for additional weapons and funds—the support that had been promised by Nixon during the Paris negotiations of two years before. But Nixon was gone now, and the United States Congress, out of a tangle of conflicting motives, refused to send another plane, another crate of ammunition, another dollar to South Vietnam. The legislators watched quietly, rather, as that Asian nation was drawn irretrievably into the Communist orbit.

Whatever the factors that influenced this American decision, many Israeli leaders, and important segments of the Israeli public, perceived in the fall of Vietnam ominous implications for their own country. Political leaders of all parties and citizens of all backgrounds were united in their determination not to abandon their last natural barriers in Sinai for a mere general assurance of future American support. Accordingly, in the last week of March, with both sides at an impasse, Sadat informed Kissinger that nothing was to be gained by prolonging the negotiations. The secretary manifestly had failed to "deliver" the Israelis. In Israel itself, Kissinger paid a last symbolic visit to the fortress of Masada on the Dead Sea, then returned to Lydda airport, where he issued a choked, tearful good-bye to Rabin and Allon.

DISENGAGEMENT AND BREATHING SPACE

On the plane back to the United States, speaking to reporters, Kissinger could barely disguise his frustration at Israeli "shortsightedness" and "intransigence." Once in Washington, too, the secretary continued to inspire "off the record" press criticism of the Jerusalem government. At his request, President Ford also dutifully informed a news conference that the time had come for the United States to "reassess" its Middle Eastern policy. To that end, and to give the Rabin government a compelling incentive to reconsider its stance, the United States now began holding back its promised arms shipments to the Israelis. Yet even at this moment of acute isolation, facing the obloquy of American and world opinion, the Israeli people experienced a sense of collective relief that they had not bargained away their territorial security for "empty concessions." If Rabin had entered the prime ministry with the narrowest base of support, his firmness in the recent shuttle negotiations now was given an unprecedented vote of confidence in the Knesset, 92 to 4. A disciplined soldier, flanked by men like Allon and Peres who also had undergone graver crises of war and siege, Rabin was not the man to break under international pressure. He and his colleagues suspected, also, that Egypt needed peace as badly as Israel.

They were not wrong. Despite vast infusions of Arab oil money, the war had cost Egypt heavily. In 1974 the Egyptian inflation rate had climbed to an ominous 40 percent and was still rising. The economy groaned under the weight of military spending—a fifth of Egypt's GNP— and Cairo was bursting with a population swollen by hundreds of thousands of fugitives from the Canal cities. By the end of the year, the Sadat government was spending $900 million in food subsidies alone. The nation was crippled by underproduction, with its public services, its transportation and sewage system, its water supply and hospitals, malfunctioning to the brink of collapse. The Soviet Union, meanwhile, angered by Cairo's new warmth toward the United States, had turned down Sadat's appeal to reschedule Egypt's debt payments to Moscow (estimated at nearly $7 billion). If, then, American help was needed for diplomatic pressure on Israel, it was hardly less indispensable to rescue and revamp Egypt's chaotic economy. To initiate that revival, Sadat had authorized mine-clearing and debris-removal from the Suez Canal in the aftermath of the first "corridor" agreement of November 1973. By the spring of 1975, with extensive American and British help, the job was almost completed. Thus it was, only three days after the failure of Kissinger's March shuttle negotiations, that the Egyptian president decided to gamble on a propaganda victory and on economic recovery. He announced that he would open the Canal on June 5, and proceed forthwith to begin the rebuilding of the Canal cities. Indeed, Sadat had no choice. As the Israelis recognized better than the Americans, the Egyptians no longer possessed either the strength or the willpower to renew the war. Sadat himself all but admitted this in a meeting with President Ford in Salzburg, on June 1. In a relaxed and cordial discussion, the Egyptian leader suggested that there was perhaps after all a certain limited room for "maneuver" with Israel.

As a sign of goodwill, meanwhile, the Israelis in turn announced on June 2 that they would match Egypt's decision to open the Canal by volunteering to pull back half their authorized tanks and troops, and all their guns, some 18 to 24 miles from the waterway. The gesture similarly had its effect in reducing tension between Jerusalem and Washington. Shortly afterward, in the second week of June, Rabin flew to Bonn, where he met with Ford and Kissinger during the course of the Americans' NATO visit to Europe. The ensuing conversations this time were frank and productive. With renewed assurance of political support at home, the Israeli leader was willing to make additional concessions. Nor did he bother to disguise his anxiety over the interruption of American military supplies. Like Sadat, Rabin confirmed that he also favored picking up the thread of indirect negotiations.

In this fashion, triangular diplomacy was quietly resumed. It did not at the outset take the dramatic form of a Kissinger shuttle in the Middle East. Rather, in ensuing months, discussions continued with the secretary in Washington, where the Israeli and Egyptian ambassadors passed on to him their governments' reactions to proposals outlined by the other side. Slowly but visibly, the gulf between the opposing positions began to narrow. There was little doubt that Israel's concessions to Egypt were the more substantial; the American "reassessment" had had its effect. In considerable degree, however, the imbalance seemingly was made good by Washington (p. 821). And when at last only a few points of detail remained to be clarified, Kissinger departed once again for the Middle East, on August 20, 1975, in full expectation of sealing the belated second-stage disengagement. This time his hopes were fulfilled. An additional week and a half of travel was needed between Tel Aviv and Alexandria to secure "clarifications" and "reclarifications"; but on September 1 the agreement finally was initialed by Sadat and Rabin.

In the manner of the earlier disengagements, the understanding consisted of a public accord between the two belligerents, and private communications between both Egypt and the United States and Israel and the United States. The territorial and military features of the Egyptian-Israeli agreement were incorporated into a public accord and annex. The technical surveillance functions to be performed by American civilians in the demilitarized zone were similarly outlined in a United States "proposal," as an integral component of the public accord, and countersigned by Egypt and Israel. Under the text of these documents, Rabin acquiesced to Sadat's demand to withdraw Israel's forces some 18 miles east of the current Israeli-held positions. The key sites of the evacuated area did indeed include the length of the Mitla and Gidi passes, and that portion of southwestern Sinai encompassing the Abu Rudeis and Ras Sudr fields.

Yet the nature of this military evacuation was highly qualified, and Israel's defensive posture was affected only minimally. For one thing, Egyptian forces would take over only a small part—between 2 and 4 miles—of the territory abandoned by Israel east of the Canal. The rest, including the passes, would be occupied by United Nations troops in a new and much wider buffer zone, except for a shrunken corridor stretching 88 miles along the coast to the Abu Rudeis and Ras Sudr installations; and these latter were placed under Egyptian civil administration, demilitarized completely, and left at the mercy of the Israeli army, stationed the full length of the strip's borders. The wording of the agreement unquestionably salvaged Egyptian *amour-propre* by declaring the passes entirely within the UN zone. But in fact Israeli forces were allowed to position themselves on hills substantially dominating the eastern entrances to the defiles. The Egyptians enjoyed no such rights. Their forces still remained nearly two and a half miles from the western edges of the passes.

More significantly yet, even the restricted zone of Egyptian advance was confined exclusively to limited forces, as was a narrow Israeli area east of the UN buffer zone. Each side in the limited-force areas was held to 8,000 troops, 75 tanks, and 60 artillery or heavy mortar pieces, none of them with ranges capable of reaching the lines of the other side. Egyptian missiles in the west were to be positioned for defensive cover only. There was time, too, to prepare new defensive lines. Under the terms of the annex to the accord, representatives of both sides were instructed to convene in a military working group to formulate a detailed protocol for Israeli evacuation. The withdrawal from Ras Sudr and from Abu Rudeis was scheduled to begin within two weeks after the signing of the protocol, and to be completed no later than eight weeks afterward. The redeployment of Israeli forces east of Mitla and Gidi, on the other hand, would not have to be consummated until five months after the signing. This gave them an opportunity to remove barbed wire, minefields, and other fortifications. The new Israeli line unquestionably was longer than the former one—about 220 miles, as against some 110 miles for the March 1974 disengagement frontier, but the discrepancy was compensated for by the wider UN buffer zone. It was of equal importance to Israel here that a small number of Israeli technical and administrative personnel would continue to man their early warning post atop Um Hashiba at the western edge of the Gidi Pass, well within the UN buffer zone. Under the circumstances, the Rabin government was willing to allow the Egyptians a parallel early warning station of their own in the UN buffer zone north of Gidi and just west of Israel's great Refidim (Bir Gafgafa) air base.

By the terms of the new accord, Israel failed to win its most coveted desideratum, a public Egyptian statement of nonbelligerency. Nevertheless, it extracted other commitments that were hardly negligible. Each side agreed to avoid "resort to the threat or use of force or military blockade against each other," a provision that dampened the likelihood not only of violence in Sinai but of an Egyptian naval blockade of Israeli ports or of such international waterways as the Straits of Tiran and Bab al-Mandeb (this undertaking was reinforced in supplementary United States–Israeli, and United States–Egyptian exchanges of letters). Both parties also agreed to "continue scrupulously to observe the cease-fire on land, sea, and air and to refrain from all military or paramilitary actions against each other." A kind of latter-day version of the Mixed Armistice Commission was reestablished to assist the UNEF in carrying out its mandate, and this offered at least some hope for physical communication between Israelis and Egyptians on a sustained basis. Rather more impressive was the Egyptian declaration that "nonmilitary cargoes destined for, or coming from, Israel" would be permitted through the Suez Canal. In a private communication to the United States, Sadat further pledged to relax the Egyptian boycott of selected foreign companies doing business with Israel, and to ease his government's pressure on African and other nations wishing to renew diplomatic ties with Israel. The accord itself provided for a noncancelable UN mandate, and—as an Egyptian-United States exchange confirmed—it would be renewed annually for a minimum of three years.

To Israel, by far the most significant aspect of the new agreement was the active role assumed by the United States to ensure both the cease-fire and the balance of power in the Middle East. This became apparent in the detailed arrangements for mutual warning in the passes. Actually, the stations included more than Um Hashiba and the projected Egyptian complex opposite Bir Gafgafa. In Israel's case, a chain of supplementary electronic monitors was an integral component of that nation's DEW line. It was not to be anticipated that the Egyptians would tolerate an extensive Israeli presence in the defiles (beyond Um Hashiba) to man the electronic sensors. Neither would Rabin consider handing over this equipment to the traditionally unreliable United Nations. For that matter, Sadat was equally unwilling to entrust his vulnerable Canal cities to UN protection. Thus, during his meeting with Ford at Salzburg, the Egyptian president himself had volunteered the striking notion of American technicians to man a group of auxiliary detection stations in the passes. Astonishing as the proposal was, it received instant endorsement from the Israelis. In their view, no other gesture would lend such credence to Washington's vested interest in Middle Eastern stability. When the idea was discussed with Kissinger, the secretary proved initially hesitant. Upon consideration, however, he agreed that a few hundred American technicians on the spot represented more than an inducement for a disengagement agreement. They signified an unparalleled opportunity for enhanced American influence in the Middle East, and with it American leverage for further progress toward peace in the area.

The concept was thereupon refined and eventually incorporated into the "United States Proposal" component of the disengagement agreement. It took the form of a carefully delimited proviso: that in order "to provide tactical early warning and to verify access" to the Israeli early warning station (Um Hashiba) and the Egyptian warning station (across Bir Gafgafa), three additional watch stations would be established by the United States at specified locations—well within the UNEF buffer zone— in the Mitla and Gidi passes. These facilities would be operated by American civilian personnel and reinforced by three supplemental un-manned electronic sensor fields. In the event of unauthorized military movement by either side, the Americans would report their findings to Egypt, Israel, and the UNEF. Additionally, small numbers of American civilian technicians would be assigned to Um Hashiba and to the Egyptian station to ensure that both outposts were conducting purely technical surveillance functions. Not to exceed 200 in number, the Americans would enjoy freedom of movement to perform their tasks and would remain at their assignments as long as the agreement itself continued in force, unless the United States government concluded that they were in jeopardy, or either of the two parties requested their departure.

Important as the commitment was for the Israelis, other American assurances proved even more vital. Since the collapse of the original March 1975 shuttle effort, the Rabin government had warned Kissinger that Israel would require meaningful compensation in exchange for abandonment of the passes and the oil of Abu Rudeis. Inasmuch as Egypt refused to provide that compensation, however, it was the United States that would have to make Israel whole. The secretary of state accepted the bargain in principle. Whatever the cost of a major American undertaking to the Israelis, a breakdown of talks would raise the far grimmer specter of a resumption of fighting, of a possible American confrontation with the Soviet Union, and the near-certainty of a major Arab oil embargo against the West. No payment seemed too high to avoid these unthinkable developments. In the ensuing negotiations of spring and summer, there-fore, Kissinger was engaged hardly more in completing triangular ne-gotiations on behalf of Jerusalem and Cairo than in refining an American-Israeli understanding.

Except for the issue of technicians, the American-Israeli "entente" was not incorporated into the public accord. Instead, Washington's commit-ments were embodied in a series of "private," unpublicized letters from President Ford and Secretary Kissinger to the Israeli government. These included, first of all, assurance of an uninterrupted flow of modern weap-ons systems, including the latest F-15 fighter aircraft, and a promise to request Congress for substantial appropriations—estimated at between $2 billion and $3 billion annually for the next five years—to help underwrite Israel's backbreaking new military and civilian expenditures. The latter included the cost of oil supplies to be acquired elsewhere, once Abu Rudeis and Ras Sudr went back to the Egyptians. In the event, too, of an oil embargo against Israel by Iranian or other suppliers, the United States would guarantee the Israelis adequate quantities of fuel, if necessary from American stocks. Of no less importance, the president assured the Rabin government that the expiration of the current disengagement agreement with Egypt would not be followed by American pressure for yet a subsequent unilateral Israeli withdrawal. It was understood henceforth that only a formal bilateral peace treaty would succeed in liquidating the Egyptian-Israeli impasse—or indeed the Jordanian-Israel impasse. By the same token, Washington would impose no financial or military embargo upon Israel in its search for additional disengagement on the Syrian front. Neither would the United States recognize or negotiate with the PLO so long as the PLO did not recognize Israel's right to exist.

Most meaningful of all to the Israelis, however, was Kissinger's and the president's undertaking that, in the event of any future threat to Middle Eastern peace either by Egypt or by an "outside Power," the United States would consult closely with Israel about the measures to be taken. This extraordinary assurance was not subject to diverse interpretation in Jerusalem. It signified more than a joint diplomatic stance, or even the promise of emergency military supplies to cope with an unprovoked Egyptian offensive. It implied, as well, an American commitment of protection in the event of Soviet military action against Israel. The promise may have been superfluous; the White House, even the Congress, would hardly countenance flagrant Soviet intercession in a Middle Eastern war. In any case, Washington's other financial and diplomatic undertakings to the Israelis, coupled with a somewhat less grandiose promise of financial and technological aid to Egypt, left no doubt that the United States was doing precisely what great and wealthy nations had always done. It was financing—in effect, buying—an interregnum of quietude for its own strategic purposes.

Yet if the Americans were forthcoming, their contributions to the Sinai disengagement merely accentuated the grudging nature of Egypt's concessions. Sadat in effect had offered the irreducible minimum for Israeli withdrawal. If no statement of nonbelligerency appeared in the draft accord, neither, as has been seen, did provision for the sale of Abu Rudeis oil to Israel, nor for third-country tourism between Egypt and Israel, nor for mixed patrols along the buffer zone. Although Israeli cargoes were to be allowed passage through the Canal, Egyptian acknowledgment of this right merely confirmed the earlier January 1974 disengagement agreement. Sadat emphasized the purely military, apolitical nature of the latest accord, moreover, by the representatives he dispatched to the signing ceremony in Geneva on September 4, 1975. They were army officers, and low-ranking ones at that. Refusing to salute their Israeli counterparts, the Egyptians did not so much as acknowledge the latter's presence at the table across the room. The subsequent joint protocol discussions were conducted in a far chillier atmosphere than at Kilometer 101 in the immediate aftermath of

MEDITERRANEAN SEA

Port Said

SUEZ

al-Qantara

**EGYPTIAN
LIMITED FORCE ZONE**
8000 TROOPS   75 TANKS
60 ARTILLERY PIECES

U.N.
BUFFER
ZONE

Ismailia

LAKE TIMSAH

CANAL

Tasa

SINAI

Bir Gafgafa
(Refidim)

GREAT BITTER LAKE

LITTLE BITTER LAKE

ISRAELI
SURVEILLANCE
STATION

EGYPTIAN
SURVEILLANCE
STATION

UM
HASHIBA

GIDI PASS

U.S. ELECTRONIC
SENSOR FIELDS

MITLA PASS

Suez

U.N.
BUFFER
ZONE

Abadiye

**ISRAELI
LIMITED FORCE ZONE**
8000 TROOPS   75 TANKS
60 ARTILLERY PIECES

Ras Sudr

GULF OF SUEZ

PENINSULA

**ISRAELI-EGYPTIAN
SEPARATION-OF-FORCES AGREEMENT,
SEPTEMBER 4, 1975**

0   MILES   25

Abu Rudeis

the Yom Kippur War. It was significant, too, that Cairo's agreement to reduce—at least, in part—the boycott on foreign companies doing business with Israel, to moderate the level of diplomatic and propaganda warfare against the Jewish republic, appeared not in the public accord, but rather in the exchange of letters with the United States. Indeed, Sadat later emphasized repeatedly that his negotiations at no time had been with the Israelis, but rather with the Americans, and that the very notion of achieving a final political understanding with the enemy was premature at the least.

These shortcomings of the agreement were not lost on Begin, Dayan, and other foes of the disengagement accord. They warned that Israel was abandoning vital strategic defenses in exchange not for Egyptian but for American concessions. Could full value be placed on American guarantees? they asked. Even then, fearing involvement in another Vietnam, members of the United States Senate were questioning the proposed dispatch of American technicians to the Sinai. The request for a continuing multibillion-dollar "payoff" to Israel similarly was encountering opposition in Congress and in the United States at large. Many Israelis were frankly doubtful that an appropriation of American funds in 1975 would guarantee similar economic transfusions for Israel the following year, or the year after that. If there were a new oil embargo against both Israel and the West, could the United States seriously be depended upon to make good the diminished supply? Certainly Kissinger's promise of "joint consultations" in the event of a renewed Middle Eastern crisis appeared to Likud and to other opponents of the disengagement accord as not less fanciful than Eisenhower's assurances, in 1957, of free Israeli passage through the Strait of Tiran. If, by chance, too, President Ford succeeded in honoring his commitments to Israel, and if, even more remarkably, Sadat honored his, were the Syrians likely to remain quiet upon failing to achieve a similar Israeli withdrawal on the Golan? At the least, Assad's forces might revive intermittent shellings and commando attacks, perhaps in tandem with a Syrian-backed PLO effort to infiltrate and seize control of neighboring Lebanon. And if full-scale warfare erupted in the north, could Sadat then effectively resist the pressure to join his fellow Arabs? For that matter, would the United States be prepared to risk the ire of the entire Arab world by heeding its "private" military and diplomatic commitments to Israel?

These apprehensions and criticisms were not without substance, nor did they fail to register, at least in some degree, on Israel's citizens. On September 2 the Likud and the NRP organized a full-scale demonstration against the accord. At one point some 25,000 marchers paraded angrily near the Knesset and the prime minister's office, an outpouring unprecedented since the German reparations crisis of twenty-three years earlier. Like that earlier confrontation, however, the scale and virulence of public protest apparently did not reflect a national consensus. On September 3, the Knesset cast its vote on the agreement and endorsed it by the unexpectedly large majority of 70 to 43. It was evident by then that the nation's willingness to venture a risk for peace was far more deeply rooted than Israel's "hawks" had anticipated.

CONTINUING DANGERS . . .

If Israel had sacrificed a valuable piece of territory for a "piece of peace," the question remained whether this or later concessions would induce the Arabs to accept any variety of formalized peace treaty. Even Rabin's supporters in Israel detected little meaningful proof that Egypt, or the other Arab countries, nurtured a serious interest in ending the state of war. Sadat himself appeared to dispel all illusions on that issue when, in an interview with a *Le Monde* correspondent on January 22, 1974, he emphasized that for the return of the occupied territories "I have nothing to offer." He then added: "I leave to the next generation the trouble of deciding if it is possible not only to coexist with the Jewish state but also to cooperate with it." Was peace even conceivable, he asked rhetorically, "as long as the Palestinian problem is not resolved?" The Egyptian president's remarks suggested that he was thinking, in classical Islamic doctrine, of a jihad, a permanent state of war, if not of continuous fighting. A cease-fire might be permissible, even an armistice, but surely not real peace. In fact, Sadat accurately reflected the mood of his country. An American journalist, Joan Peters, interviewed a wide variety of Egyptian political and professional leaders after the October war and during 1974. She wrote afterward in the magazine *Commentary:*

> We may ask . . . what does "moderate" mean in the present Middle Eastern context? To describe the Egyptian position as moderate implies an attitude of reconciliation to peaceful coexistence with Israel. I found no such attitude. To all the people to whom I spoke . . . the position we call "moderate" does not mean reconciliation, but merely an acceptance of the withdrawal of Israeli troops to the pre-June 1967 borders, with no compensatory concession from the Arab side in the form of recognition. To many Egyptians, indeed, it means . . . first, an Israeli withdrawal to the 1967 borders, and then a further push back to the lines envisioned in the 1947 partition plan, accompanied by the establishment of a Palestinian state: this, for instance, is the position of Mohammed Heykal and of Egyptian Foreign Minister Ismail Fahmy. . . . That from such truncated borders the Arabs hope that Israel will in time shrink, through war or some other means of attrition, to absolutely nothing, is the unspoken but clear implication of this position.

Whatever the "moderation" of the Egyptians, it was pacifism incarnate by contrast to Syria's malevolent and unremitting hatred of the Zionist republic. Altogether typical of this sentiment were the remarks of the Ba'athist defense minister, Mustafa T'las, before the Syrian National Assembly on December 19, 1973: "There is the outstanding case of a recruit from Aleppo who murdered twenty-eight Jewish soldiers all by himself, slaughtering them like sheep. . . . He butchered three of them with an axe and decapitated them. In other words, instead of using a gun to kill them he took a hatchet to chop their heads off. . . . He struggled face-to-face with one of them, and throwing down his axe managed to break his neck and devour his flesh in front of his comrades. This is a special case. Need I single it out to award him the Medal of the Republic? I will grant this medal to any soldier who succeeds in killing twenty-eight Jews, and I will cover him with appreciation and honor for his bravery." Two years later, when the second Egyptian-Israeli disengagement pact was at last initialed, Damascus reacted with open hostility. Public protest demonstrations excoriated Sadat's "treason."

The Israelis understood precisely the neighborhood in which they were living. For them, as a result, the question was not simply one of tactical accommodation under American pressure, but of appraising the likelihood of defending their nation in the event of renewed warfare. The prognosis was sobering. An important lesson of the Yom Kippur War was the ability even of uneducated Arab troops to perform well if they were drilled thoroughly in the use of modern and efficient weapons systems. The Egyptians and Syrians plainly had mastered electronic warfare to a degree Israel never had begun to anticipate. Unable to defeat the Jews, the Arabs at least had demonstrated the capacity to inflict heavy losses. More ominously yet, the use of missiles would enable them in any future conflict to strike Israel's population centers. Under these circumstances, Israel's strategic thinking turned increasingly defensive. After the Sinai Campaign of 1956, for example, it was Nasser who had sought to hide behind the United Nations and who had allocated Egyptian territory for that purpose. Significantly, it was Israel now that requested a buffer zone of UN troops. By insisting on a long mandate for this force, too, the Israelis acknowledged a certain loss of confidence in their deterrent power.

The economics of a future conflict similarly appeared to favor the Arabs. The influx of weaponry and the cost of rebuilding damaged areas were underwritten in large measure by the Persian Gulf oil nations. It was their funds, together with Soviet technical help, that enabled Syria within two years to rebuild all its devastated refineries, its electric stations, and other gutted plant. But the support and influence of fellow Arab nations obviously reached far beyond oil money or transshipped military supplies. As we recall, it extended also to the Third World of developing nations. There was virtually no forum in which Israel could escape this mounting diplomatic pressure. Thus, in early July 1975, the UN International Women's Year Conference in Mexico City issued a declaration, sponsored by the seventy-seven "nonaligned" countries, calling for the elimination of Zionism as one of the world's "great evils, along with colonialism, neocolonialism, imperialism, foreign domination and occupation, apartheid, and racial discrimination. . . ." And the Third World offensive had only begun. If the Arabs and their supporters failed in the summer of 1975 to evict Israel from the United Nations, they accomplished essentially the same objective, that of isolating Israel diplomatically, the following autumn. On November 10, 1975, barely twenty-eight years after voting to establish a Jewish state, the UN General Assembly endorsed a resolution describing Israel as "the racist regime in occupied Palestine," and stigmatizing Zionism as "a form of racialism and racial discrimination." The resolution's preamble additionally singled out Zionism as "a threat to world peace and security," and called upon "all countries to oppose this racist and imperialist ideology." Just prior to adopting this measure, the General Assembly also passed two other resolutions, both violently anti-Israel in language and intent. The first called for the participation of the PLO in future sessions of the Geneva Conference. The second ordained the establishment of a committee, modeled on the UN Committee against Apartheid, to promote "the exercise of the inalienable rights of the Palestinian people." In the fulfillment of its mandate, this committee was authorized "to receive and consider suggestions and proposals from any state and inter-governmental regional organization and the Palestine Liberation Organization."

Although the impact of these measures was perhaps overrated initially by the appalled Israelis and by friends of Israel in the West, who detected in the resolutions a major Arab tactical advance in the delegitimization of Israel, the General Assembly votes unquestionably were a painful humiliation for the Jewish state. The blow was exacerbated less than a month later, on December 5, when the Assembly went so far as to order Israel to return all occupied Arab land without qualification (that is, without the qualification of peace treaties), and to restore the "legitimate rights of the Palestinians." Additional diplomatic reverses could be anticipated in the future.

So, apparently, could a continuation of Soviet hostility. It was based not only upon a profound and genuine fear of Israel as a magnet for Soviet Jewish irredentism, but upon Moscow's determination to effect a strategic penetration of the Middle East. That goal was more than partially fulfilled by the 1970s, of course; the burgeoning Soviet fleet had long since ended the West's domination of the Mediterranean. By then, too, the Soviets were projecting their ambitions as far east as the Persian Gulf. Russia's main staging area for this effort was Iraq, and the principal Soviet supply line to that country was via the Syrian port of Latakia. Accordingly, Moscow was investing huge sums in both these nations in an effort to outflank the eastern extremity of NATO in Turkey, and to develop a counterthreat to the growing power of the American-equipped Iranian armed forces. Indeed, the Soviets poured more than funds into Syria and Iraq. They also provided a cornucopia of weaponry—equipment not unlikely to be used in any future confrontation with Israel.

Where, then, would Israel find its supporters? Europe had been proved a hollow shell in the moment of crisis. Nor was Europe alone in acquiescing in Arab oil blackmail. Addressing the Diet in January 1975, Prime Minister Takeo Miki of Japan, a traditional friend of Israel, called on the Israelis to withdraw from the occupied Arab territories and urged recognition of the "just rights of the Palestinians." Of the Great Powers, apparently only the United States still could be reckoned as a friend. The Israelis took heart, therefore, in June 1974, when Richard Nixon became the first

American president to pay an official visit to Israel during a state tour of the Middle East. Yet the importance of the occasion was more than slightly diminished by Nixon's palpable use of the trip to refurbish his Watergate-scarred image. More significantly, it was evident that for Kissinger, as for Dulles twenty years earlier, a revival of friendship with the Arab world was envisaged as a matter of critical American self-interest.

Washington's concern for Arab goodwill was influenced not alone by strategy, by the need to counter an invidious Soviet penetration of the Middle East, but, as has been seen, by the nagging fear of a renewed Arab oil embargo. The potential impact of such a quarantine upon the United States, while less devastating than upon Europe or Japan, nevertheless was understood to be very grave. In the meantime, the Arab governments did not conceal their determination to use their vast petro-dollar wealth as an ongoing weapon against Israel, even against Jews living in Western countries. It was discovered, for example, that Kuwaiti and other Arab finance ministries had barred more than a dozen Jewish, or partially Jewish, underwriting houses from participation in Middle Eastern bond issues. The boycott of companies doing business with Israel was an old story, of course. Although this blacklist created editorial, even presidential, outrage in the United States, there appeared to be few effective legal remedies against it.

RABIN'S YEARS OF SUFFERANCE

Meanwhile, with all the pressures on the little Jewish republic, the imminent threat of hostilities at least was dissipated the moment Sadat opened the Canal in June 1975 and transformed the Suez cities into hostages of a cease-fire. In urgent need of a hiatus in which to revive his moribund economy, the Egyptian president turned unashamedly toward the Americans, offering solid, pragmatic inducements for their funds and technology. The initial response was encouraging. By the spring of 1974, some one hundred American companies, including the Rockefeller-owned Chase National Bank and other banking firms, had agreed to finance the modernization of the Canal area. All these investments plainly were dependent upon stability in the Middle East. As they embarked on a Western-oriented program of economic development, the Egyptians did not appear likely to jeopardize their rising expectations with precipitous moves along the Canal.

On the other side of the line, the Israeli economy also appeared initially to be responding to Rabin's harsh taxes and currency devaluation. Moreover, two significant international agreements offered yet additional hope for the future. The first, in May 1975, was reached with the European Economic Community. Under the treaty's provisions, the EEC would reduce its tariffs on Israeli industrial products by 60 percent, and eliminate them altogether by 1977. The process offered a major challenge to Israeli industrial efficiency, of course, by opening its economy to Common Market products. But Rabin's economic advisers regarded the prospect as a welcome incentive for improvement. In that same May of 1975, a second economic cooperation treaty was negotiated, this one with the United States. To encourage Israel's economic development, Washington authorized lower taxes on American investors' profits from Israeli enterprises than on profits earned from comparable investments in the European Common Market. To some degree, both treaties offered the potential to counteract the Arab boycott. Almost immediately, therefore, several of the largest American corporations launched new enterprises or enlarged earlier ones in Israel, among them such giants as Motorola, Control Data Corporation, International Paper, Wito Chemicals, International Telephone and Telegraph, and General Telephone and Electronics.

In the mid-1970s, too, there were still additional developments to arouse expectations and excitement among the Israeli population. One was Soviet-Jewish immigration. Despite Moscow's offended refusal to accept the—highly qualified—United States Trade Reform Act of 1975 (p. 808), the Soviet regime apparently was unwilling to abandon all hope of wider access to American technology on a most-favored-nation basis. Thus, to encourage American goodwill, the Brezhnev government authorized a cautious increase in Jewish departure visas: to 14,000 in 1976; to 17,000 in 1977. A significant minority of the immigrants were well-educated Europeans who appeared to be exceptionally promising material for Israel's thinly stretched population.

In 1976, still another achievement generated a dramatic revival of national confidence. In early June Dr. Waddia Hadad, leader of the radical Popular Front for the Liberation of Palestine, assembled his staff in an Aden apartment to formulate plans for a daring new hijacking operation. The selected victim this time was an Air France passenger jet scheduled to depart Tel Aviv for Paris. Accordingly, on the morning of June 27, a German "couple" and two Palestinians traveling with forged passports boarded the Air France AirBus during its stopover at Athens airport. Eight minutes after the aircraft took off again, the four armed plotters seized control of its crew and its 254 passengers, and forced the captain to change course for Benghazi, Libya. Upon landing in Benghazi, the plane was refueled. It then took off again and, after six hours of additional flight, landed at Entebbe, outside the Ugandan capital of Kampala, where another team of terrorists was waiting.

The passengers—eighty-three of them Israelis—were confined in an old, disused terminal building. Soon afterward Idi Amin, Uganda's pro-Arab dictator, appointed himself intermediary between the captors and the Israeli government. On June 29, Amin revealed the hijackers' demand. It was for Israel to release fifty-three imprisoned Palestinian guerrillas and arrange for these "freedom fighters" to be flown to Entebbe; otherwise the passengers would be killed. In Israel, then, upon receiving the ultimatum, Prime Minister Rabin and Defense Minister Shimon Peres declared their willingness to negotiate. The response in fact was a play for time. On their instructions, a senior military task force launched urgent explorations of a possible rescue mission. The window for that option suddenly opened when the hijackers extended their deadline by seventy-two hours. As a gesture of "goodwill," they also decided to free some one hundred fifty of the captives. The unexpected three-day grace period gave Israel's military staff planning time. Additionally, eight of the freed hostages were returned to Paris, where they were available for intensive questioning by the Israeli Mossad intelligence agency. It was from them that the Mossad learned the precise location at Entebbe airport of the hostages, their captors, and the Ugandan troop detachment. On the morning of July 3, the military presented Rabin and Peres with a hastily prepared rescue scenario. It was accepted.

At 3:00 p.m. that afternoon, four Israeli air force Hercules transports and a long-range Boeing 707 command plane took off from Sharm es-Sheikh. After a seven-hour flight along the East African coast, the five aircraft came within range of the Entebbe radio tower. The expedition had been planned to enable the first Hercules to dovetail with a scheduled British cargo flight. Thus, as the British plane landed, the lead Israeli Hercules glided in immediately behind it in the darkness, to avoid registering its signal on the airport radar. Jumping out, an advance paratroop unit placed mobile landing lights on the runway for the other three transports. The Hercules then taxied to a dark corner of the field, and the rest of the landing party disembarked with a Mercedes and two Land Rovers— vehicles precisely matching those in President Amin's usual entourage. Without arousing suspicion, then, the automobiles drove toward the building where the hostages were confined. Bursting in, the Israelis cut down the six terrorists who stood guard, and bundled the dazed hostages out of the terminal and into the waiting Hercules.

Meanwhile, under instructions radioed from the circling Boeing command aircraft, the three other Israeli transport planes landed, discharging additional troops and several armored cars. These wiped out the Ugandan troops assigned to the new terminal. Only fifty-seven minutes after the initial landing, the first Hercules took off, loaded with freed hostages. Forty-two minutes later, the fourth and last transport departed. Soon afterward, all four of the Hercules aircraft landed in nearby Nairobi, Kenya, to refuel (Kenya's president Jomo Kenyatta, a bitter enemy of Amin, had secretly agreed to cooperate). Within a half hour, the rescue force took off again and proceeded uneventfully to Israel. Of the 104 captives evacuated, only 4 had perished in the operation. An Israeli officer, Lieutenant Colonel Yonatan Netanyahu, was the sole military casualty.

Once news of the rescue was announced, Israel's entire population all but exploded with pride and relief. The reaction manifestly was a psychological compensation after the trauma of the Yom Kippur War, of endless economic crises, and unrelieved Arab hostility. Not least, the Entebbe rescue operation inspired a belated upsurge of antiterrorist efforts well beyond Israel—in Germany, France, even Egypt—all of whose governments until then had dealt circumspectly with political kidnappers and aerial hijackers. Now, however, shamed by Israel's example, they struck back at terrorism with uncharacteristic vigor. Once again, the little Zionist republic had projected a larger-than-life image throughout the world.

LIKUD ERA BEGINS

LABOR'S FINAL EPITAPH

As matters developed, the 1975 disengagement agreement with Egypt and the sensational 1976 Entebbe operation climaxed Labor's historic domination of Israeli public life. It was the issue of the occupied territories, beyond all others, that ultimately paralyzed the executive effectiveness of the Rabin cabinet. In the immediate aftermath of the June 1967 victory, the assumption was widespread that Israel would return the largest part of the captured terrain in exchange for peace. But the "phone call" from the Arab capitals did not arrive, and the Israeli government in its equivocation began to countenance a gradual, limited settlement of Jews in the West Bank, the Golan, even in Gaza, essentially along the security contours of the "Allon Plan."

By the latter 1970s, moreover, economic factors increasingly militated against "repartition." The interaction between Israel and the territories was becoming that of a common market, with the agricultural, Palestinian, component all but sucked into the highly developed Israeli industrial economy. Indeed, fully 16 percent of all Israeli "exports" were sold in the territories, which soon emerged as a larger market for Israeli goods than Britain and Germany combined, and as half the size of Israel's entire American market (pp. 705–6). In 1976, too, Arabs from both Israel and the territories were providing a quarter of Israel's factory labor, and more than half the workers in construction and in service industries such as hotels, garages, and municipal sanitation. It was the supply of cheap labor in turn that simultaneously reduced Israel's inflation rate and its need for more extensive capital investment.

Little wonder that the future of the West Bank and Gaza should arouse more indecision among the Labor Alignment than did any other public issue. Yitzchak Rabin, representing a minority component within Labor, essentially shared the partitionist approach of his mentor, Yigal Allon. Yet, preoccupied with the task of defusing the Egyptian front, of mobilizing national support for possible additional Israeli withdrawal in Sinai, the prime minister simply dared not raise the much touchier issue of Palestine. The National Religious party, negotiating to enter his government coalition, insisted that any withdrawal proposal for "Judea and Samaria" be submitted to the referendum of a national election. For Rabin, the notion of facing the voting public was unappealing.

Labor's vacillation on the territorial issue was revealed as early as April 1968, in the arid little West Bank town of Hebron. It was there, we recall (p. 682), that a group of Jewish religionists proclaimed themselves the vanguard of a revived Jewish settlement. Rather than evict the Jewish squatters, the Eshkol cabinet agreed to construct an "alternative" settlement, Kiryat Arba, on Hebron's outskirts. The "alternative" proved rather more than a temporary foothold. In ensuing years, the number of its settlers continued to grow, reaching two thousand by the mid-1970s. Their roads and utilities actually were provided by the government of Israel itself. In fact, the Kiryat Arba pietists had been prefigured by a group to be known as the Gush Emunim (Community of Believers). Most of the Gush Emunim's initial members were young people who had been educated in state religious schools and in the pioneering religious B'nai Akiva movement. Few initially were fanatics of the Hebron variety. Yet one of their components included zealots of Jerusalem's famed Rabbi Kook Yeshiva, which nurtured an intensely annexationist spirit among its students and other disciples. For them, the right of the Jewish people to Judea and Samaria was nonnegotiable.

The Gush Emunim movement picked up momentum almost in direct ratio to the Labor government's irresolution. In 1974 and 1975, its followers launched several new settlements in the heart of Arab-inhabited territory in the West Bank. Indeed, the most provocative of the emplacements, Elon Moreh, was organized in the densely populated Samarian massif. And once again, as in the case of the Hebron squatters, the Labor cabinet reacted ambivalently. Rabin and Peres were then vying for leadership of the party, and each kept a prominent Gush Emunim spokesman in his ministry. At Peres's orders, army bases provided electric and water utilities for the Elon Moreh settlers. Rabin, in turn, although put off by the group's aggressiveness, expediently decided to laud their "pioneering zeal," and eventually to acquiesce in their faits accomplis. As in the case of the Kiryat Arba squatters, a "compromise" permitted Elon Moreh's colonists to make their homes nearby, in this case the Israeli army camp at Qadum. By early 1977, therefore, with five Gush Emunim settlements on the West Bank, it was uncertain who entertained the greater contempt for Rabin and his cabinet—the "doves," who favored substantial withdrawal from the Arab-inhabited areas, or the "hawks," who divined unerringly the equivocation of a Labor government possessed of no collective vision, not even a clue, to the disposition of "reclaimed Judea and Samaria."

Labor's record on the economy was less brilliant even than on the territories. Many of the nation's financial burdens unquestionably represented a force majeure. To compensate for the vast infusion of Soviet and French weaponry to Egypt and Syria after the Yom Kippur War, the government was obliged to double its security budget. Tens of thousands of Israelis were pulled out of the economy for extended terms of military service. Indeed, the share of defense in Israel's GNP soared from 21 percent in 1972 to 47 percent in 1976. Meanwhile, the escalating (worldwide) cost of oil and other imports exacerbated a national budget deficit exceeding $4 billion by 1976. Much of the shortfall had to be covered by loans from Washington and other sources, and the expense of servicing the debt, of covering a wider balance-of-payments gap, was reflected in an inflation rate of 30 percent in 1973 and 40 percent in 1974 and 1975. It was in this period, too, that the nation's public services were intermittently paralyzed by waves of strikes, most of these by salaried government and Histadrut professionals—engineers, physicians, teachers. With few exceptions, the cabinet surrendered to the strikers' wage demands.

Israel's social economy was further distended by plain and simple fiscal corruption. The incipient rot tinctured not only the business and professional communities (pp. 1003–4), but the highest echelons of public life. One notorious scandal involved the Israel Corporation, established in 1968 by the Eshkol government and funded by Jewish investors throughout the world. In 1975, the corporation's former managing director was indicted (and eventually convicted) for embezzling millions in company funds. A year later, the director of customs similarly was indicted for waiving import fees on private business cronies. In 1976 a senior Bank of Israel official was arrested for illicitly profiting on insider information. The former manager of Israel's oil corporation in the Sinai was convicted for diverting public funds to his own use. Then the director general of the Histadrut health insurance plan was indicted for accepting bribes from potential suppliers. Several months later, the minister of housing committed suicide after being put under investigation on suspicion of misappropriating Labor party funds. Altogether, the climate of peculation came increasingly to be identified with the Labor hierarchy.

Nor was the prime minister himself spared. By late 1976, the political and personal animus between Rabin and Peres had become all but uncontrollable, undermining the line of authority in the defense establishment, even obstructing cabinet discussions. Peres in fact already had decided to challenge Rabin for party leadership before the scheduled November 1977 elections. In turn, Rabin thought he discerned an opportunity to outflank his challenger. He had attended an airport welcoming ceremony in December 1976 for a newly delivered contingent of American jet fighters. The event intruded into the Sabbath. Learning of this "desecration," the Knesset's ultra-Orthodox Agudat Israel faction introduced a motion of no confidence in the government. It was easily defeated. Yet several members of the National Religious party, partners in Rabin's coalition government, violated cabinet discipline by abstaining from the vote. Thereupon Rabin decided to tender his government's resignation and advance the elections from November to May 1977. Presumably the crisis of an accelerated election would induce the Labor central committee to rally around its current leader. It did—but by an embarrassing, hair-thin margin. The prime minister was publicly humiliated.

In the remaining months of the campaign, more of the national financial scandals broke, including the suicide of the housing minister. Then, in March 1977, a press account disclosed that Rabin's wife had maintained two secret and illegal dollar accounts in a Washington bank. As a cosignatory, Rabin himself could not escape public opprobrium. In early April he announced his resignation as head of government and Labor chairman. Soon afterward, the party central committee selected Peres as its candidate for the premiership. By then the Israeli people were in disarray, their morale already shaken by the belated implications of the Yom Kippur War, their Arab enemies seemingly rejuvenated militarily, their economy all but hooked to the respirator of American generosity. It appeared now that the erosion of public morality had left their government not only corruption-ridden but rudderless.

AN ELECTORAL UPHEAVAL

Amid a turmoil of contending parties, the electoral campaign gave every appearance of following earlier precedents, of devolving essentially into a triangular contest between the Labor-Mapam Alignment, Likud (a coalition of Cherut, the Liberals, and several tiny residual factions), and the constellation of Orthodox elements (ranging from the centrist National Religious party to the fundamentalist Agudat Israel contingent). In the spring of 1977, as political rhetoric intensified, Labor invoked the time-worn admonition that a Likud victory would threaten democracy and workers' rights. Likud's campaign, directed by Ezer Weizman, a former air force commander, was more shrewdly managed. While rejecting territorial concessions to the Arabs, it concentrated less on foreign policy issues than on Labor's corruption scandals, its flaccidity on economic matters. The pollsters who had forecast a close Labor victory were proved wrong. When the votes were counted, Likud had increased its Knesset representation from 39 to 43 seats. The National Religious party similarly enlarged its delegation, from 10 to 12 seats (the Agudah essentially held its own, with 5 seats). Yet the true surprise was not the impressive showing of the Right but the virtual collapse of the Labor Alignment, from 51 seats in 1973 to 32 now, a disappearance of more than a third of its strength. The electoral demise of other, smaller leftist parties was equally striking.

In the political upheaval, an unanticipated role also was played by a new centrist group, the Democratic Movement for Change (DMC). The DMC had its origins in the protest demonstrations that swelled in the aftermath of the 1973 Yom Kippur War. Among the civilians and demobilized soldiers who execrated Dayan and the entire Meir government for the "blunder," there were some who perceived a more basic flaw in Israel's very political system, specifically the anachronistic party-list method of voting, with its oligarchical central committees. In their impatience, these critics (most of them educated, upper-middle-class Europeans) were determined to cast a protest vote equally against the inertia of Labor and the chauvinism of Likud.

They found their chance in 1976 when leadership of the DMC was accepted by Professor Yigael Yadin, the renowned archaeologist and military commander of Israel's war of independence. The party's cochairman was Amnon Rubinstein, dean of Tel Aviv University's law school and a founder of the Shinui ("Change") faction that now was confederated with the DMC; while other party leaders were respected former Laborites and military leaders, intellectuals and industrialists—all intent upon wielding a fresh broom for reform. The candidates and the program made their impact in the election. The DMC won an astonishing 15 seats, becoming Israel's third-largest Knesset delegation. More important, two-thirds of their votes came from Israelis who had supported the Labor Alignment in 1973.

Yet the victory of the Right was impressive enough to be taken seriously on its own account. Plainly, Menachem Begin himself no longer frightened as many citizens as in earlier elections. During his stint as a member of the "wall-to-wall" government, from 1967 to 1970, he had managed to shed his former demagogic image. His annexationist position, for that matter, did not appear to differ all that much from the painstakingly balanced territorial stance adopted by numerous Laborites. It was simply that Begin projected his vision of an "undivided Land of Israel" in the mystical-historical language of an ancient vision. In any case, the massive voter shift away from Labor signified less a territorialist commitment than a social protest, a gesture of revised political allegiance on the part of hundreds of thousands of Jews from Moslem countries. Well through the 1960s, these Jews of Oriental-Sephardic background had identified overwhelmingly with Labor. Even as late as 1969, the Labor Alignment received 55 percent of their vote. Then, in 1973, the figure dropped to 38 percent. And now, in 1977, it sank to an astonishing 32 percent. A social revolution of sorts manifestly was being registered.

Fueling the non-Europeans' repudiation of Labor, for one thing, was plain and simple resentment of the Ashkenazic elite. Despite an absolute rise in the Orientals' real income by 1977, even the emergence of a substantial bourgeoisie within their ranks, their share of white-collar jobs did not exceed half that of Ashkenazic Jews. Neither did their representation in the national government, the Histadrut, the political parties, the armed forces, and the universities. During the Ben-Gurion era, Labor had offered the Oriental communities enough welfare and patronage to ensure a majority of their votes. Yet, by the 1970s, Ashkenazic "paternalism" and "tokenism" no longer evoked their loyalty. Moreover, the non-Europeans' social resentments were exacerbated by a deeply rooted suspicion of the Arabs. It was the Orientals' forebears, after all, who had suffered immemorially under Moslem rule. Renewed contact with these former persecutors after the Six-Day War simply awakened old grievances. Indeed, ensconced vocationally a rung above the thousands of commuting West Bank and Gaza Arab laborers, Oriental Jews tended to develop a "poor-white" mentality, and thus to generate a vested interest in the economic as well as the territorial status quo. More than other elements in Israel's population, therefore, the non-Ashkenazim resonated to Begin's charismatic authoritarianism and florid nationalist invective. The 1977 election accordingly was their long awaited moment of vindication against the European establishment.

ISRAEL TURNS TO THE RIGHT

The moment was even sweeter for Menachem Begin. Now sixty-four years old, an unprepossessing, bespectacled man of slight stature and uncertain health, he was a leader driven less by ambitions of glory than by his lifelong vision of a wholly redeemed Land of Israel. It was Vladimir Jabotinsky's vision. In 1925, as a law student at the University of Warsaw, Begin first met and was overwhelmed by the great Revisionist. In fact, it was Jabotinsky's style as much as his substance that left its impact, his dynamism, his bravura oratory and flirtation with undisguised demagoguery. Begin assumed many of these characteristics in his own career, we recall, first as leader of the Betar—Revisionist—youth movement in Poland, later as commander of the dissident underground Etzel uprising against the British in mandatory Palestine, and eventually as chairman of the Cherut party in the newborn State of Israel (p. 372).

Yet, by the 1960s, Begin appeared to have mellowed. Unable to invoke the old Revisionist slogans in those years of peace and comparative tranquillity, he shed his abrasive image effectively enough to woo the Liberal party into a common parliamentary bloc with Cherut. Indeed, during the May–June 1967 crisis, Begin revealed authentic largeness of spirit by suggesting that his old enemy Ben-Gurion be called back as prime minister. Once hostilities began, however, then ended in victory, Begin's vision shifted again from national survival to territorial annexation. If he continued as a member of the "wall-to-wall" cabinet, it was only because the Labor-dominated coalition was annexing Jerusalem and building settlements in the West Bank. Begin similarly developed a workable relationship with Moshe Dayan. Within the government, the two formed the nucleus of a hawkish alliance that crossed party lines.

It was in August 1970 that the cabinet accepted the "Rogers Plan," which envisaged compliance with United Nations Resolution 242—the obligation to withdraw "from territories occupied in the recent conflict." Hereupon Begin pulled his party out of the government coalition. There would be no compromise on the issue of the "Land of Israel," then or later. Thus, preparing for elections in the spring of 1977, Begin and his colleagues formulated a terse foreign policy plank: "The right of the Jewish people to the Land of Israel is eternal and inalienable," it declared. ". . . Between the sea and the Jordan, there will be Jewish sovereignty alone." It was with this adamant commitment, after the May 1977 election, that Menachem Begin stood at last on the threshold of his nation's prime ministry.

On June 20, the new cabinet was sworn in. In addition to its own Likud delegation, the government was supported by two members of Ariel Sharon's Shlomzion (Peace of Zion) party; by Moshe Dayan, who now defected from Labor to proclaim himself an "independent"; by the twelve-member faction of the National Religious party and the five members of the right-wing Agudat Israel group. Yet the bare majority was insufficient for decisive political leadership. Begin accordingly opened talks with Yigael Yadin, leader of the fifteen-member Democratic Movement for Change. The prime minister was not yet prepared to commit himself on Yadin's key desideratum of replacing the party-list system. Even so, as an act of faith, the DMC leadership agreed to risk joining the government. Four of its members accepted cabinet portfolios, with Yadin assuming the role of deputy prime minister.

Within the Likud bloc, meanwhile, it was understood from the beginning that the Liberal party would act as senior partner on economic matters. Thus, the key portfolio of finance went to Simcha Ehrlich, his party's chairman, while the ministry of commerce and industry, and numerous directorships of state corporations, went to other Liberals. Experienced business executives, these newcomers assumed office on the platform of a "New Economic Policy," a commitment to encourage investment, to fight inflation and corruption, to reduce the national tax burden and automatic cost-of-living increases, and to reverse bureaucratic interference in the marketplace by allowing the free play of supply and demand. The changed approach in fact proved effective enough to dry up Israel's notorious black market in dollars. Yet, in the process, it spawned other, unanticipated consequences. One was the creation of windfall profits for holders of foreign currency—preeminent among them some one hundred thousand beneficiaries of German restitution payments. By allowing free convertibility into foreign currencies, moreover, Ehrlich unwittingly encouraged the lavish exchange of dollar loans for shekels (the new Israeli monetary unit), a process that fueled inflation even more alarmingly.

With free enterprise the theme, still another component of Ehrlich's master plan was to auction off government corporations to private investors. The effort failed. Since the birth of Israel, these public companies had dominated energy production, banking, transportation, mineral extraction, water development, and tourism. Their forthright purpose in those years had been nation-building, not profit-making. Yet, by the same token, with their generally adverse balance sheets, these enterprises now were less than attractive to private investors. Only one corporation, a mortgage bank, ever made it to Ehrlich's sell list. Equally unrealized was Likud's promise to nationalize health care by removing the country's single largest medical health insurance program from Histadrut domination. The measure died in committee. Similarly, when the government lowered the traditional subsidies on food, transportation, and housing, the price of these vital staples rose so sharply over the ensuing twenty months that an explosion of public protest ended all plans for additional subsidy-reductions. In any case, by then the damage had been done: The poorer classes had lost even more ground.

Altogether, the results of the New Economic Policy were calamitous enough in soaring prices and social inequities to force Ehrlich's resignation in 1980. His successor, Yigal Hurewitz, a veteran businessman, demanded across-the-board reductions in subsidies and capital gains alike. He did not get them. Continually threatening to resign, Hurewitz held on for a year. Then, in January 1981, the cabinet faced a nationwide strike of teachers, whose demand for a substantial pay hike conflicted with a key Likud election pledge to introduce compulsory arbitration of labor disputes in essential services. Earlier, as it happened, the Begin cabinet had held the line against a wildcat strike by El Al employees. But that single act of resolve did not become the norm, and when the teachers walked out in 1981 the cabinet voted to override Hurewitz and authorize the demanded wage hike. Hurewitz resigned.

Yet it was noteworthy that the government was determined to initiate a number of populist measures of its own, specifically in behalf of its lower-class Oriental supporters. Begin cared about these people. They had put him in office. He had promised a "revolution" in housing for young couples by providing financial guarantees to private builders for the large-scale construction of rental apartments. Accordingly, through the persistence of Housing Minister David Levy, the bill was passed and in fact proved modestly successful. Likud also had made a campaign commitment to introduce three additional years of tuition-free education, through high school. That promise, too, was honored. Despite their severe impact on the public treasury, both measures ranked among the few genuinely admired innovations of the Begin years.

So did a promising effort to upgrade the nation's deprived neighborhoods.

The prime minister's imaginative approach to these neglected sectors was to entreat the Diaspora's cooperation in "Project Renewal," a common undertaking of slum redevelopment. With the active participation of the Jewish Agency, a comprehensive social blueprint imaginatively "twinned" eighty-two underprivileged neighborhoods with thirty-two Jewish communities abroad in a joint effort to rebuild Israel's decrepit plant and housing, to provide loans and mortgage funds, and to renovate community and day-care centers, schools, and clinics. By November 1983, Project Renewal had spent some $130 million. Although much of the program was eroded by inflation, inefficiency, and internecine politics, the venture could be rated a qualified success. And, like rental housing and free extended secondary education, Project Renewal also was the very antithesis of the New Economic Policy. In truth, an authentically right-wing economic agenda did not have a chance—not in a state devoted to the "ingathering of the exiles."

"THE ENEMY WITHIN"

Well into the 1970s, a majority of Israel's Arab votes was cast for lists "affiliated" with Labor. In 1977, however, the Labor Alignment's "Arab" list won only a single Knesset seat. The change was partly generational. In earlier years, Labor's Arab protégés tended to be older heads of clans, often village *mukhtars.* Now a younger, disenchanted Arab generation was turning to Rakach, the Communist party. Officially an Israeli faction, with its leadership still largely Jewish, Rakach in the 1970s appealed almost exclusively to Arab voters as the one available— lawful—vehicle of protest against Zionist rule. Thus, in 1965, Rakach won 24 percent of the Arab vote; in 1969, 30 percent; in 1973, 37 percent (p. 809). In 1977, it won 50 percent.

Altogether, the Arabs numbered more than 600,000 in 1977. Counting the 130,000 Arabs of Jerusalem, the figure approached 730,000 (and would exceed 800,000 twenty years later), more than one-sixth of Israel's population of 4 million. Despite the "objective" improvement of Arab circumstances, moreover, the gap between their economy and that of the Jews was widening. Well into the late 1970s, the Arabs remained essentially a rural people, and the Jews by then had become overwhelmingly an industrial-commercial people. Even so, the agricultural production of Israeli Arabs in 1977 had dropped to 4 percent of the national farm output. The disjunction above all reflected an inequity in public services. Arab agriculture received little in the way of government or Jewish Agency support. Denied access to the Histadrut Farmers Union (until 1985), Arab farmers were obliged to resort to their own, usually inferior, marketing cooperatives. Indeed, over the years, Arab young people gradually departed the land altogether. As late as 1955, 59 percent of the Arab labor force still labored on Arab farms. By 1977, the figure had dropped to 11 percent. Although thousands of other Arabs continued to work the soil, they did so increasingly as hired laborers on Jewish farms and groves.

In the same period, Arab-owned industry absorbed perhaps a quarter of the

Arab work force, mainly in stone-quarrying and small textile and clothing manufacture. Yet in this sector, too, Arab enterprises rarely matched those of the
Jews in efficiency or profitability. By the early 1980s, as a result, some 160,000
Israeli Arabs were laboring in Jewish-owned factories and service industries,
where they comprised fully a third of all unskilled, low-wage workers in Israel
(Arab commuters from the territories added yet another fourth). Half this work
force also was obliged to undergo long and fatiguing daily journeys from their
villages to their Jewish employment sites. Few slept over in Jewish cities; landlords would not rent to them. The imbalance between the two peoples was
evident at many levels. As late as 1977, infant mortality among Israeli Arabs
remained twice as high as among Jews. The quality of Arab schooling was eroded
by the depleted base of Arab villages and by the altered school curriculum. For
years, secondary schools required more Hebrew and Jewish than Arabic studies.
So did the matriculation examination for admission to higher education. Barely
two thousand Arabs were attending universities by 1977. Upon graduation, even
this advantaged elite rarely found meaningful employment in the principal—
Jewish—economic sector (pp. 392–3).

Under these circumstances, Israeli Arab discontent mounted in the post-1967
years, and finally boiled over in the aftermath of the Yom Kippur War. With
unprecedented vehemence, Arab newspapers reviewed their litany of minority
grievances: the appropriation of Arab lands and the foreclosure of Arab national
affiliations and Arab economic opportunities. In fact, the literary expression of
that protest evinced a new refinement of Israeli Arabic writing, a qualitative
improvement that itself reflected exposure since 1967 to the richness of literature in the broader Arab world. Soon most of the old Israeli Arab wordsmiths
were forgotten. The poets Michael Hadad, Mahmud Darwish, and Sami al-
Qasim (p. 582) in the post-1967 era profoundly energized and modernized their
own and their predecessors' often one-dimensional journalese. The theme of
political aggrievement remained, to be sure, but in a new richness of allusion and
metaphor. Michael Hadad's "Lisping" was a renowned case in point:

> When they raised the last step
> on the stairs of the old house
> it cost me a white front tooth
> which chipped when I stumbled
> on that arrogant threshold,
> over its rare, slippery cement . . .
> and left me a lisp in the [Hebrew] letter "shin"
> and a complex in the "t,"
> crises of pronunciation in "Tiberias," "Tabgha," "table"—
> No one knew they existed,
> and the complex was resolved by struggle and decisiveness.

For all its emerging brilliance of style, then, Israeli Arabic literature sustained
its pre-1967 obsession with the abandoned language and homeland, the plight of
refugees, the travail of social and economic discrimination—the loss of identity.
In "The Imprisoned Poet," Sami al-Qasim goaded his afflicted compatriots with
renewed vigor and forthrightness:

You were imprisoned,
But is it possible to imprison the spirit of defiance?
Cry unto the arrogant jailer!
Torture my body with whips,
Paint my ribs and my uplifted brow with my own blood,
Smash my arm and my breast, you son of dogs!
For my spirit continues to search for freedom,
The rivers of rebellion wash out the walls of the conqueror.

It was a novel, however, *The Bizarre Chronicles of Saïd the Optipessimist*, that captured both the luminescence of the "new" Israeli Arabic literature and its ongoing mood of protest. Published in 1972 by Emile Habibi, a three-term Knesset member and editor of the Rakach journal *al-Ittihad,* the work took the form of a long anecdotal letter from a recently deceased journalist. Writing a colleague from the world beyond, Saïd is free at last to ventilate his bitterness at the Jews' ultimate affront of ignoring, and thus obliterating, Arab national dignity. But at the same time, he execrates his fellow Arabs for their passivity. Nor does he entertain illusions on the resonance of his own protest. Rather, Saïd ends his litany by acknowledging that the indictment emerging from beneath his moustache has produced all the effect of a "meowing sound, like that of a cat." A brilliant tour de force, *Saïd the Optipessimist* won acclaim as a masterpiece by the Arab world at large. So it would later by the Israeli literary establishment itself. For his life's work, Habibi would be awarded the Israel Prize in 1992.

Altogether, whether on the printed page or in private discussions, Israeli Arab protest gained in spleen precisely for lack of viable outlets. The community owned no commercial or financial institutions, no banks, no independent trade unions, no television or radio stations, not even a newspaper unconnected with Israeli political parties (Rakach was not "officially" Arab). Its anti-Zionist stance effectively disqualified it as a potential coalition-partner of the Jewish parties, and thus deprived it of meaningful influence in the Knesset. Since early statehood, meanwhile, "Arab affairs" advisers to Israel's prime ministers traditionally were former Shin Bet—secret service—officials. It was telling evidence of public distrust.

In the end, more than any other factor, it was the impact of the Yom Kippur War that decisively altered the Arab-Jewish political status quo. For the first time, Israel's reputation for invincibility was undermined on both sides of the former border. The strikes, demonstrations, and riots that broke out in the West Bank (pp. 862–3) evoked a comparable, if faintly less strident, response among the Arabs of Israel. So did Yasser Arafat's appearance before the United Nations General Assembly in 1974. In that same year, too, the National Council of Chairmen of Arab Local Authorities was founded in Israel to lead the struggle for equal rights; then the National Council of Secondary School Students; then the Rakach-sponsored National Council for the Protection of Arab Lands. Government obtuseness played its role in exacerbating this unrest. The Galilee, we recall, was a region whose substantial Arab majority posed long-term demographic risks for Israel's military security. During Rabin's prime ministry, therefore, the practice continued of expropriating selected Arab tracts for defense ·

purposes. Finally, in 1976, reacting to these sequestrations, the National Council for the Protection of Arab Lands called a general strike for "Land Day," March 30. Conceivably one-tenth of the nation's entire Arab labor force participated in the event, including crowds estimated at fifty thousand in the towns of Nazareth and Shfar'am. When the oratory provoked violent outbursts, troops had to be called in. Six demonstrators were killed, scores of others wounded. From then on, moderation was a dead issue among Israeli Arabs.

As in other ethnic upheavals, university students emerged as the vanguard of the Arab nationalist camp. In 1975, their representatives at the Hebrew University indignantly refused an administrative order to perform guard duty at the dormitories. In 1978, their student committee at Haifa University staged demonstrations against a Sadat peace initiative that left the Palestine issue unresolved (p. 863). Police harassment and arrests would not deter these young activists, neither on campuses nor elsewhere. In the 1973 national elections, 23 percent of the candidates to Arab local councils were under age forty. The proportion of that younger age group nearly doubled in the 1977 elections, and most of the newcomers were Rakach partisans.

During its incumbency, the Rabin government proved as indecisive in its response to local Arab defiance as to Jewish militance. Following the Land Day demonstrations of March 1976, the cabinet extensively reviewed its minorities policy. Soon afterward, one of its confidential memoranda was leaked to the press. The document favored the use of both carrot and stick in dealing with Arab village elites. "Loyalists" and their villages should be repaid with patronage and improved facilities; Rakach activists and "all negative [Arab nationalist] spokesmen," with defamation and harassment "at all levels and [in] all institutions." The memorandum aroused such vigorous controversy among Jews and Arabs alike that the cabinet felt obliged to repudiate it. Nevertheless, the document reflected widespread public sentiment. On the one hand, numerous Jewish intellectuals expressed a deep-rooted guilt over the Palestine refugees (pp. 595–96). On the other, most Jews remained deeply suspicious of the Arabs in their midst. Uninterested in a wider familiarity with a perennial enemy, they found it more comforting for the government simply "to take care of things."

Menachem Begin was prepared to accept that mandate. Upon assuming office, he and his advisers categorically rejected Labor's mixture of rewards and punishments. The new Likud approach was straightforward and uncompromising. Its principal architect, Amnon Linn, had once been a director of the Labor party's Arab affairs department; but more recently he had become a defector to Likud. Under Linn's harsh new guidelines, all current development aid to Arab villages was to be reduced forthwith, with heavier taxation to be imposed indiscriminately on all Arab communities throughout Israel. Arab students known for "radical" views were to be denied admission to Israeli universities; Arab teachers known to support Rakach were henceforth to be subjected to "administrative detention"; Arab demonstrations of any sort were to be met with instant and uncompromising force. Thereupon the cabinet appointed Ariel Sharon to put Linn's new approach into practical operation. The burly ex-general, then serving as minister of agriculture and chairman of the cabinet's interministerial com-

mittee on land settlement, was in a pivotal position for dealing with Arabs—
supremely the people of the land—both in the occupied territories and in Israel
proper.

Within Israel, Sharon regarded the Galilee as his initial proving ground. To
"judaize" this strategic northern region, he promptly launched into construction
of thirty miniature Jewish settlements on hills overlooking key Arab villages. The
project was completed within three years. Although by 1981 only small numbers
of Jews inhabited these Galilee outposts, they sufficed to block the growth of
adjacent Arab communities. Simultaneously, to obstruct all Arab efforts to
relieve their mounting congestion, Sharon denied their villages permits to construct new homes outside local boundaries. The Arabs did not accept these
constraints passively, however, no more than in 1976. In their frustration and
bitterness, they responded to Likud's mailed fist with demonstrations and
clashes. In January 1979, it happened that the PLO Council in Lebanon exhorted
Israeli Arabs to play a central role in the Palestinian struggle at large. Accordingly, twenty-eight chairmen of Arab local councils—more than half the Arab
mayors in Israel—together with nearly one hundred leaders of the Rakach party,
endorsed a resolution "welcoming the struggle of the Palestinian people under
the leadership of the PLO to establish its independent state." In December
1980, Rakach's leaders scheduled a major Arab congress in support of the PLO,
to take place in the northern Negev.

Neither was the prime minister about to be inhibited. Summarily banning the
intended conclave, Begin threatened to outlaw any party or organization that
ventured even to moot a similar congress in the future. No such blanket prohibition had been enacted by any Israeli government since dismantlement of the
military administration for the Arab areas thirteen years before. But no such man
as Menachem Begin had ever served as premier. For him, the ideological heir of
Vladimir Jabotinsky, the time had come to throw down Israel's gauntlet on all
Arab fronts. East or west of the former armistice line, there was one land to be
redeemed as the Jewish people's inalienable heritage. With the levers of power
in his hands at last, it seemed inconceivable to Begin that any force in the Arab
world could withstand the long-delayed fulfillment of that burning Revisionist
dream.

ACCOMMODATION

WITH EGYPT

SADAT IN QUEST OF PEACE

The shift of Israel's political and economic course in 1977 was strikingly prefigured by a comparable reorientation in Egypt. Anwar al-Sadat orchestrated the change personally. With his reputation at new heights following the October 1973 War, the Egyptian president felt secure enough to embark on a far-reaching "liberalization" of his nation's economy. There was little time to waste. Egypt's population of 42 million was growing at the rate of 750,000 a year. The desperate shortage of food and housing was producing raucous public demonstrations, even several riots. For Sadat, then, it was plain that Egypt's salvage operation could be accomplished only by dispensing with the late Nasser's cryptosocialism and introducing a program of Western-style capitalism. It could also be achieved only by negotiating peace.

The president sensed his people's war-weariness. The number of Egyptian dead and wounded in all the conflicts with Israel may have exceeded one hundred thousand. These were painful losses for a family-oriented nation. Sadat recalled of the 1973 hostilities: "I lost my younger brother, who was like a son to me, five minutes after the start of the October War. I have seen the victims of that war—young men destined to spend the rest of their lives in wheelchairs." Ironically, the successful crossing of the Suez Canal appeared to fortify the nation's desire for peace. As Sadat explained succinctly in his autobiographical *In Search of Identity*:

> We have recovered our pride and self-confidence after the October 1973 battle, just as our armed forces did. We are no longer activated by "complexes"—whether defeatist "inferiority" ones or those born out of suspicion and hate. . . . With the fighting over we [and the Israelis] harbored nothing but respect for one another.

Meanwhile, the inauguration of the Carter presidency in Washington added a personalized momentum to the search for peace. A Bible student, Jimmy Carter regarded himself as a warm friend of the Jewish people and Israel. In June 1977, during his first summer in office, he enthusiastically supported congressional passage of the Williams-Proxmire Bill, a measure that at long last would ban American companies from capitulating to the Arab boycott by refusing to do business with Israel, or with other American (or Jewish) companies on the Arab "blacklist." By the same token, however, Carter had long been persuaded that the Kissinger step-by-step approach to an Arab-Israeli settlement was played out. A broader Middle Eastern peace was required now, an agreement that conceivably might be achieved within the format of a revived Geneva Conference. Carter's guidelines were prepared for him by a special Brookings Institution task force. Under this conspectus, the Israelis would pledge in advance to withdraw from the occupied territories, and the Arabs (including representatives of the PLO) would agree in advance to sign a formal peace treaty with the Jewish state.

Initially, the president floated his notion to Yitzchak Rabin, who visited the White House in March 1977. The prime minister's response was chilly. Israel would never approve a return to the pre-1967 armistice lines or abandon "security control" over the West Bank, Rabin warned; while PLO participation at Geneva was altogether unthinkable. The subsequent election of Menachem Begin dashed even colder water on the American president's formula for Middle East peace. Visiting Washington in July 1977, Begin emphasized that all participants in a Geneva Conference first would have to commit themselves to UN Resolutions 242 and 338—the mutual recognition of each nation's right to live in peace and security. From the Arabs, and specifically from Syria, such a commitment appeared entirely unlikely.

If Jimmy Carter was sobered by the obstacles to renewed negotiations, Sadat was hardly less so. The Egyptian president already had demonstrated his willingness to achieve a modus vivendi with Israel. He had accepted the 1974–75 disengagement agreements, and had decided in June 1976 unilaterally to open the Suez Canal. But having come this far, Sadat hardly was prepared to allow his efforts to founder in a procedural quagmire at Geneva. Like Begin, he entertained no illusions about the obstructionist role the Soviets intended to play in maneuvering Egypt into a corner, forcing it to dance to the tune of Syria and the Arab rejectionist camp. Earlier, Moscow had been closed out of the disengagement negotiations by Kissinger and by Sadat himself. And now, suddenly, in October, an American president was naïvely inviting the Kremlin to issue a joint communiqué with Washington, pledging both governments to revive the suspended 1973 Geneva Conference within three months. Indeed, by sponsoring this sure and certain recipe for failure, Carter unwittingly forced Sadat's hand. For the Egyptian president, there was no alternative any longer but to act on his own.

As he evaluated his future course, Sadat was presented with an unexpected opening by the Israelis. Upon forming his cabinet, Menachem Begin had astonished his colleagues by his choice for foreign minister. It was Moshe Dayan. The former general was not a member of the ruling Likud bloc (he preferred to call himself an "independent"). Nevertheless, he enjoyed Begin's confidence. For one thing, Dayan had been the most prominent hawk within the Labor camp, a forceful advocate of Israeli control over the West Bank. Yet, as an archpragmatist, he also attached no mystical significance to the Sinai. Indeed, between 1967 and 1973, it was Dayan alone in the Labor cabinet who opposed the notion of holding fast at the Suez Canal. Before and during the War of Attrition, he had hinted at possible Israeli withdrawal from Suez in return for an Egyptian commitment to nonbelligerency. Upon assuming office, therefore, Begin similarly shared this interest in a tradeoff. But the new prime minister had in mind an exchange less for an Egyptian commitment to nonbelligerency than for an Israeli free hand in Judea and Samaria, the ideological obsession of Begin's life. Dayan, with his record as a dove in Sinai and a hawk in the West Bank, could be indispensable in selling the idea of such a tradeoff—first to Egypt, then to Israel. The prime minister thereupon outlined his strategy to Dayan, and the latter accepted it. It was on this basis that Begin nominated Dayan as foreign minister, and eventually secured Knesset approval.

Thereafter, from the earliest weeks of his incumbency, Begin set about dispatching signals to Cairo of his willingness to deal. One overture took the form of the prime minister's four-day visit to Bucharest in late August 1977. The Rumanian president, Nicolae Ceauşescu, seeking visibility as a "nonaligned" statesman, had made known his desire to help broker a Middle East settlement. It was accordingly Ceauşescu who arranged a secret parallel meeting in Bucharest between Begin and Saïd Merei, a representative of the Egyptian national assembly. To Merei, as to Ceauşescu, Begin emphasized his willingness to offer "extensive satisfaction" on the Sinai, even to negotiate some form of self-governing Arab entity for Gaza and the West Bank. Merei in turn promised to convey Begin's message to Sadat. The second signal was transmitted by Dayan. Early in September, he instructed Meir Rosenne, the foreign ministry's legal adviser, to formulate a draft Egyptian-Israeli peace treaty. Rosenne subsequently produced a forty-six-point document that elaborated upon the principles Begin had outlined in Rumania. Immediately the paper was sent off to Washington for examination. Secretary of State Cyrus Vance was impressed by it. So was Carter, who had the document telexed to Cairo. The president followed with a confidential letter to Sadat, entreating the Egyptian leader to test Begin's sincerity by acceding to an early revival of the Geneva Conference (a meeting that plainly had become a fixation with Carter).

A HEGIRA TO JERUSALEM

Sadat's reaction to these feelers was influenced by an intriguing twist of history. Since 1975, Muammar Qadafi, the Libyan dictator, had been actively seeking to detach Egypt from its American relationship and to reinstate its traditional Arab-bloc military confrontation with Israel. Sadat's interest lay distinctly in the opposite direction, of course. He ignored Qadafi's entreaties. Outraged, the latter then ordered a massing of troops along the Egyptian frontier. It was at this point, in May 1977, that General Yitzchak Hofi, director of Israel's Mossad, uncovered details of a Libyan assassination conspiracy against Sadat. The hit team evidently consisted of trained Palestinian killers, men who had long been under Israeli scrutiny. Apprised of the plot, Begin came up with a novel proposal. It was to convey the information to the Egyptians. "That may warm the atmosphere between us," the prime minister suggested.

For communication with Egypt, Morocco's King Hassan was regarded as a particularly valuable conduit. A great admirer of Jewish "genius," Hassan had made a point of treating his own Jewish minority well. Moreover, the Israelis had secretly aided Hassan's military campaign against Algerian-sponsored Polisario guerrillas in the western Sahara. From 1975 on, therefore, it was the king's pet scheme to bring Israel and Egypt together in an antiradical regional bloc. Occasionally, he had even invited eminent Israelis of North African background to Morocco as his personal guests; and in 1975 Prime Minister Rabin himself paid a secret visit to Morocco to seek the king's good offices in brokering a conference with Sadat. The effort then was premature. Now, however, in June 1977, at Israel's request, Hassan arranged a meeting in Casablanca between the Mossad's General Hofi and Egypt's director of military intelligence, General Kamal Hassan Ali. Hassan Ali was stunned by the conspiracy information the Israeli brought with him, including names and addresses of the Palestinian assassins in Cairo. Acting on the information, the Egyptian police seized the plotters; and afterward, in July, the Egyptian army conducted a pulverizing strike against a major Libyan army base, twenty-two miles across. Egypt's western frontier.

Sadat was genuinely grateful to the Israelis. He had been appalled by Begin's recent electoral victory, and by the presence in the Begin cabinet of hawks like Generals Dayan, Sharon, and Weizman. But the Libyan episode, and the subsequent overtures communicated through Ceauşescu and Saïd Merei, registered on him. Accordingly, the Egyptian president sent word through Morocco that he was prepared to listen to serious Israeli proposals. Thus, in early September 1977, Dayan flew off secretly to Fez (by way of Paris) in the Moroccan king's private jet. In Fez, Hassan informed his Israeli visitor that Sadat was indeed interested in a possible bilateral agreement. Two weeks later, on September 16, Dayan flew back to Morocco. Awaiting him this time in Rabat was Egyptian Deputy Prime Minister Hassan al-Tohami.

To Dayan, Tohami outlined Sadat's willingness to preempt the distasteful prospect of a Geneva Conference by quietly negotiating a "private" understanding on Egyptian-Israeli nonbelligerency. But Israel first would have to commit itself to returning the entire Sinai to Egypt, and to a Palestinian "arrangement" that would link the West Bank and Gaza to Jordan. On that basis, Sadat was prepared to offer Israel every possible security guarantee, including even United Nations forces on both sides of the Sinai frontier. Dayan's reaction to the proposal was characteristically straightforward. Israel was prepared to restore full Egyptian sovereignty over the Sinai, he explained, but not to abandon its key air bases near the Gulf of Aqaba or its settlements in Yamit—that is, the Rafa, northeastern, corner of the peninsula. Neither would Israel withdraw its settlements from the West Bank. Dayan acknowledged, however, that on these and other issues there was room for future "clarification." Tohami remained noncommittal. Both men in any case agreed to return to Morocco in a fortnight with more concrete proposals. Each then departed for home.

The following day, in Jerusalem, Begin listened to Dayan's account of the meeting. The prime minister was gratified. Now at last he possessed the weapon for aborting Carter's anticipated Geneva Conference. The signal from Cairo was audible enough to suggest that better options were developing. They were. Sadat was indeed contemplating a new departure. He wrote later: "It was then that I drew, almost unconsciously, on the inner strength that I had developed in Cell 54 of Cairo Central Prison [under the British]—a strength, call it a talent or capacity, for change." He would launch a fresh approach to dispel Israeli suspicions. On October 30, the Egyptian president flew to Rumania for a private discussion of his own with Ceauşescu. "I asked Ceauşescu about his impressions [of Begin]. He said: 'Begin wants a solution.'" As Dayan had intimated to Tohami, the Israeli prime minister conceivably might soften his position on the Sinai. The following day, Sadat flew on from Rumania to Iran. And here, too, the shah, long a moderate on the Arab-Israel issue (p. 950), similarly urged his guest to enter into direct negotiations with Begin. It was on this Middle Eastern trip, then, that Sadat reached an epochal decision. He would make a personal visit to Israel.

If the notion was larger-than-life, such gestures were hardly foreign to Sadat. Many of his earlier actions—his wartime spying for the Germans, his assassination plots against British and Egyptian officials—revealed an instinct for the spectacular. So did his surprise move later in expelling the Soviets from Egypt, and so did his decision to open the Suez Canal in 1975. The initiative Sadat had in mind now, however, was authentically mind-boggling. It was to invite other Arab leaders to join him at the Knesset in Jerusalem. In fact, the notion did not get far. When the Egyptian president mooted it, first in a personal meeting with Saudi Arabia's King Khaled and then with Jordan's King Hussein, it was instantly shot down. Nevertheless, Sadat determined to sustain his venture, to proceed to Jerusalem on his own. On November 9, addressing his nation's People's Assembly, Sadat concluded his remarks with the laconic announcement: "I am ready to go to the Israeli parliament itself and discuss [Israeli withdrawal] with them."

The impact of the declaration was stunning. Foreign Minister Ismail Fahmi promptly resigned. In Washington, Jimmy Carter was confused and silent. Several days passed before the White House issued a somewhat constipated endorsement of Sadat's initiative. In Israel, Begin was hardly less astounded. Yet, regaining his composure, the prime minister formally extended an invitation (through the United States embassy in Tel Aviv) for the Egyptian leader to address the Knesset on November 20. Sadat immediately accepted (through the United States embassy in Cairo). In advance, however, on November 16, he flew to Damascus to seek the understanding of Hafez al-Assad. It was a wasted effort. The Syrian leader proclaimed a day of national mourning, and the reaction was widely shared elsewhere in the Arab world. But in Israel, at least, amid intense excitement, preparations were already afoot. An advance party of Egyptian officials was invited to Jerusalem to cooperate in the elaborate security precautions. Ten thousand Israeli police were placed on alert. Hospital operating rooms were put on emergency footing, with blood reserves of the correct type for Sadat and his party. Copies of the Egyptian national anthem were hurriedly distributed to the army band.

Finally, at twilight on Saturday, November 19, 1977, Sadat departed for Israel. As his presidential jet entered Israeli air space, four Israeli fighters escorted it to Ben-Gurion Airport. Once the plane landed, millions of television viewers saw the Egyptian leader and his entourage proceed along the unfurled red carpet to the echoes of a twenty-one-gun salute, and shake hands with the line of waiting Israeli dignitaries. Afterward, Sadat and his party were sped in convoy to Jerusalem's King David Hotel. The next morning, attending the al-Aqsa Mosque for prayers, the Egyptian visitors were greeted warmly by a large congregation of

Arab notables and then, afterward, were conducted on a tour of Yad Vashem, the Holocaust Memorial (an established formality on the agenda of distinguished Gentile guests). At last, in the early afternoon, the Egyptian president was ceremonially ushered into the Knesset, to a burst of trumpets and a standing ovation.

In his forty-minute address, Sadat emphasized the breadth of his purpose. It was not, he insisted, to embark on negotiations for a separate peace between Israel and Egypt, but for a peace among Israel and *all* its Arab neighbors. Here Sadat underscored the importance of total Israeli withdrawal from the occupied territories. He concluded then by offering Israel the inducement its people had waited thirty years to hear: "In all sincerity, I tell you that we welcome you among us with full security and safety. . . . I declare to the whole world that we accept living with you in permanent peace based on justice." Following prolonged applause, Begin took the lectern to reply graciously, but also to emphasize that Jerusalem would never again be divided, or the West Bank transformed into a PLO state. The prime minister then invited all "legitimate" spokesmen of Arabs living in the "Land of Israel" to meet with him and Sadat for discussions. Sadat was less than overwhelmed by the response. That evening, however, in private conversation with the prime minister, he and Begin at least reached agreement on two key principles. War was "rejected" as a means of settling disputes, and Egyptian sovereignty would be restored over the Sinai. With mutual assurances of early future meetings, Sadat and Begin then ended their discussions. The next afternoon, November 21, the Egyptian president departed for home.

THE COLD LIGHT OF DAWN

In Cairo, nearly a million people cheered Sadat on his return drive from the airport. Exploiting the groundswell of national support, he was determined now to convene his own international meeting as a "preliminary"—but in fact an alternative—to Geneva. To that end, he dispatched invitations to other Arab countries, as well as to Israel, the Soviet Union, and the United States. The Begin cabinet understood and immediately accepted. Not so the Soviets, the Arab governments, or the PLO. Instead, gathering in an emergency session of their own in the Libyan capital of Tripoli, the assembled Arab statesmen condemned Sadat's initiative and froze diplomatic relations with Cairo. At this point, Sadat accepted the reality that negotiations henceforth would take place exclusively between Egypt, Israel, and (he hoped) the United States. Quietly, then, President Carter acquiesced in the trilateral format.

Meanwhile, in early December 1977, Dayan and Egyptian Deputy Prime Minister Tohami were conferring again in Morocco. There Dayan revealed his government's detailed proposals for the Sinai. They envisaged an early return of the peninsula to Egyptian sovereignty, linked to a deliberately calibrated Israeli evacuation, with final withdrawal to be completed in the year 2000. Tohami was affronted. It was not for a scheme of protracted Israeli evacuation that Sadat had incurred the condemnation of the Arab world, he observed coldly. Neither could a Sinai agreement be reached without a parallel resolution of the Palestine question. On that somber note, both statesmen returned home. Begin and his advisers then set to work formulating a more cosmetic package for the West Bank and Gaza. Yet, as crafted by Aharon Barak, the prime minister's legal consultant, the plan was even less forthcoming than the original Dayan-Rosenne blueprint (p. 845). Under its format, Palestinian autonomy would be limited to cultural and religious activities, to health, social welfare, commerce, and tourism. Security and public order—in effect, control of the land—would remain Israel's responsibility. Resident Arabs could opt for Israeli or Jordanian but not for "Palestinian" citizenship. Begin's single concession to Sadat was his willingness to postpone the issue of sovereignty "for the time being." As for Sinai, Israel's proposal still envisaged a two-stage evacuation, with the Rafa settlements (Yamit) and the main air bases to remain in Israeli hands until the end of the century.

Even before presenting his formula to Sadat, Begin hoped once again to sell it to Jimmy Carter. To that end, he flew to Washington in mid-December to present it to the president and Secretary Vance. The Americans reacted with caution to Begin's blueprint, observing only that the document offered a "fair basis for negotiation." Ironically, the one rebuff Begin encountered was not in Washington but in Jerusalem. Many in his own cabinet regarded the autonomy plan as a prescription for an eventual Palestinian state. Taken aback, Begin and Barak then quickly set about modifying the formula to ensure that Israel would assume responsibility not only for public law and order within the West Bank, but also for the "permanent security" of the region's borders. Refugees who had fled in the aftermath of the Six-Day War would be allowed to return only in "reasonable" numbers and by unanimous decision of a joint Israeli-Jordanian-Palestinian committee. An identical unanimity would be required for delegation of authority to a West Bank council. This, finally, was the refined and rerefined plan Begin took with him for his scheduled one-day return visit to Sadat in Ismailia, on December 25, 1977.

Until then, contact between Egyptians and Israelis had been friendly. The Ismailia encounter was not. Frigidly, Sadat informed his guest that the Sinai proposal was not suitable even for discussion. As for the Palestinian formula, it would be "studied." Unfazed, flying home that night, Begin still remained confident that an Egyptian-Israeli accommodation was within reach. A procedural understanding already had been reached. It was to divide negotiations into two tracks, military and political. The former would be conducted by Israeli and Egyptian teams in Cairo; the latter, by parallel teams in Jerusalem. Initially, Ezer Weizman, serving as minister of defense, led Israel's military delegation. A warm and flamboyant man, Weizman developed an immediate rapport with Sadat. It was to him, then, that the Egyptian president expressed consternation at Israel's stance on the Sinai. In Bucharest he, Sadat, had been assured that Begin was prepared to return the Sinai to Egyptian sovereignty. But what kind of sovereignty was this? the president asked. Thereupon Weizman explained that the Sinai bases offered Israel defense in depth not only against Egypt but against Iraq and Saudi Arabia; that only the Sinai offered Israel's air force the necessary space for deploying its combat planes. But Sadat would not budge. In mid-January 1978, discussions within the Egyptian-Israeli military committee were temporarily suspended.

The political committee began its meetings in Jerusalem four days later, in the presence of Secretary of State Cyrus Vance. Foreign Minister Ibrahim Kamil led the Egyptian delegation. Both sides had agreed in advance to a moratorium on public declamations or recriminations. But at a ceremonial banquet that evening, Begin launched into an extended polemic, extolling the virtues of a united Jerusalem, of "Judea and Samaria" linked permanently to Israel. Later that evening Kamil telephoned Sadat, insisting that Begin had foreclosed meaningful negotiations. The president agreed and recalled the Egyptian delegation only forty-eight hours after its arrival. By then Sadat was in despair. Accordingly, in July 1978, he turned to Ezer Weizman, his favorite Israeli interlocutor. The two met this time at Sadat's winter vacation retreat in Salzburg, Austria. If he could make no further progress by October, the Egyptian leader warned, he would resign. Again he insisted upon full Israeli withdrawal from the Sinai. As for the West Bank, he might accept a more limited blueprint for Palestinian quasi-autonomy; but, in the interim, he would have to obtain some unilateral gesture of good faith from Israel—possibly an Israeli turnover of al-Arish, or Mount Sinai. Weizman was listening. Flying back to Israel the next day, the defense minister explained to the cabinet that Sadat was asking for little more than a "fig leaf" on Palestine. Could the government not be more forthcoming? Yet five days later, even as Begin was contemplating Sadat's plaintive appeal, Dayan conferred in England with Egyptian Foreign Minister Kamil, and the latter evinced no willingness at all to settle for a "fig leaf" on either the Sinai or the West Bank. For Begin, consequently, there could only be one response. "Nothing for nothing," the prime minister informed a press conference. Both the intransigence and inelegance of the reply enraged Sadat. On July 27, he ordered Israel's military delegation in Cairo to depart. All communications henceforth would go through Washington.

By then, eight months had passed since the Egyptian president's dramatic trip to Jerusalem. He had gambled his personal reputation in the Arab world on an early breakthrough. Even lately, as negotiations foundered, he had drawn hope from the rising peace movement among the Israelis themselves. In March 1978, some 350 military reserve officers signed an open letter to Begin, entreating the prime minister to accept an exchange of territories for peace. From this letter, the "Peace Now" movement gained momentum, winning support among university professors, kibbutz leaders, and other prominent figures among the educated (largely Ashkenazic) middle class, as well as the endorsement of thirty Knesset members from six parties, and from six famous reserve generals (Chaim Bar-Lev and Uzi Narkiss among them). Indeed, it was specifically the generals who questioned the putative military advantage of retaining the West Bank. If anything, the army would be fragmented by the need to protect a network of Jewish settlements. Worse yet, a growing Jewish presence in Arab-populated territory would increase the danger of Arab terrorism and require an even larger Israeli troop commitment. Above all else, the Peace Now movement was animated by fear that Begin, imprisoned by his Revisionist theology, was sacrificing a unique opportunity to end the thirty-year cycle of violence and death. It was a fear that lent the Peace Now demonstrations—drawing up to thirty thousand people—their anguished, visceral quality.

Informed of these mounting pressures within Israel, Sadat might well have taken heart. Yet it was ultimately with the Begin government that he would have to reach agreement. Behind that government, too, a majority of Israel's citizens still remained profoundly distrustful of Arabs after years of isolation and threatened annihilation. Even Washington did not appear capable of dissipating that suspicion. By the summer of 1978, the Carter administration had formulated numerous draft proposals of its own for the Sinai and Palestine, including an imaginative autonomy blueprint for a five-year transitional regime in the West Bank and Gaza. Begin and his advisers remained unresponsive.

On the other hand, it was the very lack of a substantive breakthrough that evoked a critical last-minute procedural agreement between Israelis, Egyptians, and Americans. On August 8, 1978, Sadat and Begin publicly accepted Jimmy Carter's invitation to discuss their differences jointly with him at the American presidential retreat of Camp David on September 5. The sense of mutual urgency was justified. Recriminations between Cairo and Jerusalem were being loosed against a blizzard of press accusations and counteraccusations. Carter, Sadat, and Begin alike now recognized that the momentum for peace could be restored only through the active diplomatic intercession of the single most powerful government in the world.

RETREAT AND BREAKTHROUGH

On September 5, 1978, Sadat and Begin and their staffs arrived separately at Camp David in Maryland's Catoctin Mountains. Despite the carefully encouraged atmosphere of informality (all participants were requested to wear sport clothes), it soon became evident that negotiations would be difficult. The next afternoon, Sadat read his position paper aloud to Carter and Begin in the presidential cabin. It included every tough demand the Arabs had ever made on the Israelis, from return of the 1948 refugees to withdrawal to the 1967 "Green Line" and a renewed division of Jerusalem. Incensed, Begin threatened to leave the conference then and there. Moshe Dayan finally calmed him down. But two additional abrasive meetings between the Middle Eastern leaders did not narrow the gap. Neither did the ensuing four days of triangular staff discussions. In private meetings with Carter, Begin remained as inflexible in his position as did Sadat. There would be no abandonment of Israel's key airfields in Sinai, no evacuation of the Jewish enclave in the Rafa (Yamit) salient, no withdrawal of Israeli settlements from Judea and Samaria. Provoked by this obduracy, Carter warned of possible "strained relations" between Washington and Jerusalem. "Please, Mr. President, no threats," Begin countered sternly.

Persisting, Carter and his advisers submitted one draft formula after another. All potential areas of agreement were revised and refined in turn by Aharon Barak and by Dr. Osama al-Baz, Sadat's closest adviser. At last, on September 12, in a personal conversation with Sadat, Dayan sensed a possible opening. Returning to his cabin, he described his impressions to his staff. "Concentrate on the Sinai issues," the foreign minister urged his associates. "I'm sure this is what Sadat really wants." Indeed, this had been Ezer Weizman's instinct all along: the Egyptians would accept a "fig leaf" on Palestine in return for Israeli flexibility on the Sinai. In turn, sensing the shift in Dayan's emphasis, Carter similarly was prepared to separate the Sinai and West Bank issues and to focus thenceforth on two distinct agreements, one dealing with Egyptian-Israeli peace, the other with a broader-ranging settlement of the Palestine issue.

For his part, Begin still intended to hold firm on the Sinai airfields and settlements. Through Dayan, however, Carter issued a warning. In the event war broke out over Israeli occupation of the Sinai, Israel would not be able to count on American support. Sadat added his own ultimatum in a private meeting with Dayan. Exhausted and nerve-frazzled, the Egyptian leader already had asked for a helicopter to be made ready. He was prepared to depart Camp David if the impasse continued. "Kindly convey this from me to Begin," he shouted. "Settlements, never! Why are you coming to me with such ideas you know I'll never agree to? Why should we torture President Carter with us?" Unexpectedly, then, Sadat added a sweetener. It was the possibility of full diplomatic relations only nine months after the signing of a peace treaty—provided Israel agreed to evacuate the Sinai completely. This time he made no mention of Palestine. Dayan reported the conversation to his prime minister. Begin was listening.

Indeed, the next evening, meeting with Carter, Begin was given further pause as the president tightened the screws. If no agreement was reached by the next day, Carter warned, he would terminate the conference and present a full report to Congress—with the intimation that blame for the collapse would be placed on Israel. But the threat was linked with an inducement. If Israel agreed to abandon the Sinai bases, the United States at its own expense would construct in Israel's Negev Desert two military air bases of "important scope and with extensive facilities." That same evening, under pressure from Dayan, Weizman, and even from Ariel Sharon (who, at Weizman's request, telephoned Begin from Jerusalem), the prime minister decided to give in. He softened his position on the Sinai. Moreover, he was willing even to honor Sadat's request for signature of a Palestine agreement in advance of a Sinai pact, thereby avoiding the appearance of a separate Egyptian-Israeli deal at the expense of the Palestinians. To Begin and his advisers, it was substance, not style, that mattered.

THE FRAMEWORKS OF AGREEMENT

The two accords were entitled a "Framework for Peace in the Middle East," and a "Framework for the Conclusion of a Peace Treaty between Egypt and Israel." Under this curious joint rubric, the second framework related exclusively to Egyptian-Israeli matters, and provided for the phased evacuation of all Israeli bases and settlements in the Sinai. Egypt in turn recognized Israel's right of maritime passage through the Suez Canal, the Strait of Tiran, and the Gulf of Aqaba. More detailed provisions envisaged an incremental three-year Sinai withdrawal of Israeli troops; a limited Egyptian military presence in certain key sectors and United Nations forces in other specified zones; the establishment of diplomatic relations between Egypt and Israel after nine months. It was a good arrangement for both sides. The Egyptians were guaranteed return of all their land. The Israelis won assurance that, for three years after treaty ratification, 40 percent of the Sinai would remain in their hands, giving them leeway to test Egyptian behavior in the interim.

Preceding the Egyptian-Israeli accord, meanwhile, was a distinctly more complex three-stage "framework" for dealing with the West Bank and Gaza. At the outset, Egypt, Israel, and Jordan (should Jordan agree to participate) would negotiate the ground rules for establishing a "self-governing authority" in the territories. Once that authority was functioning, a transitional five-year period would allow Israel to dismantle its military government and withdraw its troops to restricted security locations. Meanwhile, not more than one year after the onset of the transitional period, discussions would be launched between Israel, Egypt, Jordan, and an elected local Palestinian authority to determine the permanent status of the territories, and to negotiate a formal Israel-Jordan peace treaty.

For Sadat and Begin, the Camp David accords represented a personal diplomatic triumph. Return of the Sinai was vindication enough for the Egyptian president. Yet Sadat also chose to interpret the West Bank and Gaza framework as a major Israeli commitment to the Palestinians. Did it not promise "full autonomy" and respect for the "legitimate rights of the Palestinian people," phrases Israel had always resisted? The framework declared, too, that peace treaties should similarly be negotiated between Israel and its other Arab enemies, thereby refuting any intimation that Sadat was retrieving the Sinai without so much as a backward glance at Jordan and Syria.

Nevertheless, in perspective, it was unlikely that Sadat had achieved (or, as Weizman had always insisted, had expected to achieve) more than a "fig leaf" on Palestine. He had agreed to a convoluted formula—essentially Israel's—that postponed the question of Israeli withdrawal for future negotiations. The degree even of Palestinian autonomy also remained to be negotiated between Egypt, Jordan, and Israel. Each of these countries in effect retained a veto over the powers to be arrogated to the "self-governing authority." Begin was not likely to countenance extensive responsibilities. Neither were the Jordanians. Additionally, Israel's right was affirmed to take "all necessary measures" to ensure "the security of Israel . . . during the transitional period and beyond." Beyond? Beyond the five-year period? Begin was sure to insist on the right to station troops permanently at critical security points in and around the West Bank, thereby restricting leeway for any genuine Palestinian self-government. The sensitive issue of Jerusalem, finally, was not so much as touched upon in the accord. At Dayan's insistence, the question was relegated to separate letters from Sadat and Begin to Carter, with the Israeli prime minister reasserting the claim to a united Jerusalem as capital of Israel, and the Egyptian president favoring Arab rule over the eastern part of the city.

Yet if Sadat had acquiesced essentially in a fig leaf for Palestine, the Camp David frameworks doubtless offered immediate, tangible advantages to his own country. The Egyptian standing army could be reduced now by at least half. The

United States was prepared to organize a Western economic consortium to invest substantially in the Egyptian economy. Here, then, were the ultimate benedictions that Sadat and the Egyptian people anticipated from Camp David. It was peace, and with peace an assurance that the nation at long last would be rescued from its marginal standard of existence. Little wonder, on September 17, 1978, after twelve days of touch-and-go negotiations, that Sadat was prepared to join Carter and Begin in a televised ceremony of signing at the White House. The following evening, the three leaders appeared again before a joint session of Congress. On this occasion, television viewers were treated to the noteworthy spectacle of Begin and Sadat embracing before an audience of cheering senators and representatives. The road to peace now seemed dramatically shorter.

Begin took the initiative on that road by immediately placing the new accords before the Knesset. There, after seventeen hours of debate, the legislators endorsed the frameworks by a margin of 84 to 19. Yet the affirmative vote included only 29 of Likud's 43 representatives. Indeed, it was specifically criticism from the Right that induced Begin to move with heightened caution even toward the final peace treaty with Egypt. Sadat, too, for that matter, was not without grave misgivings of his own. Chief among his concerns was the frigid reaction of the Arab world. Even King Hassan of Morocco, once his most faithful intermediary, this time was reserved and noncommittal. So was Hussein of Jordan. King Khaled of Saudi Arabia remained ominously silent. But in Cairo, at least, cheering crowds welcomed the president back from the United States as rapturously as they had from his original visit to Jerusalem. Manifestly, they shared their leader's conviction that peace and prosperity were in sight. The hope appeared further vindicated in late November when the 1978 Nobel Peace Prize was awarded jointly to Sadat and Begin.

To sustain that hope, one of Sadat's initial priorities now was to call a halt to his nation's endemic media-and-school propaganda campaign against Israel. Even earlier, in the immediate aftermath of Camp David, Israeli journalists, professors, scientists, and other professionals were selectively admitted into Egypt. There, they were greeted cordially by their Egyptian counterparts, and with visible emotion by ordinary Egyptians. In Israel, too, meanwhile, the vision of emancipation from the brooding peril of war and endless human and economic sacrifice was all but overwhelming. Even so, well accustomed to earlier disappointments after the Six-Day and Yom Kippur Wars, the Israeli people were hesitant to articulate that vision in detail. Fate dared not yet be tempted.

SADAT'S EQUIVOCATION, CARTER'S GAMBLE

Under the terms of the Camp David framework, Egypt and Israel were obliged within three months to complete all remaining details of their impending peace treaty. Thus, in mid-October 1978, their negotiating teams gathered in Washington. The Egyptian team was led by Defense Minister Hassan Ali and Acting Foreign Minister Butros Butros-Ghali; the Israeli delegation, by Dayan and Weizman. As always, Secretary of State Vance was an active participant. The atmosphere was encouraging. Yet, as draft after draft failed to win acceptance, it emerged that one of the stumbling blocks related not to the Sinai but to Jewish settlements on the West Bank. Before the frameworks-signing ceremony, on September 17, it had been Carter's understanding that Begin would call a halt to new settlements until the Palestinians elected their self-governing council. Within days after Camp David, however, chivied to remain honest by the hard-liners in his cabinet, the Israeli prime minister "clarified" his position. The settlement freeze, he explained, would apply only to the three months (or less) needed to complete the Egyptian-Israeli peace treaty. It was a painful affront to Carter. Privately the president wrote Begin, imploring him not to raise impediments to the peace process. The prime minister held his ground.

Sadat's concern was even more far-reaching, of course. Restiveness was beginning to surface within Egypt. Both Nasserists and members of the religious Right, including remnants of the outlawed Moslem Brotherhood, had bitterly opposed the Camp David frameworks. Within the diplomatic corps, Foreign Minister Kamil—himself a successor to Ismail Fahmi—had resigned in protest. In early November 1978, emissaries of the other Arab nations were meeting again in Baghdad. Sensitive to the pressures of the volatile Palestinian guerrilla movements, the assembled statesmen prepared a list of sanctions to be imposed on Egypt in the event a peace treaty was signed with Israel. This time Sadat was shaken. He sensed that he had let Begin off too easily by not insisting upon a formal connection between an Egyptian-Israeli treaty and elections to a Palestinian self-governing entity. Although both sides had understood and quietly accepted a certain moral linkage, in the immediate aftermath of Camp David the Israelis and Egyptians had agreed that each framework—one for Palestine, one for the Sinai—was designed to stand alone. Now Sadat felt obliged to alter that understanding. On November 2, Acting Foreign Minister Butros-Ghali suddenly announced that Egypt required a definite timetable for Palestinian autonomy before committing itself to a formal peace treaty with Israel; and that full Egyptian-Israeli diplomatic relations should be delayed until one month after establishment of that autonomy.

Begin and his cabinet rejected the new proposal out of hand. Indeed, linkage between Egyptian peace and Palestinian autonomy even then was rather too close for their tastes. Moreover, Cairo now was floating additional demands for changes in the draft treaty. One of these called for a "review" of Sinai security arrangements after five years. Another requested Israel to make the "gesture" of interim withdrawal from Sinai within six, rather than nine, months following treaty signature. Still another sought an Egyptian "presence" in Gaza during elections for the envisaged Palestinian administrative council. In each case, Israel's response was a flat negative. Instead, in their revived distrust of Sadat, Begin and his advisers submitted two new demands of their own. It had been understood at Camp David that the Egyptian-Israeli treaty would operate independently of Egypt's mutual defense commitments (against Israel) with other Arab nations. Now, however, the Egyptian government reversed itself, asserting that its original Arab defense obligations would take priority over its treaty with Israel. Getting wind of this tactic, Begin and his advisers promptly countered, insisting on a new provision in the draft treaty affirming the document's precedence over all other Egyptian commitments. The second proposed amendment related to Sinai petroleum. With unrest seething in Iran, a nation supplying over 40 percent of Israel's oil, the Begin government wanted assurance of its right to purchase supplies from the Sinai—indeed, from the very wells its own engineers had drilled, enlarged, and managed during eleven years of Israeli occupation. Cairo rejected both proposed amendments.

By December 1978, the likelihood of peace was occluded again. The three-month deadline for completion of the treaty was fast approaching. On December 11, therefore, Secretary of State Vance and his associates launched into a month of strenuous shuttle diplomacy between Cairo and Jerusalem, offering not less than ten of their own draft treaty modifications. But the deadlock remained. Neither was it resolved in a second, foreign ministers' meeting at Camp David, in late February 1979. By then, press editorials in Egypt and Israel expressed a premonitory disillusionment. Had Sadat's visit to Jerusalem signified nothing more after all than a brief, dramatic interlude in the long succession of diplomatic failures: the Rhodes Armistice of 1949, the Palestinian Conciliation Commission negotiations at Lausanne in 1949–50, the Mixed Armistice Commission contacts of the 1950s, Security Council Resolutions 242 and 338, and the disengagement agreements of 1974–75? Was Camp David too, then, simply another fading landmark on a chimerical quest for peace?

A PILGRIMAGE TO THE MIDDLE EAST

In March 1979, Jimmy Carter suddenly announced plans for a new initiative—"an act of desperation," he admitted later. The president would travel personally to Egypt and Israel in search of a final breakthrough to peace. As it developed, Carter had come up with ideas on two seemingly intractable issues. On the question of "linkage," he now proposed a "side letter" to the treaty in which Israel would agree simply to complete "negotiations" for West Bank–Gaza elections within one year of the treaty signing. In the event elections were delayed as a consequence of Jordanian or Palestinian noncooperation, Israel would be left blameless. The issue of potential Egyptian treaty conflicts in turn should be finessed. The pact with Israel would be regarded as binding, without specifying its precedence over Egyptian obligations to other Arab nations. The Israelis reacted well to these proposals. The Egyptians at least did not reject them.

On March 7, Carter and his staff departed for the Middle East, arriving in Cairo the next day. The Egyptian reception was warm, and Sadat was particularly accommodating. "Sadat accepted the troublesome texts," Carter wrote later, "and within an hour he and I resolved all the [remaining] questions." On March 10, the Americans traveled on to Israel in high spirits. But in Jerusalem their welcome was less than enthusiastic. Heckling crowds greeted Carter. The president and his entourage learned that key issues remained, including guaranteed rights to Sinai oil and the timing of an exchange of ambassadors—with the Israelis insisting on the original schedule, midway through their Sinai withdrawal. Even Carter's promise to build two air bases for Israel in the Negev would not soften Begin's adamancy. He needed further assurances of American support. Here Secretary of State Vance discerned some room for maneuver. It was to dangle a list of ordnance before the Israelis, with additional promises of some $3 billion in annual military and economic support (Egypt would receive $2 billion). The president agreed, and the next day reached a tentative understanding with Begin. Thereupon Carter departed immediately for an unscheduled stopover in Cairo, where he met with Sadat at the airport and reviewed the latest Israeli concessions. Would Sadat find them acceptable? Over his advisers' reservations, the Egyptian president concurred on the spot.

The agreement negotiated during those hectic five days in Jerusalem and Cairo included two revised accords, three annexes, an appendix, minutes, and six letters. As at Camp David, the second accord was the projected Egyptian-Israeli peace treaty itself. The first, in the guise of "side letters," outlined a comprehensive peace for Palestine under which the two leaders agreed to begin negotiations on Arab self-rule one month after ratification of the Egyptian-Israeli treaty, to make a good-faith effort (but no formal commitment) to reach agreement on autonomy within one year. If an understanding actually were reached and elections for a self-governing entity carried out, then, one month later yet, Israel would terminate its military administration in the territories and withdraw its troops to specified zones. Afterward, as agreed at Camp David, a five-year transition period would begin. This time the Jerusalem issue was not so much as mentioned.

With the issue of linkage resolved, the way similarly was opened for compromise on the Egyptian-Israeli pact. Under Article VI, the new wording read: "This treaty does not affect . . . the rights and obligations of the parties under the Charter of the United Nations." The formula enabled Sadat to proclaim his commitment to regional defense, should Israel directly attack other Arab nations. Conversely, Israel received its assurance that, "in the event of a conflict between the obligations of the parties under the present treaty and any of their [other] obligations, the obligations of this treaty will be binding and implemented." Otherwise, Camp David's three-year schedule of phased Israeli withdrawal was reconfirmed. In a precisely delimited sequence of evacuation, Israeli forces would pull back to the al-Arish–Ras Muhammad line within nine months of treaty ratification. Moreover, in an initiative suggested by Carter, Begin was prepared to be even more forthcoming. The prime minister announced that Israel's army would complete its retreat to the interim line within two months— fully seven months ahead of schedule. Sadat then "unofficially" assured Carter that he, Sadat, would exchange ambassadors one month after Israel's interim withdrawal.

The oil question was resolved literally on the eve of the signature ceremony. In attached minutes, the Egyptians agreed to permit "normal commercial sales" to Israel on the same terms as to other purchasers. This commitment in turn was reinforced by an American "Memorandum of Agreement," promising to maintain Israel's oil supplies (in the event of a boycott) for not less than fifteen years. In an even wider-ranging undertaking, the "Memorandum of Agreement" confirmed U.S. willingness, should a treaty violation threaten Israel's security, to consider "such measures as the strengthening of the United States presence in the area, the providing of emergency [military] supplies to Israel, and the

ISRAELI-EGYPTIAN PEACE TREATY
MARCH 26, 1979

Phases of Israeli Withdrawal
April 1979–April 1982

········· Positions taken by UN troops as Israelis withdraw in gradual stages, April 1979–January 1980

North-south buffer zone, January 1980–April 1982

□ Israeli settlements in Sinai

Tel Aviv-Jaffa

WEST BANK

Jordan River

Jerusalem

ISRAEL

Gaza

Dead Sea

UN Zone 1975–79

Port Saïd

Mediterranean Sea

Rafa

al-Arish

GAZA STRIP

Beersheba

Phase I 2 months

JORDAN

Suez Canal

Ismailia

N E G E V

E G Y P T

Phase V 9 months

GIDI PASS

Suez

MITLA PASS

Final Phase 3 years

S I N A I

Eilat

Gulf of Suez

Phase II 3 months

Phase III 5 months

Abu Rudeis

UN Zones 1975–79

Gulf of Aqaba

Phase V 9 months

SAUDI ARABIA

al-Tur

Phase IV 7 months

Strait of Tiran

Sharm es-Sheikh

Red Sea

0   MILES   50

SINAI AFTER ISRAELI WITHDRAWAL

A   B   C   D

Permanent Zones of Reduced Forces

Zone A Egyptian force of up to 22,000 men with heavy weapons, tanks, and armored personnel vehicles

Zone B Egyptian border units with light weapons and up to 4,000 men

Zone C UN forces and Egyptian civil police

Zone D Limited 4,000-member Israeli force with armored personnel vehicles; also UN observers exercise of maritime rights in order to put an end to the violation." The memorandum further defined Washington's obligation to veto any United Nations action that could threaten the peace treaty, and to block transference of American weapons for third-party use against Israel (Saudi Arabia and Jordan clearly were implied here). It was all but a unilateral treaty of defense for Israel.

On March 22, by a margin of 95 to 18, Israel's parliament voted to ratify the pact. Four days later, in a White House ceremony hosted by Jimmy Carter, the two Middle Eastern leaders affixed their signatures to a formal treaty of peace between their nations. Israel undertook to withdraw all its armed forces and civilian settlements from the Sinai. Egypt pledged to use Israel's evacuated airfields in the peninsula exclusively for civilian purposes. Each party would respect the other's sovereignty, territorial integrity, and right to live in peace within "secure and recognized boundaries" (another Israeli victory, implying boundaries to be negotiated in the east). Each similarly undertook to conduct normal diplomatic, economic, and cultural relations with the other, removing all discriminatory barriers to the free movement of people and goods. The document proceeded then to outline four permanent limited-force zones in the Sinai and in a narrow strip of Negev territory adjacent to the Sinai (a concession by Israel), and to allow emplacement of United Nations troops and observers in the last, eastern, two of these zones (map, opposite). Nor were these forces to be evacuated unless specifically authorized to do so by unanimous vote of the UN Security Council. The fiasco of 1967 would not be repeated. Israeli ships and cargoes were assured free access through Suez and other Egypt-bordered waterways. To avoid potentially troublesome incidents, an Egyptian liaison office in al-Arish and an Israeli liaison office in Beersheba would be connected by direct telephone "hot" line.

Not later than six months after Israel's interim withdrawal, both countries would enter into negotiations on trade and commerce, the free movement of nationals into each other's territory, the establishment of postal and telephone communications, and the construction of a highway near Eilat between Egypt, Israel, and Jordan for mutual use. Finally, in accompanying letters, Begin and Sadat emphasized to Carter their expectation that the United States would participate fully in all stages of Palestine autonomy negotiations as well as all phases of enforcing the Egyptian-Israeli treaty. Carter affirmed that assumption, promising aerial monitoring over the Sinai during the three-year period of Israeli withdrawal. Should the Security Council fail to provide acceptable United Nations personnel for the withdrawal zones, Washington would seek to provide an "alternative," that is, a substantially American, multinational force. Altogether, the extent of American commitments—economic, military, and diplomatic—to Israel and Egypt alike, underscored the importance both Jerusalem and Cairo attributed to Washington's role in orchestrating Middle Eastern peace.

On March 26, 1979, in a White House ceremony attended by the Israeli and Egyptian delegations, UN Secretary-General Kurt Waldheim, prominent American government figures, and other dignitaries (among them Henry Kissinger), Sadat and Begin affixed their signatures to a formal treaty of peace between their nations.

A week after the treaty signing, Menachem Begin embarked on his first official visit to the capital of his former enemy. He was met at Cairo airport by Vice President Hosni Mubarak. The welcoming ceremony lasted a bare ten minutes, and the crowds Begin encountered as he drove through Cairo's boulevards were far less enthusiastic than those that had greeted Sadat in Israel seventeen months before. Much acrimony and many frustrations had flowed under the bridge since then, of course. The prime minister was unperturbed. He spent most of April 3, 1979, on a guided tour of the principal tourist sites. Visiting the Sh'arei Shamayim synagogue, he was tearfully welcomed by the less than two hundred remaining members of Cairo's aging Jewish community. In the evening, Begin attended a state dinner hosted by Sadat. Again the prime minister was correctly, if coolly, received by the assembled notables. This time Begin struck a conciliatory note. He praised the Egyptian people, the courage and honor of Egypt's fighting men. His remarks drew applause. For his part, Sadat replied in a vein more cordial than any he had employed toward Israel (and Begin) since his trip to Jerusalem.

Following the twenty-eight-hour visit, the two leaders publicly confirmed the earlier, "unofficial" agreement that Israel would relinquish its control over al-Arish on May 26, 1979, seven months ahead of schedule. The joint communiqué further declared that Sadat and Begin would meet in al-Arish on that occasion, and from there would travel to Beersheba, Israel. During these visits, they would ceremonially proclaim the Egyptian-Israeli border open and then would inaugurate an air corridor between Cairo and Tel Aviv. Both men had also agreed to make of the al-Arish ceremony an occasion for the display of *sulh*, an Arabic ceremony of authentic reconciliation. To that end, Defense Ministers Weizman and Hassan Ali arranged for a symbolic meeting of veterans from both sides. A selected group of one hundred Egyptian and Israeli war wounded thereupon was brought to the Sinai coastal town on May 27. Their meeting was emotional. Presently they were joined by Sadat, Begin, and Secretary of State Vance. When the excitement subsided, Sadat addressed the audience. "Premier Begin and I have decided to give maximum impetus in the movement for peace," he declared, "and to continue together the common effort to end the suffering of the countries in this area. . . . Your sacrifices will not be in vain. The road is open to peace." Begin echoed these sentiments, pledging his nation to peace, then intoning the Hebrew prayer *Shehechiyanu*: "Praised be Thou, O Lord . . . Who hast sustained us and enabled us to reach this moment."

ROMANTIC NATIONALISM AND REALPOLITIK

THE NEW PALESTINIANS

On April 30, 1979, an Israeli freighter passed through the Suez Canal. Egyptians observed the event with mild interest. Their mood had been softened by the peace treaty of the previous March, and by Israel's gesture of goodwill, several weeks later, in returning the Sinai "capital" of al-Arish well ahead of schedule. Neither did the problem of a multinational buffer force for the al-Arish–Ras Muhammad corridor impede the momentum toward peace. Although the Soviet Union had vetoed United Nations participation, Washington plugged the gap by assigning its own troops and civilian personnel to monitor the interim Israeli withdrawal. Compromise also was reached on the price Israel was obliged to pay for Sinai oil. After some haggling, Egypt consented to accept the prevailing OPEC rate.

Nevertheless, prospects for a complete normalization of relations between the two countries remained uncertain. Israel's first ambassador to Cairo, Eliahu Ben-Elissar, found himself in near-quarantine. The entire summer of 1979 passed before a landlord would agree to rent premises for the embassy. Few Egyptian officials were prepared to meet with Ben-Elissar or his staff. Although Sadat himself was fully intent on defusing his nation's suspicions of Israel, Egypt's political and economic establishment waited cautiously for evidence of meaningful progress toward Palestinian autonomy—the single feature of the peace package capable of redeeming Egypt from pariahdom in the Arab world.

In fact, the Palestine Arabs themselves would have something to say about that package. Numbering approximately 750,000 in the West Bank, with another 450,000 in Gaza, by the summer of 1979 these people no longer fitted their earlier stereotype as hapless rustics and refugees. Indeed, their standard of living had been rising more impressively on the West Bank than anywhere else in the Arab Middle East, except for the Gulf oil kingdoms. Economically integrated into the Israel-Palestine common market, commuting to jobs in Israel or working on subcontract for Israeli industries, the Palestinians were rapidly being transformed into salaried blue-collar workers, acquiring new skills and significantly better take-home pay. Tangible evidence of that economic upsurge was the fivefold increase of electricity consumption in the territories and the elevenfold increase in private vehicle ownership. In those same years between 1973 and 1980, when Israel itself experienced an annual GNP increase of 1.4 percent, the territories averaged an annual GNP increase of 13 percent.

The rising economic trajectory brought with it, first and foremost, a quantum improvement in health care. During its first decade and a half of occupation, Israel established no fewer than 146 clinics in the West Bank, 20 in Gaza. It was universal health insurance, in turn, available at bargain rates under Israeli auspices, that gave Palestinian families access to this medical care, and if necessary even in Israel proper. Educational facilities similarly were enlarged. In 1967, nearly 50 percent of the Palestinians were illiterate. By 1980, that rate had fallen to 30 percent. By then too an extensive network of vocational schools had graduated some fifty thousand young people. It was also under Israeli rule that six universities and twenty community colleges and teacher-training seminaries were established in Palestine, with an enrollment in 1981 of approximately ten thousand students.

Economic, medical, and educational transformations in turn produced even farther-reaching social and political ramifications. Thousands of Arab women were finding cottage employment as finishers of clothing or shoes for Israeli companies. As wage earners, they were prepared increasingly to question their traditional communal subservience. Palestinian youths, better educated and better paid than their parents, also now challenged the political spokesmanship of senior eminences. Until the mid-1970s, the informal Israeli-Jordanian administration in the West Bank had consisted essentially of older *mukhtars*, heads of conservative landed families who tended to accommodate to the occupation. In rewarding their leadership, Israel and Jordan since 1967 essentially had inhibited development of a radical PLO alternative. By the late 1970s, however, a new, younger, urbanized and better-educated generation was prepared at last to challenge the status quo.

Initially, it was the Yom Kippur War that aroused this youthful restiveness. "Within a few brief minutes and hours," recalled Raymonda Tawil, a distinguished Palestinian activist-feminist (and Yasser Arafat's future mother-in-law), "we were regaining the pride and self-confidence we had lost in the course of six years of defeat and humiliation." By the same token, it was the PLO confederation that emerged as winner by default among the Palestinians over Jordan's King Hussein. The initial success of the 1973 offensive was regarded as a feat entirely independent of Hussein, who had declined to participate. And when Prime Minister Rabin in turn declined to enter negotiations with Hussein in the aftermath of the second, 1975, Sinai disengagement agreement, he also rendered the Jordanian option irrelevant. Earlier, in October 1974, the Rabat Conference of Arab nations had decided to grant the PLO recognition as "sole legitimate representative" of the Palestinian people. Now, after "Sinai II," even Hussein felt obliged to pay lip service to this formula. Within the next three years, moreover, Arafat's string of diplomatic successes further enhanced the PLO's standing among the Palestinians.

So it was in the West Bank that younger, educated PLO partisans increasingly assumed direction of resistance to Israeli land expropriations and tax assessments. Shortly after Arafat's November 1974 appearance before the United Nations, pro-PLO student demonstrations erupted in the territories, to be followed by strikes of business- and professional men in East Jerusalem. During the winter, civil disobedience extended to smaller towns (p. 809). In turn, the Israeli authorities struck back with curfews and deportations. In the midst of this turmoil, however, the Labor cabinet decided to employ the carrot as well as the stick. It authorized West Bank municipal elections for April 1976. Rabin and Peres clearly anticipated winning over the Arab population by liberalizing the former Hashemite electoral regulations and allowing men and women of the poorer classes to vote for the first time.

The decision proved spectacularly counterproductive. When the votes were tallied on April 12, the pro-Jordanian moderates had been decisively repudiated. In towns and villages alike, younger PLO supporters virtually took over the municipal councils. It was significant, too, that the political agenda of these arrivistes dealt not with municipal issues but almost exclusively with those of Palestinian national identity. Indeed, the ensuing Camp David frameworks appeared only to confirm their worst nationalist fears. The so-called autonomy plan for Palestine evidently made no provision for occupied Jerusalem, for dismantlement of the Jewish settlements, for withdrawal of Israeli troops—and least of all for Arab sovereignty in Arab-inhabited territory. "What rights will we enjoy?" asked Raymonda Tawil. "The right to collect municipal taxes and supervise our sewage works?" An émigré Palestinian scholar, Fayez Sayegh, underscored this aggrieved reaction:

> A fraction of the Palestinian people . . . is promised a fraction of its rights (not including the national right to self-determination and statehood) in a fraction of this homeland . . . and this promise is to be fulfilled several years from now, through a step-by-step process in which Israel is to exercise a decisive veto power over any agreement.

Thus, in a series of consultations and public meetings, the West Bank's mayors unanimously rejected any alternative to full "self-determination."

For Prime Minister Begin, the hostility of these new leaders provided the rationale he needed, or needed to cite, in defining his government's own intractable position. So did the ongoing sequence of guerrilla terrorism against Israelis both in Israel and in Europe (pp. 810–11). The violence erupted with particular ferocity in the aftermath of the Egyptian-Israeli disengagement agreements, of Sadat's visit to Jerusalem, and the ensuing Camp David accords and peace treaty. Between January 1974 and September 1979 alone, a total of 1,207 people, Jews and Arabs alike, were killed, and 2,950 wounded, in PLO operations that ranged from assassinations to hijackings. To Begin, then, the case for Israel's "security" control of the West Bank was ironclad.

A PARALYSIS OF DIALOGUE

Yet the prime minister's approach signified more than a reaction to guerrilla violence. Menachem Begin was still the devout apostle of Revisionist Zionism. If his obsession with an undivided Land of Israel occasionally appeared to soften, it was only for tactical negotiating purposes. "Begin had repeatedly promised full autonomy for the West Bank Palestinians," Carter recalled, "and I pushed him on how much freedom they would have. He replied that the only powers they would not be able to exercise would be those relating to immigration of Palestinian refugees and the security of Israel. This sounded like good news to me." Within days of the Camp David accords, however, in October 1978, Begin reminded his colleagues that "this government was formed in order to preserve the Land of Israel." He would never abandon that mandate, he warned, his voice breaking: "My old age will not shame my youth."

The prime minister soon left no doubt that his stance was authentic. In "side letters" from Sadat and Begin to Carter, the Middle Eastern leaders had agreed that Palestine autonomy negotiations should begin within a month following ratification of the Egyptian-Israeli peace treaty, "with the goal of completing the negotiations within one year," that is, by May 26, 1980. In advance, then, the Begin cabinet issued a statement of principles: the military government would be relocated but not dismantled; Israel would retain responsibility for law and order and for land and water resources; Jewish settlements would remain under Israeli law and sovereignty. So nakedly territorialist were these guidelines that even Dayan and Weizman declared them unworkable. In turn, vexed by the evident dovishness of the two former generals, Begin simply bypassed them to name Minister of the Interior Yosef Burg as chairman of Israel's negotiating delegation. The Prague-born Burg was leader of the National Religious party, which regarded Israel's claim to Judea and Samaria as embedded in Scripture.

Discussions with the Egyptians began on May 26, 1979, initially in the northern Negev city of Beersheba. The Palestinians boycotted the talks. So did the Jordanians. Yet it was less procedure than substance that immobilized the negotiations. At the outset, General Hassan Ali, leader of the Egyptian team, adopted the maximalist Arab demand that Israel withdraw its troops and settlements equally from the West Bank, Gaza, the Golan, and East Jerusalem. The Palestine self-governing authority should be invested with the fullest authority to enact laws, maintain public order, and hold title to public domain and water resources. East Jerusalem of course would be the appropriate site of the self-governing authority.

The Israeli prospectus was equally uncompromising. Indeed, even more than the original Rosenne version, submitted to Carter in September 1977 (p. 845), the current Israeli plan would have limited autonomy to the residents of the territories, but not to the soil itself, "which was sacred to every Jew." Intimidated by the rising backlash among the nation's right wing, the government now plainly was harking back to the old Jabotinsky formula of "personal" rather than territorial autonomy. Moreover, under the Burg committee scheme, Palestinian autonomy would be narrowly administrative, not legislative, and denied competence over such vital areas as security, land and water, and abandoned property—the very guts of any credible self-governing entity. East Jerusalem, meanwhile, with its nearly 120,000 Arabs (the single largest population concentration in the territories), was to be excluded from the tenuous jurisdiction of the self-governing entity altogether. With considerable resentment and acrimony, then, General Hassan Ali and the Egyptian delegation observed that the Israeli blueprint would be a sham in the eyes of the local population. They wanted no part of it.

Until the end of 1979, the Egyptian and Israeli negotiating teams held seven plenary sessions. These took place variously in Beersheba, Tel Aviv, Alexandria, Herzlia, Haifa—even London. Here and there agreement was reached on such purely technical matters as the organization of polling procedures or currency exchanges, but never on questions of substance. By the early spring of 1980, any hope of making the one-year deadline clearly was becoming a pipe dream. The talks limped along, staggered, fell, picked themselves up, but failed to make discernible progress. To every Egyptian proposal that the self-governing entity be invested with legislative powers, that East Jerusalemites should participate in elections to the entity, Burg and his negotiators insisted that Camp David "did not provide for that."

Sadat witnessed the paralysis with growing alarm. Publicly he continued to express optimism. By March 1980, however, the president intimated that failure to complete the discussions on schedule might produce a "new situation." Indeed, on May 12, reacting to a particularly charmless claim by Begin to "the one and indivisible Land of Israel," Sadat suspended the talks altogether. Five days later, Carter persuaded him to rescind the cancellation. The talks would resume in mid-August, Sadat announced. But on July 30 the Knesset solemnly voted a "fundamental law," declaring Jerusalem to be Israel's united and indivisible capital (p. 875). Arab outrage worldwide was all but uncontrollable. In an aggrieved personal letter to Begin, Sadat observed that the Knesset action precluded any further negotiations on Palestine. But once more Carter interceded, pleading with the Egyptian leader to continue. And again, over the objections of his advisers, Sadat concurred. Yet his proviso this time was that Carter arrange still another Camp David summit, following the American president's anticipated reelection in November 1980. Carter agreed. As matters developed, the assumptions of both presidents would expire in tandem.

A FIXATION ON SETTLEMENT

For the Begin government, security remained the most obvious rationale for territorial defense in depth. No Israeli could allow himself to forget the nation's vulnerability in the years before June 1967, when the irregular bulge of the Hashemite West Bank extended to barely nine miles from the Mediterranean. Within this narrow strip had lived 75 percent of the Jewish population. From the West Bank, Jordanian guns could have reached any target in central Israel. For more than a few senior officers, therefore, and virtually all political right-wingers, the Jordan Valley represented a logical new security frontier. Hence, the Begin cabinet now chose to interpret the Camp David formula of "defined security areas" in its broadest contours, shifting its settlements approach from the "Allon Plan" areas—that is, the West Bank's sparsely inhabited, purely strategic sites—to all corners of Judea and Samaria, including the most densely packed Arab sectors. Ariel Sharon, minister of agriculture, explained the government's new policy succinctly. The entire breadth of the West Bank sooner or later would have to be populated with not less than three hundred thousand Jews, he emphasized, to ensure that the region functioned as Israel's permanent "security shield."

For the Likud cabinet, however, security and even ideological factors were interpenetrated by political considerations. Preeminent among these was the need to accommodate the religious Right. By the time of the 1977 election, it is recalled, five Gush Emunim outposts had been established in the Samarian mountain massif. These were inhabited not only by the self-anointed millenarians of the ultra-Orthodox Agudah faction, but by members of the traditionally more moderate and domestically oriented National Religious party. In earlier years, territorial militance had not been characteristic of this centrist faction. But in the 1970s the NRP's leadership was increasingly preempted by Young Guard militants like Zevulun Hammer, chairman of the B'nai Akiva youth movement; and for the Young Guard, as for the Agudah, Judea and Samaria were the very cradle of Jewish identity. Here the patriarchs had spoken with God and dug their wells. Here the Jewish judges had judged, the Jewish prophets prophesied, the Jewish kings ruled. And here too, then, the reclaimed land must be decisively repopulated, never again to be forfeited to non-Jews.

Before the 1970s, the presence of an Arab majority on the West Bank might have intimidated even the most committed group of settlers. Not the pietists, however. Nor were they given pause by the exigencies of international opinion. In the Orthodox world view, Gentile animus was an ineradicable fact of history. Nothing was to be gained by efforts to placate it. Neither was there any need to accommodate to democratic principles. "Israel was not established to give the world another democracy," insisted the fundamentalist spokesman Shabbatai Ben-Dov. "[T]wo thousand years after destruction, it was revived for only one purpose, to redeem the nation and eventually the world." By the mid-1970s, therefore, the mounting hawkishness of the Orthodox had become an accepted feature of Israeli life. Even Prime Minister Rabin, following the second disengagement with Egypt, had been obliged to assure his NRP coalition partners that the government would never yield an inch of territory without first conducting a national plebiscite.

And now Begin, who in 1977 had formed a coalition agreement with the Orthodox, responded even more acutely to their concerns. It is recalled that, in June 1974, some twenty Gush Emunim families had illegally occupied a site in the Samarian mountains, which they called Elon Moreh (p. 832). After an eight-month confrontation with the Rabin government, a compromise was reached, allowing the settlers to remain temporarily at a nearby army camp. Begin's approach now was the opposite of compromise. Almost immediately after his election, he visited the settlers, bearing a Torah scroll in his arms, to declare emotionally that "there will be many more Elon Morehs." Indeed, following the peace treaty with Egypt in March 1979, Begin elevated the Gush Emunim into the nation's leading settlement movement, and fully endorsed its commitment to establish at least sixty communities throughout the Samarian mountains. In the words of the Burg negotiation team, "the right of Jews to settle in all parts of the Land of Israel is a matter of historical ordination."

To coordinate the settlements program, meanwhile, the government and the World Zionist Organization formulated a joint planning committee under the direction of Matityahu Drobles, chairman of the WZO rural settlements division. It was Drobles who laid out the committee's guidelines:

The disposition of the [Jewish] settlements must be carried out not only around the settlements of the minorities [indigenous Arabs] but also in between them . . . with the objective of reducing to the minimum the possibility for the development of another Arab state in these regions.

With Palestine's Arabs thus categorized as "minorities," and the West Bank itself as an integral component of "Greater Israel," the Drobles committee recommended that all public, uncultivated land be expropriated forthwith. Here was the terrain on which between sixty and seventy-five additional settlements should be established, encompassing at least one hundred thousand Jews, and eventually as many as Ariel Sharon's projected figure of three hundred thousand. With the Begin cabinet's unanimous endorsement of this document, Israel's historic governmental policy of territorial compromise was decisively and officially abandoned.

THE REALITIES OF SETTLEMENT

Various techniques were adopted to promote settlement. One was to encircle areas of extensive Arab habitation with Jewish outposts, then to penetrate and fragment these Palestinian communities with a second wave of Jewish colonists. Another technique for ensuring a dominant Jewish presence on the West Bank was to restrain "uncontrolled" Arab agricultural and industrial growth. The goal was accomplished by imposing new restrictions on Arab water use including a flat ban on the drilling of wells close to the Green Line, and limitation even on authorized drilling, with meters placed on each well and heavy penalties assessed for overuse. Yet the most forthright method of all for "incorporating Judea and Samaria" (in the plainspoken language of the Drobles committee) was exercise of the government's "right" to sequester vast tracts of Arab land for "security purposes." Typically, the Gush Emunim became the catalyst for invoking this "right." In full confidence of governmental approbation, the Elon Moreh squatters pressed for action; and in June 1979, the military commander of the West Bank duly signed an order allocating for their use some 700 dunams (175 acres) of private land, much of it under cultivation by neighboring Arab villagers.

It was at this point, however, that the Begin government encountered a sharp setback. In their outrage, the expropriated Arabs sought legal help. Their lawyers (most of them Jews) promptly appealed to the Israeli supreme court, which agreed to hear the case as a matter of national priority. Caught by surprise, the government in turn defended its action on the traditional pretext of military security, and cited earlier precedents of expropriation. But here a number of former senior army commanders, led by ex-chief of staff Chaim Bar-Lev, testified for the plaintiffs, arguing that the confiscated area was of negligible security value for Israel. The court then immediately ruled for the Arab villagers. The government's purpose was manifestly political, declared the judges; its broadened interpretation of "national security" was unacceptable under the Hague Conventions. The court then ordered the Gush Emunim settlers to depart the sequestered tract within the month, and the latter grudgingly obeyed. At this point, the Drobles blueprint for widespread future requisitions was in serious jeopardy. Even Knesset legislation could not alter the West Bank's legal status without violating the Camp David framework, which postponed final decisions on issues of sovereignty until expiration of the five-year transition period.

Nevertheless, for a single-minded government, other alternatives still were available for nailing down Israel's presence in the territories. One was the approximately 32,000 dunams of West Bank land that had been owned by Jews prior to 1948, and that still were listed under Jewish names in the land registry. These were now reclaimed. Additionally, thousands of Arabs had departed the West Bank since 1967, and the Israeli commissioner for abandoned private property had "leased out" 400,000 dunams of their vacated property to Jewish settlements. Inheriting from its Jordanian predecessor the right of eminent domain, the Israeli military government had requisitioned still another 300,000 dunams, ostensibly for purposes of "infrastructure" improvement. At the same time, all restrictions were dropped against Jewish land acquisition by private purchasers. Since 1967, a Hashemite law had forbidden such transfers to Jews. Even so, from 1979 on, numerous local Arabs secretly continued to sell their lands through intermediaries, usually for hard currency in deals that were negotiated overseas. In this fashion, by 1982, some 200,000 additional dunams had been transferred to Jewish ownership.

It was not enough for the Begin government. For Drobles and his experts, "security" confiscations of private land had offered the most convenient loophole for extensive Jewish settlement, and the Elon Moreh decision apparently had closed that loophole. In March 1980, however, a ministerial committee chaired by Ariel Sharon divined an alternative, seemingly foolproof solution. Under the Hague Conventions, the right of legal redress may have applied to illicit seizures of private lands. Yet this was not a right that applied to seizures of public, or state, land. There simply existed no recognized West Bank authority to file the action. Plainly, then, the answer for the Begin cabinet was to redefine "state" land. Hereupon the government launched into an extensive survey of the ownership-and-registration status of all terrain in the West Bank. The project was completed early in 1981. Interestingly enough, the Hashemite government had begun its own registration process, and as early as 1953. Yet this task was only half completed by the time of the Six-Day War, and even in registered areas only a small minority of the landowners had finished the paperwork necessary to receive their title deeds. In the spring of 1981, therefore, the Likud government declared all land outside the original Hashemite survey, as well as all "untitled" tracts within that area, to be "state" land. The army then immediately set about requisitioning the acreage for Israel's settlement needs. So it was, by late 1981, under this widening confluence of pretexts and loopholes, that Israel acquired not less than 31 percent of the West Bank's total land area.

By then, too, the Begin cabinet had significantly enlarged the area of Jewish settlement. Moving well beyond the original, modest Allon Plan configuration, Jewish families were taking up residence in the more densely populated hill areas of Samaria and Judea. Some forty new communities were implanted there, tripling the Jewish population in the West Bank to eighteen thousand. Ten years later, their numbers had sextupled (p. 973). Meanwhile, nowhere was the Likud cabinet's implacable annexationism more evident than in the extraterritorial rights it delegated to these settlers. In March 1979, the military government established three regional councils for the territories: one for Gaza and two for the West Bank, with three more added later, together with five local (urban) councils. The powers and functions of these bodies in every respect matched those of their counterparts in Israel proper. They enacted their own regional and municipal legislation, assessed and collected their own taxes, and at all times functioned exclusively under Israeli law, rather than under the Jordanian law otherwise still operative on the West Bank. Indeed, as the summum bonum of their autonomous status, Chief of Staff Rafael Eytan early on authorized each Jewish village or town to accept responsibility for defending itself. Hundreds of settlers thus were transferred from their regular army units to their West Bank communities, where they functioned as a kind of civil militia, replete with an extensive array of government-issue weaponry.

In this fashion, as early as 1981, the reality of Begin's Revisionism was unfolding. With the Gush Emunim millenarians as his shock troops, his government was dividing Arab-inhabited West Bank areas into smaller sectors, augmenting the Israeli presence by purchase, eminent domain, exploitation of abandoned property, and redistribution of "state" land. It was pumping $100 million a year into a vast support campaign of infrastructure construction—laying roads, linking electricity grids, controlling, and in some instances diverting, water supplies. Not least of all, by delegating powers of self-government and self-defense, the cabinet was transforming the West Bank's Jewish settlements into a widening extension of the homeland. Through the confluence of these measures, the government by late 1981 was well embarked on its pledge to incorporate Judea and Samaria irretrievably into the "redeemed Land of Israel."

A DISAFFECTION FROM REVISIONISM

In Israel itself, meanwhile, Begin's program of de facto annexation aroused widening tremolos of alarm among territorial moderates. Concern was evoked less by doubts of the Jews' legitimate claim to the Land of Israel than by pragmatic realities. One of those realities was the unprecedented chance for peace that had been opened by Sadat's dramatic 1977 initiative, and that now was in danger of being forfeited. The point was made repeatedly by Peres, Rabin, Eban, and other members of the Labor opposition. A second reality was the debilitating social and political consequences for Israel itself of rule over hundreds of thousands of Palestinian Arabs. Once again, the historian Ya'akov Talmon defined the issue in a published letter to Begin of October 1980:

> Mr. Prime Minister. . . . [T]he desire, at the end of the twentieth century, to dominate and govern a hostile foreign population that differs from us in language, history, culture, religion, consciousness, and national aspirations, as well as in its economic and social structure, is like an attempt to revive feudalism. The question is not a moral one. The idea is simply not feasible . . . as France learned in Algeria.

Talmon's warnings, and those of other distinguished Israeli intellectuals, were echoed by respected businessmen and labor leaders, by military officers, among

BEGIN'S MASTER PLAN FOR THE WEST BANK, 1981

Jewish settlement
Existing   Planned

● ○ Town
■ □ Kirya (Municipality)
▲ △ Toshava (Bedroom community)
▪ ▫ Yishuv Kehilati (Integral community)
▼ ▽ Nachal (Military/agricultural) outpost

Lake Galilee

Jordan River

Mediterranean Sea

Jenin

Tulkarem

Nablus

Qalqilia

Tel Aviv-Jaffa

ISRAEL

JORDAN

Ramallah

Jericho

Jerusalem

East Jerusalem
annexed *de facto*
by Israel, 1967

Bethlehem

Dead Sea

Hebron

0   MILES   15

them former generals Matityahu Peled and Yehoshafat Harkabi, previously chief of Israeli military intelligence (p. 636). It was the latter who outlined the ultimate demographic and guerrilla dangers presented by a large, hostile Arab population whose endemic violence would require the presence of a substantially enlarged occupying army.

For Begin, to be sure, jeremiads from the political and intellectual opposition were to be anticipated, and cavalierly to be dismissed. But of potentially greater concern were reservations mounting within the prime minister's own cabinet. A key source of these misgivings was the centrist Democratic Movement for Change. From the outset, the relationship with the DMC had been an arm's-length one. Its leader, Yigael Yadin, had persuaded his colleagues to join the government, hoping to influence it from within. The hope proved vain. On domestic issues, Yadin's most cherished "constitutional" objective was not realized; the party-list system remained intact. And on Middle Eastern issues, the DMC underwent a schism only a few weeks before Camp David. Seven of its Knesset members resumed the name of their original faction, Shinui, and moved into opposition amid charges that Begin was stalling the peace process. When Yadin and his vestigial DMC group expressed a similar concern, they were rebuffed out of hand. Finally, in the autumn of 1981, with his political influence ended, Yadin announced his retirement from public life. In the new election of that year, the DMC no longer appeared on the ballot.

Meanwhile, criticism was voiced even closer to Begin's political home. It was Moshe Dayan's pragmatism, we recall, that had played a key role in achieving the breakthrough at Camp David and Jerusalem. In common with his prime minister, Dayan had steadfastly rejected the notion of a Palestinian state or even of a Jordan–West Bank confederation. Yet neither did he entertain illusions that the Arabs would accept a truncated "administrative" council under Israeli rule, or that peace with Egypt would so much as get off the ground without a meaningful gesture on Palestinian autonomy. The foreign minister expressed his views with discretion. Within the cabinet, and as a member of the Burg negotiating team, he was listened to respectfully—and with equal courtesy fended off. In October 1979, finally, after several months of this humiliation, Dayan resigned. Soon afterward, he was joined in political exile by his former brother-in-law, Ezer Weizman. Once as militant as Begin, the ex–air force commander had been sobered by the 1968–70 War of Attrition. In that nightmare of bombardment along the Suez Canal, Weizman's son had been gravely wounded, and the father later was given to reflection: "What did we do wrong that our children too must go on fighting?" His evolving flexibility allowed him to collaborate with Dayan in engineering the Camp David and Jerusalem compromises. Now, as a member of the Burg negotiating team on Palestine, Weizman joined Dayan again, this time in a—vain—effort to win over his colleagues to moderation on Arab autonomy. Some months after Dayan's resignation, Weizman similarly departed the cabinet.

The prime minister took the discord in stride. In March 1980, Sadat discreetly sent warning of a "new situation" if the autonomy talks stalled. Here, too, Begin was not given pause. Nor was he perturbed by the widely reported observations of Egyptian Minister of State Butros-Ghali that "no economic cooperation—Egyptian or Arab-Israeli—can develop without taking the Palestine mission into account." In September 1980, four months after the autonomy date had passed, Butros-Ghali repeated his government's deeper misgivings in a Paris newspaper interview. Should war erupt between Syria and Israel, he intimated, Egypt would give priority to its security treaties with other Arab countries.

The frozen Palestine negotiations manifestly did nothing to alleviate Israel's diplomatic isolation. Even earlier, the Afro-Asian "Third World" majority had all but ensured Israel's quarantine in the United Nations. By 1980, the Jewish state no longer was represented on a single UN appointive body. Indeed, since 1967, it had been subjected to ninety-three hostile UN resolutions. The most notorious of these was a "Zionism equals Racism" resolution in November 1975. The most threatening was a 1978 Iraqi proposal in the General Assembly calling for an arms embargo against Israel, a resolution that was adopted by a vote of 72 to 30. More ominous even than the affirmative votes were the 37 abstentions, for these represented many Western nations, precisely those democracies that in earlier years had supported Israel and followed its development with sympathy and admiration. Manifestly, Israel's continued occupation of the territories, then the Yom Kippur War of 1973 and the subsequent Arab oil embargo, had begun to exert a cumulative impact. But so, too, did Begin's later foot-dragging in the autonomy negotiations of 1979–80.

Israel's best hope of international understanding traditionally remained with the United States. Yet Washington too now began shifting its emphasis from reflexive support of Israel to the quest for a broader Palestine solution. It was specifically that expectation of settlement, after Camp David and the Egyptian-Israeli treaty, that impelled Carter and his foreign policy experts to sustain the momentum of peace at all costs. Thus, Zbigniew Brzezinski, the president's National Security Council adviser, warned the Begin government that time was not on its side, that Arab oil wealth and influence in world affairs could not be ignored, that the American people soon would face an agonizing choice on their best interests. The concern was described by Alexander Haig, Ronald Reagan's first secretary of state and a warm friend of Israel. "The sympathy of world opinion," Haig recalled in 1984, "which had always before largely belonged to Israel, was in considerable measure transferred . . . to the Palestinian Arabs. Acts of terrorism against Jews . . . aroused less indignation than Israeli acts of reprisal." From his earliest months in office, Haig cautioned that the situation would only worsen. Yet even he could not have anticipated the full measure of that deterioration.

MALAISE ON THE DOMESTIC SCENE

If peace with the wider Arab world still lay beyond realization in the summer of 1980, the Likud government had anticipated other compensations at home and abroad. One of these was the continued arrival of tens of thousands of Soviet Jews. By the turn of the decade, however, that hope was exposed as premature. The Soviet newcomers were shocked by the inequities and shortcomings of Israeli life, and by the grave shortage of employment opportunities for newcomers. Often married to Gentile spouses, they were repelled by the vindictiveness of Israel's

Orthodox parties, by the obstacles the chief rabbinate created for children of mixed marriages (pp. 604–5). Accordingly, writing to family members at home, the immigrants ventilated their frustrations. The relatives, in turn, applying for their own exit visas, tended to focus increasingly on alternatives beyond Israel.

Such options were not lacking. In recent years, Washington had quietly begun admitting refugees from Communist nations on a priority basis. Once this fact became known, thousands of Soviet Jewish visa holders set about bypassing Israel for the United States. In 1977, the number of "defectors" was 8,483 out of 16,737; in 1978, 16,967 out of 28,868; in 1979, 34,056 out of 41,333; in 1980, 14,878 out of 21,478. After 1980, moreover, as the likelihood of Soviet-American détente faded, Moscow perceived no further bargaining advantage even in selective Jewish departures. The gates of emigration were all but closed.

By then thousands of veteran Israelis similarly would have welcomed broader opportunities elsewhere. The nation's economy was fragile. Few citizens were quite starving yet, but in 1979 most were spending at least 45 percent of their income on food alone. Nor was their plight exclusively the consequence of Likud's New Economic Policy. Even following the peace treaty with Egypt, Israel's defense expenditures continued to average 36 percent of the government budget from 1978 through 1980, a quarter of the little country's GNP. For years, too, the nation was consuming a third more goods and services than it produced. Without adequate revenues to sustain this level of consumption, the government was obliged to borrow abroad at progressively higher rates of interest. A foreign debt of $2 billion in 1967 had become $17 billion by the end of 1980. By then, the cost merely of servicing the debt would reach $2.6 billion annually. Little wonder that Wall Street's Standard & Poor's bond-rating service gave Israeli securities the "grade" of BBB, the firm's lowest.

As the public contemplated its uncertain diplomatic and economic circumstances, it was given further pause by evidence of governmental peculation that once had been extensively identified with the Labor establishment. In December 1980, Minister of Religions Aharon Abuhatzeira, of the National Religious party, was indicted on charges of bribe-taking. That same month, the NRP's Dr. Yosef Burg, minister of the interior, fired the national police chief for investigating charges of corruption in the interior ministry itself. Evidence of wrongdoing was surfacing elsewhere in the government, in one ministry after another, month after month, and with it a rising press clamor for an electoral accounting. Indeed, by January 1981, the crisis of governmental disarray, press criticism, and sagging public opinion polls left Begin no alternative but to advance the date of the Knesset election from November 30 to June 30, 1981.

SEIZING THE POLITICAL OFFENSIVE: JERUSALEM

The prime minister was not the man to forfeit the political initiative to his critics. Better than any of his cabinet colleagues, he knew how to mobilize the religio-nationalist passions of his constituency. The Holy City was a sure and certain talisman. During the Palestine autonomy negotiations, it is recalled, Begin ensured that the Egyptians well understood that the City of Jerusalem, in its totality and fullest geographic contours, was nonnegotiable as an integral part of the Jewish state. Jerusalem's mayor, Teddy Kollek, assuredly had been operating on that assumption from the immediate aftermath of the Six-Day War (pp. 667–9). Indeed, the Vienna-born Kollek exhibited all the imagination and dynamism that had characterized his earlier Labor party career as a diplomat and as director of Ben-Gurion's Prime Minister's Office. Orchestrating a spectacular program of improvements in the city's infrastructure, the mayor refused to be limited by the constraints of local budgets. Rather, he organized a "Jerusalem Foundation" to raise funds among Diaspora Jewry for a wide series of social and cultural projects—for community centers, theaters, playgrounds, flower gardens, and parks in virtually every neighborhood, Arab and Jewish alike.

During these same years of the late 1960s and 1970s, nevertheless, the government insisted that it had not formally annexed Jerusalem's eastern, Arab sectors; it had merely "incorporated" them into the city's administrative jurisdiction. The argument was a sophistry. Since June 1967, Israeli law had been applied to the territory of both East and West Jerusalem, and to everyone who lived there, both Jews and Arabs. Indeed, that law also granted Jews and Arabs alike the right to vote and to be elected to the city council. Although only a few thousand Arabs chose to exercise the opportunity in the municipal elections of 1969, 1973, and 1978, the ensuing era of Kollek's effervescent leadership preserved Arab dignity and encouraged a certain functional cooperation between the two peoples. In consequence, the late 1960s and early 1970s were the city's best years of coexistence. Jerusalem's population grew from 260,000 in 1967 to 400,000 by 1980, thereby overtaking Tel Aviv as Israel's largest city (although Tel Aviv remained the largest all-Jewish city). The increase represented government policy, of course, a determination to "thicken" the Jewish presence throughout the entire surrounding Judean mountain area. Even so, during this same period, the Arab population of Jerusalem, 65,000 in 1967, also nearly doubled, reaching 120,000 by 1980. Most of the growth represented an influx from the neighboring West Bank, essentially of Arabs who arrived to work in the city's booming construction industry. Indeed, by then more than 50 percent of the total population of the Judean (southern) area of the West Bank resided in Greater Jerusalem. Yet, with Jews comprising three-fifths of the total population, Israel's control of Greater Jerusalem's economy and topography at least appeared irreversible.

So did the physical unity of the city. The Egyptians, even the Jordanians, tacitly acknowledged that fact of life when the autonomy talks began in May 1979. But Sadat (and Hussein) also understood that an undivided city was one thing, Israeli rule another. No element of the Arab population was inclined to accept the permanence of Israeli annexation, formal or otherwise. From 1974 on, therefore, the Jewish New City became a target for guerrilla violence. Bombs went off in crowded Jewish shopping centers, taking a mounting toll of civilian life. In Arab East Jerusalem, the quietude of pragmatic accommodation increasingly became the silence of festering resentment. "I feel less comfortable walking the streets of the Old City today," wrote Rafik Halabi, an Israeli Druze journalist, in 1981, "than I did in 1967." There were several reasons for the deterioration of relations. The 1973 Yom Kippur War exerted its impact in East Jerusalem, of course, as elsewhere in the Arab world. So did the Burg delegation's obdurate posture in the Palestine autonomy negotiations, as it insisted that Jerusalem's Arab population must remain cordoned off politically from the West Bank hinterland.

Yet even Begin's adamancy was not commitment enough for the ultra-right-wing Techiya faction (p. 928). In July 1980, one of the party's three Knesset members, Geula Cohen, a fiery Oriental nationalist, submitted a draft law to proclaim united Jerusalem the capital of Israel. From the practical standpoint, the bill would have changed little. For thirteen years, after all, Israeli administration and law had been functioning in East and West Jerusalem alike. But a proclamation of "united" Jerusalem as the capital, once adopted by the Knesset, was tantamount to de jure annexation. It was a step even Begin had not yet dared take, and specifically not in the aftermath of the Camp David frameworks. For the Techiya group, nevertheless, submission of the bill would prod the prime minister into putting his vote where his ideology lay. Would he take the fateful step? No one could be sure, for Begin meanwhile remained inscrutable, even to his closest associates. Thus, as the date for the Knesset vote approached, Washington and Cairo appealed to him not to disrupt the peace process.

In late July, however, Begin announced that he would support the bill, although he would not impose his views on the government coalition, which presumably would vote for the measure only if it perceived a broad consensus. With this shrewd move, he put the ball in the Labor Alignment's court. And it was there, after some confusion, that Peres and his colleagues felt obliged to match the Right in their commitment to the "integrity" of Jerusalem. On July 30, 1980, the bill passed its final reading and became law. The constellation of right-wing parties was exultant. Whatever the prime minister's domestic failures, this was the kind of disdain for the Arab enemy that the nation's Oriental population appreciated. Admittedly, there were consequences elsewhere. All eleven of the foreign embassies then in Jerusalem were promptly moved back to Tel Aviv. An outraged Sadat suspended the autonomy talks. Yet Begin's posture of bemused indifference merely fortified the pride of his nation's underprivileged.

A VISITATION TO OSIRAQ

Could Washington bring the prime minister to heel? The prospects were not good at a time when the two major American political parties still were engaged in their own tough election campaign. Afterward, the new Reagan administration required several months to gain its bearings in international affairs. Its rather inactive Middle East diplomacy evoked different responses, however. Sadat was all but disconsolate at the defeat of Jimmy Carter, fearing the foreclosure of any additional American initiative in the region. Begin, on the other hand, was gratified at least to be emancipated from the pressures of the irascible Carter White House. Indeed, the new president, Ronald Reagan, often had referred to the PLO as a terrorist organization, even as Alexander Haig, his secretary of state, frequently had described the Syrians as Soviet clients.

GREATER JERUSALEM UNDER ISRAELI ADMINISTRATION 1967–1986

——— Municipal boundary, 1947

- - - - UN armistice line, 1949

━━━ Jerusalem city limits unilaterally extended by Israel, June 28, 1967

▨ Built-up areas

al-Birah
Ramallah

ATAROT AIRPORT

WEST BANK
Occupied by Israel

Mount Scopus
(demilitarized Jewish/Arab enclaves)

ISRAEL

Walled City

Jewish Quarter

Former no-man's land

WEST BANK
Occupied by Israel

Bethlehem

0   MILES   2

Yet disillusionment was rapid in both Israel and the United States. As Begin took increasingly drastic measures to strike at the PLO in Lebanon (p. 899), and to thicken Israeli settlements on the West Bank, he provoked wider American criticism. The tension became particularly acute in the summer and autumn of 1981, when the Reagan government agreed to sell a squadron of radar-carrying Advance Warning and Command Systems (AWACS) aircraft to Saudi Arabia. Begin's reaction was reflexive and emphatic. The transaction could place Israel itself under Saudi radar scrutiny, he insisted. Visiting Washington afterward, in September 1981, the prime minister took the unprecedented step of going over Reagan's head to make his case directly before the Senate Foreign Relations Committee. The president was offended. Sternly and publicly, he noted that "it is not the business of other nations to make American foreign policy." At Reagan's initiative, former presidents Nixon, Ford, and Carter declared their support for the AWACS sale to Saudi Arabia, and added their own criticism of Begin's "interference." For the first time, a number of traditionally friendly legislators turned their backs on Israel. The Senate confirmed the sale to Saudi Arabia.

The uncharacteristic eruption of anti-Israel feeling actually had been triggered earlier, on June 7, 1981, by Begin's single most forceful gesture of international defiance since assuming the premiership. The challenge related to Middle Eastern nuclear competition. It is recalled that Israel's involvement in the nuclear game began as far back as 1952, when the Ben-Gurion government established its own atomic energy commission. The program's first fruit was the tiny five-megawatt "swimming pool" research reactor at Nachal Sorek. Its second, in the later 1950s and early 1960s, was a secret Franco-Israeli undertaking to construct a twenty-four-megawatt natural uranium reactor, and an adjacent processing plant, in the northern Negev town of Dimona. Both governments well understood that the facilities were intended specifically for the production of weapons-grade plutonium. Some years later, however, upon Charles de Gaulle's accession to the presidency of France, the relationship with Israel cooled, and in 1964 Paris halted its shipments of natural uranium for the Dimona reactor. No other country was prepared to pick up the slack; for Israel, intent upon maintaining its deterrent edge, had declined to sign the nuclear nonproliferation treaty.

On their own, consequently, and often through devious routes, the Israelis in ensuing years managed to lay their hands on just enough enriched uranium to keep their Dimona processing plant functional. "Operation Plumbat" was an example of that technique. A Belgian Company, Société Générale de Belgique, produced uranium oxide—"yellow cake." SGM's sales, limited to civilian purposes, were tightly monitored by Euratom, the European Atomic Energy Commission. In 1968, however, an Israeli front company, operating out of Germany, secured Euratom's consent to purchase some two hundred tons of the Belgian company's uranium oxide, ostensibly for the manufacture of petrochemicals. Arrangements subsequently were made for the yellow cake to be shipped by boat to Italy for "special processing." In fact the cargo vessel was secretly owned and operated by Israel's Mossad; and once at sea, protected by Israeli gunboats, it brought the yellow cake to Israel. Six months passed before Euratom learned that the uranium oxide had gone astray. With this material, Israel by 1973 had managed to fabricate possibly as many as twelve atomic warheads, together with several nuclear-capable Jericho I rockets, whose strike range encompassed a wide array of Middle Eastern capitals.

Yet it was vital to Israel that none of its Arab neighbors share its nuclear capability. Earlier fears of Egypt as an atomic threat may have been dissipated. By the mid-1970s, however, Iraq's President Saddam Hussein was intent upon becoming the first Arab leader to command a nuclear arsenal. In the fulfillment of that ambition, Saddam was able to rely on cooperation with France. The Giscard d'Estaing government, seeking a wider access to Iraq's vast oil supplies and weapons market, agreed in 1976 to build Saddam two nuclear reactors. Indeed, the French contract also promised delivery of uranium 235 to fuel the two plants. News of the Franco-Iraqi deal soon reached Washington and Jerusalem. Both governments appealed to Paris to reconsider, but without success. Once the final installment of U 235 was shipped, in 1981, Iraq almost certainly would possess sufficient enriched uranium to produce at least nine weapons.

In 1979, meanwhile, President Jimmy Carter allowed Israel access to Middle East intelligence photographs taken by America's phenomenal military satellite, the KH-11. Carter's gesture was no mere act of philanthropy. By then, Israel was sharing with Washington its own highly sophisticated Middle East intelligence, including material on Iran suggesting that the shah would not survive the mounting unrest in his country. For the Israelis, in any case, the KH-11 proved a bonanza. It enabled them to acquire first-generation imagery on their enemies' military installations and equipment, among which was a brilliantly clear photograph of Iraq's new Osiraq nuclear reactor, in Tuwaitah, just outside Baghdad. Indeed, it was specifically this photographic confirmation that induced the Israelis to embark on vigorous new countermeasures to abort Iraq's nuclear development. In April 1979, Mossad agents broke into a French warehouse near Toulon and blew up the uranium-fuel casings stored there for early shipment to Basra. The setback was painful for the Iraqi regime, but not irretrievable. New casings were delivered in the autumn of 1979, followed by the first installments of enriched uranium itself in June 1980. With their Osiraq reactor scheduled to become operational early in 1981, the Iraqis could be expected to move directly into the production of weapons-grade plutonium—and then atomic bombs.

Israeli intelligence was equally aware that Saddam Hussein's Soviet-supplied bombers were nuclear-capable, that nuclear warheads could even be fitted to Iraq's Soviet-built SCUD missiles. If diplomatic intercession with France had repeatedly failed, therefore, and if the Toulon operation had proved of only limited effect, more drastic steps were required. One was taken in June 1980, when Professor Yahia al-Meshed, the Egyptian-born physicist who directed Saddam's nuclear research program, was found mysteriously murdered in his Paris hotel room. Yet, by then, Israel's Prime Minister Begin was contemplating a far more decisive measure. This was aerial bombardment of the Osiraq reactor itself. In December 1980 he discussed the notion with members of his cabinet and with Shimon Peres. Their reaction was less than enthusiastic. Unilateral action might provoke an international diplomatic quarantine, they warned. Nevertheless, within the ministerial defense committee, Begin won out. The date of the operation was set for June 1981. Military preparations began immediately and continued through the winter and spring.

In the meanwhile, François Mitterrand was elected president of France. Ironically, no political figure in Europe counted himself a better friend of the Jews and Israel. During his election campaign, Mitterrand had harshly criticized Giscard d'Estaing's pro-Arab bias. Now, as one of his first presidential acts, Mitterrand instructed his foreign ministry to produce a foolproof plan for limiting the Iraqi reactor exclusively to civilian purposes. The ministry in turn formulated a schedule for spacing out uranium deliveries, to ensure that each shipment would be immediately irradiated—in effect, consumed—by the reactor. Before the plan could be reviewed, however, the Israelis decided the issue themselves.

On June 7, 1981, at 4:00 p.m., eight Israeli F-16 jets took off from their Etzion base in the Sinai. The planes were equipped with extra fuel tanks and special racks that carried two 2,000-pound bombs. Once airborne, the F-16s moved into formation with an escort of six F-14 fighters. Accompanying the squadron were several F-15s equipped with oversize tanks to provide aerial refueling. The trip would cover more than 1,000 miles to the target and back. Any deviation from plan, any battle with enemy fighters, would require additional refueling over enemy territory. Indeed, no more room for error existed here than in the 1976 Entebbe rescue operation. Crossing the Gulf of Aqaba, then, and moving along the northern width of Saudi Arabia and the Jordanian border, the attack group flew in a tightly bunched formation to project the radar "signature" of a large commercial aircraft.

Once into Iraqi air space, the planes sped on past Baghdad and approached Tuwaitah low, to avoid detection. Subsequently, in tactics that had been refined during months of practice in the Sinai, one of the F-15s overflew the Osiraq reactor to draw antiaircraft fire. The F-16s meanwhile had swept up into the sky. With the setting sun behind them, they now dived at the target, sending the bombs hurtling toward the reactor's concrete-and-lead protective dome. The first bombs were fitted with delayed-action fuses, allowing them to penetrate the dome before exploding, opening large holes in the side. The next bombs struck only moments later, finding the holes with "stupefying accuracy," in the words of a French observer, and destroying the reactor inside. Iraqi antiaircraft fire spattered harmlessly. All Israeli planes returned safely.

The air strike's diplomatic repercussions were far-reaching, as Peres and others had warned. Obviously confused, President Reagan at first condoned, then criticized the attack, both in official statements and in support of a UN Security Council resolution of condemnation. A scheduled shipment of F-16 aircraft to Israel was halted. Israeli access to KH-11 satellite photographs was sharply curtailed. In Congress, too, criticism of Israel was unprecedented. When Begin visited Washington later to testify against the AWACS sale before the Senate Foreign Relations Committee, he was vigorously cross-examined. In Riyadh, meanwhile, reaction to Israel's violation of Saudi air space merely underscored the need for effective AWACS radar protection. In Paris, Mitterrand was aggrieved, and quietly informed the Israelis that his ability to plead their case in Europe had been weakened. In Egypt, the ramifications of the bombardment were more calamitous yet (p. 883).

But in Israel itself, news of the aerial strike evoked widespread admiration as a legitimate act of self-defense. When Begin declaimed the stirring credo Never Again, the entire nation evinced a profound, silent relief that the possibility of another Holocaust had been aborted. Moreover, the sheer audacity of the raid, as well as the brilliance of its execution, visibly enhanced the prime minister's standing only days before the Knesset election. Here was the "New Zionism" at the very apogee of its practical fulfillment. Who could doubt now that its current champion was the man for Israel's future?

CHAPTER XXIX REVISIONISM AT THE APOGEE

Notwithstanding Menachem Begin's recent feats of diplomatic and military bravado, by 1981 he appeared increasingly vulnerable on domestic issues. He had failed to carry out the largest part of his 1977 domestic program. Inflation had soared from 40 percent a year at the time of his accession to 100 percent, and appeared certain to go much higher. Following Likud's decision to reduce subsidies for food and public transportation, the number of citizens living below the poverty line had reached one hundred thousand. Early in 1981, moreover, Begin had selected Yoram Avidor as Yigal Hurewitz's replacement as finance minister. A young Likud activist, Avidor possessed commendable intellectual skills but little practical business experience. With Begin's approval, he promptly adopted a disjointed version of supply-side economics, slashing taxes and import duties on a wide range of consumer goods, then pumping the nation's modest hard-currency reserves into the banking system to shore up the value of the Israeli shekel. In the frenzied squandermania that followed, shoppers filled the stores, snapping up television sets, video cameras, and other imported luxury items. Then, on the eve of Passover 1981, the government announced that prices would be cut on a number of basic foods that lately had been removed from subsidy. In effect, these staples would be resubsidized.

The populist orgy was unadulterated economic suicide. Over the short term, however, it achieved a certain political success. Hundreds of thousands of non-European voters were persuaded that they had advanced to a new plateau of income (if not of purchasing power). In any case, economic issues still evoked less resonance among this underclass than did foreign and military affairs—precisely the arena in which Begin reigned as the dominant figure. With his aggressive rhetorical style, his uncompromising insistence on an "undivided Land of Israel," the prime minister appealed uniquely to the Orientals' frustration-rooted chauvinism. Indeed, in the 1981 election campaign, he exploited their ethnic resentments more blatantly than in any earlier election. Appearing before working-class audiences, which greeted him rapturously as "Begin, King of Israel," the prime minister invoked the image of Peres as a "saboteur," of the Ashkenazic-dominated Labor Alignment as "kibbutz millionaires, with their swimming pools and beauty parlors." When Peres in turn sought to address an election rally in Jerusalem, claques of Moroccan rowdies pelted him with tomatoes until he had to withdraw, unable to utter a word. Other

Alignment speakers often encountered the same reception. Their automobiles were overturned, their branch offices vandalized. In his exasperation, Peres described his tormenters as "Khomeinists" and suggested that they return to their own countries. It was not a productive tactic.

Ultimately the Laborites' fundamental political error lay in their concentration on foreign policy rather than on such bread-and-butter issues as inflation, declining real income, and bureaucratic mismanagement. No less than the rightists, Peres and his colleagues dismissed the notion of a Palestinian state or of a redivided Jerusalem. Yet they preferred now to emphasize the need for territorial concessions within the framework of a peace settlement. In its moderation, the approach actually made a perfect target for Begin's fiery sloganeering and withering invective. Neither was Labor's cause helped by the flagrant public dissension between Rabin and Peres (Rabin's newly published memoirs were shot through with bitter recriminations against his rival). As recently as February 1981, the polls had shown Labor winning handily. Four months later, the June 30 election revealed that the Laborites had snatched defeat from the jaws of victory. Although the Alignment actually increased its strength, from 32 to 47 Knesset seats, Likud also gained, raising its own total of seats from (the equivalent of) 43 to 48. It later became clear, in fact, that Likud had added some 375,000 popular votes to its total since the 1977 election, and more than 60 percent of these came from the Oriental communities. With the two principal blocs quite evenly balanced, therefore, the religious parties once again emerged as the fulcrum. The right-wing bloc depended for its one-seat edge specifically on their goodwill (p. 885).

Fortunately for Begin, his camp at least no longer was divided on the issue of Palestine. With Dayan, Weizman, and Yadin gone by then, the new cabinet was in a position to submit an uncompromisingly territorialist statement of principles to the Knesset. The guidelines affirmed Jerusalem's status as "the eternal capital of Israel, indivisible, entirely under Israeli sovereignty," and the "right of the Jewish people to the Land of Israel, an eternal, unassailable right that is intertwined with the right to security and peace." This time no mention was made even of cultural autonomy for the Arab population. In effect, the language was a repudiation of the Camp David framework on Palestine.

RETRIBUTION IN EGYPT

If Israeli moderates were aghast at Begin's reelection and the tactics that had achieved it, the malaise in Egypt was even more profound. Sadat himself was increasingly isolated by then, even in his own country. His promises of "regional peace," and of a "prosperous new epoch," had not yet materialized. Western investors did not appear to be hurrying to the rescue of the floundering Egyptian economy. In its desperation, therefore, the government was soliciting foreign capital on terms that were virtually usurious. The editor Muhammad Heikal later observed that "not since the days of Khedive Ismail had Egypt been the scene of looting on so massive and organized a scale." In turn, many of the nation's political parties reproved Sadat for tolerating widespread corruption in Egyptian

society. His deference to Washington, too, they regarded as sterile and dangerous. By 1980, the president went so far as to allow U.S. bombers to fly missions
out of Egypt's own air force bases at Qena, Cairo West, and Ras Banas. In
November of that year, fourteen hundred American troops, accompanied by
tactical aircraft, joined the Egyptian army in desert training exercises. Egyptians
asked themselves: What had their president gotten for this American connection? Far from exerting pressure on Israel, Washington was emphasizing a
vague Middle Eastern "strategic consensus" against a putative Soviet threat that
hardly was worth taking seriously any longer.

Meanwhile, the Israelis offered even less of substance. Superficially, relations
between the two nations were correct. In October 1980, Israel's President
Yitzchak Navon paid a state visit to Cairo. In December 1980, Egyptian Prime
Minister Mustafa Khalil and Minister of State Butros Butros-Ghali were honored
guests at Israel's Labor party convention in Tel Aviv. On June 4, 1981, Sadat and
Begin held a one-day summit meeting at Sharm es-Sheikh. Only three days later,
however, Israel carried out its bombardment of the Iraqi nuclear reactor. The
timing of the attack was mortifying to Sadat. And so, even more, was the subsequent Israeli election, and Begin's return to power. Nevertheless, intent upon
salvaging the peace process, and fearful of jeopardizing Israel's scheduled departure from Sinai in April 1982, the Egyptian leader met once more with Begin
in Alexandria in late August 1981. There the two men agreed to resume the
autonomy talks the following month, and to expand trade, cultural, and tourist
exchanges. Sadat's forbearance was poignant. Clearly, he was playing for time,
loath to admit that his daring initiative for Middle Eastern peace had foundered.

To compound Sadat's difficulties, by the early 1980s Islamic fundamentalism
was gaining renewed prestige and momentum in Egypt, as elsewhere in the
Moslem world. Indeed, of all the president's critics, none despised his materialism and pro-Westernism so much as did these zealots. Their *qadis* sermonized
against the government's corruption and its "betrayal" of Palestine, against the
"alliance" with the Americans and the Israelis. Recorded on tape cassettes, these
priestly denunciations sold by the thousands. One of the many who listened was
a young army lieutenant, Khaled Ahmad Shawqi al-Islambouli, who belonged to
a secret conventicle of fundamentalists that actually had "condemned" Sadat to
death. In September 1981, moreover, Islambouli learned that he would be
participating in the great Nasser City military parade of October 6, an annual
event commemorating the 1973 Suez Canal crossing. Sadat would be present, as
always. Immediately, then, the young officer prepared to carry out the death
sentence personally. He recruited three other soldiers to his conspiracy. When
the procession of artillery columns finally began that afternoon of October 6,
Islambouli's vehicle was nearest the reviewing stand. Drawing his pistol, the
lieutenant ordered his unsuspecting driver to stop.

It was 1:00 p.m. Sadat was enthroned on the dais. At his right sat Vice
President Hosni Mubarak, amid a galaxy of the nation's most important public
figures. Although security was elaborate, with the president and his entourage
surrounded by eight bodyguards, all heads were craning upward, watching a
display of aerial maneuvers. It was then that Islambouli leaped out of his vehicle
and hurled a grenade at the bleachers. His three comrades also began hurling

grenades and firing automatic rifles. By the time the conspirators were seized, Sadat was dead and many others slain and wounded. Miraculously, Vice President Mubarak remained unscathed.

Egyptian reaction to the assassination was curiously subdued. On the day of the funeral, half a week later, the streets of Cairo remained all but empty. The ceremony in fact was almost exclusively a Western occasion. From the United States, former presidents Carter, Ford, and Nixon attended. Britain sent Prince Charles. From France came President François Mitterrand; from Germany, Chancellor Helmut Schmidt. And from Israel came Menachem Begin, intent on paying respect to his "friend" and "partner in peace." Yet it was significant that only three members of the Arab League were represented—Sudan, Oman, and Somalia. On the day of the shooting, Radio Damascus had exulted openly: "The traitor is dead." In Lebanon and Libya, people had danced in the public squares.

In Egypt, meanwhile, continuity was the watchword. Vice President Mubarak stepped more swiftly and smoothly into Sadat's shoes than Sadat had into Nasser's. In his official statements, Mubarak pledged not to "budge an inch" from his predecessor's commitment to peace. Nevertheless, grave uneasiness remained, both in Washington and Jerusalem. The United States put its Sixth Fleet on alert, and two AWACS planes were dispatched to patrol the Egyptian-Libyan frontier. In Israel, Begin welcomed Mubarak's assurances and expressed confidence that the new Egyptian president was firmly in command. But it was hardly a secret that, if he were not, Israel's impending last-stage withdrawal from Sinai could be postponed indefinitely. Indeed, in the hearts of the Israeli people was the unspoken trepidation that the peace process might already have expired with Sadat himself.

THE RELIGIONISTS CLAIM THEIR PRICE

Following the tight election of June 1981, meanwhile, Menachem Begin was obliged to engage in lengthy horse-trading to achieve his precarious, one-seat Knesset majority. As always, the Orthodox were positioned to extract the largest concessions. During the earlier years of Labor incumbency, it had been understood that religious holidays and kosher food would be maintained in the nation's public institutions, that matters of "personal status" would be left to the rabbinate. Except for these provisions, however, the Orthodox were not prepared to challenge the religion-state status quo directly, not even during "Begin I," from 1977 to 1981. Likud could have sustained its coalition majority without them. Anyway, the National Religious party had not historically been identified with rabid extremism. Its one perceptible shift of stance in recent years was in foreign affairs, specifically on the issue of "Judea and Samaria." Yet it was only a matter of time before the NRP redirected its attention to the domestic sphere, and in the 1981 election that time had come. On the one hand, the party had lost several of its Knesset seats to a dissident Moroccan faction, Tami. On the other, the fundamentalist Agudah was threatening to preempt spokesmanship of the Orthodox cause. For the NRP leaders, therefore, the best hope of credibility within the religious bloc was to match the Agudists step by step in the militance of their demands.

It was a realistic evaluation. As early as Begin's initial election in 1977, the religion-state status quo had suddenly appeared vulnerable, and it was then that even the Agudists joined the government coalition to enlarge their share of patronage. And with Begin's hairbreadth reelection in 1981, the Orthodox moment of ultimate vindication plainly had arrived. Indeed,.the Likud coalition agreement devoted not less than fifty of its eighty-three clauses to commitments on religious matters. Most of these related to such familiar issues as incorporation of Orthodox law in the nation's jurisprudence, additional funds for religious schools, wider military exemptions for Orthodox girls. But now, too, the agreement included an undertaking to ground El Al aircraft on the Sabbath, and to "make every effort to assemble a Knesset majority" for reamending the Law of Return.

This latter was to the Agudists, and now to the NRP, a litmus test of Begin's reliability. The original Knesset amendment under the Meir government accepted the Orthodox definition of a Jew as someone either born to a Jewish mother or formally converted to Judaism (p. 607). Yet this definition rejected the Jewishness not only of Gentile wives (many of them, lately, from the Soviet Union), but of their children, who thenceforth were banned from marriage with other, "authentic," Jews and, eventually, from Jewish burial. The one remaining alternative for the wives and children was conversion. In Israel itself, plainly, conversion could be performed only by Orthodox rabbis. But what of conversions performed abroad? If the ceremonies performed by Conservative or Reform rabbis were disallowed by a new Knesset amendment, Israel risked affronting millions of Diaspora Jews. The Agudists and their NRP partners in fact had always demanded precisely this reamendment; and following the 1981 election, it became their quid pro quo for joining the coalition. In the end, Begin had to accept it. His government platform accordingly promised to seek a Knesset majority for the reamendment. As it happened, that majority did not quite materialize. Labor and the Liberal faction within the Likud bloc turned back every effort to reamend the Law of Return. Nevertheless, formal legislation hardly was necessary. With tacit cabinet approval, if not Knesset action, the ministry of religions chose simply not to recognize as Jews those wives or children who had been converted abroad under non-Orthodox auspices. The chilling import of this medievalism in turn later helped to divert thousands of Soviet Jewish immigrants from Israel to the West.

Neither did the religionists' offensive spare Israel's economy or security. Under Labor, girls from religiously observant families had been allowed to claim exemption from military service, provided they underwent strict investigation of their Orthodox bona fides and contributed an equivalent period of national service to the civilian sector. But as early as Begin's first, 1977 government, girls invoking the religious loophole were obliged to make only a token appearance before a military review committee. The numbers of exemptees consequently rose from 21 percent in 1976 to 32 percent in 1980. Few ever performed alternative service. After the nip-and-tuck 1981 election, moreover, Begin yielded to Orthodox pressures and agreed to end El Al's Sabbath flights to Europe. The company's resulting loss of revenues occurred at a period of grave economic stress for Israel. Indeed, even the poorest elements of Israeli society paid the cost of Orthodoxy's relentless offensive. In 1981, a new Knesset act amended Israel's liberal abortion law, this time disallowing "sociological considerations"—essentially, economic hardship—as a criterion for abortions performed in public hospitals. Although abortions were not barred in private clinics, poorer women had little access to the procedure.

In the end, however, the Orthodox exacted their heaviest ransom in the form of patronage, subsidies, and fiscal and military exemptions. The traditional conduit for this largess was the ministry of religions. It always had been an NRP fief, even under Labor, and its bureaucracy offered a reliable source of employment for several thousand functionaries of the chief and local rabbinates, the religious and kosher-certification councils. Now, in 1982, under Begin, the ministry of religions won a budgetary increase in real terms of of 390 percent! An even more vivid example of Orthodox muscle was the NRP takeover of yet a second ministry, education and culture, a plum that actually went to the religionists upon Begin's initial electoral victory in 1977. Its new minister, Zevulun Hammer, was a founder both of his party's Young Guard faction and of the Gush Emunim (p. 866). With this background, Hammer could scarcely have shocked the nation as he set about enlarging the ministry's budgetary allocations to state religious schools by fully a third between 1977 and 1981. But if 22 percent of Israel's children attended state religious schools, the school network of the ultra-Orthodox Agudat Israel faction comprised barely 6 percent of school-age youngsters. Moreover, Agudist institutions always had been submarginal, their teachers essentially parochial religious instructors who were unfamiliar with secular European culture or languages, or even with the salient facts of Israeli history. No one anticipated that the Agudah would claim a larger share of the budgetary pie. Nevertheless, under Hammer's aegis, the Agudist schools, too, now shared a cornucopia of subsidies that reached 12 percent of the government's total allotment for education and culture.

For that matter, even within the state—nonreligious—school system, Hammer and his colleagues doubled the teaching time allocated for purely Jewish subjects. The reorientation immediately and dramatically warped the quality of Israeli education at all levels, for it was implemented at the expense of conventional instruction in the arts and sciences. And even more invidious was a 15 percent reduction of teaching hours in junior high school and 4 percent in primary schools. In fact, the shrinkage of instructional time was by no means a result simply of pedagogic restructuring. It was a direct consequence, rather, of the government's lavish diversion of educational funds to Agudist and other religious institutions, and of even costlier tax and military exemptions for seminary students and religious teachers. The transformation of cultural priorities in any case soon became baldly evident. In July 1984, Ora Namir, chairperson of the Knesset education committee, reported an alarming drop in basic reading and writing skills at the primary school level, in the quality of technical education at the high school level. During the previous three years, at a time when military equipment was becoming far more complex and sophisticated, 17 percent of new Israeli army recruits could neither read nor write Hebrew. Thus, whatever the short-term political gain for Begin and his Orthodox allies, the longer-range consequences, in Mrs. Namir's dire warning, placed the nation's very security at risk.

THE NATIONALISTS CLAIM THEIR PRICE

On October 9, 1981, the day of Sadat's funeral, Begin and Hosni Mubarak, Sadat's successor, held a forty-minute private conversation. Mubarak pledged his government's enduring commitment to peace. Begin promised that Israel would evacuate the Sinai by the deadline of April 26, 1982. Nevertheless, in the ensuing months, Mubarak regarded the approaching evacuation date with ill-disguised anxiety. As viewed on Egyptian television, the protest demonstrations of Israel's five thousand settlers in the Rafa salient, their final Yamit enclave in the Sinai, were becoming increasingly raucous and militant. In fact, the Yamit colonists were by no means resisting evacuation for ideological reasons alone. Since 1967, they had transformed their corner of the peninsula into a green and prosperous agricultural adjunct of Israel itself. Now they expected appropriate compensation for departure. The Begin cabinet was prepared to offer that compensation; indeed, to raise its initial offer by 20 percent—to nearly $1 billion—a ludicrously high sum. Observers noted that an average Israeli factory worker would have to save all his or her wages for seventy years to match the payoff to a single Sinai evacuee. In any case, for the compact nucleus of Gush Emunim religionists among the settlers, money was irrelevant. They would resist evacuation to the end.

The end came sooner than they anticipated. In a preemptive move on February 26, 1982, Ariel Sharon (now minister of defense) suddenly ordered the army to close off the northern Sinai roads. In ensuing weeks, the military set about evicting hundreds of Yamit dwellers. Most of them offered only nominal resistance, and the largest number eventually departed in a final mass exodus on April 1. Taking up positions on rooftops, however, a small rearguard of settlers hurled burning tires and fusillades of bricks at the unfortunate soldiers. Three weeks passed before the diehards could be removed. So it was, on April 25, fifteen years after the Six-Day War, that the last of the Sinai Peninsula reverted to Egypt.

Between the two countries, only one, seemingly minuscule, territorial dispute persisted. This was the fate of Taba, a six-hundred-square-yard wedge of land just south of Eilat. Both sides invoked frontier maps to support their claims to the enclave. When direct negotiations failed, the matter was reserved for a conciliation committee, and if necessary even for arbitration. Meanwhile, the treaty's other provisions went into effect as scheduled. An Egyptian-Israeli checkpost was opened below Taba, and a Cairo–Tel Aviv bus route was inaugurated in late April. If Egyptian tourism to Israel remained as limited as in the initial aftermath of the peace treaty, several ministerial delegations at least paid dutiful visits. Otherwise, Egyptian-Israeli relations continued superficial, even coldly formal.

Begin's unbudging stance on Palestine was a decisive factor in the chill. But there were others, including the declaration of united Jerusalem as Israel's capital, the saber-rattling over Lebanon (p. 899), even the preemptive strike at the Iraqi nuclear reactor. These and additional displays of ideological and political muscle doubtless were intended as compensation for evacuating the last foothold in Sinai. Thus, in a parallel to de Gaulle's "grandeur," following the abandonment of Algeria, Begin neglected no opportunity, whether speech, interview, or ceremony, to invoke the mystique of a redeemed Land of Israel. What moderating influences were left to restrain him? His government in 1982 was very different from the one that had taken power in 1977. Dayan, Weizman, and Yadin were gone. The ruling quadrumvirate now comprised Begin himself, Defense Minister Ariel Sharon, Foreign Minister Yitzchak Shamir, and General Rafael Eytan, the military chief of staff. Committed hard-liners all, these men in turn were fully supported by the religionists, by the Cherut component within Likud, and by the vast, faceless subculture of poorer, underrecognized Israelis who responded gratefully to displays of national machismo.

As early as December 1981, in fact, anticipating the moment of truth in the Sinai, Begin had offered his nation a particularly grandiloquent gesture of compensation. This one lay in the far north, on the Golan Heights. There the Syrian-Israeli disengagement agreement of May 1974 remained in force, and Damascus continued scrupulously to fulfill its part of the agreement. With quiet reigning along the disengagement lines, Israel was free to settle the Golan, to reinforce and enlarge existing settlements, and to establish new ones. Unlike the West Bank, moreover, the Golan was not an international issue. No Western nation, not even Egypt in the Arab world, was applying pressure on Israel to withdraw from a plateau that was almost universally regarded as a legitimate defense line. In the aftermath of Camp David, to be sure, the six thousand Israeli settlers in this crucial security zone remained uneasy about their future. Thus, in late 1979 and early 1980, they circulated a petition against a future Golan withdrawal, a document that eventually was signed by more than 760,000 citizens, including 70 Knesset members, among them the Labor leaders Peres, Rabin, Allon, and Bar-Lev. Except for the right-wing Techiya party, however, few Israeli politicians spoke in terms of annexation.

Then, in December 1981, much to the astonishment of the Labor opposition, Begin asked the Knesset to approve a bill applying "Israeli law, jurisdiction, and administration" to the Golan Heights. He cited a number of precedents. One was "historic," adverting to a brief period in the distant past when the territory had been inhabited by Jews. More fundamental was the long pre-1967 record of Syrian gunfire and terrorism along the northern frontier. Even following the May 1974 disengagement agreement, insisted the prime minister, Damascus had reverted to its "hostile and belligerent posture." It had forbidden the return of civilians to al-Quneitra, spurned all negotiations with Israel, and declined to accept UN Resolution 338, renouncing force. Worse yet, the Assad regime provided military and political support for guerrilla terrorism against Israel, and against Jewish targets in Europe.

Begin's indictment actually bore little relationship to the current status quo. Once again, he was adopting a compensatory tactic for the impending Sinai withdrawal. Yet the maneuver at least caught the Labor Alignment by surprise, much as had the Jerusalem unification bill. Indeed, flouting all parliamentary rules of three readings, Begin managed to steamroller the bill through the Knesset in a single day, December 14, by a vote of 63 to 21, with 8 Alignment members supporting it. In substance, too, as well as procedure, the Golan Law was of dubious legality. It violated UN Resolutions 242 and 338, which had obliged Israel to negotiate a peace with Syria based on withdrawal from "territories" to secure and recognized boundaries. Indeed, at Camp David, Egypt and Israel had confirmed those resolutions as a basis for peace "not only between Egypt and Israel, but also between Israel and each of its neighbors which is prepared to negotiate peace with Israel on this basis." Accordingly, the damage created by Begin's coup was serious. Egypt now had to endure yet another provocation at the very moment that the Sinai withdrawal was completed. Europe, too, was further alienated. And so, apparently, was the United States.

From the time of his initial election in 1977, one of Begin's idées fixes had been to secure Washington's formal acknowledgment of Israel as a strategic ally in the Cold War. Jimmy Carter plainly would not have offered that sort of open-ended partnership. Yet the new Reagan administration was envisaged as more receptive. Doubtless the contretemps on the AWACS sale to Saudi Arabia had been an inauspicious beginning, and the bombing attack on the Iraqi nuclear reactor further exacerbated relations with the Americans. Nevertheless, Begin persisted in his overtures, and at last, in November 1981, he found his man in Secretary of State Alexander Haig. It was Haig who persuaded Reagan to formalize American-Israeli strategic cooperation in a "Memorandum of Understanding." As he explained to the president, the gesture presumably would placate Israel at a time when the United States and Egypt were conducting joint military maneuvers. In any case, the document was less than portentous. It provided for mutual help in the event of a Soviet-American confrontation in the Middle East. But Israel's modest resources would have limited its own assistance essentially to an exchange of intelligence, a process that already was ongoing. Meanwhile, the Soviets were unlikely to mount the kind of direct attack on Israel that would require an American response. And in the event that the Arabs attacked Israel, the United States was committed to nothing beyond the earlier, less-than-specific assurances it had attached to the 1975 disengagement agreement and the 1979 Egyptian-Israeli peace treaty.

Whatever its questionable value to Israel, however, the "Memorandum of Understanding" was torpedoed by Begin himself on December 14, 1981, when he rushed through the Golan annexation bill. Shocked by the effrontery of the move, Haig and Reagan announced a "temporary suspension" of the agreement—and with it of some $300 million in arms sales to Israel. Here it was Begin's turn to profess outrage. Summoning United States Ambassador Samuel Lewis to his office on December 20, the prime minister heatedly accused Washington of treating Israel like a "banana republic." Barely an hour later, Begin's press officer gave the media a verbatim account of the interview. On the very eve of withdrawal from Sinai, the prime minister once again had projected an image of his nation's pride and sovereign freedom of action.

A BLUEPRINT FOR "PRAGMATIC" SETTLEMENT

By 1981, Israel had acquired direct control of more than 31 percent of the West Bank's physical terrain. Yet the number of Jews who had settled on this land did not exceed eighteen thousand; and, of these, an important element comprised

Gush Emunim ideologues, young men and women who were prepared as a matter of principle to live in remote and isolated settlements in Arab "heartland" areas. The maximalist vision of three hundred thousand Jews in Judea and Samaria plainly would have remained unfulfilled had it depended on religio-nationalism alone. A more pragmatic technique was required. For Ariel Sharon, serving as defense minister in Begin's second government, an alternative approach came logically to mind—one animated by forthright self-interest, by the Israeli people's growing trend toward comfortable suburban living. Henceforth, emphasis should be placed on extending Tel Aviv's and Jerusalem's already substantial metropolitan suburbs beyond the Green Line into the West Bank. At Sharon's initiative, therefore, the government offered West Bank plots to commercial developers and private buyers on terms distinctly more favorable than for comparable properties in Israel proper. Settlers also could feel psychologically assured that they no longer were making their homes in "foreign" territory. After all, Israeli administrative services, even Israeli law, followed and protected them.

This combination of inducements succeeded immediately and dramatically. An example was Ariel (once the Arab village of Haris), a Jewish settlement on the West Bank, and the envisaged Jewish "capital" of Samaria. By 1982 Ariel already had grown to some 350 families, with another 1,650 committed to arrive within two years. Enjoying government guarantees, private contractors now were able to provide mortgage rates so modest that a Jewish family could purchase a four-bedroom villa in the West Bank, on a spacious plot, with well-equipped schools and a stunning view, for the price of a small apartment in a cramped Tel Aviv neighborhood. Like most of Samaria's Jewish settlements, Ariel was essentially a "bedroom" community. The majority of its wage earners commuted each day to Tel Aviv and the coastal plain, a drive of barely forty minutes. Comparable settlements were going up elsewhere in the Samarian massif—in Nofim, within commuting distance of Tel Aviv; and in Ma'aleh Adumim, a ten-minute drive east of Jerusalem. Arriving by the thousands during the early and mid-1980s, Israelis no longer were pioneering in the West Bank. They were simply improving their standard of living.

Yet it was the government itself that eventually had to underwrite the low prices and low-interest mortgages that were virtual giveaways. Between 1977 and 1983 alone, the final bill came to $850 million, a figure that included not only subsidized housing but the construction of schools, roads, sewage, water and electrical facilities, and other infrastructure. Moreover, these civilian expenditures were compounded by the numerous tax exemptions offered companies and individuals doing business in the West Bank and the salaries paid the hundreds of civil servants who dealt mainly with the new communities. Beyond public expenditures, too, individual contractors accounted for yet another $1 billion put into the settlements. With Likud reversing the previous Labor ban on private land purchases, Israeli brokers (and their Arab associates) began scouring the territories for parcels that could be bought and sold later for steep profits. In the end, the speculative frenzy became uncontrollable—and unconscionable. A 1983 state comptroller report confirmed that much of the West Bank land purchased by Jews had been fraudulently obtained from elderly and illiterate

Palestinians. Not a few of the dealers were Likud party insiders, and friends of Sharon. Indeed, Likud even was sending its pitchmen to New York (among them Ehud Olmert, a Knesset member and later mayor of Jerusalem) to promote its West Bank land sales.

By December 1983, no fewer than 103 settlements were operating on the West Bank. Although still encompassing barely 25,000 Jews, they were supplemented by 65,000 Jews who had become residents of the sprawling East Jerusalem neighborhoods. Together, their numbers reached some 100,000, or 10 percent of the territory's entire population (including the Arabs of East Jerusalem). If only the beginning, the nucleus was dense enough to generate the kind of exponential growth Sharon had in mind. In turn, the new suburbanites of the 1980s were nurturing a meaningful economic stake in the West Bank. In integral Israel, each one of the settlers had at least four Israeli relatives to support his foothold in the territories. It was a bloc of voters politically formidable enough to influence the election of ten or twelve Knesset members, possibly sufficient to ensure that any future proposals for withdrawal would face grave legislative difficulty.

CARROT AND STICK IN PALESTINE

Even as the Begin government accelerated its settlements program, the Palestinians groped for their own techniques of resisting incorporation into Greater Israel. Over the years, a literature of protest developed among them, following the lead of such Israeli Arab writers as Salem Jubran, Tawfiq Zayyad, and Mahmud Darwish. In the Jerusalem-Ramallah area, numerous theater groups sprang up, giving performances on stirring nationalist themes before enthusiastic audiences. Palestinian newspapers, too, published avowedly anti-Israel articles and essays. So did three or four new Jerusalem journals, all of them lamenting the harshness of Israeli rule and the absence of a meaningful Palestinian authority.

All of them, too, forthrightly proclaimed their ideological (if not organizational) commitment to Fatah or to other PLO factions. Indeed, by the 1970s, the guerrilla confederation had tightened its grip on the loyalties of tens of thousands of younger Palestinians. Radicals like "Abu Iyad" (Salah Khalef) now spoke for the rank and file of the movement in their undisguised intention—expressed in a resolution of the Fatah congress in June 1981—to "liquidate the Zionist entity." Among local Palestinians, to be sure, advocates of restraint were not lacking. Elias Freij, mayor of Bethlehem, spoke for numerous prominent merchants and other protégés of the former Hashemite administration, those who favored coexistence between Israel and an independent Palestinian state. Yet, in the prevailing atmosphere of PLO intimidation, the public influence of Freij and other moderates was very low.

Intransigence was particularly inflamed among students of the West Bank's six universities. The largest of these institutions was Bir Zeit, located in the Samarian hills. Most of its two thousand students came from the area's refugee camps and smaller villages. By the early 1980s, so frequent were their demonstrations, their stonings of Israeli civilian vehicles and military patrols, that the military

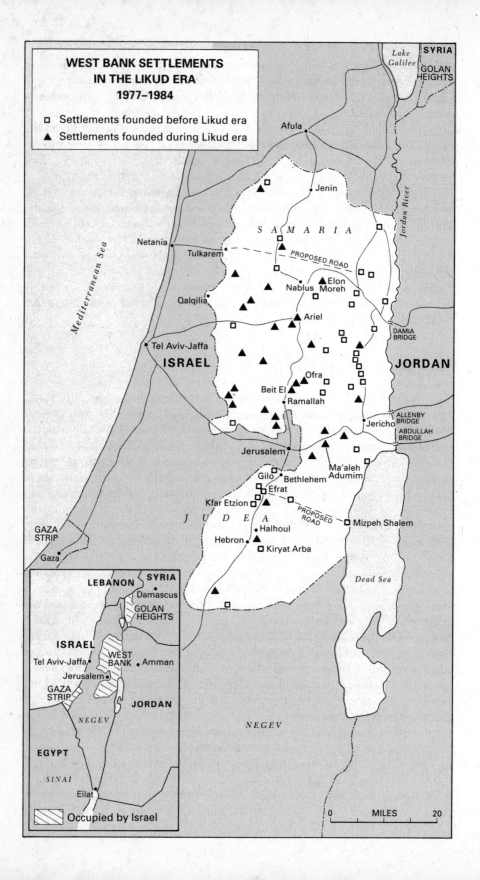

WEST BANK SETTLEMENTS
IN THE LIKUD ERA
1977–1984

□ Settlements founded before Likud era
▲ Settlements founded during Likud era

government periodically closed Bir Zeit for several days or weeks at a time. In early 1982, when Bir Zeit was shut down for an unprecedented two months, a new and substantially more violent series of demonstrations exploded throughout the West Bank. Fifteen Arab students were killed, nearly one hundred were wounded, and several hundred others were arrested. The Begin government was not prepared to deal forbearingly with this unrest. In earlier years, from 1967 to late 1973, Dayan's approach to the territories had been essentially noninterventionist and restrained. Then came the Yom Kippur War, the radicalization of Palestinian youth, and ultimately, with the municipal elections of 1976, the political ascendancy of the PLO. Even during Begin's first term, the military had adopted a hard line with the nationalist mayors, turning down or delaying their budgetary allocations and licenses and harassing them with summonses, interrogations, even house arrests.

From November 1981 on, however, during Begin's second administration, it was Ariel Sharon who set the tone of government policy in the territories. With his authority over the West Bank and Gaza further augmented in his latest incarnation as defense minister, Sharon introduced a new "civilian" administration in Palestine that in effect kept the powers of the former military government intact behind a semantic façade. The defense minister's purpose was twofold. The first was to preempt the Camp David requirement for a civilian entity by organizing a puppet regime of his own. The second was to establish links with a possible alternative—non-PLO—Arab leadership in the West Bank. For the latter objective, Sharon's favored clientele were the "Village Leagues," loose-knit collections of Palestinian farmers and rural schoolteachers that had sprung up during the late 1970s to help modernize their communities. Unlike the PLO, which had developed its links almost exclusively among the volatile and nationalist urban elites, the Village Leagues maintained no ties whatever with the cities or with PLO headquarters in Beirut. Indeed, they tended to be discreetly pro-Hashemite. These facts had caught Sharon's attention, and that of his new "civilian" director, Menachem Milson, a professor of Arabic literature at the Hebrew University.

Milson offered an open purse in his dealings with Village League spokesmen. He provided them with some $15 million in development funds for roads, electricity, water systems, schools, and clinics; assured them priority in employment and housing; and empowered them to issue all building and commercial licenses for their communities. Known PLO supporters, by contrast, were denied these benefits, even such basic necessities as drivers' licenses or travel permits to Jordan during the summer period. Towns and villages functioning under radical leadership soon began experiencing acute budgetary crises. By early 1982, the PLO's grip on the West Bank, while far from broken, appeared at least to be increasingly contested.

In applying his carrot-and-stick policy, however, Milson had assumed that the Jordanian government would approve Israel's efforts to limit PLO influence in the West Bank and to support traditionally pro-Hashemite elements. But that approval was not forthcoming. In March 1982, responding to heavy political pressure from thousands of East Bank Palestinians, Jordan's Prime Minister Mudar Badran signed a decree imposing the death penalty (in absentia) on

Village League activists. With the organization's credibility evidently sabotaged, Milson was then obliged to use the stick alone. Henceforth, if mayors refused cooperation, he dismissed them outright. At his instructions, municipal council-lors and newspaper editors were harassed, arrested, occasionally even deported for "incitement to violence."

Indeed, for Palestinians, no feature of Israeli rule evoked greater terror than the threat of deportation. "Troublemakers" and "inciters" were peremptorily seized by the army, taken to the border, and obliged to walk across. Until 1969, the principal eviction routes were the Allenby and Damiya Bridges over the Jordan River. But when the Hashemite government later refused to accept deportees, Israel shifted the venue north, to the Lebanese border. The practice had come under heavy liberal criticism in the last year of the Rabin government, and accordingly was eased somewhat. Under Begin, however, deportations were resumed and were linked precisely to the scale of Arab unrest.

A FULMINANCE OF JEWISH VIGILANTISM

That scale mounted appreciably following the prime minister's reelection in 1981. Indeed, the accelerating tempo of the settlements program raised Pales-tinian tensions to the boiling point. Hebron was a classic example. The growth of the neighboring Kiryat Arba enclave was not proceeding rapidly enough for its founder, Rabbi Moshe Levinger, and his band of fundamentalists. In 1975 Levinger's American-born wife led a sit-in at the Hadassah building, a Jewish property in the center of Hebron that dated back to the pre-1929 period. Even the Begin government initially regarded the sit-in as provocative. Once again, however, backing down under an avalanche of Orthodox and other rightist protests, the cabinet agreed finally to carry out the reconstruction of Hebron's old Jewish neighborhood, including its abandoned yeshiva. For nearly a year, the town's devoutly Moslem population seethed in frustration. Then, in the spring of 1980, a visiting yeshiva student inadvertently wandered into Hebron's casbah, and was murdered. Hereupon the Jewish settlers of Kiryat Arba raged through Hebron, indiscriminately vandalizing Arab property. When local Arab violence erupted with equal fury, five more Jews were killed and sixteen wounded. The army's own role in the mayhem was to demolish buildings suspected of shielding the Arab ambushers, then to deport Mayor Fahd Qawasmeh and two associates over the Lebanese border. The Jewish zealots meanwhile continued to wreak their own havoc, attacking Arab schoolchildren, stoning Arab houses, uprooting Arab olive trees.

At last, in February 1982, reacting to both Jewish provocations and PLO incitement, the West Bank exploded in a series of local riots unprecedented in fifteen years of Israeli occupation. During the next month and a half, eleven Palestinians were killed, and nearly two hundred wounded. In late March, Mayor Bassam al-Shak'a of Nablus and Mayor Qarim Khalef were dismissed for "inciting demonstrations." Three weeks later, in a concatenation of timing that was as disastrous as the crime itself, Allan Goodman, a recent American immi-grant doing his Israeli army service, went on a crazed rampage at the Temple

Mount, site of the venerated al-Aqsa Mosque. With his automatic rifle, Goodman shot twelve Arabs dead and wounded twelve others before Israeli troops subdued him. In the subsequent convulsion of strikes and protests, two more Arabs were killed and two hundred wounded.

Whatever the need for security measures, the treatment meted out to Arab and Jewish provocateurs was less than balanced. In mid-March 1982, an Arab teenager from the village of Sinjal was shot dead by a neighboring Israeli settler. The Israeli was never brought to trial. On March 24, Israeli civilians at Hebron shot and killed another Arab youth, one of several who had stoned the Israelis' automobiles. No full-scale investigation took place; no one was brought to trial. In late October, another stone-throwing teenager was killed by an Israeli settler. Local police briefly detained the Jew, but he was not brought to trial. During 1982, at least six other Palestinian stone-throwers were shot or stabbed by Israeli civilians, none of whom was held for questioning. Much of the flailing lawlessness could be traced to the settlers' emergent autonomy. Performing their reserve duty in their own villages on a part-time basis, they normally received the benefit of the doubt in matters of "self-defense." Within Israel itself, their political support was far-reaching. And so was their financial support in the United States (pp. 1011–12).

Yet even this mood of right-wing permissiveness was strained by a particularly grisly episode of vigilantism that occurred as early as June 1980. A month before, six Jews had been killed and sixteen wounded in an Arab ambush at Hebron. Now the alleged inciters should be made to pay. Among those marked for retribution were Mayors Bassam al-Shak'a of Nablus, Qarim Khalef of Ramallah, and Ibrahim Tawil of al-Bireh—all outspoken PLO supporters. On the night of June 1, two Jewish settlers from western Samaria drove into Nablus at night and pulled over near Mayor Shak'a's home. Under cover of darkness, they attached a bomb to the mayor's parked car. Early the next morning, Shak'a entered his automobile and turned on the ignition. His legs were blown off. In Ramallah, Mayor Khalef lost a leg from an identical bomb planted in his automobile. Simultaneously, acting on a tip, a Druze bomb-disposal expert of the Israeli defense forces examined the automobile of al-Bireh's Mayor Tawil. Brushing against a trip wire buried in a nearby flower bed, he touched off an explosion and was blinded. That same day, a grenade exploded in the Hebron market, wounding eleven Arabs.

Accusations and counteraccusations followed. Even Prime Minister Begin felt impelled to condemn the maiming of the Arab mayors. Yet, as the months passed, little progress was made in solving the crimes. Senior political officials quietly managed to block the investigation. A more fundamental obstacle, however, was the structural asymmetry of the law. Two legal systems had emerged in the territories, one intended for the Palestinians, the other for Israelis. Claude Klein, professor of jurisprudence at the Hebrew University, compared the West Bank enforcement system to the old American West under the protection of federal troops. "In case of conflict between settlers and native Indians," he asked, "who would the federal troops protect?"

It was not until four years later, in May 1984, that arrests were made for the bomb episodes. Thirty-seven Israelis, most of them Gush Emunim members, together with three senior army officers assigned to the military government, were indicted on charges ranging from attempted murder to membership in a terrorist organization. When the court hearings finally began in mid-June, the Israeli people learned that many of the defendants in fact were implicated in a network of atrocities. Beyond the maiming of the mayors, these included the murder of four Arab students, and a conspiracy, mercifully detected in time, to plant bombs on a number of buses carrying Palestinians to and from Israel during rush hours. On the eve of the trial, President Chaim Herzog, as well as numerous Knesset members, journalists, and academicians, condemned the unfolding revelations as an "unspeakable horror" and a "mortal threat" to the Israeli people.

Yet there were others of comparable eminence who took a divergent view. Addressing the Knesset, Deputy Speaker Meir Cohen-Avidor (Likud) declared: "My heart goes out to the defendants. These boys are the pride of Israel. They are the best." Minister of Science Yuval Ne'eman, chairman of the Techiya party, had refused to condemn the original maiming of the Arab mayors, and remained silent during the trial. And so, in effect, did Yitzchak Shamir, who recently had succeeded Begin as prime minister (p. 934). "It is too early to speak about clemency," was Shamir's only response to questioning on the defendants and their alleged crimes. The defendants were convicted; but none of their sentences was for life imprisonment. President Herzog's premonition manifestly was approaching realization.

Indeed, it was a proleptic vision that applied with equal urgency to the full skein of tensions bedeviling Israel: the Kulturkampf between Orthodox and non-Orthodox, the festering resentments between the nation's Oriental and European sectors, its anguished territorial moderates and the widening nucleus of implacable Jewish ideologues on the West Bank. By the spring of 1982, the nation was undergoing a malaise more profound than at any time since the aftermath of the Yom Kippur War. No one claimed that Israel's existence was yet in peril. Its character as a viable democracy, however, appeared to be approaching the threshold of gravest vulnerability.

IN LEBANON

A ROLLING THUNDER FROM THE NORTH

In early June 1982, Israel's borders were reasonably quiet. Even along the Syrian frontier, not a single episode of truce violation had occurred, either before or since Israel's annexation of the Golan Heights a half year before. The Begin government's attention was transfixed, rather, by tiny Lebanon. It was this smallest and weakest of Israel's neighbors that in recent years had become the principal breeding ground of Arab guerrilla activity. By the mid-1970s, some three hundred thousand Palestinian refugees were impacted here, in circumstances bleaker than anywhere else in the Arab world, except for the Gaza Strip. Neither "foreigners" nor "nationals," these camp dwellers were barred from productive local employment. At best, they were exploited at near-starvation wages as agricultural laborers or as an urban subproletariat. The quarantine in turn evinced Lebanese Christian fear and suspicion of the Palestinians. The nation's Maronite—Greek Catholic—elite, intent upon maintaining its domination of the nation's economy and army, its constitutionally ordained 6–5 numerical advantage in parliament, was well aware that the refugees were virtually all Sunni Moslem. Under no circumstances could they be allowed permanent integration into the demographic landscape.

In their frustrations, then, the Palestinians became fair game for the PLO. From its headquarters in West Beirut, and through a shrewd mixture of revolutionary fervor and economic acumen, the guerrilla confederation tightened its grip on Lebanon's refugee encampments. Yasser Arafat and his colleagues had at their disposal some $400 million in annual subsidies from Saudi Arabia and other Gulf oil states. With these funds, they organized in Lebanon a series of labor, welfare, and other services for their kinsmen, and operated some thirty factories employing ten thousand refugee workers who produced a wide variety of clothing and household goods. In Lebanon, too, the PLO maintained its own network of hospitals and clinics, its own news agency, radio station, and bank and telex services. Altogether, with its rule over the archipelago of refugee shantytowns, the PLO achieved a quasi-governmental autonomy for itself on Lebanese soil.

That status was further augmented by military muscle. In "Fatahland," the rocky wasteland around the foot of Mount Hermon on the borders of Syria and Israel's Upper Galilee, the guerrillas tunneled hundreds of caves as storage space for their growing array of Soviet and Libyan weaponry. In Fatahland, too, they carried out military training with approximately fifteen thousand armed men and planned their incursions into Israel, as well as even farther-ranging operations against Israelis and other Jews abroad. Between 1968 and 1974, some twelve hundred Jews and Arabs were killed and nearly three thousand wounded in these PLO operations. In turn, Israel periodically responded with air and occasional land reprisals. Casualties were by no means limited to PLO targets. The Lebanese government learned early on that it too would be held accountable for PLO violence launched or even plotted from Lebanese territory (pp. 697–8). During those years, Israeli retaliation in forty-four separate attacks killed 890 Lebanese and Palestinian civilians, together with far many more armed PLO guerrillas. Yet, if Palestinian incursions and Israeli counterincursions violated Lebanon's sovereignty and ravaged its citizenry, the undersized Lebanese army was helpless to stop or even to limit PLO violence in the south.

By the mid-1970s, as a result, Lebanon's Maronite leadership recognized that forceful action against the swelling refugee presence no longer could be postponed. Israeli retaliation was painful enough, but even graver was the radical Moslem threat to the nation's delicate sectarian balance. Accordingly, in April 1974, a Maronite "Phalangist" military unit ambushed and killed a busload of Palestinians outside Beirut. When PLO troops laid their own ambush the following day, killing several Christians, fighting spread rapidly to the capital. Groups of Lebanese Moslems then began joining the Palestinians. Soon the violence, widening in scope and savagery, approached the dimensions of a civil war. Its outcome could hardly remain a matter of indifference to the Syrians, who in thirty years had not reconciled themselves to Lebanese independence, and who regarded that nation's Moslem majority as their protégés. In late 1975, therefore, President Hafez al-Assad dispatched to Lebanon several Palestinian brigades that had been trained on Syrian soil. Thereupon the tide of fighting shifted decisively in favor of the Moslems. By year's end, after warfare that had consumed at least seventy thousand lives, Assad agreed to call a halt. Yet he imposed a daunting condition: henceforth, units of the Syrian army would remain in West Beirut and in east-central Lebanon as "peacekeepers"—in effect, as arbiters of Lebanon's public affairs.

From Jerusalem, meanwhile, the Rabin government monitored these developments with much sympathy for Lebanon's Christians. Several thousand of the latter had fled southward, where Israel had allowed them sanctuary, through the northern border town of Metulla. Food, medical care, and even employment were provided them. At the same time, early in 1976, Rabin and his colleagues ensured that President Assad understood their terms for restraint, and the Syrian president had concurred. He would not use his air force against Lebanon's Christians, or interfere with Israeli surveillance flights over southern Lebanon. Neither would Syrian—or Lebanese—forces move south in Lebanon beyond the area east of Tyre. Within that "Red Line" buffer zone, moreover, a Christian militia operated under the command of Major Sa'ad Hadad, a renegade Lebanese officer. With access to Israeli training and equipment, Haddad's militia in effect functioned as an Israeli surrogate against PLO infiltration.

The arrangement worked reasonably well for nearly two years. But in November 1977, in an effort to disrupt Sadat's peace initiative to Israel, the Syrian regime began to relax its control over the Palestinians, allowing guerrillas to infiltrate the Red Line area once more. Thus, early in March 1978, a small group of Syrian-trained fedayeen made their way from Tyre down the Israeli coast by landing craft. Disembarking about forty miles north of Tel Aviv, the Palestinians hijacked a passing interurban bus. Only two miles north of Tel Aviv, finally, the guerrillas were stopped by Israeli troops. In the exchange of fire, thirty-four Israeli civilian passengers were killed, together with the three hijackers. Hereupon Begin authorized a decisive reprisal. In the ensuing "Operation Litani," fully eight thousand Israeli troops crossed into Lebanon. Their mission was to destroy southern Lebanon's guerrilla enclaves once and for all. To that end, the expeditionary force battered through PLO positions south of Tyre. Yet the operation, unfolding cautiously and unimaginatively, proved less than a brilliant success. Few guerrillas were trapped, although scores of Lebanese villagers were killed. In the end, Operation Litani's single, limited achievement was to induce the UN Security Council to assign a three-thousand-man international force— UNIFIL —east of the Red Line zone. Yet even UNIFIL proved incapable of stopping guerrilla rocket launchings from more withdrawn emplacements.

Within three years, moreover, Lebanon's shifting sectarian balance ignited a renewed and even wider-ranging Arab-Israeli confrontation. In March 1981, a Christian Phalangist unit attacked a strategic bridge in the Syrian-dominated Beka'a Valley, inflicting heavy casualties on a Syrian army detachment. Incensed, President Assad rushed in additional troops by helicopter. Yet the use of airborne personnel violated the 1976 agreement with Israel. So later did Assad's reaction when Israeli planes destroyed two of those helicopters. He ordered surface-to-air (SAM) missiles moved into the Beka'a Valley, thereby threatening Israel's right of air surveillance. For the Begin government, the question now was of an appropriate response. At this point, the prime minister was exposed to the forceful influence of General Rafael Eytan, the military chief of staff. A legendary warrior, renowned for his courage and tenacity in blocking Syria's offensive during the Yom Kippur War, Eytan was given respectful attention as he pressed Begin for authority to bomb the SAM missiles. In fact, the prime minister needed little persuasion. Beyond sharing Eytan's distrust of the Syrians, Begin had long acknowledged an Israeli moral obligation to the Christians of Lebanon, whose impending "genocide" he equated with that of European Jewry. He was quite prepared to intercede on their behalf. But at the last moment, in May, President Reagan dispatched a special emissary to the Middle East, Assistant Secretary of State Philip Habib. Shuttling between Jerusalem and Damascus, Habib managed to persuade both governments to exercise restraint.

Then, in July 1981, after a six-week moratorium, Israel renewed its air strikes on PLO strongholds in southern Lebanon. The guerrillas in turn lashed back with a devastating rocket barrage against Naharia, a middle-size northern Israeli town, and its surroundings. Indeed, within hours, civilian activity in Israel's entire western Galilee region was all but paralyzed. Shocked and sobered, the prime minister now welcomed Habib's return. Once again, the American mediator succeeded in arranging a cease-fire. Yet the truce was humiliating for Begin. In restoring the status quo, it allowed the PLO guerrillas to replenish their arsenal and subsequently to build their front-line strength in southern Lebanon to the equivalent of five infantry brigades. Worse yet, Syria was not obliged to remove its SAM missiles from the Beka'a Valley. The ongoing threat to Israel's air force was palpable. For General Eytan, in fact, the evidence was compelling that only a larger-scale military operation could eradicate the danger. Here it was that the possible usefulness of a military partnership with Lebanon's Christian leadership became increasingly persuasive.

The idea was not new. Dayan and Ben-Gurion had explored it seriously as early as 1954 and 1955. At the time, it was rejected by Moshe Sharett, then serving as interim prime minister. Three years later, however, back in office, Ben-Gurion agreed to provide Lebanon's Christian-dominated government with a token gesture of support during a brief Lebanese civil conflict of 1958. The offering was a shipment of five hundred Uzi small arms. Then, seventeen years later, as Lebanon was convulsed by its great new civil war, the Christian-Israeli relationship was decisively revived. In March 1976 "Abu Halil," a spokesman for the Phalange, largest of the Maronite factions, boarded an Israeli missile boat off the Lebanese coast. Carried to Haifa, he met there with Prime Minister Rabin and Foreign Minister Allon. Moslem forces were about to overrun the Maronite-inhabited Mount Lebanon range, Abu Halil explained. Could Israel provide the Christians with some form of emergency aid? Rabin and Allon were sympathetic. Within the week, they dispatched two Israeli intelligence officers to a Lebanese coastal inlet, to meet secretly with Bashir Gemayel, youthful commander of the Phalangist militia and son of "Sheikh" Pierre Gemayel, the Phalangist patriarch.

A month later, Rabin himself sailed up the Lebanese coast, where he held a cordial shipboard meeting with Camille Chamoun, a former president of Lebanon and leader of a second important Maronite faction. Although Rabin tended to prefer Chamoun as a more credible ally than the Gemayels, his interim solution was simply to help both Maronite groups. Thus, during the prime minister's remaining time in office, some $150 million in Israeli weapons and other supplies were turned over to the two Christian militias. Bashir Gemayel, meanwhile, continued to meet periodically with visiting Israeli liaison officers, and even paid two visits of his own to Israel. On each occasion, he exhorted his Israeli contacts to intervene directly against the Syrian garrison in Lebanon. By perseverance and eloquence, the young Phalangist commander eventually began to win over a number of senior Israeli government officials.

In May 1977, moreover, when Likud came to power in Israel, Bashir Gemayel pressed his case even harder. Begin was cautious at first. Indeed, a year later, during Operation Litani, the Phalangists' value as putative allies appeared less than impressive. Most of their "fighters" soon disappeared. Nevertheless, by 1979, Begin was speaking openly of Israel's obligation at least to save Lebanon's Christians from "genocide." At General Eytan's request, then, the prime minister dispatched additional officers and equipment to Lebanon, and nearly one hundred Phalangist officers were accepted for training in Israel. Finally, in December 1980, Begin promised Bashir Gemayel an aerial "umbrella" in the event the Syrians launched a new offensive in Lebanon, and possibly even of additional Israeli steps to protect the Christian minority. It was a fateful blank check.

ARIEL SHARON'S MAILED FIST

Following Israel's Knesset election in June 1981, and Likud's precarious renewal in office, Ariel Sharon was awarded a new portfolio as minister of defense. Thereupon the burly ex-general set about asserting his influence over the nation's foreign and defense policies alike. Indeed, it was Sharon, more than any other Israeli, who transformed Begin's blank check for Lebanon's Christians into a full-blown military scenario. The defense minister's temperament was not one of equivocation, or even of caution. Born Ariel Scheinerman and raised on a moshav, Sharon joined the Haganah while still a teenager, then emerged as a daring company commander in the war of independence. In the 1950s, leading the elite commando Unit 101 against guerrilla infiltration, Sharon launched a series of reprisal raids across Arab borders that often were as brutal as they were audacious. During the 1956 Sinai Campaign, it was similarly Sharon's aggressiveness as a brigade commander that led to the capture of the Mitla Pass, although at heavy cost in casualties. Subsequently, as a division commander in the Six-Day War, Sharon played the decisive role in capturing the formidable Um Cataf redoubt, blasting open the gateway to the Sinai (pp. 641–2). In the postwar years, however, directed to suppress Arab unrest in the occupied Gaza Strip, Sharon resorted to methods of such unprecedented harshness in the treatment of civilians that his shocked superiors pulled him off the job.

By 1973, convinced that his future in the army was blocked, Sharon resigned to venture upon a new career in politics. Yet, within months, before he could so much as test the waters, he was returned to action as a division commander in the Yom Kippur War. Once more, then, Sharon displayed his authentic battlefield genius. It was he who conceived and executed the brilliant countercrossing of the Suez Canal. Characteristically, too, he exercised an independence of judgment and action that often was tantamount to insubordination. Indeed, Sharon made plain his indifference to official procedures, or even to public accountability, in his truculent press conference during the last stages of the fighting. "When I receive an order," he declaimed, "I treat it according to three values: the first, and most important, is the good of the state. . . . The second value is to my subordinates, and the third value is my obligation to my superiors. I wouldn't change the priority of those values in any way." The explicit challenge to military regulations provoked an immediate outcry. Sensing that he had gone too far, Sharon protested that he had been misquoted, and the issue was dropped. Soon afterward he left the army for good.

By then, in his quest for a public role, Sharon was decisively committed to politics as his single best career hope. Thus, after flirting unsuccessfully with both major blocs, he set about organizing his own faction, Shlomzion (p. 836). It won two Knesset seats in the 1977 election, then rejoined the Cherut branch of Likud soon afterward. For this act of allegiance, Sharon at last won a cabinet portfolio, as minister of agriculture in the first Begin government. It was also the post, over the ensuing four years, from which he led the vigorous settlement campaign that tripled the Jewish population in the West Bank. Sharon's efforts reflected cabinet policy, of course. He was distinguished from other ministers essentially by his style, which was characteristically frontal. Once Sharon nearly came to blows with Ezer Weizman. On another occasion, he threatened to "strip naked" Deputy Prime Minister Yigael Yadin. Even Begin was not immune to Sharon's occasional taunts of "cowardice," and for that reason the prime minister denied Sharon the defense portfolio after Weizman's resignation in 1980, preferring to assume it himself. Yet the tempestuous war hero's vast popularity, the rapture with which he was greeted in non-Ashkenazic neighborhoods, was a major asset for Begin's 1981 reelection campaign. Afterward, it was no longer possible to deny him his long-cherished plum, the defense ministry.

Sharon was fifty-three years old in 1981, a graying bear of a man whose massive paunch and lumbering stride were as intimidating as his temperament. Upon taking up his post at the defense ministry, Sharon typically wasted no time in formulating a grand design for Israel's military future. That strategy was based precisely on Sharon's forthright determination to crush the PLO as a military-political force in Lebanon. As he envisaged the initial phase of the campaign, "Operation Peace for the Galilee," the Israeli army would overrun and destroy the PLO quasi-government in Lebanon, thereby alleviating the danger of guerrilla violence against Israel's northern communities and simultaneously shattering Yasser Arafat's influence among the Arabs of Palestine. With the PLO out of the picture, "authentic" spokesmen for the Palestinians might then step forward to negotiate with Israel on the basis of the Camp David accords—as interpreted by the Begin government. That interpretation, of course, was de facto annexation.

The second phase of Sharon's master plan, "Operation Big Pines," was to make Lebanon "an independent state that will live with us in peace." Such a nation required a "responsible" government, the defense minister explained to his close associates. With a Lebanese presidential election impending for September 1982, Sharon had in mind specifically a Maronite-dominated regime under the presidency of Bashir Gemayel. Yet he acknowledged, too, that such a government could not emerge as long as the Palestinian guerrillas controlled southern Lebanon and two-thirds of the city of Beirut, while the Syrians controlled entire sections of eastern Lebanon. Sharon's master plan was characteristically straightforward, therefore, and altogether chilling in its implications. It envisaged the destruction not only of the PLO presence but of Syrian influence in Lebanon. It envisaged a full-scale invasion.

The evidence is uncertain that Begin was privy to every feature of the defense minister's scenario. Nevertheless, the two men unquestionably shared a common appraisal of the Middle East, and operated virtually as alter egos in favoring harsh retaliation for escalating guerrilla attacks on Israel's northern communities. As early as January 1982, therefore, with Begin's approval, Sharon paid a secret visit to Beirut. There he informed Bashir Gemayel that Israel was prepared to dispatch its army to the very outskirts of the Lebanese capital, if the Phalangists themselves would exploit their chance to take over the city. Bashir agreed with alacrity. The next month, Chief of Staff Eytan and a group of senior Israeli officers similarly visited Bashir at the latter's headquarters in East Beirut. They were greeted with a full-scale military parade, even a military band playing

HaTikvah, the Israeli national anthem. Bashir then entreated his guests to launch their invasion soon, for he needed at least three months in a "cleansed" Lebanon to organize his presidential campaign. Eytan in turn outlined his own strategy, including his intention to mount amphibious landings south of Beirut. By the following month, then, operational plans for the offensive were well advanced. Israeli liaison officers repeatedly visited Beirut to coordinate strategy with the Phalange. In the end, the Lebanon expedition would be the most thoroughly prepared campaign in Israel's history.

A key imponderable was the reaction of the United States. Here Begin could not ignore the ill feeling left in the wake of earlier confrontations with the Reagan administration, including the Golan annexation, the AWACS contretemps, and the bombing of the Iraqi nuclear reactor. Yet the prime minister had discerned a certain American acknowledgment of the Syrian threat to Middle East peace. Secretary of State Alexander Haig himself had alluded to that danger in his first visit to Israel in March 1981. The United States–Israel "Memorandum of Understanding," which had been quietly reinstated some months after the Golan annexation, appeared to confirm a tentative mutuality of strategic outlook. In February 1982, therefore, Foreign Minister Yitzchak Shamir arrived in Washington to sound out likely American reaction to an Israeli move against PLO nests in Lebanon. Haig seemed less than discountenanced. If terrorists continued to violate the cease-fire on any front, the secretary of state conceded, a "limited" Israeli reaction in Lebanon would be understandable. Yet Haig also emphasized, in a Washington meeting with Sharon in May, and by letter to Begin the same month, that any Israeli retaliation must be "proportionate . . . to the provocation."

By May 1982, Yasser Arafat was equally well apprised of Israel's preparations. Only the timing of the assault eluded him. The guerrilla leader's own strength was hardly negligible. Beyond the virtual rule his PLO exerted over all of western Lebanon from Beirut south to the "Red Line" buffer zone, the refugee federation's military infrastructure consisted of not less than five infantry brigades, four artillery and support units, a fledgling tank battalion, even the nucleus of a navy at the Syrian port of Latakia. Within the year, too, Arafat expected to triple his artillery strength, from 80 guns to 250. Even with this burgeoning force, however, the PLO leader remained mortally fearful of confronting a full-scale military Israeli assault. On May 15, writing as one resistance veteran to another, Arafat sent Begin a message via Brian Urquhart, a United Nations emissary: "You of all people must understand that it is not necessary to face me on the battlefield. . . . Do not try to break me in Lebanon. You will not succeed." Frozen-faced, Begin read the message, and said nothing.

The catalyst for invasion was provided in an unexpected venue. It was London. On June 3, 1982, the De La Rue Group, a British printing and publishing conglomerate, held a banquet at the Dorchester Hotel. Among the four hundred guests were several ambassadors, including Shlomo Argov of Israel. When the banquet ended, Argov left the hotel about 11:00 p.m. On the street outside, a young Palestinian, Hassan Saïd, removed an automatic weapon from his shoulder bag and fired a single shot from a distance of fifteen feet. Argov was struck in the head and collapsed. The ambassador's Israeli bodyguard then pursued Saïd down an alley, firing his pistol. Wounded, Saïd was seized and confined in a prison hospital. Within hours, police tracked down and arrested three of the assailant's Arab colleagues. A search of their rooms turned up additional quantities of weapons.

In their subsequent trial for attempted murder (Argov survived, but would remain paralyzed), it became clear that three of the defendants belonged to the Palestine National Liberation Movement (PNLM). Far from being connected with Arafat, the PNLM's leader, Sabri al-Banna, alias "Abu Nidal," was bitterly opposed to Arafat's leadership, and even had made periodic attempts on his life. The PNLM in fact was trained by Iraqi intelligence, and its undisguised objective was to provoke the Israelis into an attack on the PLO in Lebanon. Nevertheless, when the Mossad presented this information to Begin, the prime minister declined to reveal it to his cabinet.

The following day, June 4, the Israeli air force launched a massive bombardment of PLO targets in Lebanon, hitting a series of arms depots and military camps the entire distance up to Beirut. The Palestinians' reaction was to launch sporadic shelling of Israel's Upper Galilee settlements, inflicting several casualties and heavy property damage. Hereupon, at an emergency cabinet meeting of June 5, Sharon and Begin insisted that the army must strike immediately to clear a twenty-five-mile strip along the Lebanese border, forcing PLO artillery beyond range of Israel's northern communities once and for all. When several ministers expressed concern that even a limited invasion risked wider involvement, Sharon assured them that the riposte—Operation Peace for the Galilee—would be localized and completed within two or three days. The cabinet then gave its approval. So did Peres and Rabin, when Begin consulted the Labor leaders.

OPERATION PEACE FOR THE GALILEE

Sharon and General Eytan had prepared their strategy with care. At the outset, on June 6, 1982, three Israeli divisions—eighty thousand troops—closed in on the Palestinians from all sides: by a direct advance along the coastal road; by amphibious forces landed between Sidon and Damour; and by a division launched into the central sector through the Shouf Mountains. The unfolding pincer movement was intended to encircle southern Lebanon, cutting off and demolishing the Palestinian forces. At first, too, the operation went according to plan. An initial objective of the coastal advance was Beaufort Castle, a twelve-hundred-foot-high Crusader fortress that for years had served the PLO as a firing platform. Its honeycombed passages and cellars had defied all earlier Israeli attempts to bomb the Palestinians out. But now, with helicopter gunships forcing the guerrillas underground, a company of Israeli commandos climbed directly up the cliff face, moving through the interior labyrinth to ferret out and kill its Arab defenders. By the end of the first day, the Israelis were able to turn the castle over to Major Sa'ad Hadad's Christian militia. Other Israeli infantrymen proceeded toward the key PLO strongholds at Tyre, Nabatiyeh, and Sidon, overrunning the three towns by the end of the second day. Indeed, by the end of the third day, June 8, with overwhelming tactical air support, Eytan's troops had outflanked almost all PLO forces south of Beirut.

As the Israelis drove northward, however, the Syrians dispatched sixteen thousand additional troops of their own to Lebanon, increasing their contingent in the little country to nearly forty thousand. At first, these units remained comparatively inactive; President Assad was not seeking confrontation with Israel. Nevertheless, on the second day of the Israeli operation, Eytan's coastal offensive toward Beirut threatened to link up with the Phalange, and thus to separate the main body of Syrians in the Beka'a Valley from their detachments in the Lebanese capital. Still another Israeli division, commanded by the redoubtable Major General Avigdor Ben-Gal (p. 758), was moving through the Shouf Mountains in an effort to sever the Beirut-Damascus highway, and thus further to divide the two Syrian forces. At this point, President Assad either would have to withdraw his army from Lebanon entirely, as Sharon and Eytan hoped, or would have to fight back.

The issue was forced on the morning of June 7, when Ben-Gal's troops attacked Syrian units at Djezzin, a junction controlling access to the southern Beka'a Valley. It was a costly, full-scale battle, and the Israeli armored column was stopped in its tracks. For Sharon and Eytan, therefore, the single alternative now was a wider, flanking movement into the heart of the Beka'a itself, much nearer the Syrian frontier. Yet in order to achieve air supremacy in this climactic battle, the Israelis would have to strike directly against the SAM-6 missile batteries ensconced in the valley. It was a daunting prospect. Nevertheless, explaining it to the cabinet, Sharon chose not to acknowledge his maximalist purpose of eradicating the Syrian enclave in Lebanon altogether. He stressed only the need to "minimize Israeli casualties" in the Lebanese coastal zone. The cabinet then approved the attack on the missiles.

Syria's SAM-6 batteries, installed in the Beka'a Valley only the year before, were intended to deny Israel aerial supremacy over a natural invasion route into both eastern Lebanon and western Syria. Indeed, to protect that route, the Syrians had nervously fired off the missiles in earlier months whenever Israel's reconnaissance drones intermittently passed over. That was their mistake. In the few seconds between the firing and the destruction of these small, pilotless craft, the drones identified and radioed back to Israel the Syrian radar frequency. Appropriate countermeasures were taken. On June 9, 1982, the Israelis launched their attack. As their waves of fighter-bombers came over, a Hawkeye command plane, crowded with electronic gear, jammed Syrian radar. The SAMs failed to register a single hit—and all nineteen of the missile batteries were destroyed. Almost as costly for the Syrians was the beating taken by their air force. At least 20 percent of all Syrian planes crossing into Lebanese airspace were destroyed or put out of action. Between June 9 and 10 alone, ninety-six of their MiG-25 interceptors were shot down, without a single Israeli loss. By morning of June 11, therefore, the Israeli air force was free to ravage the Syrians on the ground, exacting so heavy a toll on their armor that on June 12 Assad ordered his forces to halt their active fighting in Lebanon.

With or without further Syrian participation, however, the war suddenly appeared much farther-reaching than the Israeli cabinet or people had expected.

So it did to the Great Powers. Fearing direct Soviet intervention on behalf of their Syrian client, President Reagan dispatched an urgent message to Begin on the morning of June 10. Israel's incursion into Lebanon already had far transcended its original announced purpose of liquidating PLO artillery, Reagan noted. He urged the prime minister to accede to a cease-fire immediately. Secretary of State Haig followed with his own telephoned warning. Accordingly, Begin and his ministers devised a qualified acceptance. Israel would agree to a cease-fire by noon the next day, June 11. It was assumed that the deadline would leave enough time to eradicate the PLO infrastructure and to win control of the Beirut-Damascus highway. But there was not enough time. Despite full Israeli air control, Ben-Gal's troops on the central axis were reduced to a snail's pace as they moved their armor through narrow, undulating mountain roads. The Syrians, too, although in retreat, fought vigorous defensive battles at key junctions, inflicting heavy Israeli casualties. Indeed, as Damascus accepted the cease-fire on June 11, its army remained entrenched in fully 25 percent of Lebanon, and in control of two major stretches of the Beirut-Damascus highway.

As Sharon and Eytan assessed the situation, however, there still appeared to be hope of fulfilling the second objective of Operation Peace for the Galilee. This was elimination of the PLO quasi-government in Lebanon. To that end, on June 12, the Israeli commanders launched a sustained air, artillery, and sea bombardment of Palestinian strongholds south and west of Beirut. They also maintained their infantry advance. Yet here, too, the land campaign proved unexpectedly difficult. On the coastal road, the army soon was engaged in a painful, frontal offensive against Kafr Sil, a wealthy suburb in the hills above the Beirut-Damascus highway. Here the local Syrian garrisons waged a furious resistance; for, like the Israelis, they regarded the cease-fire as inapplicable to the Beirut area. The battle of Kafr Sil consequently developed into the single most brutal of the war, continuing for a day and a half. Israel's elite Golani Brigade required prolonged artillery barrages and aerial bombardment to crack the Syrian line. Further inland, Israeli paratroops moved at an agonizing pace toward the final ridge before Beirut. Again, local Syrian forces did the heaviest fighting. Their resistance was overcome only in foot-by-foot combat, until the Israelis finally reached the eastern entrance to the capital on the afternoon of June 13.

By then, the PLO infrastructure south of Beirut had indeed been destroyed. The Syrians had been soundly thrashed, if not altogether eliminated from Lebanon. The Israelis had severed a major stretch of the Beirut-Damascus highway, and had linked up with the Phalangists in East Beirut. Besides knocking out the Syrian air force and missile system, Operation Peace for the Galilee had captured vast quantities of PLO equipment, including 1,320 armored combat vehicles, 144 artillery pieces and rocket launchers, 196 antiaircraft guns, 1,342 antitank weapons, 33,000 small arms, and several thousand tons of ammunition (much of this booty would be sold later to other nations). Begin and Sharon had contended, too, that the destruction of the PLO in southern Lebanon was an act of liberation. The claim was borne out by local Arab reaction to the Israeli invasion, as entire communities of Shi'a Moslems and Christians vied with each other in welcoming Israeli troops, inviting Israeli officers into their homes.

Yet the expedition also had proved a more harrowing psychological ordeal

**"OPERATION PEACE FOR THE GALILEE"
LEBANON, JUNE 6–11, 1982**

⟵ Israeli advances

Cease-fire line | June 12 | June 26

Phalangist Militia

Jounieh

Beirut

Ba'abda
BEIRUT AIRPORT
Kfar Sil
Khaldah
Damour

June 26
Aley Bahmadoun
Ein Sofar
June 8
June 12
Ein Dara

Rayak
Zahle
Shtura

Litani River

B E K A A   V A L L E Y

Mediterranean Sea

L E B A N O N

Awali River
June 7

A. Sultan Yakoub
June 7-8

June 12

BEIRUT-DAMASCUS HIGHWAY

Sidon
June 6

June 7
June 7

Djezzin

June 10
Karoun
Kfar Kook

June 8
June 10
Rashaiya

Zaharani River
June 7

Sarafand

June 6

Nabatiyeh
Beaufort Castle
(Ruins)

Marjayoun
Hasbaiya

June 8

M O U N T   H E R M O N

Litani River

Tyre
Rashidiyeh

June 6
June 6
Metulla

Kiryat Shmonah

SYRIA

Nakura

**GOLAN
HEIGHTS**
occupied
by Israel

G A L I L E E

Naharia

0   MILES   20

ISRAEL

than its military leadership could have anticipated. Thus, one of the army's initial objectives was the Rashidiyeh refugee camp, on the road to Tyre. Of the thirty thousand Palestinians impacted there, many were heavily armed PLO troops, and these resisted fiercely. Even after occupying the surrounding hinterland, the Israelis required nine additional days of concentrated bombing and shelling to subdue Rashidiyeh. Refugee enclaves in Tyre, Sidon, and Damour similarly had to be pounded by artillery and air bombardment. Although Israeli commanders issued repeated loudspeaker-and-leaflet appeals for civilians to flee, the cost in Palestinian dead—PLO fighters and noncombatants alike—was later estimated at more than six thousand. Indeed, soldiers entering these complexes afterward were aghast at the carnage wreaked by the bombardments. For that matter, the Israelis themselves had suffered nearly eight hundred casualties in dead and wounded. Among those killed was Major General Yekutiel Adam, the highest-ranking Israeli officer ever to fall in battle. News of these losses set off tremors of concern in Israel. No one could have predicted that far worse was to come.

OPERATION BIG PINES

After a week of war, Israel's army was in effective occupation of southern Lebanon. Its tanks and artillery surrounded Beirut, trapping at least fifteen thousand Palestinian guerrillas intermingled in the western part of the capital with a half-million local Moslems. Now was the time for Sharon to set in motion Operation Big Pines, the second phase of his carefully guarded master plan for breaking the PLO infrastructure in Beirut itself, and eventually driving the Palestinians and the Syrians out of Lebanon altogether. Once the Lebanese people were emancipated from PLO intimidation, Bashir Gemayel, the Maronite commander, presumably would be free to conduct and win his presidential campaign, then to sign a peace treaty with Israel. By the same token, now was also the moment, under the protection of Israeli air and artillery power, for Gemayel and his father, Sheikh Pierre Gemayel, to honor their part of the bargain, to send their Phalangist militia directly into West Beirut and complete the rout of the PLO.

But here the agreement hung fire. Although the Gemayels had enthusiastically welcomed Israeli paratroops at the entrance to Beirut, both father and son now pleaded the difficulty of attacking fifteen thousand combatants ensconced in the city's maze of streets and buildings. In fact, the danger for the Gemayels was as much political as military. Only two months remained before the scheduled presidential election. There appeared no need, then, in Bashir Gemayel's view, to jeopardize a possible future reconciliation with Lebanon's Moslems by engaging in active combat—even against the Palestinians. He would provide the Israelis with logistical and intelligence support, including the location of key Palestinian installations in West Beirut, but nothing more. In turn, shocked and angered by the Gemayels' "treachery," Sharon and General Eytan now faced a painful choice. The prospect of moving directly into the city and exposing their troops to street fighting was unacceptable. After a few days' hesitation, therefore, Sharon won cabinet approval for an alternative strategy. It was to uproot the PLO guerrilla enclave in Beirut by heavy aerial and artillery bombardment.

In retrospect, Begin may himself have forfeited Israel's psychological leverage during the first week of the campaign, when he publicly assured the Knesset that Israeli troops never would become embroiled in street fighting or in the occupation of a major Arab city. With this insight into his enemy's strategy, therefore, Arafat and his advisers promptly announced their intention of turning West Beirut into a Stalingrad. Presumably the Israelis in turn would quail at the notion of full-scale urban battle. Yet, by the same token, the PLO chairman committed his own psychological lapse. He had seriously underestimated Sharon's willingness to break with Israel's military tradition of short, sharp reprisals, and if necessary to embark upon a war of attrition, if not of direct conquest. Now Arafat would be enlightened. Beginning on June 14, and continuing for the ensuing two months, some four hundred Israeli tanks and one thousand guns poured salvo after salvo into West Beirut. Israel's air force systematically bombed all known PLO strongholds in the western part of the capital. By the end of June, consequently, more than five hundred buildings, shelled and bombed, lay in virtual ruin. Never in their worst nightmares had the PLO leaders imagined the Israelis capable of this kind of warfare.

The pulverizing siege continued. By mid-July, finally, the onslaught became unendurable for the Palestinian guerrillas. Arafat thereupon informed Philip Habib and other Western intermediaries that he was prepared after all to withdraw his men from the city, if appropriate terms and guarantees could be worked out. At first, the PLO leader insisted on retaining an office in Beirut, then on attaching his units to the regular Lebanese army. Begin and Sharon rejected all qualifications. There would be no interruption in the bombardment as long as a single Palestinian fighter remained in the capital. Throughout July, the Israelis tightened the siege. Intermittently, they cut off food, water, and electricity from West Beirut. On August 4, Israeli troops took over Beirut's international airport and then began inching forward ominously toward the city's western suburbs. The air force meanwhile carried out its single heaviest bombing of the campaign—127 sorties in ten hours—while naval vessels offshore joined in the bombardment.

By then, Arafat was completely unnerved, and not only by the Israeli siege. Where would his troops go? Not a single Arab government was prepared to offer them sanctuary. The Syrian and Iraqi regimes needed thousands of PLO troops on their soil as they needed the plague. Jordan's King Hussein had forcefully evicted the Palestinians in 1970–71 and hardly was eager to welcome them back now. It was not until August 10, through Philip Habib's mediation, that Syria's President Assad grudgingly consented to accept a maximum of four thousand PLO combatants. The Hashemite government also relented then, agreeing to accept two thousand. Others of Arafat's men would be dispersed through North Africa, principally in Tunisia. Under the rest of Habib's negotiated blueprint, a multilateral force of French, Italian, and American troops would enter Beirut, simultaneously with PLO and Syrian evacuation from the city; while the Israelis for their part would pull back initially some twenty-eight miles to the Awali River.

In fact, Begin and Sharon would have preferred that the multilateral force arrive only when the PLO evacuation was complete. Under heavy pressure from Washington, however, the Israeli government acquiesced on August 12. Yet, even then, as a signal to Arafat against a last-minute change of plan, Sharon ordered an unprecedented saturation bombing of West Beirut. The havoc continued for nearly a day, and killed at least three hundred people. President Reagan was appalled. "Unless the bombing stops immediately," he warned the Israeli prime minister in a personal telephone call, "I am fearful of grave consequences between our countries." Both government leaders had made their point by then. The bombardment ceased.

THE UGLY ISRAELI

The August 12 saturation attack inflicted a particularly severe blow upon Israel's image in the democratic world. Indeed, from the outset, Operation Peace for the Galilee had evoked serious misgivings. On June 6, a UN Security Council resolution demanded an immediate withdrawal of Israeli forces. In Egypt, the Mubarak government harshly condemned Israel's military operation, then announced that it was suspending its participation in the Palestine autonomy talks and postponing "normalized" relations with Israel altogether, so long as the latter's troops remained in Lebanon. The reaction in other, neutral lands hardly was more congenial. In ensuing days, Western newspaper and television reportage gave a sharply biased account of the war, often accepting PLO figures on Lebanese and Palestinian casualties. Journalists drew portentous analogies between the "genocide" of Beirut and the genocide of the Warsaw Ghetto in World War II. In Britain and France, even in Norway and Holland, there was broad governmental and public condemnation of the Israeli invasion, an attitude Begin in turn characterized as "antisemitism."

Yet the siege of Beirut also evoked concern and confusion within the Diaspora. Although the Jewish communal establishment largely accepted Israel's account of the PLO danger, some of its leaders were torn. As an act of protest, several prominent Anglo-Jewish spokesmen now resigned their offices, including Neville Sandelson, MP, vice-chairman of the British-Israel Friendship Association. From Paris, Pierre Mendès-France joined two other eminent Diaspora figures, Nahum Goldmann and Philip Klutznick of the United States, in an appeal for Israel to end the war and extend recognition to the Palestinians. Officials of several leading American Jewish communal organizations—among them, the American Jewish Committee and the (Reform) Union of American Hebrew Congregations—quietly transmitted their misgivings to Jerusalem.

A parallel shift took place in U.S. government policy. At the outset of the invasion, Secretary of State Haig displayed a certain cautious understanding, regarding Operation Peace for the Galilee as a possibly useful measure to expel all foreign troops from Lebanon. But as the scale of the campaign widened, National Security Adviser William Clark and Secretary of Defense Caspar Weinberger warned President Reagan that support of the Israeli adventure was eroding American credibility among Arab moderates. Thus, when Begin arrived in Washington to visit the president on June 21, 1982, only days before the siege of Beirut began in earnest, he was received coldly. Nor did the prime minister's irascible appearance before the Senate Foreign Relations Committee help his cause. Sharply questioned, reminded of America's unprecedented financial generosity to Israel, Begin snapped back to the senators that the United States could keep its money. Haig monitored these developments with growing chagrin, sensing that Israel was forfeiting its traditional edge in American goodwill.

Eventually, under Philip Habib's "compromise" formula, the evacuation of

PLO troops commenced on August 21. All initially went according to plan. The Palestinian units began their withdrawal precisely as three hundred French legionnaires, the first contingent of the multinational force, disembarked at Beirut. Then, after several more days of bravado, of gun-firing parades and emotional good-byes, and as American and Italian units arrived to join the peacekeeping force, additional Palestinian troops began their departure. They were hooted and jeered by thousands of Christian Lebanese onlookers. A Greek ship carried off the first load, escorted from Beirut harbor by American naval vessels. During the next twelve days, some fourteen thousand Palestinian and Syrian fighters departed the capital, either by sea or overland on the Beirut-Damascus highway. The Israelis in turn were prepared to honor their part of the bargain, to end the siege, to restore water and electricity to West Beirut, and to accelerate their retreat southward. With the largest numbers of guerrillas evacuated, the outlook for peace looked bright enough for the multinational force to carry out its own withdrawal between September 10 and 12. By then the Israelis were confident that Lebanon's newly elected government would manage to establish quiet and order at home, and simultaneously to negotiate a peace treaty with its Jewish neighbor.

THE FAILED GAMBLE

In anticipation of the Lebanese presidential election, scheduled for August 23, 1982, Bashir Gemayel set about mobilizing the required two-thirds parliamentary majority. His task was a challenging one. Numerous Moslem delegates and more than a few Christians remained in opposition. Yet here the Israelis provided Bashir a certain discreet cooperation. In their southern zone of occupation, Israeli officers "advised" Shi'a members of parliament to turn up in Beirut for the election, even supplied a helicopter for one elderly delegate in an isolated Beka'a village. The tactics worked. On August 23, Bashir Gemayel was indeed elected president of Lebanon by a comfortable majority. To the Israelis, it appeared that his government soon would be in a position to follow Egypt's lead to the peace table. "Warmest wishes from the heart on the occasion of your election," read the telegram to Bashir from Jerusalem. "May God be with you, dear friend, in the fulfillment of your great historic mission, for the liberty of Lebanon and its independence. Your friend, Menachem Begin."

In fact, Bashir did not rank a peace agreement at the top of his priorities. His initial objective now was to reestablish ties with all elements of his population—Moslem, Christian, Druze—and then with the surrounding Arab world. Politely, he sought to evade Begin's insistent appeals for an early peace conference. But the Israeli prime minister was unrelenting. On September 1, finally, Bashir agreed to be flown to Naharia in northern Israel for a summit meeting with Begin. There he was kept waiting for two hours in a guest house, until the prime minister and Sharon arrived from Jerusalem. After a few introductory amenities and an exchange of champagne toasts, Begin got down to business. "Where do we stand on the peace treaty?" he asked abruptly. In some embarrassment, Bashir proposed a nonaggression pact as an alternative. The prime minister stiffened. Alluding to Major Sa'ad Hadad, the Christian militia commander in the southern, buffer zone, Begin observed that Hadad at least knew on which side his bread was buttered, that his was an example of cooperation with Israel to be followed. Deeply offended, Bashir countered that, as president, he might well put Hadad on trial for "treason." Soon Bashir and Begin were shouting at each other. Sharon then interjected that Israel had Lebanon in its grasp, and Bashir would be wise to do as he was told. "Put the handcuffs on!" cried the latter, holding out his arms. "I am not your vassal!" The meeting ended abruptly. Returning to Beirut, the young president-elect was furious that Begin had treated him "like a bellboy." Yet he hardly needed the pretext of Begin's peremptoriness. From the outset of Phalangist-Israeli contacts, Bashir had intended to use the Israelis exclusively for his own purposes.

Publicly, nevertheless, Begin continued to express gratification at the "unqualified success" of Israel's "campaign for peace." Earlier, on June 21, during his Washington visit, the prime minister had assured a gathering of American Jewish leaders that "the day is near" when an independent Lebanon would sign a treaty with Israel, thereby linking Egypt, Israel, and Lebanon in a "triangle of peace" with open borders. In a television interview that same month, Begin asserted that Operation Peace for the Galilee had "healed the nation of the trauma of the Yom Kippur War." The evaluation was not entirely far-fetched. As late as the third week of June 1982, polls revealed that 93 percent of the Israeli public considered the military operation justified. Begin and Sharon even enjoyed a substantial increase of popularity.

Yet the illusion of healing was punctured even sooner than Begin's expectation of a friendly neighboring Lebanon. It was among Israeli troops that disenchantment set in most rapidly. Their casualties, numbering some thirteen hundred dead and wounded within the first ten days of fighting, were far heavier than anticipated. Soldiers at the front discerned no logical goal in the offensive as it pushed far beyond the twenty-five-mile line. By the time they reached the suburbs of Beirut, a number of their officers were appalled by the orders they received to make ready for a possible offensive against the city's western, Moslem sector. One of these was Colonel Eli Geva. The son of a distinguished retired general, Geva at thirty-two was the youngest brigade commander in the Israeli army. It was his tank column that would lead any assault on West Beirut. Then, in mid-July, Geva suddenly asked General Eytan to relieve him of his brigade command and allow him to serve as a mere tank officer. Should orders be issued to lead his unit into the city, Geva explained, he could not as "a matter of conscience" expose his troops and Beirut's civilian population to the heavy casualties that were sure to ensue. Shocked by the request, Eytan, then Sharon, and finally Begin himself sought to dissuade Geva, but unsuccessfully. In the end, the prime minister accepted Geva's "resignation." The episode was given widespread publicity in Israel, and evoked deepening reservations about the war altogether.

Among other officers and troops, those misgivings reflected not merely Israeli losses, but the thoroughness of Eytan's "smashup" offensive against Lebanese towns and Palestinian refugee camps alike. "Slowly the reality strikes home," recalled a noncom of the capture of Tyre. "It's not possible we did such devastation! No shop not blasted, buildings crumpled under their roofs, boats sunk in the bay . . . and above all the overwhelming stench . . . of rotting bodies in the village." When a visiting cabinet member, Ya'akov Meridor, arrived in Sidon, his recommendation for dealing with the Palestinian refugees was: "Push them out and don't let them come back." To many reserve officers, Meridor's approach reflected the apathy, even callousness, that infected the military command and government alike. Once on furlough, a number of those officers set about forming a movement, "Soldiers Against Silence," to demand an end to the war altogether. As early as July 3, the Peace Now movement (originally founded in 1978 to protest Begin's foot-dragging on peace negotiations with Egypt), organized a demonstration in Tel Aviv. An estimated one hundred thousand citizens participated. In Israel's history, no such protest ever had been mounted in wartime. Writing in the newspaper *Ma'ariv,* Abba Eban concluded that "these six weeks have been a dark age in the moral history of the Jewish people." Shortly after the July 3 Peace Now rally, to be sure, Likud organized a huge counterdemonstration of its own in Tel Aviv. Some two hundred thousand citizens attended, many bused in from other parts of the country. Addressing the rally, Begin pinned the onus of dissent exclusively on the Labor opposition. Sharon went further. Excoriating Labor for the dissent within the army, the defense minister sought (unsuccessfully) to censor all newspapers that criticized the war.

In the end, it was the outpouring of Jewish compassion for Arabs that Begin and his colleagues were at a loss to understand. Committees to provide food, clothing, and money for the Lebanese victims were springing up in one Israeli city after another. At the outset of the war, the prime minister had characterized Palestinian terrorists as "animals on two legs." Eytan termed Arab demonstrators in the West Bank "drugged roaches." These were not accidental utterances. They had long since become integrated into the terminology of rightist politicians and generals alike. In his numerous public appearances, moreover, Begin strove to place Israel's attacks and raids within the vast context of military horror. If the Israelis had bombed Tyre, what of the Allied bombing of Dresden? If the opposition urged territorial compromise in Palestine, the prime minister invoked the ghost of Neville Chamberlain and Munich. If Israeli television screened footage of a dead Lebanese child, Begin did not hesitate to counter with the 1,500,000 Jewish children sent to the ovens by the Nazis. In turn, Professor Ze'ev Manowitz, an authority on the Holocaust, reacted to these analogies in a published letter to *HaAretz* early in August:

> Are we to understand that the flattened hovels outside Sidon represent the Palestinian Dresden? . . . Begin has lost touch with reality and is pursuing phantoms born in the greatest tragedy that ever befell our people. Whatever its final outcome, the epitaph to be placed upon the war in Lebanon will read: Here lies the international stature and moral integrity of a wonderful people. Died of a false analogy.

SABRA AND SHATILA

On September 14, 1982, Bashir Gemayel turned up at a party branch office for his weekly lecture before a Maronite women's group. As the president-elect began addressing the women, a bomb secretly planted by a pro-Syrian dissident suddenly exploded, demolishing the building and killing dozens of occupants. One of the dead was Bashir himself. The shock registered almost as profoundly among Israel's government leadership as among Lebanon's Maronite community. Thus, the day after Bashir's assassination, a mortified Sharon instructed General Eytan to seize the key junctions commanding West Beirut, then to allow Phalangist militiamen direct entrance into the refugee camps. The order was implemented by the following morning. Sharon himself addressed the Phalangist commanders, assuring them that they were free to destroy all remaining PLO installations and personnel. "I don't want a single one of the terrorists left," he emphasized. The Phalangists needed no encouragement. Virtually all of them had lost family members to PLO fighters. Thus, with Israeli troops protecting their flanks, several hundred of the militiamen proceeded directly into the two largest Palestinian shantytowns, Sabra and Shatila. There they dropped out of sight of Israeli observers.

That same evening of the sixteenth, shortly before the onset of the Jewish New Year, Israel's cabinet met. Sharon, who attended the session, made no reference to Sabra and Shatila. Yet, by then, Israeli intelligence officers watching the camps from nearby roofs picked up snatches of radio conversation among the Christian militiamen. Aware that something was wrong, that indiscriminate violence might be occurring, they relayed their suspicions to army headquarters. After several hours of confusion and delay, General Amir Drori, the northern front commander, issued orders for the Phalangists to be removed from the camps. Through the initiative of several Israeli journalists, Foreign Minister Yitzchak Shamir similarly was alerted to a possible atrocity. He did not bother to investigate. Rather, on the next day, additional Phalangists managed to enter the refugee warrens to participate in the "actions." Thus it was on September 17 that a second day and night of terror settled over the camps' streets and alleys. It was not until the morning of September 18 that Sharon finally visited Sabra and Shatila personally, witnessed the evidence of mass killings, and forthwith ordered all Phalangists out.

On the evening of the eighteenth, the Israeli cabinet met again, this time specifically to inquire into the massacre. They heard Sharon, Eytan, and Drori insist that the Phalangist officers simply had "lost control of their men." Closing ranks, the ministers then issued a statement that an atrocity had been perpetrated by a "Lebanese unit" operating far from Israeli positions. Later Begin allegedly characterized the episode as "Gentiles killing Gentiles." In fact, by September 18, news of the massacre was being reported on foreign radio and television programs. The remains of some 2,300 Palestinian men, women, and children already had been found in Sabra and Shatila, and scores of additional bodies were being disinterred hourly and photographed by foreign newsmen. The Egyptian government, already deeply embarrassed at Begin's offensive into Lebanon, then announced that its ambassador to Israel, Sa'ad Mortara, would remain in Cairo for "consultations." On September 20, the United States, Italy, and France stated that their original multilateral peacekeeping force (p. 911) would return to Beirut within the week.

In Israel itself, a thread of credulity appeared to snap over that Rosh HaShanah weekend, as photographs of the bloodstained corpses appeared on national television. The war thus far had not produced a clear political or military victory. Now apparently it had reduced Israel to the level of its Arab neighbors. Almost immediately, abuse poured in on the government from every sector of the country. The press was nearly unanimous in demanding the resignation of Eytan and Sharon. The Labor Alignment demanded the resignation of the entire government. Even the cabinet's National Religious ministers joined Labor in condemning the horror and pressing for an inquiry. Most decisively of all, the nation's president, Yitzchak Navon, bravely transcended the ceremonial limits of his office by appealing for a "thorough and impartial judicial inquiry" into the massacre, and declaring that he would resign if his demand were not met. On September 24, 1982, a protest demonstration was mounted by Peace Now, by Soldiers Against Silence, and members of the Labor Alignment. From every corner of Israel, no fewer than four hundred thousand citizens poured into Tel Aviv's Municipality Square, overflowing for blocks around. No such explosion of public outrage had ever occurred in Israel's history.

On September 28, deeply shaken, Begin announced that he was appointing a commission of inquiry under the chairmanship of Yitzchak Kahan, president of the supreme court. The three-man panel began its proceedings within days, and over the next weeks took detailed testimony from Israelis and Lebanese, from local and foreign journalists, and from every possible source. Begin himself, as well as Sharon and high military officials, appeared before the panel. (The prime minister's answers to the inquiry were vague: "I don't know. . . . I'm not sure. . . . I don't recollect.") At last, in February 1983, the commission issued its report. While exonerating Begin of the decision to send the Phalangists into the refugee camps, it noted that, for "two days after the prime minister heard about the Phalangist entry, he showed absolutely no interest in their actions in the camps." The Kahan Commission was even more unsparing in its evaluation of Sharon's behavior. "As an official responsible for Israel's security affairs," declared the report, "the defense minister had the duty . . . not to disregard . . . the [possibility] . . . that the Phalangists were liable to commit atrocities."

An equivalent responsibility was imputed to General Eytan, who had concurred with Sharon in allowing the Christian militiamen entrance to Sabra and Shatila, and had ignored later reports of atrocities there. The report observed, too, that Foreign Minister Shamir "erred" in not having bothered to investigate the information when it was conveyed to him. Summarizing its findings, the Kahan Commission then recommended that, at the least, Begin "consider" the advisability of removing Sharon from office. Eytan was spared a similar recommendation only because his term of service was due to end shortly. But the commissioners urged the immediate dismissal of Eytan's generals Yehoshua Saguy, Amir Drori, and Amos Yaron.

Begin's first instinct was to hold fast against dismissing Sharon, who himself refused to budge. Yet even as the cabinet debated the Kahan Report, crowds began gathering outside the prime minister's office, shouting invectives against the government. Nor were they placated by the dismissal of Saguy, Drori, and Yaron, even by the announcement that Eytan would not be reappointed chief of staff. They wanted Sharon out, Shamir out—Begin out. On February 10, 1983, the Peace Now movement organized yet another large demonstration, this one in Jerusalem. Suddenly, a grenade was thrown into the crowd from a group of heckling Likud partisans. Ten marchers were wounded in the blast and one was killed. He was Emil Grunzweig, a thirty-three-year-old kibbutz member and paratroop officer who had fought in Lebanon. Grunzweig's funeral the next day in Haifa, attended by over ten thousand sympathizers, became a scene of even more furious antigovernment recrimination. Finally, after almost a week of widening public indictment, the prime minister's office announced a "compromise": Sharon would step down as defense minister but remain in the cabinet as a minister without portfolio.

By then the nation was polarized more acutely than at any time since the German reparations crisis of 1952. Never before had a war been so debated in purely Jewish—in contrast to Israeli—terms. Begin continued to defend it, and the casualties inflicted on a civilian Arab population, by repeatedly invoking the images and memories of World War II and the Holocaust, by equating the PLO with the Nazis. But the analogies had worn too thin. Characteristic now was an open and widely publicized letter to Begin from a bereaved father who had lost his only son in Lebanon:

> I, remnant of a rabbinical family, only son of my father, a Zionist and Socialist who died a hero's death in the Warsaw Ghetto, survived the Holocaust and settled in our country and served in the army and married and had a son. Now my beloved son is dead because of your war. Thus you have discontinued a Jewish chain of age-old suffering generations which no persecutor had succeeded in severing. The history of our ancient, wise and racked people will judge you and punish you with whips and scorpions, and let my sorrow haunt you when you sleep and when you awaken, and let my grief be the Mark of Cain upon your forehead forever!

ASSAD VETOES AN ACCORD

Bashir Gemayel had not yet been buried when the family patriarch, Sheikh Pierre, announced that Bashir's older brother Amin would seek to assume the murdered president-elect's place. On September 21, 1982, Lebanon's parliament did indeed elect Amin Gemayel president by a solid majority of 77 votes. Yet the thirty-two-year-old Amin was a weak alternative to the late Bashir. Regarded skeptically by Lebanon's welter of religious factions, unable to control even his own Maronite community, Amin was acutely conscious of the need for a consensus, for a more traditional Lebanese political alliance between a Maronite president and the Sunni Moslems of Greater Beirut.

In Jerusalem, meanwhile, as the Kahan Commission still was conducting its hearings, Defense Minister Sharon continued to think in the grandiose terms of Operation Big Pines, of a friendly Lebanese government (even under Amin Gemayel) that would assume responsibility for the security zone in the south, and would sign a final and formal peace treaty with the Jewish state. In mid-November, Sharon personally took his plan to Beirut. In its details, the formula envisaged a staged withdrawal from Lebanon of all forces—Israeli, Syrian, and PLO—with the Palestinians first departing the Beka'a Valley, the Syrians following, and the Israelis pulling back to a line twenty-five miles from their northern border. Each step would be protected by negotiated security arrangements. On the political level, meanwhile, Lebanon and Israel would sign a peace treaty. An Israeli diplomatic mission would be opened in Beirut, a Lebanese mission in Jerusalem, to forge a "normalization of Lebanese-Israeli relations on the basis of open borders."

Amin Gemayel studied the document. Then, early in December 1982, he sent word to Sharon that it was unacceptable. Like his late brother, he rejected any private deal with the Israelis that risked isolation from Lebanon's Moslems or the wider Arab world. Even so, the new president was willing to countenance "high-level" Lebanese-Israeli committee meetings, and these in fact began in January 1983. The Lebanese delegation, including representatives of that nation's various religious communities, was led by Dr. Antoine Fattal, a seasoned Maronite diplomat. David Kimche, director general of Israel's foreign ministry, headed his nation's team. The American emissaries Philip Habib and Morris Draper spelled each other as chairmen. The discussions themselves were held alternately in Khalde, Lebanon, and in Kiryat Shmonah (later in Naharia), Israel. At the outset, the Lebanese took a hard line. They rejected the very notion of a continued Israeli military presence on Lebanese soil, even on a temporary basis, or of Major Sa'ad Hadad's militia functioning as an Israeli surrogate. Neither were they prepared to sign a formal peace treaty. Plainly, the shadow of Syria was hovering over the Lebanese delegation. Syrian troops, after all, continued to maintain their hold on more than a third of Lebanon's territory.

Indeed, in ensuing weeks Damascus successfully maintained its pressure on the Gemayel government to resist any diplomatic or military concessions. Its tactic was to arm the Druze militia in Lebanon's Shouf Mountains. Fiercely independent, the Druze in turn posed a serious threat to Amin's tenuous grip on the Lebanese interior. At the same time, Syria protected its foothold in the Beka'a Valley by enlarging its garrison there to twelve hundred tanks and by accepting (on its own territory) new batteries of Soviet long-range SAM-4 missiles, together with Soviet crews to man them.

Washington recognized the acute danger of revived Middle Eastern hostilities. In late April 1983, therefore, Secretary of State George Shultz visited the region personally, determined to salvage an Israeli-Lebanese agreement through intensive shuttle diplomacy. Remarkably, he appeared to succeed. After several trips between Jerusalem and Beirut, Shultz persuaded the Begin government to abandon its insistence on a formal treaty and to accept the concept of "unofficial" relations. A joint supervisory committee would take the place of ambassadors. Amin Gemayel in turn quietly assured the Israelis that he had President Assad's promise "in writing" to pull all Syrian units out of Lebanon, on condition that the Israelis similarly withdrew. After some hesitation, Begin and his advisers consented.

This was the format that the Israeli and Lebanese delegations signed on May 17, 1983, in separate ceremonies in Khalde and Kiryat Shmonah. If less than a peace treaty, the document at least confirmed that "the state of war between [Lebanon and Israel] had been terminated," and that "the territory of each party will not be used as a base for hostile or terrorist activity against the other party, its territory, or its people." Moreover, an annex on security arrangements accepted Major Haddad's militia as a Lebanese "auxiliary force." The agreement plainly was less than Begin or Sharon had hoped to achieve by Operation Big Pines. Yet it appeared to have salvaged the essence, if not the formal lineaments, of peace.

Even in this limited form, however, the accord was doomed. It was Hafez al-Assad who ensured its demise, rejecting with contempt the very notion of pulling Syrian forces out of Lebanon with or without an identical Israeli commitment. He, the president of Syria, had not been consulted on the document's provisions (notwithstanding Amin Gemayel's assurance to the Israelis), and therefore he was not bound by it. Indeed, far from discerning advantage in a parallel Israeli evacuation, Assad regarded a trip-wire confrontation with his enemy both on the Golan and in Lebanon as politically useful. It helped mobilize Syrian nationalism, and thus diverted internal opposition to his regime. Beyond Syrian opposition, moreover, there was no likelihood that even a Maronite president would have tolerated indefinitely the quasi independence of Sa'ad Haddad's Christian militia in the south. Neither could there be guarantees against a revived PLO infiltration from the north. Sharon's maximalist vision of Operation Big Pines had overreached itself from the outset.

MENACHEM BEGIN'S MOMENT OF TRUTH

Frozen in their tracks now by a concomitant Syrian military emplacement, Israeli troops each day were exposed to the depredations of PLO and Lebanese Moslem snipers. As early as October 1982, when discussions first began with the Amin Gemayel government, 6 Israeli soldiers were killed and 22 wounded in an ambush outside Beirut. Even the Shi'a of the south, who had not initially challenged the Israeli presence, now joined in the attacks. Elsewhere, Druze snipers in the Shouf range also began taking their toll of Israeli personnel. Then, on November 1, an explosion rocked Israel's military headquarters building in Tyre. In the single worst military disaster in Israel's history, 74 soldiers and civilians were killed outright, with another 27 wounded. Altogether, during these first six months of military occupation, Israeli casualties numbered 463 killed and some 2,500 wounded. The losses mounted almost daily.

So, too, did the anguish in Israel. In December 1982 an opinion poll revealed that 41 percent of the public considered the war a mistake. On June 4, 1983, a Peace Now rally in Tel Aviv was attended by 150,000. In their opposition to the war, Israeli reservists increasingly evaded assignment to Lebanon by resorting to such excuses as a pregnant wife or a failing business. The omens for the country were not good. In July, finally, the question of withdrawal was addressed by Sharon's successor as defense minister, Moshe Arens. Normally a Likud stalwart and a hard-liner, even Arens understood that an immobilist posture could not withstand the daily attrition in casualties and public discord. At his initiative, Israeli troops exercised a pullback from the Shouf Mountains to the Awali River. Although unmatched by a reciprocal Syrian withdrawal, the maneuver did not seriously affect the security of Israeli forces.

In Lebanon itself, however, the consequences of the Israeli move were much graver. Druze irregulars in the Shouf now descended upon sixty isolated Maronite villages, slaughtering at least one thousand civilians. The Syrians meanwhile began probing westward from their enclave in the Beka'a. Soon only the religiously fractured Lebanese army and the understrength Phalangist militia remained as a "shield" for Beirut. In effect, protection of Lebanon now devolved mainly on the few hundred American marines and French legionnaires of the emergency multinational force. Yet, as the months passed, the United States, like Israel, discovered that the task of fortifying the Gemayel government was hopeless. Damascus was systematically inciting Lebanon's Moslem and Druze communities, and the marines soon found themselves the targets of snipers. By late August 1983, the American unit guarding Beirut airport came under such intensive fire that President Reagan was obliged to send a naval task force to the Lebanese coast, and even to authorize the battleship *Missouri* to fire its huge guns at Druze positions. The effort availed little. In late October, a suicide bomb killed 241 marines. Thereupon, under congressional pressure, the Reagan administration decided that its rescue effort in Lebanon had failed. In February 1984 the marines were withdrawn (the French had departed weeks earlier), and finis was written to a major American diplomatic and military fiasco.

The Begin government watched these events in dismay. With the disintegration of security in central-southern Lebanon, the daily hemorrhage in Israeli lives was becoming a Chinese water torture. In November 1983, an Israeli checkpoint was blown up by a booby-trapped vehicle, killing an additional 29 soldiers and wounding many others. By then, the cabinet understood that there was no alternative to a full withdrawal from Lebanon, even from the envisaged southern "security zone." Indeed, in this residual buffer area, Major Hadad's modest eighteen-hundred-man Christian militia was running its own daily gauntlet of sniping and casualties. In March 1984, too, Begin's and Sharon's most highly touted ambition for Operation Big Pines went up in smoke. Under Syrian pressure, the Amin Gemayel government formally and officially canceled its May 1983 accord with Israel.

Was the war then an unmitigated disaster for the Jewish nation? Doubtless the campaign provided certain tangible, short-term benefits. It removed PLO rockets from range of the Upper Galilee and destroyed the PLO state-within-a-state in Lebanon, and with it Yasser Arafat's ability to provide day-to-day guidance to his followers in the West Bank and Gaza. Leadership exercised from distant Tunis was a poor substitute for the Beirut operation, after all. Yet the longer-term results of the Lebanon invasion were entirely counterproductive. By spring 1984, more than six hundred Israeli lives had been lost, with three times that many wounded—casualties that exceeded those of the 1956 Sinai campaign. If the PLO infrastructure had been shattered, the war had left Syria's armed forces intact, and significantly more dominant in Lebanon than before the Israeli invasion. Emplaced in fully 35 percent of the little country, the Syrians were investing an immense effort in improving their antiaircraft system. Any future Israeli campaign in central-eastern Lebanon was likely to be far more difficult and costly. Not least, Israel's image throughout the democratic world, a painfully achieved amalgam of heroism and humanism, already had been grievously disfigured among well-meaning Christians and Jews alike.

Even as the mournful costs of the Lebanon expedition were becoming apparent, Menachem Begin was drawing his own conclusions from the recent war. He had been scheduled to visit Washington in July 1983. Suddenly, only a week in advance, he canceled the trip, citing "personal reasons." One of those reasons may have been the death several months earlier of his wife, to whom he had been intensely devoted. But the accumulation of public pressures and criticism almost surely exerted their influence. On August 28, visibly depressed, Begin announced his intention to step down as prime minister, and on September 15 he formally submitted his resignation to the president of the state.

Begin's was a compromised legacy. On the one hand, the peace treaty with Egypt was a magisterial diplomatic and political accomplishment. On the other, the Lebanon war, manifestly intended as the prime minister's compensation for abandonment of the Sinai, had gone all wrong. There were as well other, equally far-reaching charges to be leveled at the Begin incumbency, among them the dissipation of vital hard-currency reserves by artificially sustaining the value of the Israeli shekel, by permitting a squandermania on consumer goods and foreign holidays, and, above all, by heavily subsidizing the Israeli presence in the territories. Nevertheless, until Lebanon, the erosion of Israel's substance at least had not been measured in the lives of young soldiers, in polarized, even shattered, public morale. Indeed, Begin's premiership, like his entire earlier career, was obsessed by need for a free hand in an "undivided Land of Israel." Could the prime minister eventually have exorcised that territorialist fixation—as had Ezer Weizman and Moshe Dayan before him? Would he have dared face the electoral consequences of such a volte-face? Neither in his first nor his second government was there evidence of that kind of incipient moderation.

In the end, however, it was Begin's most egregious failure of perspective that he applied his inflammatory rhetoric not only to the nation's latent chauvinism and to its more-than-latent ethnic tensions, but to an interpretation of the Jewish experience that approached paranoia. In his diplomacy with foreign leaders no less than in his military adventurism, the prime minister adverted endlessly to the trauma of the Holocaust. The memory of that horror unquestionably was locked in Begin's heart. But its tactical application to current issues was shrill, and ultimately fatiguing. Whether it was the authorization to bombard an Iraqi nuclear reactor or a Lebanese village, the denunciation of Yasser Arafat or of Shimon Peres, the martyrological parallels delivered repeatedly to Anwar al-Sadat or to Jimmy Carter—Begin's indiscriminate invocation of the Holocaust may have been his most flagrant transgression. By word and deed, he politicized, and thereby trivialized, the single bitterest chapter in Jewish history.

A CRISIS

OF ISRAELI SPIRIT, OF

DIASPORA LOYALTY

A SOPHISTICATION OF MAJORITY CULTURE

The statistics of the nation's intellectual trajectory mounted impressively with each passing year. Throughout the 1970s and 1980s, Israel's nine institutions of higher learning maintained their growth, offering a steadily widening panoply of courses. Tel Aviv had emerged as a major center of artistic creativity and consumption. Israeli architects, sculptors, and painters were winning clientele, and prizes, from Paris to São Paulo. The country's theater audiences were the largest in the world per capita. So was its publishing industry. In 1986, its 180 firms produced more than ten million copies of 5,300 titles, four-fifths of these in Hebrew. Neither was reader interest limited essentially to "popular" literature. As many as five thousand new poems appeared in print each year, in anthologies, literary magazines, or newspaper weekend supplements. Published collections of such widely admired poets as Yehuda Amichai, Meir Wieseltier, Dahlia Ravikovitch, Natan Zach, Amir Gilboa, and Dan Pagis sold up to five thousand copies a printing, a readership that would have done credit to a nation ten times the size of Israel.

Whether in prose or poetry, the quality of Israeli writing gained steadily in range, diversity, and sheer technical sophistication during the latter twentieth century. Never before had Israeli literature offered such a welter of fictional autobiographies, childhood reconstructions, or stories told through a child's consciousness. David Shachar's Proustian cycle of novels, *Hechal HaKelim HaSh'vurim* (The Palace of Broken Vessels), signaled a breakthrough in this genre of inner narrative. In the 1970s, Yehoshua Kenaz produced his impressive *Rega Muzikali* (Musical Moment), four novellas of childhood and adolescence, and his *Hirhur Lev* (Heart Murmur), employing the inventive interaction of multiple points of view. For a growing number of Israeli authors, focus also shifted to a wider complexity of Diaspora backgrounds and influences. In 1989, the redoubtable poet-novelist A. B. Yehoshua published his most complex novel, *Mar Mani* (Mr. Mani). Consisting of five interior dialogues with an absent interlocutor, and linked by the chronicle of a single family, the stories ranged over some 150 years between eastern and central Europe, the Balkans, and Israel. For other writers, meanwhile, as for Yehoshua, a critical Diaspora influence was the effort to come to terms with the Holocaust. Books by David Schütz, Savyon Liebrecht, Nava Semel, and David Grossman dealt sensitively with the impact of that horror on survivors in Israel.

It was becoming apparent, too, that late-century Israeli literature, for all its diversity and stylistic virtuosity, had returned again to the full-hearted *engagement* of the 1950s. Although transcending that earlier period's naïve political one-dimensionalism, Israel's writers once again were forthright and articulate in their social consciousness. Indeed, theirs was a commitment not limited to writing but expressed in public forums, speeches, political conventions, signed petitions, and newspaper op-ed contributions. As much as any literary figure, Amos Oz managed to blend "modernist" technical sophistication and delicate psychological insights with an unremitting concern for contemporary public issues. Thus, having established his reputation with his initial novels of the 1960s (p. 596), Oz continued to explore his protagonists' conscious and unconscious tensions.

In the process, Oz discerned as a critical source of Israel's anxieties not only the surrounding hinterland of Arab enemies, as in his 1976 *Har HaEtzah HaRa'ah* (The Hill of Evil Counsel), but the hallucinatory vision of a Land of Israel "reborn in blood and fire." It was a danger he explored with rare sensitivity in an uninterrupted effulgence of novels and novellas, among them *Laga'at baMayim, Laga'at baRuach* (Touch the Water, Touch the Wind), in 1973; *Artzot HaTan* (Where the Jackals Howl), in 1981; *Menuchah Nechonah* (A Perfect Peace), in 1982; *Poh v'Sham b'Eretz Yisrael* (In the Land of Israel), in 1983; *Kufsah Sh'chorah* (The Black Box), in 1987; and *Lada'at Ishah* (To Know a Woman), in 1991. Ultimately Oz's works, extensively translated and widely praised in the West, became hardly less than the voice of Israel to the outside world. Among hundreds of thousands of Israelis, meanwhile, he had long since won acceptance as a virtual barometer of their collective conscience.

CONFRONTATION INTO KULTURKAMPF?

No issue touched that conscience more acutely than the burgeoning political aggressiveness of Israel's Orthodox religionists. In the 1949 Knesset elections, it is recalled, all the religious parties united as a single list and won 16 Knesset seats. By the time of the elections of the 1960s, their combined lists reached a numerical peak, 18. The religionists held that figure only intermittently through the ensuing two decades; and, in any case, until 1977 the moderate National Religious party accounted for some two-thirds of the traditionalist bloc. By the time of the 1988 election, however (p. 959), it was significant that the ratio was almost precisely reversed, with the fundamentalist, ultra-Orthodox Agudat Israel and Shas parties garnering some two-thirds of all the religious representation.

Ironically, in the earliest, formative years of Jewish revival in Palestine, no element had played a more self-sacrificing role than the Orthodox. The first Jews to return to the Holy Land in modern times were not the Zionists, after all, but precisely these religionists. Their departure from Eastern Europe in the early 1700s (p. 20), led by a vanguard of fifteen hundred devout families under Rabbi Judah the Chasid, the grim ordeal of their odyssey, the desolation that awaited the survivors among them in the Wilderness of Zin—were painful almost beyond description. A half century later, the largest number of the original Orthodox settlers had perished. Even then, however, their kinsmen did not stop coming, generation after generation. They were not a productive community. They had arrived with only one purpose in mind, to live and die within the shadow of the ancient Temple Wall. Yet neither were they a self-serving element. What, after all, was the life, and the death, of this "sleeping settlement"? Subsisting behind the medieval Turkish battlement of the Old City, they froze in winter, roasted in summer, expired by the hundreds of typhoid and typhus. In peacetime, they were taxed, tyrannized, stoned, and lynched by their Arab neighbors to within an inch of their lives. In wartime, enemy blockade reduced them to the edge of starvation. By 1880, nevertheless, the Orthodox pilgrims constituted the single largest Jewish enclave in Palestine, and, in the city of Jerusalem, the majority of the population altogether. Except for them, conceivably, there would have been no Jewish foothold in the Holy Land at all.

In later decades, to be sure, the growth of an intensely parochial nucleus of *Charedim*—fundamentalists—within Israel's traditionally more moderate and congenial Orthodox minority became a palpable fact of the nation's social and political life. At its basic level, their swelling numbers evinced plain and simple demographic mass. Rejecting birth control, these black-frocked obscurantists (virtually all of them Chasidim) not uncommonly produced families of ten or more. By the 1980s, the Charedim possibly numbered as many as one hundred thousand, most of them concentrated in and around Jerusalem and B'nai Brak. Sheer physical bulk, then, infused their political muscularity, and allowed them to emerge as primus inter pares within the Orthodox spectrum. Yet ideological factors were equally decisive. The Six-Day War was a turning point, for it sparked a growing sense of messianism, and the religionists, moderates and Charedim alike, were the first to embrace the territorialist mysticism inherent in the 1967 triumph. Nevertheless, an even more decisive factor in Orthodoxy's impact on the public scene was Likud's electoral triumph in 1977, and the unprecedented sums Menachem Begin then made available to yeshivot and other Orthodox institutions as a payoff for the religionists' swing vote in his new coalition.

From then on, their appetites whetted, it was specifically the Agudat Israel party and its Charedi constituents that would press even more relentlessly to ensure financial and political support for their self-segregation. Indeed, emerging as virtual senior partners in the Orthodox establishment, the Agudists made clear that they would not accept the dicta of the official chief rabbinate, which for decades had been identified with the more pragmatic National Religious party, but only of their own Council of Torah Sages. Self-coopting, therefore, these seventeen Chasidic rabbis owed no allegiance to anyone or any institution, and on matters of Jewish law it was their pronouncements alone—not the chief rabbinate's—that were binding on their fundamentalist adherents. The Agudists would participate in the Likud-dominated coalition, but only to share in its very tangible patronage and subsidy advantages. Otherwise, the Charedim maintained a world unto themselves, disdaining contact not only with secular Israelis but even with other Orthodox Jews. Compromise with religious pluralism in any form was not for them. Nor was it for Shas, a non-European offshoot of the Agudah that emerged to win a respectable share of the Orthodox vote in the 1984 Knesset elections and afterward. Consisting almost exclusively of North Africans, this faction had long resented the tutelage of the older, Ashkenazic-Chasidic establishment in Agudat Israel, which denied adequate representation or financial support to North African rabbis and their schools and yeshivot. Nevertheless, on issues of religion-state relations, Shas's stance for years remained as implacably right-wing as that of the Ashkenazic fundamentalists.

Charedi obduracy evoked its greatest response, we recall, in Begin's second cabinet, following the hair-thin Likud victory of 1981. It accounted for the harsh new government policy against abortion and autopsies, against recognition of non-Orthodox conversions, whether performed in the Diaspora or in Israel proper. Yet it was the sheer tension of Charedi aggressiveness that increasingly poisoned the day-to-day quality of Israeli life. No group experienced that intimidation more painfully than did Israel's women. In 1978, a Knesset commission finished a two-year study of the condition of women in the Jewish state. Its report was a shocker. Gender inequality still prevailed in the nation's public and vocational life. Notwithstanding decades of favorable legislation, women's average income for identical work remained 20 percent lower than men's. In the years after Golda Meir became prime minister in 1969, only three other women had served in the cabinet. As late as 1988, their Knesset representation was barely 8 percent. Not a single woman served as a mayor or as head of a local council.

In all countries, to be sure, social convention played a role in this anomaly. But in Israel, restrictive attitudes towards women were compounded by religious tradition. Issues of marriage and divorce fell exclusively under the jurisdiction of rabbinical tribunals, and these in turn reflected the endless coercive pressures of the Charedim. In a divorce contest, then, the male held virtually all the advantages. While still married, he could take a new partner and even father children by her, without affecting his legal position vis-à-vis his wife. Yet, if a married woman bore a child by anyone other than her husband, that child was branded a *mamzer* (illicit) and forbidden to marry, except to another mamzer. The offspring of these unions continued to bear the mamzer label for generations (p. 609). Thousands of Jewish women accordingly were subjected to blackmail. Their husbands often would agree to divorce only under oppressive conditions, demanding large sums of money or relinquishment by the wife of all property or even of child-custody rights. More common yet were the thousands of abandoned wives who were denied a rabbinical divorce until their missing husbands could be located—a near-impossibility if their men had absconded to Europe or the Americas.

Even as the Orthodox offensive gained momentum, pressing its claims for military and tax exemptions and for an unprecedented share of the nation's educational budget, it began to adopt a new and more ominous configuration. This was the shift to violence. Thus, in July 1977, Charedim in B'nai Brak's Orthodox enclave strung a chain across a public road to block Sabbath traffic, and a young motorcycle driver, striking the chain, was killed. When police sought to arrest the guilty parties, ten thousand Charedim mounted a wild, rock-throwing protest demonstration. Charedi belligerence was directed even more vehemently at working teams of archaeologists. Ironically, no cultural vocation was more highly esteemed in Israel than archaeology, for none more effectively legitimized the Jews' collective presence in the Holy Land (pp. 588–9). Yet it happened that excavations occasionally disinterred not only ancient Jewish detritus but ancient Jewish grave sites. Here existed still another area of potential confrontation with the fundamentalists.

Thus, in August 1981, as scholars resumed an excavation of Jerusalem's Temple Mount area, Israel's chief rabbis unexpectedly demanded that the entire southern slope of the Temple Mount be closed off as a collective Jewish cemetery. In fact, the demand was too far-fetched even for the National Religious party, and for its two cabinet members, the minister of the interior, Dr. Yosef Burg, and Zevulun Hammer, his colleague at the ministry of education and culture. They rejected it. Whereupon several thousand black-frocked Charedim launched clamorous demonstrations at the site of the excavation, blocking the archaeologists from entering. Agudat Israel's Council of Torah Sages went so far as to perform a kabbalistic black-candle ceremony, "excommunicating" the archaeologists. But several weeks later, the attorney general issued his official opinion that even the presence of an ancient cemetery should not halt an archaeological exploration that promised to be of "major scientific and national importance." The excavations accordingly resumed. So did the mass demonstrations, on an almost daily basis. Police cordons were necessary to guard members of the expedition from violence, until the dig finally was completed in the summer of 1985 (the site is now a major tourist attraction).

Altogether, in the Likud era, Charedi intimidation was emerging as a more palpable fact of life in Jerusalem than at any earlier period. Cultural activities were seriously affected. Theaters offering plays of "questionable" content faced the loss of kashrut licenses for refreshment concessions. Under Orthodox pressure, the city council now banned public (as distinguished from private) theatrical performances of any kind on the Sabbath. Construction plans for a soccer stadium were postponed after Charedi warnings: matches were traditionally held on the Sabbath. Soon, too, "preservation of the Sabbath" became the rationale for wider-scale public disruptions. By the early 1960s, it happened that Mea Sh'arim and others of Jerusalem's Orthodox neighborhoods already were overflowing with humanity. Then, in 1964, the Klausenberger rebbe, leader of yet another fundamentalist sect, arrived in Jerusalem to establish a new, uncrowded Charedi neighborhood that would perpetuate the name—Sanz—of his ancestral Hungarian community. The site he picked was located on the hilly, northern edge of the city. Although "Kiryat Sanz" was launched in 1965 with four hundred families, other ultra-Orthodox subcultures later attached themselves to this nucleus, transforming Kiryat Sanz within ten years into a kind of Charedi Bible belt, a dynamic, militant population of more than fifteen thousand, supporting a dense network of yeshivot, orphanages, and other institutions.

Meanwhile, in the late 1960s and early 1970s, a large non-Orthodox community, Ramot, was quietly growing up some two miles north of Kiryat Sanz. Then, in 1976, the Charedim discovered that a six-lane highway to Ramot was to be constructed precisely below their neighborhoods. Hereupon they warned City Hall that heavy traffic was likely to move down this highway on the Sabbath. Their anguish registered with Jerusalem's mayor, the legendary Teddy Kollek. An astute politician, Kollek had always displayed sensitivity to the Sabbath peace of Jerusalem's Orthodox inhabitants. Indeed, over the years, he had closed Sabbath traffic on approximately twenty streets. This time, however, the city's engineers had ruled unsafe any proposed alternate stretches around Kiryat Sanz. Immediately and reflexively, then, working themselves into hysteria, the Charedim lined the completed stretches of the Ramot thoroughfare, hurling stones, damaging scores of passing vehicles, endangering their drivers. When the police failed to act decisively, the Ramot dwellers organized their own counter-vigilante groups to open the road, even threatening to break into Kiryat Sanz with heavy trucks.

The incidents of threat and counterthreat, intimidation and retaliation, mounted in scope and violence. As in the Orthodox-secular confrontations of earlier decades (p. 600), this one eventually extended beyond Israel itself. In April 1981, an estimated nine thousand of New York City's Satmar Chasidim staged a three-hour protest before the Israeli consulate. Among their placards were some bearing the familiar slogans "Zionism—Enemy of the Jewish People," "Free the Religious Hostages," "Nazi Germany 1939—Zionist Israel 1981." Nearly a thousand policemen were needed to keep order, but the crowd succeeded in disrupting rush-hour traffic in midtown Manhattan. In Jerusalem itself, the crisis was not resolved until Mayor Kollek finally agreed that a new, permanent access road to Ramot would be built (at great expense and strategic inconvenience) to circumvent the Bible belt entirely.

The glowering hatreds and intermittent violence ultimately transcended a mere Kulturkampf. By the 1980s, the fundamentalist assault on Israel's civic values was approaching the threshold of civil strife. Yet those civic values in fact never had been deeply rooted. The concept of minority rights had failed to penetrate the nation's consciousness. What other free people, asked Shulamit Aloni, leader of the Ratz (Citizens' Rights) party, would have accepted with such passivity an Orthodox stranglehold on freedom of religion, on freedom to marry or divorce, or on women's equality?

> Step by step [warned Mrs. Aloni] . . . Israel is being converted from a democratic, humanistic state to an Orthodox, clerical community. . . . Laws with racist and discriminatory overtones are beginning to find their way onto the books, and . . . to become a sort of normative system.

In his lengthy essay *Bein Z'chut l'Z'chut* (Between Right and Right), A. B. Yehoshua traced the course of this envenomed ideological conflict through the asperities of Jewish history. The Jews had lived in exile for two thousand years not for reasons of compulsion, he argued, but by choice. All the explanations they adduced for their Diaspora existence were unconscious rationalizations. If they were inhibited from return, the cause lay in the deep-rooted folk memory of the internecine strife "between the religious and national systems" that had devoured them in antiquity, on the soil of ancient Israel. Terrified of reviving that "central and ceaseless struggle" in the Holy Land, Jews had preferred to remain in exile. So long as they were powerless to impose their will on one another, the issue of religious or national domination could be postponed.

It was only in the twentieth century, Yehoshua continued, that exile and suffering in an incorrigibly hostile Gentile world proved too great a burden. Once that agony reached its climax in the Holocaust, the decisive step finally was taken of returning to statehood. But with statehood, the old religious-secular confrontation inevitably surfaced again:

> Today, for example, the Lubavitcher Rebbe living in New York can only . . . try to persuade Jews . . . not to travel on the Sabbath, to send their children to Jewish schools, to eat kosher meat, etc. But should he come to Israel he would be able, and it would be his religious duty, to compel Jews to follow a religious life. The national framework makes coercion obligatory because it makes it possible.

Indeed, prefigurations of a new "war of the Jews" were already evident. "The national [as distinguished from the religious] component in Jewishness must now be strengthened for the sake of survival," Yehoshua pleaded. The author's cri de coeur was echoed by hundreds of thousands of other Israelis, who shared his awareness of a widening and debilitating lesion in the nation's social landscape.

A BRUTALIZATION OF CIVIC RECTITUDE

A telling insight into Orthodoxy's antipluralism was the climate of xenophobia rampant among the nation's schoolchildren. The phenomenon was particularly vivid during Zevulun Hammer's stewardship of the ministry of education. "There is an alarming spread of hatred for Arabs and a deepening belief that might makes right," declared Ora Namir as she ended her celebrated 1984 Knesset report (p. 886). "Our schools have been thrown wide open to chauvinist and antidemocratic influences." Three years later, a survey completed by Jerusalem's Van Leer Institute confirmed that nearly half the nation's high school students actually would have preferred to reduce the civil rights of Israeli Arabs, even the right to vote in Knesset elections. By then, of course, Charedi as well as other, nonfundamentalist religionists were actively "sacramentalizing" the mood of ethnic chauvinism. Rabbi Zvi Kook, spiritual father of the Gush Emunim, and himself far from the Charedi tradition, had enjoined his followers to adopt an obdurate approach to the Arab nation. "Some argue that there are Arab lands here," he scoffed. "It is all a lie and a fraud!" One of Kook's disciples, Rabbi Israel Ariel, who operated a yeshiva on the West Bank, argued: "the Torah repeats the commandment, 'you shall dispossess all the inhabitants of the land,' and Rashi [a revered talmudic commentator] explains that this means to expel them." Rabbi Eliezer Waldenberg, a noted authority on religious law, declared unequivocally in 1976: "It is forbidden for Gentiles to live in Jerusalem. . . . If we would uphold this [religious lawl] as we should, we would have to expel all non-Jews from Jerusalem and prohibit it absolutely." In 1988 Rabbi Israel Hess, formerly campus rabbi of Bar-Ilan University, argued in a published article: "the day will yet come when we will be called to fulfill the commandment of the divinely ordained war to destroy Amalek"—that is, the Arab enemy. Altogether, by the 1980s, Orthodox spokesmen for the Gush Emunim tended increasingly to equate the Arabs with Amalek, and with Amalek's ordained fate of total destruction.

Yet the notion of "encouraged" Arab departure from the West Bank was hardly less implicit in the political ideology of secular far-rightists. Their most articulate spokesmen were to be found in the Techiya party, a faction that had broken off from Likud in 1979. Techiya's guiding eminence, Dr. Yuval Ne'eman, was neither a fundamentalist zealot nor a racist demagogue. A distinguished physicist, Ne'eman had won international renown in the early 1960s for his discovery of the subatomic omega-minus particle of the atomic nucleus. In those same years, he served as chairman of Israel's atomic energy program, and briefly in the 1970s as rector of Tel Aviv University. Ne'eman's closest associate, Geula Cohen, of Yemenite-Moroccan background, held a master's degree from the Hebrew University, and her fiery nationalist rhetoric belied her estimable record as a civil-libertarian and feminist.

Upon winning three Knesset seats in the 1981 election, therefore, Ne'eman and his Techiya colleagues based their opposition to the Camp David accords and the peace treaty with Egypt exclusively on security concerns, on the danger of Israel reduced to its pre-1967 frontiers. Propounding an undisguisedly annexationist stance, Ne'eman insisted in 1981 that "world opinion [must] begin to understand that the only 'legitimate right' of the Palestinian Arabs is the right to live [as resident aliens] with the Jewish majority in Israel." By the time of the Techiya party conference of 1986, however, Ne'eman and his colleagues went rather further, openly advocating the "transfer" of at least five hundred thousand Palestinian Arabs as an indispensable requirement for any enduring peace agreement. Two years earlier, winning an unexpected five Knesset seats in the 1984 election, Techiya suddenly had arrived as a major force on the Israeli political scene.

Yet Israeli and foreign observers tended to overlook the burgeoning impact of Techiya, and the emergence of smaller, even more brutally expulsionist factions, among them General Rafael Eytan's Tsomet party, and General Rehavam Ze'evi's Moledet party. Their attention was transfixed, rather, by a far more lurid phenomenon. This was the Kach party, founded by an American-born rabbi, Meir Kahane. Ordained in a Brooklyn yeshiva, dismissed afterward from his first and only pulpit, Kahane eventually was taken on as a columnist for the Brooklyn *Jewish Press*. It was during his journalistic period in the 1960s that Kahane organized the Jewish Defense League (JDL) as a "counterterrorist organization," first against local black gangs that harassed several of New York's poor Jewish neighborhoods, then against Soviet diplomats in New York. In 1972, facing the likelihood of federal prosecution for conspiracy to commit violence, Kahane expediently moved to Israel. There, two years later, he founded his truculent Kach party.

The name, signifying "By Force," was taken from the motto of Begin's prestate Etzel underground group, and its program, as outlined in the Knesset election campaign of 1981, was to expel the Arabs from the "Land of Israel," that is, both from the State of Israel and from Judea and Samaria. A typical Kahane speech declared:

The Arabs are cancer, cancer, cancer in the midst of us. . . . I am telling you what each of you thinks deep in his heart. There is only one solution, no other, no partial solution: the Arabs are out! out! Do not ask me how. . . . Let me become defense minister for two months and you will not have a single cockroach around here!

Lest there were any doubt of his fixity of purpose, Kahane organized threatening marches upon Arab towns in Israel. The police invariably were waiting to block a confrontation, and Kahane was periodically arrested, once sentenced to nine months' imprisonment. In 1981 his initial bid for a Knesset seat failed. But the man had long since achieved his goal of national publicity.

Indeed, Kahane's demagoguery swiftly evoked resonance well beyond his party's initial hard core of non-European proletarians and West Bank Orthodox vigilantes. So too did his campaign tactics in 1984, surpassing even the rabble-rousing of 1981. Amnon Rubinstein of the moderate Shinui party, seeking to address an audience in Petach Tikvah, was obliged to run a verbal gauntlet of Kahane's yellow-shirted Kach followers and finally to take refuge behind the barricaded doors of his party office. In Tiberias, Labor's Shimon Peres was physically attacked by Kach partisans and had to be spirited away by the police. And when the election finally took place, Kach received 26,000 votes, more than enough this time to assure Meir Kahane himself a seat. It was a traumatic moment of self-recognition. Appalled, Israel's President Chaim Herzog refused to include Kahane in the traditional ceremonial reception for designated members of the Knesset. In 1985, moreover, the Knesset enacted a bill disqualifying Kach or any other party whose platform advocated "incitement to racism" (Likud grudgingly supported the bill, principally because Kach had eaten into its own constituency). Yet by then the world press had devoted an inordinate amount of space to Kach, its hooliganism and growing public support. Characteristically, the phenomenon was described as the ultimate "legitimization of bigotry in Israel."

If it was that, it also represented another, more invidious threat. Attracting public attention with his demagoguery, his flagrant appeals to racism and mob intimidation, and his eventual 1984 electoral success, Meir Kahane filled an entirely unintentional role. It was that of a diversion from the Techiya party's much larger delegation of five Knesset members. Had Professor Yuval Ne'eman and his comparatively well-mannered associates personally charted this bizarre electoral juxtaposition, they could not have been more effective. The image they projected, in common with that of numerous Gush Emunim religious spokesmen, surely was the opposite of moderation. By contrast to Kahane, however, it appeared to the Israeli public at least to be one of civility.

A WANING OF DIASPORA PATIENCE

Throughout the 1970s and 1980s, Diaspora Jewry witnessed the convulsions in Israel's domestic and diplomatic scene with growing misgivings. Of particular discomfiture to America's "mainstream" Jews was the fundamentalism of Israel's rabbinate, which blocked every effort by Western Reform and Conservative Jews to achieve legal equality for their programs in Israel. Defining its opposition as a matter of "ideological principle," the rabbinate was not uninfluenced by its monopoly of such extensive financial perquisites as marriage, divorce, burial, and kashrut supervision. As a matter of "ideological principle," then, the religious establishment for years intimidated municipal governments into denying Reform and Conservative Jews access to local facilities even for prayer and study sessions. For the while, nonetheless, in the United States and elsewhere, the Jewish (non-Orthodox) majority tended by and large to mute its criticism rather than tarnish Israel's public image.

Yet, by the late 1970s and early 1980s, American Jewish resentments no longer could be disguised. By then, too, they focused increasingly on Israel's settlements policy on the West Bank. In 1977, Nahum Goldmann, the veteran Zionist leader, called on President Jimmy Carter to urge resistance to Menachem Begin's aggressive annexationism, a policy Goldmann regarded as suicidal for Israel. Subsequently, other American Jewish eminences echoed Goldmann's concern, among them Philip Klutznick, the former B'nai B'rith president and now also a Jewish elder statesman, and Marie Syrkin, the Labor Zionist writer and editor, whose 1980 collection of essays, *The State of the Jews,* made plain her revulsion at Begin's "betrayal of the Zionist dream." The calamitous Lebanon invasion of June 1982, and its attendant Sabra and Shatila massacres, further exacerbated Diaspora Jewish reservations. Following an emergency visit to Israel, Rabbi Alexander Schindler, a leader of Reform Judaism and chairman of the Jewish Presidents Conference, acknowledged to *New York* magazine that "[American Jews] have crossed a watershed now, and our open criticism will . . . increase." It did. Bertram Gold, executive vice president of the American Jewish Committee, wondered why it was "more important to provide funds for higher education in Israel than . . . for Jewish education in the United States." Daniel Elazar, a Temple University political scientist who spent half his career teaching and writing in Israel, now described the centrality of Israel in American Jewish life as "Israelotry." Rabbi Joachim Prinz, a former president of the American Jewish Congress, warned that American Jewry's fixation with Israel was eroding spiritual Judaism in the United States.

A REAPPRAISAL OF LOYALTIES

Gestating and even spilling over periodically through the 1980s, Diaspora restiveness finally exploded into outraged protest at mid-decade. The crisis began in November 1985 with the arrest in Washington, D.C., of Jonathan Jay Pollard, a thirty-one-year-old Jewish civilian employee of the United States Naval Intelligence Service. Reared in a staunchly Zionist family, Pollard had undergone a painful childhood in South Bend, Indiana, as a bespectacled, unathletic youth, the victim of bullying and goading. Possibly his need for compensation intensified during his university years at Stanford and Tufts, and in his subsequent career as an intelligence research analyst for the navy in suburban Washington, D.C. While performing that research, too, poring over classified data, Pollard became concerned that the United States government was not honoring its intelligence exchange agreement with Israel (p. 889). "I watched the threats to Israel's security grow," he testified later, "and gradually came to the conclusion that I had to do something."

The chance "to do something" arose in May 1985, when Pollard arranged to meet with Colonel Aviem Sella, an Israeli air force hero who had arrived in Washington to speak for the Israel Bonds campaign. During their conversation, the young American offered to transmit vital intelligence data to Israel. Sella in turn relayed the offer to LAKAM, Israel's Office of Scientific Liaison. LAKAM's director, Rafael Eitan, was an ex-Mossad operative whose cloak-and-dagger exploits, including the kidnapping of Adolf Eichmann, had made him the model for "Marty Kurtz" in John Le Carré's novel *The Little Drummer Girl.* Normally a man of Eitan's experience would have rejected Jonathan Pollard's offer. Israeli intelligence had made it a point never to recruit an American Jew to spy against his own country. But Eitan's interest here was not in proprietary United States military intelligence but exclusively in Washington's information on Arab and Soviet capabilities. From the outset, this was also Pollard's understanding.

During the ensuing year, therefore, Pollard transmitted "relevant" information to Sella, via the office of Israel's scientific attaché in Washington. The material included estimates, graphs, satellite photographs, and other vital details on Middle East weapons systems, among them the location of Syrian SAM batteries and of Iraqi nuclear test sites and chemical warfare production-and-storage facilities. It also contained data on Israel's "outer ring" of enemies— Saudi Arabia, Libya, Tunisia—including the location of PLO headquarters in Tunis, a villa that Israel later destroyed in a retaliatory bombing raid (p. 962). Washington doubtless could have released much of this information to Israel, so long as parts of it were censored to protect the sources and methods used. Failing to block out any of the documents, however, Pollard unintentionally compromised a number of key United States intelligence services.

On the instructions of LAKAM's Rafael Eitan, meanwhile, Colonel Sella proceeded to follow a venerated espionage tradition. He "corrupted" Pollard by providing him with monthly cash payments. Impetuously, Pollard then began using the money to dine at expensive restaurants, to purchase jewelry for his wife, Anne, and to take vacations abroad. By the autumn of 1985, his behavior had drawn the attention of his naval superiors, who placed him under surveillance. In late November, Pollard was questioned by the FBI, then suspended from his job. He immediately informed his Israeli contacts. Within the day, Sella departed the United States. Incredibly, neither Sella nor Eitan had devised contingency plans for Pollard. When the young American telephoned the Israeli scientific attaché, he was simply instructed to come to the embassy the following morning. Pollard and his wife then hurriedly packed, expecting to be flown off posthaste to Israel. But upon reaching the embassy early on November 21, the Pollards were arrested by awaiting FBI agents, and jailed.

News of the arrest reached the media within hours, and burgeoned into a national sensation. The Reagan administration already had been embarrassed by earlier disclosures of widespread espionage. Among these was the treason committed by the John Walker family, which through the years had turned over to the Soviet Union the navy's most closely guarded secrets. This latest discovery, as a result, proved almost unbearably mortifying. Immediately, through State Department channels, the FBI proceeded to question several staff members of the Israeli embassy. They denied knowledge of Pollard. So did Prime Minister Peres and Defense Minister Rabin, upon being queried by United States embassy officials. Indeed, the Israeli leaders speculated that Pollard might have belonged to a "rogue operation." Angered by this response, Secretary of State Shultz then telephoned Peres to insist upon full Israeli cooperation. Hesitating no longer, Peres agreed to return all stolen American material, even to permit a U.S. mission to question any Israeli officials involved.

Meanwhile, learning that his wife, Anne, remained in jail as an accomplice, Jonathan Pollard also decided to cooperate with the government. In return for his information, he had been promised leniency for Anne, and a less than draconian sentence for himself. Accordingly, Pollard revealed the full extent of Israeli involvement. Peres, by contrast, did not keep his promise. Rather than punish those responsible for the "rogue operation," the prime minister allowed Sella and Eitan to be appointed to well-paying administrative jobs elsewhere. Neither of these men was made available to testify before the visiting American mission of inquiry. Nor were thousands of purloined naval intelligence documents ever returned to the United States. Outraged, Secretary of Defense Caspar Weinberger subsequently dispatched an extensive, secret affidavit to the federal district court in Washington. The memorandum apparently made its impression on Judge Aubrey Robinson. In March 1987, when the Pollards were brought into court for sentencing (after fifteen months of imprisonment), the judge meted out exceptionally harsh terms. Jonathan Pollard was sentenced to life imprisonment, and Anne Pollard to five years. The sentences equaled or exceeded those imposed on the Walkers—father, mother, and son—who for years had passed vital intelligence data to Moscow. Hustled off to a federal penitentiary in Springfield, Missouri (and later transferred to Marion, Illinois), Pollard was kept in solitary confinement "to protect his life from other inmates." Anne Pollard had been convicted only of conspiracy to receive classified property and as an accessory after the fact. Yet she too was placed in solitary confinement in a federal penitentiary, in Lexington, Kentucky.

In Israel, two separate government committees undertook investigations into the Pollard episode. Both published their summary findings in May 1987. Both acknowledged that "grave errors of judgment" had been committed. For security reasons, however, neither revealed detailed information to the public. Yet it was specifically the Israeli public that voiced consternation that the government apparently was turning its back on the Pollards, on a couple that had provided life-and-death information for Israel's security. In October 1988, two Knesset members flew to Washington to intercede with members of Congress in the prisoners' behalf, arguing that Jonathan Pollard had not spied against the United States. But the years passed. Despite a severe gastrointestinal ailment, Anne Pollard served her entire sentence and was not released until 1990. Jonathan Pollard remained in solitary confinement. Each of his appeals for a reduction of sentence was turned down.

Was the damage inflicted on Israeli-American relations irretrievable? An Anti-Defamation League survey among American Gentiles found little evidence to that effect. But the ADL's conclusion was not shared by American Jews at large. With few exceptions (polls revealed), the latter were stupefied and mortified. In their view, the Pollard case gravely threatened the goodwill for Israel that they, American Jews, had been developing assiduously for some forty years. Indeed, the danger was possibly even graver, and it was palpable in the immediate aftermath of Jonathan Pollard's arrest. Suspecting a broader Israeli espionage network in the United States, Justice Department officials repeatedly demanded that Pollard implicate various American-Jewish leaders and organizations. Hooking the prisoner to a polygraph machine, they asked him to read lists of Jewish names and to identify alleged spies (there was none). Not since the Rosenberg trial of the early 1950s had such a cloud appeared over the Jews of the United States. Thus it was, at a time when the Israeli people reacted in indignation to the "abandonment of the Pollards," that American-Jewish leaders reacted in panic, vying with one another to fly off for urgent consultations with Israeli officials in Jerusalem.

The import of these discussions was not revealed. American-Jewish press comment on the subject remained almost eerily muted. Yet, in private, the emissaries pressed for assurance that the Israeli government never again would expose them to this discomfiture. How would Washington ever entrust American Jews to positions of security responsibility? How would their neighbors ever again accept at face value the painfully achieved record of Jewish patriotism? As much as any development within Israel itself, resentment of Israel's apparent indifference to their status now profoundly exacerbated American-Jewish misgivings about their beloved Zionist homeland. After four decades of emotional inseparability, was Israel now to be relegated to the margins of American Jewish priorities? It was a chilling moment in the Israel-Diaspora partnership.

THE ERA

OF UNITY GOVERNMENTS

ELECTIONEERING ON THE ECONOMIC BRINK

No natural successor was in the wings in July 1983, when Prime Minister Menachem Begin stunned his party by announcing his resignation. As the Cherut central committee met to choose its new chairman, therefore, the contest devolved into a two-way race between David Levy, the minister of housing, and Yitzchak Shamir, the foreign minister. The latter was chosen by a solid majority, and assumed the premiership on September 15, 1983. A factor in Shamir's selection might have been the parallels between his career and Begin's. Born Yitzchak Yezrenicki in tsarist Poland, he, like Begin, had studied law at the University of Warsaw. Upon immigrating to Palestine in 1935, he too initially became a member of the Revisionist Etzel underground. A few years afterward, however, Shamir joined the ultraextremist Lech'i faction. Here Shamir and his comrades were entirely ruthless in their acts of violence. One of these was the assassination of Count Folke Bernadotte, the UN mediator, in the summer of 1948 (p. 338). Neither Shamir nor any of the other plotters was caught.

Rather, with his conspiratorial skills well honed, Shamir in 1955 joined the Mossad, where he became a member of the hit squad that eliminated selected Arab guerrilla leaders, as well as German scientists employed in Egyptian missile projects. Ten years later, Shamir tried his hand in business, but failed. In 1970, finally, at the age of fifty-six, he rejoined his former Etzel comrades in the Cherut party. Here at last he found his métier. Indeed, as a reliable technocrat, Shamir rose swiftly in Begin's esteem, and over the next decade became a perennial in the Knesset, and finally Speaker of the Knesset. In 1980, then, Begin picked him to succeed Dayan as foreign minister. The appointment raised eyebrows. Shamir was a committed hard-liner. He had voted against the peace treaty with Egypt, fearing its provision for evacuating the Sinai.

Nevertheless, belying the dire predictions of ministry professionals, Shamir settled comfortably into his office, where he displayed a quiet, affable manner, a willingness to listen that contrasted favorably with Dayan's steely gruffness. Yet it was only a matter of time before the man's hard-edged revisionism surfaced. Like Begin, he remained unshakable on the issue of Judea and Samaria. He supported the Lebanon war, and his culpability—by indifference—in the Sabra and Shatila massacres was duly noted and condemned by the Kahan Commission. And now, acceding to the premiership at the age of sixty-nine, a diminutive, brush-mustached gentleman with a deceptively ingratiating smile, Shamir evinced not the slightest willingness to budge on issues of Israel's "legitimate security," even on Jewish settler vigilantism.

Conceivably, the Knesset's moderates and the public at large would have forgiven Shamir his militance had he come up with a firm plan to extricate the nation from the Lebanon quagmire. But he did not, and that failure was eroding the army's morale, widening the reservist protest movement and evoking an unprecedented wave of draft evasions. The new prime minister appeared no less at sea in coping with the nation's metastasizing economic crisis. By 1983, we recall, Likud's shift to social populism, its West Bank settlements program, and the costs of the disastrous Lebanon war, had depleted Israel's hard currency reserves. Then, in May of that year, still during Begin's premiership, Israel's annual inflation rate was disclosed at nearly 400 percent. The news touched off a selling panic on the Tel Aviv stock exchange. In ensuing months, as billions of shekels were withdrawn from savings schemes to purchase dollars or durable goods, Israel's currency became increasingly worthless. The stage thus was set for the nation's "economic Yom Kippur," a blow that struck exactly ten years after the 1973 war.

In late September 1983, rumors circulated that the government planned drastic new curtailments on foreign-currency transactions, together with a possible major devaluation of the shekel. Immediately the public began selling off large quantities of its dollar-linked bank shares, which had long seemed to the public the safest of blue-chip investments. Yet it soon developed that the banks themselves had artificially sustained the value of those shares over the years. Moreover, to maintain that inflated value, the banks now rushed to import dollars from their subsidiaries abroad. But when these reserves soon were exhausted, the banks frantically turned to the government for help. They got it, after a fashion. On October 10, following an emergency all-night cabinet session, the treasury announced a plan for transforming limited amounts of bank shares into interest-bearing, dollar-linked government debentures, redeemable in five years. The panic eased somewhat. Nevertheless, by mid-October, tens of thousands of Israelis had disposed of their shares at a fraction of their original value. Hundreds of millions of dollars in savings were lost. And still the economic crisis was not permanently resolved. In ensuing weeks, the treasury was obliged to pump some $150 million into the stock exchange to protect its stability, and to devalue the shekel by an additional 23 percent to protect the nation's soaring balance-of-payments deficit. Other draconian measures were imposed, including tough new taxes almost everywhere, and sharply reduced currency limits on travel allowances. These emergency measures notwithstanding, by November 1983, Israel's hard-currency reserves continued to drop, approaching perilously close to the unofficial "red line" of $3 billion.

Reeling under this latest threat, offering no prospects for disengagement in Lebanon, and lacking Begin's personal charisma, Shamir appeared entirely incapable of reversing the collapse of public support for his government. Indeed, by early 1984, public opinion surveys appeared to confirm the nation's desire for a change in national leadership. The opportunity was provided in March of that year when Tami, one of the small Orthodox factions, defected from the coalition to give Labor the Knesset votes it needed for an early election. The date accordingly was set for July 23. As the politicians geared up for the campaign, Shamir and his Likud associates rushed to exploit themes that had succeeded in earlier elections. They portrayed Labor as the camp of Ashkenazic elitism, corruption, and softness on the Palestinians. Peres and his Labor colleagues in turn avoided challenging Likud directly on such "national" issues as West Bank settlements and Arab affairs, and concentrated straightforwardly on the government's record of mismanagement and economic failures. The strategy appeared to be working. Until a week before the election, polls showed the Labor Alignment leading by 10 Knesset seats.

Indeed, when the votes finally were tallied, the Labor Alignment was found to have won 46 seats, while Likud had won only 41, that is, 7 less than its earlier Knesset strength. Yet the shift by no means represented a victory for Labor, for most of the one hundred thousand voters who eventually broke with Likud ended up with other parties of the Right—with Techiya (5) and Kach (1). In the end, both major blocs had actually fought themselves to a virtual standstill. As the days passed, therefore, and as the contending leaders wheeled and dealed to put together viable coalitions, it became evident that Labor once again was incapable of forming a government without the religionists, and the latter had learned to be comfortable with their current, and generous, Likud partners. Thereupon Shamir and his associates came up with a compromise proposal. It was for a 1967-style "wall-to-wall" coalition that at least would ensure a common hard stance on the territories. The offer did not appeal to Peres.

By late September, however, even Peres had to admit the need for accommodation. Yet the formula cobbled together between the two blocs was not for a "wall-to-wall" coalition, but rather for a "national unity" government whose uniqueness would lie in the principle of rotation. Although the new constellation would encompass the largest number of established parties, Peres himself would serve initially as prime minister, while Shamir would revert to his earlier position (in the Begin government) as foreign minister. After twenty-five months, the two men would reverse roles for the final two years of their incumbency, with Shamir serving as premier and Peres as foreign minister. Rabin, meanwhile, an icon of military stability, would hold the position of defense minister under both premiers; while other portfolios would be divided evenly between the parties of the Right and Left. By any evaluation, the Government of National Unity was a strange, bicephalous arrangement, and under its constraints Peres's freedom of action seemed to be limited essentially to the search for a way out of Lebanon and the crisis of the raging inflation. For most Israelis, however, this was priority enough.

AN END TO ADVENTURISM

After years of waiting in the wings, Shimon Peres, at the age of sixty-one, at long last assumed the premiership on his own. In truth, no Israeli had ever achieved as wide-ranging an influence on the nation's public life without actually holding the title of prime minister. Born in Poland (né Perski), he moved with his family to Palestine eleven years later, where he joined a kibbutz. As a disciple of the Labor theorist Berl Katznelson (p. 159), the young man soon began a swift climb in the ranks of the Mapai party. In the early 1940s, Peres served in the Haganah, and by the end of World War II he had risen to the position of Haganah director of manpower. In 1954, at the age of thirty-two, he was appointed director-general of the ministry of defense.

In some respects, Peres's early years in the defense ministry were his most brilliant. It was then, almost single-handedly, in 1955–56, that he engineered the weapons deal with France that laid the basis for the Suez-Sinai collaboration, and afterward for the joint research-and-production program that transformed Israel into a major military power, even an incipient nuclear power. At the same time, Peres's close association with Ben-Gurion created a bond that approached the filial. When the old lion departed as prime minister in 1963, and afterward broke with the ruling Labor gerontocracy to found the dissident Rafi faction, Peres (and Dayan) risked their futures by accompanying Ben-Gurion into the political wilderness.

The opportunity for revival did not come until 1967, in the "wall-to-wall" government that emerged out of the Six-Day War crisis. In ensuing years, Peres filled a series of essentially peripheral cabinet positions that nevertheless allowed him to repair his ties with his former Labor colleagues, and to keep the party viable during the shaky aftermath of the Yom Kippur War. So it was, upon Golda Meir's resignation in April 1974, that Peres emerged as a major contender for the party chairmanship. Although his bid then was premature, and he was obliged to settle for the defense portfolio under Yitzchak Rabin, Peres eventually acceded to the party chairmanship anyway, upon Rabin's forced "leave of absence" (p. 833). It was Peres then who campaigned for the prime ministry—and lost in the 1977 upheaval.

It was also typical of the man, during his ensuing years as opposition leader, to work tirelessly in the effort to rehabilitate the Labor party, to wipe out its debts and rebuild its branches. He displayed authentic statesmanship, too, in holding his party in line to support the Camp David accords and the peace treaty with Egypt. Perhaps most impressive of all, Peres exhibited an intellectual depth uncommon in political leaders since the time of Ben-Gurion himself. Like Ben-Gurion, he shared the conviction that the nation's future depended upon skilled manpower and the imaginative exploitation of technology, upon the "scientification of Israel." It was as the supreme technocrat, therefore, the pragmatic "doer," that Peres now assumed the prime ministry in September 1984. A trim, well-tailored man of heavy features and ruddy complexion, he stood at the fullest maturity of his powers and experience.

Those talents were urgently needed, if only to end the debilitating military occupation of Lebanon. Withdrawal from the northern quagmire had begun as far back as July 1983, when the Begin government embarked on a unilateral but partial retreat to the Awali River line. Now, in January 1985, Peres was able to win cabinet approval for complete evacuation. By late June, the final stage of withdrawal was accomplished. The bulk of Israel's invading army was across the northern frontier, and home. Thus presumably ended an adventure, launched three years earlier, that had cost Israel 654 dead, 3,873 wounded, and approximately $5 billion in economic resources.

Even then, the outflow of men and funds was by no means entirely liquidated, for the evacuation required painstakingly devised future safeguards. The modified security zone in south Lebanon continued to be patrolled by the 1,800 Christian militiamen of the "South Lebanon Army." Eventually augmented to 2,600 men, the SLA for many years appeared to be a reasonably competent buffer against guerrilla penetration. Its success in turn was largely due to the "advisory" presence of approximately 200 Israeli officers and men. The collaborative venture was far from painless, however. Between 1985 and 1988 alone, the "advisers" suffered 64 dead, nearly 180 wounded—and the Lebanese militiamen many more. The financial costs also were extensive. These included the burden of providing military reinforcements and equipment, as well as subsidies for Lebanese Christian schools and clinics, even employment opportunities for SLA family members in northern Israel.

Indeed, the costs would rise in ensuing months and years, as Palestinian guerrillas gradually reinforced their strength along the northern fringes of the buffer zone. From the mid-1980s on, these armed bands drew their inspiration and practical support less from any of the PLO factions than from the government of Iran. The largest of the factions, the Hizballah (Party of God), received its training in two Iranian-operated, former Lebanese military camps near Baalbek, fifty miles north of Beirut. By the latter 1980s, the number of Hizballah trainees exceeded five thousand, and their command reported directly to the Iranian ambassador in Damascus, Mohammad Hassan Akhtari. By then, too, moving down farther to the south, the Hizballah fighters made their presence increasingly known, first in ambushes of SLA and Israeli "advisers," then in periodic rocket firings into Israel's northern frontier communities.

The danger was compounded by events elsewhere in Lebanon. Elie Hobeika, the Phalangist commander who had overseen the slaughter at Sabra and Shatila, disdained to take orders from the Beirut government, and in August 1984 led a coup that overthrew President Amin Gemayel. Soon afterward, visiting Damascus, Hobeika entered into a secret compact with the Assad regime. The Syrians promised their help in ending the factional conflict in Lebanon. Yet their price was a "tripartite pact," signed in December 1985. Under its terms, Lebanon's government at long last would reflect the nation's Moslem majority, rather than its traditional, and artificial, parliamentary even balance. Most critical of all, the new arrangement placed the nation's military and foreign policies under Syrian veto—in effect transforming Lebanon into a Syrian dependency. In February 1986, therefore, at the "invitation" of Lebanon's Moslem leadership, the Syrian army moved back into West Beirut, from which it had withdrawn under Israeli pressure four years earlier. For Israel, the long-range implications of this ensconced new Syrian hegemony were sobering.

Nevertheless, in the short term, military withdrawal from Lebanon appeared to be achieving tangible benefits, and well beyond the reduction of human and economic losses. It softened Israel's image in Europe. By 1986, Britain's Prime Minister Margaret Thatcher, a harsh critic of the Lebanon campaign, agreed to pay an official visit to Israel. That same year, Spain's Prime Minister Felipe González authorized the exchange of ambassadors with Israel. Israel's presence was reviving equally impressively in Africa. A decade earlier, in the wake of African diplomatic ruptures during the Yom Kippur War, Jerusalem had been obliged to place its emphasis upon practical, commercial ties with its former African friends. By the 1980s, however, once a peace treaty was signed with Egypt, the door was open for other African states to restore and broaden their earlier Israeli contacts. In May 1982, Zaire was the first to reestablish diplomatic ties. Liberia followed in August 1983. In ensuing years, Kenya (always secretly friendly) reopened its embassy in Israel, as did Uganda, the Central African Republic, the Ivory Coast, Cameroon, Togo, and eventually, in 1990, Ethiopia.

Indeed, for Israel, Ethiopia had always played a unique role. With its extended Red Sea coastline, the vast, 472,000-square-mile behemoth functioned as Israel's maritime gateway to the rest of Africa, as well as buffer protection against Egypt and Somalia along Israel's sea route to Asia. In turn, during the 1950s and 1960s, Ethiopia's Emperor Haile Selassie was equally appreciative of Israel's economic and military cooperation against Nasserist subversion. But in 1973, during the Yom Kippur War upheaval, even Haile Selassie had felt obliged to terminate relations with the Jewish state. Ironically, soon afterward, the emperor was himself deposed by a Marxist-oriented council of officers. Nor was Haile Selassie's successor, President Mengistu Haile Mariam, able to relinquish the Israel connection altogether. Facing an insurrection of Eritrean rebels, Mengistu and his cabal in 1976 secretly enlisted the help of Israeli military advisers; and, following the Lebanon war, Israel negotiated a substantial shipment of captured Soviet arms to Ethiopia.

The clandestine relationship ultimately transcended strategic considerations. Some 28,000 black-skinned Jews also lived in Ethiopia, most of these congregated in the highlands of Gondar province. Known to their neighbors as Falashas—"strangers"—the members of this tiny group preferred to call themselves Beta Israel. Their origins were uncertain, but it was likely that they were Ethiopians by blood, descendants of possibly as many as two or three hundred thousand Africans who had converted to Judaism in the early Middle Ages. It is certain in any case that in 1577 a Christian emperor, Sarsa Dengael, launched a systematic extermination of "infidels." Barely one hundred thousand Jews survived. In ensuing generations, persecuted and occasionally sold into slavery, barred from owning more than a mite of land, the remnant Jewish nation devolved into an impoverished pariah community of handicraftsmen and sharecroppers.

Ethiopian Jewry was not rediscovered until the nineteenth century, by the Scottish explorer James Bruce, then by a French-Jewish philologist, Joseph Halévy. Both men confirmed that the Falashas' rites by then had become a poignant amalgam of crypto-Jewish, Christian, and animist traditions. In 1903, Professor Jacques Faitlovitch, a student of Halévy's, visited the impoverished little people in their mountain retreat, and made it his mission henceforth to reintroduce them into the Jewish mainstream. Subsidized by Baron Edmond de Rothschild, Faitlovich over the years established a skeletal school system for these lost sheep of Israel. By 1948, the Falashas were well apprised of the outer Jewish world, and specifically of revived Jewish nationhood in Israel. From then on, indeed, departure to the land of their "ancestors" became their compelling dream.

It was less than a priority for the Israeli government. During the 1950s and

1960s, the Jewish state was overwhelmed by a tidal wave of immigrants from Europe, North Africa, and the Middle East. The fate of a black, primitive community, whose bona fides as Jews were not accepted by the nation's chief rabbinate, hardly seemed a burning issue. But with the overthrow of Haile Selassie in 1974, and then the debilitating Ethiopian civil war and its ensuing famine, the Falashas' very physical survival hung in the balance. Accordingly, in March 1979, through the good offices of the Carter administration in the United States, the Israeli government arranged a discreet transfer of funds to the private Swiss account of Sudan's President Ja'afar al-Numeiri. Numeiri in turn agreed to grant Ethiopian Jews temporary asylum in Sudan. It was understood that they would be quietly transported afterward to Israel. Yet even the initial migration southward was a terrifying ordeal for the Falashas. They moved entirely by foot. En route, they endured disease, starvation, robbery, rape. Once reaching Sudan, moreover, their initial fate was a wretched, vegetative confinement in the Um Raquba refugee compound. Finally, by spring of 1981, Israeli agents succeeded in constructing a dummy "tourist village" on Sudan's eastern, Red Sea coast. Over the ensuing months the Falashas were transported there by trucks, then carried by dinghies to awaiting freighters. In this fashion, approximately four thousand Ethiopian Jews reached Israel. It was anticipated that at least three times that many would follow by the end of the year.

But in the autumn of 1981, Sudan's President Numeiri canceled the arrangement. He had been unnerved by the recent assassination of Anwar al-Sadat. Some twenty-two thousand Falashas remained behind, both in Ethiopia proper and in the Sudanese refugee compound. Israel still would not give up on them. Rather, in late 1983, the Mossad devised a new scheme, "Operation Moses." The plan was to fly the remaining Falashas out of Sudan in a swift, surgical airlift. Would Numeiri agree? Once again the role of the U.S. government was decisive. Through the active intermediary effort of Vice President George Bush, Washington deposited another $100 million of Jewish Agency funds in Numeiri's Swiss bank account and in those of his personal aides. The Israelis in turn promised to spare Numeiri embarrassment with the Arab states. They would fly the refugees initially to Europe, and only afterward to Israel.

Operation Moses duly began then in November 1984. Under cover of darkness, the Falashas were trucked from Um Raquba to Khartoum airport. The carrier this time was a Mossad front, a private Belgian airline that flew the Ethiopians direct from Khartoum to Brussels, then from Brussels to Israel. From November 1984 to January 1985, as a result, some eight thousand Falashas were carried off to Israel. Yet, before the remaining fugitives could be brought out, the secret leaked, the Arab world protested, and Numeiri terminated the operation—this time permanently. As many as seventeen thousand Falashas still remained in Ethiopia proper, and the Addis Ababa government's decision now was to seal off its borders with Sudan. If only partially successful, Operation Moses still ranked as a smaller-scale version of the famed Operation Magic Carpet, the rescue of Yemenite Jewry in 1950, and as a dramatic reminder of Israel's consummate mission as a homeland for distraught and endangered Jews everywhere.

THE STRUGGLE FOR ECONOMIC STABILIZATION

Upon assuming the prime ministry in September 1984, Shimon Peres stepped into an economic chamber of horrors that would have intimidated the leader of a far wealthier nation. During the seven years of Likud rule, Israel's foreign debt had nearly doubled, from $12.5 billion in 1977 to more than $23 billion. Its annual inflation rate approached 400 percent. "Objective" circumstances doubtless played a role in this unfolding disaster. By the end of the 1970s, the price of oil worldwide was twenty times higher than at the beginning of the decade. Agricultural depression reduced demand for several of Israel's most profitable winter fruits and vegetables. So did the Common Market, which recently had admitted Spain and Portugal, with their highly competitive citrus groves. Yet, more than any other factor, it was defense that was breaking the back of Israel's economy. The cost of the Six-Day and Yom Kippur Wars, then of the Lebanon campaign, the enlargement of the standing army and reserve elements, and the vast investment for more sophisticated weapons systems—all raised defense expenditures from 9 percent of the GNP in 1966 to 22 percent by 1984. Indeed, by then, Israel's proportion of defense spending to GNP was four times greater than that of the NATO powers.

There were less "objective" influences, however, that added their burden to the nation's overheated economy. One was the Likud government's intensified West Bank settlements program. In all its dimensions, we recall, the effort was consuming some $1.5 billion a year in public funds, and possibly an additional $1 billion in private investment. David Levy's program for subsidized public housing, Zevulun Hammer's unprecedented diversion of government funds to religious institutions, Yoram Aridor's struggle to maintain the (import) buying power of the shekel—all further depleted the nation's hard currency reserves. Moreover, the wound inflicted by this combination of imperialism and populism was further exacerbated by Israel's widening vocational imbalance. As early as the mid-1970s, agriculture encompassed a bare 6 percent of the work force, and industry only 24 percent. The government, Jewish Agency, finance, transportation, storage, communications, and tourism accounted for the rest. In short, the "productive" branches of Israel's economy were overshadowed by the commercial, service, and financial sectors.

At whichever echelon, meanwhile, Israeli workers failed to achieve the productivity levels of other modern societies. The largest numbers of them did not doubt that the Histadrut would shelter them from the Western challenge of merit hiring and firing. As late as 1985, the Histadrut holding company, Chevrat Ovdim, as well as the government, continued to own a major share of the nation's industry. Even under Begin, little progress was made in government divestment of public companies (p. 837); and the combination of government and Histadrut protection remained notably uncongenial to productivity or authentic competitiveness. A case in point was Koor, largest of the Histadrut subsidiaries. At its peak, the mighty industrial-business conglomerate accounted for 10 percent of

Israel's industrial output, about 7 percent of the nation's entire GNP. Yet, by the mid-1980s, gross mismanagement and near-paralytic giantism had loaded Koor with $1.3 billion in debts, and led it to the threshold of bankruptcy.

By the mid-1980s, Israel was given additional reminder that make-work inefficiency and public-sector monopoly no longer were supportable. Its principal overseas trading partner was the Common Market. Ever since the late 1960s, the government had explored prospects for associate status with this vast entrepôt and its 320 million consumers. At last, in 1975, after lengthy negotiations, an Israel-EEC pact did indeed award Israel that status (p. 603). The agreement provided for a reciprocal phased tariff-reduction on each other's manufactured goods. The heaviest burden of competitiveness plainly would lie on Israel. In 1986, moreover, Israel and the EEC further expanded the agreement's categories of products, with the understanding that the scheduled 1992 completion of Europe's economic integration would require a parallel free entrance of additional European products into Israel. Yet, well before the target date, the strain of that competition was beginning to tell. Between 1975 and 1988, Israel accumulated a trade deficit of $15 billion with the EEC alone.

In 1985, meanwhile, a free-trade-area pact similarly was negotiated with the United States, mutually phasing out tariffs on an extended category of agricultural and industrial products. Like its predecessors, the agreement represented a heroic act of faith on Israel's part, for the smaller nation's market was certain to be open to an even wider avalanche of American goods. By then, too, Israel's dependence on the United States had reached the crisis stage. Over four decades, the Jewish republic had received an unprecedented $23 billion in assistance from Washington—$12.3 billion of it in the form of outright grants, the remaining $10.7 billion in long-term loans. The sheer effulgence of American aid in turn had come to function as a kind of narcotic for Israel, postponing the structural changes that alone would have allowed the country to face its new economic challenges from abroad.

Would the nation accept the disciplined austerity needed to return to a sounder financial basis? Until the Government of National Unity, Israelis had become accustomed to automatic wage hikes linked to an endlessly rising cost of living, to builders' payments linked to inflation, and to bank interest rates and other costs linked to the dollar. But now, at last, Shimon Peres confirmed his reputation as an archpragmatist. Like his mentor Ben-Gurion, the prime minister understood well that socialism no longer was functioning very effectively anywhere else in the world. With the government literally running out of money, and 37 percent of its budget allocated exclusively to servicing the vast foreign debt, the prime minister now pressed, and eventually won over, all major factions in his cabinet to accept a bold program of economic austerity. After additional negotiations and arm-twisting, the Histadrut leadership similarly consented to forgo its automatic wage increases. In turn, the Manufacturers' Association acquiesced in a rigorous program of price controls. The compact worked. From autumn 1985 to autumn 1986, the monthly rate of inflation dropped from 35 to 2 percent. Plainly, the withdrawal from Lebanon and ensuing reduction in defense expenditures also were vital in dampening the overheated economy. Even luck played a role. By 1985, oil prices began plunging on the international markets, and within a year Israel's annual bill for imported fuel declined by some $600 million. To compound this blessing, international interest rates fell dramatically in 1985 and 1986, further easing Israel's foreign debt burden.

Meanwhile, Peres kept his sights focused unwaveringly on dysfunctional corporations. During the four years of Unity Government, some forty of these were either dismantled or significantly attenuated, with the most drastic surgery performed on Koor. Under the government's relentless prodding, Koor's money-losing branches were cut away or down to size. So was its topheavy management and work force. By the end of the decade, Koor's debt was reduced to a more tolerable $450 million. Leaner and wiser, cost-conscious and competitive, the great labor-industrial locomotive was moving steadily into the black. Yet, in the race for viability, not all public companies were necessarily written off or downsized. El Al, although severely inhibited by the ban on Saturday flights (p. 885), managed spectacularly to improve the quality of its training, maintenance, and passenger and cargo services. By the early 1990s, the airline approached profitability. The Zim shipping line, jointly owned by the government and the Israel Corporation (a private company), flourished as a cargo carrier. Indeed, by 1988, operating eighty vessels, Zim had become the world's tenth-largest container shipping company, with annual sales of $1 billion. Tourism in Israel, although fluctuating with political and military conditions in the Middle East, generated several flourishing institutional byproducts. Thus, the Red Sea community of Eilat sustained a virtually uninterrupted record of growth, and by 1993 the once forlorn little Red Sea port, beyond its role as an important oil and shipping terminus, had become a spectacular tourist attraction, offering no fewer than six thousand hotel rooms, with another five thousand under planning or active construction. It was significant too that Arkia, Israel's inland airline, shared the pace of Eilat's tourist growth. By 1993, Arkia's annual passenger load exceeded the one-million mark.

TOWARD A SCIENTIFIC SOCIETY

In the final analysis, Israel's economic survival would depend upon a decisive leap in exports. Yet the little country's natural resources were minimal. With even its citrus exports in the 1970s and 1980s encountering stiff Common Market competition from Spain, Italy, and Greece, it was becoming evident that Israel, like Switzerland and Japan, would have to develop an export-oriented industry based essentially on skilled manpower. Fortunately, in that challenge, there was reason for cautious hope. Notwithstanding the wounds suffered by the nation's educational system during the Likud era, and the "brain drain" to the United States (p. 1007), the country still possessed an impressively large reservoir of engineering and scientific talent. Its universities and technical institutes over the years had produced more than eighty thousand graduates. The number of its working scientists and engineers approached ten thousand. Among the latter were the men and women who had pioneered Israel's spectacular dry-farming and hydrological achievements, and its equally imaginative exploitation of solar energy. Indeed, solar heating was at work in two-thirds of the nation's households. The world's largest solar pond, driving a five-megawatt generating plant along the shore of the Dead Sea, was the vanguard of a planned network of solar power stations for the entirety of Israel.

Accordingly, if not everyone shared Prime Minister Peres's optimistic designation of 1985 as Israel's "year of technology," none at least doubted the transcendent importance of an educated, highly skilled work force. Uzia Galil had discovered early on the best method of mobilizing his nation's human resources. An electronic engineer and Technion faculty member, Galil in 1961 established a laboratory in his own Haifa apartment to produce electronic equipment, with eight other faculty members and graduate students as his coworkers. They found a ready market for their products. Two years later, Galil outlined his approach to Dan Talkowsky, a former chief of the Israeli air force, then chairman of the Israel Discount Bank's investment division. Impressed, Talkowsky extended Galil a line of credit. Thereupon Galil organized a small corporation, Elron Electronics, which itself would function as a source of seed money—in effect, a holding company—for other promising high-tech ventures. The partnership between Elron Electronics and the Israel Discount Bank was destined to revolutionize Israel's industrial development.

In ensuing years, Galil and Talkowsky examined dozens of proposals for linking the nation's scientists to research-and-production enterprises. Thus, to exploit Israel's pool of doctors and engineers, Elron and the Discount Bank founded a subsidiary company, Elscint, that in turn pioneered the development of CAT scanners, later to be marketed in the United States by General Electric. Within a short period, Elscint assumed an important role in the worldwide production of medical imaging devices, including an entire family of integral camera-processors for nuclear medical applications. Meanwhile, Elron itself, Uzia Galil's original parent firm, continued to establish other subsidiaries. Among these were Bio-Technology, developed jointly with Dr. Isaac Kaplan of Tel Aviv University Medical School, and producing the world's most sophisticated surgical laser equipment, and Elmar Medical Systems, for pioneering techniques in automated hemodialysis. Not all these subsidiaries were profitable, and in 1985 Elscint found itself overextended and obliged to retrench. Yet the mother company remained unchallenged in orchestrating Israel's alliance of science and industry. Altogether, by the 1980s, high tech had come to be regarded as a panacea for an otherwise modestly endowed nation. Other competing banks now were seeking to share in the action, including Bank Leumi, Israel's oldest and largest.

Neither was the Israeli government itself laggard in encouraging science-based projects. As far back as 1968, the ministry of industry and trade was authorized to match an "approved" company's research-and-development budget, pound for pound—shekel for shekel. By 1985 the money was going into approximately six hundred ventures. Yet an important share even of Israeli government funds depended on overseas help. Here a key source was the Israel–United States Binational Industrial and Research Development Foundation—"Bird F"—underwritten jointly by the American and Israeli governments to provide low-interest loans for approved joint undertakings between American and Israeli private companies. Among the former were such giants as

Mennen Medical, Control Data, National Semiconductor, Motorola, Digital Equipment, ITT—all corporations that were eager to exploit the wealth of Israeli scientific talent, and specifically the faculties of the Technion, the Weizmann Institute, the Hebrew and Tel Aviv Universities, and other research centers. Thus, by 1985, Bird F was funding 121 joint projects. By then, too, electronics comprised 33 percent of the value of all Israeli industrial exports. By 1990, other research-and-development companies, producing solar energy, irrigation technology, computer software, and agrochemical products, helped raise that export total to 59 percent.

ISRAEL AS ARMORER

In these same years, Israel's military equipment and expertise surfaced as a uniquely profitable earner of foreign currency. The phenomenon doubtless was inevitable, in view of Israel's ongoing diplomatic and military isolation. Initially, it was the French arms embargo of 1967 that forced acceleration of Israel's own military program. From then on, development of a serious military-industrial program became a national priority. Two companies, Tadiran and Israel Aircraft Industry (IAI), accounted for three-quarters of all manufacture. Tadiran, owned by Koor and the GTE Company of the United States, produced a wide variety of military communication equipment, and of a quality and sophistication that eventually won 17 percent of the world market. IAI, organized in the early 1950s as a government enterprise, operated in its early years (when it was known as Bedek) exclusively as an aircraft maintenance-and-repair facility, but later extended its operations to the assembly and manufacture of military and civilian aircraft. By 1985, employing 25,000 people, IAI was producing jet fighter and civilian transport planes, naval vessels, missiles, and minicomputers. Still another, private firm, AEL, manufactured electronic-jamming and radar-alarm systems.

It was at the Paris International Air Show in 1981 that observers began to grasp the scope and diversity of Israeli military production. Here were first displayed IAI's Kfir fighter plane, the Arava and Westwind civilian aircraft, and the E1/M 2121 intelligence battlefield surveillance radar. Also revealed was an upgraded version of the Gabriel sea-to-sea missile, a brilliant water-skimmer that all but revolutionized the Israeli navy (p. 772); and the Tactical Command and Control system, a mobile computer equipped to provide constantly updated information in a battlefield environment. Still another product was the Barak Advanced Shipborne Point Defense Missile System, a lightweight all-weather multiple-target apparatus. IAI also introduced the Spider-11 Air Defense Artillery System, a unit capable of identifying and tracking targets, and automatically aiming and firing six twin-30mm cannon; a range of airborne electronic warfare and countermeasure systems, among them jammers, chaff dispensers, deception, and target-acquisition equipment, including a series of pilotless drones that only a year later were virtually to paralyze Syria's SAM missile system in the Lebanon war. The display—with attendant "smart" bombs, rockets, warheads, mines, and a panoply of automatic small arms, as well as laser range finders, artillery computers, and related integrated fire-control systems—left visitors gasping. And still further evidence of Israel's military scientific-industrial prowess lay ahead. In September 1988, the little nation successfully launched its first locally produced satellite, the Ofeq-1, thereby becoming the first space power in the Middle East, with the capacity independently to gather satellite intelligence on its Arab neighbors. Of greater significance yet was the satellite's missile system. It was a Shavit, based on Israel's well-proven Jericho-III solid-fuel rocket. The weapon's range was estimated at nine hundred miles, sufficient to reach any Arab capital.

Yet the competitiveness of Israel's weapons industry depended in the end upon economies of scale well beyond those of its own armed forces. Here access to the export market would prove crucial. Israel met the challenge successfully, even spectacularly. By 1987, it was exporting its locally produced weapons to some forty nations. Indeed, at its peak during the 1980s, weapons production accounted for one-fourth of Israel's exports altogether, and employed one-fourth of the nation's industrial labor force. None of the country's other products, not even citrus fruits or industrial diamonds, matched weaponry's annual export sales of $1.1 billion (although computer software would supersede weapons exports by the mid-1990s). At the same time, arms and military expertise provided Israel with advantages not less important even than profits. These were a developing nexus of vital contacts in the Third World. As examples, Singapore, Taiwan, and South Korea, efficient and authoritarian, began purchasing substantial quantities of Israeli military equipment as early as the 1960s, and thereby accepted the presence of Israel's military-trade missions on their soil at a time when formal diplomatic relations still were lacking. Battle experience also played a role in this Asian foothold, with Israel providing training for the Taiwanese secret service. In the Philippines, Israeli agents were active in the Marcos regime as early as the 1960s, helping train the Philippine dictator's private armies. Indonesia, a Moslem nation, tolerated an Israeli Mossad station in Jakarta, and in 1979 used Israel as the conduit to purchase fourteen American Skyhawk jets, and in later years to purchase other American-produced (as well as captured Soviet) military equipment. Israeli military advisers also operated in Thailand and in Sri Lanka.

As in earlier decades, Africa remained a particularly important outlet for Israeli weaponry and training. Even Ethiopia's revolutionary Mengistu regime purchased substantial quantities of Israeli light arms (p. 939). Zaire's President Joseph Mobutu continued as always to depend heavily upon Israeli weapons and military advisers, as did Morocco's King Hassan II. Altogether, Third World nations tended to find their most useful military alternative in Israel; for the Jewish state over the years had become highly adept at modernizing older equipment for local military purposes. As much as any nation, too, it had tested that equipment in combat. Moreover, Israel was prepared to deal with virtually any regime that would offer it the hand—even the left hand—of friendship. Survival was the issue, not morality. The beleaguered Jewish republic was fighting for its life.

South Africa was a case in point. In the aftermath of the Six-Day War, confronting the French embargo on Mirage jet spare parts, Israel turned to

South Africa for help. The Pretoria government was accommodating. A white enclave in an African sea, it empathized with the Israelis in their isolation. Indeed, during the 1970s, both nations enlarged their mutual diplomatic representation and cultural ties, and broadened the scope of their trade. In April 1976, at a time when other nations all but quarantined South Africa for its policy of apartheid, Prime Minister John Vorster paid an official visit to Israel and was warmly received. Subsequently, Pretoria formally approved a comprehensive set of bilateral agreements with the Jewish state. These dealt almost exclusively with weapons. On the one hand, South Africa provided the high-tensile steel for Israel's world-class Merkava tank, and for several of its heavy artillery pieces. South Africa also built Israel's newest submarine. In turn, Israel provided South Africa with substantial quantities of battle-tested equipment—patrol boats, jet aircraft, Gabriel missiles, howitzers, communications hardware, and radar systems. Thus it was, by the early 1980s, that South Africa became the Israeli military industry's single largest customer. Hundreds of South Africans were graduating from Israeli military training programs. South African naval personnel shared in training exercises on Israeli missile boats, in Israeli coastal waters, even as Israeli officers were assigned to South Africa as instructors for local commando units. The air forces of both countries worked and trained together.

In the end, it was the "Domesday Project" that represented the farthest-reaching, and most secretive, feature of the relationship. In September 1979, an American satellite recorded two distinctive bright flashes near the Prince Edward Islands, about fifteen hundred miles southeast of the Cape of Good Hope. CIA analysts were convinced that a nuclear test had taken place. It had. Indeed, the test climaxed a quarter-century of Israeli–South African nuclear cooperation. The initial fuel charge for Israel's Dimona reactor contained twenty-four tons of uranium. Of this load, ten tons came from South Africa, while Israel closely shared its basic nuclear research with the Pretoria government. By 1977, Israeli and South African scientists were also working closely on nuclear technology, and it was this cooperation, two years later, that produced the mysterious nuclear flashes in the Indian Ocean (American analysts concluded that the device was of a low-yield, two-kiloton variety—in essence, a "clean" battlefield weapon). In the meanwhile, by the early 1980s, of some two hundred foreign diplomats accredited to Pretoria, the Israeli contingent was the third largest, exceeded in size only by the American and British. Manifestly, the Israeli–South African relationship had become an alliance in all but name.

By then, in fact, Israel's relationship with conservative governments altogether was a fact of life. Thus, Central American military regimes, faced with the perennial threat of leftist guerrilla insurrections, could turn to Israel for captured Soviet weaponry, for cut-rate older Western equipment that the Israelis had skillfully modernized. No questions were asked. In return for cash, the Israelis were prepared to offer reasonably priced, battle-tested equipment, and often valuable training in counterinsurgency techniques. Guatemala was a key example. Of all the Central American juntas with which Israel dealt, Guatemala's was possibly the most reactionary. Nevertheless, during the late 1970s and early 1980s, Israel dominated the Guatemalan weapons market, providing Arava transport planes, artillery pieces, and light weapons that totally refitted the little nation's armed services. Israeli instructors similarly trained Guatemala's counterinsurgency units. In those same years, too, Israel equipped Honduras's dictatorship with extensive quantities of older, rebuilt aircraft. Indeed, Defense Minister Ariel Sharon personally visited Tegucigalpa in 1982, leading a mission of senior officers to complete the military-transfer accord. As early as 1973, too, Israel signed an agreement with El Salvador's grim military oligarchy, agreeing to rebuild the Salvadoran air force. Thus, in the ensuing two years, Israel was able to dispose of scores of its obsolescent Ouragon and Fouga jets, of twenty-five locally made Arava transports, as well as of substantial quantities of napalm and antipersonnel bombs. Israeli officers also helped train Salvadoran antiguerrilla squads. Business was not the only compelling factor in the Israeli-Salvadoran relationship, as it happened. The Salvadoran government had agreed to transfer its embassy from Tel Aviv to Jerusalem.

Beyond Central America, Israel became a major arms supplier to Chile's repressive Pinochet government. In 1977, when the Carter administration refused to deliver Chile a promised supply of Sidewinder missiles, Israel did not hesitate to fill the vacuum with its own shipment of Shafrir air-to-air rockets. In ensuing years, the Israelis also supplied Pinochet with antitank rockets, radar systems, and reconditioned American-built Hercules transport planes. A former Mossad agent, Michael Harari, "privately" trained Pinochet's secret service. Again, for the Israelis, collaboration transcended financial profit. In this case, it gave them access to Chile's French-manufactured Exocet missile, a weapon known also to be in the possession of several Arab governments. Israeli engineers were allowed to study and develop countermeasures to the Exocet. Meanwhile, in the late 1970s and early 1980s, Israel also provided the Argentine military dictatorship with some one hundred reconditioned Mirage and twenty-four Skyhawk fighters, together with three hundred Shafrir missiles, four Saar patrol boats, and fifty Gabriel sea-skimmer missiles, as well as large quantities of spare parts.

Occasionally, Jerusalem cosmeticized its relationship with these right-wing regimes by invoking its obligation to protect their substantial local Jewish communities, particularly in South Africa, Argentina, and Chile. But the decisive inducements remained hard currency, a viable arms industry, and functional diplomatic ties. In their isolation, the Israeli people had long since become inured to the brutal facts of Realpolitik, and were even prepared to brazen out criticism from the United States. That censure related not only to the unsavory regimes Israel equipped, but to the resale of American equipment and proprietary technology. Throughout the 1980s, congressional committees periodically raised the charge that Israel was illegally transshipping American-produced air-to-air missiles to China, antitank missiles to South Africa, cluster bombs to Ethiopia, and aircraft radar and jamming devices to Chile.

If the Israelis denied or dissembled, it was not exclusively for reasons of opportunism. They understood precisely the overlap of their own vital interests and Washington's. In Honduras, El Salvador, and Costa Rica, Israel in effect was acting as surrogate for the United States itself, performing "dirty work" that Washington soon would be doing on its own. Indeed, the Reagan administration was the first to exploit Israel's potential usefulness as a proxy. Although the initiative came from the Israelis, the State Department was not unresponsive to the proposal. It even discerned a certain poetic justice in using Israel's vast surplus of captured Soviet weapons to fight leftist elements throughout the world. Periodically, Washington itself footed the bill. Nor were supplies limited to established right-wing regimes. On occasion, "counterrevolutionary" guerrilla movements proved worthy of support. The latter included South African–sponsored UNITA insurrectionists in Angola, MNR rebels in Mozambique, Habré guerrillas in Chad. In the end, they would also include "Contra" guerrillas in Nicaragua.

IRAN-CONTRA: THE ISRAELI CONNECTION

Early in 1987, a Senate intelligence subcommittee under the chairmanship of John Tower (Republican, Texas) issued a report summarizing months of investigations and televised hearings. Its opening paragraph declared:

> [It has been] disclosed that in August 1985 the United States . . . participated in secret dealings with Iran involving the sale of military equipment. There appeared to be a linkage between these dealings and efforts to obtain the release of American citizens held hostage in Lebanon by . . . [Iranian-sponsored] terrorists. . . . The Attorney General [also] announced that proceeds from the arms transfer may have been diverted to United States–backed rebel forces in Nicaragua.

As the report then listed the evident violations of American law and policy against weapons sales to the hated Khomeini regime of Iran, and the diversion of profits to Contra rebels in Nicaragua, it also revealed an unexpected Israeli link with the clandestine operation.

Few Americans needed reminder that, in November 1979, Shi'a fundamentalists of Iran's revolutionary Khomeini government had seized the United States embassy in Tehran and held its staff hostage. Washington had responded then by severing diplomatic relations, freezing Iranian assets, and imposing a trade and arms embargo on Iran. That embargo would remain intact through the Iran-Iraq war of the 1980s. Nor was Washington likely to relent following the abduction in 1985 of seven Americans in Beirut, civilians who afterward were held captive by the Hizballah, the Lebanese Shi'a terrorist group funded and directed from Tehran. Even against the background of these acrimonious events, however, General Robert McFarlane, national security advisor to President Ronald Reagan, was increasingly concerned lest the imminent death of the Ayatollah Khomeini touch off a succession struggle in Iran that might lead to Soviet intervention. In June 1985, at McFarlane's request, a group of staff associates formulated recommendations for developing contacts with potentially pro-Western elements in Iran. To strengthen the latter's influence, one proposal envisaged a cautious, selective resumption of American military shipments to Iran. Defense Secretary Caspar Weinberger and Secretary of State George Shultz promptly shot the recommendation down. Even so, McFarlane was loath to abandon the scheme entirely. He knew that President Reagan was under intense pressure from the hostages' families to establish some sort of contact with Tehran.

In fact, Israel also had a vested interest in reviving its own relationship with Iran. As early as the 1960s, Israel and Iran maintained "trade missions" in each other's capitals that functioned as de facto embassies. Iran supplied nearly half of Israel's oil. El Al flew scheduled flights in and out of Tehran. During the 1960s and 1970s, Prime Ministers Ben-Gurion, Eshkol, Meir, and Begin visited Iran to meet with Iranian government figures. Numerous Iranian officials made reciprocal trips to Israel. Over the years, too, Israel trained hundreds of Iranian agronomists, irrigation engineers, hotel managers, aircraft maintenance personnel, and other technicians. Several Israeli-Iranian corporations developed joint business projects both in Iran and in Europe. Not least of all, sharing a common bête noire in Egypt's Nasser, and later in Iraq's Saddam Hussein, Israel was second only to the United States as a source of Iran's military expertise and weaponry. In the 1960s, an Israeli military mission trained the Iranian commando units engaged in suppressing dissident Shi'a tribesmen in southern Iran; offered specialized training to the SAVAK, the shah's secret police; and provided Uzi assault weapons for the Iranian army, spare parts for Iran's American-supplied fighter jets.

The relationship changed dramatically, of course, following overthrow of the shah and establishment of the Islamic Republic in 1979. All official contacts between the two countries ended. Henceforth, Israel became a "great Satan," together with the United States, and the new Khomeini regime funded and guided radical Shi'a elements in both Lebanon and Palestine. Over the years, nevertheless, key figures in Israel's foreign affairs and intelligence circles still favored an effort to resuscitate the Iranian connection. So long as Iran and Iraq were engaged in their sapping war, they argued, military help to Iran at the least would keep Saddam Hussein's armed forces bogged down to the east. Their view prevailed. It was influenced also by the fate of Iran's ninety thousand Jews. Although the new Islamic government had promised its minorities fair treatment, Iranian Jewry was frantic to escape, usually across the frontiers to Turkey or even Pakistan; and thus far, in return for an appropriate payoff, Tehran was prepared to acquiesce discreetly in their departure. The payoff was Israeli weaponry. The Iran-Iraq war had created an urgent need for replacement equipment. Indeed, between 1979 and 1982, Israel supplied Iran with some $150 million worth of ordnance—particularly Shafrir air-to-air missiles and spare parts for Iran's aging fleet of American F-4 fighter-bombers.

The conduit for much of this weaponry had been pioneered by Ya'akov Nimrodi, an Iranian-born Israeli who returned to Tehran in 1959 to serve as Israel's deputy military attaché. It was in Tehran, during the 1960s, that Nimrodi helped orchestrate the close military cooperation between the two countries. Later, in the 1970s, functioning as a private businessman in Israel, Nimrodi specialized in marketing Israeli technology to his extensive network of Iranian contacts. His partner was the American-born Al Schwimmer (who for years was the guiding genius of Israel Aircraft Industries). After the fall of the shah, therefore, in 1979, it was Nimrodi and Schwimmer who continued as the major, private source of weapons and spare parts for the successor Islamic Republic. Indeed, to broaden the relationship, the Iranian regime for its part opened an arms procurement bureau in London, where Nimrodi and Schwimmer by then similarly maintained their office. One of these Iranians, Manucher Ghorbanifar, claimed also to be in touch with moderates inside the Khomeini government, men who were eager to resume a more normal relationship with the United States. They should be contacted, he suggested. Through Nimrodi, Schwimmer, and—ultimately—David Kimche, director general of the Israeli foreign ministry, Ghorbanifar's overtures were passed on to Washington. It was the period, 1985, when National Security Advisor McFarlane was embarking on his reassessment of United States policy toward Iran. Accordingly, when McFarlane received no encouragement from George Shultz or Caspar Weinberger, he decided on his own to dispatch a personal confidant to Israel for "consultations."

The confidant, Michael Ledeen, once an associate of McFarlane's in the National Security Council, was himself a Jew who maintained numerous Israeli intelligence connections. Arriving in Jerusalem in May 1985, Ledeen consulted with Prime Minister Peres and the latter's intelligence advisers. By the time Ledeen returned to Washington, he brought with him an Israeli consensus that Iranian moderates were indeed "reachable," that it was in the U.S. interest to cultivate them through selective weapons shipments. It was even possible to circumvent the congressional ban on arms sales to Iran, Ledeen reported; Israel was prepared to sell the weaponry from its own stocks, which the Pentagon then would replenish. Soon afterward, David Kimche, the Israeli foreign ministry official, visited Washington for a followup meeting of his own with McFarlane. In the course of discussions, Kimche intimated that Iran might also be prepared to authorize release of the American hostages in Lebanon as part of an arms deal. Hereupon, deeply intrigued, McFarlane attempted to sell the concept directly to Ronald Reagan. And, over Shultz's and Weinberger's reservations, the president gave his approval.

In August 1985, then, Nimrodi and Schwimmer arranged the first delivery to Iran of 96 Israeli TOW antitank missiles. The weaponry was transported in an Israeli-chartered aircraft. Ghorbanifar, the Iranian intermediary, handled the financing; upon collecting his tidy profit, he reimbursed the Israelis, who then repurchased the TOWs from American arsenals. Much to the chagrin of Israelis and Americans alike, not a single hostage was released. Nevertheless, McFarlane and Kimche agreed to try again. In mid-September, another Israeli-chartered plane delivered 408 TOW missiles to Iran, with Ghorbanifar once more arranging payment. Soon afterward, a single hostage, the Reverend Benjamin Weir, was released in Lebanon. It was a niggardly response from the Iranians. Indeed, sensing the Americans' frustration, Kimche flew back to Washington to press for a continuation of the weapons deliveries. His concern was unwarranted. McFarlane, and for that matter, President Reagan, needed little persuasion. This time they authorized Israel to sell the Iranians one hundred Hawk antiaircraft missiles. Once again, therefore, in late September, an Israeli-chartered jet made the delivery. And once again, the operation proved a fiasco. Proclaiming the missiles to be obsolescent, the Iranians would not authorize the release of additional hostages.

For Washington, the debacle would have ended all further reliance on the Israeli connection, had not two new intermediaries suddenly appeared. The first was marine Lieutenant Colonel Oliver North, a National Security Council assistant who had recently played a key role in resolving a maritime hijacking episode. It happened that, in October 1985, four Arab terrorists seized control of the Italian cruise liner *Achille Lauro* as the vessel was en route from Alexandria to the Israeli port of Ashdod, and murdered one of its passengers, Leon Klinghoffer, an elderly American Jew. Eventually the terrorists allowed the ship to dock at Port Saïd, where they permitted its remaining four hundred occupants to disembark. In return, President Hosni Mubarak had assured the hijackers that they would be flown to safety in Tunis. When the American government challenged him on his pusillanimity, Mubarak averred that the terrorists already had departed his country. Colonel North knew otherwise. Monitoring the crisis in Washington, he had been informed by Israeli intelligence that the hijackers were still in Egypt, and about to fly off in a Misrair jet—which the Israelis precisely identified. With President Reagan's approval, then, North relayed his information to the U.S. Sixth Fleet, whose jets promptly intercepted the embarking Egyptian airliner, forcing it to land in Sicily. There the hijackers were jailed.

North emerged as a hero of the operation. By then, too, the young marine officer had established a close rapport with his Israeli counterpart, Amiram Nir, who had provided the decisive intelligence information. Almost the same age as North, holding the same military rank as well as a doctorate in defense policy, Nir had served most recently as Prime Minister Peres's adviser on counterterrorism. Like North, he was a great believer in undercover operations. Each man now pressed his respective government to sustain the Iranian connection; and in December 1985, North secured White House approval to renew the arms deliveries effort. Indeed, he even joined a team of American intelligence agents, bearing false Irish passports, on a secret visit to Tehran in May 1986. Accompanying the Americans were General McFarlane himself and (incredibly) Amiram Nir, also under an incognito. The visit was intended as a climactic breakthrough to Iranian moderates, and with it a full release of the American hostages. Once again, the venture was less than successful. Although a final planeload of five hundred TOW missiles was delivered in October 1986, only three more Americans were freed in ensuing months.

Then, in November 1986, an account of the bumbling American visit leaked to the Lebanese press. Newspapers in the United States immediately picked up the story. More embarrassing yet, as the account of illicit American-Israeli arms deals with Iran unraveled, rumors began circulating of still another, equally shocking White House dereliction. This one related to the congressional ban on the transfer of weapons or funds to Nicaragua's Contras, a guerrilla faction then engaged in a grueling military insurrection against the leftist government of President Daniel Ortega. Was it possible that the Israelis, acting as American surrogates, had secretly diverted to the Contras the profits they earned from the Iranian arms sales?

It was entirely possible. Of all Israel's extensive dealings with right-wing Central American governments, one of the oldest traced back to Nicaragua's original Anastasio Somoza regime. Infinitely bribable, it was this dictatorship in the mid-1940s that gave free reign to Haganah gun- and ship-runners, and that supported Palestine partition in the United Nations. By the 1970s, Israel was supplying President Somoza with virtually all his weaponry, from small arms to jet airplanes. Consequently, when a national uprising toppled Somoza in 1979, both Israel and the United States watched in dismay as power in Nicaragua devolved into the hands of Daniel Ortega's Marxist cabal. In the 1980s, then, the Reagan administration sought discreetly to ensure an ongoing supply of funds and weapons to a coalition of center- and right-wing Nicaraguan Contra guerrillas. But a Senate ban abruptly terminated the relationship.

Israel was more than prepared to move into the vacuum. Indeed, as early as 1982, by secret agreement with the CIA, Ariel Sharon met with Contra representatives in Honduras, and arranged to sell them extensive quantities of Soviet-bloc weapons captured in the recent Lebanon war. Several dozen Israeli advisers accompanied the equipment. Three years later, as Contra funds began to run out, it was Oliver North who discerned the logic of exploiting this Israeli connection. In January 1986, the young NSC staffer discussed with Amiram Nir the feasibility of diverting profits from the Iranian sales to support the Contras. Nir reacted enthusiastically. So, evidently, did Prime Minister Peres and Foreign Minister Shamir, who were eager to cement their "strategic" relationship with Washington. At North's direction, therefore, some $15 million of the profits was accordingly deposited in the Contras' Swiss accounts.

Details on the Reagan administration's official authorization for this move remained vague, even during the subsequent 1987 Iran-Contra hearings in the Senate. Following the weeks of unfolding public testimony, nevertheless, the Tower Commission in its final report pilloried the National Security Council for violating the congressional ban on contacts with Iran and the Nicaraguan Contras. At the same time, without directly condemning Israel, the Senate report noted acidly that "Israel's objectives and interests in this initiative were different from, and in some respects in conflict with, those of the United States." Altogether, the Iran-Contra affair, and particularly the weeks of televised Senate hearings that shocked and dismayed millions of Americans, were a source of acute embarrassment to Israel's friends in the United States. The entire unsavory episode had come in the aftermath of the Jonathan Pollard affair. If these supporters continued dutifully to characterize Israel as Washington's "ally," the price of the alliance manifestly had become increasingly unsettling. How much longer could American forbearance be tested?

A REDEEMING TERRITORIAL MODERATION

Fortunately for Israel, it was a patience influenced by several distinctly redeeming features of Peres's incumbency. The man had withdrawn Israel's army from Lebanon, after all. His palpable moderation in foreign affairs had broadened Israel's ties with the European Economic Community and restored diplomatic relations with a substantial bloc of African nations. Under Peres's aegis, too, progress on the Taba issue had all but rescued the blighted peace treaty with Egypt. Discussions on Taba had dragged on since March 1983 (p. 887). The earlier Shamir government had refused to accept the notion of Taba as an "authentic" part of the Sinai Peninsula, and had procrastinated even on submitting the issue to the International Court of Justice at the Hague. But Peres was intent on surmounting this final territorial stumbling block in Israeli-Egyptian relations. In January 1986, over the objections of Likud hard-liners in his Unity government, the prime minister finally secured a cabinet majority willing to accept arbitration. Afterward, through the mediation of U.S. Assistant Secretary of State Richard Murphy, the Egyptian and Israeli governments agreed on the international composition of the arbitration panel. They also agreed to implement promptly any decision issued by the panel. On that understanding, the road was now clear for diplomatic "normalization." In November 1986, the Egyptian ambassador returned to Tel Aviv after a hiatus of four years.

Yet the revived mood of Egyptian-Israeli cooperation—and hence of American forbearance—was influenced not alone by progress on Taba, but even more by Peres's forthright intention to dismantle Israeli rule in the occupied territories. In his earlier years, to be sure, Peres had equivocated on the thorny issue of Palestine. But after becoming chairman of the Labor party, he made plain repeatedly in 1977 and in later electoral campaigns that "our goal is territorial partition, rather than the 'freedom' to be perpetual rulers over others." As prime minister now, Peres moved toward that goal in a manner that was both shrewd and forceful. Under the rubric of salvaging the economy, he drastically slowed additional expenditures for West Bank settlements and infrastructure. Even as late as 1984 the number of Israelis who had taken up residence beyond the Green Line (except for East Jerusalem) did not exceed fifty thousand. Only a minority of these settlers were devout Gush Emunim millenarians. Most had simply responded to Ariel Sharon's pragmatic financial inducements. What money had made, money presumably could unmake.

It was with this calculation that Peres now focused his diplomatic efforts squarely on Jordan. During his years in political opposition, Peres had been one of the few Israeli political leaders to remain unswerving in his commitment to the "Jordanian option," that is, to the restoration of "dependable, moderate" Hashemite rule over the Arab-inhabited areas of the West Bank. As he saw it, the challenge was to cajole King Hussein into serious negotiations independently of the PLO. Throughout the 1970s and 1980s, to be sure, the prospect of independent negotiations with Israel was simply too daunting for the Hashemite monarch. At the least, Hussein would have risked a possible upheaval among Yasser Arafat's substantial constituency in the territories, or even in Jordan itself; at worst, he might have risked the fate of his grandfather, Abdullah (p. 452). But Peres would not be put off—not after returning to the premiership in 1984. Early the following year, at a press conference during a visit to Rome, the prime minister stated frankly: "I am ready to go to Amman. I am sure Israelis would like to see Hussein come to Jerusalem and announce whatever he has in mind."

Peres was too experienced a diplomat to anticipate a dramatic, Sadat-like personal visit from Hussein. Instead, in earlier years, as defense minister in the Rabin government, and later as chairman of the Labor opposition, he had engaged in secret, quite private negotiations with the Hashemite king. The rapport between the two men had always been cordial. Indeed, upon Peres's ascent to the premiership in September 1984, Hussein publicly alluded to the Israeli leader as "a man of vision . . . a bright light in an area of darkness." For his part, then, Peres wasted little time in sending out new overtures to Hussein, principally through United States Ambassador Thomas Pickering (a former ambassador to Amman) and Egypt's President Mubarak. The message was clear: he, Peres, had only twenty-five months of incumbency to negotiate peace, and he depended on the king to be his interlocutor.

A series of proposals and counterproposals then ensued between Jerusalem and Amman throughout late 1984 and much of 1985. In March 1985, Hussein conferred privately with Defense Minister Yitzchak Rabin in Paris, and eventually Peres and Hussein themselves met secretly in London, in October of the same year. The reunion was typically cordial. The king emphasized, however, that detailed negotiations with the Israelis were not possible except within the framework of an international peace conference. He, Hussein, could not risk a direct, bilateral Hashemite-Israeli deal without courting the fate of the late Sadat, or of his own grandfather. The PLO would have to be involved in some form of joint delegation. Peres was unprepared to accept the king's conditions. Yet he would not give up. Through intermediaries, later, the prime minister offered Hussein a variety of other formulas: bilateral talks in conjunction with discussions carried on simultaneously with other Arab states; a regional peace conference in tandem with Egypt and Saudi Arabia; a meeting in Cairo chaired by United States representatives. "My diplomatic time is running out," he warned Hussein. But the king remained adamant.

And Peres still would not give up. In consultation with Secretary of State George Shultz, a substantive plan was devised for "power sharing," a scheme allowing Israel and Jordan to engage in joint administration of the West Bank for a three-year period. During that interval, there would be a total freeze on Jewish settlement in the territories. Not less than five hundred thousand acres of government land would be transferred to Hashemite control. An Arab flag, either Hashemite or possibly Saudi, would be raised over the Moslem holy places in Jerusalem. The arrangements, entirely temporary, would not preclude Hussein at some future date from demanding sovereignty over most of the West Bank; and, in the meanwhile, the king in effect would be "reintroducing" his government to hundreds of thousands of Palestinians currently under Israeli rule. From Amman, then, the response at last was one of cautious interest. Moreover, in January 1986—again through the good offices of Richard Murphy, shuttling back and forth between Jerusalem and Amman—a certain meeting of the minds also was reached on procedure. Hussein consented to an essentially cosmetic international format, under whose "umbrella" bilateral discussions could take place between Israel and Jordan. Peres would accept a joint Hashemite-PLO delegation, provided the PLO renounced terrorism, recognized Israel, and accepted Security Council Resolutions 224 and 338.

Many issues remained to be addressed. Nevertheless, the chasm between Israel and Jordan appeared to be narrowing. And, meanwhile, even without public exposure of the negotiations, the evidence of Peres's goodwill and transparent sincerity of intent was registering not only on Hussein, on Mubarak, and on other moderates in the Arab world. It was registering on the Americans, as well, on Pickering, Murphy, and Shultz, on Reagan, on Congress—and ultimately on American public opinion. By the time Peres's not undistinguished twenty-five-month tenure expired, in October 1986, he had decisively softened the earlier, Likud-era image of the ugly Israeli. Notwithstanding the recent Jonathan Pollard and Iran-Contra episodes, the American government and the American people at large evidently still preferred to interpret Israel's missteps of recent years as errors of execution, rather than of intent. Thus far, Washington was prepared not merely to sustain its forbearance but to provide tangible, substantive proof of its friendship in an ongoing effulgence of economic generosity and diplomatic support.

THE WAGES

OF IMMOBILISM

On October 20, 1986, the Labor party honored its commitment under the National Unity format by reversing the roles of its principal leaders. Yitzchak Shamir stepped up from foreign minister to prime minister, Shimon Peres down from prime minister to foreign minister. Although other portfolios were shuffled to reflect the incoming Likud hegemony, Yitzchak Rabin continued as defense minister, and thus as a symbol of military firmness against Arab guerrilla violence. Of comparable significance (if unrecognized at the outset), Moshe Nissim became the finance minister. Nissim was a Likud stalwart, yet he affirmed his intention of maintaining Peres's uncompromising approach to financial restraint. He was as good as his word. In the ensuing two and a half years, Nissim's tightfistedness on public expenditures and wage increases held inflation to a comparatively modest 20 percent annual rate.

Resolution of the Taba issue similarly produced a measure of international goodwill for Shamir's Unity government. In September 1988, after two years of detailed study, the international arbitration panel unanimously awarded Taba to Egyptian sovereignty. Shamir had rejected all earlier Egyptian offers of compromise. Now, grudgingly, he accepted the decision. Under a complex financial arrangement, the Israeli proprietors of Taba's Sonesta Hotel and a neighboring resort village were bought out, and the Egyptians assumed full ownership. Israelis would continue to visit both facilities in ensuing years, but exclusively as foreign tourists. The terms of the Egyptian-Israeli peace treaty were fulfilled.

For Shimon Peres, however, the goal he coveted most was resolution of the Palestine question. To that end, as prime minister, he had labored painstakingly to achieve a cooperative understanding with Jordan's King Hussein. As foreign minister now, the Labor chairman assumed that he still might continue to pursue his own diplomacy. It was an assumption shared by Hussein. The king had been impressed by Peres's earlier executive decisiveness in withdrawing Israel's army from Lebanon and dampening his country's raging inflation. In April 1987, therefore, the two men met secretly yet again, once more in London. And once more they explored the vision of an international conference as an "umbrella" for direct Hashemite-Israeli negotiations. The Jordanian ruler would still have preferred the option of "referring" any deadlocked issue to the full conference. Peres continued to insist on exclusively bilateral negotiations. This time, too, he was assured of full support from Washington, and tacit support even from Cairo.

Hussein finally acquiesced. After seven hours of discussions, the two statesmen reached agreement on a format. Israel and its Arab neighbors would be invited to a conference sponsored by the five permanent members of the UN Security Council. All parties would commit themselves in advance to Security Council Resolutions 242 and 338—that is, to peace and security for all states in the area—and respect for "the legitimate rights of the Palestinian people." The participants would negotiate in bilateral committees and reach all agreements directly. The Jordanian delegation would include Palestinians from the territories, provided none was an avowed member of the PLO. Once Israel and this delegation negotiated a formula between them, the agreement would be put into effect independently of the approval or disapproval of any other Arab delegation.

On the night of April 11, 1987, Peres flew back to Israel, convinced that he had opened the road to Palestinian peace. He was assured of solid backing from his other Labor colleagues, even from Yitzchak Rabin, who initially had kept his distance from his political rival. Yet, almost incredibly, the foreign minister had not troubled to involve even a single Likud member in his diplomacy. In effect, he simply dropped the London Agreement on Shamir's desk. At the same time, Peres had the document transmitted to Washington. Reacting with enthusiasm, Secretary of State Shultz in turn promptly wrote Shamir, offering to come to the Middle East to help lay the groundwork for the envisaged peace conference. By then the prime minister had seen enough. Implacable against the very notion of compromise on the "Land of Israel," Shamir called a press conference to reveal the Labor-Hashemite formula, then to revile it as "suicidal." With or without a "referral clause," Shamir insisted, an international conclave would put unacceptable pressure on Israel to surrender territory.

For his part, Shultz was not yet willing to give up on Peres's diplomacy. Over the next eight months of 1988–89, the secretary of state pressed the London format as if it were his own. Indeed, he met with Shamir not less than four times, three in the Middle East and Europe, once during a Shamir visit to Washington. Within Israel itself, meanwhile, both Peres and Rabin were the plan's strongest enthusiasts. "If Israel remains in the rejectionist camp," warned Rabin in a press interview, "we shall be left with no political hope and in international and regional isolation." Yet, for Shamir, the entire scheme was "naïve." All the more so when Yasser Arafat similarly rejected the peace initiative and refused even to meet with Shultz during the latter's Middle East visits. By the summer of 1988, the Shultz "initiative" had petered out, even as its inspiration, the Peres-Hussein London Agreement, evidently was consigned to oblivion.

A POLITICAL ROLLOVER

In any case, Shamir had other priorities. The prime minister's two-and-a-half-year stint was running out, and in November he would be facing new elections. The campaign already had begun. As it picked up steam during the summer and early autumn of 1988, moreover, a renewed upsurge of Palestine Arab violence (pp. 965ff.) polarized Israeli political life more extensively than at any time since the Arab demonstrations of 1981. Once again, the far-rightist Techiya and Moledet parties advocated a "voluntary" transplantation of West Bank Arabs across the bridges to Jordan. On the far left, a small conventicle of "doves" favored unilateral territorial withdrawal. Likud predictably maintained its traditional emphasis on the "unity of the Land of Israel," while the Labor Alignment as always favored territorial compromise and harshly condemned Shamir for sabotaging Peres's London Agreement.

When the ballots of November 1 were counted, it was almost possible to hear a collective groan from the Israeli people. Once more, an election had resulted in a virtual political lockstep. Labor's total had dropped from 44 to 39 seats, Likud's from 41 to 40. With a single-seat margin between these two largest parties, each side then embarked on the all-too-familiar process of wheeling and dealing. And thus it was, as in so many earlier contests, that the balance of power devolved into the hands of the religious bloc. It was a formidable bloc. Indeed, the Orthodox produced their largest showing since the birth of Israel, an astonishing 50 percent increase, from 12 to 18 seats, or 15 percent of the electoral total. More surprising yet was the emergence of Agudat Israel and Shas (the Oriental offshoot of Agudat Israel) as the two largest components within the Orthodox configuration, with 6 and 5 seats, respectively. Here again was evidence of the unprecedented new muscularity of religious fundamentalism in Israel. For better or worse, therefore, it was with this element that Shamir and Peres would have to negotiate in their search for a viable coalition. Forty-two days of agonized bargaining and counterbargaining ensued. Yet on this occasion, at least, the sheer militance of the religionists' agenda, transcending even the demands they had sold Likud during the 1981 "Begin II" government, aroused widespread public revulsion. Neither Likud nor Labor could remain indifferent to that outrage.

At one point, in his eagerness to avoid capitulation to the Orthodox, Shamir was prepared to return to the National Unity format. So was Peres. Not so thirteen of thirty-nine Laborite Knesset members. Instead, by mid-December 1988, a variation of the National Unity formula was devised, one that avoided recourse to the earlier, original rotation model. The Labor leadership this time consented to a junior role. As their quid pro quo, however, they extracted Likud's promise that new Jewish settlements in the territories would be limited to eight over the next year, with each ensuing community subject to Labor's approval. Indeed, to monitor that promise, Peres chose the finance ministry for himself, a portfolio that also would enable him to oversee a wider program of economic restraint. Both sides took satisfaction, as well, that they had avoided capitulation to the Orthodox. The latter now returned to the government, but noticeably chastened in their demands.

Meanwhile, throughout the mid- and latter-1980s, even as the two political blocs achieved a certain tactical accommodation, Israel and Jordan quietly refined and enlarged a functional cooperation of their own in the West Bank. The famed "open bridges" policy had operated since 1967, of course. For more than two decades, the Jordanian dinar had remained legal tender for all business transactions, in common with Israeli currency, and Jordanian textbooks (expurgated of anti-Israel material) continued to be used in Palestinian schools. The

Hashemite government similarly continued paying the salaries of thousands of West Bank civil servants, from teachers to policemen (p. 679). Moreover, in the spirit (if not the letter) of the draft London Agreement, Hussein in 1987 announced plans to invest fully $3 billion in the territories, including funds for 23,000 housing units, eighty-six new schools, and a deep-water port for Gaza. For its part, Israel accepted Hussein's brother, Prince Hassan, as director of this extensive program of revitalization, and authorized Jordan's Central Bank to supervise all banking operations in the territories. A "condominium" in every sense of the word, the mutually supportive arrangement plainly was intended to undermine PLO influence in Palestine. Even Menachem Begin apparently had this purpose in mind when he negotiated the Camp David framework in 1978, for Jordan was mentioned in the document not less than fourteen times as Israel's anticipated interlocutor at every stage of the peace process. The tentative London Agreement of nearly a decade later presumably fortified Hussein's ensuing commitment to a final political settlement.

Then, suddenly, in July 1988, the Hashemite ruler shattered that assumption. To the astonishment of Israelis and Palestinians alike, Hussein announced that he was "bowing to the wishes" of the PLO by formally separating the West Bank from the remainder of his kingdom, and dismantling all legal and administrative links between Palestine and Jordan. Henceforth, no further subventions would be available for the Arab civil service in the territories, or for public or private institutions of any kind. The announcement was a thunderbolt. Nevertheless, conceivably it might have been anticipated. In the months since the London Agreement of April 1987, after all, Shamir had repudiated the Peres-Hussein understanding, and with it Secretary of State Shultz's rather forlorn efforts to initiate a United Nations–sponsored "umbrella" conference. Then, afterward, in the November 1988 election, Shimon Peres had failed to renew his political mandate. Even more fundamentally, however, a thunderbolt of another kind lately had struck in the territories, one that threatened to inflame Hashemite Jordan, across the river. It was a spontaneous uprising of the Palestinian people themselves.

THE STORM BEFORE THE STORM

In 1968, the Arab inhabitants of the occupied territories numbered 943,000. In 1986, their numbers had risen to 1,261,000. Of these, nearly half a million lived in Gaza, the rest in the West Bank. The increase was the consequence first and foremost of improved health and economic conditions. The surging territorial economy reflected the incorporation of Palestine into the Israeli common market, of course, with its concomitant investment of Israeli capital in Palestinian workshops and cottage industries, and the even more extensive influx of commuting Palestinian laborers directly into Israel (p. 861). Yet, by the same token, many commuting Arabs had been working in Israel long enough to contrast their circumstances in the 1980s not with those of the pre-1967 era, but with those of the Israelis who now performed comparable work around them. Even when salaries and working conditions were identical (as the Histadrut insisted, to protect Jewish labor), Palestinian fringe benefits for years remained markedly inferior.

But in practical fact, even salaries and working conditions were far from identical. Fully a third of commuting Arab laborers were "illegal" employees, hired outside the official labor exchanges by straw bosses who trucked them to menial daily jobs in Israel, in the fields, in industrial warehouses, in restaurant kitchens—and invariably at wages below the legal minimum. Whether "legal" or "illegal" workers, moreover, the Palestinians experienced the worst of their deprivations in the very process of commuting. To reach their jobs, many were obliged to depart their homes well before dawn, and correspondingly did not return until mid-evening. Thus, to avoid the exhausting trek, substantial numbers of workers eventually circumvented the law by sleeping over in or near their Israeli places of employment during the week—in basements, huts, abandoned buses, even on open beaches. These commuters were by no means the most brutalized Arabs in the Middle East. Palestinians in Lebanon and Syria suffered authentic oppression (p. 897). Nevertheless, over the years, contrasting their status with that of their Israeli fellow workers, they felt themselves the most humiliated.

And for years, too, the Palestinians were bereft of spokesmen to protest their condition. Fatah and other PLO leaders who might have provided guidance in an insurrection were concentrated in distant Tunis. Palestinian society itself was riven with ethnic, clan, sectarian, and regional divisions. Nothing in the territories appeared to offer a serious threat to the status quo. Over the decades, therefore, Israel rarely had felt the need to deploy more than twelve hundred soldiers in the West Bank and Gaza, along with a few hundred Druze border police and Shin Bet (secret service) agents. Minimal as this occupation force was, moreover, its reaction to conspiracies or deeds of violence invariably was swift, ruthless, and efficient. That response took its most draconian forms, we recall, in the destruction of Arab homes and the deportation of guerrillas or inciters to neighboring Arab countries. Then, after 1985, as assaults on Jewish settlers began to rise, a more common alternative was "administrative detention." Under this procedure, inherited from the British mandatory government, suspects could be arrested and jailed for up to six months even before formal charges were brought. In 1987, to be sure, a commission chaired by a former supreme court justice, Moshe Landau, scathingly condemned these "administrative" detentions and jailings. Nevertheless, with some modifications, they remained intact. Consciously or unconsciously, the Israeli people swallowed the fiction that their occupation of the West Bank and Gaza remained fundamentally "enlightened." Reflecting on that period, David Grossman wrote in his 1987 novel *HaZman HaTzahov* (translated into English as *The Yellow Wind*):

> I could not understand how an entire nation like mine, an enlightened nation by all accounts, is able to train itself to live as a conqueror without making its own life wretched. What happened to us? How were [the military authorities] able to pass their values on to me during those years? . . . I also became an artist of sublimation.

As late as 1982, ironically, Yasser Arafat and his Fatah supporters within the PLO had nurtured the illusion that the neighboring Arab governments eventually would bestir themselves to help emancipate the Palestinians. But the Lebanon debacle offered a decisive moment of reappraisal. Not a single Arab nation was prepared to lift a finger in behalf of the Palestinians, or initially even to give asylum to the departing PLO guerrillas. Indeed, in ensuing years, the Arab governments appeared more interested in mediating the conflict between Iraq and Iran than in tackling the Palestine issue. Arafat and his colleagues evidently were thrust back on their own resources. Those resources were less than impressive after 1982. Periodic Lebanon-based guerrilla land or sea forays against Israel were either intercepted or countered by shattering reprisals, often by Israeli aerial bombardment. Retaliation occasionally took even more emphatic form. In September 1985, Arafat's crack assault unit, "Force 17," murdered three Israeli tourists on their rented pleasure boat in Lanarca, Cyprus. Thereupon Prime Minister Peres and Defense Minister Rabin decided to exploit the intelligence data, lately provided by Jonathan Pollard, on the location of Arafat's headquarters outside Tunis. They would authorize a bombing raid on those facilities. Several weeks later, the operation was carried out with the identical surgical precision that had characterized the 1981 attack on Iraq's nuclear reactor. The complex of offices and residences was demolished, and at least sixty PLO officials were killed.

Deprived of his traditional Lebanese base, of local infrastructure in Palestine, and of significant military accomplishment, Arafat was losing influence and even "face" in the West Bank and Gaza. Some Palestinians now regarded him as a Soviet stooge; others, as a bourgeois fraud, chauffeured around in his Mercedes, far distant from the realities of the occupation. In their despair and frustration, tens of thousands of Palestinians now began developing support organizations of their own. Thus, working in urban Israel, Arab commuters explored the value of union membership, a privilege banned under former Hashemite rule. By 1987, as a result, some 20 percent of the Palestinian labor force was organized in trade unions. A women's work committee, comprised of female graduates of Bir Zeit University, gradually opened its membership to women employees of cottage industries. Its intention plainly was to draw women of all backgrounds into public and national activities. Other organizations similarly were emerging: of students, merchants, intellectuals, lawyers, most with the potential to function as self-help networks.

During these same years of the 1980s, the territories also produced a group of communal activists intent upon formulating political models of their own for Arab Palestine. Although still genuflecting respectfully to Arafat and the PLO, the best known among these spokespersons—Hanna Siniora, Sari Nuseibeh, Rashid Shahadeh, Feisal al-Husseini, Hanan Ashrawi—had come up with an innovative new scenario. It was to accept the reality of a Greater Israel. Rather than ignore the hard evidence of Israeli annexationism, they argued, it would behoove the Palestinians to integrate themselves into the "system." Over time, the sheer weight of Arab numbers, Israeli and Palestinian Arabs alike, would transform "Greater Israel" into a de facto binational state. Yet, for all its originality, the scheme underestimated the determination of Israel's rightist factions, of Likud, Techiya, Moledet, Tsomet, as well as of the religionists, to "protect" the Jewishness of Greater Israel. The approach of the hard-liners varied, but their objective was identical. It was to encourage the Palestinians either to accept Hashemite citizenship or "voluntarily" to emigrate across the Jordan.

Moreover, during the 1980s, both Peres and Shamir unwittingly contributed to a rather more violent alternative for the territories than the one advocated by Palestinian "binationalists." On the advice of the Shin Bet, the National Unity government authorized a certain limited enlargement of Moslem fundamentalist activities in Palestine. The fundamentalists' program and institutions were directed principally by Hamas, an indigenous, Gaza-based movement that drew its ideology from Egypt's famed Moslem Brotherhood (p. 209), and its funding mainly from the Gulf oil states. With unofficial Israeli approval now, these right-wing religionists were authorized to build new mosques, Islamic schools and colleges, clinics and infirmaries, and thus presumably to function as a more "spiritual" alternative to Fatah and other PLO factions in Palestine. In fact, the gamble proved ill advised. Hamas soon revealed itself as irredeemably hostile to Israel. As preached by their Sunni *qadis* in the mosques of Gaza, Beit Lahiya, Rafah, and elsewhere in the Strip, the Palestinian people could be liberated from Israeli rule only by strict adherence to Moslem religious principles and through acts of calculated violence against the Jews. It was a fiery religionationalism that struck an instant chord with students at Gaza's Islamic University, then with other young people in Palestine. By mid-decade, Hamas guerrilla cells were operating in half the refugee camps on the West Bank, and in virtually every village, town, and camp in the Gaza Strip. By 1986, too, "Abu Jihad" (Khalil al-Wazir), Arafat's military deputy, discerned in these youthful militants promising material for sabotage operations. It was to them now that Fatah supplied weapons and intermittent military leadership.

So it was that the fusion of seething Palestinian resentment, Hamas inspiration, and Fatah weaponry eventually produced an upsurge of violence in the territories, even in Israel itself. In the autumn of 1986, Arab guerrillas in Jerusalem lobbed grenades near the Western Wall during a gathering of army recruits and their families, wounding and killing nearly a dozen. In May 1987, six convicted Fatah members escaped from an Israeli prison in Gaza, killing an Israeli army captain as they fled. In the year before their capture and conviction, these young men had been spreading mayhem through the streets of Gaza, murdering and mutilating suspected informers. Their escape now represented so grave a blow to the Israeli security apparatus that Defense Minister Rabin personally rushed to Gaza and imposed a curfew on the entire Strip. Predictably, the exploit of the "Gaza Six" became the stuff of Palestinian folklore. Despite tightened security, Arab violence continued to gain momentum throughout the autumn of 1987. It took its toll in periodic stabbings in the West Bank and East Jerusalem, and in almost daily stonings of Israeli traffic passing through the territories.

Finally, on the night of November 25, the guerrilla campaign achieved its most spectacular coup. Four youthful Palestinians, all trained in Syria, took off from southern Lebanon in motor-powered hang-gliders. Under cover of darkness, the Arabs flew at a height of three thousand feet, slowly winging their way across the Israeli border. According to plan, they landed barely a mile from an Israeli army encampment. Three of the infiltrators then prepared to attack the outpost. Their commander, "Abu Tayer," directed the operation by radio. As the marauders entered the camp, they found the Israelis in pajamas. Opening fire, they killed four of the soldiers and wounded several others. Abu Tayer then signaled his men to retreat. As they withdrew, one of the attackers was shot dead; the others managed to reach their commander and their hang-gliders. They took off. A few minutes later, one of the craft was downed by ground fire. The remaining two reached their base safely. The operation was the most brilliant ever carried out by Palestinian guerrillas. News of its success immediately resonated through every public medium in the Arab world. In the West Bank and Gaza, excitement approached near-delirium.

PALESTINIAN INTIFADA, ISRAELI RETRENCHMENT

Two weeks later, on December 8, 1987, an Israeli civilian truck driver lost control of his vehicle as he passed the Gaza enclave's large refugee encampment of Jabaliya. The truck smashed into an oncoming automobile filled with local Arabs, killing four of them. Instantly riots broke out, this time of unprecedented magnitude. Wielding knives and axes and hurling rocks, huge throngs soon overwhelmed the single, isolated detachment of Israeli troops. The soldiers responded with tear gas and gunfire, wounding thirty Arabs and killing one. The crowds finally dispersed. The next day, however, violent demonstrations erupted on the West Bank, in Nablus and the Balta refugee camp. Again military gunfire inflicted several casualties. During the ensuing week, additional thousands of troops had to be rushed in to confront riots that were exploding elsewhere throughout the territories, assuming the character of a spontaneous mass *intifada*, an "awakening." In Jerusalem, the bubble of Mayor Teddy Kollek's famed coexistence burst almost immediately. Police had to erect roadblocks on the streets connecting West and East Jerusalem. As Arab youths hurled stones at neighboring Jewish residences, Israeli troop reinforcements, confused and frightened, often overreacted, clubbing indiscriminately, firing tear-gas canisters and even live ammunition into threatening crowds.

In Tunis, meanwhile, the PLO's Fatah command had been caught as much by surprise as had the Israelis by the explosion of Palestinian rage and violence. Nevertheless, their representatives in the West Bank and Gaza moved rapidly to take control and direction of the uprising. In the effort, they worked closely with the various local resistance committees that swiftly coalesced out of the network of earlier professional and self-help organizations. Veterans of mutual support, these trade unions, youth groups, feminist societies, and lawyers', academic, and student associations soon proved highly effective in offering information on Israeli police or troop movements, in providing legal counsel, medical care, hiding places, printing facilities, weapons caches. Possibly the women's committees emerged as the biggest surprise of the intifada. Shielded from the harsher forms of military repression, they were able to establish child-care centers, to visit prisoners' families, and to provide food and clothing. When West Bank schools were closed in 1988, it was the women who organized makeshift classes in mosques, churches, and homes.

In the end, however, civil disobedience proved to be the intifada's most effective weapon. It took the form initially of mass strikes by the commuting West Bank and Gaza work force—upward of sixty thousand laborers. A total stoppage could not be sustained for more than seven months. Nevertheless, within the territories themselves, thousands of Palestinian civil servants quit their jobs. Palestinian merchants and artisans closed their shops and workrooms three hours each day. Businessmen ceased paying their scheduled taxes to Israel, while the population in its entirety boycotted Israeli products. The damage to the Palestinian economy in lost wages and other income was grave, even critical. But the disruption of Israel's own economy was also very serious. As early as February 1988, the cost of augmented military forces in the territories reached $5 million a day. Losses to the Israeli business sector were much heavier, reaching $19 million daily. For lack of commuting Arab labor, Israel's construction industry and its largest citrus plantations were all but paralyzed for more than half a year. Tourism suffered a 50 percent drop by midsummer of 1988. Meanwhile, the Bank of Israel reported that, by the end of 1988, the Palestinian boycott had cost Israel $650 million in export losses, including "exports" to the Palestine common market.

Neither did the intifada leave the seven hundred thousand Arab citizens of Israel unaffected. As early as December 21, 1987, a solidarity "Day of Peace" became the occasion for a vast public outpouring. From Jaffa to Haifa to Nazareth, local Arabs waved PLO flags and stoned and cursed passing Jewish automobiles. Even Negev Bedouin joined in, erecting roadblocks, burning tires, and hurling rocks at police. The Israeli public was stunned—and terrified. It was humiliated, too, in its public image. Indeed, the uprising may have achieved its greatest success in the realm of world opinion. In their stone-throwing, barricade-erecting, and tire-burning, the demonstrators very swiftly learned to alert foreign newsmen in advance, to ensure broad television and other journalistic coverage of Israeli repression. Less thoroughly reported were Palestinian killings and sexual mutilations of suspected local Arab informers. By the end of 1989, however, fully a third of the 2,700 attacks carried out by Palestinian activists were perpetrated against fellow Arabs.

Israeli countermeasures did not err on the side of restraint. Nightly curfews were imposed on Palestinian towns and villages. Even later, upon resuming their daily treks into integral Israel, Arab commuting workers were carefully screened for new registration cards, then obliged to undergo time-consuming, often exhausting border examinations. When schools were closed in violence-prone Arab communities, some three hundred thousand children were affected. Despite the best efforts of Arab women's committees, numerous secondary-school pupils were unable to take their matriculation examinations, and accordingly were denied a possible higher education. Indeed, for more than four years, until early 1992, the West Bank's six largest colleges were themselves shut down for reasons of violent student protest. Bir Zeit eventually conducted some of its classes at the homes of teachers, in mosques and churches, even in apartments and rented stores. It was an inadequate alternative; students were not permitted use of such vital campus facilities as libraries or laboratories.

At its most sophisticated level of security intelligence, Israeli retaliation focused on the suspected PLO "brains" of the intifada. Thus, in February 1988, Mossad agents tracked down three of the Fatah's principal military commanders in Limassol, Cyprus, and assassinated them. Two months later, another group of Mossad operatives was landed off the coast of Tunis by sea, then made its way to the suburban headquarters of "Abu Jihad," Arafat's deputy and the master-mind of innumerable acts of guerrilla violence against Israel over the years. Shooting their way in, the commandos cut down Abu Jihad and seventeen of his associates. Meanwhile, in Palestine itself, Israeli Shin Bet personnel continued the hunt for PLO and Hamas militants, arresting and occasionally killing their prey in sudden break-ins and firefights.

By 1990, Israel's most palpable response to the intifada was the unprece-dented deployment of fully ten thousand soldiers in the territories. Patrolling Arab streets and alleyways, these heavily armed troops broke open padlocked shops, homes, and other buildings suspected of arms concealment, charged Arab mobs—clubbing, arresting, occasionally killing (despite the effort to rely mainly on plastic bullets). By 1990, too, according to a report issued by the Save the Children Fund, some twenty thousand Gaza and West Bank Arabs had been wounded, 722 killed. No fewer than thirteen thousand other Palestinians lan-guished in Israeli prisons, many under six-month "administrative" detention. Approximately one hundred Palestinian families, suspected of harboring guer-rillas, endured the trauma of home demolition.

In response to international criticism, the Shamir government protested that at least one hundred Israeli soldiers and civilians also had died in the violence. Yet few Israelis could be oblivious to the impact of the intifada on their own society and values. More than all others, it was young army troops who were shaken by the role assigned them of subduing civilians, often children and women, and of destroying private homes. Detesting these assignments, soldiers occasionally released their frustrations through unwonted brutality against stone-throwers and other demonstrators. But with increasing frequency, too, they resorted to expedient "unavailability" or even to conscientious refusal of service in the territories. Meanwhile, for civilians, the defacement of Israel's humanistic ideals was a source of grave unease, even anguish. It was on their behalf that the respected novelist Yizhar Smilansky declaimed, in an open letter to *HaAretz*:

> I am not blind to the fact that there are two sides to this painful situation, that it is not a question of evil oppressors persecuting the righteous oppressed. But neither am I blind to the fact that there is a way out of this quagmire . . . that in the end there will be no choice but to talk, and to negotiate a solution that will bring peace. So why not do it now instead of later—after another death, and another and another? . . . The Jew in me is crying out.

To be sure, if hundreds of thousands of Israelis were eager to have done with the occupation, there seemed to be almost as many whose atavistic suspicion and fear of Arabs dictated another, harsher course of action. Disdaining Labor's complex solutions of autonomy, these hard-liners proposed capital punishment or expulsions for terrorists, as well as tightened restrictions on the movement of all Palestinians. Nevertheless, amidst the turmoil of debate, the Israel Institute of Applied Social Research in 1988 found a "slow dovish" trend in the nation, with "each year [showing] a slight softening of attitudes." With or without the intifada, more than two decades of occupation plainly had traumatized an increasingly wider sector of Israeli society. Beyond such groups as Peace Now and Soldiers Against Silence, respected centrist newspapers of the caliber of *Ha-Aretz* and *Ma'ariv* expressed deep editorial concern about the palpable erosion of national morale.

Thus, in 1989, the Labor party adopted its firmest and least equivocal stance in favor of territorial withdrawal. Even Prime Minister Shamir, under intense pressure from both the United States and an apparently shifting Israeli public opinion, felt obliged to offer a show of moderation. In March 1989 he proposed elections among the Palestinian Arabs as early as the following May, to establish an "authorized entity" for autonomy discussions. The "entity" in turn would function during a transitional period of five years, and eventually would participate with Israel and Jordan in negotiating "final territorial dispositions." On its face, the proposal bore an apparent resemblance to the original Camp David format, and for that reason enjoyed the unofficial cosponsorship of Yitzchak Rabin, and the tentative approval of several other important Labor figures.

Yet the offer hardly was as far-reaching as it seemed. It made plain that Arab inhabitants of Greater Jerusalem, "the one and indivisible capital of Israel," would not be regarded as inhabitants of the territories. In one fell swoop, the categorization would have disfranchised some two-fifths of the Palestinians in the West Bank. Shamir was adamant, as well, that even the initial Palestinian elections could not take place until all violence stopped. A shopworn ultimatum of proven historic bankruptcy, Shamir's precondition was scorned even by Palestinian moderates. For Washington, meanwhile, James Baker, secretary of state in the newly elected Bush administration, pressed Shamir to be more forthcoming, to drop his exclusion of East Jerusalemites, to offer a model at least of limited autonomy in advance of the proposed election, and above all else to call a halt in the ongoing settlement of Jews both in the West Bank and in East Jerusalem. Baker added, too, that each side in the Palestinian-Israeli negotiations should be allowed to raise "any issue," and not be constrained by Shamir's attenuated agenda of electoral procedures. But the prime minister's reaction to the "Baker Plan" was flatly negative. He rejected each one of its innovations.

By contrast, Labor's senior figures discerned possibilities in the secretary of state's format. Once it became evident that Shamir would not budge, Shimon Peres decided to make his own move. In March 1990, as finance minister, he blocked funds for the eight West Bank settlements initially countenanced in the 1988 Likud-Labor coalition deal. Anticipating a Knesset no-confidence vote against Shamir, the Labor chairman then virtually invited Shamir to demand his resignation from the cabinet. He got it. He also got the resignation of other Labor ministers. But thereupon the tiny Shas faction, which had promised Peres its support, decided at the last moment not to join in a no-confidence vote against Shamir. Peres's maneuver had been in vain. The six-year experiment in unity government at long last collapsed under its own illogic.

All but frantic to avoid the ordeal of new elections, the parties bargained and manipulated without pause, week after week. Finally, in June 1990, Shamir managed to patch together a new coalition by including several of the smaller religious parties and those of the ultranationalist Right—Techiya, Moledet, Tsomet. Further to ensure the allegiance of hundreds of thousands of non-Ashkenazi voters, Shamir also turned over the critical foreign ministry portfolio to David Levy. It was an astonishing choice. A product of the 1950s Moroccan immigration, Levy was undereducated and proficient only in the Hebrew language. In his dealings with foreign diplomats, his lack of diplomatic experience and savoir faire rapidly became an embarrassment to his ministerial colleagues. No less shocking was still another appointment of political expediency, this one of the indestructible Ariel Sharon as minister of housing. In its impact on the territories, the post was comparable to Sharon's earlier assignment as minister of agriculture. The world was put on notice. As of June 1990, Israel's pretense to diplomatic restraint was dropped altogether. More than ever before, its government was unambiguously committed to an "undivided Land of Israel."

A RESURGENT IMMIGRATION FROM EASTERN EUROPE

It was not a coincidence that Prime Minister Shamir resumed his hard line at the moment the nation anticipated a decisive enlargement of demographic mass, indeed, a transformation capable of peopling East Jerusalem and the West Bank with tens of thousands of additional Jews. The development was related intimately to Mikhail Gorbachev's ascent to leadership in the Soviet Union in 1985, and the introduction soon afterward of economic and political liberalization throughout the Communist empire. At first, Soviet Jews shared in the heady new atmosphere. Once again, they were admitted to better universities, given employment in their traditional elite professional roles, allowed to reopen once-shuttered synagogues, and to publish books and newspapers on Jewish themes. But among other, unanticipated consequences of the new liberalization was the collapse of the Soviet economy. It was a free fall precipitous enough to unsettle a traditionally middle-class element like the Jews. Worse yet, the Soviet behemoth soon was mired in ethnic upheavals and nationalist unrest, and the Jews as always became favored targets for chauvinist extremism.

In growing numbers, therefore, they availed themselves of the single feature of liberalization that offered the cleanest solution to their future—departure. And, for his part, Gorbachev was prepared to allow it. Desperate to modernize his economy, to gain access to American trade and technology on a most-favored-nation basis, the Soviet president had learned well from his predecessors the value of American Jewish goodwill, and the price of forfeiting it. Here it was, then, that the 1972–75 struggle over the Jackson-Vanik Amendment (pp. 748, 808) at last began to pay off. After a decade and a half, the gates for Jewish emigration almost miraculously were opening again, indeed, opening wide. In 1987, 8,144 Jews were permitted to leave. In 1988, the number rose to 18,965; in 1989, to 71,000; in 1990, to 200,000!

As in the latter 1970s, however, the mounting torrent appeared likely at first to follow Soviet Jewry's well-trafficked route to the United States. Thus, in anticipation of a new avalanche, America's United Jewish Appeal leadership in 1989 focused its $75 million emergency campaign exclusively on Jewish migration to the United States. It was an unprecedented reversal of philanthropic priorities; and, upon learning of it, the government of Israel and the Jewish Agency all but exploded in outrage. So, at last, did their partisans among American Jews, who sensed that the issue of Soviet immigration was one of possibly historic demographic credibility for the little Jewish state. Moreover, the "Zionists" received unexpected support from an unexpected source, the U.S. government. It was becoming apparent to the Bush administration that the latest Soviet refugee wave also included many thousands of non-Jews—Armenians, Georgians, Estonians, Latvians—all seeking escape from Russian domination or ethnic turmoil. The anticipated influx would have placed heavy pressures on the federal government at a time of budgetary retrenchment.

For the first time in many decades, therefore, the United States Immigration Bureau announced that it would no longer automatically grant entrance to Jews unable to demonstrate a "well-founded fear of persecution." In fact, under Gorbachev, antisemitism had been dropped as government policy. By the late 1980s, most Soviet Jews were not even fleeing popular xenophobia as much as the economic malaise that afflicted all Soviet citizens in common (although they would not admit the fact). And, meanwhile, Israel's doors were wide open. Accordingly, under Washington's new directive, Soviet-Jewish applicants to the United States were obliged to provide evidence of persecution on a case-by-case basis. Only a minority appeared likely to qualify. The decision represented a major coup for Israel. Henceforth, it would be spared American Jewish competition for Soviet Jews. Better yet, the Kremlin itself now discreetly cooperated in facilitating Jewish departure for Israel. Although maintaining its ban on direct flights between Moscow and Tel Aviv (to defuse Arab protests), the Soviet government dropped objections to "indirect" flights via Budapest and Sofia. Both eastern European capitals manifestly bypassed Vienna, the transit point from which Soviet Jews earlier had switched their destination from Israel to the United States. Afterward, then, the emigration statistics revealed the full magnitude of the shift. In 1990, a total of 181,759 Soviet Jews arrived in Israel. It was a twelve-month infusion of humanity unmatched in Israel's forty-two-year history. And hundreds of thousands of other Soviet Jews, perhaps as many as half a million, were expected to arrive in the near future. For the Israeli nation, the prospect was altogether thrilling.

It was also intensely challenging. To cope with an influx of this unprecedented size and demographic potential, the nation's best physical and intellectual resources would have to be mobilized. Thus, early on, the government and the Jewish Agency decided to forgo use of the absorption center. The center in earlier years had functioned as an indispensable way station for undereducated North African and Middle Eastern Jews (p. 405), and lately for the quite primitive Falashas. It appeared inappropriate, however, for the more sophisticated Russian-speaking newcomers. Rather, on the advice of the Jewish Agency's widely experienced staff of social workers, the Soviet immigrants were cast loose in Israeli society at large. They were not left without a safety net, of course. The moment the newcomers disembarked at Ben-Gurion Airport, they were each handed 22,000 shekels to cover basic living expenses during their first year in

Israel. In addition, the Jewish Agency provided them with six months of free health insurance, as well as extensive mortgage and loan benefits.

As in the 1970s, too, make-work projects were created for several thousand immigrants. The effort was particularly useful for newcomers who brought valuable professional skills with them. In Beersheba, Ben-Gurion University's Professor Herman Branover, a renowned Soviet physicist and "veteran" of the 1970s immigration, served as unofficial godfather to hundreds of other Soviet scientists and engineers. It was Branover's scheme to raise funds for a seed-capital enterprise, SATEC, to underwrite his colleagues' ventures in developing new high-tech products. SATEC in fact proved modestly successful in fostering and marketing inventions ranging from an electronic digital power meter, a miniaturized electronic heating element, and an electronic blood-flow counter, to devices for extracting gold from industrial waste products and producing liquid ice. With public and private support, also, talented immigrant musicians often were integrated into Israeli orchestras, or into musical ensembles specifically created for their employment. Meanwhile, a spate of Russian-language dailies—*Nasha Strana, Novosti Nedeli, Vremya, Vesti*—as well as several weekly and monthly general and literary journals, attested to the newcomers' ongoing cultural acuity in Israel. With Jewish Agency and private investments, Russian-language book publishing and book imports similarly were gaining momentum. The Israeli television authority cooperated by offering Russian-language subtitles, while Friday editions of several newspapers provided Russian-language supplements.

Yet the human costs of the avalanche inevitably began to register. Even with their initial nest egg, tens of thousands of immigrants soon exhausted their funds. Appropriate employment could be provided for only a minority of the newcomers. As early as 1990, several thousand Soviet Jews, many of them holders of university degrees, were to be found laboring in the dawn hours as street sweepers in part-time municipal jobs; or standing on street corners during business hours playing violins or concertinas for the spare shekels of passersby. Hundreds of Soviet-Jewish women were known to have resorted to prostitution. Neither was it the newcomers alone who suffered the pangs of mass immigration. In one community after another, schools became gravely overcrowded with Soviet-Jewish children. Funds were inadequate for supplementary facilities or new teachers. Municipal budgets, already overstrained, could not provide for enlarged sewage or reservoir facilities. Middle- and lower-middle-income housing was in short supply. With immigrants using their government stipends to rent apartments, landlords responded to increased demand by raising rents for immigrants and veteran Israelis alike. Young married couples as a result were driven increasingly to living with parents or in-laws. In the summer of 1990, several thousand younger Israeli families actually engaged in protest demonstrations, taking up "residence" in tents or other makeshift dwellings in public parks.

The Shamir government's response to the crisis was to embark on the immediate construction of forty-five thousand public housing units, even to import some nine thousand prefabricated and five thousand trailer homes. It spurred contractors into accelerated construction with guarantees of repurchase. Yet the fundamental question loomed increasingly large: who would pay for this basket of financial inducements? With planeloads of Soviet Jews arriving virtually every night, cabinet ministers and senior Jewish Agency officials were speaking of expenditures as high as $6 billion to cope with an influx of possibly half a million immigrants within two or three years—a fifth of the current Israeli population. Where would the government find the money?

THE PRICE OF REVIVED TERRITORIALISM

Loans would have to be sought on the world market. Although the Shamir cabinet hesitated to apply yet again to the United States, it anticipated that Washington at least would guarantee repayment of as much as $10 billion in borrowed funds, by acting in effect as cosigner—thereby enabling Israel to secure less onerous interest rates elsewhere. But the expectation was coupled with still another: that the nation's expanding population would serve also as the demographic base for Greater Israel. Until recently, Laborites and other moderates had warned that permanent occupation of the territories would create a time bomb for Israel's Jewish population. Within twenty years, so the argument went, the Arabs would become the majority. By the summer of 1990, however, Shamir and his new, right-wing cabinet had the Soviet avalanche to confute this argument.

Indeed, by then, the prime minister already had embarked on a decisive shift even from Menachem Begin's commitment under the Camp David accords. By the terms of that agreement, it is recalled, Begin had muted his original Revisionist-annexationist ideology. Only later, confronting a backlash from the Right-Orthodox bloc, did he feel obliged to "interpret" his assurances to Sadat and Carter, making plain that he had always envisaged Palestinian autonomy as personal, not territorial. The Arabs would exercise jurisdiction only over civil affairs, not over territory. Yet not even Begin had rejected the participation of East Jerusalem Arabs in future Palestinian elections or autonomy negotiations, or demanded a veto-right over future Arab delegates. Shamir did.

Under the circumstances, Washington's reaction to the loan-guarantee request was chilly. President George Bush was a humanitarian. His earlier role in the rescue of Ethiopian Jewry was known and appreciated in Israel. Nevertheless, the president and Secretary of State Baker were acutely aware that the prime minister earlier had rejected the Hussein-Peres London compromise. This time they minced no words. Israel's scheme for the political neuterment of East Jerusalem Arabs was unacceptable. So was the use of American money to subsidize ongoing Jewish settlement in the West Bank and East Jerusalem. Shamir's reaction, in turn, was one of professed astonishment. Whether in the form of direct grants or guaranteed loans, he insisted, no American money would be employed to settle Israelis beyond the Green Line. But the response from Washington was equally straightforward: money reaching Israel was known to be "fungible"—that is, applicable to purely Israeli projects in a manner that released Israeli funds for territorial settlement purposes. The president would not budge.

Nor would Shamir. The prime minister was intent at all costs on accelerating his settlements program. Indeed, had he wavered from that commitment, his nation's ultra-Right might well have forced his hand. By late 1990 and early 1991, it had not escaped this element that the intifada was slowing under the weight equally of Israeli suppression and of the Palestinians' sheer economic exhaustion. On their own, then, Israeli militants prepared to resume their aggressive settlement campaign. Thus, in October 1991, hundreds of Orthodox Jews, most of them members of the Gush Emunim, stormed a cluster of six Arab homes in Silwan, an Arab village due east of Jerusalem. Recently they had purchased the land from its Arab owner. Rejecting the outraged protests of the Palestinians, who claimed right of occupation under both Israeli and Hashemite law, the settlers began forcibly evicting the Arab families. The police then arrived to block the eviction. But two months later, the Shamir cabinet retroactively approved the initial Silwan takeover, and within days the pietists returned to Silwan, with heavy police protection. Bursting into the six homes once again, they immediately expelled the Arab occupants.

The Silwan takeover in turn fitted into a wider master plan spearheaded by some three hundred members of Ateret HaCohanim, the "Priestly Crown" yeshiva. It envisaged Jewish colonization of twenty-two "unsecured"—that is, exclusively Arab-inhabited—areas of East Jerusalem. The pietists felt certain of government approval. After all, it had long been a Likud article of faith to enlarge Greater Jerusalem to a population ultimately encompassing 1 million Jews, and to link the metropolitan area with the West Bank's largest Jewish settlement, Ma'aleh Adumim, three miles to the east. In fulfillment of that scenario, the Jewish population of Greater Jerusalem already had reached 523,000 by late 1991, including 150,000 in East Jerusalem, and 35,000 in surrounding West Bank settlements. Nevertheless, in sheer unremitting militance, no effort matched that of the Ateret HaCohanim. Ensconced in the Moslem Old City as far back as 1978, these zealots were quite openly preparing for a climactic demolition of the al-Aqsa Mosque and possibly even the Dome of the Rock, the venerated Moslem holy places that had been constructed over the ruins of the ancient Second Temple. Once that Temple was rebuilt, they believed, the Messianic Age at long last could begin. Inspired by the Ateret HaCohanim, an even tighter comminution of several dozen fanatics, the "Temple Mount Faithful," gathered each autumn on the Jewish festival of Sukkot, appealing for a "massive pilgrimage" to reclaim the Temple Mount. On October 8, 1990, one such convergence of nearly three thousand Charedim led to a violent melée that caused the death of 17 Palestinians and the wounding of 150. The confrontation was given extensive media coverage worldwide and even provoked censure from the United Nations General Assembly.

The Ateret HaCohanim themselves ostensibly eschewed violence. Nevertheless, by sheer persistence and aggressiveness, they eventually fulfilled a common fundamentalist goal of enfilading Jerusalem's Moslem quarter. As early as 1987, they had succeeded in purchasing more than seventy Arab properties there, worth an estimated $10 million. Afterward, too, they began pushing their way into the Christian Quarter (also principally Arab). On April 11, 1990, during Easter Week, 150 Ateret HaCohanim partisans moved into the sixty-eight-room St. John's Hospice near the Church of the Holy Sepulchre. Owned by the Greek Orthodox Church, the building for decades had been leased to one Matyos

Matossian, an Armenian who sublet rooms to Arab families and European pilgrims. Several months earlier, however, Matossian suddenly had shifted his "clientele," renting the hospice for $3.5 million to a mysterious Panamanian company, SBC, Ltd. The latter in turn sublet the building to the Ateret HaCohanim, who promptly renamed it Ne'ot David. Ariel Sharon, who himself owned an apartment in the Moslem Quarter (purchased for him by the Ateret HaCohanim), then paid a congratulatory visit to the settlers.

The episode instantly touched off condemnation of Israel throughout the world. In protest, all major Christian churches in Israel and the West Bank, including even the Church of the Holy Sepulchre, closed on Good Friday, April 27. New York's Cardinal John O'Connor, normally a friend of Israel, denounced the takeover as an "obscene" plot. Ariel Sharon in turn accused the cardinal of antisemitism. Prime Minister Shamir limited himself to a formal denial that his government had secretly helped the settlers. Shamir was dissembling. The government had covertly channeled $1.8 million to SBC, Ltd., to underwrite the sublease. The Greek Orthodox Church in any case argued that the sublease was illegal, a claim that subsequently was upheld by an Israeli court, which ordered the settlers to vacate the property. Yet the court allowed twenty "security and maintenance employees" to remain in the hospice, pending further litigation. By no coincidence, the "employees" were Ateret HaCohanim settlers, living in the building with their families. Mayor Teddy Kollek, who had devoted his career to maintaining Jerusalem as a mosaic of pluralism, was beside himself with anguish. His dream of a multicultural city was palpably fading.

In fact, Jerusalem by 1990 was simply a microcosm of the government's wider territorial policy. Once again Ariel Sharon played a central role. As minister of housing, the aggressive ex-general now trumpeted his vision of enlarging the territories' current Jewish population of 100,000 to 300,000 within twenty years. To that end, in February 1991 he offered contractors a $5,000 bonus for each unit completed in less than eight weeks. Settlers, too, were offered new inducements. In 1991, a family buying a home in the West Bank could take out a $71,000 mortgage, all but $17,500 of it interest-free, with the remaining interest a negligible 4.5 percent; and after five years, $10,000 of the mortgage would become an outright gift. More extravagantly yet, under various financial pretexts Sharon began bypassing Israel's Land and Developments Authority to give away free plots to "preferred" settlers. In April 1992, the practice was exposed and castigated in a state comptroller's report. Sharon remained unfazed. The practice continued.

After 1990, too, with the steady growth of their militias and arsenals, the settlers exceeded all previous limits in their vigilantism. One of their private armies, operating out of Kiryat Arba, even published a guerrilla-warfare manual, calling on settlers to "impose justice [on Arabs] themselves" and recommending the use of dum-dum bullets that expanded on impact. Some militia vigilantes launched preemptive attacks on Palestinian villages at night, under the theory that the Arabs "are not afraid of the army, but are afraid of us." Rarely were the Jewish perpetrators detained, and assuredly not in the period of the reconstructed Shamir government. Indeed, from June 1990 on, the signals from that cabinet were unmistakable. In November, it happened that the Kach leader

Meir Kahane, on a return trip to New York, was murdered by an Egyptian expatriate. The next day, the Shamir government published an official statement expressing its sorrow at Kahane's death.

AN EXHAUSTION OF AMERICAN FORBEARANCE

The diplomatic consequences of Shamir's incumbency were by no means exclusively punitive. In search of Jewish and American liberal goodwill, several "neutralist" governments were prepared to establish or resume formal ties with Israel (pp. 938–9). Yet, in January 1988 the UN Security Council unanimously condemned Israel for its policy of jailing or deporting Arab demonstrators. The French reaction was even more characteristic of the West's growing frustration with Israel. When first elected president of France in 1981, François Mitterrand, a Socialist and philosemite, did not disguise his intense personal sympathy for the Jewish state. He muted his resentment over the Israeli bombing raid on Iraq's nuclear reactor. On two occasions he visited Israel, the first president of France to do so. Determined to give the Camp David accords a chance, he was the single western European statesman to dissociate himself from the European Commuity's mounting censure of Israel. Yet, by 1987, even Mitterrand felt impelled to criticize Israel's settlements policy, and afterward to extend a public reception to Yasser Arafat and other PLO officials.

It was Washington, finally, under the Bush administration, that now adopted a position toward Israel more reserved than at any time since the Eisenhower-Dulles years. That firmness in turn exploited a crevasse within American Jewry that had been opening throughout the 1970s, but that widened into a major schism with the Lebanon invasion, the Jonathan Pollard episode, and now the Palestinian intifada. Irredentism still was not lacking among this minority community. Like their counterparts in Israel, ultra-Orthodox elements tended to accept the strictures of their rabbis against withdrawal from "God-anointed" Judea and Samaria (pp. 866, 927). For many years, even such mainstream Jewish organizations as the Anti-Defamation League and the Conference of Presidents of Major Jewish Organizations maintained a public stance of unity with Israel's governments—of whichever political coloration. Nevertheless, spokesmen for Reform Judaism had emerged early on as vocal critics of Israeli territorialism, as had those of the American Jewish Congress. By 1988, as the intifada gained momentum, the frozen plateau of UJA campaigns similarly reflected the confusion and equivocation of the American Jewish public at large.

It was thus less than surprising that an initial effort to break the Arab-Israel lockstep should have emerged from a joinder of Israeli and American Jewish initiatives. For some years, a growing number of Israeli journalists, together with several left-wing members of the Knesset, had been challenging the official ban on private contacts with the PLO. Meeting with Yasser Arafat and his associates in Tunis or in Europe, they reported openly on their conversations afterward. By the late 1980s, even the Shamir government hardly bothered any longer to prosecute the violators. Then, in June 1988, Arafat and his close aide Bassam Abu Sharif circulated a document indicating that they favored direct negotiations with Israel, and were prepared at last to recognize Israel's legitimate security preoccupations. The overture was impelled by several underlying factors. One plainly was the ongoing ordeal of the Palestinians, and the likely tactical usefulness of exploiting the intifada before the uprising crested. Another was the collapse of Soviet support. Still another was the persistent rumor of a separate deal between King Hussein and Shimon Peres. An additional impulsion yet was alarm at the unprecedented influx of Soviet immigrants, and their potential for inundating the West Bank with new settlers. Possibly the most decisive factor of all, however, was the manifest indifference to the Palestinian ordeal in the Arab world at large. Thus, at a meeting of the Arab League in Amman in November 1987, the assembled statesmen had devoted most of their time evaluating the results of Iraq's continuing war with Iran (p. 977). The Palestine issue was virtually ignored.

The immediate catalyst for Arafat's overture was a series of private meetings conducted initially in Stockholm in March 1988 under the auspices of Sweden's deputy foreign minister, Pierre Schori. The interlocutors were a PLO delegation led by Bassam Abu Sharif and two American Jews, Stanley Sheinbaum and Rita Hauser. Sheinbaum was a liberal Democrat from Los Angeles and an old friend of Schori's; Hauser was a Republican lawyer from New York who had served in the Nixon administration. Both Americans were close to the International Center for Peace in the Middle East, a dovish lobby founded in 1982 by Abba Eban and Pierre Mendès-France. Before entering into their negotiations with the PLO, Hauser and Sheinbaum had consulted with Assistant Secretary of State Richard Murphy, to determine the government's minimal requirements for United States diplomatic contacts with the PLO. Murphy emphasized that Arafat must specifically accept UN Resolution 242, acknowledging "the existence of Israel as a state in the region," and the "rejection and condemnation of terrorism in all its forms."

First in Stockholm and then six months later in Geneva, Hauser and Sheinbaum pressed the PLO leadership to accept these terms. In Geneva, the circumstances were particularly favorable. There the UN General Assembly had gathered specifically to hear Arafat, who was barred as a terrorist from entering the United States. Media coverage was extensive. On December 14, therefore, at a press conference, Arafat affirmed that he accepted Resolution 242 unconditionally. "I recognize the right of all parties concerned in the Middle East conflict to exist in peace and security," he declared, ". . . including the state of Palestine, Israel, and other neighbors." The response was immediate. Within hours, Secretary of State George Shultz in Washington announced that no further obstacles remained to official contacts between the PLO and the United States. Soon afterward, those contacts were tentatively resumed for the first time since 1975 by the American ambassador in Tunis.

In Jerusalem, meanwhile, the Shamir government expressed only outrage. Then and later, it noted that Arafat's "flexibility" was less than evident in the statements the PLO leader issued publicly in the Arab world. The man, and the movement, were still to be regarded as inimical to Israel's existence. Yet it was significant that Arafat's gesture, however convoluted, was seized upon with almost palpable gratitude and relief not only by the Reagan administration but by important elements of Congress and the American media. By the late 1980s, few knowledgeable Americans needed any reminder of Israel's debt to the United States. Beyond diplomatic and military support, after all, and its preferential trade agreements with the Jewish state, Washington over the years had poured tens of billions of dollars into Israel in grants, economic support funds, and joint research projects. Whether or not Israel was the useful strategic investment its partisans claimed, the Jewish state had emerged as the recipient of more largess from the United States than any other nation in the world. Did not that record of generosity entitle Washington to some measure of flexibility from its little client?

In March 1988, in the last year of the Reagan administration, Senator Carl Levin (Democrat, Michigan), dispatched a letter to Secretary of State Shultz. Assuring Shultz of warm support for his Middle East peace initiative, the letter expressed "dismay" at Prime Minister Shamir's categorical rejection of the secretary's efforts. Among the document's twenty-nine signatories were numerous reliable pro-Israel figures of both parties, including six Jewish senators, one of them Levin himself. Two years later, in February 1990, Senator Robert Dole (Republican, Kansas), went further. Noting that the current 1991 budget bill included its traditional allocation to Israel of $3 billion in economic and military aid, Dole in an op-ed letter to the *New York Times* suggested that at least 5 percent of the sum now be diverted to newly democratic Russia and to other struggling former Soviet-bloc nations. Dole's proposal evidenced more than a reassessment of American diplomatic priorities. In later interviews, the Republican leader made plain the depth of Senate outrage at the "shooting and beating of Arab women and children." Surely, Dole insisted, the United States no longer was obliged to "reward" these excesses.

The senator's budgetary recommendation was not accepted. He had not expected that it would. In effect, he had intended it as a warning that American patience with Israel was waning. The signal was accurate. As late as 1987, public opinion polls suggested that Israel maintained a reasonably favorable—64 percent—image in the United States as a "reliable ally." But surveys taken between 1988 and 1990 revealed a sharp dropoff: to 44 percent, in a 1989 *Washington Post* poll; to 28 percent, in a 1990 Lewis Harris poll. Public opinion surveys alone could hardly determine a nation's view of its self-interest, of course. For Israel, commitment to survival was not to be confused with an overseas popularity contest. Nevertheless, by the late 1980s and early 1990s, the question had become pertinent whether Israel could grapple with its domestic and international challenges amid the mounting resentments of its own citizens, the vocal obloquy of the American government and people, and the increasingly thunderous reserve of the Diaspora at large.

A TORMENTED ROAD TO PEACE

A FIRESTORM FROM THE GULF

Iraq's President Saddam Hussein was a brutal dictator, but hardly an incompetent. During the 1970s, he exploited his nation's soaring oil profits to transform an impoverished Third World backwater into a quasi-industrial regional power. Never before had Iraq's inhabitants experienced as dramatically improved a standard of living, even such boons as free universal education and extensive medical and social-welfare benefits. For all his ruthlessness, therefore, Saddam Hussein by the early 1980s projected much of the charisma among his subjects that once had been identified with Gamal Abd al-Nasser in Egypt. He would have coveted the late Nasser's preeminence as champion of Arab nationalism, as well. Indeed, to that end, Saddam was intent upon winning for his near-landlocked nation a more extensive maritime outlet to the world's oil markets. Such was the origin of his eight-year war against Iran, from 1980 to 1988. For all its inconclusive results, the murderous, protracted contest for strategic advantage in the Persian Gulf devoured hundreds of thousands of Iraqi and Iranian lives alike. Beyond its human toll, moreover, the war cost Iraq some $500 billion and saddled its economy with a foreign debt of over $80 billion.

Saddam's black mood in the years after 1988 was influenced not merely by lack of military success. In the Iraqi president's view, his armies alone had "saved" the Arab Middle East from the hordes of the Ayatollah Khomeini. Did not that achievement entitle Iraq to financial compensation from other Arab governments, and specifically to a cancellation of Iraq's debts to them? Saddam's perspective in fact was not shared by one of the wealthiest of Iraq's creditors, the sultanate of Kuwait. It expected repayment. Worse yet, it rejected Saddam's long-standing claim to two Kuwaiti-ruled islands, Waraby and Bubiyan, directly facing the Shatt al-Arab estuary that served as Iraq's maritime outlet from Basra to the Persian Gulf. In Saddam's possession, those islands would significantly have facilitated Iraq's access to the Gulf, in some degree even have compensated for the indeterminate war against Iran. Accordingly, for a man of Saddam's temperament, there could only be one course of action. He would resolve the territorial issue and the financial issue in one fell swoop—by invading Kuwait. So it was, during the spring and early summer of 1990, that the Iraqi dictator launched a farrago of increasingly dire threats against Kuwait. Few outside observers took the warnings seriously. On August 1, however, Saddam confounded all expectations by dispatching one hundred thousand troops across the border toward Kuwait City. By dawn, the capital was encircled and the sultan of Kuwait had fled to Saudi Arabia.

The aggression, and with it the palpable danger of an even farther-ranging Iraqi thrust southward into the oil-rich Gulf, was unacceptable to western Europe and to other Arab nations alike. Assuredly, it was unacceptable to the United States. President George Bush understood precisely the threat Saddam now posed to the security of the Gulf, to the world's largest reserve of oil, to the very lifeblood of Western industry. Immediately, then, Bush set about mobilizing a coalition of European and Middle Eastern nations, including even such unlikely allies as the Soviet Union, Egypt, and Syria. It was the United States itself, moreover, that provided the bulk of the armed forces. During the ensuing six months, operating under a UN mandate, some four hundred thousand American personnel were dispatched to Saudi bases in preparation for the liberation of Kuwait.

For his part, Saddam was not about to quail before this array of military power. Even after the recent bloodbath with Iran, his army remained the fourth largest in the world. More ominously, during the 1980s, Iraq had revived its efforts to construct nuclear weapons; even as it already had acquired such other "nonconventional" weapons as poison gas and biological agents, together with an extensive array of rockets to launch them. Moreover, in a shrewd stratagem to divide the Arab front arraying against him, Saddam threatened now to loose his planes and missiles on Israel, the common Zionist enemy. The Israelis took the threat seriously. They always had. In 1981, after all, they had preemptively attacked and destroyed the Osiraq nuclear reactor. Since then, the Iraqi dictator had used poison gas to murder irredentist elements within his own country, Kurds and Arabs alike. To the Israelis, it seemed entirely probable that Saddam would also strike out against them. So it did to foreign airlines, which in the early winter of 1990 began canceling their flights to Israel. Thereupon Prime Minister Yitzchak Shamir felt impelled to warn Baghdad that Israel's air force would react massively to an Iraqi attack.

Yet the prospect of Israeli retaliation evoked a chill response, less in Iraq than within the Allied coalition. When Secretary of State James Baker first discussed this possibility with Saudi Arabia's King Fahd in November 1990, Fahd reacted unfavorably. No Arab nation, the king insisted, could be perceived as in alliance with the Zionist state. Fahd's single qualification was his acknowledgment that the Israelis could not be expected to stand by idly if they were attacked; should they choose to defend their country, Saudi armed forces would continue to fight at the Americans' side. It was a caveat that General Norman Schwarzkopf, commander of the Allied coalition, regarded as "an act of extraordinary courage and leadership." In fact, the king had in mind Israeli interception of Iraqi planes or missiles exclusively over Israeli air space, a defensive scenario that hardly was realistic for any threatened nation, least of all for Israel.

President Bush accordingly was in repeated telephone communication with Shamir, exhorting the prime minister to avoid future hostilities, and promising to supply Israel with additional quantities of Patriot surface-to-air missiles. Shamir was receptive. For the while, he agreed to coordinate with Washington any decisions on retaliation against the Iraqis. Yet, by January 1991, Israel was on full alert, with relays of pilots actually seated in the cockpits of their planes to intercept oncoming Iraqi aircraft. By then, too, gas masks had been distributed to the Israeli population. It was a nerve-racking period. As early as October 1990, and for the first time since 1973, the government began dropping cryptic hints of possible nuclear retaliation. The press, too, now was permitted to publish "leaks" on the military's alleged nuclear preparations. Even Washington obliquely encouraged this speculation, with Secretary of Defense Richard Cheney adverting to it in a press conference.

OPERATION DESERT STORM: THE ISRAELI DIMENSION

On January 17, 1991, the Allied bombardment of Iraq began. The initial strategic targets were principally in Baghdad, and they evoked little effective Iraqi fighter or antiaircraft response. But twenty-four hours later, Saddam made good on his threat to attack Israel. His instrument of choice was the Scud missile. Of Soviet invention, the long, tubular rocket was only marginally effective as a military weapon. Although the Iraqis had extended its range to approximately three hundred miles, the Scud was inaccurate for precision assaults. Nevertheless, as a terror weapon it could inflict serious harm with its 160-pound warhead. Thus, at 2:00 a.m. on January 18, eight Scuds were launched from western Iraq. Two struck in the vicinity of Haifa, the rest in and around Tel Aviv, where they destroyed several apartment buildings and wounded twelve civilians. On January 19, four more Scuds struck Tel Aviv, again causing extensive damage and wounding sixteen civilians.

Immediately, Shamir telephoned Washington to inform President Bush that the Israeli air force was prepared to launch its own counterstrike at selected Iraqi targets. At morning light, one hundred planes would attack, one hundred more in the afternoon, with helicopters to follow at nightfall, bearing commandos who would seek out and destroy the Scud launchers. But to fulfill this mission, the Israelis needed to pass through Saudi air space. Would this be possible? Hereupon Bush consulted with King Fahd, who instantly vetoed the request. To placate Shamir, however, the president agreed to divert American fighter-bombers, currently attacking targets in and around Baghdad, to a hunt for Scud launchers in western Iraq. Two additional batteries of Patriot missiles similarly would be airlifted to Israel, together with American crews. Once "Operation Desert Storm," the liberation of Kuwait, had been successfully completed, Bush added, he would request Congress to provide Israel with substantial financial help for repairs and rehabilitation. Shamir was listening. After a four-hour cabinet meeting, he was able to accept the president's compromise.

Bush kept his promise. Throughout the night of January 19–20, even as another dozen Scuds crashed into Tel Aviv, American cargo planes rushed two additional Patriot batteries to Israel, and American antiaircraft crews worked closely with their Israeli counterparts to deploy the weapons. Meanwhile, U.S. combat aircraft launched into an intensive search-and-destroy mission in western Iraq. General Schwarzkopf recalled:

We . . . [diverted] fully one third of the more than two thousand combat and support
missions scheduled each day for the strategic air campaign to the Scud hunt. F-15s
and F-16s repeatedly braved their way through concentrations of antiaircraft missiles to bomb Scud storage bunkers and suspected launch sites in western Iraq.

The hunt-and-destroy effort, continuing for ten days, significantly reduced the
number of Scud launchings, although Tel Aviv endured eighteen more attacks
until the nightmare ended, on February 25. By then, thirteen Israelis had died.
Although most of these were victims of gas-mask suffocation or heart attacks,
some two hundred others had been wounded. More than four thousand buildings had been damaged. For civilians, a much graver ordeal even than the
physical trauma was the psychological strain of waiting in specially caulked,
insulated rooms, often with gas masks donned, as the wail of alarms announced
the imminence of approaching Scuds. In its larger dimensions, of course, this
was not "Israel's" war. Yet the nation's sense of vulnerability in some respects
was more intense than in earlier years, when its vaunted armed forces effectively
shielded civilians against conventional weapons. How much more exposed would
the nation be in an authentic, full-scale war, when gas or biological agents—or
worse—might actually be used?

The Gulf War produced other sobering revelations. One was a depth of
Palestinian hatred that apparently had not been plumbed even in the intifada.
Ever since the original Iraq-Iran war of the 1980s, these people had accepted
Saddam Hussein's self-proclaimed role as hero of the Arab world. So had Yasser
Arafat and other PLO spokesmen. Indeed, with the Iraqi occupation of Kuwait,
Arafat joined in a blistering denunciation of the Gulf kingdoms for their recent
indifference to the Palestinian cause. "The time when Israel had the upper hand
in the region is now in the past," exulted the PLO chairman. And when Iraqi
Scuds began streaking across the West Bank en route to Tel Aviv, Palestinians
in both Jordan and the West Bank stood on their roofs to cheer. Their frenzy in
turn inhibited even a moderate like Jordan's King Hussein from joining the
Allied coalition (and so did Shamir's ill-judged insistence, earlier, that "Jordan is
Palestine"). Meanwhile, for a number of eminent Israeli doves, Palestinian
vindictiveness was a source of particular chagrin. A. B. Yehoshua confessed that
"[I was] especially surprised by those [Palestinians] with whom we had been
engaged in protected dialogue. I was also surprised by the [pro-Iraq] riots in
Jordan and the fact that people there were ready to mobilize, and die, for
Saddam Hussein." By the same token, the dismay of moderates like Yehoshua
appeared to be moral vindication for Shamir and the hard-liners.

In ensuing weeks, once the United States and its allies inflicted defeat on
Saddam's armed forces (p. 981), the restored Kuwaiti government took harsh
vengeance on its two hundred thousand Palestinian guest laborers. It drove them
out. The blow was a disaster for the entire Palestinian economy. Remittances
from sons or husbands working in the Gulf had made up not less than 30 percent
of the territories' GNP. But the reaction of the Israeli government was equally
severe. The moment the Scud attacks began, the cabinet imposed a tight curfew
on the Palestinians. For the ensuing three weeks in the West Bank, and six weeks
in Gaza, Arab movement was limited to shopping for necessities. Palestinian
laborers were banned from employment, either locally or in Israel. Indeed, after

the war, approximately 50 percent of the commuting Arab work force lost their jobs permanently to recent Soviet immigrants. Beyond losses in wages and production, moreover, fully 60 percent of the Palestinian grain harvest was left to rot during the curfew. In the end, deprived of remittances, subsidies, and employment, the Palestinian economy suffered a loss of $425 million. This was suffering of such magnitude that it soon revived the Israeli Left's earlier instincts of sympathy and accommodation.

OPERATION DESERT STORM: DIVIDENDS AND DEBTS

On February 24, 1991, the Allies launched their invasion of Kuwait. Within one hundred hours, the little sultanate was emancipated, and Saddam Hussein's army, together with much of his military infrastructure, was broken. For the near future, at least, the threat to the stability of the Gulf appeared dissipated. The Israelis, too, seemingly had emerged winners. Their civilian losses were minimal. Their armed forces had been spared a possibly costly expedition of their own. Moreover, by acquiescing in George Bush's appeal for restraint, the Shamir government assumed that it actually had imposed a moral claim on Washington.

The president did not see matters that way. By his calculations, Israel's need for protection had cost the United States heavily in diverted military resources. Additionally, the Gulf War had further radicalized the Palestinian population, even in Jordan. That hatred in turn had severely complicated Washington's efforts to negotiate a solid, pro-Western coalition in the region. Shamir's "moral" claim accordingly produced no shift in Bush's attitude toward ongoing Israeli settlement in the West Bank, and least of all toward the prime minister's $10 billion loan-guarantee request. Bush's approval would remain linked to a halt in Jewish settlement activity. On February 11, 1991, Secretary of State Baker bluntly warned Israel's minister of defense Moshe Arens that it "is inappropriate to request aid at a time when United States soldiers [are] dying in a war beneficial to Israel." Three days later, when Israel's ambassador Zalman Shoval publicly and intemperately criticized the White House for giving Israel the "runaround" on loan guarantees, Bush all but exploded. At his instructions, Baker accused Shoval of violating "the bounds of behavior by the ambassador of a friendly country."

Congress supported the president. Even traditionally pro-Israel senators and representatives sensed that the American people—and now a growing number of American Jews—favored a tough stance against the Likud government's settlements policy (p. 976). Meanwhile, George Bush preferred to express his "goodwill" toward Israel exclusively in humanitarian gestures. One of these was to honor his wartime promise to Shamir by approving a short-term grant of $650 million for the repair of war damage in Tel Aviv. Another was directed toward the rescue of Ethiopia's remnant Jewish population. In 1984–85, it is recalled, Operation Moses essentially had cleared the Sudanese transit camps of their eight thousand Falasha refugees. Yet as many as seventeen thousand Jews remained stranded in Ethiopia itself, their circumstances deteriorating from month to month. Consisting mainly of women, children, and the elderly, the beleaguered little minority was ravaged by drought, hunger, and the mounting political chaos that afflicted Ethiopian society altogether. Was a second Operation Moses realistic? It appeared not. Although Israel and Ethiopia had resumed diplomatic relations by 1989 (p. 939), the Mengistu regime was uninterested in provoking Arab ire. Neither did Ethiopia's mountainous terrain lend itself to secret evacuation by air.

Then, on May 24–25, 1991, a new phase of deliverance, "Operation Solomon," began to unfold. Forces hostile to the Mengistu government were rapidly converging on Addis Ababa. The Falasha community, acutely at risk, would have to be flown out without delay. In fact, over the preceding six months, Jewish Agency representatives had been conducting the Falashas from their villages to Addis Ababa, where makeshift hostels awaited them. More recently, the Israeli government had transferred some $40 million to the Swiss bank accounts of key Ethopian ministers. As in 1984, however, it was Washington's intercession that ultimately proved crucial. Responding to an urgent personal appeal from Yitzchak Shamir, President Bush exhorted the Ethiopian government to cooperate in the Falasha evacuation effort.

Even with that cooperation, the sheer logistical challenge of a mass airlift was daunting. By the night of May 23, rebel artillery could be heard outside the capital, and Israeli officials sensed that barely a day or two remained to complete the mission. In relays, then, their fleets of chartered buses rushed the Falashas to the Addis Ababa airport. Here, Israeli air force crews managed to pack the entire refugee aggregation into thirty-three military and civilian aircraft, from air force Hercules transports to El Al 747s, parked wingtip to wingtip. In this fashion, within less than two days, flying in daylight and darkness, Operation Solomon whisked 14,400 Ethiopian Jews out of Addis Ababa and brought them all to Israel. En route, Israeli army doctors and nurses ministered continually to ill and dehydrated passengers. Three babies were delivered. Once in Israel, the newcomers were accommodated in special hostels, in chartered hotels, hospitals, kibbutzim, and other temporary facilities. Plainly, their integration would be as formidable a task as that of their predecessors of 1984–85. But they were safe.

A DIPLOMATIC RESPECTABILITY

Meanwhile, following the Gulf War, the implosion of the Soviet empire and the emergence of the United States as the uncontested power broker in the Middle East decisively buttressed Israel's already formidable presence in the region. By then, the staying power of the Zionist republic compelled respect even from governments that earlier had kept Israel at arm's length. One of these was the Vatican. The status of Jerusalem, for years a serious bone of contention between the Holy See and Israel, essentially had become moot following the Six-Day War of 1967. Rather, it was the fate of Palestinians under Israeli rule that inhibited papal dealings with the Jewish state. With Catholic institutions scattered throughout the Arab world, even Pope John Paul II, who consistently had displayed goodwill to the Jewish people, hesitated to extend Israel diplomatic recognition. But in the aftermath of the 1991 Gulf War, and with a functionally wider Arab-Israel peace apparently in the offing (pp. 994–5), the Vatican no longer discerned usefulness in postponing direct engagement with the Israelis. In June 1994, following months of negotiations to ensure protection for Jerusalem's Catholic shrines, the decision was reached to exchange ambassadors with Israel. Not a single Arab country retaliated against Catholic institutions.

Other governments similarly were responding to the new American-Israeli configuration in the Middle East, and in consequence reassessing their position toward the Jewish state. Thus, in January 1992, within the space of a single fortnight, India and China established diplomatic relations with Israel. For the Israelis, the prospects of broadened, official contacts with two of the largest nations on earth were hardly less than staggering. For the Chinese, in turn, establishment of diplomatic ties simply climaxed a relationship that had begun with a self-interested access to Israeli military technology. The contact could be traced back to the early 1970s, to a period when both Moscow and Washington maintained a strict arms embargo on the Beijing regime. The Israelis then characteristically were eager to pick up the slack. In fact, they had much to offer the Chinese. Three Middle Eastern wars had enabled them to capture, study, reproduce, and upgrade some of the USSR's most important equipment, precisely the ordnance that Moscow now was denying China. Most important yet, the Israelis had devised the technology and weaponry to defeat this Soviet materiel. The Chinese wanted it. By the end of the decade, they were importing $2.5 billion worth of weapons systems from Israel. In later years, to be sure, Beijing became less dependent on Israeli equipment, and during the 1980s it began courting trade relations with the United States. Even for this purpose, however, Israel and American Jewry were regarded as useful conduits. Thus, in 1991, as an earnest of its goodwill, China cooperated with the Russians and Americans in helping to rescind the Zionism-is-Racism resolution in the United Nations (pp. 826–7). Full diplomatic relations soon followed, in January 1992. Within the next year and a half, El Al was operating weekly flights between the two countries. One of its passengers was Israel's President Chaim Herzog, who paid a state visit to China in 1993.

By then, the relationship with eastern Europe similarly had thawed. Israel's special connection with Rumania was an old story, of course (pp. 661, 732). Hungary, too, seeking an improved atmosphere in Washington, cautiously widened its mercantile contacts with Israel during the 1970s and 1980s. Then, in 1991, with the collapse of the Communist empire, the governments of Hungary, Czechoslovakia, and Poland all formally resumed diplomatic ties with Israel. Nevertheless, the farthest-reaching change in the eastern European equation plainly lay with the Soviet Union itself. Here was a regime that had poured funds and weaponry into the hands of Israel's enemies for nearly four decades, and that was left with nothing for its exertions except Arab debts totaling a catastrophic $25 billion. Even more ominously, Islamic irredentism by 1991 was emerging as a major threat to Russian hegemony within its own empire. For President Gorbachev and Foreign Minister Eduard Shevardnadze, then, the decisive impulsion in Middle East statecraft no longer was Arab goodwill but American goodwill—and with it American technology and trade. It was this priority, after all, that had induced Moscow to open the floodgates of Jewish emigration. A forbearing approach to the State of Israel appeared to be a logical corollary. Thus, in October 1991, Moscow formally reestablished the diplomatic relations with Jerusalem that had been severed in 1967.

The timing of the move was not coincidental. Gorbachev had cooperated with the United States in Operation Desert Storm. Following the defeat of Iraq, to preserve his nation's lingering visibility in the Middle East, the Soviet president also had agreed to join the United States in cosponsoring an Arab-Israeli peace conference. Israel's condition for acceptance of that cosponsorship was resumption of diplomatic ties with Moscow. For the Soviets, the price was a cheap one.

THE MADRID CONFERENCE—AND BEYOND

In the late winter of 1991, it was Secretary of State James Baker's idée fixe to sustain the diplomatic momentum that had produced the recent Gulf military victory. His intention was to exploit Arab and Israeli gratitude by maneuvering both sides into negotiations that would resolve their own historic impasse. Beginning in March 1991, therefore, Baker launched a series of whirlwind visits to the Middle East. Remarkably, under his courteous persistence, the Syrian, Lebanese, and Jordanian governments all agreed to participate in an international conference. So, in principle, did the Israelis. Shamir had anticipated that the Syrians would torpedo the conference proposal, thereby letting him off the hook. But if Hafez al-Assad had unexpectedly accepted the American offer, Shamir for his part dared not risk open confrontation with Washington, and a possibly indefinite postponement of loan guarantees.

Nevertheless, procedural issues remained to be "clarified" between Shamir and Baker. Some were disposed of early on. Both men swiftly agreed that the conclave would be held under Soviet-American cochairmanship, rather than that of the United Nations. Even this narrowly circumscribed format would serve essentially as an umbrella for direct negotiations between "regional committees." The latter would consist of Israel and each separate Arab delegation. The single exception would be the Palestinian delegation; it would be subsumed in that of the Jordanians, and, at that, would not include PLO members. Nevertheless, throughout the spring and summer of 1991, Shamir continued to place his own interpretation on both the "atmospherics" and the details of the conference. He rejected Baker's persistent appeal for a moratorium on Jewish settlement in the West Bank. Under no circumstances, either, could Arabs from East Jerusalem participate as members of the Palestinian delegation. The prime minister had never budged on these issues, and was not about to now. Finally, in August, Baker conceded both points. Shamir then won cabinet approval for participation.

The selected venue was Madrid. Eager to display Spain's bona fides as a once-historic fount of both Islamic and Jewish culture, its government had offered every assurance of security and comfort. And thus it was, on November 1, 1991, that delegations from the Soviet Union (by then rapidly in the process of dissolution), the United States, Jordan-Palestine, Lebanon, Syria, and Israel gathered in the Palacio Parcen, an elegant eighteenth-century structure that functioned currently as the Spanish ministry of justice. Bush and Gorbachev had flown in to launch the conclave, and in their opening remarks each expressed the usual pious hopes for Middle Eastern peace.

The chiefs of delegations then rose to make their opening statements. Farouq al-Shar'a, the Syrian foreign minister, was harsh and accusatory, demanding that Israel commit itself in advance to withdrawal from the entirety of the occupied Golan. The Lebanese chairman similarly demanded Israeli withdrawal from its "security zone" on Lebanese territory. By contrast, the Palestinian spokesman, Haidar Abd al-Shafi, a Gaza physician, appeared the soul of moderation. Acknowledging the reality of two nations coveting the same land, Shafi now belatedly accepted the language of the original Camp David accords, with their concept of negotiations for an initial, transitional stage of self-government. For the moment, too, he did not press the time-honored demand for a return of the 1948 Palestinian refugees, only for those displaced by the 1967 war. Manifestly chastened by Israel's staying power and the defeat of Arab extremism in the recent Gulf conflict, the Palestinians in effect were prepared to compromise.

Were the Israelis? Yitzchak Shamir, who personally led his country's sizable contingent, might easily have scuttled the conference at the outset. Yet the prime minister's opening address was unexpectedly low-key. This time he refrained from elaborating upon his nation's historic attachment to Judea and Samaria. Neither did he make Jewish settlements a nonnegotiable issue. Rather, by stating only that it would be "regrettable" to focus negotiations "exclusively on territory," Shamir suggested that talks on Palestine be linked to other issues—for example, the existential question of Israel's legitimacy. By sitting across from Haidar Abd al-Shafi, too, the prime minister clearly accepted the equal status of the Palestinians.

Afterward, the conclave adopted the format that had been refined over Baker's earlier weeks of painstaking negotiations. Its venue was shifted from Madrid to Washington. There, in the State Department's conference rooms, Arabs and Israelis conferred on a face-to-face basis: one Israeli delegation sitting with its Lebanese counterpart; another with the Syrians; a third with the Jordanian-Palestinian delegation. It was the negotiating procedure devised for this third contingent, however, that proved exceptionally complex. Agreement had been reached that no "card-carrying" Fatah or other PLO member would be accepted as a member of the Palestinian group. Neither would any resident of East Jerusalem. Thus, Feisal al-Husseini, a Jerusalemite who arrived in Madrid with the Palestinians, and who remained in continual touch with PLO headquarters in Tunis by telephone, was obliged to maintain the façade of an "adviser." Spokesmanship for the Palestinians devolved instead on Dr. Hanan Ashrawi, an eloquent, American-educated professor of English literature at Bir Zeit University, who qualified simply because she lived in Ramallah, outside Jerusalem. Yet the Israelis refused even to sit down with these Palestinians independently of the latter's Jordanian colleagues. Not until the third round of the bilateral meetings, in mid-January 1992, did both sides accept a convoluted formula under which the Israelis would negotiate essentially Israeli-Jordanian issues with a counterpart delegation comprised of nine Jordanians and two Palestinians. On issues relating essentially to the West Bank and Gaza, the Arab delegation would be restructured to consist of ten Palestinians and two Jordanians.

It was in this uneven fashion, then, that separate bilateral negotiations—Syrian, Lebanese, Jordanian, Palestinian—continued in Washington, round after round, from December 1991 through all of 1992 and well into the spring and summer of 1993. Over the months, a certain intermittent progress was achieved on procedural issues, and occasionally even on substantive matters. Thus, on an "interim" basis, the Jordanians were prepared to address such contentious problems as water, energy, environment, refugee resettlement, and arms control. The Lebanese, although pressing for Israeli withdrawal from the violence-prone "security zone," would not disguise the urgency of their hope for a permanent, mutually ensured peace. Neither was it an insurmountable shock that the Syrians remained the most obdurate and abrasive of the Arab interlocutors. In round after round, month after month, their delegation pressed for advance Israeli commitment to full and total withdrawal from the Golan plateau. For the Shamir government, it was a nonstarter; the Golan was part of Israel. Even the successor Rabin cabinet (p. 989) initially refused commitment on the Golan issue. In later months, however, the Israelis intimated that they were prepared to bend, conceding that occupation of the Golan buffer was perhaps not entirely critical in an age of missile warfare, that partial evacuation and demilitarization at least were negotiable options. Only then did the Syrians acknowledge the desideratum of full peace, rather than mere nonbelligerency, as a legitimate end product, together with "mutual security" arrangements.

In Madrid, it was the Palestinian connection that had appeared to be the most promising. But in Washington, ironically, once the procedural issue of separate delegations was resolved, an impasse soon developed on matters of substance (although excellent progress was made with the Jordanians). From the outset, the Palestinians equated the concept of an "interim" self-governing authority with a full legislative assembly, to be elected by inhabitants of all occupied territories, including Jerusalem. The Shamir government, and later the Rabin government, rejected the scenario even as a basis for negotiation. Although the Palestinians eventually softened their position, accepting the format of an administrative council rather than a legislature, no movement seemed possible on the scope of the council's authority, and assuredly not on the inclusion of Jerusalem. By the summer of 1993, the eleven intermittent Madrid rounds (which of course had become the Washington rounds) had ground to a virtual stalemate.

LABOR'S POLITICAL REINCARNATION

As the peace negotiations lurched on erratically, Israel suddenly confronted an unanticipated internal political crisis. In mid-January 1992, the militant Techiya and Moledet factions withdrew from the Likud cabinet to protest Shamir's seeming willingness to negotiate even a limited Palestinian autonomy. Stripped of his governing coalition, the prime minister then reluctantly consented to advance the date for Knesset elections from November to June of that year. The political campaigning accordingly began within six weeks. In a calculated gamble, moreover, to win back his far-rightist support, Shamir adopted a harshly aggressive approach that in fact was directed less against Labor than against the Bush administration, which he now accused of undermining both Israel's security and its economy. It was a dangerous tactic.

By then, even Israel's non-Ashkenazic voters were having second thoughts about Shamir's stewardship of national affairs. Lately there had been a palpable economic deterioration within their communities. Nearly 18 percent of the population was living below the poverty line, and the widening gap between the Jewish rich and poor was still essentially one between Europeans and non-Europeans. Moreover, in Likud's territorialist appeal to Israel's Sephardic-Oriental underclasses, a significant new demographic component was overlooked. These were the recent Soviet-Jewish immigrants, who comprised nearly a tenth of the 3.5 million Israelis eligible to vote in 1992. Europeans for the most part, and often widely cultured, the Russian immigrants found little in common with Likud's still undereducated constituency. Neither did they appreciate the chauvinist militance that Likud conscientiously exploited among this non-Ashkenazic population, or, worse yet, the Shamir government's evident willingness to neglect the immigrants' desperate housing and employment conditions in favor of Jewish settlements in the West Bank. Nor were the newcomers prepared to accept the rabbinical chamber of horrors inflicted upon them by the government's Orthodox allies. By a margin of three to one, therefore, Soviet Jews gave their votes to the Labor-Left.

For its part, Labor was shrewdly positioning itself to exploit the groundswell of popular discontent. In February 1992, the party's 150,000 registered members for the first time selected their leadership in a democratic, American-style primary election. Until then, a central executive committee of party mandarins had determined the list of Knesset candidates, and Likud and other parties still functioned within that traditional structure. It was in the Labor primary, moreover, that Shimon Peres, Labor chairman and standard bearer for fifteen years, lost out to his perennial rival, Yitzchak Rabin, by a narrow margin. None of Labor's constituents failed to appreciate Peres's historic accomplishments in reuniting the party after its 1977 debacle, ending the Lebanon disaster, bringing the nation's roaring inflation under control, and improving Israel's image abroad during his years as premier and foreign minister. Yet it was plain, in campaign after campaign, that Peres had failed to bring his party back to a decisive electoral triumph. By contrast, Rabin appealed to the nation's Oriental-Sephardic voters as a strong man, the military hero of the Six-Day War, a defense minister in the 1980s who had responded to guerrilla violence and the intifada with an iron hand. As much as any figure on the Right, he could be trusted to guard the nation's security interests. Once the sixty-nine-year-old Rabin was declared the victor in the primary election, moreover, Peres accepted the decision with unanticipated good grace. As number-two man on the Labor list, he campaigned loyally at Rabin's side. Indeed, Labor's unity this time stood in vivid contrast to the factionalism and backbiting within Likud, specifically between Shamir and his European colleagues, on the one hand, and David Levy and the non-Ashkenazim, on the other.

As the electioneering gained momentum, too, it became apparent that growing numbers of Labor and Likud voters alike shared an acute concern over the widening crisis of Israeli education. Massively underwriting the settlements program on the West Bank, Likud over the years had been obliged to reduce public funding for the nation's schools, to shorten the school day, and to divert a larger proportion of the savings to the parochial institutions of its Orthodox political allies. Thus, in 1991, a ministry of education survey revealed that 14 percent of Israel's third-graders could barely read or understand a simple text. For the first time in Israel's history, therefore, the electorate turned increasingly to the parties that put improved education near the top of their agenda. At the same time, the June election also reversed the tendency of recent years for parties to split into smaller factions. The public had had enough of it, and of the endless horse-trading in forming coalitions. This time, Israelis voted for stability. The ultra-right-wing Techiya party failed to win a single Knesset seat. Conversely, when Shinui, Mapam, and Ratz (the Citizens' Rights movement) joined forces in the Meretz bloc, they raised their number of combined seats in the Knesset by 20 percent.

Above all else, the largest majority of Israelis appeared determined to have done with the endless cycle of military confrontation and death. Even the most committed hard-liners had been sobered by the recent Gulf War, and the possibility of future rocket attacks on the nation's impacted cities. Neither was it possible to ignore the message that President Bush was transmitting straightforwardly and forcefully: Israel would have to choose between Shamir's agenda of a Greater Israel or the traditional economic and diplomatic support of the mighty United States. The prime minister alone evidently failed to grasp the importance of that peace issue. Thus, months after the election Shamir frankly acknowledged that he had intended to drag out negotiations on Palestinian self-rule for at least another ten years, "and in the meantime we would have reached half a million Jews in Judea and Samaria." By contrast, Rabin had made plain his intention of negotiating an agreement on Palestine within a year of taking office. "I am against throwing away billions of shekels on [Jewish] settlements in the territories," he emphasized during the election campaign, ". . . when we have grave problems of immigrant absorption and unemployment at home." He acknowledged forthrightly, too, his intention of "rehabilitating" Israel's relationship with Washington.

When the votes were counted on the evening of June 23, 1992, it became clear that Likud had suffered its most decisive defeat in fifteen years. Its Knesset representation fell from 40 to 32. Labor in turn increased its number of seats from 39 to 44. The dovish Meretz bloc increased its combined strength from 10 to 12 members, and these were "mobilizable" for Labor. And so were the Knesset's 5 Arab members. Rabin could not realistically include them in his government. Together with the 56 Labor and Meretz MKs, however, at least these minority votes could block Likud from turning out a Labor cabinet.

Meanwhile, to fortify his narrow electoral mandate, Rabin negotiated patiently with several unlikely political bedfellows. One of these was Shas, the disgruntled Sephardic-Orthodox faction. The other was General Rafael Eytan's Tsomet party (vigorously surviving the election by stressing its commitment to improved education). Yet even before the bargaining reached fruition, Rabin was able to assume office as prime minister. Peres resumed his earlier role as foreign minister.

No one welcomed the change of political guard more gratefully than did George Bush. Indeed, he was the first head of state to congratulate Rabin. Six weeks later, in August, Rabin visited the president at the latter's summer retreat in Kennebunkport, Maine, and committed himself to a fundamental break with his predecessor's territorialism. In turn, Bush announced his willingness to approve the long-awaited $10 billion in loan guarantees to Israel. Both the content and the cordiality of the president's remarks, including an allusion once again to the United States and Israel as "strategic partners," underscored the end of a long and deeply troubled crisis in American-Israeli relations.

BACKGROUND TO A DIPLOMATIC REVOLUTION

Rabin had an agenda. It was to revive the momentum of the bilateral Washington (originally Madrid) negotiations. Through his new ambassador in Washington, Professor Itamar Rabinovich, an expert on Syrian affairs, the prime minister signaled the Damascus government of his flexibility on the scope and timetable of Israeli withdrawal from the Golan. Israel also would drop further objections to Feisal al-Ḥuṣṣeini, a resident of East Jerusalem, as a member of the Palestinian delegation. Plainly there could be no compromise on matters of basic security or Zionist ideology. For Labor, as for Likud, it was axiomatic that Jerusalem would remain united under Israeli rule. Neither would Rabin react permissively to Arab violence, no more as prime minister than he had earlier as defense minister (this time he held both portfolios simultaneously).

It happened that in mid-December 1992, to commemorate the fifth anniversary of the intifada, Hamas guerrillas kidnapped and murdered an Israeli border policeman. The atrocity was only the latest in a series of killings that had claimed seven Israeli lives within a single week, and that evidenced Hamas's determination to sabotage the peace talks. The new prime minister reacted grimly. At his orders, some four hundred Hamas partisans, Arabs who had earlier been seized in the West Bank, were taken now from prison, carried off en masse across the Lebanese frontier, and unceremoniously dumped in the "Red Line" buffer zone. In earlier years, Palestinian expellees traditionally had found asylum with friends or relatives in Lebanon. But this time the former prisoners decided to remain where they had been dumped, month after month, living in tents, using only primitive cooking and sanitary facilities. Their purpose manifestly was to evoke international sympathy and disrupt the peace talks.

By and large, they succeeded. World criticism of Israel was harsh. The Palestinian and other Arab delegations in Washington promptly withdrew from the eighth round of the bilateral negotiations and returned home. Throughout the West Bank, moreover, riots and attacks on Israeli settlers and soldiers revived in frequency and intensity. By the same token, Jewish vigilantism also resumed, including execution-style murders of suspect local Arabs. Rabin's official response then was to seal off Gaza and the West Bank from Israel altogether. "There will be no Palestinians from the territories on the sovereign territory of Israel until further notice," warned the prime minister. It was an astonishing departure, and one that wreaked the identical financial havoc on Palestinian Arabs and Israelis alike that had occurred in the early months of the Gulf War.

In fact, Rabin's purpose transcended the immediate emergency. For many months even before the latest Palestinian explosion, he, Peres, and other Labor advisors had given intensive attention to a possibly definitive physical separation between Jews and Arabs, this time to accustom the Israeli people to the realities of political disengagement from the territories. Moreover, in late March of 1993, Rabin paid his first visit on President Bill Clinton in Washington. The president was cordial but cautious. In the event no progress was made in the bilateral discussions, he intimated, the United States government no longer could expend the time or resources to resolve the Arab-Israel impasse. Rabin hardly needed the admonition. The clock was ticking. By then, more than ten months had passed since his own election, and although he had pledged to achieve a peace settlement within a year, all bilateral talks had been suspended. Lately, increased guerrilla attacks even within Israel proper had killed six Jews and wounded fourteen others, making "black March" one of the worst months in Israel's history. The four hundred Hamas deportees were becoming folk heroes to the Arab world. In his quest to make 1993 "the year of peace," would the prime minister have an interlocutor?

This was an issue the Palestinians now had to consider among themselves. Indeed, Rabin's deportation order had placed the issue of "authoritative" spokesmanship squarely on their national agenda. Could the PLO leadership in Tunis really allow the political initiative to devolve into the hands of religious fundamentalists? Was this the authentic expectation of 1.3 million Palestinian Arabs? In view of President Clinton's obvious friendship for American Jewry and the State of Israel, would Hamas terrorism not shift Washington's policy irretrievably against the Palestinians? The recent collapse of the Soviet Empire, and the unavailability of any further Russian diplomatic or military support, had also to be considered. So too did the PLO's grievously marred image among other Arab governments after its fulsome support of Saddam Hussein in the recent Gulf War. Deprived of its traditional Gulf subsidies, the PLO no longer was capable of maintaining its own extensive civil service and welfare institutions among the Palestinians. And, meanwhile, with the ongoing influx of Soviet immigrants, the Jewish state clearly was gaining in strength, in wealth—in demographic mass. Thus it was, fearing that Israel's grip on the West Bank might soon become unshakable, that Yasser Arafat lately had dispatched signals to Cairo, seeking President Mubarak's intercession. The response was frigid. The PLO chairman would not easily be forgiven his transgression during Operation Desert Storm. For Arafat, therefore, another conduit would have to be found.

A S C A N D I N A V I A N D O O R T O P A L E S T I N E

Although unofficial discourse between Israelis and PLO members had been taking place since the 1970s, those contacts intensified only after 1992, when the Rabin government decided to eliminate all further legal constraints against them. No meetings occurred on Israeli soil. Both sides preferred other, neutral venues. One of these was Stockholm (p. 975). Another was Oslo. There the Institute for Applied Social Science, a respected think tank devoted to the resolution of international disputes, functioned under the unofficial imprimatur of the Norwegian foreign ministry. In the spring of 1992, the institute's director, Terje Rod Larsen, who had developed extensive PLO contacts in the course of field studies in the Gaza Strip, sought out Dr. Yossi Beilin, a protégé and close adviser of Shimon Peres. Larsen informed Beilin that key PLO members had confided to him their fatigue with the intifada, and their willingness to explore the accommodation Arafat had mooted as far back as the winter of 1988. Beilin was interested.

After Labor's electoral victory of June 1992, Peres appointed Beilin his deputy in the foreign ministry. Larsen's wife, Mona Juul, by then was administrative assistant to Norwegian Foreign Minister Johan Jorgen Holst and accordingly in a position to offer Beilin the services of the Norwegian government. In turn, sensing that the bilateral discussions in Washington had reached a dead end, Beilin brought the proposal to Peres. The foreign minister did not veto it. Yet he cautioned Beilin to avoid "official" Israeli involvement. Operating under this guideline, Beilin selected two "unofficial" representatives, Professor Yair Hirschfeld and Dr. Ron Pundak of Haifa University. Hereupon Arafat selected as his principal negotiator "Abu Ala'a" (Ahmed Suleiman Khoury), the PLO "minister of finance" who had long functioned virtually as the chairman's alter ego.

In January 1993, under cover of Larsen's institute, Hirschfeld, Pundak, Abu Al'a and two Palestinian aides were secretly accommodated in a luxurious private mansion outside Oslo. Discussions began. From the outset, both sets of negotiators agreed that the most realistic objective was an interim accord, essentially a declaration of principles, on Palestinian "empowerment." Both Israelis and Palestinians would require time to develop trust and mutual interests. To that limited end, negotiations then continued over the ensuing weeks, with Larsen always in the background to provide for every physical need, and on occasion to function as a mediator between the two sides. Periodically, there were serious disagreements, and both sets of negotiators returned to Jerusalem and Tunis for further consultations. Then, in late February 1993, Yitzchak Rabin finally was brought into the picture. Cautiously, the prime minister allowed the initiative to continue, although without shifting his focus on the "official" bilateral negotiations in Washington.

By then, too, both sides were concentrating on the Gaza Strip as the likeliest site for early Israeli withdrawal and Palestinian "empowerment." A suppurating pesthole, Gaza in any case evoked little historic resonance even among Israeli hard-liners. Indeed, under Peres's instructions from Jerusalem, Hirschfeld and

Pundak intimated a willingness to add Jericho to Gaza as a locale for early Israeli withdrawal. As the foreign minister saw it, Jericho's proximity to the River Jordan improved the chances of an eventual confederation between the Palestinians and Hashemite Jordan, the political scenario that Peres had always favored. To Arafat and his advisers, by the same token, the dusty little town of fourteen thousand represented a kind of preliminary lien on the West Bank. They were interested.

Thus, by late spring 1993, anticipating a breakthrough, both the Israelis and the PLO upgraded their representatives in Oslo to "official" status. Although maintaining a cover of secrecy, Beilin himself made periodic visits to share in the discussions. At the same time, Peres discreetly alerted Egypt's President Mubarak to the backdoor negotiations and won his cooperation in encouraging Arafat to move forthrightly toward an accommodation. Others who quietly fostered the negotiating process were the Americans; for Secretary of State Warren Christopher similarly had been apprised of the Oslo channel. Christopher's Middle East negotiator, Daniel Kurtzer, shuttled between Tunis and Jerusalem, seeking to narrow the gap between the PLO and the Israelis. The combined efforts eventually bore fruit. At long last, Abu Ala'a and his colleagues were authorized to diverge from the Palestinian stance in the Washington negotiations: the explosive issue of Jerusalem would be postponed. Manifestly, the distance was narrowing between security, of decisive concern to the Israelis, and self-rule, which mattered most to the Palestinians.

By August 1993, the basic outline of a "Declaration of Principles" was emerging. Yet, even then, Arafat in Tunis was fearful of taking the final step. Accordingly, Rabin and Peres sent word through Beilin that Israel would be prepared to recognize the PLO as official spokesman for the Palestinian people. The concession was exceptionally painful for the two Israeli leaders. Neither had to be reminded of the many hundreds of Israelis and other Jews who had died by guerrilla violence over the years. Yet they sensed now that public acknowledgment of Arafat's legitimacy as the one and official Palestinian spokesman was an inducement the PLO chairman could not easily reject. The gesture was a shrewd one, and it worked. So did Peres's final gamble, on August 17, of alerting the PLO leadership that the time for procrastination was over, that his own, and Rabin's, patience had expired, that the Declaration of Principles must be completed that very night. The Israeli foreign minister was in Stockholm, ostensibly to attend an international Socialist congress. Through the Norwegian foreign minister—also present—a series of back-and-forth telephone calls to Arafat in Tunis clarified the few remaining points at issue. When the PLO chairman still hesitated, Peres threatened to break off all further contacts and negotiate exclusively with Syria. Hereupon Arafat wilted. Without further demurrer, he accepted the final draft outline of the Declaration of Principles. The next day, Peres flew secretly to Oslo, and was present at the Norwegian government guest house as his appointed delegate, Uri Savir, director general of Israel's foreign ministry, signed the agreement for his government; while Abu Ala'a and his young aide Hassan Asfour signed for the PLO.

Even then, Rabin would not submit the document to his cabinet. If he had paid the bitter price of recognizing the PLO's official status, he expected repayment in kind. On September 9, he got it. It was a formal letter from Arafat. In black on white it affirmed that the PLO acknowledged Israel's right to exist in peace and security; that the PLO renounced the use of terrorism and other acts of violence; and that "[t]hose articles of the Palestinian Covenant which deny Israel's right to exist . . . are now inoperative and no longer valid." In response, the prime minister's letter of September 10 (a single, icily formal paragraph) confirmed that "the Government of Israel has decided to recognize the PLO as the representative of the Palestinian people and to commence negotiations with the PLO within the Middle East peace process."

The American government had committed itself deeply to that peace process, and specifically to the "official" bilateral negotiations that had been going on intermittently in Washington since late 1991. Although well informed on the clandestine negotiations in Oslo, the Clinton administration had not been the principal mediator in the Israeli-Palestinian compact. Yet its role, however supportive, could hardly be exposed as marginal if American financial and diplomatic leverage were to be exploited in the peace process. With some trepidation, therefore, Peres flew off to the United States to ensure Secretary of State Christopher's willingness to acknowledge the supersession of the earlier Washington bilateral talks, and the primacy of the Oslo agreement. As it developed, Peres's concern was unwarranted. Christopher was gratified, even thrilled, by the successful culmination of the Oslo negotiations, with its climactic Declaration of Principles. Both men agreed, moreover, that President Clinton should host a formal Palestinian-Israeli "peace" ceremony. On its own, the gesture would be decisive and dramatic enough to signify ongoing United States endorsement and involvement.

But if Christopher's reaction was favorable, Rabin and Arafat would learn that their own constituencies were a more formidable proposition. Thus, in late August, as the PLO chairman submitted the document to his executive committee in Tunis, he was met by an explosion of disbelief and recrimination. Two days of acrimonious give-and-take were required before Arafat won over a narrow, precarious majority. The reaction in Israel was almost as incredulous. Upon being informed, Rabin's cabinet eventually accepted the draft declaration, on August 30, with only two abstentions. But the Knesset debate afterward was a furious one. It was not only Likud and other rightist factions that vented their outrage. Within the Labor camp a significant minority of Knesset members expressed grave reservations at the very notion of recognizing the PLO. Here it was that Rabin's brief had to be the most eloquent and urgent of his political career. From the Knesset rostrum, the prime minister reviewed the months of fruitless bilateral negotiations in Washington. He concluded solemnly:

Members of the Knesset, we cannot choose our neighbors, or our enemies, not even the cruelest among them. We only have what there is. The PLO has fought against us, and we have fought against them—and with them we are today seeking a path to peace. We can lock every door, thwart every attempt at peace. We have the moral right not to sit at the negotiating table with the PLO . . . not to shake the hand that pulled the trigger. We have the power to reject with revulsion the PLO proposals—and then to be unwilling partners to the continuing cycle with which we have been forced to live until now: war, terrorism, and violence.

Rabin's majority held firm. Despite the firestorm of Likud and other rightist protest, the Knesset approved the Declaration of Principles.

AN EXPERIMENTAL PALESTINIAN EMPOWERMENT

The signing ceremony in Washington was designated for September 13, 1993. Like the long, feckless negotiations in the State Department, the event nominally took place under the joint American-Russian aegis of the original Madrid conference. Gathered in the White House Rose Garden, therefore, the participants included not only Yasser Arafat, Mahmoud Abbas, Yitzchak Rabin, Shimon Peres, President Clinton, and Secretary Christopher, but also Russian Foreign Minister Andrei Kozyrev. Indeed, once Peres and Abbas performed the act of signature, both Christopher and Kozyrev added their own signatures as "witnesses."

The twenty-three-page "Declaration of Principles on Interim Self-Government" consisted of a basic text, four annexes and agreed minutes, and the September 9–10 exchange of letters between Arafat and Rabin. Less than a comprehensive treaty, the document in effect was an agreement to reach agreement, leaving the details to be negotiated between the parties. Nevertheless, under the declaration's collective guidelines, Israel would begin its military withdrawal from Gaza and Jericho as early as December, and by April 1994 leave to a Palestinian authority virtually full self-government in these enclaves. Subsequently, a five-year transitional period would commence for the West Bank in its entirety, and early on during that time span the Israeli civil administration would transfer "empowerment" to the Palestinian authority in five carefully delimited spheres: education, health, social welfare, taxation, and tourism. It was understood, too, that the spectrum of self-government would rapidly expand into other areas, including the judiciary and water control. The Israeli army similarly would deploy outside the main West Bank population centers, although retaining authority for internal security in the region. From beginning to end, meanwhile, Israel would retain full legal jurisdiction over Jewish settlements in the territories. Two years into interim empowerment for the West Bank, negotiations would commence between Israel, the Palestinians, and Jordan on the final status and borders of the territories, as well as of Jerusalem. The process would be completed in three years. Indeed, the entire five-year timetable was based on the original Camp David accord of fifteen years before.

Yet the Declaration of Principles diverged from that earlier, 1978 document in several important respects. For one thing, it resolved the question of whether, as the Palestinians claimed, their interim empowerment would be territorial, covering the entire West Bank and Gaza areas; or whether, as Begin and Shamir had insisted, it should be exclusively personal, covering only the inhabitants of Palestine, but not the territories in which they lived. Here Rabin and Peres had affirmed that Palestinian empowerment would indeed be territorial. Except for the network of Jewish settlements and Israeli military installations, empowerment (initially in the five spheres cited above) would cover the totality of the land on which Arabs traditionally had lived, built their homes, worked, and raised their crops and families.

Of equal significance, the five-year interim period would begin immediately upon elections for a Palestinian Council and the council's formal inauguration. Camp David also had provided: "When the self-government authority [administrative council] in the West Bank and Gaza is established and inaugurated, the transitional period of five years will begin." Yet the Camp David format specified that the permanent status negotiations must be conducted between "Egypt, Israel, Jordan and the elected representatives of the inhabitants of the West Bank and Gaza." In practice, then, no agreement ever was reached on the ambit of the self-governing authority; hence the authority was never "established and inaugurated"—and thus, fifteen years after Camp David, the five-year transitional period had not yet begun. This time, the uncertainties of Arab intramural politics would not become a pretext for delay ("I do not believe that democracy can be imposed artificially on another society," Peres commented drily later). The Declaration of Principles announced an intention to move ahead to Palestinian empowerment forthrightly, vigorously, and extensively—and, in the case at least of Gaza and Jericho, immediately.

So it was, on September 13, 1993, in the bright sunshine of a Washington morning, before an audience that included former presidents Carter and Bush, former secretaries of state Kissinger, Vance, and Baker, that Rabin solemnly declaimed:

> Let me say to you, the Palestinians, we are destined to live together on the same soil in the same land. We, the soldiers who have returned from battles stained with blood; we who have seen our relatives and friends killed before our eyes; we who have attended their funerals and cannot look into the eyes of their parents; we who have come from a land where parents bury their children; we who have fought against you, the Palestinians, we say to you today in a loud and clear voice, enough of blood and tears. Enough!

Arafat responded in the same spirit, promising "to implement all aspects of UN Resolutions 242 and 338," and assuring Israel that "the right to [Palestinian] self-determination" would not "violate the rights of their neighbors or infringe on their security." In the flurry of handshakes afterward, the PLO chairman walked over to Rabin, who until that moment had avoided speaking to him or even standing next to him, and offered the Israeli prime minister his hand. After a moment's hesitation, and with a tight smile that onlookers might easily have confused with a grimace, Rabin accepted the hand and gave it two perfunctory shakes. Although no words were exchanged, the media treated the event as one of modern history's decisive watersheds.

The watershed was not to be traversed that easily. One month after the signature ceremony, Israeli-PLO negotiations began as scheduled in the Egyptian border town of Taba (and later in Cairo). Their purpose was to formulate guidelines for implementing the first, Gaza-Jericho, phase of the interim agreement. As matters developed, those negotiations would not be completed until May 4, 1994—five months behind schedule. If the original Declaration of Principles consisted of twenty-three pages, the Gaza-Jericho document encompassed not less than three hundred! In Oslo, after all, both sides had agreed that "empowerment" for Palestine would consist of "two legs" (in the words of

ISRAELI-PALESTINIAN AGREEMENTS, 1993–1999

Declaration of Principles
Washington, D.C., Sept. 13, 1993

Interim Self-Government Arrangements

GAZA-JERICHO AGREEMENT
Signed May 4, 1994

TRANSFER OF POWERS
Signed Aug. 29, 1994

Early transfer of powers and responsibilities in specified spheres, in those parts of the territories not included in the Gaza-Jericho Agreement. These spheres include:

- Education and culture
- Health
- Social welfare
- Direct taxation
- Tourism
- Other spheres as agreed

- Security arrangements
- Transfer of civil affairs
- Legal framework
- Economic framework

INTERIM AGREEMENT
Signed Sept. 28, 1995

Comprehensive agreement on the transfer of powers and responsibilities in the West Bank from Israel to an elected Palestinian Council. Milestones of implementation:

- *Dec. 31, 1995:* Redeployment from population centers in West Bank
- *Jan. 20, 1996:* Elections to the Palestinian Council
- *Jan. 17, 1997:* Redeployment from Hebron
- *Oct. 23, 1998:* **Wye River Memorandum.** Stage 1 of further redeployment implemented *Nov. 20, 1998*
- *Sept. 4, 1999:* **Sharm es-Sheikh Memorandum**

Permanent Status

PERMANENT STATUS AGREEMENT

Agreement finalizing the relationship between Israel and the Palestinians, as follows:

- Talks to begin no later than third year of interim period *(May 1996)* (DOP)
- Issues to include Jerusalem, refugees, settlements, security arrangements, and borders (DOP)
- Agreements to enter into force after fifth year of self-government (DOP)
- Permanent status talks resumed *(Erez, Sept. 13, 1999)* according to the **Sharm es-Sheikh Memorandum** (DOP)

Israel's legal adviser, Joel Singer), one longer than the other. Thus, the "longer leg," encompassing Gaza and Jericho, represented the only geographic areas in Palestine from which Israel's armed forces would withdraw entirely, and in which Israeli civil authority would be dissolved altogether. Here the Palestinians would enjoy empowerment over the widest ambit of internal affairs, even maintaining order with their own police. Here, too, the transfer of civilian responsibilities would be to a Palestinian "authority," an appointative body, as distinguished from a Palestinian Council, later to be elected for the rest of the West Bank.

Determined to preserve its security interests down to the last detail, therefore, Israel's negotiators incorporated into the document every possible guarantee of military protection. Those assurances encompassed first and foremost the entire perimeter of the Gaza Strip and Jericho, including the air space over both areas, and all approaches by sea. Israel would operate all international crossing points, and control the entry of all visitors into the autonomous Gaza and Jericho enclaves. Similarly, Israel retained "full operational authority," with its own police, to protect Jewish settlements in the Gaza Strip, which of course remained strictly under Israeli jurisdiction. Moreover, the Israelis also retained the right strictly to monitor the Palestinian police, to ensure that their numbers did not exceed seven thousand, that their weaponry remained limited to small arms, and their personnel limited to Palestinians whose background revealed no earlier guerrilla activity.

Other "protective" features of the Gaza-Jericho accord related to the economic as well as the military sphere. Thus, a complex series of agreements kept the Gaza and Jericho economies tightly linked to Israel's. Although the Palestinians would continue to enjoy access to the Israeli market, products admitted duty-free were limited (as in the past) to a specified list of agricultural goods not in direct competition with Israel's own farm output. Israel similarly reserved the right, whenever necessary for "security reasons," to close off its labor market to commuting Palestinian laborers. Altogether, then, Rabin did not exaggerate when he reminded the Knesset on May 11, 1994, that even the "longer leg"—the Gaza-Jericho sector of the new Palestine Authority—was enmeshed in a dense webwork of Israeli controls.

AN ERRATIC JOURNEY TOWARD NORMALIZATION

Yasser Arafat arrived in Gaza within days of the May 1994 signing to a tumultuous, hysterical reception from tens of thousands of awaiting Palestinians. Amid the euphoria, however, it soon became evident that the PA chairman had only a limited vision of his new Palestinian empowerment. Although the man was under no obligation at this early stage to foster democratic government, his handpicked appointees initially were little more than personal sycophants. Few were equipped to grapple with Gaza's huge refugee population and its near-universal mendicancy. Worse yet, the PA treasury itself was all but empty; the recent Gulf War had ended its subventions and remittances from Kuwait and Saudi Arabia. With Israel's encouragement, therefore, Arafat turned for help to the EEC and the World Bank. These sources in fact were prepared to arrange a $2.1 billion, five-year loan. They asked only a reasonable schedule of supervised accountability. It was a commitment Arafat was unwilling to make. Soon, then, the chairman's authoritarianism produced a confusion that approached paralysis. Arriving from Egypt with uniforms and suitcases, the Palestine police found themselves without assured salaries, even without living quarters. Months passed before Arafat finally relented, and permitted a World Bank liaison committee to share in structuring his administration. Bit by bit, funds began to arrive, including a $60 million contribution from Israel itself. Slowly, erratically, the PA began to function.

Beyond his own personal and political eccentricities, Arafat did not lack other—Arab—enemies intent upon torpedoing Palestinian-Israeli peace. During the remainder of 1993–94, Hamas terrorists carried out over three dozen random shootings, stabbings, and bombings of Israeli citizens, both along the Gaza security zone and in Israel proper. The grisliest of their violence, in October 1994, was a suicide bomb that destroyed a packed Tel Aviv bus at the height of the morning rush hour, killing twenty-two passengers and wounding forty-seven. Several months later, in January 1995, another suicide bomb would kill twenty-one soldiers at a bus stop near Netania; and in later months, still additional suicide bombings would take place in Ramat Gan and Jerusalem. In the ensuing shock and horror, it was inevitable that Likud and other right-wing political spokesmen would redouble their attacks on the Labor government, branding the entire Palestinian autonomy experiment a mortal threat to Israel's security.

Rabin and Peres would not be deterred. They had risked their electoral mandate on peace. Admittedly, the interim agreement was far more complicated than the initial accord ("Oslo I") on Gaza and Jericho, in view of the number of Palestinian cities involved, the larger territories that required allocation. The West Bank encompassed 3,634 square miles, as contrasted with the modest 135 square miles of the Gaza Strip and the minuscule 19 square miles of the town of Jericho. Perhaps inhibited by the magnitude of the challenge, Israelis and Palestinians did not so much as begin their exploratory work on the interim accord until December 1994.

Against the backdrop of suicide bombings, however, negotiations were soon accelerated. Uri Savir, director-general of Israel's foreign ministry, and Mahmoud Abbas, Arafat's "foreign minister," labored diligently through the late spring and summer of 1995 to fashion the parameters of the Oslo process's next stage. Savir and his advisers projected the largest area of the West Bank as Zone C, in which they envisaged Israel retaining both security—that is, military—and administrative authority; and a somewhat smaller area, Zone B, in which Israel would retain security authority even after transferring governmental authority to the Palestinians. Finally, in Zone A, the smallest, the Palestine Authority would take over both governmental and security responsibilities. Not surprisingly, Abbas held out for enlargement of both Zones A and B.

It was not until mid-July that a compromise was reached. Initially, the PA's security authority would still be confined to the smallest zone, A; but the zone of shared military and administrative powers, B, would be incrementally enlarged, from 22 to 27 percent of the West Bank. Most important, Israel would accelerate its military evacuation of both Zones B and C. Final military redeployment from the West Bank would be completed by mid-1997 (two years before the end of the original—five-year—redeployment schedule), thus permitting both sides an earlier opportunity to tackle the "final-status" issues of permanent borders, Jerusalem, and refugees.

During August and September 1995, in discussions conducted within the congenial premises of an Egyptian resort hotel in Taba, the most important remaining "interim" issues were apparently resolved. The Israelis consented to release five thousand Palestinians who had been imprisoned for acts of violence. Agreement was also reached on a trilateral committee of Americans, Israelis, and Palestinians to deal with the equitable allocation of water resources. Arafat committed himself to the—still unfulfilled—revision of the "Palestinian Covenant," affirming in clear and explicit language acceptance by the Palestinian Legislative Council of the legitimacy of the State of Israel. With these issues finally out of the way, the interim agreement ("Oslo II") was drafted on September 24, 1995, and three days later, on September 28, Rabin, Peres, and Arafat ceremonially signed the final document at the White House, in the presence of President Clinton, Egypt's President Mubarak, and Jordan's King Hussein.

A PARTNER TO THE EAST

In their dealings with Arafat and his advisers, Rabin and Peres wielded not only the carrot of broadened Palestinian empowerment but the stick of negotiation with an alternate partner for peace. This was their long-favored interlocutor, King Hussein of Jordan. It was true that earlier, in 1987, the London Agreement had been torpedoed by Prime Minister Shamir (pp. 957–58); and a year later, Hussein, in his exasperation with Palestinians and Israelis alike, had publicly renounced all further responsibility for the West Bank. Nevertheless, it was hardly a secret that the king would resume his connections with either or both groups if the political climate changed. In 1992, Labor's triumph in the Israeli elections offered decisive evidence of such a change. Later in the year, and extending into 1993, a series of meetings took place in London and Paris between Rabin, Peres, and Crown Prince Hassan, the king's younger brother and alter ego. The Israelis reemphasized their long-standing preference for a confederation of the Hashemite Kingdom with any future Palestinian entity. It was in Israel's interest, they suggested, and surely in Jordan's, to foster that kind of stability.

By the early winter of 1993, as a sweetener, Rabin and Peres suggested that Israel would be willing to take into account the Jordanian monarchy's former "special relationship" as protector of Jerusalem's Moslem shrines. The inducement was a powerful one, for it instantly conjured up visions of the Hashemite dynasty's past glory as Guardian of the Holy Places of Mecca and Medina.

Equally attractive for King Hussein was the opportunity to repair his ties with Washington, which had been strained by his refusal to join the American-led coalition in the recent Gulf War. Moreover, détente with Israel would enable the king to play a central, if belated, role in a peace configuration that already had encompassed Egypt and the PLO, and would soon include Morocco, Tunisia, and the Gulf Principality of Qatar (p. 1005).

Responding to these inducements, Hussein and his advisers reached a meeting of minds with their Israeli counterparts by the late winter. Only the details remained to be filled in. Thus it was, on September 14, 1993, one day after the initial Israel-PLO "Declaration of Principles" signing ceremony in the White House Rose Garden, that a second Washington ceremony took place, this one presided over by Warren Christopher in the State Department reception hall. Present were a senior Russian foreign ministry official, as well as Jordan's and Israel's ambassadors to the United States. In a portentous gesture of near equivalence to the previous morning's Rabin-Arafat handshake, the Israeli and Jordanian diplomats then signed a "Common Agenda" for peace, a commitment not only to observe UN Resolutions 242 and 338, but to negotiate such vital outstanding issues as arms control, water resources, status of refugees, and territorial democratization "without prejudice" to the internal status of the West Bank itself.

Seventeen days after that, on October 1, 1993, Shimon Peres and Prince Hassan met at the White House, ostensibly to establish a joint economic committee, but in fact to make plain, in the words of President Clinton, that their presence "symbolize[d] a new relationship between Jordan and Israel." That relationship gained a seemingly irresistible momentum on July 20, 1994, when Peres, Warren Christopher, and Jordanian Prime Minister Abd al-Salaam Majali gathered at a Jordanian resort hotel, the Dead Sea Spa, due north of Aqaba. Here were outlined, in far greater detail than in the earlier "Common Agenda," plans for trade between the two countries on a most-favored-nation basis, and for cooperation in promotional and marketing channels, scientific research, joint banking ventures, tourism, and water development.

Within the week, on July 25, 1994, as the production continued to unfold in a sequence of tableaux coordinated as artfully as a theatrical performance, the Dead Sea Spa event was succeeded in Washington by yet another ceremonial signing, this one featuring King Hussein and Prime Minister Rabin at the White House. With President Clinton again functioning as host, the two Middle Eastern leaders affixed their signatures to a "Washington Declaration." Proclaiming that "the state of belligerency between Israel and Jordan has been terminated," the declaration promised yet again to develop "good neighborly relations of cooperation between [Jordan and Israel] to ensure lasting security and to avoid threats and the use of force between them."

It was peace. The final coup de théâtre, on October 26, 1994, at the Israel-Jordan border village of Ein Evrona, was essentially a ritual of coronation. Again, Rabin was present, together with Peres and Ezer Weizman, the latter in his current eminence as president of the State of Israel. For Jordan, King

Hussein was on hand, with Prime Minister Majali and other ministers and dignitaries. Secretary of State Christopher was present, as was Russian Foreign Minister Andrei Kozyrev. Plainly, the original—Madrid—façade of joint sponsorship was to be maintained to the end.

No illusions were sustained, however, about the Great Power sponsorship that mattered most. Seated at center stage under the blinding desert sun was President Bill Clinton, whose presence at Ein Evrona once again attested to the decisive role the Israelis and Jordanians projected for the United States in their joint diplomatic and economic future. The speeches, the mutual protestations of goodwill and cooperation, were by then an old story. The peace treaty itself similarly had been refined over two years of painstaking negotiations between Israel and Jordan. Under its terms, full and formal diplomatic relations were established. The international boundary between the two countries was defined. Arrangements were completed for mutual civilian crossings and checkpoints, for postal and telecommunications links, for water allocations from the Jordan and Yarmuk rivers, from the ground sources of the Arava Rift, and from future joint water projects, and for the promotion of tourism and cultural exchanges.

It was a stirring event. Yet, for Israel, the most poignant expression of the nation's collective emotion occurred not in Ein Evrona on October 26, but in Washington three months earlier, on July 25, following the signing ceremony at the White House (described above), when Rabin and Hussein addressed a joint session of Congress. The prime minister's tribute to his "partner in peace" was gracious and respectful, and included a touching allusion to "your grandfather, King Abdullah, who sought avenues of peace with the heads of the Jewish people and the leaders of the young State of Israel." It was in his personal reflections, however, that Rabin, normally a phlegmatic soldier, achieved a dimension of authentic eloquence. Turning to a group of friends who had accompanied him from Israel, and who were seated now in the gallery of the House of Representatives, the prime minister observed:

Mr. Speaker . . . allow me to refer to some Israelis who are here with me, and with you. Amiram Kaplan, whose first brother was killed in an accident, whose second brother was killed in pursuit of terrorists, whose third brother was killed in war, and whose parents died of heartbreak. . . . Moshe Sasson, who together with his father [Eliahu] was an emissary to the talks with King Abdullah, and to other missions of peace. Today, he is also an emissary of peace.

With me [also] is a classmate of mine from elementary school, Channa Rivlin, of Kibbutz Gesher . . . who endured bitter fighting and lost a son in war. Today she looks out of her kibbutz window onto Jordan, and shares the dream of peace to come. . . . [And] Dani Mat, who fought against Jordan in the war of independence, [who] was taken a prisoner of war, and [who] devoted his life to the security of the State of Israel. He hopes that . . . his grandchildren will never know war. . . . And Mr. Talal al-Qurnawi, mayor of a Bedouin town in Israel, who looks forward to renewing his friendship with his kinsmen in Jordan. . . . And Dr. Sharon Segev, whose father was killed while pursuing terrorists in the Jordan Valley, and who yearns for peace with all his heart.

Here they are before you, people who never rejoice in the victories of war, but whose hearts are now filled with . . . the joy of peace. . . . Allow me [also] a personal note. . . . I, who served my country for twenty-seven years as a soldier, say to you, Your Majesty, this is the only battle that is a pleasure to win, the battle for peace. . . . "Blessed art Thou, O Lord, Who has preserved us and sustained us and enabled us to reach this moment." God bless the peace.

A DETERIORATION OF THE

RABIN-PERES LEGACY

A POST-RABIN VALEDICTORY

On the evening of November 4, 1995, Prime Minister Yitzchak Rabin addressed a peace rally of some 100,000 citizens that overflowed Tel Aviv's Municipality Square. Afterward, at 9:30 p.m., his spirits buoyed by the warmth of the audience's reception and its visible support for his peace diplomacy, Rabin made ready to depart. Lurking undetected near his limousine was Yigal Amir, a twenty-five-year-old law student at Bar-Ilan University, and an unregenerate opponent of territorial concessions to the Arabs. As the prime minister walked by, the young man fired three pistol shots into his back. Rabin was immediately rushed by ambulance to Tel Aviv's Ichilov Hospital, where he underwent emergency surgery. The effort was unavailing. He was pronounced dead at 11:10 p.m.

In the shocked aftermath of the assassination, the media scrupulously observed the old adage, *de mortuis nil nisi bonum,* against speaking ill of the dead. No references were made to Rabin's career as "Mr. Security" as defense minister in the Shamir "unity" government; his instructions to the Israeli army during the first, 1987, intifada to use rubber bullets, and if necessary "to break the bones" of stone-throwing Palestinian youths. As prime minister, in December 1992, Rabin had exiled 415 Gaza militants to a grim no-man's-land along the Israeli-Lebanese frontier. In the summer of 1993, he launched the army against Hizballah terrorists who had penetrated Israel's security zone in southern Lebanon, putting to flight thousands of Lebanese civilians. Even after the September 1993 "Declaration of Principles" ceremony with Arafat, the prime minister would not be hurried into impetuous concessions. In reaction against Palestinian violence, he postponed the signing of "Oslo I," with its formula for an initial Israeli withdrawal from Gaza and Jericho, until May 4, 1994; and he put off until September 28, 1995, the signing of "Oslo II," the agreement for subsequent, phased Israeli withdrawals from the territories. In the meantime, Rabin did not hesitate to approve the "thickening" of strategically valuable Jewish settlements in the West Bank.

But the United States and the European Community, even Egypt and Jordan, had reacted forbearingly to these delays and spasms of retaliation. In July 1994, Rabin and King Hussein had been granted a tumultuous reception as both addressed the United States Congress to declare the end of their two countries' state of war (described above). In October 1994, evincing Europe's overwhelming sense of relief at the prospect of an Arab-Israeli accommodation, the Nobel Committee had awarded its peace prize jointly to Rabin, Peres, and Arafat. Thus, by the mid-1990s, the aura Rabin had acquired as a hero of peace gleamed no less impressively than his repute as a hero of the 1967 Six-Day War.

Rabin had been the leader of a small country, with a population of less than seven million. Yet his funeral in Jerusalem, on November 6, 1995, was attended by presidents, prime ministers, and royalty from North and South America, from Asia, Africa, Australia, and, without a single exception, from the nations of Europe, large and small. The major powers were represented by President Jacques Chirac of France, Prime Minister Lamberto Dini of Italy, President Roman Herzog and Chancellor Helmut Kohl of Germany, Prince Charles and Prime Minister John Major of Britain, and Prime Minister Viktor Chernomyrdin of Russia. President Bill Clinton of the United States was present to deliver a moving eulogy. He was joined in the tribute by King Hussein of Jordan and President Hosni Mubarak of Egypt.

Rabin had been born in Israel. Yet his forebears and several million of his fellow citizens had drawn their initial breaths in Europe. Standing under a Middle Eastern sun, could these respectful visiting eminences have shared the sense of common loss, and a premonitory vision of their own continent, largely purged of its Jews only a half century earlier, now entwined with a nation of survivors in a possible common future destiny: of crippling oil shortages or assurance of future prosperity? Of imported Moslem terrorism or civilian tranquillity and security? Of Mediterranean volatility or regional stability? Of war or peace?

PERES'S LEGACY TO RABIN

Within the week of Rabin's interment, the central committee of Israel's ruling Labor party selected Foreign Minister Shimon Peres as his successor. An experienced veteran of the prime ministry, and a perennial foreign minister or finance minister in national-unity and rotating cabinets, Peres knew his way around the government as did few of his predecessors. He and Yossi Beilin, his former deputy at the foreign ministry, were the authentic architects of the Oslo peace process. Indeed, Peres arguably had a clearer insight than Rabin into the international dividends to be reaped by accepting a blueprint for Palestinian self-government. It was the two men's common vision, in any case, that had fostered the country's improved relations not only with the Soviet Union, India, and China (pp. 983–84) but with selected Moslem nations, as well. In October 1993, only a month after his celebrated White House handshake with Arafat, Rabin was able to visit Indonesia, the world's most populous Moslem country, where he was warmly received by President Muhammad Suharto; and then travel to Moslem Malaysia, where his welcome was equally cordial. In New York, that same autumn, Rabin met with Nelson Mandela, the president-elect of South Africa, for an amiable and extended conversation. In December 1993 the Vatican agreed in principle to open diplomatic ties with Israel (p. 983), and in March 1994 Pope John Paul II paid a respectful visit to Israel, stopping to intone a prayer at Jerusalem's Western Wall.

By 1994, ignoring the Arab League's—already frayed—economic boycott guidelines, the governments of Morocco, Tunisia, and Qatar permitted Israel to set up "interest sections" in their capitals. In December 1994, after participating in the Middle Eastern Economic Conference at Casablanca, Israel's leading corporations began receiving inquiries from business groups in Egypt, Jordan, Morocco, Algeria, Tunisia, and even Lebanon, seeking information on joint economic ventures with Israel and the Palestinians. Discussions then ascended to the governmental level, with proposals for regional cooperation in water, energy, trade, and industrial development. A few months later yet, Jacques Delors, president of the European Community's Executive Commission (functioning under the "umbrella" of the newly created European Union), reminded his follow commissioners that the EC was exerting five times the financial effort on behalf of East European, formerly Communist nations than for the southern Mediterranean countries. The asymmetry was hazardous, Delors argued, for North Africa's and the Middle East's poverty and rapid population growth, their corruption, crime, and political terrorism, above all, their metastasizing unemployment, were propelling waves of immigrants into Europe. The influx was threatening large areas of the continent with economic and social instability.

Delors's warning registered. The European Union itself then launched into intensive discussions with southern Mediterranean governments, a process that eventually culminated in November 1995 with the signing in Barcelona of a European-Mediterranean Partnership Agreement. The new venture encompassed fifteen EU nations and twelve southern Mediterranean countries extending from Algeria and Morocco to Egypt, Syria, Turkey—and Israel. Far more than a trade agreement, the "Barcelona Pact" transcended all earlier economic cooperation treaties between Europe and the Mediterranean "poor cousins." Its projected goal was nothing less than development of a Euro-Mediterranean "zone of peace and stability." The expectation was by no means fanciful. The Barcelona Pact members soon became enmeshed in a cat's cradle of multinational committees devoted to joint programs for agriculture, industry, communications, and transportation, as well as joint campaigns against terrorism and traffic in drugs and women.

The EU-Mediterranean paradigm was not designed specifically to advance the Arab-Israeli peace process. But neither was it a secret that, for the European partners, no issue of their wider agenda transcended that process. Following "Oslo I" and "Oslo II," both Peres and Arafat requested Europe's economic help for the emergent Palestinian entity. For its part, the EU almost leaped at the opportunity to offer its largesse. As early as September 8, 1993, five days even before the initial Israeli-Palestinian signing ceremony in Washington, the EU's Executive Commission proposed a $600-million aid package for the Palestinians, to be applied over the ensuing five years. Before the first year was out, the commission approved an additional $104 million grant simply to help underwrite the new Palestinian police force. In January 1996, as Arafat and his staff prepared to organize the Palestinians' first "national" election (in which Arafat was duly elected president of the Palestine Authority), the

European Union as a collectivity provided most of the funds and some three hundred monitors to help administer the actual balloting.

As Peres had envisaged, however, it was specifically his own country—its image dramatically revived as a "peacemaker," the solicitous "patron" of Palestinian empowerment—that reaped the most tangible, bread-and-butter results from Western Europe. With the Arab "secondary" economic boycott of Israel virtually moribund, all residual barriers to European investment in the Jewish state were similarly discarded. Britain was a case in point. Until lately, under the Conservative governments of Margaret Thatcher and John Major, the British had been unrelenting in their criticism of Yitzchak Shamir's hard line. In December 1987 and January 1988, Britain's ambassador to the UN Security Council supported resolutions condemning Israel's settlement activity and its policy of repression in Gaza and the West Bank. In the June 1989 meeting of the European Community's Council of Ministers, Britain's Foreign Secretary Geoffrey Howe had joined his colleagues in endorsing the condemnation.

From the advent of the Rabin government in 1992, however, and the ensuing progress toward Middle East peace, London's approach to Israel softened. In March 1995, Prime Minister Major paid his first official visit to the Jewish state. It was significant that he brought with him thirty-one leaders of British industry. Several British corporations, like Unilever and Marks & Spencer, already had explored investment opportunities in Israeli firms. Subsequently, Madge, a British network giant, made an outright purchase of Lannet, a promising Israeli computer software firm. As other British companies sought attractive purchases or joint ventures, they availed themselves of the services of the—formerly dormant—Israel-UK Business Council, as well as of the commercial office of the British embassy in Tel Aviv, which recently had grown to eight staffers.

By the same token, under the new Rabin government the relationship between the German Federal Republic and Israel surpassed even its earlier warmth. In March 1993, six months before the Rabin-Arafat handshake, the two governments established a German-Israeli Cooperation Council to foster shared research in environmental technologies. The venture was but one of the many cooperative undertakings that actually had been in place since the 1960s (pp. 561–62). In 1986, a jointly funded German-Israeli Foundation for Science Research and Development, the brainchild of Shimon Peres and Helmut Kohl, had been launched with start-up capital of $50 million. By 1993 the operating capital had doubled, and was generating sixty grants a year for approved ventures. Over the years, too, Germany's three principal political parties, its trade union federation, and eight separate German municipalities had funded an exchange program that brought selected groups of Israelis to the Bundesrepublik.

Yet, more than any single factor, it was the Oslo peace process that vastly accelerated German investment and tourism in Israel, and narrowed the balance-of-payments gap between the two countries. In 1995, the Daimler-Benz Investment Corporation had opened an office in Israel to explore likely prospects for its capital reserves. Establishing an Israeli branch for the same investment purposes, Siemens launched its initial venture by purchasing a local computer firm, Or Net, for $30 million. Volkswagen formed an investment relationship with Israel's Dead Sea Works for the extraction of magnesium, and quickly poured $350 million into the venture over the mid-1990s. In 1996, the Hendek Detergents and Cosmetics Corporation purchased a 50 percent share in So'ad, a subsidiary of Israel's Koor conglomerate. Operating jointly with Clal, Israel's single-largest public-investment company, Schneider Optical Works committed $80 million to the local high-tech firms Robomatics and ELOP Optronics. Frankfurt's FG Bank AG and Israel's Bank HaPoalim opened joint departments in Haifa and Jerusalem, specializing in Israel's foreign trade with the Bundesrepublik.

At all times, the German government gave its official encouragement to these projects. Like Israel, it authorized special tax advantages for private investors in the Jewish state. When Chancellor Kohl paid his second visit to Israel, in June 1996, he brought with him twenty German business executives. Germany's Economics Minister Gunther Rexrodt and the economics ministers of individual German Länder also were frequent visitors, attracted by Israel's high-tech industry and its educated workforce. By 1996, as well, over 200,000 private German tourists were coming to Israel annually, more than to any other nation outside Europe, except for the United States. With 125,000 Israelis also visiting Germany annually, *Geschichtspolitik*—the politics of historical memory and atonement—evidently was being paralleled by mild and pragmatic self-interest.

RABIN'S SYRIAN LEGACY

Little wonder that Israeli support for the ongoing Oslo process, even with its likely outcome of an independent Palestinian state, remained solid into the mid-1990s. So long as personal security was maintained along the areas of densest Jewish settlement, both within and beyond the pre-1967 "Green Line" of integral Israel, a majority of the population could live with Yitzchak Rabin's diplomatic coup. It was noteworthy, however, that Rabin actually did not regard an agreement with Arafat as his most pressing objective. Rather, since taking office in 1992, he had accorded priority to an accommodation with Israel's northern neighbor, Syria. On the one hand, Rabin nurtured a profound distrust and antipathy toward the Syrians, whose record of torturing and murdering captured Israeli pilots and soldiers was particularly grim. The prime minister well appreciated, too, that Syria was the one potential military threat remaining on Israel's borders. On the other hand, it was a threat that was kept on a tight leash under the Syrian president, Hafez al-Assad. A former general himself, Assad was a disciplined interlocutor. He had scrupulously observed the armistices of 1967 and 1973. However cautiously, Rabin was prepared to seek a deal with him.

In November 1992, the prime minister authorized Itamar Rabinovich, Israel's ambassador in Washington, and an expert on Syrian politics, to explore the possibility of negotiations with his, Rabinovich's, counterpart in the American capital, Syria's Ambassador Walid al-Moualem. Upon approval from Damascus, Moualem was allowed to proceed with discussions. The exchanges got off to a rocky start. In December, Hamas guerrillas killed three Israeli soldiers and a border policeman in Gaza. When Rabin in turn ordered the summary expulsion of 415 suspected Hamas and Islamic Jihad militants from Palestine (p. 989), the Syrians immediately suspended their contacts with the Israelis. It was not until April 1993, when European and American mediators produced a formula for the return of the Palestinians, that Assad hinted of his willingness to resume the Washington talks. By the summer, the Syrian president was even publicly mooting a new if rather vague equation, of "full peace for full withdrawal," that is, full diplomatic and trade relations with Israel in return for full Israeli evacuation of the Golan Heights.

Unbeknownst to Assad, by the summer of 1993 Rabin was directing his attention to the new Oslo developments, and these consumed the Israeli prime minister's diplomacy for the ensuing months. The line of communication from Damascus went silent. Toward the end of the year, however, responding to personal appeals from President Bill Clinton in Washington (and undoubtedly to the compulsion not to be left isolated in the peace process), Assad once more consented to resume serious, if oblique, negotiations with the Israelis. In January 1994, following a meeting with Clinton in Geneva, the Syrian leader declared: "[W]e want a peace of the brave, a real peace that thrives, continues, guarantees the interests of all, and gives rights to their owners. If the leaders of Israel have enough courage to respond to such a peace, a new era of security and stability and normal peace relations among all will emerge in the region. . . . We are ready to sign such a peace now." Rabin, for his part, was eager to restart discussions. Through Washington, the prime minister intimated his willingness to go a long way to accommodate Assad, even to forfeit (in incremental stages) almost the entirety of the Golan Heights and to evacuate its twelve thousand Israeli settlers—in return for authentic peace. "The depth of the withdrawal," he asserted, "will reflect the depth of the peace."

There were still delays. In December 1994, Assad's eldest son, Basil, whom the Syrian president had been grooming as his eventual successor, was killed in an automobile accident. Six weeks later, Israeli-Arab tensions flared after a demented Jewish settler gunned down twenty-nine Palestinian worshippers in a Hebron mosque (p. 1109). Nevertheless, under Clinton's discreet pressure, Israeli-Syrian ambassadorial contacts in Washington were maintained during the winter, and in April 1995 Rabin signaled his acceptance of a text seemingly agreed to by Damascus. Only details remained for clarification. Several additional months went by as the Israeli cabinet devoted its attention to "Oslo II," the ensuing stage of Palestinian empowerment; but in October the Syrian negotiations were resumed. Then, on November 4, 1995, Rabin was assassinated.

In mid-December, Dennis Ross, a member of the State Department's Middle East division and President Clinton's selected "point man" on Arab-Israeli negotiations, came to Jerusalem to divulge to Shimon Peres the late Rabin's circuitous dealings with Assad. The new prime minister had not been informed of the Syrian negotiations. Rabin, in his mistrust of Peres (his perennial rival for the Labor leadership), had insisted on conducting his negotiations with Assad exclusively through his personal staff, through Ambassador Rabinovich in Washington, and through Clinton and the president's Middle East advisers. Back in 1992, the Americans, like the Syrians, had interpreted Rabin's formula—"the depth of the withdrawal will reflect the depth of the peace"—as a commitment to a Golan evacuation with due, deliberative speed. But Rabin had subsequently insisted that the Israeli evacuation be extended over five years and, at that, be matched by the Syrians in incremental trade, consular, and finally diplomatic relations. The one concession he had lately made to Secretary of State Warren Christopher, in April 1995, was to agree, "on principle," that the withdrawal would after all be a full withdrawal, that the Golan border would be restored to the pre-1967 cease-fire line.

This was the formula Ross now revealed to Peres. The prime minister was not pleased to be locked into his predecessor's diplomatic strategy. Yet he was too experienced a statesman to risk the loss of President Clinton's direct involvement in the peace process. Somewhat reluctantly, he agreed to shift the Syrian issue back to the front burner, and to revive his country's oblique, ambassadorial negotiations with Syria in the United States. The Americans, in turn, gratified that the Middle East peace process was reaching its apparent culmination, assiduously prepared the groundwork for treaty discussions. Their selected venue, in December 1995, was the Wye Plantation, located on Maryland's eastern shore. Originally operated by the University of Maryland's School of Agriculture, the plantation was a complex of research stations, inns, and private homes. In recent years it had served as the Aspen Institute's prestigious Center for Humanistic Studies. Like Camp David, Wye was far enough from Washington to offer its guests a bucolic, restful setting for extended conversations. Besides Ambassador Rabinovich, Peres had sent Uri Savir, director-general of the Israeli foreign ministry. Syria's Ambassador Walid al-Moualem was accompanied by Savir's ministerial counterpart, Farouk al-Hareh.

Concentrated into three intensive series of meetings, the negotiations continued intermittently over ten weeks, from late December 1995 to late February 1996. Dennis Ross presided, but Clinton himself helicoptered in periodically to nudge the talks along. From the outset, the Israelis insisted upon a calibrated progression to full diplomatic and economic relations as the climax of Israel's phased withdrawal from the Golan. The Syrians bridled. If Israel had accepted a minimalist, arm's-length exchange of ambassadors with Egypt, they argued, that precedent should be sufficient for a Syrian peace treaty. Eventually Moualem and his colleagues moderated their stance to acknowledge the feasibility of progressive stages of trade and tourism. The Israelis, on the other hand, interpreted their own commitment to evacuation as a withdrawal of soldiers and civilians, but not of the electronic, early-warning sensors that their engineers had emplaced at strategic sites on the Golan. These, they insisted, should remain. But the Syrians were not having it. Toward the end of January 1996, the Wye discussions reached an impasse. Peres allowed the talks to continue desultorily for five more weeks. Yet by then he had lost interest in the Syrian option. As long as quiet reigned along the Golan, he preferred to direct his attention to another front, equally close to Israel, one that posed even more immediate dangers.

A BELATED FLEXING OF MUSCLES

With financial help lately from Iran and Islamic groups in Saudi Arabia, Musa Muhammad Abu Marzouk, chief of Hamas's political bureau in Jordan, had virtually reinvented his guerrilla network as a Palestinian shadow government, providing social, health, and educational services in Gaza and the West Bank. Marzouk himself was arrested during a visit to the United States in July 1995, and was now awaiting possible extradition to Israel on charges of terrorism. But, meanwhile, exploiting its growing prestige, Hamas did not neglect its more spectacular and sinister role as a guerrilla underground. Its suicide bombers continued to infiltrate Israeli cities, detonating their concealed explosives, taking a growing toll of civilian lives. Directed from Gaza by Yahya Ayyash, "the engineer," the escalating campaign of mayhem was fast becoming a nightmare for the traditionally battle-hardened Israeli population. In January 1996, at Peres's orders, Israeli Shin Bet (internal security) agents succeeded in disposing of Ayyash, by planting an explosive device in his cellular telephone. Yet, far from deterring Hamas violence, the act of reprisal seemed only to provoke more terror bombings. Within a space of eight days in late February and early March 1996, fifty-nine Israeli civilians were killed and hundreds injured, as four bombings mounted by Hamas and the Islamic Jihad (p. 1050) took place in the very heart of the nation—in Jerusalem, Tel Aviv, Ashkelon, and Netania.

It was this sequence of civilian massacres that convinced Peres that more draconian countermeasures were needed. His political foes in Likud and other rightist parties were assailing him for ineptitude and naïveté in his ongoing negotiations with the Syrians and Palestinians. By late winter, opinion polls suggested that the public's faith in the peace process altogether, and certainly in the prime minister's ability to deter terrorism, was fast ebbing. In addition, then, to putting his Syrian diplomacy on the back burner, Peres reacted to the bombings by cordoning off selected areas of the West Bank and Gaza, thus depriving at least sixty thousand commuting Arab laborers of their customary employment in Israel. Moreover, in the urgency of his counterterror campaign, the prime minister actually received a measure of support from Yasser Arafat. Lately sworn in as president of the new Palestine Authority, Arafat was acutely aware that Hamas suicide attacks might erode Peres's political base, and thereby deprive him, Arafat, of his most reliable partner in the ongoing Oslo peace track. To minimize this danger, he ordered his security forces to rein in Hamas. On March 5, 1996, dozens of the Islamist organization's quite formidable social institutions, its schools, philanthropic societies, hospitals, and mosques, were transferred to the PA's administrative control. In Gaza alone, some two thousand Hamas militants were placed in "detention."

Washington meanwhile shared fully in the effort to preserve the Oslo momentum. In that same March, President Clinton dispatched his CIA director, George Tenet, to the Middle East, to confer with Israeli and Jordanian intelligence officials on the scope of the Hamas network. Later that same month, Dennis Ross held a meeting with King Hussein. Presenting the Hashemite ruler with data Tenet had accumulated, Ross requested and obtained Hussein's cooperation in the effort to isolate the guerrilla leadership. At the same time, to demonstrate his support of the peace effort, and of Peres himself, Clinton persuaded Egypt's President Mubarak to join him in cohosting a summit of "peacemakers." Assembling on March 13 in the Red Sea resort of Sharm es-Sheikh, the conclave of government leaders included Russian President Yeltsin, French President Chirac, British Prime Minister Major, German Chancellor Kohl, and the presidents, kings, and emirs of North African and Gulf states, even Saudi Foreign Minister Saud—all of whom denounced terrorist activities and expressed their unreserved support of Israeli-Palestinian peace. Afterward, stopping off in Tel Aviv, Clinton addressed a crowd of three thousand schoolchildren, emphasizing his personal commitment to the Oslo process "with every fiber of my being." It is possible that these diplomatic efforts had some inhibiting effect on Hamas assaults; during ensuing weeks, suicide bombings in Israeli population centers tapered off.

Ironically, a threat along a different front suddenly took precedence among Israeli security concerns. This was in the twenty-mile-wide "security zone" of southern Lebanon where Israel's military emplacement, and its surrogate "South Lebanon Army," confronted new violence from Hizballah and Islamic Jihad. Both guerrilla factions were financed, armed, and trained under the semi-official sponsorship of the Iranian government. During late March and April 1996, they intensified their rocket firing into Israel's border "security zone" and even directly into northern Israel. Israeli warnings to the Lebanese government to control their southern frontier produced no result. On April 6, salvos of homemade "Qassem" rockets wounded thirty-six civilians in Israel's frontier communities, and drove several thousand Israeli families to the protection of reinforced shelters.

For Shimon Peres, this latest guerrilla offensive was an intolerable provocation. He discerned in the assault a threat not only to Israeli life and limb but to his own political leadership. Binyamin Netanyahu, the recently elected chairman of the Likud party (p. 1013), was denouncing Peres for "selling out" the Land of Israel to Arafat and Arab terrorism. For the prime minister, it was essential now to establish his security credentials as no less authentic than the late Rabin's. In consultations with the military general staff, therefore, Peres decided on a pulverizing hammer blow against guerrilla bases in southern Lebanon. Entitled "Operation Grapes of Wrath," the counterstrike was launched on April 11, 1996, and took the form of a massive cross-frontier artillery bombardment.

For a while, Hamas, Hizballah, and Islamic Jihad forces, extensively equipped with both homemade and first-line Iranian rockets, gave as good as they received. Israeli families in the north were compelled to huddle in their shelters over a span of sixteen days. Yet the accumulated impact of Israel's retaliatory onslaught was devastating. In addition to scores of guerrilla casualties, an even greater number of innocent Arab civilians were also killed. April 18 was a day of particular human and diplomatic catastrophe. An errant Israeli artillery salvo fell on a UN-guarded enclave adjacent to the town of Qana, where hundreds of Lebanese civilians and Palestinian refugees had taken refuge. Before the Israeli artillerists corrected their aim, 102 people, many of them women and children, lay dead or dying. When informed of the tragic mistake, Peres, deeply shaken, issued a public statement of apology.

Two days later, recognizing the potential diplomatic ramifications of the violence, President Clinton dispatched Secretary of State Christopher to the Middle East to negotiate a cease-fire. Although Christopher shuttled back and forth between Jerusalem, Beirut, and Damascus, it was eventually French diplomacy that proved decisive. On the first day of Operation Grapes of Wrath, the terrified Lebanese prime minister, Rafiq Hariri, persuaded France's President Chirac to send his foreign minister, Hervé de Charette, to Beirut. Charette promptly set about devising a formula that all parties could accept. Israel and the guerrillas mutually promised not to aim at civilian targets. In the presence of American and French observers, a joint committee of Israeli, Lebanese, and Syrian representatives would meet at Naqura, near the Israeli-Lebanese border, to verify a cease-fire scheduled for April 27. Almost miraculously, the cease-fire was put into effect, and apparently held.

Yet the cost by then had been heavy. In Lebanon, 154 civilians had been killed and 350 wounded. For Israel, the price of Operation Grapes of Wrath was paid in severe international criticism, in and out of the United Nations, and specifically in the European media. It took its toll, as well, in Israel's domestic politics. The Arabs of Israel, profoundly shocked by the Qana massacre, decided to boycott the forthcoming Israeli elections. It would be Peres and his Labor coalition that would lose these Arab votes (p. 1015). But the political cost of Operation Grapes of Wrath resonated as well among Israel's Jewish majority.

AN ANTI-OSLO BACKLASH

Until April's tragic events in Lebanon, Peres's domestic and diplomatic record could be counted a success. He had sustained Israel's economic upsurge. In 1996, the nation's GNP growth rate of 7 percent was the highest among developed nations, and foreign investors were clamoring to share in Israel's potential (pp. 1006–7). The Oslo agreements with Arafat were apparently being carried out in an orderly way, and until lately, guerrilla attacks against civilians had been reduced. But the most recent upsurge of suicide bombings in the heart of Israel's cities, and the prime minister's ill-considered and politically suspect Operation Grapes of Wrath, suddenly and dramatically eroded public confidence in the Labor coalition. So did a widespread uneasiness that Peres seemed willing to negotiate a return of the Golan Heights to Syria (in 1996, placards appeared on thousands of Israeli balconies: "We Are with the Golan").

In early February 1996, still counting on national support of Labor's record in the Oslo breakthrough, and lingering horror at the Rabin assassination, the prime minister decided to advance the scheduled date of Knesset elections from mid-October to May 29 of that year. In fact, he made his move too late. The ensuing shift of public opinion away from Labor was more cumulative than he had anticipated. It was prefigured as early as 1993, in the primary election of the Likud opposition, which that year replaced the aging Yitzchak Shamir as party chairman with a new, younger, and more charismatic figure, the forty-four-year-old Binyamin Netanyahu.

The choice of the Tel Aviv–born Netanyahu signified a reversion to the hard line of Revisionist Zionism. Indeed, the new Likud chairman came by his stance naturally. His father, Benzion Netanyahu, himself born in Palestine, had served as a political adviser to Vladimir Jabotinsky and as editor of the Revisionist daily newspaper, *HaYarden*. A historian by profession, the elder Netanyahu was unable to secure tenure at the Hebrew University, and ultimately decamped for the United States, where he taught for many years at Cornell. Benzion's historical publications served as counterpoint to his ideology, reflecting a vision of the Jews as perennial outcasts in an irredeemably hostile world, and as a people whose one and authentic salvation lay in a reclaimed and undivided Land of Israel.

After completing secondary education in the United States, Binyamin Netanyahu and his older brother, Yonatan, and his younger brother, Iddo, returned to Israel, where they all served as commandos in elite army units. Rising to captain's rank, Binyamin took part in the raid on Beirut airport in 1968 and in the storming of a hijacked Sabena airliner at Lod airport in 1972. Yonatan passed into legend as the only Israeli commando to be killed in the Entebbe rescue operation in July 1976. In his memory, the Netanyahu family set up the "Yonatan Institute" to sensitize governments and public opinion to the dangers of terrorism. Binyamin, the middle brother, returned to the United States to earn bachelor's and master's degrees at the Massachusetts Institute of Technology. After a brief career in business in the late 1970s and early 1980s, he became active in Likud politics, and soon came under the wing of Moshe Arens, foreign minister in the Shamir government. In 1982, Arens appointed Netanyahu as Israel's deputy chief of mission in Washington, and two years later as Israel's permanent representative at the United Nations. While serving in the UN, the young diplomat became a self-proclaimed expert on international terrorism, appearing on many television talk shows, where his verbal fluency and good looks could be exhibited to greatest advantage.

In 1988, Netanyahu returned to Israel. Placed high in the Likud party list, he became a member of the Knesset in the elections of that year, and was appointed deputy foreign minister in Shamir's government. In that capacity, he proved a master of sound bites in the Israeli media. In 1993, following Shamir's political defeat the year before, the dynamic, telegenic Netanyahu was selected in the Likud primary as party chairman. He hit the ground running. In ensuing months, he published a book, *A Place among the Nations: Israel and the World*. Its central theme, true to his family background, was the right of the Jewish people to the Land of Israel in its entirety. According to Netanyahu (and his father), it was not the Jews who had usurped the land from the Arabs, but the Arabs who had usurped the land from the Jews. The whole world was hostile to the State of Israel and antisemitism was the root of this hatred. The PLO was a mortal enemy. Israel, for its own self-protection, was compelled to retain security control over all territory west of the Jordan River.

With these and other provocative assertions, Netanyahu in effect repudiated the very essence of the Oslo Declaration of Principles, which was signed shortly after the book's publication. Indeed, the young diplomat-politician was not hesitant in proclaiming the entire Oslo scenario as akin to treason. Nevertheless, as recently anointed leader of the Likud opposition, and aware of the public's urgent passion for peace, Netanyahu grudgingly committed himself to observing Israel's earlier signed international agreements. He merely implied that he would delay putting them into effect. It was a stance that evoked increased support in the late winter and spring of 1996, as Palestinian guerrilla violence took its toll among Israeli civilians.

In addition to public alarm at the bombings in Israel's cities, and growing cynicism at Peres's clumsy Operation Grapes of Wrath in Lebanon, there had recently taken place a "constitutional" alteration in the rules governing Israeli elections that Netanyahu exploited to his advantage. Until 1996, elections for the Knesset had determined the appointment of the prime minister, as was customary in most Western parliamentary systems. On the other hand, Israel was the only state in the world that operated as a single electoral district, and functioned according to a party-list system (pp. 357–58). Under this formula, discerning the prospect of at least a minimal proportional representation for themselves, a surfeit of parties sprang up in Israel, thereby all but guaranteeing that none of them could ever achieve an overall Knesset majority. Rather, from the very outset of statehood, political leaders had been obliged to bargain with minor parties even to set up a government, and then to engage in protracted and increasingly venal horse-trading simply to maneuver each piece of legislation through the Knesset.

Over the years, many attempts had been made to recast legislative elections as a full or partial constituency system, in hopes of consolidating the political landscape under two or three major parties. The effort invariably was shot down by an ad hoc alliance of smaller parties, each unwilling to face potential eradication. But in 1992, under heavy public pressure and much support from both Labor and Likud, the Knesset agreed to a compromise measure. It took the form of an amendment to the "Basic Law: The Government." Scheduled to come into effect in 1996, the new version of the law provided for simultaneous, two-tier elections. Each voter would cast one ballot for the party of his choice, and a second ballot for a prime ministerial candidate of his choice. Thereafter, whichever candidate won a majority of the popular vote would occupy the prime ministry, and presumably invest that office with an augmented measure of governing stability. Yet, in passing this amendment, the Knesset assumed that the victorious prime ministerial candidate would also be the chairman of the party obtaining at least a plurality of the ballots cast. The assumption proved erroneous.

The election of May 29, 1996, turned out to be the closest in Israel's history, with Netanyahu inching ahead in the prime ministerial voting by less than 1 percent (50.4 percent against 49.5 percent for Peres), or fewer than thirty thousand votes out of the nearly three million cast. It was conceivable that Peres might yet have won the prime ministerial election, if he had mobilized the vote of Israel's traditionally pro-Labor Arab population. But in their outrage at the casualties Peres had inflicted on their Lebanese kinsmen in Operation Grapes of Wrath, Israel's Arabs boycotted the election en masse. Even then, with Netanyahu as prime minister, Labor might still have dictated the nation's legislative agenda, for it had actually won thirty-four seats to Likud's thirty-two in the balloting for the Knesset party lists, and at first seemed to be in the better position to engineer a coalition.

Yet the Labor plurality turned out to be less important than the fact that both major parties lost seats (Labor, six seats; Likud, eight seats) to new and smaller parties. Evidently the voters had sensed a new and unique opportunity to vote both for the leader of their choice and, at the same time, for the party of their ideological persuasion. The Orthodox, for example, whatever their suspicions of Netanyahu's American veneer and his secularism, supported him almost unanimously, considering him the safer bet to keep the "Land of Israel" intact. But they also felt safe in casting their Knesset ballots for one or another of their own religious parties, shrewdly sensing that whichever candidate won the prime ministerial vote would have to depend upon them to put together a coalition government.

And so it happened. In the 1996 election, the three Orthodox factions—Shas, the National Religious party, and United Torah Judaism—collectively garnered a spectacular twenty-three seats, up from their 1992 total of sixteen. This was a bloc that suddenly had burgeoned out as virtually indispensable to any governing coalition. Already predisposed to opt into a Netanyahu cabinet, the religionists were also in a position to expand their influence in crucial aspects of Israel's daily life. Meanwhile, the smaller, secular factions—Moledet and Tsomet—that were to the right even of Likud were similarly in a position to extract ministerial posts in return for their support. When the dust of the election settled, therefore, Netanyahu was obliged to fill more than half his cabinet seats from outside his own Likud party.

Yet, in one key area, Netanyahu recognized that he could have his way, and this was in altering the course of the peace process. In securing a Knesset vote of 62–52 for his government, he could take assurance that at least sixty-two Knesset members stood with him in opposing a return of the Golan Heights, or the division of Jerusalem between Israel and the Palestinians, or the establishment of a Palestinian state in the West Bank and Gaza, or the return even of a minimal number of Palestinian refugees.

THE PEACE PROCESS IN NETANYAHU'S EXTREMIS

An insight into Netanyahu's agenda could be gleaned by his deference to his perennial rival within the Likud party, David Levy (p. 968), whom he brought into his cabinet as foreign minister. For the same reasons of shoring up his right flank, Netanyahu assigned a cabinet seat to Ariel Sharon, giving the corpulent ex-general the portfolio of "national infrastructure." This was a newly created ministry that would encompass authority for roads, railways, ports, water planning, and land allocation—both in integral Israel and in Sharon's favored bailiwick of the West Bank and Gaza. With further ideological support from the Iraqi-born Yitzchak Mordechai, serving as defense minister, Netanyahu, in presenting his government to the Knesset on June 18, 1996, emphatically demonstrated his foreboding reassessment of the Oslo peace process.

Indeed, far from committing himself to the establishment of a Palestine "entity," the new prime minister scorned the very mention of subsequent territorial withdrawals from the West Bank and Gaza. Resumption of talks on permanent status, he insisted, would be conditioned on the Palestine Authority's "strict fulfillment" of its obligations to maintain the peace. Nor did Netanyahu neglect to give the back of his hand to the Syrians. Alluding to his predecessors' earlier explorations with the Assad government, he announced that he would resume those negotiations only "without preconditions"—a de facto repudiation of even the marginal progress the two sides had earlier accomplished in their Golan discussions.

The belligerence of Netanyahu's stance quite shocked Yasser Arafat. The Palestinian leader immediately sought and obtained a three-way summit in Cairo with Egypt's President Mubarak and Jordan's King Hussein. But the latter were not yet prepared to jeopardize the Oslo diplomatic process with a new Israeli government. Neither was Clinton, when Netanyahu flew to Washington on July 9 to pay his first courtesy visit to the White House (p. 1018). In turn, interpreting diplomatic forbearance as the award of a clean bill of health, the young Israeli prime minister then proceeded to elaborate on a program designed to spur the economy of the West Bank's Jewish settlements. All the financial advantages the Labor government had earlier canceled for these towns and outposts were now restored. Predictably, the mastermind of this rejuvenated policy of development was Ariel Sharon. As minister of infrastructure, Sharon had been allocated a budget of a half-billion dollars, and promptly launched into the construction of a road network to connect the West Bank's Jewish settlements—in the process further disrupting the contiguity of Arab farms and villages. Moreover, Sharon openly boasted of his plans to increase the Jewish population in the territories by fifty thousand in the ensuing four years. Not to be upstaged, Netanyahu himself then publicly announced to the Likud central committee: "There will never be a Palestinian state between the Mediterranean and the Jordan." When Arafat and the Palestinian population learned of these statements, the atmosphere became ripe for explosion.

Netanyahu provided the spark by yet another gaffe, on the night of September 23–24, 1996. The setting was the "Hasmonean Tunnel." Located in East Jerusalem, this was an underground passageway close by the Haram es-Sharif, the thirty-eight-acre plateau in the Old City's Moslem Quarter on which stood the venerated al-Aqsa Mosque, and the neighboring and equally venerated Dome of the Rock (also known as the Mosque of Omar). According to Jewish tradition, the Dome of the Rock, and, indeed, a large part of the Haram es-Sharif esplanade, allegedly formed part of the Temple Mount, the site of the revered Second Temple of biblical antiquity. The tunnel itself, verified by archaeologists as a subterranean aqueduct used by the Hasmoneans of the second century B.C.E. to bring water to the Temple, was first excavated by Israel's ministry of religions in 1987, and then connected to a pre-existing tunnel under the Jews' Western Wall. The ministry's purpose was to facilitate the movement of Israelis and foreign tourists directly from the Western Wall area into the Haram es-Sharif. The project was incomplete, however, for its logical exit would require the destruction of a small retaining buttress under the Sisters of Zion Convent. Each time the ministry sought to "unseal"—that is, demolish—the buttress, the officials of Jerusalem's Islamic Waqf launched a vigorous protest, regarding the move as an Israeli initiative to alter, in effect, to Judaize the character of the Haram es-Sharif. For a while, the ministry abstained.

In September 1996, however, anticipating a major influx of Jewish visitors intent on celebrating the autumn festival of Sukkot in Jerusalem, the city's mayor, Ehud Olmert, himself a powerful Likud politician, decided once and for all to break open the retaining buttress and provide unimpeded access to the Haram es-Sharif. Prime Minister Netanyahu, although traveling in Europe at the time, had been apprised of the decision in advance, and saw no reason to object. During the night of September 23–24, therefore, municipal work crews blasted a passage through the retaining barrier. By the next morning, as Waqf officials and other local Palestinians first noticed the new aperture leading to the Haram es-Sharif, they began to shout their protests. Informed of this reaction, Netanyahu at first described the tunnel project as a "local engineering improvement" and a "non-event."

This was not the view of Yasser Arafat. From his office in Gaza, the PA president characterized the Israeli move as a grave threat to the Haram es-Sharif and to the status quo of the entire Moslem Quarter, and then called for mass demonstrations and a general strike. Responding to Arafat's exhortation, the Arabs of East Jerusalem then exploded in violence, stoning Jewish shops and passersby, breaking windows, setting cars alight. At first, the Israeli police responded with truncheons and tear gas. But as demonstrations extended north of the city, bringing Palestinian police into the fray against Israeli police, the Israeli government called in army units. These latter soon began employing rubber-coated bullets against the rioters. At the end of the first day of unrest, 7 Arabs were dead and 253 wounded. Funerals for the slain demonstrators then became the occasions for further Palestinian violence—and Israeli repressive measures—extending throughout neighboring Palestinian communities.

Within the week, as the Israeli ministry of defense called up armored vehicles and even attack helicopters, the Arabs suffered hundreds of additional casualties. Fifteen Israeli soldiers also were killed and scores of others wounded, and the army had to deploy a cordon of tanks at strategic sites throughout the West Bank and Gaza Strip. Although a semblance of order was restored by the end of the month, the "non-event" of September 1996 represented the most vehement confrontation between Israelis and Palestinians since the 1987 intifada. Its repercussions would eventually prove even more violent and longer-lived than the first uprising. Yet, even now, the threat to the Oslo peace process had become grave enough to induce Clinton in Washington to intervene personally. The president invited Netanyahu and Arafat, as well as Egypt's President Mubarak and Jordan's King Hussein, to an emergency conference at the White House on October 2, 1996.

AN ADVENT OF CLINTONIAN DIPLOMACY

After winning the United States presidential election in November 1992, and settling into the White House, Clinton would have preferred to give his principal attention to his domestic agenda, and specifically to health care and other social-welfare issues. He was not given that luxury. On the international scene, post-Soviet Russia took up much of his attention, with the concern that the great former empire, in its economic distress, might revert to dictatorship. The collapse of Yugoslavia into a murderous civil conflict also became a high priority on the president's desk, as were the dangers of nuclear proliferation in Iran, Iraq, and North Korea. Although entertaining few illusions about the complexity of the Arab-Israeli conflict, Clinton was swiftly obliged to address this issue, as well. Thus, in his first term of office, he visited Israel and the Arab countries, established personal relations with Middle Eastern leaders, presided over the Israeli-Palestinian ceremony of mutual recognition and the Israeli-Jordanian peace signing, and attended the funeral of Yitzchak Rabin.

More recently, upon election to Israel's prime ministry, Binyamin Netanyahu lost no time in attempting to cultivate a personal relationship with the American president. It should not have been difficult. Clinton had many Jewish friends and advisers, and had appointed Jews to sensitive positions in the Middle East, including Martin Indyk as ambassador to Israel, Daniel Kurtzer as ambassador to Egypt, and Dennis Ross as principal State Department negotiator between Israel and the Palestinian leadership. Moreover, Netanyahu and Clinton were of the same generation and background—both American-educated, photogenic, media-wise. Netanyahu's first visit to the White House took place on July 9, 1996, and the prime minister emerged from it believing that he had won the president's attention and respect. But the opposite was the case. As Dennis Ross would recall, Netanyahu, by delivering an uncompromising monologue on the dangers of Arab terrorism, had bored and offended Clinton. Nevertheless, remaining outwardly cordial, the president had given assurances of his goodwill and his understanding of Israel's security needs.

The Hasmonean Tunnel violence, however, was not a development that could be ignored or minimized. Although the appearance of Mubarak and Hussein at the White House emergency meeting on October 2 was essentially cosmetic and brief, the Washington discussions swiftly developed into a serious triangular conference between Netanyahu, Arafat, and Clinton, along with their respective advisers. For his part, Netanyahu implied that he would "deactivate" the Hasmonean Tunnel. But from Clinton's perspective, the underlying urgency was of restarting the Oslo process and propelling it off dead center. To reactivate it, the president then informed Netanyahu and Arafat that he was sending Dennis Ross to the Middle East with a mandate to expedite the next link in the pending, and overdue, schedule of Israeli withdrawals.

An especially critical link in the process was the fate of Hebron. A community of some 120,000 Arabs, the town assumed particular importance in Palestinian calculations because it was the only remaining West Bank city (as distinguished from the area's essentially agricultural terrain) from which Israeli army units had not yet been redeployed. Since 1967, Jewish pietists had insisted on reviving and preserving their people's historic enclave in this venerated community (pp. 682, 831–32). In their negotiations with the earlier Peres government, Arafat and his advisers had reluctantly accepted this condition. Yet, even after the "Oslo I" and "Oslo II" agreements, the size and extraterritorial status of the Jewish presence in Hebron was still to be decided; and, meanwhile, the issue remained a bone in the Palestinians' throat. Both Arafat and Netanyahu now understood that it would have to be resolved if they were to preserve Clinton's trust and goodwill.

To that end, Dennis Ross, shuttling between Jerusalem and Gaza, devoted the next two and a half months to the search for a compromise formula. The turning point came when Jordan's King Hussein took it upon himself to fly to Gaza on December 12, then to Tel Aviv the next day, extracting concessions from both sides. Finally, on January 15, 1997, a "Hebron Protocol" was signed by Netanyahu and Arafat. The Palestinian chairman had acquired less from Netanyahu than Peres had tentatively conceded. Under Peres's formula, the Palestinians would have been left with jurisdiction over 85 percent of the city, while Hebron's approximately five hundred Jews, ensconced in their own "zone" adjacent to the town center, would have controlled 15 percent. But under the latest agreement, the percentages were altered respectively to 80 and 20 percent. Henceforth, the tiny Jewish enclave would enjoy privileged, extraterritorial status in a sector that included the venerated Cave of the Patriarchs and an access route to the nearby Jewish settlement of Kiryat Arba (p. 682), and encompassed as well some fifteen thousand Palestinians. Most galling of all to the Arabs, an Israeli army unit of some five hundred soldiers would be stationed in Hebron to guard the privileged Jewish minority.

It is of interest that even this manifestly asymmetrical formula passed the Israeli cabinet by an unimpressive eleven votes to seven. Binyamin Begin, minister of science and technology (and son of the late Menachem Begin), resigned from the government in protest. Ariel Sharon, although he remained in the cabinet, also registered his vigorous opposition. Yet the Knesset found it expedient to follow the government lead and endorse the Hebron Protocol, eighty-seven to seventeen (with fifteen abstentions). Israeli tanks then began withdrawing from Hebron, and Arafat returned to the city that he had not entered for the past thirty years. Meanwhile, Israel still remained in both administrative and security control—that is, military occupation—of fully 73 percent of the land area of the West Bank, and continued to exercise residual security control (although not administrative control) over the remaining 27 percent.

But if moderates in Israel and the United States, and virtually all Arabs in Palestine and elsewhere, severely condemned the latest "breakthrough" as entirely unacceptable, Dennis Ross and King Hussein believed that they had extracted another important concession from both sides. Netanyahu had consented in principle to resume negotiations for further Israeli withdrawals from the rural areas of the West Bank; and Arafat had accepted an extended, mid-1998 deadline for completion of these negotiations, instead of the—already delayed—timetable of mid-1997, as mandated by the "Oslo II" accord of September 1995. Other issues presumably would be resolved by mid-1998, including Israel's release of Palestinian prisoners, a "safe passage" for Palestinians between Gaza and the West Bank, and a Palestinian airport.

On March 7, 1997, armed with these scheduling alterations, the Israeli cabinet announced the next phase of its envisaged military withdrawals. The communiqué left Arafat in shock. The extent of the incremental pullback was to be a grudging 9.1 percent, not the minimum of 20 percent that in the end would have been necessary to allow the "final-status" negotiations to begin by mid-1998. No less ominously, the Netanyahu cabinet three weeks earlier had endorsed a decision of the Jerusalem municipality to embark on construction of a 6,500-unit housing project for new Jewish settlers in the Har Homa neighborhood of southwest Jerusalem, thereby all but sealing off Arab Jerusalemites from the surrounding Palestinian hinterland. This decision was similarly a violation of the Oslo II agreement, which had left the disposition of Jerusalem for final-status negotiations.

Arafat regarded both developments as a virtual declaration of war. In mid-March of 1997, he made his position clear by releasing scores of Hamas guerrillas from the Palestine Authority's prisons, at the same time ordering his security services to suspend all cooperation with their Israeli counterparts. Arafat then personally began reorganizing the Tanzim, his Fatah party's own armed militia. Subsequently, on March 21, a suicide bomber blew himself up in a Tel Aviv café, killing 3 people and wounding 48—the first such act of mayhem in over a year. It was the merest beginning. On June 30, another 16 Israelis were murdered and 178 wounded in two consecutive suicide bombings in a crowded Jerusalem market area; and a month later, also in Jerusalem, 5 Israelis were killed and 181 wounded in three simultaneous explosions in the capital's main pedestrian mall. The toll would have been even higher, but in mid-July, three Palestinian policemen, carrying bags packed with explosives, were intercepted en route to a Jewish settlement in the West Bank.

CLINTON AS SENIOR PARTNER

By the summer of 1997, well embarked upon his second term in office, Clinton had shed most of his lingering hopes for Netanyahu. The relationship between the two men had become increasingly formal with each of the Israeli prime minister's diplomatic "reinterpretations." The president also entertained growing misgivings about Arafat, whom he had come to regard as devious and demagogic. Under these circumstances, he shared the view of his newly appointed secretary of state, Madeleine Albright, that there was no alternative to his, the president's, frontal engagement in Palestinian-Israeli negotiations as a "senior" rather than an "equal" partner. In October of the same year, he summoned Netanyahu and Arafat yet again to Washington. Meeting in the White House, with Albright and Ross by his side, Clinton "suggested" to his guests that the next stage of Israeli security—that is, military—evacuation should be widened. No figure was placed on the extent of withdrawal, but Ross later intimated that the minimum the president would find acceptable was an additional 20 percent. Rather taken aback, Netanyahu then asked for time to return home and consult his cabinet. The discussions in Jerusalem subsequently consumed almost three months. Finally, in late January 1998, as Netanyahu and Arafat returned to Washington, the best withdrawal offer the prime minister could produce was an additional 10 percent. Arafat was furious. At that rate, he protested, Israel's ensuing incremental withdrawals would not begin to approach the, already extended, mid-1998 deadline for final-status negotiations.

Hereupon Clinton surprised his guests with a daring alternative proposal he had worked out in advance with Albright, Ross, and other State Department experts. If Arafat would forgo a subsequent, third, Israeli redeployment, and move forthwith to final-status negotiations, the United States would announce its official support for the goal of independent Palestinian statehood. The PA president's reaction was cautious, although not overtly negative; he would still have preferred full Israeli evacuation *before* committing himself to final-status discussions. Netanyahu's response was one of dour noncommittal. This time both men requested time to discuss the proposal with their governments. Nevertheless, once back in their respective lands and offices, and in intensive consultations with their advisers, Arafat and Netanyahu both thought better of presenting an obdurate face to a United States president.

Over the ensuing months, the two Middle Eastern leaders inched closer to a common position; and by July 1998, a functional agreement seemed within reach. Netanyahu and his cabinet agreed to extend Zone A (offering the Palestinians both administrative and security control) from 10 to 13 percent of the West Bank; and to extend Zone B (offering the Palestinians administrative control) to 40 percent. The formula offered a tremulous hope that final-status negotiations could at least begin (if not be completed) within the next few months. On that assumption, and with much cajoling and arm-twisting, Dennis Ross persuaded the Israelis and Palestinians to return to the United States in October, for a conference intended at last to produce a working outline for a conclusive treaty.

Once again, the selected venue was the Wye Plantation. Arafat and Netanyahu arrived on October 15, 1998. The Palestinian president was accompanied by his minister of information, Saeb Erekat, and the latter's aides. The Israeli prime minister was joined on October 16 by his cabinet's most vocal hardliners, Ariel Sharon, recently appointed as foreign minister, and Natan (Anatoly) Sharansky, the renowned former Russian "refusenik," currently serving as minister of industry. Although Dennis Ross served as chairman of the discussions, the president himself helicoptered to Wye on the second day, before substantive negotiations began, to summarize at length the steps both parties had already taken, and the narrowness of the gap that seemed to remain between them. With some passion, then, Clinton exhorted his guests to bridge the divide and move forthwith to the much-delayed final-status deliberations. After an hour and a half, he turned the meeting over to Ross and returned to Washington.

Yet, in Clinton's absence, the talks started off badly. The Israelis insisted on obtaining a detailed prospectus of Arafat's plans to combat terrorism, including the names of militants whom the Palestine Authority proposed to arrest. For Arafat, the demand was insulting to his authority and personal dignity. The Israeli government, he countered, must first commit itself to full and final troop evacuation. The atmosphere of mutual distrust was so palpable that Ross and his colleagues wondered if there was leeway even for preliminary discussions. For the rest of the day, and the following day, the conference room echoed to maximalist proposals and categorical rejections. Then, on October 19, an unexpected visitor arrived at Wye. It was Jordan's King Hussein. At Clinton's personal request, the diminutive monarch had been flown in by plane and helicopter directly from Rochester, Minnesota, where he had been undergoing intensive treatment for lung cancer at the Mayo Clinic. Hussein was but a shadow of his former self: pale, gaunt, bald from his recent chemotherapy. Nevertheless, during a four-day sojourn, he managed to transcend his infirmity as he pressed both sides to trim their agendas.

Clinton made a return visit to Wye on October 22. At first, it appeared that both Palestinians and Israelis were still holding their ground. In the ensuing week, however, Netanyahu, recognizing that he was testing the president's goodwill to its limits, finally came up with a proposal that Clinton could endorse, and that Arafat could grudgingly accept—although still as an "interim" measure. The Palestinians agreed to the Israeli formula of a 13 percent troop withdrawal, with an additional 40 percent transfer of administrative jurisdiction. Although Arafat did not repeat his demand for an en masse release of prisoners from Israeli custody, he still refused to turn over names of "alleged" terrorists slated for arrest by the Palestine Authority. The most he would concede was a promise of cooperation between the respective Israeli and Palestinian security agencies in interdicting suspected guerrillas. Even with this agreement in hand, Netanyahu at the last minute nearly subverted it by intimating—factitiously—that the president had agreed to consider a pardon for Jonathan Pollard (pp. 932–33). When Clinton bridled at this last-minute interpolation, Netanyahu did not pursue it.

Once back in Jerusalem, the Israeli prime minister reviewed his concessions in several lengthy, acrimonious cabinet sessions. The far-rightists, including Sharon and Scharansky, remained skeptical, and the religionists were scathing. But the concessions eventually were accepted, on November 15, 1998, and the Knesset approved the text of the agreement two days later. The "permanent-status" issues were still not touched upon; yet, for all practical purposes, the Palestinians would be left with full administrative and security control of their principal cities (except for the Jewish enclave in Hebron); an additional 13 percent security control (essentially around built-up, urban areas); and an additional 40 percent administrative control (essentially of more sparsely occupied agricultural terrain). The formula included the establishment of joint Israeli-Palestinian-American committees for verifying the PA's cooperation in suppressing terrorism, and Arafat's pledge to eliminate threatening language against

Israel in the Palestine National Covenant. Most important, both sides agreed to tackle forthwith such permanent-status issues as Jerusalem, Jewish settlements, Palestinian refugees, allocation of water supplies, and territorial boundaries.

The agreement was embellished by a highly symbolic gesture. The Palestinians were finally to be awarded their long-coveted airport at Rafa, in the southern quadrant of the Gaza Strip. Already in the process of construction, the facility was opened for operation on November 24, 1998, with the ceremonial arrival of Egyptian, Saudi, and Moroccan commercial transports, and the presence of Miguel Moratinos, the European Union's emissary to the Middle East, who made the first Arkia (Israel Inland Airways) flight from Tel Aviv's Sde Dov airpark to Rafa. On December 13, Bill Clinton himself arrived in Israel. After a brief visit to Gaza, he traveled to Jerusalem to address the Knesset, then to Nablus for a short greeting to the Palestine Executive Committee, where he called on both Israelis and Palestinians to recognize each other's security and dignity. Afterward, the president motored in an escorted cavalcade to Bethlehem, where he lit a Christmas tree in Manger Square, and then accompanied Netanyahu on a helicopter flight to the ancient Judean fortress of Masada. Following the two-day visit, as he departed for Washington in his presidential jet, Clinton shared with his staff his cautious optimism that his "seniority" of partnership in Israeli-Palestinian negotiations at long last had nudged the Oslo peace process to the threshold of fruition.

EHUD

BARAK'S TWO YEARS

A PARALYSIS OF NEGOTIATIONS, A
DETERIORATION OF LIKUD GOVERNANCE

In voting to adopt Binyamin Netanyahu's latest formula for withdrawal, on November 17, 1998, the members of Israel's cabinet made plain that they would go no further in negotiations, pending evidence of Yasser Arafat's "good faith" in suppressing terrorism. Accusations of dissimulation and corruption, if bruited by the Netanyahu government essentially for political reasons, were nonetheless close to the mark. At every level, key officials of Arafat's executive council demanded their payoffs on public contracts, and squirreled the bribes away in overseas bank accounts. The legislative incompetence of the PA Assembly had become a reeking scandal. Arafat dictated its agenda and decisions with his presidential network of Fatah cronies. The Authority's incipient police/security organizations answered directly to Arafat. Members of the Palestine judiciary who failed to do the president's bidding were peremptorily dismissed. Individual rights went by the board. Some three thousand of Arafat's political enemies languished in Palestinian jails, most of them on vague or "pending" charges. Even respected Palestinian nationalists, stalwarts like Feisal al-Husseini and Hanan Ashrawi, and Arab-American intellectuals of the stature of Professors Edward Saïd and Ibrahim Abu-Loghod, were unable to convince Arafat of the harm he was doing to their common cause.

Netanyahu's administration, in turn, was afflicted with its own distinctive version of political dysfunctionalism. Within the prime minister's governing coalition, the formidable Ariel Sharon continued to act as a spoiler. Were he at the center of power, Sharon repeatedly proclaimed, he would not have so much as paid lip service to "Oslo II." Although Netanyahu was intimidated enough by the outspoken ex-general to appoint him, successively, to the ministry of "national infrastructure," the ministry of finance, and then, briefly, the foreign ministry, it was not enough to keep Sharon's hot breath off his neck. After Netanyahu joined Arafat and Clinton in putting his signature on the "Wye River Memorandum," on October 23, 1998, he capitulated altogether to Sharon's partisans on the far right. No sooner was the ink dry on the memorandum than the prime minister found ways to delay its implementation, claiming (not always factitiously) that Arafat was reneging on his commitment to ensure peace and order in Palestine. And, in the end, the Wye Accord languished.

With the likelihood of new Israeli elections approaching (see below), and the five-year interim period for a "final-status" agreement seemingly headed for expiration, neither side made an honest attempt to resume negotiations. In Washington, meanwhile, Clinton, embroiled in political and personal struggles of his own, and increasingly exasperated with both Middle Eastern leaders, was tempted to disentangle himself altogether from involvement in the Middle Eastern peace process.

Indeed, for the president, an especially flagrant act of diplomatic irresponsibility was Netanyahu's endorsement of Sharon's proposed "Golan Law," in January 1999, requiring a formal Knesset majority vote to ratify any future Israeli-Syrian agreement for Israeli withdrawal from the Golan Heights. The tactic immediately torpedoed Washington's efforts to renew Syrian-Israeli negotiations. By that time, entering the final year of his presidency, Clinton had discounted Netanyahu as a partner in his Middle East diplomacy. Although the president met with Arafat three times after the Wye Conference, he snubbed the Israeli prime minister, and Vice President Al Gore declined to meet with Netanyahu at the economic summit in Davos, Switzerland. The implications of United States detachment soon became an open subject of commentary in the Israeli media. It was a disquieting prospect.

So was the increased evidence of Netanyahu's political ineptitude. The Israeli prime minister's feckless efforts to propitiate Ariel Sharon with an ongoing series of high-profile cabinet appointments did not accomplish their purpose. In 1998, Sharon ventured the observation that a "national-unity" government was preferable to "one man from making all policy decisions." Netanyahu meekly swallowed the provocation. Neither was the prime minister immune to charges of political chicanery. In late spring of 1998, attempting to ensure the loyalty of the Shas party for his government coalition, Netanyahu searched for a device to keep the Shas chairman, Aryeh Deri, from being tried for rampant political bribery. In the process, the prime minister came up with the unsavory tactic of nominating his personal lawyer for the post of attorney general, a man who presumably could be trusted not to prosecute Deri. When the ruse became public, Netanyahu ignominiously withdrew the nomination. (Subsequently, when Deri was forced by the Shas elders to resign both his party chairmanship and his Knesset seat, he was prosecuted, convicted, and imprisoned.)

By December 1998, a series of newspaper polls had revealed that public toleration for the rudderless government was dramatically waning. The prime minister's political opportunism had forfeited his core constituency. David Levy, his original foreign minister, Dan Meridor, his finance minister, Yitzchak Mordechai, his defense minister, Binyamin Begin, his science minister—all had left the cabinet. On January 4, 1999, sensing that his right-wing coalition would collapse altogether if more time passed before he went to the country, Netanyahu obtained the Knesset's consent to advance national elections to May 17, 1999, more than a year ahead of schedule.

West Bank Populations

—— 1967 Green Line

Palestinian Communities
Residents
- 0–350
- 351–1,400
- 1,401–5,600
- 5,601–12,600
- 12,601–22,400
- 22,401–35,000
- 35,001–50,400
- 50,401–68,600
- 68,601–89,600
- 89,601–113,400
- 113,401 and above

Israeli Settlements
Residents
- 0–350
- 351–1,400
- 1,401–5,600
- 5,601–12,600
- 12,601–22,400
- 22,401 and above

JENIN

TULKAREM

NABLUS

QALQILIYA

ARIEL

TEL AVIV–YAFO

Ben Gurion
International
Airport

MODI'IN
ILLIT

Route 443

RAMALLAH

WEST
BANK

JERICHO

Jordan River

JORDAN

ISRAEL

JERUSALEM

MA'ALE
ADUMIM

BETAR ILLIT

BETHLEHEM

EFRAT

Dead
Sea

QIRYAT ARBA

HEBRON

Sources: Israeli Ministry of the Interior, Peace Now, B'Tselem
Copyright © 2004 by the Washington Institute for Near East Policy
Reprinted with permission

0   10 mi

0   10 km

N

"THE MOST DECORATED SOLDIER"

After Labor's defeat in 1996, and Shimon Peres's subsequent resignation as party chairman, it was a virtual certainty that the Labor leadership this time would turn to an individual with unshakable security credentials. In fact, the party's choice was a former soldier of unimpeachable, even legendary, reputation in security matters. Ehud Barak was a former army chief of staff. He was also the most decorated soldier in Israel's history. Born Ehud Brog in 1942 at Kibbutz Mishmar HaSharon, he had displayed his extraordinary leadership talents as a young officer-recruit. Although he decided early on to follow a military career, Barak, upon his first leave from the army, studied at the Hebrew University, took his degree in mathematics and engineering, and subsequently won a scholarship to study for a Master's degree in physics and engineering at Stanford— at the same time that Binyamin Netanyahu was enrolled in the graduate school at MIT. Both men later participated in the 1973 Yom Kippur War. Barak, however, remaining in the army as a career soldier, rose more rapidly in the officer corps. Climbing the ladder of command, he participated in some of Israel's most daring exploits, including leadership of the raid on Arafat's headquarters outside Tunis (p. 962). In the late 1980s and early 1990s, he served as Israel's military chief of staff. In 1992, as a committed Labor partisan, Barak was awarded the ministry of the interior in Rabin's cabinet. Upon Rabin's assassination, he became foreign minister until the fall of Peres's government in 1996. When Peres subsequently resigned as Labor chairman, the party primary turned overwhelmingly to Barak as his successor.

On the campaign trail in the early months of 1999, the fifty-seven-year-old soldier-politician dutifully embraced many of Israel's national shibboleths. Like Netanyahu (and Peres and Rabin), he declared himself uncompromising on the unity of Jerusalem, on the security of Israel's borders, on Arafat's obligation to suppress terrorism. Yet Barak also lost no opportunity to remind the Israeli public that within their country the gap between rich and poor was widening steadily, and that the shortfall in social services could be traced directly to Likud's relentless and financially skewed settlements program in the territories. It had to be abandoned. Of equal importance in Barak's political agenda was evacuation of Israel's putative "security zone" in southern Lebanon. In 1983, as a consequence of Menachem Begin's ill-considered "Peace for the Galilee" campaign, the Israeli military forces had eventually pulled out of the largest part of Lebanon. With them, the Israeli government allowed almost six thousand Christian Lebanese, active or passive collaborators of the Israelis, to find shelter and intermittent employment across the "good fence" in northern Israel.

Still, a thin buffer strip was retained, just north of Israel's frontier, guarded by a modest force of between two hundred and eight hundred Israeli military "advisers" to the South Lebanon Army that functioned as a kind of "picket fence" against infiltrating Hizballah guerrillas (p. 938). Iranian-trained and -armed, the Hizballah had recently directed their rocket firings less against Israeli border communities than against the Israeli "picket fence" itself. That was attrition enough. Throughout the late 1990s, even after Peres's Operation Grapes of Wrath, almost five hundred Israeli soldiers were killed or seriously wounded by these random assaults. Speaking then with the authority of a former commander-in-chief, Barak during his election campaign declared that Israel's troop presence was serving no further purpose in Lebanon. If he came to the prime minister's office, he would evacuate these young recruits "within the year." It was a promise that resonated favorably with the Israeli public.

Barak's campaign quickly assumed serious momentum. His security bona fides were given enthusiastic endorsement by dozens of reserve generals and colonels; while the candidate at the same time shrewdly co-opted two of Labor's "sibling" factions—Gesher and Meimad—to campaign on a common slate dubbed "One Israel." As the public-opinion surveys anticipated, the elections of May 17, 1999, proved a resounding personal victory for Barak. In the voting for both party and prime minister (p. 1014), he himself won 56 percent of the vote. In the Knesset, Labor alone won a plurality of twenty-six seats, against Likud's nineteen seats, and the subsequent ascension of Meretz gave the coalition nearly three times Likud's total. On the evening of May 17, as the results of the election became clear, tens of thousands of Israelis gathered in Tel Aviv's Rabin (formerly Municipality) Square, dancing and singing in celebration, and hoisting banners proclaiming "The Nightmare Is Over. We Shall Have Peace."

Barak's single, overarching goal was to achieve that peace on all fronts: Palestinian, Syrian, and ultimately the Arab world at large. Every other consideration was subordinate to that objective, even the cherished left-centrist goal of reducing the engorged subsidies claimed by the ultra-religionists and the West Bank settlers. Barak hesitated only briefly, therefore, before inviting into his government coalition not only Labor's political allies of the left and center but the National Religious party and Natan Scharansky's hawkish Russian-immigrant party, Yisrael b'Aliyah. The leadership of the two latter factions had hinted that they would display "flexibility" in their stance on the Palestinian territories. The one surprise was Barak's marginalization of Shimon Peres, who had anticipated reinstatement in his former role as foreign minister. Determined, however, not to be overshadowed by the former Labor chairman, Barak consigned Peres instead to an anodyne sinecure, a specially created "ministry of regional cooperation"; while the foreign ministry was reserved for David Levy, who had devolved over the years from a resolute champion of Israel's Moroccan underclass into a neutered political hack.

BARAK'S SYRIAN OPTION

Even before he completed structuring his government coalition, the prime minister–elect began signaling his eagerness to restart the inanimate peace talks with Syria. In late June of 1999, he gave an interview to a British journalist, Patrick Seale, a biographer and confidant of Syrian President Hafez al-Assad. "The only way to build a stable, comprehensive peace in the Middle East," Barak insisted, "is through agreement with Syria. . . . My policy is to [concentrate] . . . on [putting] an end to the conflict with Syria." He had made a campaign promise to the Israeli people to extricate their soldiers from Lebanon within one year. But that commitment, in turn, would inevitably entail the tacit forbearance of Syria, whose thirty-thousand-troop force in Lebanon's Beka'a Valley substantially inhibited the Lebanese government's freedom to impose order on its frontiers and to choke off Hizballah guerrilla attacks against Israel (p. 938). In the end, Barak emphasized, quiet along the Lebanese border depended on the willingness of Syria to negotiate its own peace agreement with Israel.

It was specifically to explore the peace option that Barak, through Patrick Seale, now offered President Assad a bouquet of political compliments. "There is no doubt that President Assad has shaped the Syrian nation," the Israeli leader declared. "His legacy is a strong, independent, self-confident Syria, which I believe to be very important for the stability of the Middle East." Three days later, Seale transmitted Barak's remarks to Assad in Damascus. The Syrian president reciprocated Barak's overture. "I have followed his career and his statements," Assad acknowledged to Seale. "He seems to be a strong and honest man. As the election results show, he evidently has wide support. It is clear that he wants to achieve peace with Syria." Assad stressed in this interview, however, that "[i]t is not a question of starting something new but rather, now that Netanyahu has gone, of resuming [negotiations] on the basis of what was achieved before." Seale concluded from these interviews that the two Middle Eastern leaders were determined to put the Netanyahu-era stalemate behind them.

Meanwhile, in early July 1999, two weeks after his inauguration as prime minister, Barak embarked on a whirlwind of personal visits to Arab capitals. He engaged in cordial discussions with Egypt's Mubarak, with Jordan's King Hussein, and, briefly, at the Erez checkpoint between the Gaza Strip and Israel, with Yasser Arafat, to whom Barak promised "substantive, productive meetings" very soon. Nevertheless, it was ultimately through Clinton that Barak hoped to gain the crucial support for his priorities. On July 14, the prime minister and his wife traveled to Washington for their first visit with the American president. After his uncongenial experience with Netanyahu, Clinton for his part eagerly looked forward to working with Barak. The next day, the two leaders' private meeting in the White House consumed an unprecedented three hours; and afterward, as a special gesture of cordiality, the Clintons took the Baraks by helicopter to Camp David to have dinner and spend the night.

It was at Camp David, the following morning, that Barak disclosed to the president his intention to allow himself up to fifteen months to reach a "framework" agreement with the Palestinians. In the interval, however, he wished to give priority to a diplomatic agreement with Syria's Assad, whom he considered a more "reliable" interlocutor. Clinton was taken by surprise. He had expected that the new Israeli government would move immediately to implement the Wye Agreement (p. 1022), including final-status negotiations with Arafat. But when the prime minister held fast to his own formula, assuring Clinton that he, Barak, was fully committed to territorial withdrawal and Palestine statehood, the president acquiesced. Evidently congressmen of both parties shared Clinton's enthusiasm for the new prime minister, giving Barak a tumultuous reception when he was ushered into the House of Representatives to address a joint congressional session. Without hesitation, the legislators endorsed Clinton's decision to finance Israel's acquisition of a new and more effective anti-missile system, and to approve "broad cooperation" between the two governments' defense and intelligence services.

IN PURSUIT OF HAFEZ AL-ASSAD

It was with American approbation, therefore, during the late summer and autumn of 1999, that Barak gave his most intensive effort to the Syrian track. In certain respects, the new prime minister took a harder line than had Rabin. He did not consider it advisable or necessary to concede the Rabin "pocket," that is, to engage in a full territorial withdrawal to the pre-1967 armistice line of Lake Kinneret, thereby allowing the Syrians to regain their "pocket" on the lake's eastern shore. Neither did he wish to accept postponement of full diplomatic relations until the last stage of Israeli military evacuation from Syrian soil. Ambassadors should be exchanged not later than at a, yet-to-be-defined, intermediate stage. Like Rabin, the new prime minister would insist on keeping a small Israeli early-warning station on Mount Hermon, the Golan's northernmost promontory.

With the exception of these desiderata, however, Barak was prepared to "bend over backwards" to assuage Assad's nationalist insecurities. The chances for substantive progress appeared reasonably good. Dennis Ross, still operating as "point man" for the White House, conducted a series of private meetings with Syrian and Israeli foreign-ministry officials in Berne, Switzerland, and later in Washington. The issues now appeared reduced to such lingering minutiae as the number of feet (no longer miles) to be left under Israel's control on Lake Kinneret's eastern shore, and to the precise calibration of diplomatic and economic relations with Israel's phased troop withdrawal. Barak convinced himself that, with Ross's mediation, the two governments were moving toward a final agreement.

The prime minister underestimated the remaining difficulties. It was common knowledge that the Golan's approximately twelve thousand Israeli settlers were the products of secular kibbutzim and moshavim. They had established flourishing agricultural communities of their own in these former Syrian highlands, and the sons emulated the fathers in volunteering for the army's elite combat units. The Labor party regarded them as the best of the best. More important, the terrain they occupied was strategically far more important than the Palestinian West Bank. Thus, on December 13, 1999, when Barak addressed the Knesset to announce his expectation of an imminent diplomatic breakthrough with Syria, the reaction of the legislators was distinctly tepid. Only forty-seven members gave him unqualified support, and Labor MKs were among those who sat on their hands. So did Foreign Minister David Levy. Natan Scharansky, emerging as a professional maverick of both the left and the right, threatened to pull his Yisrael b'Aliyah party out of the government coalition rather than countenance an agreement to return the Golan to Syria. Barak was sobered. Nevertheless, he remained confident that his Knesset majority would remain intact long enough to endorse a formal Israeli-Syrian peace treaty.

In the same month, Bill Clinton, in Europe for a series of economic conferences, arranged to meet with Syria's President Assad in Bern, Switzerland. The talks were cordial, and Assad reassured Clinton that he was prepared to match full Israeli withdrawal from the Golan with a corresponding array of reciprocal concessions. Returning to Washington, Clinton accepted Dennis Ross's evaluation that the signals from Damascus and Jerusalem were positive enough to warrant a summit meeting of the Israeli and Syrian leadership, under American chairmanship. Both Middle Eastern governments concurred, and in the second week of January 2000, trilateral discussions began in the United States. The venue was an attractive manorial retreat in Shepherdstown, West Virginia, a two-hour drive (and a forty-minute helicopter flight) from Washington. In attendance were Clinton, who opened the proceedings, and Secretary of State Albright and Ross, for the United States; for Israel, Ehud Barak, with his foreign-ministry and military advisers; and for Syria, Foreign Minister Farouk al-Shara, leading a four-man delegation (President Assad, in increasingly frail health, was not present). It was the highest-level meeting ever held between Syrians and Israelis.

In the recollection of Dennis Ross, the negotiations got off to an unpromising start when Syrian Foreign Minister Shara refused to shake hands with Barak and the other Israelis. He maintained his glacial reserve throughout the subsequent eight days of talks, even when Clinton escorted him and Barak on casual strolls through the estate's idyllically wooded grounds. To the consternation of the Americans, moreover, it appeared that Barak had stiffened his position. Evidently the foreboding in Israel at the prospect of a Golan evacuation finally had registered on him. A recent public-opinion survey had indicated that only 13 percent of the Israeli people favored a total withdrawal from the heights. The prime minister now stood firm on retaining for Israel a thirty-foot strip of Lake Kinneret's northeast shoreline, and a correspondingly modest foothold along the Golan's Yarmuk tributary as it flowed into the Jordan River before descending into the Kinneret.

Equally critical for Barak and his military advisers was an early-warning station atop Mount Hermon, to be kept in place for an indeterminate (although negotiable) period after Israeli withdrawal from the Golan. The final provision in Barak's security arrangements would have granted Israel a minimum of three years to complete a phased military evacuation. In return, Israel would concede three zones for limited Syrian troop emplacement on the heights, although the territorial segment closest to Israel's border would have to be demilitarized. Conversely, on the Israeli side of the border, Barak would agree to a limited Israeli troop deployment—but not an equivalent zone of total demilitarization. By the prime minister's logic, Israel, once deprived of its Golan ensconcement, would be the more vulnerable of the two parties. If the Syrians wished to re-enter the high ground, they would have to pay an asymmetrical price.

Syrian Foreign Minister Shara rejected Barak's security conditions in their entirety. His country must have back every square mile of its pre-1967 frontiers, including the thirty-foot emplacements Barak was claiming on Lake Kinneret and the Jordan River. Neither would the "abomination" of a postwithdrawal Israeli early-warning station be allowed to defile Syrian territory. Although

Shara accepted the logic of demilitarized zones, Syrian national honor required that the process be totally symmetrical. The foreign minister proved equally unbudging on the "content" of peace. The Israelis had insisted that a peace treaty incorporate full diplomatic, commercial, and tourist relations *before* final military evacuation was completed. The Syrians rejected the demand instantly and categorically. They wanted the Israelis out within eighteen months, and only then would "full" peace take effect, including diplomatic and "normal" civilian relations. Not even Clinton's presence at the Shepherdstown negotiations, his intimate involvement with the minutiae of strategic and diplomatic issues, his repeated telephone calls directly to Syrian President Assad, could bridge the gap. After eight days, by mutual consent, the conference came to an end. By then, Barak and his advisers recognized that they had put excessive emphasis on the Syrian track, to the neglect of the "Oslo II" timetable with the Palestinians—and also to the withdrawal of troops from the "security zone" in Lebanon.

The Chinese water torture of Hizballah attacks on Israeli outposts in southern Lebanon had always been intimately related to the broader issue of peace with Syria. Even if Hizballah training and weaponry were supplied by Iran, its personnel movements and arms transfers went through Syria—and through Syrian military emplacements in Lebanon. Barak had pinned his hopes on cauterizing this open lesion as part of an all-embracing peace treaty with Damascus. But with those hopes apparently extinguished upon the failure of the Shepherdstown Conference, the issue of Israeli withdrawal from its Lebanese neighbor could no longer be postponed. Upon returning to Jerusalem, Barak informed his military staff that troop evacuation from the Lebanese border enclave, originally envisaged as a gradual process, must be rescheduled for the coming May and concluded by early July. The prime minister's timelines were meticulously followed. On May 3, 2000, the modest Israeli security force set about repositioning its artillery, dynamiting its fortifications and other installations, and moving its armor to a skeletal trip-wire emplacement barely a half mile north of the Israeli border. In the meantime, Israel's surrogate "South Lebanon Army," the residual 2,800-man Christian militia, fearing Hizballah reprisals, was allowed to evacuate with its families and resettle in northern Israeli encampments. By the morning of May 25, the last Israeli tanks rumbled out of the security zone. On June 17, United Nations Secretary General Kofi Annan confirmed the Israeli withdrawal to the UN Security Council.

Beyond stemming the casualties inflicted on its soldiers in this lethal border area, there was a certain diplomatic advantage for Israel in its accelerated withdrawal. It took the Syrian government by surprise. Initially, President Assad had hoped to use the withdrawal issue as a bargaining chip during his negotiations for the Golan Heights. Now it was too late. On the other hand, the Israelis would have little opportunity to exploit their "advantage." On June 10, 2000, Assad died suddenly of a heart attack. At an "election" conducted by the ruling Ba'ath party, he was succeeded as president by his thirty-four-year-old physician-son, Bashar, who lacked his father's commanding authority to make deals with the Israelis. Moreover, as both Ehud Barak's supporters and critics had feared, the Hizballah guerrillas in Lebanon flooded into the last of the abandoned Israeli positions, organized tumultuous "victory" rallies, and defiantly proclaimed themselves the de facto administrators of south Lebanon. The triumphalist message was not lost on Hamas, on Hizballah, or, least of all, on PA President Yasser Arafat.

BARAK'S PALESTINIAN OPTION

Notwithstanding his persistent quest of a deal with Hafez al-Assad, Ehud Barak had remained sentient to the importance of placating Yasser Arafat, if only to buy time for more substantive negotiations with the Syrians. In early July 1999, in a conversation in his Jerusalem office with Saeb Erekat, Arafat's spokesman, the Israeli prime minister had emphasized that he personally was committed to a Palestinian state, and to a second stage of Wye-sequence withdrawals from the Palestinian territories. He had repeated the pledge to Clinton that same month at the White House. The promise had been "sanctified," moreover, at a special ceremony on September 4, 1999, hosted by Egypt's President Mubarak, and attended by Clinton and Jordan's ailing King Hussein, at Sharm es-Sheikh. There, Barak and Arafat signed an agreement for Israeli troop withdrawal from an additional 11 percent of the West Bank (an evacuation completed by early January 2000). Moreover, on November 3, 1999, Clinton, Barak, and Arafat met yet again, in Oslo, ostensibly to commemorate the fifth anniversary of the Nobel Peace Prize award to the Israeli and Palestinian leadership, but in fact to draw up a schedule for the long-delayed final-status negotiations. A framework accord was to be concluded before February 13, 2000, and the final document signed before September of that year (a full year behind the original "Oslo II" schedule). Upon signing these commitments, however, Barak had then devoted his most intensive efforts of autumn–winter 1999–2000 to the Syrian "track."

It was only after the Syrian negotiations hit a dead end in the winter of 2000, and Barak made the decision to implement unilateral troop evacuation from Lebanon, that the Israeli prime minister reluctantly turned his full attention to a resumption of talks with the Palestinians. Dennis Ross had warned him that procrastination on this issue was threatening to ignite explosive demonstrations in the territories. Additionally, President Clinton had made it clear that he himself would broker a final-status deal, if Arafat and Barak would accept his "invitation" to come to Washington. Rejection of the offer was unthinkable. Yet the prospect of biting the final bullet on Palestine did not register well with several of Barak's cabinet colleagues. Indeed, the National Religious party and Natan Scharansky's Yisrael b'Aliyah faction left the government. After some hesitation, Foreign Minister David Levy also resigned, to be succeeded by a Labor technocrat, Shlomo Ben-Ami. In the late spring of 2000, moreover, a—nonbinding—resolution of "censure" against Barak passed the Knesset by a vote of 54–42, with 24 absentions.

Nevertheless, on the ensuing July 11, the new summit began in the informal ambience of Camp David. The prospects for success were distinctly mixed. Clinton, flanked by Madeleine Albright and Dennis Ross, hoped to re-create the 1979 atmosphere of the original Begin-Sadat-Carter summit in the same historic venue. But it soon became clear that Clinton had been overly optimistic.

Too much venom had been spewed lately between Israelis and Palestinians, and too many guerrilla attacks had been conducted against Israeli civilians. So acute was the mutual distrust that, on the opening day of "Camp David II," Barak and Arafat took pains not to address each other directly. Eventually the chill thawed somewhat, but the discussions remained tense. All the participants knew by then that proposals for incremental Israeli withdrawal were no longer relevant. Clinton did not have time for anything less than a final-status agreement. Indeed, the American president warned his guests at the outset that his second term of office was approaching its end, and as soon as campaigns for the 2000 elections got under way, his involvement in the peace process would be limited. Then, by prearrangement, he departed for Washington and the two delegations were left with Albright and Ross to ventilate their respective concerns.

These were substantial. Barak and his entourage accepted the principle of future Palestinian statehood, and with it the evacuation of the Gaza Strip and not less than 92 percent of the West Bank. But they stood firm on maintaining Israel's sovereignty over the largest of the Jewish settlement blocs, most of them directly adjacent to the Green Line, and embracing 75–80 percent of the Jews in the West Bank. Barak's "map" included the central Givat Ze'ev/Pisgat Ze'ev/Ma'aleh Adumim bloc, which effectively divided the West Bank in two, and the Efrat/Etzion/Betar Ilit bloc to the southwest of Jerusalem, which severed any coherent connection between Bethlehem and Hebron. The "map" included the city of Ariel and its satellite villages in western Samaria, which sat astride and brought under Israeli control a major West Bank aquifer. Some fifty thousand additional settlers in more dispersed enclaves would have to remain under Israeli "protection" until arrangements could be made to relocate them. Finally, the Israeli army would have to maintain its emplacements in the Jordan River Valley.

Arafat contemptuously rejected these proposals. He pointed out that under their terms, Israel's matrix of control would include most of the 220,000 settlers who had moved into the West Bank since 1967 (in addition to another 180,000–200,000 in East Jerusalem). Moreover, from the beginning of the Oslo process in 1993, Israel had constructed for settler use an elaborate network of twenty-nine highways and bypass roads. These had devoured an additional 17 percent of West Bank land. The Palestinian president noted that he had accepted incremental Israeli withdrawals so long as they were features of "interim," provisional diplomacy. But since their two governments were now engaged in final-status discussions, Israel would have to be more forthcoming. He would concede Israel's "temporary" control of the two major settlement blocs directly adjacent to the Green Line, but retention of Ariel, even on a temporary basis, let alone the more dispersed enclaves, was unacceptable. Equally unthinkable was an Israeli military presence in the Jordan Valley.

If, for both sides, these respective claims and categorical rejections were nonstarters, so was the question of Arab refugees. By the opening of the twenty-first century, their numbers had grown to between 3.5 and 4 million (estimates varied). During the earliest Oslo negotiations, Arafat had alluded to the subject of their repatriation only intermittently, but in the late 1990s he returned to the issue with growing frequency and adamancy. For the Israelis, in turn, there was no topic on which there was more unanimity among all the nation's political parties. Financial compensation for a limited number of Arab refugees was a subject for possible discussion, as long as payments were at least partially offset by the financial losses suffered by some half-million Jewish refugees from Moslem lands and by Israel's costs in absorbing these kinsmen, as well as by the establishment of an international fund to help underwrite the compensation. In addition, provision could theoretically be made for the admission to Israel of a symbolic number of some thirty to forty thousand Palestinian refugees within the framework of "family reunions." But a mass repatriation of Palestinian Arabs was as unthinkable for Barak as for all his predecessors in office.

A renewed political division of Jerusalem was equally nonnegotiable for the Israeli prime minister. He was willing to accept an American "bridging" formula, granting the Palestinians sovereignty over the Old City's Moslem quarters, while its Jewish and Armenian quarters would be annexed to Israel. Under that formula, too, as the Americans had nursed it along and refined it, the Palestinians (instead of Hashemite Jordan) would be granted "custodial" sovereignty over the Haram es-Sharif and allowed to fly the Palestinian flag there; while Israel would be assigned "residual" sovereignty over the Dome of the Rock's lower level, with its remains of the Second Temple. For the rest of East Jerusalem, however, with its—by then—tens of thousands of Jewish residents, the Americans proposed that the Palestine Authority "administer" the city's Moslem and Christian neighborhoods on an autonomous basis, but with their juridical sovereignty limited to the adjoining Arab town of Abu Dis, which the Palestinians might retitle "al-Quds" (Jerusalem). Barak was prepared to discuss the idea. Not Arafat. "I will accept no Israeli sovereign presence in [Arab] Jerusalem," the PA president asserted. His alternative plan was for Jerusalem to be designated an open and undivided city in which Arabs and Jews could move about freely. Israel would control the—pre-1967—New City, together with the Old City's Jewish quarter and Western Wall. But the rest of East Jerusalem, including the Jewish neighborhoods built there since the Six-Day War, would remain under Palestinian sovereignty.

As the talks continued, day after day, Clinton repeatedly helicoptered to Camp David in an effort to chivy both sides into compromise. He was especially concerned about Arafat's threat to declare a Palestinian state on his own if his conditions were not met. To counter that warning, Clinton telephoned President Mubarak in Cairo and King Abdullah (son of Hussein, who had succumbed to cancer the previous February) in Amman, entreating them to dissuade Arafat from precipitating a crisis. The two Arab leaders agreed. In the face of their appeals, however, Arafat remained noncommittal, and the negotiations remained deadlocked. Finally, on day eight of the summit, Clinton departed for a previously scheduled weeklong trip to the Far East, leaving Madeleine Albright and Dennis Ross to monitor discussions. In his absence, the negotiations foundered altogether, and even the president's subsequent return could not reactivate them. After a duration of more than two weeks, the Camp David conference was suspended. To Ross, the president glumly confessed that the ordeal had been "like going to the dentist without novocaine injections in your gums." Not the least of his concerns was the staying power of Barak. Clinton suspected that rumors of the prime minister's "concessions" on Jerusalem and the refugees might have eroded his political standing in Israel.

Arafat, in turn, returned to his headquarters in Gaza a hero to his followers. He had defied both Clinton and Barak. He had stood up for Palestinian rights and refused to accept a *diktat* from any party. But his obduracy was also tactical. If it registered in Palestine and the Arab world, he sensed that it had evoked only a lukewarm reaction in the West. On August 9, therefore, Arafat dispatched a placating letter to Clinton, offering to set up a "discreet" channel with the Israelis to discuss "practical" approaches to the more intractable remaining issues. Forthwith, the president dispatched Ross to Israel to join the discussions. These took place in Jerusalem's King David Hotel, with Muhammad Dahlan and Saeb Erekat, the PA's foreign-policy spokesmen, representing Arafat, and Israeli Foreign Minister Ben-Ami and Gilad Sher, the Israeli security adviser, speaking for Barak. Soon Muhammad Bassiouny, Egypt's ambassador to Israel, and Bassiouny's counterpart, United States Ambassador Martin Indyk, were brought into the talks.

Throughout the remaining weeks of August and into early September of 2000, a certain room for maneuver seemed to be developing. On the Jerusalem issue, the city was discussed neighborhood by neighborhood. Whose laws would apply in what neighborhood? How would security issues be coordinated? How could functional municipal responsibilities be allocated? Land "swaps" also were discussed, to compensate for the West Bank settlement blocs Israel was claiming for itself. As the gap between the two sides slowly narrowed, Ross suggested that Erekat and Dahlen accompany him back to Washington to continue discussions with the participation of Madeleine Albright and a wider State Department team. In the interval, Barak hosted Arafat at an informal dinner at the prime minister's Jerusalem residence. Although no diplomatic matters were touched upon, a cordial personal atmosphere was reestablished. Was a functional accommodation indeed in the offing? After the reversals and setbacks of the Netanyahu years, was the Oslo process actually regaining its former momentum?

In fact, the negotiators' worst nightmare for Middle East peace was about to materialize.

ARIEL SHARON TAKES A WALK

Its vortex was Jerusalem, traditionally the most explosive ingredient in the Palestinian-Israeli impasse; and its catalyst was Ariel Sharon, the perennial loose cannon of Israeli politics. A year earlier, following Netanyahu's electoral defeat, the Likud party had overwhelmingly selected Sharon as its new chairman (p. 1044). Since then, Sharon had escalated his personal campaign against Barak's suspected territorial concessions to Arafat. Sharon's views on Jerusalem were uncompromising. As minister of housing in the Shamir government, he had vigorously promoted and subsidized Jewish settlement in the eastern part of the city. In 1992, with much fanfare, he had made a point of buying himself a home in the heart of the Arab Old City. Now, eight years later, on September 28, 2000, the day before the onset of the Jewish New Year, Sharon set about making another point, this time in a location that both Jews and Moslems regarded as a sanctum sanctorum. He would pay a walking visit to the Temple Mount.

If the substructure of the Second Temple comprised the most venerated site in the world of Jewish Orthodoxy, that site also impinged on the site of the Dome of the Rock, the fabled setting of the Prophet Muhammad's ascent to heaven for his visitation with the Archangel Gabriel. Moreover, on the same thirty-eight-acre Haram es-Sharif esplanade stood the Dome's close neighbor, the al-Aqsa Mosque. Both these buildings were among the most sacred shrines in Islam. Indeed, on June 17, 1967, in the immediate aftermath of Israel's conquest of East Jerusalem, Minister of Defense Moshe Dayan had assembled the city's Moslem religious authorities, and reassured them that the entire Haram es-Sharif plaza would be respected by the Israeli government. Although Jews could visit the site, they would not be allowed to pray there. The Moslem dignitaries were mollified. Over the ensuing years, all Israeli governments respected the Moslem character of the Haram es-Sharif, and cooperated with Palestinian clerics in declaring its shrines under Moslem religious administration.

But now, on September 28, 2000, Sharon ostensibly had cleared his visit in advance with Ehud Olmert, the mayor of Jerusalem and a respected Likud stalwart. Olmert in turn had consulted with Jibril Rajoub, director of the Palestine Authority's security services in the West Bank. The latter foresaw no problem if the visit was brief and if Sharon did not actually enter the Dome of the Rock or the al-Aqsa Mosque. Similarly alerted, Ehud Barak understood full well the political advantage Sharon hoped to score with his "walk." Not to be outflanked, however, at a time when he was under growing public criticism for alleged weakness in his negotiations with Arafat, the prime minister decided to allow the visit, and even to provide a police escort for Sharon, Olmert, four accompanying Likud politicians, and a half-dozen news reporters. The visit in any case lasted no longer than twenty-five minutes. None of the group entered the al-Aqsa Mosque or the Dome of the Rock, although Sharon and Olmert momentarily approached the mosque's newly reconstructed entrance. Finally, just before leaving the Haram es-Sharif plateau, Sharon declared to the press: "I think we can live together with the Palestinians. I came to see what is going on here. . . . I have not committed any act of provocation." But evidently he had, and Barak, in permitting this visit by a man of Sharon's convictions and temperament, a figure anathematized by the entire Arab world as the "butcher of Sabra and Shatila," had committed perhaps his most egregious tactical error.

The next morning, Friday, September 29, Moslems began to congregate for worship at the al-Aqsa Mosque. Routinely, a cordon of Israeli police was on hand to keep Jewish passersby from straying onto the Haram es-Sharif on a Moslem holy day. But suddenly about twenty young Arabs began stoning the police. When the violence grew, police reinforcements were summoned, and soon opened fire with tear gas, then with rubber bullets. The rioting lasted several hours. Before it subsided, 4 Arabs had been killed and 164 wounded. At this point, spontaneous demonstrations erupted in the major towns of the West Bank. Although under the provisions of "Oslo II" these urban centers had been returned to Palestinian security control, hundreds of Israeli police, supported by Israeli army units, were dispatched to suppress the unrest. In turn, they encountered the resistance of PA security forces. By the end of the day, 6 more Arabs had been slain, and some 400 had been wounded. That same evening, in Ramallah, Marwan Barghouti, a trusted Arafat lieutenant, issued orders for the demonstrations to be enlarged under the direction of the Palestine Authority's reigning Fatah party. So began Palestine's second intifada, "the al-Aqsa intifada," with the name "al-Aqsa" adding a powerful religious symbolism to the Palestinians' long-held nationalist frustrations. Sharon's visit had essentially provided the spark.

Soon the West Bank and Gaza Strip were seething with violence. Joining the unrest, too, were Israeli Arabs (as they had not in the first, 1987 intifada). As it developed, the events of late September and early October 2000 were the closest the Arab citizens of Israel came to open civil revolt. Over the course of three weeks, residents of almost all of Israel's major Arab communities took to the streets, attacking cars, setting fire to gasoline stations and banks, blocking traffic, throwing stones at their Jewish neighbors and the police. The police in turn reacted against the rioters with unbridled force, using live bullets. Thirteen Israeli Arabs and one Israeli Jew were killed, and about seven hundred were injured. Plainly more than the "al-Aqsa violation" had kindled the rage of these veteran Israeli citizens. Several months later a government commission once again set about assessing the lagging economic and social conditions of Israel's Arab sector.

At all times, however, the worst of the turmoil occurred in the West Bank and Gaza, where Israeli police and troops began to suffer their own mounting casualties. On October 8, Prime Minister Barak acceded to the request of Army Chief of Staff Shaul Mofaz, and authorized the use of tanks and helicopter gunships to destroy PA security installations adjacent to Arafat's new headquarters in Ramallah, and Palestinian police stations elsewhere in the West Bank. Tightening the siege, Israeli troops closed the Gaza airport and the routes of entry into integral Israel, and set road barriers around Palestinian cities. By mid-October the toll of fatalities had climbed to 102 Palestinians and 10 Israelis, and more than 2,000 on both sides had been wounded.

Altogether, the new uprising was a public-relations disaster for Israel. Newspaper photographs and telecasts of Palestinian teenagers confronting Israeli tanks went out to the world. One image was especially haunting. It was of an Arab man and his twelve-year-old boy caught in the fusillade between Israeli and Palestinian gunners at the Netzarim road junction in the Gaza Strip. The father pleaded for the shooting to stop, but within minutes his little son was killed before his eyes. The incident created outrage among Palestinians and Europeans alike. Replayed again and again on television, it became the enduring symbol of the "al-Aqsa intifada."

On October 2, 2000, Clinton placed urgent telephone calls to Barak and Arafat. It was the American president's "suggestion" to both leaders that they meet forthwith in Paris, where Secretary of State Madeleine Albright was then holding discussions (on European matters) with France's President Chirac. Barak and Arafat agreed. On October 4, arriving at the Elysée Palace, they conferred separately with Chirac and Albright, before each was joined by Dennis Ross and UN Secretary-General Kofi Annan. It was an emotional gathering. Barak laid the full blame for the violence on the "Tanzim," the Fatah militia that took its orders directly from Arafat. Ross acknowledged that Arafat was doing nothing to restore order, but he insisted that the Israeli army was reacting with unwarranted harshness. At first, Barak and Arafat did not meet face-to-face, but eventually they were induced to accept a joint dinner conference with the secretary of state at the home of United States Ambassador Felix Rohatyn. That evening, Albright barely managed to maintain a degree of civility between the two guests. By 11:00 p.m., however, a makeshift agreement was reached. There would be two commissions, one to preside over the technical aspects of a cease-fire, and to be chaired by George Tenet, director of the United States CIA; and the other, a "neutral" commission of inquiry, to explore underlying causes of the new upsurge of violence. Albright also prevailed on Barak and Arafat to accept Egyptian President Mubarak's invitation to a summit conference at Sharm es-Sheikh, on October 16. Then the two men departed for home. The intifada continued.

The Sharm es-Sheikh conference began on schedule—one of a half-dozen since the onset of the Oslo peace process. This time Clinton was present, as well as young King Abdullah of Jordan, UN Secretary-General Kofi Annan, Miguel Moratinos, the EU's emissary to the Middle East, and Hosni Mubarak, acting as host. Barak and Arafat were accompanied by their respective foreign-policy advisers, Shlomo Ben-Ami and Saeb Erekat. The meeting was as tense as its predecessor in Paris. Indeed, when Erekat accused the Israeli government of genocide, Ben-Ami physically lunged at him and Moratinos had to intervene to separate them. During the two-day meeting, however, Clinton eventually secured a commitment from both sides to take immediate, concrete measures to end the violence. In return, the American president was willing to finesse the issue of a commission of inquiry, and instead to offer his own proposals for security cooperation between Palestinians and Israelis. Once back in Jerusalem, then, Barak gave the order to ease travel curfews within the occupied territories. From his office in Ramallah, Arafat in turn sent out word for the random sniping and rioting to be scaled down.

CLINTON'S MIDDLE EASTERN VALEDICTORY

The two leaders' orders were honored only in the breach. Throughout October and November 2000, hardly a day went by without an incident of Palestinian violence and Israeli military reprisal. By December, contacts between the Israeli government and the Palestine Authority had ceased. By then, too, the most punitive of Israel's countermeasures were economic, and specifically the closure of Israel's employment market to the Palestinians. In late October, Terje Larsen (p. 991), recently appointed as UN "coordinator" for Palestinian economic and social issues, disclosed that virtually all of the 110,000–120,000 Palestinians who ordinarily commuted to work in Israel were blocked from entry. The closure of the Israeli employment market in turn ramified through the Palestinian economy. Larsen estimated that as many as 200,000 families had lost their principal source of income. Nor was Israel's economy unaffected. It experienced heavy losses in those sectors that had relied on Palestinian labor, specifically in agriculture and in the building industry. Israeli employers were forced increasingly to import foreign workers—from Eastern Europe, Africa, and East Asia (p. 1093). Tourism in Israel declined by half.

There were diplomatic consequences, as well. A special session of the UN Commission on Human Rights, meeting in Geneva, condemned Israel for "crimes against humanity." In Cairo, the Arab League convened for an emergency session on October 21–22, its first meeting in five years. After issuing a communiqué that accused Israel of conducting "war against the Palestinian people," the prime ministers and other representatives of twenty-two Arab nations agreed to suspend all regional cooperation with the Jewish state. A month later, in retaliation for an attack on an Israeli school bus, the Israelis bombarded a suspected guerrilla base in the Gaza Strip. Thereupon the government of Egypt recalled Ambassador Muhammad Bassiouny from Tel Aviv for "consultations." The same day, the Jordanian government announced that it would delay sending its new ambassador-designate to Israel "until Israel ends its attacks and honors its commitments to the peace process." Morocco and Tunisia similarly ended the low-level commercial relations they had established with the Jewish state in the aftermath of the 1993 Oslo agreement (p. 1005). On October 12, 2000, the Sultanate of Oman ordered Israel to close its trade office in the capital city of Muscat. Qatar requested Israel to downgrade its trade delegation to a single official and a secretary.

On November 9, a week after the American national elections, Arafat visited Clinton in the White House. The Palestinian leader was pale and distraught. It had been his devoutest wish, he insisted, to secure an agreement with Israel and declare a Palestinian state while the president was still in office. Clinton responded in kind. Indeed, he still believed it possible to attain that goal, for he had two remaining months in office. Was President Arafat prepared to soften his position? he inquired. Arafat's response was disappointing. He would not relinquish his claim to the entirety of East Jerusalem, or to fully 98 percent of the rest of Israeli-occupied territory. The visit ended in impasse. Ehud Barak arrived at the White House five days later. When apprised of Arafat's terms, he summarily rejected them. Yet the prime minister agreed not to inflame the intifada further. If there was any room for additional diplomatic flexibility, he was open to suggestions.

One came in late November. Responding to an urgent call from Arafat, who was holding consultations with Moroccan government officials, Dennis Ross flew to Rabat to meet with the Palestinian president. For the first time, Arafat intimated that there still existed a thin margin for compromise. If President Clinton would summon his, Arafat's, aides and Barak's aides for private discussions in Washington, the talks might be worthwhile. Less than forty-eight hours later, the presidential invitation was forthcoming. The meeting was set for

December 19, and the designated site was Bolling Air Force Base, an hour's drive from the American capital. Thus, on December 19, Saeb Erekat arrived with the Palestinian delegation. Shlomo Ben-Ami led the Israelis. Both men were subdued, even friendly, putting their recent flare-up at Sharm es-Sheikh behind them. After three days of intensive discussions, however, progress remained negligible. The Palestinians reduced their claim for 98 percent of the West Bank to 95 percent, with the proviso that they be given "commensurate" Israeli land in exchange. But the gulf apparently remained unbridgeable on the critical issues of Jerusalem, return of refugees, and full Palestinian control of the Jordan Valley.

On December 23, the two delegations were brought to the White House. In the Cabinet Room, Clinton awaited them. As the president greeted his visitors, Ross noted that "he was as stern as I had ever seen him." Forthwith, Clinton announced that he would present his own peace formula for consideration. It had been carefully scripted in advance with Albright, Ross, and other State Department advisers. Before reading the text, the president warned that it represented the culmination of his efforts, not the beginning point of negotiations. If either side could not accept its provisions, he would withdraw the formula entirely, and in any case it would no longer exist once he left office. Finally, he informed both sides that they would have five days to respond with either a yes or a no. A conditional answer, or a failure to answer, would be taken as a no. Clinton then read off his ideas.

As Ross recounted afterward, they envisaged a range of 4 to 6 percent on Israeli territorial annexation in the West Bank, to accommodate the 80 percent of Jewish settlers who lived in the three principal blocs beyond the Green Line. In other words, between 94 and 96 percent of the West Bank, and all of Gaza, would remain in the envisaged Palestinian state. Israel would provide compensation even for its minimalist annexed strip of the West Bank by relinquishing to the Palestinians 1 to 3 percent of its own territory, as well as a permanent safe-passage zone between the West Bank and Gaza. Clinton emphasized that in proposing these guidelines, he would insist on territorial contiguity for the Palestinian state and on minimizing the number of Palestinians included in the sectors of Israeli annexation.

To monitor implementation of the scheme, the president continued, an international security force would gradually take the place of the Israeli army—although that army could remain in the Jordan Valley for a maximum of six years. Israel would also retain three electronic early-warning sites in the West Bank. The Palestinian state in turn would be demilitarized, except for a police force and a militia sufficient to guarantee internal security, and Israel would reserve the right to redeploy its army to the Jordan River in the event of a serious external threat to the Jewish state. While the Palestinians would exercise sovereignty over their airspace, they would be obliged to "accommodate" Israeli air force training and operational needs. With these exceptions, however, Israel would complete its phased military withdrawals from the allocated Palestinian territory within three years.

Clinton saved the two most emotionally charged issues for last. These dealt with Arab refugees and the future of Jerusalem, and the president's recommendations were forthright, the one favoring Israel, the other favoring the Palestinians. The solution for refugees, he declared, should be based on a recognition of the State of Palestine as the homeland of the Palestinian people, and the State of Israel as the homeland of the Jewish people. The right of Palestinian refugees to return should not be equated with a "specific right of return to Israel." Without question, Israel should acknowledge the moral and material suffering it caused the Palestinians in 1948–49, and accept as well its obligation to assist the international community in addressing the problem. Indeed, the United States itself would be prepared to lead an international effort to ease the material circumstances of the Palestinians. But, otherwise, "[t]he right of Palestinian return would pertain only to the state of Palestine. . . . Admission into Israel would be Israel's sovereign decision."

As for Jerusalem, the Palestinians would gain sovereignty over the Haram es-Sharif plateau, and all its structures, including the "superstructure" of the Dome of the Rock. The Israelis in turn would be awarded sovereignty over Jerusalem's historic Jewish Quarter, with its Western Wall, as well as the remains of the Second Temple—that is, the "substructure" of the Dome of the Rock—and both Palestinian and Israeli archaeologists would share the right of excavations in this mutually holy site. In the rest of East Jerusalem, however, Clinton proposed that Israel would exercise sovereignty only in the predominantly Jewish sectors, which should be recognized as part of the Israeli capital. Otherwise, East Jerusalem's Arab neighborhoods would be recognized as a legitimate part of a Palestinian state. No barriers would be erected to separate one community from the other.

When the president concluded his presentation, he did not ask for questions. Rather, he stated again that this was his best judgment for an equitable and viable peace settlement. He would not negotiate on it. He would expect an answer within five days. Then he wished the Palestinians and Israelis well, bade them goodbye, and left the room. After mutual handshakes, the two delegations also took their leave.

On December 27, 2000, Barak's cabinet voted to accept the president's formulation. Over the lingering misgivings of Shaul Mofaz, the military chief of staff, the assembled ministers formally accepted proposals that would have divided East Jerusalem politically, phased out Israel's military presence in the Jordan Valley, and produced a Palestinian state in roughly 94 percent of the West Bank and 100 percent of the Gaza Strip. Meanwhile, at Clinton's request, the Egyptians and Saudis, as well as virtually all the EU governments, pressed Arafat to accept the president's offer, which they declared to be a generous and fair one. But Arafat replied cautiously. He required information on the specific percentage of territories that would be annexed and exchanged. He asked for the precise number of Palestinian refugees to be admitted into Israel, and clarification on the remuneration they would receive for the land and personal property seized over the decades by Israel's Custodian of Absentee Property. He asked, too, for a shortening of the time period for Israeli withdrawal. In essence, Arafat interposed so many questions and conditions that their cumulative effect was a deal breaker.

Even then, under heavy international and Arab pressures, neither Barak nor

Arafat was prepared to give up. On January 21, 2001, they dispatched their senior advisers to Taba, Egypt, for intensive negotiations. As a gesture of good-will to the Palestinians, Yossi Beilin, the original "architect of Oslo," was included in the Israeli delegation. No Americans were present, but the Euro-pean Union sent its envoy, Miguel Moratinos. During the first two days of nego-tiations, differences between the sides were further narrowed. At Camp David, Barak had offered the Palestine Authority 92 percent of the West Bank. Now he authorized his negotiators to increase the figure to Clinton's minimal (and his cabinet's maximal) target of 94 percent; to drop altogether the demand for an Israeli military presence in the Jordan Valley; and to accept the president's formula for Jerusalem. On his own, Yossi Beilin even intimated his willingness to concede the "right" of Palestinian refugees to return to Israel, but with the "practical application" of this right limited to a reunion of families (on hearing of Beilin's tortured formulation, Barak promptly repudiated it, as did Arafat).

On January 23, Palestinian guerrillas murdered two Israeli restaurant owners who were on a buying trip in the West Bank, and Barak promptly withdrew his representatives from the Taba conference. Even then, members of both dele-gations unofficially maintained contact, and floated ideas to each other. But on the issues of Jerusalem and refugees it was clear, finally, that no compromise would be forthcoming from the Palestinian leader. To the dismay of Clinton, Barak, Jordan's Abdullah, and Egypt's Mubarak, Arafat refused to budge. For Dennis Ross, the situation called to mind an historical precedent. In 1948, a Palestinian moderate, Anwar al-Nuseibeh, had described Haj Amin Muham-mad al-Husseini, the Mufti of Jerusalem, as someone who "succeeded as a sym-bol and failed as a leader." This seemed an apt description, in Ross's words, of "the essence of Arafat fifty-three years later."

THE REINCARNATION OF ARIEL SHARON

On December 9, 2000, two weeks before Clinton issued his final proposal, Ehud Barak had surprised his country by agreeing to early elections, and scheduling them for February 6, 2001, a full two years before the Knesset's cur-rent term was due to expire. His advisers regarded the move as politically indis-pensable. The al-Aqsa intifada was in full force, violence was blazing in Gaza and the West Bank. On the one hand, Israeli polls revealed the nation's unmis-takable yearning for peace. Yet they suggested as well that at least 56 percent of Israel's Jewish population no longer trusted the prime minister to guard the nation's vital interests. He was conceding too much: on Jerusalem, on his adher-ence to Clinton's proposed schedule of evacuations, above all, on his willing-ness to discuss even a symbolic return of Arab refugees. If Barak waited much longer to go to the country, his aides insisted, his political support might de-teriorate even further.

Moreover, by calling early elections, the prime minister would avoid the prospect of facing Netanyahu again as his challenger. Israeli law barred any person except a sitting Knesset member from running against an incumbent prime minister; and Netanyahu, after his resounding 1999 electoral defeat, had resigned his seat in the Knesset, together with his party leadership. Shortly afterward, in the Likud primary, the man who was elected to replace Netanyahu as party chairman was none other than the combative Ariel Sharon. In moving up the date for elections, therefore, Barak was wagering his prime ministry that the Israeli people still would regard Sharon, his presumed opponent under the electoral amendment (p. 1014), as too aggressive and impulsive to be entrusted with government leadership.

The assumption was not unreasonable. Nothing in Sharon's record gave evidence that he had undergone a change of ideology or temperament. In 1983, he had brazened out the Kahan Report (p. 915), with its indictment of his shared responsibility for the Sabra-Shatila massacre, subsequently he had ignored his enforced resignation as defense minister to remain on in Menachem Begin's cabinet as minister without portfolio. Later, as minister of public housing in the Shamir cabinet, he had "Judaized" the West Bank with reckless disregard for the treasury's resources or world opinion. More recently yet, as a member of the Netanyahu government, Sharon had sustained his reputation as an inveterate troublemaker and power seeker. When Netanyahu at first rejected him for the critical post of finance minister, Sharon proposed that his fellow Likud party members form a national-unity government to keep "one man from making all policy decisions" (p. 1025). In September 1997, as Netanyahu made his first gestures of accepting a—modified—Oslo II schedule of withdrawals, Sharon warned the prime minister against wilting under Clinton's pressure. "If it becomes a fact," he threatened, "then we [the Likud] promise to topple you and not to elect you for a second term."

A year later, in October 1998, as Netanyahu was preparing for still another trip to Washington to negotiate further withdrawal schedules, the price Sharon claimed, and won, for his support was the portfolio of foreign minister. Sitting beside the prime minister at the Wye Plantation Conference, he ensured that Netanyahu's concessions were minimal; and once the Knesset endorsed this latest accord, Sharon set the tempo of irredentist developments on the ground. "Everyone should take action," he exhorted Jewish settlers in the West Bank. "Everyone should run, should grab more hills. We'll expand the area. Whatever is seized will be ours. Whatever isn't seized will end up in [Arab] hands." It was only upon stern admonition from the Clinton administration that the Wye River Memorandum moved toward implementation—slowly, belatedly, grudgingly (pp. 1022–23). By that time, Netanyahu was in deep political trouble, and in the ensuing election of May 1999, Israel's voting public summarily evicted him from office.

Sharon played only a perfunctory, cosmetic role in the 1999 election. It was obvious that he was saving his ammunition for the Likud primary several months later. Here he won decisively, and assumed the party chairmanship. For the ensuing two years, although out of office, he was hardly out of the limelight. Much of the attention was unwelcome. Then and later, Sharon was the focus of investigations for malfeasance: in a libel trial, he was charged with bribing a senior general to withdraw accusations that Sharon had hoodwinked the government into the disastrous 1982 Lebanon invasion; in an investigation of purported conflict of interest during his stint as minister of agriculture in the first

Begin cabinet, when he was accused of maintaining his ownership of one of the largest private ranches in Israel, and then finessing the Knesset rules by leasing out the ranch to relatives and friends.

But Sharon was impervious to all accusations, public and private. He luxuriated in opportunities to pander to the right's territorial chauvinism. In January 1999, at the start of Likud's electoral campaign, Sharon initiated the "Golan Law," requiring a Knesset majority to approve relinquishment "of any part of the Land of Israel," and forced Netanyahu expediently to endorse the legislation. In May of the same year, and a week before the Israeli 1999 elections, Sharon promised that, if Likud were returned to power, twenty thousand more Jews would be settled in the West Bank within six months. And in the campaign of early 2001, with Sharon himself as the Likud candidate, and many Labor campaigners were dubbing him a loose cannon, his partisans riposted by execrating Barak as a traitor. Rarely had Israeli politics been so polarized or poisonous.

By the close of election night, February 6, 2001, it was clear that Sharon had won the prime ministerial contest by a landslide vote of 62.5 percent to Barak's 37.5. By no means did the election signify a rejection of peace. In the last week of the campaign, polls revealed that a majority of the voters simply had concluded that the government should be "less conciliatory" in the face of Yasser Arafat's duplicity and terrorism. Barak was seen as a waffler, pretending to be firm, and then retreating. In his stead, the "bulldozer," a man who only nineteen years earlier had been almost universally execrated as the "butcher of Sabra and Shatila," and whose political future had been written off, was awarded an overwhelming national mandate to lead the government and people of Israel toward a peace, ostensibly, of realism and security.

THE BULLDOZER AS
PRIME MINISTER

ARIEL SHARON ORGANIZES A GOVERNMENT

On February 6, 2001, in the aftermath of his political triumph, Sharon as prime minister–elect had a mandatory forty-five days to form a government. The challenge was a formidable one. In consequence of the new two-tier electoral process, his personal victory, like Netanyahu's in 1996, was not matched by his party. Likud had won only nineteen Knesset seats, while Labor had won twenty-three. Although Sharon could rely on the support of the two principal religious parties, and a smaller constellation of rightist factions, it soon became apparent that he would not command a viable Knesset majority without Labor's support. Yet the hurdle was not insurmountable. By portraying himself as a "centrist," Sharon during the electoral campaign had already expressed his openness to the formation of another national-unity government. In that posture of centrism, he soon proved himself as wily a tactician on the political terrain as on the battlefield.

Thus, as an inducement to the Labor leadership, Sharon promised to honor all existing diplomatic agreements—essentially the incremental evacuation commitments that Netanyahu and Barak had signed with Arafat during the Clinton years. He further embellished the proposal by offering the defense ministry to Barak, and the foreign ministry to Shimon Peres. Peres was willing to accept on the spot, convinced that he could be a moderating influence in the new government. In an agony of indecision, Barak procrastinated. Finally, in late February, he resigned as Labor chairman, gave up his Knesset seat, and announced that he was retiring from politics altogether. Labor's central committee thereupon voted to join a government of "national unity," and on March 7, 2001, Sharon was sworn in as prime minister of the largest coalition in Israel's history, with twenty-six ministers and fourteen deputy ministers, an executive so large that the table in the cabinet room had to be extended.

Meanwhile, Sharon's political victory was greeted by the media and much of the Arab world with cries of rage and warnings of bloodshed. The European Union governments were more reserved. With studied correctness, they extended Sharon their pro forma congratulations. From Washington, George W. Bush, himself newly installed as United States president, expressed the hope of working productively with Sharon, although he had made clear earlier that he would not follow Clinton's precedent in involving himself directly in the Middle East peace process. Even Yasser Arafat telephoned to congratulate Sharon.

Sharon reciprocated the courtesy, and the two leaders engaged in a brief, amicable conversation. In fact, by the time Sharon held his first cabinet meeting on March 13, 2001, additional terror-suicide bombings had already taken place in Israeli cities. Yet the new prime minister reacted with uncharacteristic restraint. It was the price he had agreed to pay for a national-unity government. Indeed, at his orders, economic sanctions actually were eased in Gaza and the West Bank, and the army reduced the number of its armored units in the territories. Several new border crossings were opened for Palestinian businessmen en route to Israel and to Jordan and Egypt.

Sharon's forbearance was not altogether cosmetic. In mid-March, as he traveled to Washington to meet with Bush and Secretary of State Colin Powell, he was intent on selling himself to the Americans as a diplomatic realist. For their part, Bush and Powell received the prime minister with great cordiality. Although they alluded to the importance of restraint in the Middle Eastern tinderbox, they accepted at face value Sharon's declared interest in achieving détente with the Palestine Authority.

ARAFAT AND SHARON REVERT TO TYPE

Before long, however, it became clear that Yasser Arafat did not intend to act as Sharon's "policeman." He would not seek to quell an intifada that Sharon himself had fueled on the Haram es-Sharif a half-year earlier. By late March 2001, Arab guerrillas were firing on Jewish settlements and Israeli motorists in the West Bank almost on a daily basis. Not all the attackers were residents of Gaza or the West Bank, or even members of Hamas. From Lebanon, many of the cross-border operations were carried out by partisans of Hizballah, who continued to receive their funding and weaponry from Iran and their training in Syrian or north Lebanese bases. But Israeli intelligence had verified that the guerrilla campaign was also being waged increasingly by two of Arafat's personal militias, Tanzim and the al-Aqsa Martyrs Brigade. The attacks typically were launched directly from Gaza and the West Bank or from refugee encampments in Lebanon.

On March 28, then, Sharon felt obliged to send a "message" of his own to the Palestine Authority. Israeli helicopters were dispatched to fire missiles against guerrilla training camps in Ramallah and Gaza. Artillery and rockets also damaged Arafat's private helicopter pad in Gaza and the PA's radio transmitter in Ramallah. Western observers soon noted that Israel's armed forces seemed more intent on targeting Arafat's militias than on striking at the other guerrilla factions. Indeed, the prime minister coupled his "message" with an open warning to Arafat. "Under Barak," he declared, "we gave immunity to the 'A' zones [of Israeli military evacuation], and the Palestine Authority turned them into terrorist safe havens. I shall not repeat that mistake." But Arafat was not intimidated. On March 29, as he returned to Gaza from an Arab summit in Amman, his first order of business was to call for another wave of "reprisals" against Israel.

By mid-spring 2001, Palestinian ambushes, sniping, and bombings, and Israeli counterstrikes, were approaching the threshold of small-scale war. If the guerrillas had the advantage of stealth, the Israelis did not lack for imaginative countermeasures. Perhaps the most effective was a network of paid Arab inform- ers in the occupied territories as well as *mustaribim,* Arabic-speaking Israeli secret agents who provided Israeli intelligence with the location of guerrilla training bases and the whereabouts and schedules of insurgent leaders. Sharon then gave his military free rein to use conventional and unconventional techniques of reprisal, including the widespread use of attack helicopters. On April 12, after Hamas launched a series of mortar barrages on Jewish settlements in the Gaza Strip, an Israeli armored column made good Sharon's threat of ground action against the enclave's "Zone A." Tanks entered the Khan Yunis refugee camp and destroyed numerous Hamas firing emplacements. Two days later, a barrage of Hamas rockets struck S'derot, an Israeli town adjacent to the Gaza Strip. Within hours, Israeli bulldozers were dispatched to Gaza City, flattening houses sus- pected of harboring guerrillas. Armored vehicles then proceeded to cut the Strip's narrow band of coastal territory into segments, barring all movement between them. In response to European and even American protests, Sharon repeated his earlier warning, that "whether Arab areas fall within the categories of A, B, or C, it would be a mistake for terrorists to think that they are safe there."

In mid-April, however, the prime minister agreed temporarily to rein in his armor. He was responding less to foreign protests than to the entreaties of Shi- mon Peres. As foreign minister and senior member of a Labor party that was indispensable to Sharon's coalition, Peres argued for an opportunity to explore a recent offer by the Egyptian and Jordanian governments to resuscitate their suspended diplomatic relations with Israel. They would send their ambassadors back to Tel Aviv if the Israeli government lifted its blockade of Palestinian towns and desisted from "thickening" its settlements in the West Bank. Although Sharon refused to withdraw his tank columns altogether, he did sanc- tion a "breather" to allow Peres to confer with Arafat. The Peres-Arafat meet- ing accordingly took place in the third week of April, at the Erez crossing between Gaza and Israel. It lasted three hours, and its tone was businesslike— and cold. The Palestinian leader disclaimed any intent to promote violence either in the territories or in Israel proper. In fact, he was prepared to suggest a "cease-fire." Yet he reiterated his earlier refusal to serve as "policeman" for Sharon's government.

In this case, Arafat was a man of his word. During late April and May 2001, more than a thousand mortar and sniping attacks were mounted against Jewish settlements in Gaza and the West Bank. Soon the assaults began to target inte- gral Israel. On May 25, in the Israeli coastal town of Hadera, two Palestinians rammed a dynamite-laden automobile into a crowded bus. Besides the Pales- tinians themselves, the explosion killed four Israelis and wounded sixty-three others, many seriously. In the same week, two similar car bombings took place in the heart of Jerusalem. Except for the bombers, no one was killed, but twenty-four Israelis were wounded. At that point, Sharon, meeting in his office with visiting United States Assistant Secretary of State Edward Burns, insisted that he could not exercise "restraint" indefinitely. In addition to the capture or targeted assassination of Palestinian "murderers," he warned, and the selective closure of Israel's borders to commuting Arab labor, Israel's armed forces might have to draw a cordon more tightly and permanently around Palestine's major urban centers.

The prime minister would make good on his threat sooner than he anticipated. On May 31, 2001, Feisal al-Husseini, the Palestinian diplomat and unofficial spokesman for Jerusalem's Arab population, succumbed to a heart attack in his East Jerusalem headquarters at Orient House. The next day, June 1, tens of thousands of Palestinians marched in Husseini's funeral cortege, sobbing, shouting, vowing revenge against Israel for having "martyred" an Arab national hero. It was uncertain if the funeral hastened the subsequent episode of terror bombing; but at 11:00 the same night, an Arab blew himself up at the entrance to the Dolphinarium, a popular seaside Tel Aviv discotheque. The entrance to the dance floor had been crowded with teenagers, many of them from Russian immigrant families. Twenty-two of the youngsters were killed on the spot, and ninety of them were injured, some to die within the next few days. It was the most traumatic episode of civilian carnage in the state's history. A few hours after the massacre, Hamas militia leaders claimed responsibility.

In Tel Aviv the next morning, thousands of Israeli right-wingers demonstrated in the streets, mindlessly setting cars on fire, tearing up paving stones, and—in a mirror image of the mourners at Husseini's funeral—calling for "death to the Arabs." At an emergency cabinet meeting in Jerusalem, Sharon promptly secured agreement to take "definitive" measures against terrorism. The preventive steps this time would not be limited to curfews or to the selective re-occupation of Palestinian cities, or even to the blockade of roads and highways in the West Bank and Gaza. Nor would measures be restricted to the bulldozing of Palestinian homes suspected of harboring terrorists, or to the retaliatory destruction of olive groves. Now all commuting Palestinian laborers, from Gaza and the West Bank alike, were to be barred from entry into Israel. Also closed off was the movement of Palestinians into neighboring Jordan for reasons of work or family visits. The ensuing paralysis of the Palestine economy would ultimately take an even grimmer toll than the bombings, and on Jews and Arabs alike (pp. 1054–56).

In the shorter term, however, even Israel's harshest countermeasures appeared incapable of throttling the spate of suicide bombings. Many of the Hamas and Islamic Jihad perpetrators, explosives packed in belts under their shirts, availed themselves of the open funnel of an undivided Jerusalem and the porous frontier along Israel's coastal waist to move undetected from the West Bank directly into Israel's cities. On August 9, 2001, at the peak of the summertime vacation season, a Palestinian teenager blew himself up in a crowded downtown Jerusalem pizzeria. Six children and thirteen adults were killed instantly, and some ninety other people were injured. Three days later, another suicide bomber touched off an explosion in a Haifa café, injuring more than twenty persons, Israeli Arabs as well as Jews. Successive bomb attacks continued throughout the autumn of 2001, in Jerusalem markets and in Tel Aviv buses, as well as in West Bank Jewish settlements, killing and maiming scores of Israelis.

On November 29, the anniversary of the UN Partition Resolution, a Palestinian blew himself up on a bus en route from Netania to Tel Aviv, killing four people and wounding nine. As Israeli intelligence swiftly determined, the incident had been perpetrated by Arafat's own Fatah party, in cooperation with the Islamic Jihad. More was to come. On December 1, two Palestinians detonated powerful explosive devices in Jerusalem's main pedestrian mall, killing 11 people and injuring 180. Twelve hours later, another 15 Israelis were killed and 45 injured in a suicide bombing on a Haifa bus. Between October 2000 and December 2001, the total of Israelis killed stood at 685, with over 4,500 injured, many of them subsequently to die. Palestinian casualties were estimated as 1,300 killed and 9,700 wounded, most of these in firefights with Israeli military forces. The communal violence plainly was approaching the scale of the 1936–39 "time of troubles" during the British mandate.

For Sharon personally, a watershed in the terror campaign was reached on October 15, 2001. It was then that the seven-member Knesset delegation of the National Union party, a far-right-wing—secular—faction led by Rechavam Ze'evi, announced its withdrawal from the government coalition, accusing Sharon of not dealing ruthlessly enough with Arafat and the Palestine Authority. That same day, Ze'evi booked a hotel room in Jerusalem for a few days of vacation. The second night of his stay, two Palestinian gunmen waylaid him in a hotel corridor and shot him fatally. Ze'evi, aged seventy-five, a father of five and grandfather of eighteen, was a sixth-generation Jerusalemite. He had been a member of the Palmach (p. 234), and was one of the last of the senior officers who had fought in the War of Independence alongside Rabin and Sharon. From 1968 to 1973, as a major general, he had been commander of Israel's central, or coastal, sector. Leaving the army for politics in 1974, Ze'evi founded the Moledet (Homeland) party—subsequently "folded" into the National Union Party—which called expressly for the mass expulsion of Palestinians from the West Bank to Jordan. In 1993, comparing Arafat to Hitler, Ze'evi had staged a hunger strike with two other MKs to protest the signing of the Oslo accord. A swaggering gun toter, periodically visiting the West Bank without bodyguards, he had expressed only disdain for Arab commuting workers, dubbing them "lice."

Although Ze'evi had long been a prime target for Arab guerrillas, no episode in the raging intifada caused Sharon greater shock than the murder of his old comrade. He called another emergency cabinet meeting. With Peres and the Labor members concurring, the assembled ministers unanimously concluded that Yasser Arafat had approved the assassination. Even before that morning, Sharon's blueprint for a future Palestine entity was comparatively grudging: Israel would retain exclusive sovereignty over the totality of Jerusalem, as well as extensive security areas in the West Bank and the "external borders" of a demilitarized Palestine; and self-rule would be offered to only 42 percent of territorial Palestine. But now, with Ze'evi's assassination, Sharon put even this attenuated format on hold. He ordered the army to conduct intimidating forays into the West Bank's major urban centers, the so-called Zone A, that had ostensibly devolved under the direct security control of the Palestine Authority. Israeli tanks and armored troop carriers henceforth conducted periodic raids into the town squares of Ramallah, Nablus, Jenin, Tulkarem, and Bethlehem,

providing cover as Israeli soldiers erected roadblocks and imposed evening curfews on the local residents. Israel's communication with the Palestine Authority
for all practical purposes was suspended.

THE GEORGE W. BUSH ADMINISTRATION:
OVERTURE TO A MIDDLE EAST DIPLOMACY

In the final analysis, it was the tacit support of the United States president that
offered Sharon the leeway to conduct these territorial incursions. George W.
Bush and Sharon had first met in 1998, when Bush, as governor of Texas, visited Israel with a group of fellow governors, and Sharon was Israel's foreign
minister. A born-again Christian, Bush did not trouble to meet Arafat on the
same visit; and later, as president, he rejected Secretary of State Colin Powell's
suggestion for an informal handshake with Arafat on the floor of the UN General Assembly. When Bush invited Sharon as prime minister to the White
House, in March 2001, Arafat received no parallel invitation. Nevertheless, in
October of that year, in the wake of the Israeli cabinet decision virtually to re-
invade Palestine, Sharon decided that a "re-insurance" trip to Washington was
in order.

It was arranged for the second week in November. This time the president
was prepared to tender Sharon a reception even more sympathetic than in the
previous March. This was two months after the United States had suffered the
catastrophic attacks of September 11, 2001, and the tragedy seemed to have
shifted the mood of the American government and people alike. Revulsion at
Moslem terrorism was exacerbated by television and press displays of Palestinian crowds dancing in palpable jubilation (Israel's government had declared an
official day of mourning for the American victims). In the first week of November, however, before Sharon's visit could take place, Palestinian gunmen
opened fire on the bus station of Afula, a middle-sized Israeli town, killing two
civilians and wounding dozens more before being shot dead themselves.
Sharon immediately put off his American visit to December.

As it turned out, the Afula killings were but a prelude to the assault of
December 1, when Jerusalem was hit by the massive double explosions that
left eleven Israelis killed, 180 wounded. Sharon was then en route to Washington for his belated visit with Bush. When he learned of the Jerusalem carnage,
he decided again to reverse course and fly back home. Bush himself then
returned from Camp David, where he had expected to receive Sharon, and
embarked on discussions with his Middle East advisers. The next morning,
while the two governments' Middle East stance was being determined, there
came news of the Haifa bus bombing. At this point, the White House declined
to issue its usual perfunctory call for mutual restraint. Instead, it released a
statement proclaiming Israel's right to defend itself. The president by then had
already accepted an earlier recommendation by Secretary of State Colin Powell
to play a more active role in Israeli-Palestinian peacemaking. Two weeks
before, Bush had approved the secretary's proposal to appoint a special Middle

East envoy, with the task of devising mutual security arrangements between Israel and the Palestine Authority. The person selected for this mission was a senior marine officer, Major General Anthony Zinni, the former chief of America's Central Command, a twenty-six-nation region that included the Middle East.

The Zinni Mission was not the first appointed by Washington to defuse the escalating Palestinian-Israeli violence. In September 2000, at the beginning of the al-Aqsa intifada, and during an otherwise unsuccessful summit meeting attended by Clinton, Arafat, and Barak, all parties had agreed to accept an investigative commission chaired by a respected American ex-senator, George Mitchell, who had acquired previous experience mediating between Protestant and Catholic political factions in Northern Ireland. The Mitchell Commission included former senator Warren Rudman; Suleiman Demirel, a former president of Turkey; Thorbjorn Jaland, the former foreign minister of Norway; and Javier Solana, a Spanish diplomat and the European Union's current high representative for foreign and security policy.

In May 2001, after an extensive round of interviews and investigations in the Middle East, the Mitchell Commission issued a rather anodyne report, blaming Arafat for countenancing the succession of terror bombings, and the Israeli government (now Sharon's government) for its harsh military retaliation against innocent Palestinian civilians, and its encouragement of continued Jewish settlement building in the West Bank. Both sides, the report concluded, should engage in "confidence-building" measures of restraint. The following month, in the wake of the Dolphinarium discotheque bombing (p. 1049), President Bush dispatched CIA Director George Tenet to Israel for consultations on antiterrorism measures. Tenet again recommended that both sides exercise "restraint." Both suggestions, the Mitchell Commission's and Tenet's, predictably evoked dutiful commitments to peace from Arafat and Sharon, assurances that just as predictably soon fell apart.

And now, arriving in Israel on November 26, 2001, Anthony Zinni entered into his own intensive discussions with Israeli and Palestinian leaders. The talks were conducted against a continuing backdrop of suicide bombings, in Jerusalem and Tel Aviv. Within the two and a half weeks after the general's arrival, forty-four more Israelis and sixty-three Palestinians were killed. On December 14, Zinni departed for additional discussions with Egyptian and Jordanian officials. Afterward, he returned to Washington to convey his impressions to Bush, Powell, and Condoleezza Rice, the president's national security adviser.

The general's evaluation was a sobering one. The Israeli-Palestinian confrontation had escalated into a state of low-grade war. Sharon's government was hardly blameless, Zinni acknowledged. Indeed, the Israeli prime minister probably had not relinquished his cherished vision of extending Israel's sovereignty in the territories. At the same time, Arafat had prevaricated in his disclaimer of responsibility for the violence. He had not lifted a finger to dissuade his Fatah loyalists, his personal Tanzim and Force 17 militias, from attacks against Jewish settlers in the territories. It was the general's educated guess, too, that Arafat was implicated in the terror bombing of the civilian population in Israel proper.

Zinni's assessment was given confirmation within days. On January 3, 2002, Israeli naval commandos in the Red Sea stormed a chartered Iranian freighter, the *Karine A*, about three hundred miles from Eilat. It later developed that the United States CIA had helped Israel track the ship, which had embarked from the Iranian port of Bushire. The *Karine A*'s Arab crew surrendered to the Israeli boarding party without a fight. Its cargo was discovered to include some fifty tons of munitions, including Katyusha rockets, antitank missiles, mortars, and sniper rifles. Upon interrogation, the ship's captain acknowledged that his instructions were to sail through the Suez Canal to Alexandria. From there, the weaponry was to be off-loaded to three smaller vessels, which would then proceed toward the Gaza coastline under cover of darkness and float the arms and ammunition ashore in watertight containers.

The evidence of direct Iranian complicity in weapons transfers was not in itself a surprise. The previous spring, in Tehran, Iran's government had hosted a two-day "International Conference for the Support of the Intifada." The event had been attended by leaders of all major Palestinian resistance groups: Hizballah, Hamas, Islamic Jihad, Tanzim, and the al-Aqsa Martyrs Brigade. The Palestine Authority was represented by Arafat himself. Ironically, the PA president earlier had been denounced by the Iranian leadership for his willingness to sign the Oslo accords. But his more recent pledge, to "resume the path of the people" by launching the al-Aqsa intifada, had restored his standing in Iranian eyes. At the conference, Ayatollah Ali Khaminei, the nation's supreme spiritual (and political) leader, bestowed his personal benediction on Arafat. For Israel, meanwhile, if Iranian support for the intifada was an old story, more significant were the documents surrendered by the captain of the *Karine A* on January 3, 2002. These were payment receipts to Iranian suppliers bearing the signatures of PA officials, including Yasser Arafat's. Within the week, the Israeli government was able to display the captured weaponry and its paper trail to the foreign diplomatic community and the foreign press. From his headquarters in Ramallah, meanwhile, Arafat issued a somewhat confused announcement that he was forming an internal investigative panel to "look into" Israeli charges about the *Karine A*.

On January 5, in a White House press conference, George W. Bush let it be known that the Palestine Authority was sufficiently implicated in violence to raise "serious doubts" about Yasser Arafat's credibility as a partner for peace. On that assumption, the president then alluded to an ambitious program for the establishment of a "responsible Palestine entity," with the aim of reaching full agreement for "two states, living side by side." The announcement, which Bush outlined in somewhat greater detail on June 24 of the following year, was to become the basis for the "Road Map" to peace, which was drafted by the State Department and other governments, and later, in June 2003, publicly revealed in its final form (pp. 1063–65).

Although the time frame and its emphasis on Palestinian statehood were not exactly Sharon's cup of tea, Bush's public demand for Arafat's replacement and for the dismantlement of terrorist networks fully reflected Israel's position. The president and his advisers evidently had accepted Sharon's argument that Arafat, as well as the leaders of the various Palestinian militant factions, belonged in the same category with Osama bin Laden, mastermind of the destruction of Manhattan's Twin Towers. For the first time, the White House's Middle East policy was closer to that of Israel's political right than of Israel's political left.

THE RECONQUEST OF PALESTINE

From Ariel Sharon's viewpoint, there now existed sufficient diplomatic leverage for a full-scale military reoccupation of Palestine. The prime minister's strategy was not motivated exclusively by political considerations. By the late winter and early spring of 2002, security concerns would have amply dictated a pulverizing counteroffensive. In March alone, Israel underwent the most terrifying sequence of suicide bombings in its history, with explosions going off almost every other day, leaving 126 civilians killed and 411 wounded, nearly half the casualty total of the entire preceding seventeen months of the al-Aqsa intifada. One of the explosions killed 11 Israelis at Jerusalem's Moment Café, a popular gathering place for members of the Peace Now movement.

On March 27, an even more lethal attack took place in Netania. It was the eve of Passover, and 250 Israelis had arrived for a communal *seder* at the city's Park Hotel, a seaside resort. As the guests took their seats, a twenty-three-year-old Hamas guerrilla wearing a long-haired wig strolled past a security guard at the hotel's main entrance. Unobtrusively entering the dining room where the seder was just beginning, the young man detonated a bomb strapped to his waist. The explosion left 30 people killed and another 140 injured. It was later discovered that the bomber, Abd al-Basseh Odeh, was the son of a prosperous vegetable wholesaler in the West Bank city of Tulkarem. A stream of relatives and friends subsequently called on the father to congratulate him on his son's "martyrdom."

Sharon called yet another emergency cabinet meeting. This one lasted for eight hours. From evidence submitted by military intelligence, it appeared that the terrorists were obtaining access to military-grade explosives. The American-backed Zinni Mission, whose aim was to negotiate mutual security arrangements between Israel and the Palestinian Authority, was palpably foundering. Without a single dissent, therefore, the cabinet gave Sharon the green light for Israel's most formidable military campaign since the 1982 Lebanon war. Codenamed "Operation Defensive Shield," the offensive envisaged nothing less than a full-scale reoccupation of the West Bank, as if "Oslo I" and "Oslo II" had never been signed. On March 29, two days after the Passover massacre, Israeli armored columns rolled into Palestinian cities—Tulkarem, Qalqilia, Bethlehem, Nablus, Ramallah, and Jenin (where they killed some fifty-four heavily armed resisters), as well as a string of neighboring villages and refugee encampments. As the army took up positions at key intersections, its engineers set about constructing fixed emplacements that manifestly were intended for a prolonged stay.

In the course of the reoccupation, moreover, Israeli tanks surrounded Arafat's office compound in Ramallah, only three hundred yards away from the Palestine president's living quarters. Arafat was forbidden to leave this constricted perimeter. As a further precaution, Israeli troops in the Gaza Strip plowed up the runways of the Palestine Authority's newly opened airport, further reducing Arafat's ability to travel to the Arab world and Europe. Meanwhile, Israeli intelligence officers, inspecting the PA's offices, garages, and warehouses, discovered extensive bomb-making facilities together with scores of drums of plasticine explosive, hundreds of Kalashnikov automatic weapons, and stacks of counterfeit Israeli currency in bills of high denominations. They confiscated as well hundreds of documents augmenting the evidence collected earlier from the *Karine A.* In addition to paying for imported weaponry, Arafat evidently had remunerated the suicide bombers' families from his personal slush fund.

In Washington, the government muted its criticism of Sharon's Operation Defensive Shield. Although the State Department called upon Israel to show restraint, the cautionary statements were bracketed with increasingly urgent appeals for the Palestine Authority to take a firm stand against terrorism. Bush's exasperation became particularly evident in the early summer of 2002, when the sequence of suicide bombings reached its crescendo. In a speech on June 24, the president reiterated his assertion that the "peace process requires a new and different Palestinian leadership, so that a Palestinian state can be born. I call on the Palestinian people to elect new leaders, leaders not compromised by terror." Sharon, too, was under pressure within his own governing coalition to have done with the Palestine Authority, to close down PA headquarters in Ramallah, to arrest Arafat and expel him from Palestine. The prime minister was tempted to accept the proposal. He had remained unregenerate in his disdain for the Oslo agreements. A year earlier, in the spring of 2001, following Tehran's "International Conference for the Support of the Intifada," he acknowledged in a newspaper interview that he was prepared at most to recognize a limited, demilitarized Palestine "entity" in a maximum of 42 percent of the West Bank and 70 percent of the Gaza Strip—approximately the formula that Netanyahu had already offered the Palestinians (although Barak subsequently had offered much more).

Yet if Sharon hesitated to repudiate the Oslo accords altogether, or explicitly to reject President Bush's periodic allusions to future Palestinian statehood, it was hardly Washington's mild, cautionary messages that stayed his hand. Neither was it a lack of public support within Israel itself. As early as the summer of 2001, as Sharon's military counterstrikes against the terror bombings became more severe, opinion polls gave the prime minister an approval rating of an unprecedented 62 percent. Nevertheless, Sharon was still hesitant to jeopardize Labor's participation in his national-unity government. Foreign Minister Shimon Peres, in his wide diplomatic experience, understood better than Sharon that public opinion abroad, particularly in Europe, could not be ignored. Repeatedly,

Peres had warned Sharon that exclusive reliance upon a mailed-fist policy, let alone physical reprisals against Arafat himself, would evoke even wider European condemnation. It would also exacerbate the rash of suicide bombings. "Let's say we even assassinate [Arafat]," Peres had cautioned. "What happens next? With all the criticism of Arafat, he is the Palestinian who recognizes the map in which Jordan and Israel exist. In his place will only come Hamas, Islamic Jihad, and Hizballah."

The foreign minister's warnings were prescient. With Arafat holed up in his Ramallah compound and his administrative ministries paralyzed, the Palestine Authority was now incapable of delivering basic public services to its people. Sewage flowed uncontrolled in Palestinian cities, law and order were breaking down, and Arafat himself was relying increasingly on Hamas and Islamic Jihad to provide education and medical care. In July 2002, for the first time since the establishment of the Palestine Authority eight years before, thousands of Gazans took to the street to protest the PA's failure to supply them with jobs. Denied employment in Israel, fully 65 percent of the Strip's population could not support their families. Charges grew of PA lawlessness and corruption. Appeals for reform in Palestinian newspapers grew increasingly urgent. By that time, Hamas and Islamic Jihad suicide bombers were celebrated like rock stars in Gaza and the West Bank. Their "civilian" organizations at least were beginning to fill the vacuum in social services left by the PA.

It was becoming apparent, too, that Sharon's decision to close off all border entry points to the commuting Arab workforce was eroding not only the Palestinian economy but important segments of the Israeli economy. The nation's construction industry and much of its agricultural production had been dependent on this vital Palestinian labor pool. Both sectors now were hard hit. As early as July 2001, the Bank of Israel reported that foreign investment in the country during the first five months of the year had dropped by 59 percent, to $2.2 billion, compared with $5.3 billion during the first five months of 2000. Inhibited by terrorism, moreover, the number of foreign tourists in Israel had dropped by 55 percent during the same period. In the government's dealings with the Palestinians, Peres and his Labor colleagues insisted, surely the carrot ought to accompany the stick. By countenancing the virtual reoccupation of the territories, Sharon in effect was precluding that option.

AN ELECTORAL RECONFIRMATION

As Sharon's Operation Defensive Shield gained momentum, the pressure from Israel's political left became more bitter and strident. Finally, in November 2002, with Peres's reluctant acquiescence, Labor's central committee voted to withdraw the party from the coalition. The reason given was opposition to the proposed government austerity budget, which would have cut social-welfare benefits. Indeed, two of the Orthodox parties, whose constituents had become increasingly dependent on these entitlements, joined Labor in the walkout. But the underlying cause of Labor's defection was consternation at the prime minister's apparently indiscriminate use of military force in Palestine. In any case, deprived of his Knesset majority, Sharon was left with no alternative but to call for new elections. The date was set at January 28, 2003, almost two years ahead of schedule.

For Labor, the first order of business was to select a new chairman as their electoral standard-bearer. This time the party's resurgent left wing, led by Yossi Beilin, settled on Amram Mitzna, the highly respected mayor of Haifa. Mitzna was a native-born Israeli, a former kibbutz member, and a reserve army major general. It was not certain that any other candidate possessed more credible political and security bona fides, or could have made the Labor case more impressively. When measured against the charismatic Sharon, however, Mitzna was a comparative unknown to the Israeli public, and his conciliatory approach to the Palestinians even during the upsurge of guerrilla violence evoked as little popular resonance as had Barak's peace formula two years earlier. Addressing audiences and television interviewers, Mitzna made plain that he favored a maximal separation from the Palestinians. He would evacuate all settlements in Gaza, with or without a formal treaty agreement, and all West Bank settlements that were not at least directly proximate to the Green Line. As for Jerusalem, Jewish neighborhoods would remain under Israeli sovereignty, but the city's predominantly Arab neighborhoods would function under Palestinian political authority. In December 2002, one month before the election, Mitzna saw fit to announce that he would resume negotiations with the Palestinians from the same point at which Barak and Arafat had discontinued their talks at Taba on the eve of the 2001 elections (p. 1043). For large elements of the Israeli public, this final concession appeared to confirm that the Labor leadership was prepared to bargain from weakness.

Indeed, whatever the criticisms of Sharon's performance as head of government—his neglect of Israel's social and economic problems, his apparent indifference to the income gap widening between the nation's upper and lower strata—the Israeli people had always given priority to security issues over economic ones. From their viewpoint, Sharon at least was answering force with force. His Operation Defensive Shield, in its frontal brutality, its armored reoccupation of West Bank cities and towns, its enforced curfews, roadblocks, and travel bans, its assassination of suspected Palestinian terrorists and reprisal destruction of Arab homes and orchards—all constituted a response that the Palestinians evidently understood.

It was in July 2002, as the Palestinian economy lay prostrate, and as the West Bank unemployment rate hovered at an estimated 35 percent (and in Gaza at a starvation-level 50 percent), that the Gazans mounted their street protests against the PA's failures, and Palestinian newspapers amplified their appeals for reform, and for an end to an intifada that had achieved nothing. By January 2003, there appeared tentative indications that the force of the intifada was being blunted. Suicide bombers were being intercepted at a higher rate, as Israel's military-intelligence network of hired Arab informers provided increasingly accurate information about guerrilla infiltration routes. In the evaluation of large segments of Israeli's population, Sharon's bulldozer tactics may indeed have begun taking effect.

This was the American government's assessment, and perhaps its subliminal wish. Having already committed troop contingents to the search for Osama bin Laden in Afghanistan, and preparing then to launch far more extensive military operations against Saddam Hussein in Iraq, Bush and his security advisers had developed an equable, even empathetic appreciation of Ariel Sharon's vigorous response to terrorism. The president had welcomed the Israeli prime minister to Washington four times in the space of two years, and lately seemed prepared to discard his lingering reservations about Operation Defensive Shield. The "hint" resonated with the Israeli people, as well. Moreover, in his reelection campaign, Sharon for the first time expressed his own hints of his implied willingness to countenance a separate Palestinian state, once the Palestine Authority had restored peace and order in the territories. In his pose of flexibility, and surely in the perceived support he was gaining from the American president, the prime minister ingratiated himself even with traditionally moderate elements of the Israeli voting public.

On January 28, 2003, that public went to the polls for the third time in less than four years. The turnout was comparatively low, an apparent reflection of voter fatigue. Only 68 percent of the qualified electorate cast ballots. Nevertheless, the results were starkly revealing. Likud, which had suffered defeat in the 1999 elections, and in the 2001 elections actually had run behind Labor, this time staged a major comeback, doubling its Knesset representation, from nineteen to thirty-eight seats. Conversely, Labor's representation declined to nineteen seats, its lowest level in Israeli history, falling from 20.1 percent of the total vote in 2001 to 14.5 percent in 2003 (Meretz, a Labor "satellite," returned a meager six seats). Indeed, Labor met defeat in all sectors, among veteran citizens and new immigrants alike, rich and poor, Jews of European and non-European origin. Public-opinion surveys were unanimous that, in positioning itself to the left of the national consensus on security issues, the party had suffered a fatal loss of credibility.

As for Sharon, no further political compromises were necessary. Within a month he had cobbled together his Knesset majority. Dominated by Likud, the coalition included the extremist National Union mini-faction, as well as the National Religious party. Yet the prime minister rejected a partnership with Shas, the largest of the religious parties, as well as with the ultra-Orthodox United Torah Judaism. With these rejections, Sharon made possible an alliance with the Shinui (Change) party. As heir to the Democratic Movement for Change (p. 871), and several other moderate-reformist, essentially middle-class factions, Shinui in this latest election had just won an astonishing fifteen seats, thereby emerging as Israel's third-largest party, and an apparent future rival to Labor as a centrist alternative to Likud. On territorial matters, Shinui's chairman, Yosef ("Tommy") Lapid, shared with Sharon a suspicion of the Oslo process, and of Yasser Arafat as a negotiating partner. On domestic issues, however, Lapid and his fiercely secularist Shinui colleagues rejected the very notion of participating in a cabinet with the more militant Orthodox parties—and Sharon had deferred to their wishes. It was the accession of Shinui, in turn, that allowed the prime minister to jettison his marriage of convenience with Labor. With a new centrist-right coalition, he anticipated clear sailing now for his version of an imposed peace.

SHARON BUILDS A FENCE

By the winter of 2003–4, at a time when the threat of full-scale war with neigh-boring Arab countries was proving less serious than infiltration by terrorists, growing numbers of Israelis had come to regard security as dependent less on permanent military occupation of the territories than on physical separation from them. In an incisive analysis published by the Washington Institute for Near East Policy, David Makovsky, a former editor of the *Jerusalem Post*, noted that the reappraisal far predated Sharon's prime ministry. As far back as May 1992, following the murder of an Israeli teenage girl by a Palestinian terrorist from Gaza, Yitzchak Rabin had mooted the notion of "separation" as a strate-gic option. For Rabin, sheer demographic realities warranted that alternative (p. 990), and the more recent spate of guerrilla violence apparently reinforced the need for some sort of physical quarantine. Rabin used the phrase "Israel must take Gaza out of Tel Aviv," that is, the government would have to consider the establishment of two separate national entities. The prime minister's salient diplomatic strategy for accomplishing that goal was his endorsement of the Oslo peace process.

But in October 1994, when Arafat was permitted to enter Gaza and set up his quasi-government there, a string of terrorist incidents occurred within days of each other, including a suicide bombing in Tel Aviv, a shooting in Jerusalem, and the abduction of an Israeli soldier. At a press conference on October 17, therefore, Rabin invoked the notion of physical separation: "We have to decide on separation as a policy," he insisted. "There has to be a clear border." He repeated the formula at greater length in late January 1995, following a guerrilla attack in Beit Lid that killed twenty-one soldiers. On television the next day, he declared: "This path must lead to a separation, although not according to the borders prior to 1967." It was to become the prime minister's "physical disengagement" policy, and was enthusiastically endorsed by most of his Labor colleagues.

Shortly after his January telecast, therefore, Rabin appointed an interminis-terial committee, headed by Moshe Shahal, his police minister and Labor col-league, to explore the most feasible method of building a security-separation barrier. Over the ensuing months, the Shahal Committee succeeded in formu-lating a preliminary blueprint. Before it could be adopted, however, Rabin was assassinated. Afterward, both of Rabin's successors, Peres and Netanyahu, put the barrier idea on hold, although for different reasons. Peres feared that a fence would impede Israeli-Palestinian economic integration, the "New Mid-dle East" that he had always envisaged as the key to regional peace. Netanyahu rejected the idea of separation in deference to the annexationist right-wingers within his government. In any case, the diplomatic process seemed to be inter-mittently alive with the Hebron Accord of 1997 and the—grudging—territorial concessions of the Wye Accord of 1998. As for the Palestinians, they had always been hostile to the fence idea, fearing that it would restrict their access to employment in Israel.

Yet the notion of separation was revived when Ehud Barak became prime minister in 1999. In his election campaign, Barak had forthrightly defined peace in terms of disengagement, and ensured that the official Labor platform included physical separation as an integral feature of a two-state solution. Shortly before departing for the July 2000 Camp David summit, Barak in a television interview reaffirmed his commitment to a barrier between Israel and the independent Palestinian entity. "[The fence] is essential to Israel," the prime minister insisted, "in order to guarantee its Jewish identity . . . and it is [equally] essential to the Palestinian nation in order to foster its national identity . . . without being dependent on the State of Israel." In fulfillment of that scenario, Barak appointed Deputy Defense Minister Ephraim Sneh as chairman of a committee that would devise a partition line between Israel and the West Bank. Comprising senior technocrats from several ministries, Sneh's team proceeded to refine the earlier Shahal Committee's blueprint. This latest version provided for an array of crossing points between the West Bank and Israel that would remain open in times of quiet.

Moreover, the West Bank barrier, like a much smaller Gaza barrier that Barak had countenanced and was even then in the process of construction, was envisaged as a multicomponent defense layout. A wall would function merely as its most visible feature. Other features would include a bulldozed buffer zone, patrol roads, barbed-wire fences, ditches, and, above all, a series of high-tech surveillance posts. In effect, the plan served as a compromise between separation and integration. But political circumstances almost immediately aborted the compromise. The subsequent failure of the Camp David summit and the eruption of the al-Aqsa intifada in September 2000, together with Arafat's rejection of the generous Clinton proposal in December of that year, virtually destroyed Israeli hopes of a foreseeable peace. The sequence of events simultaneously underscored the urgency of a complete physical separation. It was thus ironic that Sharon, succeeding Barak in February 2001, was the prime minister who began actual construction on the West Bank fence. Indeed, as the number of suicide bombings originating from the West Bank increased, the project appeared increasingly logical. All the more so as the Gaza fence, originally built in the mid-1990s, but rebuilt in 2001 with myriad new electronic-surveillance improvements, proved successful in blocking virtually all guerrilla infiltration (although not rocket firings) from the south.

On the other hand, Jewish settlers in the Palestinian territories regarded the construction of a "security fence" with unalloyed horror. Israel Harel, secretary-general of the "Yesha" (Judea-Samaria-Gaza) Settlement Council, stated as far back as Rabin's January 23, 1995, telecast address: "We will prevent with our very bodies the construction of a separation barrier. . . . It would divide the Land of Israel, and that is impermissible." Yet the settlers' anxieties were existential as well as ideological. They feared being left on the wrong side not only of a fence but of a future border. Actually, their concerns were unwarranted. As the fence began to take shape, it became clearer that the major Jewish settlement blocs, those that had been constructed in direct proximity to the pre-1967 Green Line, would be protected. For that reason alone, public-opinion polls consistently revealed overwhelming approval of the fence concept. In late 2002, therefore, still in his first term as prime minister, Sharon authorized work on the West Bank security barrier to proceed at full speed.

Attitudes toward the construction of the West Bank fence were changing in

Washington as well. George W. Bush's Middle East advisers at first opposed the plan, especially in mid-2003, when they were persuaded by Mahmoud Abbas, the PA prime minister, that Israel's underlying purpose was to encircle the West Bank and annex large portions of it. But when Arafat in his obstructionism proceeded to subvert Abbas's moderate prime ministry (p. 1072), Bush's advisers began to reconsider the fence. In the second half of 2003, Washington initiated discreet negotiations with the Sharon government. These took the form of talks between Condoleezza Rice, Bush's national security adviser, and Dov Weisglass, Sharon's personal envoy, to ensure that the fence inflicted minimal human suffering on the Palestinians while ensuring Israel's security.

The low-key approach by and large was successful. In mid-April 2004, months of "fence diplomacy" culminated in a Washington summit between Bush and Sharon. The president, conscious of his forthcoming re-election campaign, and intent on making inroads in the traditionally Democratic Jewish electorate, openly acknowledged that it was "unrealistic" to expect a complete evacuation of "every existing major Israeli population center" in the West Bank. Clinton's peacemaking efforts during 2000–2001 had included approximately the same acknowledgment, but rather less flagrantly for domestic political advantage. Nevertheless, Bush reminded Sharon that "the barrier erected by Israel should be a security rather than a political barrier, should be temporary rather than permanent, and should not prejudice any final-status issues including borders." Most important, in charting the fence, the Israelis were enjoined to exert maximum effort to reduce the barrier's impact on the great majority of Palestinian civilians.

But whatever its actual configuration or ultimate intent, by the latter months of 2004, the fence, snaking in a zigzag pattern along the northeastern and Judean quadrants of the West Bank, was beginning to fulfill its security purposes. Where the fence did not exist, there had been 165 incidents of infiltration during 2000–2003. Of these, 58 had resulted in suicide bombings that killed 430 Israeli civilians. (Of the remaining incidents, 95 were suicide bombings that resulted in no Israeli deaths, while 12 infiltrators were intercepted before they could reach their targets.) By contrast, in those segments of the West Bank fence that were completed between mid-2003 and mid-2004, infiltrations had been reduced dramatically, to less than 10, or approximately one-thirtieth the number that had taken place in earlier years. It is noteworthy that with the apparent success of the fence concept, defense planners did not focus their principal attention on the dangers of tactical rocketry.

ALTERNATE SPONSORSHIPS FOR PEACE

However seemingly effective in protecting Israel's civilian population, Sharon's military and economic counteroffensive, and his later construction of the security barrier, inevitably exerted a debilitating impact on guerrillas and innocent Palestinians alike. The ordeal of these Arab civilians was publicized widely in the West, and specifically in Western Europe. Throughout Sharon's tenure of office, European media provided graphic accounts of Israeli tanks and helicopters blasting away at Palestinian guerrillas (almost invariably dubbed "resistance fighters") holed up in urban casbahs or in refugee shantytowns. In the spring of 2002, after the Passover bombing at Netania's Park Hotel, European journalists described Israel's retaliatory quarantine of Arafat's compound in Ramallah in minute detail, together with the actions of hundreds of foreign volunteers, most of them young people from Italy and France, who had been organized by the Palestinian "International Solidarity Movement" and "Grass-Roots International for the Palestinian People" as a protective shield for the "old warrior" (as BBC reporters tended to describe Arafat). The protesters demonstrated in front of Israeli tanks and attempted to walk through Israeli military cordons. One of them was inadvertently killed by an Israeli bulldozer.

On European television screens, moreover, the vast unemployment in the occupied Palestinian territories was depicted less in terms of statistics than in portrayals of Arab families under Israeli military curfew, of sick Arab children and pregnant mothers standing in line for hours at Israeli army checkpoints, seeking access to Israeli hospitals. Back in September 2001, a UN-sponsored World Conference against Racism, held in Durban, South Africa, condemned Zionism as "based on racial superiority," and stigmatized Israel above all other nations as a "racist, apartheid state" that was guilty of crimes against humanity (the United States delegation joined Israel's in walking out of the conference). A Belgian court subsequently declared its willingness to put Ariel Sharon on trial for human-rights abuses committed twenty years before, in Sabra and Shatila. The Danish foreign ministry, after examining the Likud background of an Israeli ambassador-designate, refused to accredit him. The Portuguese novelist José Saramago, a Nobel laureate, writing in El País, a prominent Madrid newspaper, described Israel's actions in the Palestine territories as "a crime comparable to Auschwitz." In an interview with the Egyptian newspaper Al-Ahram, an Oxford professor of literature, Thomas Paul, suggested that Jewish settlers on the West Bank and Gaza were "Nazis" who should be "shot dead." In April 2002, an open letter to Britain's left-liberal Guardian, signed by 120 university academics across Europe, asked the European Union and the European Science Foundation to impose a moratorium on grants to Israeli researchers.

In the late spring of 2003, an EU poll of 7,500 Europeans revealed that 59 percent of its respondents considered Israel the single gravest threat to world peace, exceeding even Iran or North Korea. It was the EU survey, in turn, that impelled Polly Toynbee, the Guardian's diplomatic columnist, to observe:

> For the Left, Israel was once Jerusalem the Golden, Zionist banners fluttered on peace marches, young idealists worked in socialist kibbutzim, filled with all the earnest hopes [of people of goodwill]. . . . Now the Left feels all the more betrayed by Ariel Sharon, war criminal, igniting the intifada by striding into the al-Aqsa mosque and using the trouble he caused to seize power.

Toynbee's evaluation of European disenchantment was perceptive. For the Continent's liberals and socialists, Zionism had become a dream denied, a movement obstensibly collapsing into militarism, ethnic chauvinism, and religious fanaticism.

European efforts to defuse the Israel-Palestine impasse obviously could not ignore the indiscriminate mayhem inflicted on Israeli civilians by Arab terror attacks. Miguel Moratinos, the EU representative in Israel, had conferred many times with Arafat in an effort to persuade the PA president to choke off the rash of suicide bombings. Germany's Foreign Minister Joschka Fischer, visiting the Middle East shortly after the Dolphinarium bombing, had berated Arafat unmercifully for the latter's failure to take firm action against terrorism. In private consultations with Arafat, Britain's Prime Minister Tony Blair reiterated Europe's horror at the carnage inflicted on innocent civilians, whether Palestinian or Israeli.

By the same token, the Europeans were aghast at the economic sinkhole the Palestine Authority was fast becoming. Since the onset of the Oslo accords, the EU governments had been pouring vast amounts of money into this state-in-the-making. The actual level of funds committed through June 1998 alone was $3.5 billion, of which $2.5 billion had already been disbursed. Yet a significant proportion of this transfusion was vitiated by PA corruption and Arafat's inability or unwillingness to take confidence-building measures. In February 2003, the International Monetary Fund conducted an audit of the Palestine Authority's expenditures and reported that some $900 million in public funds had been diverted to a special bank account controlled solely by Arafat and his PA economic adviser. That same year, a team of American accountants hired by the PA's own finance ministry confirmed that at least $1 billion of the Authority's funds had been deposited in a coded portfolio, and "virtually none of it was [used] for the Palestinian people." (In October 2003, the French public prosecutor opened a money-laundering probe of Suha Arafat, wife of the PA president, for untaxed transfers of $1.27 million from a numbered Swiss bank account to Mrs. Arafat's bank in Paris.)

Accordingly, in May 2003, it was the combination of Palestinian guerrilla violence, PA corruption, and Israel's unsparing military and economic reprisals that accelerated a series of conferences in Geneva between the members of the "Quartet"—that is, the UN secretary-general, the EU Foreign and Security Policy Commission, and the Russian and United States governments. The meetings solidified a consensus to establish a "Road Map" for Israel-Palestine peace. The Quartet's decision was based on three assumptions. First, the Palestine Authority would have to clean up its act, instituting a regime of strict financial accountability. Second, the economic and strategic interests of both Europe and the United States required a peaceful accommodation between Israelis and Palestinians, for the Middle Eastern confrontation in earlier decades already had proved volatile enough to generate international ramifications—in 1956, 1967, 1973, and 1982. Third, Israelis and Palestinians, like other small nationalities before them, were marinated in too much insecurity and reciprocal hatred to negotiate a lasting accommodation on their own. The Road Map for a settlement would have to be firmly "recommended" by more "objective" parties, those with heavier diplomatic clout and deeper financial pockets—in effect, by the Quartet.

As subsequently refined by the Quartet, the Road Map incorporated features of the Oslo accords, the Mitchell Report, and the sequential evacuations earlier accepted by Arafat and Prime Ministers Peres, Netanyahu, and Barak. Yet the plan transcended its predecessors, for it was based specifically on the principle of two independent states functioning side by side, a goal that former agreements had never officially endorsed but left open for negotiations between the Palestine Authority and Israel. But to accomplish this end result, the Palestine Authority would have to act decisively against terror; and Israel, for its part, would have to commit itself not only to accept "a democratic Palestinian state" as its neighbor, but to freeze, and then substantially to abandon, the construction of new Jewish settlements in the territories, based on the foundations of the Madrid Conference, on the principle of "land for peace," and on the UN Security Council's Resolutions 242, 338, and 397, as well as on agreements previously reached by the parties themselves.

Adhering closely to proposals formulated by the Middle East staffers of the United States State Department, the Quartet then laid down a "timeline" for compliance. In Phase I, beginning immediately in May 2003, the Palestine Authority would institute an unconditional cessation of violence, organize responsible security services, and resume security cooperation with Israel and its Arab neighbors. The PA would be obliged as well to undertake comprehensive political and financial reform, producing the draft of a constitution and conducting open elections. Israel, in turn, would refrain from deportations, attacks on civilians, and confiscations or demolitions of Palestinian homes and property. Most important, Israel would withdraw from Palestinian areas occupied since September 28, 2000, that is, since the beginning of the al-Aqsa intifada, and refrain from expanding all new settlements built since March 2001. These measures would be monitored by the Quartet.

In Phase II, the "transitional" phase, all efforts would be focused on creating provisional borders for the independent Palestinian state as a way station to a permanent-status settlement. This transitional phase would commence in June 2003, after Palestinian elections and the formation of a viable Palestinian government, and end in December of the same year with the declaration of an independent state within its "provisional" borders. If these goals were met, the Quartet would then undertake to "support Palestinian economic recovery," and to convene an international conference of all Arab states, with the view of concluding a comprehensive Middle East peace between all the remaining belligerents, including measures for regional water, trade, and other economic agreements.

In the final stage, Phase III, the Quartet at the outset of 2004 would review and help consolidate the establishment of Palestinian governmental institutions and security arrangements. At the same time, the Quartet would endorse, "in consultation with the parties," the agreement for an independent Palestinian state, and launch a process leading to a final-status treaty by 2005, including the decisive configuration of borders and settlements, an "agreed, just, fair, and realistic solution to the refugee issue," and a resolution of the status of Jerusalem that would take into consideration "the political and religious concerns of both sides, and protection of the religious interests of Jews, Christians, and Muslims worldwide."

It was a tidy, seemingly unexceptionable blueprint.

By spring 2003, under mounting pressure from the Quartet (and specifically from Washington), neither Arafat nor Sharon was inclined any longer to raise serious objections to the Road Map. Even the politically loaded references—the end of occupation, the freezing of Jewish settlement activity, the solution of the refugee and Jerusalem issues—were phrased in sufficiently general terms to allow both sides to accept the document's parameters. In almost every paragraph, after all, the Road Map managed to link its final-status objectives to Palestinian and Israeli "negotiations" to "consultations between the parties," to "international conferences." Obviously, there was ample precedent for Sharon and Arafat to maneuver, to procrastinate, to interpret, to insist that the other side had not lived up to its commitments. Domestically, too, Sharon discerned political advantage in adopting a stance of moderation. It might regain Labor's support for his diplomacy.

Thus, in March 2003, upon Arafat's agreement to appoint a known moderate, Mahmoud Abbas, as prime minister of the Palestine Authority (p. 1073), George W. Bush was optimistic enough to add a two-day Middle East visit to his scheduled trip to Europe and Russia. In anticipation of the president's arrival, on June 2, Sharon as a gesture of goodwill ordered the release of 942 Palestinian political prisoners. The atmosphere of compromise extended to Cairo, where Bush on June 3 first met with the government leaders of Egypt, Saudi Arabia, Jordan, and Bahrein, and with Palestinian Prime Minister Abbas. All these figures announced their support for the Road Map and promised to cut off financial transfers to "terrorists." The next day, Bush headed to Aqaba, Jordan, to confer directly with Sharon and Abbas, both of whom reaffirmed their commitment to the Road Map.

To underscore that commitment, Sharon and Abbas met in Jerusalem on July 1, 2003, to hold a ceremonial, if much belated, signing of the Road Map. The event was televised throughout the Middle East in Arabic and Hebrew. Abbas agreed that violence between their two peoples had gone on too long. Sharon, as a tangible gesture of his own, ordered Israeli troops pulled out of Bethlehem and full security control of the city returned to the Palestine Authority. At the same time, following a carefully drafted script, Washington announced the delivery of a $50-million aid package to Abbas, to help in rebuilding the PA's demolished infrastructure. Was this, then, the beginning of authentic peace? Even the most optimistic of its participants wondered if the Road Map actually had a chance when so many of its previous incarnations had turned out to be mirages.

THE BULLDOZER
AS STATESMAN

OVERTURE TO A TACTICAL WITHDRAWAL

The early prognosis for the Road Map at best was guarded. From Gaza, intermittent rocket attacks continued against Israeli border towns. From the West Bank, suicide bombers continued their attempt to infiltrate Israel's cities. For his part, offering lip service to the document's terms, Sharon from the moment of signature appeared equally intent upon violating its spirit. Far from calling a halt to the growth of new Jewish settlements in the territories, the prime minister allowed construction to proceed on the West Bank in the guise of "natural growth." Neither did he honor his promise to Bush and the other members of the Quartet to dismantle some 105 skeletal outposts built deep in Palestinian territory after March 1, 2001. As the months went by, his government continued to haggle with Washington about the proper interpretation of a settlement freeze, insisting that the Road Map did not bar construction within existing "built-up areas," but only outside them. The disclaimer was without merit. The Quartet's terminology was specific in banning construction both within and outside "built-up" areas.

The example of Ma'aleh Adumim was typical. In late November 2004, Sharon announced that Israel was preparing to construct 3,500 new housing units within the "municipal boundaries" of this West Bank town, a community that had been developing for some thirty years just over the Green Line, adjacent to Greater Jerusalem. The government's plan was to house up to 14,000 new settlers in Ma'aleh Adumim. In fact, the projection of large municipal boundaries around smaller communities was by then a standard Israeli device to create the illusion that new construction was merely a process of "thickening" existing settlements. Thus, the official municipal boundaries established for Ma'aleh Adumim were grandiose, stretching nearly to the Palestinian city of Jericho. Even as late as spring 2005, its population of 32,000—the largest Jewish community in the West Bank—occupied only about 15 percent of the town's "official" area.

Given Ma'aleh Adumim's proximity to Greater Jerusalem, moreover, the passions it evoked were intense among both Israelis and Palestinians. The Sharon government wanted the construction to provide contiguity for the outlying Jewish population between East Jerusalem and the West Bank. The prime minister was adamant on this point. "It is the Israeli position," he had declared in April 2004, during a visit to Washington, "that the major Israeli population centers will remain in Israel's hands under any future final-status agreement, with all related consequences." George W. Bush meekly concurred. In November 2004, writing to Sharon on the eve of the American congressional elections, the president noted that it was "unrealistic," even in the longer term, to expect a complete evacuation of every "existing major Israeli population center" in the West Bank.

Two and a half years earlier, in despair at the Likud government's evident intransigence, Yossi Beilin, leader of Labor's contingent of "doves," and the original architect of the Oslo process (pp. 991–92), had been hard at work devising an alternate territorial scenario. Using the parameters suggested by Clinton in his last-moment December 2000 proposal to the Israelis and Palestinians, Beilin initially conducted his—private, unofficial—negotiations with the former PA information minister, Yasser Abed Rabbo. Their meetings continued for eighteen months, in both Jerusalem and Geneva, and in the early autumn of 2003 the two men unveiled their peace formula. Under the "Geneva Accord," Israel would commit itself in advance, rather than in gradual "transitional" phases, to yield fully 98.5 percent of the West Bank (as opposed to the 94 to 96 percent proposed by Clinton). The formula envisaged withdrawal from two large, established communities, Ariel (population seventeen thousand) and Efrat (population seven thousand), key ganglia of smaller, outlying communities that, once deprived of their cores, would similarly begin emptying out.

In short, the Geneva document proposed Israel's eventual relinquishment of some 109,000 Jews, nearly half the West Bank's total, either to be withdrawn from the emergent fence's protective envelope or (less likely) to stay on, but under Palestinian control. Even those 110,000–115,000 Jews remaining under Israeli political rule immediately beyond the Green Line would reside on a far more attenuated strip of West Bank land than formerly; and the Palestine Authority would be compensated for this strip through a "land swap" elsewhere along the common border, an innovation that originally had appeared in the Clinton plan. The Geneva Accord also reflected the Clinton proposal in its somewhat nebulous provisions for Palestinian refugee compensation and for a token "reunion" of a few thousand Palestinian families. Predictably, Ariel Sharon dismissed the Geneva blueprint with a sulfurous blast. A final-status commitment on frontiers before gauging the consequences of a staged withdrawal, he warned, would be "suicidal," "catastrophic," for Israel.

Yet, at the same time, the prime minister was not oblivious to the likelihood that permanent Israeli sovereignty over the Gaza Strip and even 40 percent of the West Bank (his original blueprint) was becoming unviable. On May 27, 2003, he acknowledged publicly that continued "occupation" of the Palestinian territories was "a terrible thing for Israel and for the Palestinians [which] . . . cannot continue indefinitely." If the statement aroused shock among the parties of the far right, it was no more than an experienced soldier's unsentimental appraisal of evolving demographic realities. By then, the approximately 225,000 Israeli settlers in the West Bank, the 190,000 in East Jerusalem, and the 9,000 in the Gaza Strip represented a mere 10 percent of the territories' Arab population (2.9 million in the West Bank, 200,000 in East Jerusalem, 1.2 million in the Gaza Strip). The asymmetry was becoming more evident every year. So were the voices of protest within Israel. As early as February 2002, more than one hundred senior reserve officers, from colonel up to the rank of major general, published their intention of refusing to serve in the territories. Israel's military rule over a predominantly Arab population, insisted the signatories, was tantamount to "dominating, expelling, starving, and humiliating an entire people," and was "leading to the corruption of all Israeli society."

Moreover, as the intifada smoldered on intermittently into 2003 and even 2004, and Peace Now demonstrations became a perennial feature of the national landscape, it appeared for the first time that a majority of Israelis was becoming reconciled to a substantial disentanglement from the territories. An *HaAretz* poll of February 2004 suggested that 64 percent of Israelis believed that the government should unilaterally withdraw at least from the hilltop settlements that were not clustered directly adjacent to the Green Line. There was evidence, too, that a growing number of Likud members, even Likud ministers in Sharon's cabinet, were beginning to accept a less maximalist territorial agenda. Ehud Olmert, former Likud mayor of Jerusalem and lately deputy prime minister in Sharon's second government, acknowledged in December 2003 that the cabinet was coming to grips with hard demographic facts, and would probably not hold on to the smaller Jewish settlements deep in Judea and Samaria.

Olmert was speaking for Sharon. If the prime minister had not mellowed ideologically over the years, he was acquiring at least a more seasoned experience in both the potentialities and the limitations of statecraft. Above all, he had grasped more readily than had his Likud predecessors, Shamir and Netanyahu, the crucial importance of retaining the support of the United States. In George W. Bush's second term, the president's key foreign-policy aides, Secretary of State Condoleezza Rice and National Security Adviser Stephen Hadley, were becoming increasingly (if privately) critical of Israel's counterterrorism actions, the helicopter rocketing of suspected guerrillas, the checkpoints and curfews deep within the Palestinian territories, the armored incursions into Palestinian towns, the seizure and prolonged "administrative" imprisonment of eight thousand Palestinian militants (of whom some two thousand were confirmed terrorists). Sharon's latest trip to Washington took place in April 2005. At a joint press conference, Bush reiterated his commitment to the central principles of the Road Map, and his expectation of a reciprocal acknowledgment from "both Israelis and Palestinians."

In fact, the prime minister by then was preparing his own preliminary, and dramatic, gesture of reciprocity.

A POLITICAL RECONFIGURATION

From the inception of his own second term of office, in February 2003, Ariel Sharon had been giving heed to the cautionary advice of his military advisers. Defense Minister Shaul Mofaz and other senior officials agreed that one sector of Israeli occupation, the acutely impoverished Gaza Strip, had become a snake pit of refugee desperation and fury. Measuring just twenty-seven miles in length and five miles in width, overflowing with some 1.2–3 million Palestinian refugees and their descendants, and lacking in significant Jewish historical associations, the sector had been regarded as expendable as early as the "Oslo I" agreement in 1994, when Gaza City had been transformed into Yasser Arafat's provisional capital. Yet, even under the early Oslo peace process, the fate of a thin necklace of twenty-one Jewish settlements in Gaza, most of them located in the "Katif Bloc," in the Strip's southwest corner, had been reserved for final-status negotiations.

It was the government of Menachem Begin that had originally encouraged the establishment of these Jewish outposts, essentially as a land swap for the twelve hundred Jewish settlers of Yamit, in the Sinai Peninsula, when Israel returned this little cluster of farm colonies to Egypt in 1982 (p. 887). Doubtless these initial Yamit evacuees accepted their transplantion to Gaza for reasons of undiminished Zionist idealism. So did approximately two thousand Jewish religionists who later joined them. But the majority of Gaza's nine thousand Jewish settlers were responding to a more pragmatic compulsion. For them, the Katif Bloc's newly built villas, quiet streets, and flourishing schools evoked an older, more innocent time in Israel's history. During the ensuing years, guarded by the army, they could leave their doors unlocked, and parents remained unconcerned about where their children were at night. Many inhabitants, former residents of Israel's charmless lower-middle-class towns, occasionally referred to their Gaza communities as a "Garden of Eden."

More problematic, however, in the same period of the 1980s when the Katif Bloc was taking root, was the relationship between Jews living in integral Israel and Arabs living in the Gaza Strip. Over the years, the approximately sixty thousand Arabs who commuted from Gaza to Israel had become an inseparable and routine presence in the Israeli landscape. As described by the *HaAretz* correspondent Aluf Benn:

> They found employment in the Jewish nation's municipal garbage-disposal and street-cleaning services, in gasoline stations, restaurant kitchens, citrus plantations, vegetable fields, and construction sites. Assembly points for their services (distastefully called "slave markets") flourished at the entrances to Israel's cities, where a large proportion of Gaza's commuting Arabs depended upon local Israeli *padrones* to pick them up for daily work. Indeed, the main road from Gaza to Ashkelon and northward was one long traffic jam of Arab job-seekers. Vanquished, passive, hangdog in their demeanor, they paid the price of defeat in the Israeli marketplace.

In those circumstances, the establishment of Gaza's Jewish settlements did not seem a precarious enterprise. "The [Strip's] Arabs," recalled Aluf Benn, "who had not even been recognized yet as 'Palestinians,' accepted everything back then." True, Gaza was crowded and squalid, Benn acknowledged, but its Arab inhabitants seemed comparatively quiescent during the first decades of Israeli rule, even reasonably grateful for their new and better-paying employment opportunities in the Jewish state. In December 1987, when the first intifada began in Gaza, should the Israelis really have been alarmed when thousands of the sector's Arabs erupted in vehement protest demonstrations, some of them becoming ardent recruits of Hamas and Islamic Jihad guerrilla confederations? Possibly not even then, for the vortex of the uprising appeared to be shifting to the West Bank. Between December 1987 and the Rabin-Arafat "Declaration of Principles" in September 1993, some three hundred Palestinians were killed by the Israeli army in the Gaza Strip, against over twice that many in the West Bank; and during the Oslo era, between September 1993 and September 2000, when Gaza had come under the governance of the Palestine Authority, a comparatively "modest" total of 92 Palestinians were killed in the Strip, against 203 in the West Bank.

It was only when the second, al-Aqsa, intifada was winding down, in 2003, as Sharon's Operation Defensive Shield devolved into a semipermanent military presence around the cities and along the principal road intersections of the West Bank, that the numbers and proportions of Arab dead and injured mounted again in Gaza. This time, however, the violence took the form less of guerrilla penetration into integral Israel—the Gaza "fence" by then had effectively sealed off these incursions—than of a dramatic increase of Qassam rocket firings into the Strip's Katif Bloc of Jewish settlements, and subsequently into such Israeli frontier communities as S'derot, along the Gaza border. Since the beginning of the al-Aqsa intifada, some four thousand mortar shells and rockets launched from the Strip had fallen on these border towns. To flush out the guerrillas' firing nests, the Israeli army was obliged to increase its incursions into the Strip's refugee casbahs. Although the military command was discreet about its casualties, the physical and psychological attrition among the troops in Gaza was becoming serious. It was also becoming counterproductive. Even for an "imperialist" like Sharon, the evidence was mounting that the Gaza sinkhole had largely exhausted its strategic value. It was losing its political value as well, for the majority of Jews living in Israel proper did not attribute sentimental importance to this congested and volatile stretch of coastal land. In the spring of 2003, therefore, with the concurrence of his key military and political advisers, Sharon discreetly began laying the groundwork for an evacuation of Gaza's Jewish settlements, together with a scattering of rickety "hilltop" emplacements deep in the West Bank.

In making this decision, the prime minister was aware that he would face difficulties with the ardent right-wingers in his own Likud party, as well as among the Knesset's religious factions. Indeed, in their party conclaves, the Likud rank and file voted to stand fast in all the territories. Public-opinion surveys among the Israeli population at large, however, conveyed a different reaction. The latest poll, in April 2004, revealed that 73 percent of those queried favored relinquishment of the Gaza settlements. For Sharon, it was evident that nothing was to be gained by procrastination, and much to be gained in increased goodwill on the part of the Bush administration, which was exerting quiet pressure for an Israeli gesture of moderation. If Palestinian hostility and desperation could be mitigated, the argument went, without endangering Israel's basic security, the better the chances were for the emergence of a more temperate and trustworthy alternative to Arafat's political leadership.

In May 2004, therefore, Sharon introduced a Knesset resolution proposing unilateral disengagement from the Gaza Strip by late July of the following year. The prime minister warned his cabinet that he would regard disloyalty on this issue as tantamount to a vote of no-confidence in his leadership. Indeed, he soon made good on the threat. On June 4, 2004, he dismissed two National Union ministers, the ultra-rightists Avigdor Lieberman and Binyamin Elon, for their opposition to Gaza withdrawal. Two days later, the Knesset accepted Sharon's resolution by a two-thirds majority, although over the opposition of a third of the Knesset's Likud members, and of all the members of the religious parties.

In the following months, as the—preliminary—July 2005 deadline approached for evacuation of the Gaza settlements, Sharon ignored persistent appeals from Likud and Orthodox MKs to hold a popular referendum on the issue, and invited the resignation of other cabinet members who appeared to be wavering. Those who did resign, often on the pretext of voting against the government budget, included Yosef ("Tommy") Lapid, whose centrist Shinui party regarded withdrawal from Gaza as premature in the absence of reciprocal gestures from Arafat; Natan Scharansky, on the same grounds; and finally, Binyamin Netanyahu, Likud's minister of finance, who after initially supporting Sharon on the Gaza withdrawal, thought better of his stance at the last moment, and on August 9, 2005, gave up his cabinet seat.

These defections normally would have robbed the prime minister of his Knesset majority. But six months earlier, on January 10, 2005, he had availed himself of an alternate political weapon. For most of Sharon's first term, from 2001 to 2003, Shimon Peres, elder statesman of the Labor party, had been pressing the prime minister to commit himself to the dismantlement of the Gaza settlements. By his second term, in agreeing finally to take this step, Sharon would have preferred to have the support of Likud and his coalition partners. In the summer of 2004, however, failing to mobilize their allegiance, he entered into serious coalition negotiations with Peres and the Labor leadership. Neither side made far-reaching commitments to the other's territorial or domestic agenda. Labor's left wing actually would have favored a maximal evacuation of the West Bank as well as Gaza, and a substantial shift of financial resources to domestic social-welfare programs (pp. 1096–97). The evacuation of the Gaza settlements, together with a cluster of West Bank hilltop outposts, was their one issue of congruence. For the time being, however, it was enough for leaders of both parties. On January 10, 2005, upon being assured a senior cabinet partnership as deputy prime minister, as well as six other portfolios for his party colleagues, Peres led Labor's Knesset faction return to Sharon's coalition. The prime minister now had repaired his governing majority.

JEWLESS IN GAZA

Even earlier, another political development had allayed Sharon's reservations about the Gaza evacuation. This one occurred on the Palestinian side. On October 25, 2004, during a meeting with his confidants in his Ramallah office, Yasser Arafat suddenly turned pale and began vomiting blood. His condition deteriorated in the following days, and he experienced periods of unconsciousness. With Israeli government permission, the PA president was transferred to a hospital in Amman, Jordan. There he received treatment by a succession of physicians, including specialists rushed in from Egypt and Tunisia. His condition steadily worsened, however, and the PA cabinet decided to accept an offer by France's President Jacques Chirac to have Arafat flown to Paris for treatment. On October 31, the patient was put aboard a French air force transport and duly carried off from Amman to Paris, where he was admitted to a French military hospital the same day.

Within the week, Arafat was diagnosed as suffering from "idiopathic thrombocytopenic purpura," a traumatic decrease of red-cell platelets. Despite a series of blood transfusions, the seventy-five-year-old PA president lapsed into a coma. On November 11, he died. Although rumors about the cause of death (most of them originating in Israel) ranged from AIDS to liver cirrhosis to ricin poisoning, Arafat's widow forbade an autopsy. Professing security concerns, the Israeli government in turn refused Arafat's oft-expressed wish to be buried in Jerusalem's al-Aqsa Mosque. Instead, following a state funeral in Cairo attended by a gathering of Arab potentates and presidents, his body was "temporarily" interred within his former headquarters at Ramallah.

Arafat's death was a pivotal event that was greeted with ill-concealed relief by Sharon and his political advisers. If the reaction was more guarded in Washington, it was nevertheless an open secret that the Bush administration similarly thought the moment propitious for alternate, more moderate Palestinian leadership. Both governments, moreover, Israeli and American, had identified that alternative. It seemed to be Mahmoud Abbas, the veteran PLO "foreign minister." Palestinian-born, Abbas had moved with his refugee family to Syria after the rise of Israel. After graduating from the University of Damascus, he went on to earn a doctorate in history at Moscow's Institute of Oriental Studies. Subsequently joining Arafat's Fatah party, Abbas won a reputation as an ingratiating spokesman for the Palestinian cause. At the White House peace accord with Israel, on September 13, 1993, it was he who signed the "Declaration of Principles" on behalf of the PLO. By early 2003, after the *Karine A* episode, as Sharon wrote Arafat off as a negotiating partner, Abbas's reputation as a pragmatist won him favor equally with the Bush administration and with important elements of the Palestinian legislature, those who were increasingly disillusioned with the corruption and violence that reigned under Arafat. In March 2003, in a rare play for Western goodwill, Arafat himself reluctantly had appointed Abbas prime minister, and even delegated him some measure of initiative in economic dealings with the European Union.

But as the year wore on, numerous power conflicts surfaced between the two men. A particularly contentious issue was that of security control. Abbas's modus operandi was to inhibit guerrilla action, to display patience in dealings with both the Israelis and the Americans. It was a stance that was anathema to Hamas, Islamic Jihad, and other Palestinian splinter groups. To avoid an internecine conflict, Abbas attempted negotiating with these guerrilla factions, and initially he won their pledge to observe a cease-fire with Israel. After a few weeks, however, they resumed attacks against Israeli civilians. Israel then responded with targeted assassinations. At this point, Abbas, intending a crackdown against the militants, demanded full control of the PA's security services. Arafat bridled, and soon countenanced demonstrations, even death threats, against the prime minister. In September 2003, his position untenable, Abbas resigned his post. The Palestinians in turn were left with nothing but their political isolation, Israeli military reprisals, and mounting economic desperation.

But now, a year later, Arafat was dead and buried. It took only a fortnight after that for the Fatah party's Revolutionary Council to endorse Mahmoud Abbas as its candidate for the Palestinian presidential election, scheduled for January 9, 2005. Once again, as in his previous stint as prime minister, Abbas launched his campaign appealing for an end to the unrest and a return to "peaceful resistance"—in effect, to negotiations with the Israeli government. The entreaty perhaps registered with the Palestinian "silent majority," which plainly was exhausted by the intifada and Israeli retaliation, and eager, above all, for political and economic reform. Abbas was elected by a landslide vote. Directly after his inauguration, the new president circumspectly invoked the memory of the *shahid* (martyr) Yasser Arafat, and vowed to protect "freedom fighters" wanted by Israel as "so-called terrorists." But he also cautioned his people that "the little *jihad* is over, and we have [before us] the larger *jihad*, the battle for achieving internal security and economic growth."

From the declaration of Abbas's candidacy, on November 25, 2004, until his election as president on January 9, 2005, guerrilla violence and Israeli reprisals continued to flicker along Israel's borders, killing six Israeli civilians and twice that many Palestinians. On January 23, 2005, however, Israel Radio announced that Abbas had secured a commitment from Hamas and the Islamic Jihad to a thirty-day cease-fire. Although even then intermittent attacks and counterattacks persisted, Abbas once again had verified his moderationist intentions to the governments of Israel and the United States. On May 9, he traveled to Washington and met with George W. Bush in the White House, a gesture that the American president had never extended to Arafat. Clearly gratified by Abbas's commitment to a peaceful solution of the Middle Eastern impasse, Bush reiterated his own government's support of Palestinian statehood, and then confirmed his earlier pledge of $50 million in aid to the Palestine Authority. It was Washington's first grant directly to the PA. All previous subventions had gone through the European Union or to nongovernmental organizations.

For Ariel Sharon, the time had come to make good on a commitment of his own. At his initiative, on February 16, the Knesset voted to approve a reserve fund of $884 million for the compensation of Gaza's soon-to-be-evacuated Jewish families. Although the formula varied according to location, house size, and number of children, the individual payments would average out to a not ungenerous $230,000 per family. Later on the same day, in a frantic rearguard move, a group of Likud hard-liners once again introduced an amendment to submit the evacuation to a popular referendum. The proposal was overwhelmingly rejected. Sharon's one concession, on March 9, was to postpone the evacuation, originally scheduled for July 20, 2005, to August 15, to avoid conflicting with the Orthodox mourning periods of Yud Zayin Tammuz and Tisha b'Av, dates memorializing the Roman army's breach of Jerusalem's walls and the destruction of the Second Temple of antiquity.

The government's deference to religious tradition did not appease the far-rightists. On May 16, 2005, they mounted a countrywide "day of protest," with some 40,000 demonstrators obstructing major traffic arteries throughout Israel. The demonstration was sponsored by a self-proclaimed "National Front," led mainly by the Orthodox parties. More than forty key road junctions were blocked, among them the entrance to Jerusalem, and five major street intersections within Jerusalem. On July 18, another protest was organized in the town of Netivot, adjacent to the Gaza Strip. Here the crowd swelled to 70,000 over three days, and dispersed only when police reinforcements prevented it from marching on Gaza. On August 10, in response to a summons from the nation's religious leaders, including three former chief rabbis, 70,000–80,000 Israelis gathered for a protest rally centered at Jerusalem's Western Wall. This time the crowd overwhelmed the site and extended into the rest of the Old City and its surrounding neighborhoods. Even this demonstration was dwarfed the following day, as fully 150,000 protesters massed in and around Tel Aviv's Rabin Square for still another anti-disengagement rally.

When August 15 dawned, prayers were intoned in mosques throughout Gaza and the West Bank, evincing Palestinian suspicion that the disengagement would not take place. But it did, albeit two days late, to allow for supplementary anti-riot equipment to be brought up. With a presence of not less than fourteen thousand police and soldiers (who had been trained and retrained to act with minimum force against settler resistance), the evacuations began in the early morning of August 17. The inhabitants of the Katif Bloc had long since been apprised that the government was entirely serious, that the dismantlement would take place. Every settler family by then had been offered financial compensation. Yet the government's plans for alternative locations and new homes had been formulated only recently, and were imprecise. In mingled anger and confusion, at least half of the settlers made a show of protest and resistance. There were scenes of troops dragging screaming inhabitants from houses and synagogues. Many of the protesters had instructed their children to leave their homes with their hands up, or wearing yellow Star of David badges, to link the actions of Israel with those of Nazi Germany.

With few exceptions, however, resistance did not approach the level that characterized the Yamit evacuation of 1982 (p. 887). The settlers' resistance was vocal but not particularly violent. The troops were forbearing, occasionally allowing families one or two extra days to complete their packing. By August 22 the ordeal was over. The last of the Jewish occupants were out of Gaza. The day marked the end of a thirty-eight-year-long Israeli presence in the Strip, although military bulldozers continued to work there for the ensuing two weeks, demolishing the settlers' villas, community centers, and synagogues (by agreement with the Palestine Authority, which preferred to use the vacated space for more economical high-rise apartment buildings). On September 12, the Israeli flag was lowered on the army's Gaza headquarters, and the remaining troops pulled out of the Strip.

Although it almost escaped public notice, the evacuation of four West Bank "hilltop" settlements was similarly accomplished, on August 23, 2005. The residents of two of these skeletal communities, Ganim and Kadim, were middle-class, secular Jews, and they had long since abandoned their trailer homes. But several dozen families and about two thousand outsiders tried to prevent the dismantlement of Sa-Nur and Chomesh, most of whose settlers were religious traditionalists. Yet, even among these, the evacuation was completed relatively peacefully. On September 22 the army was able to withdraw its detachments from the vicinity, and the land was proclaimed available for Palestinian use. Sharon had kept his promise. He had allowed no public Israeli demonstrations, political threats, or settler resistance to deter him.

The issue of the Gaza Strip was not to be resolved through Israeli evacuation alone. In ensuing weeks, an unexpected complication threatened to dissipate the brief reciprocity of goodwill Sharon had evoked from Mahmoud Abbas and the PA government. This was the issue of freedom of movement in and out of Gaza. The Palestinians had not awaited the relinquishment of Israeli occupation simply to remain penned in a coastal ghetto. They had anticipated the opportunity to trade and travel in Egypt, in Israel, in the West Bank. But the Israeli government so far had made no commitments on this issue. Defense Minister Mofaz had persuaded Sharon that it was vital for Israeli troops to remain at the town of Rafah, on the border between Gaza and Egypt, to block a likely influx of weaponry from the Sinai. On September 1, therefore, following lengthy negotiations, agreement was reached between Egyptians and Israelis, allowing a contingent of three hundred Egyptian police to ensure order on the Egyptian side of Rafah. Yet it seemed equally important for Israeli security personnel to be stationed on the Palestinian side to monitor the possible infiltration of guerrillas and weapons from Sinai. Mahmoud Abbas surely was no more interested than Sharon or Egypt's Hosni Mubarak in a revival of terrorism, but he considered the residual presence of Israeli troops on Gazan soil an affront to Palestinian liberty and dignity. His own security services would monitor the Rafah crossing, he insisted.

Abbas's protest was echoed by the Quartet's recently appointed "Special Envoy for Gaza Disengagement," James Wolfensohn. Wolfensohn had been reared in Australia, the son of a middle-class Jewish family. After his graduation from Sydney University, he earned an MBA degree at Harvard, and remained in the United States to develop a spectacular career in international finance. In 1995, at the recommendation of the Clinton administration, he was appointed president of the World Bank. Upon serving ten years at the bank, however, Wolfensohn resigned and specifically requested the Gaza assignment, which he regarded as crucial to Middle Eastern peace. Thus, in his new capacity as the Quartet's "point man" for Palestine, Wolfensohn warned repeatedly that the peace process would remain dead on the paper if the Gazans were not free to develop links with the West Bank, and to seek employment and markets for their produce in Israel proper.

In its second term of office, the Bush administration was listening. Condoleezza Rice, the new secretary of state, was assuming a more active role in the Israel-Palestine negotiations than had her predecessor, Colin Powell. She was keenly aware that the Gaza breakthrough could not be allowed to stall. The elections for the Palestine legislature were scheduled for January 2006, and both Americans and Israelis had a vested interest in strengthening Abbas's standing and the cause of Palestinian moderation. In the second week of November 2005, Rice flew to Israel to engage in urgent consultations with Israeli and Palestinian leaders. On November 14, although scheduled to join Bush's entourage for a series of visits to the Far East, the secretary remained in Jerusalem through the night of the 14–15. In her suite in Jerusalem's David Citadel Hotel, accompanied by Wolfensohn, she engaged in intensive— separate—discussions with senior aides to Sharon and Abbas. With both the Israelis and the Palestinians apparently intransigent, Wolfensohn wilted early and departed for a night's rest, muttering that he would resign his post if the two sides "want to blow each other up." But at 4:00 a.m. on the fifteenth, Rice was able to announce that an agreement had been reached.

As outlined in her formal communiqué, the Strip's Rafah terminal would open in ten days. Its Sinai entrance would be placed under the exclusive control of the Egyptians, and its Palestine side under the exclusive control of the Palestine Authority. Israeli officers would not be present at Rafah. Instead, they would be stationed two and a half miles distant, at a control station under the command of the European Union, together with representatives from the Palestinian security services, jointly to monitor telecasts from remote-control cameras set up at the Rafah crossing. If the Israelis detected a suspicious figure on the monitor, and wanted him detained, they would then request their Palestinian counterparts to take him into custody. If the Palestinians refused, an appeal could be made within fifteen minutes to the EU team of police experts, led by an Italian general, and the suspect could then be held for a maximum of six hours pending the EU decision. It was a cumbersome arrangement, leaving much to be desired in practical operation. Nevertheless, Sharon endorsed it.

In addition, the Israelis had committed themselves to permit at least 150 truckloads of Palestinian agricultural produce to be imported from Gaza daily through the northeastern, Karni, crossing into Israel proper (up from the 35 daily truckloads permitted before Israel's evacuation), and not less than 400 truckloads daily by the end of 2006. As of December 15, 2005, moreover, individual Palestinians would be allowed to travel back and forth in bus convoys between Gaza and the West Bank. Finally, with Secretary Rice's vigorous endorsement, the Israeli government acquiesced in the construction of a Gaza seaport and the repair and enlargement of the original Gaza airport (p. 1023). Although the two projects would depend upon substantial foreign investment, and require several years of planning and building, the acceptance of sea and air avenues for Palestine was arguably the most important concession of any Israeli government since the initial, halcyon days of the Oslo peace process—all the more so for having been approved by the government of Ariel Sharon.

As in so many earlier Israeli-Palestinian agreements, however, the concessions of both sides, in common with Wolfensohn's tenure as the Quartet's "point man" in Palestine, would soon be placed in direst jeopardy by the ensuing Palestinian parliamentary elections (p. 1114).

AND FOR THE REST OF PALESTINE . . . ?

Deeper suspicions of the Israeli prime minister remained. Amira Hass, a veteran Israeli journalist, had spent the late 1990s investigating the conditions of Palestinian life under both Israeli and Palestinian rule. Although equally cynical about both Arafat and Sharon, Hass in a November 2004 article in *HaAretz* reserved her sharpest criticism for Shimon Peres. The Labor chairman was even then completing negotiations to return his party to Sharon's government coalition. Was Peres really willing to make this commitment, Hass asked, for the miserably limited objective of a Gaza evacuation? Just the month before, on October 6, *HaAretz* had quoted a senior Sharon aide, Dov Weisglass, as boasting that the Gaza disengagement would preclude a Palestinian state for years to come. "The significance of the disengagement plan," Weisglass had explained, "is the freezing of the peace process, and if you freeze that process, you prevent the establishment of a Palestinian state, and you prevent a discussion on the refugees, the borders, and Jerusalem."

Hass then proceeded to expand on the West Bank settlement scenario that, in her view, the coalition negotiations were camouflaging:

> While the media waves are foaming around the coalition talks, on the ground . . . Israeli bulldozers work tirelessly throughout the West Bank, opposite the village of Hizmah, south of Pisgat Ze'ev, in the settlement of Betar, at the . . . [Tapuach] junction, on the Uzon road and in the northern Jordan Valley near the village of Bardela. In one place . . . it is to expand a settlement that is "in the consensus." In another, it is to build an extra detour road or to expand one, or for a road to some fresh new outpost. Everything is for the "public benefit," that is, for the benefit of the Jewish [settlers]. . . . Everything here is at the expense of the territorial contiguity of [a possible] Palestinian state and against the logic of a peaceful solution.

But were Sharon's annexationist expectations still as engorged as in earlier years of Likud governance? Was Amira Hass's dire prognosis still relevant? The previous spring, the prime minister had been speaking to his Likud confidants about the "shattering of a dream" of a Greater Israel. "Facts on the ground are a function of the number of settlers," he observed with evident resignation. "If I had been able to implant a million Jews in the territories, instead of just a quarter of a million, things would have been different." Doubtless the prime minister was coming to terms with the "facts" of plain and simple demography. So was Ehud Olmert, the deputy prime minister, the first member of Sharon's cabinet to acknowledge that Israel probably would not find it possible to hold on to the necklace of Jewish settlements deep in Judea and Samaria, let alone in Gaza (p. 1068).

On November 11, 2005, Israel's Central Bureau of Statistics confirmed Sharon's and Olmert's misgivings. The proportion of Jews in Israel or in territories under Israel's control had dropped to 50 percent. Some 5.639 million Jews lived in Israel, East Jerusalem, and the Palestinian territories. At the same time, in Israel and East Jerusalem lived almost 1.39 million Arabs. Although those living in Jerusalem were not Israeli by citizenship, neither were they listed as Palestinian citizens, but simply under the anomalous status of "Jerusalem residents." Added to their numbers were the approximately 2.9 million Arabs who resided in the West Bank. Israel's recent evacuation of the Gaza Strip may have excised some 1.2 million Gazans from the ambit of direct Israeli rule. But inasmuch as this coastal enclave was not yet officially attached to a sovereign Palestinian state, Israel's Central Bureau of Statistics continued to list it as among the "administered territories," and its population thereby contributed to the emerging Palestine-Israel non-Jewish majority. Meanwhile, in the eyes of those concerned with maintaining a Jewish majority, even the 1.39 million Arabs of Israel and East Jerusalem were a ticking demographic time bomb.

Sharon's initial priority, meanwhile, was to guard the security of Israel's citizens from suicide bombers and other infiltrators. At his initiative, a television-monitored system of concrete barricades, electrified wire, and militarized checkpoints continued to snake its way through the Judean hinterland of East Jerusalem, up into the former "Little Triangle" of the West Bank, and into the Samarian massif. By and large, the "temporary" barrier fulfilled its intended purpose, of protecting the life and limb of the citizens both of pre-1967 Israel and of "Greater Israel." With only occasional diverticulations eastward, the "fence" adhered reasonably closely to the largest Jewish settlement clusters just east of the Green Line. But was security the fence's only purpose? Was it the Green Line or the fence's obliquities that signified the government's ultimate territorial ambitions? The Israel human-rights organization B'Tselem (p. 1091) was convinced that it was the latter. In its annual report published in September 2005, B'Tselem noted that the government's strategy was to build "subsidiary" encirclement fences, and Israeli-dominated highways and access roads around various large clusters of Palestinian towns and villages throughout the entire West Bank. If completed, this strategy would give Israel logistical if not physical control of approximately 47 percent of the West Bank, leaving the Palestinians with contiguity and control only of the remaining 53 percent.

Yet if Sharon's critics remained skeptical that Likud's political leadership had at last come to grips with ethnographic realities, they perhaps underestimated Washington's quiet "fence diplomacy." Entrapped as it was in the mire of Iraq, the Bush administration was determined to abort a recrudescence of intifada in Palestine. Sharon's frequent visits to the White House, his detailed consultations with the president and the latter's advisers, had made clear that Bush's support for a modified security fence was conditional. It indeed envisaged an expansion of the fence's contours, but only to encompass the three major settlement clusters directly east of the 1967 Green Line. Before and after the president's election to a second term, he and his advisers refused to deviate from this limited scenario. For them, the security fence's "temporary" route manifestly was envisaged as a prefiguration of final, diplomatically established borders. In its new flexibility, Sharon's diplomatic stance during 2004–5 reflected this American pressure. The maximalist Likud territorial blueprint would have to be drastically revised.

Under the altered guidelines, presumably, the completed fence (and final-status borders) would incorporate between 10 percent and 12.5 percent of West

Bank territory beyond the Green Line, but include within its contours a mere 1 percent—some 12,000 or 13,000 individuals—of the West Bank's Arab population. Even this residual Arab minority would eventually be "gerrymandered" in a land exchange with Israel to preserve the Palestinians' basic ethnic contiguity. At the same time, the fence would leave about 14 percent of Israel's settlers beyond its protection, and thus would put them under pressure to uproot themselves from their "hilltop" settlements and move into the three larger, protected clusters. Indeed, Ehud Olmert had already voiced the previously unspoken suggestion that these remaining "hilltop" settlers should not wait for a final-status agreement, but even then prepare for a voluntary evacuation.

In the end, however, the understanding, the hint, perhaps even the subliminal wish, for an accelerated settler relocation depended less upon logic or logistics than upon psychology. Among the 415,000 Jews settled in the West Bank and East Jerusalem, some 270,000 had taken up residence beyond the 1967 frontiers predominantly for economic and "quality of life" reasons, often in response to generous financial inducements offered by the government, including under then Housing Minister Ariel Sharon in the early 1990s (p. 973). It was estimated that another 80,000 had settled in East Jerusalem's outlying quasi suburbs for the same pragmatic inducements, although they sustained as well a pietistic commitment to the "holy city." But at least 65,000 Jews in East Jerusalem and in the precarious Judean and Samarian hinterland were militant Orthodox territorialists. Any lingering assumption that they would peacefully relinquish their outposts was sanguine to the point of surrealism. In embracing a scaled-down territorial blueprint, therefore, Ariel Sharon could not have doubted that he was facing the most daunting challenge of his political, and perhaps even his military, career.

ISRAEL FACES

THE TWENTY-FIRST CENTURY

A RUSSIAN SUCCESS STORY

Between 1989 and 2002, more than 900,000 immigrants flooded into Israel from the former Soviet Union. Added to the 120,000 Soviet citizens who had arrived in the previous three and a half decades, these newcomers soon comprised the largest Jewish ethnic bloc in the country, surpassing the Moroccans and Hungarians of the early postindependence era. Yet, as many as 35 percent of them were accompanied by non-Jewish spouses and their children. Israel's absorption officials were understandably reluctant to discuss the figures. Full disclosure would have revealed that the several hundred Jewish Agency emissaries who were recruiting these people in Russia and elsewhere in Eastern Europe had always been aware of the high quotient of non-Jews among them. But as long as Gentile family members were eligible for Israeli citizenship even under the 1970 amendment to the Registration of Inhabitants Law (p. 607), the emissaries indiscriminately registered them for dispatch to Israel.

An unexpected price was to be paid for this pell-mell inclusivity. The 1970 amendment simultaneously defined Jewish identity (as distinct from Israeli citizenship) according to the guidelines of the Halachah, that is, accepting as a Jew only a person who either was born to a Jewish mother or had undergone the ritual of—specifically—Orthodox conversion. During the years of the "first" Russian immigration, primarily in the 1970s and 1980s, the rabbinical campaign to impose strictly Orthodox criteria for conversion produced as much tribulation for the newcomers in marital, divorce, and burial issues as among other Israelis of mixed heritage. Indeed, it created even more psychological distress. Jews of Soviet background were a highly secularized and assimilated element, and both they and their numerous Gentile spouses recoiled at the notion of Orthodox conversion, with its requirements not only of concentrated study courses in Judaism but of male circumcision and female immersion in ritual baths.

During the late 1980s and early 1990s, however, the rabbinate's standards for conversion tended to ease somewhat. The reasons were strictly political. When the Soviet empire began to founder, and to produce its attendant tidal wave of Russian-Jewish immigration, Israel was governed by Yitzchak Shamir's coalition of Likud and Orthodox parties. In years past, the religionists were the factions that had objected most vigorously to the absorption of arriving Gentiles, and to the threat these newcomers posed to Jewish religiocultural homogeneity. But Israel in 1989 was in the midst of a polarizing ideological struggle: whether permanently to incorporate the occupied territories into a Greater Land of Israel by fostering massive Jewish settlement in the West Bank, or else to divide the Holy Land's terrain between Israelis and Palestinians. The issue fractured Israeli society at a time when the first intifada was at its height in 1989.

It was in the context of this political impasse that the flood of Russian immigrants proved a godsend for the coalition of Likud and religious annexationists. Addressing a Likud party convention in January 1990, Prime Minister Shamir justified his opposition to any territorial compromise by proclaiming that "big immigration also requires a big Israel." The Orthodox, who as recently as 1989 were adhering to strict halachic definitions of "authentic" Jewishness, also began to sense the desirability of welcoming all newcomers, even those of questionable identity, as "Jews returning to their homeland." Later, during the ensuing Rabin-Peres government of the early and mid-1990s, the Orthodox parties resumed their former adamance on the conversion issue and attendant halachic requirements. Yet the Russians by then could not be intimidated. Whatever the marital or burial penalties, their conversions in that decade did not exceed several hundred a year. The newcomers sensed the groundswell of their public acceptance. To them, after all, hundreds of thousands of "veteran" Israelis gratefully attributed an increased toleration for secular activities, for open shopping malls on Saturdays, for the wider availability of non-kosher food in Israeli stores, for weddings and burials that reduced the halachic component to more modest dimensions.

In turn, it was the Russians' educational level that, for the most part, accounted for their commitment to secularism. By the opening of the twenty-first century, 50 percent of their immigrants were professionals (compared to 28 percent of Israel's "veteran" citizens). In the years 1990–95 alone, 68,000 engineers arrived, together with 50,000 teachers, 40,000 musicians, 20,000 journalists, 20,000 research scientists, and 10,000 doctors and dentists. More than 60 percent of the Russians had undergone at least thirteen years of education, compared to 24 percent of Israel's general population. Unlike the immigrant majority of Israel's early years, the Russians were simply moving from one industrialized, high-tech society to another. In dealing with them, consequently, the government from the outset decided to abandon its former absorption techniques. With few exceptions, it would refrain from aggressively channeling the Russians to development areas. Rather, furnished with baskets of government "start-up" money, the newcomers were given their preference of settling in the country's urban population centers, where their skills could more readily be employed and their cultural appetites fulfilled.

The Russians' early years were still far from a bed of roses (pp. 969–71). Yet, in their case, the innovative techniques adopted by the government and the Jewish Agency were supplemented by those of other institutions and individuals. In the last years of his tenure as Jerusalem's mayor, Teddy Kollek and his Municipality of Jerusalem Development Authority set about developing a series of high-tech industrial parks in and around the city. By the mid-1990s, the project was operational, renting out space to companies and providing them with advanced services including computing centers, mail and messenger facilities, and conference and lecture halls. A decade and a half earlier, the industrial-parks scheme had been successfully pioneered in Rehovot by the Weizmann Institute, and in northern Israel by a visionary industrialist, Stefan Wertheimer (p. 1006). But Kollek's undertaking was unique in its dedication specifically to the employment of Russian immigrants. Its emphasis upon light industry took into account the mathematical and computing talents of the newcomers. And, indeed, like Herman Branover's seed-capital project (p. 970), this one too became a modest success. During the 1990s, some fifteen thousand Russian scientists and technicians found employment in the industrial-parks project, in the Hebrew University and Jerusalem's teachers' seminars, and in a growing belt of independent small high-tech firms.

Beyond Israel's enhanced military security and its palpable demographic and economic growth, other factors accelerated the Russians' process of absorption. Salient among these was commercial self-help, the newcomers' vigorous initiative in organizing themselves as caregivers for fellow immigrants. During the mid-1990s, dozens of Russian voluntary associations sprang up. A number of these were "nurturing" groups for individuals with problems of age or health. Others were cultural organizations to bridge the gap between the veteran and immigrant communities. There were not lacking, as well, associations whose main functions were to lobby for political and economic causes. Possibly the most effective of them was the Soviet-Jewish Zionist Forum. Pioneered by groups of former "refuseniks" and "Prisoners of Zion," the forum by the end of the twentieth century embraced forty-two constituent organizations and sixty thousand members, and had become powerful enough to mobilize scores of thousands of Russian immigrants on behalf of causes specific to their needs and outlook.

One of the forum's most important accomplishments was the establishment of a political party, Yisrael b'Aliyah (Israel Ascending). It was formed in 1995, when the Russian influx already had swelled to over six hundred thousand persons, and when leaders emerged, "veterans" of the 1970s and 1980s, who were by then acculturated to Israeli politics and understood the system's operation. The process developed in stages. The first was in the 1992 elections, when Labor's victory was attributed in large measure to the Russian immigrant vote, thereby giving the newcomers a sense of latent power. Afterward, the Russians capitalized on the discovery by organizing their own Yisrael b'Aliyah faction, under the leadership of Natan (Anatoly) Scharansky, a famed "refusenik" of the Soviet era. The party won an astonishing seven Knesset seats in the 1996 elections. In 2006, the party's constituency was effectively superseded by another, even more assertive Russian faction, Yisrael Beitenu (Israel Our Home). In the Knesset elections of 2006, under the chairmanship of the aggressively nationalistic Avigdor Liberman, Yisrael Beitenu captured eleven seats, and emerged as a formidable component of the political landscape. Together, the two parties effectively lobbied for their special interests in housing, schooling, and government employment.

Augmenting the newcomers' political and economic progress was the concomitant growth of a sophisticated Russian-language press. Staffed both by veteran Russian-speaking citizens and by more recent immigrants, some fifty

Russian-language daily and weekly newspapers were being published by the mid-1990s (p. 970). Later, however, the number gradually diminished, in common with German-language, Yiddish-language, and other varieties of "ethnic" publications. The phenomenon bespoke perhaps the most decisive influence in the absorption of Russian immigrants. It was cultural. Among the influx from the collapsing Soviet Union were no less than fifty thousand teachers (p. 1081). Appalled by the frequently marginal quality of Israeli education, many of these professionals believed that they had something to contribute. At first, they were unable to find employment in the Hebrew-speaking school system. In 1992, however, a group of teachers who had taught at elite schools in Moscow and Leningrad opened their own *gymnasium* (secondary school) for immigrant children, bearing the acronym MOFET (Good Example).

The MOFET's initial facilities, in a dilapidated former school building, were undistinguished. Nevertheless, specializing in mathematics, physics, and "general culture," the new secondary courses proved an instant success. Shortly afterward, the MOFET program was accepted for extracurricular instruction in other schools around the country, with special emphasis on immigrants (the parents paid privately). Most of these classes initially were conducted in Russian, but after several years, Hebrew also came into use. At the insistence of veteran Israeli families, state schools also began introducing the MOFET program into the curriculum of public education. By the turn of the century, 140 such classes were operating in state high schools and 3,000 classes in elementary schools throughout Israel, and the state religious-school system was also increasingly adopting major elements of the MOFET program.

With these resources of support and self-help, it was not unnatural that the Russians took pride in sustaining their European cultural identity for years after arrival in Israel. Reinforcing their determination was Moscow's decision in 1992 to allow emigrating Jews to maintain dual Russian and Israeli citizenship. Perhaps as many as half the Russians took advantage of this accommodation. Some among them even managed to vote in Russian elections. The newcomers kept in touch with Russian developments through Israel's Russian-language media, or else through periodic trips to their first homeland. Far from adopting the stance of Russians in exile, they tended to regard themselves as Israeli Russians or Russian Israelis. Remarkably, this vigorous pluralism did not appear to inhibit the immigrants' assimilation into Israeli life. They sponsored many literary evenings in which Hebrew literature was read in Russian translation. Tel Aviv's Gesher (Bridge) Theater described itself as an "Israeli-Russian" theater that specialized in a repertoire of both Russian and Israeli plays. It produced Russian works with simultaneous Hebrew translations, as well as Israeli works with simultaneous Russian translations.

ECONOMIC LIBERALIZATION, TECHNOLOGICAL INNOVATION

In addition to the notable success of the Russian immigration, there were other hopeful auguries for Israel's future. The country was making impressive economic progress. Integral to the achievement was privatization, including the sell-off of Histadrut companies and a variety of Histadrut social services. Concomitantly, the government reduced its traditional support for pension funds, relaxed its currency controls, and privatized several large public corporations. Notwithstanding the lingering reservations of Labor veterans, who still nourished social-democratic principles, the process of divestiture achieved solid results. A reliable indicator was the quantum expansion of Tel Aviv's stock exchange, with its attendant stimulus to private investment. Whatever the effect on the widening income gap between rich and poor (p. 1094), Binyamin Netanyahu's tenure as prime minister, and then, later, his campaign of privatization as finance minister in the Sharon government, contributed to the pace of economic expansion. By 2005, the national economy, sluggish during the second, al-Aqsa, intifada, had rebounded, ascending to a 5 percent annual growth rate of the gross domestic product. By then, too, the country's economic expansion was reflected in a per capita GDP exceeding that in many West European countries.

On the debit side, however, Israel remained chronically vulnerable to deficiencies in natural resources. In January 1991, the nation was reminded of the most important of these. In her annual report, State Comptroller Miriam Ben-Porat warned the Knesset that twenty-five years of neglect and wastage had left the nation on the verge of a "catastrophic" water shortage. The overuse of recent decades not only had gravely depleted Israel's "strategic" water reserve but had seriously damaged its quality. Existing aquifers had dropped far below the safe level, enabling saline water and pollutants to infiltrate these natural reservoirs, and thus to threaten the long-term productivity of Israeli agriculture. As Mrs. Ben-Porat noted, however, the powerful agricultural lobby itself shared responsibility for the crisis by keeping farmers' water prices artificially low as an investment in "national character." It was her recommendation that water management be removed from the ministry of agriculture and placed under an "objective" state authority. The Knesset acted on this recommendation within the year.

Yet the fundamental cause of the water shortage was less political than "objective." Beyond the universal phenomenon of global warming, the critical environmental danger for Israel was the sheer growth in population, both of Jews and of Arabs—and both west of the 1967 Green Line and in the Palestinian territories. The population of integral Israel actually was drawing water not only from its own resources, from annual reserves totaling approximately 1.65 billion cubic meters, but from the West Bank, whose principal aquifer in fact was shared by Israel, and whose usable annual reserves were estimated at barely 620 million cubic meters. The fate of these supplies clearly was a matter of profound economic and political significance to Israelis, Palestinians, and Jordanians alike. By the early twenty-first century, periodic adjustments between Israel and Jordan appeared to be working. The 1994 Israel-Jordan peace treaty had promised a good-faith effort to resolve outstanding claims between the two countries, and their joint water committee by and large confirmed that expectation.

It was the issue rather of shared resources between Israelis and Palestinians that clouded the optimism of their initial 1993 "Declaration of Principles."

Here the difficulty did not lie in the West Bank's network of Jewish settlements; these communities were using in total barely 5 percent of the area's water. But integral Israel was tapping for its own use fully 30 percent of the common Palestinian aquifer. Until the outbreak of the al-Aqsa intifada, negotiations between the Palestine Authority and Israel produced some incremental adjustments in the Arabs' favor, but a definitive water formula still remained as inaccessible as a final territorial agreement. Hardly less troublesome was the availability of water from the north—from the Golan. Approximately 15 percent of Israel's (post-1967) supply flowed down from these heights. If a future peace deal could ever be struck with the Syrians, it was improbable that more than a nominal share of this water would be available for Israeli use.

Israel's hydrologists and engineers were not sleeping, of course. In earlier years, they had accomplished near miracles of exploration, drilling, sewage treatment, and hydroponics (pp. 519–22). Could they now devise a practicable method of desalinating Mediterranean seawater? The technology was available. Indeed, by the early twenty-first century, a pilot desalinization plant was operating in Ashkelon. Yet the expense of large-scale desalinization presented a serious challenge for a nation of Israel's still modest economic resources. Other alternatives were under continual study. One of the most persistent was a scheme to divert the flow of the Jordan River from the Dead Sea (where it evaporated uselessly) to agricultural use. In turn, the level of the Dead Sea would be preserved by "feeding" it with an equivalent quantity of Mediterranean water, to be conveyed inland via an artificial canal. The project would have been surrealistically costly, perhaps even more so than desalinization. Nevertheless, every few years Israeli economists and engineers reevaluated the scheme, either modifying it—for example, substituting the Red Sea for the Mediterranean—or postponing it, but never quite abandoning it.

Another possible alternative was the importation of water from Turkey, either by tanker or by using huge plastic "medusa bags" towed by coastal steamers, and pumping the transported water into Israeli pipelines at the port of Ashdod. For its part, Turkey was more than eager to exploit its surfeit of Taurus Mountain runoff by selling it to foreign buyers. Israel would have been a logical customer, inasmuch as the two nations already enjoyed extensive military, commercial, and tourist relations. As recently as 2005, their governments actually had signed letters of intent to go forward with the transaction on an experimental basis. But for Israel, the envisaged costs of shipping and pumping water remained as intimidating as for desalinization or canal dredging, and the prognosis for a long-term contract with Turkey remained unclear. It was all but certain, in any case, that one or another of these options would eventually be adopted. More than oil or even local food supplies, water for Israel, as for the surrounding Arab world, was the one indispensable resource that would determine the nation's viability, and perhaps its very survival.

In the short term, to be sure, and notwithstanding limited water resources, imaginative irrigation and dry-farming techniques had allowed Israel to remain largely self-sufficient in agriculture, and even a perennial exporter to Europe of fruits, vegetables, cut flowers, and poultry products. Between 1999 and 2004, the value of the country's agricultural exports to the European Union rose by

29 percent. Yet agriculture still comprised a bare 5 percent of Israel's GDP. Rather, the nation's economic future was increasingly to be found elsewhere. As late as 2000, the annual value of Israel's industrial exports was a modest $23.5 billion, still $6.5 billion short of its industrial imports. In the same year, however, Bank of Israel analysts confirmed that the nation's industry, despite its late start, was contributing almost two-fifths of the nation's GDP. In product diversity, output was still uneven. Textile manufacture, for decades a pillar of Israel's light industry, had largely atrophied, the victim (as elsewhere) of Chinese competition. But other industrial enterprises were gaining impressive ground, among them, plastics, electronics, and optical and medical equipment. Diamond cutting as always remained a flourishing export industry, together with pharmaceuticals and military, aviation, and satellite equipment (pp. 945–46). On the verge of surpassing all exports, moreover, even the "export" of tourism, was computer software programming, which burgeoned out in the late twentieth century, in tandem with the immigration of Russian computer scientists, into a spectacular foreign-currency earner. One Israeli software-systems provider, Amdocs, with offices worldwide, serviced an important share of Europe's and America's telephone billings (including those of metropolitan New York). Altogether, Israel ranked third only to the United States and Canada in the number of its high-tech companies listed on New York's NASDAQ.

"CONSTITUTIONAL" LIBERALIZATION

Over the course of nearly six decades of independence, meanwhile, Israelis could boast that their country, for all its political shortcomings, at least had been spared the kind of military coups perennially afflicting other recently established nations. The claim was legitimate. Yet it was also true that political office-holding had become an increasingly attractive career for senior Israeli military officers (p. 746). Between 1949 and 1994, of some 250 Israeli generals of various ranks, more than one-third took up political vocations or assumed important administrative directorships in government or Histadrut companies. The phenomenon became particularly widespread after the Six-Day War, when military heroes were "parachuted" into the Knesset and cabinet almost from the moment they doffed their uniforms. Men such as Ezer Weizman, the former air force commander, moved directly from the armed services to the cabinet in 1969, as did Chaim Bar-Lev in 1972. Even earlier, Moshe Dayan had served as minister of agriculture, then as minister of defense. In 1974, Yitzchak Rabin became prime minister, and Yigal Allon deputy prime minister and foreign minister.

The trend continued, even accelerated, from the late 1980s on. The former generals Raphael Eytan and Rechavam Ze'evi emerged as leaders of their own factions in the Knesset, and later as cabinet ministers in coalition governments. In 1992, Rabin came back as prime minister. Eventually the political courting of generals became so rampant that, in its primary election of 1999, the Labor party selected another former military chief of staff and defense minister, Ehud Barak, as its instant candidate for the prime ministry, and yet a second reserve general, Amram Mitzna, as its instant party leader and candidate in 2003. Perhaps the most spectacular feat of political sleight of hand, however, was the emergence of Ariel Sharon from the moral quarantine imposed on him by the Kahan Commission Report in 1983 (pp. 915–16) to a succession of increasingly influential cabinet posts, and ultimately to the prime ministry.

The practice of competitive political bidding for military "stars" appeared likely to survive as long as a nation already rent by religious and territorialist schisms continued decade after decade to operate under the corroded party-list electoral process. In no Knesset since the establishment of the state had there been fewer than ten political parties represented, and in none had a single party ever won a majority. The roots of this system, it is recalled, lay within the pre-1948 Zionist experience, where proportional representation allowed the Zionist Organization to keep every Zionist faction involved in the struggle for the Jewish homeland. If a party's votes after Israeli independence were diluted in coercive power, at least they were not entirely wasted, as in nations with single-member districts and majority victories.

Yet, as matters developed, Israeli citizens after 1948, and especially after 1967, were not selecting a government so much as authorizing an intricate obstacle course of coalition bargaining. No voter knew until after an election, and usually after weeks of intensive horse-trading (a process that in later years became as financially venal as it was politically cynical), for whom or what he had cast his ballot. With the various parties themselves frequently the products of coalitions, Israeli government soon became a politician's nightmare of double and triple helixes. Indeed, in a classic study of the electoral systems of twenty Western democracies, political scientist Douglas Rae found Israel's to be the most dysfunctional. The blackmail leverage of smaller factions increasingly tipped the balance of operative government, with all major cabinet decisions influenced by the need simply to assure stability. The result was a built-in disincentive to decision making and risk taking. After the Six-Day War, that disincentive most frequently was associated with the risks of territorial compromise in Palestine and the termination of Orthodox educational and military-exemption entitlements (pp. 1104–5).

By the early 1990s, popular and editorial criticism of the nation's political catatonia had become scathing enough to register on important elements of Israel's two major parties. In March 1992, therefore, a combination of Labor majority and Likud minority votes allowed the Knesset to approve electoral change. Although the parties' various lists of candidates would remain on the ballot, the prime minister in a separate ballot would be chosen directly by the voters. Put into effect in the 1996 election for the Fifteenth Knesset, the innovation was expected to provide Israel with a reasonable degree of executive stability, as in France's Fifth Republic. In Israel, however, the expectation was misconceived. Split-ticket voting actually decreased the prime minister's ability to steer legislation through the Knesset, for it produced an even larger morass of contentious parties and special-interest factions (pp. 1014–15). Eventually, in March 2001, the Knesset passed a bill to jettison the failed experiment.

More promising, however, than the amendment or its later replacement by the original electoral process were two other governmental developments of the late 1980s and early 1990s. These were juridical. In the first, the Supreme Court under the presidency of Chief Justice Aharon Barak declared that the eleven "Basic Laws" that the Knesset had individually enacted over time would be regarded henceforth as the nation's "constitution." The second—correlated—ruling was even more far-reaching. In earlier years, the Supreme Court had functioned essentially in the manner of Britain's highest court of appeal, the House of Lords. Its impact on governmental policy had been negligible, for it deferred to the Knesset in the enactment and practical application of legislation. But now, in a truly seminal decision, the court asserted its authority to conduct an American-style process of judicial review that would extend to Knesset legislation and governmental administrative procedures alike. If the assumption of this power was sweeping, it reflected less the court's proactive interpretation of its juridical authority than Israel's desperate need to break the continuing lockstep of Knesset and coalition politics.

The enhanced role of the Supreme Court was particularly evident when the justices sat in their alternate role as the "High Court of Justice," in effect, as a chancery court of equity. In this incarnation, the court in the late 1980s and beyond used its discretion increasingly to protect and advance individual rights. The new activism was first manifested in a long-overdue expansion of civil liberties in religious affairs. In 1988, the justices ruled against the local rabbinical councils' exclusion of women members solely on the basis of their gender. In 1994, the court similarly cracked the whip on the rabbinical court system, declaring that rabbinical tribunals must adopt the criteria used by civil courts when deciding property settlements in divorce cases. "The common property laws," the justices declared, "are part of the general civil law, and as such the rabbinical courts must rule according . . . to those laws."

In the 1990s, too, the justices laid particular emphasis on their leeway to interpret one specific Basic Law, that of "Human Dignity and Liberty." Adopted by the Knesset in 1992, the "constitutional" provision served Israel as the equivalent of the American Bill of Rights. In this case, the law's very phraseology implied that the court could reverse Knesset laws or administrative regulations that failed to meet common standards of fairness and human decency. By the opening of the twenty-first century, the Supreme Court was applying this law to protect both Israel's secular majority and its Arab minority. Thus, in 2003, the justices ruled that the government was obligated to allow Arabs the same rights extended to Jews to purchase homes on public land—that is, state or Jewish National Fund land. Did the Basic Law of Human Dignity and Liberty apply to areas of the West Bank and Gaza still under Israeli occupation? During the prime ministries of Rabin, Peres, and Barak this had not been the government's interpretation. But in 2003, the court, sitting as the High Court of Justice, decreed that the route of the emerging "security fence" should be altered in a way that would not impose gratuitous hardships on the Palestinian civilian population. The government—the *Sharon* government—accepted this ruling, and agreed to modify the fence route. The concession was a modest one, but pregnant with implications for "human dignity and freedom," and perhaps even for the peace process.

STYLISTIC ARTISTRY, MORAL SOPHISTICATION

The consciences of Israel's most eminent literary artists in some measure paralleled those of its senior jurists and many of its senior academics. To be sure, the publishing industry in Israel responded to the same economic inducements as did its Western counterparts. It, too, had evolved into a market of best sellers in which a small list of books was purchased and read by a great many people, and benefited from concentrated media attention. By the 1970s and 1980s, this "Westernization" of publishing influenced the readership of Israeli fiction both at home and, increasingly, in Europe and the United States. An audience was growing for Hebrew fiction in translation—most notably in English, French, and German. If sales of Israeli fiction were unspectacular, the works of such heavyweight novelists as S. I. Agnon, Amos Oz, A. B. Yehoshua, Aharon Apelfeld, Aharon Meged, and David Grossman were taken with growing seriousness in cultural circles abroad.

Well before the twenty-first century, too, a notable development in the "Westernization" of Israeli fiction was the emergence of a vibrant minority of women writers. These included Savyon Liebrecht, Michal Govrin, Dorit Peleg, Yehudit Katzir, Ruth Almog, and Ronit Matalon. A major catalyst in this gender breakthrough was Amalia Kahana-Carmon, whose first collection of stories, *Tachat Gag Echad* [Under One Roof], was published as early as 1966. Together with her male colleagues, Kahana-Carmon was part of the "New Wave" in Hebrew fiction that used modernist techniques to grapple with Israel's social issues, and most particularly with social issues unique to Israeli women. In the latter twentieth century, Yehudit Hendel and Shulamith Hareven, whose fiction overlapped that of Kahana-Carmon's generation, similarly tended to address the nation's contemporary issues from a feminine perspective.

Over and above specific themes—Zionism, post-Zionism, feminism—the sheer technical virtuosity of Israeli fiction also reflected comparable developments overseas. Apelfeld and Yehoshua were profoundly influenced by Franz Kafka, Ruth Almog by Virginia Woolf. Ya'akov Shabtai and Dan Benaya-Sera veered toward Latin America's Gabriel García Márquez and Jorge Amado, while the stories of Binyamin Tammuz and Yitzchak Ben-Ner expressed a "symbolic" realism akin to the techniques of Max Frisch and Albert Camus. Altogether, Hebrew literature by the twenty-first century had assimilated elements from an array of sources, if only because the best of American, European, and (more recently) Latin American literature had been translated into Hebrew. Yet the specific politics and geography of Israel gave this literature its own indigenous personality. In a country where life was lived at "pressure-cooker intensity," suggested Gershon Shaked, dean of Israeli literary critics, all the elements of world literature were "radicalized and exacerbated . . . more compressed, impacted, and as a consequence more acute." (Decades before, the Israeli poet Natan Alterman had characterized Israeli literature as "a whole world in a dewdrop.")

Even more than diversity of themes or sophistication of techniques, however, Israeli literature year by year evinced a moral imperative that functioned in tandem with that of its senior intellectuals, whether on the high court bench or in a majority of its university classrooms. Political chauvinism was rarely more pungently exposed than in Hanoch Levin's and Hillel Mittelpunkt's theatrical productions, a succession of caustic indictments that portrayed Golda Meir as an intransigent diplomatic haggler, Menachem Begin as a bombastic territorialist, Shimon Peres as a political opportunist, and Israeli leadership altogether as peopled by criminals and moral cripples. From the narrow military escape of the Yom Kippur War through the Palestinian intifadas and Israel's frequently indiscriminate military counterblows, the nation's literary establishment engaged in a veritable chain reaction of jeremiads.

In earlier years, in the twilight of the "Palmach generation" and the beginning of the "New Wave," such novelists as A. B. Yehoshua and Amos Oz already had warned of the hazards posed by insensitivity to the plight of the nation's Arab minority (pp. 596–97). Yet, after the Six-Day War, the warning was expanded to the far more complex plight of the occupied Palestinian territories. The icons of the Israeli literary firmament—A. B. Yehoshua, Amos Oz, David Grossman—stepped increasingly from the realm of fiction and metaphor to the newspaper op-ed page, the lecture platform, television interviews, book-length personal reminiscences and direct observations. Mordechai Bar-On, a noted educator, chronicled the role of literary *engagés* among the Peace Now movement, from its inception after the Sabra and Shatila massacres (pp. 914–15), to its proliferation into protest organizations as diverse as "End the Occupation," "Mothers for Peace," and "Re-Set" (the women's peace network).

Arguably the most effective of these groups was "B'Tselem" (In the Image of God). Founded in 1989 by Dedi Zucker, one of the original members of Peace Now, B'Tselem consisted of prominent litterateurs, academics, lawyers, army officers, and Knesset members who set out initially to monitor and document human-rights abuses that were inflicted in the course of suppressing the first Palestinian intifada. In ensuing years, with funds raised locally and from American Jews, B'Tselem developed a wider-ranging agenda, including the publication of a series of monthly and annual reports, and periodic booklets and essays containing information on the demolition of Palestinian houses, injuries to children, deportations, censorship of newspapers, and the effects of the "security fence" on commuting Palestinian workers and their families, as well as the ongoing activities of Israeli real-estate firms that illegally acquired Palestinian lands from Arab accomplices and resold them to Jewish settler associations. Like the anguished belletristic warnings of Israel's most respected literary figures, these publications reminded the world that a "moral" voice was still vigorous and resonant in the Zionist republic.

STEPCHILDREN OF ISRAEL

As in all countries, it was still an elitist voice. Indeed, if the Israeli majority's prevailing fear of the Palestinians had an analogue, it was in a lingering distrust of the state's own Arab citizens. In 2006, Arabs comprised 22 percent of Israel's population of 7.1 million, and were gaining both in absolute numbers and in demographic proportion. Their resentments were not a secret. The income gap between the two peoples was wide, and becoming wider. Although the imbalance was reflective more of the Arabs' comparatively unskilled workforce, the evidence of discrimination also remained palpable. Even during the best of the country's economic circumstances, in the mid-1990s, Israeli Arabs continued to suffer both in the private sector and in the budgetary allocation of public funds. Moreover, despite their significant electoral influence—their unwillingness to vote in 1996 spelled defeat for Peres and the Labor party—and the presence of five or six Arab MKs in virtually every Knesset, not a single Arab ever had been appointed a minister in the Israeli government. Although the Arab electorate had given Ehud Barak sweeping support in his 1999 political victory, when Barak as prime minister–elect embarked on negotiations to form his government, he virtually ignored the Arab parties. The 2005 *Israeli Democracy Index*, a comparative analysis of the nation's political and cultural indicators, revealed that the overwhelming majority of Israeli Jews supported the premise that Israeli was the "state of the Jewish people," rather than the shared homeland of Jews and Arabs. For most of Israel's history, and specifically in the recent years of Arab "Land Day" protests (p. 841), the largest number of Jewish Israelis continued to regard their Arab neighbors as a potential fifth column, and were hesitant to venture more than superficial contacts with them.

The "ethnic" gap remained wide not only between Arab and Jew but between Israel's "veteran" population (whether of European or of Sephardic/Oriental background) and the recent influx of Ethiopian "Falashas." Arriving in two rescue stages, in the 1980s and 1990s (pp. 940, 981–82), approximately seventy thousand of these African Jews had been resettled in Israel by the turn of the century. Despite energetic measures exerted on their behalf, no other immigration wave had ever proved less adaptable to a modern society. The Falashas initially were housed in absorption centers. Unlike the *ma'abarot* of Israel's early statehood, however, these facilities were not allowed to devolve into indefinite way stations. Rather, after twelve or fifteen months, the Ethiopians were transferred to their own trailer homes, and within usually a year after that to subsidized apartments, principally in the development communities of southern Israel. Medical and dental care was provided for the newcomers, as well as vocational guidance, classes in Hebrew, and their first, albeit uniformly unskilled, employment opportunities.

· Notwithstanding these efforts, the absorption program foundered badly in its first decades. The Ethiopians had been transplanted from the bottom rung of a primitive society to the economy of a developed, rapidly industrializing nation. People who had never encountered bathrooms or refrigerators in their native villages were now exposed to crash courses in modern urban living. Perhaps 20 percent of the Falashas, essentially from among their younger generation, managed to adjust to the new society within their first years in Israel, but the rest tended to drop out of the functional economy. Even into the first years of the twenty-first century, more than half of Falasha households did not include a single employed person. They remained totally dependent on government or Jewish Agency relief.

As in the case of the more backward Kurdish immigrants, the problems of relocation were exacerbated by the patriarchal traditions of Ethiopian society. Once in Israel, the Falashas encountered a social-welfare system that permitted both husband and wife to receive equal shares of unemployment pensions. The consequent erosion of the husband's authority led to familial tensions, including male drunkenness and wife beating, and often to the husband's abandonment of the home altogether. The divorce rate among the Ethiopians soared to five or six times that of Israeli society as a whole. Some 30 percent of their children were school dropouts. Although the government released no statistics, for many years it was common knowledge that the rate of suicides among Falasha army conscripts was dramatically higher than among other Israeli soldiers.

The Falashas' general disorientation assuredly was not eased by Israel's chief rabbinate, which had long disdained these Africans' bona fides as Jews. Thus, when the Ethiopians began to arrive in Israel, they were required to undergo a special conversion ceremony that included a *mikveh* (ritual immersion) for women, and for men a symbolic circumcision (consisting of a shallow incision producing a few drops of blood). Although most Ethiopians initially accepted the procedures, their resistance quickly grew. As early as their first immigration wave, in 1985, a group of Falasha men camped out for two months in front of the chief rabbinate's headquarters in Jerusalem to protest the humiliating rigor of these demands. Under public pressure, the requirement of circumcision was gradually dropped. Yet Israeli rabbis still refused to preside at the nuptials of Falasha couples unless both bride and groom agreed beforehand to mikveh immersion. In 1989, indignation at the policy led the Supreme Court to appoint David Chelouche, the Sephardic chief rabbi of Netania, as marriage registrar for the Ethiopians. Known for his permissiveness, Chelouche did not require symbolic immersion, and Falashas who were married under his auspices were finally accepted as authentic Jews.

By the last years of the twentieth century, while incremental progress was also made in reducing the Falasha suicide rate in the army, a new and equally frightening issue surfaced to disrupt the newcomers' integration into Israeli life. Many of the Falashas were discovered to be HIV-positive. A furor erupted, moreover, when the press disclosed that Israeli health officials had been secretly disposing of all blood donated by Ethiopians. In their outrage, charging racism, thousands of Falashas and their supporters turned out in January 1996 for a protest rally in front of the office of Prime Minister Peres. A few months afterward, a state commission recommended against the indiscriminate rejection of donated Falasha blood, and only then was the practice dropped. The unsettling episode had at least one unexpected "diplomatic" aftermath, however. Nine years later, aware that AIDS was ravaging the population of Ethiopia, and that Israel's physicians had developed a unique familiarity with the disease in their treatment of infected Falashas, an American Jew had an inspiration. This was Richard Schifter, a prominent Washington lawyer and former ambassador to the UN Commission for Human Rights. At Schifter's suggestion, the State Department agreed to underwrite an AIDS training seminar in Israel's hospitals for visiting Ethiopian doctors and nurses. The project may have enhanced Israel's—and America's—image in at least one corner of Africa.

As a second and then a third generation of Falashas were exposed to Israeli life, evidence of a more effective acculturation became discernible. By the early twenty-first century, some one hundred Ethiopians were enrolled in Israeli universities, and a handful among them had graduated as lawyers and physicians. A Falasha was appointed an Israeli consul in Chicago. By 2006 the Falashas had even organized their own party, Atid Echad (One Future), and another Falasha was represented on Labor's electoral list. Nevertheless, even at that late date, 70 percent of the Falashas remained below the poverty line, and 55 percent of them were unemployed altogether. In light of the vicissitudes they had endured in their native Ethiopia, and the racial prejudices and economic/cultural challenges they faced later in the Jewish homeland, the odyssey of this rescued community could hardly be counted an Israeli success story.

Neither could Israel's experience with its scores of thousands of imported non-Jewish workers. The decision to recruit foreign labor was a consequence of the Palestinian intifada, the terror bombings, and Israel's ensuing closure of its employment market to its former commuting Arab workforce. Eventually, the government approved the expedient of filling the economy's vacuum of unskilled and semi-skilled labor, whether in agriculture, construction, or practical nursing, with short-term labor from abroad. By the early 1990s, the principal sources for these transients were such Third World countries as the Philippines, Thailand, Ghana, and Nigeria, or the impoverished formerly Communist nations of Rumania, Poland, Ukraine, Belarus, and Moldova. A decade later, the number of foreign workers in Israel had grown to approximately 240,000. In fact, not more than 100,000 of them were legally in the country. The rest had come as tourists and remained on, or (more commonly) had arrived legally as foreign workers and overstayed their visas. Either way, by 2005 they comprised fully 13 percent of Israel's labor force.

Foreigners with valid work permits arrived usually by contract agreement with employers, and at a guaranteed wage level that permitted them to send remittances to their families at home. The "illegals," however, frequently were exploited by local straw bosses, who paid them subsistence wages and deprived them of health insurance and other minimal social benefits. A majority of these undocumented workers found lodgings in Tel Aviv, and for many years the living conditions in their slum quarters, particularly around the city's old central bus terminal, were squalid and crime-ridden. In 2001, however, under increasing criticism from Israel's press and social agencies, and eventually from the UN Commission for Human Rights, the Knesset passed a "Law for the Prevention of Trade in Human Beings," which authorized stiff fines for employers who denied their workers (legal or illegal) a living wage, or social benefits meeting "accepted norms." Together with this legislation, the Sharon government began taking more vigorous action to prevent unauthorized immigration, both through closer inspection of documents at Israel's ports of entry and periodic follow-up interrogation of employers by the ministry of the interior. By March 2006, government estimates placed the foreign-worker population (again, legal and illegal) at between 180,000 and 190,000. The decline, if unspectacular, at least reflected acknowledgment of conditions that were palpably inimical to the criteria of basic decency, and surely to the moral health of the Israeli nation.

A SOCIAL DISEQUILIBRIUM

By the early years of the twenty-first century, that nation was increasingly polarized not only by issues of intifada, ethnic homogeneity, and divergent political scenarios for Palestine, but by the growing evidence of an economically fractured society. The 2005 *Israeli Democracy Index*'s comparative surveys of advanced industrial nations revealed an ominous statistic. With the exception of the United States, the gap in Israel between rich and poor had become the largest in the "Western" world. In December 2006, an estimated 1.34 million Israelis lived below the poverty line. In a mere five years, since December 1999, the poverty rate had climbed from 18 percent of Israel's population to 21 percent. In the same period, by the calculations of Israel's ministry of social welfare, the suffering of the poor had become so acute that the number of homeless had climbed from 908 to 2,874, an increase of 217 percent. At least 236 of the "street people" had died of hunger and exposure. Meanwhile, the resources to assist these derelicts were steadily shrinking. The state comptroller's investigation of seven large and middle-sized municipalities revealed that the plight of the homeless was at the bottom of their priorities—or capabilities. As the finance ministry diverted an increasing share of its budget to homeland defense and settlement enlargement in the West Bank, or to domestic infrastructure improvement, funds even for the most basic national and local social-welfare services were drying up. All over Israel, soup kitchens for the hungry, supported by private philanthropies, were becoming too numerous to attract further notice.

It was during Binyamin Netanyahu's program of privatization, when even social-security funds became eligible for partial diversion to the stock market, and the GDP was averaging 5.2 percent in 2004 and 2005, that Israel's public became seized of the dramatically widening gulf between rich and poor. Accordingly, with the "security fence" beginning to contain the worst of terrorist penetration, social issues regained a measure of their former prominence on Israel's political horizon. The most telling confrontation with these realities took place on November 9, 2005. Although the central committee of the Labor party apparently stood fast with Sharon, the rank and file of the labor movement proved increasingly restive under the leadership of their political spokesmen. The latter, it seemed, had lost touch with the average working family, and was failing to address the plight of the hundreds of thousands of lunch-pail Israelis subsisting below the poverty line. Thus, on November 9, when the Labor party conducted its nationwide primary election, Shimon Peres, Labor's elder statesman, suffered a shocking repudiation. The party chose as its new chairman Amir Peretz, a hard-driving union activist.

Peretz, then age fifty-three, was born in Morocco. He was four years old when his family immigrated to Israel in 1956 and settled in the development town of S'derot—inhabited predominantly by North African immigrants— adjacent to the Gaza Strip. In S'derot, Peretz's father was a vegetable farmer. Although the son's education stopped after high school, he displayed leadership in the army and was accepted for officer training. During the Yom Kippur War he was badly wounded and spent nearly a year recovering in a military hospital. Peretz's ensuing career as a politician began in 1983, when he ran for the mayoralty of S'derot on the Labor ticket. After winning handily, he embarked on an aggressive and innovative program of improvements in the town's school system. Peretz's municipal achievements and his reputation for personal incorruptibility soon attracted national attention. By 1994, he had risen to the post of deputy chairman of the Histadrut, and two years later he became chairman. In that capacity, a militant advocate for the blue-collar class, Peretz led his unions in a series of crippling strikes until his workers achieved their wage demands. Subsequently elected to the Knesset, he waged a furious rearguard campaign against Finance Minister Netanyahu's free-market policies.

Despite his fiery rhetoric, Peretz was no demagogue. His priorities were authentic. Salient among them was a restoration of Israel's social-welfare program, and the eradication of the chasm between the nation's forgotten underclass and the top fifteen or sixteen families who controlled perhaps 30 percent of the nation's private capital. Military security was indispensable, Peretz conceded, but continuing occupation of the Palestinian territories was leaching Israel of the funds needed to save its society. He matched his actions to his words. Within a week of his November 2005 victory in the Labor primaries, Peretz browbeat the party's central committee into withdrawing (again) from Sharon's coalition. The consequences were mathematically predictable. Stripped of his governing majority in the Knesset, Sharon was left with no alternative but to call for a new election. It was scheduled for March 28, 2006.

Sharon had won his military reputation in Israel's wars by adopting unexpected and daring tactics against Arab armies and guerrillas. In politics, too, he had outflanked his opponents in 1977 by organizing his own faction, Shlomzion (p. 836), then using his bargaining leverage to win a succession of influential portfolios in the Likud governments of Begin, Shamir, and Netanyahu. Eventually, as prime minister, Sharon adapted his characteristically ruthless methods to guerrilla terrorism and domestic politics alike. Breaking the back of the second, al-Aqsa, intifada, he proceeded afterward to confound his Likud supporters by accepting the military and demographic logic of withdrawal from the Gaza Strip. Now Sharon would similarly undertake to divide the Labor camp. The Gaza evacuation, he knew, had only enhanced his credibility with Shimon Peres and other senior members of the Labor leadership. He was also aware that many of these stalwarts were distinctly reluctant to follow Amir Peretz's lead in abandoning the government coalition. For his part, the prime minister was willing to meet the Peres faction halfway—indeed, more than halfway.

For the preceding two years the most troublesome thorn in Sharon's side had not been his Labor partners but his own Likud party. At gatherings of Likud MKs and party rank and file alike, tremolos of concern had been registered at the prime minister's cautious stance on the West Bank settlements, and his evident willingness to accede to Washington's pressure for an abridged version of his security fence (p. 1078). In February 2005, when the prime minister declared his intention to evacuate the Gaza Strip, he evoked howls of protest from Likud hard-liners. In ensuing months, a sizable minority of the party's Knesset contingent backed motions to submit the Gaza issue to a nationwide referendum. It was only with the help of Labor votes that the motions were defeated. But in the autumn, after the Gaza evacuation was completed, the right-wingers' attacks on the prime minister grew in decibel power and vitriol. At a Likud party conference in October, Sharon was heckled and his microphone was shut down when he attempted to address the audience. Inasmuch as Labor, under Amir Peretz's new leadership, had recently voted to withdraw its nineteen MKs from the government, it was evident by then that Sharon's coalition was hanging by a thread.

The prime minister met the challenge head-on. On November 21, 2005, after consulting with Deputy Prime Minister Ehud Olmert and others of his closest political advisers, he released an electrifying press announcement. He could no longer lead a party, he asserted, whose ideology conflicted with his own vision of a demographically homogeneous Jewish state. "If I were to stay in Likud," Sharon continued, "I could probably still win the [forthcoming] election. This would be the safest move for me personally. However, it is not the way to serve the State of Israel." The prime minister then declared his intention formally to resign from Likud to form a new "centrist" party, which he would entitle "Kadima" (Forward).

Sharon's strategic instincts were unerring. Caught entirely by surprise at his flank attack, two-thirds of Likud's Knesset members needed only a week to decide where their political futures lay. By the opening of December, twenty-seven of them (out of forty) had announced their allegiance to Sharon and his new Kadima "umbrella." The defectors' rationale was, variously, their embrace of a "two-state" solution to the Palestine impasse, or their professed, and belated, recognition that the nation's social problems needed urgent attention. By mid-December, Likud's Knesset representation was further reduced to eleven. The ensuing competition for the party's chairmanship then devolved between Foreign Minister Silvan Shalom, a borderline moderate, and Binyamin Netanyahu, ever on the qui vive for a political comeback among Likud's residual core of territorial hard-liners. It was no contest. Shalom capitulated to Netanyahu before a final vote was taken.

On the other side of the Knesset aisle, Shimon Peres, chagrined at his summary repudiation as Labor chairman in favor of a union boss like Amir Peretz, did not think twice before leading a critical defection of his Knesset followers to Kadima. At that moment, Labor, with its already shrunken Knesset representation, was similarly reduced to eleven seats. Sharon's political audacity could not fail to impress observers. But for some of these, distraught by the fault line that had been widening in Israel's society, it was the evidence of Labor's attrition that was particularly ominous. In the pages of *HaAretz*, the renowned novelist and social humanist A. B. Yehoshua issued an impassioned plea to his countrymen not to abandon a party that, for all its lapses and debilities, had been the traditional voice of Israeli social democracy. Yehoshua nurtured few illusions that Labor could unseat Sharon in the impending election. But the next government, he insisted,

will not be able to correct the [nation's] social injustices without the encouragement and pressure of a strong and substantial partnership with those [Laborites] who have been long concerned with this phenomenon and have lived with it and studied it day in and day out for years, and not only as a matter of routine, but out of a profound belief in social and economic change. . . . The poverty and distress in Israel are not only painful, and not only undermine the dignity of us all. They also unravel the social fabric and the values of national solidarity that have been painstakingly and painfully built up here over the . . . decades of our national existence.

By then, the lament was an old one; yet in recent years, measured against the perennial threat to Israel's peace and security, it seemed to evoke an increasingly uncertain resonance in the country at large.

CHAPTER XL A MOTTLED

LANDSCAPE

A COLD PEACE, AN EXISTENTIAL THREAT

Israel had achieved peace treaties with two of its neighbors, Jordan and Egypt. Neither of them now posed a threat to the Jewish state. Jordan's young, British-educated king, Abdullah II, who had succeeded his father, Hussein, upon the latter's death in 1999, genuinely hoped to sustain productive relations with the Israelis. With its meager economic resources, and a population smaller than Israel's, the Hashemite Kingdom in any case was a much reduced factor in the Middle Eastern equation. On Israel's southern border, Hosni Mubarak, Egypt's president, similarly felt no compulsion to repudiate the late Sadat's peace diplomacy. Mubarak was better served by concentrating upon his country's surfeit of domestic problems, the most ominous of which, lately, was the recrudescence of Islamic terrorism. Meanwhile, the Egyptian *rais* scrupulously observed almost every provision of the 1979 treaty with Israel. Over the years, Israel's merchant ships had continued to pass unhindered through the Suez Canal. Egyptian troop deployments in the Sinai did not exceed their modest treaty limits (p. 859). In Israel's tortuous diplomacy with the Palestinian leadership, Mubarak had played a generally constructive role. His government had cooperated in facilitating Israel's recent withdrawal from the Gaza Strip. Although the relations between the two nations were those of a "cold peace," bereft of significant trade relations or cultural exchanges, Israeli tourists were gratefully welcomed at the Sinai resorts of Sharm es-Sheikh and Taba, and even in Cairo.

The most problematic of Israel's immediate neighbors remained Syria. The inscrutable Hafez al-Assad died in 2000. His son Bashar, who had been groomed by his father and the Ba'ath party as his successor, was duly "elected" as president by the Syrian parliament. Like the new Jordanian king, Bashar had been educated in England, where he had recently completed his medical studies. At first, the Israeli government entertained cautious hopes that the young president, with his Western background, would adopt a more forthcoming approach to peace negotiations. The hopes proved misplaced. Insecure in his political base, Bashar in 2005 was persuaded to approve the assassination of Lebanese public figures who ventured to criticize Syria's military "peacekeeping" force ensconced in their country. Among the victims was a prominent Lebanese journalist, as well as Rafik Hariri, a widely popular former Lebanese prime minister. Indeed, the murder of Hariri aroused such a firestorm of Lebanese and international condemnation that Bashar was obliged to beat a hasty retreat, agreeing to withdraw Syrian army contingents from eastern Lebanon. Chagrined and humiliated, the new president afterward did not feel politically strong enough to resume his late father's elliptical negotiations with the Israelis. Rather, he allowed Syria to continue functioning as an overland conduit for the delivery of Iranian weapons to the Palestinian guerrilla networks and Hizballah in south Lebanon.

For Israelis, that transit function was peril enough. Their gravest security concern at the opening of the twenty-first century was less the threat posed by the Syrian army, or by the army of any other Arab state, than by Palestinian guerrilla activity—and the potential threat of future Iranian belligerency and nuclear capability. The two dangers were interrelated. Although a substantial number of Palestinian militants belonged to Hamas, which drew its original ideology from the Egyptian-based Moslem Brotherhood, other guerrilla factions included the Hizballah, the Islamic Jihad, and even (after the 2006 Palestinian election) the late Arafat's Fatah mercenaries, the al-Aqsa Martyrs Brigade. But for all these groups, their onslaught of civilian carnage, achieving its fullest intensity in the al-Aqsa intifada, depended on the beneficence of Iran's Revolutionary Council for money, weaponry, and propaganda.

Altogether, by the twenty-first century, the Iranian Islamic Republic, with its population of sixty-eight million, had emerged as the principal reservoir of Islamic fundamentalism. Its uncompromising version of Shi'ite Islam, demonizing all institutions Jewish, Christian, and Western, soon was revealed as a threat to government stability as far afield as Algeria, Tunisia, Egypt, Ethiopia, Somalia, and Eritrea. For that matter, even Iran's anti-Israel offensive was not limited to the Middle East or exclusively to Israeli citizens. In March 1992, the Israeli embassy in Buenos Aires was blown apart by a car bomb, with the loss of twenty-nine lives. Hizballah claimed responsibility. Two years later, in July 1994, a bomb exploded outside Buenos Aires's twelve-story Jewish Federation building, killing eighty-five Argentine Jews, as well as five non-Jewish passersby. Both Israeli and Argentine intelligence services discerned a significant pattern of Iranian involvement.

The Iranian threat transcended guerrilla violence, however. "Strategic" weaponry also played an increasing role. As early as 1992, the authoritative *Jane's Defense Weekly* estimated that Iran had embarked on a $50 billion effort to acquire sophisticated military hardware, including long-range ballistic missiles from China and intermediate-range missiles from North Korea. Preeminent among Iranian suppliers, too, were the Soviet Asian successor governments of Kazakhstan, Azerbaijan, Uzbekistan, and Turkmenistan, whose inherited conventional and ballistic equipment was available to buyers for the right price. The Iranian government was willing to pay that price. Indeed, it was ready to fund the development of even more fearful weaponry. Dr. Abd al-Qadir Khan, the "father" of Pakistan's nuclear bomb, was engaged as the principal (although secret) adviser to Iran's nuclear-energy scientists. By the opening of the twenty-first century, the Islamic Republic was known to have made significant headway in the construction of ten nuclear research-and-development centers, most of them in underground facilities widely dispersed from Tabriz in the north to Bushire on the Persian Gulf.

It was only in 2004, however, that the International Atomic Energy Agency began issuing public warnings that Iran, a nation that earlier had been a signatory to the Nuclear Non-Proliferation Treaty, was embarked on a program whose end objective could only be the development of nuclear weapons. In response, the Iranian government repeatedly assured the IAEA that its atomic research was dedicated exclusively to the production of "alternate, peaceful" energy supplies. But the protestations rang increasingly hollow in light of Western intelligence assessments. With growing urgency, the American and European governments pressed Tehran to allow IAEA inspectors access to its nuclear facilities. All the requests were met with procrastination, dissimulation, or, increasingly, flat refusal. By early 2006, too, the newly elected president of Iran, Mahmoud Ahmadinejad, was openly and repeatedly proclaiming his conviction that Israel "should be wiped off the face of the earth."

In the short term, Israel was capable of winning a battlefield war against any foreseeable constellation of Arab enemies, and probably of defending itself even against Iran. Yet the qualitatively superior Israeli air force each year became a less certain shield for the nation's civilian population. A preemptive bombing strike against a monolith like Iran was not a serious option. Against incoming rockets, Israeli warplanes and pilots would be at a severe disadvantage. Indeed, accepting that reality, Israel's defense ministry in 1987 abandoned its $1.6 billion, eight-year investment in a locally manufactured fighter-bomber, the Lavie. In its stead, shortly after the 1991 Gulf War, Minister of Defense Moshe Arens completed negotiations with the first Bush administration to develop an anti-ballistic rocket, the Arrow. Envisaged as an upgraded version of the American-produced Patriot missile (p. 979), the Arrow was intended to strike at longer-range enemy missiles, those capable of approaching Israeli targets at a higher trajectory and speed.

Within a few years, however, Israeli military intelligence officials began to reevaluate the Arrow project as well. They expressed growing doubts that the Iranian regime actually was contemplating the use of nuclear-tipped rockets against Israel. The Israelis, had after all, developed their own nuclear and ballistic capability, and were successfully manufacturing and launching into orbit their own state-of-the-art spy satellites. Moreover, Israel's population included 1.5 million Arabs (in addition to the neighboring populations of the Palestinian territories) who would similarly be exposed to radiation in the event of a nuclear attack. The Iranian nuclear threat, intelligence officials conjectured, was to be regarded essentially as one of diplomatic pressure of the kind that had created the nuclear standoff between the United States and the former Soviet Union, or between India and Pakistan. The question more pertinently remained, therefore, whether a country of Israel's limited demographic and geographic defense in depth could endure that kind of impasse, either economically, politically—or psychologically.

In the autumn of 2004, with the developing evidence of Iran's nuclear program, Prime Minister Sharon had appointed a military-civilian committee under the chairmanship of Dan Meridor, a respected former minister in a succession of Likud governments. The committee's mandate was to devise an appropriate defensive posture in light of "significant" changes in the Middle

Eastern security equilibrium. The members took their responsibility seriously, meeting fifty-two times in the ensuing eighteen months. On April 23, 2006, the committee's draft report was submitted to Shaul Mofaz (still defense minister in Ehud Olmert's interim government). It ran to 260 pages, and most of its details were classified. Yet, with government permission, three of its conclusions were released. First, Israel should maintain its policy of "nuclear ambiguity," neither confirming nor denying its ability or willingness to take appropriate action to counter a nuclear threat. Second, the military's conventional land and air power should be scaled back in favor of more advanced satellite intelligence relating to "operations from outer space." Third, Israel's National Security Council should become the government's central military-planning authority. In that role, the council's responsibilities would include for the first time the development of countermeasures to perhaps the most lethal danger of all. This was widespread civilian terror, pandemonium, and flight in anticipation of imminent attack by "nonconventional weapons."

CRIME AND BRUTALIZATION

In his heartfelt plea for his countrymen to give heed to the poverty and distress in Israel (pp. 1096–97), A. B. Yehoshua warned that these social lesions were "already causing the burgeoning crime and corruption that are bringing Israel to an unprecedentedly low ranking among the countries of the Western world." Yehoshua was not exaggerating the danger of "crime and corruption." Yet the phenomenon did not arise from poverty and distress alone. Israel's very existence traced back to its people's disregard of the law. In the late nineteenth century, when the Ottoman regime imposed restrictions on Jewish land purchase, and, later, when the British mandatory government repudiated the Balfour Declaration, the Yishuv in turn developed an overarching contempt for "legalism." Steadily, relentlessly, "illegal" activity became the moral norm, countenancing "illegal" immigration, "illegal" defense, "illegal" settlement, "illegal" weapons and money shipments. An entire generation of young Zionists, later to assume leading roles in Israel, was trained in this defiant tradition of illegalism. It was a heritage that characterized the nation's existential struggle for security, and from the government down: from dissemblement and resistance to international inspection in the production of atom bombs, to clandestine arms deals with such unsavory clients as apartheid South Africa, right-wing Latin American dictatorships, and Communist China, to such harebrained schemes as the Lavon and Pollard affairs.

Under the harshly austere economic conditions of the state's first years, tens of thousands of Israelis, refugees from European and Moslem countries, kept their heads above water by fudging on their tax records and tax payments. Veterans and immigrants alike moonlighted exclusively for cash, often at the expense of their salaried employment. Hidden currency accounts or questionable "investments" overseas became commonplace. The need for and temptation of these underground alternatives, together with an ongoing disdain for the law altogether, infected public officials and their relatives as well as private citizens. Indeed, the former set the tone for the latter: from Prime Minister Rabin, who allowed his wife to squirrel money away in two illegal bank accounts in the United States; to Knesset member Omri Sharon, the son of Prime Minister Sharon, who was indicted and convicted for accepting illegal campaign contributions on behalf of his father; to Aryeh Deri, chairman of the Shas party, who spent prison time for extorting bribes while serving as minister of the interior (in later years, three other Shas Knesset members would also serve prison sentences). By 2006, as Israel prepared for its March elections, fifteen MKs—no less than 12 percent of the current Knesset membership—were under investigation or actual indictment for crimes of political or financial turpitude.

As early as August 1977, a committee chaired by a senior police official, Michael Bochner, drew up a "crime map," a 184-page report that suggested white-collar crime had become virtually a collaborative enterprise between the public bureaucracy and the nation's citizenry. Derelictions ranged from kickbacks for state transactions to illicit purchase of licenses from municipal authorities. No sector of the public domain remained untouched by peculation, not even national defense. Within the armed services, discoveries periodically were made of graft, embezzlement, and wholesale theft of property, including weapons and ammunition. Although corruption was uncovered at all levels, possibly no episode was quite as sordid as that of Brigadier General Rami Dotan. Chief of the equipment branch of Israel's air force, Dotan over a period of eight years accepted $10 million in bribes from suppliers in Israel and the United States. Caught dead to rights in 1991, Dotan implicated a half-dozen fellow officers and civilian colleagues, all of whom were convicted and imprisoned.

Was the moral delinquency subject to improvement with growing prosperity, or had it become irreversible? In 2005, the World Bank published data that identified Israel's government as one of the most inefficient among the West's "developed" countries in its oversight mechanisms. However reluctantly, the *Israeli Business Data Index* of that year corroborated the World Bank's estimate. And so did Israeli public opinion. Indeed, the Israeli people were their own harshest critics. The 2005 *Israeli Democracy Index* suggested that, in public perception of government integrity, Israel scored 80.8 percent, compared to an average 91.4 percent among other developed nations. In 2006, a Harvard study of globalization ranked Israel no higher than the middle tier of government oversight efficiency. Whether merely "inefficient" or deliberately constrained, government oversight was a vacuum waiting to be exploited.

Neither was there a qualitative distinction to be made between the venality of Israel's secular and its religious officialdom. The elaborate apparatus of religious courts and councils, of kashrut commissions and burial societies, had long proved a uniquely lucrative source of income, both legal and illegal. The notorious corruptibility of these Orthodox personnel generated a veritable folklore of pungent anecdotes. In 1979, seven rabbis, members of Jerusalem's religious-court system, together with Rabbi Moshe Mizrachi, deputy chairman of Tel Aviv's religious council, were convicted of "expediting" divorce and conversion processes in return for bribes. If it had not been for accusations of "antireligious bias," dozens of other Orthodox officials would have been prosecuted.

But in 1981 the attorney general's office found it impossible to overlook the case of Aharon Abuhatzeira, minister of religions. That year Abuhatzeira was tried and summarily convicted for embezzlement of the ministry's trust funds. In 1998, there was the Aryeh Deri bribery episode (p. 1025). In 2006, the attorney general recommended the dismissal of Ashkenazic Chief Rabbi Yona Metzger from his post for having repeatedly billed the government and the chief rabbinate itself for extensive family vacations in a series of luxury hotels. With these examples before them, it was less than surprising that private citizens often cheated on their taxes and business deals. In 1976, the overworked police were solving only 17 percent of white-collar crimes. Thirty years later, in an age of more sophisticated computer tracking, the rate of police success had improved only slightly, to a still-meager 28 percent.

It was all but predictable, too, that among the hundreds of thousands of late-twentieth-century immigrants from the defunct Soviet Union—including in their ranks Georgians, Tajiks, Uzbeks, Azerbaijanis, and other former Soviet subcommunities (Jews and non-Jews alike)—who had survived and even thrived in the dysfunctional Communist economy by skirting the law, a substantial minority now adapted readily to the "culture of illegalism" on the sands of Israel. Some of them became major perpetrators of hard-core felonies. In the manner of many North African immigrants before them, the newcomers developed an expertise in extortion. In Tel Aviv's Carmel Market, thugs hired themselves out as "watchmen" of the market's hundreds of fruit and vegetable stalls. Few vendors rejected their services, for those who did were likely to experience mysterious episodes of vandalization or arson. More sinister yet was the growth of drug trafficking. Initially, the trade emerged from the capture of Arab territories in 1967. Israelis, many of them originally fugitives from the Arab world, swiftly developed a lucrative connection with the Middle Eastern drug industry. Much of their purchased cocaine and opium was smuggled out to Europe, but enough remained in Israel itself to contribute to an upsurge of robberies and physical assaults, particularly in slum neighborhoods and development towns.

Indeed, the Bochner Report had presented a harrowing account of thuggery and extortion in restaurants, bars, and a growing diversity of smaller retail establishments, even in upscale neighborhoods. Intimidation occasionally included the murder of witnesses and informers. Police officials were appalled by the large quantities of illicit weapons circulating in Israel. Altogether, crimes of violence, often among rival crime "families," multiplied more rapidly than any other category of felonies, up over 200 percent from 1977 to 1989. In 1989 alone, 110 murders (unrelated to Arab violence) were committed in Israel. Among developed countries, only the United States, the Netherlands, Italy, and Germany listed higher per capita murder rates.

In 1985, Professor Shlomo Shoham, a renowned criminologist teaching at Tel Aviv University Law School, issued a chilling forecast: "We are at five minutes to midnight," he warned. "The symbiotic relationship between the criminal classes and the authorities that has developed in the United States may not have fully developed here, but we are on the verge of transition to the relationship." The challenge was formidable if only because the roots of the problem were deeply entangled in a number of historic sources that paralleled the "culture of illegalism." The emotional disorientation of Holocaust survivors was a critical determinant in the state's first years. So was plain and simple economic desperation in a period of mass immigration and severe austerity. The crisis was further exacerbated when police were continually diverted from "normal" issues of local crime to the struggle against violence in the occupied territories. And, integral to the quest for a solution of the Palestine problem, there loomed the brutalizing effects of incessant warfare, Arab guerrilla violence, and progressively harsher Israeli retaliatory measures. It was the congruence of these historic and sociological influences that appeared to confirm Shlomo Shoham's unsparing evaluation. If crime in the Zionist republic was not proportionately more widespread than in Italy, Germany, the Netherlands, the United States, or many other Western countries, it was the kind of parity that Israel, in its ongoing struggle for security and cohesion, needed even less than did other larger, wealthier, and more secure nations.

A BURGEONING KULTURKAMPF

Long before the twenty-first century, it had become apparent that another threat to Israel's social viability was the growing political influence of religious extremists. One manifestation of that leverage was Charedi success in extorting government funding for their parochial (and frequently submarginal) school systems. Another was the preferential tax benefits and outright government subventions that the ultra-Orthodox secured for their limitless proliferation of offspring. It had not always been so. Until the late 1970s, the Orthodox by and large had maintained a stance of political forbearance. In those years, the comparatively moderate National Religious party functioned as the principal spokesman for the religious camp, and its desiderata related mainly to the exemption of Orthodox girls from military service, and assurance that kashrut would be observed in the dining facilities of the army and other state institutions. As primus inter pares among the various religious factions, the NRP consistently received between ten and twelve seats in the Knesset, and preserved a functional relationship with the major secular parties, especially Labor.

The political upset of 1977, when Likud replaced Labor as the coalition-forming party, effected a major change in this comparatively benign secular-religious configuration. Menachem Begin's expedient new deference to the Orthodox profoundly influenced not only the NRP but the Agudat Israel (or Agudah), a faction consisting exclusively of Charedim. Winning its customary five seats, the Agudah for the first time since 1952 elected to join a coalition government—Begin's government—as a full member. Henceforth, the NRP would no longer be the single religious party participating in the cabinet. Moreover, in the ensuing national election, in 1981, the NRP lost half of its electoral strength, down from twelve Knesset seats to six; and by the time of the 1988 elections, the NRP had also lost its senior standing among the religionists. Together, the Agudah and (North African) Shas parties—that is, the right-wing Orthodox bloc—garnered two-thirds of all the religious representation in the Knesset.

The summit of Orthodox political muscularity was apparently reached in the late 1990s. In the 1996 Knesset election, the religious factions between them accounted for an astonishing twenty-three seats. Three years later, in the 1999 election, which otherwise brought Labor and Ehud Barak to power, Shas alone emerged with seventeen seats, thereby becoming the third-largest party in the Knesset, after Labor and Likud. Inasmuch as the smaller Charedi party, United Torah (encompassing the recently joined Agudah and Degel HaTorah factions), won five seats, the ultra-Orthodox parties together now held an unprecedented twenty-two seats. Indeed, with the virtual collapse of the traditionally more moderate NRP, to a meager five seats, less than one-sixth of the religionists in the Knesset might be considered even marginally flexible on doctrinal issues. No longer could the NRP sustain its former role as spokesman for the Orthodox in the public sphere. That function henceforth was fulfilled by the Charedim and the constituents of Shas—the more than 60 percent of Orthodox men who comprised Israel's lowest-income group, whether marginally employed or so extensively subsidized by the government as "yeshiva scholars" and/or fathers of burgeoning families that thousands of them disdained remunerative employment of any kind.

These electoral mutations undermined the very basis of Israel's tradition of ideological compromise, transforming Orthodox extremism from a nostalgia to a political, and eventually to a security, threat. One of its most notable features was the growing success achieved by many Agudah and Shas adherents in winning exemption of their young men from military service under the category of "yeshiva students" (pp. 885–86). Even as a majority of religiously observant young men continued to serve in the armed forces (often with great heroism), in 1996 the ministry of defense revealed that 27,500 males, overwhelmingly of ultra-Orthdox background, had been granted deferment that year, a growth of 16 percent over the previous year. Of potential female conscripts in 1996, a full 32 percent similarly claimed—and were granted—exemption on religious grounds. Beyond security considerations, as late as the 1980s military service had been defined as the central feature of the Israeli "experience," as the single most effective force integrating and bonding the nation's Jewish citizens, of all backgrounds. No longer.

FROM KULTURKAMPF TO INCIPIENT CIVIL WAR

The messianic impulsions of the ultra-Orthodox ramified well beyond integral Israel. As painful as evacuation was for the 9,000 Jewish settlers of the Gaza Strip, their numbers obviously were negligible compared to the approximately 190,000–200,000 Israelis living in annexed and expanded East Jerusalem, let alone the 225,000 Israelis residing in the West Bank. Demographers listed 365,000 of these people as either secular or "moderately" religious. Most of them had taken up residence across the pre-1967 Green Line essentially in response to inducements of attractive mortgages and a more spacious quality of life, either in Jerusalem's eastern suburbs or in exurban West Bank "garden communities" (pp. 890–91). But some 80,000–90,000 of the settlers were committed Orthodox religionists, a majority of them affiliated with the Gush Emunim movement, and on the West Bank they tended to live in smaller enclaves and outposts beyond the route of the envisaged "security fence." For these pietists, Judaism itself was indissolubly entwined with the "biblical Land of Israel."

It was understandable, then, that Rabin's and Peres's Oslo Accords stunned the Yesha Council of West Bank and Gaza settlers, particularly the Gush Emunim members among them (p. 832). At first, these latter were slow to react. By 1994, however, they had moved into a vigorous countercampaign against the government. It started in March of that year, when the Rabin government revealed that it was considering the evacuation of the tiny Jewish enclave—comprising seven ultra-Orthodox families—in Tel Rumeida, a small hill in central Hebron. The militants were appalled. In their minds, if the government could evacuate Tel Rumeida, it could evacuate all the settlements in the West Bank. The import of this looming "disaster" swiftly produced one of the dramatic mobilization efforts in settler history. The Yesha Council prepared contingency plans to bring thousands of sympathizers, fundamentalists, and moderate traditionalists alike to block the Hebron evacuation, if necessary by planting their bodies on the ground.

Most notable was the action of Israel's senior rabbis, among them Shlomo Goren, Avraham Shapiro, Shaul Yisraeli, and Moshe Zvi Neria, who issued a "ruling":

> The criminal initiative to evacuate Hebron ought to be met with "total attention." The ruling on such a heinous crime, like the ruling on saving life, is "Be killed but do not sin.". . . . According to Halachah, the destruction of Hebron, God forbid . . . would be akin to the killing of people, which requires *kriah* [cutting one's clothes], as for the dead. . . . This is why we have to give our lives in the struggle against the government's vicious plan . . . and be ready to die rather than to allow the destruction of Hebron.

More startling than the substance of the rabbinical pronunciamento was its issuance to the army, and specifically to the army's thousands of religiously traditionalist soldiers, who were instructed to disobey their commanding officers. Indeed, the rabbinical injunction created a public uproar. A majority of the population considered it the most frontal attack ever made on Israel's still fragile democracy, more reprehensible perhaps than Menachem Begin's threat in 1952 against Knesset members who voted to accept German reparations (pp. 372–73). The attorney general declared his intention to consider a charge of criminal incitement. Even prominent Likud members this time expressed unease.

Although the government eventually decided against evacuating Tel Rumeida, the rabbinical injunction remained in effect. In May 1994, the Israel Rabbinical Union, representing most of the nation's yeshivot and more than a thousand of its rabbis, denounced the Oslo peace process altogether with the proclamation: "The so-called peace agreement . . . may lead, God forbid, to great danger to human life. This is why anyone who can overturn this 'agreement' and does not do so, breaks the rule: 'You shall not stand idle when there is danger to your brother.' " Small and large rabbinical protest meetings continued into 1995, and mobilized virtually the entire religious sector, even the formerly moderate National Religious party.

In February 1995, following a series of Hamas and Islamic Jihad suicide bombings inside Israel that killed 86 Israeli civilians and wounded 202—mainly in revenge for the Baruch Goldstein massacre (p. 1109)—the heads of Yesha's Rabbinical Council explored with Talmudic experts the feasibility of putting the government on trial in accordance with the principles of *din moser* and *din rodef. Din moser* was a medieval rabbinical ruling against any Jew who sought to provide Gentiles with secret information about other Jews, or who illegally sought to transfer to Gentiles the property of Jews, including any part of the Land of Israel. In such cases, Jews were obliged to kill the *moser. Din rodef* was an equally draconian ruling from the Talmud against a person who similarly was intent upon committing the murder of another Jew. He too was to be killed immediately, and preemptively. The rabbis' letter of "inquiry" to their colleagues was an unprecedented incitement. Equally so were the affirmative replies from hundreds of individual rabbis across Israel. By the autumn of 1995, demonstrations, posters, and slogans—"Rabin and Peres Are Traitors," "Assassins," "Collaborators of Terror"—were the order of the day, both in the territories and in Israel proper.

Yigal Amir, a young law student at Bar-Ilan University, had earlier been traumatized by the threatened evacuation of Tel Rumeida. He took the rabbinical incitements seriously. As he acknowledged later at his trial: "If not for a halachic ruling of *din rodef,* it would have been very difficult to murder. . . . If I had not gotten the support [of the rabbis] . . . and had I not been representing many more people, I would not have acted." But on the evening of November 4, 1995, act he did, by loading his pistol, making his way to Tel Aviv's Municipality Square, and pumping three bullets into the back of Prime Minister Yitzchak Rabin.

A DIASPORA IRREDENTISM

By the late 1980s and early 1990s, still another ingredient fueled Israel's right-wing territorialism. This was its defense in depth among a sizable minority of Jews abroad. Indeed, the ultra-Orthodox and other Israeli annexationists drew some of their most ardent partisans, and an increasingly large part of their financial support, from their substantial Orthodox constituency in the United States. A case in point was the Ateret HaCohanim (Temple Mount Faithful) yeshiva, which nurtured a program of infiltrating the Moslem and Christian quarters of Jerusalem's Old City. This conventicle of zealots could mobilize on short notice Brooklyn's *Jewish Press* and other right-wing American-Jewish media to recruit prominent politicos as guest speakers at its banquets (among them, New York's ex-mayor Edward Koch and Senator Alfonse D'Amato). Thus, the "Friends of Ateret HaCohanim" in the United States raised more than $7.5 million between 1988 and 1993. Other American-Jewish foundations sprang up after 1993 to oppose negotiations for Palestinian self-rule. The Gush

Emunim established two of them in New York, and their donations in turn helped fund the "logistics" of clamorous protest demonstrations in both Israel and the United States.

By 2003, an estimated 10–12 percent of the settlers on the West Bank and—extended—East Jerusalem came originally from North America. With few exceptions, these tended to be Orthodox, and often *ba'alei t'shuva* (recently "converted" pietists), for whom redemption of the Land of Israel was a halachic obligation. Over the years, they received imaginative support from the Likud government. In the early 1980s, in a step that was a collateral offshoot of "Project Renewal" (p. 838), Menachem Begin had encouraged Orthodox congregations in North America to adopt as "twins" poor, predominantly religious neighborhoods in and about Jerusalem, and other Orthodox neighborhoods in both Israel and the West Bank. Within a decade, hardly an Orthodox settlement in the territories failed to receive substantial financial contributions from its Orthodox "twin" in the United States.

Altogether, the relationship between right-wing militants in Israel and their American supporters was becoming increasingly seamless. In earlier decades, the precedent of philanthropic help to fraternal communities in Israel had been established largely by the extensive American-Jewish network of Labor Zionist institutions, and that tradition still endured. But the dimension of imported support for territorialist violence was essentially a new phenomenon. Although some of these American right-wingers, in Israel and the United States, were quite well educated, and included a scattering of doctors and lawyers, most were of lower-middle-class background, and of these a vibrant subcommunity were devotees of Rabbi Meir Kahane and of Kach-inspired movements (pp. 928–29). By the mid-1980s, the rabble-rousing Kahane, banned from the Knesset in 1985 for his incendiary anti-Arab racism, had organized four tax-exempt foundations in the United States to promote his political program. In 1987, at a typical fund-raising banquet in his honor in Manhattan's Lincoln Square (Orthodox) Synagogue, Kahane assured his supporters that their tax-exempt donations would help Kach candidates win ten seats in the 1988 Knesset elections and compel the government to accept them. Although his political comeback proved illusory, by 1989, he was bringing $500,000 a year into Israel.

In November 1990, Kahane was shot to death by an Arab partisan in New York. His movement survived, however, and its largest offshoot, Kahane Chai (Kahane Lives), based in the West Bank settlement of Kfar Tapuach, was led by the murdered rabbi's youngest son, Rabbi Binyamin Kahane. Seeking to run candidates for the 1992 Knesset elections, Kahane Chai, like its predecessor, was disqualified by the Supreme Court on the identical grounds of racism. But the "party's" most important activities in any case were not political. In November 1992, four of its teenage partisans hurled a grenade into the East Jerusalem shop of an Arab shoemaker, killing the owner and wounding ten other Palestinians. Soon afterward, Kahane Chai organized a front group in the United States, the "Committee for the Freedom of the Youths," to solicit contributions for the young terrorists' legal defense fund. In addition, Kahane Chai succeeded in raising hundreds of thousands of dollars on its own behalf, largely from its offices in Brooklyn and from advertisements in the *Jewish Press*. The money was used both to operate the Kfar Tapuach settlement and to establish a paramilitary training camp in New York's Catskill Mountains, as well as to purchase weapons on Israel's black market. Over the years, Kahanists in the West Bank were involved in numerous episodes of violence, many of them directed less against guerrilla terrorists than against peaceful Palestinian villagers.

Their militancy reached an apotheosis of sorts in February 1994. It was then that a young American-born physician, Baruch Goldstein, managed to gain entrance to Hebron's Ibrahami Mosque during a packed Arab religious service. With his automatic rifle, Goldstein loosed volley after volley, killing twenty-nine Arabs and wounding more than a hundred before other worshippers subdued him and beat him to death. Goldstein had been a member of the neighboring settlement of Kiryat Arba (pp. 682, 832), whose vigilante groups had been attacking Palestinians long before the first intifada. An ardent Kahanist, insisting that there was no possibility of coexistence with Arabs, "the Nazis of today," Goldstein had been outraged by the Oslo peace process. In fact, he achieved his purpose of disrupting that process. His act of mass murder resulted in the postponement of Israel's political transfer of Gaza and Jericho to the Palestine Authority. Before Yasser Arafat agreed to resume discussions, Prime Minister Rabin for several months had to accept the presence of foreign observers to "monitor" the process of transition.

The episode ominously prefigured a right-wing scheme for sabotaging the later phases of Palestinian "empowerment." By the mid- and late 1990s, Kahane Chai, with its mounting war chest of American-raised funds, was only one among the growing network of settler vigilante groups that managed to purchase weaponry, including mortars and rocket launchers. "We had the idea of civil war," declared Kfar Tapuach's mayor, David Axelrod, another American. "We will never accept giving up Jewish land to Gentiles." In their campaign to subvert any possibility of Palestinian statehood in the West Bank, it was conceivable that these and other Jewish militants eventually would launch indiscriminate Algerian *colon*–style attacks on Arab civilians. If the most recent, August 2005, experience of withdrawal from Gaza was a precedent, then a future and even more violent confrontation with the Israeli army was distinctly possible. In that fearsome prospect of civil conflict, it would be the North American minority among the Jewish settlers that was likely to provide a critical new dynamic in manpower, funds, and weaponry, and, above all, in the classically irredentist brand of ideological fanaticism.

JERUSALEM: A DEFUSABLE TIME BOMB?

In the aftermath of "Oslo I" and "Oslo II," as Israelis and Palestinians set about devising a formula intended to extend and complete the peace process, they grappled endlessly for a solution to the single most complex issue in the entire Arab-Israeli impasse. This was no longer the status of Palestine. With or without violence, some version of Israeli dismantlement and Palestinian "empowerment" was a foregone conclusion. It was rather the future status of

Jerusalem that challenged the skills even of both sides' most resourceful and well-intentioned negotiators.

At first, the prospects for a diplomatic breakthrough had not appeared unrelievedly bleak. In September 1993, as he participated in the "Declaration of Principles" ceremony at the White House, Yitzchak Rabin made clear his willingness to reach an accommodation on Jerusalem. Sensitive to Arab concerns, he well recognized that the future of the Holy City was the final nuclear component in achieving Israeli-Palestinian peace. Moreover, a backlog of imaginative blueprints for Jerusalem was available. One of these was the concept of a "Greater Jerusalem Metropolitan Area," stretching beyond the city limits to include the towns of Ramallah in the north and Bethlehem in the south, as well as the Jewish settlements of Ma'aleh Adumim in the east and Givat Ze'ev in the northwest. Under this rubric, with its nominal objective of "easing road and sewage congestion," the Palestinians might establish the seat of their Palestinian government outside East Jerusalem proper, but within the "Greater Jerusalem Metropolitan Area." Another alternative, supported in the 1970s and 1980s by Jerusalem's Deputy Mayor Meron Benveniste, was a London-style collection of separate "cities" within a Greater Jerusalem equivalent of a "county council." Each "city"—Jewish, Moslem, Christian—would operate its own mini-administration, even its own city hall.

Yet there lingered at least two formidable barriers to a resolution of the Jerusalem issue. The first was political. During the twenty-eight years of his incumbency, from 1965 to 1993, Teddy Kollek, the city's energetic mayor, strove heroically to improve the quality of life both for the city's Jewish inhabitants and, following the Six-Day War, for its annexed Arab population. After the 1977 Knesset election, however, which brought Likud to power, Kollek's considerable efforts on behalf of Jerusalem's Arabs fell increasingly short. In part, the fault lay with the national government, which under Menachem Begin and Yitzchak Shamir encouraged the massive settlement of Jews in East Jerusalem. By the beginning of the twenty-first century, some 190,000 Jews had moved across the city's former dividing line. Under political pressure, Kollek was obliged to accommodate this influx, in many instances by confiscating "public" land (albeit for buyout compensation), and commissioning private Israeli investors to develop East Jerusalem for Jewish residential and commercial purposes. Over the decades, in these Jewish-designated sectors, new housing developments sprang up, roads were paved, sewage and electricity were installed, schools and synagogues were constructed, parks and playgrounds were laid out—all for the needs of the surging Jewish population.

In East Jerusalem's traditional Arab quarters, meanwhile, public utilities at first were conscientiously linked to those of Israel's New (Jewish) City. Arab public employees were taken on by Kollek's unified municipal administration (pp. 668–69). For Arab residents and tradesmen, however, the only visible boom was in human congestion. Kollek's initial burst of energy unquestionably provided East Jerusalem with a range of basic facilities superior to those earlier supplied by Hashemite Jordan. Yet, during the entire period of Kollek's mayoralty, not a single new Arab neighborhood was built, and existing ones frequently lagged behind their Jewish counterparts in upgraded sewage lines, paved roads, sidewalks, and streetlights. Kollek's pleas to the national government to provide more funding for the Arab sectors rarely were successful. His efforts to build even a symbolic park, a playground, a community center for East Jerusalem's Arab residents came to naught. When eventually, in the 1993 mayoral election, the city's Jewish population voted Kollek out of office, the Arabs sat on their hands. Under Ehud Olmert's subsequent right-wing municipal administration, the sequestration of "public" land on the fringes of East Jerusalem served both to ghettoize the city's Arab inhabitants and to cordon them off from their West Bank hinterland.

Yet it was not political considerations alone that blocked the attempts of Israelis and Palestinians to resolve the Jerusalem issue. The clash of religio-nationalist ideologies played by far the greater role. After 1967, the largest numbers of Jews who settled in East Jerusalem were religious traditionalists, including a rapidly expanding core of Charedim. To these latter especially, the very notion of forswearing their claim on the "City of David" was unthinkable. As Ehud Barak soon discovered, any Israeli politician who revealed so much as a theoretical willingness to compromise on the "undivided capital of Israel" guaranteed himself political oblivion. For the Palestinians, meanwhile, al-Quds—"the Holy Place," Jerusalem—and its Moslem shrines had long since acquired an equivalent iconic symbolism. If the riots of 1921 and 1929 did not give sufficient evidence of the fact, the al-Aqsa intifida of 2000–2003 emphatically did. Wherever in the Israeli-Palestinian impasse there appeared to be leeway for diplomatic compromise—in the evacuation of Gaza, the occasional repositioning of the "security fence," the configuration of an "ethnographic" Israeli-Palestinian border—the prospect of even the narrowest incremental accommodation on Jerusalem remained seemingly beyond the diplomatic horizon.

In September 1993, the Rabin-Arafat Declaration of Principles had reserved the future of Jerusalem for "final-status" negotiations. In hindsight, Israelis and Palestinians would have been better advised to exploit the initial momentum for peace by tackling the issue of Jerusalem head-on, and without postponement.

A TALE OF TWO ELECTIONS

The collapse of the Oslo process was only one factor in this cheerless prognosis. The force majeure of a medical accident also played a role. On the late afternoon of December 18, 2005, Ariel Sharon, at home in his Jerusalem apartment, complained of weakness and difficulty in speaking. His aides transported him forthwith to the nearby Hadassah hospital. Carrying out a battery of tests, a team of neurologists promptly concluded that the prime minister had suffered a mild stroke, the result evidently of a blood clot. A subsequent angiogram traced the difficulty to a small congenital opening in one of Sharon's heart ventricles. At a press conference the next day, the hospital director gave assurances that medication had already dissipated the worst effects of the stroke. Following a three-week period of rest and diet, he asserted, the prime minister would have a stent threaded into the ventricle hole and be "as good as new." Meanwhile, Sharon was kept on heparin, an anticoagulant. At his own insistence, he was allowed to recuperate at his Negev ranch.

On January 4, 2006, however, Sharon suffered a complete collapse, and he was rushed back by helicopter to Jerusalem. At the Hadassah hospital, another series of MRI scans indicated that he had suffered a massive brain hemorrhage, the probable result of his medication. Over the next few days, neurosurgeons were obliged to perform three marathon craniotomies to stanch Sharon's bleeding. Although his vital signs gradually stabilized, he remained comatose, and in late January physicians confirmed that the prime minister had suffered extensive brain damage.

Recovering from their own state of shock, meanwhile, the Israeli people quickly reconciled themselves to Sharon's departure from public life. Would they reassess their party loyalties? Not Amir Peretz and his Knesset Labor faction. With Sharon gone, they envisaged new opportunities for Labor's political recovery. On the political right, similarly discerning a revived chance of leading his followers to victory, Binyamin Netanyahu would not give even a moment's thought to abandoning his recently confirmed Likud chairmanship. Nor would Shimon Peres relinquish his new Kadima affiliation. One of the earliest senior politicians to defect from Labor to the new party, Peres discerned in Kadima's centrism, with or without Sharon at the helm, the likeliest approach to a negotiated peace with the Palestinians. Nor, finally, would Ehud Olmert, Sharon's deputy prime minister, who was now duly confirmed by the attorney general as *acting* prime minister (and later as *interim* prime minister) for the term of Ariel Sharon's incapacitation.

From the outset of Sharon's first election, in January 2001, Olmert, even as mayor of Jerusalem, had served as the prime minister's closest adviser and political alter ego. In November 2005, he was by then a member of Sharon's second government, and the first Likud member to join the prime minister in founding the Kadima party. After Sharon was felled by his stroke, Olmert discreetly refrained from occupying the prime minister's chair when presiding at cabinet meetings. But in mid-January of 2006, the acting prime minister made the decision to put himself forward as Kadima chairman, and personally to lead the new party in its campaign for the March 28 election. Public-opinion polls were running in Kadima's favor, after all, and Olmert was by no means an unknown.

Sixty years old in 2006, he was already a seasoned politician. As a member of the Likud "young guard," he served in the Yitzchak Shamir government from 1990 to 1992, holding the portfolio of health. In 1993, out of office, he had waged an impressive campaign to defeat the much-respected Teddy Kollek as mayor of Jerusalem. Subsequently forging an alliance with the Orthodox parties, Olmert had managed the Jerusalem city council successfully enough to root out the municipal government's rancid backlog of corruption. In 2003, as manager of Ariel Sharon's second election campaign, he was reputedly the political eminence gris of the Kadima party. Perhaps most important, Olmert, for years a committed right-winger, evidently had mellowed in national office. With Sharon, he was among the earliest in the Likud leadership to grasp the need for the evacuation of Gaza, and for territorial compromise in the West Bank. Indeed, he was the first to moot these proposals on Sharon's behalf.

But functioning since 2003 as adviser and stalking horse for a prime minister was less hazardous than the challenge of acting as prime minister in one's own right. In Israel, the public mood was notoriously volatile, as Shimon Peres and Ehud Barak had learned to their dismay. Above and beyond all qualifications, the Israelis wanted a leader with proven credentials on security matters. Rabin and Barak obviously had possessed those bona fides. Perhaps even more charismatically then both, however, Sharon had personified the strength, not to speak of the brutality, to deal with Palestinian violence. In the cynical appraisal of Egypt's President Mubarak, "only Sharon is able to make peace with the Palestinians." Could a civilian like Olmert, however experienced a politician, draw a territorial demarcation line on the West Bank and proclaim to a chronically unstable Palestine Authority, itself rent with civil strife: Here is where we Israelis will live, and there, on ninety percent of this historic land, your people will live? To the Jews living in Jerusalem, could he utter the plainspoken challenge: This is now our capital, but we must find a way to give the Palestinians at least a symbolic governmental presence in the neighborhoods where they have lived for generations? Every Israeli Jew and Palestinian Arab knew that Sharon could have used that language, and animate it both through political ultimata and fearless and frontal action.

The Israeli people would soon have their answer. The March 28, 2006, Knesset elections provided some moderate surprises. Kadima did indeed win a plurality of votes, although its aggregation of twenty-nine Knesset seats was rather less decisive than the pollsters had foreseen. Conversely, Labor had recovered enough from its autumn 2005 defections to achieve second place with nineteen seats, and thereby to emerge as Olmert's likeliest coalition partner. But all predictions of a comparatively brief interlude of party negotiations, resembling the aftermath of Sharon's overwhelming second-term election, were belied. Truer to Israel's political traditions, the process of intramural bargaining was protracted and contentious. In order to achieve the parliamentary majority needed to form a government, one or more of the smaller parties—Shas (twelve seats), the newly formed Pensioners party (seven seats), the right-wing, predominantly Russian, Yisrael Beitenu (eleven seats), even the ultra-Orthodox United Torah Judaism (six seats)—would have to join in the coalition. Meanwhile, all of Kadima's potential partners, including Labor, drove a hard bargain, each demanding ministries specific to their ideologies and patronage expectations. The hardest nut to crack was Amir Peretz's claim upon the finance ministry. The portfolio would have offered Labor its best chance to restore the nation's social-democratic agenda of the pre-1977 era. For Olmert, however, there was no turning back the political calendar. The economy of Israel would remain a market economy, although provided with a generous social-welfare safety net. In the end, Peretz and the Labor leadership accepted that compromise, although not without the accompanying Likud concession to Labor of fully seven ministries, including the crucial portfolios of education and defense, the latter to Peretz himself.

Once he had fashioned the marriage between Kadima and Labor, the prime minister–designate found the task rather easier of wooing into his coalition the Shas religionists, without giving way to their aggressive demands for increased family and school subsidies. When the dust settled, Olmert had well and truly outflanked Likud. The government he presented to the Knesset on May 4 was approved by a vote of 65 to 49. Besides Olmert's own Kadima, it encompassed Labor, Shas, and the Pensioners party. Yet the prime minister had paid a heavy price in government "workability." Although he retained for Kadima the key portfolios of finance, interior, and foreign affairs, his cabinet reached the engorged size of twenty-six members, surpassing the total for any democracy in the West (including the largest of them).

Meanwhile, on March 29, 2006, the day after the Israeli electorate went to the polls, the Palestinians made a political decision of their own. Two months earlier, on January 25, 2006, they had cast their ballots for the Palestine Authority's Legislative Council—the Palestinian parliament. In a massive repudiation of the Fatah party's legacy of administrative and financial corruption, the Palestinians voted overwhelmingly for the Hamas faction. When the returns were tabulated, they revealed that Hamas had captured 74 out of 132 parliamentary seats. The following day, the incumbent Fatah prime minister, Ahmed Qurei, and his cabinet submitted their resignations. In the next weeks, urgent political consultations ensued, as the Hamas leadership decided on the composition of their cabinet. Their first instinct was to incorporate Fatah into their ruling coalition, and thereby present a "respectable" face to the West. But Mahmoud Abbas and his Fatah associates declined the offer. They wanted no part of a Hamas government. On March 29, then, the very day after Israel's Knesset elections, the Palestine Authority's new Hamas cabinet was sworn in by Mahmoud Abbas (who remained on as president, if with diminished governing authority).

For their part, the Israelis regarded the accession of the new Palestinian government as a critical blow to the peace process. In the nineteen years of its existence, this militantly Islamicist party had been responsible for more Israeli civilian deaths than all other Palestinian guerrilla factions combined. Unlike the Fatah of Yasser Arafat, Hamas had preserved intact its political charter, calling for the eradication of the State of Israel, and the transformation of the entirety of Palestine into an Islamic state. Its new prime minister, Ismail Haniyeh, apparently would set the tone of the Palestinian administration. Born in 1963, Haniyeh was a son of Palestinian refugees, and had been reared in the UN's al-Shati camp in Gaza. In 1987, upon graduating from Gaza's Islamic University, Haniyeh had thrown himself heart and soul into the resistance movement. Two years later, the Israelis arrested him and sentenced him to a three-year prison term for incitement and weapons possession. Following his release in 1992, he was deported to Lebanon.

Haniyeh's record from then on was the trajectory of Hamas itself. Although maintaining a low profile for several years, even managing to return from Lebanon to accept the deanship of the Islamic University, he rapidly emerged as a senior strategist in both Hamas's social-welfare and guerrilla activities. In 1997, after the release from prison of the movement's spiritual leader, the aged and ill Sheikh Ahmed Yassin, Haniyeh was picked to direct the sheikh's office. It was a relationship that cemented the younger man's operative control of Hamas guerrilla operations, even as it spurred intermittent Israeli military strikes against him. In December 2005, by then a national hero among the Palestinians, the forty-four-year-old Haniyeh was elected to first place on the Hamas list of candidates, and then went on to guide the party to its stunning January 25, 2006, electoral victory. On March 29, he took the oath of office as the Palestine Authority's prime minister.

A stocky, dynamic figure of considerable personal charm, quick to smile and promise help to his constituents, Haniyeh proved rather less ingratiating as he announced his legislative agenda. It was not only to bring order out of chaos and honesty out of corruption, but to reaffirm his government's commitment to nonrecognition of Israel, to spurn all negotiations with Israel, to refrain from interdicting or punishing acts of guerrilla violence against Israel—in short, to adhere relentlessly to Hamas's charter of sustaining war against Israel until the Jewish state ceased to exist. To that end, one of Haniyeh's first acts as prime minister was to approve the appointment of a notorious Hamas guerrilla, Jamal Abu Samhadana, as chief of his government security forces, "to restore order in Palestine." In response, the Israeli government leadership, supported by the Bush administration in the United States, reciprocated Hamas's policy of non-recognition. They shun any underground contacts with the Hamas regime, even on the narrowest, functional level; would not commit themselves to observance of earlier diplomatic agreements with the Palestine Authority; would ban imports or exports from Palestinian territory; would not transfer to the Hamas government taxes that in earlier years they had collected on the PA's behalf.

Two and a half weeks later, on April 17, during the Passover holiday, a Palestinian suicide bomber made his way into Tel Aviv, and detonated a bomb in the crowded site of the city's old central bus station. Nine people were killed and over sixty were wounded (two to die later), the largest number of Israeli civilian casualties from a single act of terrorism in seventeen months. The bomber had been a member of the Iranian-funded Islamic Jihad. That very day, the Palestine Authority issued a statement declaring the attack on Israel to be a "legitimate" measure of self-defense, and that none of the Islamic Jihad's members would be arrested. For the moment, the Israeli government stayed its hand. Several days later, however, it issued a terse official communiqué. Israel's proclaimed stance of reciprocity, it declared, might well include the "restoration of order" in Palestine on its own.

CHAPTER XLI   A MIDDLE

EASTERN HOUR OF DECISION

THE ROCKETS OF LEBANON

The contingency of reciprocity materialized sooner than the Israeli government could have predicted. During the spring of 2006, Hamas guerrillas in the Gaza Strip intermittently fired off short-range Qassam rockets over the frontier toward the Israeli development town of S'derot. At first, damage was comparatively minimal, but the psychological pressure on S'derot's inhabitants was intense. Almost each day, families were obliged to take cover in bomb shelters, and children were deprived of schooling. Toward late June, moreover, Hamas ordnance specialists increased the range of the Qassams, and the rockets began to penetrate as far south as Ashkelon. Then, on June 25, ten months after Ariel Sharon had completed Israel's withdrawal from the Strip, Hamas guerrillas tunneled under the Gaza border post of Kerem Shalom, killing two Israeli soldiers and abducting a third.

Later that day, Palestinian Prime Minister Ismail Haniyeh announced that the Israeli captive, Gilad Shalit, a nineteen-year-old corporal, would be held as hostage for some nine thousand Palestinians currently languishing in Israeli prisons for acts of violence or suspected violence against Israel's citizenry. To these Hamas acts of murder, abduction, and extortion, as well as to the ongoing ordeal of rocket attacks, the Israeli government gave an unequivocal and emphatic response. It took the form of systematic artillery and tank shelling of suspected Hamas guerrilla concentrations, as well as the punitive closure of Israeli border stations to Gaza's commuting laborers and agricultural exports.

Far from achieving its goal of securing Corporal Shalit's unconditional release, however, or deterring further Palestinian assaults and abductions, Israel's retaliation seemed only to provoke wider and more daring acts of guerrilla mayhem. On July 12, seventeen days after the Hamas incursions, and fully six years after Ehud Barak had withdrawn the residual Israeli "picket fence" contingent from Lebanon, Hizballah militia members in south Lebanon staged an even more extensive and carefully planned raid on an Israeli military patrol just across the Lebanese border. The price for Israel this time was the death of eight soldiers, the abduction of two more, and an extensive shower of Katyusha rockets into Israel's northern border communities of Kiryat Shmonah, Metulla, and Rosh Pina.

Inasmuch as Hizballah drew its support from Iran, could the timing of the

July 12 raid have reflected the decision of Sheikh Hassan Nasrallah, Hizballah's spiritual leader in Lebanon, three days before the scheduled "G-8" summit of industrial nations in St. Petersburg, Russia, to divert attention from Iran's secret nuclear-development program? If this was Nasrallah's purpose, it did not succeed. Upon convening in St. Petersburg, the G-8 powers finally reached their long-delayed agreement on a UN Security Council resolution to condemn Iran's evasion of IAEA inspections, and to warn of possible (although unde-fined) sanctions.

Yet it was equally conceivable that Hassan Nasrallah's provocation against Israel constituted a more limited gamble, comparable to Hamas's June 25 raid on the Gaza border post. In years past, Hizballah had demonstrated its muscu-larity in bombing the United States marine barracks in Beirut in 1983, killing 241 American servicemen. In 1992, Hizballah agents bombed the Israeli embassy in Argentina, killing 29 Israelis and local Jews, and wounding 222 oth-ers, Jews and non-Jews. Two years later yet, a car bomb planted by Hizballah saboteurs blew up outside Buenos Aires's Jewish Community Center, killing 85 people and injuring 150. It was six years after that, in 2000, that the accu-mulation of Hizballah guerrilla attacks persuaded Ehud Barak to withdraw Israel's "picket fence" from Lebanon. Since then, Hizballah had emerged not only as the strongest local force in Lebanon altogether, with some thirteen thousand members by 2006, but also as a political party that held fourteen seats in the country's parliament and two seats in the Lebanese cabinet. Should it now remain inert while a Hamas militia in the congested and impoverished Gaza Strip proved capable of striking a humiliating blow against the Israeli army?

In the last week of July, moreover, by the time full-scale fighting had erupted between Israel and Hizballah (see below), John Anderson, an American jour-nalist writing for the *New Yorker* magazine, secured an interview in Beirut with Ali Fayyed, a senior member of the Hizballah politburo. In Fayyed's explana-tion to Anderson, Sheikh Nasrallah's purpose in authorizing the July 12 raid and abduction was "to get Israel to return Lebanese lands"—his reference to the Sheba'a Farms, a small strip of territory occupied by Israel since 1967—"and to release three of our prisoners. We've made many efforts to have them returned, and have tried everything, including diplomacy, with no results. . . . The idea was 'prisoners for prisoners.' And we have exchanged prisoners with Israel in the past." The assertion was valid. So was the expectation of Israeli forbearance. In recent years, Hizballah had indeed mounted similar raids into Israel. In 2005, moreover, Prime Minister Sharon's military intelligence advisers had alerted him to Hizballah's accumulating stockpile of rockets. The Meridor Committee recently had confirmed that appraisal (pp. 1100–1101). Neverthe-less, although sorely tempted to react to the Hizballah threat with his custom-ary pulverizing aggressiveness, Ariel Sharon was unwilling to create problems for the new Lebanese premier, Fuad Siniora, who had recently evicted the thirty-thousand-man Syrian military force that had long occupied his country. In any case, the Israeli prime minister had his hands full with his evacuation of the Gaza Strip and his projected master plan for a future withdrawal from the largest part of the West Bank.

But whatever its ulterior purpose in mounting the raid of July 12, 2006, Hizballah's gamble this time had unintended consequences. If Ariel Sharon, with his formidable military reputation, could afford to exercise restraint, the recently elected Ehud Olmert was not willing to exhibit the same forbearance. Olmert and his newly appointed minister of defense, the dovish Laborite Amir Peretz, had come to their portfolios as civilians, and as advocates of retrenchment in Palestine. Their security credentials, if not suspect, at least were unproved. Thus, on July 13, after an emergency cabinet session, Olmert warned the Beirut government that "the sky will fall on Lebanon" if the Hizballah were not reined in and the abducted soldiers not repatriated. Meanwhile, the military high command ordered armored columns to assemble and to begin shelling Hizballah rocket positions in southern Lebanon. Simultaneously, the air force attacked suspected launching sites as far north as Beirut. The runways of Beirut airport were also bombed, to prevent weaponry from being flown in from Syria, or even directly from Iran. But when more than a week of intensive shelling failed to reduce the rocket attacks, the Israeli "security" cabinet again went into emergency session with General Dan Halutz, the military chief of staff, and senior military intelligence officers. In the early evening of July 19, Olmert confirmed the decision to send units of the elite Golani Brigade into south Lebanon. The troops' limited, "surgical" objective would be to clean out suspected Hizballah firing points and then return to Israel. It was a strategy that Israeli commentators later described as "half coffee, half tea."

Supported by armored columns and fighter-bombers, the ground force initially targeted the Hizballah stronghold of Bint Jbeil, a Lebanese hilltop village less than three miles across the international border. In successive attacks, from July 25 to July 29, the Israeli troops encountered resistance that one of them later described (from his hospital bed) as a "hell on earth." The Hizballah "fired from all directions," "from 180 degrees," from underground bunkers, from behind hillocks, from barns and farmhouses where the Israelis sought shelter. Fifteen soldiers were mowed down in cunningly laid enemy ambushes. Eleven others were killed in face-to-face combat. Many of the casualties were sustained when troops attempted to retrieve the bodies of slain comrades. Several Israeli tanks, in an effort to provide covering fire, were themselves turned into fiery coffins by Hizballah laser-guided rockets. After three days of close-order combat, in which scores of casualties were sustained on each side, the Israelis returned to base, their "surgical" objective still unfulfilled.

The murderous encounter at Bint Jbeil was repeated the same week in two neighboring Lebanese villages, Ayt al-Sha'ab and Jebel. Although Israeli infantrymen eventually overran these redoubts, the fierceness of Hizballah resistance once again shocked and horrified them. Over the years since 2000, when Prime Minister Ehud Barak had evacuated the Israeli "picket fence," the Hizballah militia had electrified and air-conditioned their underground bunkers, and reinforced them with enough concrete to withstand any but direct hits from air or artillery attack. They had been stocked with enough ammunition and food to last for weeks at a time. During pauses in the close-order combat and aerial bombardment, Hizballah guerrillas were able to emerge from deep within the bunkers to fight again, and to inflict scores of casualties on the Israelis.

By the third week of July, it was apparent to the Israeli general staff that bombing, shelling, and small-scale infantry assaults were not adequate to destroy Hizballah defenses. Yet Olmert and his cabinet still were reluctant to mobilize the additional thousands of reserve troops that would be required for success in a prolonged and debilitating land war. The reasons were by no means exclusively political or economic. Whatever precarious success could be achieved in neutralizing short-range Katyushas in the Lebanese borderland, other versions of Iranian-manufactured rockets were being transported through Syria to northern and central Lebanon. These included the highly sophisticated Fajr-3, with a greater range and a much heavier payload of explosives than the Katyusha. Even fired from Beirut, in central Lebanon, the Fajr-3 was rumored to be capable of reaching well beyond the much-battered Israeli border communities of Kiryat Shmonah and Metullah, and Naharia.

Indeed, as early as the second week of the war, the rumor was verified. As they began setting up and firing Fajr-3s from their launching sites in south Beirut, Hizballah militiamen managed to score direct hits in populated areas of Haifa, Israel's third-largest city. One of the missiles exploded in the maintenance shed of the Haifa railroad terminal, killing eight workers. Two days later, another missile crashed into a Haifa apartment courtyard, killing two residents, and sending thousands of families into air-raid shelters. A few days later yet, a Fajr-3 launched from Sidon traveled well beyond Haifa, exploding just outside the northern Israeli town of Afula. Both Katyusha and Fajr-3 rockets, moreover, were fired in cascades of 8 or 10. By the third week of July, the extravaganza of projectiles reached 125–150 a day. Meanwhile, from his clandestine headquarters in the basement of the Iranian embassy in Beirut, Sheikh Hassan Nasrallah warned that new and even larger varieties of missiles would soon be directed at Tel Aviv. It was significant, too, that Nasrallah made no claim that his militia's developing ballistic campaign was directed at military targets. Rather, it was waged specifically as an instrument of terror against Israel's population centers. By the third week of July, some 100,000 residents of the country's northern cities had joined a civilian exodus southward, and the number would quadruple within days. For those civilians—the majority—who remained behind, as many as half a million were obliged to huddle intermittently in public air-raid shelters or in the "safe" rooms of their homes.

These were the circumstances, by July 22, in which Israel's military command reached a consensus that continued priority had to be given to the aerial campaign against the enemy's longer-range rocket launchers, squirreled away in Beirut and other Hizballah strongholds in central Lebanon. Chief of Staff Dan Halutz, himself a former air force commander, presented his strategy to the cabinet. In making his case, Halutz actually was repeating views he had expressed in recent years in ongoing debate with the intelligence staff and infantry and armored-force commanders. "A land force is not sent into action as long as there is an effective alternative," he had said in a lecture at Israel's National Defense College in January 2001. "Victory means achieving the strategic goal and not necessarily territory. I maintain that we also have to part with the concept of a land battle. . . . Victory is a matter of consciousness. Only air power affects the adversary's consciousness significantly." In ensuing years, he

The New York Times
Graphics: Map of Israel
(Mideast Update),
The New York Times,
August 16, 2006.
Reprinted by permission
of The New York Times
Graphics.

saw no need to relinquish that principle. And now, in mid-July of 2006, as Halutz and his senior officers presented their strategy to Olmert, Peretz, and the inner "security" cabinet, there seemed to be no apparent alternative to a sustained air campaign. It was only by means of "clean," surgical air strikes, targeting Lebanon's infrastructure, including highways, bridges, and fuel depots, that Israel could interdict the transport of rockets from Syria and Iran to Hizballah sector stations and arsenals. Olmert and his colleagues were convinced. As the prime minister saw it, relentless bombing might even succeed in turning Lebanon's large Christian and Sunni populations against the Hizballah.

From July 14 to July 29, in their intensified campaign, Israel's fighter-bombers registered a certain success in eliminating the Fajr-3s, as well as transforming virtually all remaining highway networks and even back roads between Syria and Lebanon into cratered moonscapes. By the end of July, Israeli aircraft were even able to give renewed attention to the Katyushas hidden in Lebanese population centers south of the Litani River. Thus, on July 30, an F-16 jet was directed to aim its laser-guided "smart" bomb at a suspect apartment building in Qana, a town of some ten thousand people, five miles southeast of Tyre. The pilot followed instructions, dropped his ordnance, and the building crumbled. Whatever success the attack may have achieved against hidden rocket launchers, however, the effect on the residents was devastating. The Lebanese government initially announced that over fifty civilians had lost their lives in the bombing, twenty-three of them children (although later reports scaled down the number of casualties by half).

Whatever the final toll of killed and wounded, the Qana bombing horrified Western opinion as did no other single episode in the war. In Britain, the anti-

Israel bias of BBC reportage, and public opinion generally, was an old story. But now Foreign Minister Margaret Beckett joined in denouncing the attack as "absolutely dreadful," and "quite appalling." France's President Jacques Chirac harshly condemned "this unjustified action." Among Europe's major powers, Germany had traditionally evinced the greatest understanding of Israel's security needs (pp. 559–62); yet this time Foreign Minister Frank-Walter Steinmeier felt impelled to issue a cautionary statement that "every use of military force, even in the framework of self-defense, must be proportionate. . . . Victims among the civilian population must particularly be avoided." From the Vatican, Pope Benedict XVI expressed his shock. "In the name of God," the pontiff declaimed, "I call on all those responsible for this spiral of violence . . . to lay down [their weapons] on all sides." In the Middle East, the leaders of the "moderate" Arab states, Hosni Mubarak of Egypt and King Abdullah II of Jordan, joined Lebanese Prime Minister Fuad Siniora in expressing unreserved condemnation of Israel and countenancing pro-Hizballah popular demonstrations in their capitals (Mubarak's eldest son departed for Tehran to participate in a mass international solidarity rally for Lebanon's "freedom fighters"). Not least of all, thousands of Israeli Arabs, even in communities that had themselves suffered casualties from rocket avalanches, risked prosecution by conducting pro-Hizballah demonstrations and carrying Hizballah banners.

SEEKING A DIPLOMATIC BREATHING SPACE

On July 30, several hours after the initial death toll in Qana was tallied, Lebanon's Prime Minister Siniora bracketed his condemnation of the "Israeli massacres" with a heartfelt plea: "[T]here is no place on this sad morning for any discussion other than [of] an immediate and unconditional cease-fire." The same thought surely had occurred to others. When the leaders of the G-8 powers had first convened in St. Petersburg, on July 15, their discussions from the outset had been preoccupied not only with the challenge of Iran's nuclear development program but with the escalating Hizballah-Israeli hostilities in Lebanon. On the sixteenth, the assembled prime ministers and presidents issued a joint resolution, condemning Hizballah for provoking the hostilities in Lebanon, but urging Israel to exercise "the utmost in restraint." Beyond releasing this rather anodyne appeal, however, most of the G-8 leaders did not disguise their preference for seeking an immediate UN Security Council cease-fire resolution.

The most important dissenter was George W. Bush. If the American president was unwilling to let Iran win domination of the Persian Gulf through its Shi'ite proxies in Iraq, he had no intention of allowing those proxies to win a foothold in Lebanon. Britain's Prime Minister Tony Blair shared the president's concerns. Yet he prevailed upon Bush to send Secretary of State Condoleezza Rice directly from St. Petersburg to Lebanon and Israel to explore a cessation of Israeli air strikes and Hizballah missile launchings, as well as a mutual withdrawal of ground forces. The content of subsequent discussions between Rice and the president has not yet been revealed. On July 24, however, just before the secretary departed for the Middle East, she and Bush evidently agreed that Israel would not be pressed to cease its attacks on Hizballah militants until its army had registered demonstrable success and an effective security force could then be interposed between Lebanon and Israel.

Stopping off in Beirut for a few hours on the first segment of her Middle East journey, Rice held intensive consultations with Prime Minister Siniora. The two were friends. Siniora was a gallant liberal and steadfast defender of his nation's independence against Syrian intimidation. The year before, Rice had enthusiastically welcomed his election to Lebanon's prime ministry. But now, Siniora complained, Israel's air force was bombing his homeland to smithereens. He entreated the secretary to persuade Olmert to forbear; he, Siniora, would personally intercede with Hassan Nasrallah for an exchange of prisoners. In turn, Rice assured the prime minister that she too favored a cease-fire, but that the crisis manifestly had gone far beyond the issue of prisoners. Any cease-fire that functioned merely as camouflage for a Hizballah return to south Lebanon would produce at most a temporary lull in hostilities.

Arriving in Jerusalem a few hours later, the secretary conferred through the late afternoon and the morning of the twenty-fifth with Prime Minister Olmert, Defense Minister Peretz, and General Halutz. President Bush, she explained, shared Israel's view that a simple truce, followed by a unilateral Israeli retreat from Lebanese territory, would leave an intolerable vacuum for Hizballah, and Iranian, exploitation. Washington would reject such a formula. But in the interval, Rice insisted, Israel's bombing campaign must not be seen to emulate the indiscriminate terrorism of Hizballah rocket launchings. It must be demonstrably surgical in its choice of military targets. Olmert took only meager consolation from the secretary's proposal. As he and his colleagues explained, a more restricted air bombardment suggested the alternative of a bitter land campaign, possibly as far inland as the Litani River (see map, p. 1120). That contingency, in turn, would require a more widespread mobilization of Israel's reserves. It was an unappealing prospect. Rice was sympathetic, but continued to advocate restraint. However, she promised to work out a viable diplomatic solution, one that would be acceptable to Israel. On that conciliatory note, she then departed for Washington.

During the ensuing week and a half, the secretary explored diplomatic alternatives with Nicholas Burns, her principal Middle East adviser, and with National Security Adviser Stephen Hadley. George W. Bush had returned from Russia by then, and periodically Rice and the president held news conferences, explaining the need for linking a UN Security Council cease-fire resolution with a formula to preclude Hizballah's return to Israel's northern border. Rice's explanations were phrased in restrained, diplomatic language, citing the urgency of defusing the explosive Israeli-Lebanese frontier once and for all. But in his own public statements, Bush was characteristically one-dimensional in equating Israel's military campaign in Lebanon with America's purpose of "preempting" Iranian domination in Iraq. The Europeans did not react well to the president's conflation of the two issues.

The Qana episode, however, on the night of July 29–30, may be regarded as a fault line in the Lebanon war. When Rice proposed an immediate return visit to Beirut, Lebanese Prime Minister Siniore declined to receive her. Under mounting international pressure, then, Rice, Burns, and Hadley searched urgently for a prospective cease-fire resolution that would satisfy other permanent members of the UN Security Council. It was France, specifically, that was regarded as the key to an agreement. With its historic ties to Lebanon, and its success in negotiating the Israeli-Lebanese cease-fire agreement of April 1996, following Shimon Peres's Operation Grapes of Wrath, France was manifestly the interlocutor of choice. During the first week of August, therefore, John Bolton, the United States ambassador to the UN, and his French counterpart, Jean-Marc de La Sablière, conferred several times daily, and often into the late evening hours, trying to achieve a meeting of minds. By August 6, it appeared that a tentative agreement had been reached. The Security Council would pass a cease-fire resolution stipulating that Hizballah and Israeli forces would cease all hostilities in Lebanon. Subsequently, another Security Council resolution would be issued, authorizing the formation of a "robust" multinational UN force of some fifteen thousand troops, France presumably supplying the largest contingent, to take over Hizballah positions from the Litani River to the "blue line," the Lebanese-Israeli border. Once this deployment was complete, perhaps over a period of several weeks, Israel would then evacuate its army units altogether from Lebanese territory.

No sooner had France accepted the proposal, however, and the United States had secured the Israeli government's concurrence, than the Hizballah leadership, together with the Lebanese and other Arab governments, began issuing vehement objections. On August 8, representatives of the Arab League flew to New York to echo Lebanese Prime Minister Siniora's indignation. The UN resolution, they protested, was unacceptably one-sided. It would have left Israeli troops in place on Lebanese soil until the composition of a UN expeditionary force was negotiated with the relevant governments. Moreover, the complicated logistics and emplacement of such a multilateral detachment would have to be resolved. The process might take weeks, even months. In turn, swayed by these Arab objections, the French delegation radically shifted its position, and proposed that both Hizballah and Israeli troops withdraw from the Litani River forthwith, and simultaneously.

For the United States, and Israel, such a proposal was equivalent to a blank check for Hizballah to reoccupy and restock their fortifications. They were not having it. The previous week, Prime Minister Olmert had secured his cabinet's permission to call up thirty thousand additional troops from Israel's pool of reserves. At first, even after donning their uniforms, taking up arms, and undergoing last-minute refresher training, the reserves were held back from active battle. But on August 9, the army command began deploying the new units just over the Lebanese frontier. Indeed, on that day, in a reprise of the military's once-vaunted tactical panache, Israeli helicopters leapfrogged the front lines, disgorged two squads of commandos near the Litani River, and burst into a Hizballah sector command post, killing its officers. At the same time, the air force resumed its heavy aerial and artillery bombardment.

The strategy registered on Western diplomats. Late on the evening of August 10, after round-the-clock discussions at the UN between the French and American ambassadors, as well as with Condoleezza Rice, who had come up from Washington to press negotiations to a conclusion, the outline of a compromise Franco-American agreement was reached, and won approval from the Lebanese and Israeli governments. It developed later that Fuad Siniora had himself provided a critical inducement for the compromise (see below). Early the next morning, the plenum of the UN Security Council was called into session. The proceedings consumed fully eight hours, giving the various delegations time to phone home to their governments. But by mid-evening of Friday, August 11, the resolution passed unanimously.

Entitled UN Security Council Resolution 1701, the document required Hizballah to cease all attacks against Israel and for Israel to "end its offensive operations" in Lebanon. The resolution refrained from precisely defining "offensive operations," but the United States and Israel had reached a private agreement that the Israelis would be entitled to respond to Hizballah actions against the Jewish state's civilian population. In its text, moreover, the resolution extended until 2007 the mandate of the UN Interim Force in Lebanon (UNIFIL)—a modest, two-thousand-man contingent that had been stationed along the Israeli-Lebanese frontier since 1978—to enable it to fulfill a new task, the "robust enforcement" of peace, rather than, as heretofore, simply the monitoring of frontiers. To fulfill this new role, the UNIFIL detachments (henceforth to be called UNIFIL II) would gradually be expanded to fifteen thousand troops, and equipped with armaments and communications sufficient to carry out its mandate from the Lebanese-Israeli border as far north as the Litani River. Moreover, as negotiations proceeded for the expansion of UNIFIL II, the resolution "welcome[d]" the Lebanese government's decision to deploy fifteen thousand of its own troops in south Lebanon. It was only when this combined total of thirty thousand UN and Lebanese soldiers was actively in the process of formation, and embarked on its mission of patrolling the sector between the international border and the Litani River, that Israel would be obliged to begin withdrawing its army from Lebanese soil, a sequential process that would be completed once the UNIFIL II units reached full strength.

It was indicative of the exhaustion and damage suffered by both sides that the release of the Israeli captives was not included in the provisions of the cease-fire. Indeed, Ehud Olmert belied his earlier insistence that his government would never bargain with either the Hizballah or the Hamas over Israeli hostages. Sobered by the cost of the recent war, the prime minister intimated that he was now prepared after all to enter negotiations over the release of the two soldiers kidnapped in Lebanon on July 12. In return, however, he restricted the prospective quid pro quo to the release of the handful of Lebanese prisoners currently incarcerated in Israeli jails, including some twenty Hizballah guerrillas. Yet it was later apparent that even this limitation would not long endure.

Under the terms of the August 11 resolution, the cease-fire was to go into effect at 1:00 a.m. on August 14. But, until then, hostilities reached a new crescendo of ferocity. After a brief (post-Qana) lull, Israeli artillery and jets blasted away at every suspected Hizballah installation, from the international border up to Beirut. From Lebanon, in turn, an unprecedented total of some 250 missiles rained down on Haifa and other northern Israeli population centers. Manifestly, Hizballah's arsenal was far from depleted. And then, almost miraculously, in the darkness of 1:00 a.m. on August 14, the fighting stopped. Except for a few isolated instances of small-arms fire, it did not resume. In ensuing days, units of the Lebanese army began to take up makeshift positions south of the Litani River. Some half of the estimated thirty-five thousand Israeli ground forces in southern Lebanon were ordered home.

THE RECKONING

In the immediate aftermath of the cease-fire, both the Lebanese and the Israeli governments engaged in somber assessments of the war's costs. Without question, the people of Lebanon had endured the more fearsome ordeal. A peace-loving nation, traditionally the least belligerent of Israel's neighbors, it had suffered over 1,187 civilian dead, and more than three times that many wounded (the number of Hizballah guerrilla casualties was not made public). Approximately 700,000–800,000 Lebanese, a quarter of the nation's entire population, had been uprooted. Of these, about 200,000 fled for refuge to neighboring Syria, but most were obliged to find shelter in basements, tents, or even open fields, where they faced acute privation, especially in food and water. From Beirut south, entire towns and villages—their homes and workplaces, their utilities and sanitary facilities—had been reduced to rubble. The Lebanese government tentatively projected the cost even of the most elementary physical reconstruction of infrastructure, housing, and commercial buildings at between $6 billion and $10 billion.

For Israel, too, of course, the war had taken a serious toll. By the time of the cease-fire, the number of dead was listed as 161, of whom 44 were civilians, the rest soldiers. The number of wounded combatants reached some 1,350; of civilians, over 4,200—all of the latter from rocket strikes against Israel's northern communities. On August 13, Israel's ministry of finance tentatively projected the economic cost of the war as $5.5 billion. Of this sum, $2.85 billion consisted of defense spending and the expense of covering direct and indirect civilian damage (including the loss of summer tourism), the rest went for the provision of temporary housing, compensation for lost civilian income, and a $500 million one-time payment to local governments in the north. The finance ministry warned, too, that the expense of the recent fighting would result in at least a 1.5 percent decline in gross domestic product, equivalent to approximately $2.5 billion, including the loss of $500 million in tax income and the future increase of the defense budget.

In the end, however, loss of economic resources, even loss of life, proved less crippling a blow than the malaise of spirit that descended like a fog on the citizens of Israel. Their military and political commentators did not hesitate to appraise the war's ominous portents. To be sure, Israel had not won all its wars. Indeed, it had not won a decisive victory since 1967. Nevertheless, even in the Yom Kippur War of 1973, the armed forces, crippled at the outset by the notorious intelligence "blunder" (pp. 744–46), managed at least to escape defeat by the time of the cease-fire. But in the Lebanon war of 2006, the nation for the first time experienced the unmistakable and bitter taste of failure. The government of Ehud Olmert could not discern, or so much as explore, the possible limited purpose behind a single border foray, or devise a more imaginative solution to it than a reflexive and full-blown spasm of retaliation against the weakest of Israel's Arab neighbors. Once that retaliatory campaign was launched, moreover, escalating into the longest Arab-Israeli conflict since the original War for Independence of 1948–49, General Halutz's air offensive proved incapable of destroying perhaps more than a quarter of a vast, residual enemy stock of ballistic missiles. When Israel's government and military command belatedly approved the mobilization of thousands of reserve troops, and even more belatedly dispatched them into southern Lebanon, the ensuing ground offensive proved inadequate to wrest decisive control of enemy emplacements more than half the distance to the Litani River.

For that matter, who were the enemy? Whatever their cornucopia of logistical and ordnance support from Iran and Syria, the Hizballah on the battlefield consisted of not more than ten thousand irregulars concentrated in the trans-Litani's honeycomb of fortifications, with possibly a maximum of three thousand support personnel farther north to transport and fire rockets. If it was this modest network that fought the vaunted Israeli military machine to a standstill, others among Israel's Arab neighbors were likely to draw tempting conclusions. Even those, like Egypt and Jordan, that had already signed treaties of peace with Israel could not be indifferent to the implications of the Jewish state's unexpected vulnerability. In the Middle East, perceptions of weakness too often had induced Israel's enemies to take precipitous gambles. Only one of them had to succeed.

On August 18, three days after the first contingent of some two hundred Lebanese soldiers deployed south of the Litani River, the battalion's commander announced that "[t]he army will deploy on the wounded Lebanese land *alongside* the men of the resistance." Manifestly, the Lebanese army had no plans to drive Hizballah out of the south, or even to disarm them. The following day, Émile Lahoud, president of Lebanon and commander-in-chief of its army, confirmed that Hizballah militiamen would not be compelled to give up their weapons. Hassan Nasrallah may have promised the Lebanese government that his men would not carry their weapons openly, but he gave no assurances that they would refrain from rebuilding and rearming their bunkers. Indeed, his guerrillas were photographed openly patrolling in the villages of southern Lebanon, recording the positions and movements of the nearby Israeli army, and giving boastful interviews to Arab television crews.

More forebodingly yet, only one week after the UN Security Council had passed Resolution 1701, with its commitment to provide a "robust" international force of fifteen thousand soldiers to monitor and enforce the Hizballah-Israeli cease-fire, the pledge began fraying. It was the United States' and Israel's understanding that France, with its historic solicitude for Lebanon, would provide a substantial component of the UN troops. On August 18, however, President Chirac informed UN Secretary-General Kofi Annan that France was already providing two hundred monitors for the preexisting UNIFIL contingent, and was prepared to augment that allotment by only an additional two hundred. Although Chirac hedged this message by vague assurances of "ongoing reappraisal" in the event "rules of engagement and administrative control" were clarified, Annan reacted with undisguised shock and dismay. So did George W. Bush. In a press conference two days later, the president all but overtly accused the French government, "our friend and ally," of reneging on a solemn promise. Meanwhile, as UN Deputy Secretary-General Mark Malloch Brown urgently set about canvassing other governments for troop commitments, a few—Spain, Malaysia, Nepal, Turkey—seemed equally hesitant to provide more than a few hundred UNIFIL supernumeraries.

Eventually, however, Ehud Olmert, Kofi Annan, and George W. Bush prevailed on an unexpected source, the government of Italy, to commit a minimum of three thousand troops for the UNIFIL II buffer force. By assuming European leadership in a critical area of world tension, Prime Minister Romano Prodi's newly established coalition cabinet evidently discerned an opportunity to win a certain degree of prestige for their nation. Polls conducted among the Italian people at large supported this view. In turn, embarrassed at being upstaged by the Italians in an historic sphere of French concern, Jacques Chirac reconsidered his earlier equivocation, and decided to project a rather more statesmanlike image. Yet the French president's vision of statesmanship did not extend beyond the offer of a thousand additional troops. For its part, the German government then took on the responsibility of supplying five naval frigates and some two thousand sailors to patrol Lebanon's coastal waters and interdict transference of weaponry by sea. Nevertheless, a combined UNIFIL II contingent of six or seven thousand troops and sailors was less than half the size anticipated by the UN Security Council in its cease-fire resolution of August 11. To be sure, UNIFIL II was supplemented by fifteen thousand Lebanese regular army troops, but this lackluster contingent was too ill trained and timorous to perform as more than a civilian constabulary.

In the end, however, UNIFIL II's most glaring lacuna was not modesty of numbers. It was the force's refusal to interpret its Security Council mandate—of functioning as a "robust" peacekeeper—to apply to the disarmament of Hizballah. Even if the transference of Iranian weaponry could be interdicted (itself a daunting challenge), Hizballah's ample stocks of short- and medium-range rockets, laser-guided antitank projectiles, radar-directed anti-boat missiles, and other sophisticated weaponry presumably would remain intact. Israel's more astute military commentators, together with members of the political right, had long suspected that it would come to this. In their mordant appraisal, no credible military presence appeared likely to deter the reestablishment and consolidation of a virtual "mini-Iran" in south Lebanon.

Was Israel's fate after all to be one of unremitting warfare and human sacrifice?

A LINGERING VACUUM OF GREAT POWER STATESMANSHIP

It need not have been. The lesson of earlier confrontations should long since have been internalized by the "Quartet." Rarely in modern history had contentious smaller nations, those whose relationships had been drenched in rancor and blood, managed successfully to "negotiate" boundaries or enduring peace treaties on their own. For precedent, it was necessary only to hark back to the sequence of nineteenth- and early-twentieth-century Great Power conclaves (Vienna, London, Paris, Berlin, among others) that established the independence of countries as diverse as Greece, Belgium, Serbia, Bulgaria, Rumania, or Albania; or to the Paris Peace Conference of 1919–20, which sculpted an aggregation of European successor states and Asian mandates from the debris of the prewar empires.

Which of this seething heterogeneity of races and cultures, of ethnic and religious communities, "negotiated" their sovereignties or autonomies, their boundaries or their respective financial claims, among themselves? It was unthinkable that any of these political neophytes, suppurating in an immemorial folklore of cultural and national hatreds, could have achieved a voluntary meeting of minds with their neighbors. Periodic diplomatic negotiations between them tended at best to be unproductive; at worst, inflammatory. More recently, when Egypt's President Anwar al-Sadat and Lebanon's President-elect Bashir Gemayel moved on their own to deal bilaterally with Israel, they paid with their lives, and with their peace initiatives exposed as minefields of diplomatic fragility. It required the Gulf War, and a conference jointly sponsored by the United States and the Soviet Union in Madrid (later in Washington) to devise the framework for a so-called negotiated settlement between Israel and Hashemite Jordan. With few exceptions—the Oslo agreement plainly was not the success story among them, or even the ultimately toothless guidelines of the Quartet's "Road Map"— it had been the initiatives of the Great Powers alone that legitimized the sovereign identities of perenially hostile smaller nations, that defined their mutual borders and arbitrated their reciprocal claims and grievances.

Did Great Powers have a celestial dispensation, then, to impose their own territorial and ethnographic templates upon the world's minor players? To this cri de coeur, loosed with much anguish in the "Revolt of the Small Powers" at the 1919 Paris Peace Conference, French Premier Clemenceau, British Prime Minister Lloyd George, and United States President Wilson responded in almost identical language. It was specifically the danger of being sucked into a future conflict of irredentist claims and counterclaims, they emphasized, that obliged them to perform their own diplomatic surgery upon Europe's fulminance of regional animosities. Had it not been for the Allies' military sacrifices, after all, the very political existence of the successor states, whatever their ultimate dimensions, would have remained moot.

By the same token, neither an Israeli nor a Palestinian state would have been even faintly conceivable if dependent upon a meeting of minds among Jews and Arabs alone. After World War I, it was the victorious Western Powers that formulated the essential geopolitical contours of both the Arab nations and the Jewish homeland. After World War II, it was the United Nations that sanctioned the partition of Palestine into sovereign Jewish and Arab entities. No one contended that these dispensations begat a paradigm of justice and equity, let alone a guidebook for neighborly comity; but their conceptual framework, like that of the European successor states, had survived a chain reaction of regional challenges, and within its ethnographic lineaments two national organisms, one de jure, the other de facto, had finally achieved a near-parallel recognition.

Moreover, without an effulgence of American and German financial aid, and a semiofficial membership in the Common Market, Israel early on would have foundered in bankruptcy. Its armed forces, deprived of access to French and American military equipment, would have been hard-pressed to resist a tightening Soviet ring of Arab proxies. Similarly, had the Palestine Authority not been assured the fullest measure of European diplomatic support, and the EU's guarantee of open-ended financial subsidies, the late Yasser Arafat's nascent government would long before have imploded in the morass of its own ineptitude and corruption.

Altogether, the United States and Europe had paid their dues in their respective commitments to Israelis and Palestinians. And each of these benefactors now faced grave dangers to its own economic and political interests should the Middle Eastern conflict, like the Balkan crisis of 1914, continue to metastasize at its own genetic pace. Each Arab-Israeli war—in 1948, 1956, 1967, 1973, 1982, 2001–2—had incrementally widened the risks of Great Power confrontation, of blocked international waterways, of large-scale energy stoppages, of political assassinations, of institutionalized terrorism, and, lately and most ominously, of resort to weapons of mass destruction.

In the years immediately preceding Hamas's political victory in Palestine, United States State Department and Quartet technocrats had been quietly at work refining and mediating proposals for an Israel territorially augmented by limited and reciprocal security-frontier adjustments, and a Palestine demographically configured to encompass a near totality of its Arab population. But with the discussions and even their negotiating agenda lately collapsing in cross-border violence and retaliations, it was the "heavyweights," the Great Powers themselves, who at long last were faced with the challenge of borrowing from historical precedent and functioning less as mediators than as principals. Their own statesmen now confronted the responsibility of putting the final touches on a detailed blueprint for the Holy Land that reflected the prestige and weight of their own best collective judgment.

Skeptics may inquire whether a treaty fashioned under these auspices could be imposed in practical fact on Israelis and Palestinians. And even if both parties, storming and raging, were chivied into accepting a functional document of accommodation, could the agreement then actually be put into force under American and European diplomatic and economic incentives and penalties? The query should be reversed. Without Great Power diplomatic benediction and economic life support, would there have been a Palestine or an Israel upon which to impose and enforce a treaty in the first place? Without an assured continuum of American and European patronage, could either of these diminutive claimants to international recognition and goodwill sustain its political credibility or financial viability—even into the intermediate future? Finally, without the force majeure of uncompromising and unrelenting Great Power pressure, could Israelis and Palestinians accept a compromise formula for mutual quietude that each otherwise would reject as politically unpalatable? Not remotely likely.

A TENUOUS HORIZON

In any case, the advent of a Hamas-governed Palestine Authority and the growing militancy of Iran's Hizballah proxies in Lebanon may not have been the acutest of dangers confronting the Zionist republic. Peace treaties had been signed, after all, with the governments of Egypt and Jordan, and both countries shared Israel's abhorrence of Islamic terrorism. In its post-Soviet incarnation, Russia had abdicated its former role as the arsenal of Arab revanchism. The en masse immigration of Russian Jewry, a formerly unimaginable development, was swiftly augmenting Israel's population, and its reservoir of military manpower and scientific skills. From late 2002, the nation was seemingly on an economic upturn. Notwithstanding serious inequities of distribution in per capita terms, its 5.2 percent GDP growth rate from 2003–5 was among the most impressive in the Western world. For all its heavy defense expenditures and bloated settlements programs, Israel still had managed to forge ahead in its infrastructure improvements, in the expansion of its superb highway and light-rail systems, the modernization of its airports and growing fleet of airliners, the construction of new schools and hospitals.

In the private sector, Israel's accomplishments could be gauged in economic statistics, not least among them Warren Buffet's 2006 $4 billion purchase of Stefan Wertheimer's Iscar shares. They could be measured as well in the very profile of the nation's landscape: in the lush, imaginatively irrigated fields and orchards of its countryside; in the thriving business districts of its cities, with their towering and architecturally avant-garde skyscrapers and shopping malls; in the proliferation of its residential neighborhoods, many of them the last word in urban and suburban planning, their apartment complexes incorporating amenities that would have been impressive in any Western city. To a significant degree, Israel's cultural vitality had kept pace with its material achievements. An insight into the nation's priorities were its five Nobel Prize laureates, the diversity of its art, archaeological, and historical museums, its widening network of universities and polytechnical institutions, its theaters, its symphony and chamber orchestras, its vibrant publishing industry—as well as the passionate, even frenetic, enthusiasm with which citizens of both affluent and modest circumstances availed themselves of these intellectual and aesthetic resources. Assuredly, Israelis were not standing still in a rictus of fear and uncertainty of their neighbors' intentions.

Whatever the threat of intensified guerrilla violence, or even the awesome new dimension of ballistic warfare, a concatenation of other, equally dangerous promontories and pitfalls lurked in Israel's future. These were not external. The little country's struggle for social viability and international respect was to be conducted first and foremost among its own citizens: between a forbearing and tolerant majority and an aggressive minority of fundamentalist zealots; territorial moderates and colonialist militants; advocates of pluralistic democracy and inciters of mob intimidation; guardians of civic rectitude and transgressors of public morality; steadfast defenders of a resurrected homeland and migratory adventurers—at least 800,000 of them by 2006!—in an expatriate hinterland. Altogether, as the State of Israel approached its seventh decade, its battle was to be waged as much against the incipient blight within its own borders as against the fulmination of hatred beyond its frontiers.

In the early years of the twentieth century, the poet Yitzchak Lamdan had exhorted his fellow pioneers of the Third Aliyah in words that echoed no less hauntingly now, at the onset of the twenty-first century:

> In the hands of the few on the wall
> This dream and its solvent were stored.
> If this time you are merciless, Lord,
> And desire not the dream at all,
> Its sacrificial answer do not regard—
> Even now,
>   God,
>   Save Masada.

Acknowledgments are limited to translations and extended direct quotations from Western secondary sources only. Ascriptions to authors in Hebrew appear in the text.

p. 74: Bialik translation by Shalom Spiegel, *Hebrew Reborn*. New York, 1930.
p. 152: Shlonsky translation by A. M. Klein, in Reuben Wallenrod, *The Literature of Modern Israel*. New York, 1956.
p. 153: Lamdan translation by Richard Schenkerman, in Howard M. Sachar, *Aliyah*. Cleveland, 1961.
p. 154: Greenberg translation by Charles Cowen, in Wallenrod, *The Literature of Modern Israel*.
pp. 203, 207, 222: Weizmann meetings with Coupland, Eddé, and MacDonald described in Meyer Weisgal and Joel Carmichael, eds., *Chaim Weizmann: A Biography by Several Hands*. New York, 1963.
p. 209: Ben-Gurion's letter to Shertok quoted in Michael Bar-Zohar, *Ben-Gurion: The Armed Prophet*. Englewood Cliffs, N.J., 1967.
p. 241: Weizmann-Churchill meeting of 1943 quoted in Yehuda Bauer, *From Diplomacy to Resistance*. Philadelphia, 1970.
p. 253: Attlee quotation from Edward Francis-Williams, ed., *A Prime Minister Remembers*. London, 1962.
p. 307: Qawukji's response to Abd al-Qadr al-Husseini quoted in Netanel Lorch, *The Edge of the Sword*. New York, 1961.
p. 321: Abdullah's statement quoted in Jon Kimche and David Kimche, *Both Sides of the Hill*. London, 1960.
p. 323: Abdullah–Golda Meyerson conversation quoted in Zeev Sharef, *Three Days*. London, 1962.
p. 367: Ben-Gurion quotation from Moshe Pearlman, *Ben-Gurion Looks Back*. London, 1965.
p. 413: Almogi quotation from Sachar, *Aliyah*.
p. 453: Darwazah quotation from Yehoshafat Harkabi, *Arab Attitudes to Israel*. Jerusalem, 1972.
pp. 440, 450: Eban quotations from Robert St. John, *Eban*. New York, 1972.
pp. 484, 492, 493: Fauré, Mollet, and Pineau quotations from Michael Bar-Zohar, *Embassies in Crisis*. Englewood Cliffs, N.J., 1970.
pp. 503, 510: Eban-Dulles conversation from St. John, *Eban*.
p. 839: Hadad translation by Anton Shammas, in *Ariel*, Autumn 1973.
p. 840: Qasim translation by Avraham Yinon, in *HaMizrach HeChadash*, Winter–Spring 1975.
p. 1131: Lamdan translation by Richard Schenkerman, in Sachar, *Aliyah*.

BIBLIOGRAPHY

This compendium is presented topically. Some works are listed, as appropriate, under more than one heading. *The Encyclopedia of Zionism and Israel* (2nd ed., 2 vols., New York, 1995) and the *Encyclopedia Judaica* (2nd ed., 18 vols., New York, 1995) will also provide useful, brief reference information on the majority of topics. A more detailed account of the period from 1974 to 1984 will be found in the author's *A History of Israel: From the Aftermath of the Yom Kippur War* (New York, 1987). Material relating to the Lebanon War of 2006 is extensively adapted from the Israeli press and other contemporary Israeli media, with the kind assistance of Bradford Rothschild.

ZIONISM AND THE YISHUV BEFORE WORLD WAR I

I. *The Rise of Jewish Nationalism*

Ahad HaAm. *Selected Essays.* Philadelphia, 1948.
———. *Ten Essays on Zionism and Judaism.* London, 1922.
Avineri, Shlomo. *Moses Hess: Prophet of Communism and Zionism.* New York, 1985.
Avi-Yonah, M. *The Holy Land.* London, 1972.
Baron, Salo W. *Modern Nationalism and Religion.* New York, 1947.
Bavli, Hillel. *The Growth of Modern Hebrew Literature.* New York, 1939.
Bein, Alex, ed. *Arthur Ruppin: Memoirs, Diaries, Letters.* New York, 1972.
Ben-Gurion, David. *Recollections.* London, 1970.
Berlin, Isaiah. *The Life and Opinions of Moses Hess.* Cambridge, Mass., 1959.
Bernstein, Y. *M'Pi Rishonim v'Acharonim* [From the Lips of the First and the Last]. Jerusalem, 1968.
Blumberg, Arnold. *Zion before Zionism, 1938–1880.* Syracuse, N.Y., 1986.
Böhm, Adolf. *Die zionistische Bewegung.* Vol. I. Berlin, 1935.
Brainin, Reuven. *Perez Smolenskin* [in Hebrew]. Warsaw, 1896.
Chomsky, William. "Did Hebrew Ever Die?" *Jewish Frontier,* Sept. 1950.
———. "Hebrew as a Medium of Jewish Religion and Culture," *Reconstructionist,* Dec. 1950.
Citron, S. L. *Toldot Chibat Zion* [A History of the Chibat Zion]. Odessa, 1914.
Cohen, Israel. *A Short History of Zionism.* London, 1951.
———. *The Zionist Movement.* New York, 1946.
Dinaburg (Dinur), B. Z., et al., eds. *Chibat Zion* [in Hebrew]. 2 vols. Tel Aviv, 1922–24.
———. *Sefer HaZionut* [The Book of Zionism]. Vol. I. Tel Aviv, 1938.

Druyanov, A. *K'tavim l'Toldot Chibat Zion* [Writings from the History of the Chibat Zion]. Odessa, 1919.

———. *Pinsker u'Zmano* [Pinsker and His Time]. Jerusalem, 1953.

Efros, Israel, ed. *Hayyim Nahman Bialik: Complete Poetic Works*. Vol. I. New York, 1948.

Eliasburg, Y. *B'Olam HeHafichot* [In a World of Revolutions]. Jerusalem, 1965.

Elon, Amos. *The Israelis: Fathers and Sons*. New York, 1971.

Epel, Y., ed. *B'Toch Reshit HaT'chiyah: Zichronot u'Ch'tavim m'Y'mei Chovevei Zion* [From the Beginning of the Awakening: Memoirs and Writings from the Days of the Chovevei Zion]. Tel Aviv, 1935.

Freundlich, Charles H. *Peretz Smolenskin: His Life and Thought*. New York, 1966.

Gelber, N. M., ed. *Die Kattowitzer Konferenz*. Brno, 1918.

———. *Zur Vorgeschichte des Zionismus: Judenstaats projekte in den Jahren, 1695–1845*. Vienna, 1927.

Gordon, Y. L. *Igarot* [Correspondence]. 2 vols. Warsaw, 1894.

Gruenbaum, Y. *HaT'nuah HaZionit b'Hitpatchutah* [The Zionist Movement and Its Development]. 4 vols. Jerusalem, 1942–54.

Gur-Arieh, Y. *HaRav Y. H. Alkalai* [Rabbi Y. H. Alkalai]. Tel Aviv, 1929.

———. *HaRav Zvi Kalischer* [Rabbi Zvi Kalischer]. Jerusalem, n.d.

Halkin, Abraham S., ed. *Zionism in Jewish Literature*. New York, 1961.

Halpern, Ben. *The Idea of the Jewish State*. Cambridge, Mass., 1961.

Halpern, Y. *HaAliyot HaRishonot shel HeChasidim l'Eretz Yisrael* [The First Immigration of Chasidim to Palestine]. Jerusalem, 1946.

Heller, Joseph. *The Zionist Idea*. New York, 1949.

Hertzberg, Arthur, ed. *The Zionist Idea*. Garden City, N.Y., 1959.

Hess, Moses. *Rome and Jerusalem*. New York, 1943.

Kalischer, Hirsch (Zvi). *Drishat Zion* [The Lure of Zion]. Berlin, 1958.

Klausner, Joseph. *A History of Modern Hebrew Literature*. London, 1932.

———. *HaT'nuah l'Zion: HaAliyah HaRishonah m'Rusia* [The Migration to Zion: The First Aliyah from Russia]. Jerusalem, 1962.

Kobler, Franz. *The Vision Was There*. London, 1956.

Kook, Avraham, *Chazon HaG'ulah* [The Vision of Redemption]. Jerusalem, 1941.

Kressel, A., ed. *HaRav Yehuda Alkalai, HaRav Zvi Hirsch Kalischer: Mivchar Kitveihem* [Rabbi Yehuda Alkalai, Rabbi Zvi Hirsch Kalischer: Selected Writings]. Tel Aviv, 1945.

Kressel, Getzel. *M'Hofa'at "Roma v'Yerushalayim" ad Moto shel Herzl* [From the Appearance of *Rome and Jerusalem* until the Death of Herzl]. Jerusalem, 1944.

Lachover, F. *Toldot HaSifrut HaIvrit HeChadashah* [A History of Modern Hebrew Literature]. 4 vols. Tel Aviv, 1927–33.

Laqueur, Walter. *A History of Zionism*. New York, 1972.

Levinson, Avraham, ed. *Bibliografia Zionit* [A Zionist Bibliography]. Jerusalem, 1943.

Lilienblum, Moshe Leib. *Kol Kitvei M. L. Lilienblum* [The Complete Writings of M. L. Lilienblum]. Odessa, 1913.

———. *The Regeneration of Israel on the Land of Its Forefathers*. London, 1884.

Meisl, Josef. *Haskalah*. Berlin, 1919.

Pinsker, Leo. *Auto-Emancipation*. New York, 1956.

———. *The Road to Freedom*. New York, 1944.

Rozen, Dov. *Sh'ma Israel* [Hear O Israel]. Jerusalem, 1968.

Sachar, Howard M. *Farewell España: The World of the Sephardim Remembered*. New York, 1994.

Schulman, Mary. *Moses Hess: Prophet of Zionism*. New York, 1963.

Shmueli, M. *P'rakim b'Toldot HaZionut u'T'nuat HaAvodah* [Chapters in the History of Zionism and the Labor Movement]. Vol. I. Tel Aviv, 1946.

Silberner, Edmund. *Moses Hess: Geschichte seines Lebens.* Leiden, 1966.

———, ed. *The Works of Moses Hess.* London, 1958.

Simon, Sir Leon. *Studies in Jewish Nationalism.* New York, 1920.

Smolenskin, Perez. *Ma'amarim* [Articles]. 3 vols. 1925–26.

Sokolow, Nahum. *Chibat Zion* [in Hebrew]. Jerusalem, 1935.

———. *A History of Zionism.* Vol. I. New York, 1919.

Spiegel, Shalom. *Hebrew Reborn.* New York, 1930.

Stein, Leonard, ed. *The Letters and Papers of Chaim Weizmann.* London, 1968.

Vital, David. *The Origins of Zionism.* London, 1975.

Winer, Gerson. *The Founding Fathers of Israel.* New York, 1971.

Yavnieli, Shmuel. *Sefer HaZionut* [The Book of Zionism]. Vol. I. Jerusalem, 1961.

Yoeli, Y. L. *M'vaser HaT'chiyah HaLe'umit* [The Herald of National Revival]. Tel Aviv, 1942.

Zehavi, Y. *M'Hitbolelut l'Zionut* [From Assimilationism to Zionism]. Jerusalem, 1972.

Zlocisti, Theodor. *Moses Hess.* Berlin, 1921.

II. *Herzl and the Growth of the Zionist Movement*

Ahad HaAm. *Essays, Letters, Memoirs.* New York, 1948.

———. *Nationalism and the Jewish Ethic.* New York, 1912.

———. *Selected Essays.* Philadelphia, 1948.

Balakan, D. *Die Sozialdemokratie und das jüdische Proletariat.* Czernowitz, 1905.

Bauer, O. *Die Nationalitätenfrage und die Sozialdemokratie.* Vienna, 1907.

Bein, Alex. "David Wolffsohn" [in Hebrew], *Zion,* Aug. 1942.

———. *Theodor Herzl: A Biography.* Philadelphia, 1956.

———. "Theodor Herzl and Walter Rathenau: Exchange of Letters," *Zion,* Aug. 1951.

Ben-Ehud, R. *Zionismus oder Sozialismus.* Warsaw, 1899.

Ben-Horin, Meir. "Max Nordau: A Study in Human Solidarity." Unpublished doctoral dissertation, Columbia University, 1952.

Ben-Zvi, Rachel Yanait. *Coming Home.* Tel Aviv, 1963.

Bick, Abraham, ed. *Exponents and Philosophy of Religious Zionism.* New York, 1942.

Birnbaum, Nathan. *Ausgewählte Schriften zurjüdischen Frage.* 2 vols. Czernowitz, 1910.

Blumenfeld, Kurt. *Erlebte Judenfrage: Ein Vierteljahrhundert deutscher Zionismus.* Stuttgart, 1962.

Bodenheimer, Channa. *Toldot Tochnit Basle* [A History of the Basel Platform]. Jerusalem, 1947.

Bodenheimer, Max I. *Prelude to Israel.* New York, 1963.

Böhm, Adolf. *Die zionistische Bewegung.* Vol. I. Berlin, 1935.

Borochow, Ber. *K'tavim* [Writings]. 3 vols. Tel Aviv, 1955–66.

———. *Nationalism and the Class Struggle.* New York, 1937.

Breuer, R. *Nationaljudentum, ein Wahnjudentum.* Mainz, 1903.

Brod, M., and F. Weltsch. *Zionismus als Weltanschauung.* Berlin, 1925.

Buber, Martin. *Israel and Palestine: The History of an Idea.* London, 1952.

Cohen, Emil B. *David Wolffsohn.* New York, 1944.

Cohen, Hermann. *Religion und Zionismus.* Krefeld, 1916.

Cohen, Israel. *A Short History of Zionism.* London, 1951.

———. *Theodor Herzl: Founder of Political Zionism.* New York, 1959.

De Haas, Jacob. *Theodor Herzl: A Biographical Study.* 2 vols. New York, 1927.

Dinaburg (Dinur), B. Z., et al., eds. *Sefer HaZionut* [The Book of Zionism]. Vol. I. Tel Aviv, 1938.

Ebner, M. "Memories of the First Zionist Congress," *Zion,* Aug. 1951.

Eliav, Mordecai. *Die Juden Palästinas in der deutschen Politik, 1842–1914.* Tel Aviv, 1973.

Elon, Amos. *Herzl.* New York, 1975.

Fishman, J. L. *The History of the Mizrachi Movement.* New York, 1928.

Fraenkel, Josef. *Duhnow, Herzl, and Ahad HaAm.* London, 1963.

Gal, Allon. *Socialist-Zionism: Theory and Issues in Contemporary Jewish Nationalism.* Cambridge, Mass., 1983.

Goldmann, F. *Zionismus oder Liberalismus.* Frankfurt a/M., 1911.

Gottheil, Richard. *Zionism.* Philadelphia, 1914.

Gottschalk, Alfred. *Achad Habm: 'Ha-Ruach Hasemi* [Achad Ha-Am and the Hebrew National Spirit]. Jerusalem, 1992.

Gruenbaum, Y. *HaT'nuah HaZionit* [The Zionist Movement]. Vols. II, IV. Jerusalem, 1949, 1954.

Güdemann, Moritz. *Nationaljudentum.* Vienna, 1897.

Haber, Julius. "When Herzl Died," *Land and Life,* Spring 1955.

Halpern, Ben. *The Idea of the Jewish State.* Cambridge, Mass., 1961.

Hermann, Leo. *Nathan Birnbaum: Sein Werk und seine Wandlung.* Berlin, 1914.

Herzl, Theodor. *The Jewish State.* Garden City, N.Y., 1959.

———. *Old-New Land.* Haifa, 1960.

———. *The Tragedy of Jewish Immigration: Evidence Given before the British Royal Commission in 1902.* New York, 1920.

Kellner, Leon, ed. *Theodor Herzl: Zionistische Schriften.* Berlin, 1920.

Klausner, Joseph. *Menahem Ussishkin: His Life and Work.* New York, 1942.

Klausner, Y. *Opozitzia l'Herzl* [Opposition to Herzl]. Tel Aviv, 1959.

Kraus, K. *Eine Krone für Zion.* Vienna, 1898.

Landau, Saul R. *Sturm and Drang im Zionismus.* Vienna, 1937.

Laqueur, Walter. *A History of Zionism.* New York, 1972.

Learsi, Rufus. *Fulfillment: The Epic Story of Zionism.* Cleveland, 1951.

Leftwich, Joseph. *Israel Zangwill.* New York, 1957.

Levin, N. Gordon, ed. *The Zionist Movement in Palestine and World Politics, 1880–1918.* New York, 1974.

Levin, Shmaryahu. *Forward from Exile.* Philadelphia, 1967.

Lewisohn, Ludwig, ed. *Theodor Herzl: A Portrait for the Ages.* Cleveland, 1955.

Lipsky, Louis. *A Gallery of Zionist Profiles.* New York, 1956.

Litvinoff, Barnet, ed. *The Letters and Papers of Chaim Weizmann.* Vols. II, III. London, 1971, 1972.

Lowenthal, Marvin, ed. *The Diaries of Theodor Herzl.* New York, 1962.

Luz, Ehud. *Parallels Meet: Religion and Nationalism in the Early Zionist Movement, 1888–1904.* Philadelphia, 1988.

Medzini, Moshe. *HaM'diniyut HaZionit m'Reshitah v'ad Moto shel Herzl* [Zionist Diplomacy from Its Origins to the Death of Herzl]. Jerusalem, 1934.

Mosse, George. *Germans and Jews.* New York, 1969.

Nathan, P. *Palästina und Palästinisches Zionismus.* Berlin, 1914.

Nedava, Joseph. "The Tragedy of the House of Herzl," *Zionist Quarterly,* Spring 1952.

Nordau, Anna, and Maxa Nordau. *Max Nordau: A Biography.* New York, 1943.

Nordau, Max. *Zionism and Anti-Semitism.* New York, 1904.

———. *Zionistische Schriften.* Berlin, 1923.

Nussenblatt, Thio. *Zeitgenossen über Herzl.* Brno, 1929.

Patai, Raphael, ed. *The Complete Diaries of Theodor Herzl.* New York, 1960.

———, ed. *Herzl Year Book.* 6 vols. New York, 1958–65.

Pines, D. "Nachman Syrkin: His Essential Teachings," *Israel Youth Horizon,* Sept. 1951.

Rabinowicz, Oskar K. *Fifty Years of Zionism.* London, 1951.

———. "Herzl and England," *Jewish Monthly*, Nov.–Dec. 1951.

———. *Herzl, Architect of the Balfour Declaration*. New York, 1958.

———. "New Light on the East Africa Scheme," in Israel Cohen, ed., *The Rebirth of Israel*. London, 1952.

Reinharz, Jehuda. *Chaim Weizmann: The Making of a Zionist Leader*. Vol. I. New York, 1985; *The Making of a Stateman*. Vol. II. New York, 1993.

Robinsohn, A. *David Wolffsohn*. Berlin, 1921.

Rose, Norman. *Chaim Weizmann: A Biography*. New York, 1986.

Ruppin, Arthur. *Pirkei Chayai* [Chapters from My Life]. Vol. I. Tel Aviv, 1968.

Sacher, Harry. *Zionist Portraits and Other Essays*. London, 1959.

Simon, Sir Leon. *Ahad HaAm: Asher Ginzberg: A Biography*. Philadelphia, 1960.

———. *Studies in Jewish Nationalism*. New York, 1920.

Singer, M. *B'Reshit HaZionut HaSozialistit* [The Beginnings of Labor Zionism]. Haifa, 1958.

Sokolow, Nahum. *A History of Zionism*. Vol. I. New York, 1919.

Syrkin, Marie. *Nachman Syrkin, Socialist Zionist*. New York, 1961.

Syrkin, Nachman. *Essays in Socialist Zionism*. New York, 1935.

Teller, Judd L. "The Making of the Ideals That Rule Israel," *Commentary*, Jan.–Feb. 1954.

Ussishkin, Menachem. *Kol HaAdamah* [The Voice of the Earth]. Tel Aviv, n.d.

Vital, David. *Zionism: The Crucial Phase*. New York, 1987.

Vlavianos, Basil J., and Feliks Gross, eds. *Struggle for Tomorrow: Modern Political Ideologies of the Jewish People*. New York, 1954.

Weisgal, Meyer, and Joel Carmichael, eds. *Chaim Weizmann: A Biography by Several Hands*. New York, 1963.

Weizmann, Chaim. *Trial and Error*. New York, 1949.

Zipperstein, Steven J. *Elusive Prophet: Ahad Ha'Am and the Origins of Zionism*. Berkeley, Calif., 1993.

Zweig, Stefan. *The World of Yesterday*. Lincoln, Neb., 1964.

III. *The Rise of the Yishuv*

Ahad HaAm. *Essays, Letters, Memoirs*. New York, 1948.

Avi-Yonah, Michael, ed. *A History of the Holy Land*. London, 1969.

Bardin, Shlomo. *Pioneer Youth in Palestine*. New York, 1932.

Barkai, Haim. *The Public, Histadrut, and Private Sectors in the Israeli Economy*. Jerusalem, 1964.

Bavli, Hillel. *The Growth of Modern Hebrew Literature*. New York, 1939.

Bein, Alex, ed. *Arthur Ruppin: Memoirs, Diaries, Letters*. New York, 1972.

———. *The Return to the Soil*. Jerusalem, 1952.

Ben-Arieh, Y. *Eretz Yisrael b'Mea HaYod-Tet* [Palestine in the Nineteenth Century]. Jerusalem, 1970.

Ben-Avi, Itamar. *Im Shachar Atzma'utenu* [With the Dawn of Our Nationhood]. Tel Aviv, 1962.

Ben-Gurion, David. *Recollections*. London, 1970.

Ben-Shalom, Avraham. *Deep Furrows: Pioneer Life in Palestine*. New York, 1937.

Ben-Yehuda, Eliezer. *HeChalom v'Shivro* [The Dream and Its Meaning]. Jerusalem, 1942.

Ben-Zion, S. *Die Bilu auf dem Weg*. Tel Aviv, 1935.

Ben-Zvi, Rahel Yanait. *Coming Home*. Tel Aviv, 1963.

Ben-Zvi, Yitzchak. *Eretz Yisrael v'Yishuvah b'Y'mei HaShilton HaOtomani* [Palestine and Its (Jewish) Settlement under Ottoman Rule]. Jerusalem, 1955.

———. *HaYishuv HaYehudi b'Chfar Peki'in* [The Jewish Settlement in Peki'in Village]. Tel Aviv, 1922.

Bermant, Chaim. *Israel.* New York, 1967.

Blanc, Chaim. "The Growth of Israeli Hebrew," *Middle Eastern Affairs,* Dec. 1954.

Böhm, Adolf. *Die zionistische Bewegung.* Vol. I. Berlin, 1935.

Braslavsky, M. *T'nuat HaPoalim HaEretz Yisreelit* [The Palestine Workers Movement]. Vol. I. Tel Aviv, 1946.

Brenner, Y. Ch. *Kol K'tavav* [Complete Works]. 9 vols. Tel Aviv, 1924–30.

Burstein, Moshe. *Self-Government of the Jews in Palestine since 1900.* Tel Aviv, 1934.

Chabas, Bracha, ed. *Sefer HaAliyah HaShniyah* [The Book of the Second Aliyah]. Tel Aviv, 1949.

Dayan, Deborah. *Pioneer.* Tel Aviv, 1968.

Dayan, Shmuel. "A Picture of the Second Aliyah," *Jewish Frontier,* Feb. 1955.

De Haas, Jacob. *A History of Palestine.* New York, 1934.

Druck, David. *Baron Edmond de Rothschild.* New York, 1928.

Eliav, Mordecai. *Die Juden Palästinas in der deutschen Politik, 1842–1914.* Tel Aviv, 1973.

Elon, Amos. *The Israelis: Fathers and Sons.* New York, 1971.

Epel, Y., ed. *B'Toch Reshit HaT'chiyah: Zichronot u'Ch'tavim m'Y'mei Chovevei Zion* [At the Beginning of the National Renaissance: Memoirs and Writings from the Days of Chovevei Zion]. Tel Aviv, 1935.

Even-Shoshan, Z. *Toldot T'nuat HaPoalim b'Eretz Yisrael* [A History of the Palestinian Workers Movement]. Vol. I. Tel Aviv, 1965.

Fein, Harry, ed. *A Harvest of Hebrew Verse.* Boston, 1934.

Fellman, Jack. *The Revival of a Classical Tongue: Eliezer Ben Yehuda and the Modern Hebrew Language.* The Hague, 1973.

Franco, Moïse. *Essai sur l'histoire des Israélites de l'Empire Ottoman depuis des origines jusqu'à nos jours.* Paris, 1897.

Frankel, Ludwig August. *Nach Jerusalem: Eine Reisebericht.* Berlin, 1935.

Galanté, Abraham. *Turcs et Juifs: Étude historique, politique.* Istanbul, 1932.

Gordon, A. D. *K'tavim* [Writings]. 5 vols. Tel Aviv, 1925–29.

———. *Selected Essays.* New York, 1938.

Heyd, Uriel. *Eretz Yisrael b'T'kufat HaShilton HaOtomani* [Palestine in the Era of the Ottoman Empire]. Jerusalem, 1969.

Horowitz, David. *HaEtmol Sheli* [My Yesterday]. Tel Aviv, 1970.

Hyamson, Albert. *The British Consulate in Jerusalem in Relation to the Jews of Palestine, 1838–1914.* 2 vols. London, 1939–41.

Judelevich, D., ed. *Sefer Rishon l'Zion* [The Book of Rishon l'Zion]. Rishon l'Zion, 1941.

Katznelson, Berl. *Drachim l'Aretz* [The Roads to Israel]. Tel Aviv, 1948.

———. *Revolutionary Constructivism.* New York, 1937.

Klausner, Joseph. *Eliezer Ben-Yehuda: Toldotav u'Mifal Chayav* [Eliezer Ben-Yehuda: His Life and Career]. Tel Aviv, 1939.

———. *A History of Modern Hebrew Literature.* London, 1932.

Kobler, Franz. *The Vision Was There.* London, 1956.

Kressel, A., ed. *Sefer Petach Tikvah* [The Book of Petach Tikvah]. Petach Tikvah, 1952.

Kurland, Samuel. *Biluim: Pioneers of Zionist Colonization.* New York, 1943.

Lachover, F. *Bialik: Chayav v'Y'tzirotav* [Bialik: His Life and Works]. Tel Aviv, 1950.

Laqueur, Walter. *A History of Zionism.* New York, 1972.

Lask, I. M. "Three Decades of Hebrew Writing," *Zion,* April 1954.

Levontin, S. D. *L'Eretz Avotenu* [To the Land of Our Fathers]. Tel Aviv, 1964.

Mandel, Neville. "Turks, Arabs, and Jewish Immigration into Palestine, 1882–1914," in *St. Antony's Papers,* No. 17. London, 1968.

Ma'oz, Moshe. *Ottoman Reform in Syria and Palestine, 1850–1861.* London, 1968.

Margalith, Israel. *Le baron Edmond de Rothschild et la colonization juive en Palestine, 1882–1899.* Paris, 1957.

Marmorstein, Emile. "European Jews in Muslim Palestine," *Middle Eastern Studies,* Jan. 1975.

Meerovitch, Menashe. *B'Y'mei Bilu* [In the Days of the Bilu]. Jerusalem, 1942.

———. *Zichronot Acharon HaBiluim* [Memoirs of the Last of the Biluists]. Jerusalem, 1946.

Montefiore, Sir Moses. *Diaries of Sir Moses and Lady Montefiore.* 2 vols. London, 1890.

Naiditch, Israel. *Edmond de Rothschild.* Washington, D.C., 1945.

Nathan, P. *Palästina und Palästinisches Zionismus.* Berlin, 1914.

Oliphant, Laurence. *Haifa.* Edinburgh, 1897.

———: *The Land of Gilead.* New York, 1881.

Parkes, James. *A History of Palestine from 135 A.D. to Modern Times.* London, 1949.

Pearlman, Moshe. *Ben-Gurion Looks Back.* London, 1965.

Preuss, Walter. *The Labour Movement in Israel: Past and Present.* Jerusalem, 1965.

Rose, Herbert H. *The Life and Thought of A. D. Gordon.* New York, 1954.

Roth, Samuel, ed. *New Songs of Zion: A Zionist Anthology.* New York, 1914.

Rubaschow, Rachel Katznelson, ed. *The Plough Woman: Records of the Pioneer Women of Palestine.* New York, 1932.

Ruppin, Arthur. *The Agricultural Colonization of the Zionist Organization in Palestine.* London, 1926.

———. *Building Israel: Selected Essays, 1907–1935.* New York, 1949.

———. *Pirkei Chayai* [Chapters from My Life]. Vols. I, II. Tel Aviv, 1968.

———. *Three Decades of Palestine.* Jerusalem, 1936.

Sachar, Howard M. *Aliyah: The Peoples of Israel.* Cleveland, 1961.

Samsonov, A., ed. *Sefer Zichron Ya'akov* [The Book of Zichron Ya'akov]. Tel Aviv, 1943.

Samuel, Maurice. *Harvest in the Desert.* New York, 1944.

Sanders, Ronald. *Israel: The View from Masada.* New York, 1966.

Sefer HaShomer [The Book of HaShomer]. Tel Aviv, 1957.

Shapiro, Z. *Bialik v'Y'tzirotav* [Bialik and His Works]. Jerusalem, 1950.

Shazar, Zalman. *Morning Stars.* Philadelphia, 1967.

Shmueli, M. *P'rakim b'Toldot HaZionut u'Ch'tavim m'Y'mei Chovevei Zion* [Chapters and Writings of the History of Zionism from the Days of the Chovevei Zion]. Tel Aviv, 1935.

Shva, Shlomo. *Shevet HaNoazim* [The Tribe of the Bold]. Tel Aviv, 1949.

Singer, M. *B'Reshit HaZionut HaSotzialistit* [The Beginnings of Labor Zionism]. Haifa, 1958.

Smilansky, Moshe. *P'rakim b'Toldot HaYishuv* [Chapters from the History of the Yishuv]. Vol. I. Tel Aviv, 1943.

Szereszewski, Robert. *Essays on the Structure of the Jewish Economy in Palestine and Israel.* Jerusalem, 1968.

Trager, Hannah. *Pioneers in Palestine: Stories of the First Settlers in Petach Tikvah.* London, 1923.

Vlavianos, Basil J., and Feliks Gross, eds. *Struggle for Tomorrow: Modern Political Ideologies of the Jewish People.* New York, 1954.

Wallenrod, Reuben. *The Literature of Modern Israel.* New York, 1956.

Wilhelm, Kurt, ed. *Roads to Zion: Four Centuries of Travelers' Reports.* New York, 1948.

Willbush, Nahum. *The Industrial Development of Palestine.* London, 1920.

Yaari, Avraham. *The Goodly Heritage.* Jerusalem, 1958.

Yaari-Poleskin, Y. *M'Chayei Yosef Chaim Brenner* [From the Life of Joseph Chaim Brenner]. Tel Aviv, 1922.

Yalkut Poalei Zion [The Poalei Zion Travel Bag]. 2 vols. Jerusalem, 1947–54.

Yavnieli, Shmuel. *Sefer HaZionut* [The Book of Zionism]. Vol. I. Jerusalem, 1961.

Yellin, Y. *Zichronot l'ven Yerushalayim* [Jerusalem Memories]. Jerusalem, 1924.

THE JEWISH NATIONAL HOME

I. *The Balfour Declaration. The Establishment of the Mandate*

Aaronsohn, Alexander. *With the Turks in Palestine.* Boston, 1916.

Abdullah, King of Jordan. *Memoirs.* New York, 1950.

Adler, Selig. "The Palestine Question in the Wilson Era," *Jewish Social Studies,* Spring–Summer 1948.

Andrews, Fannie F. *The Holy Land under Mandate.* 2 vols. Boston, 1931.

Antonius, George. *The Arab Awakening.* Philadelphia, 1938.

Ashbee, C. R. *A Palestine Notebook, 1918–1923.* New York, 1923.

Attias, Moshe, ed. *Sefer HaT'udot shel HaVa'ad HaLe'umi Knesset Yisrael b'Eretz Yisrael* [Documents from the Palestine *Va'ad HaLe'umi*]. Jerusalem, 1963.

Balfour, Arthur James. *Speeches on Zionism.* London, 1928.

Bentwich, Norman, and Helen Bentwich. *Mandate Memories, 1918–1948.* London, 1965.

Ben-Zvi, Yitzchak. *The Hebrew Battalions.* Jerusalem, 1969.

Bericht über die Tätigkeit des Kopenhagener Büros des zionistischen Organization von Februar 1915 bis Dezember 1918. Copenhagen, 1919.

Bodenheimer, Max. *Die Zionisten und das kaiserliche Deutschland.* Stuttgart, 1962.

Bowles, John. *Viscount Samuel.* London, 1957.

Brecher, Frank W. "Woodrow Wilson and the Arab-Jewish Conflict," *American Jewish Archives,* April 1987.

Burstein, Moshe. *Self-Government of the Jews in Palestine since 1900.* Tel Aviv, 1934.

Churchill, Winston. *The World Crisis.* Vol. IV. London, 1929.

Cohen, Naomi W. *American Jews and the Zionist Idea.* New York, 1975.

Conjoint Foreign Committee of the Jewish Board of Deputies and the Anglo-Jewish Association. *Correspondence with His Majesty's Government Respecting the Eventual Peace Negotiations.* London, 1917.

Dodd, C. H., and Mary Sales, eds. *Israel and the Arab World.* London, 1970.

Dugdale, Blanche. *Arthur James Balfour.* 2 vols. London, 1936.

Elmailach, A. *Eretz Yisrael v'Suriya b'Y'mei Milchemet HaOlam* [Palestine and Syria during the World War]. Jerusalem, 1927.

Engel, Anita. *The Nili Spies.* London, 1959.

Esco Foundation for Palestine. *Palestine: A Study of Jewish, Arab, and British Policies.* Vol. I. New Haven, Conn., 1947.

Feinberg, Nathan. *Some Problems of the Palestine Mandate.* Tel Aviv, 1936.

Friedman, Isaiah. *The Question of Palestine, 1914–1918: British-Jewish-Arab Relations.* New York, 1973.

Frischwasser-Ra'anan, H. F. *The Frontiers of a Nation.* London, 1955.

Gardner, Brian. *Allenby of Arabia.* New York, 1966.

Gilbert, Martin. *The Arab-Israeli Conflict: Its History in Maps.* London, 1974.

Grose, Peter. *Israel in the Mind of America.* New York, 1983.

Halpern, Ben. *The Idea of the Jewish State.* Cambridge, Mass., 1961.

Hanna, Paul S. *British Policy in Palestine.* Washington, D.C., 1942.

Hourani, Albert. *Great Britain and the Arab World.* London, 1945.

———. *Syria and Lebanon.* London, 1946.

Howard, Harry N. *The King-Crane Commission.* Beirut, 1963.

Hurwitz, J. C., ed. *Diplomacy in the Near and Middle East: A Documentary Record.* Vol. II. Princeton, N.J., 1956.

Hyamson, Albert. *Palestine under the Mandate.* London, 1950.

Ingrams, Doreen. *Palestine Papers, 1917–1922: Seeds of Conflict.* London, 1972.

Jabotinsky, Vladimir. *N'umim* [Lectures]. Vol. I. Jerusalem, 1947.

———. *The Story of the Jewish Legion.* New York, 1945.

Joseph, Bernard. *British Rule in Palestine.* Washington, D.C., 1948.

Kedourie, Elie. *Britain and the Middle East, 1914–1921.* London, 1956.

———. "Sir Herbert Samuel and the Government of Palestine," *Middle Eastern Studies,* Jan. 1969.

Kimche, Jon. *The Second Arab Awakening.* London, 1970.

———. *The Unromantics: The Great Powers and the Balfour Declaration.* London, 1968.

Kirkbride, Sir Alan. *A Crackle of Thorns.* London, 1956.

Klieman, Aaron S. *Foundations of British Policy in the Arab World: The Cairo Conference of 1921.* Baltimore, 1970.

Klieman, Aaron S., and Adrian Klieman, eds. *American Zionism: A Documentary History.* 17 vols. New York, 1990.

Kling, Simha. *Nahum Sokolow: Servant of His People.* New York, 1960.

Laqueur, Walter, and Barry Rubin, eds. *The Israel-Arab Reader: A Documentary History of the Middle East Conflict.* New York, 1985.

Laserson, Max M., ed. *On the Mandate: Documents, Statements, Laws and Judgments Relating to and Arising from the Mandate for Palestine.* Tel Aviv, 1937.

Leslie, Shane. *Mark Sykes: His Life and Letters.* London, 1923.

Levin, N. Gordon, ed. *The Zionist Movement in Palestine and World Politics, 1880–1918.* New York, 1974.

Levin, Shmaryahu. *M'Zichronot Chayai* [Memoirs of My Life]. Vol. IV. Tel Aviv, 1942.

Lichtheim, Richard. *Sha'ar Yashuv* [The Remainder of the Yishuv]. Tel Aviv, 1938.

Lipovetzky, Pesah. *Joseph Trumpeldor: Life and Works.* Jerusalem, 1953.

Livneh, Eliezer. *Aaronsohn: HaIsh u'Z'mano* [Aaronsohn: The Man and His Times]. Tel Aviv, 1969.

Lloyd George, David. *Memoirs of the Peace Conference.* Vol. II. London, 1938.

Magnus, L. *Zionism and the Neo-Zionists.* London, 1917.

Manuel, Frank E. "The Palestine Question in Italian Diplomacy," *Journal of Modern History,* Sept. 1955.

———. *The Realities of American-Palestine Relations.* Washington, D.C., 1949.

Medzini, Moshe. *Eser Shanim shel M'diniyut Eretz Yisreelit* [Ten Years of Palestinian (Jewish) Diplomacy]. Tel Aviv, 1928.

Meinertzhagen, Richard. *Middle East Diary, 1917–1956.* London, 1959.

Montefiore, Claude G. *Liberal Judaism and Jewish Nationalism.* London, 1917.

Nevakivi, Jukka. *Britain, France, and the Arab Middle East, 1914–1920.* London, 1969.

Nicolson, Harold. *Peacemaking, 1919.* London, 1933.

Patterson, Colonel J. H. *With the Judeans in the Palestine Campaign.* New York, 1922.

———. *With the Zionists in Gallipoli.* New York, 1916.

Pearlman, Moshe. "Chapters in Arab-Jewish Diplomacy, 1918–22," *Jewish Social Studies,* Spring 1944.

Pichon, Jean. *Le partage du Proche-Orient.* Paris, 1938.

Poznansky, Menachem. *M'Chayei Yosef Trumpeldor* [The Life of Joseph Trumpeldor]. Tel Aviv, 1945.

Puryear, Vernon J. *France and the Levant.* Berkeley, Calif., 1941.

Rabinowicz, Oskar K. *Fifty Years of Zionism.* London, 1951.

Reinharz, Jehuda. *Chaim Weizmann: The Making of a Zionist Leader.* Vol. I. New York, 1985; *The Making of a Zionist Statesman.* Vol. II. New York, 1993.

Rose, Norman. *Chaim Weizmann: A Biography.* New York, 1986.

Sachar, Howard M. *The Emergence of the Middle East, 1914–1924.* New York, 1969.

————. *A History of the Jews in America.* New York, 1992.

Sacher, Harry. *Zionism and the Jewish Future.* London, 1916.

Sadaka, Nagib. *La question syrienne pendant la guerre de 1914.* Paris, 1940.

Samuel, Viscount Herbert L. S. *Memoirs.* London, 1955.

Schechtman, Joseph B. *Vladimir Jabotinsky.* Vol. I. New York, 1956.

Schmidt, Sarah. "The Zionist Conversion of Louis D. Brandeis," *Jewish Social Studies,* Winter 1975.

Sidebotham, Herbert. *Great Britain and Palestine.* London, 1937.

Sokolow, Nahum. *A History of Zionism.* Vol. II. New York, 1919.

Stein, Leonard. *The Balfour Declaration.* London, 1961.

Storrs, Sir Ronald. *Orientations.* London, 1937.

Stoyanovsky, Jacob. *The Mandate for Palestine.* London, 1928.

Sykes, Christopher. *Crossroads to Israel, 1917–1948.* New York, 1956.

————. *Two Studies in Virtue.* New York, 1953.

Tuchman, Barbara W. *Bible and Sword.* New York, 1956.

Upthegrove, Campbell L. *Empire by Mandate: A History of the Relations of Great Britain with the Permanent Mandates Commission of the League of Nations.* New York, 1954.

Urofsky, Melvin I. *American Zionism from Herzl to the Holocaust.* Garden City, N.Y., 1975.

Weisgal, Meyer, and Joel Carmichael, eds. *Chaim Weizmann: A Biography by Several Hands.* New York, 1963.

Weizmann, Chaim. *Trial and Error.* New York, 1949.

Wise, Stephen S. *Challenging Years.* New York, 1949.

Yaari-Poleskin, Y. *M'raglim o Giborei HaMoledet?* [Spies or Heroes of the Homeland?]. Tel Aviv, 1930.

Yehuda, Avraham Shalom. *HeHaganah al HaYishuv b'Milchemet HaOlam HaRishonah* [Defense of the Yishuv in World War I]. Jerusalem, 1951.

Zechlin, E. *Die deutsche Politik und die Juden im ersten Weltkrieg.* Göttingen, 1969.

Zeine, Zeine N. *The Struggle for Arab Independence.* Beirut, 1960.

II.   *The Development of the Jewish National Home*

Abramovitz, Z. *B'Sherut HaT'nuah* [In the Service of the Movement]. Merchavia, 1965.

Arlosoroff, Chaim. *K'tavim* [Writings]. Tel Aviv, 1934.

————. *Yoman Yerushalayim* [Jerusalem Diary]. Tel Aviv, 1949.

Aronovitz, Y. *K'tavim* [Writings]. Tel Aviv, 1941.

Bardin, Shlomo. *Pioneer Youth in Palestine.* New York, 1932.

Barkai, Haim. *The Public, Histadrut, and Private Sectors in the Israeli Economy.* Jerusalem, 1964.

Bauer, Yehuda. *My Brother's Keeper: A History of the American Joint Distribution Committee.* Philadelphia, 1974.

Bavli, Hillel. *The Growth of Modern Hebrew Literature.* New York, 1939.

Bein, Alex. *The Return to the Soil.* Jerusalem, 1952.

Ben-Ari, N. *P'rakim l'Toldot T'nuat HaPoalim b'Eretz Yisrael* [Chapters from the History of the Labor Movement in Palestine]. Warsaw, 1936.

Ben-Gurion, David. *M'Ma'amad l'Am* [From Self-Respect to Nationhood]. Tel Aviv, 1933.

————. *Recollections.* London, 1970.

Ben-Shalom, Avraham. *Deep Furrows: Pioneer Life in Palestine.* New York, 1937.

Bentwich, Joseph B. *Education in Israel.* Philadelphia, 1965.

————. *Fulfillment in the Promised Land, 1917–1937.* London, 1938.

Ben-Zvi, Yitzchak. *Kitvei Yitzchak Ben-Zvi* [Writings]. Tel Aviv, 1936.

Berlin, George L. "The Brandeis-Weizmann Dispute," *American Jewish Historical Quarterly*, Sept. 1970.

Bermant, Chaim. *Israel*. New York, 1967.

Brandeis, Louis. *Brandeis on Zionism*. Washington, D.C., 1942.

Braslavsky, M. *T'nuat HaPoalim HaEretz Yisreelit* [The Palestine (Jewish) Labor Movement]. Vols. II, III. Tel Aviv, 1952, 1959.

Cana'an, D. *Beinam l'vein Artzenu* [Between the Others and Our Homeland]. Tel Aviv, 1955.

Dan, Hillel. *B'Derech Lo Slulah* [On an Unpaved Road]. Tel Aviv, 1963.

Darin-Drabkin, Haim. *The Other Society*. New York, 1963.

De Haas, Jacob. *Louis D. Brandeis: A Biographical Sketch*. New York, 1929.

Edelman, Maurice. *Ben-Gurion: A Political Biography*. London, 1964.

Edidin, Ben. *Rebuilding Palestine*. New York, 1939.

Eisenstadt, S. N. *P'rakim b'Toldot T'nuat HaPoalim HaYehudit* [Chapters from the History of the Jewish Labor Movement]. 2 vols. Merchavia, 1944.

Elon, Amos. *The Israelis: Fathers and Sons*. New York, 1971.

Erez, Yehuda, ed. *Sefer HaAliyah HaShlishit* [The Book of the Third Aliyah]. 2 vols. Tel Aviv, 1964.

Esco Foundation for Palestine. *Palestine: A Study of Jewish, Arab, and British Policies*. Vol. II. New Haven, Conn., 1947.

Even-Shoshan, Z. *Toldot T'nuat HaPoalim b'Eretz Yisrael* [A History of the Labor Movement in Palestine]. 3 vols. Tel Aviv, 1963–66.

Fein, Harry, ed. *A Harvest of Hebrew Verse*. Boston, 1934.

Fineman, Irving. *Woman of Valor: The Life of Henrietta Szold*. New York, 1961.

Fishman, Ya'akov, ed. *BaSa'ar* [In the Storm]. Tel Aviv, 1943.

Gaethon, Ari L. *National Income and Outlay in Palestine, 1936*. Jerusalem, 1941.

Gelber, N. M. "Zionist Congresses," *Zion*, Aug. 1941.

Goldenberg, N. *General Zionism*. London, 1937.

Goldman, Guido G. *Zionism under Soviet Rule, 1917–1928*. New York, 1960.

Granott, Avraham. *Agrarian Reform and the Record of Israel*. London, 1956.

Great Britain. *Palestine: Report on Immigration, Land Settlement and Development* (Hope Simpson Report). Cmd. 3686–7. 2 vols. London, 1930.

Greenberg, Uri Zvi. *Chazan Achad HaLigyonot* [The Vision of One of the Legionnaires]. Tel Aviv, 1927.

———. *Eimah G'dolah v'HaYareach* [The Great Terror and the Moon]. Tel Aviv, 1925.

Haber, Julius. *The Odyssey of an American Zionist*. New York, 1956.

Halkin, Simon. *Modern Hebrew Literature*. New York, 1950.

Halpern, Ben. "The Americanization of Zionism, 1880–1930," *American Jewish History*, Sept. 1979.

———. *A Clash of Heroes: Brandeis, Weizmann, and American Zionism*. New York, 1987.

———. *The Idea of the Jewish State*. Cambridge, Mass., 1961.

Himadeh, Saïd, ed. *The Economic Organization of Palestine*. Beirut, 1936.

Horowitz, David. *Aspects of Economic Policy in Palestine*. Tel Aviv, 1936.

Infeld, Herma Z. *The Jewish State in the Making: Its Structure, Institutions and Parties*. Johannesburg, 1946.

Jewish Agency. *Palestine: Land Settlement, Urban Development and Immigration. Memorandum to Sir John Hope Simpson, July 1930*. London, 1930.

Kabak, Aharon, ed. *Kitvei Berl Katznelson* [Collected Writings of Berl Katznelson]. 12 vols. Tel Aviv, 1946–49.

———. *M'Asaf* [Collections]. Tel Aviv, 1940.

Klausner, Joseph. *A History of Modern Hebrew Literature*. London, 1932.

————. *Shaul Tchernichovsky: HaAdam v'HaM'shorer* [Saul Tchernichovsky: The Man and the Poet]. Jerusalem, 1947.

Kleinmann, M. *HaZionim HaKlalim* [The General Zionists]. Jerusalem, 1945.

Kochan, Lionel, ed. *The Jews in Soviet Russia since 1917*. London, 1970.

Kurzweil, Baruch. *Bein Chazon l'vein HaAbsurdi* [Between the Vision and the Absurd]. Jerusalem, 1968.

————. *Bialik v'Tchernichovsky* [Bialik and Tchernichovsky]. Jerusalem, 1967.

Lachover, S., ed. *Avraham Shlonsky* [in Hebrew]. Tel Aviv, 1951.

————. *Toldot HaSifrut HaLvrit HeChadashah* [A History of Modern Hebrew Literature]. 4 vols. Tel Aviv, 1927–33.

Lamdan, Yitzchak. *Masada*. Tel Aviv, 1927.

Laqueur, Walter. *A History of Zionism*. New York, 1972.

Leon, Dan. *The Kibbutz*. London, 1969.

Levenberg, S. *The Jews and Palestine: A Study in Labour Zionism*. London, 1945.

Levin, Marlon. *Balm in Gilead: The Story of Hadassah*. New York, 1975.

Lewkowitz, B. *Der Weg des Misrachi*. Vienna, 1936.

Lipovetzky, Pesah. *Joseph Trumpeldor: Life and Works*. Jerusalem, 1953.

Lipschitz, A. *Uri Zvi Greenberg: M'shorer Adnut HaUmah* [Poet of the Tender Nation]. Tel Aviv, 1945.

Litvinoff, Barnet. *To the House of Their Fathers*. London, 1965.

Lubianiker (Lavon), Pinchas. *Y'sodot* [Foundations]. Tel Aviv, 1941.

Meir, Golda. *My Life*. New York, 1975.

Meyer, Isador S., ed. *The Early History of Zionism in America*. New York, 1958.

Münzer, Gerhard. *Jewish Labour Economy in Palestine*. London, 1945.

Nardi, Noach. *Zionism and Education in Palestine*. New York, 1934.

Neumann, Emanuel. *In the Arena: An Autobiographical Memoir*. New York, 1976.

Ostrowski, M. *Toldot HaMizrachi b'Eretz Yisrael* [A History of the Mizrachi Movement in Palestine]. Jerusalem, 1943.

Palestine Economic Review: A Survey. Jan.–July 1936.

Patai, Raphael, and Zvi Wohlmuth, eds. *Mivchar HaSipur HaEretz Yisreeli* [Selected Israeli Stories]. Jerusalem, 1956.

Pearlman, Moshe. *Ben-Gurion Looks Back*. London, 1965.

Pines, Dan. *HeChalutz b'Chur HaMahapechah* [Pioneering Youth in the Forge of Revolution]. Tel Aviv, 1938.

Poznansky, Menachem. *M'Chayei Yosef Trumpeldor* [From the Life of Joseph Trumpeldor]. Tel Aviv, 1945.

Preuss, Walter. *The Labour Movement in Israel: Past and Present*. Jerusalem, 1965.

Rabinowitz, Ezekiel. *Justice Louis D. Brandeis: The Zionist Chapter of His Life*. New York, 1966.

Rabinowitz, Oskar K. *Fifty Years of Zionism*. London, 1951.

Reznikoff, Charles, ed. *Louis Marshall, Champion of Liberty: Selected Papers and Addresses*. 2 vols. Philadelphia, 1957.

Ruppin, Arthur. *Building Israel: Selected Essays, 1907–1935*. New York, 1949.

————. *Three Decades of Palestine*. Jerusalem, 1936.

Sachar, Howard M. *Aliyah: The Peoples of Israel*. Cleveland, 1961.

Sacher, Harry. *Zionist Portraits and Other Essays*. London, 1959.

Samuel, Maurice. *Harvest in the Desert*. New York, 1944.

Sanders, Ronald. *Israel: The View from Masada*. New York, 1966.

Schechtman, Joseph. *Zionism and Zionists in Soviet Russia*. New York, 1966.

Schmorak, Emil. *The Economic Development of Palestine.* Tel Aviv, 1943.

Shalom, Shin. *Yoman baGalil* [Galilee Diary]. Tel Aviv, 1932, 1933.

Shapiro, Yonathan. *Leadership of the American Zionist Organization, 1897–1930.* Urbana, Ill., 1971.

Shlonsky, Avraham. *BaGalil* [In the Galilee]. Tel Aviv, 1927.

———. *D'vai* [Sorrow]. Tel Aviv, 1924.

———. *L'Abba, Ima* [To Father, to Mother]. Tel Aviv, 1929.

Silberschlag, Eisig. *Saul Tschernichowsky.* Ithaca, N.Y., 1968.

Simon, Sir Leon, and Edward Stein, eds. *Awakening Palestine.* London, 1923.

Spiegel, Shalom. *Hebrew Reborn.* New York, 1930.

Stern, Boris. *The Kibbutz That Was.* Washington, D.C., 1965.

Szereszewski, Robert. *Essays on the Structure of the Jewish Economy in Palestine and Israel.* Jerusalem, 1968.

Tchernichowsky, Saul. *Selected Poems.* London, 1929.

"Tel Aviv: Forty Years of Progress," *Israel Life and Letters,* April 1950.

Teller, Judd L. "The Making of the Ideals That Rule Israel," *Commentary,* Jan.–Feb. 1954.

Uchmani, A. *L'Ever HaAdam* [Toward Man]. Merchavia, 1953.

Uman, S. *The World of Isaac Lamdan.* New York, 1961.

Urofsky, Melvin I. *American Zionism from Herzl to the Holocaust.* Garden City, N.Y., 1975.

Viteles, Harry. *A History of the Cooperative Movement in Israel.* Vols. I, II. London, 1966, 1968.

Wallenrod, Reuben. *The Literature of Modern Israel.* New York, 1956.

Weiner, Herbert. "Rav Kuk's Path to Peace within Israel," *Commentary,* March 1954.

Weintraub, D., M. Lissak, and Y. Azmon. *Moshava, Kibbutz, and Moshav.* Ithaca, N.Y., 1969.

Weisgal, Meyer, and Joel Carmichael, eds. *Chaim Weizmann: A Biography by Several Hands.* New York, 1963.

Weizmann, Chaim. *Trial and Error.* New York, 1949.

Wise, Stephen S. *Challenging Years.* New York, 1949.

———. *Personal Letters.* Boston, 1956.

Yaari, Avraham. *The Goodly Heritage.* Jerusalem, 1958.

Yeivin, Y. *Uri Zvi Greenberg: HaM'shorer M'chokek* [Uri Zvi Greenberg: The Poet-Legislator]. Tel Aviv, 1938.

Yoffe, A. B. *Avraham Shlonsky: HaM'shorer u'Z'mano* [Avraham Shlonsky: The Poet and His Time]. Merchavia, 1966.

Yudkin, L. I. *Isaac Lamdan.* London, 1971.

Zenziper, Arieh. *Eser Sh'not R'difot* [Ten Years of Persecution]. Tel Aviv, 1930.

Ziman, Joshua. *The Revival of Palestine.* New York, 1946.

Zmora, Y. *Sifrut al Parashat Dorot* [Literature at the Crossroads of the Generations]. Tel Aviv, 1950.

III. *The Arab-Jewish Confrontation. Britain Repudiates the Jewish National Home*

Abcarius, M. F. *Palestine through the Fog of Propaganda.* London, 1946.

Abramovitz, Z., and I. G'ulfat. *HaMeshek HaAravi* [The Arab Economy]. Tel Aviv, 1944.

Achimeier, A. *HaZionut HaMahapchanit* [Revolutionary Zionism]. Tel Aviv, 1966.

———. *Im Kriat HaGever* [At Daybreak]. Tel Aviv, 1940.

Allon, Yigal. *The Making of Israel's Army.* London, 1970.

Arab Higher Committee for Palestine. *A Collection of Official Documents Relating to the Palestine Question, 1917–1947*. Submitted to the General Assembly of the United Nations, Nov. 1947.

Arlosoroff, Chaim. *Yoman Yerushalayim* [Jerusalem Diary]. Tel Aviv, 1949.

Ashbee, C. R. *A Palestine Notebook, 1918–1923*. New York, 1923.

Assaf, Michael. *The Arab Movement in Palestine*. New York, 1937.

———. *Toldot HaAravim b'Eretz Yisrael* [A History of the Arabs of Palestine]. 3 vols. Tel Aviv, 1935–70.

Avigur, Shaul. *Im Dor HaHaganah* [With the Generation of the Haganah]. Tel Aviv, 1962.

Bar-Zohar, Michael. *Ben-Gurion: The Armed Prophet*. Englewood Cliffs, N.J., 1967.

Bauer, Yehuda. "The Arab Revolt of 1936," *New Outlook*, July–Sept. 1966.

———. *From Diplomacy to Resistance: A History of Jewish Palestine, 1939–1945*. Philadelphia, 1970.

Ben-Gurion, David. *Anachnu v'Shechnenu* [We and Our Neighbors]. Tel Aviv, 1931.

———. *The Peel Report and the Jewish State*. Jerusalem, 1938.

———. *P'gishot im Manhigim Arviyim* [Meetings with Arab Leaders]. Tel Aviv, 1967.

Ben-Meir, Chaim. *HaRevizionizm: Sakanah laAm* [Revisionism: A Danger to the Nation]. Tel Aviv, 1938.

Bentwich, Norman. *For Zion's Sake: A Biography of Judah L. Magnes*. Philadelphia, 1954.

———. *Jewish Youth Comes Home: The Story of the Youth Aliyah, 1933–1943*. New York, 1975.

Ben-Yerucham, Chaim, ed. *Sefer HaBetar* [The Book of the Betar Movement]. Vol. I. Tel Aviv, 1938.

Ben-Zvi, Yitzchak. *HaT'nuah HaAravit* [The Arab Movement]. Jaffa, 1921.

Bin-Nun, Y. *Jew and Arab on the Border*. New York, 1940.

Boustany, W. F. *The Palestine Mandate: Invalid and Impracticable*. Beirut, 1938.

Buber, Martin, Judah L. Magnes, and Moses Smilansky. *Palestine: A Bi-National State*. New York, 1946.

Canaan, Tawfiq. *Conflict in the Land of Peace*. Jerusalem, 1936.

Cohen, Aharon. *Israel and the Arab World*. New York, 1970.

Cohen, Michael J. *Churchill and the Jews*. London, 1985.

Courtney, Roger. *Palestine Policeman*. London, 1939.

Dinur, B. Z., et al., eds. *Sefer Toldot HaHaganah* [The History of the Haganah]. Vol. I. Tel Aviv, 1956.

Elath, Eliahu. *Haj Mohammed Amin al-Husseini* [in Hebrew]. Jerusalem, 1968.

Elsberg, P. "HaSh'elah HaAravit b'M'diniyut HaHanhalah HaZionit Lifnei 1914 [The Arab Question in Zionist Diplomacy before 1914]," *Shivat Zion*, No. 4, 1956.

Elston, David. *No Alternative*. London, 1960.

Erskine, Beatrice. *Palestine of the Arabs*. London, 1935.

Esco Foundation for Palestine. *Palestine: A Study of Jewish, Arab, and British Policies*. Vol. II. New Haven, Conn., 1947.

Ever-Hadani, Aharon. *Am b'Milchamto* [A People at War]. Tel Aviv, 1948.

Feiwell, T. R. *No Ease in Zion*. London, 1939.

Furlonge, Geoffrey. *Palestine Is My Country: The Story of Musa Alami*. London, 1969.

Gilad, Zerubavel, ed. *Magen B'Seter* [The Secret Defense]. Jerusalem, 1951.

Goldberg, Reuven, ed. *B'Dam v'Esh* [In Blood and Fire]. Jerusalem, 1937.

Golomb, Eliahu. *Shivion Oz* [An Equality of Courage]. Tel Aviv, 1944.

Great Britain. *Palestine Partition Report* (Woodhead Report). Cmd. 5854. London, 1938.

———. *Palestine: Report on Immigration, Land Settlement and Development* (Hope Simpson Report). Cmd. 3686–7. 2 vols. London, 1930.

———. *Palestine: Royal Commission Report* (Peel Report). Cmd. 5479. London, 1937.

————. *Palestine: Statement of Policy* (White Paper). Cmd. 6019. London, 1939.

Hadawi, Sami. *Bitter Harvest: Palestine between 1914–1967.* New York, 1967.

Haganah: HaMagen HaIvri. *Chaverim M'saprim. I: B'Y'mei M'ora'ot* [Comrades Relate: I. In the Days of the (Arab) Uprising]. Tel Aviv, 1945.

Hanna, Paul. *British Policy in Palestine.* Washington, D.C., 1942.

Hattis, Susan Lee. *The Bi-National Idea in Palestine during Mandatory Times.* Jerusalem, 1970.

Hurewitz, J. C. *The Struggle for Palestine.* New York, 1950.

Hyamson, Albert. *Palestine under the Mandate, 1920–1948.* London, 1950.

Jabotinsky, Vladimir. *K'tavim* [Writings]. Vols. IV, VII. Jerusalem, 1947, 1953.

Jeffries, J. M. N. *Palestine: The Reality.* London, 1939.

Jewish Agency. *The Jewish Case against the White Paper: Documents Submitted to the Permanent Mandates Commission.* London, 1939.

Jewish Frontier Association. *The Broken Pledge: The Case against the White Paper on Palestine.* New York, 1944.

Khalidi, Thabit al-. *Arab Clan Rivalry in Palestine.* Jerusalem, 1945.

Kimche, Jon. *There Could Have Been Peace.* New York, 1973.

Kisch, Frederick H. *Palestine Diary.* London, 1938.

Klausner, Joseph, ed. *Ze'ev Jabotinsky: K'tavim Nivcharim* [Vladimir Jabotinsky: Selected Writings]. 2 vols. Jerusalem, 1943.

Landau, Jacob. *The Arabs in Israel.* London, 1969.

Laqueur, Walter. *A History of Zionism.* New York, 1972.

Laqueur, Walter, and Barry Rubin, eds. *The Israel-Arab Reader.* New York, 1985.

Machon Jabotinsky, ed. *Brit HaBiryonim* [The League of Hooligans]. Tel Aviv, 1953.

Magnes, Judah L., ed. *Arab-Jewish Unity.* Jerusalem, 1946.

————. *Like All Nations?* Jerusalem, 1930.

Marder, Munya. *Haganah.* New York, 1966.

Marlowe, John. *The Seat of Pilate: An Account of the Palestine Mandate.* London, 1959.

Medzini, Moshe. *Eser Shanim shel M'diniyut Eretz Yisreelit* [Ten Years of Palestinian (Jewish) Diplomacy]. Tel Aviv, 1928.

Meinertzhagen, Richard. *Middle East Diary, 1917–1956.* London, 1959.

Nation Associates. *The Arab Higher Committee: Its Origins, Personnel, and Purposes.* New York, 1947.

Naufah, Sayyid. "A Short History of the Arab Opposition to Zionism and Israel," *Islamic Review,* Feb. 1965.

Nedava, Joseph. *Jabotinsky b'Chazon HaDor* [Jabotinsky in the Vision of the Generation]. Tel Aviv, 1950.

Pearlman, Maurice. *Mufti of Jerusalem: The Story of Haj Amin al-Husseini.* London, 1947.

Polk, W. R., D. M. Stamler, and E. Asfour. *Backdrop to Tragedy: The Struggle for Palestine.* Boston, 1974.

Porath, Yehoshua. *The Emergence of the Palestinian-Arab National Movement, 1918–1929.* London, 1974.

Rabinowicz, Oskar K. *Vladimir Jabotinsky's Conception of a New Nation.* New York, 1946.

Razzaq, Asad. *Greater Israel: A Study in Zionist Expansionist Thought.* Beirut, 1970.

Reinharz, Jehuda. *Chaim Weizmann: The Making of a Zionist Statesman.* Vol. II. New York, 1993.

Roi, Ya'akov. "HaEmdah HaZionit Klapei HaAravim, 1908–1914 [The Zionist Standpoint toward the Arabs, 1908–1914]," *Keshet,* Nos. 42–43, 1969.

Rose, Norman. *Chaim Weizmann: A Biography.* New York, 1986.

————. "The Debate on Partition, 1937–38: The Anglo-Zionist Aspect—I: The Proposal,"

Middle Eastern Studies, Oct. 1970; "II: The Withdrawal," *Middle Eastern Studies,* Jan. 1971.

———. *The Gentle Zionist: A Study in Anglo-Zionist Diplomacy, 1929–1939.* London, 1972.

Sachar, Howard M. *Aliyah: The Peoples of Israel.* Cleveland, 1961.

———. *Europe Leaves the Middle East, 1936–1954.* New York, 1972.

Samuel, Maurice. *On the Rim of the Wilderness: The Conflict in Palestine.* New York, 1931.

———. *What Happened in Palestine: The Events of August, 1929.* Boston, 1929.

Schechtman, Joseph. *Vladimir Jabotinsky.* Vol. II. New York, 1961.

Schechtman, Joseph, and Yehuda Benari. *A History of the Revisionist Movement.* Vol. I. Tel Aviv, 1970.

Sereni, Enzo, and R. E. Ashery, eds. *Jews and Arabs in Palestine.* New York, 1936.

Shimoni, Ya'akov. *Arevei Eretz Yisrael* [The Arabs of Palestine]. Tel Aviv, 1947.

Slutzki, Yehuda. *A History of the Haganah.* Jerusalem, 1954.

Stein, Avraham. *HaNoter HaIvri, 1936–1946* [The Hebrew Watchman, 1936–1946]. Tel Aviv, 1946.

Sykes, Christopher. *Crossroads to Israel, 1917–1948.* New York, 1965.

———. *Orde Wingate.* London, 1959.

Teveth, Shabtai. *Moshe Dayan.* London, 1972.

Tibawi, Abdul Latif. *Arab Education in Mandatory Palestine.* London, 1956.

———. "Educational Policy and Arab Nationalism in Contemporary Palestine," *Welt des Islams,* 1955.

Waschitz, Y. *HaAravim b'Eretz Yisrael* [The Arabs of Palestine]. Tel Aviv, 1947.

Weizmann, Chaim. *Trial and Error.* New York, 1949.

Weizmann, Vera. *The Impossible Takes Longer.* London, 1967.

Yisraeli, David. "The Third Reich and Palestine," *Middle Eastern Studies,* Oct. 1971.

IV. *World War II and Its Aftermath. The Yishuv Repudiates the Mandate*

Adler, Selig. "American Policy vis-à-vis Palestine in the Second World War." Paper presented to the National Archives Conference on Research on the Second World War. Washington, D.C., June 14, 1971.

Agar, Herbert. *The Saving Remnant.* New York, 1960.

Allon, Yigal. *The Making of Israel's Army.* London, 1970.

Arsenian, Seth. "Wartime Propaganda in the Middle East," *Middle East Journal,* Summer 1948.

Avigur, Shaul. *Im Dor HaHaganah* [With the Generation of the Haganah]. Tel Aviv, 1962.

Banai, Ya'akov. *Chayalim Almonim* [Unknown Soldiers]. Tel Aviv, 1958.

Bartov, Hanoch. *The Bridge.* Philadelphia, 1967.

Batal, James. "Truman Factors in the Middle East," *Middle East Forum,* Dec. 1956.

Bauer, Yehuda. *Flight and Rescue: Bricha.* New York, 1970.

———. *From Diplomacy to Resistance: A History of Jewish Palestine, 1939–1945.* Philadelphia, 1970.

Begin, Menachem. *BaMachteret* [In the Underground]. 2 vols. Tel Aviv, 1946.

———. *The Revolt: The Story of the Irgun.* New York, 1951.

Ben-Avraham, Y. *HaHe'avkut al Tzava Yehudi* [The Battle for a Jewish Army]. Tel Aviv, 1946.

Ben-Gurion, David. *B'Hilachem Yisrael* [While Israel Fought]. Tel Aviv, 1949.

Brenner, Y. S. "The 'Stern Gang,' 1940–48," *Middle Eastern Studies,* Oct. 1965.

Bullock, Alan. *The Life and Times of Ernest Bevin.* Vol. I. London, 1960.

Cana'an, Haviv. *B'Tzet HaBritim* [The Departure of the British]. Tel Aviv, 1958.

Caroe, Sir Olaf K. *Wells of Power: The Oilfields of South-West Asia.* New York, 1951.

Charteris, M. N. C. "A Year as an Intelligence Officer in Palestine," *Journal of the Middle East Society,* 1946.

Charters, David A. *The British Army and Jewish Insurgency in Palestine, 1945–47.* New York, 1989.

Churchill, Winston. *The Second World War.* Vols. III, IV. Boston, 1950, 1951.

Cohen, Israel. *Britain's Nameless Ally.* London, 1942.

Cohen, Michael J. *Churchill and the Jews.* London, 1985.

Crossman, R. H. S. *Palestine Mission.* London, 1946.

Crum, Bartley C. *Behind the Silken Curtain.* New York, 1947.

Dayan, Moshe. "M'Y'mei HaPlishah HaSurit [From the Days of the Syrian Invasion]," *Bitaon HaPalmach,* July 1944.

———. *The Story of My Life.* New York, 1976.

Dekel, Ephraim. *Alilot Shai* [The Exploits of Shai (Haganah Intelligence)]. Tel Aviv, 1953.

Dinur, B. Z., et al., eds. *Sefer Toldot HaHaganah* [The History of the Haganah]. Vols. I, II. Tel Aviv, 1956, 1964.

Edelman, Maurice. *Ben-Gurion: A Political Biography.* London, 1964.

Elath, Eliahu. *Zionism at the U.N.: A Diary of the First Days.* Philadelphia, 1976.

Eppler, Johann. *Rommel ruft Kairo: Aus dem Tagebuch eines Spiones.* Bielefeld, 1959.

Ever-Hadani, Aharon. *Am b'Milchamto* [A People at War]. Tel Aviv, 1948.

———. *B'Ruach u'v'Chalil* [With Spirit and Zephyr]. Tel Aviv, 1952.

Farran, Roy. *Winged Dagger: Adventures in Special Service.* London, 1948.

Feingold, Henry L. *The Politics of Rescue: The Roosevelt Administration and the Holocaust, 1938–1945.* New Brunswick, N.J., 1970.

Fitzsimons, M. A. *The Foreign Policy of the British Labour Government, 1945–1951.* South Bend, Ind., 1953.

Francis-Williams, Edward. *Ernest Bevin.* London, 1952.

———, ed. *A Prime Minister Remembers: The War and Post-War Memoirs of the Rt. Hon. Earl Attlee.* London, 1962.

Frank, Gerold. *The Deed.* New York, 1963.

Frankenstein, Ernst. *Palestine in the Light of International Law.* London, 1946.

Friedman, Philip. *Martyrs and Fighters.* New York, 1954.

Ganin, Zvi. *Truman, American Jewry, and Israel, 1945–1948.* New York, 1979.

Gilad, Zerubavel, ed. *Magen B'Seter* [The Shield of Secrecy]. Jerusalem, 1951.

———, ed. *Sefer HaPalmach* [The Book of the Palmach]. 2 vols. Tel Aviv, 1955.

Graves, R. M. *Experiment in Anarchy.* London, 1949.

Great Britain. *Proposals for the Future of Palestine: July, 1946–Feb., 1947.* Cmd. 7044. London, 1947.

———. *Report of the Anglo-American Committee of Inquiry Regarding the Problems of European Jewry and Palestine, Lausanne; 20th April, 1946.* Cmd. 6808. London, 1946.

Habas, Braha. *The Gate Breakers.* New York, 1963.

Halperin, Samuel. *The Political World of American Zionism.* Detroit, 1961.

Hentig, Otto von. *Mein Leben: Eine Dienstreise.* Göttingen, 1962.

Hilberg, Raoul. *The Destruction of the European Jews.* Chicago, 1961.

Hirschmann, Ira. *Life-Line to the Promised Land.* New York, 1946.

Hirszowicz, Lukasz. *The Third Reich and the Arab East.* London, 1966.

Hodson, H. V. "British Interests in the Middle East," *Listener,* Jan. 20, 1949.

Hurewitz, J. C. *The Struggle for Palestine.* New York, 1950.

Jabotinsky, Vladimir. *The War and the Jew.* New York, 1942.

Jewish Agency. *Activities in Palestine during the War.* London, 1945.

Kaplan, Eliezer. *Report on Seven Years of Palestine, 1939–1946.* New York, 1947.

Katz, Doris. *The Lady Was a Terrorist.* New York, 1953.

Katz, Samuel. *Days of Fire.* New York, 1966.

Kedourie, Elie. "Panarabism and British Policy," *British Quarterly,* April–June 1957.

Kimche, Jon. *The Second Arab Awakening.* London, 1970.

———. *Seven Fallen Pillars: The Middle East, 1915–50.* London, 1950.

Kimche, Jon, and David Kimche. *The Secret Roads: The "Illegal" Migration of a People, 1938–48.* London, 1954.

Kirk, George. *The Middle East, 1945–1950.* London, 1954.

Lamdan, Yitzchak. *Kovetz Sefer HaHitnadvut* [The Volunteer Files]. Tel Aviv, 1946.

Landsborough, T. *HaKomando shel Tobruk* [The Tobruk Commando]. Tel Aviv, 1959.

Laqueur, Walter, and Barry Rubin, eds. *The Israel-Arab Reader.* New York, 1985.

Lazar, David. *L'opinion français et la naissance de l'État d'Israël 1, 1945–1949.* Paris, 1972.

Lifshitz, Y., ed. *Sefer HaBrigada* [The Book of the (Jewish) Brigade]. Tel Aviv, 1957.

Litvinoff, Barnett. *Ben-Gurion Looks Back.* London, 1954.

Lugol, Jean. *Egypt and World War II.* Cairo, 1945.

Machon Jabotinsky. *David Raziel* [in Hebrew]. Tel Aviv, 1956.

Marlowe, John. *Rebellion in Palestine.* London, 1946.

Meir, Golda. *My Life.* New York, 1975.

Monroe, Elizabeth. "British Interests in the Middle East," *Middle East Journal,* Winter 1948.

———. "Mr. Bevin's Arab Policy," in *St. Antony's Papers,* No. 11. London, 1961.

Nation Associates. *The Record of Collaboration of King Farouk of Egypt with the Nazis, and Their Ally, the Mufti.* New York, 1948.

Niv, David. *Ma'arachot HaIrgun HaZ'vai HaLe'umi* [The Struggles of the Etzel]. 2 vols. Tel Aviv, 1965.

Parzen, Herbert. "The Roosevelt Palestine Policy, 1943–1945," *American Jewish Archives,* April 1974.

Rabinowitz, L. *Soldiers from Judea.* London, 1945.

Rahn, Rudolf. *Ruheloses Leben.* Düsseldorf, 1949.

Rose, Norman. "Weizmann, Ben-Gurion, and the 1946 Crisis in the Zionist Movement," *Studies in Zionism,* No. 1, 1990.

Royal Institute of International Affairs. *British Security.* London, 1946.

Sachar, Howard M. *Europe Leaves the Middle East, 1936–1954.* New York, 1972.

———. *From the Ends of the Earth: The Peoples of Israel.* Cleveland, 1964.

———. *A History of the Jews in America.* New York, 1992.

———, ed. *The Rise of Israel: A Documentary History.* 39 vols. New York, 1988.

Schechtman, Joseph B. *The Mufti and the Führer.* New York, 1965.

———. *The United States and the Jewish State Movement: The Crucial Decade, 1939–49.* New York, 1966.

———. *Vladimir Jabotinsky.* Vol. II. New York, 1961.

Schwartz, Leo W. *The Redeemers.* New York, 1953.

Shamir, A. *Yehudim Ochazim b'Neshek* [Arms-Bearing Jews]. Tel Aviv, 1946.

Sharett, Moshe. *B'Sh'ar HaUmot, 1946–1949* [On the Threshold of Nationhood, 1946–1949]. Tel Aviv, 1958.

Silver, Abba Hillel. *Vision and Victory.* New York, 1949.

Steffen, H. von. *Salaam: Geheimkommando zum Nil–1943.* Neckargemund, 1960.

Stein, Avraham. *HaNoter HaIvri, 1936–1946* [The Hebrew Watchman, 1936–1946]. Tel Aviv, 1946.

Steiner, Gershon. *Patria* [in Hebrew]. Tel Aviv, 1964.

Stone, I. F. *Underground to Palestine.* New York, 1946.

Sykes, Christopher. *Crossroads to Israel, 1917–1948.* New York, 1965.

Syrkin, Marie. *Blessed Is the Match.* Philadelphia, 1947.

Tavin, Y. *HaMa'avak HaZ'vai v'HaM'dini shel HaIrgun HaZ'vai HaLe'umi b'Europa, Yuni 1946–Yanuar 1949* [The Etzel's Military and Diplomatic Struggle in Europe, June 1946–January 1949]. Jerusalem, 1963.

Teveth, Shabtai. *Moshe Dayan.* London, 1972.

Tornovsky, V. *Tochnit HaYishuv b'Aretz l'Zman HaMilchamah* [The Yishuv's Program during the War]. Tel Aviv, 1941.

Trevor, Daphne. *Under the White Paper.* Jerusalem, 1948.

Truman, Harry S. *Memoirs.* 2 vols. New York, 1953–55.

United States. Department of State. *Foreign Relations of the United States:* 1943, Vol. IV; 1945, Vol. VII; 1946, Vol. VIII. Washington, D.C., 1965.

Van Paassen, Pierre. *The Forgotten Ally.* New York, 1943.

Waters, M. P. (Moshe Pearlman). *Haganah: Jewish Self-Defence in Palestine.* London, 1946.

Weinshall, Ya'akov. *HaDam Asher BaSaf* [The Blood on the Doorstep]. Tel Aviv, 1956.

Weissberg, Alex. *Desperate Mission: Joel Brand's Story.* New York, 1958.

Weizmann, Chaim. "Palestine's Role in the Solution of the Jewish Problem," *Foreign Affairs,* Jan. 1942.

Wilson, R. D. *Cordon and Search: With the Sixth Airborne Division in Palestine.* Aldershot, 1949.

Woodward, Sir E. Llewellyn. *British Foreign Policy in the Second World War.* London, 1962.

Yakobovitz, M. *M'Palmach ad Tzahal* [From Palmach to the Army of Israel]. Tel Aviv, 1953.

Zasloff, Joseph H. *Great Britain and Palestine: A Study of the Problem before the United Nations.* New York, 1952.

THE ESTABLISHMENT AND GROWTH OF THE STATE

I. *The Birth of Israel and War of Independence*

Abdullah, King of Jordan. *My Memoirs Completed.* Washington, D.C., 1954.

Acheson, Dean. *Present at the Creation.* New York, 1969.

Allon, Yigal. *The Making of Israel's Army.* London, 1970.

Arab Higher Committee. *A Collection of Official Documents Relating to the Palestine Question, 1917–1947.* Submitted to the General Assembly of the United Nations, Nov. 1947.

Avinoam, Reuven, ed. *Such Were Our Fighters.* New York, 1965.

Avnery, Uri. *B'Sadot Pleshet 1948* [In Philistine Fields, 1948]. Tel Aviv, 1950.

Banai, Ya'akov. *Chayalim Almonim* [Unknown Soldiers]. Tel Aviv, 1958.

Bar-Yosef, Uri. *The Best of Enemies: Israel and Transjordan in the War of 1948.* London, 1987.

Bar-Zohar, Michael. *Ben-Gurion: The Armed Prophet.* Englewood Cliffs, N.J., 1967.

———. *Gesher al HaYam HaTichon* [Bridge over the Mediterranean]. Tel Aviv, 1964.

Batal, James. "Truman Factors in the Middle East," *Middle East Forum,* Dec. 1956.

Begin, Menachem. *The Revolt: Story of the Irgun.* New York, 1951.

Ben-Gurion, David. *B'Hilalchem Yisrael* [In the Struggle for Israel]. Tel Aviv, 1949.

———. *Israel: A Personal History.* New York, 1971.

Bernadotte, Folke. *To Jerusalem.* London, 1951.

Brodie, Bernard. "American Security and Foreign Oil," *Foreign Policy Reports,* March 1, 1948.

Cana'an, Haviv. *B'Tzet HaBritim* [The Departure of the British]. Tel Aviv, 1958.

Carmel, Moshe. *Ma'arachot Tzafon* [The Northern Battle Fronts]. Ein Harod, 1949.

Childers, Erskine. "The Other Exodus," *Spectator,* May 12, 1961.

Chorshi, Arieh. *HaAchad-Asar m'Rishon l'Zion* [The Rishon Zion Eleven]. Rishon l'Zion, 1969.

Clifford, Clark. "President Truman's Decision to Recognize Israel," *American Heritage,* Spring 1977.

Cohan, Naomi W. *American Jews and the Zionist Idea.* New York, 1975.

Cohen, Michael J. *Truman and Israel.* Berkeley, Calif., 1990.

Crossman, R. H. S. *A Nation Reborn.* New York, 1960.

Cunningham, General Sir Andrew. "Palestine—the Last Days of the Mandate," *International Affairs,* Aug. 1948.

Dayan, Moshe. *The Story of My Life.* New York, 1976.

Dinur, B. Z., et al., eds. *Sefer Toldot HaHaganah* [The History of the Haganah]. Vol. II. Tel Aviv, 1964.

Eban, Abba. *Personal Witness.* New York, 1993.

Elston, David. *Israel: The Making of a Nation.* New York, 1963.

Feis, Herbert. *The Birth of Israel: The Tousled Diplomatic Bed.* New York, 1969.

Feuer, Leon. "The Birth of the Jewish Lobby: A Reminiscence," *American Jewish Archives,* Nov. 1976.

Friedman, Saul. "The Palestinian Issue and the Arab Refugee Problem," *Middle East Information Series,* Nov. 1971.

Gabbay, Rony E. *A Political Study of the Arab-Jewish Conflict.* Geneva, 1959.

Galili, Israel. *Rishonim Tamid* [Always in the Lead]. Tel Aviv, 1953.

Ganin, Zvi. *Truman, American Jewry, and Israel, 1945–1948.* New York, 1979.

Garcia-Granados, Jorge. *I Saw the Birth of Israel.* New York, 1948.

Gilad, Zerubavel, ed. *Sefer HaPalmach* [The Book of the Palmach]. Vol. II. Tel Aviv, 1955.

Gilbert, Martin. *The Arab-Israeli Conflict: Its History in Maps.* London, 1974.

Glick, Edward B. *Latin America and the Palestine Problem.* New York, 1958.

Glubb, Lieutenant General Sir John B. *A Soldier with the Arabs.* London, 1957.

Golan, Aviezer. *Milchemet HaAtzma'ut* [The War of Independence]. Tel Aviv, 1968.

Gruber, Ruth. *Destination Palestine.* New York, 1948.

Hadawi, Sami. *Bitter Harvest: Palestine between 1914–1967.* New York, 1967.

———. *Palestine: Loss of a Heritage.* San Antonio, Tex., 1963.

Heckelman, A. Joseph. *American Volunteers and Israel's War of Independence.* New York, 1974.

Horowitz, David. *State in the Making.* New York, 1953.

Hourani, Albert. "The Decline of the West in the Middle East," *International Affairs,* July 1953.

Hurewitz, J. C. *The Struggle for Palestine.* New York, 1950.

Israel. Ministry of Defense. *K'nafei Nitzachon* [The Wings of Victory]. Tel Aviv, 1966.

———. Ministry of Defense. *Toldot Milchemet HaKomemiyut* [A History of the War of Independence]. Tel Aviv, 1959.

Joseph, Dov (Bernard). *The Faithful City: The Siege of Jerusalem, 1948.* New York, 1960.

Khalidi, Walid. "Why Did the Palestinians Leave?" *Middle East Forum,* July 1959.

Kimche, Jon, and David Kimche. *Both Sides of the Hill: Britain and the Palestine War.* London, 1960.

Knohl, Dov, ed. *Siege in the Hills of Hebron: The Battle of the Etzion Bloc.* New York, 1958.

Krammer, Arnold. *The Forgotten Friendship: Israel and the Soviet Bloc, 1947–53.* Urbana, Ill., 1974.

Kurzman, Dan. *The First Arab-Israeli War.* Cleveland, 1970.

Lankin, Eliahu. *The Story of the Altalena.* Tel Aviv, 1967.

Lapierre, Dominique, and Larry Collins. *O Jerusalem.* London, 1972.

Lazar, David. *L'opinion français et la naissance de l'État d'Israël, 1945–1949.* Paris, 1972.

Leonard, Leonard L. *The United Nations and Palestine.* New York, 1949.

Lie, Trygve. *In the Cause of Peace.* New York, 1954.

Lorch, Netanel. *The Edge of the Sword: Israel's War of Independence.* New York, 1961.

Ma'oz, Moshe, and Allen Weinstein, eds. *Truman and the American Commitment to Israel.* Jerusalem, 1981.

McDonald, James G. *My Mission in Israel.* New York, 1951.

Morris, Benny. *Israel's Border Wars.* New York, 1994.

Niv, David. *Ma'arachot HaIrgun HaZ'vai HaLe'umi* [The Struggles of the Etzel]. Vol. II. Tel Aviv, 1969.

Peretz, Don. *Israel and the Palestine Arabs.* Washington, D.C., 1958.

Pinner, Walter. *How Many Arab Refugees?* New York, 1953.

Postal, Bernard, and Henry W. Levy. *And the Hills Shouted for Joy: The Day Israel Was Born.* Philadelphia, 1973.

Proskauer, Joseph. *A Segment of My Time.* New York, 1950.

Reynier, Jacques de. *À Jerusalem un drapeau flottait sur la ligne de feu.* Neûchatel, 1950.

Rifaat Bey, Muhammed. "The Story of el Faluge," *Islamic Review,* June 1949.

Robinson, Jacob. *Palestine and the United Nations.* Washington, D.C., 1947.

Rosenne, Shabtai. *Israel's Armistice Agreement with the Arab States.* Tel Aviv, 1951.

Sachar, David B. "David K. Niles and United States Policy toward Palestine." Unpublished honors thesis, Harvard University, 1959.

Sachar, Howard M. *Aliyah: The Peoples of Israel.* Cleveland, 1961.

———. *Europe Leaves the Middle East, 1936–1954.* New York, 1972.

———. *From the Ends of the Earth: The Peoples of Israel.* Cleveland, 1964.

———. *A History of the Jews in America.* New York, 1992.

Sacher, Harry. *Israel: The Establishment of a State.* London, 1952.

Safran, Nadav. *The United States and Israel.* Cambridge, Mass., 1963.

Sakran, Frank C. *Palestine Dilemma: Arab Rights versus Zionist Aspirations.* Washington, D.C., 1948.

Schechtman, Joseph B. *The United States and the Jewish State Movement: The Crucial Decade, 1939–49.* New York, 1966.

Schwartz, Yoachim. *Milchemet HaShichrur shel Am Yisrael* [Israel's War of Independence]. Jerusalem, 1953.

Sela, A. "Transjordan, Israel and the 1948 War: Myth, Historiography, and Reality," *Middle East Studies,* No. 4, 1992.

Sharef, Zeev. *Three Days.* London, 1962.

Sharett, Moshe. *B'Sh'ar HaUmot, 1946–1949* [On the Threshold of Nationhood, 1946–1949]. Tel Aviv, 1958.

Silverberg, Robert. *If I Forget Thee O Jerusalem: American Jews and the State of Israel.* New York, 1970.

Singer, Mendel. *215 Yamim P'nei Moledatenu* [215 Days toward Nationhood]. Haifa, 1966.

Slater, Leonard. *The Pledge.* New York, 1970.

Smolansky, O. M. "Soviet Policy in the Arab East, 1945–47," *Journal of International Affairs,* Summer 1959.

Snetsinger, John. *Truman, the Jewish Vote, and the Creation of Israel.* Stanford, Calif., 1974.

Steinberg, Alfred. *The Man from Missouri: The Life and Times of Harry S. Truman.* New York, 1962.

Stevens, Richard P. *American Zionism and U.S. Foreign Policy.* New York, 1962.

Talmi, Ephraim. *Yisrael b'Ma'arachah* [Israel on the Battle Front]. Tel Aviv, 1952.

Teveth, Shabtai. *Ben-Gurion and the Palestinian Arabs: From Peace to War.* New York, 1985.

———. *Moshe Dayan.* London, 1972.

———. "The Palestine Arab Refugee Problem and Its Origins," *Middle East Studies,* No. 2, 1990.

Truman, Harry S. *Memoirs.* Vol. II. New York, 1953.

United Nations. Document A/648. *Report of the United Nations Mediator, Count Folke Bernadotte.* New York, 1948.

United States. Department of State. *Foreign Relations of the United States, 1947.* Vol. V. Washington, D.C., 1972.

Weinberg, Zvi. *Heim Halchu* [They Went Forward]. Tel Mond, 1955.

Yakobovitz, M. *M'Palmach ad Tzahal* [From Palmach to the Army of Israel]. Tel Aviv, 1953.

Yizhar, S. (Smilansky). *Midnight Convoy and Other Stories.* Jerusalem, 1969.

Zaar, Isaac. *Rescue and Liberation: America's Part in the Birth of Israel.* New York, 1954.

Zarour, M. "Ramallah: My Home Town," *Middle East Journal,* Autumn 1953.

II.   *Government and Politics. The Arab Minority*

Abramov, S. Z. *Perpetual Dilemma: Jewish Religion in the Jewish State.* Cranbury, N.J., 1976.

Abu Muna, Butrus. "Spotlight on Arab Students," *New Outlook,* March 1965.

Akzin, Benjamin, and Yechezkel Dror. *Israel: High-Pressure Planning.* Syracuse, N.Y., 1966.

Amster, Shmuel. *Yisrael shel Metach* [Israel under Pressure]. Tel Aviv, 1959.

Arian, Alan. *The Choosing People: Voting Behavior in Israel.* Cleveland, 1973.

———. *Ideological Change in Israel.* Cleveland, 1968.

Avi-Hai, Avraham. *Ben-Gurion: State Builder.* New York, 1974.

Badi, Joseph. *The Government of the State of Israel.* New York, 1963.

———. *Religion in Israel Today: The Relationship between State and Religion.* New York, 1969.

Begin, Menachem. *BaMachteret* [In the Underground]. Vol. II. Tel Aviv, 1962.

Ben-Dor, Gabriel. *The Druze in Israel.* Boulder, Colo., 1979.

Ben-Gurion, David. *D'varim k'Havayatam* [Things as They Develop]. Tel Aviv, 1965.

———. *Israel: A Personal History.* New York, 1971.

———. *Israel: Years of Challenge.* Tel Aviv, 1963.

———. *Recollections.* London, 1970.

Ben-Porat, Yoram. *The Arab Labor Force in Israel.* Jerusalem, 1966.

Bernstein, Marver. *The Politics of Israel.* Princeton, N.J., 1967.

Birnbaum, Ervin. *The Politics of Compromise: State and Religion in Israel.* Rutherford, N.J., 1970.

Caiden, Gerald E. *Israel's Administrative Culture.* Berkeley, Calif., 1970.

Chasin, Eliahu, and Don Horowitz. *HaParashah* [The Affair]. Tel Aviv, 1961.

Christman, Henry M., ed. *The State Papers of Levi Eshkol.* New York, 1969.

Cohen, Abner. *Arab Border Villages in Israel.* Manchester, England, 1965.

Cohen, Haim H., ed. *Jewish Law in Ancient and Modern Israel.* New York, 1971.

Cohen, Yona. *HaKnesset* [The Knesset]. Tel Aviv, 1972.

Colbi, Saul. *Christianity in the Holy Land: Past and Present.* Tel Aviv, 1969.

Deshen, Shlomo. *Immigrant Voters in Israel: Parties and Congregations in a Local Election Campaign.* Manchester, England, 1970.

Domb, I. *The Transformation: The Case of the Neturei Karta.* London, 1958.

Dror, Yechezkel, and Emanuel Gutmann, eds. *The Government of Israel.* Jerusalem, 1964.

Edelman, Maurice. *Ben-Gurion: A Political Biography.* London, 1964.

Ehad, Nissim. "Can Arabs Identify with Israel?" *New Outlook,* Jan. 1967.

Elazar, Daniel, and Chaim Kalchheim, eds. *Local Government in Israel.* Jerusalem, 1988.

Eliachar, E. *Israeli Jews and Palestinian Arabs.* Jerusalem, 1970.

Elizur, Yuval, and Eliahu Salpeter. *Who Rules Israel?* New York, 1973.

Emanuel, Muriel, ed. *Israel.* London, 1971.

Fein, Leonard. *Politics in Israel.* Boston, 1968.

Freudenheim, Yehoshua. *Government in Israel.* Dobbs Ferry, N.Y., 1967.

Gilon, M., ed. *Norms for Public Administration.* Jerusalem, 1969.

Goldman, Eliezer. *Religious Issues in Israel's Political Life.* Jerusalem, 1964.

Goodrich, M. George. *Management in the Government of Israel.* Tel Aviv, 1958.

Hadawi, Sami. *Israel and the Arab Minority.* New York, 1959.

Harel, M. *Yane'eli: Kfar Druzi baGalil* [Yane'eli: A Druze Village in the Galilee]. Jerusalem, 1959.

Horowitz, Don. *M'Yishuv ad Medina* [From Yishuv to State]. Jerusalem, 1972.

Hussein, Rashid. "The Arab School in Israel," *New Outlook,* Nov.–Dec. 1957.

Israel. Office of Information. *The Arabs in Israel.* Jerusalem, 1953.

———. Office of Information. *The Knesset: Its Origin, Form, and Procedure.* Jerusalem, 1958.

———. State Comptroller's Office. *State Control in Israel.* Jerusalem, 1965.

Janowsky, Oscar, ed. *Foundations of Israel.* Philadelphia, 1959.

Jiryis, Sabri. *The Arabs in Israel, 1948–1966.* Beirut, 1966.

Katan, Victoria. "A Silent Revolution," *New Outlook,* Jan. 1960.

Kleinberger, Aharon F. *Society, Schools, and Progress in Israel.* London, 1969.

Kodesh, Shlomo. *HaEzrach b'Yisrael* [The Israeli Citizen]. Jerusalem, 1959.

Kraines, Oscar. *Government and Politics in Israel.* Boston, 1961.

Lahav, P. "The Supreme Court of Israel: Formative Years, 1948–1955," *Studies in Zionism,* No. 1, 1990.

Landau, Jacob. *The Arabs in Israel.* London, 1969.

Layish, Aharon. "The Muslem Waqf in Israel," *Asian and African Studies,* Spring 1965.

Lazar, David. *Mishtar M'dinat Yisrael* [The State Administration of Israel]. Jerusalem, 1970.

Lehrman, Hal. *Israel: The Beginning and Tomorrow.* New York, 1951.

Leslie, S. Clement. *The Rift in Israel: Religious Authority and Secular Democracy.* New York, 1971.

Levi, Shlomit, and Louis Guttman. *T'guvot HaTzibur l'Ba'ayot HaSha'a* [Public Reaction to Current Problems]. Jerusalem, 1971.

Likhovski, Eliahu S. *Israel's Parliament: The Law of the Knesset.* London, 1971.

Lorch, Netanel. *The Knesset.* Jerusalem, 1988.

Manoach, Y. *Elbono shel Chofesh HaVikuach* [The Sacrifice of Freedom of Debate]. Tel Aviv, 1964.

Marmorstein, Emile. *Heaven at Bay: The Jewish Kulturkampf in the Holy Land.* London, 1969.

Marx, Emanuel. *Bedouin of the Negev*. Manchester, England, 1967.

Medding, Peter Y. *Mapai in Israel: Political Organization and Government in a New Society*. London, 1972.

Naamani, Israel. *Israel: A Profile*. New York, 1972.

Oded, Y. "Land Losses among Israel's Arab Villagers," *New Outlook*, Sept. 1964.

Pearlman, Moshe. *Ben-Gurion Looks Back*. London, 1965.

Peretz, Don. *Israel and the Palestine Arabs*. Washington, D.C., 1958.

Perlmutter, Amos. *Anatomy of Political Institutionalization: The Case of Israel and Some Comparative Analyses*. Cambridge, Mass., 1970.

Rosetti, Moshe. *The Knesset: Its Origins, Forms, and Procedures*. Jerusalem, 1966.

Rosoglio, David. *Ten Years of the Civil Service in Israel, 1948–58*. Jerusalem, 1958.

Sachar, Howard M. *Aliyah: The Peoples of Israel*. Cleveland, 1961.

———. *From the Ends of the Earth: The Peoples of Israel*. Cleveland, 1964.

Samuel, Edwin. *British Traditions in the Administration of Israel*. London, 1957.

———. *Problems of Government in the State of Israel*. Jerusalem, 1957.

Sanders, Ronald. *Israel: The View from Masada*. New York, 1966.

Segev, Samuel. *The Parliamentary System of Israel*. Syracuse, N.Y., 1985.

Seligman, Lester G. *Leadership in a New Nation: Political Development in Israel*. New York, 1964.

Shalev, Moshe, and Menachem Portugali. *HaShitah* [The System]. Tel Aviv, 1972.

Shamir, Shimon. "Changes in Village Leadership," *New Outlook*, March–April 1962.

Sharef, Zeev. *Three Days*. London, 1962.

Shubat, Ibrahim. "The Twenty-five Years Seen through Arab Eyes," *New Middle East*, July 1965.

Teller, Judd L. *Government and the Democratic Process*. New York, 1969.

Vilnay, Ze'ev. *HaMiyutim b'Yisrael* [The Minorities in Israel]. Jerusalem, 1959.

Vitti, Eduardo. *The Conflict of Laws in Matters of Personal Status in Palestine*. Tel Aviv, 1947.

Vlavianos, Basil J., and Feliks Gross, eds. *Struggle for Tomorrow: Modern Political Ideologies of the Jewish People*. New York, 1954.

Watad, Muhammad. "Combatting Unemployment in the Arab Village," *New Outlook*, May 1967.

Zidon, Asher. *The Knesset*. New York, 1967.

Zu'bi, Abdul Aziz. "Discontent of Arab Youth," *New Outlook*, Jan. 1958.

III.   *Immigration, Economic and Social Change, 1948–1967*

Agar, Herbert. *The Saving Remnant*. New York, 1960.

Akzin, Benjamin, and Yechezkal Dror. *Israel: High-Pressure Planning*. Syracuse, N.Y., 1966.

Antonovsky, Aaron, and Alan Arian. *Hopes and Fears of Israelis*. Jerusalem, 1972.

Avineri, Shlomo. "Israel: Two Nations?" *Midstream*, March 1972.

Balabkins, Nicholas. *West German Reparations to Israel*. New Brunswick, N.J., 1971.

Bank of Israel. *HaShilumim v'Hashpa'atam al HaMeshek HaYisreeli* [The Reparations and Their Influence on the Israeli Economy]. Tel Aviv, 1965.

Baranès, Sauveur. *Nouveau précis de l'immigration d'expression française en Israël*. Jerusalem, 1969.

Barer, Shlomo. *The Magic Carpet*. London, 1952.

Barkai, Haim. *The Public, Histadrut, and Private Sectors in the Israeli Economy*. Jerusalem, 1964.

Bar-Yosef, Rivka, and Dorit Padan. *HaAspekt HaKalkali ba'Givush HaChevrah HaYisreelit* [The Economic Consolidation of Israeli Society]. Jerusalem, 1968.

Bavly, Sarah. *Levels of Nutrition in Israel, 1963–64: Urban Wage and Salary Earners.* Jerusalem, 1966.

Becker, Aharon. *HaM'tziut HaKalkalit v'HaPoel* [Economic Reality and the Worker]. Tel Aviv, 1954.

Ben-Gurion, David. *Israel: Years of Challenge.* Tel Aviv, 1963.

Ben-Meir, G. "Oriental Jews in Israel: Problems and Prospects," *Jewish Forum,* Oct. 1966.

Bensimon-Donath, Doris. *Immigrants d'Afrique du Nord en Israël.* Paris, 1970.

Ben-Tov, Mordechai. *Kalkalat Yisrael al Parashat D'rachim* [The Israeli Economy at the Crossroads]. Tel Aviv, 1965.

Bentwich, Joseph B. *Education in Israel.* Philadelphia, 1965.

Ben-Zvi, Yitzhak. *The Exiled and the Redeemed.* Philadelphia, 1957.

Berger, L. J. *The Impact of Aliya on Israel's Development.* Jerusalem, 1969.

Berler, Alexander. *Yachsei Ir-Kfar b'Yisrael* [Town-Village Relations in Israel]. Jerusalem, 1969.

Berman, Morton M. *The Bridge to Life: The Saga of Keren HaYesod, 1920–1970.* Tel Aviv, 1970.

Braham, Randolph L. *Israel: A Modern Education System.* Washington, D.C., 1966.

Brutzkus, Eliezer. *Physical Planning in Israel.* Jerusalem, 1964.

Chouraqui, André. *Les Juifs d'Afrique du Nord.* Paris, 1953.

Cohen, A. "The Emergence of the Public Sector of the Israeli Economy," *Jewish Journal of Sociology,* Dec. 1968.

Cohen, Chaim. *HaP'ilut HaZionit b'Iraq* [Zionist Activity in Iraq]. Jerusalem, 1969.

Cohen, Hayyim. *The Jews of the Middle East, 1860–1972.* Jerusalem, 1973.

Curtis, Michael, and Mordecai S. Chertoff, eds. *Israel: Social Structure and Change.* New Brunswick, N.J., 1973.

Darin (Drabkin), Chaim. *Shikun u'Klitah b'Yisrael* [Housing and Absorption in Israel]. Tel Aviv, 1955.

Darin-Drabkin, Haim. *The Other Society.* New York, 1963.

Dash, Jacob. *The Israel Physical Master Plan.* Jerusalem, 1964.

Derogy, Jacques, and Edouard Saab. *Les deux exodes.* Paris, 1968.

Deshen, Shlomo, and Moshe Shokeid. *The Predicament of Homecoming: Cultural and Social Life of North African Immigrants in Israel.* Ithaca, N.Y., 1974.

Eisenstadt, S. N. *The Absorption of Immigrants.* London, 1954.

———. *Israeli Society.* London, 1967.

Eisenstadt, S. N., Rivka Bar-Yosef, and Chaim Adler, eds. *Integration and Development in Israel.* London, 1970.

Emanuel, Yitzchak. *HaPa'ar* [The Gap]. Cholon, 1968.

Evenari, Michael, Leslie Shanan, and Naphtali Tadmor. *The Negev: The Challenge of a Desert.* Cambridge, Mass., 1971.

Falk Project for Economic Research in Israel. *A Ten-Year Report: 1954–63.* Jerusalem, 1964.

"Fifteen Years That Changed the Face of Israel," *Jewish Observer and Middle East Report,* Nov. 19, 1965.

Frankenstein, Carl, ed. *Between Past and Future: Essays and Studies on Aspects of Immigrant Absorption in Israel.* Jerusalem, 1953.

Gaudard, Gaston. *Les bases économiques de l'État d'Israël.* Freiburg, 1957.

Gil, Benjamin. *Settlement of New Immigrants in Israel, 1948–1953.* Jerusalem, 1957.

Ginor, Fanny. *Uses of Agricultural Surpluses.* Jerusalem, 1963.

Gotthelf, Y. *HaChevrah HaYisreelit b'Mivchan HaT'kufah* [Israeli Society under Ongoing Evaluation]. Tel Aviv, 1964.

———. *HaM'dinah, HaChevrah, v'HaHistadrut* [State, Society, and Histadrut]. Tel Aviv, 1961.

Granott, Avraham. *Agrarian Reform and the Record of Israel.* London, 1956.

Greenwald, Carl Schwartz. *Recession as a Policy Instrument: Israel, 1965–1969.* Rutherford, N.J., 1973.

Grinker, Y. *Aliyatam shel Yehudei HaAtlas* [The Immigration of the Atlas Mountain Jews]. Tel Aviv, 1973.

Halevi, Nadav, and Ruth Klinov-Malul. *The Economic Development of Israel.* New York, 1968.

Halperin, Haim. *Agricultural Production and Mass Immigration in Israel.* Tel Aviv, 1953.

———. *Agrundus: Integration of Agriculture and Industries.* New York, 1963.

———. *Moshvei Olim* [Immigrant Moshavim]. Jerusalem, 1957.

Henrietta Szold Institute. *Children and Families in Israel.* New York, 1970.

Hillel, Marc. *Israël en danger de paix.* Paris, 1969.

Horowitz, David. *The Economics of Israel.* London, 1967.

———. *The Enigma of Economic Growth: A Case Study of Israel.* New York, 1972.

Hovne, Avner. "The Economic Scene in Israel," *Midstream,* May 1967.

Ilan, Akiba. *The Use of a Capital Investment Law as a Means to Promote and Direct Industrial Development in Israel.* New York, 1973.

Israel. Central Bureau of Statistics. *Statistical Abstract, 1949–1974.* 25 vols. Jerusalem, 1950–75.

———. Investment Authority. *Israel Industry, 1970.* Tel Aviv, 1970.

———. Ministry for Foreign Affairs. *Facts about Israel.* Jerusalem, 1973.

———. Ministry of Commerce. *Programme for Israel's Economic Development . . . 1965–1970.* Jerusalem, 1974.

———. Ministry of Finance. *Takzivei HaPituach l'Shanot 1949–1954* [Development Budgets for the Years 1949–1954]. Jerusalem, 1954.

———. Ministry of Housing. *Israel Builds, 1948–1968.* Tel Aviv, 1968.

———. *N'tunim, Indikatorim, v'Tachziyot Rishonot al Hitpachtut HaMeshek, 1965–1970* [Data Indicators and Initial Projections of Economic Development, 1965–1970]. Jerusalem, 1970.

———. Prime Minister's Office. *Israel Economic Development: Past Progress and Plan for the Future.* Jerusalem, 1968.

Jewish Agency. *Immigration and the Problems of the Middle Class in Israel.* Jerusalem, 1960.

Kanev, Yitzhak. *Health Services in Israel, 1948–58.* Jerusalem, 1960.

———. *Social Policy in Israel.* Tel Aviv, 1964.

Katznelson, Kalman. *Yisrael Acharei Mivtzat Sinai* [Israel after the Sinai Campaign]. Tel Aviv, 1957.

Klayman, Maxwell I. *The Moshav in Israel.* New York, 1970.

Kleinberger, Aharon F. *Society, Schools and Progress in Israel.* London, 1969.

Labour Zionist World Movement. *Israel Today: A New Society in the Making.* Tel Aviv, 1967.

Landshut, Siegfried. *Jewish Communities in the Muslim Countries of the Middle East.* Jerusalem, 1950.

Lehrman, Hal. *Israel: The Beginning and Tomorrow.* New York, 1951.

Levitas, Gideon. "The Other Israel: Is Poverty the Price of Security?" *New Middle East,* Nov. 1968.

Lissak, Moshe. *Social Mobility in Israeli Society.* Jerusalem, 1969.

Matras, Judah. *Social Change in Israel.* Chicago, 1965.

Mayer, Menahem. *Les entreprises en Israël.* Paris, 1971.

Meir, Y. *M'Ever l'Midbar* [From Across the Desert]. Tel Aviv, 1973.

Morris, Yaakov. *Masters of the Desert.* New York, 1961.

Mushkat, Marion, and Ludwig Berger. *Some Problems of Israel's Development.* Hamburg, 1971.

Naamani, Israel. *Israel: A Profile.* New York, 1972.

Naftali, Fritz. *Demokratia Kalkalit* [Economic Democracy]. Tel Aviv, 1965.

Pack, Howard. *Structural Change and Economic Policy in Israel.* New Haven, Conn., 1971.

Patai, Raphael. *Cultures in Conflict.* New York, 1961.

———. *Israel between East and West.* Philadelphia, 1953.

Patinkin, Don. *The Israel Economy: The First Decade.* Jerusalem, 1953.

Pincus, Chasya. *From the Four Winds: The Story of Youth Aliyah.* New York, 1970.

Preuss, Walter. *The Labour Movement in Israel: Past and Present.* Jerusalem, 1965.

Rabin, Albert I. *Growing Up in a Kibbutz.* New York, 1965.

Raphael, Marc Lee. *A History of the United Jewish Appeal, 1939–1982.* Chico, Calif., 1982.

Rejwan, Nissim. "The Myth of the Black Panthers," *New Middle East,* Oct. 1971.

Ronen, Yosef, ed. *Kalkalat Yisrael* [The Israeli Economy]. Tel Aviv, 1964.

Rubner, Alex. *The Economy of Israel.* New York, 1959.

Sachar, Howard M. *From the Ends of the Earth: The Peoples of Israel.* Cleveland, 1964.

Samuel, Edwin. "Is Israel a Welfare State?" *Jewish Frontier,* Oct. 1965.

———. *The Structure of Society in Israel.* New York, 1969.

Samuel, Maurice. *Level Sunlight.* New York, 1953.

Sanders, Ronald. *Israel: The View from Masada.* New York, 1966.

Schechtman, Joseph B. *On Wings of Eagles: The Plight, Exodus, and Homecoming of Oriental Jewry.* New York, 1961.

Schoenbrun, David, Robert Szekely, and Lucy Szekely. *The New Israelis.* New York, 1973.

Segre, V. D. *Israel: A Society in Transition.* London, 1971.

Selzer, Michael. *The Outcasts of Israel: Communal Tensions in the Jewish State.* Jerusalem, 1965.

Shai, Donna. *Neighborhood Relations in an Immigrant Quarter.* Jerusalem, 1970.

Shelach, Ilana, Channa Harlap, and Shifra Weiss. *The Social Structure of Israel: A Bibliography.* Jerusalem, 1971.

Shuval, Judith T. *Immigrants on the Threshold.* New York, 1963.

Sicron, Moshe. *Immigration to Israel, 1948–1953.* Jerusalem, 1957.

Sitton, Shlomo. *Israël: Immigration et croissance, 1948–1958.* Paris, 1963.

Smilanski, Moshe. *Child and Youth Welfare in Israel.* Jerusalem, 1960.

Spiegel, Erika. *New Towns in Israel: Urban and Regional Planning and Development.* New York, 1967.

Spiro, Medford. *Children of the Kibbutz.* Cambridge, Mass., 1958.

Szereszewski, Robert. *Essays on the Structure of the Jewish Economy in Palestine and Israel.* Jerusalem, 1968.

Urofsky, Melvin I. *We Are One: American Jewry and Israel.* Garden City, N.Y., 1978.

Viteles, Harry. *A History of the Cooperative Movement in Israel.* Vol. II. London, 1968.

Weingarten, Murray. *Life in a Kibbutz.* New York, 1965.

Weingrod, Alex. *Israel: Group Relations in a New Society.* New York, 1965.

———. *Reluctant Pioneers.* Ithaca, N.Y., 1966.

Weitz, Ra'anan, and Avshalom Rokach. *Agricultural Development Planning and Implementation: An Israeli Case Study.* New York, 1968.

Willner, Dorothy. *Nation-Building and Community in Israel.* Princeton, N.J., 1969.

Yaari, Meir. *Israel 1968: On the Road to Socialism.* Tel Aviv, 1968.

Zaslavsky, David. *Shikun Ovdim b'Yisrael* [Workers' Housing in Israel]. Tel Aviv, 1954.

Zweig, Ferdynand. *The Israeli Worker.* New York, 1959.

IV.   **Foreign Relations, 1948–1967**

Abdullah, King of Jordan. *My Memoirs Completed.* Washington, D.C., 1954.

Adenauer, Konrad. *Memoirs, 1945–53.* Chicago, 1966.

Alami, Musa al-. "The Lesson of Palestine," *Middle East Journal,* Summer 1949.

Allon, Yigal. *Masach shel Chol* [Sand Screen]. Tel Aviv, 1959.

Alteras, Isaac. *Eisenhower and Israel: U.S.-Israeli Relations, 1953–1960.* Gainesville, Fla., 1993.

American Friends of the Middle East. *The Jordan Water Problem.* Washington, D.C., 1954.

Arendt, Hannah. *Eichmann in Jerusalem.* New York, 1962.

Aron, Raymond. *De Gaulle, Israel, and the Jews.* New York, 1968.

Balabkins, Nicholas. *West German Reparations to Israel.* New Brunswick, N.J., 1971.

Bar-Yaakov, Nissim. *The Israel-Syrian Armistice: Problems of Implementation, 1949–1966.* Jerusalem, 1967.

Bar-Zohar, Michael. *The Avengers.* London, 1968.

———. *Gesher al HaYam HaTichon* [Bridge over the Mediterranean]. Tel Aviv, 1964.

Be'eri, Eliezer. "A Note on Coups d'État in the Middle East," *Journal of Contemporary History,* Feb. 1970.

Bell, W. Bowyer. *The Long War: Israel and the Arabs since 1946.* Englewood Cliffs, N.J., 1969.

Ben-Asher, A. *Yachsei Chutz shel Israel* [Israel's Foreign Relations]. Tel Aviv, 1955.

Ben-Gurion, David. *Israel: A Personal History.* New York, 1971.

———. *Israel: Years of Challenge.* Tel Aviv, 1963.

Berger, Earl. *The Covenant and the Sword: Arab-Israeli Relations, 1948–1956.* London, 1965.

Bilby, Kenneth. *New Star in the Near East.* Garden City, N.Y., 1950.

Bovis, H. Eugene. *The Jerusalem Question, 1917–1968.* Stanford, Cal., 1971.

Brecher, Michael. *Decisions in Israel's Foreign Policy.* New Haven, Conn., 1974.

———. *The Foreign Policy System of Israel.* London, 1972.

Brook, David. *Preface to Peace: The United Nations and the Arab-Israel Armistice System.* Washington, D.C., 1964.

Burns, E. L. M. *Between Arab and Israeli.* New York, 1963.

Byford-Jones, W. *Forbidden Frontiers.* London, 1958.

Cohen, Aharon. *Israel and the Arab World.* New York, 1970.

Crosbie, Sylvia K. *A Tacit Alliance: France and Israel from Suez to the Six-Day War.* Princeton, N.J., 1974.

Dagan, Avigdor. *Moscow and Jerusalem: Twenty Years of Relations between Israel and the Soviet Union.* London, 1970.

Dayan, David. *Bitachon l'Lo Shalom* [Security without Peace]. Tel Aviv, 1968.

Deutschkron, Inge. *Bonn and Jerusalem: The Strange Coalition.* Philadelphia, 1970.

Dodd, C. H., and Mary Sales, eds. *Israel and the Arab World.* London, 1970.

Eban, Abba. *Personal Witness.* New York, 1993.

Elath, Eliahu. *Israel and Her Neighbors.* Cleveland, 1957.

Eytan, Walter. *The First Ten Years: A Diplomatic History of Israel.* New York, 1958.

Feinberg, Nathan. *Eretz Yisrael b'T'kufat HaMandat u'M'dinat Yisrael* [Palestine in the Time of the Mandate and of the State of Israel]. Jerusalem, 1962.

Gabbay, Rony E. *A Political Struggle of the Arab-Jewish Conflict.* Geneva, 1959.

Giniewski, Paul. *Israël devant l'Afrique et l'Asie.* Paris, 1958.

Goldmann, Nahum. *Sixty Years of Jewish Life.* New York, 1969.

Grossman, Kurt. *Germany's Moral Debt: The German-Israel Agreement*. Washington, D.C., 1954.

Hadawi, Sami. *Palestine: Loss of a Heritage*. San Antonio, Tex., 1963.

Harel, Isser. *The House on Garibaldi Street*. Boston, 1975.

Harkabi, Yehoshafat. *Arab Attitudes to Israel*. Jerusalem, 1972.

Herman, S. N., Y. Peres, and E. Yuchtman. "Reactions to the Eichmann Trial in Israel," *Scripta Hierosolymitana*, 1965.

Hurewitz, J. C. *Middle East Politics: The Military Dimension*. New York, 1969.

Hutchison, E. H. *Violent Truce*. New York, 1956.

India. Ministry of External Affairs. *India and Israel: The Evolution of a Policy*. New Delhi, 1972.

Israel. Ministry for Foreign Affairs. *Egypt and the Suez Canal, 1948–1956*. Jerusalem, 1956.

———. Ministry for Foreign Affairs. *Egypt's Unlawful Blockade of the Gulf of Aqaba*. Jerusalem, 1967.

———. Ministry for Foreign Affairs. *Israel's Programme of International Cooperation*. Jerusalem, 1967.

———. Office of Information. *Israel's Struggle for Peace*. New York, 1960.

———. Office of Information. *Jerusalem and the United Nations*. New York, 1953.

Jansen, Godfrey. *Zionism, Israel, and Asian Nationalism*. Beirut, 1971.

Kaplan, Deborah. *The Arab Refugees*. Jerusalem, 1959.

Kenen, I. L. *Israel's Defense Line: Her Friends and Foes in Washington*. Buffalo, N.Y., 1981.

Khoury, Jacques G. *La Palestine devant le monde*. Paris, 1953.

Krammer, Arnold. *The Forgotten Friendship: Israel and the Soviet Bloc, 1947–53*. Urbana, Ill., 1974.

Kreinin, Mordecai. *Israel and Africa*. New York, 1964.

Laqueur, Walter, and Barry Rubin, eds. *The Israel-Arab Reader*. New York, 1985.

Laufer, Leopold. *Israel and the Developing Countries*. New York, 1967.

Man, Peter. *Eichman b'Yadai* [Eichmann Is in My Hands]. Tel Aviv, 1983.

Margalit, Dan. *Sheder m'HaBayit HaLavan* [Broadcasting from the White House]. Tel Aviv, 1971.

Marwen, Iskander. *The Arab Boycott of Israel*. Beirut, 1966.

McDonald, James G. *My Mission in Israel*. New York, 1951.

Meir, Golda. *My Life*. New York, 1975.

Namir, Mordechai. *Shlichut b'Moskva* [Moscow Mission]. Tel Aviv, 1971.

Peres, Shimon. *David's Sling*. New York, 1970.

Peretz, Don. *Israel and the Palestine Arabs*. Washington, D.C., 1958.

Pinner, Walter. *How Many Arab Refugees?* New York, 1953.

Rao, Sudha. *The Arab-Israeli Conflict: The Indian View*. New Delhi, 1972.

Roberts, Samuel J. *Survival or Hegemony: The Foundation of Israeli Foreign Policy*. Baltimore, 1973.

Rosenne, Shabtai. *Israel's Armistice Agreement with the Arab States*. Tel Aviv, 1951.

Sachar, Howard M. *Israel and Europe: An Appraisal in History*. New York, 1999.

Safran, Nadav. *From War to War: The Arab-Israeli Confrontation, 1948–1967*. New York, 1969.

———. *The United States and Israel*. Cambridge, Mass., 1963.

Sagi, Nana. *German Reparations: A History of the Negotiations*. New York, 1987.

Saliba, Samir. *The Jordan River Dispute*. The Hague, 1968.

Sarna, Aaron J. *Boycott and Blacklist: A History of Arab Economic Warfare against Israel*. Totowa, N.J., 1986.

Scheidle, Franz-Josef. *Deutschland, der Staat Israel and die deutsche Wiedergutmachung.* Vienna, 1963.

Seelbach, Jörg. *Die Aufnahme der diplomatischen Beziehungen zu Israel als Problem der deutschen Politik seit 1955.* Meisenheim am/Glan, 1970.

Sharett, Moshe. *Yoman M'dini* [Diplomatic Diary]. Tel Aviv, 1968.

Shinnar, Felix. *B'Ol Korach v'Rag'shut b'Shlichut HaM'dinah: Yachsei Yisrael-Germania 1951 ad 1966* [In the Mandate and Mission of the State: Israeli-German Relations from 1951 to 1966]. Jerusalem, 1967.

Soustelle, Jacques. *La longue marche d'Israël.* Paris, 1968.

Stevens, Georgiana G. *Jordan River Partition.* Stanford, Calif., 1965.

Teller, Judd L. *The Jews, the Kremlin, and the Middle East.* Syracuse, N.Y., 1957.

Tibawi, A. L. "Visions of the Return: The Palestine Arab Refugees in Arab Poetry and Art," *Middle East Journal,* Summer 1963.

Wishart, D. "The Breakdown of the Johnston Negotiations over the Jordan Waters," *Middle East Studies,* No. 4, 1990.

Zurayk, Constantine. *The Meaning of the Disaster.* Beirut, 1956.

v.   *The Growth of Israel's Defense Forces: The 1956 Sinai War*

Allon, Yigal. *The Making of Israel's Army.* London, 1970.

Avneri, Arieh. *P'shitot HaTagmul* [Retaliation Raids]. Tel Aviv, 1969.

Bar-Am, Micha, and Azaria Alon. *Al P'nei Sinai* [On the Terrain of Sinai]. Tel Aviv, 1957.

Barer, Shlomo. *The Weekend War.* Tel Aviv, 1959.

Barker, A. J. *The Seven Day War.* London, 1964.

Bar-Zohar, Michael. *Ben-Gurion: The Armed Prophet.* Englewood Cliffs, N.J., 1967.

———. *Gesher al HaYam HaTichon* [Bridge over the Mediterranean]. Tel Aviv, 1964.

———. *Suez: Ultra Secret.* Paris, 1964.

Beaufré, André. *L'expédition de Suez, 1956.* Paris, 1968.

Bell, W. Bowyer. *The Long War: Israel and the Arabs since 1946.* Englewood Cliffs, N.J., 1969.

Ben-Gurion, David. *Israel: A Personal History.* New York, 1971.

———. *Ma'arechet Sinai* [The Sinai Campaign]. Tel Aviv, 1959.

Ben-Shaul, M. *Alufei Yisrael* [Israel's Generals]. Tel Aviv, 1968.

Berger, Earl. *The Covenant and the Sword: Arab-Israeli Relations, 1948–1956.* London, 1965.

Braslavi, Y. *M'R'zuat Aza ad Yam Suf* [From the Gaza Strip to the Red Sea]. Tel Aviv, 1956.

Brecher, Michael. *Decisions in Israel's Foreign Policy.* New Haven, Conn., 1974.

Bromberger, Merry, and Serge Bromberger. *Les secrets de l'expédition d'Egypte.* Paris, 1957.

Burns, E. L. M. *Between Arab and Israeli.* New York, 1963.

Chasin, Eliahu, and Don Horowitz. *HaParashah* [The Affair]. Tel Aviv, 1961.

Childers, Erskine B. *The Road to Suez.* London, 1962.

Churchill, Randolph. *The Rise and Fall of Anthony Eden.* London, 1959.

Crosbie, Sylvia K. *A Tacit Alliance: France and Israel from Suez to the Six-Day War.* Princeton, N.J., 1974.

Dagan, Avigdor. *Moscow and Jerusalem: Twenty Years of Relations between Israel and the Soviet Union.* London, 1970.

Dayan, Moshe. *Diary of the Sinai Campaign.* New York, 1965.

———. *The Story of My Life.* New York, 1976.

Eban, Abba. *Personal Witness.* New York, 1993.

Edelman, Maurice. *Ben-Gurion: A Political Biography.* London, 1964.

Eden, Anthony. *Full Circle.* London, 1960.

Evron, Yosef. *B'Yom Sagrir* [On an Inclement Day]. Tel Aviv, 1968.

Eytan, Walter. *The First Ten Years: A Diplomatic History of Israel.* New York, 1958.

Fisher, S. N., ed. *The Military in the Middle East.* Columbus, Ohio, 1963.

Fox, Moshe. "Backing the 'Good Guys': American Governmental Policy, 'Jewish Influence,' and the Sinai Campaign of 1956," *American Jewish Archives,* April 1988.

Gardosh, Kariel. *Hagadat Sinai* [Sinai Narrative]. Tel Aviv, 1957.

Gepner, B., ed. *Sefer Milchemet Sinai* [The Book of the Sinai War]. Tel Aviv, 1957.

Gilbert, Martin. *The Arab-Israeli Conflict: Its History in Maps.* London, 1974.

Golan, Aviezer. *Ma'arechet Sinai* [The Sinai Campaign]. Tel Aviv, 1966.

Henriques, Robert. *100 Hours to Suez.* New York, 1957.

Israel. Ministry for Foreign Affairs. *Egypt's Unlawful Blockade of the Gulf of Aqaba.* Jerusalem, 1967.

———. Office of Information. *Israel's Struggle for Peace.* New York, 1969.

Johnson, J. J., ed. *The Role of the Military in Undeveloped Countries.* New York, 1962.

Kagan, Benjamin. *Combat secret pour Israël.* Paris, 1963.

Katz, Shmuel. *M'Dan v'ad Sinai* [From Dan to Sinai]. Tel Aviv, 1957.

Kravi, Y. *Toldot Tzahal* [A History of Israel's Defense Forces]. Tel Aviv, 1957.

Lartéguy, Jean. *Les murailles d'Israël: Les secrets de l'armée la plus secrète du monde.* Paris, 1970.

League of Arab States. *Israel's Aggression prior to the Israeli Attack of October 29, 1956, on Egypt.* Cairo, 1957.

Levey, Z. "Israel's Pursuit of French Arms, 1942–1958," *Studies in Zionism,* No. 2, 1993.

Love, Kenneth. *Suez: The Twice-Fought War.* New York, 1969.

Luttwak, Edward, and Don Horowitz. *The Israeli Army.* London, 1975.

Marshall, S. L. A. *Sinai Victory.* New York, 1958.

Meir, Golda. *My Life.* New York, 1975.

Milstein, Uri. *Chel HaTzanchanim* [The Parachutists' Branch]. Tel Aviv, 1969.

Morris, Benny. *Israel's Border Wars.* New York, 1994.

Nutting, Anthony. *Nasser.* New York, 1972.

O'Ballance, Edgar. *The Sinai Campaign, 1956.* New York, 1960.

Ofek, Uriel, ed. *Min HaMilchamah* [Since the War]. Tel Aviv, 1969.

Oren, Baruch. *MiSipurei Bayit Echad* [Tales of One Household]. Tel Aviv, 1960.

Peres, Shimon. *David's Sling.* New York, 1970.

Perlmutter, Amos. *Military and Politics in Israel.* London, 1969.

Reingold, Uriel. *HaMasa el Sharm el-Sheikh* [The Trail to Sharm al-Sheikh]. Tel Aviv, 1966.

Robertson, Terence. *Crisis: The Inside Story of the Suez Conspiracy.* New York, 1965.

Rolbant, Samuel. *The Israeli Soldier.* New York, 1970.

Safran, Nadav. *From War to War: The Arab-Israeli Confrontation, 1948–1967.* New York, 1969.

Soustelle, Jacques. *La longue marche d'Israël.* Paris, 1968.

Stock, Ernest. *Israel on the Road to Sinai, 1949–1956.* Ithaca, N.Y., 1967.

Talmi, Ephraim. *Milchamot Yisrael, 1949–1969* [The Wars of Israel, 1949–1969]. 2 vols. Tel Aviv, 1969.

Teveth, Shabtai. *Masah Tzahal b'Sinai* [The Military's Odyssey in Sinai]. Tel Aviv, 1957.

———. *Moshe Dayan.* London, 1972.

Thomas, Hugh. *Suez.* London, 1966.

Tournoux, J. R. *Secrets d'État.* Paris, 1960.

Tsur, Ya'akov. *Prélude à Suez: Journal d'une ambassade, 1953–1956.* Paris, 1968.

Vatikiotis, P. J. *The Egyptian Army in Politics.* Bloomington, Ind., 1961.

Wheelock, Keith. *Nasser's New Egypt.* New York, 1960.

Wint, Guy, and Peter Calvocoressi. *Middle East Crisis.* Baltimore, 1957.

VI.   *Cultural, Ideological, and Religious Currents*

(Additional material on this topic may be found in the Israeli journals *Gilyonot, Moznayim, Prozdor, Keshet, Gesher, Ariel, P'tachim,* among others)

Aaroni, A., ed. *Selected Stories of Hayim Hazaz.* New York, 1971.

Abramov, S. Z. *Perpetual Dilemma: Jewish Religion in the Jewish State.* Cranbury, N.J., 1976.

Abu Muna, Butrus. "Spotlight on Arab Students," *New Outlook,* March 1965.

Agnon. S. Y. *The Bridal Canopy.* New York, 1937.

———. *A Guest for the Night.* London, 1968.

———. *T'mol Shilshom* [Yesterday and the Day Before]. Tel Aviv, 1950.

Alter, Robert. *America and Israel: Literary and Intellectual Trends.* New York, 1970.

———. "New Israeli Fiction," *Commentary,* June 1969.

———. "On Lea Goldberg and S. Y. Agnon," *Commentary,* May 1970.

———. "The Shalit Case," *Commentary,* July 1970.

America-Israel Cultural Foundation. *Omanut Yisrael* [Israeli Art]. Tel Aviv, 1964.

Amichai, Yehuda. *Shirim, 1948–62* [Poems, 1948–62]. Tel Aviv, 1964.

Amiel, Mordechai. *Chamishim Omanim* [Fifty Artists]. Tel Aviv, 1958.

"Arab Intellectuals on Israel," *New Outlook,* Nov.–Dec. 1962.

Avishai, M. *Shorashim b'Tzameret* [Roots at the Top]. Tel Aviv, 1969.

Baal-Teshuva, Jacob, ed. *The Mission of Israel.* New York, 1963.

Badi, Joseph. *Religion in Israel Today.* New York, 1969.

Band, Arnold J. "Between Fiction and Historiography," *Midstream,* June 1964.

———. *Nostalgia and Nightmare: A Study in the Fiction of S. Y. Agnon.* Berkeley, Calif., 1968.

Bar-Am, Benyamin. *20 Shanah b'Musika HaYisreelit* [Twenty Years of Israeli Music]. Tel Aviv, 1968.

Bar-Natan, Moshe. "The Rabbinate in Israel," *Jewish Frontier,* Nov. 1964.

Bartov, Hanoch. *Wounds of Maturity.* New York, 1968.

Ben-Chaim, S. "Progressive Judaism in Israel—A Balance Sheet," *Journal of the Central Conference of American Rabbis,* Oct. 1968.

Ben-Gurion, David. *Recollections.* London, 1970.

Ben-Or, A. *Toldot HaSifrut HaIvrit b'Dorenu* [A History of Hebrew Literature in Our Generation]. Vol. III. Tel Aviv, 1955.

Bentwich, Joseph B. *Education in Israel.* Philadelphia, 1965.

Birnbaum, Ervin. *The Politics of Compromise: State and Religion in Israel.* Rutherford, N.J., 1970.

B'nai Yeshivot. *Sh'elot u'T'shuvot b'Ein Chazon* [Questions and Answers without Vision]. Jerusalem, 1969.

Burla, Yehuda, ed. *Masechet* [A Treatise]. Tel Aviv, 1951.

Chel-Or, Yom-Tov. *HaT'chiyah HaRuchanit-Musarit* [The Spiritual and Moral Renaissance]. Jerusalem, 1971.

Cohen, A. *Sofrim Ivriyim B'nai Zmanenu* [Contemporary Hebrew Writers]. Tel Aviv, 1964.

Cohen, Haim H., ed. *Jewish Law in Ancient and Modern Israel.* New York, 1971.

Cohen, Jack J. "Religion in Israel," *Jewish Frontier,* Oct. 1967.

Ehud, Nissim. "Can Arabs Identity with Israel?" *New Outlook,* Jan. 1967.

Eisenstadt, S. N. *Israeli Society.* London, 1967.

Falk, Ze'ev. *Halachah v'Ma'aseh b'M'dinat Yisrael* [Jewish Law and Practice in the State of Israel]. Jerusalem, 1967.

Fisch, Harold. "Faith in Israel," *Commentary*, Feb. 1969.

Frank, Moses Z. *Controversial Themes in Israeli Society*. London, 1969.

———, ed. *Sound the Great Trumpet*. New York, 1955.

Gamzu, Haim. *Painting and Sculpture in Israel*. Tel Aviv, 1958.

Geller, Benjamin. *Mizrachi Ideology: A Reassessment*. Jerusalem, 1964.

Gellman, Leon. *B'Darchei Noam* [On Pleasant Paths]. Jerusalem, 1968.

Goldberg, Leah. *M'Beiti HaYashan* [From My Old Home]. Tel Aviv, 1944.

Gradenwitz, Peter. "Israeli Music," *Ariel*, Summer 1968.

———. *Music and Musicians in Israel*. Tel Aviv, 1959.

Gurfein, R. *M'Karov u'm'Rachok* [From Near and Far]. Tel Aviv, 1964.

Guri, Chaim. *Multa HaZ'chuchit* [Multa the Glass]. Tel Aviv, 1962.

HaCohen, Mordechai, ed. *Taharat HaMishpachah b'Yisrael* [Family Disorder in Israel]. Jerusalem, 1959.

Hafetz, Baruch, ed. *Ogdan* [A Compilation]. Jerusalem, 1957.

Halkin, Simon. *Modern Hebrew Literature*. New York, 1950.

Halpern, Israel. *HaMahapechah HaYehudit* [The Jewish Revolution]. Jerusalem, 1967.

Hazaz, Hayim. *Gates of Bronze*. Philadelphia, 1975.

———. *HaYoshevet baGanim* [At Rest in the Gardens]. Tel Aviv, 1944.

———. *Mori Sa'id*. New York, 1956.

Herman, Simon. *Israelis and Jews: The Continuity of an Identity*. New York, 1970.

Hochman, B. *The Fiction of S. Y. Agnon*. Ithaca, N.Y., 1970.

Hussein, Rashid. "The Arab School in Israel," *New Outlook*, Nov.–Dec. 1957.

Israel. Ministry for Foreign Affairs. *Facts about Israel*. Jerusalem, 1973.

———. Ministry of Education and Culture. *Al Admatam: Tzayarim Yisreelim* [On Their Own Soil: Israeli Painters]. Tel Aviv, 1959.

Kahana, K. *The Case for Jewish Civil Law in the Jewish State*. London, 1960.

Kaniuk, Yoram. *Himmo, Melech Yerushalayim* [Himmo, King of Jerusalem]. Tel Aviv, 1969.

Kenyon, K. *Archaeology in the Holy Land*. New York, 1965.

Kimche, Dov. *Mivchar Sipurei Eretz Yisrael* [A Selection of Israeli Stories]. Tel Aviv, 1956.

Kleinberger, Aharon F. *Society, Schools and Progress in Israel*. London, 1969.

Kohansky, Mendel. "The First Twenty Years: Art and Culture," *Jewish Frontier*, May 1968.

———. *The Hebrew Theater—Its First Fifty Years*. Jerusalem, 1968.

Kook, Zvi. *L'N'tivot Yisrael* [Israeli Pathways]. Jerusalem, 1966.

Kurzweil, Baruch. *Masot al Sipurav shel Shai Agnon* [Essays on the Tales of S. Y. Agnon]. Jerusalem, 1965.

———. *Sifrutenu HeChadashah* [Our New Literature]. Jerusalem, 1959.

Landau, Jacob. *The Arabs in Israel*. London, 1969.

Lask, I. M. "Three Decades of Hebrew Writing," *Zion*, April 1954.

Leiter, S. J., ed. *Selected Stories of S. Y. Agnon*. New York, 1970.

Leslie, S. Clement. *The Rift in Israel: Religious Authority and Secular Democracy*. New York, 1971.

Levinson, A. *Tarbut Yotzeret* [A Creative Culture]. Tel Aviv, 1950.

Mansour, Atallah. "Arab Intellectuals Not Integrated," *New Outlook*, June 1964.

Marmorstein, Emile. *Heaven at Bay: The Jewish Kulturkampf in the Holy Land*. London, 1969.

Meged, Aharon. *HaMatmon* [The Treasure]. Tel Aviv, 1963.

Meged, Mati. "The Jewish Intellectual in Israel," *Commentary*, Jan. 1961.

Mintz, Ruth Finer, ed. *Modern Hebrew Poetry*. Berkeley, Calif., 1966.

Miron, D. *Chaim Hazaz* [in Hebrew]. Merchavia, 1959.

Moreh, S. "The Arabic Literary Revival in Israel," *Ariel,* Summer 1962.

———. "Arabic Literature in Israel," *Middle Eastern Studies,* April 1967.

Naamani, Israel. *Israel: A Profile.* New York, 1972.

Ofek, Uriel, ed. *Min HaMilchamah* [From the War]. Tel Aviv, 1969.

Oz, Amos. *Elsewhere, Perhaps.* New York, 1973.

———. *My Michael.* New York, 1972.

Patai, Raphael, and Zvi Wohlmuth, eds. *Mivchar HaSipur HaEretz-Yisreeli* [A Selection of Israeli Stories]. Jerusalem, 1956.

Penueli, S. Y., and A. Ukhmani, eds. *An Anthology of Hebrew Short Stories.* 2 vols. Tel Aviv, 1965.

———. *An Anthology of Modern Hebrew Poetry.* Jerusalem, 1966.

Picker, Shlomo. *T'filah baAretz* [Prayer in Israel]. Jerusalem, 1961.

Religious Kibbutz Movement. *HaYachid v'HaTzibur baChaim HaDatiyim shel HaKvutzah* [The Individual and the Community in the Religious Life of the Kvutzah]. Tel Aviv, 1970.

Samuel, Edwin. "Religious Conflict in Israel," *Jewish Heritage,* Autumn 1965.

Schweid, Eliezer. *Israel at the Crossroads.* Philadelphia, 1973.

———. *Shalosh Ashmorot* [Three (Night) Watches]. Tel Aviv, 1964.

Shaked, Gershon. "The Double Confrontation of a Renascent Literature," *Ariel,* Summer 1968.

———. *Gal Chadash baSiporet HaIvrit* [A New Trend in Hebrew Prose]. Merchavia, 1970.

———, ed. *HaMachazeh HaIvri* [Hebrew Drama]. Jerusalem, 1966.

Shamir, Moshe. *King of Flesh and Blood.* London, 1957.

———. *My Life with Ishmael.* London, 1970.

Shanaan, A. "Developments in Israeli Literature," *Israel,* No. 4, 1968.

Shragai, Shlomo. *B'Sugiot HaDor* [Issues of the (Contemporary) Generation]. Jerusalem, 1970.

Shulewitz, Malka Hillel. "The B'nei Israel versus the Rabbinate," *Jewish Frontier,* Oct. 1963.

Smilansky, Yizhar. *Arba'ah Sipurim* [Four Stories]. Tel Aviv, 1966.

———. *Y'mei Ziklag* [The Days of Ziklag]. 2 vols. Tel Aviv, 1958.

Smoira-Roll, Michal. *Folk Song in Israel.* Tel Aviv, 1963.

Steiner, J. J. "Trends and Ideas in Modern Hebrew Literature," *Judaism,* Summer 1955.

Tal, Miriam. "Israel Art Comes of Age," *Ariel,* Summer 1971.

Uchmani, Azriel, ed. *Dor baAretz* [A Generation in Israel]. Merchavia, 1958.

———. *L'Ever HaAdam* [Toward Man]. Merchavia, 1953.

Wallenrod, Reuben. *The Literature of Modern Israel.* New York, 1956.

Weiner, Herbert. *The Wild Goats of Ein Gedi: A Journal of Religious Encounters in the Holy Land.* Garden City, N.Y., 1961.

Yehoshua, A. B. *Mul HaYa'arot* [Opposite the Forests]. Tel Aviv, 1968.

Zimmer, Uriel. *Torah-Judaism and the State of Israel.* London, 1961.

Zimmerman, Y. *B'Einav shel Ma'amin* [In the Eyes of the Believer]. Tel Aviv, 1970.

Zinger, Z. "How Irreligious Are the Israelis?" *Jewish Life,* Nov.–Dec. 1964.

Zinger, Z., and Avraham Avi-Hai, eds. *Trends in Religion, Culture, and Political Thought in Eretz Yisrael in the 20th Century.* Jerusalem, 1971.

Zmora, I. *Shnei M'saprim: Ch. Hazaz v'Ya'akov Horowitz* [Two Storytellers: Chaim Hazaz and Ya'akov Horowitz]. Tel Aviv, 1940.

Zohar, Zevi. *Israel among the Nations.* Jerusalem, 1966.

Zucker, Norman L., and Naomi F. Zucker. *The Coming Crisis in Israel: Private Faith and Public Policy.* Cambridge, Mass., 1973.

VII. *The Six-Day War*

Abu-Loghod, Ibrahim, ed. *The Arab-Israeli Confrontation of June 1967: An Arab Perspective*. Evanston, Ill., 1970.

Arbel, Naftali, ed. *Milchamah v'Nitzachon* [War and Victory]. Tel Aviv, 1967.

Aron, Raymond. *De Gaulle, Israël, et les Juifs*. Paris, 1968.

Associated Press. *Lightning out of Israel: The Six-Day War in the Middle East*. New York, 1967.

Avneri, Arieh. *HaYom HaKatzar b'Yoter* [The Shortest Day]. Tel Aviv, 1967.

———. *P'shitot HaTagmul* [Retaliatory Raids]. Tel Aviv, 1969.

Barkay, Mordechai. *Written in Battle: The Six Day War as Told by the Fighters Themselves*. Tel Aviv, 1969.

Bar-On, Mordecai, ed. *Israel Defence Forces: The Six Day War*. Philadelphia, 1969.

Bar-Yaakov, Nissim. *The Israeli-Syrian Armistice: Problems of Implementation, 1949–1866*. Jerusalem, 1967.

Bar-Zohar, Michael. *Embassies in Crisis: Diplomats and Demagogues behind the Six-Day War*. Englewood Cliffs, N.J., 1970.

———. *Spies in the Promised Land: Iser Harel and the Israeli Secret Service*. Boston, 1972.

Bell, W. Bowyer. *The Long War: Israel and the Arabs since 1946*. Englewood Cliffs, N.J., 1969.

Ben-Hanan, Eli. *Our Man in Damascus: Eli Cohen*. New York, 1969.

Ben-Shaul, Moshe. *Alufei Yisrael* [Israel's Generals]. Tel Aviv, 1968.

Brecher, Michael. *Decisions in Israel's Foreign Policy*. New Haven, Conn., 1974.

———. *The Foreign Policy System of Israel*. London, 1972.

Christman, Henry M., ed. *The State Papers of Levi Eshkol*. New York, 1969.

Churchill, Winston, and Randolph Churchill. *The Six Day War*. Boston, 1967.

Cohen, Samy. *De Gaulle, les gaullistes et Israël*. Paris, 1974.

Crosbie, Sylvia K. *A Tacit Alliance: France and Israel from Suez to the Six Day War*. Princeton, N.J., 1974.

Dagan, Avigdor. *Moscow and Jerusalem: Twenty Years of Relations between Israel and the Soviet Union*. London, 1970.

Dan, Uri. *De Gaulle contre Israël*. Paris, 1969.

———. *L'embargo*. Paris, 1970.

Dan, Uri, and Y. Ben-Porat. *The Secret War: The Spy Game in the Middle East*. New York, 1970.

Dayan, David. *Strike First! A Battle History of Israel's Six Day War*. New York, 1968.

Dodd, C. H., and Mary Sales, eds. *Israel and the Arab World*. London, 1970.

Draper, Theodor. *Israel and World Politics: Roots of the Third Arab-Israel War*. London, 1968.

Eban, Abba. *Personal Witness*. New York, 1993.

Ehrlich, Y. *B'Ma'alot Giborim* [In Praise of Heroes]. Tel Aviv, 1969.

Eshkol, Joseph. *The Six Days' War*. Jerusalem, 1967.

Feinberg, Nathan. *The Arab-Israel Conflict in International Law*. Jerusalem, 1970.

Gamzu, Y. *B'Shesh Acharei HaMilchamah* [Six O'Clock after the War]. Tel Aviv, 1967.

Gilboa, Moshe. *Shesh Shanim, Shishah Yamim* [Six Years, Six Days]. Tel Aviv, 1969.

Golan, Aviezer. *Shishah Y'mei T'hilah* [Six Days of Glory]. Tel Aviv, 1967.

Gur, Mordechai. *Har HaBayit B'Yadenu* [The Temple Mount Is in Our Hands]. Tel Aviv, 1973.

Harel, Yehuda. *El Mul HaGolan* [Looking at the Golan]. Tel Aviv, 1967.

———. *HaKrav al HaYam* [The Sea Battle]. Tel Aviv, 1970.

Harkabi, Yehoshafat. *Arab Attitudes to Israel.* Jerusalem, 1972.

———. *Emdat Yisrael baSichsuch Yisrael-Arav* [Israel's Position in the Arab-Israel Conflict]. Tel Aviv, 1967.

Hashavia, Arye. *A History of the Six-Day War.* Tel Aviv, 1969.

Herzog, Chaim. *HaYamim HaG'dolim* [The Great Days]. Tel Aviv, 1967.

Israel. Ministry for Foreign Affairs. *Egypt's Unlawful Blockade of the Gulf of Aqaba.* Jerusalem, 1967.

Johnson, Lyndon B. *The Vantage Point.* New York, 1972.

Kashtan, Mordechai. *Kach Nitzachnu* [Thus We Triumphed]. Tel Aviv, 1967.

Kimche, David, and Dan Bavly. *The Sandstorm.* London, 1968.

Kosut, Hal, ed. *Israel and the Arabs: The June 1967 War.* New York, 1967.

Lall, Arthur. *The United Nations and the Middle East Crisis, 1967.* New York, 1968.

Laqueur, Walter, and Barry Rubin, eds. *The Israel-Arab Reader.* New York, 1985.

———. *The Road to Jerusalem.* New York, 1968.

Lutz, Wolfgang. *The Champagne Spy.* London, 1972.

Margalit, Dan. *Tzanchanim b'Kele Suri* [Parachutists in a Syrian Prison]. Tel Aviv, 1968.

Marshall, S. L. A. *Swift Sword.* New York, 1967.

Mezerik, Avraham, ed. *The Arab-Israel Conflict and the United Nations.* New York, 1969.

Nakdimon, Shlomo. *Likrat Sh'at HaEfes* [The Call of Zero Hour]. Tel Aviv, 1968.

Nutting, Anthony. *Nasser.* New York, 1972.

O'Ballance, Edgar. *The Third Arab-Israeli War.* Hamden, Conn., 1972.

Oren, Michael B. *Six Days of War: June 1967 and the Making of the Modern Middle East.* New York, 2001.

Peres, Shimon. *David's Sling.* New York, 1970.

Perlmutter, Amos. "Assessing the Six-Day War," *Commentary,* Jan. 1970.

Prittie, Terence. *Eshkol: The Man and the Nation.* New York, 1969.

Quandt, William. "Lyndon Johnson and the June 1967 War: What Color Was the Light?" *Middle East Journal,* Winter 1992.

Rabinovich, Abraham. *The Battle for Jerusalem, June 5–7, 1967.* Philadelphia, 1972.

Radio Free Europe. *The Arab-Israeli Conflict and Public Opinion in Eastern Europe.* Washington, D.C., July 1967.

Robinson, Donald B. *Under Fire: Israel's 20-Year Struggle for Survival.* New York, 1968.

Rolbant, Samuel. *The Israeli Soldier.* New York, 1970.

Saber, Ali. *Nasser en procès face à la nation arabe.* Paris, 1968.

Sachar, Howard M. *Israel and Europe: An Appraisal in History.* New York, 1999.

Safran, Nadav. *From War to War: The Arab-Israeli Confrontation, 1948–1967.* New York, 1969.

Schiff, Ze'ev, and Raphael Rothstein. *Fedayeen.* London, 1972.

Schleiffer, Abdullah. *The Fall of Jerusalem.* New York, 1972.

Segev, Samuel. *Israël, les arabes et les grandes puissances, 1967–1968.* Paris, 1968.

———. *Sadin Adom* [Red Sheet]. Tel Aviv, 1967.

Stevens, R. *Nasser.* London, 1971.

Teveth, Shabtai. *Moshe Dayan.* London, 1972.

———. *The Tanks of Tammuz.* London, 1969.

Vance, Vince, and Pierre Lauer, eds. *Hussein of Jordan: My "War" with Israel.* New York, 1969.

Velie, Lester. *Countdown in the Holy Land.* New York, 1969.

Wilson, Evan. *Jerusalem, Key to Peace.* Washington, D.C., 1970.

Yaari, Ehud. *Strike Terror: The Story of Fatah.* New York, 1970.

VIII. *Israel as Empire*

Abid, Ibrahim al-. *Israel and Human Rights.* Beirut, 1969.

Ages, Arnold. "New Arab Propaganda," *Jewish Frontier,* June 1970.

Arab Women's Information Committee. *The Arabs under Israeli Occupation.* Beirut, 1969.

Arad, Yitzchak, ed. *1000 Yamim: 12 Yuni 1967–8 Agust 1970* [A Thousand Days: June 12, 1967–August 8, 1970]. Tel Aviv, 1972.

Avineri, Shlomo. "The Palestinians and Israel," *Commentary,* June 1970.

Avnery, Uri. *Israel without Zionists.* New York, 1968.

Bank of Israel. *The Economy of the Occupied Territories.* Jerusalem, 1970.

Bavly, Dan, and David Farhi. *Israel and the Palestinians,* London, 1970.

Benvenisti, Meron. "Reunion without Reconciliation: Jews and Arabs in Jerusalem," *New Middle East,* March 1973.

Blum, Y. Z. *Secure Boundaries and Middle Eastern Peace.* Jerusalem, 1971.

Bovis, H. Eugene. *The Jerusalem Question, 1917–1968.* Stanford, Calif., 1971.

Brecher, Michael. *The Foreign Policy System of Israel.* London, 1972.

Christman, Henry M., ed. *The State Papers of Levi Eshkol.* New York, 1969.

Cohen, Yerucham. *Tochnit Alon* [The Allon Plan]. Tel Aviv, 1972.

Dan, Uri. *De Gaulle contre Israël.* Paris, 1969.

———. *L'embargo.* Paris, 1970.

Dayan, Moshe. *Mapah Chadashah* [A New Map]. Tel Aviv, 1969.

Dib, George, and Fuad Jabber. *Israel's Violation of Human Rights in the Occupied Territories.* Beirut, 1970.

Dodd, C. H., and Mary Sales, eds. *Israel and the Arab World.* London, 1970.

Eliav, Arieh. *K'fitzat HaDerech* [The Parting of the Way]. Tel Aviv, 1970.

———. *Land of the Hart.* Tel Aviv, 1972.

———. "A Palestinian Arab State: Scenario for Peace," *New Middle East,* Nov. 1972.

Eran, Oded, and Jerome Singer. "Exodus from Egypt and the Threat to Kremlin Leadership," *New Middle East,* Nov. 1972.

Fawdah, Izz al-Din. *Israel's Belligerent Occupation and Palestinian Armed Resistance in the Light of International Law.* Beirut, 1970.

Gilbert, Martin. *The Arab-Israeli Conflict: Its History in Maps.* London, 1974.

Gottkelf, Yehuda, ed. *Israel and the New Left.* Tel Aviv, 1969.

Hadawi, Sami. *Crime and No Punishment: Zionist Israeli Terrorism, 1939–1972.* Beirut, 1972.

Harkabi, Yehoshafat. *Fedayeen Action and Arab Strategy.* London, 1968.

Heymont, Col. Irving. "The Israeli Defense of the Suez Canal," *Middle East Information Series,* April 1971.

Horelick, Arnold L. "Soviet Involvement in the Middle East and the Western Response," *Middle East Information Series,* June 1972.

Institute for Palestine Studies. *The Palestinian Refugees: A Collection of United Nations Documents.* Beirut, 1970.

Israel. Central Bureau of Statistics. *Statistical Abstract.* Jerusalem, 1967–74.

———. Information Center. *Facts about the Administered Areas.* Jerusalem, 1975.

———. Ministry of Defense. *Four Years of Military Administration, 1967–71.* Tel Aviv, 1972.

———. Ministry of Information. *Government Yearbook.* Jerusalem, 1967–74.

Kanovsky, Eliahu. *The Economic Impact of the Six-Day War.* New York, 1970.

Kenan, Amos. *Israel: A Wasted Victory.* Tel Aviv, 1970.

Kochav, David. "Israel's Second Front: How to Pay for Defence," *New Middle East,* Jan.–Feb. 1973.

Kollek, Teddy. "Undivided but Still Diverse: The Mosaic That Is Jerusalem," *New Middle East*, Jan.–Feb. 1973.

Korn, David A. *Stalemate: The War of Attrition and Great Power Diplomacy in the Middle East, 1967–1990*. Boulder, Colo., 1992.

Lifshitz, Ya'akov. *HaHitpatchut HaKalkalit baSh'tachim HaMuchzakim* [Economic Development in the Administered Territories]. Tel Aviv, 1970.

Meir, Golda. *My Life*. New York, 1975.

Melman, Yossi. *Lo Tihyeh Hitkadmut l'Lo N'sigah* [No Advance without Retreat]. Jerusalem, 1969.

Na'or, Mordechai. *HaMilchamah l'achar HaMilchamah* [The War after the War]. Tel Aviv, 1972.

National Religious Party. *Mahut HaShalom* [The Nature of Peace]. Tel Aviv, 1970.

O'Neill, Brad. *Revolutionary Warfare in the Middle East: The Israelis versus the Fedayeen*. Boulder, Colo., 1974.

Oren, Uri. *Al Shloshah Pishei Dameseq* [For the Three Sins of Damascus]. Jerusalem, 1970.

Prittie, Terence. *Eshkol: The Man and the Nation*. New York, 1969.

Pryce-Jones, David. *The Face of Defeat: Palestinian Refugees and Guerrillas*. New York, 1972.

Pundik, Herbert. "Israel's Arabs Establish Their Identity," *New Middle East*, Aug. 1969.

Ra'anan, Uri. "Soviet Global Policy and the Middle East," *Midstream*, May 1969.

Reich, Bernard. *Israel and the Occupied Territories*. Washington, D.C., 1973.

Rejwan, Nissim. "Arab Intellectuals and Israel," *New Outlook*, Aug. 1971.

———. "Palestinians under Israeli Occupation: The Search for Identity," *Midstream*, Feb. 1971.

Remba, Oded. "Israel and the Occupied Areas: Common Market in the Making," *New Middle East*, Nov. 1970.

Rodinson, Maxime. *Israel: A Colonialist Settler State?* New York, 1974.

———. *Israel and the Arabs*. New York, 1968.

Schiff, Ze'ev. *K'nafayim m'al Suez* [Wings over Suez]. Haifa, 1970.

Schroeter, Leonard. "The Status of East Jerusalem," *Midstream*, Aug.–Sept. 1972.

Segal, Ronald. *Whose Jerusalem? The Conflicts of Israel*. London, 1973.

Segev, S. *Israël, les arabes et les grandes puissances, 1967–1968*. Paris, 1968.

Shamir, Moshe. *My Life with Ishmael*. London, 1970.

Sharabi, Hisham B. *Palestine Guerrillas: Their Credibility and Effectiveness*. Washington, D.C., 1970.

Stevens, R. *Nasser*. London, 1971.

Syrkin, Marie. *Golda Meir: Israel's Leader*. New York, 1969.

Tabenkin, Y. *Lekach Sheshet HaYamim* [The Lesson of the Six-Day (War)]. Tel Aviv, 1970.

Talmon, J. L. "Is Force an Answer to Everything?" *Dispersion and Unity*. Jerusalem, 1970.

———. *Israel among the Nations*. London, 1970.

———. "Reciprocal Recognition or Mutual Destruction," *Jewish Digest*, May–June 1970.

Teveth, Shabtai. *The Cursed Blessing*. London, 1969.

Uri, Pierre. "Israel and the European Economic Community: The Prospects for Integration," *Middle East Information Series*, Dec. 1972.

Weigert, Gideon. *Arabs and Israelis: Life Together*. Jerusalem, 1973.

Whetton, Lawrence L. "June 1967 to June 1971: Four Years of Canal War Reconsidered," *New Middle East*, June 1971.

Yaari, Ehud. "The Decline of Al-Fatah," *Midstream*, May 1971.

———. *Strike Terror: The Story of Fatah*. New York, 1970.

Zander, Walter. *Israel and the Holy Places of Christendom*. London, 1971.

Zweig, Ferdynand. *Israel: The Sword and the Harp*. London, 1969.

IX.   *Israel and World Jewry*

Agus, Jacob B. *Guideposts to Modern Judaism.* New York, 1954.

Alexander, Zvi (Netzer). "Immigration to Israel from the USSR," *Israel Yearbook on Human Rights.* Jerusalem, 1977.

Alter, Robert. "Zionism for the '70s," *Commentary,* Feb. 1970.

American Council for Judaism. *An Approach to American Judaism.* New York, 1958.

Avi-Hai, Avraham. "Israel-Centrism and Diasporism," *Jewish Journal of Sociology,* June 1976.

Avnery, Uri. *Israel without Zionists.* New York, 1968.

Avni, Haim. "Argentine Jewry: Its Socio-Political Status and Organizational Patterns," *Dispersion and Unity,* 1971, 1972.

Azbel, Mark Ya. *Refusenik: Trapped in the Soviet Union.* Boston, 1981.

Beller, Jacob. "Jews in Argentina," *Jewish Frontier,* April 1966.

———. *Jews in Latin America.* New York, 1969,

Ben-Ami (Arieh Eliav). *Between Hammer and Sickle.* Philadelphia, 1967.

Ben-Gurion, David. "How Is Israel Different?" *Jewish Frontier,* Aug. 1962.

Benjamin, Joseph. *Besieged Bedfellows: Israel and the Land of Apartheid.* Westport, Conn., 1988.

Berman, Morton M. *The Bridge to Life: The Saga of Keren HaYesod, 1920–1970.* Tel Aviv, 1970.

Blumenfeld, S. N. "Israel and Jewish Education in the Diaspora," *Jewish Education,* Oct. 1968.

Bokser, Ben-Zion. *Jews, Judaism, and the State of Israel.* New York, 1974.

Chinitz, Zelig S. "Reconstituting the Jewish Agency," *Jewish Frontier,* Dec. 1969.

Cohen, Arik. *Seker HaMiyutim b'Yisrael* [A Survey of Minorities in Israel]. Jerusalem, 1972.

Cohen, Richard, ed. *Let My People Go.* New York, 1971.

Dinur, B. Z. *Israel and the Diaspora.* Philadelphia, 1969.

Domb, I. *The Transformation: The Case of the Neturei Karta.* London, 1968.

Eckman, Lester S. *Soviet Policy towards Jews and Israel, 1917–1974.* New York, 1974.

Eliashivili, Natan. *HaYehudim HaGruzim B'Gruziyah u'v'Eretz Yisrael* [Georgian Jews in Georgia and in Israel]. Tel Aviv, 1975.

Elkin, Judith L. *Jews of the Latin American Republics.* Chapel Hill, N.C., 1980.

Friedberg, Maurice. "Soviet Jewry Today," *Commentary,* Aug. 1969.

———. *Why They Left: A Survey of Soviet Jewish Emigrants.* New York, 1972.

Gitelman, Zvi. "Baltic and Non-Baltic Immigrants in Israel: Political and Soviet Attitudes and Behavior," *Studies in Comparative Communism,* Spring 1979.

Goldmann, Nahum. *Sixty Years of Jewish Life.* New York, 1969.

Goodman, Philip. *Sixty-six Years of Benevolence: The Story of PEF Israel Endowment Funds.* New York, 1989.

Gurin, Arnold. "The Impact of Israel on American Jewish Community Organizations and Fund-Raising," *Jewish Social Studies,* Spring–Summer 1957.

Halkin, Hillel. "Americans in Israel," *Commentary,* May 1972.

Halpern, Ben. *The American Jew: A Zionist Analysis.* New York, 1956.

Halpern, Ben, and Israel Kolatt. *Amadot Mishtanot b'Yachsei M'dinat Yisrael u'HaT'futzot* [Changing Relations between Israel and the Diaspora]. Jerusalem, 1969.

Hauslich, Arieh. "A Million Tourists a Year by 1970?" *Jewish Observer and Middle East Review,* Jan. 30, 1970.

Herman, Donald L. *The Latin-American Community of Israel.* New York, 1984.

Herman, Simon. *American Students in Israel.* Ithaca, N.Y., 1970.

————. *Israelis and Jews: The Continuity of an Identity.* New York, 1970.

Hertzberg, Arthur. "America Is Galut," *Jewish Frontier,* July 1964.

Jewish Agency. *Immigration from the Soviet Union.* Jerusalem, 1973.

Kaplan, Mordecai M. *A New Zionism.* New York, 1959.

Karp, Abraham J. "Reaction to Zionism and to the State of Israel in the American Jewish Religious Community," *Jewish Social Studies,* Winter 1966.

————. *To Give Life: The UJA in the Shaping of the American Jewish Community.* New York, 1981.

Klutznick, Philip. *No Easy Answers.* New York, 1961.

Kochan, Lionel, ed. *The Jews in Soviet Russia since 1917.* London, 1970.

Korey, William. *The Soviet Cage.* New York, 1973.

Korn, Yitzchak. *Dor b'Ma'avako* [A Generation in Struggle]. Tel Aviv, 1970.

Lapide, P. E. *A Century of U.S. Aliya.* Jerusalem, 1961.

Lazaris, Vladimir. "The Saga of Jewish Samizdat," *Soviet Jewish Affairs,* Jerusalem, 1979.

Lendvai, Paul. *Anti-Semitism without Jews: Communist Eastern Europe.* Garden City, N.Y., 1971.

Lerner, Natan. *Jewish Organizations in Latin America.* Tel Aviv, 1974.

Levi, Shlomit. *HaZionut v'HaAm HaYehudi* [Zionism and the Jewish People]. Jerusalem, 1971.

Levine, E. "Israel as Jewish Theology," *American Zionist,* Sept. 1969.

Levyne, E. *Judaism contre Sionisme.* Paris, 1969.

Liebman, Charles. "The Role of Israel in the Ideology of American Jewry," *Dispersion and Unity.* Jerusalem, 1970.

Livneh, Eliezer. *Yahadut Amerika* [American Jewry]. Ramat Gan, 1967.

Markish, Esther. *The Long Return.* New York, 1978.

Marrus, M. E. *The Politics of Assimilation.* London, 1971.

Mashal, Shaul. *Minchat HaKlitah b'Yisrael b'Shanim 1964–1970* [The Management of Absorption in the Years 1964–1970]. Jerusalem, 1971.

Maybaum, I. *The Faith of the Jew in the Diaspora.* London, 1956.

Meerson-Aksenov, Michael. "The Jewish Exodus and Soviet Society," *Midstream,* April 1979.

Meyer, P., D. Weinryb, E. Duschinsky, and N. Sylvain. *The Jews in the Soviet Satellites.* Westport, Conn., 1971.

Morris, Yaakov. *On the Soil of Israel: Americans and Canadians in Agriculture.* Tel Aviv, 1965.

————. *Pioneers from the West: A History of Colonization in Israel by Settlers from the English-Speaking Countries.* Westport, Conn., 1972.

Neusner, Jacob. "Israel and Yavneh: The Perspective of Time." Address to the Philadelphia Board of Jewish Education, Jan. 26, 1975.

"New Aid Program," *Near East Report,* May 9, 1973.

Orbach, William W. *The American Movement to Aid Soviet Jews.* Amherst, Mass., 1979.

Penalosa, Fernando. "Pre-Migration Background and Assimilation of Latin American Immigrants in Israel," *Jewish Social Studies,* Spring 1972.

Petuchowski, Jacob J. *Zion Reconsidered.* New York, 1966.

Rawidowicz, Simon. *Bavel v'Yerushalayim* [Babylon and Jerusalem]. London, 1957.

Rosenheim, Y. *Kol Ya'akov* [The Voice of Jacob]. Tel Aviv, 1954.

Rubin, Jacob A. *Partners in State-Building: American Jewry and Israel.* New York, 1969.

Rusenik, Alla. *Like a Song, Like a Dream.* New York, 1969.

Sachar, Howard M. *Diaspora: An Inquiry into the Contemporary Jewish World.* New York, 1985.

————. *A History of the Jews in America.* New York, 1992.

Samuel, Maurice. *Light on Israel.* New York, 1968.

Schechtman, Joseph B. *Zionism and Zionists in Soviet Russia.* New York, 1966.

Schroeter, Leonard. *The Last Exodus.* New York, 1974.

Schwarz, Solomon. *The Jews in the Soviet Union.* Syracuse, N.Y., 1951.

Schweid, Eliezer. *Ad HaMashber* [Until the Crisis]. Jerusalem, 1969.

Selzer, Michael. *Zionism Reconsidered.* New York, 1970.

Shapiro, Judah J. "Dezionizing the Jewish Agency," *New Middle East,* Aug. 1969.

———. "Israel's Influence," *Jewish Frontier,* May 1969.

———. "Zionism in America since the Establishment of the State," *Jewish Frontier,* May 1973.

Shimoni, Gideon. *Jews and Zionism: The South African Experience, 1910–1949.* London, 1980.

Sklare, Marshall. *The Impact of Israel on American Jewry.* New York, 1969.

———. *The Jews: Social Patterns of an American Group.* Glencoe, Ill., 1958.

Steiner, George. "From Without," *Congress Bi-Weekly,* Feb. 24, 1969.

Talmon, J. L. *Israel among the Nations.* London, 1970.

Weinstock, N. *Le Sionism contre Israël.* Paris, 1969.

Weisbrod, Robert G. "The Dilemma of South African Jewry," *Journal of Modern African Studies,* No. 5, 1967.

Zeitlin, Aharon. *Al Yachsei HaGomlin bein HaM'dinah laGolah* [On Reciprocal Relations between Israel and the Diaspora]. Tel Aviv, 1966.

"Zionism: Soviet Scapegoat," *Jewish Frontier,* Oct. 1970.

Zukerman, William. *The Voice of Dissent.* New York, 1964.

x. *The Yom Kippur Earthquake—and Aftershocks*

Ablin, R. "A Lost Decade of Israeli Growth? Economic Policy since 1973," *Economic Review,* May 1980.

Abramov, S. Z. "The Agranat Report and Its Aftermath," *Midstream,* June–July 1974.

Alexander, Zvi (Netzer). "Immigration to Israel from the USSR," *Israel Yearbook on Human Rights.* Jerusalem, 1977.

Altshuler, Mordechai. *Ma'amadah shel M'dinat Yisrael b'Kerev Yehudei B'rit HaMo'atzot* [The Position of Israel among Soviet Jewry]. Jerusalem, 1983.

An-Nahar Arab Report. *The October War.* Beirut, 1974.

Anthony, John Duke. "The Red Sea: Control of the Southern Approach," in *Problem Papers of the Middle East Institute.* Washington, D.C., 1974.

Astrachan, Anthony. "The October War at the United Nations," *Midstream,* Dec. 1973.

Avnery, Uri. "Inside the PLO," *New Outlook,* Oct.–Nov. 1977.

Barker, A. J. *The Yom Kippur War.* New York, 1974.

Ben-Ami (Arieh Eliav). *Between Hammer and Sickle.* Philadelphia, 1967.

Ben-Chanan, E., A. Bar-Amon, and I. Tashlit. *Yisrael: Oktober 1973* [Israel: October 1973]. Tel Aviv, 1974.

Ben-Horin. *Ma Koreh Sham: Sipuram shel Yehudei B'rit HaMo'atzot* [What Is Happening There: The Story of Soviet Jewry]. Tel Aviv, 1970.

Ben-Meir, Dov. *Mashber baChevrah HaYisreelit* [A Crisis in Israeli Society]. Jerusalem, 1973.

Ben-Porat, Yeshayahu, Eitan Haber, and Ze'ev Schiff. *Entebbe Rescue.* New York, 1977.

———. *HaMechdal* [The Blunder]. Tel Aviv, 1973.

Chibwe, Ephraim C. *Afro-Arab Relations in the New World Order.* New York, 1978.

Cobban, Helena. *The Palestine Liberation Organization: People, Power, Politics.* New York, 1984.

Cohen, Yaacov. *Israel and the EEC, 1958–1977.* Tel Aviv, 1977.

Dowty, Alan. "Israel's Palestinian Policy," *Midstream,* April 1975.

Draper, Theodor. "The United States and Israel: Tilt in the Middle East?" *Commentary,* April 1975.

Dubberstein, W. "Sinai II in Retrospect," *Strategic Review,* No. 2, 1977.

Duclos, J. S. "Un essai de rapprochement égypto-israélien," *Maghreb-Machrak,* Jan. 1976.

Eisenstadt, Shmuel. "Israeli Society Transformed," *Jerusalem Quarterly,* Winter 1985.

Farago, U. "The Ethnic Identity of Russian Immigrant Students in Israel," *Jewish Journal of Sociology,* Dec. 1978.

Fishelson, Gideon. *The Economic Integration of Israel into the EEC.* Tel Aviv, 1977.

Forrestal, F. "The Sinai-American Connection," *MERIP Reports,* Dec. 1977.

Friedberg, Maurice. "From Moscow to Jerusalem—and Points West," *Commentary,* May 1978.

Friedman, Michel. *Ils on fui la liberté: la tragique odyssée des juifs qui veulent retourner en U.R.S.S.* Paris, 1979.

Gitelman, Zvi. "Moscow and the Soviet Jews: A Parting of the Ways," *Problems of Communism,* Jan. 1980.

Gitelson, Susan A. "Africa's Rupture with Israel," *Midstream,* Feb. 1974.

Handel, Michael. *Israel's Political and Military Doctrine.* Cambridge, Mass., 1974.

Hart, Harold H. *Yom Kippur Plus 100 Days.* New York, 1974.

Heikal, Mohamed. *The Road to Ramadan.* New York, 1975.

Herzog, Chaim. *The War of Atonement.* London, 1975.

Jacobs, Dan N., and Ellen Frankel Paul, eds. *Studies in the Third Wave: The Recent Migration of Soviet Jews to the United States.* Boulder, Colo., 1981.

Jacobs, Paul. "Let My People Go—But Where?" *Present Tense,* Winter 1979.

Kalb, Marvin, and Bernard Kalb. *Kissinger.* New York, 1974.

Kimche, Jon. "The Riddle of Sadat," *Midstream,* April 1974.

Klinghoffer, Arthur J., and Judith Apter. *Israel and the Soviet Union.* Boulder, Colo., 1975.

Kohler, Foy D. *The Soviet Union and the October 1973 Middle East War.* Coral Gables, Fla., 1974.

Korey, William. "The PLO's Conquest of the U.N.," *Midstream,* Nov. 1979.

Laqueur, Walter. *Confrontation: The Middle East War and World Politics.* London, 1974.

Leshem, El'azar. *Noshrim v'Olim b'Kerev Yotzei B'rit HaMo'atzot* [Dropouts and Immigrants among Soviet Jews]. Jerusalem, 1980.

Levins, Hoag. *Arab Reach.* Garden City, N.Y., 1983.

Luttwak, Edward, and Don Horowitz. *The Israeli Army.* London, 1975.

Marcus, Joel. "October, 1973: An Israeli Perspective," *Midstream,* Jan. 1974.

Medzini, Meron. "Israel and Africa—What Went Wrong?" *Midstream,* Jan. 1974.

———. "Reflections on Israel's Asian Policy," *Midstream,* June–July 1972.

Meerson-Aksenov, M. "The Jewish Exodus and Soviet Society," *Midstream,* April 1979.

Merari, Ariel, and Shlomo Elad. *The International Dimension of Palestinian Terrorism.* Boulder, Colo., 1987.

Morraflet, Claude. *Otages à Kampala.* Paris, 1976.

Na'or, Mordechai, and Ze'ev Anner. *Y'mei Oktober* [The Days of October]. Tel Aviv, 1974.

National Council for Soviet Jewry. *Hostages for Trade: Soviet Jews.* Miami, Fla., 1979.

Neff, Donald. *Warriors against Israel: How Israel Won the Battle to Become America's Ally.* New York, 1973.

———, ed. *Gush Emunim: Political Inspiration and Settlement Prospects.* New York, 1984.

Ofry, Dan. *The Yom Kippur War.* Tel Aviv, 1974.

Oren, Stephen. "The December Elections in Israel," *Midstream*, Feb. 1974.

———. "The Rabin Government," *Midstream*, Aug.–Sept. 1974.

Peretz, Don. "The War Election and Israel's Eighth Knesset," *Middle East Journal*, Winter 1974.

Peters, Jean. "In Search of Moderate Egyptians," *Commentary*, May 1975.

Rabinovich, Abraham. *The Yom Kippur War.* New York, 2004.

Rabinovich, Itamar. "The Limitations of Power: Syria under al-Assad," *New Middle East*, March 1973.

Rafael, Gideon. *Destination Peace.* New York, 1981.

Rass, Rebecca. *From Moscow to Jerusalem.* New York, 1976.

Roth, Stanley. *Middle East Balance of Power after the Yom Kippur War.* Cambridge, Mass., 1974.

Sachar, Howard M. *Diaspora: An Inquiry into the Contemporary Jewish World.* New York, 1985.

———. *Egypt and Israel.* New York, 1981.

———. *A History of Israel: From the Aftermath of the Yom Kippur War.* New York, 1987.

Scharansky, Avital. *Next Year in Jerusalem.* New York, 1979.

Schiff, Ze'ev. *October Earthquake: Yom Kippur, 1973.* Tel Aviv, 1974.

Schroeter, Leonard. *The Last Exodus.* Seattle, 1981.

Sevela, Ephraim. *Farewell, Israel.* South Bend, Ind., 1977.

Sheehan, Edward R. F. "How Kissinger Did It: Step by Step in the Middle East," *Foreign Policy*, Spring 1976.

Sobel, Lester A., ed. *Israel and the Arabs: The October 1973 War.* New York, 1974.

Sunday Times Correspondents. *Insight on the Middle East War.* London, 1974.

Tahtinen, Dale R. *The Arab-Israeli Military Balance since October, 1973.* Washington, D.C., 1974.

United States. Congress. House Committee on Foreign Affairs. *The Impact of the October Middle East War.* Washington, D.C., 1974.

Voronel, A. "The Immigration of Russian Intelligentsia," *Economic Review of Problems of Aliyah and Absorption*, Oct. 1975.

Wheen, F. "No Exit for Jews," *New Statesman and Nation*, April 27, 1979.

AN AMBIVALENT QUEST FOR PEACE

I. The Likud Era Begins

Adle, A., and R. Hodge. "Ethnicity and the Process of Status Attainment in Israel," *Israel Social Science Research*, No. 1, 1983.

Aloni, Shulamit. "Legal Discrimination," *New Outlook*, May–June 1978.

Amit, M. "Israel: The Bases of Economic Growth," *Washington Quarterly*, Spring 1979.

Arian, Asher. *Politics in Israel: The Second Generation.* Chatham, N.J., 1985.

Ata, I. "The West Bank Palestinian Family after 1967 and the Political Socioeconomic Structure," *Arab Perspectives*, May 1985.

Avruch, K. "Gush Emunim: Politics, Religion, and Ideology in Israel," *Middle East Review*, No. 2, 1978–79.

Bar-Gal, Y., and A. Soffer. *Geographical Changes in the Traditional Arab Village in Israel.* Durham, England, 1981.

Barkai, C. "The Israeli Economy in the Past Decade," *Jerusalem Quarterly*, Summer 1984.

Bar-Nir, Dov. *MiJabotinsky ad Begin* [From Jabotinsky to Begin]. Tel Aviv, 1982.

Barzilay, I. "The Arab in Modern Hebrew Literature: Image and Problems," *Hebrew Studies*, No. 18, 1977.

Begin, Menachem. *BaMachteret* [In the Underground]. 4 vols. Tel Aviv, 1959–61.

———. *The Revolt*. New York, 1951.

———. *White Nights*. New York, 1957.

Ben-Porat, Y. "Israeli Dilemmas: Economic Relations between Jews and Arabs," *Dissent*, No. 4, 1984.

Ben-Rafael, Eliezer. *The Emergence of Ethnicity: Cultural Groups and Social Conflict in Israel*. Westport, Conn., 1982.

Ben-Zadok, and G. Goldberg. "A Socio-Political Change in the Israeli Development Town: An Analysis of Voting Patterns of Oriental Jews," *Plural Society*, No. 14, 1983.

Bitan, Arieh. *T'murot Yeshuviyot baGalil HaTachton HaMizrachi, 1800–1978* [Settlement Changes in Eastern Lower Galilee, 1800–1978]. Jerusalem, 1982.

Brinner, W. "The Arabs of Israel: The Past Twenty Years," *Middle East Review*, No. 2, 1987.

Caspi, Dan. "Ta'amulat HaB'chirot v'Totza'at HaB'chirot: Hashva'ah bein Ma'arachot b'Yisrael [Electoral Propaganda and the Electoral Result: A Comparison of Campaigns in Israel]," *M'dina, Mimshal, v'Yachasim Beinle'umiyim*, Nos. 19–20, 1982.

Caspi, Dan, et al. *The Roots of Begin's Success*. New York, 1984.

Doron, A. "The Histadrut, Social Policy, and Equality," *Jewish Quarterly*, No. 47, 1985.

Dutter, L. E. "Eastern and Western Jews: Ethnic Divisions in Israeli Society," *Middle East Journal*, Summer 1977.

Eisenstadt, S. N. *Hitpatchutah shel HaBa'ayah HeAdatit b'Yisrael* [The Development of the Ethnic Problem in Israeli Society]. Jerusalem, 1986.

Eliachar, E. "The Sephardi Non-Presence," *New Outlook*, Jan.–Feb. 1977.

Esmar, Fouzi al-. *To Be an Arab in Israel*. Beirut, 1978.

Falahi, G. "Israeli State Policy toward Bedouin Sedentarization in the Negev," *Journal of Palestine Studies*, No. 4, 1989.

———. "Israel's 'Judaization' Policy in Galilee," *Journal of Palestine Studies*, No. 4, 1991.

Giladi, G. *Discord in Zion: Conflict between Ashkenazic and Sephardic Jews in Israel*. London, 1990.

Ginor, Fanny. *Socio-Economic Disparities in Israel*. Tel Aviv, 1979.

Goering, K. "Israel and the Bedouin of the Negev," *Journal of Palestine Studies*, No. 4, 1979.

Gonem, A. "Geografikat Hitacharut B'chirot bein HaMa'arachiah v'HaLikud b'Arim Ye-hudiyot b'Yisrael, 1965–1981 [The Geography of the Electoral Competition between the Labor Alignment and the Likud in Jewish Cities of Israel, 1965–1981]," *M'dina, Mimshal, v'Yachasim Beinle'umiyim*, Nos. 19–20, 1982.

Haber, Eitan. *Menahem Begin*. New York, 1978.

Haidar, Aziz. *Social Welfare Services for Israel's Arab Population*. Boulder, Colo., 1991.

Hareven, A., and A. Radian. "The Likud Government and Domestic Policy Change," *Jerusalem Quarterly*, Winter 1981.

Hoffman, J., and N. Rouhana. "Young Arabs in Israel: Some Aspects of a Conflicted Social Identity," *Journal of Social Psychology*, June 1977.

Israeli, A. "Mahapechat HaTa'asukah bein HaMiyutim HaLoYehudiyim b'M'dinat Yisrael [The Employment Revolution among the Non-Jewish Minorities of Israel]," *HaMizrach HeChadash*, Nos. 3–4, 1976.

Jurays, Sabri. *The Arabs in Israel*. New York, 1976.

Karni, E. "The Israeli Economy, 1973–1976," *Economic Development and Cultural Change*, Oct. 1979.

Khalidi, Raja. *The Arab Economy in Israel.* London, 1988.

Khouri, R. G. "Israel's Imperial Economics," *Journal of Palestine Studies,* No. 2, 1979.

Koenig Report. "Demographic Racism in Israel," *MERIP Reports,* Oct. 1976.

Kreimer, S. "Entrepreneurism in Israel's Arab Communities," *New Outlook,* July–Aug. 1987.

Kretzer, David. *The Legal Status of the Arabs in Israel.* Boulder, Colo., 1990.

Landau, Jacob. *The Arab Minority in Israel, 1967–1991: Political Aspects.* Oxford, 1993.

Lesch, Ann M. "Israeli Settlements in the Occupied Territories," *Journal of Palestine Studies,* No. 3, 1977.

Lustick, Ian. *Arabs in the Jewish State.* Austin, Tex., 1980.

Moragh, Gilead. "The Arab as 'Other' in Israeli Fiction," *Middle East Review,* Fall 1989.

Nachmias, David, and David Rosenbloom. *Bureaucratic Culture: Citizen and Administration in Israel.* New York, 1978.

Nisan, Mordechai. *Israel and the Territories.* Ramat Gan, 1978.

Ofer, G. "Israel's Economy: Diagnosis and Cure," *Jerusalem Quarterly,* Summer 1981.

Peled, E. "Equality in Israel's Educational Policy," *Jerusalem Quarterly,* Winter 1981.

Peretz, Don. "The Earthquake—Israel's Ninth Knesset Elections," *Middle East Journal,* Autumn 1985.

Rabin, Yitzchak. *The Rabin Memoirs.* New York, 1979.

Radian, A., and I. Sharkansky. "Tax Reform in Israel," *Policy Analysis,* No. 3, 1979.

Ramras-Rauch, Gila. *The Arab in Israeli Literature.* Bloomington, Ind., 1989.

Rehkess, E. "The Israeli Arab Intelligentsia," *Jerusalem Quarterly,* Spring 1979.

Roumani, Maurice. "The Sephardic Factor in Israeli Politics," *Middle East Journal,* Spring 1988.

Sachar, Howard M. *A History of Israel: From the Aftermath of the Yom Kippur War.* New York, 1987.

Schnall, David. "Gush Emunim: Messianic Dissent and Israeli Politics," *Judaism,* Summer 1977.

———. *Radical Dissent in Contemporary Israeli Politics.* New York, 1979.

Shamir, M., and A. Arian. "HaB'chirah HaEdatit baB'chirot 1977 b'Yisrael [The Ethnic Vote in Israel's 1977 Elections]," *M'dina, Mimshal, v'Yachasim Beinle'umiyim,* Nos. 19–20, 1982.

Shammas, Anton. "Arabic Literature in Israel," *Ariel,* Winter 1978.

Shapiro, Yonathan. *The Road to Power: Herut Party in Israel.* Albany, N.Y., 1991.

Silver, Eric. *Begin: The Haunted Prophet.* New York, 1984.

Smooha, Sammy. "Existing and Alternative Policies toward the Arabs in Israel," *Ethnic and Racial Studies,* Jan. 1982.

———. *Israel: Pluralism and Conflict.* London, 1979.

Suleiman, K. *Palestine and Modern Arab Poetry.* London, 1985.

Teicher, Morton. "Project Renewal," *Midstream,* Jan. 1991.

Temko, Ned. *To Win or to Die: A Personal Portrait of Menachem Begin.* New York, 1987.

Winter, M. "Arab Education in Israel," *Jerusalem Quarterly,* Summer 1979.

Yaniv, A. "Jews and Arabs on Campus," *Jerusalem Quarterly,* Spring 1984.

Yaniv, A., and F. Pascal. "Doves, Hawks, and Other Birds of a Feather: The Distribution of Israeli Parliamentary Opinions on the Future of the Occupied Territories, 1967–1977," *International Journal of Middle Eastern Studies,* April 1980.

Yinon, A. "Nosim b'Sifrut Arvei Yisrael [Themes in the Literature of Israeli Arabs]," *HaMizrach HeChadash,* No. 1, 1975.

Yishai, Y. "Israel's Right-Wing Jewish Proletariat," *Jewish Journal of Sociology,* Dec. 1982.

II. *An Accommodation with Egypt*

"After the Peace Treaty: The Military Situation in the Middle East," *Journal of Palestine Studies*, No. 4, 1979.

Ajami, Fuad. "The Struggle for Egypt's Soul," *Foreign Policy*, Fall 1979.

Ali, M. "Jordan's Stance toward the Camp David Agreements," *Pakistan Horizon*, No. 31, 1978.

Arad, Ruth, Ze'ev Hirsch, and Alfred Tovias. *The Economics of Peacemaking: Focus on the Egyptian-Israeli Situation.* New York, 1983.

Aruri, N. H. "Kissinger's Legacy to Carter," *Middle East,* March 1977.

Bar-Yaacov, N. "Keeping the Peace between Egypt and Israel, 1973–80," *Israel Law Review,* April 1980.

Carter, Jimmy. *The Blood of Abraham.* New York, 1985.

———. *Keeping Faith.* New York, 1982.

Dayan, Moshe. *Breakthrough to Peace.* London, 1981.

Egypt. Ministry of Foreign Affairs. *Egypt and the Palestinian Question, 1945–1982.* Cairo, 1982.

"Egyptian Oil in 1977," *Middle East Economic Survey,* July 19, 1978.

Gilboa, Eytan. "Educating Israeli Officers in the Process of Peacemaking in the Middle East," *Journal of Peace Research,* No. 2, 1979.

Hasan, Sana. *Enemy in the Promised Land.* New York, 1986.

Hirst, David, and Irene Beeson. *Sadat.* London, 1981.

Kanovsky, Eliahu. "Economic Aspects of Peace between Israel and the Arab Countries," *New Outlook,* Oct. 1987.

Katz, Shmuel. *The Hollow Peace.* Jerusalem, 1981.

Kreinin, M. "On the Potential Trade Pattern between Egypt and Israel," *Middle East Review,* No. 3, 1980.

Kubursi, Atif. *The Economic Consequences of the Camp David Agreements.* Kuwait City, 1979.

Lapidoth, R. "The Camp David Agreements: Some Legal Aspects," *Jerusalem Quarterly,* Autumn 1979.

Lipschitz, Ora. *Sinai.* Tel Aviv, 1978.

Mansour, A. "Getting to Know You," *New Outlook,* May–June 1979.

Markus, Yoel. *Camp David: Petach l'Shalom* [Camp David: Gateway to Peace]. Tel Aviv, 1979.

Nes, D. "Egypt Breaks the Deadlock," *Journal of Palestine Studies*, No. 2, 1979.

Peres, Shimon. "Dampening the Fire in the Middle East: A Strategy for a Transition Period," *International Security,* No. 3, 1978.

Peric, M. "Camp David—Damascus—Baghdad," *Review of International Affairs,* Nov. 1978.

Preuss, Teddy. *Begin b'Shilton* [Begin in Office]. Jerusalem, 1984.

Quandt, William. *Camp David: Peacemaking and Politics.* Washington, D.C., 1986.

Rabinovich, Itamar. "Israel: The Impact of the Treaty," *Current History,* Jan. 1980.

Rondot, P. "Après la signature du traité de paix égypto-israélien. Les limits du refus arabe," *Politique Étrangère,* No. 2, 1979.

Ron-Feder, G'lilah. *Moshe Dayan* [in Hebrew]. Vol. II. Jerusalem, 1984.

Roy, D. "Egyptian Liberalization: The First Decade, 1973–1983," *Middle East Executive Reports,* Dec. 1983.

Sachar, Howard M. *Egypt and Israel.* New York, 1981.

———. *A History of Israel: From the Aftermath of the Yom Kippur War.* New York, 1987.

Sadat, Anwar al-. *Egypt in Search of Identity.* New York, 1977.

Sayegh, Fayez. *Palestine and the Camp David Accords.* London, 1979.

Segev, Shmuel. *Sadat, HaDerech l'Shalom* [Sadat, the Road to Peace]. Tel Aviv, 1978.

Shamay, M. "La communauté juive en Egypte," *Peuples Méditerranéens,* No. 16, 1981.

Shamir, Shimon. *Mitzrayim b'Hanhagat Sadat* [Egypt under the Leadership of Sadat]. Tel Aviv, 1978.

Shoukhri, Ghali. *Egypt: Portrait of a President: Sadat's Road to Jerusalem.* London, 1981.

Sid-Ahmed, Mohamed. *After the Guns Fall Silent: Peace or Armageddon in the Middle East.* London, 1978.

Taub, Y. "Israel's Economy: The Challenge of Peace," *Jerusalem Quarterly,* Autumn 1979.

Torgovnik, E. "Accepting Camp David: The Role of Party Factions in Israeli Policy-Making," *Middle East Review,* No. 2, 1978–79.

Waterbury, John. *Egypt: Burdens of the Past, Options for the Future.* Bloomington, Ind., 1978.

Weizman, Ezer. *The Battle for Peace.* New York, 1981.

Wissa, Karim. *The Oil Question in Egyptian-Israeli Relations.* Cairo, 1990.

Yariv, Aharon. "Strategic Depth," *Jerusalem Quarterly,* Spring 1980.

Yinon, Moshe. *Mishva'at HaShalom* [The Peace Equation]. Haifa, 1981.

Zelniker, Shimshon, and Zaki Shalom. *Cooperation between Israel and Egypt: Positions and Trends.* Tel Aviv, 1981.

Zion, Sidney, and Uri Dan. "The Untold Story of the Mideast Talks," *New York Times Magazine,* Jan. 21, 28, 1979.

III. *Romantic Nationalism and Revisionism*

Abboushi, W. *The Unmaking of Palestine.* Cambridge, England, 1986.

Alexander, Yona. "The Nature of the PLO: Some International Implications," *Middle East Review,* No. 3, 1980.

Antonius, S. "Fighting on Two Fronts: Conversations with Palestinian Women," *Journal of Palestine Studies,* No. 3, 1979.

Arian, A. "Elections 1981: Competitiveness and Polarization," *Jerusalem Quarterly,* Autumn 1981.

———, ed. *The Elections in Israel 1981.* Tel Aviv, 1981.

Aronoff, Myron. *Israeli Visions and Divisions: Cultural Change and Political Conflict.* New Brunswick, N.J., 1989.

Aruri, N. H. "Repression in Academica: Palestinian Universities versus the Israeli Military," *Arab Perspectives,* April 1981.

———. "Resistance and Repression," *Journal of Palestine Studies,* No. 2, 1978.

Ashrawi, H. M. "The Contemporary Palestinian Poetry of Occupation," *Journal of Palestine Studies,* No. 1, 1978.

"Attainment in Israel," *Israel Social Science Research,* No. 1, 1983.

Aviad, J. *The Return to Judaism: Religious Renewal in Israel.* Chicago, 1983.

Bahiri, Simcha. *Industrialization in the West Bank and Gaza.* Boulder, Colo., 1988.

Bailey, Clinton. "Changing Attitudes toward Jordan in the West Bank," *Middle East Journal,* Winter 1978.

Bar-Yaacov, N. "Keeping the Peace between Egypt and Israel, 1973–1980," *Israel Law Review,* April 1980.

Bar-Zohar, Michael, and Eitan Haber. *The Quest for the Red Prince.* New York, 1983.

Bassiouni, M. C. "An Analysis of Egyptian Policy toward Israel," *New Outlook,* Jan. 1981.

Beinin, J. "The Cold Peace," *MERIP Reports,* Jan. 1984.

Benveniste, Meron. "First Steps to a Solution," *New Outlook,* May 1981.

———. *Jerusalem: Study of a Polarized Community.* Jerusalem, 1983.

———. *Jerusalem: The Torn City.* Minneapolis, 1976.

————. *West Bank Data Project, 1986, 1987.* Jerusalem, 1986, 1987.

"Bir Zeit: Palestinian University Confrontations," *Palestine Bulletin,* Jan. 1979.

Bisharat, George E. *Palestinian Lawyers and Israeli Rule.* Austin, Tex., 1984.

Blaisse, Mark. *Anwar Sadat: The Last Hundred Days.* London, 1981.

Byran, S. "Advancing U.S.–Israeli Strategic Cooperation," *Middle East Review,* No. 2, 1984.

Butros-Ghali, Butros. "The Foreign Policy of Egypt in the Post-Sadat Period," *Foreign Affairs,* April 1982.

Capitanchik, D. "Religion and Politics in Israel," *Jewish Journal of Sociology,* July 1983.

Caplan, Gerald, and Ruth Caplan. *Arab and Jew in Jerusalem: Explorations in Community Mental Health.* Cambridge, Mass., 1980.

Caspi, Dan, Avraham Diskin, and Emanuel Gutmann. *The Roots of Begin's Success: The 1981 Israeli Elections.* London, 1984.

Cattan, Henry. *The Question of Jerusalem.* London, 1980.

Chertok, Haim. "Ferment from Russian Jews," *Midstream,* May 1992.

Cohen, S. "Jerusalem's Unity and West Bank Autonomy—Paired Principles," *Middle East Review,* Nos. 3–4, 1981.

Cohn, A. "The Changing Patterns of West Bank Politics," *Jerusalem Quarterly,* Autumn 1977.

Dajani, Ahmad al-. "The PLO and the Euro-Arab Dialogue," *Journal of Palestine Studies,* No. 3, 1980.

Darin-Drabkin, H. "From Settlement to Colonization," *New Outlook,* Feb.–March 1978.

Davies, P. "The Educated West Bank Palestinians," *Journal of Palestine Studies,* No. 3, 1979.

Davis, Uri. *The Golan Heights under Israeli Occupation, 1967–81.* Durham, England, 1983.

Dehter, Aaron. *How Expensive Are West Bank Settlements?* Boulder, Colo., 1987.

Don-Yehiya, E. "Jewish Orthodoxy, Zionism, and the State of Israel," *Jerusalem Quarterly,* Autumn 1984.

————. "Religious Leaders in the Political Arena: The Case of Israel," *Middle Eastern Studies,* April 1984.

Egypt. Ministry of Foreign Affairs. *Egypt and the Palestinian Question, 1945–1982.* Cairo, 1982.

Eisenberg, Dennis, Uri Dan, and Eli Landau. *The Mossad.* New York, 1979.

Elon, Amos. *Jerusalem: City of Mirrors.* Boston, 1989.

Evron, B. "Mad Settlers on the West Bank," *Nation,* April 21, 1979.

————. "Occupation Corrupts Israeli Justice," *New Outlook,* March 1988.

Feintuch, Yossi. *United States Policy on Jerusalem.* Westport, Conn., 1987.

Freedman, L. "Israel's Nuclear Policy," *Survival,* May–June 1975.

Friedberg, Maurice. "From Moscow to Jerusalem—and Points West," *Commentary,* May 1978.

Friedman, M. "Mifleget HaMafdal b'Mashber [The National Religious Party in Crisis]," *M'dina, Mimshal, v'Yachasim Beinle'umiyim,* Nos. 19–20, 1982.

Gazit, Mordechai. "Israeli Military Procurement from the United States," in Gabriel Sheffer, ed. *Dynamics of Dependence: United States–Israel Relations.* Boulder, Colo., 1987.

Ghareibeh, Fawzi A. *The Economics of the West Bank and Gaza Strip.* Boulder, Colo., 1985.

Golan, Gila. *The Soviet Union and the Palestine Liberation Organization.* New York, 1980.

Goldberg, G., and E. Ben-Zadok. "Gush Emunim in the West Bank," *Middle East Studies,* No. 1, 1986.

Goldstein, M. "Israeli Security Measures in the Occupied Territories: Administrative Detention," *Middle East Journal,* Autumn 1978.

Halabi, Rafik. *The West Bank Story.* New York, 1981.

Harkaby, Yehoshafat. *The Bar Kochba Syndrome.* Chappaqua, N.Y., 1982.

———. *Palestinians and Israel.* New York, 1977.

Harkavy, Robert C. *Spectre of a Middle East Holocaust: The Strategic and Diplomatic Implications of the Israeli Nuclear Weapons Program.* Denver, 1977.

Harris, William W. *Taking Root: Israeli Settlement in the West Bank, the Golan, and Gaza-Sinai, 1967–1980.* New York, 1980.

Hattis, S. "Jabotinsky's Parity Plan for Palestine," *Middle Eastern Studies,* Jan. 1977.

Heikal, Mohammed. *Autumn of Fury: The Assassination of Sadat.* New York, 1983.

Hersh, Seymour. *The Samson Option: Israel's Nuclear Arsenal and American Foreign Policy.* New York, 1991.

Hirschfeld, R. "The Village Leagues," *Christian Century,* April 6, 1983.

Inbar, E. "American Arms Transfers to Israel," *Middle East Review,* Nos. 1–2, 1982–83.

International Center for Peace in the Middle East. *Human Rights in the Occupied Territories.* Tel Aviv, 1984.

Isaac, Eric, and Raul Jean Isaac. "The Impact of Jabotinsky on Likud's Policies," *Middle East Review,* Autumn 1977.

Jahbra, Joseph. "The Palestinian Exile as Writer," *Journal of Palestine Studies,* No. 2, 1979.

Kalter, D. "The Truth about Elon Moreh," *New Outlook,* July–Aug. 1979.

Kieval, Gershon R. *Party Politics in Israel and the Occupied Territories.* Westport, Conn., 1983.

Kimche, Jon. "Taba or Masada?" *Midstream,* April 1985.

Kollek, Teddy. *For Jerusalem.* New York, 1978.

———. "Jerusalem," *Foreign Affairs,* July 1977.

Kraemer, Joel L. *Jerusalem: Problems and Prospects.* New York, 1980.

Krausz, E., and M. Bar-Lev. "Varieties of Orthodox Religious Behavior," *Jewish Journal of Sociology,* July 1978.

Langer, Felicia. *With My Own Eyes: Israel and the Occupied Territories, 1967–1973.* London, 1975.

Lapidoth, R. "The Autonomy Talks," *Jerusalem Quarterly,* Spring 1984.

Lesch, Ann. "The Politicization of the Occupied Territories, 1967–1977," *New Outlook,* Dec. 1977–Jan. 1978.

Lesch, Ann, and M. Tessler. *Israel, Egypt, and the Palestinians: From Camp David to Intifada.* Bloomington, Ind., 1989.

Liebman, Charles. "The Religious Component in Israeli Ultra-Nationalism," *Jerusalem Quarterly,* Winter 1987.

Liebman, Charles, and Eliezer Ben-Yehuda. *Civil Religion in Israel.* Berkeley, Calif., 1983.

Litani, Y. "Leadership in the West Bank and Gaza," *Jerusalem Quarterly,* Winter 1980.

Lustick, Ian. "Israel and the West Bank after Elon Moreh: The Mechanics of De Facto Annexation," *Middle East Journal,* Summer 1981.

MacKinley, John. *The Peacekeepers: An Account of Peacekeeping Operations at the Arab-Israel Interface.* London, 1989.

Ma'oz, Moshe, and Mordechai Nisan. *Palestinian Leadership in the West Bank: The Changing Role of the Mayors under Jordan and Israel.* London, 1984.

Meron, Raphael. *The Economy of the Administered Areas, 1977–78.* Jerusalem, 1980.

Metzger, J. *Israeli Policy in the West Bank and Gaza Strip.* Washington, D.C., 1986.

———. *This Land Is Our Land: The West Bank under Israeli Occupation.* London, 1983.

Migdal, Joel S., et al. *Palestine Society and Politics.* Princeton, N.J., 1980.

Milson, Menachem. "How Not to Occupy the West Bank," *Commentary*, April 1986.

———. "How to Make Peace with the Palestinians," *Commentary*, May 1981.

———. "The Palestinians and the Peace Process," *Forum*, Nos. 42–43, 1981.

Nachmias, David, and E. Zureik, eds. *The Sociology of the Palestinians.* New York, 1980.

Nakdimon, S. *First Strike: The Exclusive Story of How Israel Foiled Iraq's Attempt to Get the Bomb.* New York, 1987.

Neff, Donald, ed. *Gush Emunim: Political Inspiration and Settlement Prospects.* New York, 1984.

Negbi, M. "The Israeli Supreme Court and the Occupied Territories," *Jerusalem Quarterly,* Winter 1983.

Newman, David. "Gush Emunim between Fundamentalism and Pragmatism," *Jerusalem Quarterly,* Autumn 1986.

———, ed. *The Impact of Gush Emunim: Politics and Settlements in the West Bank.* New York, 1985.

Ostrovsky, Victor. *By Way of Deception.* New York, 1990.

Peace Now. *Government Investment in the Settlements in the Occupied Territories.* Jerusalem, 1991.

Pelcovits, Nathan. *Peacekeeping on Arab-Israeli Fronts: Lessons from the Sinai and Lebanon.* Boulder, Colo., 1984.

Peretz, Don. "Israel's Tenth Knesset Elections," *Middle East Journal,* Summer 1981.

———. *The West Bank: History, Politics, Society, and Economy.* Boulder, Colo., 1986.

Peri, Yoram. "Mushroom over the Middle East," *New Outlook,* May 1982.

Perlmutter, Amos, Michael Handel, and Uri Bar-Joseph. *Two Minutes over Baghdad.* London, 1982.

Perry, G. "Israeli Involvement in Inter-Arab Politics," *International Journal of Islamic and Arabic Studies,* Winter 1984.

Plaut, S. E. "Perverse Suburbanization in Jerusalem," *Israel Social Science Research,* No. 1, 1983.

Posner, Steve. *Israel Undercover: Secret Warfare and Hidden Diplomacy in the Middle East.* Syracuse, N.Y., 1987.

Pry, Peter. *Israel's Nuclear Arsenal.* Boulder, Colo., 1984.

Quester, G. H. "Nuclear Weapons and Israel," *Middle East Journal,* Summer 1983.

Raafat, W. "The Taba Case," *Revue Egyptienne de Droit International,* No. 39, 1983.

Ramati, Yochanan. "Analyzing Israel's Election," *Midstream,* Oct. 1981.

Ramberg, W. "Attacks on Nuclear Reactors: The Implications of Israel's Strike on Osiraq," *Political Science Quarterly,* Winter 1982–83.

Reich, Walter. *A Stranger in My House.* New York, 1984.

Reiser, Stewart. *The Politics of Leverage: The National Religious Party of Israel and Its Influence on Foreign Policy.* Cambridge, Mass., 1984.

Rokach, Livia. *Israel's Sacred Territorism.* Belmont, Mass., 1980.

Romann, Michael, and Alex Weingrad. *Living Together Separately: Arabs and Jews in Contemporary Jerusalem.* Princeton, N.J., 1991.

Roumani, Maurice. "Jews and Arabs in Jerusalem," *Jerusalem Quarterly,* Spring 1982.

Rubinstein, D. "The Occupied Territories 15 Years Later," *New Outlook,* June–July 1982.

Sachar, Howard M. *A History of Israel: From the Aftermath of the Yom Kippur War.* New York, 1987.

Saint-Prot, Charles. *La France et le renouveau arabe. De Charles de Gaulle à Giscard d'Estaing.* Paris, 1980.

Saliyah, Emile. *In Search of Leadership: West Bank Politics since 1967.* Washington, D.C., 1988.

Salmon, Y. "Religious Zionism between Tradition and Modernity," *Jerusalem Quarterly,* Spring 1980.

Sayigh, Rosemary. *The Palestinians: From Peasants to Revolutionaries.* London, 1979.

Schölsch, Alexander, ed. *Palestinians over the Green Line: Studies on the Relations between Palestinians on Both Sides of the Armistice Line since 1967.* London, 1983.

Shadid, Mohammed, and Rec Seltzer. "Political Attitudes of Palestinians in the West Bank and Gaza Strip," *Middle East Journal,* Autumn 1982.

Shahak, I. "A History of the Concept of 'Transfer' in Zionism," *Journal of Palestine Studies,* No. 3, 1989.

Shemesh, M. "The West Bank: Rise and Decline of Traditional Leadership," *Middle Eastern Studies,* July 1984.

Shiloach Institute, ed. *Tahalich Nirmul HaYachasim bein Israel l'vein Mitzrayim* [The Process of Normalization of Relations between Israel and Egypt]. Tel Aviv, 1981.

Shinar, Dov, and Danny Rubinstein. *The Palestinian Press in the West Bank.* Boulder, Colo., 1988.

Shipler, David. *Arab and Jew: Wounded Spirits in the Promised Land.* New York, 1986.

Shuaibi, Issa al-. "The Development of Palestinian Entity-Consciousness," *Journal of Palestine Studies,* No. 3, 1979.

Silberstein, Laurence J., ed. *Jewish Fundamentalism in Comparative Perspective.* New York, 1993.

Siniora, Hanna. "The Hope for Peace and a Homeland: A Palestinian View," *Middle East Insight,* June 1988.

Spector, Leonard S., with Jacqueline R. Smith. *Nuclear Ambitions.* Boulder, Colo., 1990.

Sprinzak, Ehud. *The Ascendance of Israel's Radical Right.* New York, 1991.

————. "Gush Emunim: The Tip of the Iceberg," *Jerusalem Quarterly,* Autumn 1981.

Sullivan, A. "Palestinian Universities under Occupation," *Arab Studies Quarterly,* Nos. 3–4, 1990.

Swirski, S. "The Oriental Jews in Israel: Why Many Tilted toward Begin," *Dissent,* No. 1, 1984.

Tal, Uriel. "Foundations of a Political Messianic Trend in Israel," *Jerusalem Quarterly,* Autumn 1988.

Talmon, Ya'akov. "The Homeland Is in Danger: An Open Letter to Menachem Begin," *Dissent,* No. 3, 1980.

Tamarin, G. "Jewish-Arab Relations in Israel Following the 1973 War," *Pluralism and Society,* No. 4, 1976.

Tawil, Raymonda. *My Home, My Prison.* New York, 1979.

United States. House of Representatives. Committee on Foreign Affairs. *The Multinational Force and Observers (MFO) for the Sinai.* Washington, D.C., May 1982.

Urieh, Nachman. *Aliyatah u'N'filatah shel Dash* [The Rise and Fall of the Democratic Movement for Change]. Tel Aviv, 1982.

Vitullo, Anita. "Israel's War by Bureaucracy: We'll Blow Your House Down," *Dissent,* No. 1, 1984.

Weisburd, D. *Jewish Settler Violence: Deviance as Social Reaction.* University Park, Pa., 1989.

Weiss, S. "Israeli Non-Violent Khomeinism," *New Outlook,* Feb. 1984.

Weissman, Steve, and Herbert Krosney. *The Islamic Bomb.* New York, 1981.

Yehoshua, A. B. *Between Right and Right.* New York, 1981.

Yiftah, S. "The Middle East Nuclear Race: An Israeli View," *New Outlook,* May 1982.

Yishai, Y. "Israeli Annexation of East Jerusalem and the Golan Heights: Factors and Processes," *Middle Eastern Studies,* Jan. 1985.

Yishai, Y., and A. Yaniv. "Israeli Settlements on the West Bank: The Politics of Intransigence," *Journal of Politics*, No. 2, 1978.

Yitzhaki, A. "Milson's Year on the West Bank," *Middle East Review*, No. 2, 1985.

Zelnicker, S., and M. Kahan. "Religion and Nascent Cleavages: The Case of Israel's National Religious Party," *Comparative Politics*, Oct. 1976.

Zu'bi, N. "The Development of Capitalism in Palestine: The Expropriation of the Palestinian Direct Producers," *Journal of Palestine Studies*, No. 1, 1984.

IV.   *Israel in Lebanon*

Allen, David, and Alfred Pijpers, eds. *European Foreign Policy-Making and the Arab-Israel Conflict.* The Hague, 1984.

Alper, Joseph, ed. *Israel's Lebanon Policy: Where To?* Tel Aviv, 1984.

Barkai, H. "Reflections on the Economic Cost of the Lebanon War," *Jerusalem Quarterly*, Autumn 1986.

Bauberot, J., et al. *Palestine et Liban: Promesses et mensonges de l'Occident.* Paris, 1977.

Benzimon, Uri. *Sharon: An Israeli Caesar.* New York, 1985.

Bulloch, Keith. *Final Conflict: The War in Lebanon.* London, 1983.

Caplan, N., and I. Black. "Israel and Lebanon: Origins of a Relationship," *Jerusalem Quarterly*, Summer 1983.

Chafetz, Z. "Beirut and the Great Media Coverup," *Commentary*, Sept. 1984.

Davidson, L. "Lebanon and the Jewish Conscience," *Journal of Palestine Studies*, No. 2, 1983.

Dawisha, A. "The Motives of Syria's Involvement in Lebanon," *Middle East Journal*, Winter 1984.

Depuy, Trevor N., and Paul Martell. *Flawed Victory: The Arab-Israeli Conflict and the 1982 War in Lebanon.* Fairfax, Va., 1986.

Eban, A. "The Trauma in Beirut," *Jewish Frontier*, Aug.–Sept. 1982.

Evron, Yair. *War and Intervention in Lebanon: The Israeli-Syrian Deterrence Dialogue.* Baltimore, 1987.

Feldman, S., and H. Rechnitz-Kijner. *Deception, Consensus and War: Israel in Lebanon.* Boulder, Colo., 1984.

Friedman, Thomas L. *From Beirut to Jerusalem.* New York, 1989.

Gabriel, Richard. *Operation Peace for the Galilee.* New York, 1984.

Gamson, Josh. "The Limits of Conscience," *Nation*, June 9, 1984.

Gordon, David C. *Lebanon: The Fragmented Nation.* Stanford, Calif., 1980.

HaKibbutz HaMe'uhad. *Milchemet Levanon* [The Lebanon War]. Tel Aviv, 1983.

Haig, Alexander. *Caveat.* New York, 1984.

Halabi, Rafik. *Yesh G'vul* [There's a Limit]. Jerusalem, 1983.

Hall-Cathala, David. *The Peace Movement in Israel, 1967–87.* New York, 1990.

Heller, P. "The Syrian Factor in the Lebanese Civil War," *Journal of South Asian and Middle Eastern Studies*, Jan. 1980.

———, ed. *The Middle East Military Balance.* New York, 1984.

Hof, Fredric C. *Galilee Divided: The Israel-Lebanon Frontier, 1916–1984.* Boulder, Colo., 1985.

Hudson, Michael C. "The Palestinian Factor in the Lebanese Civil War," *Middle East Journal*, Spring 1978.

Inbar, E. "Great Power Mediation: The USA and the May 1983 Israeli-Lebanese Agreement," *Journal of Peace Resolution*, No. 1, 1991.

Israel. Ministry of Foreign Affairs. *Te'udot l'M'diniyut HaChutz shel M'dinat Yisrael* [Documents on Israeli Foreign Policy]. Vols. II–III. Jerusalem, 1981–84.

————. Ministry of Information. *Mivtzat "Shalom HaGalil"* [Operation Peace for the Galilee]. Jerusalem, 1983.

Israeli, Raphael. *The PLO in Lebanon.* New York, 1983.

Jansen, Michael. *The Battle of Beirut: Why Israel Invaded Lebanon.* Boston, 1983.

Jones, M. "Verdict in London," *Present Tense,* Summer 1983.

Karetzky, Stephen. *The Media's War against Israel.* New York, 1986.

Khalidi, R. "The Palestinians in Lebanon: Social Repercussions of Israel's Invasion," *Middle East Journal,* Winter 1984.

Levins, Hoag. *Arab Reach: The Secret War against Israel.* Garden City, N.Y., 1983.

Lissak, Moshe, ed. *Israeli Society and Its Defense Establishment: The Social and Political Impact of a Protracted Violent Conflict.* London, 1984.

Lubrani, Uri. "Israel, Syria, and Lebanon—an Israeli Perspective," *Middle East Insight,* March 1985.

MacBride, Sean, et al. *Israel in Lebanon: The Report of an International Commission.* London, 1983.

Ma'oz, Moshe. "Israel and the Arabs after the Lebanese War," *Jerusalem Quarterly,* Summer 1983.

Morris, R. "Beirut—and the Press—under Siege," *Columbia Journalism Review,* Nov.–Dec. 1982.

Muir, J. "Lebanon: Arena of Conflict, Crucible of Peace," *Middle East Journal,* Winter 1984.

Oz, Amos. *M'Mordot Levanon* [From the Slopes of Lebanon]. Tel Aviv, 1984.

Pail, M. "Lebanon: A Military Analysis," *New Outlook,* Aug.–Sept. 1982.

Pallis, E. "The Widening Rift between Israel and the Diaspora," *Middle East Insight,* Aug. 1983.

Peleg, Ilan. *Begin's Foreign Policy, 1977–1983.* Westport, Conn., 1987.

————. "Jabotinsky's Legacy and Begin's Foreign Policy," *Israel and the World,* Oct. 1983.

Pipes, Daniel. "The Media and the Middle East," *Commentary,* Jan. 1984.

Quandt, William. "Reagan's Lebanon Policy: Trial and Error," *Middle East Journal,* Winter 1984.

Rabinovich, Itamar. *The War for Lebanon, 1970–1983.* Ithaca, N.Y., 1984.

Randal, Jonathan C. *Going All the Way.* New York, 1983.

Rasler, K. "International Civil War: A Dynamic Analysis of the Syrian Intervention in Lebanon," *Journal of Conflict Resolution,* Sept. 1983.

Ron, Moshe. *Milchemet Levanon* [The Lebanon War]. Tel Aviv, 1983.

Rubenberg, C. "The Civilian Infrastructure of the Palestine Liberation Organization," *Journal of Palestine Studies,* No. 3, 1983.

Sachar, Howard M. *A History of Israel: From the Aftermath of the Yom Kippur War.* New York, 1987.

Sadowski, Y. "The Sands Run Out in Lebanon," *Nation,* June 18, 1983.

Sahliyeh, Emile. *In Search of Leadership: West Bank Politics since 1967.* Washington, D.C., 1988.

Salpeter, E. "The Geva Case," *New Leader,* Sept. 6, Nov. 29, 1982.

Schiff, Ze'ev. "Dealing with Syria," *Foreign Policy,* Summer 1984.

————. "Green Light, Lebanon," *Foreign Policy,* Autumn 1983.

————. *A History of the Israeli Army.* New York, 1985.

Schiff, Ze'ev, and Ehud Ya'ari. *Israel's Lebanon War.* New York, 1984.

Schueftan, D. "The PLO after Lebanon," *Jerusalem Quarterly,* Autumn 1983.

Segev, Shmuel. *Mivtsat "Yachsin"* [Operation "Yachsin"]. Tel Aviv, 1984.

Shiffer, Shalom. *Kadur Sheleg* [Snowball—The Lebanon War]. Jerusalem, 1984.

Shlain, A. "Conflicting Approaches to Israel's Relations with the Arabs: Ben-Gurion and Sharett," *Middle East Journal,* Winter 1983.

Simon, R. "The Print Media's Coverage of the War in Lebanon," *Middle East Review*, No. 1, 1983.

Smith, P. A. "European Reactions to Israel's Invasion," *Journal of Palestine Studies*, No. 1, 1982.

Tabbarah, R. B. "Background to the Lebanese Conflict," *International Journal of Comparative Sociology*, May–June 1979.

Tucker, R. W. "Lebanon: The Case for the War," *Commentary*, Oct. 1982.

Weinberger, N. "Peacekeeping Operations in Lebanon," *Middle East Journal*, Spring 1983.

Ya'ari, E. "Israel's Dilemma in Lebanon," *Middle East Insight*, April–May 1984.

Ya'ari, E., and R. Lieber. "Personal Whim or Strategic Imperative? The Israeli Invasion of Lebanon," *International Security*, No. 2, 1983.

Yaniv, Avner. *Dilemmas of Security: Politics, Strategy, and the Israeli Experience in Lebanon*. New York, 1987.

Yermiha, D. *My War Diary: Lebanon, June 5–July 1, 1982*. Boston, 1984.

Zagorin, A. "A House Divided," *Foreign Policy*, Autumn 1982.

Zamir, M. "Smaller and Greater Lebanon: Squaring the Circle?" *Jerusalem Quarterly*, Winter 1982.

v.   *A Crisis of Israeli Spirit, of Diaspora Loyalty*

Alter, Robert. "The Israeli Novel and Post–World War II Fiction," *Tel Aviv Review*, No. 3, 1991.

Anderson, Elliott, ed. *Contemporary Israeli Literature*. Philadelphia, 1977.

Arieli, Yehoshua. "On Being a Secular Jew in Israel," *Jerusalem Quarterly*, Winter 1988.

Aronoff, Myron, ed. *Cross-Cultures in Israeli Culture and Politics*. New Brunswick, N.J., 1984.

Avishai, Bernard. "Looking Over Jordan," *New York Review of Books*, April 28, 1983.

Beit-Hallami, B. "Israel's Ultra-Orthodox," *MERIP Reports*, June 1992.

Ben-Dov, Nitza. "Why They Write: The Political Impulse of Israeli Writers," *Middle East Review*, No. 1, 1987–88.

Ben-Ezer, E. "Cross-Cultural Misunderstandings," *Israel Social Science Review*, No. 3, 1985.

———. "War and Siege in Israeli Literature after 1967," *Jerusalem Quarterly*, Winter 1978.

Blitzer, Wolf. *Territory of Lies: The Exclusive Story of Jonathan Jay Pollard*. New York, 1989.

———. "Why Did He Spy?" *Washington Jewish Week*, March 10, 1988.

Capitanchik, D. "Religion and Politics in Israel," *Jewish Journal of Sociology*, Jan. 1986.

Cohen, M. "Islam and the Jews," *Jerusalem Quarterly*, Autumn 1986.

Cohen, Stephen M. *The Attitude of American Jews toward Israel and Israelis*. New York, 1983.

Cohen, Y., et al. "Occupational Sex-Segregation in Israel, 1972–83," *Israel Social Science Review*, Nos. 1–2, 1987.

Eliav, Arieh. *A New Heart and a New Spirit: Biblical Humanism for Modern Israel*. New York, 1980.

Feldman, Yael S. "The 'Other' within Contemporary Israeli Fiction," *Middle East Review*, Fall 1989.

———. "Recreating the Past in Contemporary Israeli Fiction," *Ariel*, Fall 1988.

Flegenheimer, Arnold J. *Archaeological Adventure in Israel: A Practical Guide*. Roslyn Heights, N.Y., 1986.

Fuchs, E. "Israeli Mythologies: Women in Contemporary Hebrew Fiction," *International Journal of Middle Eastern Studies*, Feb. 1989.

Galnoor, I. "The Failure of Religious Zionism," *Jerusalem Quarterly*, Winter 1986.

Gertz, Nurith. "Israeli Novelists," *Jerusalem Quarterly*, Autumn 1980.

Gilboa, Eytan. "Attitudes of American Jews toward Israel: Trends over Time," *American Jewish Yearbook*, 1986.

Glinert, L. *The Grammar of Modern Hebrew*. Cambridge, Mass., 1989.

Halter, Aloma. "Translating Israel," *Ariel*, Spring 1986.

Hareven, Aluph. "Are We Still the People of the Book?" *Jerusalem Quarterly*, Winter 1984.

Harkabi, Yehoshafat. *Israel's Fateful Hour*. New York, 1988.

Hartman, H. "Economic and Familial Roles of Women in Israel," *Israel Social Science Research*, No. 2, 1985.

Heidelberger Kunstverein. *Dani Karavan: Modelle und Projekte*. Heidelberg, 1983.

Hoffman, Charles. *The Smoke Screen: Israel, Philanthropy, and American Jews*. Silver Spring, Md., 1989.

Huppert, Uri. *Back to the Ghetto: Zionism in Retreat*. Buffalo, N.Y., 1988.

Israel. Council on Higher Education. *The Higher Education System in Israel*. Jerusalem, 1984.

Israel Composers League. *Aspects of Music in Israel*. Tel Aviv, 1980.

Jabbour, S. "Le conflit entre religieux et laïques en Israël," *Revue D'Études Palestiniennes*, No. 22, 1987.

Katz, Elihu, and Michael Gurevitch. *The Secularization of Leisure: Culture and Communication in Israel*. Cambridge, Mass., 1976.

Kenny, Herbert A. *Israel and the Arts*. Boston, 1988.

Keren, Michael. *The Pen and the Sword: Israeli Intellectuals and the Making of the Nation-State*. Boulder, Colo., 1989.

Mergui, Raphael. *Israel's Ayatollahs: Meir Kahane and the Far Right*. London, 1987.

Nundi-Israeli, Dafna. "Israeli Women in the Work Force," *Jerusalem Quarterly*, Spring 1983.

Oz, Amos. *In the Land of Israel*. San Diego, 1983.

Pollock, D. "The Politics of Pressure: American Arms and Israeli Policy since the Six-Day War," *Middle East Studies Association*, July 1983.

Pomerantz, Marsha. "The Jerusalem Book Fair," *Ariel*, Spring 1983.

Rabinowicz, H. *Hasidism and the State of Israel*. Rutherford, N.J., 1982.

Ramras-Rauch, Gila. *The Arab in Israeli Literature*. Bloomington, Ind., 1989.

Ravitzky, A. "The Roots of Kahanism," *Jerusalem Quarterly*, Autumn 1986.

Regev, Reviga. "Contemporary Israeli Sculpture," *Ariel*, Spring 1989.

Rosovsky, Nitza. *The Museums of Israel*. New York, 1989.

Sachar, Howard M. *A History of the Jews in America*. New York, 1992.

Salmon, Y. "Religious Zionism between Tradition and Modernity," *Jerusalem Quarterly*, Winter 1990.

Seiden, M. "Who Is a Jew?" *Forum*, Nos. 57–58, 1985–86.

Shechori, Ran. *Art in Israel*. Tel Aviv, 1974.

Sheffer, Gabriel. "The Elusive Question: Jews and Jewry in Israeli Foreign Policy," *Jerusalem Quarterly*, Spring 1988.

———. "The Uncertain Future of American Jewry–Israel Relations," *Jerusalem Quarterly*, Summer 1984.

Shohat, Ella. *Israeli Cinema*. Austin, Tex., 1989.

Silberman, Neil. *Between Past and Present: Archaeology, Ideology, and Nationalism in the Modern Middle East*. New York, 1989.

Silberstein, Laurence J., ed. *Jewish Fundamentalism in Comparative Perspective.* New York, 1993.

Somet, M. "Who Is a Jew? 1958–1977," *Jerusalem Quarterly,* Autumn 1986.

Sprinzak, Ehud. *The Ascendance of Israel's Radical Right.* New York, 1991.

Stock, Ernest. *Beyond Partnership: The Jewish Agency and the Diaspora, 1959–1971.* New York, 1992.

Stone, I. F. *Underground to Palestine and Reflections Thirty Years Later.* New York, 1978.

Swirski, Barbara. *Banot Havah, Banot Lilit: Al Chayei Nashim b'Yisrael* [Daughters of Eve, Daughters of Lilith: On the Life of Women in Israel]. Givatayim, 1984.

Syrkin, Marie. *The State of the Jews.* New York, 1980.

Weiler, Gershon. *Jewish Theocracy.* Leiden, Netherlands, 1988.

Weill, Asher. "Book Publishing in Israel," *Ariel,* Spring 1993.

Wigoder, Geoffrey. "Beth Ha-Tefutsoth," *Ariel,* Spring 1979.

Wolfsfield, Gad. *The Politics of Provocation: Participation and Protest in Israel.* Albany, N.Y., 1988.

Zehavi, Alex. "Israel's Literature of the Eighties," *Ariel,* Summer 1991.

VI. *The Era of Unity Governments*

Abu Fadal, M. "The Tail That Wagged the Dog: Tower Commission Spotlights Israel," *Middle East,* April 1987.

Adams, J. *Israel and South Africa: The Unnatural Alliance.* New York, 1985.

Alexander, Edward. "Operation Moses," *Commentary,* Nov. 1985.

Allen, David, and Alfred Pijpers, eds. *European Foreign Policy-Making and the Arab-Israel Conflict.* The Hague, 1984.

Avimor, S. "Israel's Relations with Southeast Asia," *Middle East Review,* No. 2, 1989–90.

Avraham, Shmuel. *Treacherous Journey: My Escape from Ethiopia.* New York, 1986.

Aynor, H. "Black Africa's Rediscovery of Israel," *Jerusalem Journal of International Relations,* Jan. 1990.

Bahbah, Bishara, with Linda Bahbah. *Israel and Latin America: The Military Connection.* New York, 1986.

Bahiri, Simcha. "Military and Colonial Aspects of the Israeli Economy since 1967," *New Outlook,* June 1987.

Bar-El, Raphael, ed. *Rural Industrialization in Israel.* Boulder, Colo., 1987.

Bar-Zohar, Michael. *Facing a Cruel Mirror.* New York, 1990.

Beit-Hallami, B. *The Israeli Connection: Who Israel Arms and Why.* New York, 1987.

Black, Ian, and Benny Morris. *Israel's Secret Wars: A History of Israel's Intelligence Services.* New York, 1991.

Bragman, A. "The Slowdown of Industrial Productivity," *Bank of Israel Economic Review,* No. 56, 1985.

Clark, B. "Israel's Science-Based Industries Come of Age," *Kidma,* No. 3, 1983.

Cohen, Yaacov. *Israel and the EEC, 1958–1977.* Tel Aviv, 1977.

Curtis, M. "Africa, Israel, and the Middle East," *Middle East Review,* No. 4, 1984.

Decter, M. "The Arms Traffic with South Africa," *Midstream,* Feb. 1977.

Doron, A. "The Histadrut, Social Policy, and Equality," *Jewish Quarterly,* No. 4, 1985.

Efrat, Elisha. *The Transformation of Israeli Society.* Boulder, Colo., 1985.

———. *Urbanization in Israel.* New York, 1984.

Elazar, Daniel, and Shmuel Sandler. *Israel's Odd Couple: The 1984 Knesset Elections and the National Unity Government.* Detroit, 1990.

Elenbogen, Dina. "From Moses to Solomon," *Midstream,* Dec. 1991.

Feuerwerger, Marvin C. *Congress and Israel: Foreign Aid Decision-Making in the House of Representatives, 1969–1976.* Westport, Conn., 1979.

Gavron, Daniel. *Israel after Begin.* Boston, 1984.

Golan, Matti. *Shimon Peres.* New York, 1982.

Goldfield, S. "Israel in Central America," *Strategic Studies,* Feb. 1986.

Gradus, Y., and R. Israelowitz. "The Negev: An Examination of Expectations and Realities," *Forum,* Nos. 57–58, 1985–86.

Gruber, Ruth. *Rescue: The Exodus of Ethiopian Jews.* New York, 1987.

Halper, J. "The Absorption of Ethiopian Immigrants," *Israel Social Science Research,* Jan. 1984.

Harmon, L. "COSTI: Israel's Centre of Scientific and Technological Information," *Kidma,* No. 4, 1980.

Hazan, R. "Peaceful Conflict Resolution in the Middle East: The Taba Negotiations," *Journal of the Middle East Studies Society,* Jan. 1988.

Hunter, Jane. *Israeli Foreign Policy: South Africa and Central America.* Boston, 1987.

Inbar, Efraim. "The Israeli Navy," *Naval War College Review,* Summer 1990.

Israel Economist. *Electronics—1985: High Technology and Science-Based Industries in Israel.* Jerusalem, 1985.

"Israel's Electronics Industry," *Israel Economist,* Nov.–Dec. 1980.

"Israel's Security Products Industry," *Israel Economist,* Nov.–Dec. 1980.

Jahbra, Joseph, and Nancy Jahbra. *Elusive Peace: The Collapse of the Lebanese-Israeli Troop Withdrawal Accord of 17 May 1983.* Toronto, 1985.

Jonas, George. *Vengeance.* New York, 1984.

Kievel, Gershon, ed. *Israeli National Security Policy.* New York, 1985.

———. *Party Politics in Israel and the Occupied Territories.* Westport, Conn., 1983.

Kievel, Gershon, and Bernard Reich, eds. *Israeli Politics in the 1990s.* Westport, Conn., 1991.

Kimche, Jon. *The Last Option.* New York, 1991.

King, E. "Solar Energy and Israel," *Jewish Frontier,* Dec. 1980.

Klieman, Aaron. *Israel's Global Reach: Arms Sales as Diplomacy.* New York, 1985.

Lake, J. "The Israel Defense Industry: An Overview," *Defense Electronics,* Sept. 1983.

Land, T. "Black Africa Poised to Restore Relations with Israel," *New Outlook,* March 1980.

Lanir, Zvi, ed. *Israeli Security Planning in the 1980s: Its Politics and Economics.* New York, 1984.

Lapidoth, R. "The Taba Controversy," *Jerusalem Quarterly,* Autumn 1986.

Lavie, Arie, and Robert L. Kuhn. *Industrial Research and Development in Israel: Patterns and Portents.* Westport, Conn., 1988.

Levenfeld, D. "Israel and Black Africa," *Midstream,* Feb. 1984.

Le Vine, V. "The African-Israeli Connection 40 Years Later," *Middle East Review,* No. 1, 1988.

Lissak, Moshe. *Israeli Society and Its Defense Establishment.* London, 1984.

Mahler, Gregory, ed. *Israel after Begin.* Albany, N.Y., 1990.

Marshall, J. "Israel, the Contras, and the North Trial," *MERIP Report,* Feb. 1989.

Melman, Yossi, and Dan Raviv. *The Imperfect Spies: The History of Israeli Intelligence.* London, 1989.

Mintz, Alex. "Arms Production in Jerusalem," *Jerusalem Quarterly,* Spring 1987.

Nacklemann, E. "Israel and Black Africa: A Rapprochement," *Journal of Modern African Studies,* No. 5, 1981.

Norton, A. "Occupational Risks and Planned Retirement: The Israeli Withdrawal from South Lebanon," *Middle East Insight,* March 1985.

Oded, A. "Africa, Israel, and the Arabs: On the Restoration of Israeli-African Diplomatic Relations," *Jerusalem Journal of International Relations*, No. 6, 1982.

Ojo, Olusola. *Africa and Israel: Relations in Perspective*. Boulder, Colo., 1988.

Ostrowsky, Victor. *By Way of Deception*. New York, 1990.

Peres, Shimon. *From These Men*. London, 1979.

———. "The Vision of Labor," *Jewish Frontier*, April 1982.

Peretz, Don, and Sammy Smooha. "Israel's Eleventh Knesset Election," *Middle East Journal*, Autumn 1985.

Peters, Joel. *Israel and Africa*. London, 1992.

Rapoport, Louis. *Redemption Song: The Story of Operation Moses*. New York, 1986.

Reiser, Stewart. *The Israeli Arms Industry*. New York, 1989.

Room, J. "Science and Development in Israel," *Kidma*, Jan.–April 1979.

Sanders, S. W. "Begin Leaves behind an Economic Mess," *Business Week*, Sept. 26, 1983.

Sandler, Shmuel. "Israel's 1988 Knesset Elections and the Transformation of the Israeli Polity," *Middle East Review*, No. 1, 1989/90.

Schiff, Ze'ev. "The Israel Defense Forces after Lebanon," *Middle East Insight*, Sept. 1985.

Schoenbaum, David. *The United States and the State of Israel*. New York, 1993.

Segev, Samuel. *The Iranian Triangle: The Untold Story of Israel's Role in the Iran-Contra Affair*. New York, 1988.

Sharkansky, Ira. *The Political Economy of Israel*. New Brunswick, N.J., 1987.

Sherman, Arnold, and Paul Hirschhorn. *Israel High Technology*. Jerusalem, 1984.

Sobhani, Sohrab. *The Pragmatic Entente: Israeli-Iranian Relations, 1948–1988*. New York, 1989.

Tabor, M. "Solar Energy Development in Israel," *Kidma*, May–Aug. 1979.

Tahiri, Amir. *Nest of Spies: America's Journey to Disaster in Iran*. New York, 1988.

"The Technion Looks to the Future," *Israel Economist*, June 1983.

Tower Commission Report. Washington, D.C., 1987.

Tschirgi, Dan. *The American Search for Mideast Peace*. Westport, Conn., 1989.

Vardi, J. "Energy in Israel," *Kidma*, Sept.–Dec. 1978.

Wagaw, Teshome G. "The Emigration and Settlement of Ethiopian Jews in Israel," *Middle East Review*, No. 1, 1987–88.

Winn, I., and A. Peranio. "Israel's Energy Dilemma," *Bulletin of the Atomic Scientists*, April 1980.

Ya'alon, D. "Soil Sciences in Israel, Past and Present," *Kidma*, Sept.–Dec. 1978.

Zahlan, Antoine. *Science and Higher Education in Israel*. Beirut, 1970.

Zussman, Pinchas. *Ma'arechet HaBitachon v'T'rumatah laKidmah HaTechnologit* [The Defense System and Its Contribution to Technological Advancement]. Tel Aviv, 1983.

VII. *The Wages of Immobilism*

Alexander, Jonah, and Joshua Suna. *Terrorism: The PLO Connection*. New York, 1989.

Alperson, Myra. "Pro-Israel PACs," *Present Tense*, Spring 1984.

Arian, Asher, and Michael Shamir. *The Elections in Israel, 1988*. Boulder, Colo., 1990.

Aulas, M. "The Daily Life of Palestinians," *Arab Studies Quarterly*, No. 6, 1984.

Avneri, Ariel. *David Levy* [in Hebrew]. Tel Aviv, 1983.

Bard, M. "Israel's Standing in American Public Opinion," *Commentary*, April 1985.

Bar-Zohar, Michael. *Facing a Cruel Mirror*. New York, 1990.

Bennis, Phyllis. *From Stones to Statehood: The Palestinian Uprising*. Brooklyn, N.Y., 1989.

Ben-Rafael, Eliezer. *Israel-Palestine: A Guerrilla Conflict in International Politics*. New York, 1987.

Ben-Zvi, Avraham. *The United States and Israel: The Limits of the Special Relationship.* New York, 1993.

Binur, Yoram. *My Enemy, My Self.* New York, 1989.

Branover, Herman. *HaDerech HaTzarah* [The Narrow Road]. Tel Aviv, 1984.

Clarke, Duncan L. "The PLO and the Intifada," *Middle East Journal,* Winter 1990.

Cohen, Roberta. *Soviet Jewish Emigration to Israel.* Washington, D.C., 1990.

Cohler, Larry. "Lobbying Congress Hard Going during Crisis," *Washington Jewish Week,* Mar. 10, 1988.

Dayan, Aryeh. "More Than We Can Handle," *New Outlook,* Jan.–Feb. 1990.

Dumper, Michael. "Israeli Settlement in the Old City of Jerusalem," *Journal of Palestine Studies,* No. 2, 1992.

Findley, Paul. *They Dare to Speak Out: People and Institutions Confront Israel's Lobby.* Westport, Conn., 1985.

Freedman, Robert O. "Religion, Politics, and the Israeli Elections of 1988," *Middle East Journal,* Winter 1989.

———. *Soviet Policy toward Israel under Gorbachev.* New York, 1991.

———, ed. *The Intifada: Its Impact on Israel, the Arab World, and the Superpowers.* Miami, Fla. 1991.

Gabriel, Judith. "The Economic Side of the *Intifadah,*" *Journal of Palestine Studies,* No. 4, 1988.

Gittelman, Zvi. *Becoming Israelis: The Political Resocialization of Soviet and American Immigrants.* Bloomington, Ind., 1984.

Goldberg, David H. *Foreign Policy and Ethnic Interest Groups: American and Canadian Jews Lobby for Israel.* Westport, Conn., 1990.

Green, Stephen. *Taking Sides: America's Secret Relations with Militant Israel.* New York, 1984.

Han, X. "Sino-Israeli Relations," *Journal of Palestine Studies,* No. 2, 1993.

Hefetz, Mikhail. "The Russian Press in Israel," *Ariel,* Spring 1993.

Hiltermann, Joost. *Behind the Intifada: Labor and Women's Movements in the Occupied Territories.* Princeton, N.J., 1991.

Hunter, F. Robert. *The Palestinian Uprisings.* Berkeley, Calif., 1991.

Inbar, Efraim. "Israel's Small War: The Military Response to the Intifada," *Armed Forces and Society,* No. 1, 1991.

Jerusalem Media and Communication Centre. *Soviet Jewish Immigration and Israeli Settlement in the West Bank and Gaza Strip.* Jerusalem, 1990.

Johnson, P., L. O'Brien, and J. Hiltermann. "The West Bank Rises Up," *Mid-East Reports,* No. 3, 1988.

Kaniuk, Yoram. "The Intifadah and the Peace Camp in Israel," *Journal of Palestine Studies,* No. 4, 1988.

Kelman, H. "The Palestinization of the Arab-Israeli Conflict," *Jerusalem Quarterly,* Winter 1988.

Kievel, Gershon, and Bernard Reich, eds. *Israeli Politics in the 1990s.* Westport, Conn., 1991.

Kimche, Jon. *The Last Option.* New York, 1991.

Klieman, Aaron. *Statecraft in the Dark: Israel's Practice of Quiet Diplomacy.* Boulder, Colo., 1988.

Ledeen, B., and M. Ledeen. "The Temple Mount Plot," *New Republic,* June 18, 1984.

Levy, G. "Hewers of Wood and Drawers of Water: Arab Workers in Israel," *New Outlook,* April 1985.

Melman, Yossi. *The New Israelis.* New York, 1992.

Melman, Yossi, and Dan Raviv. *Beyond the Uprising: Israelis, Jordanians, and Palestinians.* Westport, Conn., 1989.

Meron, Raphael. *The Economy of the Administered Areas, 1977–78.* Jerusalem, 1980.

Nakleh, Emile A. "The West Bank and Gaza: Twenty Years Later," *Middle East Journal,* Winter 1988.

Nazzal, L. "Demise of the Intifada?" *Israel and Palestine,* No. 161, 1990.

Negbi, M. "On Occupation, Intifada, and Constitutional Crisis in Israel," *Jerusalem Quarterly,* Summer 1989.

Peleg, Ilan, and Ofira Seliktar, eds. *The Emergence of a Binational Israel: The Second Republic in the Making.* Boulder, Colo., 1989.

Peretz, Don. *The West Bank: History, Politics, Society, and Economy.* Boulder, Colo., 1986.

Peretz, Don, and Sammy Smooha. "Israel's Twelfth Knesset Election: An All-Loser Game," *Middle East Journal,* Spring 1989.

Peteet, Julie M. *Gender in Crisis: Women and the Palestinian Resistance Movement.* New York, 1992.

Qurah, Nazih. "The Rise of Palestinian Revolutionary Cinema," *Palestine,* April 1983.

Rabie, Mohammed. *The Politics of Foreign Aid: U.S. Foreign Assistance and Aid to Israel.* New York, 1988.

Ro'i, Y. "The Historical Link between Soviet Domestic Developments and Jewish Emigration," *Jerusalem Quarterly,* Summer 1990.

Rouhana, Nadim. "The Political Transformation of the Palestinians in Israel: From Acquiescence to Challenge," *Journal of Palestine Studies,* No. 2, 1989.

Rubinstein, D. "The Political and Social Impact of the *Intifada* on Palestinian Arab Society," *Jewish Quarterly,* No. 2, 1989.

Ruby, Walter. "Whom Do the Pro-Israel PACs Help?" *Washington Jewish Week,* Oct. 30, 1986.

Sachar, Howard, M. *A History of the Jews in America.* New York, 1992.

Sandler, Shmuel. "Israel's 1988 Knesset Elections and the Transformation of the Israeli Polity," *Middle East Review,* No. 2, 1989.

Schiff, Ze'ev. "Israel after the [Gulf] War," *Foreign Affairs,* Feb. 1991.

Schiff, Ze'ev, and Ehud Ya'ari. *Intifada.* New York, 1990.

Shapira, Shimon. "The Origins of Hizballah," *Jerusalem Quarterly,* Spring 1988.

Sheetrit, Meir. "Russian Jews in Israel: The Housing Crisis," *Midstream,* Jan. 1991.

Shindler, Colin. *Ploughshares into Swords? Israelis and Jews in the Shadow of the Intifada.* London, 1991.

Sosebee, S. "The Palestinian Women's Movement and the Intifada," *American Arab Affairs,* No. 32, 1990.

Sullivan, A. "Palestinian Universities under Occupation," *Arab Studies Quarterly,* Nos. 3–4, 1990.

Wood, Pia Christina. "France and the Israeli-Palestinian Conflict: The Mitterrand Policies," *Middle East Journal,* Autumn 1993.

VIII. A Tormented Road to Peace. Breaking the Palestine Lockstep, An Appraisal at Half Century

Abed, George T. "The Palestinians and the Gulf Crisis," *Journal of Palestine Studies,* No. 43, 1991.

Almog, Z. "Israel's Naval Theater," *Israel Defense Forces Journal,* No. 2, 1986.

Alpher, J. "From Wagner to Arafat: Demonology and Survival," *Jerusalem Quarterly,* Autumn 1983.

Amir, Menachem. *P'shiah, Avaryanut, Meniah, v'Tikun b'Yisrael* [Crime; Delinquency, Prevention, and Rehabilitation in Israel]. Jerusalem, 1979.

Amirav, M., and H. Siniora. "Jerusalem: Resolving the Unresolvable," *International Spectator*, No. 3, 1992.

Arad, V. *The Mediterranean–Dead Sea Project*. Jerusalem, 1990.

Arad, V., and E. Rosenthal, eds. *Water in Israel, 1970–1982*. Tel Aviv, 1985.

Arens, Moshe. *Broken Covenant: American Foreign Policy and the Crisis between the United States and Israel*. New York, 1995.

Arian, Asher. "Israeli Democracy, 1984," *Jerusalem Journal of International Relations*, No. 2, 1985.

Arian, Asher, Ilan Talmud, and Tamar Hermann. *National Security and Public Opinion in Israel*. Boulder, Colo., 1988.

Ashkenazy, Daniella, ed. *The Military in the Service of Society and Democracy*. Westport, Conn., 1994.

Avineri, Shlomo. "The Impact of Changes in the Soviet Union and Eastern Europe in the Arab-Israeli Conflict," *Mediterranean Quarterly*, No. 1, 1991.

Avi-Ran, Reuven. "The Syrian Military-Strategic Interest in Lebanon," *Jerusalem Quarterly*, Spring 1988.

Avishai, Bernard. "Israel's Future: Brainpower, High Tech—and Peace," *Harvard Business Review*, Nov.–Dec. 1991.

Avnery, Uri. *My Friend, My Enemy*. Westport, Conn., 1986.

Benantar, A. "La question de l'eau dans les négotiations arabo-israéliennes," *Revue d'études Palestiniennes*, No. 47, 1993.

Benjamin, G. "Israel: Too Much Democracy?" *Midstream*, April 1977.

Ben-Meir, A. "The Israeli-Syrian Battle for Equitable Peace," *Middle East Policy*, No. 1, 1994.

Bensinger, Gad. *Justice in Israel: A Survey of Criminal Justice*. Chicago, 1989.

Berger, E. "A Tangled Web: Israel and the Gulf," *Arab Studies Quarterly*, Nos. 1–2, 1991.

Beschorner, N. "L'eau et le processus de paix israélo-arabe," *Politique Étrangère*, No. 4, 1992.

Brian, Asher, and Michael Samir, eds. *The Elections in Israel: 1992*. Albany, N.Y., 1995.

Brichta, A. "Forty Years of Struggle for Electoral Reform in Israel, 1948–1988," *Middle East Review*, No. 1, 1988.

Carmon, Yigal. "The Story behind the Handshake," *Commentary*, March 1984.

Caspi, D. "How Representative Is the Knesset?" *Jerusalem Quarterly*, Winter 1980.

Clarke, Duncan L. "The Arrow Missile: The United States, Israel, and Strategic Cooperation," *Middle East Journal*, Spring 1994.

Clarke, Duncan L., and Alan S. Cohen. "The United States, Israel, and the Lavi Fighter," *Middle East Journal*, Autumn 1985.

Cooley, J. J. "The War over Water," *Foreign Policy*, Summer 1979.

Corbin, Jane. *Gaza First: The Secret Norway Channel to Peace between Israel and the PLO*. London, 1994.

Dedein, David. "Ethnic Minority—or Fifth Column?" *Midstream*, May 1992.

Dellapergola, Sergio. "Mass Aliyah: A Thing of the Past?" *Jerusalem Quarterly*, Spring 1989.

Dillman, Jeffrey D. "Water Rights in the Occupied Territories," *Journal of Palestine Studies*, Autumn 1989.

Drezon-Tepler, Marcia. "Contested Waters and the Prospects for Arab-Israeli Peace," *Middle Eastern Studies*, April 1994.

Elizur, Dov. "Israelis in the United States," *American Jewish Yearbook*, Philadelphia, 1980.

Farid, Abdel Majid, and Hussein Sirriyeh, eds. *Israel and Arab Water*. London, 1985.

Felsenthal, D. "Aspects of Coalition Payoffs: The Case of Israel," *Comparative Political Studies*, July 1979.

Ferrari, Silvio. "The Vatican, Israel, and the Jerusalem Question (1943–1984)," *Middle East Journal*, Winter 1985.

Feuerwerger, Marvin C. *The Arrow Next Time? Israel's Missile Defense Program for the 1990s.* Washington, D.C., 1991.

Frenkel, H., and A. Meiri, eds. *Soil Salinity: Two Decades of Research in Irrigated Agriculture.* New York, 1985.

Friedberg, A., and A. Kfir. "Jewish Emigration from Israel," *Jewish Journal of Sociology*, Jan. 1988.

Friedlander, Dov, and Calvin Goldscheider. *The Population of Israel.* New York, 1979.

Friedman, Robert I. "The Brooklyn Avengers," *New York Review of Books,* June 23, 1994.

Garnham, D. "Explaining Middle Eastern Alignments during the Gulf War," *Jerusalem Journal of International Relations*, Autumn 1991.

Ghilan, M. "Madrid," *Israel and Palestine Political Reports,* No. 168, 1992.

Giniewski, Paul. "Demography—The Chief Arab Weapon," *Midstream*, Jan. 1988.

Golan, Gila. *Moscow and the Middle East: New Thinking on Regional Conflict.* London, 1992.

Goldstein, Jonathan. "Israel and the Great People of China Today," Midstream, Aug.–Sept. 1993.

Goodman, Hirsh, and W. Seth Carus. *The Future Battlefield and the Arab-Israeli Conflict.* New Brunswick, N.J., 1990.

Gowers, Andrew, and Tony Walker. *Behind the Myth: Yasser Arafat and the Palestinian Revolution.* New York, 1992.

Grinwald, Zvi. *Mayim b'Yisrael* [Water in Israel]. Tel Aviv, 1980.

Hadar, I. "The 1992 Electoral Earthquake and the Fall of the Second Israeli Republic," *Middle East Journal*, Autumn 1992.

Hoch, Gary. "The Politics of Water in the Middle East," *Middle East Insight,* March–April 1993.

Horowitz, Dan, and Moshe Lissak. "Democracy and Security in a Protracted Conflict," *Jerusalem Quarterly*, Summer 1989.

Hurwitz, Bruce A. "The Multilateral Peace Process," *Midstream*, Aug.–Sept. 1994.

Irani, George E. *The Papacy and the Middle East: The Role of the Holy See in the Arab-Israeli Conflict.* Notre Dame, Ind., 1986.

Israel. Ministry of Commerce and Industry. *Kivunim baMechkar HaHidrologit b'Yisrael* [Approaches to Hydrologic Research in Israel]. Jerusalem, 1981.

———. Ministry of Police. *The Prevention of Crime and the Treatment of Offenders in Israel.* Jerusalem, 1990.

Jaffee Center for Strategic Studies. *The Middle East Military Balance, 1992–1993.* Tel Aviv, 1994.

———. *War in the Gulf—Implications for Israel.* Tel Aviv, 1992.

Kally, Elisha, and Gideon Fishelson. *Water and Peace: Water Resources and the Arab-Israeli Peace Process.* Westport, Conn., 1993.

Kaplan, Steven, and Chaim Rosen. "Ethiopian Immigrants in Israel: Between Preservation of Culture and Invention of Tradition," *Jewish Journal of Sociology,* June 1993.

Klieman, Aaron, and Reuven Pedatzur. *Rearming Israel: Defense Procurement through the 1990s.* Boulder, Colo., 1992.

Krausz, Ernest. *Vatican Policy on the Palestinian-Israeli Conflict: The Struggle for the Holy Land.* Westport, Conn., 1990.

Kuttab, Daoud. "In the Aftermath of the War," *Journal of Palestine Studies*, No. 2, 1991.

Lehman-Wilzig, Sam. "Israel's 1992 Election: The Real Message," *Midstream*, Oct. 1992.

Leket, Y. "The Problem of Yerida," *Jewish Frontier,* Aug.–Sept. 1981.

Ma'oz, Moshe. "Syrian-Israeli Relations and the Middle East Peace Process," *Jerusalem Journal of International Law,* Spring 1992.

Melamed, Aharon. *No'ar b'Metzukah* [Youth in Distress]. Haifa, 1983.

Mendes, Meir. *HaVatikan v'Yisrael* [The Vatican and Israel]. Jerusalem, 1983.

Montoisy, J. "Israël-Vatican: Le nouveau dialogue," *Studia Diplomatica,* No. 6, 1981.

Murphy, Emma. "Structural Inhibitions to Economic Liberalization in Israel," *Middle East Journal,* Spring 1992.

Muslih, Muhammad. "The Golan: Israel, Syria, and Strategic Calculations," *Middle East Journal,* Summer 1993.

Ne'eman, Yuval. "The Water Which Flows Towards the Eastern Region," *Ariel,* Winter 1983.

Peres, Shimon. *Battling for Peace.* London, 1995.

Peres, Shimon, with Arye Na'or. *The New Middle East.* New York, 1993.

Peri, Yoram. *Between Battles and Ballots: The Israeli Military in Politics.* London, 1983.

Perry, Mark. *A Fire in Zion: The Israeli-Palestinian Search for Peace.* New York, 1994.

Rokach, Livia. *The Catholic Church and the Question of Palestine.* London, 1987.

Rolef, Susan Hattis. "The Ramon Affair," *Jewish Frontier,* May–June 1994.

Roy, Sara. *The Gaza Strip: A Demographic, Economic, Social, and Legal Survey.* Jerusalem, 1987.

Saltiel, M. "Is Israel a Democracy?" *Israel and Palestine,* No. 157, 1990.

Schiff, Ze'ev. "Israel after the [Gulf] War," *Foreign Affairs,* Feb. 1991.

———. "The Spectre of Civil War in Israel," *Middle East Journal,* Winter 1985.

Schnall, D. "Yored Is Also a Noun," *Midstream,* Feb. 1978.

Schwarzkopf, Norman. *It Doesn't Take a Hero.* New York, 1992.

Segal, G. "China and Israel: Pragmatic Politics," *SAIS Reviews,* No. 2, 1987.

Shakak, I. "The Israeli Elections of 1992: An Analysis," *Middle East Policy,* No. 3, 1992.

Shalev, Aryeh. *Israel and Syria: Peace and Security on the Golan.* Boulder, Colo., 1994.

Sharfman, Daphna. *Living without a Constitution: Civil Rights in Israel.* Armonk, N.Y., 1993.

Shoham, Shlomo. *Israel Studies in Criminology.* Vols. II, III. New Brunswick, N.J., 1976.

Shokeid, Moshe. *Children of Circumstances: Israeli Emigrants in New York.* Ithaca, N.Y., 1988.

Shuval, Hillel. "Le problème du partage de l'eau entre Israël et les Palestiniens: à la recherche d'une solution équitable," *Maghreb-Machrek,* 1992.

Sicherman, Harvey. *Palestinian Autonomy, Self-Government, and Peace.* Boulder, Colo., 1993.

Smooha, Sammy, and Don Peretz. "Israel's 1992 Knesset Elections: Are They Critical?" *Middle East Journal,* Spring 1993.

Sobel, Zvi. *Migrants from the Promised Land.* New Brunswick, N.J., 1986.

Soffer, A. "Demography in Eretz-Israel: 1988 and the Year 2000," *Jerusalem Quarterly,* Autumn 1989.

Sprinzak, Ehud. "Illegalism in Israeli Political Culture," *Jerusalem Quarterly,* Summer 1988.

Stock, Ernest. *HaZ'ramim HaDatiyim baGolah u'Shluchoteihem b'Yisrael* [The Religious Trends in the Diaspora and Their Constituent Groups in Israel]. Jerusalem, 1983.

Susser, Bernard, and Jacob Schreiber. "We the Israeli People: A Draft Constitution for Israel," *Midstream,* Aug.–Sept. 1988.

Tamari, Anita. *Sealed In: An Israeli Diary of the Gulf War.* Konstanz, 1991.

"Theoretical and Historical Footnotes," *Jerusalem Quarterly,* Summer 1988.

Van Leer Institute. *Echad m'Kol Shishah Yisraelim* [One of Every Six Israelis]. Jerusalem, 1981.

Waxman, C. "American Israelis in Judea and Samaria," *Middle East Review,* No. 2, 1982–83.

Yaniv, Avner. *Deterrence without the Bomb: The Politics of Israeli Strategy.* Lexington, Mass., 1987.

———. *Israel's Nuclear Dilemma.* Ithaca, N.Y., 1994.

Zamir, D. "Generals in Politics," *Jerusalem Quarterly,* Autumn 1981.

THE STRUGGLE FOR ISRAELI-PALESTINIAN COEXISTENCE

I. *A Tormented Road to Peace*

Abbas, Mahmoud. *Through Secret Channels: The Road to Oslo.* Reading, England, 1995.

Abed, George T. "The Palestinians and the Gulf Crisis," *Journal of Palestine Studies,* No. 43, 1991.

Arens, Moshe. *Broken Covenant: American Foreign Policy and the Crisis between the United States and Israel.* New York, 1995.

Avineri, Shlomo. "The Impact of Changes in the Soviet Union and Eastern Europe in the Arab-Israeli Conflict," *Mediterranean Quarterly,* No. 1, 1991.

Berger, E. "A Tangled Web: Israel and the Gulf," *Arab Studies Quarterly,* Nos. 1–2, 1991.

Brian, Asher, and Michael Samir, eds. *The Elections in Israel: 1992.* Albany, N.Y., 1995.

Carmon, Yigal. "The Story behind the Handshake," *Commentary,* March 1994.

Chaïbi, Denis. *Le droit humanitaire et les territoires sous occupation: Le cas des territoires palestiniens.* Louvain-la-Neuve, Belgium, 1993.

Clarke, D., and E. Flohr. "Christian Churches and the Palestine Question," *Journal of Palestine Studies,* No. 4, 1992.

Clinton, Bill. *My Life.* New York, 2004.

Corbin, Jane. *Gaza First: The Secret Norway Channel to Peace between Israel and the PLO.* London, 1994.

Cramer, Richard Ben. *How Israel Lost: The Four Questions.* New York, 1994.

Flamhaft, Ziva. *Israel on the Road to Peace: Accepting the Unacceptable.* Boulder, Colo., 1995.

Freedman, Robert O. "Israeli-Russian Relations since the Collapse of the Soviet Union," *Middle East Journal,* Spring 1995.

Garnham, D. "Explaining Middle Eastern Alignments during the Gulf War," *Jerusalem Journal of International Relations,* Autumn 1991.

Gazit, Shlomo. *Trapped Fools: Thirty Years of Israeli Policy in the Territories.* London, 2003.

Ghilan, M. "Madrid," *Israel and Palestine Political Reports,* No. 168, 1992.

Golan, Gila. *Moscow and the Middle East: New Thinking on Regional Conflict.* London, 1992.

Goldstein, Jonathan. "Israel and the Great People of China Today," *Midstream,* Aug.–Sept. 1993.

Gowers, Andrew, and Tony Walker. *Arafat: The Biography.* New York, 2005.

Hadar, I. "The Last Days of Likud: The American-Israeli Big Chill," *Journal of Palestine Studies,* No. 4, 1992.

———. "The 1992 Electoral Earthquake and the Fall of the Second Israeli Republic," *Middle East Journal,* Autumn 1992.

Hurwitz, Bruce A. "The Multilateral Peace Process," *Midstream,* Aug.–Sept. 1994.

Irani, George E. *The Papacy and the Middle East: The Role of the Holy See in the Arab-Israeli Conflict.* Notre Dame, Ind., 1986.

Jaffee Center for Strategic Studies. *The Middle East Military Balance, 1992–1993.* Tel Aviv, 1994.

————. *War in the Gulf—Implications for Israel.* Tel Aviv, 1992.

Klieman, Aaron. *Statecraft in the Dark: Israel's Practice of Quiet Diplomacy.* Boulder, Colo., 1988.

Kumaraswamy, P. R. "Israel-India Relations: Seeking Balance and Realism," *Israel Affairs,* Autumn/Winter 2004.

Kuttab, Daoud. "In the Aftermath of the [Gulf] War," *Journal of Palestine Studies,* No. 2, 1991.

Lehman-Wilzig, Sam. "Israel's 1992 Election: The Real Message," *Midstream,* Oct. 1992.

Lukacs, Yehuda. *Israel, Jordan, and the Peace Process.* Syracuse, N.Y., 1997.

Makovsky, David. *Making Peace with the PLO: The Rabin Government's Road to Oslo.* Boulder, Colo., 1996.

Miller, Rory. "The PLO Factor in Euro-Israeli Relations, 1964–1992," *Israel Affairs,* Autumn/Winter 2004.

Morag, N. "Unambiguous Ambiguity: The Opacity of the Oslo Peace Process," *Israel Affairs,* Summer 2000.

Pappé, Ilan. "A Palestinian State in Zionist and Israeli Thought," *Palestine-Israel Journal,* Autumn 1999.

Peres, Shimon. *Battling for Peace.* London, 1995.

Peres, Shimon, with Arye Na'or. *The New Middle East.* New York, 1993.

Perry, Mark. *A Fire in Zion: The Israeli-Palestinian Search for Peace.* New York, 1994.

Reich, Bernard, Noah Dropkin, and Meyrav Wurmser. "Soviet Jewish Immigration and the Palestinian Revolution," *Middle East Journal,* Summer 1993.

Rubinstein, Elyakim. *The Peace between Israel and Jordan: An Anatomy of Negotiations.* Tel Aviv, 1996.

Sachar, Howard M., *Israel and Europe: An Appraisal in History.* New York, 1999.

Savir, Uri. *The Process.* New York, 1998.

Schiff, Ze'ev. "Israel after the [Gulf] War," *Foreign Affairs,* Feb. 1991.

Schwarzkopf, Norman. *It Doesn't Take a Hero.* New York, 1992.

Segal, G. "China and Israel: Pragmatic Politics," *SAIS Reviews,* No. 2, 1987.

Shakak, I. "The Israeli Elections of 1992: An Analysis," *Middle East Policy,* No. 3, 1992.

Shamir, Yitzchak. *Summing Up: An Autobiography.* London, 1994.

Sicherman, Harvey. *Palestinian Autonomy, Self-Government, and Peace.* Boulder, Colo., 1993.

Silver, Hillary Wollpert, Simcha Bahiri, and Ronen Sacher. *The Economy of Jordan and Possibilities for Economic Cooperation between Israel and Jordan: An Overview.* Tel Aviv, 1989.

Smooha, Sammy, and Don Peretz. "Israel's 1992 Knesset Elections: Are They Critical?" *Middle East Journal,* Spring 1993.

Tamari, Anita. *Sealed In: An Israeli Diary of the Gulf War.* Konstanz, 1991.

Vassiliev, Alexei. *Russian Policy in the Middle East: From Messianism to Pragmatism.* Reading, England, 1993.

Waage, Hilde Henriksen. "Explaining the Oslo Back Channel: Norway's Political Past in the Middle East," *Middle East Journal,* Autumn 2002.

Welch, D. "The Politics and Psychology of Restraint: Israeli Decision-Making in the Gulf War," *International Journal,* No. 2, 1992.

World Bank. *Developing the Occupied Territories: An Investment in Peace.* Vols. I–VI. Washington, D.C., 1993.

Zak, Moshe. *Arbaim Sh'not Dusiach im Moskva* [A Forty-Year Dialogue with Moscow]. Ramat Gan, 1996.

II. A Deterioration of the Rabin-Peres Legacy

Arens, Moshe. *Broken Covenant: American Foreign Policy and the Crisis between the United States and Israel.* New York, 1995.

Avi-Ran, Reuven. "The Syrian Military-Strategic Interest in Lebanon," *Jerusalem Quarterly,* Spring 1988.

Barnea, Tamara, et al., eds. *Israeli-Palestinian Cooperation in the Health Field, 1994–1998.* Jerusalem, 2000.

Beilin, Yossi. *Touching Peace: From the Oslo Accord to a Final Agreement.* London, 1999.

Ben-Meir, A. "The Israeli-Syrian Battle for Equitable Peace," *Middle East Policy,* No. 1, 1994.

Bentsur, Eytan. *Making Peace: A First-Hand Account of the Arab-Israeli Peace Process.* Westport, Conn., 2001.

Bickerton, Ian J., and Carla L. Klausner. *A Concise History of the Arab-Israeli Conflict.* 3rd ed. Upper Saddle River, N.J., 1998.

Breger, Marshall L., and Thomas Idinopolis. *Jerusalem's Holy Places and the Peace Process.* Washington, D.C., 1998.

Ciment, James. *Palestine/Israel: The Long Conflict.* New York, 1997.

Clinton, Bill. *My Life.* New York, 2004.

Cobban, Helena. *The Israeli-Syrian Peace Talks: 1991–96 and Beyond.* Washington, D.C., 1999.

Dumper, Michael. *The Politics of Jerusalem since 1967.* New York, 1997.

———. *The Politics of Sacred Space: The Old City of Jerusalem in the Middle East Conflict.* Boulder, Colo., 2002.

Elon, Amos. *Jerusalem: City of Mirrors.* Boston, 1989.

European Parliament. Directorate-General for Research. *The Middle East Peace Process and the European Union.* Brussels, 1999.

Ezrahi, Yoram. *Rubber Bullets: Power and Conscience in Modern Israel.* New York, 1997.

Gazit, Shlomo. *Trapped Fools: Thirty Years of Israeli Policy in the Territories.* London, 2003.

Gold, Dore. *Israel as a Non-NATO Ally: Parameters of Defense-Industrial Cooperation in a Post–Cold War Relationship.* Boulder, Colo., 1993.

Gorenberg, Gershom. *The End of Days: Fundamentalism and the Struggle for the Temple Mount.* New York, 2000.

Gresh, Alain. *The PLO, the Struggle Within: Towards an Independent Palestinian State.* Atlantic Highlands, N.J., 1988.

Haj, Majid al-. "The Impact of the Intifada on the Arabs in Israel: The Case of Double Periphery," in A. Cohen and G. Wolfsfeld, eds., *Framing the Intifada: Media and People.* Englewood Cliffs, N.J., 1993.

Kadri, Ali. "A Survey of Commuting Labor from the West Bank to Israel," *Middle East Journal,* Autumn 1998.

Kammer, Reuven. *The Politics of Protest: The Israeli Peace Movement and the Palestinian Intifada.* Brighton, England, 1996.

Karsh, Efraim. *Arafat's War.* New York, 2003.

Klein, Menachem. *Jerusalem: The Contested City.* New York, 2001.

Kober, Avi. *Coalition Defection: The Dissolution of Arab Anti-Israel Coalitions in War and Peace.* Westport, Conn., 2002.

Levy, Gid'on. *Ezor HaDimdumim* [Twilight Zone: Life and Death under Israeli Occupation, 1988–2003]. Tel Aviv, 2004.

Ma'oz, Moshe. "From Conflict to Peace? Israel's Relations with Syria and the Palestinians," *Middle East Journal,* Summer 1999.

————. *Suria v'Yisrael* [Syria and Israel]. Tel Aviv, 1996.

————. "Syrian-Israeli Relations and the Middle East Peace Process," *Jerusalem Journal of International Relations,* Summer 1992.

Matar, I. "Israeli Policy in Jerusalem: A Chronology of Dispossession," *Palestine-Israel Journal,* Nos. 3–4, 2000.

Muslih, Muhammad. "The Golan: Israel, Syria, and Strategic Calculations," *Middle East Journal,* Summer 1993.

Netanyahu, Binyamin. *A Durable Peace: Israel and Its Place among the Nations.* New York, 2000.

Neuberger, B. "The Arab Minority in Israeli Politics: From Marginality to Influence," *Foreign Policy,* No. 3, 1995.

Peleg, Ilan. *Human Rights in the West Bank and Gaza: Legacy and Politics.* Syracuse, N.Y., 1995.

Peres, Shimon, with Arye Na'or. *The New Middle East.* New York, 1993.

Peretz, Don, and Gideon Doron. "Israel's 1996 Elections: A Second Political Earthquake," *Middle East Journal,* Winter 1996.

Rabinovich, Itamar. *The Brink of Peace: The Israeli-Syrian Negotiations.* Princeton, N.J., 1998.

Rekhess, E. "Resurgent Islam in Israel," *Foreign Policy,* No. 3, 1995.

Ross, Dennis. *The Missing Peace: The Inside Story of the Fight for Middle East Peace.* New York, 2003.

Sachar, Howard M. *Israel and Europe: An Appraisal in History.* New York, 1999.

Sadeh, Tal. "Some Trade Effects of the EMU Process on Israel," *Israel Affairs,* Autumn/Winter 2004.

Seale, Patrick. "Syria and Israel: No Progress Towards Peace," *Middle East International,* Dec. 1997.

Shalev, Aryeh. *Israel and Syria: Peace and Security on the Golan.* Boulder, Colo., 1994.

Shaoul, Raquel. "Japan and Israel: An Evaluation of Relationship-Building in the Context of Japan's Middle East Policy," *Israel Affairs,* Autumn/Winter 2004.

Slonim, Shlomo. *Jerusalem in American Foreign Policy, 1947–1997.* The Hague, 1998.

Smooha, Sammy. *The Orientation and the Politicization of the Arab Minority in Israel.* Haifa, 1984.

Tovias, Alfred. "From Twelve to Fifteen: The Impact of the Last European Union's Enlargement on Israel's Political Economy," *Israel Affairs,* Winter 1995.

Wasserstein, Bernard. *Divided Jerusalem: The Struggle for the Holy City.* New Haven, Conn., 2001.

Zertal, Idith, and Akiva Eldar. *Adone HaArets: HaMitnahalim u-medinat Yisrael, 1967–2004.* Tel Aviv, 2005.

Zilberfarb, Ben-Zion. "The Israeli Economy in the 1990s: Immigration, the Peace Process and the Medium-Term Prospects for Growth," *Israel Affairs,* Autumn 1996.

Zisser, Eyal. *HaSuria shel Assad b'Hitztalvut* [Assad's Syria at a Crossroads]. Tel Aviv, 1999.

III. *Ehud Barak's Two Years*

Assaraf, Robert. *Drame d'Israël: De la paix à la guerre.* Paris, 2001.

Avi-Ran, Reuven. "The Syrian Military-Strategic Interest in Lebanon," *Jerusalem Quarterly,* Spring 1998.

Beilin, Yossi. *Touching Peace: From the Oslo Accord to a Final Agreement.* London, 1999.

Bentsur, Eytan. *Making Peace: A First-Hand Account of the Arab-Israeli Peace Process.* Westport, Conn., 2001.

Benzimon, Uri. *Sharon: An Israeli Caesar.* New York, 1985.

Bucaille, Laetitia. *La violence de la paix: La violence arabe-israëlienne en Gaza et Palestine*. Paris, 1998.

Clawson, Patrick, and Zoë Danon. *Dollars and Diplomacy: The Impact of U.S. Initiatives on Arab-Israeli Negotiations*. Washington, D.C., 1999.

Clinton, Bill. *My Life*. New York, 2004.

Cobban, Helena. *The Israeli-Syrian Peace Talks: 1991–96 and Beyond*. Washington, D.C., 1999.

Elazar, Daniel J., and M. Ben Mollov. "Introductions: Elections 1999—The Interplay Between Character, Political Culture and Centrism," *Israel Affairs*, Winter/Spring 2001.

Feiler, Gil, and Simon Lassman. "The House of Assad's Capitalism of Convenience: Economics as a Political Weapon," in Elie Podek and Asher Kaufman, eds., *Essays in Honour of Moshe Ma'oz*. Sussex, England, 2006.

Fischbach, Michael A. *Records of Dispossession: Palestine Refugee Property and the Arab-Israeli Conflict*. New York, 2003.

Gerges, F. A. "Israel's Retreat from South Lebanon," *Middle East Policy*, No. 8, 2001.

Gilbar, Gad, and Onn Winckler. "The Economic Factor of the Arab-Israeli Peace Process: The Cases of Egypt, Jordan, and Syria," in Elie Podek and Asher Kaufman, eds., *Essays in Honour of Moshe Ma'oz*. Sussex, England, 2006.

Hanieh, Akram. "The Camp David Papers," *Journal of Palestine Studies*, Winter 2001.

Harel, Amos, and Avik Isacharoff. *HaMilchama HaShivit* [The Seventh War]. Tel Aviv, 2004.

Howe, Stephen. "The Israeli Left," *New Statesman*, Dec. 9, 2002.

Ma'oz, Moshe. "From Conflict to Peace? Israel's Relations with Syria and the Palestinians," *Middle East Journal*, Summer 1999.

———. *Suria v'Yisrael* [Syria and Israel]. Tel Aviv, 1996.

Morris, Benny. *The Birth of the Arab Refugee Problem Revisited*. Cambridge, England, 2004.

Muslih, Muhammad. "The Golan: Israel, Syria, and Strategic Calculations," *Middle East Journal*, Summer 1993.

Peretz, Don, and Gideon Doron. "Sectarian Politics and the Peace Process: The 1999 Israeli Elections," *Middle East Journal*, Winter 2000.

Podek, Elie, and Asher Kaufman, eds. *Essays in Honour of Moshe Ma'oz*. Sussex, England, 2006.

Rabil, Robert. "The Ineffective Role of the U.S. in the U.S.-Israeli-Syrian Relationship," *Middle East Journal*, Summer 2001.

Rabinovich, Itamar. *The Brink of Peace: The Israeli-Syrian Negotiations*. Princeton, N.J., 1998.

———. "The Evolution of U.S.-Israeli-Syrian Peace Negotiations," in Elie Podek and Asher Kaufman, eds., *Essays in Honour of Moshe Ma'oz*. Sussex, England, 2006.

———. *Waging Peace: Israel and the Arabs, 1938–2003*. New York, 2003.

Ross, Dennis. *The Missing Peace: The Inside Story of the Fight for Middle East Peace*. New York, 2003.

Rubinstein, Dani, et al. *Kemp Daivid 2000: Mah b'emet karah sham?* [Camp David 2000: What Actually Happened There?]. Tel Aviv, 2000.

Sharon, Ariel, with David Chanoff. *Warrior: An Autobiography*. New York, 1989.

Shikaki, Khalil. "Refugees and the Legitimacy of Palestinian-Israeli Peace-Making," in Elie Podek and Asher Kaufman, eds., *Essays in Honour of Moshe Ma'oz*. Sussex, England, 2006.

Shindler, Colin. *Israel, Likud and the Zionist Dream: Power, Politics and Ideology from Begin to Netanyahu*. London, 1995.

Zisser, Eyal. *HaSuria shel Assad b'Hitztalvut* [Assad's Syria at a Crossroads]. Tel Aviv, 1999.

IV. **Ariel Sharon as Prime Minister and Statesman**

Almog, Don. "The West Bank Fence: A Vital Component in Israel's Strategy of Defense," *Washington Institute for Near East Policy*, Feb. 2004.

Arnon, A., I. Luski, A. Spivak, and J. Weinblatt. *The Palestinian Economy: Between Imposed Integration and Voluntary Separation*. Leiden, Netherlands, 1997.

Assaraf, Robert. *Le drame d'Israël: De la paix à la guerre*. Paris, 2001.

Beilin, Yossi. *The Path to Geneva: The Quest for a Permanent Agreement*. London, 2004.

Borenstein, Avram. *Crossing the Green Line: Between the West Bank and Israel*. Philadelphia, 2002.

Della Pergola, Sergio. *Demography in Israel/Palestine: Trends, Prospects, Political Implications*. Jerusalem, 2000.

Enderlin, Charles. *Shattered Dreams: The Failure of the Peace Process in the Middle East*. New York, 2003.

Eytan, Freddy. *Ariel Sharon: A Life in Times of Turmoil*. Plattsburgh, N.Y., 2006.

Ezrahi, Yoram. *Rubber Bullets: Power and Conscience in Modern Israel*. New York, 1997.

Hafez, Nvi, and Gadi Bloom. *Ariel Sharon: A Life*. New York, 2006.

Harel, Amos, and Avi Isacharoff. *HaMilchama HaShivit* [The Seventh War]. Tel Aviv, 2004.

Hass, Amira. *Drinking the Sea at Gaza: Days and Nights in a Land under Siege*. New York, 1999.

Kadri, Ali. "A Survey of Commuting Labor from the West Bank to Israel," *Middle East Journal*, Autumn 1998.

Karsh, Efraim. *Arafat's War*. New York, 2003.

————. *Fabricating Israeli History: The "New Historians."* London, 1997.

Kimmerling, Baruch. *Politicide: Ariel Sharon's War against the Palestinians*. New York, 2001.

Kober, Avi. "Arab Perceptions of Post–Cold War Israel: From a Balance of Threats to a Balance-of-Power Thinking," *Review of International Affairs*, Summer 2002.

Levitt, Matthew. *Politics, Charity, and Terrorism in the Service of Jihad*. New Haven, Conn., 2006.

Levy, Gid'on. *Ezor HaDimdumim* [Twilight Zone: Life and Death under Israeli Occupation]. Tel Aviv, 2004.

Lustik, Ian. "To Build and to Be Built By: Israel and the Hidden Logic of the Iron Wall," *Israel Studies*, Spring 1996.

Makovsky, David. "A Defensible Fence: Fighting Terror and Enabling a Two-State Solution," *Washington Institute for Near East Policy*, April 2004.

Miller, Anita, Jordan Miller, and Sigalit Zetouni. *Sharon: Israel's Warrior-Politician*. Chicago, 2002.

Peretz, Don, Rebecca Kook, and Gideon Doron. "Knesset Elections 2003: Why Likud Regained Dominance and Labor Continued to Fade Out," *Middle East Journal*, Autumn 2003.

Samuels, David. "In a Ruined Country," *Atlantic Monthly*, Sept. 2005.

Susser, Leslie. "The Privatization of Peacemaking," *Jerusalem Report*, Aug. 26, 2002.

Zertal, Idith, and Akiva Eldar. *Adonei HaAretz: HaMitnachlim u'Medinat Yisrael, 1967–2004* [Lords of the Land: The Settlers and the State of Israel, 1967–2004]. Tel Aviv, 2005.

V. **Israel Faces the Twenty-first Century**

Alcalay, Ammiel, ed. *Keys to the Garden: New Israeli Writing*. San Francisco, 1996.

Alter, Robert. *Hebrew and Modernity*. Indianapolis, Ind., 1994.

Arad, V. *The Mediterranean–Dead Sea Project*. Jerusalem, 1990.

Arian, Asher. *The Second Republic: Politics in Israel*. Chatham, N.J., 1998.

Ashkenazy, Daniella, ed. *The Military in the Service of Society and Democracy*. Westport, Conn., 1994.

Barak, Aharon. *The Judge in a Democracy*. Princeton, N.J., 2006.

Bar-On, Mordechai. *In Pursuit of Peace: A History of the Israeli Peace Movement*. Washington, D.C., 1996.

Benantar, A. "La question de l'eau dans les négotiations arabo-israéliennes," *Revue d'études Palestiniennes*, No. 47, 1993.

Ben-Bassat, Avi. *The Israeli Economy, 1985–1998: From Government Intervention to Market Economics*. Cambridge, Mass., 2002.

Benita, E., and G. Noam. "The Absorption of Ethiopian Immigrants," *Israel Social Science Review*, No. 10, 1995.

Beschornar, N. "L'eau et le processus de paix israélo-arabe," *Politique Étrangère*, No. 4, 1992.

Borthwick, Bruce. "Water in Israeli-Jordanian Relations: From Conflict to the Danger of Ecological Disaster," *Israel Affairs*, Spring 2003.

Brichta, Avraham. *Political Reform in Israel: The Quest for Stable and Effective Government*. Brighton, England, 2001.

B'Tselem. "The Settlement Process: A Study in Illegality," *Palestine-Israel Journal*, Nos. 3–4, 2000.

Caplan, Neil. "Israeli Historiography: Beyond the 'New Historians,'" *Israel Affairs*, Winter 1995.

Carey, Roane, and Jonathan Shainin, eds. *The Other Israel: Voices of Refusal and Dissent*. New York, 2002.

Cohen, H. A., and S. Plaut. "Quenching the Levant's Thirst," *Middle East Quarterly*, No. 3, 1995.

Dedein, David. "Ethnic Minority—or Fifth Column?" *Midstream*, May 1992.

Dor, Moshe. *The Stones Remember: Native Israeli Poetry*. Washington, D.C., 1991.

Doron, Abraham. "Social Welfare Policy in Israel: Developments in the 1980s and 1990s," *Israel Affairs*, Summer 2001.

Drezon-Tepler, Marcia. "Contested Waters and the Prospects for Arab-Israeli Peace," *Middle East Studies*, No. 2, 1994.

Edelman, M. "The New Israeli Constitution," *Middle East Studies*, Autumn 2000.

Emusa, Sharif C. *The Water Issue and the Palestinian-Israeli Conflict*. Washington, D.C., 1993.

Ezrahi, Yoram. *Rubber Bullets: Power and Conscience in Modern Israel*. New York, 1997.

Farid, Abdel Majid, and Hussein Sirriyeh, eds. *Israel and Arab Water*. London, 1985.

Fuchs, Esther. *Israeli Mythogynies: Women in Contemporary Hebrew Fiction*. Albany, N.Y., 1987.

Ghanem, As'ad. *The Palestine Arab Minority in Israel, 1948–2000*. Albany, N.Y., 2001.

Goldstein, Douglas. *Building Wealth in Israel: A Guide to International Investment and Financial Planning*. Jerusalem, 2006.

Grossman, David. *Death as a Way of Life: From Oslo to the Geneva Agreement*. London, 2003.

Hacohen, Dvora. "Mass Immigration and the Demographic Revolution in Israel," *Israel Affairs*, Autumn 2002.

Haddad, Marwin, Eran Feitelson, and Taher Nasseredin. *Joint Management of Shared Aquifers: Final Report of Phase II*. Washington, D.C., 1998.

Haidar, Aziz. *On the Margins: The Arab Population in the Israeli Economy*. London, 1995.

Hall-Cathala, David. *The Peace Movement in Israel, 1967–87*. New York, 1990.

Hillel, Daniel. *Rivers of Eden: The Struggle for Water and the Quest for Peace in the Middle East*. New York, 1994.

Hoch, Gary. "The Politics of Water in the Middle East," *Middle East Insight*, Mar.–Apr. 1993.

Inbar, Efraim. *The Israeli-Turkish Strategic Partnership*. Ramat Gan, 2003.

Joseph, Herbert S., ed. *Modern Israeli Drama: An Anthology*. Rutherford, N.J., 1983.

Kahan, David. *Agriculture and Water Resources in the West Bank and Gaza, 1967–1987*. Jerusalem, 1987.

Kally, Elisha, and Gideon Fishelson. *Water and Peace: Water Resources and the Arab-Israeli Peace Process*. Westport, Conn., 1993.

Kammer, Reuven. *The Politics of Protest: The Israeli Peace Movement and the Palestinian Intifada*. Brighton, England, 1996.

Kaplan, Steven, and Chaim Rosen. "Ethiopian Immigrants in Israel: Between Preservation of Culture and Invention of Tradition," *Jewish Journal of Sociology*, June 1993.

Karsh, Efraim, and Dan Urian, eds. *In Search of Identity: Jewish Aspects in Israeli Culture*. London, 1999.

Landau, Jacob. *The Arab Minority in Israel, 1960–1991: Political Aspects*. Oxford, 1993.

Liel, A. "Turkish Water: Bringing Peace to the Middle East," *Insight Turkey*, Vol. 2. 1999.

Lissak, Moshe, and Eli Leshem. "The Russian Intelligentsia in Israel: Between Ghettoization and Integration," *Israel Affairs*, Winter 1995.

Litwin, Howard. *Uprooted in Old Age: Soviet Jews and Their Social Networks in Israel*. Westport, Conn., 1995.

Lowi, Miriam R. *Water and Power: The Politics of a Scarce Resource in the Jordan River Basin*. Cambridge, England, 1994.

Margalit, Avishai. *Jews in Review: Politics and Culture in the State of the Jews*. New York, 1998.

Menahem, Gila. "Water Policy in Israel, 1948–2000: Policy Paradigms, Policy, Networks and Public Policy," *Israel Today*, Summer 2001.

Mintz, Alan L., ed. "The Boom in Contemporary Israeli Fiction," *Jerusalem Report*, Oct. 15, 1997.

———, ed. *Reading Hebrew Literature: Critical Discussion of Six Modern Texts*. Hanover, N.H., 2002.

Morris, Benny. *Righteous Victims: A History of the Zionist-Arab Conflict, 1881–1999*. New York, 1999.

Murphy, Emma. "Structural Inhibitions to Economic Liberalization in Israel," *Middle East Journal*, Spring 1992.

Neuberger, B. "The Arab Minority in Israeli Politics: From Marginality to Influence," *Foreign Policy*, No. 3, 1995.

Rae, Douglas W. *The Political Consequences of Electoral Laws*. 2nd ed. New Haven, Conn., 1971.

Ramraz-Ra-Ukh, Gita. *The Arab in Israeli Literature*. Bloomington, Ind., 1989.

Rouyer, A. R. "The Water Accords of Oslo II: Averting a Looming Disaster," *Middle East Policy*, Vol. 7. 1999.

Saltiel, M. "Is Israel a Democracy?" *Israel and Palestine*, No. 157, 1990.

Schake, Korni N., and Judith S. Yaphe. "The Strategic Implications of a Nuclear-Armed Iran," *Institute for National Strategic Studies*, 2001.

Schnell, Izhak, Michael Sofer, and Israel Drori. *Arab Industrialization in Israel*. Westport, Conn., 1995.

Shaheen, M. "Questioning the Water-War Phenomenon in the Jordan Basin," *Middle East Policy*, Vol. 7. 2000.

Shaked, Gershon. *Hebrew Writers: A General Directory*. Tel Aviv, 1997.

———. *Modern Hebrew Fiction, 1880–1980*. Bloomington, Ind., 2000.

Shapland, Greg. *Rivers of Discord: International Water Disputes in the Middle East*. New York, 1997.

Sharfman, Daphna. *Living without a Constitution: Civil Rights in Israel*. Armonk, N.Y., 1993.

Starr, Joyce R., and Daniel C. Stoll, eds. *The Politics of Scarcity: Water in the Middle East.* Washington, D.C., 1988.

Wagaw, Teshome G. *For Our Soul: Ethiopian Jews in Israel.* Detroit, 1993.

Wolkinson, Benjamin W. *Arab Employment in Israel: The Quest for Equal Employment Opportunity.* London, 1999.

Yaish, Meir. "Class Structure in a Deeply Divided Society: Class and Ethnic Equality in Israel," *British Journal of Sociology,* Sept. 2001.

Yona, Amnon. *Missions with No Traces: Sixty Years of Israeli Underground National Security.* Jerusalem, 2001.

Yudkin, Leon. *Public Crisis and Literary Response: The Adjustment of Modern Jewish Literature.* London, 2001.

VI.   A Mottled Landscape; A Middle Eastern Hour of Decision

Amir, Menachem. *P'shiah, Avaryanut, Meniah, v'Tikun b'Yisrael* [Crime, Delinquency, Prevention, and Rehabilitation in Israel]. Jerusalem, 1979.

Amirav, M., and H. Siniora. "Jerusalem: Resolving the Unresolvable," *International Spectator,* No. 3, 1992.

Bensinger, Gad. *Justice in Israel: A Survey of Criminal Justice.* Chicago, 1989.

Breger, Marshall L., and Thomas A. Indinopolis. *Jerusalem's Holy Places and the Peace Process.* Washington, D.C., 1998.

Cheshin, Amir, Bill Hutman, and Avi Melamed. *Separate and Unequal: The Inside Story of Israeli Rule in East Jerusalem.* Cambridge, Mass., 1999.

Clarke, Duncan L. "The Arrow Missile: The United States, Israel, and the Lavi Fighter," *Middle East Journal,* Spring 1994.

Cohen, Asher, and Bernard Susser. *Israel and the Politics of Jewish Identity: The Secular-Religious Impasse.* Baltimore, 2000.

Cohen, Avner. *Israel and the Bomb.* New York, 1998.

———. *The Opaque Bomb: The Political History of the Israeli Nuclear Bomb.* New York, 1996.

Cohen, S. A. "Military Service in Israel: No Longer a Cohesive Force?" *Jewish Journal of Sociology,* Nos. 1–2, 1997.

Cramer, Richard Ben. *How Israel Lost: The Four Questions.* New York, 2004.

Dowek, Ephraim. *Israeli-Egyptian Relations, 1980–2000.* London, 2001.

Dumper, Michael. *The Politics of Jerusalem since 1967.* New York, 1997.

———. *The Politics of Sacred Space: The Old City of Jerusalem in the Middle East Conflict.* Boulder, Colo., 2002.

Feuerwerger, Marvin C. *The Arrow Next Time? Israel's Missile Defense Program for the 1990s.* Washington, D.C., 1991.

Friedberg, A., and A. Kfir. "Jewish Emigration from Israel," *Jewish Journal of Sociology,* Jan. 1988.

Friedland, Roger, and Richard Hecht. *To Rule Jerusalem.* Cambridge, England, 2006.

Friedman, Robert I. "The Brooklyn Avengers," *New York Review of Books,* June 23, 1994.

Goldberg, David H. *Foreign Policy and Ethnic Interest Groups: American and Canadian Jews Lobby for Israel.* Westport, Conn., 1990.

Gorenberg, Gershom. *The End of Days: Fundamentalism and the Struggle for the Temple Mount.* New York, 2000.

Hazoni, Yoram. *The Jewish State: The Struggle for Israel's Soul.* New York, 2001.

Israel Ministry of Police. *The Prevention of Crime and the Treatment of Offenders in Israel.* Jerusalem, 1990.

Kimmerling, Baruch. "Between Hegemony and Dormant *Kulturkampf* in Israel," *Israel Affairs*, Spring/Summer 1998.

Klein, Menachem. *Jerusalem: The Contested City*. New York, 2001.

Kook, Rebecca, Michael Harris, and Gideon Doron. "In the Name of G-D and Our Rabbi: The Politics of the Ultra-Orthodox in Israel," *Israel Affairs*, Autumn 1998.

Liebman, Charles S. *Religion, Democracy, and Israeli Society*. Amsterdam, 1997.

Melamed, Aharon. *No'ar b'Metzukah* [Youth in Distress]. Haifa, 1983.

Mishal, Shaul, and Avraham Sela. *The Palestinian Hamas*. New York, 2000.

Mittelberg, David. *The Israeli Connection and American Jews*. Westport, Conn., 1999.

Negbi, Moshe. *K'Sdom Hayinu: Ba'Midron mi'M'dinat Chok LaRepublikat Bananot* [We Were Like Sodom: Down the Slope from a Law-Abiding State to a Banana Republic]. Tel Aviv, 2004.

Ravitzky, Eliezer. *Religious and Secular Jews in Israel*. Jerusalem, 1997.

———. *Zionism and Jewish Religious Radicalism*. Chicago, 1996.

Shahak, Israel. *Open Secrets: Israeli Nuclear and Foreign Policies*. London, 1997.

Shahak, Israel, and Norton Mezvinsky. *Jewish Fundamentalism in Israel*. London, 1999.

Sharkansky, Ira. *The Politics of Religion and the Religion of Politics: Looking at Israel*. Lanham, Md., 2001.

Shoham, Shlomo. *Israel Studies in Criminology*. Vols. II, III. New Brunswick, N.J., 1976.

Shokeid, Moshe. *Children of Circumstances: Israeli Emigrants in New York*. Ithaca, N.Y., 1988.

Sobel, Zvi. *Migrants from the Promised Land*. New Brunswick, N.J., 1986.

Sprinzak, Ehud. *The Ascendance of Israel's Radical Right*. New York, 1992.

———. *Brother against Brother: Violence and Extremism in Israeli Politics from Altalena to the Rabin Assassination*. New York, 1999.

———. "Illegalism in Israeli Political Culture," *Jerusalem Quarterly*, Summer 1988.

Stock, Ernest. *HaZ'ramim HaDatiyim baGolah u'Shluchoteihem b'Yisrael* [The Religious Trends in the Diaspora and Their Constituent Groups in Israel]. Jerusalem, 1983.

Wald, Kenneth, et al. "Reclaiming Zion: How American Religious Groups View the Middle East," *Israel Affairs*, Spring/Summer 1996.

Wasserstein, Bernard. *Divided Jerusalem: The Struggle for the Holy City*. New Haven, Conn., 2003.

Waxman, C. "American Israelis in Judea and Samaria," *Middle East Review*, No. 2, 1982–83.

Yaniv, Avner. *Israel's Nuclear Dilemma*. Ithaca, N.Y., 1994.

Zakheim, Dov. *Flight of the Lavi: Inside a U.S.-Israel Crisis*. London, 1996.

INDEX

A NOTE ON THE TYPE

This book was set in Caledonia, a face designed by W. A. Dwiggins (1880–1956). It belongs to the family of printing types called modern face by printers—a term used to mark the change in style of the type letters that occurred around 1800. Caledonia borders on the general design of Scotch Roman but it is more freely drawn than that letter.

Composed by Creative Graphics, Allentown, Pennsylvania
Printed and bound by R. R. Donnelley & Sons, Harrisonburg, Virginia

Maps by Jean Paul Tremblay and George Colbert
Designed by Camilla Filancia